# COLLINS
## POSTCODE ATLAS
# BRITAIN
## & NORTHERN IRELAND

## CONTENTS

| | | | |
|---|---|---|---|
| Key to map symbols | ii | London key to map pages and symbols | 123 |
| Structure of postcodes | iii | London mapping | 124-131 |
| Postcode areas | iv-v | (3.2 inches to 1 mile) | |
| Britain maps | 2-107 | Administrative areas information | 132-145 |
| (4.1 miles to 1 inch) | | Administrative areas map | 146-151 |
| Northern Ireland map | 108-109 | (19.7 miles to inch) | |
| (9 miles to 1 inch) | | London boroughs map | 152-153 |
| Urban maps (1.6 miles to 1 inch) | 110-122 | (2.6 miles to 1 inch) | |
|   London (1.3 miles to 1 inch) | 110-113 | Index to London street names | 154-166 |
|   West Midlands | 114-115 | Index to Great Britain place names | 167-223 |
|   Manchester | 116-117 | Index to Northern Ireland place names | 224 |
|   Leeds and Bradford | 118-119 | | |
|   Liverpool | 120 | | |
|   Newcastle upon Tyne | 121 | | |
|   Glasgow | 122 | | |

**Collins**

Published by Collins
*An imprint of* HarperCollins Publishers
77-85 Fulham Palace Road, Hammersmith, London W6 8JB

www.harpercollins.co.uk

Copyright © HarperCollins Publishers Ltd 2009

Collins® is a registered trademark of HarperCollins Publishers Limited

Mapping generated from Collins Bartholomew digital databases

Postcode boundaries and codes copyright © Royal Mail Group plc

The postcode boundary information published in this atlas is compiled from the Postcode Address File (PAF) and reproduced with the permission of Royal Mail Group plc. The copyright and database rights in PAF are owned by Royal Mail Group plc. Details included in this atlas are subject to change without notice.

The grid on this map is the National Grid taken from the Ordnance Survey map with the permission of the Controller of Her Majesty's Stationery Office.

British population figures are derived from the 2001 census.
Source: National Statistics website: www.statistics.gov.uk
Crown copyright material is reproduced with the permission of the Controller of HMSO.
Northern Ireland populations derived from the 2001 Census.
Source: Northern Ireland Statistics and Research Agency www.nisra.gov.uk
Reproduced by permission.

All rights reserved. No part of this publication may be reproduced, stored in a retrieval system, or transmitted, in any form or by any means, electronic, mechanical, photocopying, recording or otherwise, without the prior written permission of the publisher and copyright owners.

The contents of this publication are believed correct at the time of printing. Nevertheless, the publisher can accept no responsibility for errors or omissions, changes in the detail given, or for any expense or loss thereby caused.

The representation of a road, track or footpath is no evidence of a right of way.

Printed in China

ISBN 978 0 00 731200 9   Imp 001   WV12437   RDR

e-mail: roadcheck@harpercollins.co.uk

# Key to map symbols

## Postcode information

- **PL** — Area code
- Area boundary
- **35** — District code
- District boundary

## Britain map symbols (pages 2-107)

- M4 — Motorway
- M6 Toll — Toll Motorway
- Motorway junction with full / limited access
- Motorway service areas (off road, full, limited access)
- A48 — Primary route dual / single carriageway
- A5 — 'A' road dual / single carriageway
- B1403 — 'B' road dual / single carriageway
- Minor road
- Restricted access due to road condition or private ownership
- Roads with passing places
- Roads proposed or under construction
- Multi-level junction (occasionally with junction number)
- Roundabout
- Road tunnel
- Steep hill (arrows point downhill)
- Level crossing
- Toll
- Car ferry route with journey times
- Railway line and station
- Preserved railway line and station
- Railway tunnel
- Airport with / without scheduled services
- Heliport
- Built up area
- Towns, villages and other settlements
- National boundary
- County / Unitary Authority boundary
- Spot / Summit height in metres
- Lake, dam and river
- Canal / Dry canal / Canal tunnel
- Beach

1:260,000 (approx)
0  2  4  6  8  10 miles
0  2  4  6  8  10  12  14  16 km
4.1 miles to 1 inch   2.6 km to 1 cm

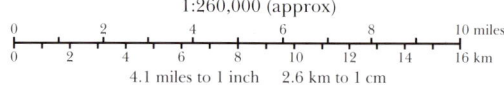

## Northern Ireland map symbols (pages 108-109)

- M1 — Motorway
- Motorway junction with full / limited access
- A28 / N4 — Primary / National primary route
- A29 / N52 — 'A' road / National secondary route
- B113 / R408 — 'B' road / Regional road
- Minor road
- Road under construction
- Multi-level junction / roundabout
- Steep hill (arrows point downhill)
- Car ferry route
- International / domestic airport
- Canal
- International boundary
- District / County boundary
- 754 — Summit height (in metres)
- Built up areas
- Beach

## Conurbation map symbols (pages 110-122)

- M73 — Motorway
- M6 Toll — Toll motorway
- Motorway junctions with full / limited access
- FRANKLEY SERVICES — Motorway service area
- A725 — Primary route dual / single carriageway
- A4054 — 'A' road dual / single carriageway
- B7078 — 'B' road dual / single carriageway
- Minor road dual / single carriageway
- Roundabout
- Car ferry
- Railway line and station
- London Underground / Subway / Metro / Light rail station
- Railway tunnel
- Airport with scheduled services
- Built up areas
- Public building
- County / Unitary Authority boundary
- Woodland / Park
- 266 — Spot height in metres
- Congestion charging zone
- Extended congestion charging zone (from Feb 2007)

# Structure of postcodes  iii

Postcodes operate at five levels.

Level 1. Areas are denoted by the first one or two letters of the code, eg GL. These areas are then divided into districts.

Level 2. Districts are denoted by the number or numbers in the first part of the postcode, eg GL52. Districts are further subdivided into sectors.

Level 3. Subdistricts are a further special division of districts and only occur in London, eg EC1A.

Level 4. Sectors are denoted by the number in the second part of the postcode, eg GL52 5.

Level 5. The final two letters of the code denote a group of houses or an individual building, eg GL52 5HH.

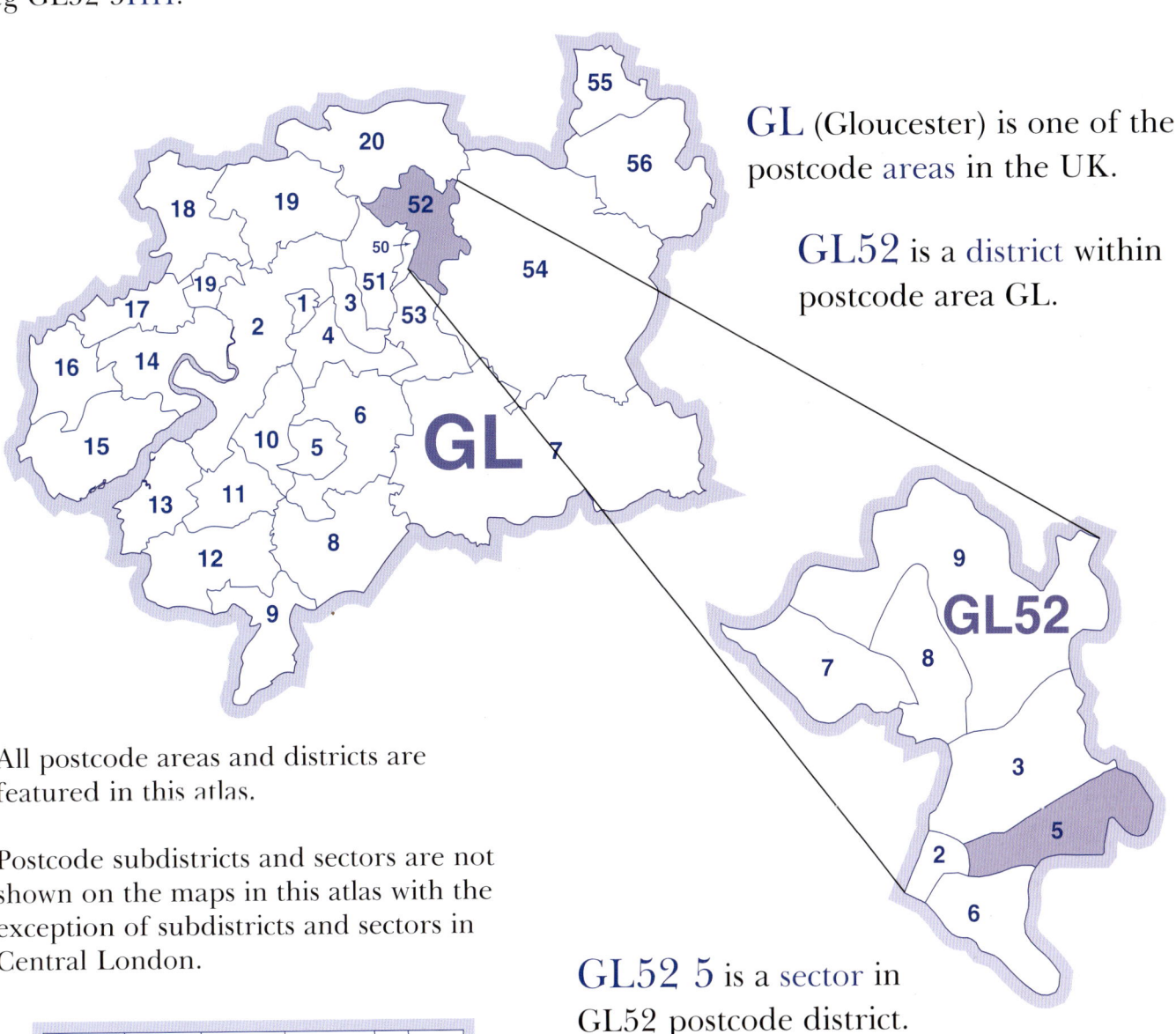

GL (Gloucester) is one of the postcode areas in the UK.

GL52 is a district within postcode area GL.

All postcode areas and districts are featured in this atlas.

Postcode subdistricts and sectors are not shown on the maps in this atlas with the exception of subdistricts and sectors in Central London.

GL52 5 is a sector in GL52 postcode district.

GL52 5HH is the postcode. It pinpoints a group of houses and in some cases individual business premises.

# Postcode areas

| Postcode | & Area |
|---|---|
| SA | Swansea |
| SE | London SE |
| SG | Stevenage |
| SK | Stockport |
| SL | Slough |
| SM | Sutton |
| SN | Swindon |
| SO | Southampton |
| SP | Salisbury |
| SR | Sunderland |
| SS | Southend-on-Sea |
| ST | Stoke-on-Trent |
| SW | London SW |
| SY | Shrewsbury |
| TA | Taunton |
| TD | Galashiels |
| TF | Telford |
| TN | Royal Tunbridge Wells |
| TQ | Torquay |
| TR | Truro |
| TS | Teesside |
| TW | Twickenham |
| UB | Southall |
| W | London W |
| WA | Warrington |
| WC | London WC |
| WD | Watford |
| WF | Wakefield |
| WN | Wigan |
| WR | Worcester |
| WS | Walsall |
| WV | Wolverhampton |
| YO | York |
| ZE | Shetland |

| Postcode | & Area |
|---|---|
| AB | Aberdeen |
| AL | St Albans |
| B | Birmingham |
| BA | Bath |
| BB | Blackburn |
| BD | Bradford |
| BH | Bournemouth |
| BL | Bolton |
| BN | Brighton |
| BR | Bromley |
| BS | Bristol |
| BT | Northern Ireland |
| CA | Carlisle |
| CB | Cambridge |
| CF | Cardiff |
| CH | Chester |
| CM | Chelmsford |
| CO | Colchester |
| CR | Croydon |
| CT | Canterbury |
| CV | Coventry |
| CW | Crewe |
| DA | Dartford |
| DD | Dundee |
| DE | Derby |
| DG | Dumfries |
| DH | Durham |
| DL | Darlington |
| DN | Doncaster |
| DT | Dorchester |
| DY | Dudley |
| E | London E |
| EC | London EC |
| EH | Edinburgh |
| EN | Enfield |
| EX | Exeter |
| FK | Falkirk |
| FY | Blackpool |
| G | Glasgow |
| GL | Gloucester |
| GU | Guildford |
| GY | Guernsey |
| HA | Harrow |
| HD | Huddersfield |
| HG | Harrogate |
| HP | Hemel Hempstead |
| HR | Hereford |
| HS | Hebrides |
| HU | Kingston upon Hull |
| HX | Halifax |
| IG | Ilford |
| IM | Isle of Man |
| IP | Ipswich |
| IV | Inverness |
| JE | Jersey |
| KA | Kilmarnock |
| KT | Kingston-upon-Thames |
| KW | Kirkwall |
| KY | Kirkcaldy |
| L | Liverpool |
| LA | Lancaster |
| LD | Llandrindod Wells |
| LE | Leicester |
| LL | Llandudno |
| LN | Lincoln |
| LS | Leeds |
| LU | Luton |
| M | Manchester |
| ME | Medway |
| MK | Milton Keynes |
| ML | Motherwell |
| N | London N |
| NE | Newcastle upon Tyne |
| NG | Nottingham |
| NN | Northampton |
| NP | Newport |
| NR | Norwich |
| NW | London NW |
| OL | Oldham |
| OX | Oxford |
| PA | Paisley |
| PE | Peterborough |
| PH | Perth |
| PL | Plymouth |
| PO | Portsmouth |
| PR | Preston |
| RG | Reading |
| RH | Redhill |
| RM | Romford |
| S | Sheffield |

v

6
A
B
C
D
E
1
2
3
4
5
6
7
EX
North West Point
LUNDY
34
Shutter Rock
Rat Island
Heddon's Mouth
Widmouth Head
Ilfracombe
Hele
Berrynarbor
Combe Martin
Martinhoe
Trentishoe
Hunter's Inn
Kemacott
Killington
Parracombe
Churchill
Bull Point
Rockham Bay
Morte Point
Mortehoe
Woolacombe
Morte Bay
Lee
Slade
Mullacott Cross
Seymour Villas
Trimstone
Cheglinch
West Down
Dean Cross
Bradwell
Sterridge
Berry Down Cross
Kentisbury
Blackmoor Gate
Challacombe
Patchole
Kentisbury Ford
Arlington Beccott
Arlington
East Down
Clifton
Bittadon
Baggy Point
Putsborough
Pickwell
North Buckland
Croyde Bay
Georgeham
Croyde
33
Knowle
Lobb
Halsinger
Winsham
Boode
Middle Marwood
Marwood
Milltown
Muddiford
Upcott
Higher Muddiford
Shirwell Cross
Shirwell
Kingsheanton
Prixford
Pippacott
Loxhore
Lower Loxhore
Knightacott
Bratton Fleming
Benton
Stoke Rivers
Saunton
Saunton Sands
Braunton
Heanton Punchardon
West Ashford
Ashford
Wrafton
Braunton Burrows
Toll
Chivenor
BARNSTAPLE
Bickington
Fremington
Yelland
Pilton
Bradiford
Newport
Lilly
Goodleigh
Willesleigh
Gunn
32
Stoodleigh
West Buckland
East Buckland
Charles
Landkey
Swimbridge Newland
Yarnacott
Riverton
Swimbridge
Bishop's Tawton
Tawstock
Lake
St John's Chapel
BARNSTAPLE BAY (BIDEFORD BAY)
The Neck
Appledore
Instow
Bickleton
Westward Ho!
Northam
Tapeley
Westleigh
Eastleigh
Horwood
Lower Lovacott
Newton Tracey
Hiscott
Harracott
Ensis
Herner
Chapelton
Cobbaton
Stowford
Filleigh
Chittlehampton
Umberleigh
Eastacott
Hudscott
Warkleigh
Satterleigh
Hartland Point
Titchberry
Windbury Point
Gallantry Bower
Clovelly
Clovelly Bay
Abbotsham
East-the-Water
Bideford
Gammaton
Gammaton Moor
Woodtown
Alverdiscott
Hartland Quay
Stoke
Hartland
Slerra
Dyke
Clovelly Cross
Buck's Mills
Buck's Cross
Horns Cross
Fairy Cross
Ford
Yeo Vale
Alwington
Littleham
Landcross
Huntshaw Water
Huntshaw
Yarnscombe
Fishleigh Barton
Atherington
Langridge
Langridgeford
Huntshaw Cross
High Bickington
Chittlehamholt
Milford
Edistone
Philham
Tosberry
Elmscott
Goldworthy
Parkham
Parkham Ash
Cranford
Woolfardisworthy
Buckland Brewer
Saltrens
Monkleigh
Weare Giffard
High Bullen
Sherwood Green
37
39
South Hole
Knaps Longpeak
Welcombe
Mead
Almiston Cross
Melbury
Frithelstock Stone
Frithelstock
Great Torrington
Dodscott
St Giles in the Wood
Kingscott
Roborough
Head Bridge
Northcote Manor
Darracott
Ashmansworthy
Meddon
Powler's Piece
Taddiport
38
Little Torrington
Burrington
Gooseham
Woolley
Eastcott
Kismeldon Bridge
East Putford
Langtree
Langtree Week
Villavin
Morwenstow
Higher Sharpnose Point
East Youlstone
West Youlstone
Dinworthy
West Putford
Stibb Cross
Great Potheridge
Little Potheridge
Beaford
Shop
Woodford
Lower Sharpnose Point
Bradworthy
Haytown
Bulkworthy
Berry Cross
Peters Marland
Winswell
Woolleigh
Riddlecombe
Ashreigney
Taylors Cross
Coombe
Kilkhampton
Thurdon
Alfardisworthy
Sutcombe
Brendon
Abbots Bickington
Newton St Petrock
Little Marland
Merton
Heanton Satchville
Huish
Dolton
Hollacombe Town
Ashley
Stibb
Upper Tamar Lake
Lower Tamar Lake
Soldon
Soldon Cross
Sutcombemill
Vennggreen
Milton Damerel
Dowland
Hollacombe
Eggesford Barton
23
Youldonmoor Cross
Youldon
Holsworthy Beacon
Shebbear
North Town
Petrockstowe
Ash Barton
19
Iddesleigh
Wembworthy
Maer
Bude Haven
Poughill
Flexbury
Hersham Bush
Grimscott
Woodacott
Thornbury
Buckland Filleigh
Meeth
Winkleigh
Bude
Stratton
Launcells Cross
Lana
Chilsworthy
Brendon
Bradford
Lashbrook
Sheepwash
Ingleigh Green
D
Brushford
Launcells
Red Post
Pancrasweek
22
Cookbury
Middlecott
Hele Bridge
Monkokehampton
Broadwood Kelly
Cookbury Wick
Black Torrington
Bondleigh
Helebridge
Marhamchurch
Derril
Rydon
Holsworthy
Anvil Corner
Brandis Corner
Highampton
Hatherleigh
Lowton
Widemouth Bay
Bridgerule
Pyworthy
Derriton
Chasty
Whimble
Dunsland Cross
Hollacombe
Graddon Moor
Chilla
Lydacott
Odham
Basset's Cross
Honeychurch
Exbourne
Sampford Courtenay
North Tawton
Titson
Box's Shop
Yeomadon
Halwill Forest
21
Jacobstowe
Shilstone
Week Orchard
Coppathorne
Poundstock
Tregole
Treskinnick Cross
Tinney
Clawton
Halwill
Halwill Junction
Beaworthy
Whiddon
Northlew
Inwardleigh
Oak Cross
Belstone Corner
Trecott
Rowden
Whitstone
Corfcott Green
East Kimber
Ashbury
Trewint
Penlean
Week St Mary
North Tamerton
Upcott
Patchacott
Folly Gate
CORNWALL
Quoditch
Higher Prestacott
Broadbury
20
Chichacott
Taw Green
Trebarrow
Tetcott
Lana
Ashwater
Eworthy
Thorndon Cross
Southcott
Okehampton
Yelland
Sticklepath
South Tawton
Jacobstow
Higher Whiteleigh
West Curry
Luffincott
Henford
Germansweek
Boasley Cross
Belstone
South Zeal
Trengune
Maxworthy
Clubworthy
Northcott
Chapmans Well
Hewton
Okehampton Camp
Whiddon Down
Canworthy Water
Langdon
Boyton
Bennacott
Virginstow
Bratton Clovelly
Meldon
Yes Tor
High Willhays
Cawsand Hill
Throwleigh
Warbstow
Troswell
Brazacott
Hele
West Panson
East Panson
St Giles on the Heath
Ebsworthy Town
Forda
Sourton
4
Tremaine
Penrose
North Petherwin
15
Langdon
Bridgetown
Broadwoodwidger
Bridestowe
Bidlake
Gidleigh
Halworthy
Treneglos
Trebeath
Ladycross
Polapit Tamar
Werrington
Cross Green
Kellacott
Thrushelton
Southerly
Bridestowe and Sourton Common
Okement Hill
Hangingstone Hill
Murchington
Chagford
Three Hammers
Tresmeer
Tregeare
Egloskerry
Langore
Trussott
Yeolmbridge
Dutson
Lowford
Lewdown
Portgate
Allerford
Lobhillcross
Shortacombe
Great Kneeset
Whitehorse Hill
Cold Northcott
Badgall
St Stephens
Newport
PL
Launceston
Lifton
Tinhay
Sprytown
Lewtrenchard
Lydford
Amicombe Hill
Frenchbeer
Red Down
Pipers Pool
Tregadillett
Downhead
Laneast
Trewen
Trebullett
Polyphant
Kennards House
Daw's House
Lawhitton
16
Marystow
Coryton
Liddaton Green
Chillaton
Downton
Beardon
Sittaford Tor
Fernworthy Reservoir
Black Ridge
Cut Hill
White Ridge
Warren House
Tregunnon
Altarnun
Trewint
Tredaule
Fivelanes
South Petherwin
Trecrogo
Lewannick
Kelly
Bradstone
Meadwell
North Brentor
Brent Tor
Black Down
Willsworthy
Lynch Tor
Rough Tor
Higher White Tor
DARTMOOR
Hawks Tor
South Brentor
Felldownhead
Plusha
Horndon
Cocks Hill
Cowsic Head
Postbridge
Bray Down
Lezant
Dunterton
Blackdown
Mary Tavy
Cudlipptown
Peter Tavy
Cox Tor
Great Mis Tor
Lamerton
19
Bellever
Trebartha
Coad's Green
Bealsmill
Treburley
0 2 4 6 miles
0 2 4 6 8 10 km

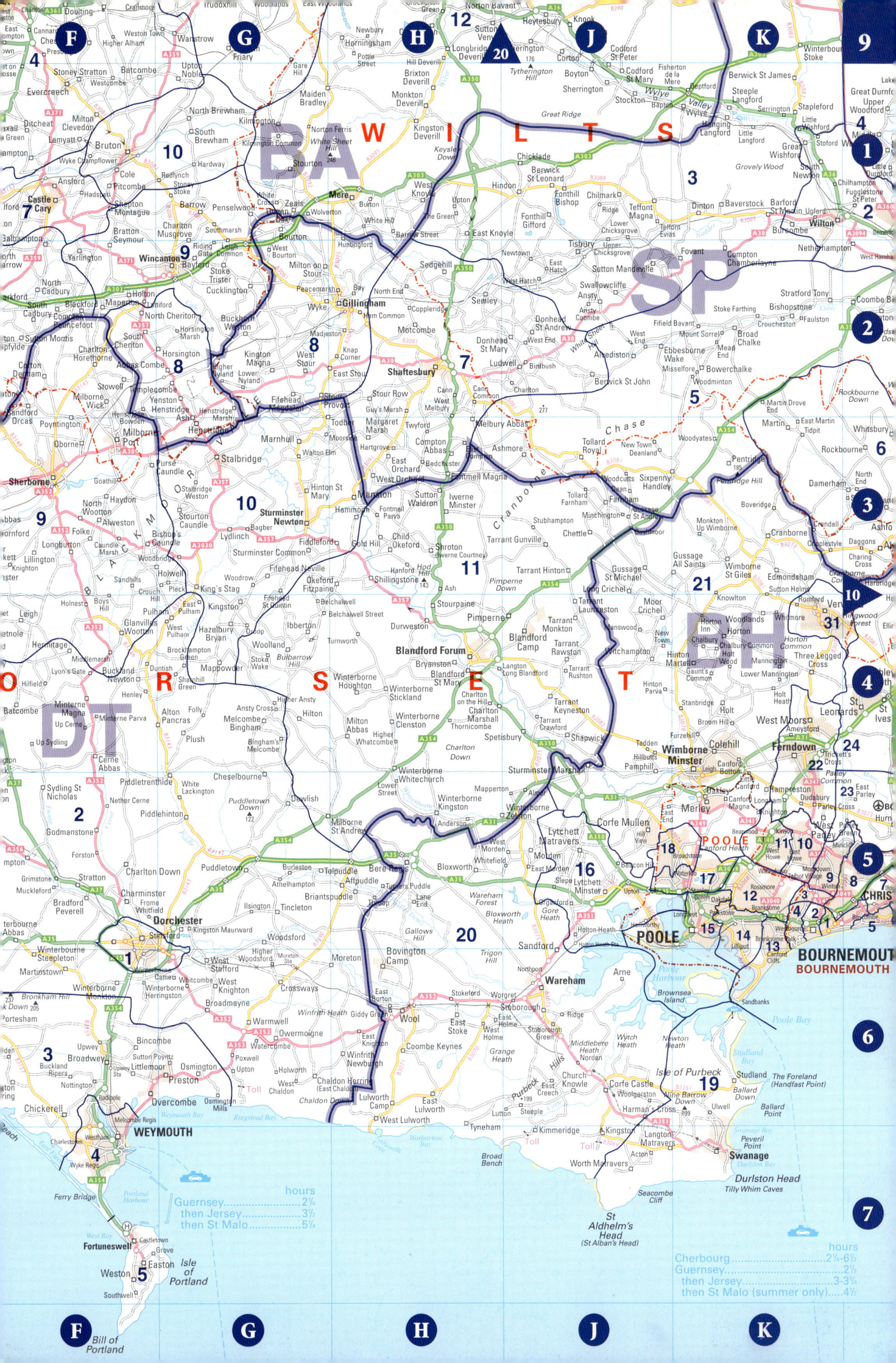

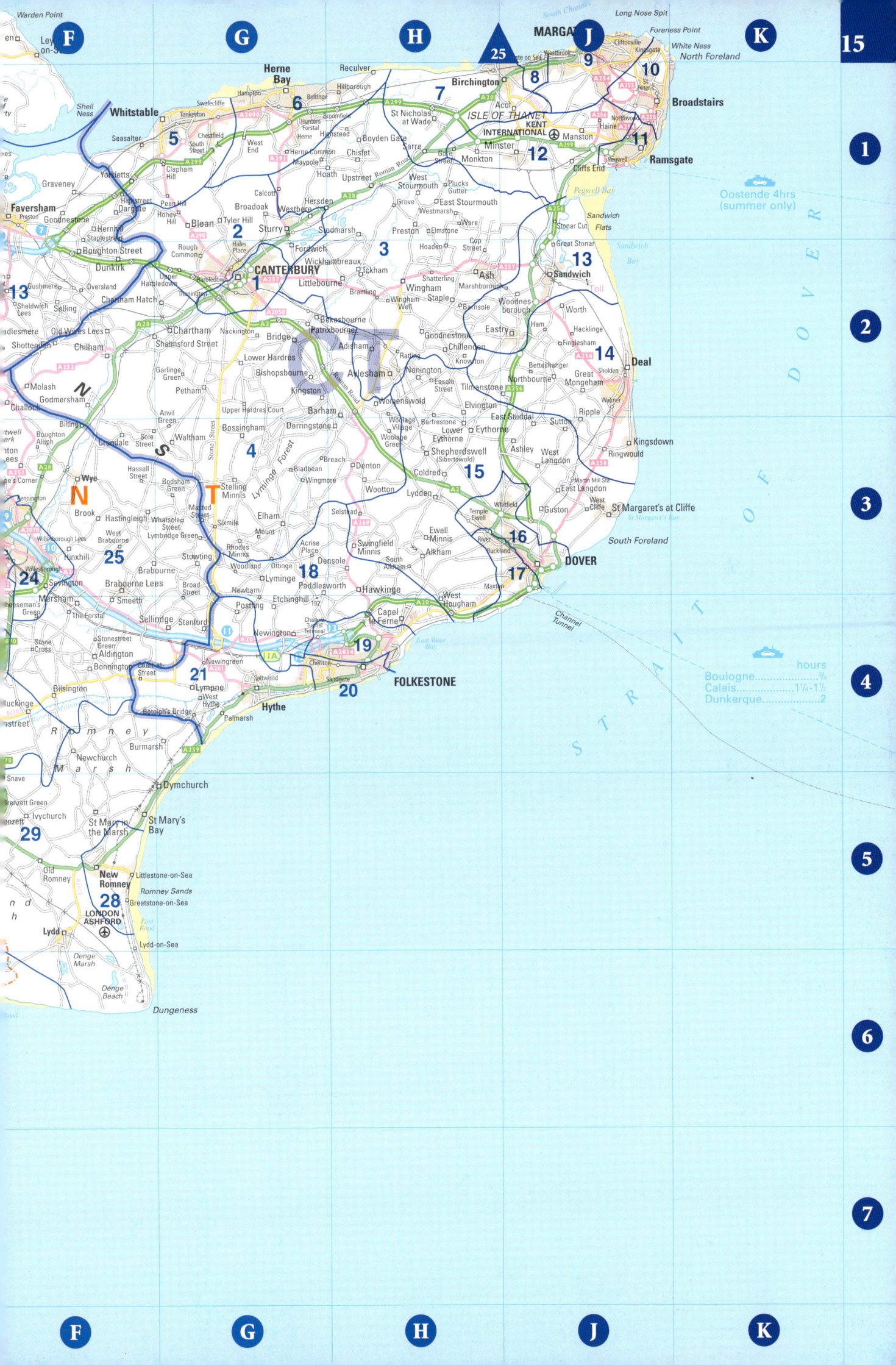

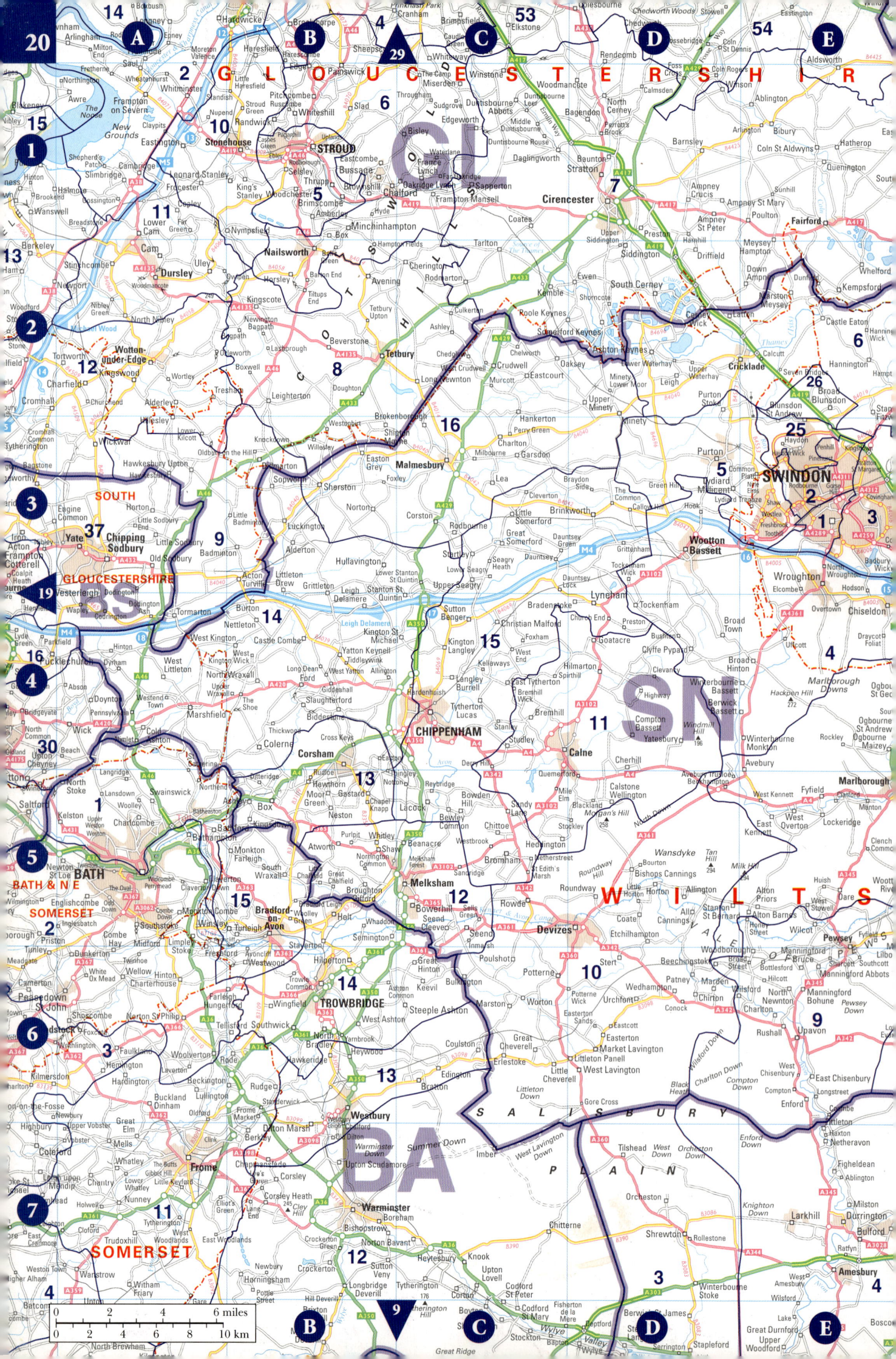

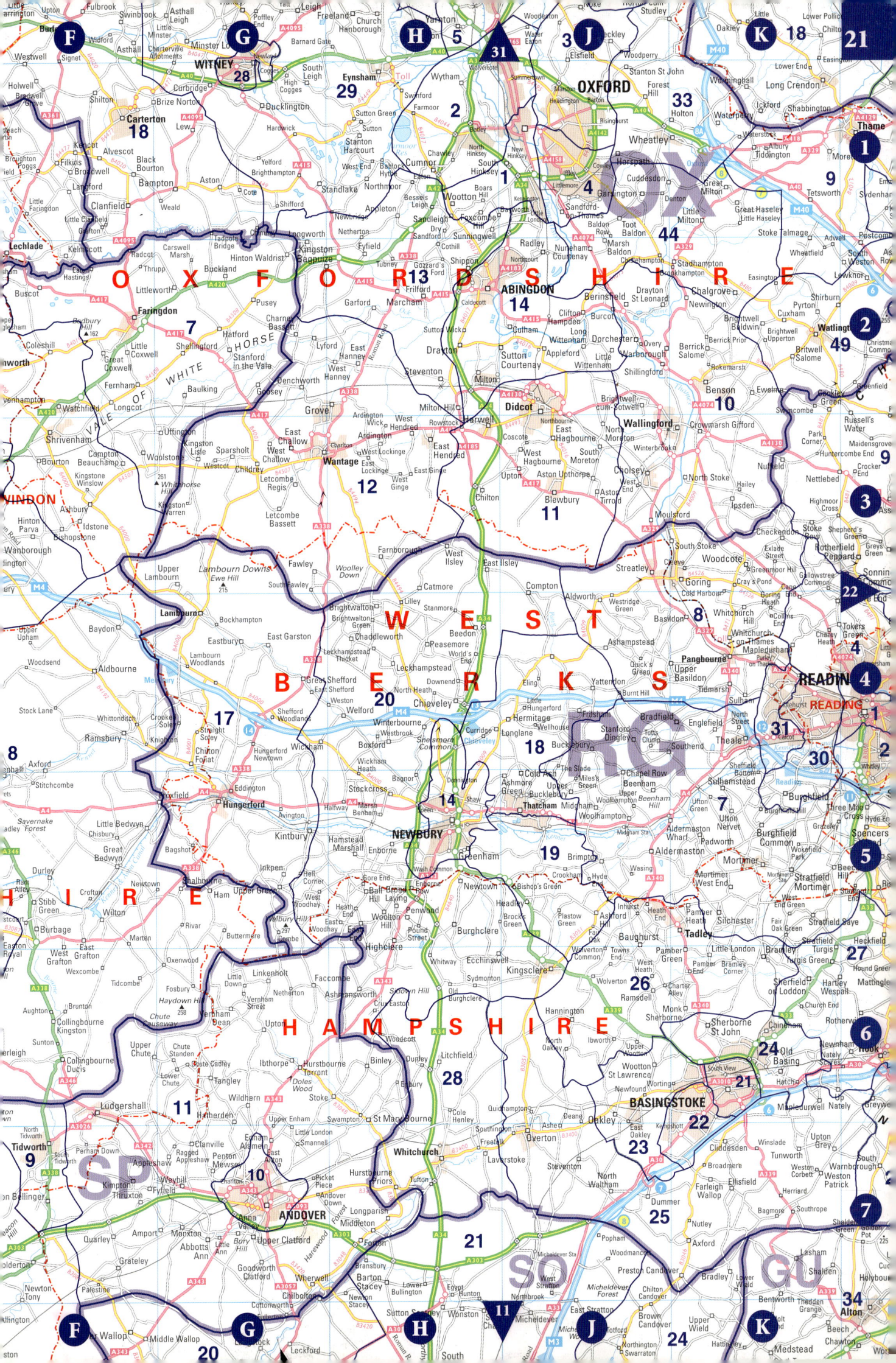

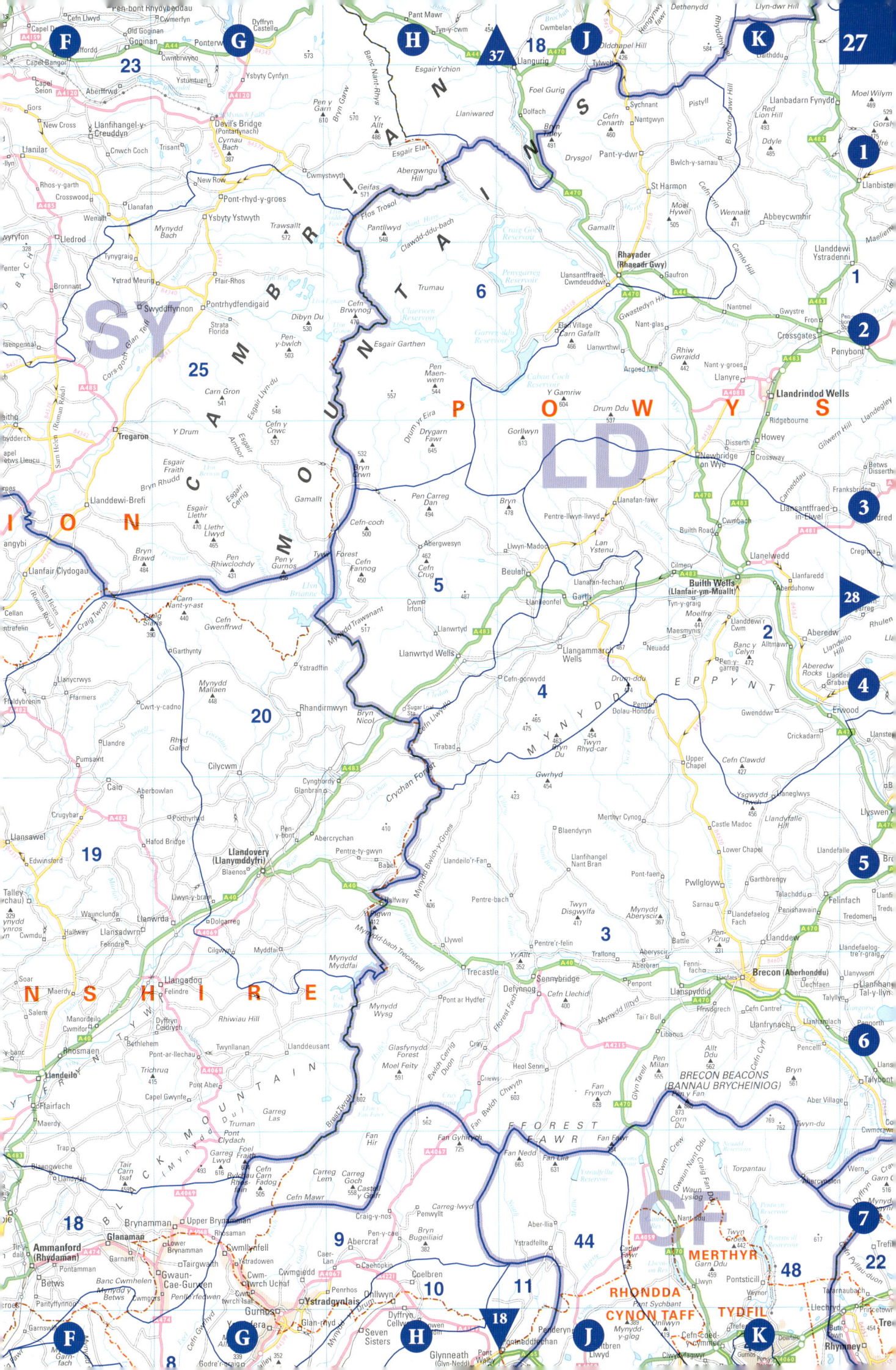

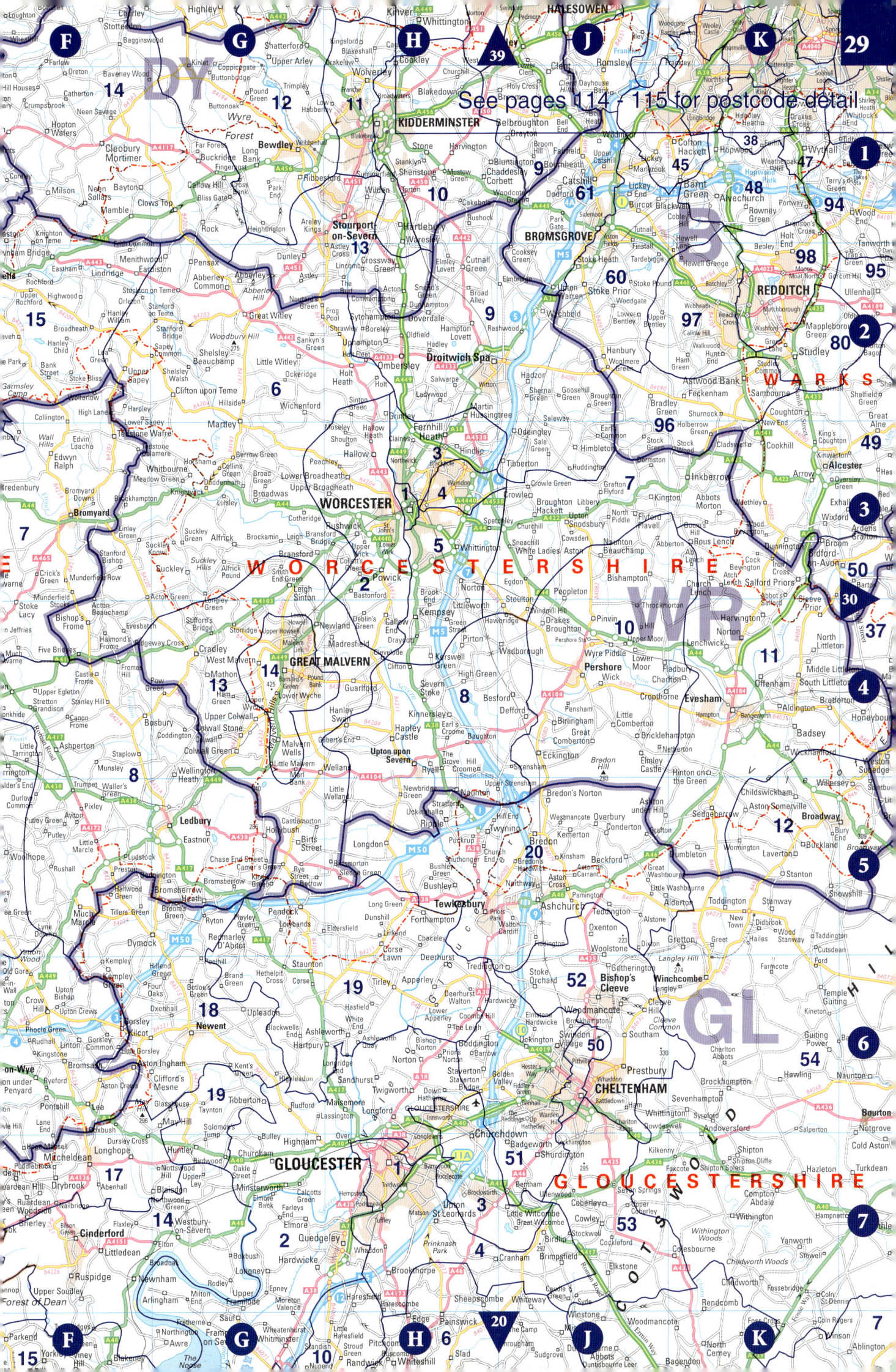

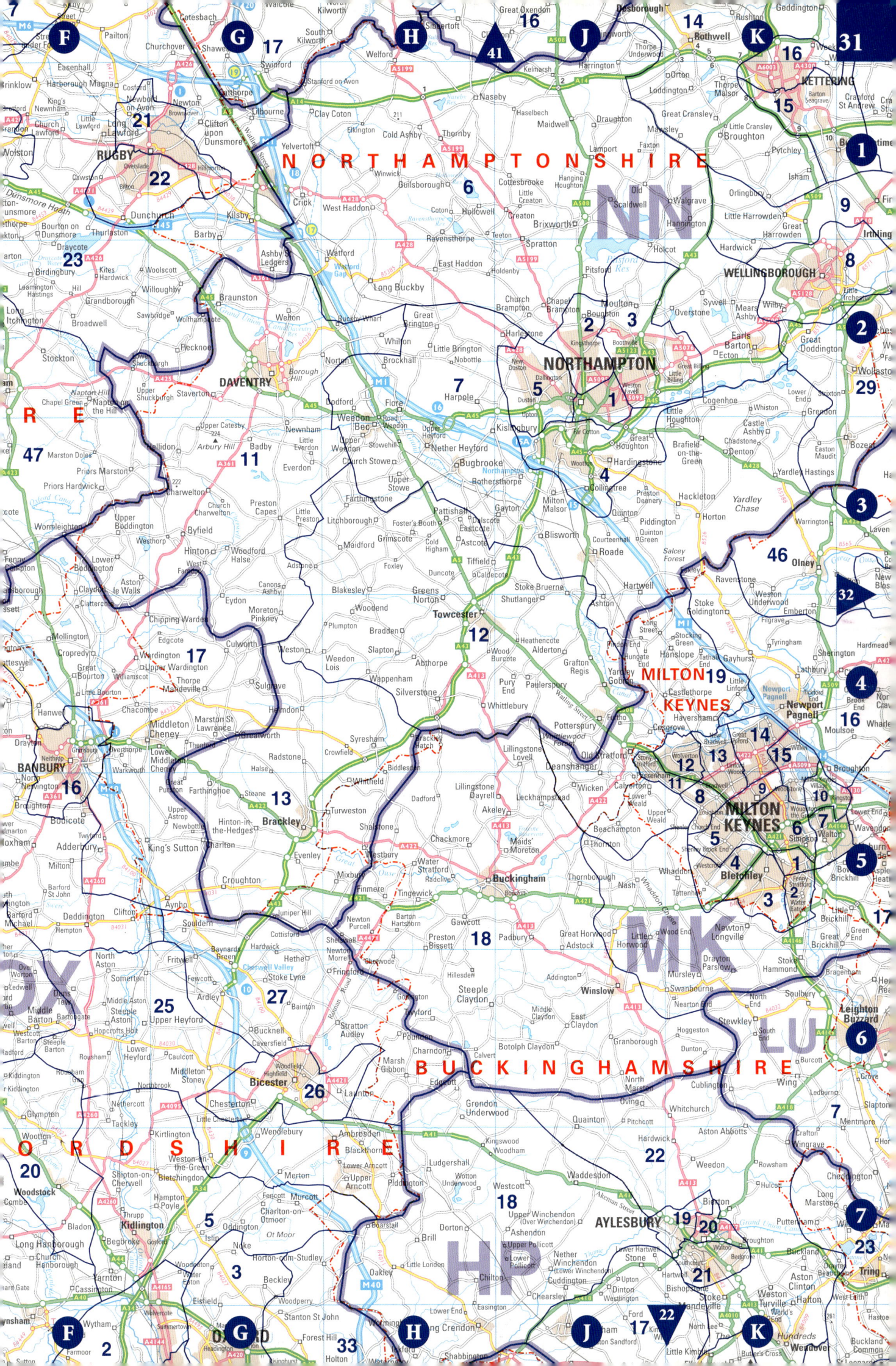

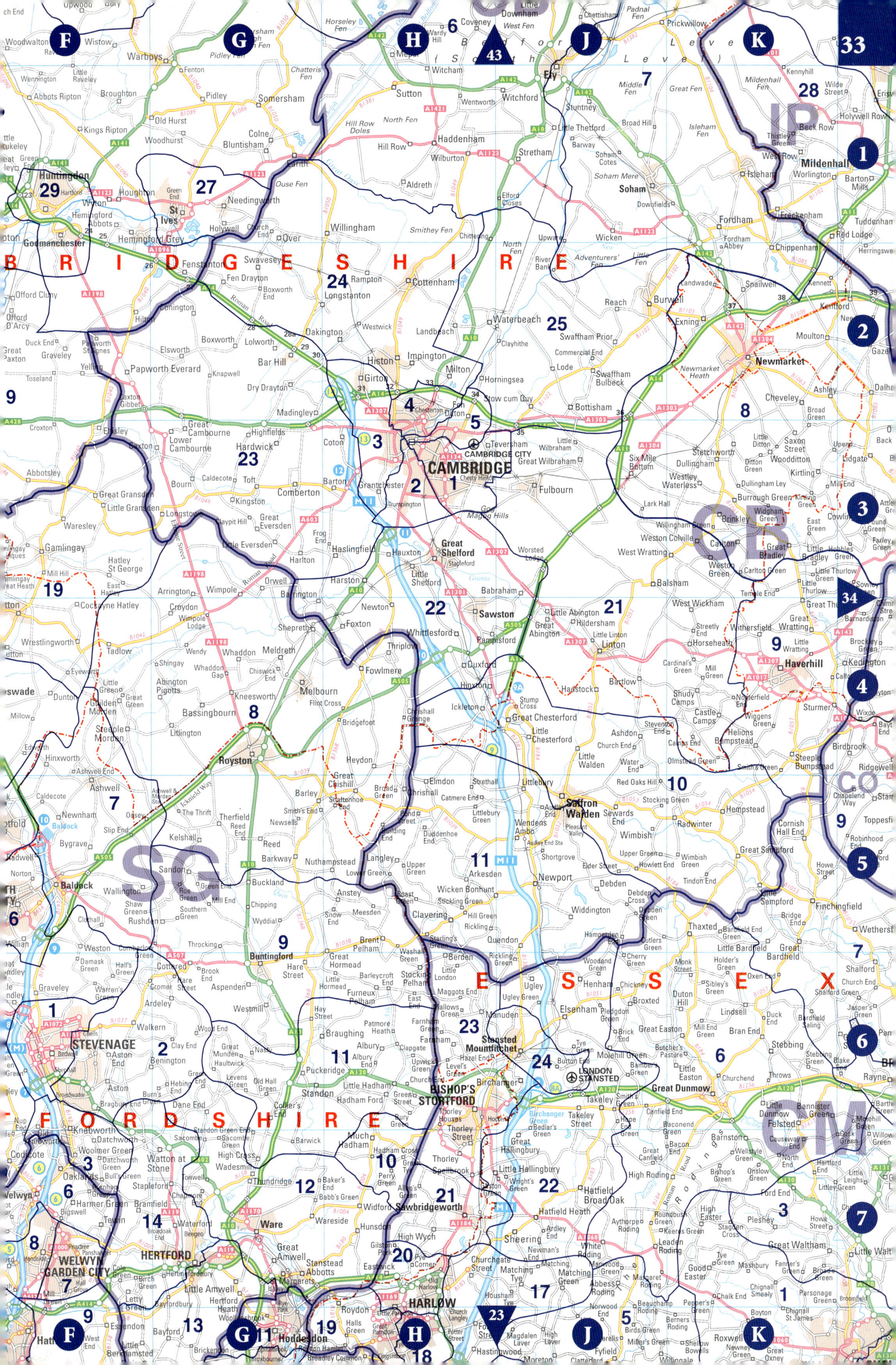

33
43
34
23
CAMBRIDGESHIRE
HERTFORDSHIRE
ESSEX
SG
CB
CO
CM
IP
Huntingdon
Godmanchester
St Ives
Ely
Soham
Mildenhall
Newmarket
Haverhill
CAMBRIDGE
CAMBRIDGE CITY
Histon
Girton
Cottenham
Waterbeach
Great Shelford
Sawston
Linton
Royston
Baldock
STEVENAGE
WELWYN GARDEN CITY
HERTFORD
Ware
Hoddesdon
HARLOW
Sawbridgeworth
BISHOP'S STORTFORD
Stansted Mountfitchet
LONDON STANSTED
Great Dunmow
Thaxted
Saffron Walden
Buntingford
Melbourn
Bassingbourn
Papworth Everard
Great Cambourne
Fulbourn
Bottisham
Burwell
Fordham
Chippenham
Steeple Bumpstead
Finchingfield
Felsted
Hatfield Broad Oak
Sheering
Great Waltham

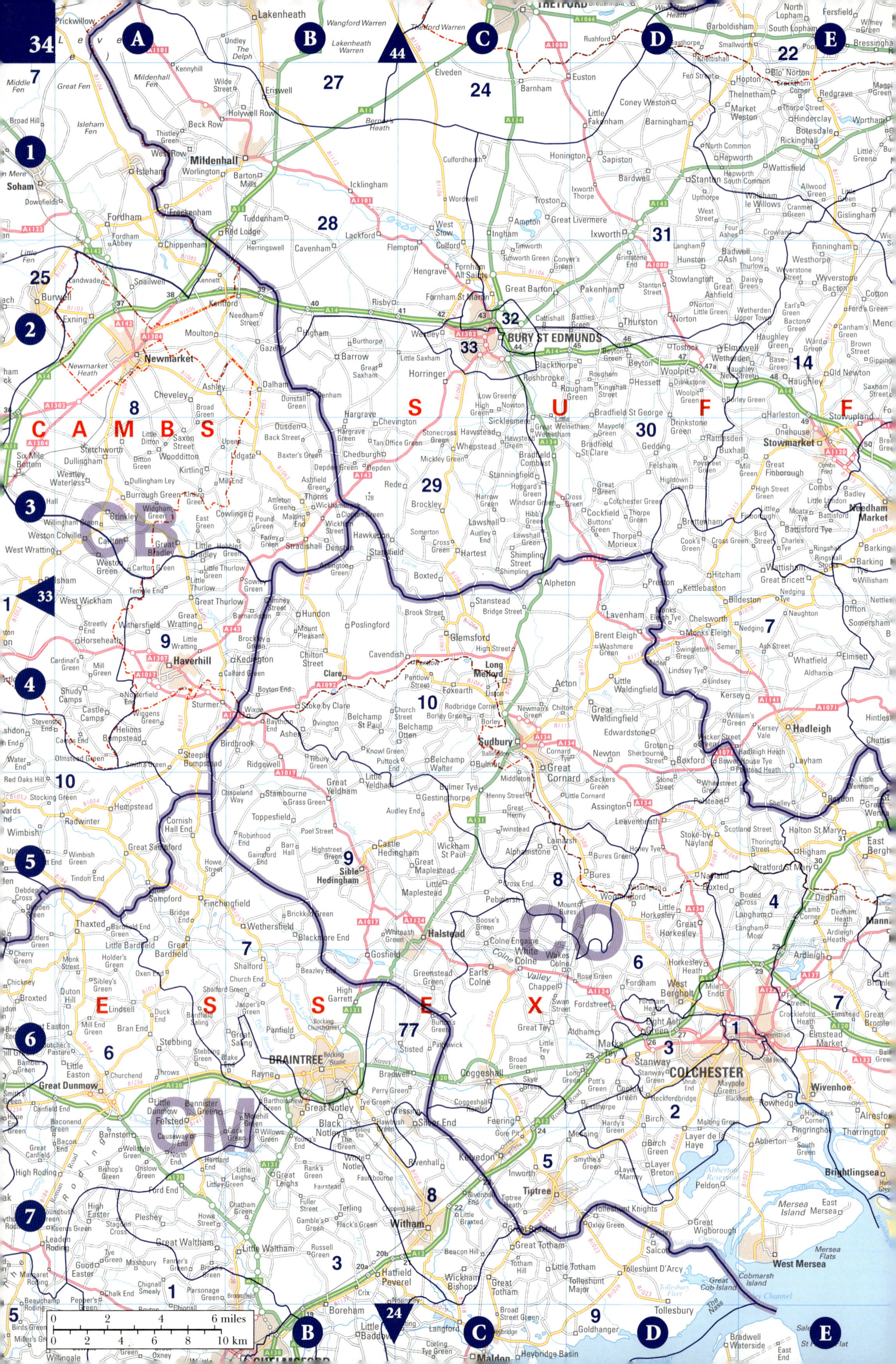
34
44
24
33
A
B
C
D
E
1
2
3
4
5
6
7
CAMBS
SUFFOLK
ESSEX
CB
CO
CM
Lakenheath
Wangford Warren
Lakenheath Warren
Thetford Warren
Thetford
Elveden
Barnham
Euston
Garboldisham
North Lopham
South Lopham
Fersfield
Prickwillow
Mildenhall Fen
Eriswell
Undley
Middle Fen
Great Fen
Kenny Hill
Wilde Street
Holywell Row
Beck Row
Thistley Green
West Row
Mildenhall
Worlington
Barton Mills
Isleham Fen
Isleham
Broad Hill
Soham
Fordham
Fordham Abbey
Chippenham
Freckenham
Red Lodge
Tuddenham
Icklingham
Herringswell
Cavenham
Lackford
Flempton
West Stow
Culford
Ingham
Ampton
Great Livermere
Troston
Ixworth
Ixworth Thorpe
Honington
Sapiston
Bardwell
Coney Weston
Barningham
Little Fakenham
Hopton
Thelnetham
Market Weston
Stanton
Hepworth
Wattisfield
Walsham le Willows
Hinderclay
Redgrave
Botesdale
Rickinghall
Wortham
Gislingham
Finningham
Westhorpe
Wyverstone
Bacton
Cotton
Badwell Ash
Hunston
Stowlangtoft
Pakenham
Great Barton
Fornham All Saints
Fornham St Martin
Hengrave
Risby
Kentford
Newmarket
Exning
Burwell
Snailwell
Landwade
Moulton
Gazeley
Higham
Barrow
Westley
Little Saxham
Great Saxham
Horringer
BURY ST EDMUNDS
Rougham
Beyton
Thurston
Norton
Tostock
Elmswell
Woolpit
Wetherden
Haughley
Old Newton
Stowmarket
Onehouse
Harleston
Buxhall
Rattlesden
Drinkstone
Bradfield St George
Great Whelnetham
Bradfield Combust
Hessett
Felsham
Gedding
Cockfield
Lawshall
Hawstead
Whepstead
Chevington
Hargrave
Ousden
Dalham
Denham
Ashley
Cheveley
Newmarket Heath
Stetchworth
Dullingham
Kirtling
Lidgate
Cowlinge
Wickhambrook
Stradishall
Denston
Chedburgh
Depden
Rede
Brockley
Hartest
Stanningfield
Thorpe Morieux
Preston
Brettenham
Hitcham
Kettlebaston
Bildeston
Nedging
Chelsworth
Monks Eleigh
Brent Eleigh
Lavenham
Alpheton
Shimpling
Boxted
Glemsford
Stansfield
Hawkedon
Cavendish
Poslingford
Hundon
Clare
Stoke by Clare
Kedington
Haverhill
Withersfield
Great Wratting
Little Wratting
Great Thurlow
Little Thurlow
Great Bradley
Brinkley
Carlton
Weston Colville
West Wickham
Horseheath
Castle Camps
Shudy Camps
Sturmer
Steeple Bumpstead
Helions Bumpstead
Birdbrook
Ridgewell
Belchamp St Paul
Belchamp Otten
Belchamp Walter
Long Melford
Foxearth
Borley
Acton
Sudbury
Great Cornard
Little Cornard
Bures
Lavenham
Newton
Boxford
Groton
Edwardstone
Kersey
Hadleigh
Layham
Polstead
Stoke-by-Nayland
Nayland
Leavenheath
Assington
Higham
Stratford St Mary
Dedham
Ardleigh
Langham
Great Horkesley
Little Horkesley
Wormingford
Mount Bures
Wakes Colne
White Colne
Earls Colne
Colne Engaine
Halstead
Gosfield
Sible Hedingham
Castle Hedingham
Great Maplestead
Little Maplestead
Pebmarsh
Alphamstone
Lamarsh
Great Yeldham
Toppesfield
Stambourne
Finchingfield
Wethersfield
Shalford
Great Sampford
Little Sampford
Radwinter
Hempstead
Thaxted
Great Bardfield
Little Bardfield
Lindsell
Great Dunmow
Stebbing
Rayne
BRAINTREE
Bocking
Great Notley
Black Notley
Cressing
Silver End
Coggeshall
Feering
Kelvedon
Rivenhall
Witham
Terling
Hatfield Peverel
Wickham Bishops
Great Totham
Little Totham
Tiptree
Tolleshunt Knights
Tolleshunt D'Arcy
Tolleshunt Major
Goldhanger
Tollesbury
Heybridge Basin
Maldon
Langford
Boreham
Little Baddow
Little Waltham
Great Waltham
Pleshey
Good Easter
High Easter
Barnston
Felsted
Great Leighs
Little Leighs
Fordham
West Bergholt
Aldham
Marks Tey
Stanway
COLCHESTER
Wivenhoe
Rowhedge
Elmstead Market
Alresford
Thorrington
Brightlingsea
Abberton
Layer de la Haye
Birch
Layer Marney
Peldon
Mersea Island
East Mersea
West Mersea
Salcott
Great Wigborough
Inworth
Messing
Copford
Eight Ash Green
Great Tey
Chappel
Needham Market
Barking
Offton
Somersham
Battisford
Combs
Great Finborough
Wattisham
Elmsett
Whatfield
Semer
Lindsey
0 2 4 6 miles
0 2 4 6 8 10 km

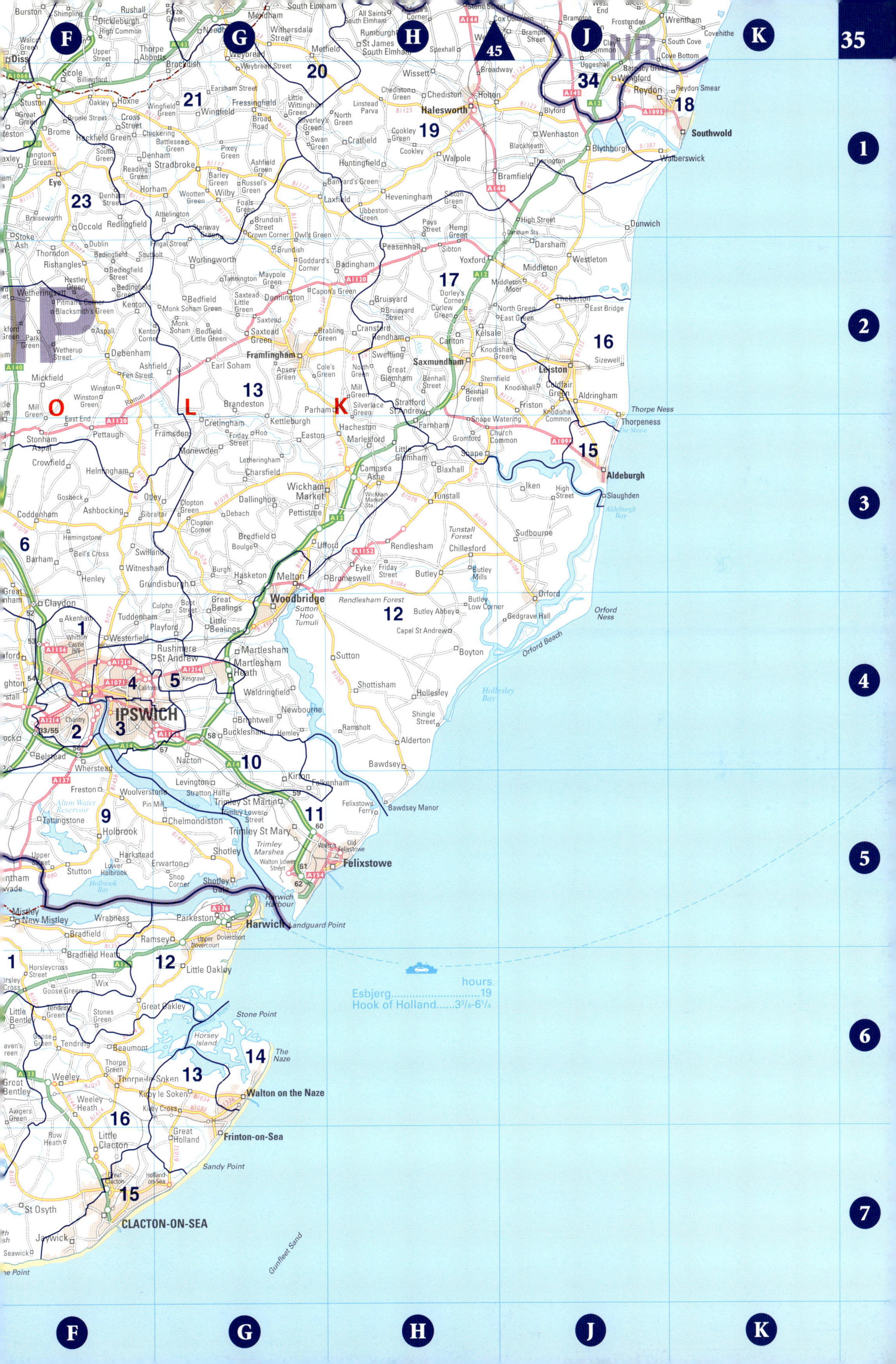
F
G
H
J
K
45
1
2
3
4
5
6
7
Diss
Scole
Hoxne
Eye
Stradbroke
Wingfield
Fressingfield
Weybread
Mendham
Metfield
Halesworth
Holton
Wenhaston
Walpole
Bramfield
Southwold
Walberswick
Blythburgh
Reydon
Wrentham
Covehithe
Dunwich
Westleton
Yoxford
Middleton
Theberton
Leiston
Sizewell
Aldringham
Thorpe Ness
Thorpeness
Aldeburgh
Slaughden
Snape
Saxmundham
Kelsale
Carlton
Framlingham
Debenham
Kettleburgh
Parham
Marlesford
Wickham Market
Campsea Ashe
Tunstall
Rendlesham
Chillesford
Sudbourne
Orford
Orford Ness
Orford Beach
Butley
Woodbridge
Melton
Ufford
Sutton Hoo Tumuli
Rendlesham Forest
Sutton
Shottisham
Hollesley
Hollesley Bay
Shingle Street
Alderton
Bawdsey
Bawdsey Manor
Felixstowe Ferry
Felixstowe
Trimley St Martin
Trimley St Mary
Kirton
Falkenham
Nacton
Levington
Martlesham
Martlesham Heath
Rushmere St Andrew
Kesgrave
Westerfield
Claydon
IPSWICH
Belstead
Wherstead
Freston
Woolverstone
Pin Mill
Chelmondiston
Holbrook
Tattingstone
Alton Water Reservoir
Stutton
Harkstead
Erwarton
Shotley
Shotley Gate
Harwich Harbour
Harwich
Landguard Point
Parkeston
Ramsey
Dovercourt
Mistley
New Mistley
Wrabness
Bradfield
Bradfield Heath
Wix
Little Oakley
Great Oakley
Stone Point
Horsey Island
The Naze
Walton on the Naze
Thorpe-le-Soken
Kirby le Soken
Kirby Cross
Frinton-on-Sea
Great Holland
Weeley
Weeley Heath
Little Clacton
Sandy Point
CLACTON-ON-SEA
St Osyth
Jaywick
Seawick
Gunfleet Sand
hours
Esbjerg..............................19
Hook of Holland......3³/₄-6¹/₄

A
B
C
D
E
46
1
2
3
4
5
6
7
54
51
49
52
53
LLEYN PENINSULA (PEN LLŶN)
TREMADOG BAY
CARDIGAN BAY (BAE CEREDIGION)
Pontllyfni
Trwyn Maen Dylan
Aberdesach
Talysarn
Llanllyfni
Nebo
Nasareth
Pant Glas
Garneddgoch
Craig Cwm Silyn
Beddgelert Forest
Gyrn Goch
Bwlch Mawr
Gyrn Ddu
Bwlch-derwin
Trefor
Trwyn y Gorlech
Yr Eifl
Llanaelhaearn
Llithfaen
Garndolbenmaen
Dolbenmaen
Golan
Cennin
Bryncir
Glan-Dwyfach
Pen-sarn
Cefn-caer-Ferch
Pencaenewydd
Llangybi
Llanarmon
Carreg Ddu
Porth Dinllaen
Pistyll
Morfa Nefyn
Nefyn
Edern
Groesffordd
Garn Boduan
Tan-y-graig
Ceidio Fawr
Hendre
Boduan
Fron
Llwyndyrys
Rhos-fawr
Y Ffôr
Chwilog
Llanystumdwy
Criccieth
Pentrefelin
Wern
Penmorfa
Tremadog
Moel-y-Gest
Porthmadog
Morfa Bychan
Borth-y-Gest
Black Rock Sands
Harlech Point
Morfa Harlech
Porth Ysgaden
Rhos-y-llan
Tudweiliog
Llannor
Abererch
Afon Wen
Penychain Sta
Pen-ychain
Efailnewydd
Denio
Pwllheli
Carreg yr Imbill
Dinas
Carn Fadryn
Garnfadryn
Rhyd-y-clafdy
Porth Colmon
Penllech
Porth Colmon
Pen-y-Graig
Bryn-mawr
Llaniestyn
Llangwnnadl
Penrhyn Mawr
Sarn Meyllteyrn
Penrhos
Ty-hen
Bryncroes
Botwnnog
Rhedyn
Nanhoron
Llanbedrog
Y Gamlas
Methlem
Rhydlios
Llandegwning
Mynytho
Trwyn Llanbedrog
Porth Oer
Capel Carmel
Mynydd Rhiw
Rhoshirwaun
Rhiw
Llangian
Abersoch
Braich Anelog
Llawr-y-dref
Mynydd Anelog
Anelog
Rhydolion
Llanengan
St Tudwal's Road
Pwlldefaid
Aberdaron
Llanfaelrhys
Sarn Bach
Bwlchtocyn
Porth Neigwl (Hell's Mouth)
Braich y Pwll
Aberdaron Bay
St Tudwal's Islands
Uwchmynydd
Ynys Gwylan-fawr
Porth Ceiriad
Trwyn yr Wylfa
Pen y Cil
Cilan Uchaf
Trwyn Cilan
Bardsey Island (Ynys Enlli)
Bardsey Sound (Swnt Enlli)
Llandanwg
Coed Ystumgwern
Dyffryn Ardudwy
Llanddwywe
Tal-y-bont
Barmouth (Bae Bermo)
Llangelynin
Rhoslefain
Llanfendigaid
Tonfanau
Aber Dysynni
Tywyn
Aberdyfi
Sarn Cynfelyn
Aberystwyth
The Bar
Rhydyfelin
Allt Wen
A487
A499
A497
B4417
B4354
B4413
B4415
B4411
0 2 4 6 miles
0 2 4 6 8 10 km

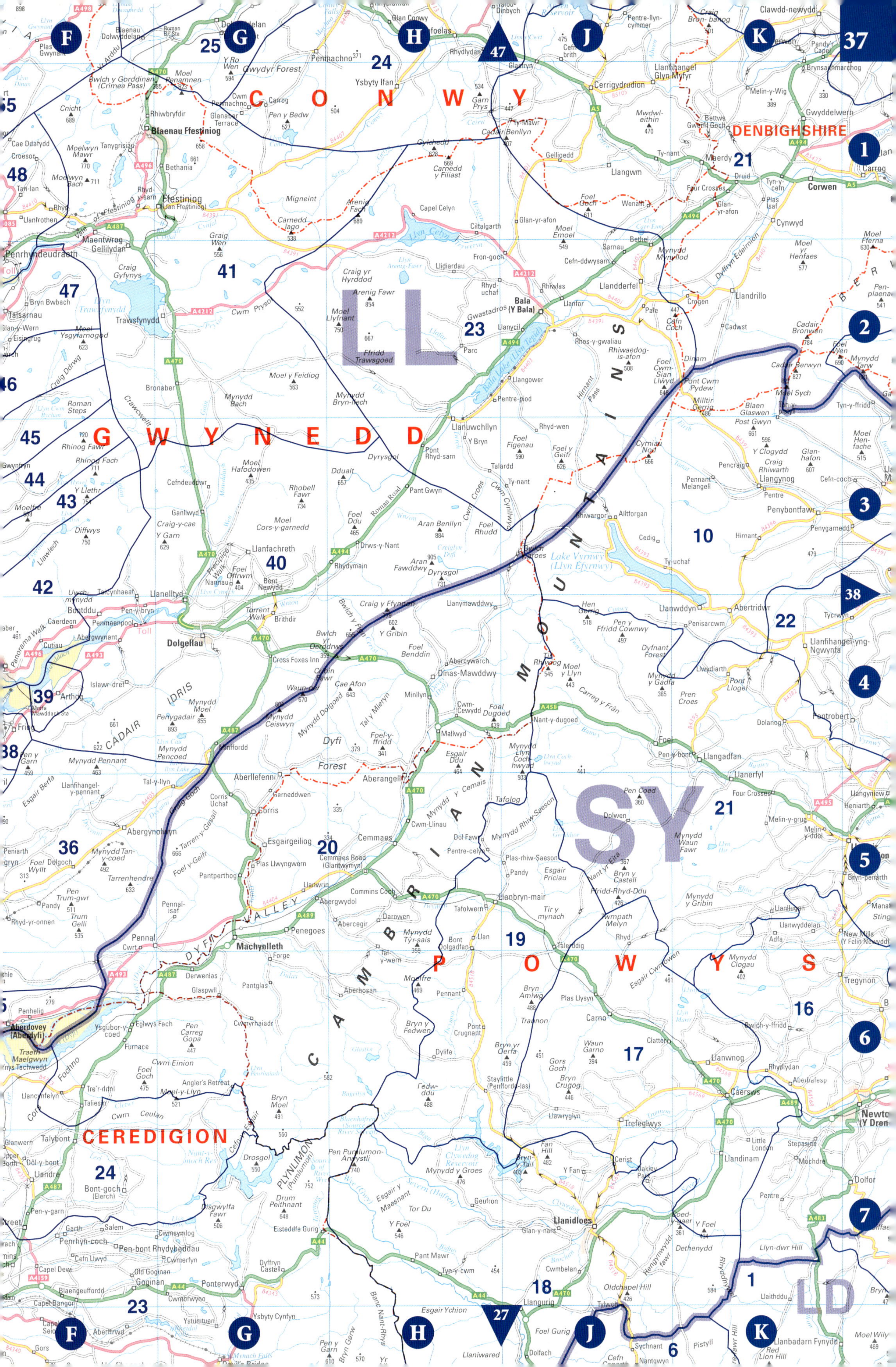
CONWY
GWYNEDD
DENBIGHSHIRE
POWYS
CEREDIGION
LL
SY
LD
CAMBRIAN MOUNTAINS
BERWYN
CADAIR IDRIS
DYFI VALLEY
Dyfi Forest
PLYNLIMON (Pumlumon)
F
G
H
J
K
1
2
3
4
5
6
7
47
27
38
Dolwyddelan
Blaenau Dolwyddelan
Roman Br Sta
Pentrefoelas
Glan Conwy
Dinbych
Alwen Reservoir
Pentre-llyn-cymmer
Craig Bron-banog
Clawdd-newydd
Gwydyr Forest
Pentrachno
Ysbyty Ifan
Rhydlydan
Glasfryn
Cerrigydrudion
Llanfihangel Glyn Myfyr
Brynsaithmarchog
Melin-y-Wig
Bwlch y Gorddinan (Crimea Pass)
Moel Penamnen
Cwm Penmachno
Carrog
Pen y Bedw
Garn Prys
Ty-Mawr
Cadair Benllyn
Mwdwl-eithin
Bettws Gwerfil Goch
Gwyddelwern
Cnicht
Rhiwbryfdir
Blaenau Ffestiniog
Glanaber Terrace
Cylchedd
Carnedd y Filiast
Gellioedd
Llangwm
Ty-nant
Maerdy
Druid
Corwen
Carrog
Cae Ddafydd
Croesor
Moelwyn Mawr
Tanygrisiau
Bethania
Moelwyn Bach
Tan-lan
Rhyd-y-sarn
Ffestiniog (Llan Ffestiniog)
Migneint
Arenig Fach
Capel Celyn
Foel Goch
Wenallt
Four Crosses
Glan-yr-afon
Tyn-y-cefn
Plas Isaf
Cynwyd
Rhyd
Llanfrothen
Vale of Ffestiniog
Maentwrog
Gellilydan
Carnedd Iago
Llyn Celyn
Ciltalgarth
Glan-yr-afon
Moel Emoel
Sarnau
Bethel
Mynydd Mynyllod
Moel yr Henfaes
Moel Fferna
Penrhyndeudraeth
Graig Wen
Fron-goch
Cefn-ddwysarn
Dyffryn Edeirnion
Craig Gyfynys
Lidiardau
Craig yr Hyrddod
Arenig Fawr
Rhyd-uchaf
Rhiwlas
Llandderfel
Llandrillo
Pen-plaenau
Bryn Bwbach
Trawsfynydd
Cwm Prysor
Llanfor
Crogen
Bala (Y Bala)
Talsarnau
Glan-y-Wern
Eisingrug
Ysgyfarnogod
Moel Llyfnant
Gwastadros
Llanycil
Rhos-y-gwaliau
Cefn Coch
Palé
Cadwst
Cadair Bronwen
Ffridd Trawsgoed
Parc
Bala Lake (Llyn Tegid)
Rhiwaedog-is-afon
Dinam
Cadair Berwyn
Moel Wen
Mynydd Tarw
Craig Ddrwg
Moel y Feidiog
Llangower
Foel Cwm-Sian Llwyd
Pont Cwm Pydew
Moel Sych
Bronaber
Crawcwellt
Mynydd Bach
Mynydd Bryn-llech
Pentre-piod
Hirnant Pass
Milltir Gerrig
Blaen Glaswen
Tyn-y-ffridd
Roman Steps
Llanuwchllyn
Rhyd-wen
Post Gwyn
Rhinog Fawr
Pont Rhyd-sarn
Y Bryn
Foel Figenau
Foel y Geifr
Cyrniau Nod
Y Clogydd
Glan-hafon
Moel Hen-fache
Rhinog Fach
Moel Hafodowen
Dyrysgol
Talardd
Pencraig
Craig Rhiwarth
Llangynog
Cefn-coch
Y Llethr
Cefndeuddwr
Dduallt
Rhobell Fawr
Pant Gwyn
Ty-nant
Pennant Melangell
Pentre
Moelfre
Roman Road
Cwm Cynllwyd
Croes
Penybontfawr
Ganllwyd
Craig-y-cae
Moel Cors-y-garnedd
Foel Ddu
Aran Benllyn
Foel Rhudd
Rhiwargor
Alltforgan
Cedig
Hirnant
Penygarnedd
Diffwys
Y Garn
Llanfachreth
Drws-y-Nant
Bwlch y Groes
Lake Vyrnwy (Llyn Efyrnwy)
Ty-uchaf
Llawlech
Precipice Walk
Foel Offrwm
Aran Fawddwy
Dyrysgol
Rhydymain
Nannau
Bont Newydd
Uwch-mynydd
Tal-cynhaeaf
Llanelltyd
Craig y Ffynnon
Llanymawddwy
Hen Gerrig
Llanwddyn
Abertridwr
Tycrwyn
Bontddu
Pen-y-bryn
Torrent Walk
Brithdir
Penisarcwm
Pen y Ffridd Cownwy
Llanfihangel-yng-Ngwynfa
Caerdeon
Penmaenpool
Panorama Walk
Abergwynant
Toll
Dolgellau
Bwlch yr Oerddrws
Y Gribin
Foel Benddin
Dyfnant Forest
Cutiau
Cross Foxes Inn
Aberrywarch
Dinas-Mawddwy
Rhiwarog
Moel y Llyn
Mynydd y Gadfa
Llwydiarth
Pont Llogel
Arthog
Islawr-dref
Craig Fawr
Cae Afon
Waun-oer
Minllyn
Carreg y Frân
Pren Croes
Mawddach Sta
Friog
Mynydd Moel
Penygadair
Mynydd Ceiswyn
Mynydd Dolgoed
Tal-y-Mieryn
Cwm-Cewydd
Foel Dugoed
Nant-y-dugoed
Pentrobert
Dolanog
Mallwyd
Foel-y-ffridd
Esgair Ddu
Mynydd Llyn Coch-hwyad
Foel
Pen-y-bont
Llangadfan
Pen y Garn
Mynydd Pencoed
Mynydd Pennant
Minffordd
Aberllefenni
Aberangell
Llanerfyl
Llanfihangel-y-pennant
Tal-y-llyn
Llyn Coch-hwyad
Pen Coed
Four Crosses
Llangyniew
Esgair Berfa
Corris Uchaf
Garneddwen
Tafolog
Dolwen
Heniarth
Corris
Craig Goch
Mynydd y Cemais
Mynydd Rhiw-Saeson
Melin-y-grug
Abergynolwyn
Cwm-Llinau
Dol Fawr
Melin-y-ddôl
Tarren-y-Gesail
Esgairgeiliog
Cemmaes
Pentre-celyn
Mynydd Waun Fawr
Peniarth
Mynydd Tan-y-coed
Foel Dolgoch
Foel Wyllt
Tarrenhendre
Foel y Geifr
Cemmaes Road (Glantwymyn)
Plas Llwyngwern
Plas-rhiw-Saeson
Pandy
Esgair Priciau
Nant yr Eira
Bryn y Castell
Bryn-penarth
Pantperthog
Llanwrin
Commins Coch
Llanbryn-mair
Fridd-Rhyd-Ddu
Mynydd y Gribin
Pen Trum-gwr
Trum Gelli
Pennal-isaf
Abergwydol
Tafolwern
Tir y mynach
Wmpath Melyn
Llanllugan
Pandy
Rhyd-yr-onnen
Darowen
Abercegir
Penegoes
Mynydd Tyr-sais
Bont Dolgadfan
Llan
Rhyd
Llanwyddelan
Pennal
Cwrt
Machynlleth
Forge
Tal-y-wern
Talerddig
Adfa
New Mills (Y Felin Newydd)
Mynydd Clogau
Esgair Cwmowen
Tregynon
Derwenlas
Pantglas
Moelfre
Pennant
Bryn Amlwg
Plas Llysyn
Glaspwll
Aberhosan
Trannon
Carno
Bwlch-y-ffridd
Penhelig
Aberdovey (Aberdyfi)
Ysgubor-y-coed
Eglwys Fach
Cwmyrhaiadr
Pen Carreg Gopa
Bryn y Fedwen
Pont Crugnant
Dylife
Bryn yr Oerfa
Waun Garno
Gors Goch
Clatter
Traeth Maelgwyn
Ynys Tachwedd
Furnace
Cwm Einion
Llanwnog
Rhydlydan
Aberhafesp
Fochno
Foel Goch
Angler's Retreat
Staylittle (Penffordd-las)
Bryn Crugog
Caersws
Llancynfelyn
Tre'r-ddôl
Taliesin
Moel-y-Llyn
Fedw-ddu
Llawryglyn
Trefeglwys
Newtown (Y Drenewydd)
Cors
Cwm
Ceulan
Bryn Moel
Glanwern
Talybont
Blaenhafren Source of River Severn
Fan Hill
Little London
Stepaside
Dôl-y-bont
Llandre
Bont-goch (Elerch)
Nant-y-moch Reservoir
Drosgol
Pen Pumlumon-Arwystli
Llyn Clywedog Reservoir
Mynydd y Groes
Bryn-y-Tail
Cerist
Y Fan
Oakley Park
Llandinam
Mochdre
Dolfor
Pen-y-garn
Disgwylfa Fawr
Drum Peithnant
Esgair y Maesnant
Severn (Hafren)
Geufron
Pentre
Tor Du
Llanidloes
Coed-y-gaer
Y Foel
Salem
Garth
Cwmsymlog
Penrhyn-coch
Eisteddfa Gurig
Y Foel
Glan-y-nant
Hengynwydd-fawr
Dethenydd
Llyn-dwr Hill
Pen-bont Rhydybeddau
Cefn Llwyd
Cwmerfyn
Capel Dewi
Old Goginan
Goginan
Dyffryn Castell
Pant Mawr
Tyn-y-cwm
Cwmbelan
Oldchapel Hill
Rhydyfelin
Blaengeuffordd
Ponterwyd
Cwmbrwyno
Llangurig
Tylwch
Llaithddu
Capel Bangor
Ysbyty Cynfyn
Esgair Ychion
Ystumtuen
Aberffrwd
Banc Nant-Rhys
Foel Gurig
Sychnant
Pistyll
Llanbadarn Fynydd
Moel Wily
Gors
Pen y Garn
Bryn Garw
Llaniwared
Dolfach
Cefn
Nantgwyn
Red Lion Hill
Devil's Bridge
A5
A494
A470
A487
A496
A4212
A458
A489
A493
A483
A495
A44
A4159
B4391
B4401
B4402
B4393
B4396
B4395
B4404
B4518
B4569
B4568
B4343
B4340
B4353
B4405
B4407
B4410

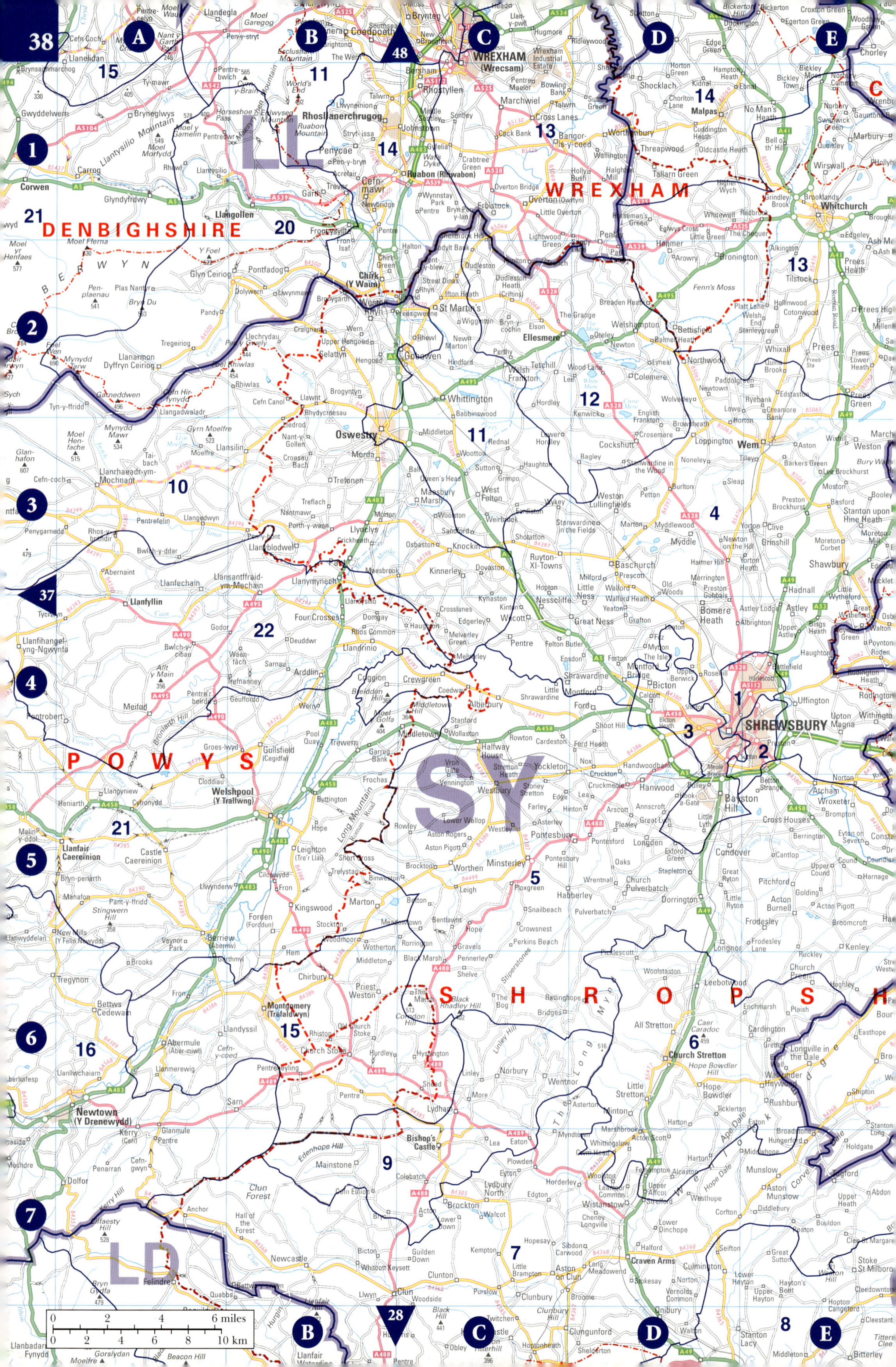
38
48
37
28
A
B
C
D
E
1
2
3
4
5
6
7
LL
SY
LD
DENBIGHSHIRE
WREXHAM
POWYS
SHROPSHIRE
WREXHAM (Wrecsam)
Corwen
Llangollen
Chirk (Y Waun)
Oswestry
Ellesmere
Whitchurch
Malpas
Wem
SHREWSBURY
Welshpool (Y Trallwng)
Llanfair Caereinion
Montgomery (Trefaldwyn)
Newtown (Y Drenewydd)
Bishop's Castle
Church Stretton
Clun
Llanfyllin
Ruabon (Rhiwabon)
Rhosllanerchrugog
Overton (Owrtyn)
Gobowen
Pontesbury
Minsterley
Chirbury
Lydbury North
Craven Arms
B E R W Y N
Clun Forest
Long Mountain
The Long Mynd
Wenlock Edge
0 2 4 6 miles
0 2 4 6 8 10 km

F
G
H
J
K
49
40
29
STOKE-ON-TRENT
NEWCASTLE-UNDER-LYME
STAFFORDSHIRE
STAFFORD
Stone
Uttoxeter
Cheadle
Market Drayton
Eccleshall
Newport
TELFORD & WREKIN
TELFORD
Shifnal
Penkridge
CANNOCK
Rugeley
Hednesford
LICHFIELD
Burntwood
Brownhills
Aldridge
WOLVERHAMPTON
WALSALL
WEST MIDLANDS
WEST BROMWICH
DUDLEY
OLDBURY
SMETHWICK
BIRMIN
STOURBRIDGE
HALESOWEN
KIDDERMINSTER
Bridgnorth
Broseley
Albrighton
Codsall
Wombourne
See pages 114 - 115 for postcode detail
CW
ST
TF
WS
WV
DY
DE

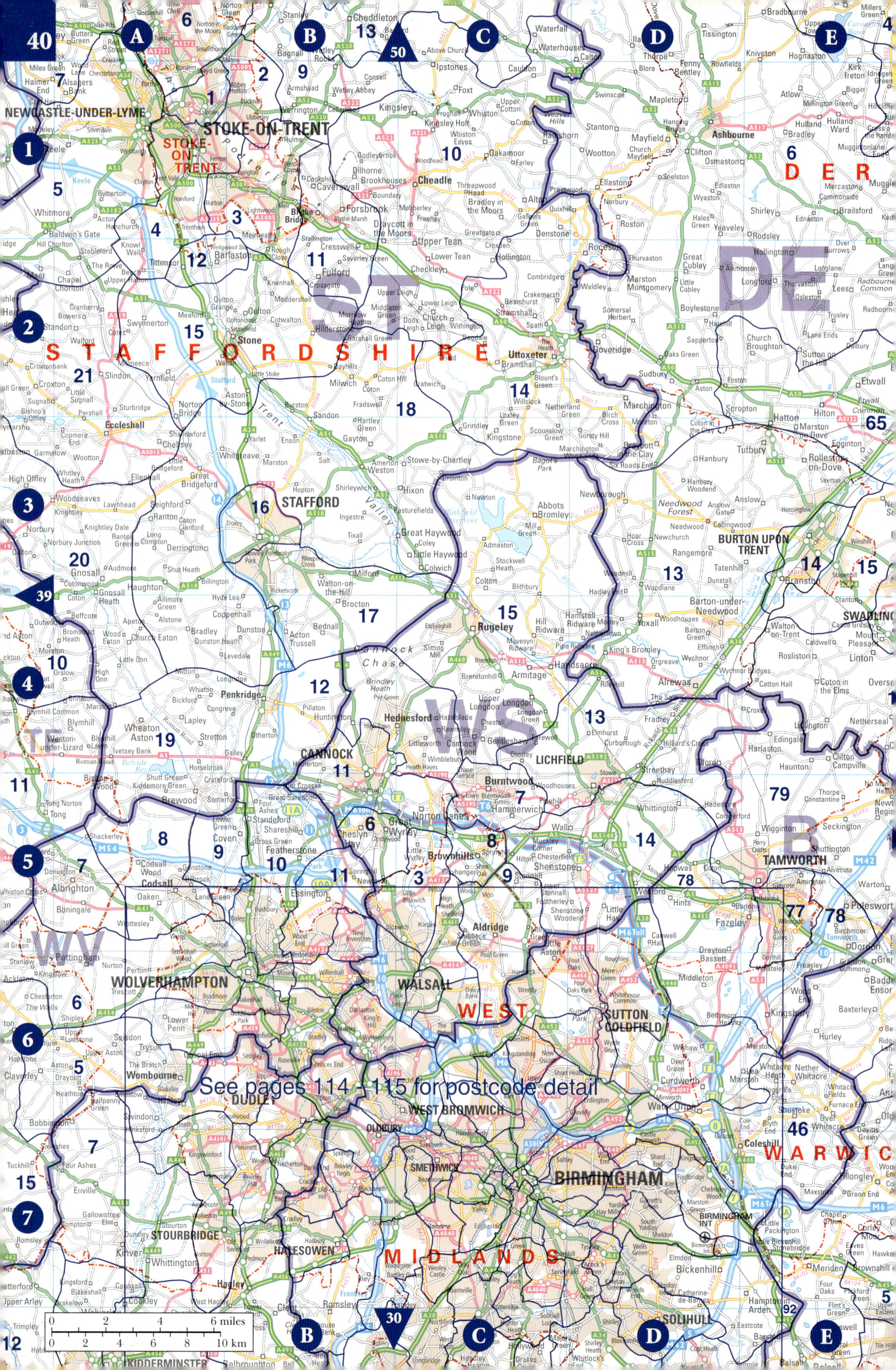
NEWCASTLE-UNDER-LYME
STOKE-ON-TRENT
STAFFORDSHIRE
Cheadle
Ashbourne
Stone
Uttoxeter
Eccleshall
STAFFORD
BURTON UPON TRENT
Penkridge
Rugeley
CANNOCK
Hednesford
LICHFIELD
Burntwood
TAMWORTH
Brownhills
Aldridge
WOLVERHAMPTON
WALSALL
SUTTON COLDFIELD
WEST MIDLANDS
See pages 114 - 115 for postcode detail
DUDLEY
WEST BROMWICH
OLDBURY
SMETHWICK
BIRMINGHAM
Coleshill
WARWIC
BIRMINGHAM INT
STOURBRIDGE
HALESOWEN
SOLIHULL
KIDDERMINSTER
0 2 4 6 miles
0 2 4 6 8 10 km

NOTTINGHAM
NOTTINGHAMSHIRE
NG
DERBY
SHIRE
LEICESTER
LEICESTERSHIRE
LE
CV
NN
NORTHANTS
LOUGHBOROUGH
MELTON MOWBRAY
COALVILLE
HINCKLEY
NUNEATON
WIGSTON
Oadby
Market Harborough
Market Bosworth
Ashby de la Zouch
Ilkeston
Beeston
West Bridgford
Long Eaton
Hucknall
Arnold
Carlton
Bingham
Ripley
Heanor
Belper
Eastwood
Kimberley
Stapleford
Sandiacre
Shepshed
Syston
Narborough
Lutterworth
Bedworth
Atherstone
Melbourne
Castle Donington
NOTTINGHAM EAST MIDLANDS
Ruddington
Keyworth
Radcliffe on Trent
Cotgrave
Quorn
Sileby
Mountsorrel
Rothley
Anstey
Groby
Desford
Earl Shilton
Barwell
Broughton Astley
Countesthorpe
Whetstone
Blaby
Enderby
Braunstone
Kibworth Harcourt
Fleckney
Great Glen
Husbands Bosworth
Burbage
Hathern
Kegworth
Ibstock
Measham
Swadlincote
Bottesford
Asfordby
Desborough
Rothwell
F
G
H
J
K
51
31
42
25
24
23
1
2
3
4
5
6
7

NOTTS
LINCOLNSHIRE
RUTLAND
LEICESTERSHIRE
NORTHAMPTONSHIRE
PETERBOROUGH
NG
LE
NN
GRANTHAM
Sleaford
Bingham
MELTON MOWBRAY
Oakham
Uppingham
Stamford
Bourne
Market Deeping
CORBY
Market Harborough
Desborough
Rothwell
KETTERING
Oundle
Thrapston
Rutland Water
Vale of Belvoir
Vale of Catmose
Bottesford
Ancaster
Colsterworth
Castle Bytham
Cottesmore
Empingham
Ketton
Wansford
Kings Cliffe
Rockingham
Weldon
Brigstock
Islip
Woodford
Great Oxendon
Braybrooke
Hallaton
Billesdon
Tilton on the Hill
Leadenham
Cranwell
Ruskington
Heckington
Helpringham
Folkingham
Billingborough
Corby Glen
Swayfield
Morton
Thurlby
Langtoft
Deeping St James
Alwalton
Winwick
Upton
Alconbury Weston
Old Weston
A1
A6
A17
A15
A47
A43
A52
A606
A607
A6003
A151
A153
A427
A6116
A14
0 2 4 6 miles
0 2 4 6 8 10 km
24
52
13
31
32
33
34
14
10
9
15
17
16
18
8
5
7
41
A
B
C
D
E
1
2
3
4
5
6
7

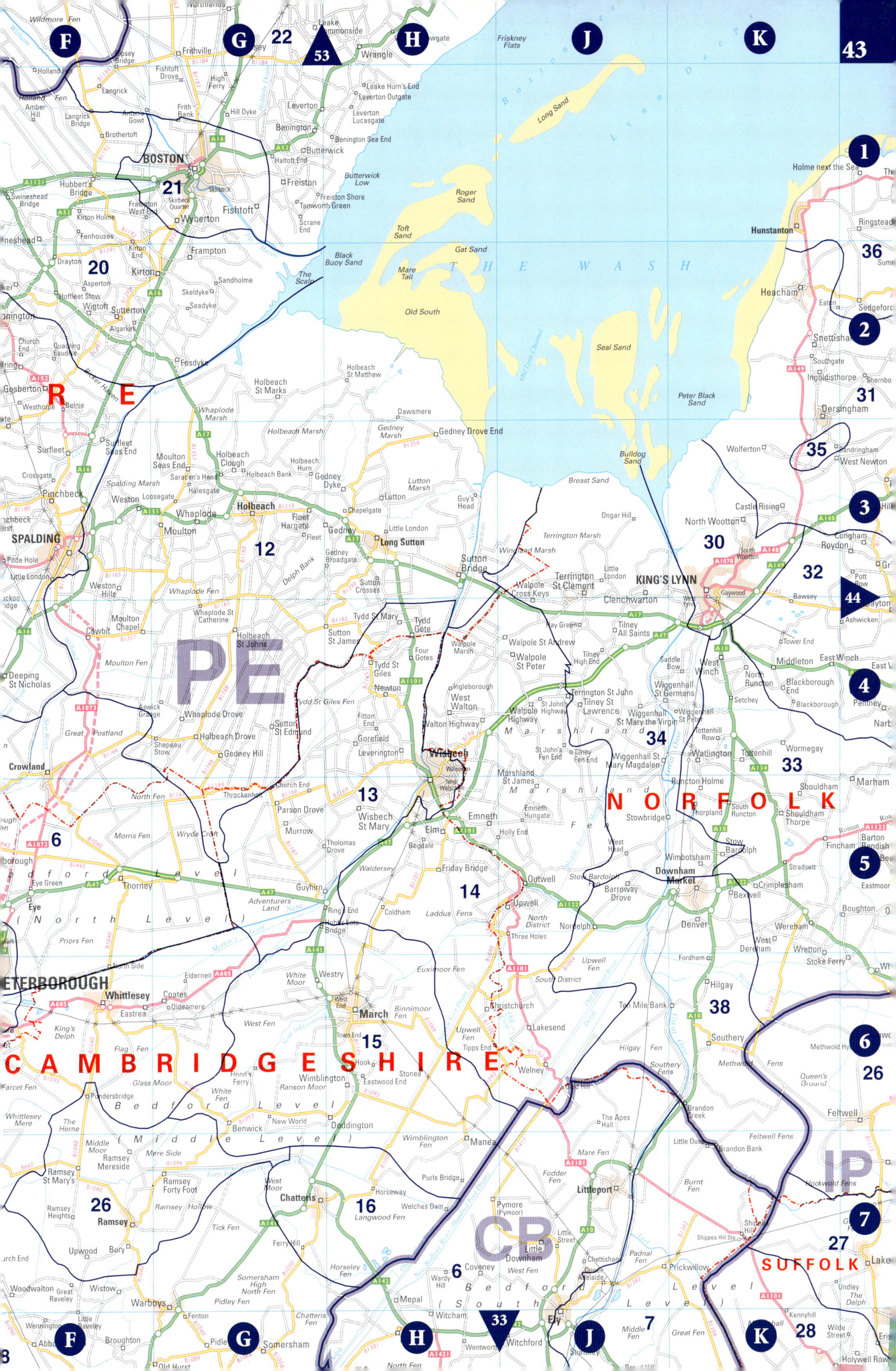

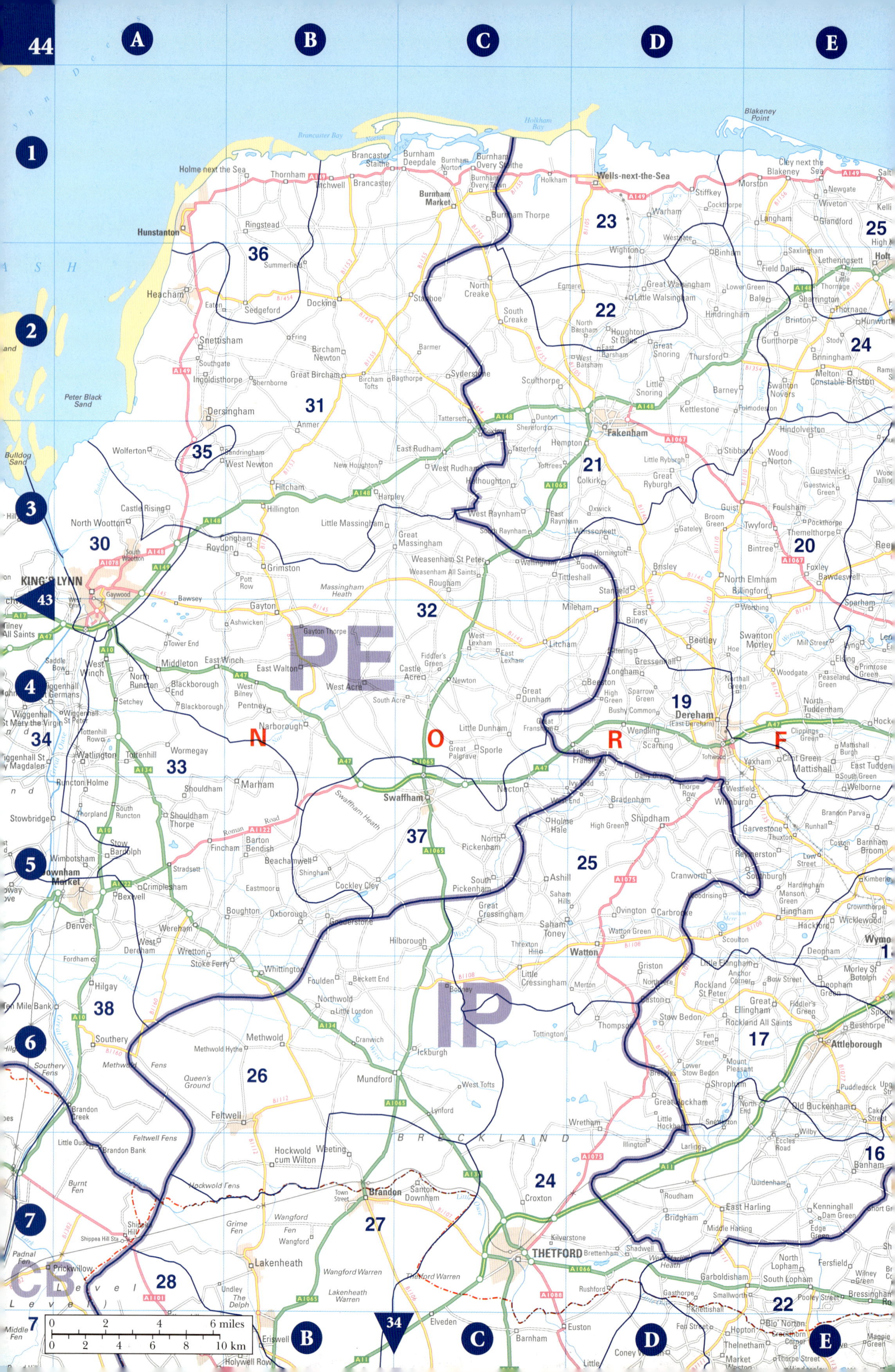
A
B
C
D
E
1
2
3
4
5
6
7
Brancaster Bay
Holkham Bay
Blakeney Point
Holme next the Sea
Thornham
Titchwell
Brancaster
Brancaster Staithe
Burnham Deepdale
Burnham Norton
Burnham Overy Staithe
Burnham Overy Town
Burnham Market
Burnham Thorpe
Holkham
Wells-next-the-Sea
Stiffkey
Cockthorpe
Morston
Blakeney
Cley next the Sea
Salt
Newgate
Wiveton
Kelli
Glandford
Langham
Hunstanton
Ringstead
36
Summerfield
Heacham
Sedgeford
Docking
Stanhoe
North Creake
South Creake
Egmere
Great Walsingham
Little Walsingham
Wighton
Binham
Warham
Westgate
23
22
Field Dalling
Saxlingham
Letheringsett
Holt
25
Bale
Lower Green
Hindringham
Sharrington
Thornage
Little Thornage
Brinton
Hunworth
Gunthorpe
Stody
24
Briningham
Melton Constable
Briston
Swanton Novers
Snettisham
Fring
Bircham Newton
Barmer
Southgate
Ingoldisthorpe
Shernborne
Great Bircham
Bircham Tofts
Bagthorpe
Syderstone
Sculthorpe
North Barsham
Houghton St Giles
East Barsham
West Barsham
Great Snoring
Thursford
Little Snoring
Barney
Kettlestone
Fulmodeston
Peter Black Sand
Dersingham
31
Anmer
Tattersett
Dunton
Shereford
Fakenham
Hempton
Tatterford
Toftrees
Hindolveston
Wolferton
35
Sandringham
West Newton
East Rudham
West Rudham
New Houghton
Helhoughton
21
Colkirk
Little Ryburgh
Great Ryburgh
Stibbard
Wood Norton
Guestwick
Guestwick Green
Bulldog Sand
Flitcham
Harpley
Castle Rising
Hillington
West Raynham
East Raynham
Oxwick
Guist
Foulsham
Broom Green
Pockthorpe
Themelthorpe
North Wootton
30
Little Massingham
South Raynham
Whissonsett
Gateley
Twyford
Bintree
20
Congham
Roydon
South Wootton
Great Massingham
Horningtoft
Reepham
KING'S LYNN
Gaywood
Pott Row
Grimston
Weasenham St Peter
Weasenham All Saints
Godwick
Tittleshall
Brisley
Foxley
Bawdeswell
43
Bawsey
Massingham Heath
Rougham
Stanfield
North Elmham
Billingford
Gayton
32
Mileham
East Bilney
Worthing
Sparham
Tilney All Saints
Ashwicken
Gayton Thorpe
PE
West Lexham
East Lexham
Litcham
Beetley
Swanton Morley
Mill Street
Lyng
Tower End
Fiddler's Green
Castle Acre
Newton
Gressenhall
Hoe
Elsing
Primrose Green
Saddle Bow
West Winch
Middleton
East Winch
East Walton
Longham
Beeston
Woodgate
Peaseland Green
North Runcton
Blackborough End
Blackborough
West Bilney
Pentney
West Acre
South Acre
Great Dunham
High Green
Sparrow Green
Bushy Common
19
Northall Green
Dereham (East Dereham)
North Tuddenham
Wiggenhall St Germans
Wiggenhall St Mary the Virgin
Wiggenhall St Peter
Setchey
Narborough
Little Dunham
Great Fransham
Wendling
Scarning
Clippings Green
Hockering
Tottenhill Row
34
Watlington
Tottenhill
Wormegay
N
O
R
F
Great Palgrave
Sporle
Little Fransham
Toftwood
Yaxham
Clint Green
Mattishall Burgh
Mattishall
East Tuddenham
Wiggenhall St Mary Magdalen
33
Marham
Swaffham
Necton
Ivy Todd
Dale Green
Thorpe Row
Westfield
South Green
Welborne
Runcton Holme
Shouldham
Swaffham Heath
West End
Bradenham
Whinburgh
Stowbridge
Thorplands
South Runcton
Shouldham Thorpe
Roman Road
Holme Hale
High Green
Shipdham
Garvestone
Thuxton
Runhall
Brandon Parva
Stow Bardolph
Fincham
Barton Bendish
37
North Pickenham
25
Reymerston
Coston
Barnham Broom
Wimbotsham
Downham Market
Stradsett
Beachamwell
Shingham
Ashill
Cranworth
Southburgh
Low Street
Kimberley
Crimplesham
Bexwell
Eastmoor
Cockley Cley
South Pickenham
Saham Hills
Woodrising
Hardingham
Manson Green
Hingham
Crownthorpe
Wicklewood
Denver
Boughton
Oxborough
Gooderstone
Great Cressingham
Ovington
Carbrooke
Scoulton Mere
Hackford
Wereham
West Dereham
Wretton
Saham Toney
Watton Green
Scoulton
Wymondham
Fordham
Stoke Ferry
Hilborough
Threxton Hill
Watton
Deopham
Hilgay
38
Whittington
Beckett End
Fouldon
Little Cressingham
Griston
Little Ellingham
Anchor Corner
Morley St Botolph
Ten Mile Bank
Northwold
Little London
Bodney
IP
Merton
North Acre
Bow Street
Rockland St Peter
Deopham Green
Caston
Great Ellingham
Fiddler's Green
Stow Bedon
Spooner Row
Southery
Methwold
Cranwich
Thompson
Rockland All Saints
Besthorpe
Attleborough
17
Methwold Hythe
Ickburgh
Tottington
Fen Street
Southery Fens
Methwold
Fens
Queen's Ground
26
Mundford
West Tofts
Mount Pleasant
Lower Stow Bedon
Breckles
Shropham
Puddledock
Brandon Creek
Feltwell
Lynford
Great Hockham
Little Hockham
North End
Old Buckenham
Cake Street
Snetterton
Wilby
Little Ouse
Feltwell Fens
Brandon Bank
Hockwold cum Wilton
Weeting
B R E C K L A N D
Wretham
Illington
Larling
Eccles Road
16
Banham
Burnt Fen
Hockwold Fens
Town Street
Brandon
Santon Downham
24
Croxton
Quidenham
Roudham
East Harling
Kenninghall
Dam Green
Short Green
Shippea Hill
Shippea Hill Sta
Grime Fen
Wangford Fen
Wangford
27
Kilverstone
Bridgham
Middle Harling
Edge Green
THETFORD
Brettenham
Shadwell
West Harling Heath
North Lopham
Fersfield
Padnal Fen
Prickwillow
CB
28
Lakenheath
Wangford Warren
Thetford Warren
Garboldisham
South Lopham
Wilney Green
Level
Undley
The Delph
Lakenheath Warren
Rushford
Gasthorpe
Smallworth
Knettishall
22
Pooley Street
Bressingham
Middle Fen
Eriswell
34
Elveden
Barnham
Euston
Fen Street
Hopton
Blo' Norton
Thelnetham
Market Weston
Thorpe Street
Holywell Row
Coney Weston
Maggie Green
0 2 4 6 miles
0 2 4 6 8 10 km

F
G
H
J
K
1
2
3
4
5
6
7
Sheringham
West Runton
East Runton
Cromer
Overstrand
Sidestrand
Trimingham
Northrepps
Southrepps
Mundesley
Aylmerton
Gresham
Roughton
Bacton
Keswick
Walcott
Happisburgh
North Walsham
Eccles-on-Sea
Sea Palling
Waxham
Aylsham
Cawston
Stalham
Hickling
Hickling Green
Horsey
Winterton-on-Sea
Hemsby
Martham
Ormesby St Margaret
Caister-on-Sea
Coltishall
Wroxham
Hoveton
Horning
NORFOLK
BROADS
NR
Taverham
Costessey
Hellesdon
NORWICH
NORWICH INTERNATIONAL
Acle
Blofield
Brundall
Cringleford
Hethersett
Poringland
Loddon
GREAT YARMOUTH
Gorleston-on-Sea
Belton
Hopton
Corton
Lowestoft Ness
LOWESTOFT
Carlton Colville
Kessingland
Kessingland Beach
Beccles
Bungay
Harleston
Long Stratton
Diss
Halesworth
Wrentham
Reydon
SUFFOLK
O
L
K
26
27
11
28
12
10
29
8
6
3
7
5
2
1
4
13
30
14
31
15
32
35
33
34
20
19
21
18

A
B
C
D
E
1
2
3
4
5
6
7
The Skerries
West Mouse
Middle Mouse
Carmel Head
Bull Bay (Porth Llechog)
Point Lynas
Amlwch
Cemaes
Llanbadrig
Tregele
Llanfairynghornwy
Llaneilian
Ynys Dulas
HOLYHEAD BAY
hours
Dublin............1¾-3¼
Dún Laoghaire......1¾
ISLE OF
ANGLESEY
ANGLESEY
(YNYS MON)
Moelfre
Benllech
Red Wharf Bay
Puffin Island (Priestholm)
Penmon
North Stack
Holyhead Mountain
Holyhead (Caergybi)
Salt Island
South Stack
Penrhyn Mawr
HOLY ISLAND
Trearddur
Four Mile Bridge
Rhoscolyn
Valley
Llangefni
Llanddona
Llangoed
Beaumaris (Biwmares)
Dutchman Bank
Lavan Sands
Llanfairfechan
Rhosneigr
Aberffraw
Malltraeth
Newborough (Niwbwrch)
Newborough Warren
Llanddwyn Island
Abermenai Point
Llanfairpwllgwyngyll
Menai Bridge (Porthaethwy)
Bangor
Port Penrhyn
Llandygai
Tal-y-bont
Bethesda
Y Felinheli
Caernarfon
Llanberis
Llanrug
Dinas Dinlle
Llandwrog
Penygroes
Pontllyfni
Trwyn Maen Dylan
Aberdesach
CAERNARFON BAY
GWYNEDD
SNOWDONIA (ERYRI)
Snowdon (Yr Wyddfa)
Beddgelert
Beddgelert Forest
Nant Peris
Pass of Llanberis
Glyder Fach
Pen-y-Pass
Yr Aran
Plas Gwynant
Rhyd-Ddu
Moel Tryfan
Mynydd Mawr
Garneddgoch
Pant Glas
Bwlch Mawr
Trefor
67
68
66
69
70
72
73
74
71
78
76
75
58
65
77
59
64
63
62
60
56
61
57
55
54
36
41
0 2 4 6 miles
0 2 4 6 8 10 km

Birkenhead to    hours
Belfast.....................8
Dublin.......................8
Liverpool to     hours
Douglas..............2½-4
Dublin.......................8

LIVERPOOL BAY

A
B
C
D
E
1
2
3
4
5
6
7
55
47
38
SOUTHPORT
Formby
Formby Point
Hightown
CROSBY
BOOTLE
LITHERLAND
LIVERPOOL
WALLASEY
BIRKENHEAD
BEBINGTON
Hoylake
West Kirby
Heswall
Neston
ORMSKIRK
Maghull
Kirkby
Knowsley
HUYTON
ST HELENS
Prescot
WIGAN
Skelmersdale
CHORLEY
LEYLAND
Standish
Newton-le-Willows
WIDNES
RUNCORN
HALTON
Frodsham
ELLESMERE PORT
CHESTER
Connah's Quay
Shotton
Queensferry
Flint (Y Fflint)
Holywell (Treffynnon)
Mold (Yr Wyddgrug)
Buckley (Bwcle)
WREXHAM
WREXHAM (Wrecsam)
Ruthin (Rhuthun)
Talacre
Point of Ayr
Mostyn
Hilbre Island
LIVERPOOL JOHN LENNON
L A N C A S H I R E
M E R S E Y S I D E
FLINTSHIRE
DENBIGHSHIRE
CHESHIRE
WEST & CHESTER
PR
WN
L
CH
WA
LL
SY
LIVERPOOL BAY
Birkenhead to hours
Belfast 8
Dublin 8
Liverpool to hours
Douglas 2½-4
Dublin 8
See page 120 for postcode detail
0 2 4 6 miles
0 2 4 6 8 10 km

49
50
56
39
See pages 116 - 117 for postcode detail
BLACKBURN WITH DARWEN
GREATER MANCHESTER
WARRINGTON
WEST YORKS
DERBYSHIRE
CHESHIRE EAST
STAFFS
BL
OL
HX
HD
WA
SK
CW
ST
DE
S
BOLTON
BURY
ROCHDALE
OLDHAM
SALFORD
MANCHESTER
STOCKPORT
STRETFORD
SALE
ALTRINCHAM
ASHTON-UNDER-LYNE
HUDDERSFIELD
MACCLESFIELD
CREWE
WINSFORD
Darwen
Rawtenstall
Littleborough
Milnrow
Heywood
Middleton
Chadderton
Royton
Shaw
Prestwich
Radcliffe
Whitefield
Walkden
Swinton
Pendlebury
Failsworth
Denton
Hyde
Dukinfield
Stalybridge
Glossop
Marple
Hazel Grove
Poynton
Bramhall
Cheadle
Gatley
Hale
Urmston
Irlam
Partington
Leigh
Atherton
Tyldesley
Hindley
Westhoughton
Horwich
Farnworth
Ramsbottom
Edgworth
Tottington
Wilmslow
Knutsford
Alderley Edge
Prestbury
Bollington
Whaley Bridge
Chapel-en-le-Frith
New Mills
Buxton
Leek
Biddulph
Congleton
Kidsgrove
Alsager
Sandbach
Middlewich
Holmes Chapel
Northwich
Nantwich
Meltham
Marsden
Slaithwaite
Holmfirth
Hollingworth
Mossley
Uppermill
F
G
H
J
K
E
1
2
3
4
5
6
7

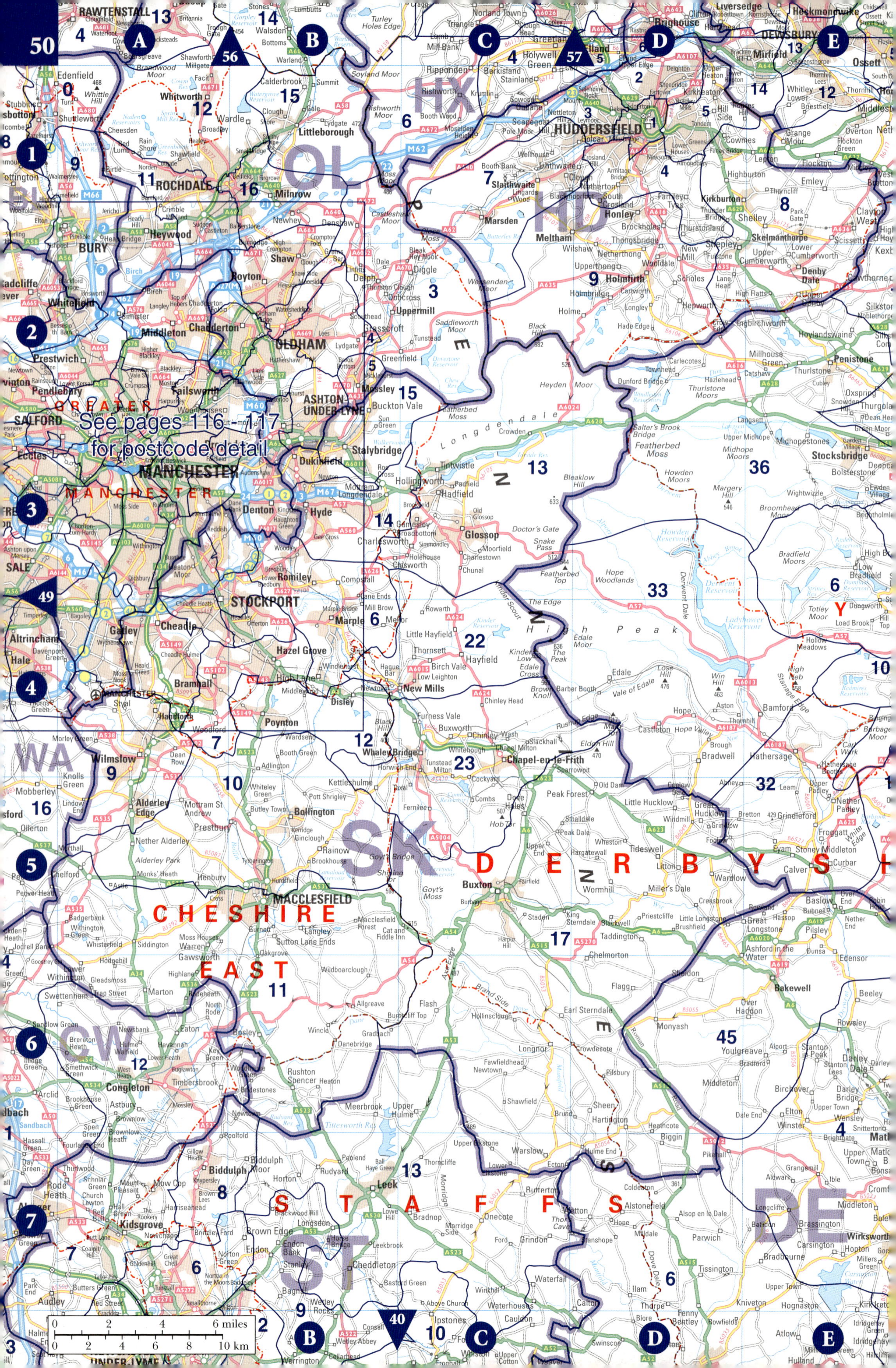
A
B
C
D
E
1
2
3
4
5
6
7
56
57
49
40
RAWTENSTALL
ROCHDALE
BURY
Heywood
Milnrow
Middleton
Chadderton
OLDHAM
Royton
Shaw
Prestwich
Whitefield
Pendlebury
SALFORD
MANCHESTER
GREATER
MANCHESTER
See pages 116 - 117
for postcode detail
ASHTON-UNDER-LYNE
Stalybridge
Dukinfield
Hyde
Denton
Stockport
STOCKPORT
Cheadle
Gatley
Hazel Grove
Bramhall
Altrincham
Hale
SALE
Eccles
Poynton
Disley
New Mills
Glossop
Hadfield
Hollingworth
Mossley
Marple
Romiley
Wilmslow
Alderley Edge
Knutsford
MACCLESFIELD
Bollington
CHESHIRE
EAST
Congleton
Kidsgrove
Biddulph
Leek
Cheddleton
Buxton
Chapel-en-le-Frith
Whaley Bridge
Hayfield
Chinley
Bakewell
Hathersage
Castleton
Bradwell
Tideswell
Youlgreave
Hartington
Longnor
Brassington
Wirksworth
HUDDERSFIELD
Brighouse
Mirfield
DEWSBURY
Holmfirth
Meltham
Marsden
Slaithwaite
Honley
Kirkburton
Skelmanthorpe
Penistone
Stocksbridge
Denby Dale
Littleborough
Whitworth
Ripponden
Elland
HX
OL
HD
SK
WA
CW
ST
DE
DERBYS
STAFFS
High Peak
Longdendale
0 2 4 6 miles
0 2 4 6 8 10 km

WEST YORKSHIRE
NORTH YORKSHIRE
EAST RIDING OF YORKSHIRE
SOUTH YORKSHIRE
NORTH LINCOLNSHIRE
LINCOLNSHIRE
NOTTINGHAMSHIRE
DERBYSHIRE
WF
DN
NG
S
58
52
41
F
G
H
J
K
1
2
3
4
5
6
7
Normanton
Pontefract
Featherstone
Knottingley
Goole Fields
Marshland
Rawcliffe Bridge
West Cowick
Cowick
Pollington
Whitley
Ackworth
Hemsworth
Upton
South Elmsall
South Kirkby
Fitzwilliam
Crofton
Walton
Sharlston
Royston
Shafton
Brierley
Grimethorpe
Cudworth
BARNSLEY
Darfield
Worsbrough
Wombwell
Hoyland
Dodworth
Thurnscoe
Goldthorpe
Bolton upon Dearne
Wath upon Dearne
Mexborough
Swinton
Conisbrough
Rawmarsh
ROTHERHAM
Adwick le Street
Askern
Carcroft
Bentley
DONCASTER
Sprotbrough
Cantley
Bessacarr
Rossington
New Rossington
Tickhill
Bawtry
Harworth
Bircotes
Maltby
Hatfield
Hatfield Woodhouse
Stainforth
Thorne
Moorends
Crowle
Epworth
Haxey
Misterton
Finningley
ROBIN HOOD DONCASTER SHEFFIELD
Blaxton
Auckley
Armthorpe
SHEFFIELD
Chapeltown
Ecclesfield
Dronfield
Eckington
Killamarsh
Renishaw
Staveley
CHESTERFIELD
Brimington
Bolsover
Clowne
Creswell
Whitwell
Dinnington
North Anston
South Anston
WORKSOP
Carlton in Lindrick
Langold
Blyth
Retford (East Retford)
Gringley on the Hill
Beckingham
Saundby
North Wheatley
South Wheatley
Clarborough
North Leverton with Habblesthorpe
Tuxford
New Ollerton
Ollerton
Boughton
Edwinstowe
Market Warsop
Shirebrook
Mansfield Woodhouse
MANSFIELD
Clipstone
Rainworth
Blidworth
Ravenshead
Southwell
Farnsfield
Bilsthorpe
Sutton in Ashfield
KIRKBY IN ASHFIELD
Hucknall
Alfreton
South Normanton
Pinxton
Somercotes
Ripley
Belper
Clay Cross
North Wingfield
Tibshelf
Holmewood
Wingerworth
Grassmoor
NEWARK ON TRENT
Collingham
Cromwell
Caunton
Kelham
North Muskham
South Muskham
The Dukeries
Clipstone Forest
Hatfield Moors
Thorne Waste (Thorne Moors)
Isle of Axholme
SHERWOOD FOREST

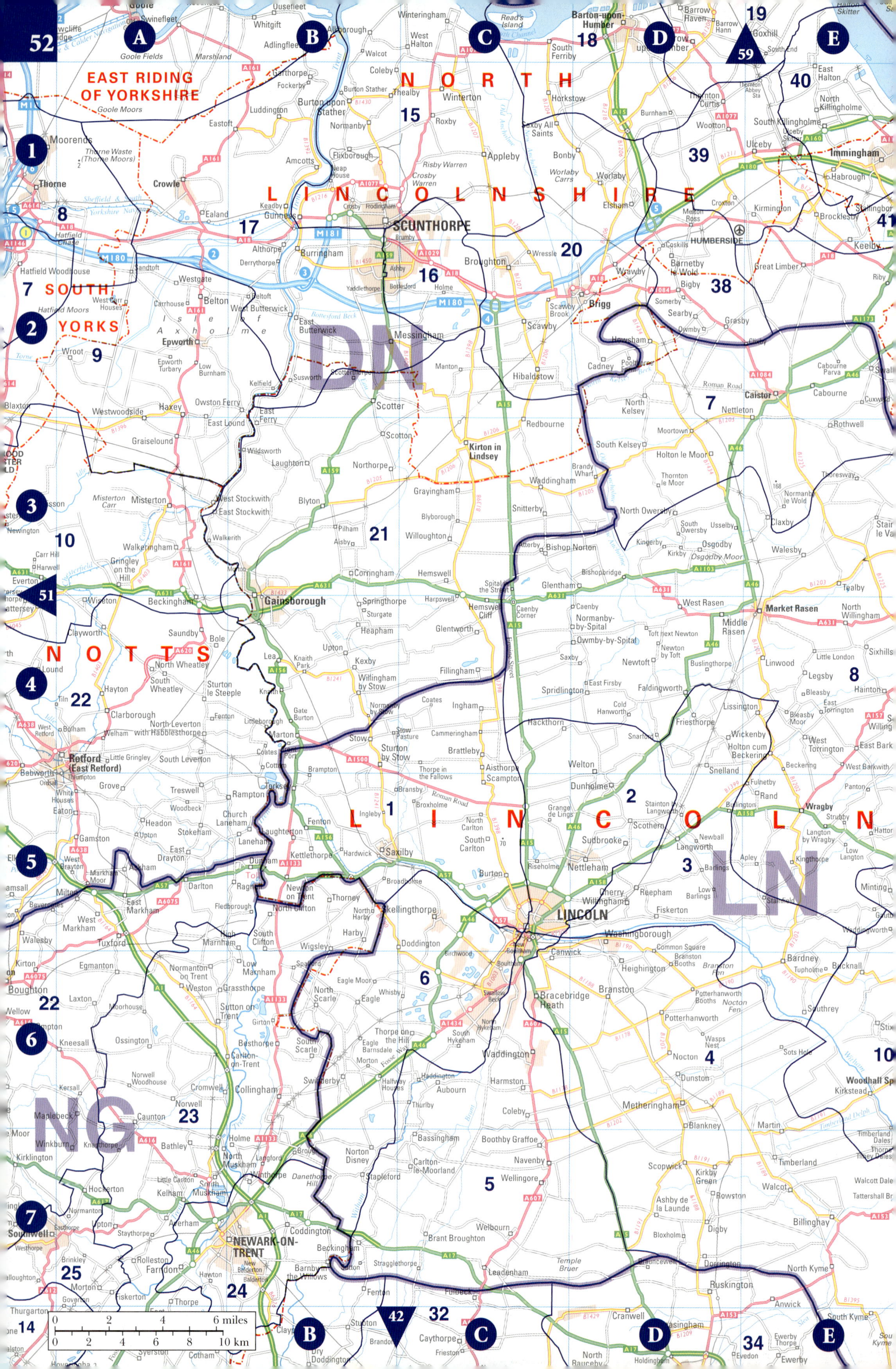

EAST RIDING OF YORKSHIRE
NORTH LINCOLNSHIRE
SOUTH YORKS
NOTTS
LINCOLN
DN
LN
NG
SCUNTHORPE
LINCOLN
NEWARK-ON-TRENT
Gainsborough
Retford (East Retford)
Barton-upon-Humber
Brigg
Caistor
Market Rasen
Saxilby
Kirton in Lindsey
HUMBERSIDE
Immingham
Goole
Goole Fields
Thorne
Moorends
Crowle
Epworth
Haxey
Misterton
Messingham
Scotter
Broughton
Winterton
Appleby
Hibaldstow
Wragby
Waddington
Bracebridge Heath
North Hykeham
Metheringham
Nettleham
Welton
Dunholme
Collingham
Tuxford
Southwell
Isle of Axholme
51
59
42
1
2
3
4
5
6
7
A
B
C
D
E
0 2 4 6 miles
0 2 4 6 8 10 km

F
G
H
J
K
1
2
3
4
5
6
7
HU
EAST RIDING OF YORKSHIRE
NORTH
EAST
LINCOLNSHIRE
PE
THE WOLDS
THE WASH
Kingston upon Hull to hours
Rotterdam..................................12
Zeebrugge..................................14
Patrington
Patrington Haven
Welwick
Out Newton
Weeton
Easington
Skeffling
Skeffling Clays
Sunk Island
Sunk Island Sands
Old Hall
Kilnsea
Kilnsea Clays
Spurn Head
Mouth of The Humber
Healing
Great Coates
West Marsh
Little Coates
GRIMSBY
Cleethorpes
Nunsthorpe
Bradley
Laceby
Scartho
Humberston
Barnoldby le Beck
Waltham
New Waltham
Holton le Clay
Tetney Lock
Brigsley
Ashby cum Fenby
Tetney
North Cotes
Ravendale
North Thoresby
Marshchapel
Donna Nook
Wragholme
Grainthorpe
Meals
North Somercotes
Fulstow
Covenham Res
Ludney
Conisholme
Church End
Skidbrooke North End
Ludborough
Covenham St Bartholomew
Covenham St Mary
South Somercotes
Saltfleet
Utterby
North Ormsby
Yarburgh
South Somercotes Fen Houses
Skidbrooke
Saltfleetby St Clements
Little Grimsby
Fotherby
Alvingham
North Cockerington
Saltfleetby All Saints
North Elkington
Keddington Corner
South Cockerington
Saltfleetby St Peter
Theddlethorpe St Helen
South Elkington
Keddington
Grimoldby
Louth
Stewton
Theddlethorpe All Saints
Manby
Burgh on Bain
Gayton le Wold
Hallington
Little Carlton
Great Carlton
Mablethorpe
Raithby
Legbourne
North Reston
South Reston
Gayton le Marsh
Trusthorpe
Biscathorpe
Donington on Bain
Withcall
Maltby
Tathwell
Little Cawthorpe
Strubby
Withern
Thorpe
Sutton on Sea
Sutton le Marsh
Sandilands
Stenigot
Haugham
Muckton
Authorpe
Tothill
Maltby le Marsh
Market Stainton
Cawkwell
Asterby
Maidenwell
Woodthorpe
Beesby
Hagnaby
Hannah
Goulceby
Ranby
Scamblesby
Burwell
Farforth
Ruckland
Walmsgate
Belleau
Claythorpe
Aby
Greenfield
Saleby
Markby
Oxcombe
Worlaby
White Pit
Swaby
South Thoresby
Ailby
Thoresthorpe
Asserby
The Grange
Bilsby
Thurlby
Huttoft
Anderby Creek
Anderby
Flint Hill
Belchford
Tetford
Little London
South Ormsby
Ketsby
Calceby
Driby
Haugh
Rigsby
Alford
Bilsby Field
Farlesthorpe
Mumby
Authorpe Row
Hemingby
Farthorpe
Midthorpe
Fulletby
Salmonby
Brinkhill
Ulceby Cross
Well
Mawthorpe
Cumberworth
West Ashby
Ashby Puerorum
Somersby
Harrington
Sutterby
Ulceby
Skendleby Psalter
Bonthorpe
Helsey
Hogsthorpe
Chapel St Leonards
Edlington
Bag Enderby
Willoughby
Low Toynton
Horncastle
Greetham
Aswardby
Langton
Claxby St Andrew
Sloothby
Thimbleby
High Toynton
Scrafield
Hagworthingham
Sausthorpe
Dalby
Skendleby
Welton le Marsh
Hasthorpe
Addlethorpe
Ingoldmells
Ingoldmells Point
Partney
Candlesby
Orby
Lusby
Raithby
Scremby
Gunby
Orby Marsh
Mareham on the Hill
Hameringham
Asgarby
Spilsby
Ashby by Partney
Mavis Enderby
Hundleby
Halton Holegate
Burgh le Marsh
Winthorpe
Seathorne
Dalderby
Great Steeping
Bratoft
Irby in the Marsh
Skegness
Old Bolingbroke
East Keal
Toynton All Saints
Roughton
Wood Enderby
Moorby
Miningsby
West Keal
Firsby
Haltham
Wilksby
East Kirkby
Hagnaby
Toynton Fen Side
Toynton St Peter
Little Steeping
Croft
Mareham le Fen
Revesby
Keal Cotes
Thorpe Culvert
Thorpe St Peter
Revesby Bridge
Stickford
Fendike Corner
Croft Marsh
Seacroft
Havenhouse Sta
Wainfleet All Saints
Wainfleet Bank
Gibraltar
Gibraltar Pt
Coningsby
Moor Side
New Bolingbroke
New Leake
Key's Toft
Wainfleet St. Mary
Tumby Woodside
Stickney
Midville
Friskney Eaudyke
Hawthorn Hill
New York
Sandy Bank
Carrington
East Fen
Friskney
Wainfleet Sand
Scrub Hill
Bunker's Hill
Lade Bank
West Fen
Northlands
Boston Deeps
Wildmore Fen
Frithville
Leake Commonside
Wrangle Lowgate
Friskney Flats
Sibsey
Wrangle
Gipsey Bridge
Old Leake
Lynn Deeps
Holland Fen
Langrick
Fishtoft Drove
High Ferry
Leake Hurn's End
Leverton Outgate
Langrick Bridge
Frith Bank
Leverton
Leverton Lucasgate
Long Sand
Dyke
Amber Hill
11
12
13
9
19
22
23
24
25
31
32
33
34
35
36
43
20
A16
A18
A46
A52
A153
A155
A157
A158
A1031
A1104
A1111
A1028

# 54

## Isle of Man

**IM**

same scale as main map

0 2 4 6 miles
0 2 4 6 8 10 km

hours
Belfast (summer only).............. 2¾
Dublin (summer only).......... 2¾–4¾
Heysham................................ 2–3½
Liverpool.............................. 2½–4

CUMBRIA
LA
LANCASHIRE
PR
BB
BLACKPOOL
BLACKBURN WITH DARWEN
MORECAMBE BAY
Forest of Bowland
Kendal
Sedbergh
Killington Lake
Ulverston
Barrow-in-Furness
Grange-over-Sands
Cartmel
Flookburgh
Allithwaite
Arnside
Milnthorpe
Kirkby Lonsdale
Silverdale
Carnforth
Bolton-le-Sands
Morecambe
Heysham
Lancaster
Hest Bank
Halton
Caton
High Bentham
Ingleton
Galgate
Glasson
Cockerham
Garstang
Fleetwood
Cleveleys
Thornton
Poulton-le-Fylde
Knott End-on-Sea
Preesall
Pilling
Hambleton
Great Eccleston
St Michael's on Wyre
Kirkham
Longridge
Chipping
Slaidburn
Waddington
Ribchester
Wilpshire
Clayton-le-Dale
Blackburn
Darwen
Preston
Bamber Bridge
Leyland
Chorley
Lytham St Anne's
Blackpool International
Southport
Freckleton
Hutton
Longton
Tarleton
Eccleston
Samlesbury
Goosnargh
Broughton
Douglas 2-3½ hrs
Larne 8 hrs
M6
M55
M61
M65
F
G
H
J
K
1
2
3
4
5
6
7
48
56
60

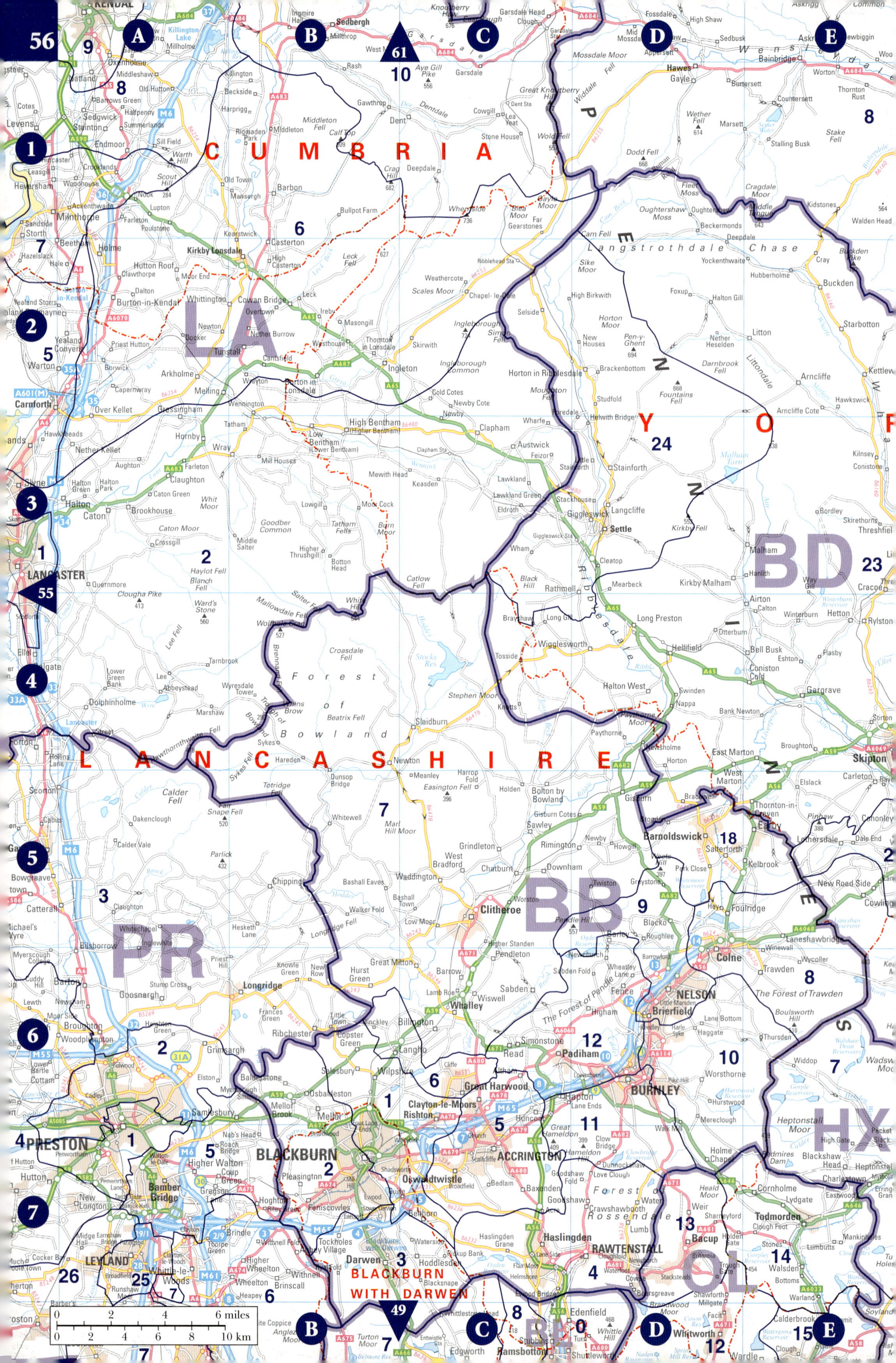

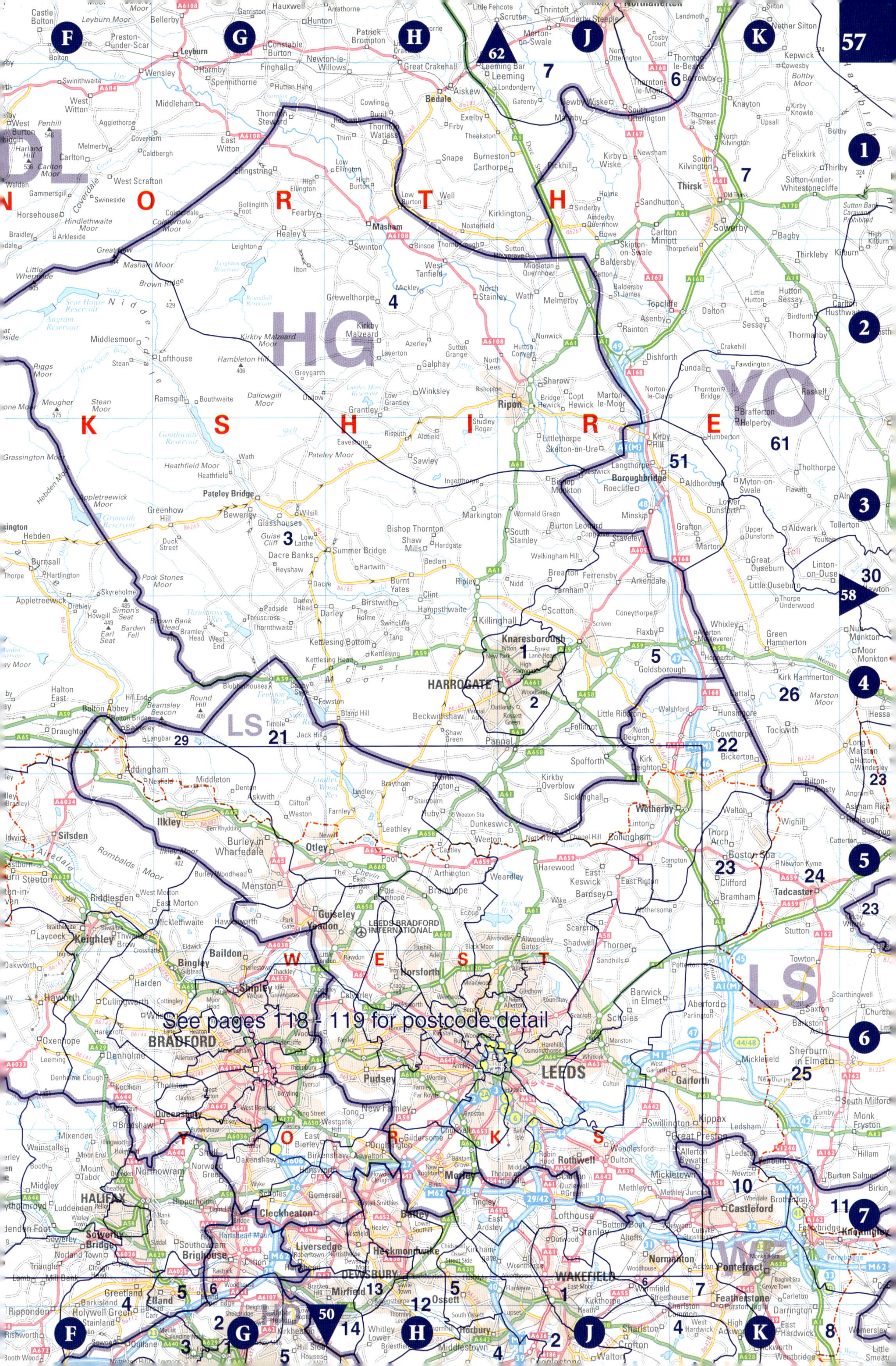
F
G
H
J
K
62
58
50
1
2
3
4
5
6
7
DL
HG
YO
LS
WF
NORTH YORKSHIRE
WEST YORKS
See pages 118 - 119 for postcode detail
Leyburn
Bedale
Leeming
Northallerton
Thirsk
Masham
Ripon
Boroughbridge
Knaresborough
HARROGATE
Pateley Bridge
Wetherby
Tadcaster
Ilkley
Otley
Keighley
Bingley
Shipley
BRADFORD
LEEDS
Pudsey
Guiseley
Yeadon
LEEDS BRADFORD INTERNATIONAL
Horsforth
Morley
Rothwell
Garforth
Castleford
Pontefract
WAKEFIELD
DEWSBURY
Batley
HALIFAX
Brighouse
Elland
Cleckheaton
Heckmondwike
Mirfield
Ossett
Normanton
Knottingley
Sherburn in Elmet
Boston Spa
Skipton-on-Swale
Sowerby
Great Ouseburn
Kirby Hill
Pannal
Spofforth
Bolton Abbey
Silsden
Haworth
Queensbury
Sowerby Bridge

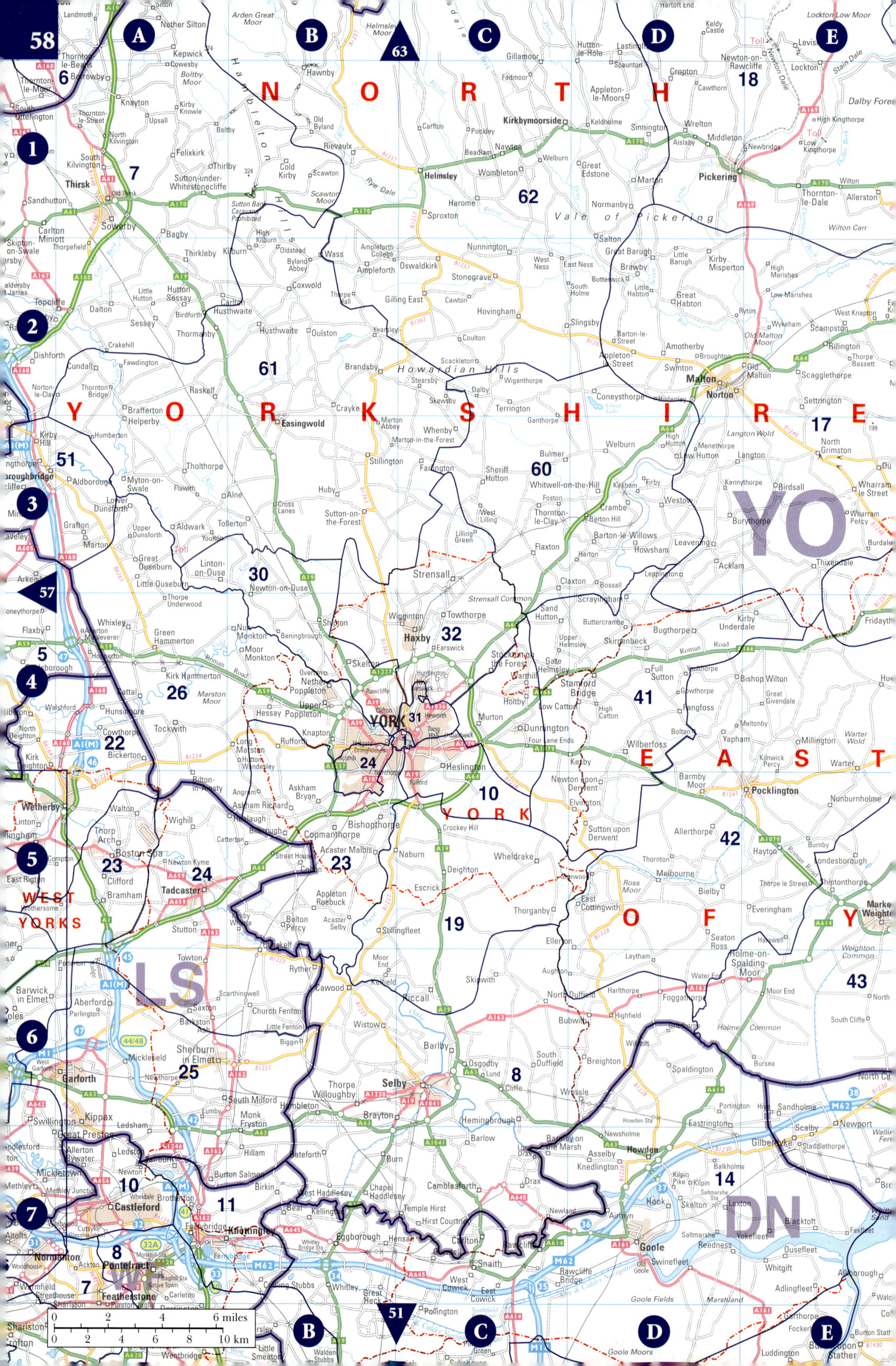

F
G
H
J
K
1
2
3
4
5
6
7
Burniston
Cromer Point
Silpho
Suffield
Langdale End
Hackness
Scalby
Everley
Wrench Green
Newby
SCARBOROUGH
South Bay
Black Rocks
Irton Moor
Falsgrave
Wykeham Forest
13
West Ayton
East Ayton
Hutton Buscel
Osgodby
Cayton Bay
Sawdon
Crossgates
Irton
Eastfield
Cayton
Seamer
Wykeham
Ruston
Snainton
Brompton
Lebberston
Gristhorpe
The Wyke
Filey Brigg
12
11
Filey
Flixton
Folkton
Staxton
Muston
West Flotmanby
Filey Bay
Willerby
Potter Brompton
Ganton
Sherburn
East Heslerton
West Heslerton
Hunmanby
14
Reighton
Reighton Sands
Speeton
Crab Rocks
Sherburn Wold
Fordon
Buckton
Bempton
15
Flamborough Head
Burton Fleming
Foxholes
Wold Newton
Grindale
16
Flamborough
Marton
Butterwick
Helperthorpe
Weaverthorpe
Octon
Thwing
East Lutton
West Lutton
Swaythorpe
Boynton
Sewerby
Grindalythe
Langtoft
Rudston
Gypsey Race
Bridlington
West Hill
Bessingby
Hilderthorpe
Cowlam Manor
Carnaby
Roman Road
Haisthorpe
West End
Kilham
Wilsthorpe
Thornholme
Carnaby Moor
Ruston Parva
Burton Agnes
BRIDLINGTON BAY
Harpham
Fraisthorpe
W O L D S
Garton-on-the-Wolds
25
Lowthorpe
Nafferton
Gransmoor
Barmston
Wetwang
Elmswell
Driffield
Great Kelk
Lissett
Little Driffield
Kelleythorpe
Gembling
Ulrome
Tibthorpe Wold
Wansford
Foston on the Wolds
Skipsea
Tibthorpe
Kirkburn
Eastburn
Southburn
Skerne
Beeford
Upton
Skipsea Brough
Old Sunderlandwick
Brigham
Hutton Cranswick
Church End
North Frodingham
Dunnington
Bainton
Rotsea
Middleton-on-the-Wolds
R I D I N G
Cawkeld
Hempholme
North End
Atwick
Kilnwick
Watton
Watton Carrs
Bewholme
Lund
Beswick
Burshill
18
Hornsea
Lockington
Little Burton
Brandesburton
Thorpe
Seaton
Holme on the Wolds
Aike
Leven
Hornsea Mere
South Dalton
Scorborough
New Arram
Arram
Catwick
Sigglesthorne
Goxhill
Rolston
Mappleton
Little Catwick
Etton
Little Hatfield
Leconfield
Routh
Great Hatfield
Great Cowden
Gardham
Cherry Burton
17
Long Riston
Rise
Arras
Y O R K S H I R E
Tickton
North End
Arnold
Withernwick
Molescroft
Bishop Burton
New Ellerby
Bishop Burton Wold
BEVERLEY
Weel
Skirlaugh
Marton
East Newton
Aldbrough
Old Ellerby
11
West Newton
Woodmansey
Etherdwick Grange
Walkington
North Newbald
Wawne
Thearne
Flinton
South Newbald
7
Swine
Garton
Grimston
Bentley
Dunswell
High Bransholme
Coniston
Risby
Humbleton
High Hunsley
Ganstead
Thirtleby
Sproatley
Fitling
Hilston
Skidby
16
6
Bransholme
20
Little Weighton
Wyton
Lelley
Dowthorpe
Owstwick
Tunstall
Cottingham
Sutton-on-Hull
8
Bilton
Riplingham
Eppleworth
Newland
Elstronwick
Sutton Ings
HU
Haltemprice Farm
9
Burton Pidsea
North End
South Cave
Roos
Preston
East End
KINGSTON UPON HULL
Willerby
10
5
Marfleet
Dairy House
Waxholme
Brantingham
Kirk Ella
2
Hedon
Wadworth Hill
West Ella
3
Rimswell
Anlaby
Withernsea
Ellougthon
Burstwick
Halsham
Welton
Swanland
14
1
Brough
Melton
KINGSTON UPON HULL
Thorngumbald
East End
4
12
19
13
North Ferriby
Hessle
Paull
Camerton
Keyingham
Hollym
Ryehill
Humber Bridge
Redcliff Channel
Paull Holme
Ottringham
Winestead
Paull Holme Sands
Holmpton
New Holland
East Halton Skitter
Read's Island
Barrow Haven
19
Barrow Hann
Patrington
Barton-upon-Humber
Cherry Cobb Sands
Out Newton
18
Barrow upon Humber
Goxhill
Salthaugh Grange
Welwick
South Ferriby
Patrington Haven
South End
Weeton
NORTH LINCOLNSHIRE
52
East Halton
Foulholme Sands
Skeffling
Easington
Sunk Island
F
G
40
H
J
K
Winteringham
Horkstow
Thornton Curtis
Rotterdam 12hrs
Zeebrugge 14hrs
Immingham
Old Hall
Skeffling Clays
Burnham
Killingholme
A165
A171
A170
A64
A1039
A614
A166
A164
A1035
A1079
A1174
A1033
A63
A15
A1077
B1229
B1255
B1259
B1253
B1249
B1252
B1246
B1242
B1244
B1243
B1248
B1238
B1240
B1362
B1445
B1206
B1204

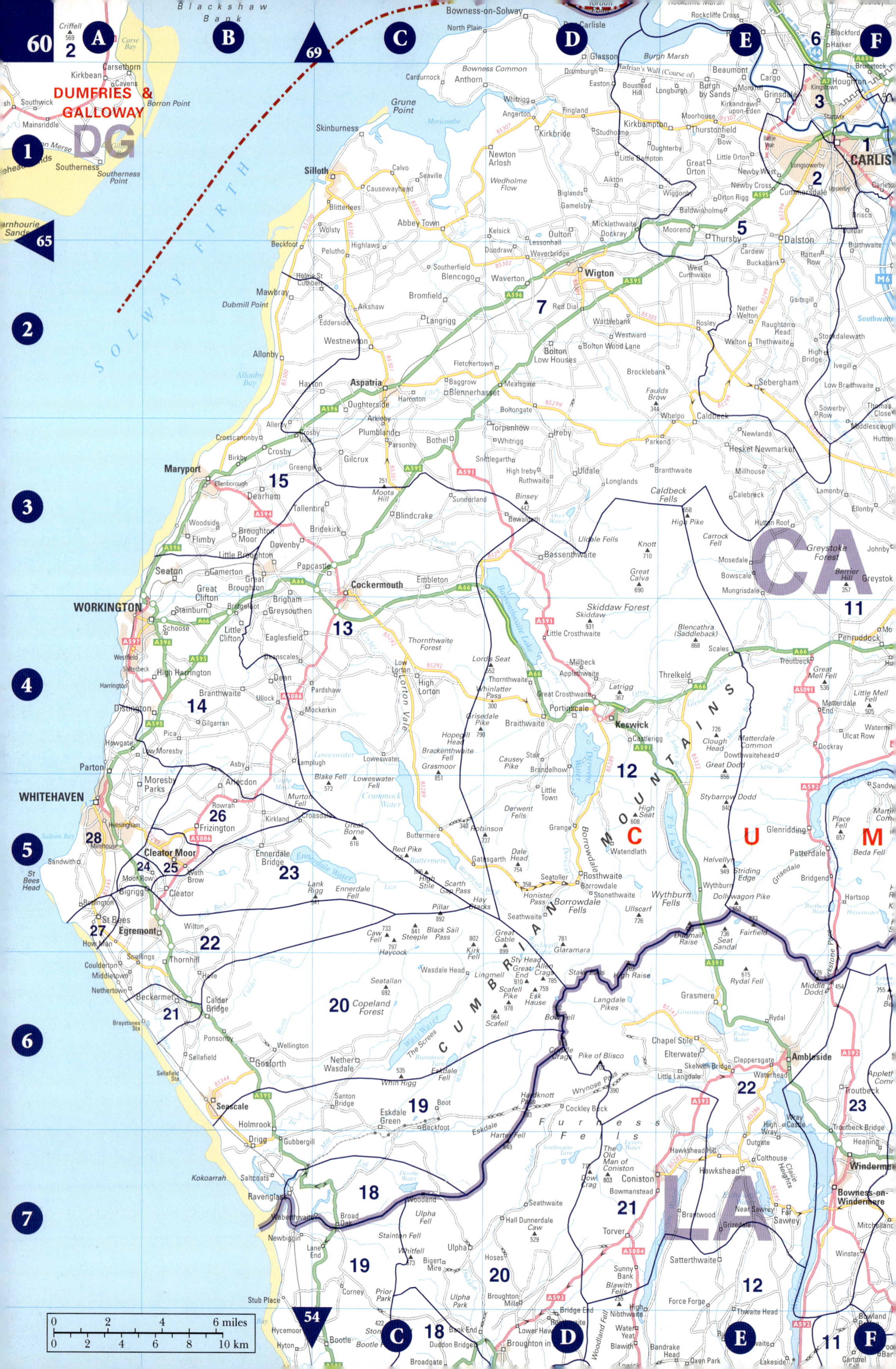

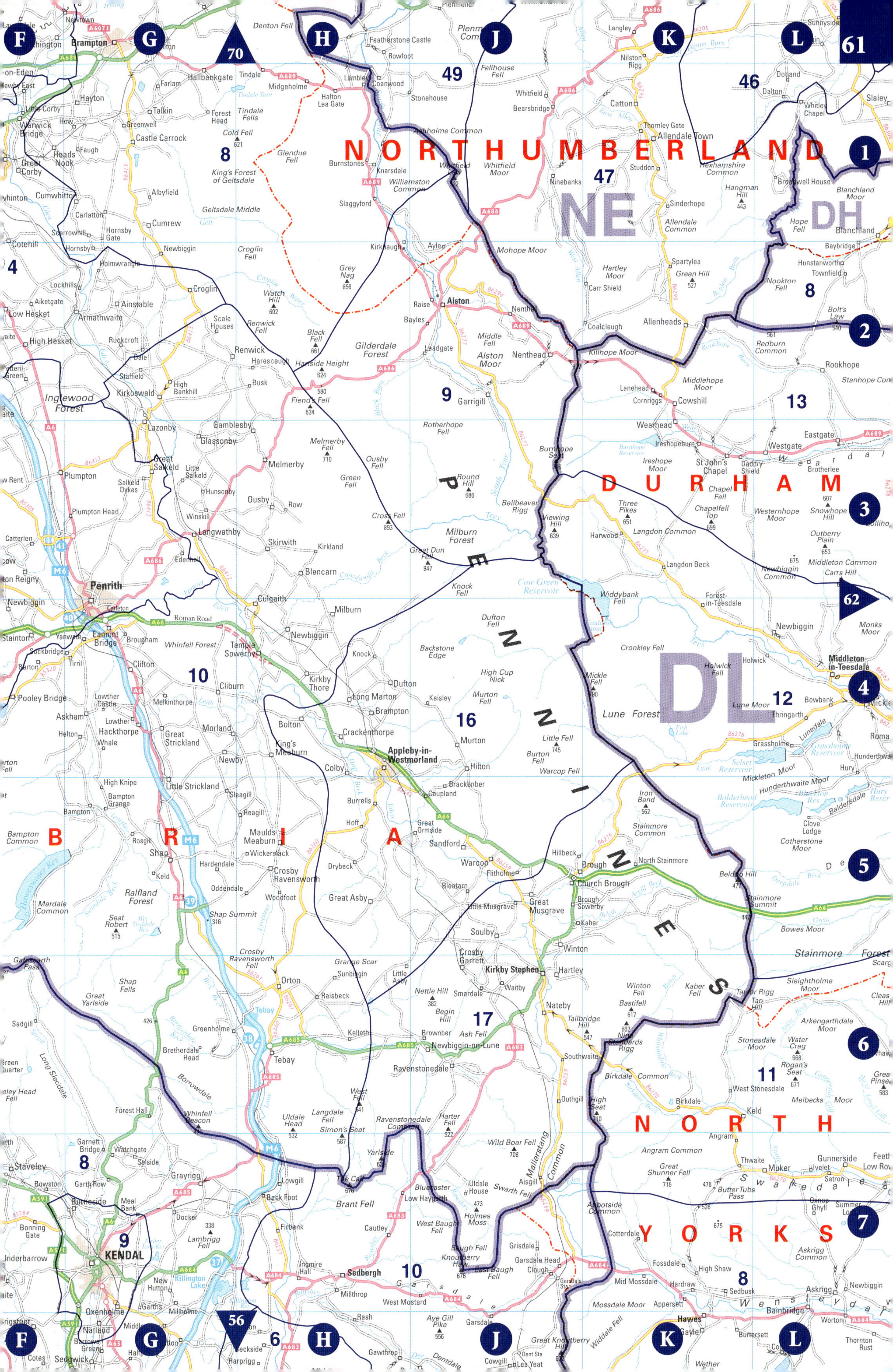

62
71
61
57
See page 121 for postcode detail
NORTHUMBERLAND
NE
DH
DL
D U R H A M
N O R T H
DARLINGTON
TYNE
WEAR
CONSETT
Whickham
Blaydon
Prudhoe
Felling
WASHINGTON
CHESTER-LE-STREET
Stanley
Annfield Plain
Lanchester
DURHAM
Houghton le Spring
Hetton-le-Hole
Sherburn
Spennymoor
Crook
Willington
Ferryhill
Sedgefield
Bishop Auckland
Shildon
Newton Aycliffe
Wolsingham
Stanhope
Middleton-in-Teesdale
Barnard Castle
Staindrop
DARLINGTON
Richmond
Catterick Garrison
Leyburn
Bedale
Northallerton
Hurworth-on-Tees
Middleton St George
Scotch Corner
Weardale
Swaledale
Wensleydale
Stainmore Forest
Hamsterley Forest
0 2 4 6 miles
0 2 4 6 8 10 km

F
G
H
J
K
same scale as main map
1
2
3
4
5
6
7
13
UNDERLAND
SR
Seaham
Nose's Point
Hawthorn
Easington Colliery
Easington
Horden
Peterlee
Blackhall Colliery
Blackhall Rocks
Hesleden
High Hesleden
Monk Hesleden
Crimdon Park
Hutton Henry
Sheraton
Hart
27
Elwick
26
24
The Headland
Hartlepool Bay
HARTLEPOOL
Dalton Piercy
HARTLEPOOL
Tees Bay
Seaton Carew
25
Embleton
22
Claxton Grange
Greatham
Newton Bewley
Wolviston
Billingham
Cowpen Bewley
TS
Seal Sands
2
20
23
Haverton Hill
Port Clarence
MIDDLESBROUGH
1
3
MIDDLESBROUGH
4
18
Thornaby-on-Tees
17
5
Acklam
Stainton
Maltby
8
Yarm
Hilton
Seamer
15
Crathorne
Hutton Rudby
Rudby
Enterpen
Potto
East Rounton
West Lees
Swainby
Ingleby Arncliffe
Ingleby Cross
Cleveland Tontine Inn
Osmotherley
Whorlton Moor
Ellerbeck
Thimbleby
Over Silton
Nether Silton
Kepwick
7
Cowesby
Boltby Moor
Kirby Knowle
Thornton-
10
Warrenby
Coatham
Redcar
Dormanstown
Kirkleatham
Marske-by-the-Sea
Saltburn-by-the-Sea
Warsett Hill
11
New Marske
Yearby
Wilton
Lazenby
6
South Bank
Grangetown
Eston
Normanby
Upleatham
Dunsdale
Skelton
Brotton
Skinningrove
Carlin How
Loftus
North Skelton
Kilton
Kilton Thorpe
Boulby
Staithes
Easington
13
REDCAR
AND
CLEVELAND
Guisborough
14
Boosbeck
Margrove Park
12
Lingdale
Charltons
Stanghow
Moorsholm
Liverton
Handale
Roxby
Borrowby
Dalehouse
Port Mulgrave
Hinderwell
Kettle Ness
Runswick Bay
Kettleness
Newton Mulgrave
Ellerby
Roxby Low Moor
Scaling
Freebrough Hill
Pinchinthorpe
Newton under Roseberry
Roseberry Topping
Gisborough Moor
Commondale Moor
Commondale
Moorsholm Moor
Danby Low Moor
Danby Beacon
Roxby High Moor
Lealholm Moor
Scaling Reservoir
Mickleby
West Barnby
East Barnby
Lythe
Sandsend
Sandsend Ness
Whitby
East Row
Dunsley
Newholm
Ugthorpe
Hutton Mulgrave
Aislaby
Ruswarp
Briggswath
Egton Low Moor
Sleights
Ugglebarnby
Sneaton
Stainsacre
7
Nunthorpe
Great Ayton
Langbaurgh
Little Ayton
Easby Moor
Newby
Marton
Stokesley
Easby
Battersby
Kildale
Kildale Moor
Baysdale
Westerdale
Castleton
Danby
Ainthorpe
21
Houlsyke
Lealholm
Egton
Grosmont
Egton Bridge
Glaisdale
Sleights
Moor
22
Littlebeck
Beck Hole
Goathland
Brawith
Great Broughton
Kirkby
Ingleby Greenhow
Great Busby
Carlton-in-Cleveland
9
Faceby
Whorlton
Urra
Round Hill
Seave Green
Chop Gate
Baysdale Moor
Westerdale Moor
Danby High Moor
Glaisdale Moor
Egton High Moor
Pike Hill Moss
Farndale Moor
Rosedale Moor
Cockayne Ridge
Cockayne
Snilesworth Moor
Arnsgill Ridge
Bilsdale West Moor
Bilsdale East Moor
Church Houses
Thorgill
Hill Cottages
Rosedale Abbey
Cropton Forest
Wheeldale Moor
Hunt House
YO
Lockton High Moor
Allerston High Moor
Burn Howe Rigg
Fylingdales Moor
Flask Inn
Saltergate
Lockton Low Moor
18
Levisham
Lockton
Kelty Castle
Newton-on-Rawcliffe
Cawthorn
Dalby Forest
High Kingthorpe
Spaunton Moor
Hartoft End
Lastingham
Spaunton
Appleton-le-Moors
Gillamoor
Fadmoor
Low Mill
Kirkbymoorside
62
58
Helmsley Moor
Arden Great Moor
Black Hambleton
Jeater Houses
O
R
K
S
H
I
R
E
CLEVELAND
HILLS
Rudland Rigg
Blakey Ridge
Castleton Ridge
Glaisdale Rigg
Bransdale
Farndale
Rosedale
Hambleton
Stain Dale
Newton Dale
Whitby
Saltwick Bay
High Hawsker
Low Hawsker
Ness Point (North Cheek)
Robin Hood's Bay
Fylingthorpe
Sneatonthorpe
Raw
Low Moor
Old Peak (South Cheek)
Ravenscar
Staintondale
NORTH
YORKS
Harwood Dale
Cloughton Newlands
Cloughton Wyke
Cloughton
Burniston
Cromer Point
Scalby Ness Rocks
Scalby
Broxa Forest
Broxa
Suffield
Hackness
13
Langdale End
Sleights
Grosmont
Egton Bridge
Bock Hole
Goathland
Falling Foss
Mulgrave
Runswick Bay
Kettle Ness

A
B
C
D
E
1
2
3
4
5
6
7
67
66
Ailsa Craig
Dowhill
Dipple
Kilkerran
Craig
Craigengillan
Chapeldonan
Low
Craighead
Dailly
Grangeston
Tairlaw
Water of Girvan
Old Dailly
Hadyard Hill
324
Garleffin Fell
429
Penkill
Penwhapple Reservoir
Linfern Loch
Loch Bradan Reservoir
Loch Finlas
Girvan
Houston
Saugh Hill
296
SOUTH
Glengennet
North Balloch
Craiglee
523
Glendoune
Black Neuk
Glendrissaig
South Balloch
Waterhead
Pinminnoch
Changue Forest
Shiel Hill
508
Ardwell
297
Kennedy's Pass
Nick of the Balloch Pass
341
Grey Hill
Barr
Shalloch
Starr
CARRICK
Pinmore
565
Polmaddie Hill
479
Shalloch on Minnoch
Lendalfoot
Aldons
Carleton Fishery
AYRSHIRE
Daljarrock
26
Kirriereoch Hill
786
Bennane Head
Poundland
Pinwherry
Colmonell
Dalreoch
KA
Merrick
843
Glenduisk
Knockdolian
265
Craigneil
Black Clauchrie
Garwall Hill
349
Ballochmorrie
Mains of Tig
Palgowan
Ballantrae Bay
Craignaw
Ballantrae
Auchairne
Balkissock
Shiel Hill
230
Barrhill
Buchan Hill
493
Glenapp Castle
Downan Point
Eldrick
Smyrton
Lochton
Corwar House
Glen Trool Lodge
Beneraird
439
Craigie Fell
Millfore
656
Carlock Hill
323
Milljoan Hill
403
Altimeg Hill
Chirmorrie
Drumlamford House
Glentrool
Bargrennan
Mulldonoch
557
Lamachan Hill
716
Larg Hill
675
Glen App
Finnarts Point
Markdhu
Clachaneasy
Larg
Milleur Point
Miltonise
Polbae
Garlick Hill
445
Barnhills
Glenwhilly
Knockville
Cordorcan
Knowe
Dalnigap
Urrall Fell
184
8
Penninghame
Cairnryan
Kirkcolm
Corsewall
Garlies Castle
Dallash
Ervie
Airies
Cairn Point
Boreland
Glenrazie
Carseriggan
Cumloden
Artfield Fell
Challoch
St Mary's Croft
Brad Fell
235
Newton Stewart
Minnigaff
Creebridge
Bargaly
DUMFRIES AN
Leswalt
Soleburn
Balminnoch
213
Culvennan Fell
Blackcraig
Tarf Bridge
New Luce
Benfield
Cairnsmore
THE RINNS OF GALLOWAY
Innermessan
Shennanton
Nether Barr
Palnure
Auchmantle
Lochinch Castle
Galdenoch
Barraer
Craig Fell
164
Baltersan
Kirkcowan
Craighlaw
Spittal
Stranraer
Carscreugh
Barlae
Castle Kennedy
Causeway End
Portslogan
Dunragit Moor
Whitecairn
Carsegowan
Barholm Mains
9
Creetown
Dunragit
Glenluce
Spittal
Whiteleys
Lochans
Cairn Pat
182
Whitecrook
Knock Moss
Culquhirk
Wigtown Sands
Genoch
Kildrochet House
Dinvin
Colfin
Knock Fell
175
Portpatrick
Genoch Square
Milton
Bladnoch
Wigtown
Carsluith
Sands of Luce
Awhirk
Stoneykirk
Crow's Nest
Culmalzie
Auchenmalg
Baldoon Sands
Braehead
Port of Spittal Bay
Culshabbin
Barnbarroch
Kirkinner
Balgreggan
Sandhead
Auchenmalg Bay
Alticry
Whauphill
Stewarton
Cairngarroch Bay
Barrachan
Loch Heed
Money Head
Elrig
Kirkland of Longcastle
LUCE BAY
Sorbie
Clachanmore
Airyhassen
Mochrum
Ardwell
Barr Point
Ardwell Bay
Chapel Rossan
THE MACHARS
Barwinnock
Logan
Balgowan
Port William
Cults
Castlewigg
New England Bay
Mull of Logan
Barsalloch Point
Monreith
Craigdhu
Port Logan
Terally
Monreith Bay
Whithorn
Glasserton
Portyerrock
Cairndoon
Clanyard Bay
Kilstay
Fell of Carleton
Drummore
Laggantalluch Head
Kirkmaiden
Kidsdale
Isle of Whithorn
Cailiness Point
St. Ninian's Cave
Damnaglaur
Cutcloy
Crammag Head
Dunman
160
Maryport
Port Castle Bay
Devil's Bridge
Burrow Head
Nick of Kindram
East Tarbet
West Tarbet
Mull of Galloway
A77
A714
A751
A75
A747
A716
A718
A712
B734
B7044
B7027
B7043
B738
B7077
B7084
B7042
B7065
B7041
B733
B735
B7005
B7052
B7085
B7004
B7021
B7063
A746

F
G
H
J
K
65
68
69
60
1
2
3
4
5
6
7
GALLOWAY
Benbrack 448
Windy Standard 698
Countam 475
Cairnkinna Hill 552
Breconside
Gateslack
Earncraig Hill
Queensberry 697
Drumjohn
Cairnsmore of Carsphairn 797
Dodd Hill 498
Colt Hill 598
Countam 500
Auchenbrack
Holm of Drumlanrig
Rashy Height 380
Wee Queensberry 512
Minnygap Height 399
Carronbridge
Dabton
Thornhill
Gatelawbridge
A713
Black Shoulder 688
Benbuie
Bail Hill 516
Torbraehead 400
Auchenhessnane
Burnhead
Penpont
Brochloch
Craig of Knockgray 383
Bennan
Keir Mill
A76
Forest of Ae
Garryhorn
Carsphairn
Knockgray
Wether Hill
Cornharrow Hill
Clonrae
Tynron
Closeburn
Great Hill 353
Bardennoch
Marscalloch Hill 381
Carroch
Moniaive
Kirkland
A702
Keir Hills
Croalchapel
B729
Craigdarroch
Crawfordton
Dalshangan
Glencrosh
Crossford
Barndennoch
Dalswinton Common
Ae Village
Parkgate
A701
Glenhead
Blackwood
Forrest Lodge
Wether Hill 385
Castlefairn
Bogrie Hill 432
Auldgirth
Burnhead
Holmhead
Lochurr
217
Crawston Hill
Knocknalling
Sundaywell
Dunscore
Allanton
Friars Carse
Dalswinton
Glenae
Loch Dungeon
Loch Urr
Milton
Stroquhan
Duncow
Amisfield Town
Corriedoo
Waterhead
Tinwald
Garroch
St John's Town of Dalry
406
Blackcraig Hill
Craigenputtock
Speddoch
Kirkton
Glenlee
Bogue
Blackcraig
Drumwhirn
Newtonairds
Holywood
Locharbriggs
Bennan 381
A713
Slongaber
Skeoch Hill
Gribton
New Bridge
Garcrogo Forest
Knocklearn
Balmaclellan
A762
New Galloway
Clatteringshaws Loch
Gibbshill
A712
Margreig
Scaur
Terregles
Lincluden
Lochar Moss
282
Larglear Hill
398
Corsock
Cairnsmore of Dee 493
DUMFRIES
A780
Collin
Clatteringshaws
Glen
Shawhead
Maxwelltown
A756
Noblehill
Henderland
A75
Cargenbridge
Forest Drive (summer only)
Crofts
Brae
Merkland
Round Fell 402
Fell of Fleet 471
Shaw Hill 385
Glenlair
Brooklands
Crocketford or Ninemile Bar
Lochfoot
Goldielea
Dalskairth
Kingholm Quay
Bennan Cottage
Drumrash
Square Point
Milton Loch
Cargen
Netherwood
Toll
Mossdale
Parton
Kirkpatrick Durham
Mabie
Kelton
Walton Park
Gillfoot
Auchencloy Hill 209
Airie Hill 291
Springholm
Milton
Whinny Hill
Slogarie
Auchendolly
Beeswing
Glencaple
Craig
Old Bridge of Urr
Hermitage
Stonehouse
321
Lotus Hill
Kirkconnell
Crossmichael
Kirkgunzeon
Shambellie
Clarebrand
Mollance
Kinharvie
Townhead of Greenlaw
Haugh of Urr
New Abbey
White Top of Culreoch 344
Laurieston
Glenlochar
Hillowton
A711
Cuil Hill
Darngarroch
Castle Douglas
Craignair
Criffell 569
A710
Buchan
Dalbeattie
Carse Bay
Castramont
Bridge of Dee
Carsethorn
Glenquicken Moor
Low Barlay
Glengap
Rhonehouse (Kelton Hill)
Breoch
Kirkbean
Cavens
Rusko
Gelston
Dalbeattie Forest
Borron Point
Glen
Lauchentyre
Doldawn
Argrennan House
Palnackie
Southwick
Gatehouse of Fleet
Ringford
Airieland
Barnbarroch
Fairgirth
Caulkerbush
Mainsriddle
Cairnharrow 456
Barcaple
Valleyfield
Screel Hill 343
Kippford (Scaur)
Anwoth
Netherthird
Preston Merse
Gillfoot Bay
Ardwall
Barwhinnock
391
Bengairn
Sandyhills
Southerness
Cardoness
Girthon
Twynholm
Tongland
Rough Firth
Colvend
Mersehead Sands
Southerness Point
Kirkdale House
Cumstoun
Rockcliffe
Port o' Warren
Sandgreen
Barharrow
Castlehill Point
Fleet Bay
Langlands
Auchencairn
Almorness Point
Lennox Plunton
High Borgue
Kirkcudbright
Auchencairn Bay
Hestan Island
Barnhourie Sands
Murray's Isles
Islands of Fleet
Knockbrex
Bombie
Bankhead
Hazlefield
Balcary Point
Ardwall Island
St Mary's Isle
Auchnabony
Borgue
Rascarrel
Barlocco Island
Dundrennan
Rascarrel Bay
Kirkandrews
Orroland
Townhead
Senwick
Barlocco Bay
WIGTOWN BAY
Ringdoo Point
Borness
Kirkcudbright Bay
Port Mary
Ross
Balmae
Abbey Head
Little Ross
SOLWAY FIRTH
Maryport
Seaton
WORKINGTON
Stainburn
Schoose
Westfield
14
11

A
B
C
D
E
1
2
3
4
5
6
7
9
Bellochantuy
Killocraw
Corrylach
Saddell Forest
Sgreadan Hill
397
Saddell
Bunlarie
Saddell Bay
ARGYLL
AND
BUTE
KINTYRE
Tangy
Skeroblingarry
Drumgarve
Glen Lussa
Ballochgair
Ugadale Point
Westport
Low Ballevain
Calliburn
Peninver
Ardnacross Bay
Kilchenzie
Machrihanish Bay
East Darlochan
A83
CAMPBELTOWN
Kilmichael
Drumore
Campbeltown
Machrihanish
Dalivaddy
Witchburn
Davaar Island
Drumlemble
B843
Kilkerran
Davaar
Chiscan
Knocknaha
Glenramskill
Oatfield
Kilchrist
Beinn Ghuilean
352
New Orleans
Earadale Point
The Slate
385
28
Cnoc Moy
446
Killellan
312
Arinarach Hill
Largybaan
273
Cnoc Reamhar
Cnoc Odhar
277
Conie Glen
Glen Kerran
Feochaig
Ru Stafnish
Sheanachie
PA
Glen Breackerie
Brecklate
Keprigan
Kildavie
Strone Glen
Carrine
Macharioch
Polliwilline Bay
Beinn na Lice
428
Southend
Garveld
Keil
Feorlan
Carskey Bay
Mull of Kintyre
Borgadelmore Point
Sanda Sound
Sheep Island
Sanda Island
KILBRANNAN SOUND
Tormore
Machrie Water
A841
Ballymichael
512
Beinn Bhreac
73
Torbeg
Shiskine
Cnoc a' Chapuill
417
Benlister Glen
Glenkiln
Lamlash
Lamlash Bay
Holy Island
Clauchlands
ARRAN
NORTH AYRSHIRE
27
458
Tighvein
Blackwaterfoot
Drumadoon Bay
Kilpatrick
Brown Head
Glen Scorrodale
Knockenkelly
Kingscross Point
Kingscross
Whiting Bay
Kiscadale
Whiting Bay
Largymore
Ashdale
Glen
KA
Corriecravie
Sliddery
Largybeg
Largybeg Point
Dippen
Dippin Head
Kilmory
Kilmory Water
Levencorroch
Lagg
Shannochie
Kildonan
Bennan Head
Sound of Pladda
Pladda
Ailsa Craig
Bennane Head
Ballantrae Bay
Ballantrae
Glenapp Castle
Downan Point
Carlock Hill
Glen App
Finnarts Point
Milleur Point
Corsewall Point
Larne 1-1¾ hrs
Belfast 1¾-3¼ hrs
Barnhills
North Cairn
South Cairn
B738
Kirkcolm
Corsewall
Dounan Bay
Airies
Ervie
Loch Connell
A718
St Mary's Croft
Portobello
Knocknain
Leswalt
Soleburn
B7043
Innermessan
A77
Cairnryan
Cairn Point
LOCH RYAN
THE RHINS
Stranraer
Broadsea Bay
Portslogan
Whiteleys

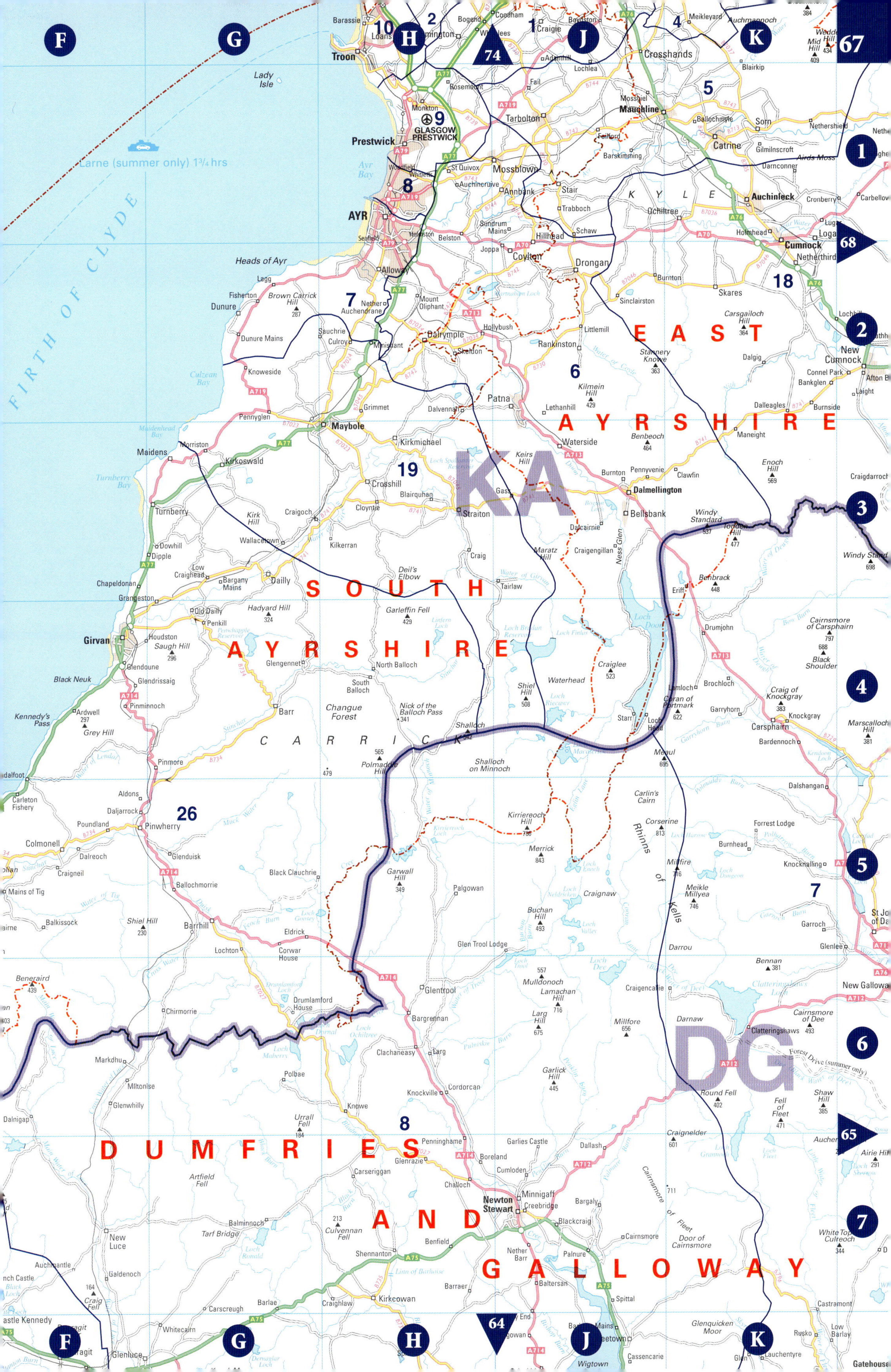

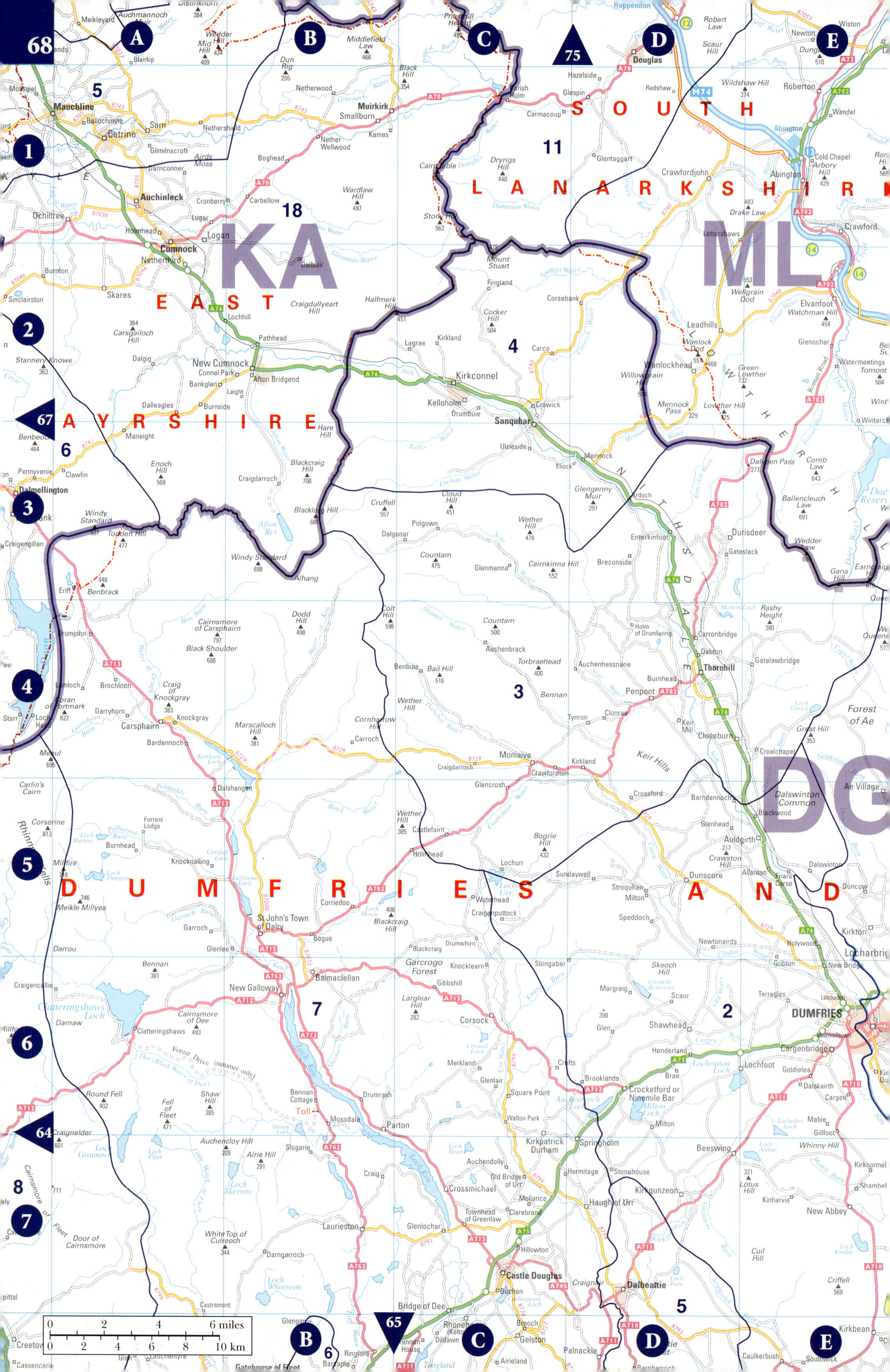

A
B
C
D
E
75
1
2
3
4
5
6
7
8
67
64
65
Auchmannoch Muir
Meikleyard
Blairkip
Mid Hill 409
Wedder Hill 434
Dun Rig 255
Middlefield Law 466
Priesthill Height 492
Black Hill 354
Happendon
Robert Law
Scaur Hill
Douglas
Hazelside
Wiston
Newton
Dungavel 510
Mossgiel
Mauchline
Ballochmyle
Sorn
Catrine
Gilmilnscroft
Netherwood
Muirkirk
Smallburn
Kames
Nethershield
Nether Wellwood
Airds Moss
Parish Holm
Glespin
Carmacoup
Redshaw
Wildshaw Hill 374
Roberton
Wandel
Abington
Cold Chapel
Arbory Hill 429
SOUTH
LANARKSHIRE
11
Dryrigs Hill 440
Cairn Table
Glentaggart
Crawfordjohn
Duneaton Water
Drake Law 483
Crawford
Boghead
Darnconner
Auchinleck
Cronberry
Carbellow
Wardlaw Hill 497
18
Ochiltree
Lugar
Logan
Holmhead
Cumnock
Netherthird
Dalblair
Stony Hill 562
Mount Stuart 478
Fingland
Corsebank
Leadhills
Wellgrain Dod 553
Elvanfoot
Watchman Hill 454
KA
ML
Burnton
Skares
Sinclairston
EAST
Craigdullyeart Hill
Halfmerk Hill 451
Cocker Hill 504
Lochhill
Carsgailoch Hill 364
Pathhead
Stannery Knowe 363
Dalgig
New Cumnock
Connel Park
Bankglen
Afton Bridgend
Laight
Lagrae
Kirkland
Kirkconnel
Kelloholm
Drumbuie
Carco
Wanlockhead
Wanlock Dod 551
Willowgrain Hill
Green Lowther 732
Mennock Pass
Lowther Hill 725
Glenochar
Watermeetings
Tomont 504
Dalleagles
Burnside
AYRSHIRE
Benbeoch 464
Maneight
Hare Hill
Crawick
Sanquhar
Ulzieside
Eliock
Mennock
Dalveen Pass
Comb Law 643
Enoch Hill 569
Pennyvenie
Clawfin
Dalmellington
Craigdarroch
Blackcraig Hill 700
Cruffell 557
Cloud Hill 451
Glengenny Muir 291
Ardoch
Ballencleuch Law 691
Windy Standard 631
Todden Hill 471
Blacklorg Hill 681
Afton Res
Polgown
Dalgonar
Wether Hill 478
Enterkinfoot
Durisdeer
Gateslack
Wedder Law 668
Craigengillan
Windy Standard 698
Alhang
Countam 475
Glenmanna
Cairnkinna Hill 552
Breconside
Gana Hill 668
Eriff
Benbrack 448
Colt Hill 598
Rashy Height 380
Cairnsmore of Carsphairn 797
Dodd Hill 498
Countam 500
Holm of Drumlanrig
Carronbridge
Drumjohn
Black Shoulder 688
Auchenbrack
Torbraehead 400
Dabton
Gatelawbridge
Lamloch
Brochloch
Benbuie
Bail Hill 516
Auchenhessnane
Burnhead
Thornhill
Craig of Knockgray 383
Wether Hill
Penpont
Forest of Ae
Moorbrock
Garryhorn
Carsphairn
Knockgray
Marscalloch Hill 381
Cornharrow Hill
Carroch
Tynron
Clonrae
Keir Mill
Closeburn
Great Hill 353
Bardennoch
Moniaive
Crawfordton
Kirkland
Keir Hills
Croalchapel
Meaul 695
Craigdarroch
Carlin's Cairn
Dalshangan
Glencrosh
Crossford
Barndennoch
DG
Dalswinton Common
Blackwood
Ae Village
Forrest Lodge
Wether Hill 385
Castlefairn
Bogrie Hill 432
Glenhead
Auldgirth 217
Crawston Hill
Corserine 813
Burnhead
Holmhead
Lochurr
Allanton
Dalswinton
Millfire
Knocknalling
Sundaywell
Dunscore
Friars Carse
Duncow
DUMFRIES AND
Meikle Millyea 746
Corriedoo
Waterhead
Craigenputtock
Stroquhan
Milton
Blackcraig Hill 406
Speddoch
Kirkton
Garroch
St John's Town of Dalry
Bogue
Newtonairds
Holywood
Locharbriggs
Darrou
Glenlee
Blackcraig
Drumwhirn
Skeoch Hill
Gribton
New Bridge
Bennan 381
Garcrogo Forest
Knocklearn
Slongaber
Terregles
Craigencallie
Balmaclellan
Gibbshill
Margreig
Scaur
Lincluden
New Galloway
Larglear Hill 282
Clatteringshaws Loch
Darnaw
7
Cairnsmore of Dee 493
Corsock
398
Glen
Shawhead
2
DUMFRIES
Maxwelltown
Clatteringshaws
Merkland
Crofts
Henderland
Cargenbridge
Lochfoot
Goldielea
Forest Drive (summer only)
Glenlair
Brooklands
Brae
Dalskairth
Round Fell 402
Fell of Fleet 471
Shaw Hill 385
Bennan Cottage
Toll
Drumrash
Square Point
Crocketford or Ninemile Bar
Milton Loch
Cargen
Walton Park
Milton
Mabie
Gillfoot
Craignelder 601
Mossdale
Parton
Kirkpatrick Durham
Springholm
Beeswing
Whinny Hill
Auchencloy Hill 209
Airie Hill 291
Slogarie
Auchendolly
Stonehouse
Kirkconnel
Loch Grannoch
Craig
Old Bridge of Urr
Hermitage
Lotus Hill 321
Shambelly
Cairnsmore of Fleet 711
Crossmichael
Kirkgunzeon
Kinharvie
Mollance
Haugh of Urr
New Abbey
Laurieston
Glenlochar
Townhead of Greenlaw
Clarebrand
Door of Cairnsmore
White Top of Culreoch 344
Darngarroch
Hillowton
Cuil Hill
Loch Kindar
Castle Douglas
Craignair
Dalbeattie
Criffell 569
Castramont
Buchan
Bridge of Dee
Creetown
Glengap
Rhonehouse or Kelton
Breoch
Gelston
Palnackie
Kirkbean
Caulkerbush
Southwick
Cassencarie
Ringford
Tongland
Gatehouse of Fleet
Airieland
Barharrow
Loch Ken
Loch Whinyeon
0 2 4 6 miles
0 2 4 6 8 10 km

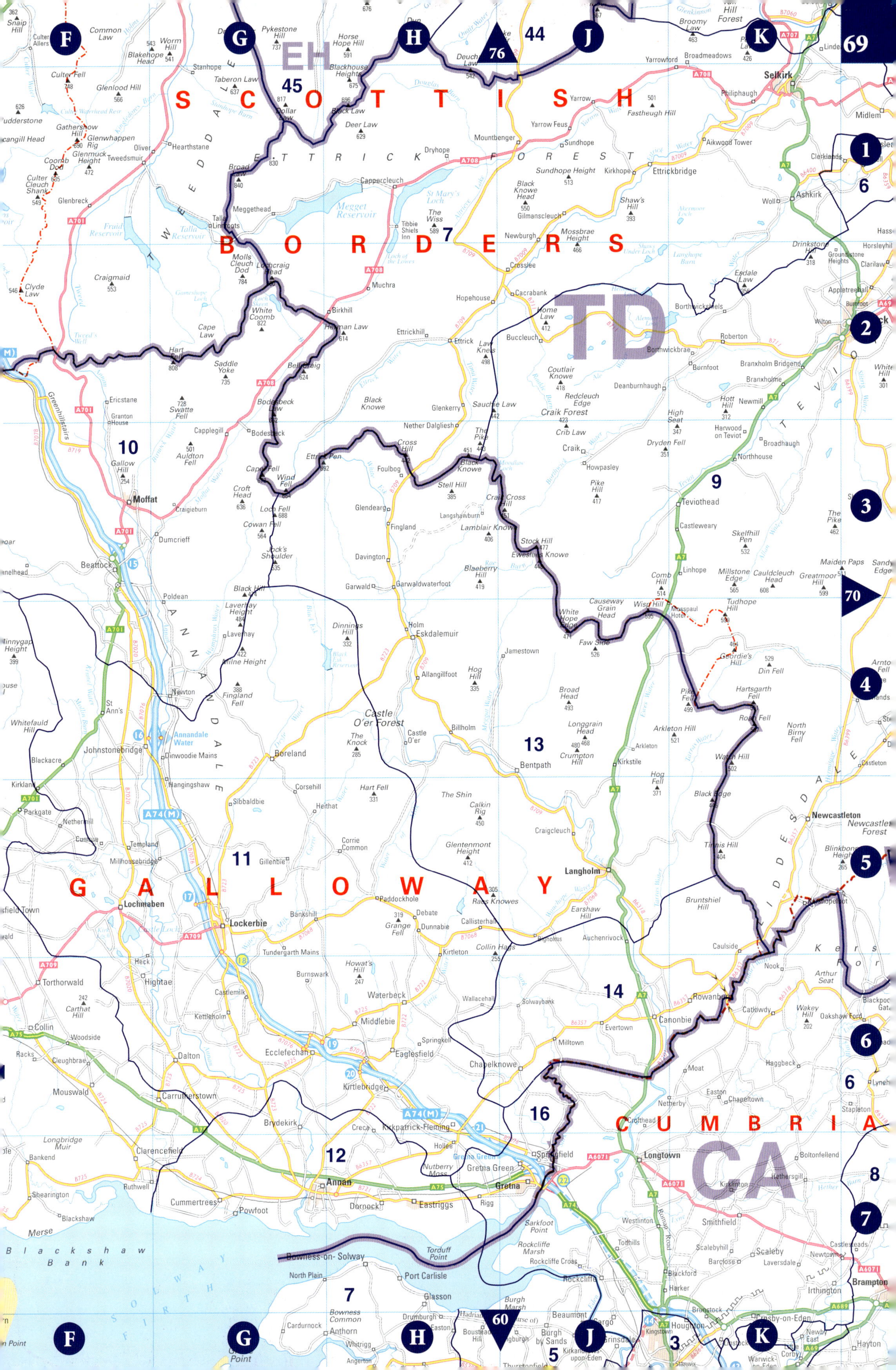
69
76
70
60
F
G
H
J
K
44
45
EH
TD
CA
SCOTTISH
BORDERS
GALLOWAY
CUMBRIA
ETTRICK FOREST
TWEEDDALE
ANNANDALE
TEVIOTDALE
LIDDESDALE
SOLWAY FIRTH
Kershope Forest
Snaip Hill 362
Common Law
Culter Allers
Culter Fell 748
Worm Hill 541
Blakehope Head 543
Pykestone Hill 737
Horse Hope Hill 591
Blackhouse Heights 675
Stanhope
Taberon Law 637
Glenlood Hill 566
Dollar Law 817
Black Law
Deer Law 629
Deuchar Law 542
Glenkinnon
Broomy Law 463
Hill Forest
Yarrowford
Broadmeadows
Selkirk
Philiphaugh
Midlem
Linde
Yarrow
Yarrow Feus
Fastheugh Hill 501
Mountbenger
Sundhope
Aikwood Tower
Gathersnow Hill 690
Glenwhappen Rig
Glenmuck Height 472
Tweedsmuir
Oliver
Hearthstane
Dryhope
Broad Law 840
Coomb Dod 635
Culter Cleuch Shank 549
Glenbreck
Cappercleuch
Megget Reservoir
Meggethead
Talla Reservoir
Talla Linnfoots
St Mary's Loch
Tibbie Shiels Inn
The Wiss 589
Sundhope Height 513
Kirkhope
Ettrickbridge
Black Knowe Head 550
Gilmanscleuch
Shaw's Hill 393
Ashkirk
Woll
Fruid Reservoir
Molls Cleuch Dod 784
Lochcraig Head
Loch of the Lowes
Newburgh
Mossbrae Height 466
Crosslee
Drinkstone Hill 318
Groundistone Heights
Hassendean
Horsleyhill
Clarilaw
Craigmaid 553
Muchra
Cacrabank
Esdale Law 356
Appletreehall
Clyde Law 546
White Coomb 822
Birkhill
Hopehouse
Home Law 412
Borthwickshiels
Cape Law
Hartfell 808
Herman Law 614
Ettrickhill
Ettrick
Law Kneis 498
Buccleuch
Alemoor Loch
Roberton
Borthwickbrae
Bornfoot
Branxholm Bridgend
Saddle Yoke 735
Bell Craig 624
Coutlair Knowe 418
Redcleuch Edge
Branxholme
White Hill 301
Hott Hill 312
Newmill
Deanburnhaugh
Craik Forest
Ericstane
Granton House
Swatte Fell 728
Bodesbeck Law
Black Knowe
Glenkerry
Sauchie Law 442
High Seat 347
Harwood on Teviot
Broadhaugh
Nether Dalgliesh
Crib Law 423
Capplegill
Bodesbeck
The Pike 443
Craik
Dryden Fell 351
Northhouse
Auldton Fell 501
Gallow Hill 254
Ettrick Pen 692
Cross Hill
Black Knowe 451
Howpasley
Capel Fell 678
Wind Fell 664
Foulbog
Stell Hill 385
Moffat
Croft Head 636
Craigieburn
Pike Hill 417
Teviothead
Craik Cross Hill
Loch Fell 688
Glendearg
Langshawburn
Lamblair Knowe 406
Fingland
Castleweary
Skelfhill Pen 532
The Pike 462
Dumcrieff
Cowan Fell 564
Stock Hill 477
Ewesless Knowe
Davington
Jock's Shoulder 535
Blaeberry Hill 419
Maiden Paps
Sandy Edge
Beattock
Comb Hill 514
Linhope
Millstone Edge 565
Cauldcleuch Head 608
Greatmoor Hill 599
Garwald
Garwaldwaterfoot
Tudhope Hill 599
Poldean
Black Hill
Laverhay Height 489
White Hope Edge
Causeway Grain Head
Wisp Hill 595
Mosspaul Hotel
Laverhay
Dinnings Hill 332
Holm
Eskdalemuir
Faw Side 526
Jamestown
Arnton Fell
Minnygap Height 399
Milne Height 422
Allangillfoot
Hog Hill 335
Geordie's Hill
Din Fell 529
Fingland Fell 388
Newton
Broad Head 493
Pike Fell 499
Hartsgarth Fell
St Ann's
Castle O'er Forest
Whitefauld Hill
Longgrain Head 480 468
Arkleton Hill 521
Roan Fell
North Birny Fell
The Knock 285
Castle O'er
Billholm
Annandale Water
Johnstonebridge
Boreland
Dinwoodie Mains
Arkleton
Blackacre
13
Bentpath
Crumpton Hill
Watch Hill 502
Castleton
Kirkstile
Kirkland
Hangingshaw
Corsehill
Hart Fell 331
Hog Fell 371
Sibbaldbie
The Shin
Calkin Rig 450
Parkgate
Heithat
Black Edge
Newcastleton
Netherhill
Newcastleton Forest
Craigcleuch
Corrie Common
Templand
Glentenmont Height 412
Tinnis Hill 404
Cumrue
11
Gillenbie
Millhousebridge
Blinkbonny Height 265
Langholm
Lochmaben
Paddockhole
Raes Knowes 305
Bruntshiel Hill
Kershopefoot
Earshaw Hill
Lockerbie
Bankshill
Debate
Grange Fell 319
Dunnabie
Callisterhall
Castle Loch
Auchenrivock
Tundergarth Mains
Kirtleton
Collin Hags 255
Canonbie
Caulside
Heck
Howat's Hill 247
Burnswark
Nook
Arthur Seat
Torthorwald
Hightae
14
Waterbeck
Wallacehall
Solwaybank
Rowanburn
Catlowdy
Wakey Hill 202
Oakshaw Ford
Carthat Hill 242
Castlemilk
Kettleholm
Middlebie
Evertown
Collin
Woodside
Springkell
Milltown
Racks
Cleughbrae
Dalton
Ecclefechan
Eaglesfield
Chapelknowe
Haggbeck
Moat
Mouswald
Kirtlebridge
Lyneholmeford
Carrutherstown
Eston
Chapeltown
Netherby
Stapleton
16
Brydekirk
Crofthead
Longbridge Muir
Creca
Kirkpatrick-Fleming
Bankend
Clarencefield
Hollee
Springfield
Longtown
Boltonfellend
12
Gretna Green
Nutberry Moss
Shearington
Ruthwell
Annan
Gretna
Kirklinton
Hethersgill
Cummertrees
Dornock
Eastriggs
Rigg
Powfoot
Blackshaw
Sarkfoot Point
Westlinton
Smithfield
Merse
Blackshaw Bank
Torduff Point
Todhills
Scaleby
Castlesteads
Rockcliffe Marsh
Scalebyhill
Newtown
Bowness-on-Solway
Rockcliffe Cross
Barclose
Laversdale
Brampton
North Plain
Port Carlisle
Rockcliffe
Blackford
Harker
Irthington
Glasson
Burgh Marsh
Brunstock
Crosby-on-Eden
7
Bowness Common
Cardurnock
Anthorn
Drumburgh
Hadrian's Wall
Easton
Boustead Hill
Beaumont
Burgh by Sands
Kirkandrews-upon-Eden
Grinsdale
Kingstown
Houghton
Warwick
Newby East
Hayton
Corby
Whitrigg
Angerton
Thurstonfield
Grune Point
3
5
8
10
1
2
4
6
9

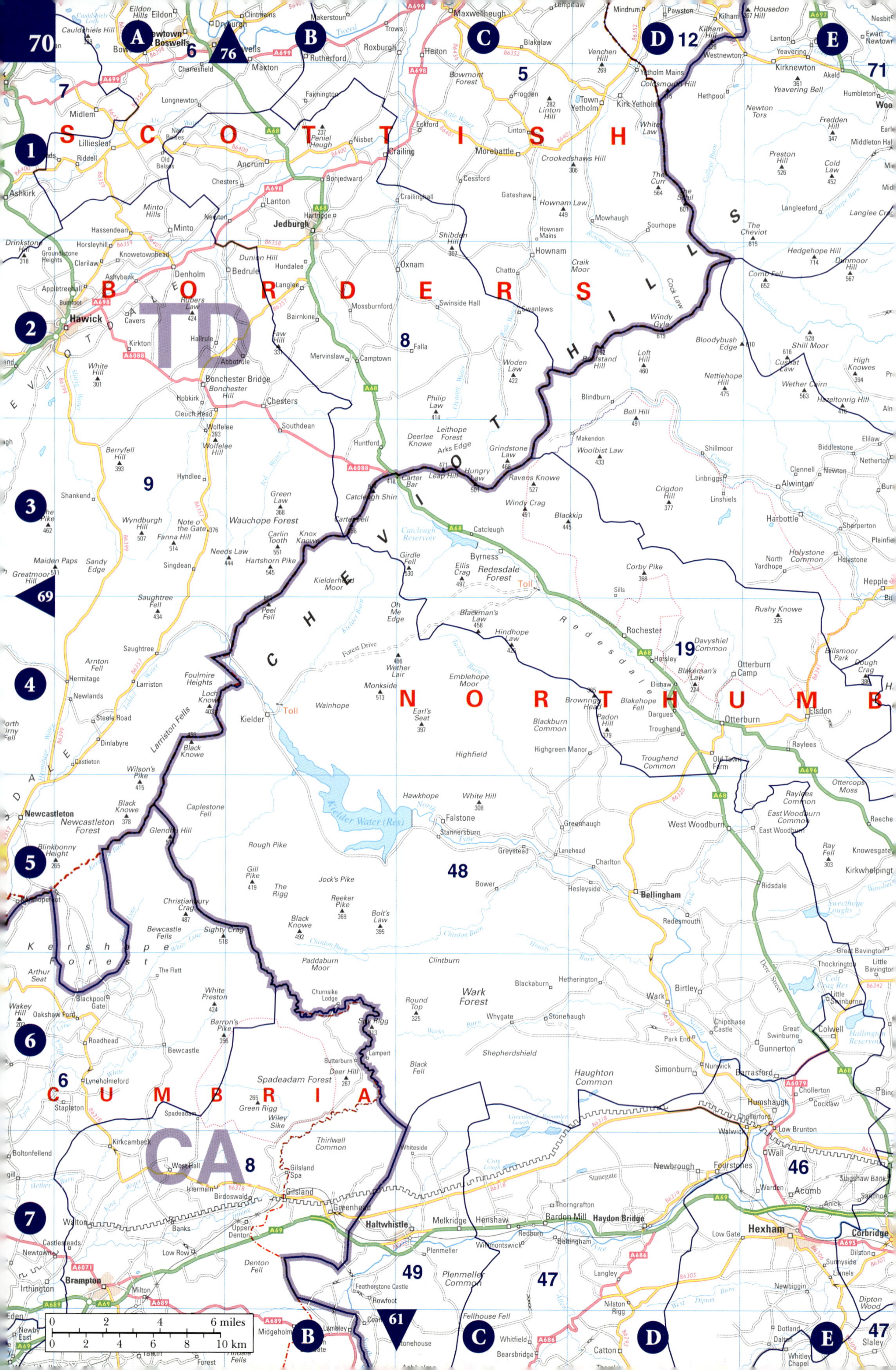
A
B
C
D
E
1
2
3
4
5
6
7
76
69
61
71
12
5
7
8
9
19
48
6
49
47
46
SCOTTISH
BORDERS
TD
CHEVIOT HILLS
CHEVIOT
NORTHUMB
CUMBRIA
CA
TEVIOTDALE
LIDDESDALE
Kershope Forest
Cauldshiels Loch
Cauldshiels Hill
Eildon Hills
Eildon
Newtown St Boswells
Dryburgh
Clintmains
Makerstoun
Tweed
Trows
Maxwellheugh
Lempitlaw
Mindrum
Pawston
Kilham
Kilham Hill
Housedon Hill
Nesbit
Ewart
Newtown
Bowden
Charlesfield
Maxton
Rutherford
Roxburgh
Heiton
Blakelaw
Vencher Hill
Yetholm Mains
Westnewton
Lanton
Yeavering
Kirknewton
Akeld
Coldsmouth Hill
Hethpool
Yeavering Bell
Humbleton
Midlem
Longnewton
Fairnington
Bowmont Forest
Frogden
Linton Hill
Town Yetholm
Kirk Yetholm
Newton Tors
Fredden Hill
Middleton Hall
Lilliesleaf
Riddell
New Belses
Old Belses
Peniel Heugh
Nisbet
Crailing
Eckford
Kale Water
Linton
Morebattle
White Law
Crookedshaws Hill
Preston Hill
Cold Law
Ashkirk
Ancrum
Chesters
Bonjedward
Cessford
The Curr
The Schil
Langleeford
Langlee Crags
Minto Hills
Minto
Lanton
Crailinghall
Gateshaw
Hownam Law
Mowhaugh
Sourhope
The Cheviot
Hassendean
Newton
Jedburgh
Hartrigge
Hownam Mains
Drinkstone Hill
Horsleyhill
Groundistone Heights
Knowetownhead
Dunion Hill
Bedrule
Hundalee
Oxnam
Shibden Hill
Hownam
Chatto
Craik Moor
Hedgehope Hill
Dunmoor Hill
Clarilaw
Denholm
Ashybank
Appletreehall
Langlee
Comb Fell
Buittock
Hawick
Cavers
Rubers Law
Bairnkine
Mossburnford
Swinside Hall
Swanlaws
Cock Law
Windy Gyle
Bloodybush Edge
Shill Moor
Kirkton
Hallrule
Abbotrule
Faw Hill
Mervinslaw
Camptown
Falla
Beefstand Hill
Loft Hill
Cushat Law
High Knowes
White Hill
Bonchester Bridge
Bonchester Hill
Woden Law
Nettlehope Hill
Wether Cairn
Hobkirk
Chesters
Philip Law
Blindburn
Hazeltonrig Hill
Cleuch Head
Southdean
Bell Hill
Wolfelee
Wolfelee Hill
Leithope Forest
Deerlee Knowe
Arks Edge
Makendon
Woolbist Law
Shillmoor
Biddlestone
Elilaw
Netherton
Berryfell Hill
Huntford
Grindstone Law
Hyndlee
Hungry Law
Carter Bar
Leap Hill
Ravens Knowe
Clennell
Newton
Linbriggs
Alwinton
Crigdon Hill
Linshiels
Shankend
Catcleugh Shin
Green Law
Windy Crag
Blackkip
The Pike
Wyndburgh Hill
Note o' the Gate
Wauchope Forest
Carter Fell
Catcleugh
Catcleugh Reservoir
Harbottle
Sharperton
Plainfield
Fanna Hill
Carlin Tooth
Knox Knowe
Needs Law
Hartshorn Pike
Girdle Fell
Byrness
Holystone Common
Holystone
North Yardhope
Maiden Paps
Sandy Edge
Greatmoor Hill
Singdean
Kielderhead Moor
Ellis Crag
Redesdale Forest
Toll
Corby Pike
Sills
Hepple
Saughtree Fell
Peel Fell
Oh Me Edge
Blackman's Law
Hindhope Law
Rochester
Rushy Knowe
Redesdale
Saughtree
Forest Drive
Wether Lair
Horsley
Davyshiel Common
Billsmoor Park
Dough Crag
Arnton Fell
Hermitage
Larriston
Foulmire Heights
Loch Knowe
Emblehope Moor
Monkside
Elishaw
Blakeman's Law
Otterburn Camp
Newlands
Kielder
Wainhope
Earl's Seat
Brownrigg Head
Blakehope Fell
Dargues
Otterburn
Elsdon
Steele Road
Larriston Fells
Black Knowe
Padon Hill
Blackburn Common
Troughend
Dinlabyre
Highfield
Highgreen Manor
Raylees
Castleton
Troughend Common
Old Town Farm
Wilson's Pike
Ottercops Moss
Newcastleton
Newcastleton Forest
Black Knowe
Caplestone Fell
Hawkhope
White Hill
Falstone
Kielder Water (Res)
North Tyne
Raylees Common
East Woodburn Common
Raechester
Greenhaugh
West Woodburn
East Woodburn
Glendhu Hill
Stannersburn
Blinkbonny Height
Rough Pike
Greystead
Lanehead
Ray Fell
Knowesgate
Charlton
Kirkwhelpington
Kershopefoot
Gill Pike
The Rigg
Jock's Pike
Bower
Hesleyside
Bellingham
Ridsdale
Christianbury Crag
Reeker Pike
Bolt's Law
Redesmouth
Sweethope Loughs
Bewcastle Fells
Sighty Crag
Black Knowe
Chirdon Burn
Arthur Seat
The Flatt
Paddaburn Moor
Clintburn
Great Bavington
Thockrington
Little Bavington
Blackpool Gate
White Preston
Churnsike Lodge
Blackaburn
Hetherington
Wark Forest
Colt Crag Res
Little Swinburne
Wakey Hill
Oakshaw Ford
Round Top
Wark
Birtley
Dere Street
Colwell
Barron's Pike
Spy Rigg
Whygate
Stonehaugh
Chipchase Castle
Great Swinburne
Hallington Reservoir
Roadhead
Lampert
Park End
Gunnerton
Bewcastle
Shepherdshield
Butterburn
Deer Hill
Black Fell
Haughton Common
Simonburn
Nunwick
Barrasford
Lyneholmeford
Spadeadam Forest
Chollerton
Stapleton
Green Rigg
Humshaugh
Cocklaw
Spadeadam
Wiley Sike
Greenlee Lough
Broomlee Lough
Chollerford
Walwick
Low Brunton
Kirkcambeck
Thirlwall Common
Whiteside
Crag Lough
Wall
Boltonfellend
West Hall
Gilsland Spa
Newbrough
Fourstones
Stanegate
Warden
Acomb
Sandhoe
Irthington
Birdoswald
Gilsland
Greenhead
Thorngrafton
Anick
Walton
Banks
Upper Denton
Haltwhistle
Melkridge
Henshaw
Bardon Mill
Haydon Bridge
Hexham
Corbridge
Castlesteads
Newtown
Low Row
Plenmeller
Willimontswick
Redburn
Beltingham
Low Gate
Dilston
Brampton
Denton Fell
Plenmeller Common
Langley
Sunnyside
Linnels
Irthington
Milton
Featherstone Castle
Rowfoot
Nilston Rigg
West Dipton Burn
Newbiggin
Dipton Wood
Coanwood
Fellhouse Fell
Midgeholme
Lambley
Whitfield
Dotland
Dalton
Slaley
Whitley Chapel
Bearsbridge
Catton
Newby East
Tindale Fells
A699
A698
A68
A6088
A697
A7
A696
A6079
A69
A686
A695
A6071
A689
B6400
B6359
B6358
B6357
B6399
B6352
B6401
B6436
B6318
B6320
B6319
B6305
B6342
B6307
0 2 4 6 miles
0 2 4 6 8 10 km

See page 121 for postcode detail

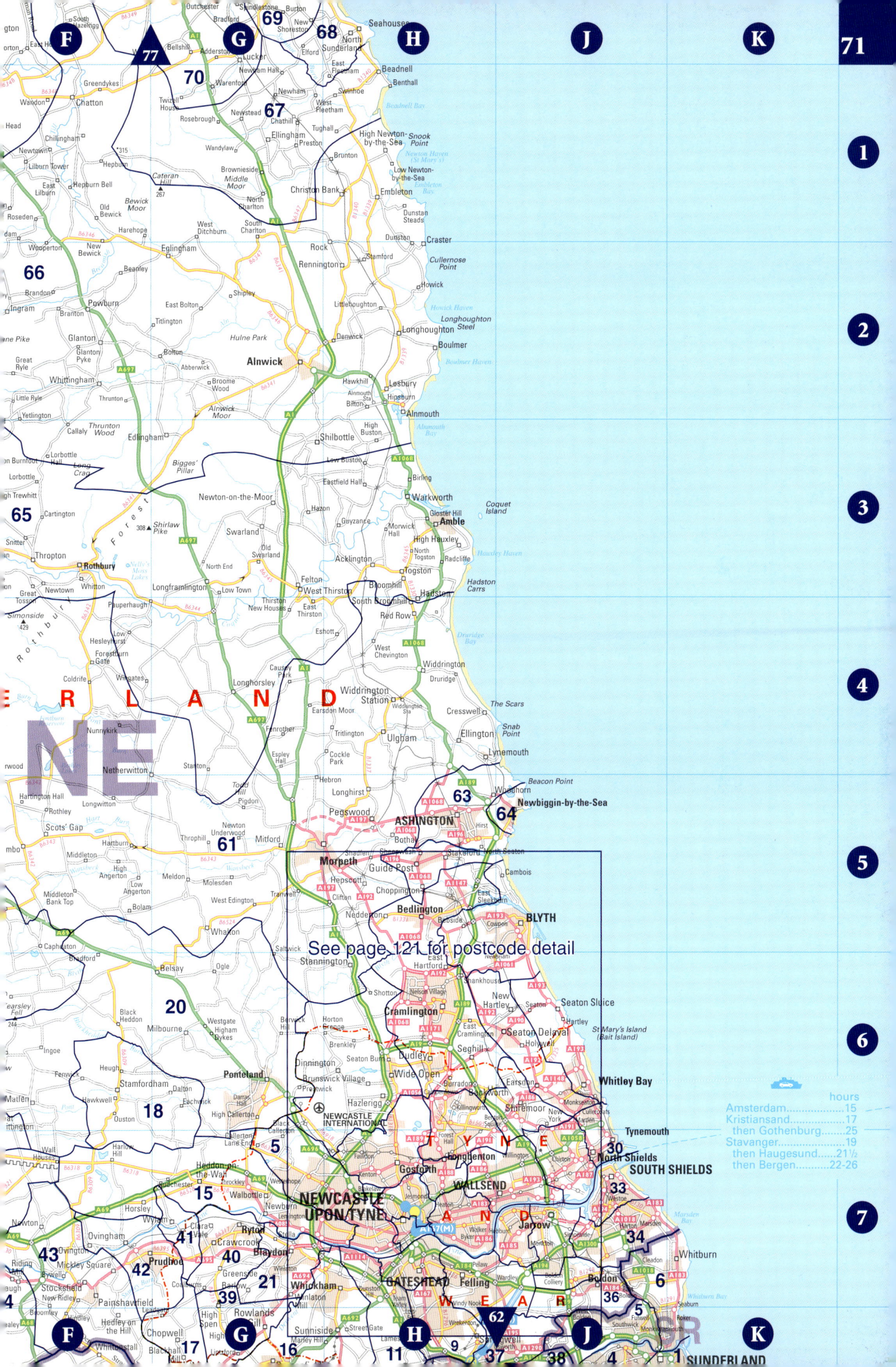

hours
Amsterdam..................15
Kristiansand.................17
then Gothenburg........25
Stavanger.....................19
then Haugesund......21½
then Bergen..........22-26

# 72

## A 78 B C D E

### 1
**COLONSAY**
- Balnahard
- Kiloran Bay
- Kiloran
- Upper Kilchattan
- Lower Kilchattan
- Port Mòr
- Colonsay House
- Scalasaig
- **61**
- Machrins
- Port Lobh
- Eilean Mhuacaig
- Garvard
- Balerominmore
- Balerominidubh
- Rubha Dubh
- Rubh' a' Geodha
- Port Ceann a' Gharraidh
- Oban 2¼ hrs

Rubh' a' Bàgh Gleann Speireig
Glengarrisdale Bay
Glengarrisdale
Ben Garrisdale 365
Cruach Ionnastail 295
Lealt

### 2
**ISLAY** (same scale as main map)
- Tormisdale
- Dubh Eilean
- Lossit
- Kelsay
- Rubha na Faing
- **47**
- Easter Ellister
- Portnahaven
- Port Wemyss
- Orsay
- Rinns Point

- Oronsay
- Eilean nan Ron
- Eilean Ghaoideamal
- Rubha Bàn

1½ hrs (summer only)

**JURA**
- Rainberg Mòr 453
- Dubh Bheinn
- Cruach Sganadail
- Shian Bay
- Loch Righ Mòr
- Gleann Aoistail
- **60**
- Lussagiven
- Ardlussa
- Inverlussa
- Lussa Point
- Eilean an Rubha
- Beinn Sgaillinish 190
- Tarbert
- Tramaig Bay

### 3
- Rubh' a' Mhàil
- Rubha Bholsa
- Nave Island
- Ardnave Point
- Ardnave
- Carraig Bhàn
- Ton Mhòr
- Sanaigmore
- Eilean Mòr
- Rubha Lamanais
- Smaull
- Braigo
- Ballinaby
- Tayovullin
- Kilnave
- Gortantaoid Point
- Killinallan
- Killinallan Point
- Sgarbh Breac 364
- Margadale Hill 283
- **46**
- Giurbheinn 316
- Beinn Bhreac
- Bunnahabhainn
- Ardnahoe

- Glenbatrick
- Scrinadle 506
- Beinn Bhreac 439
- Beinn Tarsuinn 416
- Jura Forest
- Beinn an Òir 785
- Beinn Shiantaidh 755
- Beinn a' Chaolais 734
- Paps of Jura
- Gleann Asdale
- Glas Bheinn 561
- Corran
- Lagg
- Rubh' a' Chamais
- Gate House
- Achamore
- Ardmenish
- Knockrome
- An Dùnan
- Rubh' an Leim
- Loch Tarbert
- Rubh' a' Chrois-aoinidh
- Creag Nam Fiadh Mòr 262
- Tarbert Bay
- Keillmore
- Danna Island
- Corr Eilean
- Eilean Mòr
- Point o

### 4
**ARGYLL**
- Leckgruinart
- Aoradh
- Craigens
- Carnduncan
- Grainel
- **44**
- **ISLAY**
- Loch Cam
- Loch Gruinart
- Loch Finlaggan
- Keils
- Balulive
- **45**
- Loch Ballygrant
- Kilmeny
- Ballygrant
- Ardnahoe
- Port Askaig
- Feolin Ferry
- Feolin
- Keils
- Dubh Bheinn 530
- Craighouse
- Eilean nan Gabhar
- Small Isles
- Eilean Bhride
- Point
- Machrie
- Saligo
- Loch Gorm
- Aruadh
- Foreland
- **49**
- Rockside
- Conisby
- Kilchoman
- Machir Bay
- Lyrabus
- Blackrock
- Islay House
- Moin'a'choire
- Eskinish
- Redhouses
- Beinn Dubh 267
- Cachlaidh Mhòr
- Sgorr nam Faoileann
- Am Fraoch Eilean
- Brosdale Island
- Brat Bheinn 342
- Cabrach
- Ardfin
- Jura House
- Rubha na Caillich
- Crackaig
- Sannaig
- Na Cùiltean
- Kilberry

### 5
- Bruichladdich
- Kilchiaran
- **48**
- Port Charlotte
- Gearach
- Carn
- Beinn Tart a' Mhill 232
- Tormisdale
- Lossit
- Kelsay
- Nerabus
- Easter Ellister
- **47**
- A847
- Bowmore
- Gartnatra
- Ronnachmore
- Gartbreck
- **43**
- A846
- Cruach
- Neriby
- Barr
- Cattadale
- Cluanach
- Glas Bheinn 471
- Proaig
- McArthur's Head
- Beinn Uraraidh 454
- Beinn Bhan 471
- Beinn Bheigeir 491
- Ardtalla
- Rubha Liath
- Claggain Bay

Loch Indaal
Kilenno
Laggan
Lossan
Kintour

2 hrs

### 6
Rinns Point
- Laggan Bay
- Machrie
- Leorin
- Kintra
- Glenegedale
- **ISLAY**
- **42**
- Sgorr Bhogachain 347
- Beinn Sholum
- Ardmore Point
- Ardmore
- Eilean a' Chuirn
- Eilean Bhride
- Rubha Mòr
- Maol Buidhe 165
- Cornabus
- Carnmore
- Lower Killeyan
- Risabus
- Inerval
- **THE OA**
- Mull of Oa
- Ardbeg
- Lagavulin
- Laphroaig
- Port Ellen
- The Ard
- Texa
- Rubha na Gainmhich
- Port Chubaird
- Rubha nan Leacan

2⅝ hrs

- West Tarbert Bay
- East Tarbert Bay
- Tarbert
- Ardailly
- Creag Bhàn 100
- Druimyeon Bay
- Rhunahaorin Point
- **Gigha**
- **41**
- Ardminish
- Craro Island
- Grob Bagh
- Cara Island
- Mull of Cara
- Tayinl
- Muasdale

### 7
- Glenacardoch Point
- Bellochantuy
- Bellochantuy Bay
- Killocraw
- Glenbarr
- A83
- Tangy

## A B C D E

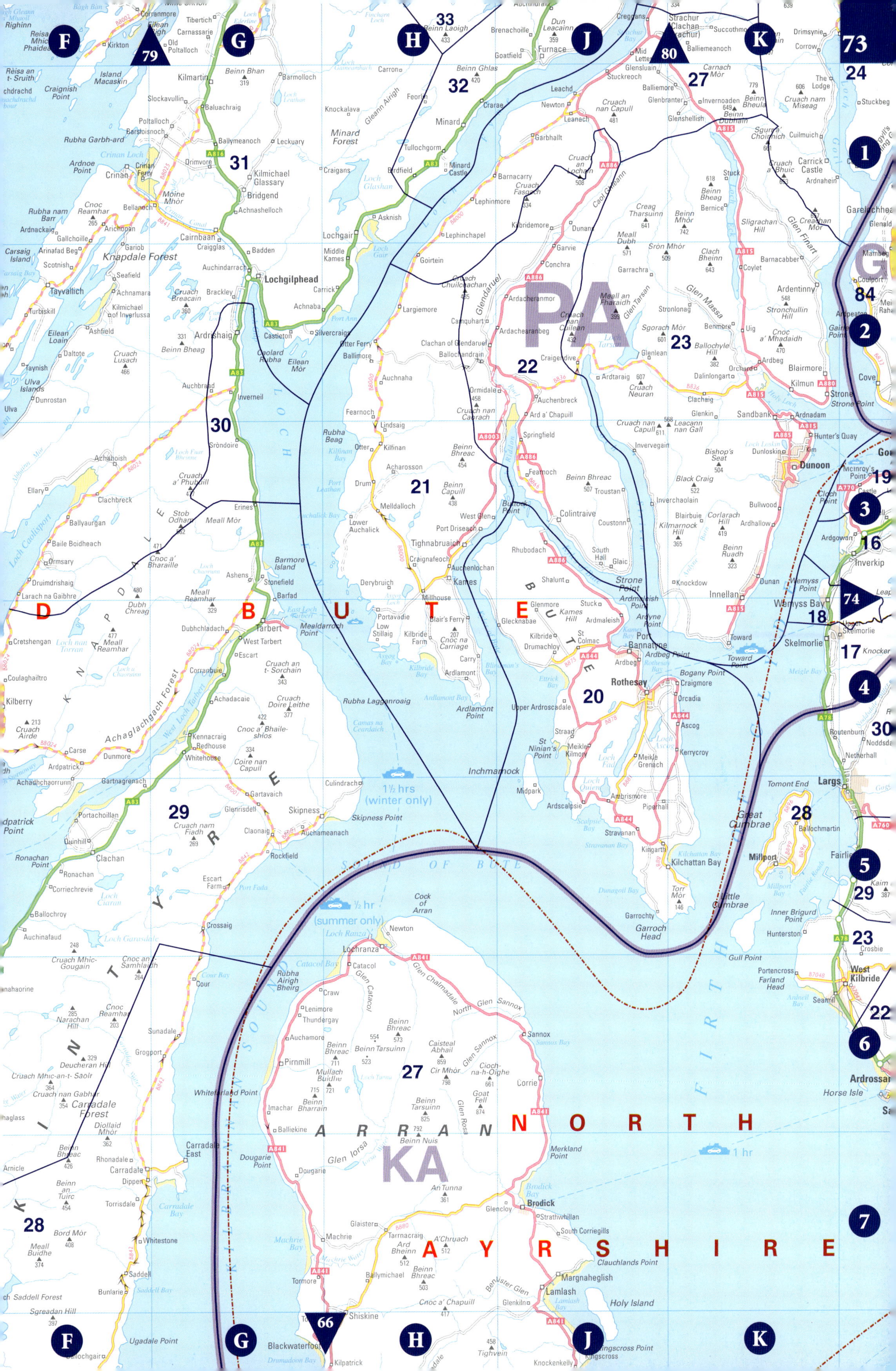

A
B
C
D
E
1
2
3
4
5
6
7
24
Lochgoilhead
The Brack
Ardgartan
Stuckgowan
Tullich Hill
Ben Reoch
Beinn Bhreac
Glen Douglas
Doune Hill
Inverbeg
Rowardennan Lodge
Kinlochard
Ledard
Pass of Aberfoyle
Milton
Aberfoyle
Achray Forest
Port of Menteith
Torrie Forest
Thornhill
Ruskie
Blairhoyle
8
Loch Ard Forest
Gartmore
Cobleland
Flanders Moss
Dykehead
Easter Poldar
Arnprior
Kippen
Cauldhame
Buchlyvie
Garden
Arngibbon
Wrightpark
S T I R L I N G
A R G Y L L
83
A N D
84
B U T E
Glenmallan
Finnart
Portincaple
Garelochhead
Glen Luss
Luss
Inchtavannach
Inchconnachan
Inchcruin
Inchfad
Inchcailloch
Balmaha
Milarrochy
Pass of Balmaha
Cashel Farm
Garadhban Forest
Milton of Buchanan
Buchanan Castle
Drymen
Balfron
Balfron Station
Boquhan
Killearn
63
Corrie of Balglass
Fintry
Craigton
Gonachan Cottage
Mambeg
Faslane
Balernock
Shandon
Glen Fruin
Coulport
Meikle Rahane
Clynder
Rhu
Rosneath
Kilcreggan
Helensburgh
Craigendoran
Cardross
Colgrain
Ardmore
Geilston
Cove
Strone
Dunoon
Hunter's Quay
Gourock
Ashton
19
Greenock
15
Port Glasgow
Langbank
16
I N V E R C L Y D E
Inverkip
Wemyss Bay
73
18
Kilmacolm
13
Bridge of Weir
Houston
11
Skelmorlie
17
Knockencorsan
Peat Hill
30
Routenburn
Noddsdale
Largs
Fairlie
28
29
Kaim Hill
A Y R S H I R E
23
West Kilbride
22
Seamill
Ardrossan
21
Saltcoats
Horse Isle
Brodick 1 hr
20
Stevenston
Kilwinning
12
IRVINE
Dreghorn
Springside
11
Crosshouse
Kilmarnock
KILMARNOCK
Dundonald
10
Troon
Larne (summer only) 1¾ hrs
Lady Isle
Barassie
SOUTH
AYRSHIRE
67
Monkton
Symington
Craigie
Crosshands
Mauchline
Mossblown
Alexandria
Balloch
Jamestown
Bonhill
Renton
WEST
DUNBARTONSHIRE
82
Dumbarton Muir
Kilpatrick Hills
DUMBARTON
Milton
60
Bowling
Old Kilpatrick
81
Erskine
Bishopton
7
6
Georgetown
Houston
3
Linwood
PAISLEY
Johnstone
Elderslie
Kilbarchan
10
R E N F R E W S H I R E
Howwood
9
Lochwinnoch
12
25
N O R T H
Kilbirnie
Beith
14
15
Glengarnock
Dalry
24
Gateside
Barrmill
Burnhouse
Dunlop
K A
Stewarton
13
Kingsford
3
Fenwick
Waterside
Kilmaurs
G
PA
Clydebank
Renfrew
GLASGOW
See page 122 for postcode detail
Barrhead
Neilston
78
E A S T
R E N F R E W S H I R E
Newton Mearns
Eaglesham
76
77
75
Milngavie
Bearsden
Kirkintilloch
Lenzie
EAST
DUNBARTONSHIRE
Lennoxtown
Milton of Campsie
Torrance
Rutherglen
Cambuslang
Blantyre
EAST KILBRIDE
Carmunnock
Nerston
Strathblane
Blanefield
C A M P S I E F E L L S
Ballagich Hill
Kingswell
Lochgoyn
Chapelton
10
L
E A S T
A Y R S H I R E
17
Darvel
Newmilns
Galston
Priestland
Greenholm
16
4
Hurlford
Crookedholm
Riccarton
Crossroads
Drumclog
Mill Rig
Distinkhorn
Blairkip
5
18
Dun Rig
Loudoun Hill

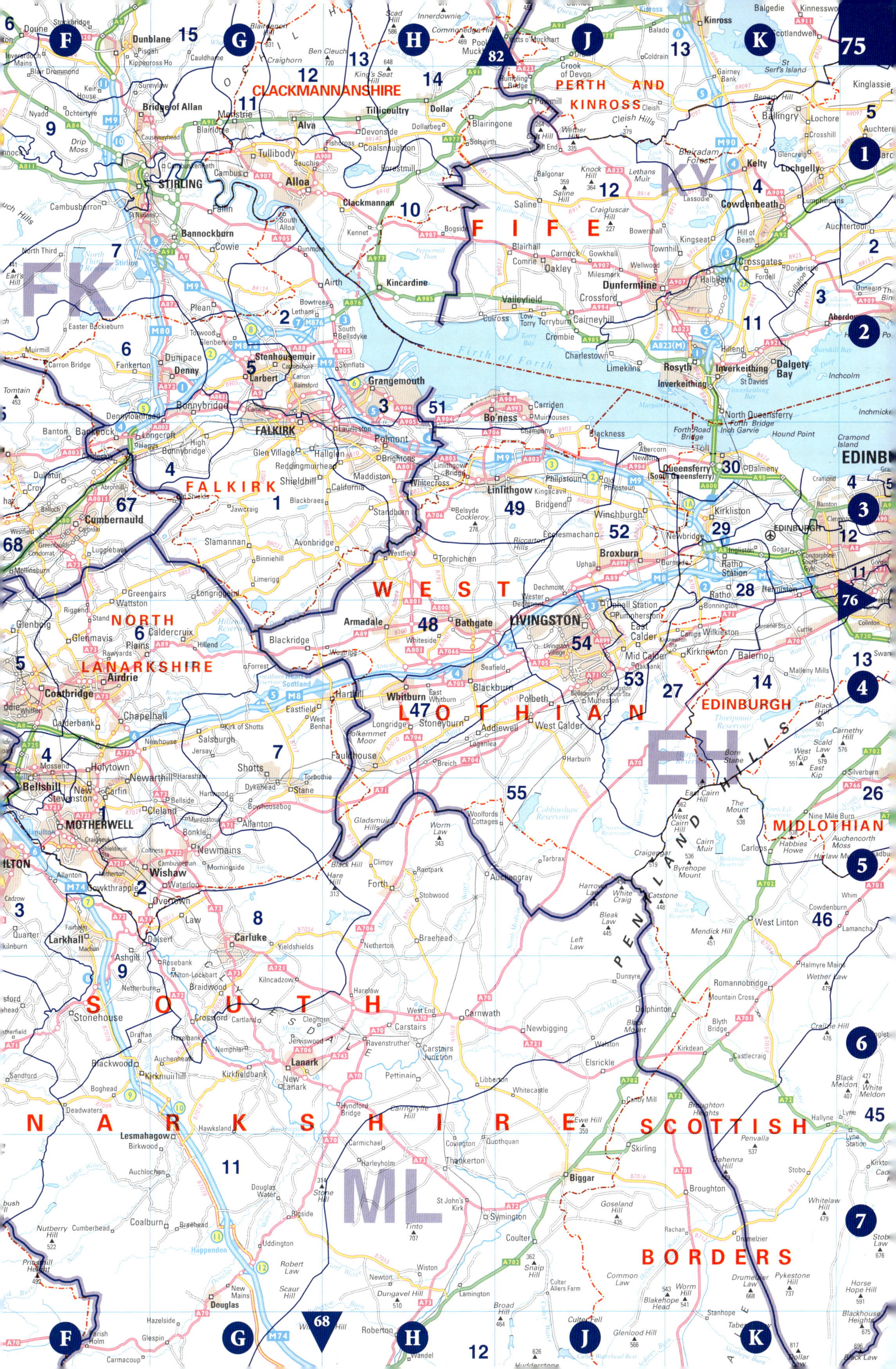

FIFE
KY
Glenrothes
Markinch
Kennoway
Leven
Methil
Buckhaven
Lundin Links
Upper Largo
Largo Bay
Ruddons Point
Kincraig Point
Earlsferry
Chapel Ness
Kilconquhar
St Monans
Pittenweem
Anstruther
Sauchar Point
Isle of May
South Ness
Kinglassie
Thornton
Lochore
Crosshill
Auchterderran
Cardenden
Cluny
East Wemyss
Coaltown of Wemyss
West Wemyss
Dysart
Kirkcaldy
Auchtertool
Kinghorn
Burntisland
Pettycur
Aberdour
Hawkcraig Point
Inchcolm
Inchkeith
Inchmickery
FIRTH OF FORTH
Zeebrugge 17½ hrs
Fidra
Lamb
North Berwick
Craigleith
Bass Rock
St Baldred's Boat
Scoughall
St Baldred's Cradle
Tyne Mouth
Belhaven Bay
Dirleton
Gullane Point
Gullane
Auldhame
Fenton Barns
North Berwick Law
Kingston
Whitekirk
Aberlady Bay
Aberlady
Luffness
Drem
Craigielaw Point
Gosford Bay
Mungoswells
Ballencrieff
East Fortune
Athelstaneford
Preston
East Linton
Tyninghame
West Barns
EAST LOTHIAN
EDINBURGH
Cramond Island
Cramond
Granton
Leith
Black Rocks
Portobello
Musselburgh
Cockenzie and Port Seton
Prestonpans
Longniddry
Spittal
Garleton Hills
Haddington
Tranent
Macmerry
Gladsmuir
Elvingston
Penston
New Winton
Samuelston
Wallyford
Whitecraig
Elphinstone
New Town
Bolton
Garvald
Whitelaw Hill
Traprain
Pitcox
Stenton
Spott
Halls
Deuchrie Dod
Dunbar Common
Bransly Hill
Clints Dod
Corstorphine
Currie
Balerno
Colinton
Swanston
Liberton
Gilmerton
Dalkeith
Danderhall
Millerhill
Crossgatehall
Cousland
Ormiston
Pencaitland
West Saltoun
East Saltoun
Gifford
Danskine
Longyester
Rangely Kip
Newlands Hill
Spartleton Edge
Whiteadder Reservoir
Penshiel Hill
Cranshaws Hill
Lammer Law
Hopes Reservoir
Meikle Says Law
Peastonbank
Pathhead
Humbie
Gilchriston
Mayfield
Easthouses
Newtongrange
Eskbank
Bonnyrigg
Lasswade
Loanhead
Roslin
Bilston
Polton
Rosewell
Auchendinny
Penicuik
Carrington
Gorebridge
Arniston Engine
Newlandrig
Crichton
Fala
Fala Dam
Tynehead
Borthwick
North Middleton
Middleton
Temple
MIDLOTHIAN
Milton Bridge
Carnethy Hill
Scald Law
West Kip
East Kip
Silverburn
Nine Mile Burn
Cauldhame Moor
Howgate
Auchencorth Moss
Leadburn
Whim
Cowdenburn
Lamancha
Westloch
Torfichen Hill
Heriot
MOORFOOT HILLS
EH
Fala Moor
Soutra
Dun Law
Gilston
Falahill
Turf Law
LAMMERMUIR
SCOTT
Oxton
Carfraemill
Hogs Law
Collie Law
Inchkeith Hill
Scoured Rig
Edgarhope Wood
Westruther
Lauder
Lauder Common
Thirlestane
Whiteburn
Houndslow
LAUDERDALE
Halmyre Mains
Wether Law
Eddleston
Dewar
Blackhope Scar
Dun Law
Ladyside Height
Fountainhall
Torquhan
Galabank
Killochyett
Stow
Torsonce
Cringletie
Redscarhead
Crailzie Hill
Totto Hill
Whitehope Law
Eastside Heights
Windlestraw Law
Dunslair Heights
Glentress Forest
Black Law
Black Knowe
Colquhar
Black Meldon
White Meldon
Hallyne
Lyne
Peebles
Lyne Station
Kings Muir
Glentress
Cardrona
Kirkburn
Cardrona Forest
Priesthope Hill
Lee Pen
Seathope Law
Innerleithen
Walkerburn
Elibank and Traquair Forest
Traquair
Wallace's Hill
Kirkton Manor
Cademuir Hill
Stobo
Whitelaw Hill
Preston Law
Hundleshope Heights
Stob Law
Horse Hope Hill
Blackhouse
Dun Rig
Blake Muir
Deuchar Law
Minch Moor
Yardstone Knowe
Great Law
Blackhaugh
Knowes Hill
Thornylee
Clovenfords
Caddonfoot
Ashiestiel Hill
Ashiestiel
Yair Hill Forest
Broomy Law
Peat Law
Broadmeadows
Yarrowford
Fastheugh Hill
Philiphaugh
Selkirk
Lindean
BORDERS
William Law
Buckholm
Galashiels
Meigle Hill
Gala Hill
Boleside
Langshaw
Glendearg
Gattonside
Melrose
Darnick
Newstead
Eildon Hills
Eildon
Cauldshiels Hill
Bowden
Newtown St Boswells
St Boswells
Dryburgh
Bemersyde
Clintmains
Charlesfield
Maxton
Rutherford
Earlston
Drygrange
Leaderfoot
Redpath
Smailholm
Makerstoun
Nether Blainslie
Legerwood
Birkhill
Huntlywood
East Morriston
West Morriston
Gordon
Fans
Longnewton
Midlem
Black Law
Dollar Law
0 2 4 6 miles
0 2 4 6 8 10 km
A B C D E
1 2 3 4 5 6 7
75 83 69

F
G
H
J
K
1
2
3
4
5
6
Barns Ness
Skateraw
Thorntonloch
Reed Point
Cove
Bilsdean
Cockburnspath
Siccar Point
Wheat Stack
Telegraph Hill
Lumsdaine
Coldingham Moor
St Abb's Head
Northfield
St Abbs
Coldingham Bay
Coldingham
Eyemouth
Blackburn Rig
Grantshouse
Houndwood
Cairncross
Horseley Hill
Reston
Burnmouth
Ayton
Ayton Hill
Hilton Bay
Lamberton Beach
Auchencrow
Drakemire
Marygold
Cockburn Law
Abbey St Bathans
Laughing Law
Ecclaw
Ecclaw Hill
Meikle Black Law
Millerton Hill
Lamberton
Mordington Holdings
Clappers
Halidon Hill
Marshall Meadows
Needles Eye
Sharper's Head
Berwick-upon-Tweed
Tweedmouth
Spittal
Highfields
East Ord
Redshin Cove
Scremerston
Cheswick Black Rocks
Cheswick
Goswick
Cheswick Buildings
Holy Island (Lindisfarne)
Emmanuel Head
Holy Island
Castle Point
Holy Island Sands
Guile Point
Fenham Flats
Preston
Lintlaw
Blanerne
Chirnside
Chirnsidebridge
Edrom
Duns
Allanton
Foulden
Hutton
Paxton
Blackadder
Whitelaw
Sunwick
Fishwick
Horncliffe
Longridge Towers
Murton
Gavinton
Choicelee
Polwarth
Sinclair's Hill
Whitsome
Horndean
Thornton Park
Thornton
West Allerdean
Ancroft
Haggerston
Beal
West Mains
Fogo
Fogorig
Swinton
Swinton Quarter
Ladykirk
Upsettlington
Norham
Shoreswood
Shoresdean
Grindon
Felkington
Duddo
Berrington
Bowsden
Swintonmill
Simprim
Purves Hall
Leitholm
Orange Lane
Lambden
Eccles
Lennel
Castle Heaton
Barmoor Lane End
Lowick
West Kyloe
East Kyloe
Fenwick
Buckton
Kyloe Hills
Coldstream
Birgham
Carham
Wark
Cornhill on Tweed
New Heaton
Pallinsburn House
Crookham Eastfield
Crookham
Etal
Ford
West Learmouth
East Learmouth
Branxton
Mardon
Ednam
Hendersyde Park
Hadden
Sprouston
Pressen
Flodden
Kimmerston
Detchant
Holburn
Elwick
Low Middleton
Middleton
Ross
Budle Bay
Budle Point
Easington
Waren Mill
Cockenheugh
North Hazelrigg
South Hazelrigg
Belford
Outchester
Bamburgh
Glororum
Shoreston
Burton
New Shoreston
North Sunderland
Seahouses
Monks House Rocks
Inner Sound
Staple Sound
Kelso
Maxwellheugh
Lempitlaw
Downham
Mindrummill
Mindrum
Pawston
Howtel
Milfield
Fenton
Nesbit
Doddington
Housedon Hill
Kilham
Kilham Hill
Westnewton
Lanton
Coupland
Ewart Newtown
West Horton
East Horton
Roman Road
Warenton
Bellshill
Adderstone
Lucker
Bradford
Elford
East Fleetham
Newham Hall
Blakelaw
Venchen Hill
Yetholm Mains
Yeavering
Kirknewton
Yeavering Bell
Akeld
Wooler
Greendykes
Chatton
Wandon
Twizell House
Newham
Swinhoe
West Fleetham
Newstead
Rosebrough
Town Yetholm
Kirk Yetholm
Hethpool
Newton Tors
Frogden
Linton Hill
NORTHUMBERLAND
TD
NE
Longstone
Farne Islands
Farne Island
Ross
Budle Point
Bamburgh
Spindlestone
Lucker
same scale as main map
A1
A1107
A6105
A6112
A698
A697
A1167
11
12
13
14
15
66
67
68
69
70
71

# 78

## A B C D E

### 1
SEA OF THE HEBRIDES

Lochboisdale 5–7
Castlebay 5¼ hrs

Eag na Maoile
Rubha Mòr
Rubh' a' Bhinnein
Cliad Bay
Bousd
Rubha Sgor-Innis Sorisdale
Torastan
Bàgh na Cèille

### 2
INNER HEBRIDES

Grishipoll
Grishipoll Bay
Clabhach
Ballyhaugh
Hogh Bay
Ben Hogh ▲104
Totronald
Totamore
Arileod
Acha
Uig
**78**
C O L L
Arinagour
Eilean Ornsay
Loch Eatharna
2¾ hrs
Caliach Point
Port na Long
Sunipol
Langamull
Mornish
Cruach Sleibhe ▲166

Calgary Point
Crossapol
Gorton
Crossapol Bay
Port Mine
Feall Bay
Port a' Mhuirin
Soa
Rubha Fasachd
Friesland Bay
3½–4¼ hrs
1 hr
Rubha nan Oirean
Calgary
Calgary Bay

### 3
Gunna
Urvaig
Sgeir Bharrach
Miodar
Salum Bay
Salum
Caolas
Ruaig
Rubha Dubh
Port Bàn
Rubha Liath
Soa

Hogh Bay
The Green
Clachan Mòr
Kilkenneth
Moss
Sandaig
Barrapoll
Heylipol
Crossapol
Balephetrish Bay
Balephetrish Hill
Kenovay
**77**
T I R E E
TIREE
B8065
Scarinish
Hynish
Baugh
Hynish Bay
B8067
Balemartine
Mannal

Treshnish Point
Treshnish
Ensay
Rubh' a' Chaoil
Rubh' an t-Suibhein
▲191 Beinn Duill
**74**
Burg
B8073
Loch Tuath

Cairn na Burgh Mòre
Cairn na Burgh Beg
Treshnish Isles
Sgeir a' Chaisteil
Fladda
Lunga
Eilean Dioghlum
Gometra
Gometra House
Rubha Maol na Mine
Maisgeir

### 4
Rinn Thorbhais
Balephuil

Bac Mòr (Dutchman's Cap)
Bac Beag

Little Colonsay
Staffa
Eilean Dubh
Fingal's Cave

**A R**

### 5
Réidh Eilean
Eilean Chalbha
Port an Daime Mhuarbh
Dùn I ▲100
**76**
Ruanaiche
Baile Mòr
Stac an Aoineidh
I O N A
Rubha na Carraig-gèire
Sound of Iona

Kintra
Beinn Chladan ▲81
Fionnphort
Aridhglas
Fidden
**66**
Knockvologan
Torr Fada ▲87
Erraid
Eilean Dubh
Eilean a' Chalmain
Aird Mòr ▲89
Eilean Mòr
Ardalanish
**67**
Rubh' Ardalanish
Ardo
Port M

Rubha nan Cearc
Eo
Loch na Lathaich
Bu
R o s s  o f  M
A849
Kilor

### 6
Soa Island

Dearg Sgeir
Ruadh Sgeir
Torran Rocks
Na Torrain
West Reef
McPhail's Anvil
Torran Sgoilte
Sgeir Ghobhlach
Otter Rock

### 7
Dubh Artach

0 2 4 6 miles
0 2 4 6 8 10 km

F
G
H
J
K
86
1
2
3
4
5
6
7
80
73
Druimnich
Ockle
Sanna Point
Sanna
Fascadale
Achateny
Kilmory
Swordle
Branault
Achnaha
Portuairk
Achosnich
Grigadale
Meall nan Con 437
Beinn an Leathaid 401
357 Beinn Bhreac
36
Meall an Tarmachain 404
ARDNAMURCHAN
313 Beinn nan Losgann
Caim
Beinn na Seilg 342
Kilchoan
Ormsaigmore
Ben Hiant 528
Beinn Bhuidhe 278
Glenbeg
Sròn Bheag
Maclean's Nose
Ardslignish
Eilean Mòr
Glenborrodale
Laga
Ben Laga 512
122 Carn Mòr
Ardtoe
Kentra
Kentra Bay
Arivegaig
Gorteneorn
Acharacle
Ardshealach
Leac Shoilleir 440
Salen
Tarbert
Beinn Bhreac 240
Ardtoe
Shielfoot
Cliff
Dalnabreck
Kinlochmoidart
Glen Moidart
Dalelia
Claish Moss
Resipole
Beinn Resipol 845
Glen Forslan
Gaskan
Gorstanvorran
Sgurr an Tarmachain 756
Sgurr na Greine 497
37
Polloch
Achnanellan
Glenhurich
Kinlochan
Glen Hurich
Druim Garbh
Carn na Nathrach 786
Sgurr Dhomhnuill 888
Scamodale
Mòr 759
Glen
Tighnacoma
SUNART
PH
Scotstown
Ardery
Anaheilt
Drumnatorran
Strontian
Sgurr nan Cnamh 701
33
Garbh Bheinn 885
Ranachan
Woodend
Ardnastang
Achnalea
Glen Tarbert
Gearr Chreag 340
LOCH SUNART
A861
Eilean Mòr
Meall a' Bhroin 303
Liddesdale
Achleek
Meall a' Choirein Luachraich 539
Ardmore Point
½ hr (summer only)
Auliston Point
Oronsay
Risga
Carna
Glencripesdale
HIGHLAND
Sorne Point
Meall an Inbhire
Mishnish
Tobermory
Calve Island
Quinish
75
'S Airdhe Beinn
Achnadrish
Dervaig
Beinn Ghormaig 452
Rahoy
Meall a' Chaise 522
Barr
571 Beinn Iadain
Kinloch
Achleanan
Drimnin
Ardantiobairt
MORVERN
Beinn Bhuidhe 451
Beinn na h-Uamha 464
Gleann Dubh
Achagavel
Taobh Dubh 352
Glas Bheinn 620
Creach Bheinn 853
Fuar Bheinn 765
Meall nan Each 591
Lochuisge
Kilmalieu
Meall a' Chaorainn
Beinn Chlaonleud 475
Clounlaid
Beach
Loch Uisge 512
Sgurr Shalachain 531
Beinn na Cille 651
Glengalmadale
Rubha na h-Airde Uinnsinn
Camasnacroise
Loch a' Choire
Ceanna Mòr
Durinemast
Sidhean na Raplaich 550
34
739 Beinn Mheadhoin
Sgurr a' Bhuic 569
Alltachonaich
Gleann Geal
38
Shuna Island
Rhemore
AROS
Speinne Mòr 444
Ardnacross
Loch Frisa
Cruachan na' Ghairbh 261
Aonacraig
Lettermore
Salen Forest
Meall na Caorach
Claggan
Killundine
Beinn an t-Sruthain 267
Creag Bhan Ard 339
Beinn Bhan 400
Bràigh na Glaice Moire
Meall Damh 339
Beinn a' Chaisil 437
Larachbeg
Ardtornish
Glensanda
nan Clach-corra 315
73
Druim an Fhraoich Mhin 318
Cnoc an da Chinn 390
Fanmore
Ballygown
Beinn Bhuidhe 387
Meall an Fhiar Mhaim 309
Ledmore
Tenga
Glen Aros
A848
Funary Forest
Funary
Tighachnoic
Achnaha
Lochaline
Eileanan Glasa
Glais Bheinn 479
Mam a' Chullaich 462
Meall a' Chaorainn 481
513
An Sleaghach
Eignaig
Eilean Ramsay
Eilean Loch Oscair
Port Ramsay
Ardtur
Appin
Kilbrennan
Beinn na Drise 424
72
Salen
Salen Bay
Fishnish Point
Fishnish
¼ hr
Ardtornish Point
Inninbeg
Clachan
Appin Rocks
Eriska
Eilean Dubh
South Shian
North Shian
Seabank
Rubha nan Gall
Lagganulva
Beinn nan Carn 333
Killiechronan
Kellan
Pennygown
Killbeg
Glen Forsa
Balmeanach
Garmony
Beinn Chreagach Mhor 579
Lynn of Morven
Lismore
Achnacroish
Baligrundle
Achatonich
A'Chrannag
Killiemor
Gruline
Cruach Torran Lochain 348
71
Loch Ba
Beinn Bhuidhe 412
Na Binneinean 329
Beinn Mheadhon 637
Salen Forest
Rubha an Ridire
Bernera
34
Kilcheran
Eilean Dubh
80
Culcharan
Benderloch
Ledaig
Balure
37
Samalan Island
Eorsa
Loch Na Keal
Knock
Beinn a' Ghraig 591
Gaodhail
Beinn na Duatharach 455
Scallastle
Craignure Bay
Pladda Island
Rubha Garbh-àird
South Ledaig
Inch Kenneth
MULL
Clachandhu
Balnahard
68
Dhiseig
Beinn Fhada 702
Gortenbuie
PA
Beinn Talaidh 761
Dun da Ghaoithe 766
65
Sgurr Dearg 741
Craignure
Maol nan Uan 429
Duart Point
Eilean Musdile
Craignure ¾ hr
Eilean Mòr
North Ledaig Point
Connel
Lochdon
Lady's Rock
Dunbeg
Achaleven
Balmeanach
Coirc Bheinn 581
ARGYLL AND BUTE
Ben More 966
Cruachan Dearg 704
Guibean Uluvailt 328
Corra-bheinn 704
Cruach Choireadail 618
Beinn Chaisgidle 504
Glen More
Ishriff
Oakbank
Gorten
Maiden Island
Rubh' a' Bhearnaig
Pennyfuir
Ardchonnel
Beinn na Sreine 519
Maol na Coille Moire 288
Balevulin
Derercach
Craig
Uluvalt
Ardachoil
Ardnadrochit
64
Grass Point
Eilean nan Gamhna
Ardentrive
Glencruitten
Strontoiller
Gib Bheinn
Aird of Kinloch
Creag na h-Iolaire 506
Beinn Fhada 501
Glas Bheinn 491
Ardura
Cruach Ardura 216
Auchnacraig
Carn Bàn 248
Ruba na Lice
Kerrera
Balliemore
Oban
Soroba
Glenamachrie
69
70
LOCH SCRIDAIN
Pennyghael
Cruach nan Con 496
Ben Buie 717
Creach Beinn 698
Kinlochspelve
Fellonmore
Loch Spelve
Croggan
Rubha na Faoilinn
Upper Gylen
Ardmore
Bach Island
Kilbride
Gallanach
Lerags
Dunach
Cleigh
Kilmore
Glenfeochan
Maol nan Uan 274
Beinn na Croise 503
Killunaig
A849
Lochbuie
Loch Buie
Glenbyre
62
Creag nam Fitheach 314
Maol Bàn 338
63
Dalnaha
Portfield
Rubha Seanach
Dubh Sgeir
Minard Point
Ardentallan
Knipoch
34
A'Chruach 368
Brolass
Cruachan Min 376
Beinn Chreagach 376
Carsaig
Beinn a' Bhainne 377
Druim Fada 405
Rubha Dubh
Barnacarry
Eilean Dùin
Duachy
Kilninver
Glen Euchar
Shellachan
Scammadale
Bragleenbeg
Nuns' Pass
Creachan Mòr 331
Frank Lockwood's Island
Rubha Garbh Airde
Ardencaple House
Ardfad
Insh Island
Clachan-Seil
Ardshellach
Corrielorne
Rubha nam Bràithrean
Malcolm's Point
Easdale
Dùn-Mòr
Seil
Easdale
Balvicar
Henderson's Rock
Caddleton
Cruach nam Fearna 332
Melfort
Pass of Melfort
6
Garvellachs
Cullipool
Torsay Island
Kilchoan
Degnish
Ardanstur
Kilmelford
Maolachy
35
Isles of the Sea
A'Chùli
Garbh Eileach
Eilean Dubh Mòr
Belnahua
Glas Eilean
Ardinamar
Eilean Gamhna
Degnish Point
Tullich
Lagalochan
Luing
Kames
Arduaine
Tom Soillier 365
Carn Dubhan 401
Inverliever Forest
Eileach an Naoimh
Lunga
Toberonochy
Shuna
Barravullin
Gleann Domhain
Cruach an Eachlaich 350
Guirasdeal
Craobh Haven
Lunga
Eilean Arsa
Gemmil
Shuna Point
Arichamish
Inverliever
Colonsay 2¼ hours
Cruach Scarba 449
Scarba
Kintraw
Torran
Ardfern
Ford
Barrackan
Eilean Mhic Chrion
Corranmore
Tibertich
Eilean Righ
Carnassarie
Rubha Righinn
Reisa Mhic Phaidean
Kirkton
Old Poltalloch
Eurach
31
Eilean Dubh
Rubh' a' Geodha
Beinn nan Capull 252
60
Rèisa an t-Sruith
Island Macaskin
Kilmartin
Barmolloch
Cruach na Seilcheig 296
Kinuachdrachd
Kinuachdrachd Harbour
Ardnoe Point
Ockavullin
Baluachraig
Knockalava
Glengarrisdale
Poltalloch

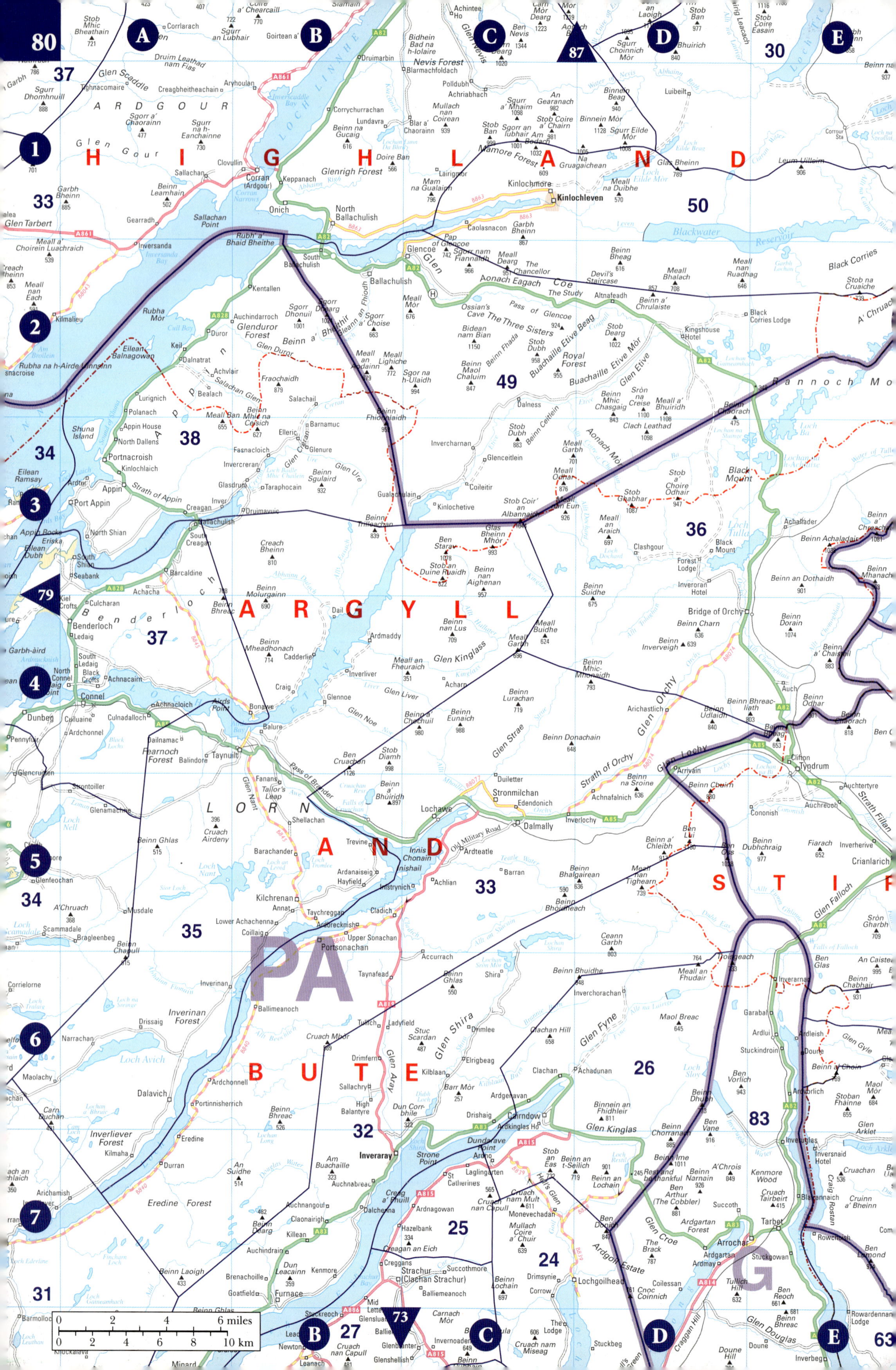

A
B
C
D
E
87
Stob Mhic Bheathain 721
Corrlarach
Sgurr an Lubhair
Goirtean a'
A82
Achintee Ho
Glen Nevis
Ben Nevis 1344
Càrn Mòr Dearg 1223
Bidhein Bad na h-Iolaire
Nevis Forest
Blarmachfoldach
Druimarbin
Sgurr Choinnich Mòr
Stob Ban 977
Stob Coire Easain
30
Druim Leathad nam Fias
37
Glen Scaddle
Tighnacomaire
Creagbheitheachain
Aryhoulan
A861
Sgurr Dhomhnuill 888
ARDGOUR
Inverscaddle Bay
LOCH LINNHE
Corrychurrachan
Polldubh
Achriabhach
Mullach nan Coirean 939
Sgurr a' Mhaim 1098
An Gearanach 982
Binnein Beag 940
Binnein Mòr 1128
Sgurr Eilde Mòr 1008
Luibeilt
Sgorr a' Chaorainn 477
Sgurr na h-Eanchainne 730
Lundavra
Blar a' Chaorainn
Sgor an Iubhair
Am Bodach 1032
Stob Coire a' Chàirn 981
Stob Ban 999
Glen Gour
HIGHLAND
Beinn na Gucaig 616
Doire Ban 566
Mamore Forest
Na Gruagaichean
Glas Bheinn 789
Leum Uilleim 906
701
Clovullin
Sallachan
Corran (Ardgour)
Keppanach
Glenrigh Forest
Lairigmor
Loch Eilde Mòr
33
Garbh Bheinn 885
Beinn Leamhain 502
Corran Narrows
Onich
Mam na Gualainn 796
Kinlochmore
Kinlochleven
Meall na Duibhe 570
50
Glen Tarbert
Gearradh
Sallachan Point
North Ballachulish
B863
Caolasnacon
Garbh Bheinn 867
Blackwater Reservoir
A861
Meall a' Choirein Luachraich 539
Inversanda
Inversanda Bay
Rubh' a' Bhaid Bheithe
A82
South Ballachulish
Glencoe
Pap of Glencoe 742
Sgorr nam Fiannaidh 966
Meall Dearg 951
The Chancellor
Beinn Bheag 616
Meall Bhalach 708
Meall nan Ruadhag 646
Black Corries
Meall nan Each
Ballachulish
Glen Coe
Aonach Eagach
The Study
Devil's Staircase
Altnafeadh
Beinn a' Chrulaiste
Stob na Cruaiche 739
Kentallen
Rubha Mòr
Kilmalieu
Sgorr Dhonuil 1001
Sgorr Dhearg 1024
Sgorr a' Choise 663
Meall Mòr 676
Ossian's Cave
The Three Sisters
Pass of Glencoe
Stob Dearg 1022
Black Corries Lodge
Kingshouse Hotel
A' Chruach
A828
Auchindarroch
Glenduror Forest
Duror
Cuil Bay
Beinn a' Bheithir
Gleann an Fhiodh
Bidean nam Bian 1150
Stob Dubh 958
Buachaille Etive Beag
Royal Forest 955
Buachaille Etive Mòr
Glen Duror
Keil
Eilean Balnagowan
Rubha na h-Airde Uinnsinn
Dalnatrat
Achvlair
Meall an Aodainn 879
Meall Lighiche 772
Sgor na h-Ulaidh 994
Beinn Fhada
Beinn Maol Chaluim 847
49
Glen Etive
Rannoch Moor
Fraochaidh 879
Bealach
Salachan Glen
Salachail
Lurignich
Polanach
Shuna Island
Appin House
North Dallens
Meall Ban 655
Beinn Mhic na Ceisich 627
Beinn Fhionnlaidh 959
Dalness
Beinn Ceitlein
Beinn Mhic Chasgaig 843
Sròn na Creise 1100
Meall a' Bhuiridh 1108
Clach Leathad 1098
Beinn Chaorach 475
Loch Bà
38
Barnamuc
Elleric
Glen Creran
Glenure
Glen Ure
Fasnacloich
Invercreran
Portnacroish
Kinlochlaich
34
Eilean Ramsay
Beinn Sgulaird 932
Stob Dubh 883
Invercharnan
Glenceitlein
Aonach Mòr
Meall Garbh 701
Meall Odhar 876
Stob Ghabhar 1087
Stob a' Choire Odhair 947
Black Mount
Ardtur
Appin
Strath of Appin
Glasdrum
Taraphocain
Port Appin
Gualachulain
Coileitir
Kinlochetive
Stob Coir' an Albannaich 1044
Meall nan Eun 926
Achallader
Beinn a' Chreachain 1081
Inver
Creagan
Druimavuic
Ballachulish
Beinn Trilleachan 839
Glas Bheinn Mhòr 993
Meall an Araich 697
Clashgour
36
Loch Tulla
Black Mount
Beinn Achaladair 1038
Appin Rocks
Eriska
North Shian
South Creagan
Eilean Dubh
South Shian
Seabank
Creach Bheinn 810
Ben Starav 1078
Stob an Duine Ruaidh
Beinn nan Aighenan 957
Forest Lodge
Beinn an Dothaidh 901
Beinn Mhanach
79
Barcaldine
Achacha
A828
Kiel Crofts
Culcharan
Benderloch
Ledaig
Beinn Mholurgainn 690
Beinn Bhreac 708
ARGYLL
Dail
Beinn Suidhe 675
Inveroran Hotel
Bridge of Orchy
Beinn Dorain 1074
37
Beinn Mheadhonach 714
Cadderlie
Ardmaddy
Beinn nan Lus 709
Meall Buidhe 624
Beinn Chaorach 636
Beinn Inverveigh 639
Beinn a' Chaisteil 883
Garbh-àird
Ardmucknish
South Ledaig
Black Crofts
Achnacairn
North Connel
Connel
Meall an Fheuraich 351
Glen Kinglass
Inverliver
Meall Garbh 696
Beinn Mhic-Mhonaidh 793
Auch
Craig
Glen Liver
Acharn
Beinn Lurachan 719
Glen Orchy
Arichastlich
Beinn Bhreac-liath 803
Beinn Odhar 901
Dunbeg
Achnacloich
Airds Point
Bonawe
Glennoe
Beinn a' Chochuill 980
Beinn Eunaich 988
Beinn Udlaidh 840
Beinn Chaorach 818
Pennyfuir
Cuiluaine
Culnadalloch
Ardchonnel
A85
Dailnamac
Fearnoch Forest
Balindore
Taynuilt
Balure
Glen Noe
Glen Strae
Beinn Donachain 648
Beinn Bheag 653
Glencruitten
Ben Cruachan 1126
Stob Diamh 998
Strath of Orchy
Glen Lochy
Arrivain
Clifton
Tyndrum
Strontoiller
Glenamachrie
Fanans
Taynuilt
Pass of Brander
Glen Nant
Tailor's Leap
Beinn a' Bhuiridh 897
Duiletter
Stronmilchan
Edendonich
Beinn na Sroine 636
Achnafalnich
Beinn Chùirn 880
A82
Auchtertyre
Strath Fillan
Loch Nell
LORN
396 Cruach Airdeny
Shellachan
Lochawe
B8077
Dalmally
Inverlochy
A85
Cononish
Auchreoch
Beinn Ghlas 515
Barachander
Trevine
AND
Innis Chonain
Inishail
Old Military Road
Ardteatle
Beinn a' Chleibh 916
Ben Lui 1130
Ben Oss 1029
Beinn Dubhchraig 977
Fiarach 652
Inverherive
Crianlarich
5
Glenfeochan
Loch Nant
Ardanaiseig
Hayfield
Achlian
33
Barran
Beinn Bhalgairean 636
Meall nan Tighearn 739
STIRLING
34
Kilchrenan
Annat
Instrynich
Cladich
Beinn Bhoidheach
Glen Falloch
A'Chruach
Musdale
Taychreggan
Sròn Gharbh 709
Scammadale
368
Lower Achachenna
Coillaig
Ardbrecknish
35
PA
Upper Sonachan
Portsonachan
Ceann Garbh 803
Bragleenbeg
Beinn Chapull 615
B840
Accurrach
Troisgeach
Ben Glas
An Caisteal 995
Corrielorne
Inverinan
Taynafead
Shira
Beinn Ghlas 550
Beinn Bhuidhe 948
764
Meall an Fhudair
Inverarnan
Beinn Chabhair 931
Inverchorachan
Ballimeanoch
A819
Inverinan Forest
6
Drissaig
Tullich
Ladyfield
Glen Shira
Stuc Scardan 487
Clachan Hill 658
Glen Fyne
Maol Breac 645
Garabal
Ardlui
Ardleish
Glen Gyle
Narrachan
Cruach Mhòr 589
Drimfern
Glen Aray
Elrigbeag
Doune
Stuckindroin
Loch Awe
Loch Avich
Maolachy
BUTE
Kilblaan
Clachan
Achadunan
26
Loch Sloy
Ben Vorlich 943
Beinn a' Choin 769
Dalavich
Ardchonnell
Sallachry
Barr Mòr 257
Ardgenavan
Ardvorlich
Maol Mòr 684
Portinnisherrich
High Balantyre
Dun Corr-bhile 322
Drishaig
Cairndow
Binnein an Fhidhleir
Beinn Dubh 783
Stoban Fhàinne 655
Carn Dubhan 491
Beinn Bhreac 526
32
A83
Ardkinglas Ho
Glen Kinglas
83
Glen Arklet
Inverliever Forest
Kilmaha
Eredine
Inveraray
Strone Point
Dundarave Point
A815
Ardno
Beinn Chorranach 885
Ben Vane 916
Inveruglas
Inversnaid Hotel
Durran
An Suidhe 514
Am Buachaille 323
Auchnabreac
St Catherines
Laglingarten
Stob an Eas 732
Beinn an t-Seilich 719
901
Beinn an Lochain
Beinn Ime 1011
Rest and be thankful
Beinn Narnain 926
A'Chrois 849
Kenmore Wood
Cruachan
Arichamish
Eredine Forest
Auchnangoul
Creag a' Phuill
Ardnagowan
Dalchenna
Cruach nam Mult 611
Cruach nan Capull
Monevechadan
Hell's Glen
Ben Arthur (The Cobbler) 881
Succoth
Cruach Tairbeirt 415
Craig Rostan
Cruinn a' Bheinn
7
Beinn Dearg 482
Claonairigh
Killean
Hazelbank 334
25
Mullach Coire a' Chuir 639
Ben Donich 847
Glen Croe
Ardgartan Forest
Arrochar
A83
Tarbet
Rowchoish
Auchindrain
Creagan an Eich
24
The Brack 787
Ardgartan
Ardmay
Stuckgowan
Ben Lomond 974
Dun Leacainn 359
Kenmore
Creggans
Strachur (Clachan Strachur)
Succothmore
Beinn Lochain 697
Drimsynie
Lochgoilhead
Ardgoil Estate
Coilessan
A814
Beinn Laoigh 433
Brenachoille
Goatfield
Furnace
Balliemeanoch
Corrow
Cnoc Coinnich 761
Tullich Hill 632
Ben Reoch 661
31
Mid Letter
Stuckreoch
A886
Glenshellish
Carnach Mòr
The Lodge
681
Beinn Bhreac
Rowardennan Lodge
Barmollock
Lead
B
27
Ballie
Glenbranter
73
Invernoaden
C
Cruach nam Miseag
Stuckbeg
D
Craggan Hill
Glen Douglas
E
63
Cruach nan Capull 481
Newton
Leanach
Glenshellish
Knockalava
Minard
Doune
Doune Hill
Inverbeg
0 2 4 6 miles
0 2 4 6 8 10 km

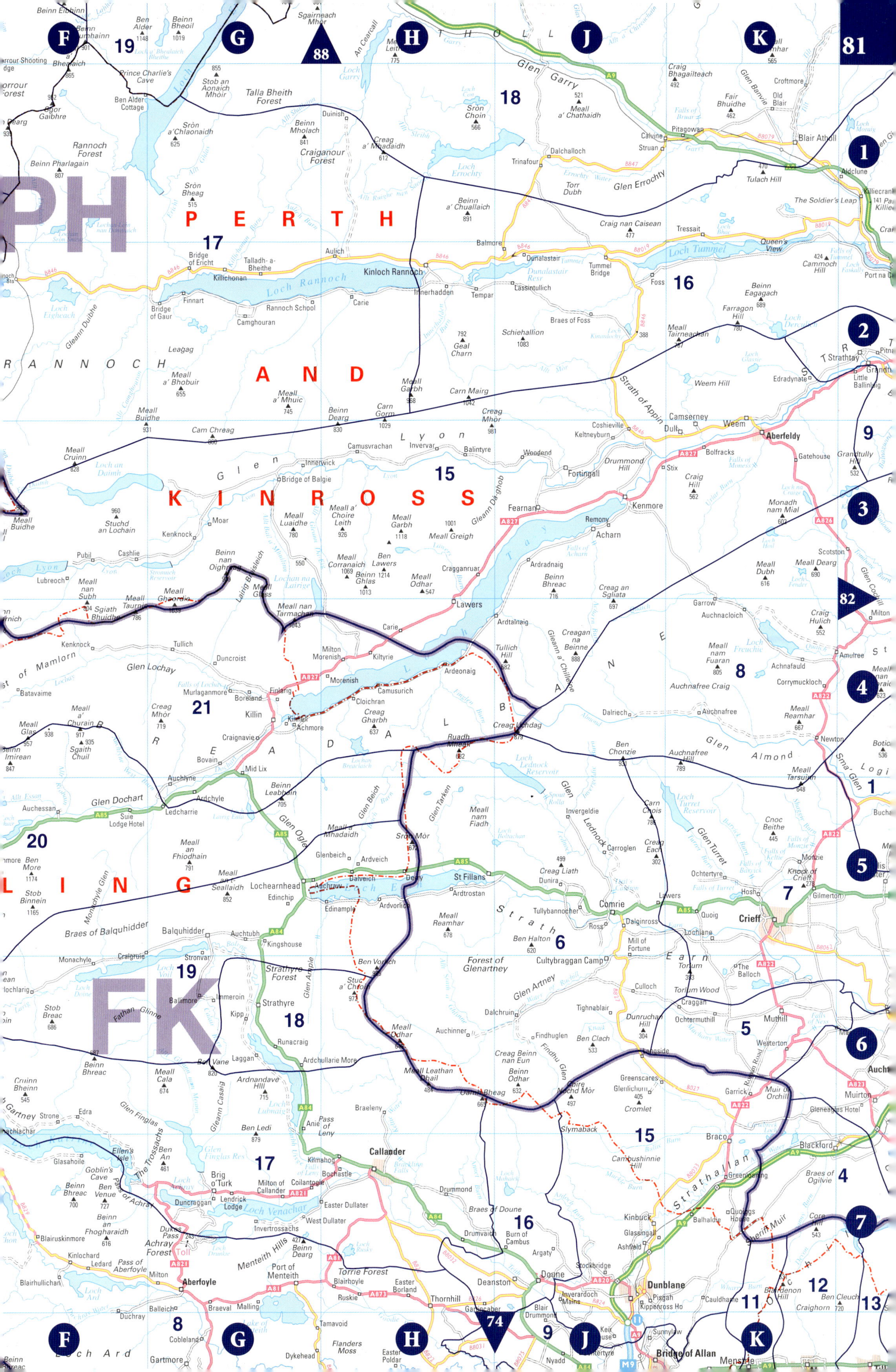
PERTH AND KINROSS
PH
FK
RANNOCH
ATHOLL
STIRLING
BREADALBANE
Rannoch Forest
Talla Bheith Forest
Craiganour Forest
Beinn Pharlagain
Loch Rannoch
Kinloch Rannoch
Bridge of Ericht
Killichonan
Talladh-a-Bheithe
Aulich
Finnart
Carie
Rannoch School
Camghouran
Bridge of Gaur
Loch Eigheach
Gleann Dubhe
Leagag
Meall a' Bhobuir
Meall a' Mhuic
Meall Buidhe
Cam Chreag
Beinn Dearg
Carn Gorm
Meall Garbh
Carn Mairg
Creag Mhòr
Schiehallion
Geal Charn
Braes of Foss
Tempar
Innerhadden
Lassintullich
Dunalastair
Dunalastair Resr
Tummel Bridge
Foss
Loch Tummel
Queen's View
Tressait
Craig nan Caisean
Glen Errochty
Loch Errochty
Trinafour
Dalchalloch
Torr Dubh
Meall a' Chathaidh
Glen Garry
Sròn Choin
Loch Con
Creag a' Mhadaidh
Beinn Mholach
Duinish
An Cearcall
Sgairneach Mhòr
Beinn Eibhinn
Ben Alder
Beinn Bheoil
Beinn Bheòil
Loch Ericht
Ben Alder Cottage
Prince Charlie's Cave
Stob an Aonaich Mhòir
Sròn a' Chlaonaidh
Sròn Bheag
Ogor Gaibhre
Blair Atholl
Calvine
Struan
Pitagowan
Old Blair
Fair Bhuidhe
Croftmore
Craig Bhagailteach
Glen Banvie
Aldclune
Killiecrankie
Tulach Hill
The Soldier's Leap
Cammoch Hill
Port na Craig
Beinn Eagagach
Farragon Hill
Meall Tairneachan
Strath of Appin
Strathtay
Edradynate
Weem Hill
Little Ballinluig
Camserney
Dull
Weem
Aberfeldy
Coshieville
Keltneyburn
Drummond Hill
Fortingall
Bolfracks
Stix
Craig Hill
Gatehouse
Grandtully Hill
Monadh nam Mial
Kenmore
Fearnan
Remony
Acharn
Glen Lyon
Lyon
Invervar
Balintyre
Woodend
Camusvrachan
Innerwick
Bridge of Balgie
Loch an Daimh
Meall Buidhe
Stuchd an Lochain
Moar
Kenknock
Pubil
Cashlie
Loch Lyon
Lubreoch
Meall nan Subh
Beinn nan Oighreag
Meall Ghaordie
Meall Taurnie
Sgiath Bhuidhe
Meall Luaidhe
Meall a' Choire Leith
Meall Garbh
Meall Greigh
Meall Corranaich
Ben Lawers
Beinn Ghlas
Meall Odhar
Meall nan Tarmachan
Lochan na Lairige
Lairig Breisleich
Gleann Da-Eig
Cragganruar
Lawers
Loch Tay
Ardradnaig
Beinn Bhreac
Creag an Sgliata
Ardtalnaig
Tullich Hill
Creagan na Beinne
Gleann a' Chilleine
Carie
Milton Morenish
Kiltyrie
Morenish
Ardeonaig
Camusurich
Cloichran
Creag Gharbh
Killin
Finlarig
Kinnell
Achmore
Boreland
Murlaganmore
Glen Lochay
Duncroist
Tullich
Kenknock
Glen of Mamlorn
Batavaime
Creag Mhòr
Meall a' Churain
Sgiath Chuil
Meall Glas
Beinn Imirean
Craignavie
Bovain
Mid Lix
Glen Dochart
Auchlyne
Ardchyle
Ledcharrie
Suie Lodge Hotel
Auchessan
Beinn Leabhainn
Glen Ogle
Meall an Fhiodhain
Meall an t-Seallaidh
Ben More
Stob Binnein
Monachyle Glen
Lochearnhead
Edinchip
Glenbeich
Ardveich
Meall a' Mhadaidh
Glen Beich
Sròn Mòr
Glen Tarken
Loch Earn
Dalveich
Derry
St Fillans
Ardtrostan
Edinample
Ardvorlich
Creag Uchdag
Ruadh Mheall
Loch Lednock Reservoir
Meall nam Fiadh
Glen Lednock
Invergeldie
Carroglen
Creag Liath
Dunira
Comrie
Tullybannocher
Ross
Dalginross
Mill of Fortune
Strath Earn
Ben Halton
Forest of Glenartney
Cultybraggan Camp
Glen Artney
Dalchruin
Auchinner
Findhuglen
Ben Clach
Dunruchan Hill
Tighnablair
Culloch
Tomm Hill
Torlum Wood
Craggan
Ochtermuthill
Muthill
Crieff
Gilmerton
Hosh
Quoig
Lochlane
The Balloch
Knock of Crieff
Monzie
Ochtertyre
Glen Turret
Loch Turret Reservoir
Carn Chois
Creag Each
Cnoc Beithe
Glen Almond
Newton
Auchnafree Hill
Auchnafree
Auchnafree Craig
Dalreich
Ben Chonzie
Meall nam Fuaran
Loch Freuchie
Achnafauld
Corrymuckloch
Amulree
Meall Reamhar
Meall Tarsuinn
Craig Hulich
Garrow
Auchnacloich
Meall Dubh
Meall Dearg
Scotston
Glen Cochill
Milton
Sma' Glen
Balquhidder
Braes of Balquhidder
Auchtubh
Kingshouse
Stronvar
Craigruie
Monachyle
Loch Voil
Loch Doine
Inverlochlarig
Stob Breac
Ballimore
Fathan Glinne
Immeroin
Kipp
Strathyre
Strathyre Forest
Glen Ample
Ben Vorlich
Stuc a' Chroin
Meall Odhar
Runacraig
Laggan
Ben Vane
Beinn Bhreac
Ardchullarie More
Meall Leathan Dhail
Uamh Bheag
Creag Beinn nan Eun
Beinn Odhar
Coire Buidhe Mòr
Findhu Glen
Langside
Greenscares
Glenlichorn
Cromlet
Slymaback
Braco
Cambushinnie Hill
Garrick
Muir of Orchill
Gleneagles Hotel
Blackford
Greenloaning
Braes of Ogilvie
Strathallan
Sheriff Muir
Quoiggs House
Balhaldie
Kinbuck
Glassingall
Ashfield
Dunblane
Pisgah
Kippenross Ho
Cauldhame
Bridge of Allan
Sunnylaw
Keir House
Blair Drummond
Doune
Deanston
Stockbridge
Inveraroch Mains
Gargunnock
Argaty
Burn of Cambus
Braes of Doune
Drumvaich
Drummond
Callander
Kilmahog
Bochastle
Anie
Pass of Leny
Braeleny
Ardnandave Hill
Meall Cala
Gleann Casaig
Ben Ledi
Glen Finglas
Glen Finglas Res
Ben An
The Trossachs
Ellen's Isle
Glasahoile
Goblin's Cave
Ben Venue
Beinn Bhreac
Beinn an Fhogharaidh
Strone
Edra
Cruinn Bheinn
Loch Katrine
Brig o' Turk
Milton of Callander
Coilantogle
Duncraggan
Lendrick Lodge
Loch Vennachar
Easter Dullater
West Dullater
Invertrossachs
Duke's Pass
Achray Forest
Pass of Achray
Toll
Menteith Hills
Beinn Dearg
Port of Menteith
Torrie Forest
Blairhoyle
Easter Borland
Ruskie
Thornhill
Lake of Menteith
Malling
Braeval
Aberfoyle
Milton
Pass of Aberfoyle
Ledard
Kinlochard
Blairuskinmore
Blairhullichan
Loch Ard
Duchray
Balleich
Cobleland
Gartmore
Tamavoid
Flanders Moss
Dykehead
Easter Poldar
Nyadd
Menstrie
Craighorn
Ben Cleuch
Blairdenon Hill
Ochil Hills
Core Hill
Muirton
F
G
H
J
K
1
2
3
4
5
6
7
88
82
74

A
B
C
D
E
1
2
3
4
5
6
7
89
81
75
PH
KY
FK
PERTH AND KINROSS
FIFE
ANGUS
DUNDEE
Blair Atholl
Carn Liath
975
Ben Vuirich
903
Meall Breac
Glen Girnaig
Ben Vrackie
841
Aldclune
Killiecrankie
The Soldier's Leap
Pass of Killiecrankie
Craigower
Moulin
Pitlochry
Port na Craig
Cammoch Hill
424
Strathtay
Pitnacree
Ballechin
Grandtully
Little Ballinluig
Bishopric
Logierait
Balnaguard
Ballinluig
Tulliemet
Balmacneil
Kindallachan
Guay
Kincraigie
Dowally
Gatehouse
Grandtully Hill
532
Meall Reamhar
506
Elrick More
517
Dalguise
Craigvinean Forest
Dalmarnock
Craig a' Barns
337
Creag an Eunaich
459
Dunkeld
Little Dunkeld
Birnam
Newtyle Hill
Inver
Dunkeld & Birnam Sta
Birnam Hill
Scotston
Meall Dearg
690
Glen Cochill
Druim Mòr
367
Ballinlick
Drumour
Aldville
Trochry
Milton
Craig Hulich
552
Strathbraan
Obney Hills
403
Creag Liath
Amulree
Meall nan Caoraich
623
Findowie Hill
Creag na Criche
455
Crochan Hill
506
Little Glenshee
Craig Lea
Botich
536
Newton
Meall Tarsuinn
648
Logiealmond
Harrietfield
Chapelhill
Tulchan
Pickston
Buchanty
Glen Almond
Grundcruie
Busby
Keillour
Methven
Murray's Hill
246
Fowlis Wester
Forebrae
Braegrum
Keillour Forest
Gilmerton
Huntingtower
Tibbermore
Newmiln
Madderty
Dubheads
Findo Gask
Crossgates
Clathy
St David's
Kirkton
Gask
Chapelbank
Broom of Dalreach
Millearne
Kinkell Bridge
Machany
Aberuthven
Duncrub
Dunning
Auchterarder
Muirton
Gleneagles Hotel
Craig Rossie
410
Kippen
Blackford
Braes of Ogilvie
Gleneagles House
Eastbow Hill
476
Steele's Knowe
485
Glen Eagles
Glendevon Forest
Glen Devon
Innerdownie
611
Scad Hill
586
Commonedge Hill
Pool of Muckhart
King's Seat Hill
Ben Cleuch
720
Craighorn
Glendevon
Burnfoot
Lendrick Hill
Yetts o' Muckhart
Crook of Devon
Drum
Pitcairns
Path of Condie
Balquhandy Hill
Common of Dunning
Innerdouny Hill
497
Slungie Hill
Middle Rigg
Dochrie Hill
Carnbo
Warroch
Dalqueich
Middleton
Milnathort
Kinross
Balado
Coldrain
Glenfarg
Glenfarg Reservoir
Duncrievie
Arngask
Newton of Balcanquhal
Gateside
Burnside
Kinross
Loch Leven
St Serf's Island
Wester Balgedie
Easter Balgedie
Kinnesswood
Bishop Hill
Scotlandwell
Auchmuirbridge
Ballingry
Lochore
Powmill
Cleish
Cleish Hills
Gairney Bank
Kinglassie
Thornton
Glenrothes
Leslie
Cadham
Markinch
Milton of Balgonie
Coaltown of Balgonie
Windygates
Kennoway
Buckhaven
Methil
Balcurvie
Bonnybank
Star
New Inn
Bandon
Freuchie
Falkland
East Lomond
Lomond Hills
West Lomond
Newton of Falkland
Kettlebridge
Kingskettle
Ladybank
Pitlessie
Springfield
Craigrothie
Cupar
Howe of Fife
Strathmiglo
Dunshalt
Auchtermuchty
Pitmedden Forest
Collessie
Letham
Monimail
Pleasance
Lindores
Newburgh
Ormiston Hill
Dunbog
Mugdrum Island
Glenduckie Hill
Luthrie
Norman's Law
Moonzie
Mount Hill
Abernethy
Aberargie
Glenfoot
Ayton
Balmanno Hill
Glen Farg
Dron
Forgandenny
Forteviot
Kintillo
Bridge of Earn
Aberdalgie
Milltown of Aberdalgie
Craigend
Moncreiffe Hill
Rhynd
Elcho
Kinfauns
Kinnoull Hill
Friarton
Tarsappie
Perth
Scone
Old Scone
Almondbank
Pitcairngreen
Luncarty
Moneydie
Stormontfield
Colenden
Newmill
Scones Lethendy
Guildtown
Balbeggie
St Martins
Stanley
West Tofts
Tullybelton
Strathord Forest
Airntully
Laguna
Bankfoot
Upper Obney
Waterloo
Murthly
Ardoch
Muir of Thorn
Caputh
Gellyburn
Spittalfield
Stenton
Thornton
Delvine
Meikleour
Kinclaven
Cargill
Wolfhill
Dunsinnan
Kinrossie
Collace
Kirkton of Collace
Cargie
Whitefield
Woodside
Burrelton
Coupar Angus
Keithick
Kettins
Campmuir
Pitcur
Lundie
Abernyte
Pitmiddle Wood
King's Seat
377
Hallyburton Forest
Springfield
Carse of Gowrie
Braes of the Carse
Kinnaird
Ballindean
Craigdallie
Inchture
Rait
Kilspindie
Pitroddie
Pole Hill
288
Kinfauns Forest
Glendoick
Glencarse
St Madoes
Chapelhill
Inchyra
Port Allen
Errol
Grange
Carthagena Bank
Dog Bank
Longforgan
Kingoodie
Invergowrie
Benvie
Denhead of Gray
Liff
Muirhead
Birkhill
Fowlis
Blacklaw Hill
284
Littleton
Knapp
Rossie Priory
Auchterhouse
Thriepley
Dronley
Leoch
Kinpurney Hill
345
Newbigging
Newtyle
Ardler
Auchtertyre
Kirkinch
Meigle
Keillor
Kinloch
Arthurstone
Balkeerie
Eassie
Castleton
Charleston
Glamis
Ark Hill
340
Nether Handwick
Auchterhouse Hill
426
Bonnyton
Kirkton of Auchterhouse
Blairgowrie
Rattray
Rosemount
Muirton of Ardblair
Carsie
Kinloch
Lornty
Craigie
Clunie
Loch of Clunie
Loch of Drumellie
Kirkton of Lethendy
Butterstone
Forneth
Concraigie
Achalader
Middleton
Riechip
319
Arlick
Deuchary Hill
509
Benachally
486
Forest of Clunie
Blackcraig Forest
Cochrage Muir
Blackcraig Hill
479
Bridge of Cally
Rochallie
Netherton
Ashmore
Persie House
Ballintuim
Balmyle
Knock of Balmyle
444
Ballinluig
Kirkmichael
Strathardle
Creag nam Mial
561
Meall Reamhar
Milton of Dalcapon
Badyo
Creag Dhubh
Dalnacarn
Glen Brerachan
Tarvie
Straloch
Kindrogan Field Centre
Ennochdhu
Balvarran
Creag an t Sithein
635
Gleann Fearnach
Meall Choire Chuidhe
868
Dalmunzie House Hotel
Ben Earb
801
Spittal of Glenshee
Ben Gulabin
Meall Uaine
794
Glen Shee
Lamh Dhearg
575
Carn an Daimh
755
Monamenach
807
Auchavan
Mealna Letter (Duchray Hill)
Finegand
Dalnaglar Castle
Lair
Cray
Forter
Mount Blair
Alrick
Meall Mor
Blacklunans
Cairn Gibbs
520
489
Knockton
Dalrulzian
Forest of Alyth
Drumderg
422
Tullymurdoch
Hill of Alyth
295
Alyth
Tullyfergus
New Alyth
Jordanstone
Balhary
Parkhill
Shanzie
Bamff
Balduff Hill
Bridge of Craigisla
Bridge of Brewlands
Kirkton of Glenisla
Glenisla Forest
Glen Isla
Folda
Druim Dearg
453
Bellaty
Badandun Hill
740
Mid Hill
774
Cairn Daunie
631
Hare Cairn
516
Glen Finlet
Glen Damff
Backwater Reservoir
Creigh Hill
Balmtore
Dykend
Loch of Lintrathen
Bridgend of Lintrathen
Auchrannie
Kirkton of Airlie
Lindertis
Baldovie
Kirkton of Kingoldrum
Kinnordy
Kirriemuir
Westmuir
Craigton
Ruthven
Balendoch
Cairn Baddoch
589
Mount Bouie
585
Glen Prosen
Runtaleave
Eskielawn
Tombain
Glenhead Farm
Corwharn
611
Glen Uig
Cairn of Barns
Glen Logie
Glen Clova
Clova
Wheen
Rottal
The Drums
Balnaboth
Glenprosen Village
Hill of Couternach
512
Glenarm
Easter Lednathie
Tulloch Hill
Cat Law
678
Pearsie
Mile Hill
409
Ascreavie
Balloch
Dykehead
Cortachy
Lochee
Dundee
Kirkton
Balmerino
Bottom
Coultra
Kilmany
Balhelvie
Hazelton Walls
Brunton
Creich
Rathillet
A9
A93
A924
A923
A984
A94
A85
A912
A90
A91
A92
A913
A914
A916
A911
A922
A977
A823
A824
A822
A827
A926
A928
A929
M90
B8019
B950
B951
B954
B947
B8063
B8062
B9099
B934
B935
B9141
B9112
B8081
B996
B920
B9097
B936
B937
0 2 4 6 miles
0 2 4 6 8 10 km

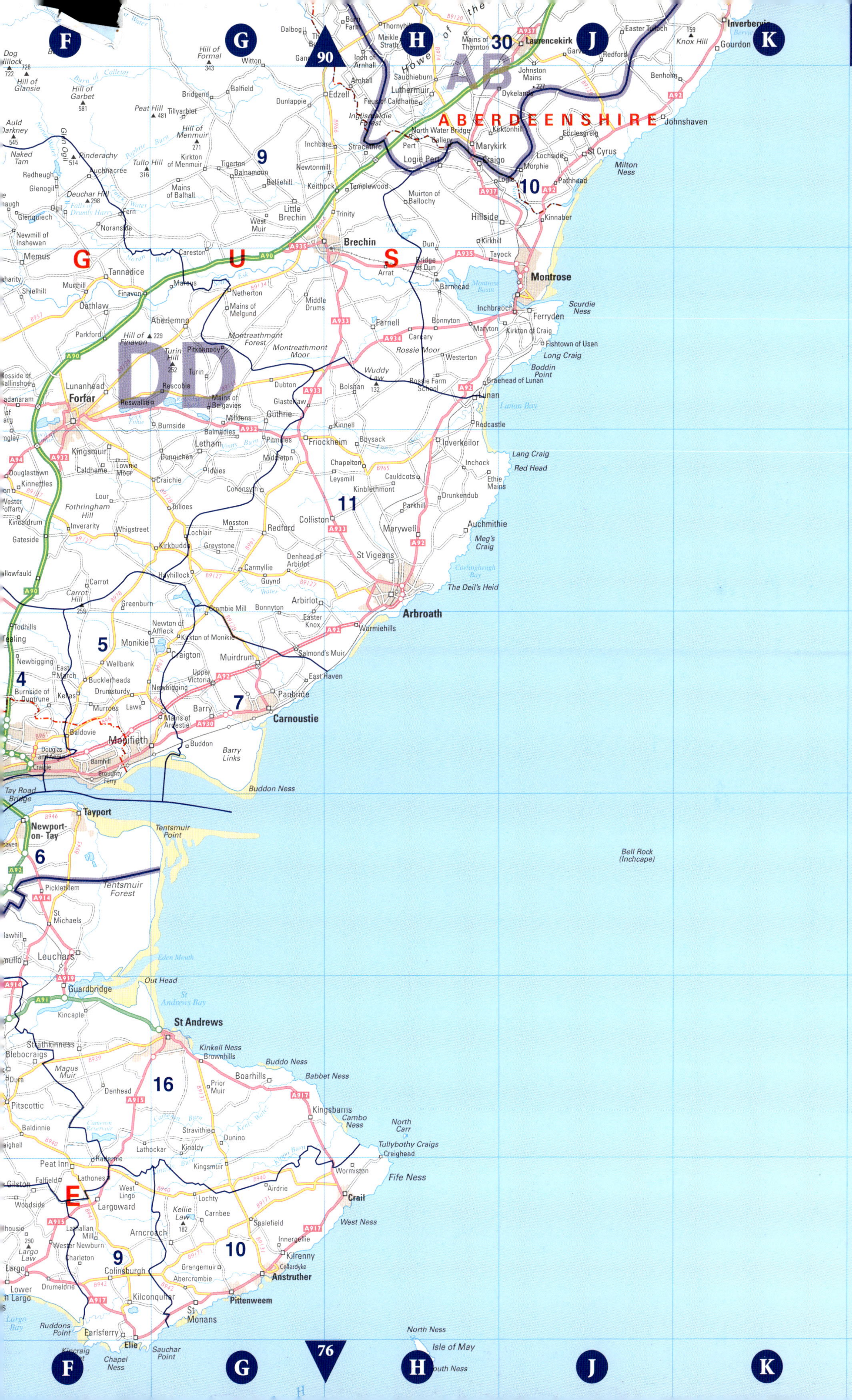

A
B
C
D
E
1
2
3
4
5
6
7
92
WESTERN
ISLES
(NA H-EILEANAN AN IAR
OUTER HEBRIDES
HS
8
SOUTH
UIST
(UIBHIST
A DEAS)
9
BARRA
(BARRAIGH)
Geirinis
Drimore
Groigearraidh
Stilligarry
(Stadhlaigearraidh)
Drimsdale
(Dreumasdal)
Homore
(Tobha Mòr)
Peighinn nan Aoireann
Snishival (Sniseabhal)
Rubha
Aird-
mhicheil
Staoinebrig
Ormacleit
Rubha Ardvule
Bornais
Kildonan
(Cilldonnain)
Gearraidh Bhailteas
Askernish
(Aisgernis)
Dalabrog
Cille Pheadair
Baghasdal
Orosay
Leth Meadhanach
Gearraidh na Monadh
Smerclet
Ceann a'
Gharaidh
Poll a' Charra
Cille
Bhrighde
Tarbert
Loch Sgioport
Ornish Island
Hecla
606
Ben
Corodale
527
Beinn
Mhòr
620
Rubha
Rossel
Rubha
Bhilidh
Prince's Cave
Rubha Hellisdale
Arinambane
Ben
na Hoe
258
Rubha Bolum
Sheaval
223
Minngearraidh
Arnaval
252
Rubha
na Gibhte
Stulaval
374
Stuley
Triuirebheinn
357
Beinn Ruigh
Choinnich
275
Rubha na Creige Mòire
Rubha na Cruibe
Crois
Dughaill
Lochboisdale
(Loch Baghasdail)
Calvay
Rubha Meall na Hoe
Taobh a' Deas
Loch Baghasdail
Trosairidh
Easaval
Oitir na Cudaig
Rubha na h- Ordaig
Ludag
Roneval
201
Bunmhullin
Sound of Eriskay
Haunn
Ben
Scrien
185
Balla
Eriskay
(Eiriosgaigh)
Ben
Stack
122
Rubha Liath
Hartamul
Lingay
Sound of Barra
Fiaray
Scurrival Point
Hornish
Eolaigearraidh
80
Fuday
Heinish
Stack Islands
Traigh Eais
102
Orosay
Greanamul
BARRA
(TRAIGH MHÒR)
Greian
Head
Cleat
Ben Cliad
207
Ardmhòr
Gighay
95
73
Hellisay
Ardveenish
Allathasdal
Cuidhir
Northbay
Borve
Point
Bruernish
107
Flodday
Buaile nam
Bodach
Fuiay
Borgh
Ruleos
A888
Bruernish Point
1¾ hrs
Doirlinn
Head
Ben
Tangaval
333
Heaval
383
Earsairidh
Brevig
Castlebay
(Bàgh a'Chaisteil)
Leideag
Aird a' Chaolais
Rubha Mòr
Caolas
Heishival
Mòr
190
Uidh
Vatersay
(Bhatarsaigh)
Vatersay
(Bhatarsaigh)
100
Am
Meall
Muldoanich
153
Flodday
Sound of Sandray
Cairn
Galtair
207
Sandray
(Sanndraigh)
Lingay
Sound of
Pabbay
Pabbay
(Pabaigh)
The Hoe
171
Sound of Mingulay
Guarsay
Mòr
Macphee's
Hill
224
Mingulay
(Miughalaigh)
273
Càrnan
Mingulay
Bay
Sròn an
Dùin
Sound of Berneray
Skate Point
191
Nisam Point
Berneray
(Bearnaraigh)
A865
B890
0 2 4 6 miles
0 2 4 6 8 10 km
B
C
D
E

Map of the Inner Hebrides and Isle of Skye region.

Grid references: F, G, H, J, K (columns); 1–7, 85, 86, 93, 78 (rows/markers)

**SKYE**
- Hoe Rape, The Hoe, Lorgill
- Healabhal Bheag (Macleod's Table South) 488
- Ben Connan 244, Beinn na Boineid 371, Ben Idrigill 340
- Harlosh Point, Harlosh Island, Idrigill Point
- MacLeod's Maidens, An Dubh Sgeir
- Tarner Island, Wiay, Oronsay, Rubha nan Clach
- Ose, Ebost, Bracadale, Struan, Ullinish, Coillore
- Ben Duagrich 304, Mugeary, Stroc-bheinn 400
- Beinn Totaig, Roineval 439, Meall an Fhuarain 291
- Loch Duagrich, Ardtreck Point, Portnalong, Fernilea
- Ben Lee 445, Peinchorran, Lower Ollach, Upper Ollach
- Carbost, Drynoch, Glen Drynoch, Glen Varragill
- Arnaval 369, Gleann Oraid, Talisker, Merkadale
- Sligachan, Glamaig 775
- Stockval 416, Talisker Bay
- Biod Mòr 383, Beinn Bhreac
- Eynort, Glen Eynort, Loch Eynort
- Beinn Bhreac 445, Gruta, Beinn a' Bhraghad 461
- Cuillin Hills, Bruach na Frithe 958, Am Basteir 935, Sgurr nan Gillean 965
- Beinn Staic 411, Sgurr Thuilm 879, Sgurr a' Mhadaidh 918, Harta Corrie
- An Cruachan 435, Sgurr a' Ghreadaidh 973
- Sgurr na Banachdich 965, Sgurr Dearg (Inaccessible Pinnacle) 986, Sgurr Mhic Choinnich 948
- Bualintur, Glenbrittle, Sgurr Alasdair 993, Sgurr Dubh Mòr 944
- Rubha Thearna Sgurr, Loch Coruisk, Sgurr na Stri 497
- Beinn an Eòin 312, Coiramean, Sgurr nan Eag 924, Gars-bheinn 895
- Strathaird, Camasunary
- Ceann na Beinne 225
- Rubh' an Dùnain
- Leac nam Faoileann, Beinn Bhreac 141
- Soay, Molchlach, Camas nan Gall
- Elgol, Prince Charles's Cave

**CUILLIN SOUND**

**SEA OF THE HEBRIDES** / INNER HEBRIDES

**CANNA** 44
- Camas Tharbernish, Carn a' Ghaill 210, Compass Hill 140
- Garrisdale Point, A'Chill, Canna Harbour
- Sròn Ruail, Tarbert Bay, Sanday, Humla

**RUM (RHUM)** 43
- Rubha Shamhnan Insir, Kilmory
- Kinloch, Rubha na Roinne
- Sgaorishal 278, Mullach Mòr 304
- Bloodstone Hill 388, A'Bhrideanach, Orval 571
- Sgor Reidh 263, An Dornabac, Barkeval 591
- Harris, Hallival, Askival 723, Ainshval 812
- Rubha Sgor an t-Snidhe, ival 528, Sgurr nan Gillean 764
- Rubha nam Meirleach

Garbh Sgeir, Oigh-sgeir

**EIGG** 42
- Cleadale, Rubha an Fhasaidh, An Cruachan 299
- Beinn Tighe 315, Laig, Bay of Laig
- Kildonnan, An Sgurr 393, Galmisdale
- Sound of Eigg

**MUCK** 41
- Eilean nan Each, Gòdag
- Rubh' a' Leam na Làraich, Beinn Airein 137, Port Mòr

**SOUND OF RUM**

Oban 5–7 hrs
Oban 5¼ hrs

Sanna Point, Sanna, Portuairk, Point of Ardnamurchan, Achnaha, Fascadale, Achateny
Meall nan Con 401, Beinn na Leathaid

**HIGHLAND IV**
**PH**

SKYE
RAASAY
Scalpay
Pabay
Longay
Crowlin Islands
Soay
SLEAT
KNOYDART
NORTH MORAR
SOUTH MORAR
ARISAIG
MOIDART
EIGG
Muck
Sound of Rum
Sound of Sleat
Sound of Eigg
Sound of Arisaig
Loch Nevis
Loch Morar
Loch Eishort
Loch Slapin
Loch Scavaig
Loch Alsh
Loch Shiel
Cuillin Hills
Portree
Sligachan
Sconser
Broadford
BROADFORD
Kyleakin
Kyle of Lochalsh
Plockton
Balmacara
Stromeferry
Glenelg
Kylerhea
Isleornsay
Teangue
Armadale
Ardvasar
Aird of Sleat
Point of Sleat
Elgol
Torrin
Kilbride
Luib
Dunan
Drynoch
Merkadale
Glenbrittle
Camasunary
Strathaird
Kinloch
Mallaig
Morar
Arisaig
Back of Keppoch
Glenuig
Kinlochmoidart
Lochailort
Inverailort
Ardnish
Acharacle
Kentra
Ockle
Kilmory
Inverie
Camusrory
Tarbet
Kinlochmorar
Arnisdale
Corran
Ardintoul
Letterfearn
Dornie
Sandaig
Achmore
Duirinish
Erbusaig
Drumbuie
Kirkton
Nostie
Ardelve
IV
PH
A87
A863
A850
A851
A830
A861
A890
B8083
1 2 3 4 5 6 7
A B C D E
94
85
79
56
36
H
I
G
½ hr
0 2 4 6 miles
0 2 4 6 8 10 km

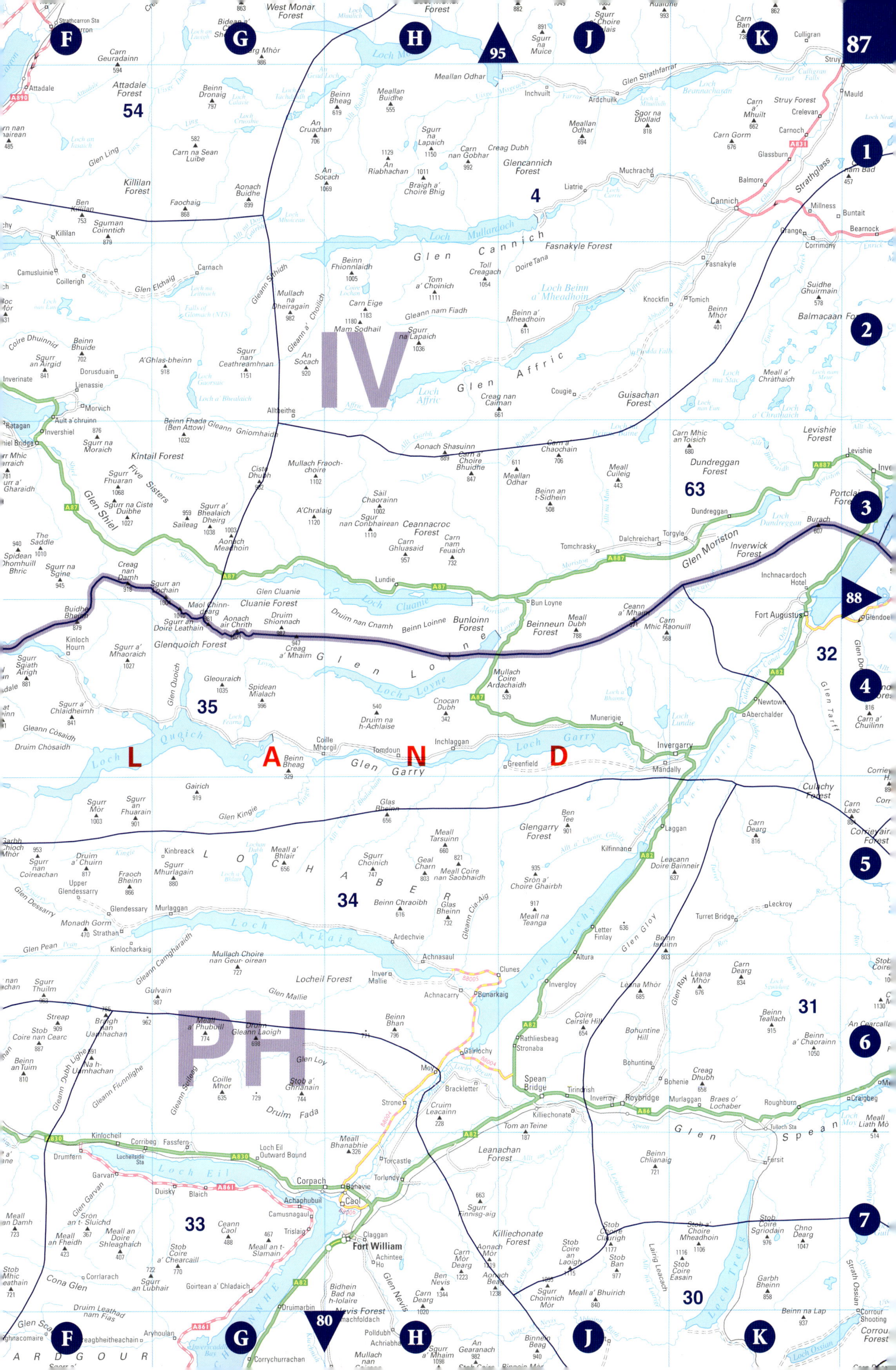

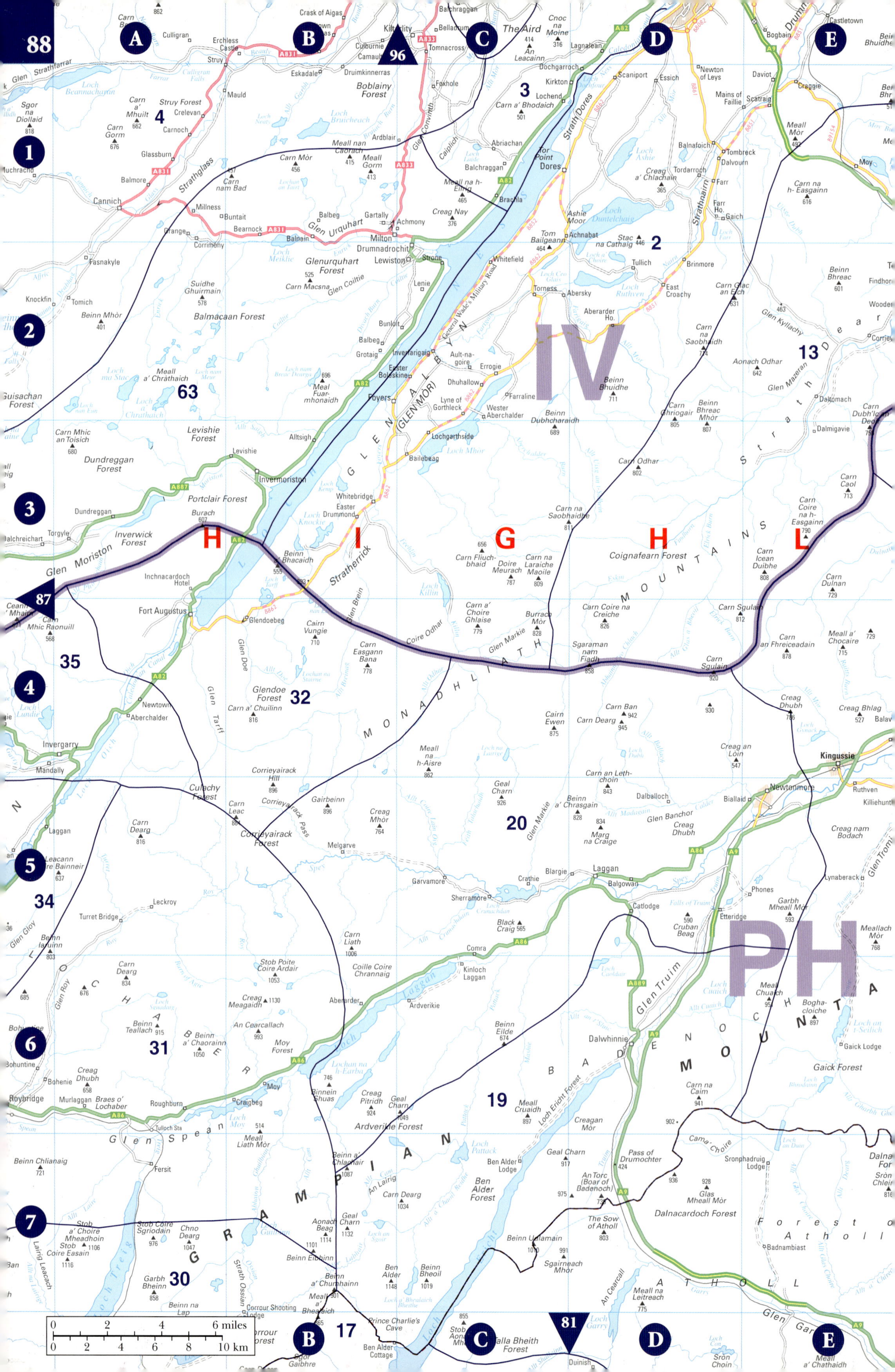
A
B
C
D
E
1
2
3
4
5
6
7
96
87
81
Glen Strathfarrar
Loch Beannacharan
Sgor na Diollaid 818
Carn a' Mhuilt 662
Carn Gorm 676
Culligran
Struy
Erchless Castle
Mauld
Struy Forest
Crelevan
Carnoch
Glassburn
Balmore
Cannich
Strathglass
Crask of Aigas
Kiltarlity
Culburnie
Camault
Eskadale
Druimkinnerras
Boblainy Forest
Loch Bruicheach
Belladrum
Tomnacross
Foxhole
Balchraggan
The Aird
Cnoc na Moine 316
An Leacainn
Lagnalean
Dochgarroch
Kirkton
Lochend
Carn a' Bhodaich 501
Scaniport
Essich
Newton of Leys
Mains of Faillie
Scatraig
Daviot
Craggie
Castletown
Bogbain
Meall Mòr 492
Moy
Balnafoich
Tombreck
Dalvourn
Tordarroch
Strathnairn
Farr
Gaich
Carn na h- Easgainn 616
Loch Ashie
Creag a' Chlachain 365
Abriachan
Caiplich
Glen Convinth
Ardblair
Meall nan Caorach 415
Meall Gorm 413
Carn Mòr 456
Carn nam Bad
Millness
Buntait
Bearnock
Balbeg
Gartally
Achmony
Glen Urquhart
Balnain
Milton
Drumnadrochit
Corrimony
Grange
Fasnakyle
Loch Meiklie
Lewiston
Strone
Glenurquhart Forest
Carn Macsna 525
Glen Coiltie
Lenie
Meall na h-Eilrig 465
Creag Nay 376
Brachla
Dores
Tor Point
Strath Dores
Ashie Moor
Tom Baigeann 464
Achnabat
Loch Duntelchaig
Stac na Cathaig 446
Whitefield
Tullich
Brinmore
Torness
Abersky
Loch Ruthven
East Croachy
Aberarder Ho.
Carn Glac an Eich 631
Beinn Bhreac 601
Findhorn
Glen Kyllachy
Knockfin
Tomich
Beinn Mhòr 401
Suidhe Ghuirmain 578
Balmacaan Forest
Bunloit
Balbeg
Grotaig
Invefarigaig
Easter Boleskine
Foyers
Ault-na-goire
Errogie
Dhuhallow
Farraline
Lyne of Gorthleck
Wester Aberchalder
Lochgarthside
Loch Mhor
Bailebeag
General Wade's Military Road
GLEN MOR
GLEN ALBYN
IV
Carn na Saobhaidh 774
Beinn Bhuidhe 711
Aonach Odhar 642
Glen Mazeran
13
Strathdearn
Dalmigavie
Dalmagavie
Beinn Dubhcharaidh 689
Carn Ghriogair 805
Beinn Bhreac Mhòr 807
Carn Odhar 802
Carn Caol 713
Carn Coire na h-Easgainn 790
Meall a' Chràthaich
Loch ma Stac
Guisachan Forest
63
Meal Fuar-mhonaidh 696
Alltsigh
Carn Mhic an Toisich 680
Levishie Forest
Levishie
Dundreggan Forest
Invermoriston
Portclair Forest
Dundreggan
Torgyle
Burach 607
Inverwick Forest
Glen Moriston
Whitebridge
Easter Drummond
Loch Knockie
Beinn Bhacaidh
Stratherrick
H
I
G
H
L
Carn na Saobhaidhe 811
Carn Fliuch-bhaid 656
Doire Meurach 787
Carn na Laraiche Maoile 809
Coignafearn Forest
MOUNTAINS
Carn Icean Duibhe 808
Carn Dulnan 729
Inchnacardoch Hotel
Fort Augustus
Glendoebeg
Carn Mhic Raonuill 568
Loch Killin
Cairn Vungie 710
Carn a' Choire Ghlaise 779
Burrach Mòr 828
Carn Coire na Creiche 826
Carn Sgulain 812
Coire Odhar
Glen Markie
Sgaraman nam Fiadh 858
Carn Sgulain 920
Carn an Fhreiceadain 878
Meall a' Chocaire 715
MONADHLIATH
35
Newtown
Aberchalder
Glen Doe
Carn Easgann Bana 778
Glendoe Forest
32
Carn a' Chuilinn 816
Glen Tarff
Cairn Ewen 875
Carn Ban 942
Carn Dearg 945
Creag Dhubh 786
Creag Bhlag 527
Invergarry
Mandally
Corrieyairack Hill 896
Corrieyairack Pass
Gairbeinn 896
Meall na h-Aisre 862
Creag an Loin 547
Kingussie
Newtonmore
Ruthven
Culachy Forest
Carn Leac 884
Corrieyairack Forest
Creag Mhòr 764
Geal Charn 926
Carn an Leth-choin 843
Dalballoch
Biallaid
Laggan
Carn Dearg 816
20
Glen Markie
Beinn a' Chrasgain 828
Marg na Craige
Glen Banchor
Creag Dhubh
Creag nam Bodach
Melgarve
Leacann nan Bainnir 637
Garvamore
Sherramore
Crathie
Blargie
Laggan
Balgowan
Lynaberack
Phones
Garbh Mheall Mòr 593
Meallach Mòr 768
34
Leckroy
Turret Bridge
Black Craig 565
Catlodge
Falls of Truim
Etteridge
590 Cruban Beag
PH
Glen Gloy
Beinn Iaruinn 803
Carn Liath 1006
Stob Poite Coire Ardair 1053
Coille Coire Chrannaig
Comra
Kinloch Laggan
Carn Dearg 834
Glen Roy
Creag Meagaidh 1130
Aberarder
Ardverikie
Glen Truim
Meall Chuaich 951
Bogha-cloiche 897
Beinn Teallach 915
31
Beinn a' Chaorainn 1050
An Cearcallach 993
Moy Forest
Beinn Eilde 674
Dalwhinnie
Gaick Lodge
Gaick Forest
Bohuntine
Creag Dhubh 658
Bohenie
Moy
Binnein Shuas 746
Lochan na h-Earba
Creag Pitridh 924
Geal Charn 1049
Meall Cruaidh 897
19
Loch Ericht Forest
BADENOCH
MOUNTAINS
Carn na Caim 941
Roybridge
Murlaggan
Braes o' Lochaber
Roughburn
Craigbeg
Tulloch Sta
Glen Spean
Meall Liath Mòr
Ardverikie Forest
Creagan Mòr
Cama' Choire
Dalnaspidal Forest
Beinn Chlianaig 721
Fersit
Beinn a' Chlachair 1087
Loch Pattack
Ben Alder Lodge
Geal Charn 917
Pass of Drumochter 424
Sronphadruig Lodge
Ben Alder Forest
An Lairig
Carn Dearg 1034
An Torc (Boar of Badenoch) 739
975
936
928 Glas Mheall Mòr
Dalnacardoch Forest
GRAMPIAN
Stob a' Choire Mheadhoin 1106
Stob Coire Easain 1116
Stob Coire Sgriodain 976
Chno Dearg 1047
Aonach Beag 1114
Geal Charn 1132
Beinn Udlamain 1010
The Sow of Atholl 803
Forest of Atholl
Badnambiast
Lairig Leacach
Loch Treig
Garbh Bheinn 858
30
Strath Ossian
Beinn Eibhinn 1101
Ben Alder 1148
Beinn Bheoil 1019
Sgairneach Mhòr 991
An Cearcall
ATHOLL
Beinn a' Chumhainn
Meall a' Bhealaich 901 865
Corrour Shooting Lodge
Beinn na Lap
Corrour Forest
17
Prince Charlie's Cave
Ben Alder Cottage
Sgor Gaibhre
Stob Aonach Mhor
Talla Bheith Forest
Duinish
Meall na Leitreach 775
Loch Garry
Sròn Choin
Glen Garry
Meall a' Chathaidh
0 2 4 6 miles
0 2 4 6 8 10 km

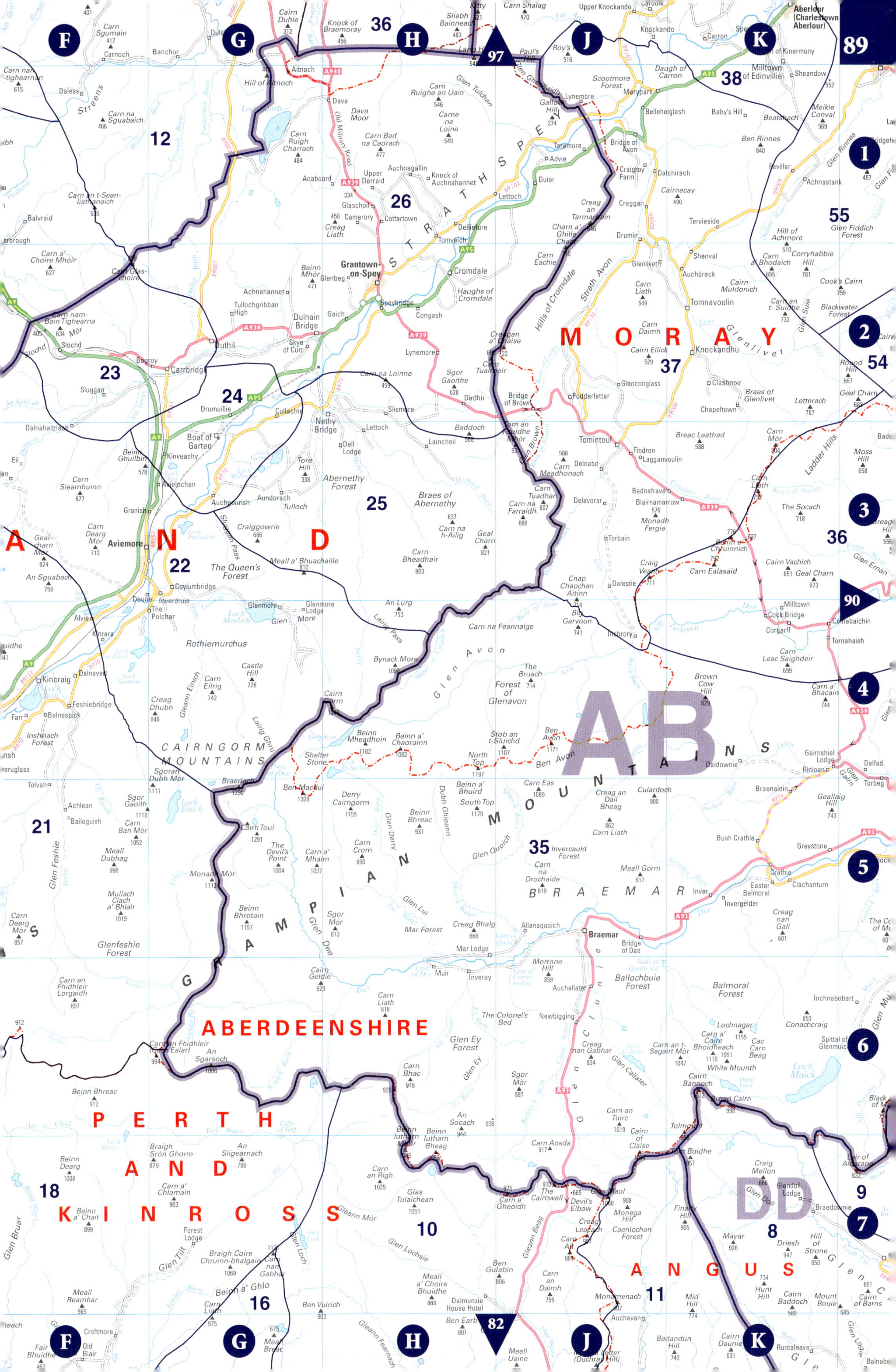

A
B
C
D
E
1
2
3
4
5
6
7
98
89
83
MORAY
ABERDEENSHIRE
ANGUS
GRAMPIAN MOUNTAINS
AB
DD
PH
CROMAR
Strathbogie
Garioch
Howe of Alford
Glenlivet
Aberlour (Charlestown of Aberlour)
Dufftown
Huntly
Rhynie
Lumsden
Alford
Tarland
Aboyne
Ballater
Insch
Kincardine O'Neil
Torphins
Strathdon
Braemar
Clova
Tarfside
Glen Esk
Glen Clova
Glen Muick
Loch Muick
Loch Lee
Balmoral Forest
Ballochbuie Forest
Forest of Glentanar
Clashindarroch Forest
Glen Fiddich Forest
Corrennie Forest
Blackhall Forest
Tomnavoulin
Knockandhu
Tomintoul
Cock Bridge
Corgarff
Colnabaichin
Boultenstone Hotel
Logie Coldstone
Dinnet
Kildrummy
Muir of Fowlis
Lumphanan
Edzell
Fettercairn
Mount Keen 939
Lochnagar 1155
Morven 871
Ben Rinnes 840
Mount Battock 778
Mayar 928
Driesh 947
Cairn Bannoch 1012
Broad Cairn 998
White Mouth
Bennachie
Millstone Hill 408
Coilliochbhar Hill
Ladder Hills
The Fungle Road
A93
A97
A939
A944
A980
A941
A96
A920
A95
B976
B9119
B9002
33
34
35
36
37
38
52
54
55
8
9
11
31
0 2 4 6 miles
0 2 4 6 8 10 km

F
G
H
J
K
1
2
3
4
5
6
7
99
Buchan Ness
Boddam
Murdoch Head
Cruden Bay
Port Erroll
Bay of Cruden
The Skares
Whinnyfold
The Veshels
Ellon
Formartine
Oldmeldrum
Inverurie
Kintore
Pitmedden
Udny Green
Udny Station
Newburgh
Newburgh Bar
Sands of Forvie
Forvie Ness (Hackley Head)
Collieston
St Catherine's Dub
Kirktown of Slains
Balmedie
Menie House
Skelly Rock
Blackdog Rock
hours
Kirkwall.................6-7¼
Lerwick..............12-12½
Dyce
ABERDEEN
Bridge of Don
Girdle Ness
Nigg Bay
Greg Ness
Souter Head
Cove Bay
Westhill
Kingswells
Peterculter
Portlethen
Findon Ness
Newtonhill
Muchalls
Doonie Point
Castle Rock of Muchalls
Garron Point
Cowie
Stonehaven
Stonehaven Bay
Catterline
Todhead Point
Inverbervie
Gourdon
Laurencekirk
Fordoun
Auchenblae
Fetteresso Forest
Durris Forest
Drumoak
Echt
Dunecht
Fyvie
Methlick
Tarves
Newmachar
Kemnay
DD

# WESTERN ISLES
## (NA H-EILEANAN AN IAR)

F
G
H
J
K
100
94
85
1
2
3
4
5
6
7
Tirga Mòr
Ullaval 659
Oreval 662
Stulaval 579
Leosaval 412
Forest of Harris
NORTH HARRIS
(CEANN A TUATH NA HEARADH)
Cleiseval 511
Uisgnaval Mòr 729
Mulla-fo-dheas 743
Clisham 799
Clett Ard 328
Aird a' Mhulaidh
Ath Linne
Abhainnsuidhe
Soay Beg
Soay Mòr
Miabhag
Tolmachan
Bun Abhainn Eadarra
Sgaoth Aird 559
Straiaval 389
Toddun 528
Maraig (Maaruig)
Kenmore
Caiteshal 449
Beinn na h-Uamha 389
Beannan Mòr 242
Beinn Mhòr 572
Park
Corlabhadh 298
Eisgean
Orasaigh
Leumrabhagh
Gob na Mi
Srianach
Eilean Iubhard
Uisenis 371
Mulhagery
Crionaig 470
Tathas Mhòr
Bhalamus
Rhenigidale (Reinigeadal)
Gob Rubh' Uisenis
Rubha Bhrollum
Rubh' a' Bhaird
Sgeir na h-Eigheach
Eilean Mòr a' Bhàigh
WEST LOCH TARBERT
Ben Raah 267
Aird Asaig
Beinn Dhubh 506
Taobh Siar
Tarbert (Tairbeart)
Beesdale
Ceann Reamhar 467
Urgha
Uieseval 334
Beinn a' Chaolais
Paible
Losgaintir
Corran Seilebost
South Harris Forest 287
Carragrich
Kyles Scalpay (Caolas Scalpaigh)
Sgeotasaigh
Scalpay
Ben Scoravick 104
Scalpay (Eilean Scalpaigh)
Kennavay
Meall Challibost
East Loch Tarbert
Miabhag
Drinisiader
Kennacley
Plocropol
Seilebost
Clett Nisabost 158
HS
A859
175 East Stocklett
Bulabhall 354
Heileasbhal Mòr 384
An Coileach 386
Aird Mhige
Greosabhagh
Liceasto
Lacklee (Leac a' Li)
Scadabhagh
Cluer (Cluthair)
Stockinish (Stocinis)
Geocrab
Beacravik
Rubha Bocaig
Rubha Cluer
SOUTH HARRIS
(CEANN A DEAS NA HEARADH)
Bleaval 398
Na-Buirgh
a Romagi
Bràigh-nam-bàgh
Manish (Manais)
Aird Leimhe
Fleoideabhagh
Ard Manish
Aird Mhighe
Màs Garbh
Finsbay (Fionnsbhagh)
Quidinish (Cuidhtinis)
Rubha Quidnish
Roneval 459
Strondeval 211
Borseam
Ceann a' Bhàigh
Lingarabay Island
Rodel (Roghadal)
Rubha Vallarip
Renish Point
Garbh Eilean 161
Eilean Mhuire
Eilean an Tighe
Shiant Islands
SOUND OF SHIANT
1¾ hrs
Fladda-chuain
Gaeilavore Island
Gearran Island
Eilean Trodday
Gilsay
Rubha Hunish
Rubha na h- Aiseig
Tulm Island
The Aird
Kilmaluag
Balmaqueen
Duntulm
Galta Mòr
Ru Bornaskitaig
Borniskeitaig
Hunglader
Kilmuir
Flodigarry
Sgeir Eirin
Eilean Flodigarry
Quiraing
Meall na Suiramach 543
The Needle
Digg
Staffin Island
Kilvaxter
Suidh' a' Mhinn 350
Balgown
Staffin
Rubha Garbhaig
Stenscholl
Monkstadt
Linicro
Bioda Buidhe 466
Kilbride Point
Totscore
Stack of Skudiburgh
Maligar
Ben Gorm
Marishader
Idrigil
Uig
Rubha Idrigil
Balnaknock
Beinn Edra 611
Garros
Earlish
Culnaknock
Rubha Chorachan
Ascrib Islands
South Ascrib
Vaternish Point
Sròn Ocrhulan 251
Ben Geary 284
Geary
Trumpan
Vaternish
LOCH SNIZORT
Lealt
Ardmore Point
Halistra
Gillen
Stac a' Bhothain
Cuidrach
Peinlich
Glenuachdarach
Creag a' Lain 608
Trotternish
Baca Ruadh 637
Hallin
Isay
Mingay Island
Bìod nan Laogh
Greshornish Point
Lyndale Point
Beinn a' Sga 452
Hartaval 668
Rigg
Dunvegan Head
Rubha Maol
Stein
Lusta
Lampay Islands
Ben Diubaig 214
Kingsburgh
Lyndale Ho.
The Storr 719
Ben Skriaig 307
Galtrigill
313
Borreraig
Claigan
Beinn Bhreac 327
Beinn Chreagach 326
Greshornish
Flashader
Treaslane
Romesdal
Eyre
51
Uig
Husabost
Totaig
A850
The Aird
HIGHLAND
Edinbane
Bernisdale
Kensaleyre
Ben Dearg 552
Milovaig
Ferinquarrie
Upper Milovaig
Lephin
Colbost
55
Ben Horneval 264
IV
Ben Uigshader 246
Tote
Borve
Waterstein Head 296
264
Beinn na Creiche
Skinidin
Uiginish
Dunvegan
Kilmuir
Lonmore
Ben Sca 286
Cruachan Beinn a' Chearcaill 271
Skeabost
Carbost
Drumuie
Sithean Bhealaich Chumhaing 392
Neist Point
Glen Dale
Ben Corkeval
Healabhal Mhòr (Macleod's Table North) 468
Roskhill
Ben Aketil 265
Beinn a' Ghlinne Bhig 208
Uigshader
Torvaig
Ramasaig
Roag
A863
SKYE
Orbost
Vatten
Glengrasco
Portree
Hoe Rape
The Hoe 233
Lorgill
Healabhal Bheag (Macleod's Table South) 488
Harlosh
Balmore
Glen Ose
Beinn na Cloiche 232
Am Maol 212
56
Ben Connan 244
Ose
417
Beinn na Greine
Penifiler
Ben Tianavaig 413
Harlosh Point
Beinn na Boineid 371
Ben Idrigil 340
Ebost
Glenmore
Mugeary
400
Ben Duagrich 304
Camastianavaig
Harlosh Island
Ullinish
Struan
Coillore
Lower Ollach
An Dubh Sgeir
LITTLE MINCH
A855
A87
A850
B884
B885

A
B
C
D
E
1
2
3
4
5
6
7
WESTERN ISLES
(NA H-EILEANAN AN IAR)
HS
Stornoway 2¾ hrs
Gob na
Srianach
Eilean Iubhard
Mulhagery
Garbh Eilean
Eilean Mhuire
161
Eilean an Tighe
Shiant Islands
Greenstone Point
Opinan
Rubha Mòr
Mellon Udrigle
Achgarve
Slaggan Bay
Eilean Furadh Mòr
Rubha Reidh
Cove
Mellon Charles
Bualnaluib
Ormiscaig
Aultbea
Isle of Ewe
An Cuaidh
296
Melvaig
Aultgrishan
Inverasdale
Midtown
Cnoc Breac
293
Peterburn
Naast
North Erradale
Boor
Londubh
Poolewe
Big Sand
Mial
Meall A' Ghiubhais
Carn Dearg
Smithstown
Longa Island
Gairloch
Auchtercairn
Charlestown
Eilean Horrisdale
Port Henderson
Badachro
Kerrysdale
Opinan
Shieldaig
Meall Aundrary
329
South Erradale
Mullach nan Cadhaichean
294
Red Point
Maol Ruadh
21
Red Point
Meall na h-Uamha
288
Baosbheinn
875
Shieldaig Forest
Beinn Bhreac
624
Craig
Rubha na Fearn
An Ruadh-mheallan
672
Lower Diabaig
Upper Diabaig
Sgurr Mhòr
985
922
Fearnmore
Fearnbeg
Beinn Alligin
Arinacrinachd
Cuaig
Kenmore
Alligin Shuas
Inveralligin
Ardheslaig
Rubha na Feola
Callakille
Inverbain
Shieldaig Island (NTS)
Shieldaig
Balgy
Lonbain
An Garbh-mheall
493
Croic-bheinn
493
Ben Shieldaig
516
Ben-damph Forest
An Fur
387
Meall na Fhuaid
518
Glenshieldaig
Forest
626
An Staonach
513
Meall na Saobhaidhe
368
Applecross Forest
Hartfield
646
Beinn Bhan
896
Applecross
Milton
Camusteel
Bealach na Ba
626
776
Camusterrach
Sgurr a' Chaorachain
792
Meall Gorm
710
Culduie
Russel
Lochcarron
Ardarroch
Toscaig
Meall Loch Airigh
Airigh-drishaig
Achintraid
Bad a' Chreamha
Eilean Trodday
Rubha Hunish
Rubha na h- Aiseig
The Aird
Kilmaluag
Balmaqueen
Duntulm
Galta Mòr
Hunglader
Flodigarry
Sgeir Eirin
Eilean Flodigarry
Kilmuir
Quiraing
Meall na Suiramach
543
Digg
Staffin Island
Kilvaxter
Suidh' a' Mhinn
350
The Needle
Balgown
Stenscholl
Staffin
Rubha Garbhaig
Linicro
Totscore
Bioda Buidhe
466
Elishader
Maligar
Uig
Ben Gorm
Marishader
Rubha nam Brathairean
Balnaknock
Beinn Edra
611
Garros
Culnaknock
Earlish
Lealt
Trotternish
Peinlich
Glenuachdarach
Creag a' Lain
608
Baca Ruadh
637
Leac Tressirnish
Beinn a' Sga
452
Hartaval
668
Rigg
SKYE
The Storr
719
Romesdal
Eyre
51
Treaslane
The Aird
Kensaleyre
Ben Dearg
552
Bernisdale
Tote
Borve
Skeabost
Carbost
Prince Charles's Cave
Sithean Bhealaich Chumhaing
392
Drumuie
Uigshader
Glengrasco
Torvaig
Portree
Am Maol
212
Beinn na Greine
417
Penifiler
Ben Tianavaig
413
Glenmore
Camastianavaig
SOUND OF RAASAY
Dry Harbour
RONA
125
Eilean Tigh
111
Eilean Fladday
Beinn na h-Iolaire
254
Torran
Manish Point
Arnish
Brochel
RAASAY
385
Glame
40
Balachuirn
Dun Caan
443
86
Rubha na' Leac
Beinn na' Leac
Sròn na h-Airde Bhaine
INNER SOUND
LOCH TORRIDON
LOCH EWE
Gair Loch
Lower Ollach
93
0 2 4 6 miles
0 2 4 6 8 10 km
A832
A855
A87
A850
A896
B8021
B8056
B8057
B885

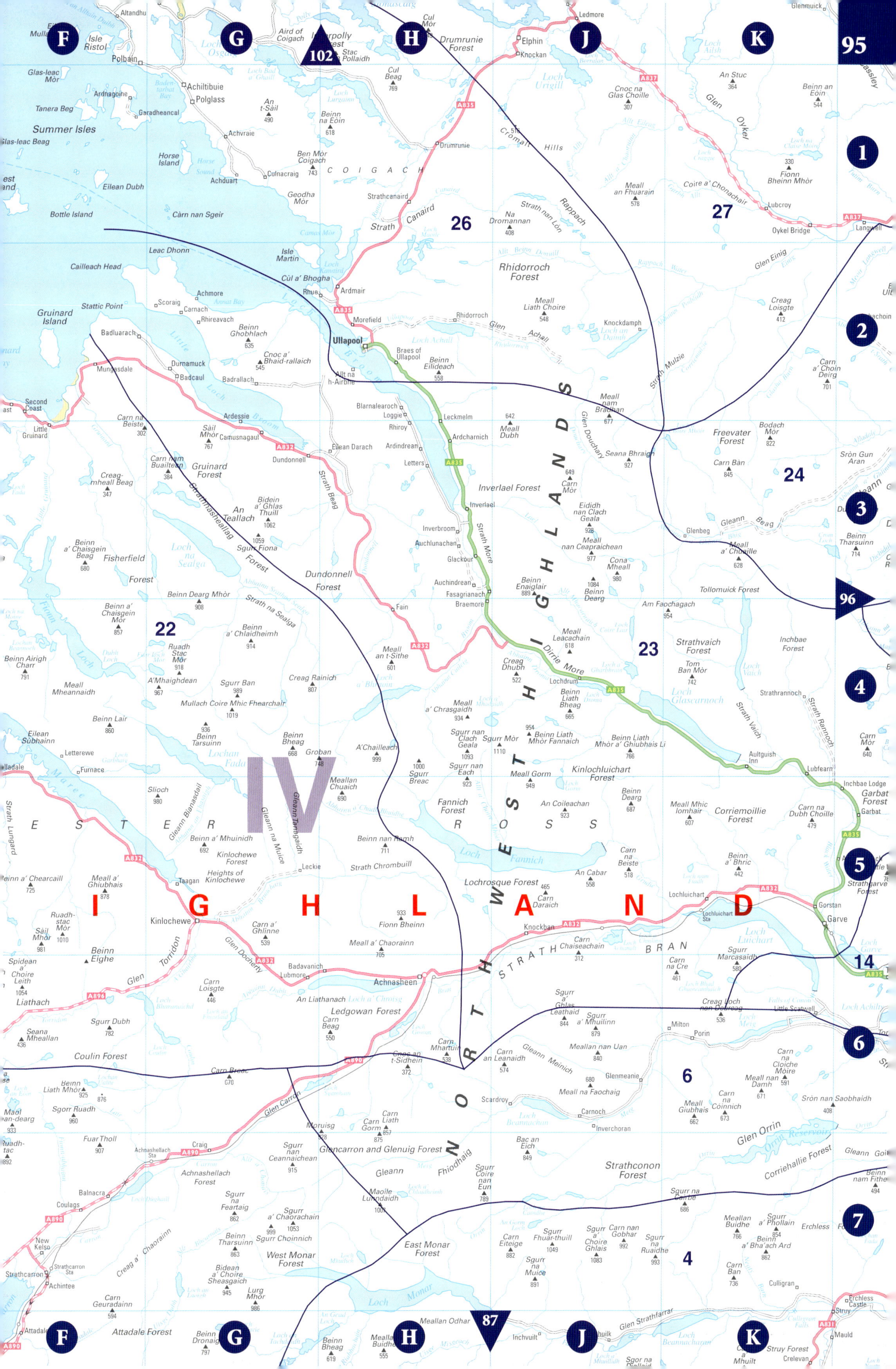
F
G
102
H
J
K
1
2
3
4
5
6
7
96
87
14
IV
Isle Ristol
Polbain
Altandhu
Aird of Coigach
Stac Pollaidh
Cul Mòr
Drumrunie Forest
Ledmore
Elphin
Knockan
Loch Urigill
Glenmuick
Glas-leac Mòr
Achiltibuie
Polglass
Ardnagoine
Tanera Beg
Garadheancal
Summer Isles
Glas-leac Beag
Achvraie
Horse Island
Culnacraig
Achduart
Eilean Dubh
Bottle Island
Càrn nan Sgeir
Cul Beag
769
An t-Sàil
490
Beinn na Eòin
618
Ben Mòr Coigach
743
C O I G A C H
Geodha Mòr
Drumrunie
Cromalt Hills
Strathcanaird
Strath Canaird
26
Na Dromannan
408
Strath nan Lòn
Rappach
Cnoc na Glas Choille
307
An Stuc
364
Beinn an Eòin
544
Glen Oykel
330
Fionn Bheinn Mhòr
Coire a' Chonachair
Meall an Fhuarain
578
27
Lubcroy
Oykel Bridge
Langwell
A837
A835
Leac Dhonn
Isle Martin
Cailleach Head
Cùl a' Bhogha
Rhue
Ardmair
Achmore
Scoraig
Carnach
Rhireavach
Stattic Point
Gruinard Island
Rhidorroch Forest
Meall Liath Choire
548
Rhidorroch
Glen Achall
Knockdamph
Creag Loisgte
412
Glen Einig
Morefield
Ullapool
Braes of Ullapool
Beinn Eilideach
558
Badluarach
Beinn Ghobhlach
635
Cnoc a' Bhaid-rallaich
545
Durnamuck
Badcaul
Badrallach
Mungasdale
Allt na h-Airbhe
Loch Broom
Little Loch Broom
Strath Mulzie
Carn a' Choin Deirg
701
Meall nam Bradhan
677
Second Coast
Little Gruinard
Blarnalearoch
Loggie
Rhiroy
Leckmelm
Ardcharnich
642
Meall Dubh
Carn na Beiste
302
Ardessie
Sàil Mhòr
767
Camusnagaul
A832
Eilean Darach
Ardindrean
Dundonnell
Letters
Freevater Forest
Bodach Mòr
822
Carn nam Buailtean
384
Gruinard Forest
Seana Bhraigh
927
Carn Bàn
845
Sròn Gun Aran
24
Creag-mheall Beag
347
Strath Beag
Inverlael Forest
649
Carn Mòr
Glen Douchary
Inverlael
An Teallach
Bidein a' Ghlas Thuill
1062
Eididh nan Clach Geala
928
Gleann Beag
Glenbeg
Beinn a' Chaisgein Beag
680
Fisherfield Forest
Loch na Sealga
1059
Sgurr Fiona
Inverbroom
Auchlunachan
Glackour
Strath More
Meall nan Ceapraichean
977
Cona' Mheall
980
Meall a' Chuaille
628
Beinn Tharsuinn
714
Dundonnell Forest
Auchindrean
Fasagrianach
Braemore
Fain
Beinn Enaiglair
889
1084
Beinn Dearg
Tollomuick Forest
Beinn Dearg Mhòr
908
Strath na Sealga
Beinn a' Chaisgein Mòr
857
22
Beinn a' Chlaidheimh
914
Ruadh Stac Mòr
918
Am Faochagach
954
Meall Leacachain
618
23
Strathvaich Forest
Inchbae Forest
Meall an t-Sithe
601
A'Mhaighdean
967
Creag Rainich
807
Creag Dhubh
522
Dirrie More
Lochdrum
Tom Ban Mòr
742
Loch Glascarnoch
Strath Vaich
Beinn Airigh Charr
791
Meall Mheannaidh
Sgurr Ban
989
Mullach Coire Mhic Fhearchair
1019
Beinn Liath Bheag
665
Meall a' Chrasgaidh
934
Strathrannoch
Strath Rannoch
Beinn Lair
860
936
Beinn Tarsuinn
954
Beinn Liath Mhòr Fannaich
Beinn Liath Mhòr a' Ghiubhais Li
766
Eilean Subhainn
Letterewe
Furnace
Lochan Fada
Beinn Bheag
668
Groban
748
A'Chailleach
999
Sgurr nan Clach Geala
1093
Sgurr Mòr
1110
Aultguish Inn
Lubfearn
Carn Mòr
640
Slioch
980
Meallan Chuaich
690
1000
Sgurr Breac
Sgurr nan Each
923
Meall Gorm
949
Kinlochluichart Forest
Inchbae Lodge
Garbat Forest
Garbat
Gleann Bianasdail
Gleann na Muice
Gleann Tanagaidh
Fannich Forest
An Coileachan
923
Beinn Dearg
687
Meall Mhic Iomhair
607
Corriemoillie Forest
Carn na Dubh Choille
479
W E S T E R R O S S
Beinn a' Mhuinidh
692
Kinlochewe Forest
Heights of Kinlochewe
Leckie
Beinn nan Ramh
711
Loch Fannich
Carn na Beiste
518
Beinn a' Bhric
442
Strathgarve Forest
Strath Chrombuill
An Cabar
558
Lochrosque Forest
465
Carn Daraich
Lochluichart
Meall a' Ghiubhais
878
Taagan
Beinn a' Chearcall
725
I G H L A N D
Gorstan
Garve
Lochluichart Sta
Ruadh-stac Mòr
1010
Sàil Mhòr
981
Kinlochewe
Carn a' Ghlinne
539
933
Fionn Bheinn
Knockban
Carn Chaiseachain
312
Loch Luichart
Meall a' Chaorainn
705
S T R A T H B R A N
Carn na Cre
461
Sgurr Marcasaidh
580
Spidean a' Choire Leith
1054
Beinn Eighe
Glen Torridon
Glen Docherty
Badavanich
Lubmore
Achnasheen
Liathach
A896
A890
An Liathanach
Loch a' Chroisg
Ledgowan Forest
Sgurr a' Ghlas Leathaid
844
Sgurr a' Mhuilinn
879
Creag Loch nan Dearcag
536
Little Scatwell
Carn Loisgte
446
Seana Mheallan
436
Sgurr Dubh
782
Carn Beag
550
Milton
Porin
Coulin Forest
Carn Breac
670
Carn Mhartuin
538
Cnoc an t-Sidhein
372
Carn an Leanaidh
574
Gleann Meinich
Mealan nan Uan
840
Carn na Cloiche Moire
591
Beinn Liath Mhòr
925
876
680
Glenmeanie
Meall na Faochaig
6
Meall nan Damh
671
N O R T H W E S T H I G H L A N D S
Sgorr Ruadh
960
Glen Carron
Scardroy
Carn na Coinnich
673
Meall Giubhais
662
Sròn nan Saobhaidh
408
Maol Chean-dearg
933
Moruisg
928
Carn Gorm
875
Carn Liath
857
Carnoch
Inverchoran
Fuar Tholl
907
Craig
Achnashellach Sta
Sgurr nan Ceannaichean
915
Glencarron and Glenuig Forest
Bac an Eich
849
Glen Orrin
Orrin Reservoir
Gleann Goibhre
Achnashellach Forest
Gleann Fhiodhaig
Sgurr Coire nan Eun
789
Strathconon Forest
Corriehallie Forest
Beinn nam Fitheach
494
Balnacra
Sgurr na Feartaig
862
Maoile Lunndaidh
1007
Sgurr na Fearstaig
686
Coulags
Sgurr a' Chaorachain
1053
999
Sgurr Choinnich
Carn Eiteige
882
Sgurr Fhuar-thuill
1049
Sgurr a' Choire Ghlais
1083
Carn nan Gobhar
992
Sgurr na Ruaidhe
993
Meallan Buidhe
766
Sgurr a' Phollain
854
Beinn a' Bha'ach Ard
862
Erchless Forest
New Kelso
Creag a' Chaorainn
Beinn Tharsuinn
863
West Monar Forest
East Monar Forest
4
Sgurr na Muice
891
Carn Ban
736
Culligran
Strathcarron
Strathcarron Sta
Achintee
Bidean a' Choire Sheasgaich
945
Lurg Mhòr
986
Loch Monar
Erchless Castle
Struy
Carn Geuradainn
594
Meallan Odhar
Inchvuilt
Glen Strathfarrar
A831
Mauld
Attadale
Attadale Forest
Beinn Dronaig
797
Beinn Bheag
619
Meallan Buidhe
555
Struy Forest
Crelevan
Sgor na Diollaid
Carn a' Mhuilt

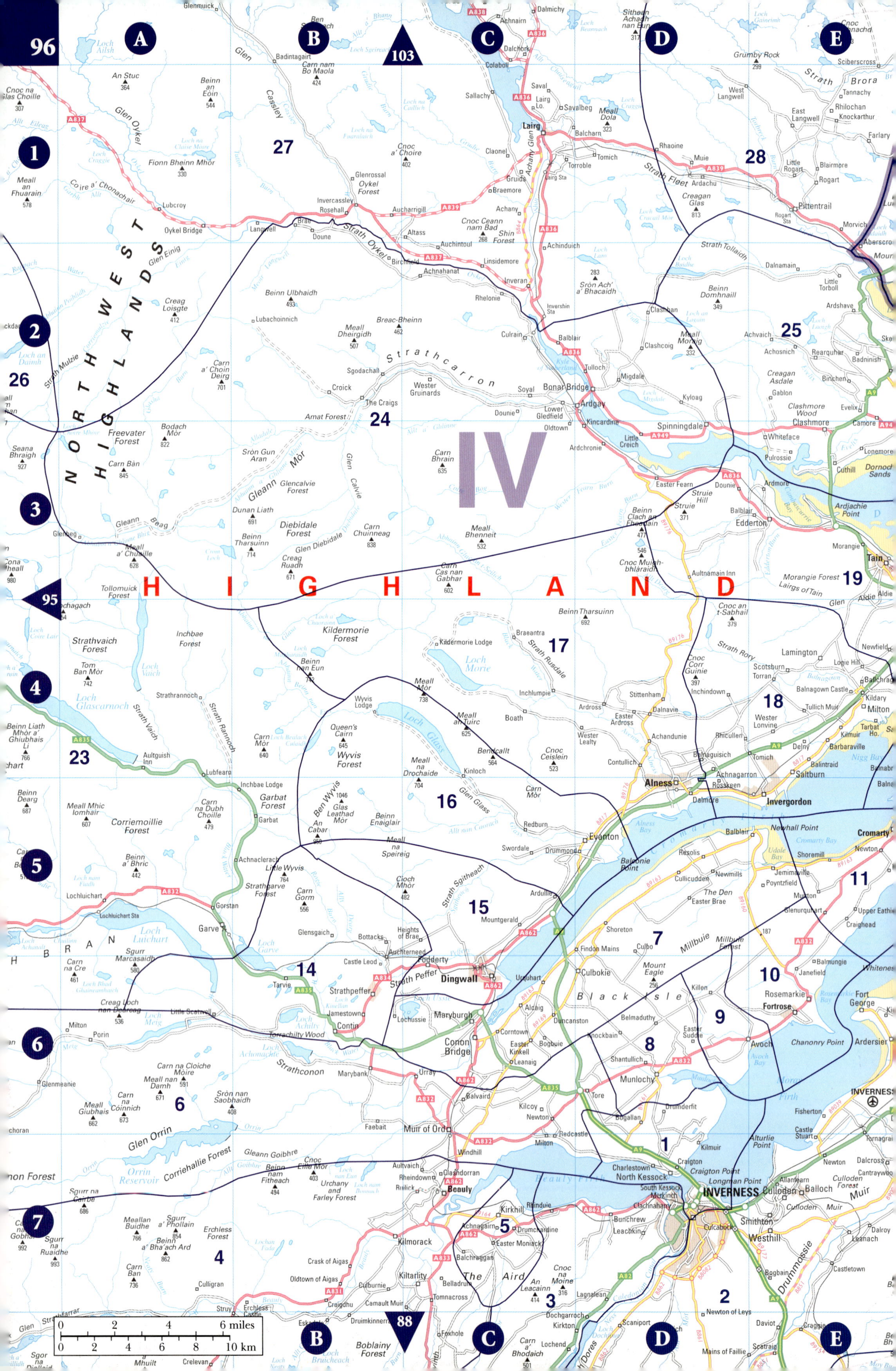

F
G
H
J
K
1
2
3
4
5
6
7
104
98
89
KW
IV
AB
PH
9
20
31
30
32
36
12
38
55
26
37
M O R A Y
Culgower
Lothmore
Kilmote
Creag a' Chrionaich
Col-bheinn
538
Lothbeg
Lothbeg Point
Gordonbush
Carrol Rock
Kintradwell
East Clyne
Greenhill
Dalchalm
Killin Rock
Carrol
West Clyne
Clynelish
Cagar Feosaig
378
East Brora
Brora
Doll
Backies
Dunrobin Castle Sta
Golspie
Embo
Tarbat Ness
Wilkhaven
Port Mòr
Hilton
Portmahomack
Bindal
Innis Mhòr
Whiteness Sands
Innis Bheag
Balcherry
Inver
Rockfield
Balnagall
Tarrel
Lochslin
Rhynie
Hill of Fearn
Fearn
Geanies Ho.
Cadboll
Tullich
Hilton of Cadboll
Balintore
Shandwick
Chapelhill
Hill of Nigg
Castlecraig
North Sutor
M O R A Y   F I R T H
Halliman Skerries
Covesea Skerries
Clashach Point
Covesea
Stotfield
Branderburgh
Lossiemouth
Hopeman
Burghead
Cummingstown
Duffus
Gordonstoun
Oakenhead
Boar's Head Rock
Lossie Forest
Innes Links
Roseisle
Roseisle Forest
Burghead Bay
Salterhill
Buthill
Findrassie
Lochhill
Findhorn
Hempriggs
Quarrywood
Bishopmill
Urquhart
Muirhead
Coltfield
Miltonhill
Ardgye
ELGIN
Culbin Forest
Wellhill
Kinloss
Alves
Palmerscross
New Elgin
Lhanbryde
Kintessack
Inverene
Grange Hall
Toreduff
Clovel
Pittendreich
Moss of Barmuckity
Muir of Lochs
Moy House
Springfield
Forres
Hillside
Miltonduff
Mosstodloch
Muirtown
The Bar
Dyke
Mains of Burgie
Monaughty Forest
Paddockhaugh
Blackhills
Clackmarras
Orbliston
Longmorn
Kingsteps
Macbeth's Hillock
Newton of Dalvey
Heldon Hill
Auchtertyre
Fogwatt
Altonside
Nairn
Tradespark
Hilton of Delnies
Blervie Castle
Califer
Barnhill
Thomshill
Whitewreath
Rafford
Tulloch
Crofts of Buinach
Teindland Forest
Househill
Auldearn
Boghole Fm
Dallas Forest
Kellas
Leanoch
Coleburn
Findlay's Seat
Whitemire
Hill of the Wangie
Glenlatterach
Bardon
Laiken Forest
Conicavel
Altyre Woods
Newtyle Forest
Briach
Edinvale
Craigend
Brylach Hill
Glen of Rothes
Wood of Dundurcas
Moss-side
Miltonn
Phorp
Branchill
Dallas
Mill Buie
Pikey Hill
Auchinroath
Torrich
Regoul
Darnaway Forest
Mains of Sluie
Romach Hill
Ardoch
Meikle Hill
Cairn Uish
The Kettles
Rothes
Piperhill
Culcharry
Fornighty
Lethen Bar
Presley
Drumine Forest
Mill Buie
Littlemill
Logie
Tomnamoon
Craigroy
Cawdor
Hill of Tomechole
Urchany
Relugas
Carnachie
Carn na Cailliche
Hill of Stob
Cairn Cattoch
Hunt Hill
Whiteacen
Dandaleith
Achindown
Redburn
Carn Ghiubhas
Elchies Forest
Clunas
Bruachmary
Mount
Tomdow
Archiestown
Robertstown
Craigellachie
Ferness
Ringorm
Balmore
Carn a' Chrasgie
Dallra
Carn Kitty
Carn Shalag
Upper Knockando
Cardow
Aberlour (Charlestown of Aberlour)
Cairn Duhie
Knock of Braemoray
Sliabh Bainneach
Knockando
Carron
Speyview
Daugh of Kinermony
Milltown of Edinvillie
Carn Sgumain
Delnie
Milltown
Banchor
Hill of Aitnoch
Aitnoch
Larig Hill
Paul's Hill
Roy's Hill
Daugh of Carron
Sheandow
Dufftown
Carn nan Tighearnan
Dava
Dava Moor
Carn Ruighe an Uain
Glen Tulchan
Carne
Gallow Hill
Scootmore Forest
Marypark
Belleheiglash
Baby's Hill
Beatshach
Meikle Conval
Carn na Sguabaich
Streens
Ben Aigan
Knock More
Knock
Boot o' Brig
Kinchill
A9
A96
A941
A940
A939
A95
B9040
B9012
B9010
B9013
B9089
B9011
B9007
B9090
B9091
B9101
B9165
B9166
B9163
B9135
B9103
B9102
B9015

A
B
C
D
E
1
2
3
4
5
6
7
Halliman Skerries
Covesea Skerries
Covesea
97
Stotfield
Branderburgh
Lossiemouth
Gordonstoun
Oakenhead
31
Lossie Forest
Boar's Head Rock
Innes Links
Salterhill
Loch Spynie
Kingston
Spey Mouth
Spey Bay
Lochhill
Garmouth
Nether Dallachy
Portgordon
Bishopmill
ELGIN
Urquhart
Upper Dallachy
Mains of Tannachy
Slackhead
Arradoul
Newton
Bogmoor
Auchenhalrig
Muir of Lochs
Palmerscross
New Elgin
Lhanbryde
Moss-of Barmuckity
Pittendreich
Newlands of Tynet
Bridge of Tynet
Broadley
Clochan
Mosstodloch
Fochabers
Paddockhaugh
Cloddach
Longmorn
Blackhills
Clackmarras
Braes of Enzie
Dipple
Orbliston
Whiteash Hill
30
Thomshill
Fogwatt
Whitewreath
Altonside
Inchberry
32
Ordiequish
Wood of Ordiequish
Speymouth Forest
Teindland Forest
M
O
R
A
Y
Glenlatterach
Bardon
Coleburn
Findlay's Seat
Thief's Hill
Forgie
North Bogbain
Hill of Mulderie
Aultmore
Brylach Hill
Glen of Rothes
Wood of Dundurcas
Boat o' Brig
Pikey Hill
The Kettles
Auchinroath
Kirdhill
Mulben
Cairn Uish
Rothes
Knock More
Tauchers
Rosarie
Auchlunkart
Carn na Cailliche
Hill of Stob
Ben Aigan
Rosarie Forest
Hill of Towie
Cairn Cattoch
Hunt Hill
38
Whiteacen
Dandaleith
Knockan
Towiemore
Craigellachie
Maggieknockater
55
Drummuir Castle
Drummuir
Braehead
Archiestown
Robertstown
Ringorm
Aberlour (Charlestown of Aberlour)
Cardow
Knockando
Speyview
Carron
Daugh of Kinermony
Tullich
Parkmore
Milltown of Edinvillie
Dufftown
Sheandow
Daugh of Carron
Marypark
Belleheiglash
37
Baby's Hill
Beatshach
Meikle Conval
Ben Rinnes
Dalchirach
Favillar
Achnastank
Cairnacay
Craggan
Tervieside
Hill of Achmore
Glen Fiddich Forest
Drumin
Glenlivet
Carn Liath
Muldonich
Meikle Conval
Laggan
Bridgehaugh
Laird's Seat
Glen Fiddich
The Scalp
Glacks of Balloch Pass
Ballochford
Carn Chrom
Bridgend
Inverharroch Farm
Ardwell
Meikle Balloch Hill
Balloch Wood
Blackhillock
Glen of Coachford
Edintore
Coachford
Hillend
Aultnapaddock
Daugh of Invermarkie
Milltown of Auchindoun
Bakebare
Keithmore
Haugh of Glass
Dumeath
Backside
Succoth
Tomnaven
Black Hill
Mount of Haddoch
90
Findochty
Portknockie
Portessie
Ianstown
Bauds of Cullen
Buckie
Rathven
Scar Nose
Cullen Bay
Logie Head
Cullen
Seatown
Sandend
Sandend Bay
Redhythe Point
Portsoy
Boyne Bay
Knock Head
Whitehills
Bin of Cullen
56
Hill of Maud
Slate Haugh
Drybridge
Weston
Linthill
Clune
Milton
Mains of Glassaugh
Fordyce
Durn Hill
Fordyce Hill
Kirktown of Deskford
Ardiecow
Berryhillock
Hoggie
Black Hill
Shiel Muir
Addie Hill
Craibstone
Millstone Hill
Aultmore
Backies
Lurg Hill
Deerhill
Broadrashes
Garralburn
Grange Crossroads
Cranoch
Bracobrae
Sillyearn
Knock Hill
Knock
Drumnagorrach
Floors
Newmill
Fife Keith
Keith
Davoch of Grange
Farmtown
Knabbygates
Canterbury
Cornhill
Gordonstown
Glen Barry
Park
Wether Hill
Culvie
Old Crombie
Moss-side
Mayno
Haughs
Milltown of Rothiemay
Redhill
Fourman Hill
Ruthven
Newton
Cairnie
The Bin
The Bin Forest
Drumdelgie
Daugh of Cairnborrow
Milton of Cairnborrow
Torry
Huntly
A B E R D E
Cairnargat
Clashmach Hill
54
Muckle Long Hill
Bailiesward
Tillathrowie
Bridgend
Strathbogie
Coynachie
Clashindarroch Forest
Cransmill Hill
Quarry Hill
Clashindarroch
Kirkney
Gartly
Newnoth
Tap o' Noth
Kennethmont
Milton of Noth
Towie
Rhynie
Belhinnie
Aldunie
Boyndie
Auds
Blairshinnoch
Wester Culbeuchly
Easter Whyntie
Hill of Culbirnie
45
Oldtown of Ord
Fattahead
Weachyburn
Linhead
Milbethill
Kebholes
Finnygaud
Knowes of Elrick
Gallow Hill
Boghead
Auchintoul
Aberchirder
Crannach
Marnoch
Clunie
Carnousie
Hilltrae
Yonder Bognie
Bognebrae
Inverkeithny
Auchininna
Fortrie
Cobairdy
Conland
Drumblair
Crichie
Corse of Kinnoir
Lessendrum
Frendraught
Largue
Denmoss
Aucharnie
Drumblade
Corse
Mosshead
Brideswell
Beggshill
Denend
Ythanwells
Slioch
Thomastown
Millburn
Kirkstile
Winds Eye
Bainshole
Hill of Tillymorgan
Backburn
Wishach Hill
Glens of Foudland
Hill of Foudland
Skares
Kirkton of Culsalmond
Cairnhill
Culdrain
Knockandy Hill
Cults
Largie
Wrangham
Colpy
Slack
Wardhouse
Upper Boddam
Glanderston
Aulton
52
Rothney
Insch
Hill of Christ's
Ardoyne
0 2 4 6 miles
0 2 4 6 8 10 km
A96
A98
A941
A95
A990
A942
A920
A97
B9040
B9012
B9135
B9013
B9015
B9103
B9104
B9016
B9017
B9018
B9014
B9115
B9009
B9008
B9102
B9022
B9023
B9025
B9117
B9139
B9002
B9001

F
G
H
J
K
1
2
3
4
5
6
7
Kinnairds Head
Fraserburgh
Fraserburgh Bay
Cairnbulg Point
Rosehearty
Pittulie
Sandhaven
Broadsea
Quarry Head
Troup Head
Crovie Head
Crovie
Northfield
Pennan Head
Pennan
Aberdour Bay
Head of Garness
Gardenstown
Gamrie Bay
Melrose
Protstonhill
Dubford
Towie
New Aberdour
Upper Boyndlie
Coburty
Peathill
Percyhorner
Pitblae
Cardno
Mid Ardlaw
Tyrie
Broomhead
Memsie
Cairnbulg
Inverallochy
Whitelinks Bay
Charlestown
St Combs
Inzie Head
South Inch
Strathbeg Bay
Gowanhill
Cairness
Coralhill
Craigellie
Rathen
Longmanhill
Wester Greenskares
Gamrie
Cushnie
Lennans
Windyheads Hill
Woodhead
Ladysford
Whitewell
Whitebog
43
Minnonie
Netherbrae
Overbrae
Bracklamore Hill
Hill of Fishrie
Bracklamore
Nether Glasslaw
Craigmaud
Bogfold
Turclossie
Hillhead of Auchentumb
Waughtonhill
Waughton Hill
Mormond Hill
Newburgh
Lonmay
Crimonmogate
Loch of Strathbeg
Old Rattray
Seatown
Rattray Head
Foulzie
Balgreen
Gorrachie
Castleton
Plaidy
Milltown of Craigston
Cairnywhing
New Pitsligo
Knowhead
Whitestripe
Strichen
New Leeds
Dartfield
Crimond
Blackhill
North Essie
Rattray Bay
Gas Terminal
AB
New Byth
Fintry
Brackens
Wester Badentyre
Garmond
Balthangie
Muiryfold
Craigculter
Whitehill
Bonnykelly
Ironside
Oldwhat
Adziel
Carnichal
Longhill
Denhead
Leys
Backfolds
St Fergus Moss
Rora Moss
Hythie
Kirktown
St Fergus
Scotstown Head
Fetterangus
Toux
Cuttyhill
Rora
Kirkton Head
Turriff
Delgaty Forest
Cuminestown
Hill of Corsegight
Corsegight
Middlehill
Mains of Fedderate
B U C H A N
Forest of Deer
Mains of Pitfour
Lunderton
Millbank
Craig Ewen
Mill of Colp
Gask
Darra
53
Howe of Teuchar
Hatton Castle
West Cairncake
Waggle Hill
Northburnhill
Muirtack
North Commonty
Grainhow
New Deer
Mains of Cush
Maud
Waterhill of Bruxie
Old Deer
Mintlaw
Longside
Torterston
Inverugie
Thunderton
Peterhead
Buchanhaven
Birkenhills
South Redbriggs
Deer's Hill
Maryhill
Drymuir
Backhill of Clackriach
Bulwark
Clockhill
Stuartfield
Inverquhomery
Keith Inch
Peterhead Bay
Tillyfar
North Millbrex
Moss of Belnagoak
Crichie
Netherton
Millbreck
42
Hillhead of Cocklaw
Little Dens
Burnhaven
Sandford Bay
Invernettie
Newmill
Knaven
Kinnadie
Clola
Nether Kinmundy
Blackhill
Boddam
Stirling
Buchan Ness
E N S H I R E
Steinmanhill
Mackerry
Inverythan
Gourdas
Darnabo
Monkshill
Lethenty
Burnend
Cairnorrie
Cottown
South Upper Barrack
Auchnagatt
Skelmuir
Skelmuir Hill
Newton
Kinknockie
Smallburn
Carse of Balloch
Moss of Cruden
Sandfordhill
Coldwells
Tifty
Backhill
Brownhill
Monteach
Hill of Skilmafilly
Mill of Elrick
Aldie
Gask
Teuchan
Murdoch Head
Gordonstown
Rothiebrisbane
Woodhead
Ardo
Skelmonae
Quilquox
Inkhorn
Loanhead
Upper Hawkhillock
Ardallie
Greenheads
North Haven
Fyvie
Crofts of Haddo
Greenmyre
Methlick
Milton of Coldwells
Hill of Dudwick
Muirtack
Auchiries
Petty
Rothienorman
Collynie
Drumwhindle
Arthrath
Mains of Dudwick
Hatton
Erollston
Cruden Bay
Cromblet
St Katherines
Barthol Chapel
Hillbrae
Tanglandford
41
Blindburn
Waterloo
Chapel Hill
Port Erroll
Springleys
South Flobbets
Eastford
Craigie Brae
Toll of Birness
Bogbrae
Bay of Cruden
Folla Rule
Core Hill
The Banking
Sovermoss
Inverebrie
Hilton Croft
Bearnie
Kiplaw Croft
The Skares
Whinnyfold
Cross of Jackston
South Blackbog
Balgove
Wedderlairs
Thornroan
Raxton
Cookston
Broomfield
Leask
51
Jackstown
Tulloch
Tarves
Artrochie
The Veshels
Pitinnan
Craigdam
Yithsie
Kinharrachie
Ellon
Auchmacoy
Cluchtow
F o r m a r t i n e
Mounie Castle
Auquhorthies
Esslemont
91
Mains of Glack
Whitefield
Fingask
Oldmeldrum
Pitmedden
Cairnhill
Kirkton
Logie Buchan
Meikle Tarty
Waterside
Slains
St Catherine's Dub
A98
A90
A981
A950
A952
A947
A948
A982
A975
A920
B9031
B9032
B9033
B9093
B9170
B9005

# WESTERN ISLES
## (NA H-EILEANAN AN IAR)

# 101

## F G H J K

### Butt of Lewis (Rubha Robhanais)
Port a' Stoth
Eoropaidh · Còig Peighinnean
Bad an Fhithich · Lionel (Lional) · Port of Ness (Port Nis)
Swainbost (Suaineabost) · Habost (Tabost)
Aird Dhail · Eorodal
South Dell (Dail Bho Dheas) · North Dell (Dail Bho Thuath) · Cross (Cros) · Sgiogarstaigh · Port Skigersta
Toa Galson · Ness (Niss) · Meall Geal
Gabhsunn Bho Thuath · Glen Cross · Port Alasdair
Gabhsunn Bho Dheas · Airigh na Glaice · Cuidhaseadair · Laimhrig
Melbost Borve (Mealabost) · Airighean Beinn nan Caorach
Roinn a' Bhuic · Ben Dell · Cellar Head
Borve (Borgh) · High Borve · Loch Langabhat
Siadar Iarach · Airighean Loch Breihavat
Rubha Leathann · Siadar Uarach · Diaval
Baile an Truiseil
A857
Upper Barvas
Brue (Brù) · Barvas (Barabhas) · Glen Shader
A858 · Loch Gress
Muirneag 248 · Port Geiraha
Tolastadh Ùr
Tolastadh
Tolsta Head
Port nam Botlag
Gleann Tholastaidh
Port Ban a' Ghlùime
E OF LEWIS (EILEAN LEODHAIS) · Gress (Griais)
Roishal Mòr 174 · Bac · Creag Fhraoch
Beinn Mholach 292 · Col
Col Uarach · Breibhig · Rubha Bhataisgeir
Tiumpan Head (Rubha an Tiumpain) · 102
Tunga · Aird Thunga · Portnaguran (Port nan Giùran) · Portvoller
New Valley · Newmarket · Sròn Ruadh · Flesherin · Rubha Deas
Laxdale · Melbost Sands · Loch a' Tuath (Broad Bay) · Aird
Stornoway (Steòrnabhagh) · Stenis · STORNOWAY · East Roisnish · Siulaisiadar · Seisiadar
Marybank · Sandwick (Sanndabhaig) · Melbost · Garrabost · Eye Peninsula (An Rubha)
**1** · Melbost Pt · Aiginis · Rubha na Greine
A859 · Holm (Tolm) · Suardail · Rubha na Bearnaich
Beinn a' Bhuna · Arnish Moor · Arnish Pt · Branahuie Banks · Upper Bayble (Pabail Uarach) · **2**
149 · Rubh' a' Bhaigh Uaine · Ceann na Circ · Lower Bayble (Pabail Iarach)
Achadh Mòr · Beagh Phabail
Leurbost (Liurbost) · Grimshader (Griomsiadar) · Loch Grimsiadar
Crosbost · Ranish (Rànais) · Raerinish Point
Keose (Ceòs) · Tabhaigh Mhòr · Ullapool 2¾ hrs
Eilean Chaluim Chille · Cromore · Orasaigh
Cearsiadar · Cabhastadh · Torraigh
Tabost · Gearraidh Bhaird · Marbhig
Calbost
Rubha Iosal
Grabhair
Tom an Fhuadain · Rubha Odhrain
Kebock Head · Leumrabhagh · Gob na Milaid
Srianach
Eilean Iubhard
Uisenis 371 · Mulhagery

SOUND OF SHIANT
Gob Rubh' Uisenis
Rubha Bhrollum
bh' a' Bhaird · Garbh Eilean 161 · Eilean an Tighe

## F G H J K

# 102

## Grid references
A B C D E
1 2 3 4 5 6 7

### Locations

**Cape Wrath area (E1–E2):**
Duslic, Cape Wrath, Stra Kea, Kear, Bay of Keisgaig, Cnoc a' Ghiubhais 297, Geodha Ruadh na Fola, Am Balg, Sandwood Bay, Beinn Dea 423, Creag Riabhach 485, Am Buachaille, Sandwood Loch, An Grianan 467, Rubh' an Fhir Leithe, Mea Mo 46, Strath Shinary

**Kinlochbervie area (D3–E3):**
Sheigra, Blairmore, Beinn a' Chraisg 257, Balchrick, Oldshore Beg, Oldshoremore, An Socach 358, Eilean an Ròin Mòr, Kinlochbervie, Badcall, Rubha na Leacaig, Loch Clash, A838, Bàgh Loch an Ròin, Achriesgill

**Scourie / Laxford (C4–E4):**
Achlyness, Ardmore Point, Rubha Ruadh, Ceathramh Garbh, Rhiconich, Fanagmore, Tarbet, Foindle, A838, Handa Island, Laxford Bridge, Badnabay, A894, Scourie More, Scourie, Loch an Lurg Aird, Gorm Loch, Rubh' Aird an t-Sionnaich, Badcall, Ben Stack 721, Loe Sta

**Eddrachillis Bay area (C5–E5):**
Eilean a' Bhreitheimh, Rubh' a' Mhucard, Ben Auskaird 386, Loch Crocach, Strath Achl St, Reay Forest, H, Meall Mòr, Meall Beag, Calbha Beag, Calbha Mòr, Point of Stoer, Sgeir nan Gall, Oldany Island, Eddrachillis Bay, Ardvar, Ben Strome 426, Cirean Geardail 161, Rubha nan Còsan, Gleann Dhu Forest, Kylestrome, Culkein, Eilean Chrona, Clashnessie Bay, Drumbeg, Loch Nedd, Kylesku, a', Cluas Deas, Raffin, Achnacarnin, B869, Nedd, Gleann Leireag, Sàil Gorm 776, Unapool, Newton, Clashmore, Balchladich, Clashnessie, Loch Poll, Quinag 808, Loch an Gainmh, Bo

**Stoer / Lochinver (C5–E6):**
Rubh' a' Mhill Dheirg, Stoer, Loch Poll Dhuadh, Loch an Leothaid, Spidean Coinich 764, A894, Bay of Stoer, Clachtoll, Loch Crocach, Loch Beannoch, A837, Glas Bheinn 776, Rubha Leumair, B869, Beir Uidt 740, Achmelvich Bay, Rhicarn, Little Assynt, Loch Assynt, Achmelvich, Ardroe, Rubha Rodha, Baddidarach, Lochinver, Beinn Gharbh 540, Inchnada, Soyea Island, Loch Inver, Kirkaig Point, Badnaban, Strathan, Loch Fada Leothaid, Inchnadamph, Gleann D, A'Chleit, Inverkirkaig, Glencanisp Forest, Suilven 731, Canisp 846, Stronechrubie

**Southern section (B7–E7):**
Rubha na Brèige, Rubha Coigeach, Eilean Mòr, Rheagreanoch, A837, Feochag Bay, Enard Bay, Rubh' a' Choin, Polly Bay, Loch Veyatie, Cam Loch, Me Bhre, Ledbeg, Ledmore, Rubha Mòr, Camas Coille, Camas Eilean Gùlais, Reiff, Loch an Alltain Duibh, Brae of Achnahaird, 26, Altandhu, Aird of Coigach, Cul Mòr, Cul Beag, Drumrunie Forest, Elphin, Loch Urigill, Cnoc na Glas Choille 307, Eilean Mullagrach, Isle Ristol, Polbain, Inverpolly Forest, Stac Pollaidh 613, Loch Bad a' Ghaill, Knockan, A835, Glas-leac, Tanera Beg, Ardnagoine, Gearadheancal, Achiltibuie, Polglas, An t-Sàil, Beinn Lurgainn, Loch Urigill

### Ferry
Ullapool – Stornoway 2¾ hrs

### Scale
0 2 4 6 miles
0 2 4 6 8 10 km

### Sea labels
THE MINCH

### Page links
101, 95, 26

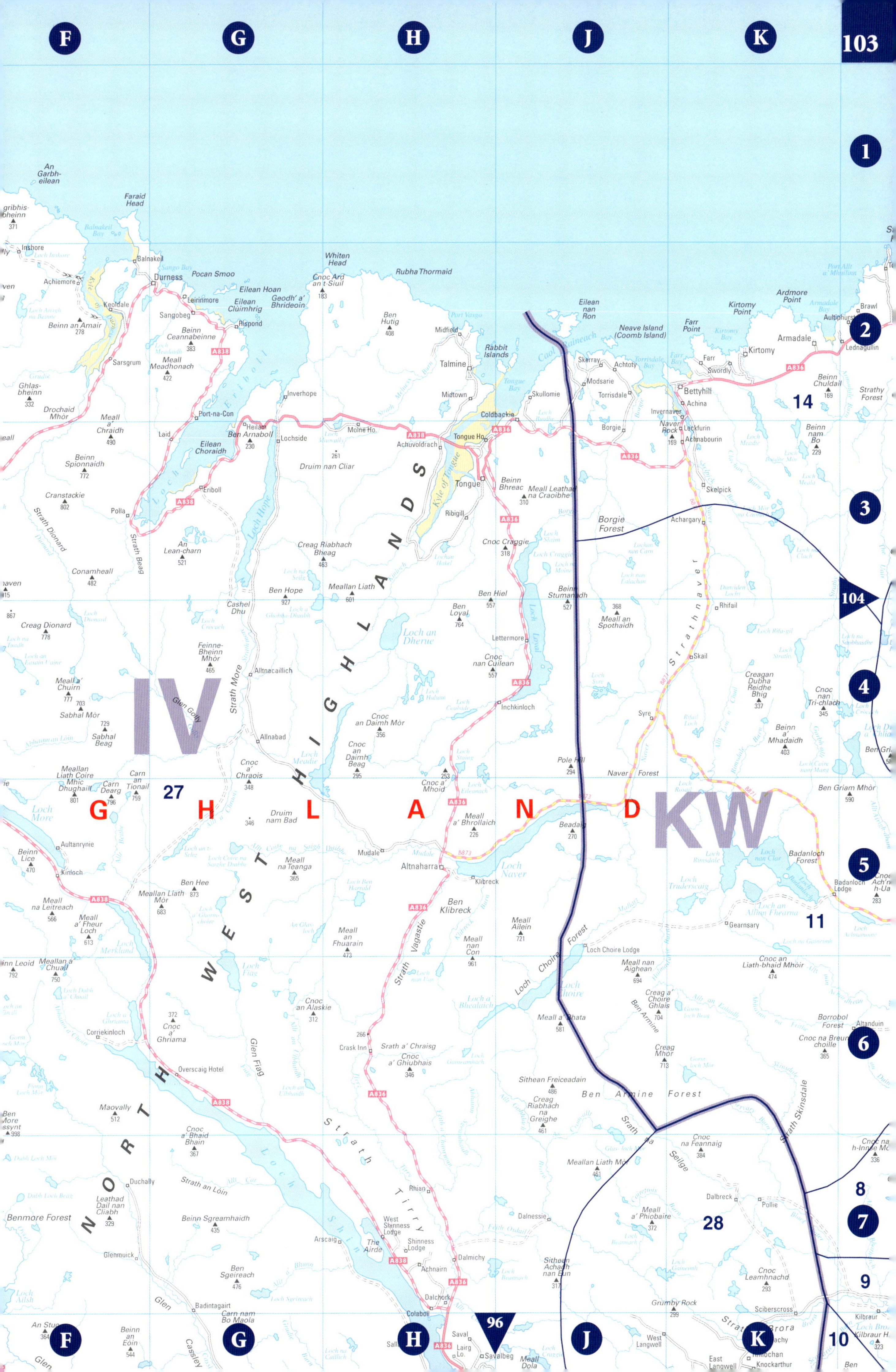
F
G
H
J
K
1
2
3
4
5
6
7
8
9
10
104
96
An Garbh-eilean
Faraid Head
Balnakeil Bay
Balnakeil
Durness
Sango Bay
Pocan Smoo
Inshore
Loch Inshore
Achiemore
Keoldale
Kyle of Durness
Beinn an Amair
278
Sarsgrum
Leirinmore
Sangobeg
Eilean Hoan
Eilean Clùimhrig
Rispond
Geodh' a' Bhrideoin
Whiten Head
Cnoc Ard an t-Siuil
183
Rubha Thormaid
Beinn Ceannabeinne
383
Meall Meadhonach
422
A838
Loch Eriboll
Port-na-Con
Eilean Choraidh
Laid
Eriboll
Polla
Ghlas-bheinn
332
Drochaid Mhòr
Meall a' Chraidh
490
Beinn Spionnaidh
772
Cranstackie
802
Strath Dionard
Conamheall
482
An Lean-charn
521
Strath Beag
Heilam
Ben Arnaboll
230
Inverhope
Lochside
Loch Hope
Moine Ho.
261
Druim nan Cliar
Ben Hutig
408
Midfield
Port Vasgo
Rabbit Islands
Talmine
Midtown
Coldbackie
Tongue Bay
Skullomie
Achuvoldrach
Tongue Ho.
Kyle of Tongue
Tongue
Ribigill
Beinn Bhreac
Meall Leathad na Craoibhe
310
Creag Riabhach Bheag
463
Cnoc Craggie
318
Loch Craggie
Ben Hope
927
Meallan Liath
601
Cashel Dhu
Loch Dionard
Creag Dionard
778
Feinne-Bheinn Mhòr
465
Strath More
Alltnacaillich
Loch an Dherue
Ben Hiel
557
Ben Loyal
764
Lettermore
Loch Loyal
Cnoc nan Cuilean
557
A836
Inchkinloch
Meall a' Chuirn
777
703
Sabhal Mòr
729
Sabhal Beag
IV
Glen Golly
Allnabad
Cnoc an Daimh Mòr
356
Cnoc an Daimh Beag
295
Cnoc a' Chraois
348
Loch Meadie
253
Cnoc a' Mhoid
Meallan Liath Coire Mhic Dhughaill
801
Carn Dearg
796
Carn an Tionail
759
27
Loch More
Druim nam Bad
346
Meall a' Bhrollaich
226
NORTH WEST HIGHLANDS
Aultanrynie
Beinn Lice
470
Kinloch
Mudale
Altnaharra
Meall na Teanga
365
Loch Naver
Klibreck
Ben Hee
873
Meallan Liath Mòr
683
Meall na Leitreach
566
Meall a' Fheur Loch
613
Loch Merkland
Ben Klibreck
Meall an Fhuarain
473
Meall nan Con
961
Strath Vagastie
Loch Fiag
Meallan a' Chuail
750
Cnoc an Alaskie
312
372
Cnoc a' Ghriama
Corriekinloch
Glen Fiag
266
Crask Inn
Strath a' Chraisg
Cnoc a' Ghiubhais
346
Overscaig Hotel
Maovally
512
Cnoc a' Bhaid Bhain
367
Strath Tirry
Loch Shin
Duchally
Strath an Loin
Leathad Dail nan Cliabh
329
Benmore Forest
Beinn Sgreamhaidh
435
Rhian
West Shinness Lodge
Arscaig
The Airde
Shinness Lodge
Glenmuick
Dalmichy
Ben Sgeireach
476
Achnairn
Badintagairt
Carn nam Bo Maola
Dalchork
Colaboll
An Stuc
364
Beinn an Eoin
544
Cassley
Glen
Saval
Lairg Lo.
Savalbeg
Meall Dola
Eilean nan Ron
Coal Raineach
Skerray
Achtoty
Neave Island (Coomb Island)
Torrisdale Bay
Farr Point
Farr Bay
Kirtomy Point
Kirtomy Bay
Ardmore Point
Armadale Bay
Port Allt a' Mhuilinn
Brawl
Aultiphurst
Armadale
Lednagullin
Kirtomy
Farr
Swordly
Modsarie
Torrisdale
Bettyhill
Achina
Beinn Chuldail
169
Strathy Forest
14
Borgie
Invernaver
Naver Rock
169
Leckfurin
Achnabourin
Beinn nam Bo
229
Skelpick
Borgie Forest
Achargary
Beinn Stumanadh
527
Rhifail
368
Meall an Spothaidh
Strathnaver
Skail
Creagan Dubha Reidhe Bhig
337
Cnoc nan Tri-chlach
345
Syre
Beinn a' Mhadaidh
403
Pole Hill
294
Naver Forest
B873
Ben Griam Mhòr
590
GHLAND
KW
Beadaig
270
Loch nan Clàr
Badanloch Forest
Loch Rimsdale
Badanloch Lodge
283
Gearnsary
11
Meall Ailein
721
Loch Choire Forest
Loch Choire Lodge
Loch Choire
Meall nan Aighean
694
Cnoc an Liath-bhaid Mhòir
474
Creag a' Choire Ghlais
704
Ben Armine
Meall a' Bhata
581
Borrobol Forest
Altanduin
Cnoc na Breun-choille
385
Creag Mhor
713
Sithean Freiceadain
486
Ben Armine Forest
Creag Riabhach na Greighe
461
Strath na Seilge
Strath Skinsdale
Cnoc na Feannaig
384
Meallan Liath Mòr
461
Dalbreck
Pollie
Meall a' Phiobaire
372
28
Dalnessie
Sithean Achadh nan Eun
317
Cnoc Leamhnachd
293
Grumby Rock
299
Sciberscross
Strath Brora
West Langwell
East Langwell
Knockarthur
Kilbraur
323

A
B
C
D
E
1
2
3
4
5
6
7
Strathy Point
Totegan
Whiten Head
Cnoc Ard an t-Siuil
183
Rubha Thormaid
Geodh' a' Bhrideoin
Ben Hutig
408
Port Vasgo
Midfield
Rabbit Islands
Eilean nan Ron
Neave Island (Coomb Island)
Farr Point
Kirtomy Point
Ardmore Point
Port Allt a' Mhuilinn
Brawl
Strathy Bay
Baligill
Melvich Bay
Portskerra
Red Point
Fresgoe
Sandside Bay
Dounreay
Talmine
Tongue Bay
Torrisdale Bay
Skerray
Achtoty
Modsarie
Torrisdale
Farr
Swordly
Kirtomy
Armadale
Aultiphurst
Lednagullin
Strathy
Melvich
Bighouse
Sandside House
Isauld
Reay
Drum Hollistan
Inverhope
Midtown
Skullomie
Bettyhill
Achina
Beinn Chuldail
169
Strathy Forest
Bowside Lodge
Kirkton
Golval
Beinn Ratha
242
14
Lochside
Moine Ho.
Coldbackie
Tongue Ho.
Achuvoldrach
A838
A836
A897
Borgie
Invernaver
Naver Rock
169
Lackfurin
Achnabourin
Beinn nam Bo
229
Beinn Ruadh
254
261
Druim nan Cliar
Achiemore
Upper Bighouse
Craigtown
Tongue
Kyle of Tongue
Beinn Bhreac
310
Meall Leathad na Craoibhe
Skelpick
Ribigill
Borgie Forest
Achargary
Dalhalvaig
Croick
Trantlemore
Trantlebeg
Cnoc an Fhuarain Bhain
243
Creag Riabhach Bheag
483
Cnoc Craggie
318
Cnoc Badaireach na Gaoithe
213
NORTH WEST HIGHLANDS
Meallan Liath
601
Ben Hope
927
103
Ben Hiel
557
Beinn Stumanadh
527
368
Meall an Spothaidh
Rhifail
13
Ben Loyal
764
Loch an Dherue
Loch Loyal
Lettermore
Strathnaver
Forsinain
Cnoc nan Cuilean
557
Skail
Strath Halladale
Sletill Hill
280
HIGHLA
Creagan Dubha Reidhe Bhig
337
Cnoc nan Tri-chlach
345
Inchkinloch
Forsinard
Cnoc an Daimh Mòr
356
Syre
Beinn a' Mhadaidh
403
Loch Druim a' Chliabhain
Ben Griam Beg
580
Cnoc nan Gall
375
Cnoc an Daimh Beag
295
Pole Hill
294
Meall a' Bhealaich
337
Loch Meadie
Naver Forest
253
Cnoc a' Mhoid
Ben Griam Mhòr
590
Cnoc Cromuillt
365
Achentoul Forest
Druim nam Bad
Meall a' Bhrollaich
226
B871
B873
Beadaig
270
Loch an Ruathair
Mudale
Loch nan Clar
Badanloch Forest
Lochside
Altnaharra
Loch Naver
Knockfin Heights
438
27
Klibreck
Badanloch Lodge
Cnoc Ach'na h-Uai
283
Achentoul
Ben Klibreck
Loch an Alltan Fhearna
11
Meall Ailein
721
Gearnsary
Kinbrace
Gobernuisgeach
Meall an Fhuarain
473
Meall nan Con
961
Loch Choire Lodge
Forest
Cnoc Coire na Fearna
437
Strath Vagastie
Meall nan Aighean
694
Cnoc an Liath-bhaid Mhòir
474
Burnfoot
Loch Choire
Cnoc an Eireannaich
517
Cnoc an Alaskie
312
Loch a' Bhealaich
Creag a' Choire Ghlais
704
Ben Armine
Meall a' Bhata
581
Borrobol Forest
Altanduin
266
Crask Inn
Strath a' Chraisg
Cnoc a' Ghiubhais
346
Creag Mhòr
713
Cnoc na Breun-choille
365
Creag nam Fiadh
387
Cnoc Salislade
483
Creag Scalabsdale
555
Strath of Kildonan
Sithean Freiceadain
486
Ben Armine Forest
IV
Kildonan Lodge
Creag Riabhach na Greighe
461
Strath Skinsdale
Beinn Dubhain
Duible
414
Strath na Seilge
Cnoc na Feannaig
384
Craggie
Cnoc na h-Innse Mòire
336
Torrish
Strath Tirry
Meallan Liath Mòr
461
8
Cnoc Meadhonach
345
Rhian
Dalbreck
Pollie
The Craggan
482
Ben Uarie
623
Beinn Dhorain
628
Meallan Liath Beag
479
Beinn Mhealaich
592
West Shinness Lodge
Dalnessie
Meall a' Phiobaire
372
28
Arscaig
The Airde
Shinness Lodge
Loch Shin
Dalmichy
Achnairn
Sithean Achadh nan Eun
317
Cnoc Leamhnachd
293
Glen Sletdale
Creag a' Chrionaich
339
Glen Loth
Col-bheinn
538
Lothmore
Culgower
Lothbeg
A9
Dalchork
Colaboll
Grumby Rock
Sciberscross
Kilbraur
Gordonbush
Loch Brora
Kilbraur Hill
323
9
Lothbeg Point
96
Brora
West Langwell
East Langwell
Knockarthur
Carrol Rock
208
Killin
Kintradwell
Ben
0 2 4 6 miles
0 2 4 6 8 10 km

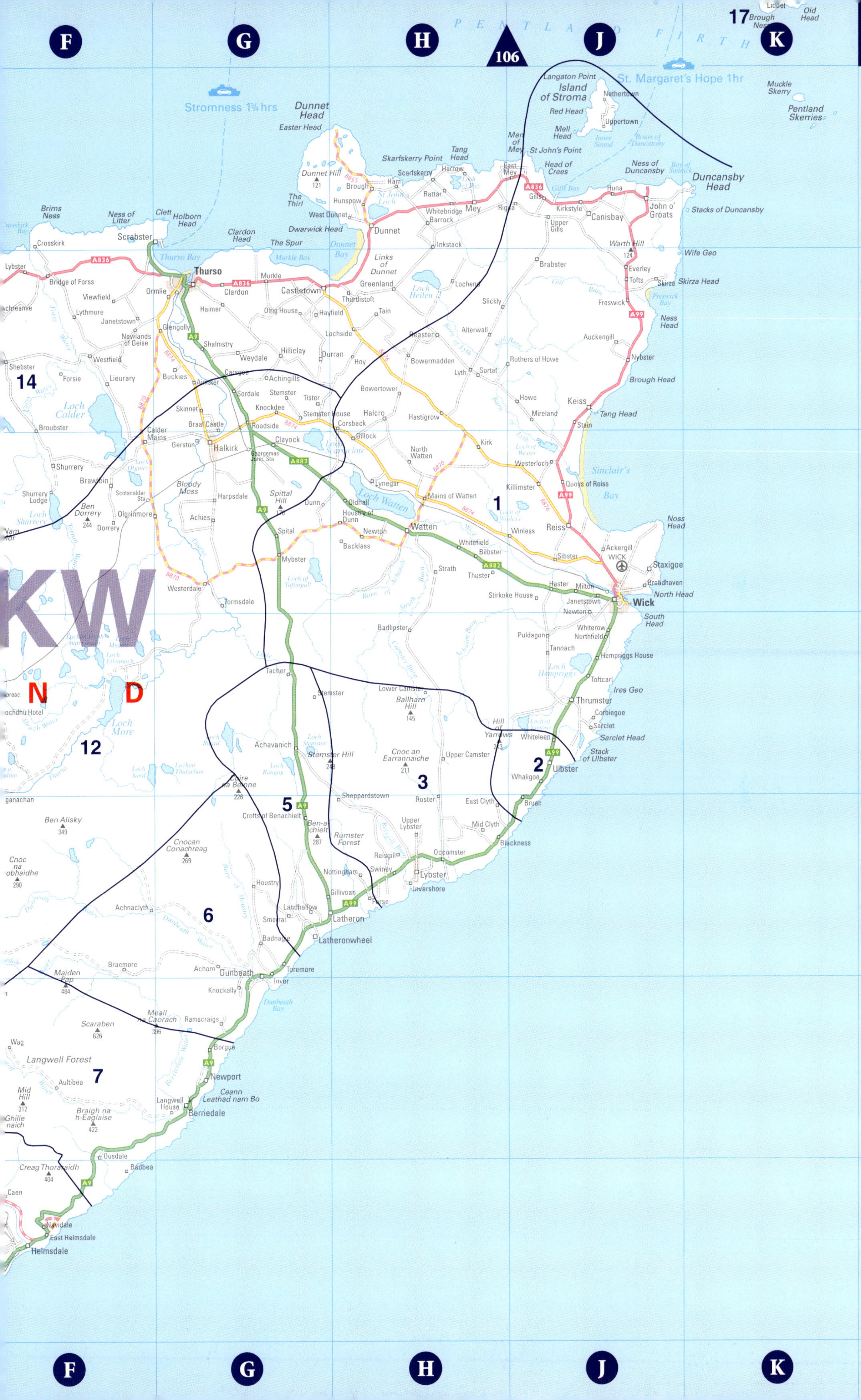

A B C D E F G H
1 2 3 4 5 6 7 8 9 10 11
ORKNEY ISLANDS
North Ronaldsay
Point of Sinsoss
NORTH RONALDSAY
Hollandstoun
Strom Ness
North Ronaldsay Firth
Mull Head
Papa Westray
PAPA WESTRAY
Holland
Bow Head
WESTRAY
Noup Head
Rackwick
Pierowall
WESTRAY
Midbea
Skelwick
Stanger Head
Rapness
Berst Ness
THE NORTH SOUND
3 hrs
Tofts Ness
Sandquoy
Linklet Bay
Burness
Otters Wick
Start Point
Newark
Roadside
Broughtown
SANDAY
SANDAY
Kettletoft
Quoy Ness
Tres Ness
Calf of Eday
Calfsound
Braeswick
Westray Firth
Faray
1½ hrs
Guith
Millbounds
EDAY
EDAY
Backaland
Loth
Spur Ness
SANDAY SOUND
Eday Sound
Sacquoy Head
ROUSAY
Wasbister
Sourin
Westness
Brinian
Egilsay
Costa Head
Brough Head
Birsay
Costa
Loch of Swannay
Marwick Head
Marwick
Twatt
Isbister
Evie
Redland
Woodwick
Wyre
Gairsay Sound
Tingwall
Gairsay
KW
Dounby
Quoyloo
Skaill
Yesnaby
Voy
Loch of Stenness
Settiscarth
Bimbister
Finstown
Bay of Firth
Wide Firth
STRONSAY
Papa Stronsay
Whitehall
Linga Holm
STRONSAY
STRONSAY FIRTH
Rothiesholm
Aith
Everbay
Grobister
Burgh Head
Lamb Head
Edmonstone
SHAPINSAY
Balfour
Sandgarth
Auskerry
Lerwick 7¾ hours
Shapinsay Sound
Kirkwall
Rerwick Head
Stromness
Hoy Sound
Ward Hill
Kirbister
Clestrain
Houton
Gyre
Scapa
Greenigo
Hobbister
KIRKWALL
Toab
Mull Head
Skaill
Gritley
Point of Ayre
Upper Sanday
MAINLAND
ORKNEY
Graemsay
Linksness
Ward Hill
479
Bring Deeps
½ hr
St Mary's
Cornquoy
Copinsay
Rose Ness
SCAPA FLOW
Rackwick
Rora Head
Rack Wick
Knap of Trowieglen
399
HOY
Sneuk Head
Cava
Rysa Little
Hunda
Burray
Southtown
Fara
Oil Terminal
Flotta
Bow
Lyness
Heldale Water
St Margaret's Hope
Grim Ness
Herston
Widewall
Longhope
Melsetter
Tor Ness
Cantick Head
South Walls
SOUTH RONALDSAY
Lythes
Ward Hill
118
1¾ hrs
Swona
Burwick
Cleat
Brough Ness
Old Head
Aberdeen 6-7¼ hrs
PENTLAND FIRTH
1hr
Island of Stroma
Mell Head
Muckle Skerry
Dunnet Head
Pentland Skerries
Scarfskerry
Brough
Ham
Rattar
Hunspow
Gills
Gills Bay
Ness of Duncansby
Duncansby Head
Huna
Kirkstyle
Canisbay
John o' Groats
Mey
Barrock
Clett
Scrabster
Holborn Head
Dunnet Bay
Dunnet
St John's Loch
Inkstack
Thurso Bay
Thurso
Murkle
Loch Heilen
Lochend
Castletown
Warth Hill
Skirza
Tofts
Freswick Bay
Freswick
Ness Head
Olrig House
Slickly
Alterwall
Auckengill
Bowermadden
Lyth
Sortat
HIGHLAND
Sordale
Bowertower
Knockdee
Hastigrow
Howe
Keiss
Lieurary
Braal Castle
Roadside
Halcro
Mireland
Halkirk
Gillock
North Watten
Kirk
Westerloch
Killimster
Watten
Noss Head
105
0 2 4 6 miles
0 2 4 6 8 10 km
A9
A836
A99
A966
A967
A986
A965
A964
A961
A960
B9064
B9068
B9069
B9070
B9063
B9066
B9062
B9061
B9055
B9047
B9044
B9043
B9042
B9052
B9058
B876
B874
B870
B855

J K L M N P Q R
1 2 3 4 5 6 7 8 9 10 11
SHETLAND ISLANDS
FAIR ISLE
ZE
2
Bu Ness
FAIR ISLE
Stonybreck
FOULA
Strem Ness
418
The Sneug
Ham
FOULA
South Ness
same scale as main map
Out Stack
Muckle Flugga
Herma Ness
Saxa Vord
285
Lamba Ness
Norwick
Burrafirth
Valsgarth
Haroldswick
UNST
Baliasta
Baltasound
Balta
UNST
Westing
A968
Belmont
Uyeasound
Mu Ness
Uyea
Gloup
Cullivoe
Gutcher
Sellafirth
Colvister
North Sandwick
Ramna Stacks
Gruney
Nev of Stuis
Point of Fethaland
Uyea
Grimister
Oddsta
Vord Hill
158
Hascosay
Camb
FETLAR
Strandburgh Ness
Brough Lodge
FETLAR
Houbie
Tresta
Aith
Funzie
Mid Yell
Isbister
North Roe
West Sandwick
YELL
Yell Sound
The Snap
Colgrave Sound
The Faither
A970
Housetter
Ronas Hill
450
North Collafirth
Aywick
Otterswick
Gossabrough
West Yell
Ulsta
Hamnavoe
Ollaberry
Burravoe
Esha Ness
Urafirth
Copister
Stenness
Hillswick
Bardister
Toft
Samphrey
Sullom Voe Oil Terminal
A968
Mossbank
Gunnister
Firth
Muckle Skerry
Sullom
Sullom Voe
Out Skerries
OUT SKERRIES
Graven
Frora Ness
Hamnavoe
Haggrister
Trondavoe
Lunna
1½ hrs
ST MAGNUS BAY
Brae
Burravoe
Collafirth
¾ hr
Busta
Lunning
Skaw Taing
Ve Skerries
Roesound
West Linga
Brough
WHALSAY
Muckle Roe
Wethersta
Vidlin
Isbister
WHALSAY
Papa Stour
Hillside
Laxo
Marrister
Voe
Skellberry
Symbister
½ hr
PAPA STOUR
Vementry
Gonfirth
Dury Voe
Melby
West Burrafirth
East Burrafirth
Brettabister
Sandness
Clousta
Unifirth
281
Scalla Field
South Nesting Bay
249
Sandness Hill
Aith
MAINLAND
SHETLAND
Skellister
Twatt
Benston
Mu Ness
Dale of Walls
Bridge of Walls
Effirth
Bixter
Freester
2½ hrs
Weisdale
Gletness
Wats Ness
Tresta
Semblister
Girlsta
Walls
Gruting
Wadbister
Sandsound
Garderhouse
Haggersta
Vaila
Whiteness
Score Head
Culswick
TINGWALL (LERWICK)
Veensgarth
Bressay
Reawick
Wester Skeld
Skeld (Easter Skeld)
Westerwick
Heogan
Maryfield
Lerwick
Isle of Noss
The Deeps
Sound
Scalloway
Trebister
Grindiscol
226
Kirkabister
Gulberwick
Ward of Bressay
Brindister
Bard Head
Hamnavoe
Wester Quarff
Quarff
Bridge End
East Burra
Fladdabister
Burra
Bergen (summer only)............12½
hours
Royl Field
293
Cunningsburgh
Helli Ness
South Havra
Mail
Maywick
Leebotten
Mousa
Hoswick
Sandwick
Ireland
St Ninian's Isle
Bigton
Levenwick
Scousburgh
Boddam
hours
Aberdeen..........................12-12½
Kirkwall...............................5½-7½
Seydisfjordur (summer only)....31
Torshavn (summer only)..........13
Quendale
283
Fitful Head
Exnaboe
Toab
SUMBURGH
Grutness
Sumburgh
Sumburgh Head
Sumburgh Roost

A
B
C
D
E
1
2
3
4
5
6
7
8
DONEGAL
LONDONDERRY (DERRY)
LIMAVADY
STRABANE
OMAGH
FERMANAGH
DUNGANNON
LEITRIM
MONAGHAN
CAVAN
BT
Tory Island
An Baile Thiar (West Town)
Tory Sound
Inishbofin
Bloody Foreland
Bun na Leaca (Brinlack)
Gola Island
Owey I.
Cionn Caslach (Kincaslough)
Donegal
Dunfanaghy
Horn Head
Na Dúnaibh (Downies)
Rosguill
Melmore Head
Earra Thíre na Binne (Arryheernabin)
Fanad Head
Portsalon
Carraig Airt (Carrickart)
Cranford
Creeslough
An Fál Carrach (Falcarragh)
Gort an Choirce (Gortahork)
Gweedore
Doirí Beaga (Derrybeg)
Gaoth Dobhair (Gweedore)
An Bun Beag (Bunbeg)
Cloghaneely
Errigal 752
Anagaire (Annagry)
Croithlí (Crolly)
Dún Lúiche (Dunlewy)
Derryveagh Mts
Glendowan Mts
The Rosses
Loch an Iúir (Loughanure)
Ailt an Chorráin (Burtonport)
Clochán Liath (Dungloe)
Gleann Doimhin (Glendowan)
Church Hill
Kilmacrenan
Termon (An Tearmann)
Lough Salt Mountain 471
Milford
Carrowkeel
Rathmullan
Ramelton (Ráth Mealtain)
Letterkenny (Leitir Ceanainn)
Newtowncunningham
Dunaff Head
Dunaff
Dumhaigh Bhig (Doagh Beg)
Gleann Bhairr (Glenvar)
Lough Swilly
Ballyliffin
Clonmany
Malin Head
Ballygorman
Glengad Head
Portaleen
Malin
Culdaff
Carndonagh
Gleneely
Inishowen
Slieve Snaght 615
Drumfree
Buncrana (Bun Cranncha)
Fahan
Tooban
Burnfoot
Muff
Bridge End
Culmore
Coolkeeragh
LONDONDERRY (DERRY)
48
Inishowen Head
Greencastle
Moville (Bun an Phobail)
Magilligan
Redcastle
Carrowkeel
Lough Foyle
Ballymagaraghy
Downhill
49
Aghanloo
Bolea
Ballykelly
Limavady
City of Derry
Eglinton
Greysteel
Lackagh
Glenhead
Drumsurn
Drumahoe
Lettershendony
Gortnahey
Ervey Cross Roads
New Buildings
Magheramason
Benbradagh 468
Foreglen
Dungiven
Boviel
Claudy
Craigdarragh
47
Feeny
Manorcunningham
St Johnstown
Carrigans
Pluck
Old Town
Rashedoge
Knockbrack
Raphoe (Ráth Bhoth)
Bready
Cloghcor
Artigarvan
Ballymagorry
Donemana
Liscloon
Ballyneaner
Park
Ballynamallaght
Craig
Mullaghclogha 635
Sawel Mt.
Sperrin Mountains
Mullaghmore
Money
Draperstown
Mount Hamilton
The Six Towns
Dunmore Head
Portnoo
Narin
Clooney
Maas
Leitir Mhic an Bhaird (Lettermacaward)
An Dúchoraidh (Doochary)
Baile na Finne (Fintown)
Béal an Átha Móir (Bellanamore)
Drumnacross
An Clochán (Cloghan)
An Coimín (Commeen)
Stranorlar (Srath an Urláir)
Kilross
Convoy
Cloghfin
Ballindrait
Lifford (Leifear)
Strabane
82
Liscooly
Castlefinn
Killygordon
Clady
Glebe
Sion Mills
Victoria Bridge
Plumbridge
Cranagh
Butterlope
Ballybofey (Bealach Féich)
Glenties
Kilrean
Ardara (Ard an Rátha)
Glengesh Pass
Blue Stack 676
Blue Stack Mts
Croaghnageer 546
Croagh
Frosses
Letterbarra
Donegal (Dún na nGall)
Inver
Mountcharles
Killybegs (Na Cealla Beaga)
St John's Point
Donegal Bay
Laghey
Bridgetown
Ballintra
Rossnowlagh
Coolmore
Ballyshannon (Béal Átha Seanaidh)
Bundoran (Bun Dobhráin)
Mullaghmore Head
Mullaghmore
Tullaghan
Single Street
Kinlough
Cliffoney
Belleek
Leggs
Letter
Pettigo
Clonelly
Kesh
Croaghnameal 440
Killeter
81
Killen
Castlederg
Spamount
Drumlegagh
Ardstraw
Newtownstewart
Gortin
Rousky
Glenhull
Greencastle
Dunnamore
Mullaghcarn 542
Creggan
Mountfield
79
Loughmacrory
80
Mountjoy
Drumquin
Killyclogher
Omagh
Drumnakilly
Carrickmore
Pomeroy
78
Clanabogan
Ballynahatty
Keeran
Lack
Ederny
Dromore
Beragh
Gortaclare
Sixmilecross
Cappagh
70
Donaghmore
Castlecaulfield
Seskinore
Mullaghmassa
The Diamond
Fintona
Garvaghy
Eskragh
Ballymackilroy
Ballygawley
77
Carnteel
Aughnacloy
Augher
Clogher
69
Crilly
68
Lower Lough Erne
Lisnarrick
Drumduff
Irvinestown
Rosscor
93
Church Hill
Killadeas
Blaney
Trillick
Kilskeery
Ballinamallard
Ballycassidy
Derrygonnelly
Tullybrack 376
Monea
Springfield
Boho
Trory
Tempo
94
Garvary
Enniskillen
74
Murley
Clabby
Creagh
Fivemiletown
75
76
Slieve Beagh
Cooneen
Carrickroe
Emyvale
Glaslough
Tedavnet
Letterbreen
Culkey
Bellanaleck
Lisbellaw
Brookeborough
Knockatallan
Holywell
Blacklion
Belcoo
Arney
Tamlaght
Maguiresbridge
Eshnadarragh
Scotstown
Bellanode
Monaghan (Muineachán)
Drummacabranagher
Mackan
Lisnaskea
Rosslea
Drumcard
Tully
92
Donagh
Magheraveely
Smithborough
Three Mile House
Cavanagarven
Mullan
Swanlinbar
Derrylin
Newtownbutler
Clones (Cluain Eois)
Anlore
Killeevan
Newbliss
Swan's Cross Roads
Upper Lough Erne
Teemore
Derrynacreeve
Bawnboy
Ballyconnell
Belturbet
Redhills
Scotshouse
Drum
Rockcorry
Cloverhill
Cootehill
Ballyhaise
Milltown
Ardlougher
Butlers Bridge
Killeshandra
Drung
Tullyvin
Tullcoe
Cavan (An Cabhán)
Stradone
Lavey
Poles
Canningstown
Shercock
Crossdoney
Ballinagh
Crosskeys
Derrylane
Cornafean
Carrigallen
Arghavas
Corriga
Mohill
Fenagh
Gowna
Drumlea
Greagh
Ballinamore
Newtown Gore
Drumcong
Drumshanbo
Corraleehan
Slieve Anierin 586
Iron Mountains
Glengavlen
Dowra
Corry
Lough Allen
Arigna
Keadew
Gubaveeny
Glenfarne
Manorhamilton
Killarga
Dromahair
Ballintogher
Drumkeeran
Drummacool
Geevagh
Riverstown
Ballyfarnon
Ballinafad
Kilmactranny
Knockvicar
Cootehall
Leitrim
Drumsna
Jamestown
Sligo (Sligeach)
Rathbraghan
Drumcliff
Dartry Mountains
Truskmore 643
Benbulben 525
Glencar
Glenade
Moneylahan
Ballaghnatrillack
Buckode
Rossinver
Garrison
Scribbagh
Lough Melvin
Kiltyclogher
Dough Mt. 461
Ballygawley
Toberscanavan
Ballymote
Castlebaldwin
Kesh
Culfadda
Gurteen
Mullaghroe
Edmondstown
0 5 10 15 20 miles
0 5 10 20 30 km

NORTH CHANNEL
IRISH SEA
MOYLE
BALLYMONEY
BALLYMENA
LARNE
CARRICKFERGUS
NEWTOWNABBEY
NORTH DOWN
ANTRIM
COOKSTOWN
CRAIGAVON
BELFAST
CASTLEREAGH
ARDS
LISBURN
DOWN
BANBRIDGE
NEWRY & MOURNE
LOUTH
See inset for postcode detail
Cairnryan 1-1¾ hours
Troon (summer only) 1¾ hours
Fleetwood 8 hrs
Stranraer 1¾-3¼ hrs
Douglas (summer only) 2¾ hours
Birkenhead 8 hours

LONDON WEST

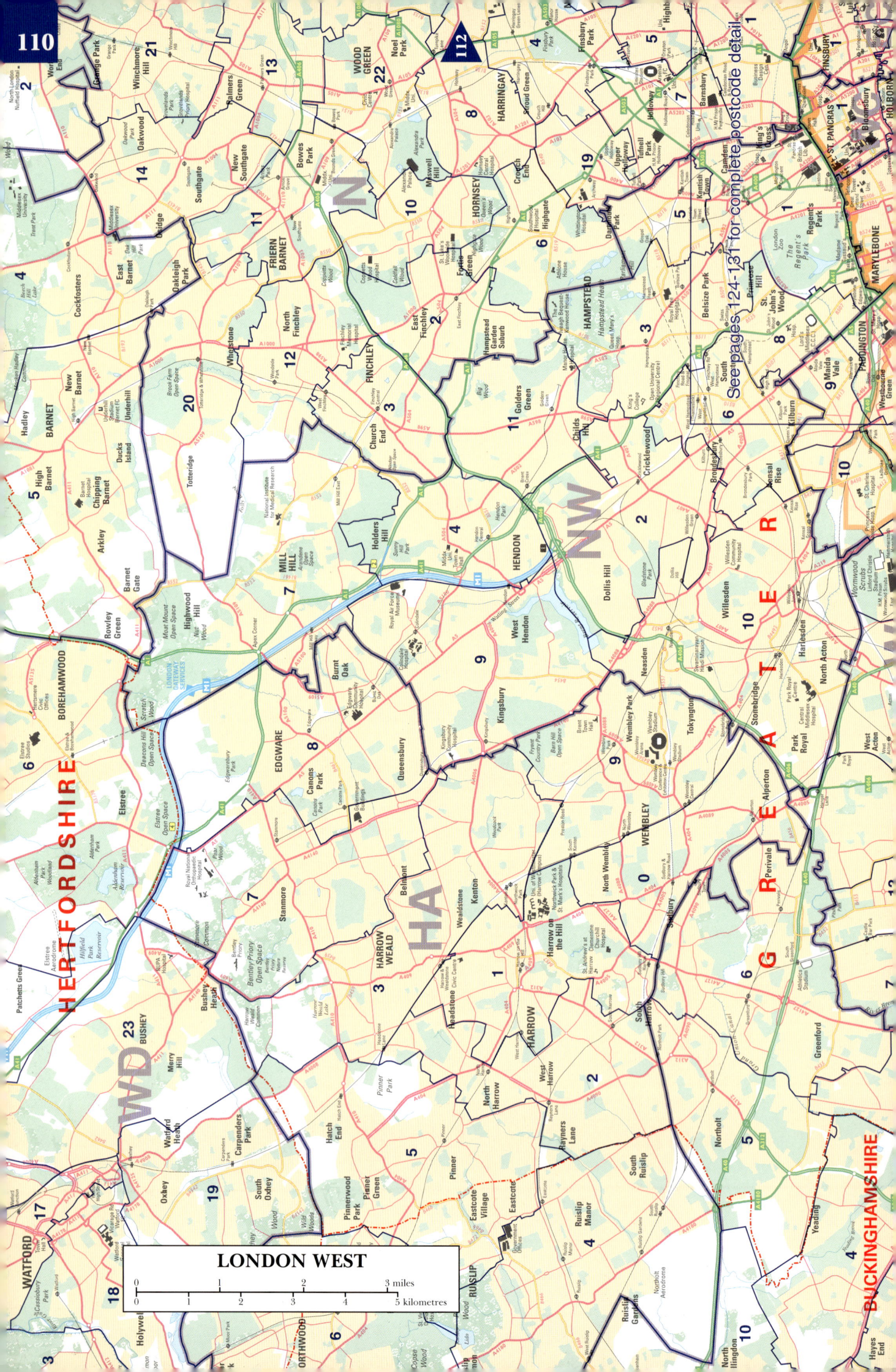

111

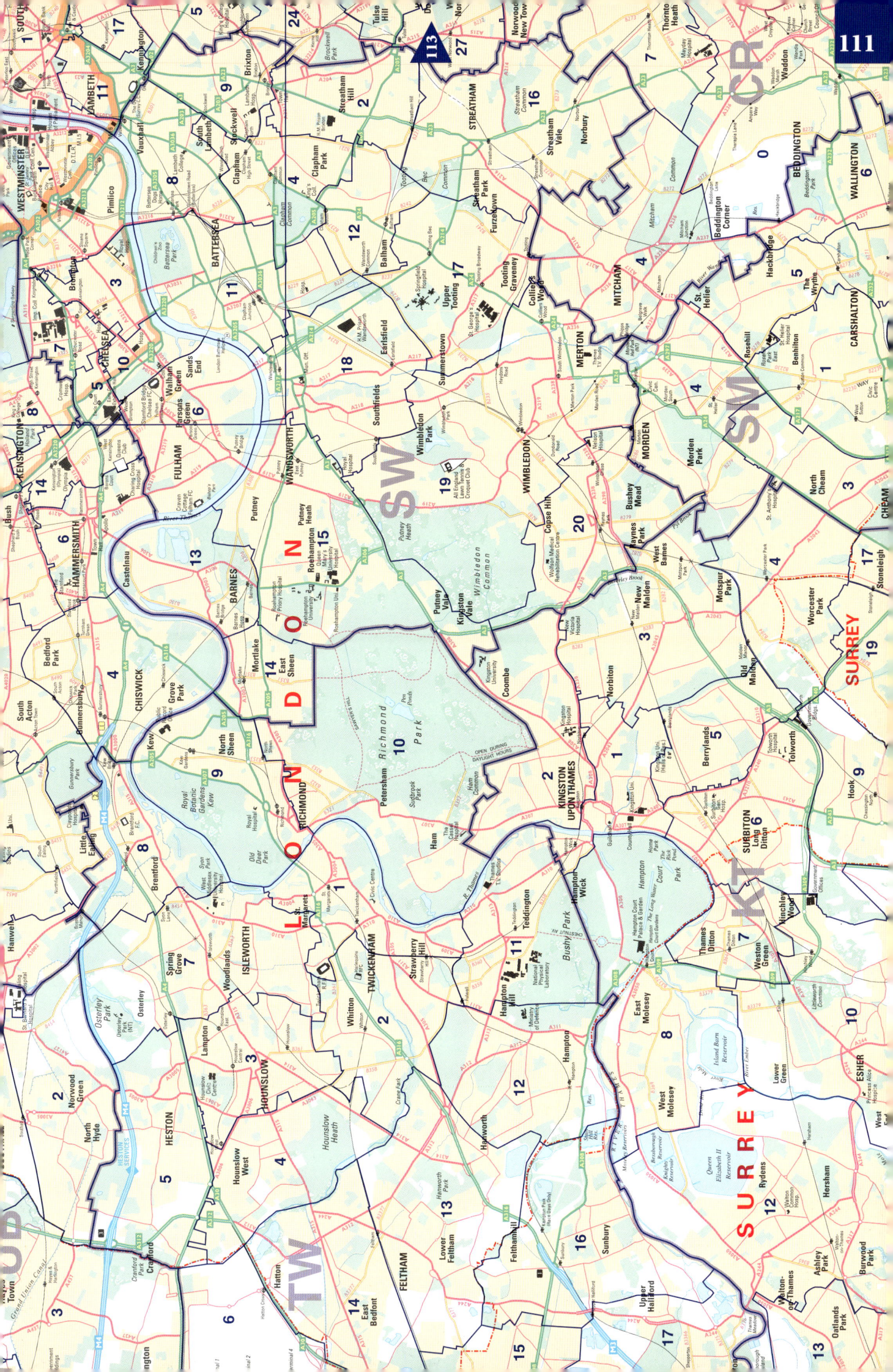

LONDON EAST

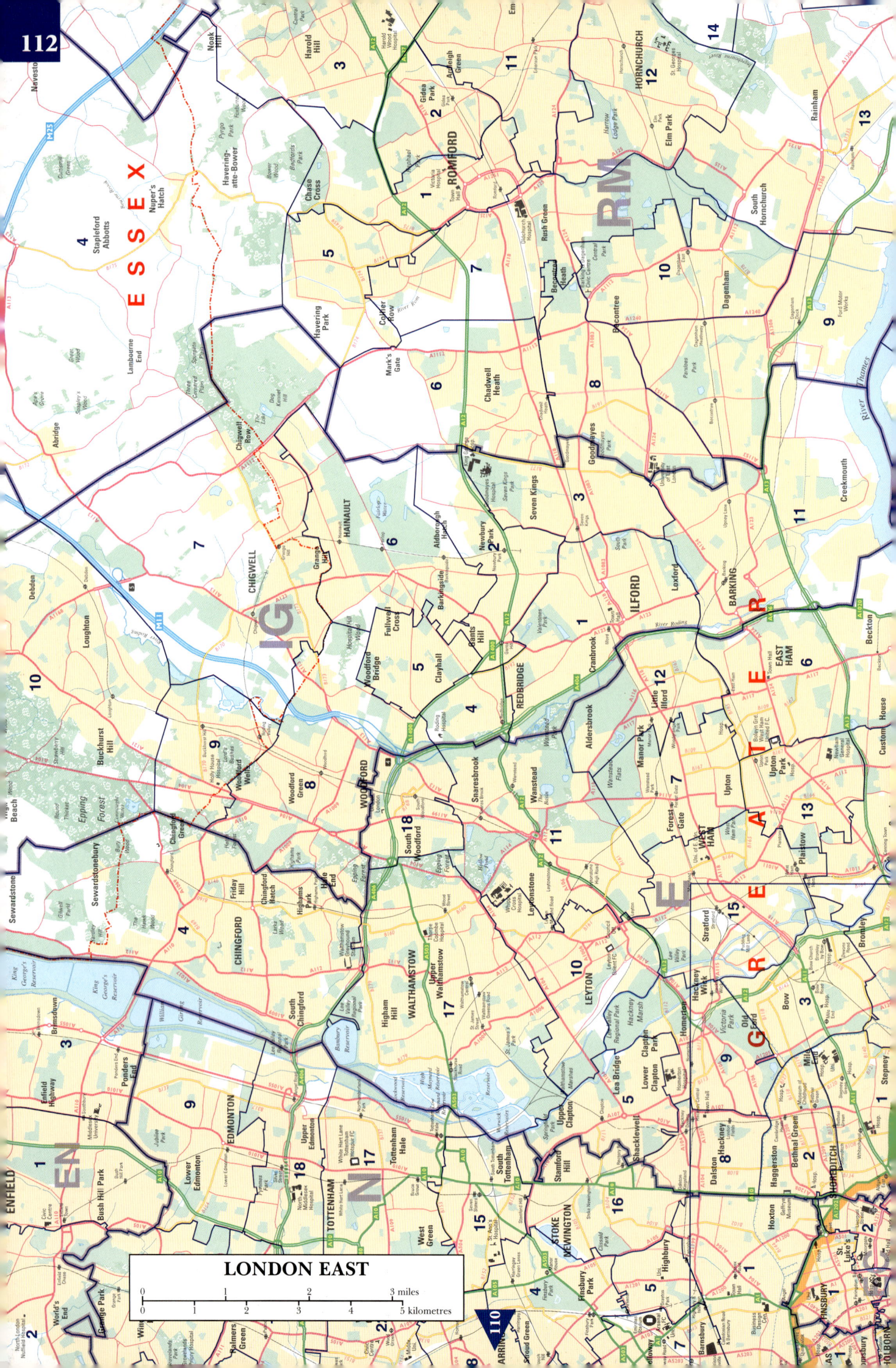

See pages 124-131 for complete postcode detail

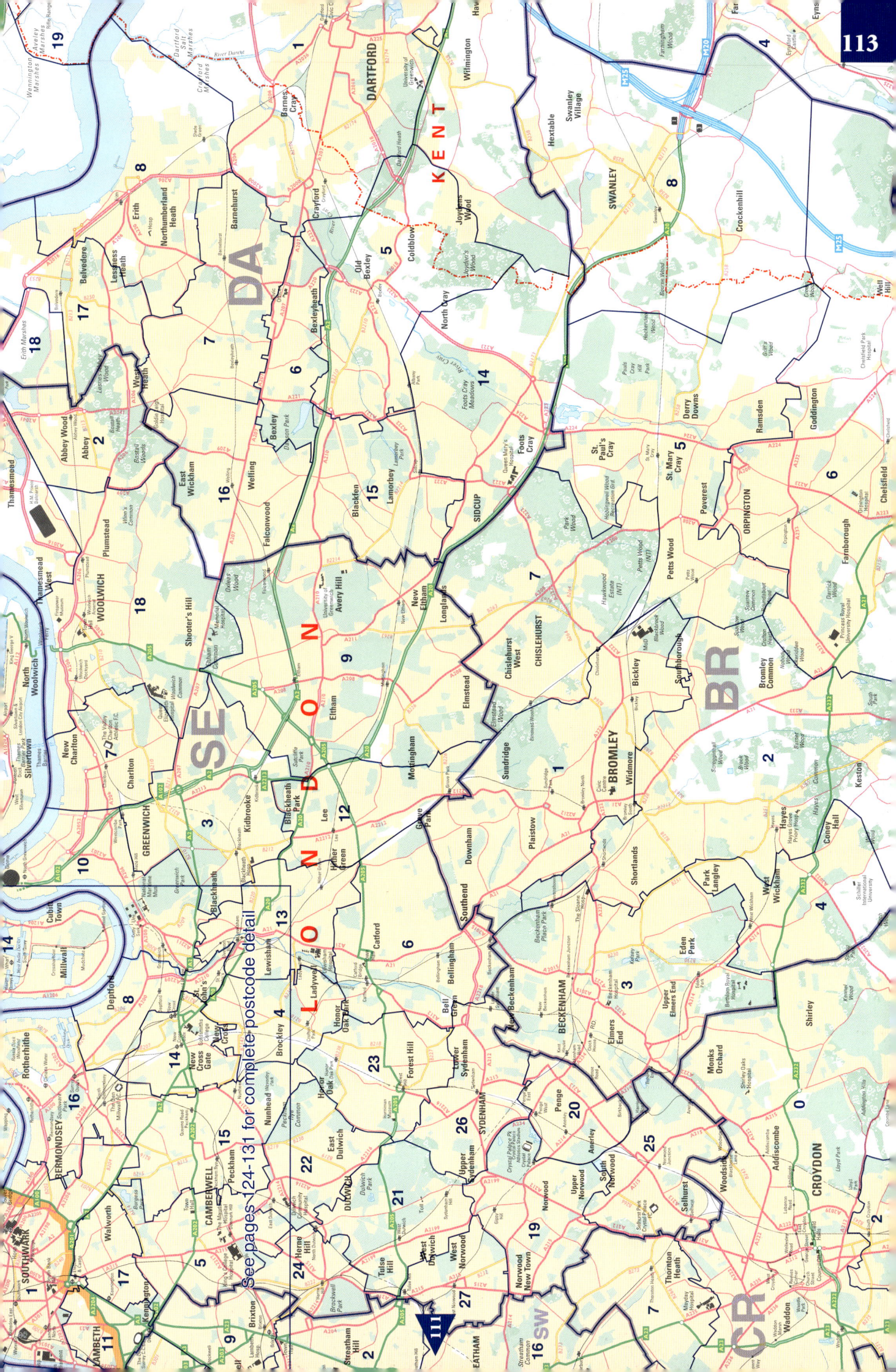

WEST MIDLANDS
0 1 2 3 4 miles
0 1 2 3 4 5 6 kilometres
WV
DY
STAFFORDSHIRE
WORCESTERSHIRE
WOLVERHAMPTON
DUDLEY
STOURBRIDGE
HALESOWEN
WEST BROMWICH
SANDWELL
KIDDERMINSTER
Bilbrook
Codsall
Lane Green
Moseley
Essington
Pelsall Wood
Oaken
Fordhouses
Bushbury
Wallington Heath
Little Bloxwich
Heath End
Wrottesley
Oxley
Old Fallings
Ashmore Park
Wood Hayes
Wood End
Bloxwich
Blakenall Heath
Harden
Claregate
Perton
Tettenhall
Dunstall Hill
Wednesfield
New Invention
Leamore
Coal Pool
Tettenhall Wood
Park Village
Heath Town
Ashmore Lake
Lane Head
Nurton
Springfield
Willenhall
Birchills
Bentley
Compton
Old Purton
Monmore Green
Moseley
Portobello
Darlaston Green
Castlecroft
Bradmore
Merry Hill
Stow Lawn
Pleck
Caldmore
Palfrey
Bescot
Trescott
Blakenhall
Priestfield
Darlaston
Fallings Heath
Kings Hill
Wood Green
Wednesbury
Goldthorn Park
Parkfield
Bilston
Woods Bank
The Delves
Lower Penn
Penn
Colton Hills
Lanesfield
Ettingshall
Ettingshall Park
Spring Vale
Moxley
The Woods
Spring Hill
Bradley
Church Hill
Mesty Croft
Cinder Hill
Lower Bradley
Friar Park
Orton
Seisdon
Coseley
Wednesbury Oak
Stone Cross
Trysull
Gospel End
Sedgley
Hurst Hill
Princes End
Ocker Hill
Balls Hill
Hateley Heath
Roseville
Wallbrook
Summer Hill
Golds Green
Hill Top
Charlemont
The Batch
Bramford
Bloomfield
Toll End
Black Lake
Dunsdale
Wombourne
Tipton
Tipton Green
Harvills Hawthorn
Churchfield
Giggetty
Upper Gornal
Horseley Heath
Lyndon
Blakeley
Smestow
Himley
Ruiton
Woodsetton
Swan Village
Guns Village
New Town
Lower Gornal
Redhall
Dudley Port
Gornalwood
London Fields
Eve Hill
Burnt Tree
Swindon
Wall Heath
Tividale
Brades Village
Hinksford
Russell's Hall
Kate's Hill
Dixon's Green
Oakham
Darby's Hill
Rounds Green
Ashwood
Pensnett
Waterfront
Oldbury
Langley
Rood End
Kingswinford
Summer Hill
Baptist End
Netherton
Bromley
Brockmoor
Mount Pleasant
The Knowle
Darby End
Portway
Rowley Regis
Causeway Green
Langley Green
Smethwick
Primrose Hill
Ross
Wordsley
Buck-pool
Brierley Hill
Bowling Green
Dudley Wood
Bristnall Fields
Bearwood
Prestwood
Hawbush
Old Hill
Blackheath
Audnam
Withymoor Village
Quarry Bank
Cradley Heath
Warley
Amblecote
Amblecote Bank
Cockshot
Haden Cross
Hurst Green
Netherend
Coombeswood
Gallowstree Elm
Stourton
Wollaston
Holloway End
Dunn's Bank
Overend
Cradley
High Park
Lye
The Hayes
Hawne
Belle Vale
Quinton
Ridgacre
Harborne
Kinver
Potters Cross
Dunsley
Stambermill
Wollescote
Gigmill
Lapal
Norton
Swindford
Hasbury
Spring Hill
Moor Street
California
Whittington
Pedmore
Woodgate
Bartley Green
Weoley Castle
Hunnington
Illey
Blakeshall
Caunsall
Hagley
Shenley Fields
Cookley
Lower Clent
West Hagley
Romsley
Churchill
Clent
Frankley
Wolverley
Romsley Hill
Blakedown
Broadwaters
Broome
Holy Cross
Dayhouse Bank
Greenhill
Bell Heath
Rubery
Bell End
Rednal
Longbridge
Fairfield
Cofton Hackett
Stone

STAFFORDSHIRE
WARWICKSHIRE
WEST MIDLANDS
TAMWORTH
SUTTON COLDFIELD
BIRMINGHAM
SOLIHULL
Oak
Stonnall
Shenstone
Weeford
The Leys
Bolehall
Kettlebrook
Glascote
Walsall Wood
Vigo
Leighswood
Druid's Heath
Aldridge
Pool Green
Mill Green
Thornes
Lower Stonnall
Footherley
Shenstone Woodend
Little Hay
Hints
Mile Oak
Bonehill
Fazeley
Drayton Manor Park
Belgrave
Two Gates
Wilnecote
Drayton Bassett
Hockley
Dosthill
Whateley
Little Aston
Four Oaks
Hardwick
Streetly
Roughley
Mere Green
Ley Hill
Little Sutton
Four Oaks Park
Doe Bank
Tudor Hill
Whitehouse Common
Sutton Park
Middleton
Daisy Bank
Pheasey
Banners Gate
Maney
Falcon Lodge
Reddicap Heath
Kingsbury
Bodymoor Heath
Great Barr
Queslett
Kingstanding
New Oscott
Boldmere
Wylde Green
Old Oscott
Perry Beeches
Thimble End
Over Green
Wishaw
Marston
Walmley
Lea Marston
Hamstead
Tower Hill
Perry
Perry Common
Short Heath
Chester Road
Minworth
Curdworth
Perry Barr
Upper Witton
Erdington
Whitacre Heath
Nether Whitacre
Handsworth Wood
Brown's Green
Pype Hayes
Tyburn
Castle Vale
Hoggrill's End
Witton
Water Orton
Birchfield
Gravelly Hill
Birches Green
Handsworth
Gibson
Cole End
Shustoke
Nechells
Castle Bromwich
Bromford
Lozells
Washwood Heath
Hodgehill
Buckland End
Shard End
Coleshill
Aston
Newtown
Ward End
Colehall
Kingshurst
Winson Green
Gib Heath
Hockley
Saltley
Vauxhall
Glebe Farm
Kitt's Green
Bacon's End
Rotton Park
Stechford
Fordbridge
Alum Rock
Tile Cross
Chelmsley Wood
Lea Hall
Edgbaston Reservoir
Ladywood
Little Bromwich
Bordesley
Digbeth
Yardley
Garrett's Green
Marston Green
Lee Bank
Chad Valley
Highgate
Small Heath
Lyndon Green
Sparkbrook
Hay Mills
South Yardley
Gilbertstone
Balsall Heath
Birmingham International Airport
Edgbaston
Sheldon
Little Packington
Middle Bickenhill
Sparkhill
Tyseley
Acock's Green
Stonebridge
Bournbrook
Moseley
Elmdon
Moor Green
Wake Green
Olton
Bickenhill
King's Heath
Kineton Green
Hall Green
Ulverley Green
Hampton in Arden
Stirchley
Elmdon Heath
Worlds End
Billesley
Cotteridge
Brandwood End
Catherine-de-Barnes
Billesley Common
Lode Heath
Yardley Wood
King's Norton
Warstock
Hasluck's Green
Shirley Street
Sharmans Cross
Shirley
Eastcote
Highter's Heath
Walkers Heath
Blossomfield
Barston
Copt Heath
Hawkesley
Major's Green
Shirley Heath
Hollywood
Headley Heath
Trueman's Heath
Balsall Common
Drakes Cross
Knowle
Whitlocks End
Bateman's Green
Dickens Heath
Tilehouse Green
Grimes Hill
Wythall
Tidbury Green
Cheswick Green
Bentley Heath
Temple Balsall
Sedgemere
M6 Toll
M6
M42
A38(M)
ASTON EXPRESSWAY
WS
B
CV

Horwich
Wallsuches
Bottom o th' Moor
Barrow Bridge
Delph Hill
Doffcocker
Halliwell
Markland Hill
Astley Br.
Harwood
Walshaw
Ainsworth
Breightmet
BOLTON
Tonge Fold
BOLTON WEST SERVICES
Blackrod
Haigh
Scot Lane End
Aspull
New Springs
Marylebone
Wigan
Ince-in-Makerfield
Hindley
Westhoughton
Wingates
Water's Nook
Chequerbent
Hunger Hill
Chew Moor
Lostock
Deane
Heaton Cemetery
Furnhill
Daubhill
Lever Edge
Great Lever
Darcy Lever
Burnden
Little Lever
Harper Green
Moses Gate
Nob End
Farnworth
New Bury
Highfield
Hollins
Edge Fold
Over Hulton
Prestolee
Stoneclough
Kearsley
Cinder Hill
Ringley
Daisy Hill
Atherton
Greenheys
Little Hulton
Hill Top
Walkden
Linnyshaw
Kearsley Moss
Clifton
Shakerley
Tyldesley
Hindsford
Howe Bridge
Hindley Green
Platt Bridge
Dangerous Corner
Bickershaw
Tamer Lane End
Westleigh
Abram
Hawkley
WN
BL
Parr Brow
Mosley Common
Astley
Ellenbrook
Worsley
Roe Green
Wardley
Swinton
Hazelhurst
Moorside
Boothstown
Higher Folds
Gin Pit
Blackmoor
Lark Hill
LEIGH
Firs Lane
Bedford
Pennington
Plank Lane
The Flash
Town Lane
Higher Green
Astley Green
Moss Side
Alder Forest
Monton
Winton
Patricroft
Eccles
Ashton in Makerfield
Golborne
Lowton
Lowton St Mary's
Aspull Common
Pocket Nook
Lane Head
Glazebury
Astley Moss
Worsley Moss
Botany Bay Wood
Brookhouse
Peel Green
Barton Airport
Barton upon Irwell
Dumplington
Barton Moss
Chat Moss
M
Haydock Park
Town of Lowton
Twiss Green
Fowley Common
Kenyon
New Lane End
Culcheth
Little Town
HM Prison Risley
Croft
Larkhill
Irlam Moss
Higher Irlam
Irlam
Cadishead Moss
Lower Irlam
Crofts Bank
Davyhulme
URMSTON
Flixton
Newton-le-Willows
Wargrave
Vulcan Village
Winwick
Holcroft Moss
Glazebrook
Cadishead
Carrington
Chemical Works
Carrington Moss
Partington
Risley
Risley Moss
Birchwood
Woolston Moss
Houghton Green
Hulme
Cinnamon Brow
Longford
Orford
Padgate
Callands
Dallam
Bewsey
Old Hall
Rixton Moss
Hollins Green
Warburton
Mossbrow
Sinderland Green
Woodhouses
Broadheath
Oldfield Brow
WARRINGTON
Great Sankey
Sankey Bridges
Howley
Westy
Victoria Park
Latchford
Heatley
Carr Green
Dunham Woodhouses
Dunham Town
Statham
Rushgreen
Lymm
Little Bollington
Bowdon
Rosehill
Bowgreen
Ashley Heath
Stockton Heath
Lower Walton
Hillcliffe
Cobbs
WA
Broomedge
Arthill
Booth Bank
Higher Walton
Moore
Appleton Reservoir
Appleton Park
Hatton
Daresbury
Stretton
High Legh
Hulseheath
Rostherne Mere
Rostherne
Bucklow Hill
Ashley
CHESHIRE EAST
CW
M
MANCHESTER
0 1 2 3 4 miles
0 1 2 3 4 5 6 kilometres

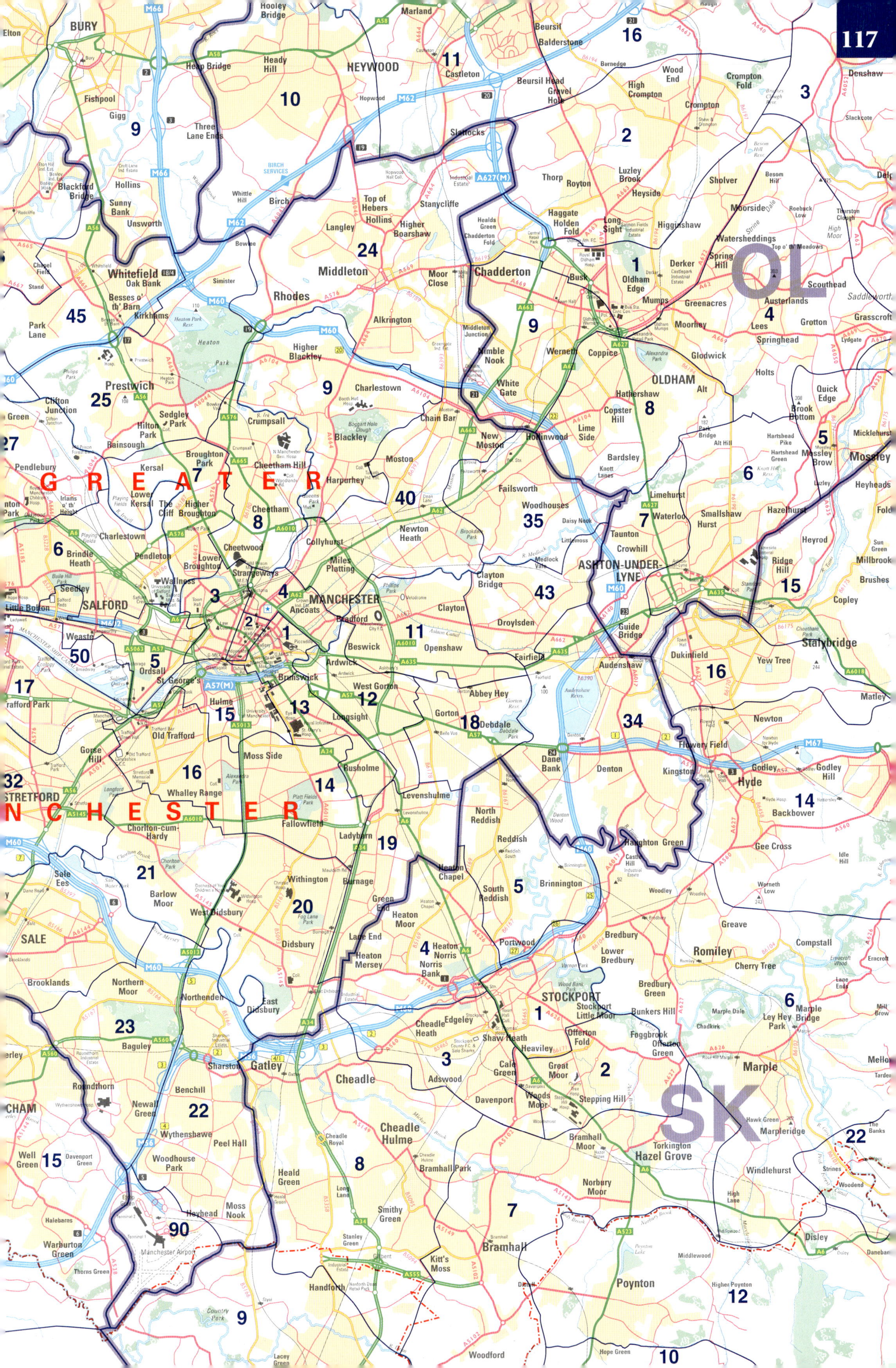

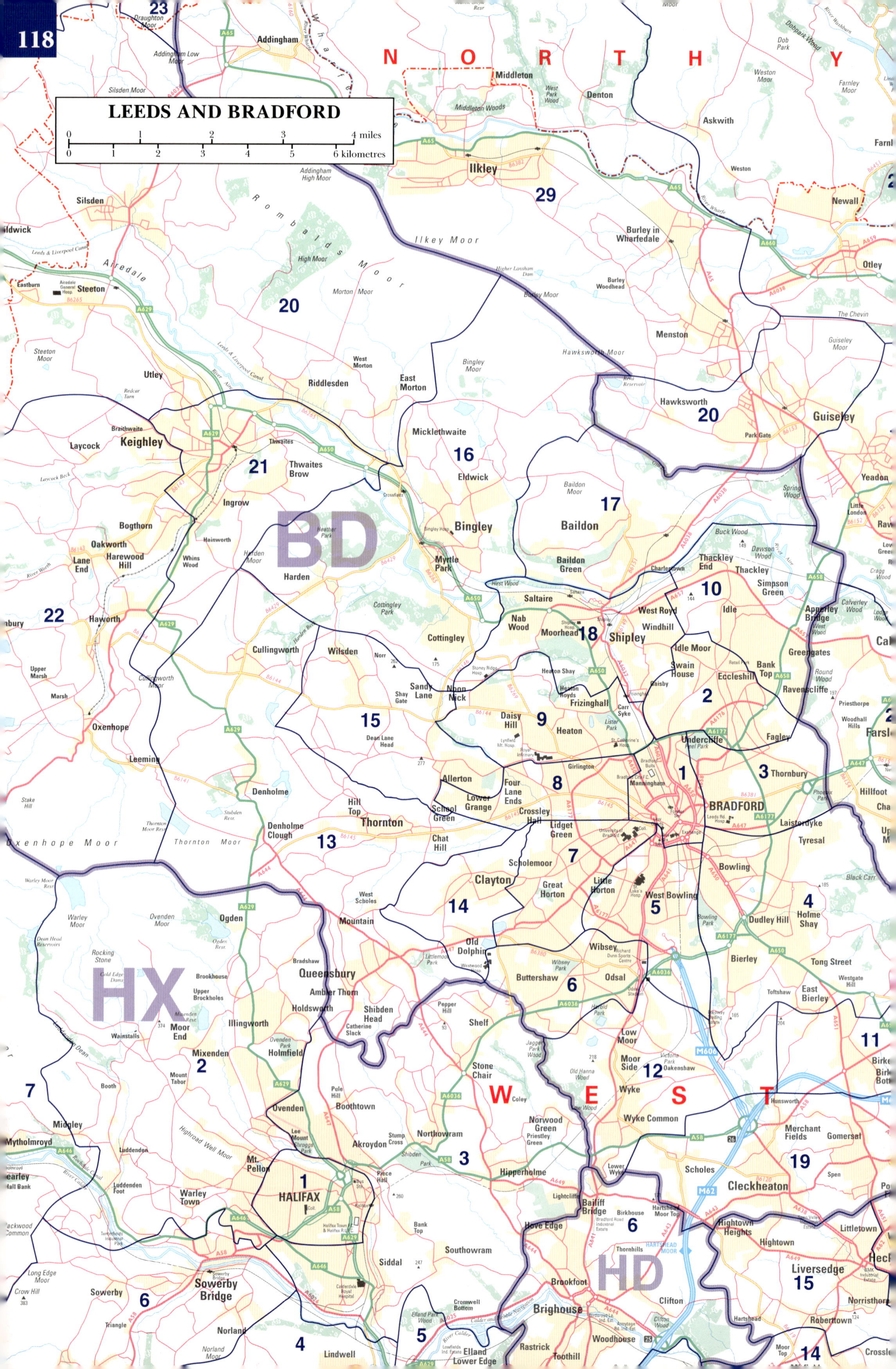
LEEDS AND BRADFORD
0 1 2 3 4 miles
0 1 2 3 4 5 6 kilometres
N O R T H Y
W E S T
BD
HX
HD
Draughton Moor
Addingham
Addingham Low Moor
Silsden Moor
Middleton
Middleton Woods
West Park Wood
Denton
Askwith
Dob Park
Weston Moor
Farnley Moor
Ilkley
Addingham High Moor
Weston
Newall
Silsden
Rombalds Moor
Ilkey Moor
Burley in Wharfedale
Otley
Leeds & Liverpool Canal
Airedale
High Moor
Higher Lanshaw Dam
Burley Woodhead
Burley Moor
Eastburn
Airedale General Hosp.
Steeton
Morton Moor
Menston
The Chevin
Steeton Moor
Guiseley Moor
Hawksworth Moor
West Morton
Bingley Moor
Utley
Redcar Tarn
Riddlesden
East Morton
Reva Reservoir
Hawksworth
Guiseley
Braithwaite
Laycock
Keighley
Thwaites
Micklethwaite
Park Gate
Thwaites Brow
Yeadon
Laycock Beck
Eldwick
Baildon Moor
Spring Wood
Crossflatts
Ingrow
Little London
Bogthorn
Heather Park
Bingley
Baildon
Hainworth
Bingley Hosp.
Oakworth
Buck Wood
Harewood Hill
Whins Wood
Harden Moor
Myrtle Park
Baildon Green
Thackley End
Dawson Wood
Thackley
Lane End
River Worth
Harden
Charlestown
Cragg Wood
Hirst Wood
Simpson Green
Calverley Wood
Saltaire
Idle
Apperley Bridge
Haworth
Cottingley Park
West Royd
West Wood
Nab Wood
Windhill
Moorhead
Shipley
Cottingley
Cullingworth
Wilsden
Norr
Idle Moor
Greengates
Upper Marsh
Stoney Ridge Hosp.
Heaton Shay
Swain House
Retail Park
Bank Top
Round Wood
Cullingworth Moor
Ravenscliffe
Marsh
Heaton Royds
Frizinghall
Daisby
Eccleshill
Priesthorpe
Sandy Lane
Noon Nick
Carr Syke
Shay Gate
Daisy Hill
Heaton
Lister Park
Woodhall Hills
Oxenhope
Dean Lane Head
Lynfield Mt. Hosp.
St. Catherine's Hosp.
Undercliffe
Peel Park
Fagley
Royal Infirmary
Leeming
Girlington
Bradford Bulls
Thornbury
Allerton
Bradford City F.C.
Manningham
Four Lane Ends
Hillfoot
Denholme
Lower Grange
BRADFORD
Phoenix Park
Stake Hill
Hill Top
Leeds Rd. Hosp.
Stubden Resr.
School Green
Crossley Hall
Laisterdyke
Thornton Moor Resr.
Denholme Clough
Thornton
Lidget Green
University of Bradford
Exchange
Oxenhope Moor
Thornton Moor
Chat Hill
Tyresal
Scholemoor
Bowling
Warley Moor Resr.
Clayton
Great Horton
Little Horton
Black Carr
West Scholes
St. Luke's Hosp.
West Bowling
Holme Shay
Warley Moor
Ovenden Moor
Ogden
Mountain
Bowling Park
Dudley Hill
Dean Head Reservoirs
Ogden Resr.
Old Dolphin
Wibsey
Richard Dunn Sports Centre
Bierley
Littlemoor Park
Westwood Hosp.
Rocking Stone
Bradshaw
Tong Street
Queensbury
Cold Edge Dams
Buttershaw
Wibsey Park
Odsal
Odsal Stadium
Westgate Hill
Brookhouse
Amber Thorn
Toftshaw
East Bierley
Upper Brockholes
Holdsworth
Shibden Head
Pepper Hill
Mixenden Resr.
Harold Park
Illingworth
Catherine Slack
Shelf
Moor End
Wainstalls
Ovenden Park
Low Moor
Jagger Park Wood
Holmfield
Mixenden
Mount Tabor
Moor Side
Victoria Park
Oakenshaw
Old Hanna Wood
Stone Chair
Booth
Wyke
Coley
Hunsworth
Pule Hill
Boothtown
Ovenden
Highroad Well Moor
Norwood Green
Wyke Common
Merchant Fields
Gomersal
Midgley
Priestley Green
Lee Mount
Akroydon
Stump Cross
Northowram
Mytholmroyd
Luddenden
Shibden Park
Mt. Pellon
Hipperholme
Scholes
Spen
Lower Wyke
Rochdale Canal
River Calder
Luddenden Foot
HALIFAX
Piece Hall
Warley Town
Cleckheaton
Lightcliffe
Bailiff Bridge
Birkhouse
Hartshead Moor Top
Bradford Road Industrial Estate
Hove Edge
Hightown Heights
Littletown
Tenterfields Industrial Park
Bank Top
Halifax Town F.C. & Halifax R.L.F.C.
Thornhills
HARTSHEAD MOOR
Hightown
Southowram
Long Edge Moor
Siddal
Liversedge
BMK Industrial Estate
Sowerby Bridge
Brookfoot
Calderdale Royal Hospital
Crow Hill
Sowerby
Clifton
Norristhorpe
Cromwell Bottom
Brighouse
Calder and Hebble Navigation
Clifton Wood
Hartshead
Elland Park Wood
Triangle
Birdsroyd La. Ind. Est.
Armytage Rd. Ind. Est.
Roberttown
Norland
Woodhouse
Rastrick
Lowfields Ind. Estate
Elland
Norland Moor
Lindwell
Lower Edge
Toothill
Moor Top
A65
A629
A650
A660
A6038
A657
A658
A6037
A6177
A647
A6181
A641
A6036
A650
A58
A646
A649
A644
A643
A638
M606
M62
A6025
23
20
29
20
21
16
17
10
22
18
2
15
9
1
3
8
13
7
14
5
4
6
12
11
2
7
1
3
19
6
15
6
5
4
14

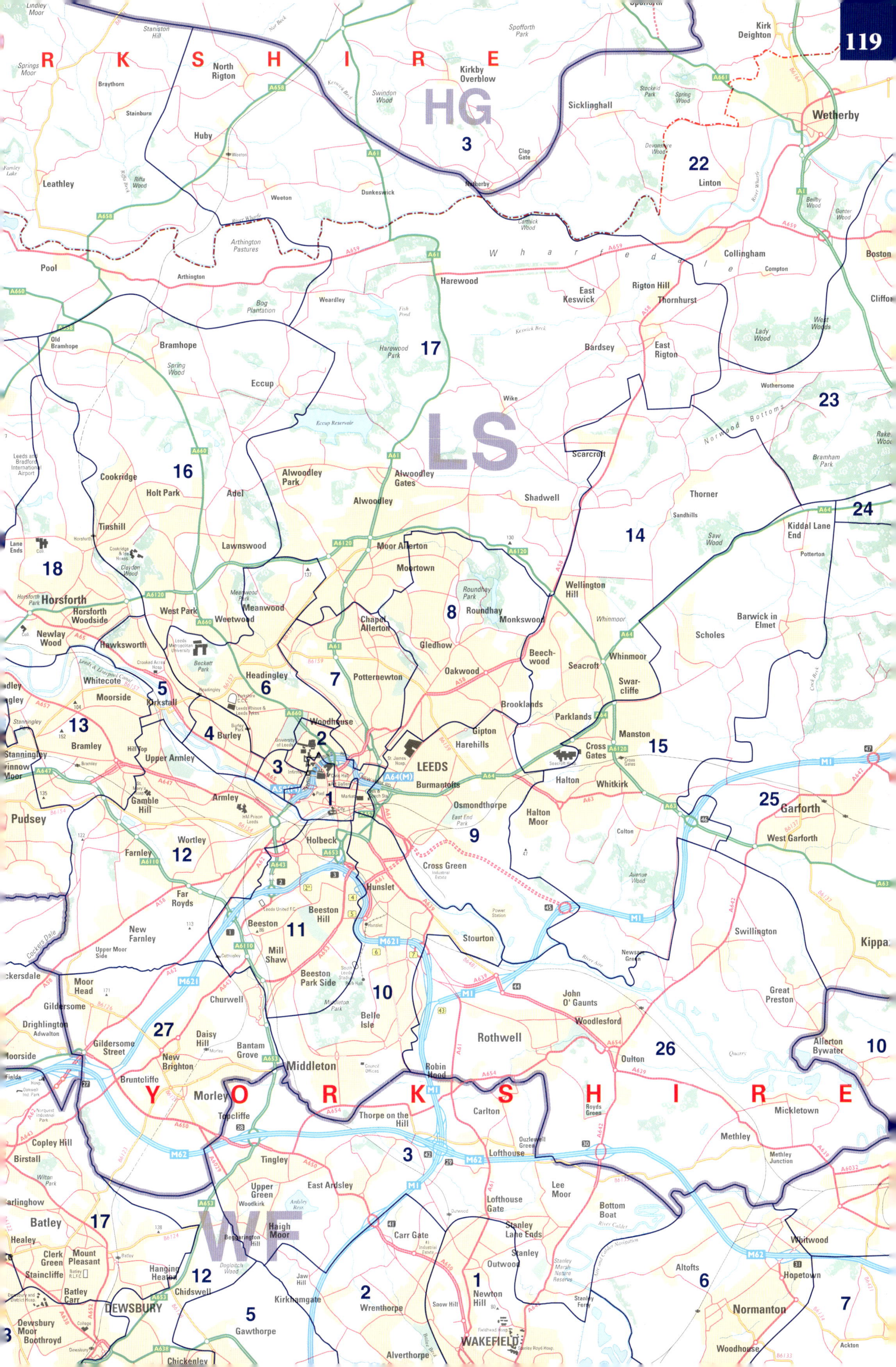

Y O R K S H I R E
HG
3
LS
WF
Lindley Moor
Staniston Hill
North Rigton
Springs Moor
Braythorn
Stainburn
Huby
Weeton
Leathley
Riffa Wood
Kirkby Overblow
Swindon Wood
Spofforth Park
Kirk Deighton
Sicklinghall
Stockeld Park
Spring Wood
Wetherby
Clap Gate
Dunkeswick
Rigton Hill
Devonshire Wood
22
Linton
Netherby
Carthick Wood
River Wharfe
Arthington Pastures
Pool
Arthington
Harewood
Wharfedale
Collingham
Compton
Boston
Clifford
East Keswick
Thornhurst
Weardley
Bog Plantation
Fish Pond
Old Bramhope
Bramhope
Harewood Park
17
Bardsey
East Rigton
Lady Wood
West Woods
Spring Wood
Eccup
Keswick Beck
Eccup Reservoir
Wike
Wothersome
23
Norwood Bottoms
Rake Wood
Bramham Park
Scarcroft
Leeds and Bradford International Airport
Cookridge
16
Alwoodley Park
Alwoodley Gates
Holt Park
Adel
Alwoodley
Shadwell
Thorner
Sandhills
24
Kiddal Lane End
Potterton
Tinshill
Saw Wood
14
Lane Ends
18
Lawnswood
Moor Allerton
Moortown
Horsforth
Horsforth Park
Horsforth Woodside
West Park
Meanwood
Weetwood
Roundhay Park
Roundhay
Monkswood
8
Wellington Hill
Whinmoor
Barwick in Elmet
Scholes
Newlay Wood
Hawksworth
Chapel Allerton
Gledhow
Beech-wood
Seacroft
Swarcliffe
Leeds Metropolitan University
Beckett Park
Headingley
6
7
Potternewton
Oakwood
Brooklands
Parklands
Manston
15
Whitecote
Moorside
Kirkstall
5
Woodhouse
Gipton
Harehills
Cross Gates
13
Bramley
4
Burley
2
3
LEEDS
Burmantofts
Halton
Whitkirk
25
Garforth
Stanningley
Upper Armley
Hill Top
Armley
1
Osmondthorpe
Halton Moor
West Garforth
Pudsey
Gamble Hill
HM Prison Leeds
Wortley
12
Farnley
Holbeck
East End Park
9
Colton
Cross Green
Hunslet
Far Royds
Beeston Hill
Beeston
11
Mill Shaw
Stourton
Avenue Wood
Swillington
New Farnley
Upper Moor Side
Beeston Park Side
10
Belle Isle
Middleton Park
Newsam Green
River Aire
Kippax
Moor Head
Gildersome
Drighlington
Adwalton
Churwell
John O' Gaunts
Woodlesford
Great Preston
27
Daisy Hill
Gildersome Street
Bantam Grove
New Brighton
Rothwell
Middleton
Robin Hood
Oulton
26
Allerton Bywater
Bruntcliffe
Morley
Topcliffe
Thorpe on the Hill
Carlton
Royds Green
Mickletown
Methley
Methley Junction
Copley Hill
Birstall
Wilton Park
Tingley
East Ardsley
Ouzlewell Green
Lofthouse
Upper Green
Woodkirk
Ardsley Resr.
Lee Moor
Lofthouse Gate
Bottom Boat
Batley
Healey
Clerk Green
Mount Pleasant
Staincliffe
Batley Carr
Beggarington Hill
Haigh Moor
Carr Gate
Stanley Lane Ends
Stanley
Outwood
Whitwood
Hopetown
Altofts
Hanging Heaton
Chidswell
Jaw Hill
Kirkhamgate
Wrenthorpe
Snow Hill
Newton Hill
Stanley Ferry
Normanton
DEWSBURY
Dewsbury Moor
Boothroyd
Gawthorpe
Chickenley
Alverthorpe
WAKEFIELD
Woodhouse
Ackton
A61
A64(M)
M1
M62
M621
A58
A65
A660
A6120
A647
A6110
A643
A653
A654
A639
A642
A63
A659
A658
A661
A1

LIVERPOOL
0 1 2 3 4 miles
0 1 2 3 4 5 6 kilometres
MERSEYSIDE
LANCS
CHESHIRE WEST & CHESTER
LIVERPOOL BAY
Crosby Channel
River Mersey
Birkenhead to hours
Belfast 8
Dublin 8
Liverpool to hours
Douglas 2½-4
Dublin 8
Ince Blundell
Hightown
Little Crosby
Blundellsands
Thornton
Great Crosby
CROSBY
Waterloo
Waterloo Park
Seaforth
Litherland
Buckley Hill
Maghull
Lydiate
Aughton
Town Green
Bowker's Green
Stanley Gate
SKELMERSDALE
Barrow Nook
Aintree
Orrell
Fazakerley
Walton
BOOTLE
Kirkdale
Anfield
Clubmoor
Tuebrook
Everton
Stoneycroft
Fairfield
LIVERPOOL
Old Swan
Knotty Ash
Swanside
Dovecot
Page Moss
Roby
Huyton with Roby
Huyton
Huyton Park
Huyton Quarry
Whiston Cross
Windy Arbor
Prescot
Longview
Woolfall Heath
Fincham
West Derby
Norris Green
Dog and Gun
Croxteth
Gillmoss
Kirkby
Westvale
Southdene
Northwood
Knowsley
Knowsley Park
Court Hey
Bowring Park
Childwall
Wavertree
Edge Hill
Princes Park
Toxteth
Dingle
St Michael's
Hamlet
Mossley Hill
Calderstones
Aigburth
Grassendale
Otterspool
Allerton
Gateacre
Belle Vale
Netherley
Woolton
Halewood
Hunts Cross
Garston
Speke
Liverpool John Lennon Airport
New Brighton
WALLASEY
Liscard
Egremont
Poulton
Seacombe
Bidston
Bidston Hill
Ford
Upton
Claughton
BIRKENHEAD
Noctorum
Oxton
Tranmere
Arrowe Hill
Woodchurch
Prenton
Rock Ferry
Landican
Higher Bebington
Woodhey
New Ferry
Bromborough Pool
Storeton
BEBINGTON
Lower Bebington
Port Sunlight
Thingwall
Barnston
Brimstage
Heswall
Poulton
Bromborough
Eastham
Brookhurst
Thornton Hough
Gayton
Raby
Parkgate
Neston
Willaston
Hooton
Childer Thornton
Overpool
ELLESMERE PORT
Little
M58
M57
M62
M53
A59
A570
A506
A580
A565
A5036
A562
A561
A41
A550
A5300
A58
A57
A5047
A5049
A5089
A554
A551
A552
A5139
A5080
L
WA
CH
WN
1
2
3
4
5
6
7
8
9
10
11
12
13
14
15
16
17
18
19
20
21
22
23
24
25
26
27
28
29
30
31
32
33
34
35
36
37
38
39
40
41
42
43
44
45
46
49
60
61
62
63
64
65
66

# NEWCASTLE UPON TYNE

GLASGOW
0 1 2 3 4 miles
0 1 2 3 4 5 6 kilometres
STIRLING
EAST DUNBARTONSHIRE
GLASGOW
NORTH LANARKSHIRE
EAST RENFREWSHIRE
SOUTH LANARKSHIRE
CAMPSIE FELLS
G
PA
ML
Strathblane
Blanefield
Carbeth
West Carbeth
Auchengillan
Clachan of Campsie
Haughhead
Lennoxtown
Lennox Forest
Mugdock
Milngavie
Milton of Campsie
Kinkell
Birdston
Twechar
Queenzieburn
Baldernock
Dougalston
Bardowie
Torrance
Balmore
Cadder
Kirkintilloch
Harestanes
Gallowhill
Oxgang
Waterside
Lenzie
Bearsden
Drumchapel
Buckhey
Kenmure
Bishopbriggs
Milton
Woodhill
Crowhill
Auchinloch
Bridgend
Moodiesburn
Chryston
Muirhead
Gartcosh
Stepps
Craigendmuir
Millerston
Summerston
Knightswood
Temple
Maryhill
Gilshochill
Lambhill
Springburn
Auchinairn
Balornock
Barmulloch
Yoker
Scotstounhill
Anniesland
Kelvindale
Kelvinside
Scotstoun
Possilpark
Dowanhill
Partick
Whiteinch
Shieldhall
Dean Park
Finnieston
Provanmill
Royston
Riddrie
Ruchazie
Garthamlock
Lochwood
Easterhouse
Dennistoun
Carntyne
Springboig
Barlanark
Swinton
Baillieston
Barrachnie
Garrowhill
Crosshill
Shettleston
Muirhead
Mount Vernon
Broomhouse
Hillington
Cardonald
Craigton
Govan
Ibrox
Bridgeton
Parkhead
Glasgow
Oldhall
Ralston
Crookston
Pollokshields
Dumbreck
Oatlands
Braidfauld
Mosspark
Pollok
Crossmyloof
Govanhill
Polmadie
Rutherglen
Carmyle
Hawkhead
Shawlands
Langside
Mount Florida
Birkenshaw
Kylepark
Uddingston
Hurlet
Pollokshaws
Battlefield
Cathcart
King's Park
Eastfield
Newton
Hallside
Nitshill
Priesthill
Mansewood
Newlands
Croftfoot
High Crosshill
Arden
Carnwadric
Merrylee
Muirend
Burnside
Cambuslang
Flemington
Darnley
Thornliebank
Giffnock
Netherlee
Castlemilk
Barrhead
Low Blantyre
Stamperland
Williamwood
Carmunnock
Crookfur
Whitecraigs
Clarkston
Sheddens
Broom
Busby
Blantyre
High Blantyre
Springwells
Nerston
Rogerton
Stewartfield
Calderwood
East Mains
West Mains
East Kilbride
St. Leonards
Hillhouse
Earnock
Malletsheugh
Netherplace
Newton Mearns
Mearns
Braehead
Thorntonhall
Waterfoot
Westwood
The Murray
Birniehill
Auchentibber
Lawmuir
Jackton
Greenhills
Eaglesham
Torrance House
Cumberland Farm
63 65 66 81 62 64 23 15 61 22 20 21 13 12 14 4 11 33 69 34 3 2 1 31 51 52 5 40 32 41 42 43 53 73 44 72 45 46 78 76 74 75 77 10

# London key to map pages

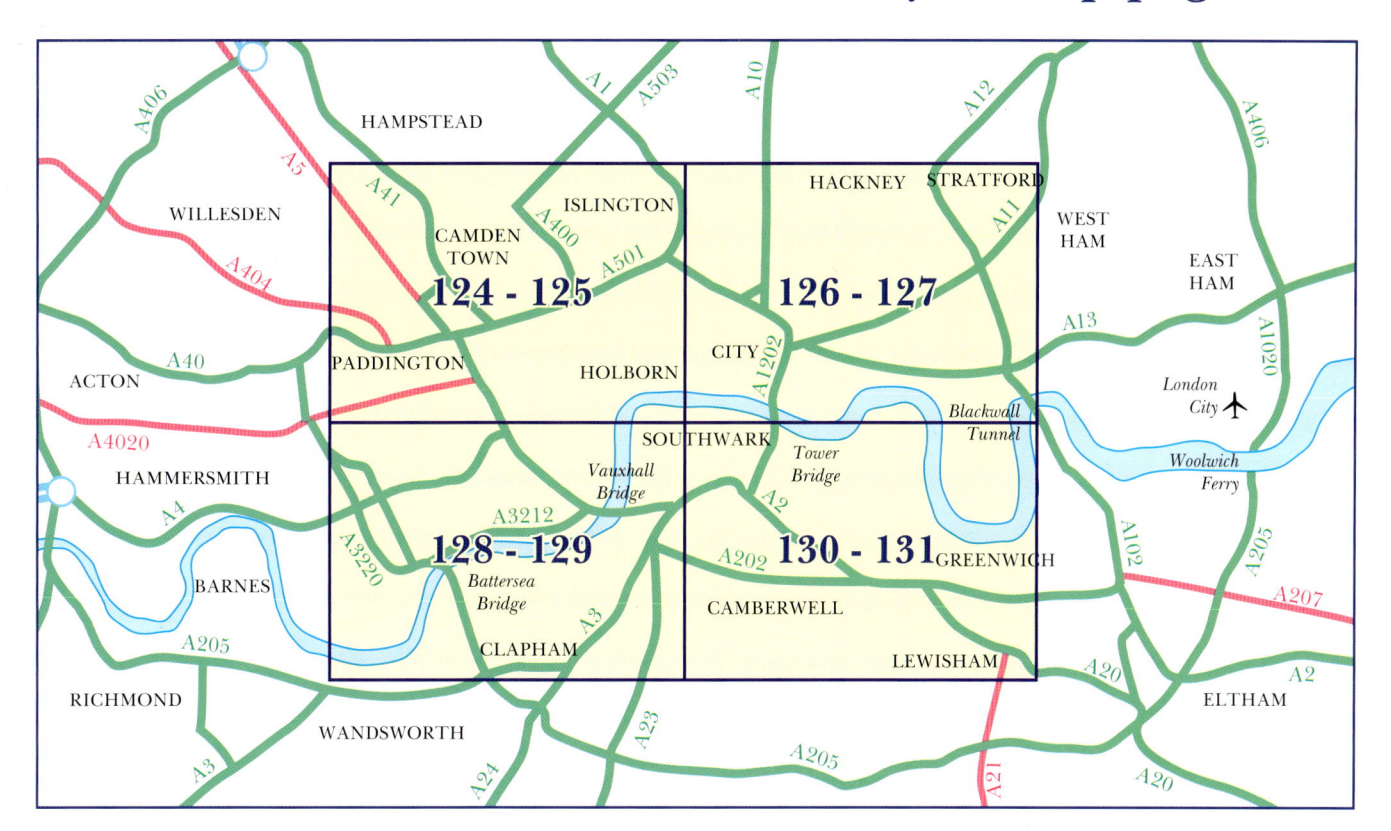

| | |
|---|---|
| 124 - 125 | 126 - 127 |
| 128 - 129 | 130 - 131 |

# London key to symbols

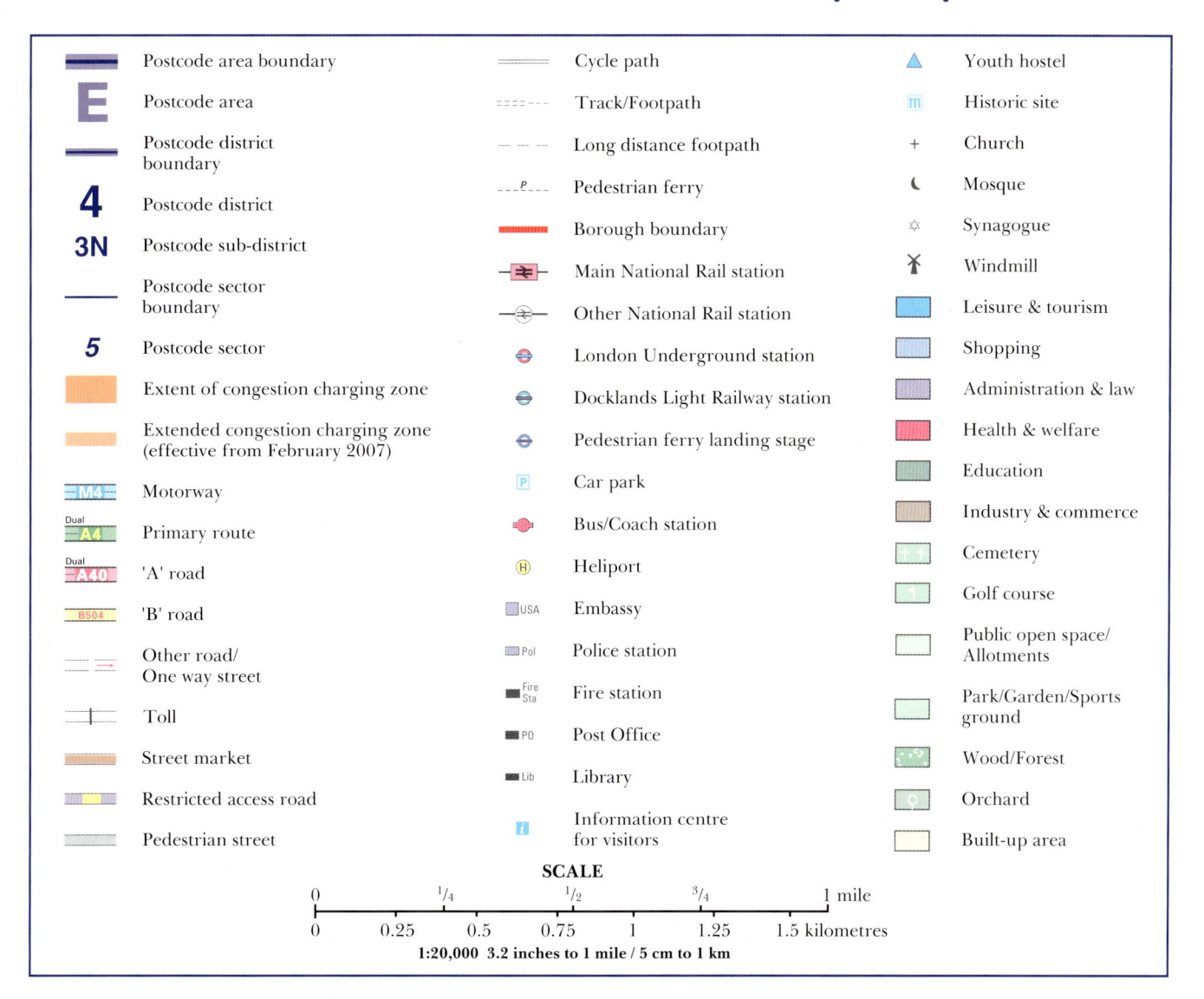

|  |  |
|---|---|
| | Postcode area boundary |
| E | Postcode area |
| | Postcode district boundary |
| 4 | Postcode district |
| 3N | Postcode sub-district |
| | Postcode sector boundary |
| 5 | Postcode sector |
| | Extent of congestion charging zone |
| | Extended congestion charging zone (effective from February 2007) |
| M4 | Motorway |
| Dual A4 | Primary route |
| Dual A40 | 'A' road |
| B504 | 'B' road |
| | Other road/One way street |
| | Toll |
| | Street market |
| | Restricted access road |
| | Pedestrian street |
| | Cycle path |
| | Track/Footpath |
| | Long distance footpath |
| ---P--- | Pedestrian ferry |
| | Borough boundary |
| | Main National Rail station |
| | Other National Rail station |
| | London Underground station |
| | Docklands Light Railway station |
| | Pedestrian ferry landing stage |
| P | Car park |
| | Bus/Coach station |
| H | Heliport |
| USA | Embassy |
| Pol | Police station |
| Fire Sta | Fire station |
| PO | Post Office |
| Lib | Library |
| i | Information centre for visitors |
| | Youth hostel |
| m | Historic site |
| + | Church |
| | Mosque |
| | Synagogue |
| | Windmill |
| | Leisure & tourism |
| | Shopping |
| | Administration & law |
| | Health & welfare |
| | Education |
| | Industry & commerce |
| | Cemetery |
| | Golf course |
| | Public open space/Allotments |
| | Park/Garden/Sports ground |
| | Wood/Forest |
| | Orchard |
| | Built-up area |

**SCALE**

0 — 1/4 — 1/2 — 3/4 — 1 mile
0 — 0.25 — 0.5 — 0.75 — 1 — 1.25 — 1.5 kilometres

1:20,000  3.2 inches to 1 mile / 5 cm to 1 km

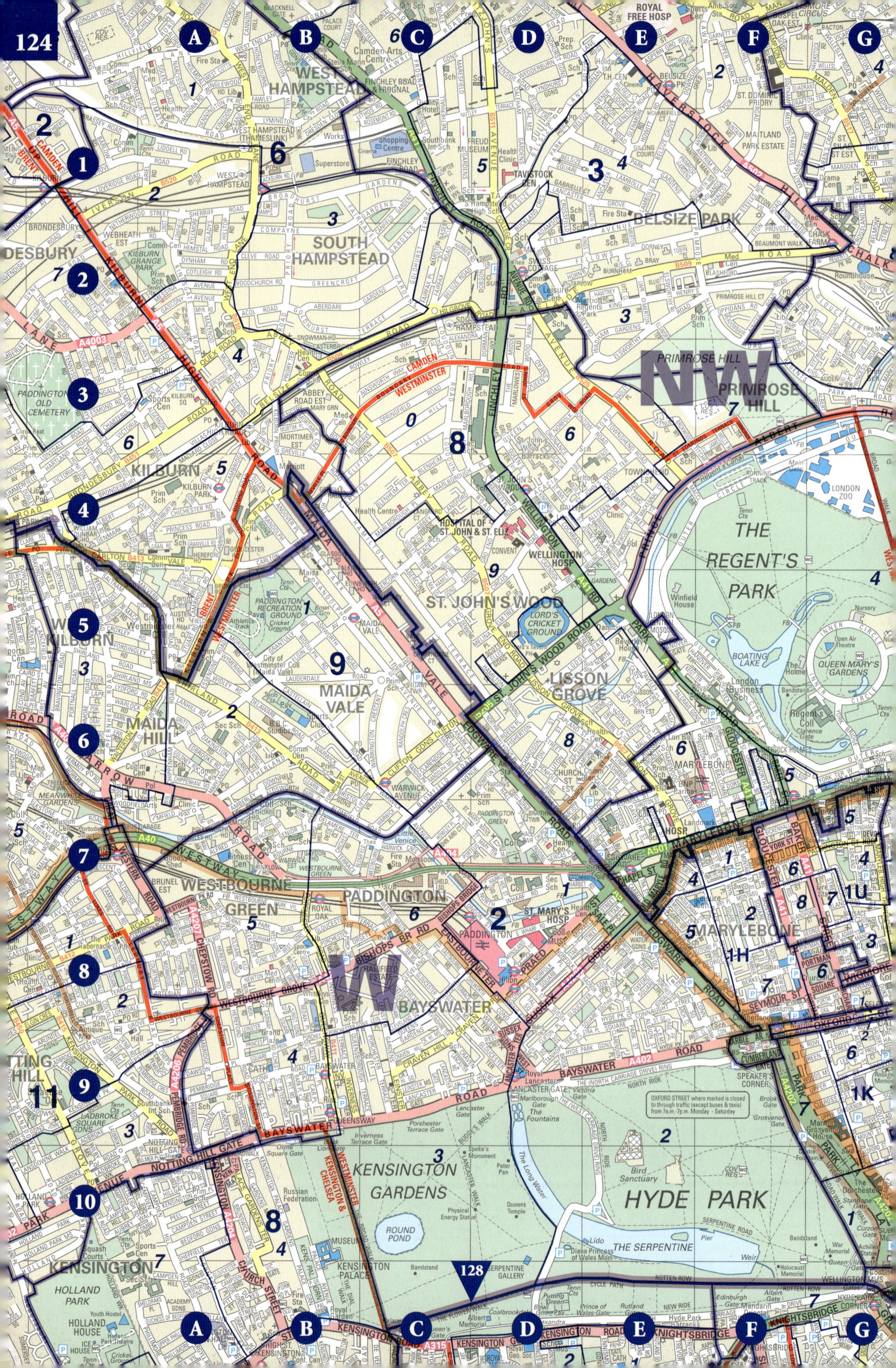

A
B
C
D
E
F
G
1
2
3
4
5
6
7
8
9
10
WEST HAMPSTEAD
SOUTH HAMPSTEAD
BELSIZE PARK
PRIMROSE HILL
NW
KILBURN
ST. JOHN'S WOOD
THE REGENT'S PARK
LORD'S CRICKET GROUND
LISSON GROVE
MAIDA VALE
MAIDA HILL
WESTBOURNE GREEN
PADDINGTON
MARYLEBONE
W
BAYSWATER
KENSINGTON GARDENS
HYDE PARK
THE SERPENTINE
ROUND POND
KENSINGTON
HOLLAND PARK
WESTWAY
NOTTING HILL GATE
BAYSWATER ROAD
KNIGHTSBRIDGE
LONDON ZOO
QUEEN MARY'S GARDENS
BOATING LAKE
HOSPITAL OF ST. JOHN & ST. ELIZ
WELLINGTON HOSP
ST. MARY'S HOSP
ROYAL FREE HOSP
128

H
J
K
L
M
N
P
HOLLOWAY
LOWER HOLLOWAY
HIGHBURY
KENTISH TOWN
CANONBURY
CALEDONIAN PARK
PENTONVILLE PRISON
BARNSBURY
KING'S CROSS
ISLINGTON
N
CAMDEN TOWN
SOMERS TOWN
BRITISH LIB
EUSTON
ST. PANCRAS
FINSBURY
PENTONVILLE
CLERKENWELL
EC
126
WC
BLOOMSBURY
BRITISH MUSEUM
HOLBORN
SOHO
STRAND
CHARING CROSS
EMBANKMENT
VICTORIA EMBANKMENT
RIVER
BLACKFRIARS
SHAKESPEARE GLOBE THEATRE
TATE MODERN
SOUTHWARK
SE
LAMBETH
WATERLOO
ST. JAMES'S
THE GREEN PARK
ST. JAMES'S PARK
SW
129
BUCKINGHAM PALACE
THE BOROUGH
CITY
1
2
3
4
5
6
7
8
9
10

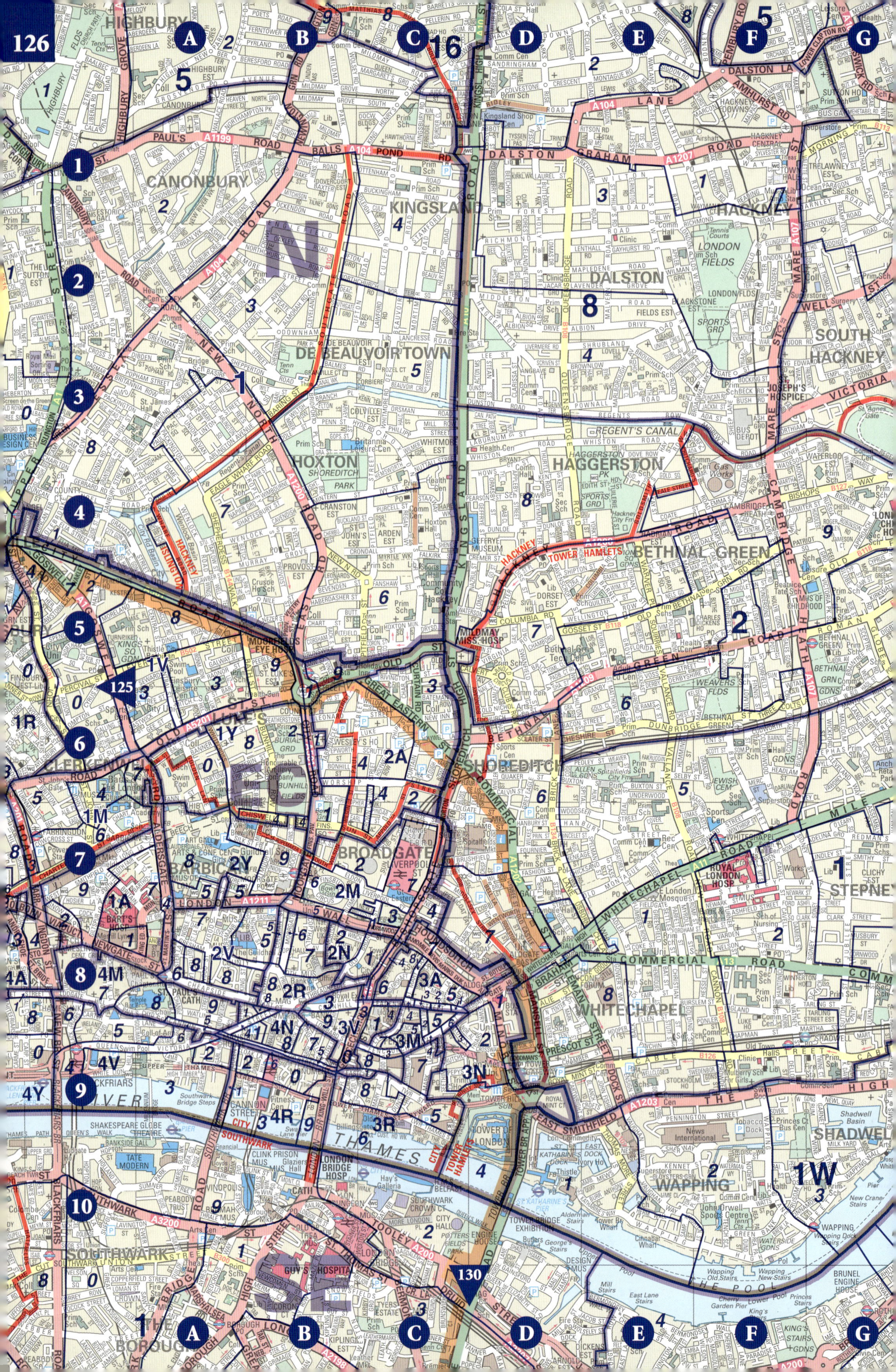

HOMERTON
HACKNEY WICK
STRATFORD
STRATFORD INTERNATIONAL (under construction)
Channel Tunnel Rail Link (under construction)
VICTORIA PARK
OLD FORD
BOW
MILE END
ROYAL LON. HOSP (ST. CLEMENTS)
TOWER HAMLETS CEMETERY PARK
BROMLEY
LIMEHOUSE
POPLAR
RIVER THAMES
ISLE
EAST INDIA DOCKS
The Dome Redevelopment (Open 2007)
NORTH GREENWICH
TOWER HAMLETS
NEWHAM
SOUTHWARK
GREENWICH
LEE VALLEY PARK
MILE END PARK
MILE END STADIUM
EAST INDIA DOCK BASIN NATURE RES
ELECTRA BUSINESS PARK
CANARY WHARF
Blackwall Basin
Poplar Dock
GROVE HALL PARK
LANGDON PARK
BARTLETT PARK
ST. ANDREW'S HOSP
MILE END HOSP
Queen Mary University of London
E
SE
131
H
J
K
L
M
N
P
1
2
3
4
5
6
7
8
9
10

A
B
C
D
E
F
G
KENSINGTON GARDENS
HYDE PARK
ROUND POND
124
THE SERPENTINE
KENSINGTON
HOLLAND PARK
W
SW
KENSINGTON ROAD
KENSINGTON GORE
KNIGHTSBRIDGE
SOUTH KENSINGTON
NATURAL HISTORY MUSEUM
VICTORIA & ALBERT MUSEUM
CROMWELL ROAD
BROMPTON
BELGRAVIA
EARLS COURT
EARLS COURT EXHIBITION CENTRE
WEST BROMPTON
BROMPTON CEMETERY
CHELSEA
ROYAL MARSDEN HOSP
ROYAL BROMPTON HOSP
ROYAL HOSPITAL CHELSEA
CHELSEA & WEST. HOSP
KING'S ROAD
FULHAM ROAD
CHELSEA EMBANKMENT
BATTERSEA PARK
CHELSEA REACH
STAMFORD BRIDGE CHELSEA FC
WALHAM GREEN
PARSONS GREEN
SANDS END
WANDSWORTH BRIDGE
HURLINGHAM PARK
HURLINGHAM CLUB
HAMMERSMITH & FULHAM
WANDSWORTH
KENSINGTON & CHELSEA
WESTMINSTER
LONDON BATTERSEA HELIPORT
CLAPHAM JUNCTION
LAVENDER HILL
WANDSWORTH COMMON
CLAPHAM COMMON
BOLINGBROKE HOSP

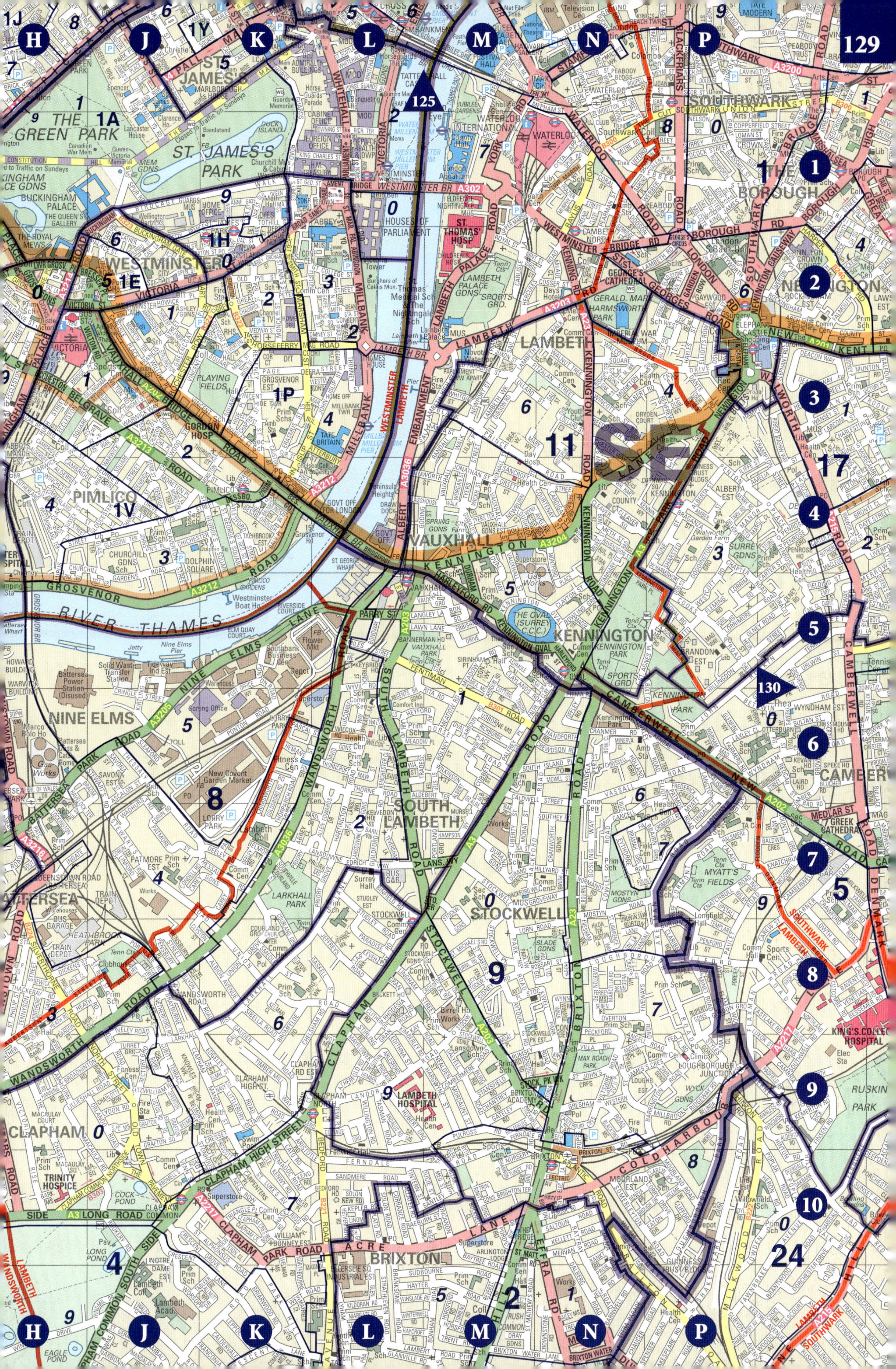

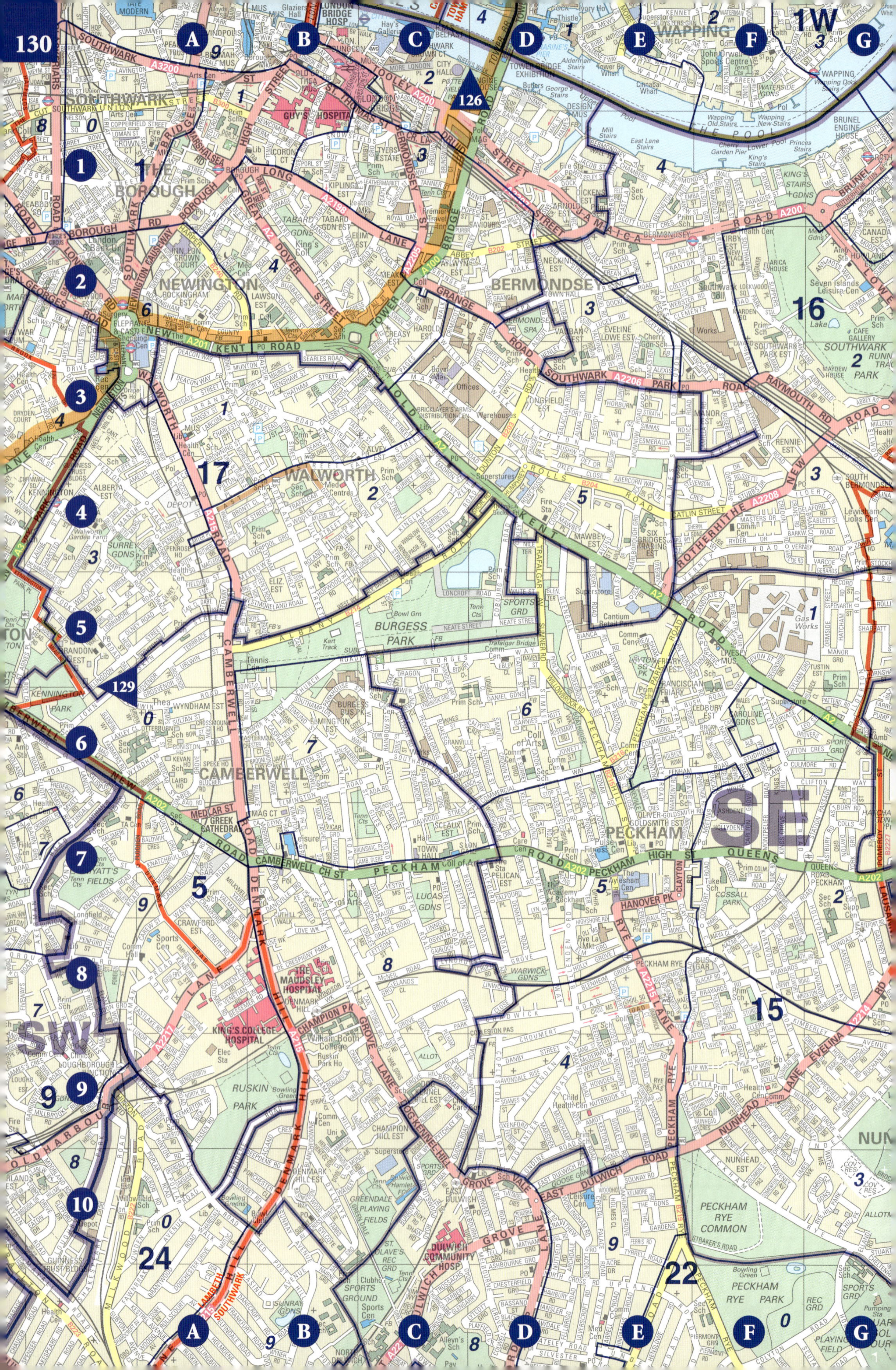
A
B
C
D
E
F
G
1W
WAPPING
SOUTHWARK
THE BOROUGH
GUY'S HOSPITAL
NEWINGTON
BERMONDSEY
16
SOUTHWARK PARK
WALWORTH
17
BURGESS PARK
CAMBERWELL
PECKHAM
SE
15
SW
KING'S COLLEGE HOSPITAL
MAUDSLEY HOSPITAL
RUSKIN PARK
PECKHAM RYE COMMON
PECKHAM RYE PARK
DULWICH COMMUNITY HOSP
22
24
126
129
1
2
3
4
5
6
7
8
9
10

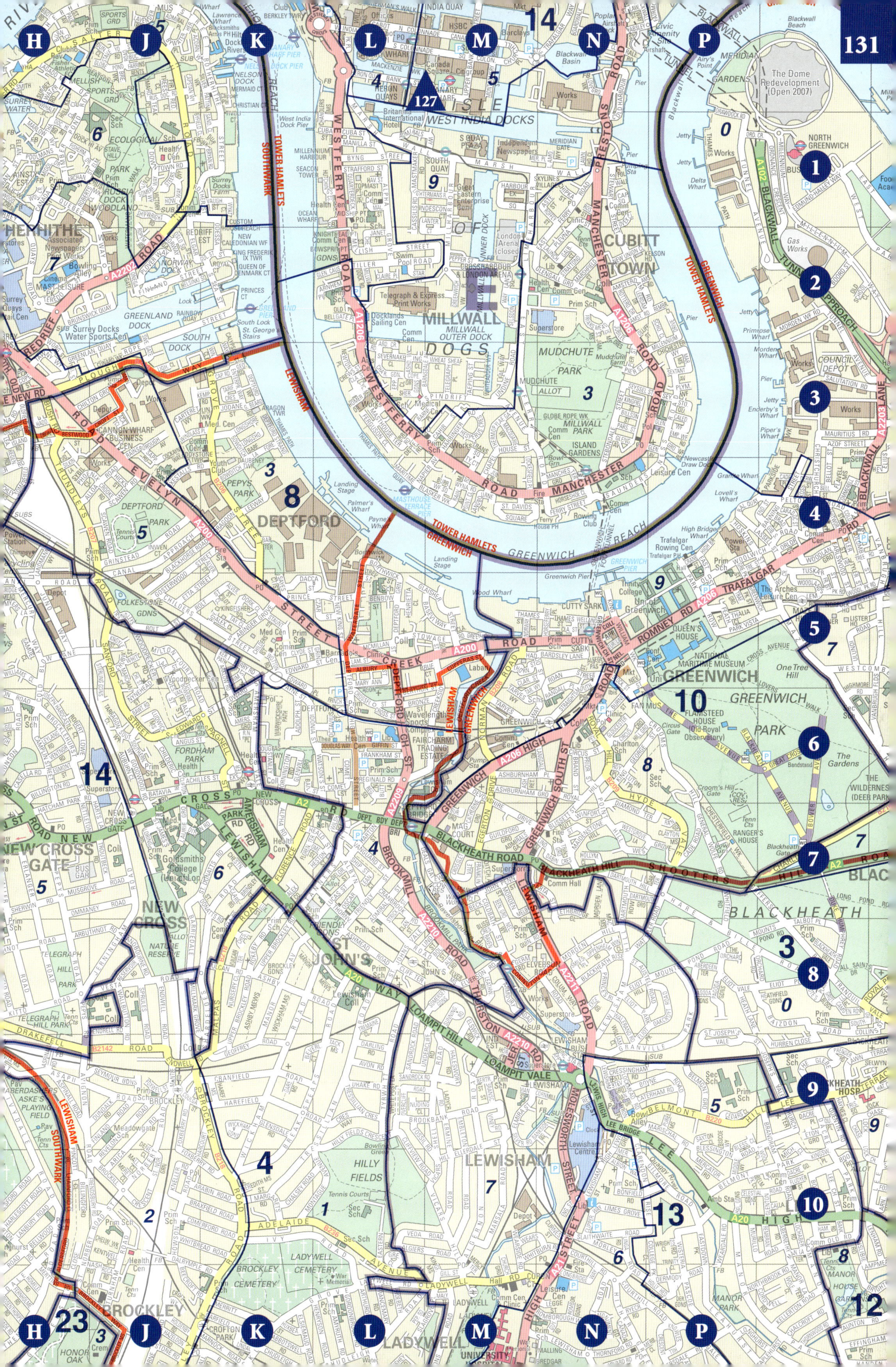
14
127
13
23
ROTHERHITHE
SURREY QUAYS
SURREY DOCKS WATER SPORTS CEN
GREENLAND DOCK
SOUTH DOCK
WEST INDIA DOCKS
CANARY WHARF
ISLE OF DOGS
MILLWALL
MILLWALL OUTER DOCK
MILLWALL INNER DOCK
MUDCHUTE PARK
CUBITT TOWN
ISLAND GARDENS
NORTH GREENWICH
The Dome Redevelopment (Open 2007)
BLACKWALL TUNNEL APPROACH
DEPTFORD
DEPTFORD PARK
PEPYS PARK
CUTTY SARK
GREENWICH
GREENWICH PARK
NATIONAL MARITIME MUSEUM
QUEEN'S HOUSE
FLAMSTEED HOUSE (Old Royal Observatory)
NEW CROSS
NEW CROSS GATE
ST JOHN'S
BLACKHEATH
LEWISHAM
HILLY FIELDS
BROCKLEY
BROCKLEY CEMETERY
LADYWELL
LADYWELL CEMETERY
TOWER HAMLETS
SOUTHWARK
GREENWICH
LEWISHAM
GREENWICH REACH

# Administrative areas

**Notes:** Listed below are the administrative areas for Great Britain, Northern Ireland and Isle of Man used in this Postcode Atlas. Where an area is dual language, the English form is given first, followed by the alternative in parenthesis. Each entry includes its standard abbreviation in *italics* which will appear in the index. Population figures are derived from 2001 Census information. A brief description of the area then follows, which includes: adjoining administrative areas; main centres (based on descending order of population); historical, physical and economic characteristics. For English counties or former Metropolitan counties, each district, city or borough authority is listed under the heading, **Districts**.

**Aberdeen** *Aberdeen* Population: 212,125.
Unitary authority surrounding Aberdeen, Scotland's third largest city, on the NE coast and neighbouring Aberdeenshire. Aberdeen is the major commercial and administrative centre for N Scotland. It is the second largest fishing port in Scotland, with docks at the mouth of the River Dee, and is the oil and gas capital of Europe.

**Aberdeenshire** *Aber.* Population: 226,871.
Unitary authority on the NE coast of Scotland neighbouring Aberdeen, Angus, Highland, Moray and Perth & Kinross. Main centres are Peterhead, Fraserburgh, Inverurie, Stonehaven, Ellon, Banchory, Portlethan and Huntly. Aberdeenshire is split geographically into two main areas. The W is dominated by the Grampian Mountains and is largely unpopulated. The undulating lowlands of the E are mainly rural and are populated by farming and fishing communities. The major rivers are the Dee, which flows through Royal Deeside, and the Don.

**Angus** *Angus* Population: 108,400.
Unitary authority on the E coast of Scotland neighbouring Aberdeenshire, Dundee and Perth & Kinross. The chief centres are Arbroath, Forfar, Montrose, Carnoustie, the ancient cathedral city of Brechin, Kirriemuir and Monifieth. Angus occupies an area of 2200 square km and is an important agricultural area. It combines ancient relics and castles with highland terrain and market towns. Rivers include the North Esk, Isla and Prosen Water.

**Antrim** *Antrim* Population: 48,366
Covering around 4% of the total area of Northern Ireland, Antrim borders the eastern and northern shores of Lough Neagh, the largest freshwater lake in the United Kingdom. Major towns include Antrim, Crumlin, Templepatrick, Toombridge, internationally famous for its eel industry and Randalstown. Chief industries are heavy engineering, construction, transport and distribution, plus agriculture and tourism.

**Ards** *Ards* Population: 73,244
Designated as an Area of Outstanding Natural Beauty (AONB). Over half the area is a peninsula created by Strangford Lough. Newtownards is the largest town, with smaller ones being Donaghdee, Portaferry, where the ferry can be caught to the other side of the lough, Kircubbin, Ballygowan, Comber, Millisle and Portavogie. The Copeland Islands lie about a mile offshore and there are several small islands in Strangford Lough itself. Main industries are agriculture and tourism.

**Argyll & Bute** *Arg. & B.* Population: 91,306.
Unitary authority on the W coast of Scotland combining mainland and island life and neighbouring Highland, Inverclyde, North Ayrshire, Perth & Kinross, Stirling and West Dunbartonshire. The main towns are Helensburgh, Dunoon, Oban, Campbeltown, Rothesay and Lochgilphead. It includes the former districts of Argyll and Bute as well as the islands of Islay, Jura, Colonsay and Mull. The main industries are fishing, agriculture, whisky production and tourism.

**Armagh** *Armagh* Population: 54,263.
The southern border of Armagh abuts the Republic of Ireland and the city of Armagh is home to the Archbishops of both the Church of Ireland and the Roman Catholic Church. Other towns include Keady, Tandragee, Richill, Loughgall and Markethill. Chief industries are agriculture (particularly orchard fruits), food processing, small scale manufacturing and tourism, with IT as an emerging sector.

**Bath & North East Somerset** *B. & N.E.Som.* Population: 169,040.
Unitary authority in SW England neighbouring Bristol, North Somerset, Somerset, South Gloucestershire and Wiltshire. It surrounds the city of Bath, and includes the towns of Keynsham, Radstock and Midsomer Norton. The Georgian spa of Bath is considered to be one of the most beautiful cities in Britain, and is an important commercial and ecclesiastical centre popular with tourists. The River Avon flows through the area.

**Ballymena** *Ballymena* Population: 58,610.
The river Bann, which forms the western border, affords some of the best coarse fishing in Europe. To the east are the Antrim Hills. The main town is Ballymena, where around half the population live. Other towns include Broughshane, Cullybackey and Ahogill. Main industries are agriculture, textiles, manufacturing and tourism.

**Ballymoney** *Ballymoney* Population: 26,894.
This predominantly rural district contains much of the Antrim Coast & Glens AONB, in the north-east corner of Northern Ireland. Ballymoney is the principle town, lying on the main A26 road. Many small villages dot the area, with agriculture being the main industry. There are a high proportion of self-employed and small businesses, along with textiles and pharmaceuticals.

**Banbridge** *Banbr.* Population: 41,392.
Crossed by the river Bann and dotted with glacial drumlins, Banbridge is a peaceful, unspoilt district, with the rugged Slieve Croob mountain in the east. Banbridge is the main town, while the historic cathedral town of Dromore on the river Lagan is the other major settlement. Other villages include Scarva, Loughbrickland and Gilford. Main industries are textiles (linen), construction, light engineering and agriculture.

**Bedford** *Bed.* Population: 154,700
Unitary authority in England formed in April 2009 from the northern part of Bedfordshire county. Bounded by Milton Keynes, Northamptonshire, Cambridgeshire and Central Bedfordshire. The main centres are Bedford and Kempston. The main river is the Great Ouse.

**Belfast** *Belfast.* Population: 277,391.
Belfast has the highest population and population density of all the Northern Ireland Districts. The city of Belfast sits on the river Lagan at the mouth of Belfast Lough and is a lively, vibrant city. There are no other settlements of significance within the area. A busy port, shipbuilding is still a major industry, the Titanic was built here, along with aircraft manufacturing, textiles, construction, oil refining, brewing, retail and tourism. Belfast city airport handles tourist and business flights.

**Blackburn with Darwen** *B'burn.* Population: 137,470.
Unitary authority in NW England surrounding Blackburn and Darwen and neighbouring Greater Manchester and Lancashire. Blackburn is a market and retail centre with a wide spread of industry including textiles, brewing and electronic engineering.

**Blackpool** *B'pool* Population: 142,283.
Unitary authority on the NW coast of England surrounding Blackpool and neighbouring Lancashire. Blackpool receives around 7.2 million visitors each year, making it the most popular seaside resort in Europe. Attractions including the Tower, Pleasure Beach, Winter Gardens and Illuminations.

**Blaenau Gwent** *B.Gwent* Population: 70,064.
Unitary authority in S Wales bounded by Caerphilly, Monmouthshire, Powys and Torfaen. The chief towns are Ebbw Vale, Tredegar, Bryn-mawr and Abertillery. The area was previously dependent upon coal, iron and steel industries but has since developed a broader industrial base. Part of the Brecon Beacons are in the N of the area.

**Bournemouth** *Bourne.* Population: 163,444.
Unitary authority on the S coast of England surrounding Bournemouth and neighbouring Dorset and Poole. Bournemouth is a major resort, conference and commercial centre.

**Bracknell Forest** *Brack.F.* Population: 109,617.
Unitary authority to the W of Greater London and bounded by Hampshire, Surrey, Windsor & Maidenhead and Wokingham. Bracknell is the chief town, while to the N of the area there are the villages of Winkfield and Binfield. To the S lies forest and heathland, and the towns of Crowthorne and Sandhurst. Bracknell has many hi-tech industries, and is a shopping and leisure centre.

**Bridgend** (Pen-y-Bont ar Ogwr). *Bridgend* Population: 128,645.
Unitary authority in S Wales bounded by Neath Port Talbot, Rhondda Cynon Taff, Vale of Glamorgan and the sea. Main centres are Bridgend, Maesteg and Porthcawl. The area is mountainous to the N, having ribbon development along river valleys; there is greater urbanisation in the S.

**Brighton & Hove** *B. & H.* Population: 247,817.
Unitary authority on the S coast of England neighbouring East Sussex and West Sussex. It encompasses the seaside resort of Brighton, which is a major commercial and conference centre, and the surrounding area which includes Hove, Portslade-by-Sea, Portslade, Rottingdean, Saltdean and part of the South Downs.

**Bristol** *Bristol* Population: 380,615.
Unitary authority in SW England neighbouring Bath & North East Somerset, North Somerset, South Gloucestershire and the Bristol Channel. The area includes the city of Bristol and surrounding urban area, including Avonmouth. Bristol is an important industrial and commercial centre of W England. A former major port, its character varies from docks and a busy city centre, to parks and gardens and Georgian terracing. The city hosts the Balloon Fiesta and Harbour Regatta. River Avon forms part of the W border of the area.

**Buckinghamshire** *Bucks.* Population: 479,026.
S midland county of England bounded by Central Bedfordshire, Greater London, Hertfordshire, Northamptonshire, Oxfordshire, Surrey, Windsor & Maidenhead and Wokingham. Chief towns are High Wycombe, the county town of Aylesbury, Amersham, Chesham, Marlow and Beaconsfield, around which, and other smaller towns, is a variety of light industry, as well as extensive residential areas. The chalk downs of the Chiltern Hills traverse the S part of the county, which is otherwise mostly flat. The River Thames flows along its S border.
**Districts**: Aylesbury Vale; Chiltern; South Bucks; Wycombe.

**Caerphilly** (Caerffili). *Caerp.* Population: 169,519.
Unitary authority in S Wales bordered by Blaenau Gwent, Cardiff, Merthyr Tydfil, Rhondda Cynon Taff and Torfaen. The chief centres are Caerphilly, Gelligaer, Risca, Bargoed, Blackwood and Bedwas. The geography of the area varies from open moorland to busy market towns. The former mining industry has been replaced by electronics and automotive companies, with tourism also being important to the local economy. Rivers include the Rhymney and Sirhowy.

**Cambridgeshire** *Cambs.* Population: 552,658.
County of E England bounded by Bedford, Central Bedfordshire, Essex, Hertfordshire, Lincolnshire, Norfolk, Northamptonshire, Peterborough and Suffolk. Cambridgeshire is mostly flat, with fenland to N and E, although there are low chalk hills in the S and SE. Chief centres are the city and county town of Cambridge, Wisbech, St. Ives, March, Huntingdon, St. Neots and the cathedral city of Ely. Agriculture is a major industry with sugar beet, potatoes and corn all important crops; soft fruit and vegetable cultivation and canning are also significant rural industries. There has been recent growth of medical, pharmaceutical and hi-tech industries around Cambridge. Rivers include the Cam, Nene, and Great Ouse.
**Districts**: Cambridge; East Cambridgeshire; Fenland; Huntingdonshire; South Cambridgeshire.

**Cardiff** (Caerdydd). *Cardiff* Population: 305,353.
Unitary authority in S Wales surrounding the city of Cardiff and bordered by Caerphilly, Newport, Rhondda Cynon Taff, Vale of Glamorgan and the Bristol Channel. Cardiff, the capital of Wales, is a major administrative, commercial, cultural and tourism centre. It contains the Welsh Office, Welsh National Stadium, remains of medieval castle, cathedral at Llandarff and university. Cardiff docks, which were formerly used to export Welsh coal, are part of an ongoing major redevelopment. The city has excellent shopping facilities, notably at the St. David's Centre. The birthplace of Roald Dahl.

**Carmarthenshire** (Sir Gaerfyrddin). *Carmar.* Population: 172,842.
Unitary authority in S Wales bounded by Ceredigion, Neath Port Talbot, Pembrokeshire, Powys, Swansea and the sea. The chief towns are Llanelli, Carmarthen and Ammanford. The geography varies from the Brecon Beacons in the E, to the river valleys in the N, and the fishing villages, beaches and coastal towns in the S. The 50m coastline runs along the S of the area. Rivers include the Tywi, Cothi, Gwendaeth Fach and Gwendaeth Fawr.

**Carrickfergus** *Carrick.* Population: 37,659.
A small district, with Belfast Lough at its eastern boundary. The main town of Carrickfergus is an ancient harbour with the impressive Carrickfergus Norman Castle built on a volcanic dyke. Smaller towns include Greenisland and Whitehead. Main industries are construction, manufacturing, retailing and tourism.

**Castlereagh** *Castle.* Population: 66,488.
To the south-east of Belfast, the main town of the district is Castlereagh, with other towns being Carryduff and Dundonald, which still has a Norman motte. Agriculture is the main industry but many people work in the shipbuilding and aircraft industries in Belfast.

**Central Bedfordshire** *Cen Beds.* Population: 249,200
Unitary authority in England formed in April 2009 from the southern part of Bedfordshire county (the former districts of Mid and South Bedfordshire). Bounded by Milton Keynes, Bedford, Cambridgeshire, Hertfordshire, Luton and Buckinghamshire. The main centres are Dunstable, Leighton Buzzard and Biggleswade. It includes the N end of the Chiltern Hills but is otherwise flat.

**Ceredigion** *Cere.* Population: 74,941.
Unitary authority in W Wales bounded by Carmarthenshire, Gwynedd, Pembrokeshire, Powys and the sea at Cardigan Bay. The main towns are Aberystwyth, Cardigan, Aberaeron, Lampeter, Tregaron and Llandysul. Part of the Cambrian Mountains lie in the E of the area and the 50m coast has many sandy beaches. Tourism and agriculture are the most important industries. The main river is the Teifi.

**Cheshire East** *Ches.E.* Population: 359,000
Unitary authority of NW England formed in April 2009 from three former districts of the county of Cheshire. Bounded by Warrington, Greater Manchester, Derbyshire, Staffordshire, Shropshire and Cheshire West & Chester. Chief centres are Crewe, Macclesfield, Nantwich, Wilmslow and Congleton. The foothills of the Pennines enter the NW of the area.

**Cheshire West & Chester** *Ches.W & C.* Population: 327,600
Unitary authority of NW England formed in April 2009 from three former districts of the county of Cheshire. Bounded by Merseyside, Halton, Warrington, Cheshire East, Shropshire and the Welsh authorities of Wrexham and Flintshire. Chief centres are the cathedral city of Chester and the towns of Ellesmere Port, Northwich and Winsford. The country is mainly flat with the rural areas of the S and W noted for dairy products. To the N and W are the estuaries of the River Dee and River Mersey.

**Clackmannanshire** *Clack.* Population: 48,077.
Unitary authority in central Scotland neighbouring Fife, Perth & Kinross and Stirling. The N includes the Ochil Hills, while the lowland surrounding the Forth estuary contains the chief towns which are Alloa, Tullibody, Tillicoultry and Alva. Clackmannanshire has over 50 sites of nature conservation and five historic castles and towers. The main rivers are the Devon and the Forth.

**Coleraine** *Coleraine* Population: 56,315.
This beautiful district borders the coast on its northern edge,

with the ports of Portrush, Portstewart and Portballintrae. The resorts of Downhill and Castlerock are popular with tourists, the latter at the outlet of the River Bann. Coleraine is the main town, an ancient but busy shopping centre. Smaller towns include Garvagh and Kilrea. Industries centre on agriculture and tourism.

**Conwy** *Conwy* Population: 109,596.
Unitary authority in N Wales bordered by Denbighshire, Gwynedd and the sea. The chief towns are Colwyn Bay, Llandudno, Abergele, Rhôs-on-Sea and Conwy. Around 40 per cent of Conwy is within Snowdonia National Park and there are 29m of coastline. The coastal resorts attract tourism which is a key industry, but agriculture and light manufacturing are also important to the local economy. The main river is the Conwy.

**Cookstown** *Cookstown* Population: 32,581.
With Lough Neagh at its eastern border and the foothills of the Sperrin Mountains to the west, Cookstown has been designated an AONB. The main town of Cookstown has the longest main street in Northern Ireland, with one mile of shops. Another town of significance is Moneymore, with other settlements being scattered, smaller villages. Industries are based around small businesses, agriculture and tourism.

**Cornwall** *Cornw.* Population: 499,114.
Unitary authority of SW England bounded by Devon and the sea. Chief centres are St. Austell, Falmouth, Penzance, the cathedral city and administrative centre of Truro, Redruth, Camborne and Newquay. The coastline is wild and rocky; headlands and cliffs are interspersed with large sandy beaches in the N, and deeply indented with river estuaries in the S. The interior is dominated by areas of moorland, notably the granite mass of Bodmin Moor in the NE. There are also farmlands providing rich cattle-grazing, and deep river valleys. The climate is mild, and flower cultivation is carried on extensively. The many derelict tin mines are witness to the former importance of this industry; there has recently been a partial revival. The chief industry is tourism. China clay is produced in large quantities in the St. Austell area, and there is some fishing. Rivers include the Tamar, forming the boundary with Devon; Fowey, East and West Looe, Fal, Camel, and Lynher.

**Craigavon** *Craigavon* Population: 80,671.
Craigavon's northern boundary is the southern shore of Lough Neagh. The M1 motorway crosses east-west, providing a link to Lisburn, Belfast and Antrim. Its principle towns are Craigavon itself, Lurgan, home to the Carnegie library and Portadown. Main industries include manufacturing, retail, public service and construction.

**Cumbria** *Cumb.* Population: 487,607.
County of NW England bounded by Durham, Lancashire, Northumberland and North Yorkshire; the Scottish authorities of Dumfries & Galloway and Scottish Borders; and the Solway Firth and Irish Sea. Chief centres are the city of Carlisle and the towns of Barrow-in-Furness, Whitehaven, Workington, Kendal, Penrith and Ulverston. A narrow strip of flat country along the coast widens to a plain in the N and around Carlisle. Otherwise the county is composed of mountains, moorland and lakes, and includes the scenically famous Lake District. Cumbria is mostly rural and uncultivated, with industry centred on Carlisle and the urban centres. Whitehaven, Workington, and Maryport all once relied on coal, while Barrow-in-Furness developed due to shipbuilding and heavy industry. There are links with nuclear technology: Calder Hall, N of Seascale, was Britain's first atomic power station, Sellafield is the site of a nuclear reprocessing plant and Trident submarines were built at Barrow-in-Furness. Tourism in the Lake District and sheep farming are also important industries. The area is noted for its radial drainage, with Windermere and Ullswater being the largest of the lakes and the River Eden being the chief of many rivers.
**Districts**: Allerdale; Barrow-in-Furness; Carlisle; Copeland; Eden; South Lakeland.

**Darlington** *Darl.* Population: 97,838.
Unitary authority in NE England surrounding Darlington and neighbouring Durham, North Yorkshire and Stockton-on-Tees. Darlington has a variety of industries, including iron, steel and textiles. The River Tees forms the S border.

**Denbighshire** (Sir Ddinbych). *Denb.* Population: 93,065.
Unitary authority in N Wales neighbouring Conwy, Flintshire, Gwynedd, Powys, Wrexham and the sea. The chief towns are Rhyl, Prestatyn, Denbigh, Ruthin, the ancient city of St. Asaph, and Llangollen. Main industries are tourism, centred on the coastal resorts of Rhyl and Prestatyn, and agriculture. Rivers include the Morwynion.

**Derby** *Derby* Population: 221,708.
Unitary authority in central England surrounding the city of Derby and bordered by Derbyshire. Derby has a history dating back to Roman times and is now important in the rail industry; other key industries are manufacturing and aerospace engineering. The River Derwent passes through the area.

**Derbyshire** *Derbys.* Population: 734,585.
Midland county of England bounded by Cheshire East, Derby, Greater Manchester, Leicestershire, Nottinghamshire, South Yorkshire, Staffordshire and West Yorkshire. Chief towns are Chesterfield, Long Eaton, Swadlincote, Ilkeston, Staveley, Dronfield, Alfreton, Heanor and Buxton. The high steep hills in the N, which include the dramatic scenery of The Peak, are the S extremity of The Pennines, and provide grazing for sheep and cattle. There is some textile industry in the towns of the N and W, while the S of the county is dominated by heavy industry, mining, and quarrying. Tourism is based on the scenic Peak District National Park, most of which falls in the county. Principal rivers are the Dove, forming much of the boundary with Staffordshire and noted for its scenery and fishing, and the Derwent; the Trent flows through the S corner of the county.
**Districts**: Amber Valley; Bolsover; Chesterfield; Derbyshire Dales; Erewash; High Peak; North East Derbyshire; South Derbyshire.

**Devon** *Devon* Population: 704,493.
Large county in SW peninsula of England bounded by Cornwall, Dorset, Plymouth, Somerset, Torbay and the Bristol and English Channels. The chief centres are the city of Exeter, Exmouth, Barnstaple, Newton Abbot, Tiverton, Bideford and Teignmouth. The county includes the W end of Exmoor and the whole of the granite mass of Dartmoor, whose summit, High Willhays, is the highest point in S England. Moorland areas apart, the county is largely given over to agriculture, and on the coast, to fishing and tourism. On Dartmoor there are quarries and a military training area; there are china clay workings in the S. Daffodils are grown commercially in River Tamar valley. Chief rivers are Exe, Teign, Dart, Avon, Erme, Tamar and Tavy in the S; and Taw and Torridge in the N. The granite island of Lundy is included in the county for administrative purposes.
**Districts**: East Devon; Exeter; Mid Devon; North Devon; South Hams; Teignbridge; Torridge; West Devon.

**Dorset** *Dorset* Population: 390,980.
County in SW England bounded by Bournemouth, Devon, Hampshire, Poole, Somerset, Wiltshire and the English Channel. The chief towns are Weymouth, Christchurch, Wimborne Minster, the county town of Dorchester, Bridport, Swanage and Blandford Forum. The county is hilly, with chalk downs and impressive geological formations along the coastline. Sand, gravel, stone and oil extraction takes place around the Isle of Portland and the Isle of Purbeck. Dorset is also noted for its agricultural and dairy produce. Tourism is an important industry due to the beautiful scenery, the proliferation of prehistoric and Roman remains, and the connection with Thomas Hardy's Wessex. Among numerous minor rivers are the Stour, Frome, and Piddle or Trent.
**Districts**: Christchurch; East Dorset; North Dorset; Purbeck; West Dorset; Weymouth & Portland.

**Down** *Down* Population: 63,828.
The southern tip of Down includes part of the beautiful Mourne Mountains, and the eastern edge consists of a long coastline, with the long sandy beach of Dundrum Bay and the shores of Strangford Lough. The main town is Downpatrick, others being Ballynahinch, Crossgar and Saintfield along with the coastal towns of Killyleagh, Newcastle and Ardglass. Industries include engineering and agriculture.

**Dumfries & Galloway** *D. & G.* Population: 147,765.
Unitary authority in SW Scotland neighbouring East Ayrshire, Scottish Borders, South Ayrshire, South Lanarkshire, the English county of Cumbria and the sea. It comprises the former counties

of Dumfries, Kirkcudbright and Wigtown. Chief towns are Dumfries, Stranraer, Annan, Dalbeattie, Lockerbie, Castle Douglas, Newton Stewart and Kirkcudbright. The hilly area to the N is largely given over to sheep-grazing and afforestation, while farther S there is some good-quality arable farmland. At the extreme W of the area is the peninsula known as the Rinns of Galloway, and the port of Stranraer, which provides passenger and car ferry services to Larne in Northern Ireland. Main rivers are the Esk, Annan, Nith, Dee and Cree which descend S to the Solway Firth from the Tweedsmuir Hills, Lowther Hills and the Rhinns of Kells in the N.

**Dundee** *Dundee* Population: 145,663.
Unitary authority on the E coast of Scotland surrounding the city of Dundee and neighbouring Angus and Perth & Kinross. Dundee is Scotland's fourth largest city and is a centre of excellence in a variety of areas from telecommunications to medical research. The Firth of Tay borders Dundee to the S.

**Dungannon** *Dungannon* Population: 47,735.
Dungannon includes the scenic Clogher valley, and the Republic of Ireland forms its southern boundary. The north-east corner meets Lough Neagh and the main A4 road bisects it east-west. Dungannon town has almost a quarter of the whole population, with the rest of the area being basically rural. Coalisland still has a linen industry and Tyrone Crystal is famous worldwide. Industries include agriculture, construction, retail and manufacturing.

**Durham** *Dur.* Population: 493,470.
Unitary authority in NE England bounded by Cumbria, Darlington, Hartlepool, Northumberland, North Yorkshire, Stockton-on-Tees, Tyne & Wear and the North Sea. Chief centres are the cathedral city of Durham; and the towns of Chester-le-Street, Peterlee, Newton Aycliffe, Bishop Auckland, Seaham and Consett. The W part includes The Peninnes and consists mostly of open moorlands which provide rough sheep-grazing and water for the urban areas from a number of large reservoirs. Economic activity is concentrated on the lowland in the E which is more heavily populated, and was formerly a centre for coal-mining and heavy industry. Diversification has since provided a broad industrial base. The principal rivers are the Tees and the Wear.

**East Ayrshire** *E.Ayr.* Population: 120,235.
Unitary authority in SW Scotland bounded by Dumfries & Galloway, East Renfrewshire, North Ayrshire, South Ayrshire and South Lanarkshire. The principal towns are Kilmarnock, Cumnock, Stewarton, Galston and Auchinleck. Traditional industries centred on textiles and lace in the Irvine valley, coal mining and engineering. Dairy farming is also an important industry, particularly beef and sheep production. The area is a popular tourist destination, with several castles, battle sites and associations with Robert Burns and Keir Hardie. Rivers include the Irvine, Annick and Cessnock.

**East Dunbartonshire** *E.Dun.* Population: 108,243.
Unitary authority in central Scotland bounded by Glasgow, North Lanarkshire, Stirling and West Dunbartonshire. The chief centres are Bearsden, Bishopbriggs, Kirkintilloch and Milngavie. Much of the urban and industrial development occurs on the N periphery of Greater Glasgow. The Campsie Fells lie in the N of the area.

**East Lothian** *E.Loth.* Population: 90,088.
Unitary authority in central Scotland neighbouring Edinburgh, Midlothian, Scottish Borders and the North Sea. The main towns are Musselburgh, Haddington, Tranent, Prestonpans, Dunbar, North Berwick and Cockenzie and Port Seton. There are 43m of varied coastline and the topography includes the Lammermuir Hills in the S, and the ancient volcanoes at North Berwick and Traprain. Much of the urban and industrial development is in the NW and N of the area. Rivers include Whitehead Water, the Tyne, Peffer Burn and Gifford Water.

**East Renfrewshire** *E.Renf.* Population: 89,311.
Unitary authority in SW Scotland bounded by East Ayrshire, Glasgow, Inverclyde, North Ayrshire, Renfrewshire and South Lanarkshire. The principal centres are Newton Mearns, Clarkston, Barrhead and Giffnock, which lie on the S periphery of Greater Glasgow. Over two-thirds of East Renfrewshire is farmland; the rest being mostly residential, with some light industry.

**East Riding of Yorkshire** *E.Riding* Population: 314,113.
Unitary authority on the E coast of England neighbouring Kingston upon Hull, North Lincolnshire, North Yorkshire, South Yorkshire and York. The chief centres are Bridlington, Beverley, Goole, Great Driffield, Hornsea, Brough, Hedon and Withernsea. The area is mostly low-lying, except for the central ridge which forms part of The Wolds. The coastline is subject to much erosion, with material being moved from Flamborough Head to the large spit of Spurn Head, at the mouth of the River Humber. Key industries in the area include agriculture, aerospace, gas and oil industries.

**East Sussex** *E.Suss.* Population: 492,324.
County of SE England bounded by Brighton & Hove, Kent, Surrey, West Sussex and the English Channel. Main towns are Eastbourne, Hastings, Bexhill, Seaford, Crowborough, Hailsham, Peacehaven and the county town of Lewes; Rye is a small historic town in the E of the county. In the W, the coast is backed by the chalk ridge of the South Downs, ending with the white cliffs of the Seven Sisters and Beachy Head, just W of Eastbourne. E of this point, there are extensive areas of reclaimed marshland, which provide good sheep-grazing. Inland is the heavily wooded Weald, a former centre of the iron industry, interspersed with hill ridges, the largest being the open heathland of Ashdown Forest. Rivers, none large, include the Cuckmere, Ouse, Rother, and upper reaches of the Medway.
**Districts**: Eastbourne; Hastings; Lewes; Rother; Wealden.

**Edinburgh** *Edin.* Population: 448,624.
Unitary authority on the E coast of central Scotland surrounding the city of Edinburgh and neighbouring East Lothian, Midlothian, West Lothian and the sea at the Firth of Forth. Edinburgh as the capital of Scotland, is a major administrative, cultural, commercial and tourist centre. It contains most of Scotland's national and cultural institutions. Its historic core is centred around Edinburgh Castle and the Royal Mile, attracting much tourism. The city is also a centre for education and scientific research; other important industries are electronics and food and drink production. The river Water of Leith runs through the city to the docks at Leith.

**Essex** *Essex* Population: 1,310,835.
County of SE England bounded by Cambridgeshire, Greater London, Hertfordshire, Southend, Suffolk, Thurrock and the sea at the Thames estuary and North Sea. Chief towns are Basildon, the county town of Chelmsford, Colchester, Harlow, Brentwood, Clacton-on-Sea, Loughton, Canvey Island, Billericay and Braintree. The landscape is mostly flat or gently undulating, and the low-lying coast is deeply indented with river estuaries. Along the county's S and W sides, there is a concentration of urban development, with a mixture of light engineering and service industries. In the N and central parts are farmlands, orchards, market and nursery gardens. The NE coast has the busy passenger and container port of Harwich, and the popular seaside resort of Clacton-on-Sea. Rivers include the Stour, forming part of the boundary with Suffolk, the Lea, forming part of the boundary with Hertfordshire, and the Blackwater.
**Districts**: Basildon; Braintree; Brentwood; Castle Point; Chelmsford; Colchester; Epping Forest; Harlow; Maldon; Rochford; Tendring; Uttlesford.

**Falkirk** *Falk.* Population: 145,191.
Unitary authority in central Scotland surrounding Falkirk and neighbouring Clackmannanshire, Fife, North Lanarkshire, Stirling and West Lothian. Main towns are Falkirk, Grangemouth, Polmont, Stenhousemuir and Bo'ness. Petrochemical and chemical industries are important to the local economy, as well as bus manufacturing, toffees and paper-making. The Firth of Forth borders Falkirk to the N. Other rivers include the Carron and Pow Burn.

**Fermanagh** *Ferm.* Population: 57,527.
One third of this district is water, mainly taken up by Upper and Lower Lough Erne. Consequently, there are around 150 inland islands, and the population density is one of the lowest in Northern Ireland. Large areas have been planted with conifers for timber. The north-west and south-west boundaries border the Republic of Ireland. The main town of Enniskillen lies on the

River Erne at the junction of the two major loughs and other towns include Irvinestown, Rosslea and Lisnaskea. Main industries are agriculture and tourism, engineering and timber milling.

**Fife** *Fife* Population: 349,429.

Unitary authority in E Scotland neighbouring Clackmannanshire and Perth & Kinross, and lying between the Firth of Tay and Firth of Forth. Main towns are Dunfermline, Kirkcaldy, Glenrothes, Buckhaven, Cowdenbeath and St. Andrews. Fife comprises the former county of the same name, known since ancient times as the Kingdom of Fife, and is noted for its fine coastline with many distinctive small towns and fishing ports. The historic town of St. Andrews, on the coast between the two firths, is a university town, and the home of the world's premier golf club. Inland, the area is outstandingly fertile, with agriculture being an important industry. The SW of the area is a former coal-mining area.

**Flintshire** (Sir y Fflint). *Flints*. Population: 148,594.

Unitary authority in N Wales neighbouring Conwy, Denbighshire, Wrexham, Cheshire West & Chester and the mouth of the River Dee. Main towns are Buckley, Connah's Quay, Flint, Hawarden, Shotton, Queensferry, Mold and Holywell. Known as the Gateway to N Wales, the landscape varies from the mountains which form the Clwydian Range, to small villages and woodlands.

**Glasgow** *Glas*. Population: 577,869.

Unitary authority in SW Scotland surrounding Glasgow and bounded by East Dunbartonshire, East Renfrewshire, North Lanarkshire, Renfrewshire, South Lanarkshire and West Dunbartonshire. Glasgow is Scotland's largest city and its principal industrial and shopping centre. The city developed significantly due to heavy industry, notably shipbuilding, being centred on the Clyde. While such industry has declined, Glasgow has emerged as a major cultural centre of Europe, due to its impressive arts and cultural scene. The River Clyde runs through the city.

**Gloucestershire** *Glos*. Population: 564,559.

County of W England bounded by Herefordshire, Oxfordshire, South Gloucestershire, Swindon, Warwickshire, Wiltshire, Worcestershire and the Welsh authority of Monmouthshire. Main centres are the cathedral city and county town of Gloucester and the towns of Cheltenham, Stroud, Cirencester and Dursley. The limestone mass of the Cotswold Hills dominates the centre of the county, and provides the characteristic pale golden stone of many of its buildings. The River Severn forms a wide valley to the W, ending in a long tidal estuary, beyond which are the hills of the Forest of Dean. Industry is centred on the fertile Severn Vale, with aerospace, light engineering, food production, and service industries in and around the towns; in rural areas market gardening and orchards dominate. The River Thames rises in the county, and forms part of its S boundary in the vicinity of Lechlade. Apart from the Severn and the Thames, there is the River Wye, which forms part of the boundary with Monmouthshire, and many smaller rivers, among them the Chelt, Coln, Evenlode, Leach, Leadon, and Windrush.

**Districts**: Cheltenham; Cotswold; Forest of Dean; Gloucester; Stroud; Tewkesbury.

**Greater London** *Gt.Lon*. Population: 7,172,091.

Former metropolitan county of 32 boroughs and the City of London which together form the conurbation of London, the capital of the UK. Greater London is the largest financial, commercial, cultural, distribution and communications centre in the country, including all but primary industrial sectors. London developed from the City of London, a walled Roman settlement on the Thames, and Westminster, which was a Saxon religious settlement and later a Norman seat of government. The Great Fire of 1666 destroyed most of the medieval city, and was followed by a period of rebuilding and rapid, unplanned expansion. Industrialisation and improved public transport over the last two centuries have caused major suburban growth, and the absorption of most of the surrounding settlements and countryside. Tourism is a major industry, with most attractions situated in and around the historic core, and along the Thames bankside. Other notable tourist areas include Greenwich, Hampstead, Kew and Richmond. Industrial activity is widespread, with major concentrations in the E along the Thames. Leisure facilities include national and major sports stadiums, and many big parks and gardens. Airports at Heathrow and docklands. The main river is the Thames.

**Districts**: Barking & Dagenham; Barnet; Bexley; Brent; Bromley; Camden; City of London; City of Westminster; Croydon; Ealing; Enfield; Greenwich; Hackney; Hammersmith & Fulham; Haringey; Harrow; Havering; Hillingdon; Hounslow; Islington; Kensington & Chelsea; Kingston upon Thames; Lambeth; Lewisham; Merton; Newham; Redbridge; Richmond upon Thames; Southwark; Sutton; Tower Hamlets; Waltham Forest; Wandsworth.

**Greater Manchester** *Gt.Man*. Population: 2,482,328.

Former metropolitan county of NW England neighbouring Blackburn with Darwen, Cheshire East, Derbyshire, Lancashire, Merseyside, Warrington and West Yorkshire. It comprises the near-continuous urban complex which includes the adjoining cities of Manchester and Salford; and towns including Bolton, Stockport, Oldham, Rochdale, Wigan, Bury and Sale. The conurbation is framed by the wild moorland of The Pennines to the N and the Peak District and Cheshire Plain to the S. Development occurred during the 18c and 19c, creating a series of cotton producing textile towns, while Manchester established itself as the commercial and trading hub, later becoming an inland port linked to Liverpool via the canal network. As textile production declined, the industrial base of the area broadened to include brewing, food production, electronics, plastics, printing, light engineering, financial, leisure and service sectors. Retail is based on town shopping centres and malls such as the Arndale and Trafford Centres. There are many major sporting venues in the area, and cultural facilities include the G-MEX centre, numerous universities, museums and galleries and a diverse nightlife. The area is served by Manchester Airport. Main rivers are Irwell and Mersey.

**Districts**: Bolton; Bury; Manchester; Oldham; Rochdale; Salford; Stockport; Tameside; Trafford; Wigan.

**Gwynedd** *Gwyn*. Population: 116,843.

Unitary authority in NW Wales bounded by Ceredigion, Conwy, Denbighshire, Isle of Anglesey, Powys and the sea. Main centres are the cathedral city of Bangor, Caernarfon, Ffestiniog, Blaenau Ffestiniog, Llanddeiniolen, Pwllheli, Llanllyfni, Bethesda and Porthmadog. The whole mainland area, except the Lleyn Peninsula in the NW, is extremely mountainous and contains the scenically famous Snowdonia National Park. There is slate-quarrying in the Ffestiniog valley, otherwise sheep-farming and tourism are the principal occupations; the coastline has been much developed for the holiday trade. The area contains many lakes and reservoirs, among them are Llyn Trawsfynedd, Llyn Celyn and Llyn Tegid. Of the many rivers, the Wnion and the Dyfi, which flows through part of the area, are most significant.

**Halton** *Halton* Population: 118,208.

Unitary authority in NW England neighbouring Cheshire West & Chester, Merseyside and Warrington. The principal towns are Runcorn and Widnes, separated by the River Mersey. The area is industrialised, being dominated by petro-chemicals and chemicals industries due to the nearby salt mines and port facilities.

**Hampshire** *Hants*. Population: 1,240,103.

County of S England bounded by Bracknell Forest, Dorset, Portsmouth, Southampton, Surrey, West Berkshire, West Sussex, Wiltshire, Wokingham and the English Channel. Main towns are Basingstoke, Gosport, Waterlooville, Farnborough, Aldershot, Eastleigh, Havant, the ancient city and county town of Winchester, Andover and Fleet. The centre of the county consists largely of chalk downs interspersed with fertile valleys. In the SW is the New Forest, while in the NE is the military area centred on Aldershot. The much indented coastline borders The Solent and looks across to the Isle of Wight. Main industries are in the service sector, with chemicals and pharmaceuticals also important. The chief rivers are the Itchen and Test, both chalk streams flowing into Southampton Water, and the Meon flowing into The Solent.

**Districts**: Basingstoke & Deane; East Hampshire; Eastleigh; Fareham; Gosport; Hart; Havant; New Forest; Rushmoor; Test Valley; Winchester.

**Hartlepool** *Hart*. Population: 88,611.

Unitary authority on the NE coast of England surrounding Hartlepool and bordering Darlington, Durham, Stockton-on-Tees and the North Sea. Fishing is a major industry and a marina has been created from part of the old docks. The mouth of the River Tees forms part of the E border.

**Herefordshire** *Here.* Population: 174,871.
Unitary authority in W England bounded by Gloucestershire, Shropshire, Worcestershire and the Welsh authorities of Monmouthshire and Powys. Main centres are the cathedral city of Hereford and the towns of Ross-on-Wye, Leominster and Ledbury. Herefordshire lies between the Malvern Hills to the E and the Black Mountains to the W. It is mainly rural, with dairy farming, orchards and market gardening in evidence. The main river is the Wye, which provides excellent fishing.

**Hertfordshire** *Herts.* Population: 1,033,977.
S midland county of England bounded by Central Bedfordshire, Buckinghamshire, Cambridgeshire, Essex, Greater London and Luton. Chief centres are Watford, the cathedral city of St. Albans, Hemel Hempstead, Stevenage, Cheshunt, Welwyn Garden City, Hoddesdon, Hitchin, Letchworth and Hatfield; the county town is Hertford. The Chilterns rise along the W border, and there are chalk hills in the N around Royston; otherwise the landscape is mostly flat or gently undulating. There is a mixture of rural and urban life, with agricultural and hi-tech industries represented. While the urban centres in the S lie on the N periphery of the Greater London conurbation, there are many villages with the traditional large green or common. The more urban S part of the county includes a dense network of major roads bypassing, and leading N from London. Rivers include the Colne, Ivel, and Lee.
**Districts**: Broxbourne; Dacorum; East Herts; Hertsmere; North Hertfordshire; St. Albans; Stevenage; Three Rivers; Watford; Welwyn Hatfield.

**Highland** *High.* Population: 208,914.
Unitary authority covering a large part of N Scotland and neighbouring Aberdeenshire, Argyll & Bute, Moray and Perth & Kinross. It contains a mixture of mainland and island life, comprising the former districts of Badenoch and Strathspey, Caithness, Inverness, Lochaber, Nairn, Ross and Cromarty, Skye and Lochalsh and Sutherland. Main towns are Inverness, Fort William, Thurso, Nairn, Wick, Alness and Dingwall. Overall, Highland is very sparsely inhabited, being wild and remote in character. It is scenically outstanding, containing as it does part of the Cairngorm Mountains, Ben Nevis, and the North West Highlands. Many of the finest sea and inland lochs in Scotland are also here, such as Loch Ness, Loch Linnhe, Loch Torridon and Loch Broom. The discovery of North Sea oil has made an impact on the towns and villages around the Moray Firth. Elsewhere, tourism, crofting, fishing and skiing are important locally.

**Inverclyde** *Inclyde* Population: 84,203.
Unitary authority on the W coast of central Scotland, on the S bank of the River Clyde. It is bordered by North Ayrshire, Renfrewshire and the Firth of Clyde. The chief towns are Greenock, Port Glasgow, Gourock and Kilmacolm.

**Isle of Anglesey** (Sir Ynys Môn). *I.o.A.* Population: 66,829.
Unitary authority island of NW Wales divided from Gwynedd and the mainland by the Menai Strait, and with Holy Island lying to the W. Main towns are Holyhead, Llangefni, Amlwch and Menai Bridge. Anglesey has 125m of coastline and 16 beaches. Agriculture is an important industry to the island, with other industries including aluminium smelting and food processing. Holyhead is an important port terminus for the Republic of Ireland. Rivers include the Braint and Cefni.

**Isle of Man** *I.o.M.* Population: 76,315.
Self-governing island in the Irish Sea, situated in the centre of the British Isles. The chief towns are Douglas, Ramsey, Peel, Castletown, Port St. Mary, Port Erin and Laxey. Apart from the N tip, the topography is generally mountainous, rising to a peak at Snaefell. The main industries are agriculture, fishing and tourism as well as financial services and manufacturing. The island is synonymous with motorsport, being the home of the internationally renowned Tourist Trophy Circuit. Rivers include the Glen Auldyn and Neb.

**Isle of Wight** *I.o.W.* Population: 132,731.
County and island with an area of 147 square miles or 381 square km, separated from the S coast of England by The Solent. Chief towns are the capital, Newport, Ryde, Cowes, Shanklin, Sandown, Ventnor and Yarmouth. The island is geologically diverse, composed of sedimentary rocks and contains many important fossil remains. Tourism flourishes owing to the mild climate and the natural beauty of the island. There are Royal associations as Queen Victoria lived and died at Osborne House in the N of the island. There is a strong naval tradition, with the island historically acting as a defence for Portsmouth. Cowes is internationally famous for yachting. There are ferry and hovercraft connections at Cowes, Ryde, and Yarmouth (ferry to Lymington). Chief river is the Medina.

**Isles of Scilly** *I.o.S.* Population: 2153.
Group of some 140 islands 48m/45km SW of Land's End, Cornwall, of which five are inhabited: Bryher, St. Agnes, St. Martin's, St. Mary's and Tresco. Chief industries are fishing, and the growing of early flowers and vegetables due to the exceptionally mild climate.

**Kent** *Kent* Population: 1,329,718.
South-easternmost county of England bounded by East Sussex, Greater London, Medway, Surrey and the sea at the Thames estuary and the Strait of Dover. Chief centres are the county town of Maidstone, Royal Tunbridge Wells, Dartford, Margate, Ashford, Gravesend, Folkestone, Sittingbourne, Ramsgate, the cathedral city of Canterbury, Tonbridge and Dover. The chalk ridge of the North Downs runs along the N side, then SE to Folkestone and Dover. The River Medway cuts through the chalk in the vicinity of Maidstone, and there are low lying areas to the E of Canterbury and of Tonbridge, on Romney Marsh in the S, and bordering the Thames estuary in the N. Chief industrial areas are around Maidstone, Ashford and Tonbridge; Dover and Folkestone are major ports, with the Channel Tunnel terminus to the N of Folkestone; Sheerness is a port of growing importance. Industrial activity includes mineral extraction, cement manufacture and papermaking. On the highly productive agricultural land, Kent's reputation as the Garden of England is earned, with market gardening, fruit and hop production. Romney Marsh is used for extensive sheep-grazing. Rivers include the Medway, Stour, and Beult.
**Districts**: Ashford; Canterbury; Dartford; Dover; Gravesham; Maidstone; Sevenoaks; Shepway; Swale; Thanet; Tonbridge & Malling; Tunbridge Wells.

**Kingston upon Hull** *Hull* Population: 243,589.
Unitary authority on the E coast of England surrounding the city of Kingston upon Hull and bounded by East Riding of Yorkshire and the mouth of the River Humber. Kingston upon Hull is a major sea port and a great industrial city, with key industries including chemicals, food processing, pharmaceuticals and engineering. The River Hull passes through the area, and the River Humber forms the S border.

**Lancashire** *Lancs.* Population: 1,134,974.
County of NW England bounded by Blackburn with Darwen, Cumbria, Greater Manchester, Merseyside, North Yorkshire, West Yorkshire and the Irish Sea. Chief centres are the administrative city of Preston, Burnley, Morecambe, the historic county town of Lancaster, Skelmersdale, Lytham St. Anne's, Leyland, Accrington and Chorley; Fleetwood and Heysham are ports. The inland side of the county is hilly and includes the wild and impressive Forest of Bowland. The W side contains the coastal plain, where vegetables are extensively cultivated. The S is largely urban; industries include cotton spinning and weaving, chemicals, glass, rubber, electrical goods, and motor vehicles. The principal rivers are the Lune and the Ribble.
**Districts**: Burnley; Chorley; Fylde; Hyndburn; Lancaster; Pendle; Preston; Ribble Valley; Rossendale; South Ribble; West Lancashire; Wyre.

**Larne** *Larne* Population: 30,832.
On the east coast of Northern Ireland, Larne port is one of the main points of entry to Northern Ireland and is also an important centre for freight. The northern part of the district contains the southern tip of the Antrim Hills and the coastline has an amazing range of geological features, from the most ancient rocks, to remains from the last glaciation. Other towns include Carnlough, Ballygalley and Portmuck on the coast, and Kilwaughter, Ballynure and Ballycarry inland. Industries are based around freight, agriculture and tourism.

**Leicester** *Leic.* Population: 279,921.
Unitary authority in central England surrounding Leicester and bounded by Leicestershire. It is one of the leading shopping

regions in the Midlands. Traditional industries such as hosiery and footwear, as well as hi-tech industries, are important to the local economy. Leicester is aiming to be one of the most environmentally-friendly cities in Europe. It is involved in pioneering electronic toll road schemes in order to encourage the use of public transport. The Rivers Sence and Soar run through the area.

**Leicestershire** *Leics.* Population: 609,578.
Midland county of England bounded by Derbyshire, Leicester, Lincolnshire, Northamptonshire, Nottinghamshire, Rutland, Staffordshire and Warwickshire. Chief towns are Loughborough, Hinckley, Wigston, Coalville, Melton Mowbray, Oadby, Market Harborough, Shepshed and Ashby de la Zouch. The landscape is mostly of low, rolling hills. E and W of Leicester are areas of higher ground, notably Charnwood Forest. The W is largely industrial; industries include light engineering, hosiery, and footwear. The E is rural, with large fields and scattered woods, and is noted for field sports and food production. Part of the legacy left by the Roman occupation of Leicestershire are the Great North Road, Watling Street and Fosse Way which dissect the county. River Soar traverses the county from S to N, while River Welland forms part of the boundary with Northamptonshire to the S.
**Districts**: Blaby; Charnwood; Harborough; Hinckley & Bosworth; Melton; North West Leicestershire; Oadby & Wigston.

**Limavady** *Limavady* Population: 32,422.
There are two AONBs in this district, which contains the Sperrin mountains to the south and the wide, fertile valley of the river Roe in the centre. To the north is Lough Foyle and the long, sandy beach of Magilligan Strand. Main towns are Limavady, Dungiven and Ballykelly and a car ferry runs across Lough Foyle from Magilligan Point to the Inishowen Peninsula in the Republic of Ireland. Industries include agriculture, services, small-scale manufacturing, construction and tourism.

**Lincolnshire** *Lincs.* Population: 646,645.
County of E England bounded by Cambridgeshire, Leicestershire, Norfolk, Northamptonshire, North East Lincolnshire, North Lincolnshire, Nottinghamshire, Peterborough, Rutland and the North Sea. Main towns are the cathedral city and county town of Lincoln and the towns of Boston, Grantham, Gainsborough, Spalding, Stamford, Skegness and Louth. Much of the county is flat and includes a large area of The Fens in the S. This reclaimed marshland is richly fertile, producing large crops of peas (for canning), sugar beet, potatoes, corn, and around Spalding, flower bulbs. Two ranges of hills traverse the county N and S: the narrow limestone ridge, a continuation of the Cotswold Hills, running from Grantham to Scunthorpe, and the chalk Wolds, about 12m/20km wide, running N from Spilsby and Horncastle. Apart from agriculture, industries include manufacture of agricultural machinery and tourism, which is centred on historic Lincoln, and the coastal resorts of Skegness and Mablethorpe. The rivers, of which the chief are the Witham and Welland, are largely incorporated into the extensive land-drainage system, and scarcely distinguishable from man-made channels.
**Districts**: Boston; East Lindsey; Lincoln; North Kesteven; South Holland; South Kesteven; West Lindsey.

**Lisburn** *Lisburn* Population: 108,694.
This district borders Belfast in the east and touches Lough Neagh in the west. Lisburn city itself sits in the valley of the River Lagan, with other towns being Dunmurry, Hillsborough, Magheraberry and Derriaghy. The Giants' Ring is a massive 656 feet (200m) diameter earthwork near the village of Drumbo. Industries include textiles (linen) and light engineering.

**Londonderry/Derry** *London.* Population: 105,066.
The city of Londonderry (Derry) is an important seaport and the second city of Northern Ireland, sitting astride the wide estuary of the river Foyle. The city walls, erected in 1619, are complete and some of the finest in Europe. Other towns include New Buildings and Eglinton, with several small villages scattered in the rural areas. In the south, are the forested glens of the Sperrin Mountains. Agriculture is the main industry, along with textiles (linen), distilling and chemicals.

**Luton** *Luton* Population: 184,371.
Unitary authority in SE England surrounding Luton and bounded by Central Bedfordshire and Hertfordshire. Luton is one of the major centres of employment and manufacturing in SE England, with automotive, electrical and retail industries among the most important. The production and export of high fashion and straw hats remains a feature of the local economy. London Luton Airport is situated in the SE of the area, and the River Lea rises nearby.

**Magherafelt** *Magh.* Population: 39,780.
The Sperrin Mountains form the western boundary and the River Bann, the eastern. The main town of Magherafelt is the administrative and marketing centre of the district and is also well known for its arts festival. Other small towns include Maghera and Draperstown. Agriculture is the main industry, along with some manufacturing and construction.

**Medway** *Med.* Population: 249,488.
Unitary authority on SE coast of England S of the River Thames estuary and neighbouring Kent. The chief centres are Gillingham, the naval base of Chatham, Strood and the cathedral city of Rochester. The S part of the area, surrounding the River Medway, is largely urban and industrialised. The marshland to the N includes Kingsnorth Power Station and the Isle of Grain, but is mostly rural, and contains Northward Hill Nature Reserve which is a haven for birds.

**Merseyside** *Mersey.* Population: 1,362,026.
Former metropolitan county of NW England. It neighbours Cheshire West & Chester, Greater Manchester, Halton, Lancashire, Warrington and the sea. It comprises the near-continuous urban complex which includes the city of Liverpool and the towns of St. Helens, Birkenhead, Southport, Bootle, Wallasey, Bebington, Huyton and Crosby. The county straddles the long, wide estuary of the River Mersey, which accounts for the development of the area. During the 18c, growing Imperial trade of goods and slaves, led to the explosion of urban development surrounding the docks at Liverpool, Birkenhead and Bootle. Liverpool went on to become Britain's premier transatlantic port and a significant terminus during the migration flows of the 19c, leading to an ethnically diverse city culture. Over the last century the docks have declined, leaving behind an impressive waterfront and cityscape as testament to a mercantile and maritime heritage. Inland, the urban spread has reached the industrial town of St. Helens which is famed for glass production. To the N are the residential areas of Crosby, Formby and the coastal resort of Southport. The area includes race courses at Aintree and Haydock, and an airport at Speke.
**Districts**: Knowsley; Liverpool; St. Helens; Sefton; Wirral.

**Merthyr Tydfil** *M.Tyd.* Population: 55,981.
Unitary authority in S Wales bounded by Caerphilly, Powys and Rhondda Cynon Taff. Main centres are the town of Merthyr Tydfil and the villages of Treharris, Abercanaid and Troedyrhiw. The area stretches from the Brecon Beacons, along the Taff Valley, to the centre of the former Welsh coal mining district. The local economy has diversified from primary industry, with Merthyr Tydfil being an important centre for public administration, shopping and employment for the region. The River Taff flows through the area.

**Middlesbrough** *Middbro.* Population: 134,855.
Unitary authority in NE England surrounding Middlesbrough and bounded by North Yorkshire, Redcar & Cleveland and Stockton-on-Tees. Middlesbrough is an industrial town, with chemical and petro-chemical industries in evidence. It is also an important sub-regional shopping and entertainment centre between Leeds and Newcastle upon Tyne.

**Midlothian** *Midloth.* Population: 80,941.
Unitary authority in central Scotland neighbouring East Lothian, Edinburgh and Scottish Borders. Main towns are Penicuik, Bonnyrigg, Dalkeith, Gorebridge and Loanhead. The area is mostly rural, including the rolling moorland of the Pentland Hills and Moorfoot Hills in the S. To the N, the urban area is comprised of satellite towns to the SE of Edinburgh. Rivers include Tyne Water and South Esk.

**Milton Keynes** *M.K.* Population: 207,057.
S midland unitary authority of England bounded by Bedford,

Central Bedfordshire, Buckinghamshire and Northamptonshire. The area includes the city of Milton Keynes, Bletchley, Newport Pagnell, Great Linford, Stony Stratford and Wolverton. Over the past 30 years, the area has undergone the fastest rate of growth in the country, attracting numerous industries. The Great Ouse and Ouzel rivers pass through the area.

**Monmouthshire** (Sir Fynwy). *Mon.* Population: 84,885.
Unitary authority in SE Wales bounded by Blaenau Gwent, Newport, Powys, Torfaen, the English areas of Gloucestershire, Herefordshire and the Bristol Channel. The main towns are Abergavenny, Caldicot, Chepstow and Monmouth. Part of the Brecon Beacons are found in NW Monmouthshire, whereas the SW area is mainly flat. Agriculture, mineral extraction and the service sector are important to the local economy. Rivers include the Wye, which forms part of E border, and the Usk, Trothy and Monnow.

**Moray** *Moray* Population: 86,940.
Unitary authority in N Scotland neighboured by Aberdeenshire, Highland and the sea. Main towns are Elgin, Forres, Buckie, Lossiemouth and Keith. The area is mainly mountainous, including part of the Cairngorm Mountains in the S. It is dissected by many deep river valleys, most notably that of the River Spey. Along with the local grain and peat, the abundant waters provide the raw materials for half of Scotland's malt whisky distilleries, leading to the Whisky Trail and much tourism through Speyside.

**Moyle** *Moyle* Population: 15,933.
This is Northern Ireland's smallest district by population but it is famous for the amazing basalt columns of the Giant's Causeway on the north coast, a UNESCO World Heritage Site. The entire Causeway Coast has been designated as an AONB. Ballycastle is the largest town, others being Cushendun, Cushendall and Bushmills, which has the world's oldest licensed distillery. Off the north coast is Rathlin Island where Northern Ireland's largest seabird colony breeds under the management of the RSPB. The main industry is agriculture, with some light industry and tourism.

**Neath Port Talbot** (Castell-nedd Port Talbot). *N.P.T.* Population: 134,468.
Unitary authority in S Wales neighbouring Bridgend, Powys, Rhondda Cynon Taff, Swansea and the sea. The chief centres are Neath, Port Talbot, Pontardawe, Baglan, Glyncorrwg and Briton Ferry. The area is mostly mountainous, divided up by the river valleys of the Tawe, Neath, Afan and Dulais, which all flow out to sea at Swansea Bay. The lower valley of the River Neath is heavily industrialised.

**Newport** (Casnewydd). *Newport* Population: 137,011.
Unitary authority on the S coast of Wales, N of the mouth of the River Severn, and bounded by Caerphilly, Cardiff, Monmouthshire and Torfaen. Main centres are Newport, Liswerry, Malpas and Caerleon. Steel manufacturing and hi-tech industries are important to the local economy. The rivers Ebbw and Usk run through the area.

**Newry & Mourne** *N. & M.* Population: 87,058.
Bordering the Republic of Ireland on its southern edge, the district contains the beautiful Mourne mountains in the east and has two areas designated as AONBs. Newry is the main town and has been an important centre for cross-border trade development. Warrenpoint is a modern port. Other towns include Killkeel, with its important fishing industry, Rostrevor, Bessbrook and Annalong. Besides fishing, industries are mainly agriculture and tourism.

**Newtownabbey** *Newtown.* Population: 79,995.
Bordering the north-western shore of Belfast Lough, this small district is a mix of the urban and rural. It has a high population density compared to the rest of Northern Ireland. The main town is Newtownabbey, others being Ballyclare, which hosts one of the oldest horse fairs in Ireland, Mossley and Mallusk which is a busy commercial centre. There are many small businesses in the area as well as agriculture.

**Norfolk** *Norf.* Population: 796,728.
County of E England bounded by Cambridgeshire, Lincolnshire, Suffolk and the North Sea. Chief centres are the cathedral city and county town of Norwich, Great Yarmouth on the E coast, the expanding port of King's Lynn near the mouth of the Great Ouse and The Wash, Thetford, which is known as the Breckland 'capital', East Dereham and Wymondham. Norfolk is mainly flat or gently undulating, with fenland in the W characterised by large drainage channels emptying into The Wash. In the SW is Breckland, an expanse of heath and conifer forest used for military training; other afforested areas are near King's Lynn and North Walsham. NE of Norwich are The Broads, an area of meres and rivers popular for boating; reeds for thatching are grown here. The N Norfolk coastline is an Area of Outstanding Natural Beauty and Heritage Coast, and includes the popular resorts of Cromer and Sheringham. Otherwise the county is almost entirely agricultural, with farming an important activity; service and manufacturing industries are also significant. Rivers include the Great Ouse, Bure, Nar, Wensum, Wissey, and Yare; the Little Ouse and Waveney both enter the county briefly, but mainly form the boundary with Suffolk.
**Districts**: Breckland; Broadland; Great Yarmouth; King's Lynn & West Norfolk; North Norfolk; Norwich; South Norfolk.

**North Ayrshire** *N.Ayr.* Population: 135,817.
Unitary authority in central Scotland including the islands of Arran, Great Cumbrae and Little Cumbrae. It is bounded by East Ayrshire, East Renfrewshire, Inverclyde, Renfrewshire, South Ayrshire and the sea. The principal towns are Irvine, Kilwinning, Saltcoats, Largs, Ardrossan, Stevenston and Kirbirnie. The area includes mountains and part of Clyde Muirshiel Regional Park in the N, and the lower lands of Cunninghame in the S. There is a maritime heritage to the area; ferry routes operate from Largs and Ardrossan. Rivers include the Garnock, Dusk Water and Noddsdale Water.

**North Down** *N.Down* Population: 76,323.
On the southern shore of Belfast Lough, this is another high population density district. The main town of Bangor is an important maritime resort with a large, modern marina and shopping centre. Other towns are Helen's Bay and Holywood. Main industries include light engineering, food processing, retail and tourism.

**North East Lincolnshire** *N.E.Lincs.* Population: 157,979.
Unitary authority in NE England, S of the mouth of the River Humber and bounded by Lincolnshire, North Lincolnshire and the North Sea. Chief towns are Grimsby, Cleethorpes and Immingham. Grimsby and Cleethorpes together are the shopping and commercial centres of the area. Fishing, food, tourism, chemical and port industries are all important to the local economy. The main rivers are the Humber and Freshney.

**North Lanarkshire** *N.Lan.* Population: 321,067.
Unitary authority in central Scotland neighbouring East Dunbartonshire, Falkirk, Glasgow, South Lanarkshire, Stirling and West Lothian. The chief centres are Cumbernauld, Coatbridge, Airdrie, Motherwell, Wishaw and Bellshill. North Lanarkshsire contains a mixture of urban and rural areas, and formerly depended heavily upon the coal, engineering and steel industries. Regeneration and diversification have occurred in recent years.

**North Lincolnshire** *N.Lincs.* Population: 152,849.
Unitary authority in NE England neighbouring East Riding of Yorkshire, Leicestershire, Norfolk, North East Lincolnshire, Nottinghamshire, Peterborough, Rutland, South Yorkshire and the River Humber. The main centres are Scunthorpe, Bottesford, Barton-upon-Humber and Brigg. The area is mainly rural, but does include oil refineries, steel and manufacturing industries; the River Humber provides pool and wharf facilities. Rivers include the Humber, Trent and the Old Ancholme.

**North Somerset** *N.Som.* Population: 188,564.
Unitary authority in W England, S of the mouth of the River Severn, and neighbouring Bath & North East Somerset, Bristol, Somerset and the Bristol Channel. Chief towns are Weston-super-Mare, Clevedon, Nailsea and Portishead. The area is largely rural with tourism, centred on the coastal resort of Weston-super-Mare, being a major industry. Bristol International Airport is located in the E of the area.

**North Yorkshire** *N.Yorks.* Population: 569,660.
Large county of N England bounded by Cumbria, Darlington,

Durham, East Riding of Yorkshire, Lancashire, Middlesbrough, Redcar & Cleveland, South Yorkshire, Stockton-on-Tees, West Yorkshire, York and the North Sea. Main centres are Harrogate, Scarborough, Hetton, Selby, the cathedral city of Ripon, the county town of Northallerton, Whitby, Skipton and Knaresborough. Apart from the wide plain around York, through which flow River Ouse and its tributaries, and the smaller Vale of Pickering, watered by the Derwent and its tributary the Rye, the county is dominated by two ranges of hills; The Pennines in the W and the Cleveland Hills in the NE. The plains are pastoral and agricultural, while the hills provide rough sheep-grazing. The county includes the popular resorts of Scarborough and Whitby, and the majority of the North York Moors and Yorkshire Dales National Parks which promote tourism. Other economic activities include light engineering, service and hi-tech industries. Principal rivers are the Ouse, fed by the Derwent, Swale, Ure, Nidd and Wharfe, and draining into the Humber; the Esk, flowing into the North Sea at Whitby; and in the W, the Ribble, passing out into Lancashire and the Irish Sea.
**Districts**: Craven; Hambleton; Harrogate; Richmondshire; Ryedale; Scarborough; Selby.

**Northamptonshire** *Northants*. Population: 629,676.
Midland county of England bounded by Bedford, Buckinghamshire, Cambridgeshire, Leicestershire, Lincolnshire, Milton Keynes, Oxfordshire, Peterborough, Rutland and Warwickshire. Chief towns are Northampton, Corby, Kettering, Wellingborough, Rushden and Daventry. The county consists largely of undulating agricultural country rising locally to low hills, especially along the W border. Large fields and scattered woods provide terrain for field sports. Northamptonshire still retains its rural and agricultural charm, despite undergoing rapid population growth recently. There are many villages of architectural, scenic and historic interest. Industrial development is modest, concentrating on the traditional footwear manufacture. Corby is undergoing regeneration following the decline of its steel industry. Tourism is set to increase due to the county's natural Middle England ambience, and the seasonal opening of the Althorp Estate, the family home and resting place of Diana, Princess of Wales. The principal rivers are the Nene and Welland.
**Districts**: Corby; Daventry; East Northamptonshire; Kettering; Northampton; South Northamptonshire; Wellingborough.

**Northumberland** *Northumb*. Population: 307,190.
Northernmost unitary authority of England bounded by Cumbria, Durham and Tyne & Wear, the Scottish authority of Scottish Borders and the North Sea. The principal towns are Blyth, Ashington, Cramlington, Bedlington, Morpeth, Berwick-upon-Tweed, Prudhoe and Hexham. There is some industry in the SE coastal area, otherwise it is almost entirely rural, the greater part being high moorland, culminating in the Cheviot Hills along the Scottish border. The most spectacular stretches of Hadrian's Wall traverse the area to the N of Haltwhistle and Hexham. There is extensive afforestation, including Kielder Forest Park and part of the Northumberland National Park in the NW; parts of these forests are used for military training. The large reservoir, Kielder Water, also occurs in the NW of the area. Rivers include the Aln, Blyth, Breamish, Coquet, East and West Allen, North and South Tyne, Till, and Wansbeck. The Tweed forms part of the Scottish border and flows out to sea at Berwick-upon-Tweed.

**Nottingham** *Nott*. Population: 266,988.
Unitary authority in central England surrounding the city of Nottingham and bounded by Nottinghamshire. The city of Nottingham has a long history, having been granted many Royal Charters; Nottingham Castle and Wollaton Hall are among its many historical buildings. It is also an industrial and engineering centre, and a university city. Its main industries include the manufacture of chemicals, tobacco, cycles, lace and hosiery. The River Trent flows through the city.

**Nottinghamshire** *Notts*. Population: 748,510.
Midland county of England bounded by Derbyshire, Leicestershire, Lincolnshire, North Lincolnshire, Nottingham and South Yorkshire. Principal towns are Mansfield, Carlton, Sutton in Ashfield, Arnold, Worksop, Newark-on-Trent, West Bridgford, Beeston, Stapleford, Hucknall and Kirkby in Ashfield. Much of the county is rural, with extensive woodlands in the central area of The Dukeries, part of the larger Sherwood Forest. Cattle-grazing is the chief farming activity. Around the large towns there is much industry, including iron and steel, engineering, knitwear, pharmaceuticals, and coal-mining. The county has associations with Robin Hood, at Sherwood Forest, and D.H. Lawrence, at Eastwood. The most important river is the Trent.
**Districts**: Ashfield; Bassetlaw; Broxtowe; Gedling; Mansfield; Newark & Sherwood; Rushcliffe.

**Omagh** *Omagh*. Population: 47,952.
One of the largest districts by area of Northern Ireland, the borders are mainly hills, with the town of Omagh in a central valley, at the confluence of several rivers where almost one third of the total population live. The area is primarily rural, with small towns and villages scattered throughout the landscape. These include Fintona, Dromore and Carrickmore. Agriculture is the main industry.

**Orkney** *Ork*. Population: 19,245.
Group of some fifteen main islands and numerous smaller islands, islets and rocks. Designated an Islands Area for administrative purposes, and lying N of the NE end of the Scottish mainland across the Pentland Firth. Kirkwall is the capital, situated on the island Mainland, 24m/38km N of Duncansby Head. Stromness is the only other town. About twenty of the islands are inhabited. In general the islands are low-lying but have steep, high cliffs on W side. The climate is generally mild for the latitude but storms are frequent. Fishing and farming (mainly cattle-rearing) are the chief industries. The oil industry is also represented, with an oil terminal on the island of Flotta, and oil service bases at Car Ness and Stromness, Mainland and at Lyness, Hoy. Lesser industries include whisky distilling, knitwear and tourism. The islands are noted for their unique prehistoric and archaeological remains. The main airport is at Grimsetter, near Kirkwall, with most of the populated islands being served by airstrips. Ferries also operate from the Scottish mainland, and between islands in the group.

**Oxfordshire** *Oxon*. Population: 605,488.
S midland county of England bounded by Buckinghamshire, Gloucestershire, Northamptonshire, Reading, Swindon, Warwickshire, West Berkshire, Wiltshire and Wokingham. Chief centres are the county town, cathedral and university city of Oxford and towns of Banbury, Abingdon, Bicester, Witney, Didcot, Thame and Henley-on-Thames. Burford and Chipping Norton are small Cotswold towns in the W and NW respectively. The landscape is predominantly flat or gently undulating, forming part of the Thames Valley. High ground occurs where the Chiltern Hills enter the county in the SE and the Cotswold Hills in the NW. The county is largely agricultural, with industries centred on the towns. Scientific, medical and research establishments are attracted by the proximity of Oxford's universities. Printing and publishing industries have their greatest concentration outside London. The motor industry is well represented with car manufacture at Cowley, Oxford, and the county has the world's largest concentration of performance car development and manufacturing. Tourism, attracted to stately homes, notably Blenheim Palace, and Oxford city centre, is also important. Chief rivers are the Thames (or Isis), Cherwell, Ock, Thame, and Windrush.
**Districts**: Cherwell; Oxford; South Oxfordshire; Vale of White Horse; West Oxfordshire.

**Pembrokeshire** (Sir Benfro). *Pembs*. Population: 114,131.
Unitary authority in the SW corner of Wales neighbouring Carmarthenshire, Ceredigion and the sea. The chief centres are Haverfordwest, Pembroke Dock, Pembroke, Tenby, Saundersfoot, Neyland, Fishguard and the ancient cathedral city of St. David's. Key industries are tourism, agriculture and oil refining. The deep estuarial waters of Milford Haven provide a berth for oil tankers. A large part of Pembrokeshire's coastline forms Britain's only coastal National Park. Ferries sail from Fishguard and Pembroke Dock to Rosslare in the Republic of Ireland.

**Perth & Kinross** *P. & K*. Population: 134,949.
Unitary authority in Scotland bounded by Aberdeenshire, Angus, Argyll & Bute, Clackmannanshire, Fife, Highland and Stirling. Chief centres are the city of Perth, Blairgowrie, Crieff, Kinross, Auchterader and Pitlochry. The area is mountainous, containing large areas of remote open moorland, especially in the N and W; the vast upland expanses of Breadalbane, Rannoch and Atholl,

form the S edge of the Grampian Mountains. The lower land of the S and E is more heavily populated and is dominated by the ancient city of Perth. The area is rich in history as it links the Highlands to the N with the central belt and lowlands to the S via important mountain passes, most notably the Pass of Dromochter. The area has many castles, and Scottish Kings were traditionally enthroned at Scone Abbey, to the N of Perth. There are many lochs, including Loch Rannoch and Loch Tay. Main industries are tourism and whisky production. The world famous Gleneagles golf course is in the S of the area. Rivers include the Tay, Almond and Earn.

**Peterborough** *Peter.* Population: 156,061.
Unitary authority in E England neighbouring Cambridgeshire, Lincolnshire, Northamptonshire and Rutland. The area includes the city of Peterborough, which lies at the heart of an important agricultural area. Developing as a railway hub, it has become a major industrial, distribution and shopping centre. The River Nene passes through Peterborough.

**Plymouth** *Plym.* Population: 240,720.
Unitary authority on the SW coast of England surrounding the city of Plymouth and neighbouring Cornwall and Devon. Plymouth stands at the mouth of the River Tamar and is the largest city on the S coast of England. It has strong mercantile and naval traditions; it is closely linked with Sir Francis Drake, and has maintained a Royal Naval Dockyard for 300 years. Plymouth is a regional shopping centre and a popular resort.

**Poole** *Poole* Population: 138,288.
Unitary authority on S coast of England surrounding Poole and bordered by Bournemouth and Dorset. Poole Harbour is the second largest natural harbour in the world, which enabled Poole to prosper through trading, especially with Newfoundland. Poole has now attracted a variety of industries including boat-building, fishing, pottery, engineering and electronics. Ferries run to the Channel Islands and France.

**Portsmouth** *Ports.* Population: 186,701.
Unitary authority on the S coast of England surrounding the city of Portsmouth and bordered by Hampshire. Portsmouth developed as a strategic port around Portsmouth Harbour, and it is still the home of the Royal Navy. It has become a culturally diverse centre, attracting a wide range of industries which include leisure, tourism, financial services, distribution, manufacturing and hi-tech industries.

**Powys** *Powys* Population: 126,354.
Large unitary authority in central Wales bordering Blaenau Gwent, Caerphilly, Carmarthenshire, Ceredigion, Denbighshire, Gwynedd, Merthyr Tydfil, Monmouthshire, Neath Port Talbot, Rhondda Cynon Taff, Wrexham and the English areas of Herefordshire and Shropshire. Main centres are Newtown, Gurnos, Brecon, Welshpool, Ystradgynlais, Llanllwchaiarn, Llandrindod Wells, Knighton, Llanidloes, Builth Wells and Machynlleth. Powys is almost entirely rural, with mountainous terrain; most of the Brecon Beacons National Park falls within the S part of the area, while the Cambrian Mountains are in the W. There is considerable afforestation, and a number of large reservoirs, including Lake Vyrnwy. To the N of Brecon, on Mynydd Eppynt, is an extensive military training area. Main economic activities are agriculture, which is predominantly based around hill farming. Tourism is significant, owing to the natural beauty of the area, and innovative attractions such as the Centre for Alternative Technology. Industrial development is gradually increasing. Among the many rivers, the largest are the Severn, Usk, and Wye.

**Reading** *Read.* Population: 143,096.
Unitary authority in S England to W of Greater London, surrounding Reading and bordered by Oxfordshire, West Berkshire, Windsor & Maidenhead and Wokingham. Reading developed as a crossing point of the River Thames and River Kennet. Traditional industries include brewing and food production, notably biscuits. These are accompanied by an increasing sector of hi-tech and computer-based companies, attracted by Reading's location in the M4 corridor. Reading has also established itself as a major entertainments centre.

**Redcar & Cleveland** *R. & C.* Population: 139,132.
Unitary authority on the NE coast of England neighbouring Hartlepool, Middlesbrough and North Yorkshire. The main centres are Redcar, South Bank, Eston, Guisborough, Marske-by-the-Sea, Saltburn-by-the-Sea, Loftus and Skelton. The area is one of great contrasts. It combines rural villages, market towns and coastal resorts, along with heavily populated urban areas and industrialised port facilities. Industries include steel-making, due to the local ironstone, and chemicals, based around the River Tees to the NW of the area. The coastal towns attract some tourism. The River Tees forms part of the border to the W.

**Renfrewshire** *Renf.* Population: 172,867.
Unitary authority in central Scotland bordering East Renfrewshire, Glasgow, Inverclyde, North Ayrshire, West Dunbartonshire and the Firth of Clyde. Main centres are Paisley, Renfrew, Johnstone, Erskine and Linwood. The area emerges W from the Greater Glasgow periphery into a contrasting countryside of highlands, lochs and glens. Industry is centred on the urban area and includes electronics, engineering, food and drink production and service sectors; in rural areas to the W, agriculture is still important. The W part of the area includes some of Clyde Muirshiels Regional Park; Glasgow Airport is in the E.

**Rhondda Cynon Taff** (Rhondda Cynon Taf). *R.C.T.* Population: 231,946.
Unitary authority in S Wales bounded by Bridgend, Caerphilly, Cardiff, Merthyr Tydfil, Neath Port Talbot, Powys and Vale of Glamorgan. The principal towns are Treorchy, Aberdare, Pontypridd, Ferndale and Mountain Ash. Rhondda Cynon Taff is a mountainous area, dissected by deep narrow valleys, with urbanisation typified by ribbon development. The area was the former heart of the Welsh coal mining industry, and has experienced a sharp economic decline as pits closed. Diversification into light engineering and service sectors are gradually improving the industrial base. Main rivers are the Rhondda and Cynon.

**Rutland** *Rut.* Population: 34,563.
Unitary authority in E England neighbouring Leicestershire, Lincolnshire, Northamptonshire and Peterborough. The main town is Oakham. Agriculture is the main industry; other important industries are engineering, cement-making, plastics, clothing and tourism. The area includes the large reservoir, Rutland Water, which is an important feature for leisure, tourism and wildlife.

**Scottish Borders** *Sc.Bord.* Population: 106,764.
Administrative region of SE Scotland bordering Dumfries & Galloway, East Lothian, Midlothian, South Lanarkshire, West Lothian, the English counties of Cumbria and Northumberland and the North Sea. It comprises the former counties of Berwick, Peebles, Roxburgh and Selkirk. Main towns are Hawick, Galashiels, Peebles, Kelso, Selkirk and Jedburgh. It extends from the Tweedsmuir Hills in the W to the North Sea on either side of St. Abb's Head in the E, and from the Pentland, Moorfoot and Lammermuir Hills in the N to the Cheviot Hills and the English border in the S. The fertile area of rich farmland between the hills to N and S is known as The Merse. The area around Peebles and Galashiels is noted for woollen manufacture. Elsewhere, the electronics industry is of growing importance. The River Tweed rises in the extreme W and flows between Kelso and Coldstream, finally passing into England, 4m/6km W of Berwick-upon-Tweed.

**Shetland** *Shet.* Population: 21,988.
Group of over 100 islands, lying beyond Orkney to the NE of the Scottish mainland; Sumburgh Head being about 100m/160km from Duncansby Head. Designated an Islands Area for administrative purposes, the chief islands are Mainland, on which the capital and chief port of Lerwick is situated, Unst and Yell. Some twenty of the islands are inhabited. The islands are mainly low-lying, the highest point being Ronas Hill, on Mainland. The oil industry has made an impact on Shetland, with oil service bases at Lerwick and Sandwick, and a large terminal at Sullom Voe. Other industries include cattle and sheep-rearing, knitwear and fishing. The climate is mild, considering the latitude, but severe storms are frequent. The islands are famous for the small Shetland breed of pony, which is renowned for its strength and hardiness. There is an airport at Sumburgh, on S part of Mainland.

**Shropshire** *Shrop.* Population: 283,173.
W midland unitary authority of England bounded by Cheshire East, Cheshire West & Chester, Herefordshire, Staffordshire, Telford & Wrekin, Worcestershire and the Welsh authorities of Powys and Wrexham. Main towns are Shrewsbury, Oswestry, Bridgnorth, Market Drayton, Ludlow and Whitchurch. The S and W borders are hilly, with large areas of open moorland, including The Long Mynd and Wenlock Edge, which provide good sheep-grazing. Elsewhere the county undulates towards the Severn Valley, which provides fertile agricultural land served by prosperous market towns. Agricultural output includes dairy, poultry and pig farming, along with corn crops. As the former heart of the Marches of Wales, Shropshire contains the remains of numerous border defences. There are also the remains of several monasteries, for instance, at Much Wenlock and Buildwas. The most important river is the Severn, which flows across the county from W to SE; others include the Clun, Corve, Perry, Rea Brook, and Teme.

**Slough** *Slo.* Population: 119,067.
Unitary authority in SE England to the W of London, surrounding Slough and bordering Buckinghamshire, Greater London, Surrey and Windsor & Maidenhead. Slough has grown significantly over the past 30 years, and is a major regional shopping centre. Industry is centred on the large Slough Trading Estate, which was planned after World War I. Numerous sectors are represented in Slough, among them is confectionery.

**Somerset** *Som.* Population: 498,093.
County in SW England bounded by Bath & North East Somerset, Devon, Dorset, North Somerset, Wiltshire and the Bristol Channel. The chief centres are the county town of Taunton, Yeovil, Bridgwater, Frome, Chard, Street, Burnham-on-Sea, Highbridge, the small cathedral city of Wells, Wellington and Minehead. Somerset consists of several hill ranges, including the Mendip, Polden, Quantock, Brendon Hills, along with most of Exmoor. These uplands are separated by valleys, or, on either side of the River Parrett, by the extensive marshy flats of Sedgemoor. Economic activity is mainly based on agriculture in the fertile vales, with manufacturing, distribution and service industries centred on the urban areas. Tourism is important with attractions including Exmoor National Park, a holiday complex at Minehead and the county's natural rural charm. Somerset also holds one of Europe's largest music festivals at Glastonbury. The chief rivers are Axe, Brue, Parrett, and Tone, draining into the Bristol Channel; and Barle and Exe, rising on Exmoor and flowing into Devon and the English Channel.
**Districts**: Mendip; Sedgemoor; South Somerset; Taunton Deane; West Somerset.

**South Ayrshire** *S.Ayr.* Population: 112,097.
Unitary authority in SW Scotland bounded by Dumfries & Galloway, East Ayrshire, North Ayrshire and the sea. The chief towns are Ayr, Troon, Prestwick, Girvan and Maybole. The area consists of a long coastline, with lowlands surrounding Ayr Bay and higher ground to the S. Agriculture is a major economic activity on the uplands. To the N, aerospace and hi-tech industries are located near Prestwick International Airport and Ayr, the main retail centre. Notable sporting venues include a race course at Ayr and open championship golf courses at Troon and Turnberry. Tourism is a major feature of the local economy. The area was the birthplace of Robert the Bruce and Robert Burns; it contains Scotland's first country park at Culzean Castle; and it has a holiday camp on the coast near Ayr. Rivers include the Ayr, Water of Girvan and Stinchar.

**South Gloucestershire** *S.Glos.* Population: 245,641.
Unitary authority in SW England neighbouring Bath & North East Somerset, Bristol, Gloucestershire and Wiltshire. The chief centres are Kingswood, Chipping Sodbury, Mangotsfield, Frampton Cotterell, Yate, Thornbury, Patchway and Filton. The S part of the area lies on the N and E fringes of Bristol. The Cotswold hills are in the E, and the Severn Vale in the W. Main industries are in the S, and include aerospace engineering; the N is mainly agricultural. South Gloucestershire includes the English side of both Severn road bridges. Badminton Park in the E of the area, is the location for the Badminton Horse Trials. The River Severn borders the area to the NW.

**South Lanarkshire** *S.Lan.* Population: 302,216.
Unitary authority in central Scotland bordering Dumfries & Galloway, East Ayrshire, East Renfrewshire, Glasgow, North Lanarkshire, Scottish Borders and West Lothian. The main towns are East Kilbride, Hamilton, Blantyre, Larkhall, Carluke, Lanark and Bothwell. Urban development is mainly in the N, merging with the SE periphery of Greater Glasgow. The S part is mostly farmland and not highly populated. Tourism is mainly centred on the picturesque valley of the upper Clyde; there is a race course at Hamilton. The area has associations with the industrial philanthropist, Robert Owen, who built a model village at New Lanark. Rivers include the Clyde, Avon and Dippool Water.

**South Yorkshire** *S.Yorks.* Population: 1,266,338.
Former metropolitan county of N England bordered by Derbyshire, East Riding of Yorkshire, North Lincolnshire, North Yorkshire, Nottinghamshire and West Yorkshire. It comprises the industrial and urban area around the city of Sheffield and the towns of Rotherham, Barnsley and Doncaster. Located at the heart of a major coalfield, South Yorkshire prospered through the development of heavy industry. Barnsley and Rotherham were coal mining towns, with steel and fine cutlery centred on Sheffield. The decline of these industries has led to the area redefining itself. Sheffield has become a centre of learning, tourism and conferences, aided by its environmental improvements. Barnsley, Rotherham and Doncaster have increased their industrial base, especially via light industries. Leisure and recreation are an important feature of the area, with venues including Barnsley's Metrodome, Doncaster's race course and Dome, and Sheffield's Arena and Don Valley Stadium. Retail has increased with city and town centre redevelopment, and the Meadowhall complex. The surrounding countryside includes country parks at Rother Valley and Thrybergh, with part of the Peak District National Park W and NW of Sheffield. The chief river is the Don.
**Districts**: Barnsley; Doncaster; Rotherham; Sheffield.

**Southampton** *S'ham.* Population: 217,445.
Unitary authority on the S coast of England surrounding the city of Southampton, and bordered by Hampshire. Southampton owes much to the deep waters of Southampton Water, which have enabled the development of Europe's busiest cruise port. Water and the waterfront remain very important to the local economy, with marine technology, oceanography, boat shows and yacht races all prominent. The city is also a leading media, recreational, entertainment and retail centre. The chief river is the Itchen.

**Southend** *S'end* Population: 160,257.
Unitary authority in SE England, N of the mouth of the River Thames, surrounding Southend-on-Sea and bordering Essex. Southend is a commerical, residential, shopping and holiday centre, with tourism among its main industries. It includes a 7m shoreline from Leigh-on-Sea to Shoeburyness, a famous pier and a sea life centre.

**Staffordshire** *Staffs.* Population: 806,744.
Midland county of England bounded by Cheshire East, Derbyshire, Leicestershire, Shropshire, Stoke-on-Trent, Telford & Wrekin, Warwickshire, West Midlands and Worcestershire. Chief centres are Newcastle-under-Lyme, Tamworth, the county town of Stafford, Burton upon Trent, Cannock, Burntwood, the cathedral city of Lichfield, Kidsgrove, Rugeley and Leek. The urban development occurs around the West Midlands conurbation in the S, where main industries include engineering, iron and steel, rubber goods and leather production, while to the N, there is an urban concentration around Stoke-on-Trent. Burton upon Trent is noted for brewing. The ancient hunting forest and former mining district of Cannock Chase is in the centre of the county and contains preserved tracts of moorland. In the NE lies part of the Peak District National Park. The rest of the county is predominantly agricultural, with milk, wheat and sugar beet produced. To the E of Leek, moorland broken up by limestone walls extends across the Manifold valley to the Derbyshire border. In additon to the Trent, which dominates much of the county, rivers include the Blithe, Manifold, Sow and Tame. River Dove forms the boundary with Derbyshire.
**Districts**: Cannock Chase; East Staffordshire; Lichfield; Newcastle-under-Lyme; South Staffordshire; Stafford; Staffordshire Moorlands; Tamworth.

**Stirling** *Stir.* Population: 86,212.
Unitary authority in central Scotland neighbouring Argyll & Bute, Clackmannanshire, East Dunbartonshire, Falkirk, North Lanarkshire, Perth & Kinross and West Dunbartonshire. The chief centres are Stirling, the ancient cathedral city of Dunblane, Bannockburn, Bridge of Allan and Callander. The fertile agricultural lands of the Forth valley are in the centre of the area, bounded by mountains: The Trossachs and the mountain peaks of Ben Lomond, Ben More and Ben Lui in the N, while in the S are the Campsie Fells. Tourism is an important industry with Stirling including many sites of historical significance to Scotland, particularly during the struggle to retain independence. There are associations with Rob Roy, and the battle site of Bannockburn. Other features include The Trossachs, part of the Loch Lomond Regional Park and the Queen Elizabeth Forest Park. There are several lochs, including Loch Lomond, which forms part of the W border, and Loch Katrine. Scotland's only lake named as such, Lake of Menteith, is also in Stirling. The main river is the Forth.

**Stockton-on-Tees** *Stock.* Population: 178,408.
Unitary authority in NE England neighbouring Darlington, Durham, Hartlepool, Middlesbrough, North Yorkshire and Redcar & Cleveland. The main centres are Stockton-on-Tees, Billingham, Thornaby-on-Tees, Eaglescliffe, Egglescliffe and Yarm. The area has a diverse mix of picturesque villages, large-scale urbanisation and heavy industry. The area has recently undergone major renewal and regeneration, with industries now including electronics, food technology and chemical production. Stockton is the main shopping centre for the area, and includes the Teesside Retail Park. The main river is the Tees, which is controlled by the Tees Barrage. This has created Britain's largest purpose-built whitewater canoeing course.

**Stoke-on-Trent** *Stoke* Population: 240,636.
Unitary authority in England surrounding the city of Stoke-on-Trent and neighbouring Staffordshire. The city has six town centres: Burslem, Fenton, Hanley, Longton, Stoke-upon-Trent and Tunstall. Hanley is where most current city centre activities are located. The area forms The Potteries, and is the largest claywear producer in the world, although now it is largely a finishing centre for imported pottery. There are a wide variety of other industries, including steel, engineering, paper, glass and furniture. Stoke-on-Trent is a centre of employment, leisure and shopping for the surrounding areas. It is noted for its environmental approach, particularly with land reclamation which accounts for around 10 per cent of the city area; sites include Festival Park, Central Forest Park and Westport Lake. The River Trent flows through the area.

**Strabane** *Strabane* Population: 38,248.
To the east lie the Sperrin Mountains (an AONB) with the Republic of Ireland border and the River Mourne to the west. The main town of the district is Strabane, an historic market town. Other towns include Castlederg in the Derg valley, Newtonstewart, with Baronscourt Forest nearby, Sion Mills, with its model linen village, Plumbridge and Mount Hamilton. Main industries are agriculture, manufacturing and tourism.

**Suffolk** *Suff.* Population: 668,553.
Easternmost county of England bounded by Cambridgeshire, Essex, Norfolk and the North Sea. Main towns are the county town of Ipswich, Lowestoft, Bury St. Edmunds, Felixstowe, Sudbury, Haverhill, Newmarket, Stowmarket and Woodbridge. The county is low-lying and gently undulating. It is almost entirely agricultural, with cereal crops and oil seed rape in abundance. The low coastline, behind which are areas of heath and marsh, afforested in places, is subject to much erosion; it is deeply indented with long river estuaries which provide good sailing. The NW corner of the county forms part of Breckland. The central region includes many notable historic Wool Towns, for instance, Lavenham. Apart from agriculture, industries include electronics, telecommunications, printing and port facilities. Lowestoft is a prominent fishing port and Felixstowe is a container port of growing importance. River Stour forms the S boundary with Essex, and the Little Ouse and Waveney form most of the N boundary with Norfolk. The many other small rivers include the Alde with its estuary the Ore, Deben, and Gipping with its estuary the Orwell, in the E and Lark in the W.
**Districts**: Babergh; Forest Heath; Ipswich; Mid Suffolk; St. Edmundsbury; Suffolk Coastal; Waveney.

**Surrey** *Surr.* Population: 1,059,015.
County of SE England bounded by Bracknell Forest, East Sussex, Greater London, Hampshire, Kent, Slough, West Sussex and Windsor & Maidenhead. The principal towns are Woking, the cathedral and university town of Guildford, Staines, Leatherhead, Farnham, Epsom, Ewell, Sunbury, Walton-on-Thames, Weybridge, Egham, Redhill, Reigate, Esher, Camberley, Frimley and Godalming. The chalk ridge of the North Downs, gently sloping on the N side but forming a steep escarpment on the S, traverses the county from E to W. Extensive sandy heaths in the W are much used for military training. The county is heavily wooded, and contains many traces of the former iron industry in the predominantly rural S. Much of the urbanised E and N areas include commuter or dormitory towns which form the residential outskirts of the Greater London conurbation. Industries include the agricultural activites of dairy farming and horticulture. Tourism and recreation are also important, with Surrey including numerous stately homes, Wentworth golf course, four race courses, and a theme park at Thorpe Park. The chief river is the Thames, into which flow the Wey and the Mole.
**Districts**: Elmbridge; Epsom & Ewell; Guildford; Mole Valley; Reigate & Banstead; Runnymede; Spelthorne; Surrey Heath; Tandridge; Waverley; Woking.

**Swansea** (Abertawe). *Swan.* Population: 223,301.
Unitary authority in S Wales bordering Carmarthenshire, Neath Port Talbot and the sea. Main centres are the city of Swansea, Gorseinon, The Mumbles, Sketty, Cockett and Clydach. The area includes mountains in the N, the urban centre surrounding Swansea, and the Gower peninsula in the S. Swansea originally developed as a port serving the W coalfield of S Wales. The area gained an international reputation for tin-plating and copper and nickel production. Swansea is now a regional shopping and commercial centre, including a university and marina development. The Gower peninsula attracts many tourists with its fine beaches and cliff scenery; hang-gliding is popular at Rhossili Down, and there are associations with Dylan Thomas. The Mumbles is a popular resort, formerly connected to Swansea via a tramway. The chief river is the Tawe.

**Swindon** *Swin.* Population: 180,051.
Unitary authority in SW England neighbouring Gloucestershire, Oxfordshire and Wiltshire. Main centres are Swindon, Stratton St. Margaret, Highworth and Wroughton. The area is located between the Cotswold Hills and Wiltshire Downs, on the fringes of the Thames Valley. Originally a railway town, Swindon has experienced rapid recent growth and is now a centre for car manufacture and central commercial operations. The town is a regional shopping centre with a redeveloped town centre and the Designer Outlet Village. The River Thames borders the area to the N and the River Cole to the E.

**Telford & Wrekin** *Tel. & W.* Population: 158,325.
Unitary authority in W England bordered by Shropshire and Staffordshire. Main centres are Telford, Wellington, Madeley, Donnington, Oakengates, Hadley and Newport. The area was the cradle of the Industrial Revolution, with notable firsts including Darby's discovery of the iron smelting process at Coalbrookdale, the casting and construction of the first cold blast iron bridge at Ironbridge, and the construction of the first iron ship. The new town of Telford, named after the famous engineer, surveyor and road builder, Thomas Telford, is the major commercial centre. The River Severn runs S through the area.

**Thurrock** *Thur.* Population: 143,128.
Unitary authority in SE England, N of the mouth of the River Thames. It is bounded by Essex and Greater London. The main centres are Grays, South Ockendon, Stanford-le-Hope, Corringham and Tilbury. The area is a mix of old and modern, rural and urban. In the N there are historic villages set in agricultural land, while in the S, there are the modern urban developments, and industrial activities surrounding oil refining and the container port of Tilbury. Grays is the commercial centre of Thurrock, with the major retail centre being Thurrock Lakeside. The area includes the N stretch of the Dartford Tunnel and Queen Elizabeth II Bridge, both of which cross the River Thames.

**Torbay** *Torbay* Population: 129,706.
Unitary authority located on the SW coast of England

neighbouring Devon. The major towns are Torquay, Paignton and Brixham. The area, situated on Tor Bay, is among Britain's main holiday resorts, and is widely regarded as the English Riviera. Tourism is the main industry, with Torbay receiving over 1.5 million visitors per year. Excellent leisure, recreation and conference facilities are added attractions.

**Torfaen** (Tor-faen). *Torfaen* Population: 90,949.
Unitary authority in S Wales bounded by Blaenau Gwent, Caerphilly, Monmouthshire and Newport. The principal towns are Cwmbran, Pontypool and Blaenavon. Torfaen contains rugged mountains with a 12-mile-long valley running N to S from Blaenavon to Cwmbran. The area is a manufacturing centre which includes electronics, engineering and automotive companies. The industrial past of the area has led to the growth of tourist attractions, with notable sites including The Valley Inheritance at Pontypool, and Big Pit National Mining Museum of Wales and 19c ironworks at Blaenavon. The river Afon Llwyd runs through the area.

**Tyne & Wear** *T. & W.* Population: 1,075,938.
Maritime county of NE England bordered by Durham and Northumberland. It comprises the urban complex around the cities of Newcastle upon Tyne and Sunderland, South Shields, Gateshead, Washington and Wallsend. Named after its two important rivers, the area developed largely through the coal mining and ship-building industries. As these industries declined, the area has undergone urban and industrial regeneration. Newcastle upon Tyne is now a commercial, university and cultural centre, with a historic heart including a cathedral, 12c castle and the Tyne Bridge; the historic Quayside has recently been developed. Sunderland gained city status in 1992, and is now a centre for car manufacture, with recreational facilities including the Crowtree Leisure Complex and the National Glass Centre. Elsewhere, Wallsend has hi-tech and off-shore industries; South Tyneside has electronics industries, and tourism, via its Catherine Cookson links. Gateshead has an international athletics stadium, Europe's largest undercover shopping centre, the Metrocentre, and the modern symbol of renewal, the Angel of the North. The area is served by the Port of Tyne and Newcastle International Airport.
**Districts**: Gateshead; Newcastle upon Tyne; North Tyneside; South Tyneside; Sunderland.

**Vale of Glamorgan** (Bro Morgannwg). *V. of Glam.* Population: 119,292.
Unitary authority on the S coast of Wales neighbouring Bridgend, Cardiff and Rhondda Cynon Taff. The chief towns are Barry, Penarth and Llantwit Major. Vale of Glamorgan is a lowland area between Cardiff and Bridgend, with some agricultural activities, and tourism at the resorts of Barry and Penarth. Cardiff International Airport is situated in the SE near Rhoose. Main river is the Ely, which passes through the area.

**Warrington** *Warr.* Population: 191,080.
Unitary authority in NW England surrounding Warrington and bounded by Cheshire East, Cheshire West & Chester, Greater Manchester, Halton and Merseyside. The area developed as a main crossing point of the River Mersey and latterly the Manchester Ship Canal. During industrialisation it became an important strategic trading centre for the NW region. In 1968, Warrington was granted New Town status, leading to traditional industries such as chemicals, brewing and food processing being joined by hi-tech industries and research and development facilities. Warrington retains its importance as a regional shopping, leisure and commercial centre. The River Mersey flows through the area.

**Warwickshire** *Warks.* Population: 505,860.
Midland county of England bounded by Gloucestershire, Leicestershire, Northamptonshire, Oxfordshire, Staffordshire, West Midlands and Worcestershire. Chief towns are Nuneaton, Rugby, Royal Leamington Spa, Bedworth, the county town of Warwick, Stratford-upon-Avon and Kenilworth. Warwickshire consists of mostly flat or undulating farmland, although the foothills of the Cotswold Hills spill over the SW border. Main manufacturing activites occur in an industrial belt extending NW from Rugby to the boundary with Staffordshire. They include motor and component industries, service sectors, electrical and general engineering. Tourism is centred on the historic town of Warwick with its medieval castle, and Stratford-upon-Avon with its Shakespeare associations. The principal river is the Avon.
**Districts**: North Warwickshire; Nuneaton & Bedworth; Rugby; Stratford-on-Avon; Warwick.

**West Berkshire** *W.Berks.* Population: 144,483.
Unitary authority in S England bordered by Hampshire, Oxfordshire, Reading, Wiltshire and Wokingham. The chief centres are Newbury, Thatcham and Hungerford. West Berkshire is a mixture of old market towns, historic buildings and waterways, and includes the famous Newbury racecourse. Rivers include the Kennet and the Pang.

**West Dunbartonshire** *W.Dun.* Population: 93,378.
Unitary authority in central Scotland bordered by Argyll & Bute, East Dunbartonshire, Glasgow, Inverclyde, Renfrewshire and Stirling. The chief towns are Clydebank, Dumbarton, Alexandria and Bonhill. The area is mountainous, containing the Kilpatrick Hills, and is bounded by Loch Lomond in the N and the Firth of Clyde in the S. The urban SE area of West Dunbartonshire forms part of the NW periphery of Greater Glasgow. There is a broad base of light manufacturing and service sector industries. Tourism and leisure are a feature, with the SE tip of Loch Lomond Regional Park and the whole of Balloch Castle Country Park falling within the area. West Dunbartonshire includes the Erskine Bridge which spans the River Clyde, other rivers include the Leven.

**West Lothian** *W.Loth.* Population: 158,714.
Unitary authority in central Scotland neighbouring Edinburgh, Falkirk, Midlothian, North Lanarkshire, Scottish Borders and South Lanarkshire. The chief towns are Livingston, Bathgate, Linlithgow, Broxburn, Whitburn and Armadale. The area undulates to the S of the Firth of Forth, and rises to moorland at the foot of the Pentland Hills in the S. The main urban areas are situated along commuter corridors between Glasgow, Edinburgh and Falkirk; elsewhere the area is mostly rural. Hi-tech and computing industries are in evidence.

**West Midlands** *W.Mid.* Population: 2,555,592.
Former metropolitan county of central England bordered by Staffordshire, Warwickshire and Worcestershire. It comprises the urban complex around the cities of Birmingham and Coventry, and the towns of Wolverhampton, Dudley, Walsall, West Bromwich, Sutton Coldfield and Solihull. The West Midlands developed as a manufacturing and engineering centre which specialised in the metalworking and motor trades. The area around Dudley, Walsall and Wolverhampton became known as the Black Country, with heavy industry centred on the local deposits of coal, iron ore and limestone. Other local trades included glassware, saddlery and lock-making. Birmingham became Britain's second city by specialising in 1001 trades from confectionery to cars, and has developed into the major business, industrial, commercial and cultural centre for the area. As the traditional industries have declined, there has been a shift towards service, leisure and recreation sectors of the economy; several significant corporate service centres and venues, such as the National Exhibition Centre and the Indoor Arena, are in the West Midlands. The area is served by Birmingham International Airport. Rivers include the Tame and the Cole.
**Districts**: Birmingham; Coventry; Dudley; Sandwell; Solihull; Walsall; Wolverhampton.

**West Sussex** *W.Suss.* Population: 753,614.
County of S England bounded by Brighton & Hove, East Sussex, Hampshire, Surrey and the English Channel. Main towns are Worthing, Crawley, Bognor Regis, Littlehampton, Horsham, Haywards Heath, East Grinstead, the cathedral city and county town of Chichester, Burgess Hill and Shoreham-by-Sea. N of a level coastal strip run the South Downs, a steep-sided chalk ridge which is thickly wooded in parts. The remaining inland area, The Weald, is largely well-wooded farmland, although there is industrial development around Crawley, Gatwick (London) Airport, Horsham, and Haywards Heath, as well as among the predominantly residential towns on the coast. Tourism is a major activity throughout the county. There are many castles and stately homes, such as Arundel Castle and Goodwood House, the popular seaside resorts of Bognor Regis and Worthing, race courses at Goodwood and Fontwell, Chichester Harbour, which is a centre for yachtsmen and wildfowl, historic Chichester itself,

and numerous picturesque villages. The N of the county includes Gatwick (London) Airport. The rivers, none large, include the Adur and Arun, with its tributary the Rother; the Medway rises in the E of the county.
**Districts**: Adur; Arun; Chichester; Crawley; Horsham; Mid Sussex; Worthing.

**West Yorkshire** *W.Yorks.* Population: 2,079,211.
Former metropolitan county of N England bordering Derbyshire, Greater Manchester, Lancashire, North Yorkshire and South Yorkshire. It comprises the area around the cities of Leeds, Bradford and Wakefield, and the towns of Huddersfield, Halifax, Dewsbury, Keighley, Batley, Morley, Castleford, Brighouse, Pudsey, Pontefract and Shipley. West Yorkshire developed as a centre for wool and textiles, manufacturing and engineering, creating an industrial urban landscape set against rural moorland. As the traditional industries have declined, the area has undergone regeneration and diversification, moving towards tertiary economic sectors. Leeds is the industrial, administrative, commercial and cultural centre of the area, containing regional government offices and many corporate service centres and head offices. Emerging economic activities across West Yorkshire have included printing, distribution, chemicals, food and drink production, hi-tech industries and financial services. Haworth with its Brontë associations, Holmfirth and the moorlands are the centres of tourism. The area includes Leeds Bradford International Airport. The chief rivers are the Aire and the Calder, while the Wharfe forms its N boundary below Addingham.
**Districts**: Bradford; Calderdale; Kirklees; Leeds; Wakefield.

**Western Isles** (Na h-Eileanan an Iar. Also known as Outer Hebrides.) *W.Isles* Population: 26,502.
String of islands off the W coast of Scotland and separated from Skye and the mainland by The Minch. They extend for some 130m/209km from Butt of Lewis in the N, to Barra Head in the S. Stornoway, situated on the Isle of Lewis, is the main town; elsewhere, there are mainly scattered coastal villages and settlements. The chief islands are Isle of Lewis, North Uist, Benbecula, South Uist and Barra. North Harris and South Harris form significant areas in the S part of the Isle of Lewis. The topography of the islands consists of undulating moorland, mountains and lochs. The main industries are fishing, grazing and, on the Isle of Lewis, tweed manufacture. There are airfields with scheduled passenger flights on the Isle of Lewis, Benbecula and Barra.

**Wiltshire** *Wilts.* Population: 432,973.
Unitary authority of S England bounded by Bath & North East Somerset, Dorset, Gloucestershire, Hampshire, Oxfordshire, Somerset, South Gloucestershire, Swindon and West Berkshire. Main centres are the cathedral city of Salisbury, Trowbridge, Chippenham, Warminster, Devizes and Melksham. Wiltshire consists of extensive chalk uplands scattered with prehistoric remains, notably at Avebury and Stonehenge, and interspersed with wide, well-watered valleys. The N of the county is dominated by the Marlborough Downs which are much used for racehorse training, while in the S, the chalk plateau of Salisbury Plain is an important military training area. Between these two upland areas lies the fertile Vale of Pewsey where dairy production and bacon-curing are important agricultural activities. Other industries include electronics, computing, pharmaceuticals, plastics, telecommunications and service sector activities. Wiltshire attracts tourism with its prehistoric remains, stately houses and picturesque market towns and villages. Rivers include the so-called Bristol and Wiltshire Avons, Ebble, Kennet, Nadder, Wylye, and the upper reaches of the Thames.

**Windsor & Maidenhead** *W. & M.* Population: 133,626.
Unitary authority in SE England to the W of Greater London, and bounded by Bracknell Forest, Buckinghamshire, Slough, Surrey and Wokingham. The towns of Maidenhead and Windsor are the main centres for industry, leisure and recreation. The area is particularly noted for its strong Royal connections as it includes Windsor Castle and the former Royal hunting estate of Windsor Great Park. Other popular tourist attractions include Ascot race course, Windsor Legoland and Eton College. The River Thames forms the N boundary.

**Wokingham** *W'ham* Population: 150,229.
Unitary authority in SE England, to the W of Greater London. The area encompasses Wokingham and is bordered by Bracknell Forest, Buckinghamshire, Hampshire, Oxfordshire, Reading, West Berkshire and Windsor & Maidenhead. The area includes riverside villages in the N, with undulating ridges covered by woodlands and commons in the S. Wokingham is a growing centre for hi-tech and computer industries. The River Thames forms the N border, and the River Blackwater forms the border to the S.

**Worcestershire** *Worcs.* Population: 542,107.
S midland county of England neighbouring Gloucestershire, Herefordshire, Shropshire, Warwickshire and West Midlands. Main centres are the cathedral city and the county town of Worcester, and the towns of Redditch, Kidderminster, Great Malvern, Bromsgrove, Droitwich Spa, Stourport-on-Severn and Evesham. The urban areas in the N of the county form part of the periphery and commuter belt of the West Midlands conurbation, and attract much of the industrial development. The central and S sections of the county are largely rural, containing the fertile Severn Valley and Vale of Evesham, with market gardening and orchard-growing being the main agricultural activities. Tourism is an important industry, much of it being centred on historic Worcester, with its cathedral, the triennial Three Choirs Festival, Worcester Sauce and china factories. Other popular attractions include boating on the River Severn and visiting the Vale of Evesham whilst the flowers are in full bloom. The main river is the Severn.
**Districts**: Bromsgrove; Malvern Hills; Redditch; Worcester; Wychavon; Wyre Forest.

**Wrexham** (Wrecsam). *Wrex.* Population: 128,476.
Unitary authority in NE Wales bordering Denbighshire, Flintshire, Powys and the English counties of Cheshire and Shropshire. Main centres are Wrexham, Rhosllanerchrugog, Gwersyllt, Cefn-mawr and Coedpoeth. The area is mountainous in the SW, containing part of the Berwyn range; the Dee valley lies in the NE. The area was formerly dominated by the iron, coal and limestone industries. Food manufacture, brewing, plastics and hi-tech industries are now important to the local economy. Wrexham is the largest commercial and shopping centre in N Wales. The River Dee flows through the area.

**York** *York* Population: 181,094.
Unitary authority in N England surrounding the historic cathedral city of York and bordered by East Riding of Yorkshire and North Yorkshire. York is a major archaeological, episcopal, industrial, commercial and cultural centre, situated at the confluence of the River Foss and the River Ouse. The city has a unique history dating from the original Roman military camp, which has led to it becoming one of the main museum and tourist centres in the country. The historic core, situated around the centrepiece of the medieval Minster, is well preserved. Other major attractions include the Jorvik Viking Centre, the medieval city walls and the National Railway Museum. Economic sectors include the confectionery industry, company head offices, Government departmental offices, and research and development establishments. The main river is the Ouse.

## WALES Counties

- BLAENAU GWENT
- BRIDGEND
- CAERPHILLY
- CARDIFF
- CARMARTHENSHIRE
- CEREDIGION
- CONWY
- DENBIGHSHIRE
- FLINTSHIRE
- GWYNEDD
- ISLE OF ANGLESEY
- MERTHYR TYDFIL
- MONMOUTHSHIRE
- NEATH PORT TALBOT
- NEWPORT
- PEMBROKESHIRE
- POWYS
- RHONDDA CYNON TAFF
- SWANSEA
- TORFAEN
- VALE OF GLAMORGAN
- WREXHAM

## ENGLAND Counties & Districts

- BATH AND NORTH EAST SOMERSET
- BEDFORD
- BOURNEMOUTH
- BRACKNELL FOREST
- BRIGHTON & HOVE
- BRISTOL
- BUCKINGHAMSHIRE
  1. Aylesbury Vale
  2. Wycombe
  3. Chiltern
  4. South Buckinghamshire
- CAMBRIDGESHIRE
  1. Fenland
  2. Huntingdonshire
  3. East Cambridgeshire
  4. South Cambridgeshire
  5. Cambridge
- CENTRAL BEDFORDSHIRE
- CHESHIRE EAST
- CHESHIRE WEST & CHESTER
- CORNWALL
- DERBY
- DERBYSHIRE
  1. High Peak
  2. Derbyshire Dales
  3. North East Derbyshire
  4. Chesterfield
  5. Bolsover
  6. Amber Valley
  7. Erewash
  8. South Derbyshire
- DEVON
  1. North Devon
  2. Torridge
- 3 Mid Devon
- 4 East Devon
- 5 Exeter
- 6 Teignbridge
- 7 West Devon
- 8 South Hams
- DORSET
  1. North Dorset
  2. East Dorset
  3. Christchurch
  4. Purbeck
  5. West Dorset
  6. Weymouth & Portland
- EAST SUSS
  1. Lewes
  2. Wealden
  3. Eastbourne
  4. Rother
  5. Hastings

Scale: 1:1,250,000 — 20 miles to 1 inch / 12.5 km to 1 cm

146

## 147

**ESSEX**
Uttlesford
Braintree
Colchester
Tendring
Maldon
Chelmsford
Epping Forest
Harlow
Brentwood
Basildon
Rochford
Castle Point

**GLOUCESTERSHIRE**
Forest of Dean
Gloucester
Tewkesbury
Cheltenham
Cotswold
Stroud

**GREATER LONDON**
See pages 152-153 for map of boroughs

**HAMPSHIRE**
1 Basingstoke & Deane
2 Hart
3 Rushmoor
4 Test Valley
5 Winchester
6 East Hampshire
7 New Forest
8 Eastleigh
9 Fareham
10 Gosport
11 Havant

**HEREFORDSHIRE**

**HERTFORDSHIRE**
1 North Hertfordshire
2 Stevenage
3 East Hertfordshire
4 Broxbourne
5 Welwyn Hatfield
6 St Albans
7 Dacorum
8 Three Rivers
9 Watford
10 Hertsmere

**ISLE OF WIGHT**

**ISLES OF SCILLY**

**KENT**
1 Dartford
2 Gravesham
3 Swale
4 Canterbury
5 Thanet
6 Dover
7 Shepway
8 Ashford
9 Maidstone
10 Tonbridge & Malling
11 Sevenoaks
12 Tunbridge Wells

**LEICESTER**

**LEICESTERSHIRE**
1 North West Leicestershire
2 Charnwood
3 Melton
4 Harborough
5 Oadby & Wigston
6 Blaby
7 Hinckley & Bosworth

**LINCOLNSHIRE**
1 West Lindsey
2 Lincoln
3 East Lindsey
4 North Kesteven
5 Boston
6 South Kesteven
7 South Holland

**LUTON**

**MEDWAY**

**MILTON KEYNES**

**NORFOLK**
1 Kings Lynn & West Norfolk
2 North Norfolk
3 Great Yarmouth
4 Broadland
5 Norwich
6 South Norfolk
7 Breckland

**NORTH SOMERSET**

**NORTHAMPTONSHIRE**
1 East Northamptonshire
2 Corby
3 Kettering
4 Daventry
5 Wellingborough
6 Northampton
7 South Northamptonshire

**NOTTINGHAMSHIRE**
1 Bassetlaw
2 Mansfield
3 Newark & Sherwood
4 Ashfield
5 Gedling
6 Broxtowe
7 Rushcliffe

**OXFORDSHIRE**
1 Cherwell
2 West Oxfordshire
3 Oxford
4 Vale of White Horse
5 South Oxfordshire

**PETERBOROUGH**

**PLYMOUTH**

**POOLE**

**PORTSMOUTH**

**READING**

**RUTLAND**

**SHROPSHIRE**

**SLOUGH**

**SOMERSET**
1 West Somerset
2 Taunton Deane
3 Sedgemoor
4 Mendip
5 South Somerset

**SOUTH GLOUCESTERSHIRE**

**SOUTHAMPTON**

**SOUTHEND**

**STAFFORDSHIRE**
1 Newcastle-under-Lyme
2 Staffordshire Moorlands
3 Stafford
4 East Staffordshire
5 South Staffordshire
6 Cannock Chase
7 Lichfield
8 Tamworth

**STOKE-ON-TRENT**

**SUFFOLK**
1 Forest Heath
2 St Edmundsbury
3 Mid Suffolk
4 Waveney
5 Suffolk Coastal
6 Ipswich
7 Babergh

**SURREY**
1 Spelthorne
2 Runnymede
3 Surrey Heath
4 Woking
5 Elmbridge
6 Epsom & Ewell
7 Reigate & Banstead
8 Tandridge
9 Mole Valley
10 Guildford
11 Waverley

**SWINDON**

**TELFORD AND WREKIN**

**THURROCK**

**TORBAY**

**WARWICKSHIRE**
1 North Warwickshire
2 Nuneaton & Bedworth
3 Rugby
4 Warwick
5 Stratford-on-Avon

**WEST BERKSHIRE**

**WEST MIDLANDS**
(Former Metropolitan County)
1 Walsall
2 Wolverhampton
3 Dudley
4 Sandwell
5 Birmingham
6 Solihull
7 Coventry

**WEST SUSSEX**
1 Chichester
2 Horsham
3 Crawley
4 Mid Sussex
5 Adur
6 Worthing
7 Arun

**WILTSHIRE**

**WINDSOR AND MAIDENHEAD**

**WOKINGHAM**

**WORCESTERSHIRE**
1 Wyre Forest
2 Bromsgrove
3 Redditch
4 Wychavon
5 Worcester
6 Malvern Hills

SCOTLAND
KINROSS
ARGYLL AND BUTE
STIRLING
WEST DUNBARTONSHIRE
EAST DUNBARTONSHIRE
INVERCLYDE
RENFREWSHIRE
EAST RENFREWSHIRE
NORTH LANARKSHIRE
SOUTH LANARKSHIRE
FALKIRK
CLACKMANNANSHIRE
WEST LOTHIAN
GLASGOW
NORTH AYRSHIRE
EAST AYRSHIRE
SOUTH AYRSHIRE
DUMFRIES & GAL
Tiree
Mull
Iona
Colonsay
Jura
Islay
Arran
Bute
Ailsa Craig
Firth of Lorn
Sound of Jura
Loch Fyne
Kilbrannan Sound
Firth of Clyde
Solway Firth
Oban
Taynuilt
Lochaline
Craignure
Fionnphort
Scalasaig
Port Askaig
Bowmore
Portnahaven
Port Ellen
Lochgilphead
Tarbert
Carradale
Campbeltown
Lochranza
Brodick
Dunoon
Helensburgh
Lochgoilhead
Garelochhead
Dalmally
Crianlarich
Tyndrum
Killin
Lochearnhead
Callander
Aberfoyle
Dunblane
Bridge of Allan
Stirling
Alloa
Dollar
Tillicoultry
Crieff
Auchterarder
Gleneagles
Dunfermline
Kincardine
Grangemouth
Bo'ness
Falkirk
Linlithgow
Denny
Kilsyth
Cumbernauld
Kirkintilloch
Bathgate
Whitburn
Alexandria
Dumbarton
Greenock
Port Glasgow
Milngavie
Bearsden
Clydebank
Paisley
Johnstone
Barrhead
Coatbridge
Airdrie
Motherwell
Wishaw
Hamilton
East Kilbride
Carluke
Lanark
Carnwath
Strathaven
Douglas
Abington
Newton Mearns
Largs
Millport
Wemyss Bay
Beith
Dalry
Dunlop
Stewarton
Kilwinning
Stevenston
Ardrossan
Saltcoats
Irvine
Kilmarnock
Galston
Troon
Prestwick
Glasgow Prestwick
Ayr
Mauchline
Cumnock
Muirkirk
New Cumnock
Dalmellington
Maybole
Girvan
Ballantrae
Sanquhar
Thornhill
Moniaive
Dumfries
Lochmaben
New Galloway
Cairnryan
Stranraer
Portpatrick
Newton Stewart
Glenluce
Sandhead
Wigtown
Port William
Whithorn
Drummore
Kirkcudbright
Maryport
Workington
Whitehaven
Egremont
ISLE OF MAN
Andreas
Ramsey
Kirk Michael
Peel
Laxey
Dalby
Foxdale
Onchan
Douglas
Port Erin
Port St Mary
Castletown
Isle of Man
IRISH SEA
North Channel
ISLE OF ANGLESEY
Anglesey
Holyhead
Holy Island
Amlwch
Llangefni
Menai Bridge
Bangor
Caernarfon
Llandudno
Colwyn Bay
Abergele
CONWY
NORTHERN IRELAND Districts
ANTRIM
ARDS
ARMAGH
BALLYMENA
BALLYMONEY
BANBRIDGE
BELFAST
CARRICKFERGUS
CASTLEREAGH
COLERAINE
COOKSTOWN
CRAIGAVON
DOWN
DUNGANNON
FERMANAGH
LARNE
LIMAVADY
LISBURN
LONDONDERRY (DERRY)
MAGHERAFELT
MOYLE
NEWRY & MOURNE
NEWTOWNABBEY
NORTH DOWN
OMAGH
STRABANE
0 10 20 30 40 kilometres
0 10 20 30 miles
NORTHERN IRELAND
Inishtrahull Sound
Rathlin Island
Lough Foyle
Lough Swilly
Lough Neagh
Carndonagh
Moville
Buncrana
Letterkenny
Portrush
Portstewart
Bushmills
Ballycastle
Armoy
Coleraine
Ballymoney
Limavady
Ballykelly
Eglinton
City of Derry
Londonderry (Derry)
Dungiven
Garvagh
Kilrea
Ballymena
Broughshane
Carnlough
Larne
Maghera
Magherafelt
Draperstown
Randalstown
Antrim
Ballyclare
Whitehead
Carrickfergus
Newtownabbey
Belfast
Belfast City
Bangor
Donaghadee
Newtownards
Dundonald
Comber
Kirkcubbin
Portavogie
Ards Peninsula
Portaferry
Strangford
Killinchy
Saintfield
Crossgar
Downpatrick
Ardglass
Dundrum
Newcastle
Ballynahinch
Dromore
Lisburn
Dunmurry
Crumlin
Lurgan
Craigavon
Portadown
Tandragee
Armagh
Markethill
Keady
Banbridge
Rathfriland
Newry
Warrenpoint
Kilkeel
Annalong
Cookstown
Moneymore
Dungannon
Donaghmore
Pomeroy
Sixmilecross
Beragh
Omagh
Dromore
Newtownstewart
Castlederg
Strabane
Sion Mills
Lifford
Ballybofey
Glenties
Donegal
Ballyshannon
Enniskillen
Belcoo
Manorhamilton
Lisbellaw
Fivemiletown
Lisnaskea
Newtownbutler
Augher
Aughnacloy
Ballygawley
Clones
Monaghan (Muineachán)
Ballyconnell
Castleblayney
Cavan
Carrickmacross
Carrick-on-Shannon
Mohill
Arvagh
Dundalk (Dun Dealgan)
Dundalk Bay
Ardee
Dunleer
Virginia

## ENGLAND Counties & Districts

**BLACKBURN WITH DARWEN**

**BLACKPOOL**

**CHESHIRE**
1. Ellesmere Port & Neston
2. Vale Royal
3. Macclesfield
4. Chester
5. Congleton

**CUMBRIA**
1. Carlisle
2. Allerdale
3. Eden
4. Copeland
5. South Lakeland
6. Barrow-in-Furness

**DARLINGTON**

**DERBYSHIRE**
1. High Peak
2. Derbyshire Dales
3. North East Derbyshire
4. Chesterfield
5. Bolsover

**DURHAM**

**EAST RIDING OF YORKSHIRE**

**GREATER MANCHESTER**
(Former Metropolitan County)
1. Wigan
2. Bolton
3. Bury
4. Rochdale
5. Oldham
6. Tameside
7. Stockport
8. Manchester
9. Salford
10. Trafford

**HALTON**

**HARTLEPOOL**

**ISLE OF MAN**

**KINGSTON UPON HULL**

**LANCASHIRE**
1. Lancaster
2. Wyre
3. Fylde
4. Preston
5. Ribble Valley
6. Pendle
7. Burnley
8. Rossendale
9. Hyndburn
10. Chorley
11. South Ribble
12. West Lancashire

**LINCOLNSHIRE**
1. West Lindsey
2. Lincoln
3. East Lindsey
4. North Kesteven

**MERSEYSIDE**
(Former Metropolitan County)
1. Wirral
2. Sefton
3. Liverpool
4. Knowsley
5. St Helens

**MIDDLESBROUGH**

**NORTH EAST LINCOLNSHIRE**

**NORTH LINCOLNSHIRE**

**NORTH YORKSHIRE**
1. Scarborough
2. Ryedale
3. Hambleton
4. Richmondshire
5. Craven
6. Harrogate
7. Selby

**NORTHUMBERLAND**

**NOTTINGHAM**

**NOTTINGHAMSHIRE**
1. Bassetlaw
2. Mansfield
3. Newark & Sherwood
4. Ashfield

**REDCAR AND CLEVELAND**

**SOUTH YORKSHIRE**
(Former Metropolitan County)
1. Barnsley
2. Doncaster
3. Rotherham
4. Sheffield

**STOCKTON-ON-TEES**

**TYNE AND WEAR**
(Former Metropolitan County)
1. Newcastle upon Tyne
2. North Tyneside
3. South Tyneside
4. Gateshead
5. Sunderland

**WARRINGTON**

**WEST YORKSHIRE**
(Former Metropolitan County)
1. Calderdale
2. Bradford
3. Leeds
4. Wakefield
5. Kirklees

**YORK**

WESTERN ISLES
(NA H-EILEANAN AN IAR)
Port of Ness
Portnaguran
Stornoway
Garrynahine
Lewis
North Harris
Tarbert
South Harris
Rodel
North Uist
Lochmaddy
Benbecula
South Uist
Lochboisdale
Barra
Castlebay
Vatersay
The Minch
Little Minch
Durness
Tongue
Bettyhill
Rhiconich
Laxford Bridge
Scourie
Sutherland
Kinbrace
Lochinver
Ledmore
Summer Isles
Brora
Golspie
Ullapool
Bonar Bridge
Dornoch Firth
Portmahomack
Aultbea
Poolewe
Gairloch
Easter Ross
HIGHLAND
Wester Ross
Kinlochewe
Achnasheen
Garve
Strathpeffer
Dingwall
Invergordon
Cromarty Firth
Cromarty
Moray Firth
Nairn
Fortrose
Inverness
Muir of Ord
Beauly
Uig
Skye
Portree
Raasay
Inner Sound
Shieldaig
Dunvegan
Lochcarron
Stromeferry
Sligachan
Kyle of Lochalsh
Kyleakin
Broadford
Elgol
Drumnadrochit
Grantown-on-Spey
Carrbridge
Aviemore
Invermoriston
Fort Augustus
Canna
Rum (Rhum)
Ardvasar
Sound of Sleat
Invergarry
Kingussie
Newtonmore
Mallaig
Arisaig
Eigg
Dalwhinnie
Glenfinnan
Spean Bridge
Fort William
Salen
Kinlochleven
Rannoch Sta
Kinloch Rannoch
Blair Atholl
Coll
Tobermory
Ballachulish
Loch Linnhe
PERTH
KINRO
Aberfeldy
Tiree
Lochaline
Bridge of Orchy
SCOTLAN
Mull
Craignure
Killin
Tyndrum
Oban
Taynuilt
Dalmally
Crianlarich
Lochearnhead
Crieff
Iona
Fionnphort
ARGYLL AND BUTE
STIRLING
Firth of Lorn
Callander
Dunblane
Bridge of Allan
Aberfoyle
CLACKMANNANSHIRE
Alloa
Stirling
Colonsay
Scalasaig
Lochgoilhead
Kincardine
Jura
Lochgilphead
Garelochhead
Denny
Helensburgh
WEST DUNBARTONSHIRE
Kilsyth
Falkirk
FALKIRK
Alexandria
EAST DUNBARTONSHIRE
Cumbernauld
Greenock
Dumbarton
Milngavie
Bearsden
Kirkintilloch
Dunoon
Port Glasgow
INVERCLYDE
Clydebank
GLASGOW
NORTH LANARKSHIRE
Bathgate
Port Askaig
Islay
Sound of Jura
Loch Fyne
Tarbert
Wemyss Bay
Johnstone
RENFREWSHIRE
Paisley
Coatbridge
Airdrie
Barrhead
Hamilton
Motherwell
Wishaw
Largs
Bute
Bowmore
Millport
Beith
Newton Mearns
EAST RENFREWSHIRE
East Kilbride
Carluke
Portnahaven
Port Ellen
Lochranza
Dalry
Dunlop
Stewarton
Kilwinning
Strathaven
Lanark
NORTH AYRSHIRE
Ardrossan
Saltcoats
Stevenston
Irvine
Kilmarnock
SOUTH LANARKSHIRE
Carradale
Kilbrannan Sound
Brodick
Galston
Douglas
Arran
Troon
Prestwick
Mauchline
EAST AYRSHIRE
Muirkirk
Firth of Clyde
Ayr
Cumnock
Inishtrahull Sound
Campbeltown
New Cumnock
Sanquhar
Maybole
Dalmellington
SOUTH AYRSHIRE
DUMFRIES &
Rathlin Island
Carndonagh

# 151

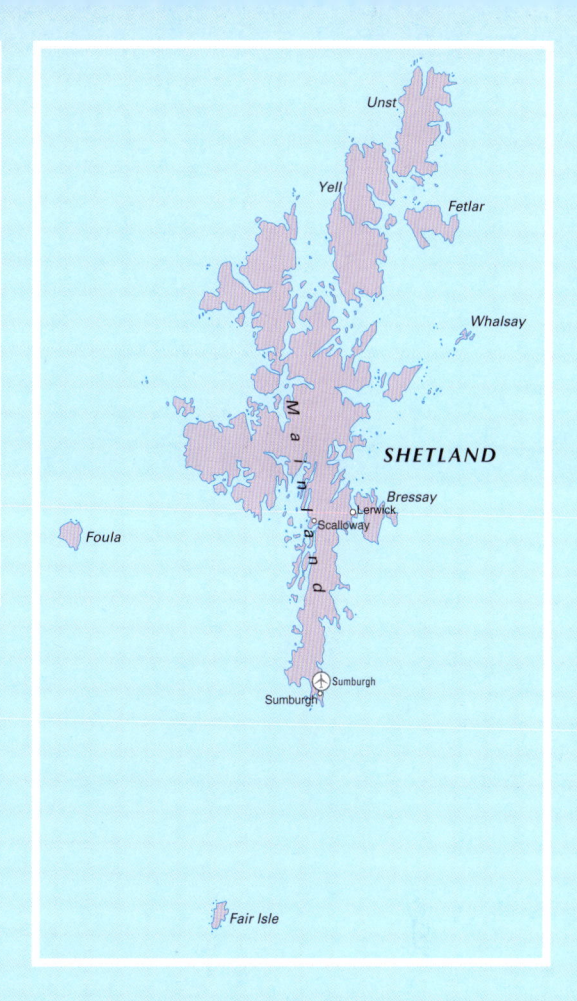

## ORKNEY
- Papa Westray
- Westray
- North Ronaldsay
- Rousay
- Sanday
- Eday
- Stronsay
- Shapinsay
- Mainland
- Kirkwall
- Stromness
- Hoy
- Lyness
- St Margaret's Hope
- South Ronaldsay
- Pentland Firth
- Scrabster
- Thurso
- John o' Groats

## SHETLAND
- Unst
- Yell
- Fetlar
- Whalsay
- Mainland
- Bressay
- Lerwick
- Scalloway
- Foula
- Sumburgh
- Fair Isle

## SCOTLAND Councils
ABERDEEN
ABERDEENSHIRE
ANGUS
ARGYLL AND BUTE
CLACKMANNANSHIRE
DUMFRIES AND GALLOWAY
DUNDEE
EAST AYRSHIRE
EAST DUNBARTONSHIRE
EAST LOTHIAN
EAST RENFREWSHIRE
EDINBURGH
FALKIRK
FIFE
GLASGOW
HIGHLAND
INVERCLYDE
MIDLOTHIAN
MORAY
NORTH AYRSHIRE
NORTH LANARKSHIRE
ORKNEY
PERTH AND KINROSS
RENFREWSHIRE
SCOTTISH BORDERS
SHETLAND
SOUTH AYRSHIRE
SOUTH LANARKSHIRE
STIRLING
WEST DUNBARTONSHIRE
WEST LOTHIAN
WESTERN ISLES (NA H-EILEANAN AN IAR)

1:1,250,000  20 miles to 1 inch/12.5 km to 1 cm

# Map of Greater London and Surrounding Areas

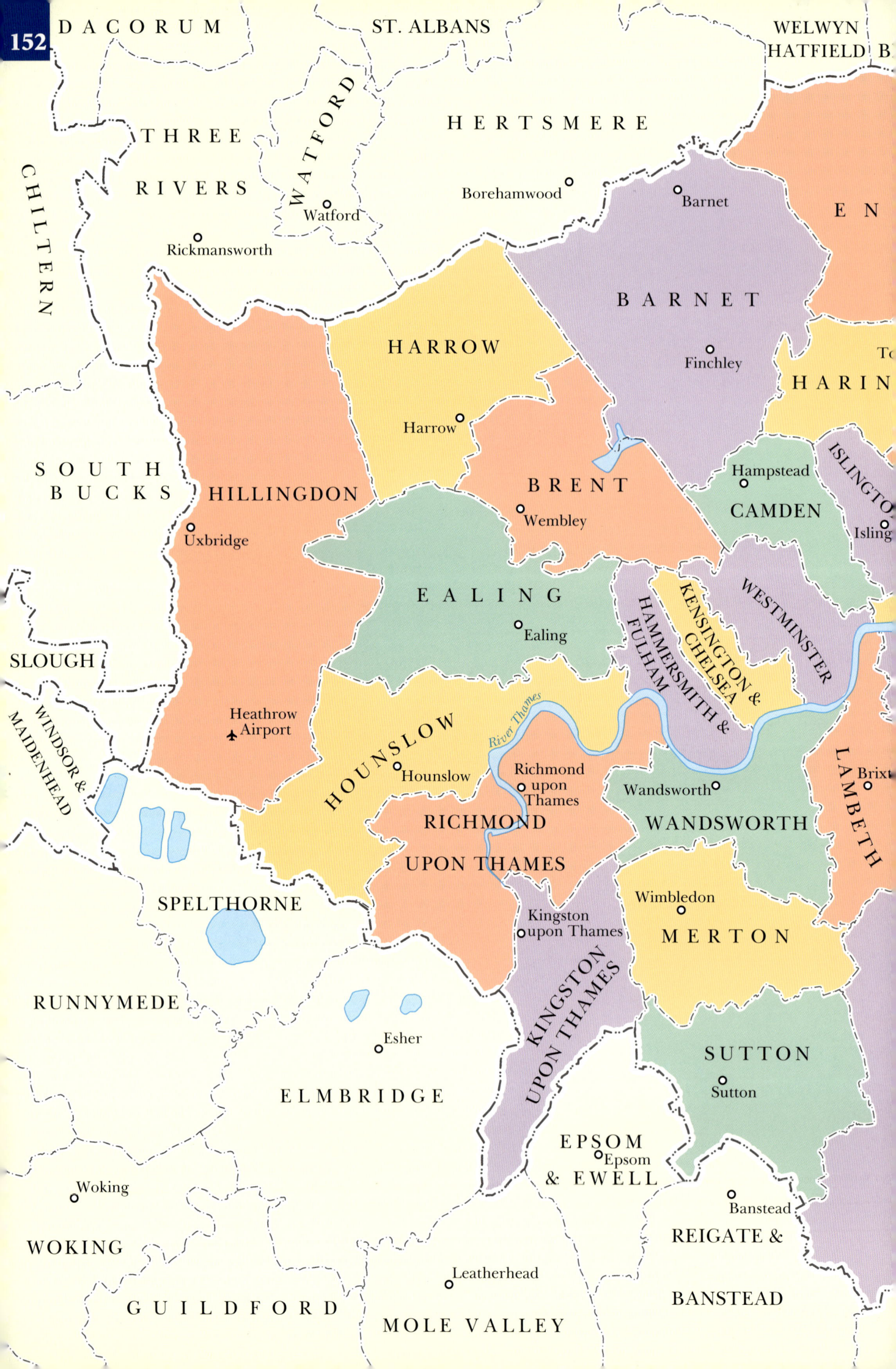

**Surrounding districts (outside Greater London):**
- DACORUM
- ST. ALBANS
- WELWYN HATFIELD B...
- CHILTERN
- THREE RIVERS (Watford, Rickmansworth)
- WATFORD
- HERTSMERE (Borehamwood)
- SOUTH BUCKS
- SLOUGH
- WINDSOR & MAIDENHEAD
- SPELTHORNE
- RUNNYMEDE
- WOKING (Woking)
- GUILDFORD
- ELMBRIDGE (Esher)
- MOLE VALLEY (Leatherhead)
- EPSOM & EWELL (Epsom)
- REIGATE & BANSTEAD (Banstead)

**London Boroughs:**
- HILLINGDON (Uxbridge, Heathrow Airport)
- HARROW (Harrow)
- BARNET (Finchley)
- EN... (Enfield)
- HARIN... (Haringey)
- BRENT (Wembley)
- CAMDEN (Hampstead)
- ISLINGTON (Islington)
- EALING (Ealing)
- HAMMERSMITH & FULHAM
- KENSINGTON & CHELSEA
- WESTMINSTER
- HOUNSLOW (Hounslow)
- RICHMOND UPON THAMES (Richmond upon Thames)
- WANDSWORTH (Wandsworth)
- LAMBETH (Brixton)
- KINGSTON UPON THAMES (Kingston upon Thames)
- MERTON (Wimbledon)
- SUTTON (Sutton)

*River Thames*

152

## 153

### Map of Eastern Greater London Boroughs

**Boroughs and places shown:**

- BOURNE
- EPPING FOREST
  - Waltham Abbey
- BRENTWOOD
  - Brentwood
- ENFIELD
  - Edmonton
- WALTHAM FOREST
  - Walthamstow
- REDBRIDGE
  - Woodford
  - Ilford
- HAVERING
  - Romford
  - Upminster
- HACKNEY
  - Hackney
- NEWHAM
  - West Ham
  - Beckton
- BARKING & DAGENHAM
  - Barking
  - Dagenham
- TOWER HAMLETS
  - Stepney
- London City Airport
- River Thames
- THURROCK
  - Tilbury
- SOUTHWARK
  - Southwark
- GREENWICH
  - Greenwich
- LEWISHAM
  - Lewisham
- BEXLEY
  - Bexley
- DARTFORD
  - Dartford
- GRAVESHAM
- BROMLEY
  - Bromley
- CROYDON
- SEVENOAKS
  - Sevenoaks
- TONBRIDGE & MALLING
- ANDRIDGE

### GREATER LONDON BOROUGHS

| | |
|---|---|
| BARKING & DAGENHAM | HOUNSLOW |
| BARNET | ISLINGTON |
| BEXLEY | ROYAL BOROUGH OF KENSINGTON & CHELSEA |
| BRENT | ROYAL BOROUGH OF KINGSTON UPON THAMES |
| BROMLEY | |
| CAMDEN | |
| CORPORATION OF LONDON (CITY) | LAMBETH |
| CROYDON | LEWISHAM |
| EALING | MERTON |
| ENFIELD | NEWHAM |
| GREENWICH | REDBRIDGE |
| HACKNEY | RICHMOND UPON THAMES |
| HAMMERSMITH & FULHAM | SOUTHWARK |
| HARINGEY | SUTTON |
| HARROW | TOWER HAMLETS |
| HAVERING | WALTHAM FOREST |
| HILLINGDON | WANDSWORTH |
| | WESTMINSTER |

# INDEX TO CENTRAL LONDON

## General Abbreviations

| | | | | | | | | | |
|---|---|---|---|---|---|---|---|---|---|
| All | Alley | Conv | Convent | Gar | Garage | Mkts | Markets | Sch | School |
| Allot | Allotments | Cor | Corner | Gdn | Garden | Ms | Mews | Sec | Secondary |
| Amb | Ambulance | Coron | Coroners | Gdns | Gardens | Mt | Mount | Shop | Shopping |
| App | Approach | Cors | Corners | Govt | Government | Mus | Museum | Sq | Square |
| Apts | Apartments | Cotts | Cottages | Gra | Grange | N | North | St. | Saint |
| Arc | Arcade | Cov | Covered | Grd | Ground | NT | National Trust | St | Street |
| Av/Ave | Avenue | Crem | Crematorium | Grds | Grounds | Nat | National | Sta | Station |
| Bdy | Broadway | Cres | Crescent | Grn | Green | PH | Public House | Sts | Streets |
| Bk | Bank | Ct | Court | Grns | Greens | PO | Post Office | Sub | Subway |
| Bldgs | Buildings | Cts | Courts | Gro | Grove | Par | Parade | Swim | Swimming |
| Boul | Boulevard | Ctyd | Courtyard | Gros | Groves | Pas | Passage | TA | Territorial Army |
| Bowl | Bowling | Dep | Depot | Gt | Great | Pav | Pavilion | TH | Town Hall |
| Br/Bri | Bridge | Dev | Development | Ho | House | Pk | Park | Tenn | Tennis |
| Bus | Business | Dr | Drive | Hos | Houses | Pl | Place | Ter | Terrace |
| C of E | Church of England | Dws | Dwellings | Hosp | Hospital | Pol | Police | Thea | Theatre |
| Cath | Cathedral | E | East | Hts | Heights | Prec | Precinct | Trd | Trading |
| Cem | Cemetery | Ed | Education | Ind | Industrial | Prim | Primary | Twr | Tower |
| Cen | Central, Centre | Elec | Electricity | Int | International | Prom | Promenade | Twrs | Towers |
| Cft | Croft | Embk | Embankment | Junct | Junction | Pt | Point | Uni | University |
| Cfts | Crofts | Est | Estate | La | Lane | Quad | Quadrant | Vil | Villa, Villas |
| Ch | Church | Ex | Exchange | Las | Lanes | Rbt | Roundabout | Vw | View |
| Chyd | Churchyard | Exhib | Exhibition | Lib | Library | RC | Roman Catholic | W | West |
| Cin | Cinema | FB | Footbridge | Lo | Lodge | Rd | Road | Wd | Wood |
| Circ | Circus | FC | Football Club | Lwr | Lower | Rds | Roads | Wds | Woods |
| Cl/Clo | Close | Fld | Field | Mag | Magistrates | Rec | Recreation | Wf | Wharf |
| Co | County | Flds | Fields | Mans | Mansions | Res | Reservoir | Wk | Walk |
| Coll | College | Fm | Farm | Mem | Memorial | Ri | Rise | Wks | Works |
| Comm | Community | Gall | Gallery | Mkt | Market | S | South | Yd | Yard |


1 Canada Sq **E14** 127 M10

A

Abbey Cl **SW8** 129 K7
Abbey Gdns **NW8** 124 C4
Abbey La **E15** 127 N4
Abbey Orchard St **SW1** 129 K2
Abbey Rd **NW6** 124 B2
Abbey Rd **NW8** 124 C4
Abbey Rd Est **NW8** 124 B3
Abbey St **SE1** 130 C2
Abbeyfield Rd **SE16** 130 G3
Abbot St **E8** 126 D1
Abbots Manor Est **SW1** 129 H3
Abbot's Pl **NW6** 124 B3
Abbotsbury Cl **E15** 127 N4
Abbotsbury Ms **SE15** 130 G9
Abbotshade Rd **SE16** 127 H10
Abbotswood Rd **SE22** 130 C10
Abbott Rd **E14** 127 N7
Abchurch La **EC4** 126 B9
Aberavon Rd **E3** 127 J5
Abercorn Cl **NW8** 124 C5
Abercorn Pl **NW8** 124 C5
Abercorn Way **SE1** 130 E4
Abercrombie St **SW11** 128 E8
Aberdare Gdns **NW6** 124 B2
Aberdeen Pl **NW8** 124 D6
Aberdeen Ter **SE3** 131 P8
Aberdour St **SE1** 130 C3
Aberfeldy St **E14** 127 N8
Abingdon Rd **W8** 128 A2
Abingdon St **SW1** 129 L2
Abingdon Vil **W8** 128 A2
Abinger Gro **SE8** 131 K5
Ablett St **SE16** 130 G4
Acacia Cl **SE8** 131 J3
Acacia Pl **NW8** 124 D4
Acacia Rd **NW8** 124 D4
Academy Gdns **W8** 128 A1
Acanthus Dr **SE1** 130 E4
Acanthus Rd **SW11** 128 G9
Acfold Rd **SW6** 128 B7
Achilles Cl **SE1** 130 E4
Achilles St **SE14** 131 J6
Ackmar Rd **SW6** 128 A7
Ackroyd Dr **E3** 127 K7
Acland Cres **SE5** 130 B10
Acol Rd **NW6** 124 A2
Acorn Wk **SE16** 127 J10
Acre Dr **SE22** 130 E10
Acre La **SW2** 129 L10
Acton Ms **E8** 126 D3
Acton St **WC1** 125 M5
Ada Gdns **E14** 127 P8
Ada Pl **E2** 126 E3
Ada Rd **SE5** 130 C6
Ada St **E8** 126 F3
Adam & Eve Ms **W8** 128 A2
Adam St **WC2** 125 L9
Adams Row **W1** 124 G9
Adamson Rd **NW3** 124 D2
Adderley St **E14** 127 N8
Addington Rd **E3** 127 L5
Addington Sq **SE5** 130 A6
Adelaide Av **SE4** 131 K10
Adelaide Rd **NW3** 124 D2
Adelina Gro **E1** 126 G7
Adeline Pl **WC1** 125 K7
Adler St **E1** 126 E8
Admiral Pl **SE16** 127 J10
Admiral Sq **SW10** 128 D7
Admiral St **SE8** 131 L8
Admiral Wk **W9** 124 A7
Admirals Gate **SE10** 131 M7
Admirals Way **E14** 131 L1
Adolphus St **SE8** 131 K6
Adpar St **W2** 124 D6
Adrian Ms **SW10** 128 B5
Adys Rd **SE15** 130 D9
Afghan Rd **SW11** 128 E8
Agar Gro **NW1** 125 J2
Agar Gro Est **NW1** 125 K2
Agar Pl **NW1** 125 J2
Agar St **WC2** 125 L9
Agdon St **EC1** 125 P6
Agnes St **E14** 127 K8
Ailsa St **E14** 127 N7
Ainger Rd **NW3** 124 F2
Ainsdale Dr **SE1** 130 E4
Ainsley St **E2** 126 F5
Ainsty Est **SE16** 131 H1
Ainsworth Rd **E9** 126 G2
Ainsworth Way **NW8** 124 C3
Air St **W1** 125 J9
Airdrie Cl **N1** 125 M2
Akerman Rd **SW9** 129 P8
Albany Mans **SW11** 128 E6
Albany Rd **SE5** 130 B5
Albany Rd **SE17** 130 B5
Albany St **NW1** 125 H4
Albatross Way **SE16** 131 H1
Albemarle St **W1** 125 H9
Albert Av **SW8** 129 M6
Albert Br **SW3** 128 E5
Albert Br **SW11** 128 E5
Albert Br Rd **SW11** 128 E6
Albert Embk **SE1** 129 L4
Albert Gdns **E1** 127 H8
Albert Gate **SW1** 128 F1
Albert Pl **W8** 128 B1
Albert Sq **SW8** 129 M6
Albert St **NW1** 125 H3
Albert Ter **NW1** 124 G3
Albert Way **SE15** 130 F6
Alberta Est **SE17** 129 P4
Alberta St **SE17** 129 P4
Albion Av **SW8** 129 K8
Albion Dr **E8** 126 D2
Albion Est **SE16** 130 G1
Albion Ms **N1** 125 N3
Albion Ms **W2** 124 E8
Albion Pl **EC1** 125 P7
Albion Riverside Bldg **SW11** 128 E6
Albion Sq **E8** 126 D2
Albion St **SE16** 130 G1
Albion St **W2** 124 E8
Albion Ter **E8** 126 D2
Albion Way **SE13** 131 N10
Albrighton Rd **SE22** 130 C9
Albury St **SE8** 131 L5
Albyn Rd **SE8** 131 L7
Aldbridge St **SE17** 130 C4
Aldebert Ter **SW8** 129 L6
Aldenham St **NW1** 125 K4
Alder Cl **SE15** 130 D5
Aldermanbury **EC2** 126 A8
Alderney Ms **SE1** 130 B2
Alderney Rd **E1** 127 H6
Alderney St **SW1** 129 H3
Aldersgate St **EC1** 126 A7
Alderton Rd **SE24** 130 A9
Aldford St **W1** 124 G10
Aldgate **EC3** 126 C8
Aldgate High St **EC3** 126 D8
Aldsworth Cl **W9** 124 B6
Aldwych **WC2** 125 M9
Alexander Pl **SW7** 128 E3
Alexander Sq **SW3** 128 E3
Alexander St **W2** 124 A8
Alexandra Av **SW11** 128 G7
Alexandra Cl **SE8** 131 K5
Alexandra Cotts **SE14** 131 K7
Alexandra Pl **NW8** 124 C3
Alexandra Rd **NW8** 124 C2
Alexandra St **SE14** 131 J6
Alexis St **SE16** 130 E3
Alfred Ms **W1** 125 K7
Alfred Pl **WC1** 125 K7
Alfred Rd **W2** 124 A7
Alfred St **E3** 127 K5
Alfreda St **SW11** 129 H7
Algernon Rd **NW6** 124 A3
Algernon Rd **SE13** 131 M10
Algiers Rd **SE13** 131 L10
Alice La **E3** 127 K3
Alice St **SE1** 130 C2
Alie St **E1** 126 D8
Aliwal Rd **SW11** 128 E10
All Saints St **N1** 125 M4
Allardyce St **SW4** 129 M10
Allen Edwards Dr **SW8** 129 L7
Allen Rd **E3** 127 K4
Allen St **W8** 128 A2
Allensbury Pl **NW1** 125 K2
Allingham St **N1** 126 A4
Allington St **SW1** 129 H2
Allitsen Rd **NW8** 124 E4
Alloa Rd **SE8** 131 H4
Alloway Rd **E3** 127 J5
Allsop Pl **NW1** 124 F6
Alma Gro **SE1** 130 D3
Alma Sq **NW8** 124 C5
Alma St **E15** 127 P1
Alma St **NW5** 125 H1
Almeida St **N1** 125 P2
Almeric Rd **SW11** 128 F10
Almond Cl **SE15** 130 E8
Almond Rd **SE16** 130 F3
Almorah Rd **N1** 126 B2
Alpha Gro **E14** 131 L1
Alpha Pl **NW6** 124 A4
Alpha Pl **SW3** 128 E5
Alpha Rd **SE14** 131 K7
Alpha St **SE15** 130 E8
Alpine Gro **E9** 126 G2
Alpine Rd **SE16** 131 H4
Alsace Rd **SE17** 130 C4
Alscot Rd **SE1** 130 D3
Alscot Way **SE1** 130 D3
Altenburg Gdns **SW11** 128 F10
Althea St **SW6** 128 B8
Alton St **E14** 127 M7
Alverton St **SE8** 131 K4
Alvey Est **SE17** 130 C3
Alvey St **SE17** 130 C4
Alwyne Pl **N1** 126 A1
Alwyne Rd **N1** 126 A2
Alwyne Sq **N1** 126 A1
Alwyne Vil **N1** 125 P2
Alzette Ho **E2** 127 H5
Ambergate St **SE17** 129 P4
Amberley Rd **W9** 124 A7
Ambrosden Av **SW1** 129 J2
Ambrose Ms **SW11** 128 E8
Ambrose St **SE16** 130 F3
Amelia St **SE17** 129 P4
Amersham Gro **SE14** 131 K6
Amersham Rd **SE14** 131 K6
Amersham Vale **SE14** 131 K6
Amiel St **E1** 126 G6
Amies St **SW11** 128 F9
Amott Rd **SE15** 130 E9
Amoy Pl **E14** 127 L8
Ampton St **WC1** 125 M5
Amsterdam Rd **E14** 131 N2
Amwell St **EC1** 125 N5
Anchor Retail Pk **E1** 126 G6
Anchor St **SE16** 130 F3
Andalus Rd **SW9** 129 L9
Anderson Rd **E9** 127 H1
Anderson St **SW3** 128 F4
Anderton Cl **SE5** 130 B9
Andover Pl **NW6** 124 B4
Andrew St **E14** 127 N8
Andrew's Rd **E8** 126 F3
Anerley St **SW11** 128 F8
Angel Ct **EC2** 126 B8
Angel La **E15** 127 P1
Angel Ms **N1** 125 N4
Angel St **EC1** 126 A8
Angell Pk Gdns **SW9** 129 N9
Angell Rd **SW9** 129 N9
Angler's La **NW5** 125 H1
Anglia Ho **E14** 127 J8
Anglo Rd **E3** 127 K4
Angrave Ct **E8** 126 D3
Angus St **SE14** 131 J6
Anhalt Rd **SW11** 128 E6
Ann La **SW10** 128 D6
Ann Moss Way **SE16** 130 G2
Anna Cl **E8** 126 D3
Annabel Cl **E14** 127 M8
Annie Besant Cl **E3** 127 K3
Annis Rd **E9** 127 J1
Ansdell Rd **SE15** 130 G8
Ansdell St **W8** 128 B2
Anselm Rd **SW6** 128 A5
Anstey Rd **SE15** 130 E9
Antill Rd **E3** 127 J5
Antill Ter **E1** 127 H8
Antrim Gro **NW3** 124 F1
Antrim Mans **NW3** 124 E1
Antrim Rd **NW3** 124 F1
Apollo Pl **SW10** 128 D6
Appleby Rd **E8** 126 E2
Appleby St **E2** 126 D4
Appold St **EC2** 126 C7
Approach Rd **E2** 126 G4
Aquila St **NW8** 124 D4
Arabin Rd **SE4** 131 J10
Aragon Twr **SE8** 131 K3
Arbery Rd **E3** 127 J5
Arbour Sq **E1** 127 H8
Arbuthnot Rd **SE14** 131 H8
Arbutus St **E8** 126 C3
Arcadia St **E14** 127 L8
Arch St **SE1** 130 A2
Archangel St **SE16** 131 H1
Archery Cl **W2** 124 E8
Archibald Ms **W1** 124 G9
Archibald St **E3** 127 L5
Arden Cres **E14** 131 L3
Arden Est **N1** 126 C4
Ardleigh Rd **N1** 126 B1
Argon Ms **SW6** 128 A6
Argyle Rd **E1** 127 H6
Argyle Sq **WC1** 125 L5
Argyle St **WC1** 125 L5
Argyle Way **SE16** 130 E4
Argyll Rd **W8** 128 A1
Argyll St **W1** 125 J8
Arica Ho **SE16** 130 F2
Arica Rd **SE4** 131 J10
Ariel Rd **NW6** 124 A1
Aristotle Rd **SW4** 129 K9
Arklow Rd **SE14** 131 K5
Arlesford Rd **SW9** 129 L9
Arlington Av **N1** 126 A4
Arlington Lo **SW2** 129 M10
Arlington Rd **NW1** 125 H3
Arlington Sq **N1** 126 A3
Arlington St **SW1** 125 J10
Arlington Way **EC1** 125 N5
Armadale Rd **SW6** 128 A6
Armagh Rd **E3** 127 K3
Armoury Rd **SE8** 131 M8
Armstrong Rd **SW7** 128 D2
Arne St **WC2** 125 L8
Arnhem Pl **E14** 131 L2
Arnold Circ **E2** 126 D5
Arnold Est **SE1** 130 D1
Arnold Rd **E3** 127 L5
Arnould Av **SE5** 130 B10
Arnside St **SE17** 130 A5
Arran Wk **N1** 126 A2
Arrow Rd **E3** 127 M5
Artesian Rd **W2** 124 A8
Artillery La **E1** 126 C7
Artillery Row **SW1** 129 K2
Arundel Pl **N1** 125 N1
Arundel Sq **N7** 125 N1
Arundel St **WC2** 125 M9
Ascalon St **SW8** 129 J6
Ash Gro **E8** 126 F3
Ashbridge St **NW8** 124 E6
Ashburn Gdns **SW7** 128 C3
Ashburn Pl **SW7** 128 C3
Ashburnham Gro **SE10** 131 M6
Ashburnham Pl **SE10** 131 M6
Ashburnham Retreat **SE10** 131 M6
Ashburnham Rd **SW10** 128 C6
Ashbury Rd **SW11** 128 F9
Ashby Gro **N1** 126 A2
Ashby Ms **SE4** 131 K8
Ashby Rd **SE4** 131 K8
Ashcombe St **SW6** 128 B8
Ashcroft Rd **E3** 127 J5
Ashdene **SE15** 130 F7
Ashdown Wk **E14** 131 L3
Asher Way **E1** 126 E10
Ashfield St **E1** 126 F7
Ashland Pl **W1** 124 G7
Ashley Cres **SW11** 128 G9
Ashley Gdns **SW1** 129 J2
Ashley Pl **SW1** 129 J2
Ashmead Rd **SE8** 131 L8
Ashmere Gro **SW2** 129 L10
Ashmill St **NW1** 124 E7
Ashmole Pl **SW8** 129 M5
Ashmole St **SW8** 129 M5
Ashmore Cl **SE15** 130 D6
Ashton St **E14** 127 N9
Ashwin St **E8** 126 D1
Ashworth Rd **W9** 124 B5
Aspen Way **E14** 127 L9
Aspinall Rd **SE4** 131 H9
Aspinden Rd **SE16** 130 F3
Assembly Pas **E1** 126 G7
Astbury Rd **SE15** 130 G7
Aste St **E14** 131 N1
Astell St **SW3** 128 E4
Astle St **SW11** 128 G8
Aston St **E14** 127 J8
Astoria Wk **SW9** 129 N9
Astwood Ms **SW7** 128 B3
Asylum Rd **SE15** 130 F6
Athelstane Gro **E3** 127 K4
Atherfold Rd **SW9** 129 L9
Atherstone Ms **SW7** 128 C3
Atherton St **SW11** 128 E8
Athlone St **NW5** 124 G1
Athol Sq **E14** 127 N8
Atlantic Rd **SW9** 129 N10
Atlas Ms **N7** 125 M1
Atley Rd **E3** 127 L3
Atterbury St **SW1** 129 K3
Auburn Cl **SE14** 131 J6
Auckland Rd **SW11** 128 E10
Auden Pl **NW1** 124 G3
Audley Cl **SW11** 128 G9
Audrey St **E2** 126 E4
Augusta St **E14** 127 M8
Augustus St **NW1** 125 H4
Aulton Pl **SE11** 129 N4
Austen Ho **NW6** 124 A5
Austin Friars **EC2** 126 B8
Austin Rd **SW11** 128 G7
Austin St **E2** 126 D5
Austral St **SE11** 129 P3
Autumn St **E3** 127 L3
Avalon Rd **SW6** 128 B7
Ave Maria La **EC4** 125 P8
Aveline St **SE11** 129 N4
Avenue, The **SE10** 131 P6
Avenue Cl **NW8** 124 E3
Avenue Rd **NW3** 124 D2
Avenue Rd **NW8** 124 D2
Avery Row **W1** 125 H9
Avignon Rd **SE4** 131 H9
Avis Sq **E1** 127 H8
Avon Rd **SE4** 131 L9
Avondale Ri **SE15** 130 D9
Avondale Sq **SE1** 130 E4
Avonley Rd **SE14** 130 G6
Avonmouth St **SE1** 130 A2
Aybrook St **W1** 124 G7
Aylesbury Rd **SE17** 130 B4
Aylesbury St **EC1** 125 P6
Aylesford St **SW1** 129 K4
Aylesham Cen, The **SE15** 130 E7
Aylward St **E1** 126 G8
Aylwyn Est **SE1** 130 C2
Ayres St **SE1** 130 A1
Aytoun Pl **SW9** 129 M8
Aytoun Rd **SW9** 129 M8
Azenby Rd **SE15** 130 D8

B

Baches St **N1** 126 B5
Back Ch La **E1** 126 E9
Back Hill **EC1** 125 N6
Bacon Gro **SE1** 130 D2
Bacon St **E1** 126 D6
Bacon St **E2** 126 D6
Baddow Wk **N1** 126 A3
Badsworth Rd **SE5** 130 A6
Bagley's La **SW6** 128 B7
Bagshot St **SE17** 130 C4
Baildon St **SE8** 131 K6
Bainbridge St **WC1** 125 K8
Baker St **NW1** 124 F6
Baker St **W1** 124 F7
Baker's Row **EC1** 125 N6
Bakery Cl **SW9** 129 M7
Balaclava Rd **SE1** 130 D3

## Bal - Bro

Balcombe St **NW1** 124 F6
Balcorne St **E9** 126 G2
Balderton St **W1** 124 G8
Baldock St **E3** 127 M4
Baldwin Cres **SE5** 130 A7
Baldwin Ter **N1** 126 A4
Baldwin's Gdns **EC1** 125 N7
Bale Rd **E1** 127 J7
Balfe St **N1** 125 L4
Balfern St **SW11** 128 E7
Balfour St **SE17** 130 B3
Balladier Wk **E14** 127 M7
Ballance Rd **E9** 127 H1
Ballantine St **SW18** 128 C10
Ballast Quay **SE10** 131 P4
Ballater Rd **SW2** 129 L10
Balls Pond Rd **N1** 126 B1
Balmer Rd **E3** 127 K4
Balmes Rd **N1** 126 B3
Balmoral Gro **N7** 125 M1
Balmore Cl **E14** 127 N8
Balniel Gate **SW1** 129 K4
Baltic St E **EC1** 126 A6
Baltic St W **EC1** 126 A6
Balvaird Pl **SW1** 129 K4
Banbury Rd **E9** 127 H2
Banbury St **SW11** 128 E8
Bancroft Rd **E1** 126 G5
Banfield Rd **SE15** 130 F9
Bank End **SE1** 126 A10
Bank St **E14** 127 L10
Bankside Av **SE13** 131 M9
Bankton Rd **SW2** 129 N10
Banner St **EC1** 126 A6
Bannerman Ho **SW8** 129 M5
Banstead St **SE15** 130 G9
Bantry St **SE5** 130 B6
Barbers Rd **E15** 127 M4
Barbican, The **EC2** 126 A7
Barchester St **E14** 127 M7
Barclay Cl **SW6** 128 A6
Barclay Rd **SW6** 128 A6
Bardsley La **SE10** 131 N5
Barfleur La **SE8** 131 K3
Barford St **N1** 125 N3
Barforth Rd **SE15** 130 F9
Baring St **N1** 126 B3
Bark Pl **W2** 124 B9
Barker Dr **NW1** 125 J2
Barker Ms **SW4** 129 H10
Barker St **SW10** 128 C5
Barkston Gdns **SW5** 128 B3
Barkworth Rd **SE16** 130 F4
Barlborough St **SE14** 130 G6
Barleycorn Way **E14** 127 K9
Barnaby Pl **SW7** 128 D3
Barnard Ms **SW11** 128 E10
Barnard Rd **SW11** 128 E10
Barnby St **NW1** 125 J4
Barnes St **E14** 127 J8
Barnes Ter **SE8** 131 K4
Barnet Gro **E2** 126 E5
Barnfield Pl **E14** 131 L3
Barnham St **SE1** 130 C1
Barnsbury Gro **N7** 125 M2
Barnsbury Pk **N1** 125 N2
Barnsbury Rd **N1** 125 N4
Barnsbury Sq **N1** 125 N2
Barnsbury St **N1** 125 N2
Barnsbury Ter **N1** 125 M2
Barnsdale Av **E14** 131 L3
Barnsley St **E1** 126 F6
Barnwood Cl **W9** 124 B6
Baron St **N1** 125 N4
Barons Pl **SE1** 129 N1
Barrett St **W1** 124 G8
Barriedale **SE14** 131 J7
Barrington Rd **SW9** 129 P9
Barrow Hill Rd **NW8** 124 E4
Barset Rd **SE15** 130 G9
Barter St **WC1** 125 L7
Bartholomew Cl **EC1** 126 A7
Bartholomew Cl **SW18** 128 C10
Bartholomew Rd **NW5** 125 J1
Bartholomew Sq **EC1** 126 A6
Bartholomew St **SE1** 130 B2
Bartholomew Vil **NW5** 125 J1
Bartlett Cl **E14** 127 L8
Basevi Way **SE8** 131 M5
Basil St **SW3** 128 F2
Basing Ct **SE15** 130 D7
Basingdon Way **SE5** 130 B10
Basinghall Av **EC2** 126 B7
Basinghall St **EC2** 126 A7
Basire St **N1** 126 A3
Basnett Rd **SW11** 128 G9
Bassett St **NW5** 124 G1
Bastwick St **EC1** 125 P6
Basuto Rd **SW6** 128 A7
Batavia Rd **SE14** 131 J6
Batchelor St **N1** 125 N4
Bateman's Row **EC2** 126 C6
Bath St **EC1** 126 B5
Bath Ter **SE1** 130 A2
Bathurst St **W2** 124 D9
Batten St **SW11** 128 E9
Battersea Br **SW3** 128 D6
Battersea Br **SW11** 128 D6
Battersea Br Rd **SW11** 128 E6
Battersea Ch Rd **SW11** 128 D7
Battersea High St **SW11** 128 D7
Battersea Pk **SW11** 128 F6
Battersea Pk Rd **SW8** 129 H7
Battersea Pk Rd **SW11** 128 E8
Battle Br La **SE1** 126 C10
Battle Br Rd **NW1** 125 L4
Batty St **E1** 126 E8
Bavent Rd **SE5** 130 A8
Bawtree Rd **SE14** 131 J6
Baxendale St **E2** 126 E5
Baxter Rd **N1** 126 B1
Bayford St **E8** 126 F2
Bayham Pl **NW1** 125 J3
Bayham St **NW1** 125 J3
Bayley St **WC1** 125 K7
Baylis Rd **SE1** 129 N1
Baynes St **NW1** 125 J2
Bayswater Rd **W2** 124 D9
Baythorne St **E3** 127 K7
Baytree Rd **SW2** 129 M10
Bazely St **E14** 127 N9
Beachy Rd **E3** 127 L2
Beacon Gate **SE14** 131 H9
Beaconsfield Rd **SE17** 130 B4
Beak St **W1** 125 J9
Beale Pl **E3** 127 K4
Beale Rd **E3** 127 K3
Beanacre Cl **E9** 127 K1
Bear Gdns **SE1** 126 A10
Bear La **SE1** 125 P10
Beaton Cl **SE15** 130 D7
Beatrice Pl **W8** 128 B2
Beatrice Rd **SE1** 130 E3
Beatson Wk **SE16** 127 H10
Beatty St **NW1** 125 J4
Beauchamp Pl **SW3** 128 E2
Beauchamp Rd **SW11** 128 E10
Beaufort Gdns **SW3** 128 E2
Beaufort St **SW3** 128 D5
Beaufoy Wk **SE11** 129 M3
Beaulieu Cl **SE5** 130 B9
Beaumont Gro **E1** 127 H6
Beaumont Pl **W1** 125 J6
Beaumont Sq **E1** 127 H6
Beaumont St **W1** 124 G7
Beaumont Wk **NW3** 124 F2
Beccles St **E14** 127 K9
Beck Cl **SE13** 131 M7
Beck Rd **E8** 126 F3
Beckett Ho **SW9** 129 L8
Beckway St **SE17** 130 B3
Bedale St **SE1** 126 B10
Bedford Av **WC1** 125 K7
Bedford Gdns **W8** 124 A10
Bedford Ho **SW4** 129 L10
Bedford Pl **WC1** 125 L7
Bedford Rd **SW4** 129 L9
Bedford Row **WC1** 125 M7
Bedford Sq **WC1** 125 K7
Bedford St **WC2** 125 L9
Bedford Way **WC1** 125 K6
Beech St **EC2** 126 A7
Beechmore Rd **SW11** 128 F7
Beechwood Rd **E8** 126 D1
Beehive Cl **E8** 126 D2
Beehive Pl **SW9** 129 N9
Beeston Pl **SW1** 129 H2
Belfort Rd **SE15** 130 G8
Belgrave Gdns **NW8** 124 B3
Belgrave Ms N **SW1** 128 G2
Belgrave Ms S **SW1** 128 G2
Belgrave Ms W **SW1** 128 G2
Belgrave Pl **SW1** 128 G2
Belgrave Rd **SW1** 129 H3
Belgrave Sq **SW1** 128 G2
Belgrave St **E1** 127 H8
Belgrove St **WC1** 125 L5
Belinda Rd **SW9** 129 P9
Belitha Vil **N1** 125 M2
Bell La **E1** 126 D7
Bell St **NW1** 124 E7
Bell Wf La **EC4** 126 A9
Bell Yd **WC2** 125 N8
Bellefields Rd **SW9** 129 M9
Bellenden Rd **SE15** 130 D8
Bellevue Pl **E1** 126 G6
Bells All **SW6** 128 A8
Bellwood Rd **SE15** 131 H10
Belmont Cl **SW4** 129 J9
Belmont Gro **SE13** 131 P9
Belmont Hill **SE13** 131 P9
Belmont Pk **SE13** 131 P10
Belmont Pk Cl **SE13** 131 P10
Belmont Rd **SW4** 129 J9
Belmont St **NW1** 124 G2
Belmore St **SW8** 129 K7
Belsham St **E9** 126 G1
Belsize Av **NW3** 124 D1
Belsize Gro **NW3** 124 E1
Belsize La **NW3** 124 D1
Belsize Pk **NW3** 124 D1
Belsize Pk Gdns **NW3** 124 E1
Belsize Rd **NW6** 124 B3
Belsize Sq **NW3** 124 D1
Belsize Ter **NW3** 124 D1
Belton Way **E3** 127 L7
Beltran Rd **SW6** 128 B8
Belvedere Ms **SE15** 130 G9
Belvedere Pl **SE1** 129 P1
Belvedere Rd **SE1** 125 M10
Belvedere Twr, The **SW10** 128 C7
Bemerton Est **N1** 125 M2
Bemerton St **N1** 125 M3
Ben Jonson Rd **E1** 127 J7
Benbow St **SE8** 131 L5
Benedict Rd **SW9** 129 M9
Bengeworth Rd **SE5** 130 A9
Benham Cl **SW11** 128 D9
Benhill Rd **SE5** 130 B6
Benjamin Cl **E8** 126 E3
Benjamin St **EC1** 125 P7
Benledi St **E14** 127 P8
Benn St **E9** 127 J1
Bennett Gro **SE13** 131 M7
Bennett Rd **SW9** 129 N8
Bentham Rd **E9** 127 H1
Bentinck St **W1** 124 G8
Benworth St **E3** 127 K5
Berger Rd **E9** 127 H1
Berkeley Ho **E3** 127 L6
Berkeley Sq **W1** 125 H9
Berkeley St **W1** 125 H9
Berkley Rd **NW1** 124 F2
Berkshire Rd **E9** 127 K1
Bermondsey Sq **SE1** 130 C1
Bermondsey Wall E **SE16** 130 E1
Bermondsey Wall W **SE16** 130 E1
Bernard St **WC1** 125 L6
Bernays Gro **SW9** 129 M10
Berners Ms **W1** 125 J7
Berners Pl **W1** 125 J8
Berners Rd **N1** 125 N4
Berners St **W1** 125 J7
Bernhardt Cres **NW8** 124 E6
Berry St **EC1** 125 P6
Berryfield Rd **SE17** 129 P4
Berthon St **SE8** 131 L6
Bertrand St **SE13** 131 M9
Berwick St **W1** 125 J8
Bessborough Gdns **SW1** 129 K4
Bessborough Pl **SW1** 129 K4
Bessborough St **SW1** 129 K4
Bessemer Rd **SE5** 130 A8
Besson St **SE14** 130 G7
Bestwood St **SE8** 131 H3
Bethnal Grn Est **E2** 126 G5
Bethnal Grn Rd **E1** 126 D6
Bethnal Grn Rd **E2** 126 D6
Bethwin Rd **SE5** 129 P6
Betterton St **WC2** 125 L8
Bevan St **N1** 126 A3
Bevenden St **N1** 126 B5
Beverley Ct **SE4** 131 K9
Bevington St **SE16** 130 E1
Bevis Marks **EC3** 126 C8
Bewdley St **N1** 125 N2
Bewick Ms **SE15** 130 F6
Bewick St **SW8** 129 H8
Bianca Rd **SE15** 130 D5
Bickenhall St **W1** 124 F7
Bicknell Rd **SE5** 130 A9
Bidborough St **WC1** 125 K5
Bidbury Cl **SE15** 130 C5
Biddulph Rd **W9** 124 B5
Bidwell St **SE15** 130 F7
Biggerstaff Rd **E15** 127 N3
Bigland St **E1** 126 F8
Billing Pl **SW10** 128 B6
Billing Rd **SW10** 128 B6
Billing St **SW10** 128 B6
Billingford Cl **SE4** 131 H10
Billington Rd **SE14** 131 H6
Billiter St **EC3** 126 C8
Billson St **E14** 131 N3
Bina Gdns **SW5** 128 C3
Binfield Rd **SW4** 129 L7
Bingfield St **N1** 125 L3
Bingham St **N1** 126 B1
Binney St **W1** 124 G8
Birchfield St **E14** 127 L9
Birchin La **EC3** 126 B8
Birchington Rd **NW6** 124 A3
Bird in Bush Rd **SE15** 130 E6
Birdcage Wk **SW1** 129 J1
Birdhurst Rd **SW18** 128 C10
Birdsfield La **E3** 127 K3
Birkbeck St **E2** 126 F5
Birkenhead St **WC1** 125 L5
Birley St **SW11** 128 G8
Biscoe Way **SE13** 131 P9
Bishop St **N1** 126 A3
Bishops Br **W2** 124 C8
Bishops Br Rd **W2** 124 B8
Bishop's Rd **SW11** 128 E6
Bishops Ter **SE11** 129 N3
Bishops Way **E2** 126 F4
Bishopsgate **EC2** 126 C8
Bisson Rd **E15** 127 N4
Black Friars La **EC4** 125 P9
Black Prince Rd **SE1** 129 M3
Black Prince Rd **SE11** 129 M3
Blackburn Rd **NW6** 124 B1
Blackburne's Ms **W1** 124 G9
Blackfriars Br **EC4** 125 P9
Blackfriars Br **SE1** 125 P9
Blackfriars Rd **SE1** 125 P10
Blackheath Av **SE10** 131 P6
Blackheath Hill **SE10** 131 N7
Blackheath Ri **SE13** 131 N8
Blackheath Rd **SE10** 131 M7
Blackhorse Rd **SE8** 131 J4
Blacklands Ter **SW3** 128 F3
Blackpool Rd **SE15** 130 F8
Blackstone Est **E8** 126 F2
Blackthorn St **E3** 127 L6
Blacktree Ms **SW9** 129 N9
Blackwall Trd Est **E14** 127 P7
Blackwall Tunnel **E14** 127 P10
Blackwall Tunnel Northern App **E3** 127 L4
Blackwall Tunnel Northern App **E14** 127 L4
Blackwall Way **E14** 127 N9
Blackwood St **SE17** 130 B4
Blair Cl **N1** 126 A1
Blair St **E14** 127 N8
Blake Gdns **SW6** 128 B7
Blaker Rd **E15** 127 N3
Blakes Rd **SE15** 130 C6
Blanchard Way **E8** 126 E1
Blanchedowne **SE5** 130 B10
Blandford Sq **NW1** 124 E6
Blandford St **W1** 124 G7
Blantyre St **SW10** 128 D6
Blashford **NW3** 124 F2
Blasker Wk **E14** 131 L4
Blenheim Gro **SE15** 130 E8
Blenheim Rd **NW8** 124 C4
Blenheim Ter **NW8** 124 C4
Blessington Cl **SE13** 131 P9
Blessington Rd **SE13** 131 P9
Bletchley Ct **N1** 126 B4
Bletchley St **N1** 126 A4
Bliss Cres **SE13** 131 M8
Blissett St **SE10** 131 N7
Blithfield St **W8** 128 B2
Blomfield Rd **W9** 124 C7
Blomfield St **EC2** 126 B7
Blomfield Vil **W2** 124 B7
Blondel St **SW11** 128 G8
Blondin St **E3** 127 L4
Bloomfield Pl **W1** 125 H9
Bloomfield Ter **SW1** 128 G4
Bloomsbury Pl **WC1** 125 L7
Bloomsbury Sq **WC1** 125 L7
Bloomsbury St **WC1** 125 K7
Bloomsbury Way **WC1** 125 L8
Blossom St **E1** 126 C7
Blount St **E14** 127 J8
Blucher Rd **SE5** 130 A6
Blue Anchor La **SE16** 130 E3
Blue Anchor Yd **E1** 126 E9
Blundell St **N7** 125 L2
Blythe St **E2** 126 F5
Boardwalk Pl **E14** 127 N10
Boathouse Wk **SE15** 130 D6
Bobbin Cl **SW4** 129 J9
Bocking St **E8** 126 F3
Bohemia Pl **E8** 126 F1
Bohn Rd **E1** 127 J7
Bolden St **SE8** 131 M8
Bolina Rd **SE16** 130 G4
Bolingbroke Gro **SW11** 128 E10
Bolingbroke Wk **SW11** 128 D6
Bolney St **SW8** 129 M6
Bolsover St **W1** 125 H6
Bolton Cres **SE5** 129 P5
Bolton Gdns **SW5** 128 B4
Bolton Gdns Ms **SW10** 128 B4
Bolton Rd **NW8** 124 B3
Bolton St **W1** 125 H10
Boltons, The **SW10** 128 C4
Boltons Pl **SW5** 128 C4
Bombay St **SE16** 130 F3
Bonar Rd **SE15** 130 E6
Bond Ct **EC4** 126 B8
Bondway **SW8** 129 L5
Bonfield Rd **SE13** 131 N10
Bonhill St **EC2** 126 B6
Bonita Ms **SE4** 131 H9
Bonner Rd **E2** 126 G4
Bonner St **E2** 126 G4
Bonnington Sq **SW8** 129 M5
Bonny St **NW1** 125 J2
Bonsor St **SE5** 130 C6
Boot St **N1** 126 C5
Borland Rd **SE15** 130 G10
Borough High St **SE1** 130 A1
Borough Rd **SE1** 129 P2
Borthwick St **SE8** 131 L4
Boscobel Pl **SW1** 128 G3
Boscobel St **NW8** 124 D6
Boston Pl **NW1** 124 F6
Boswell St **WC1** 125 L7
Boulcott St **E1** 127 H8
Boulevard, The **SW6** 128 C7
Boundary La **SE17** 130 A5
Boundary Rd **NW8** 124 B3
Boundary St **E2** 126 D6
Bourdon St **W1** 125 H9
Bourne Est **EC1** 125 N7
Bourne St **SW1** 128 G3
Bourne Ter **W2** 124 B7
Bournemouth Cl **SE15** 130 E8
Bournemouth Rd **SE15** 130 E8
Bousfield Rd **SE14** 131 H8
Boutflower Rd **SW11** 128 E10
Bouverie Pl **W2** 124 D8
Bouverie St **EC4** 125 N8
Bovingdon Rd **SW6** 128 B7
Bow Back Rivers Wk **E15** 127 M2
Bow Br Est **E3** 127 M5
Bow Common La **E3** 127 K6
Bow Ind Pk **E15** 127 L2
Bow La **EC4** 126 A8
Bow Rd **E3** 127 K5
Bow St **WC2** 125 L8
Bowden St **SE11** 129 N4
Bowditch **SE8** 131 K4
Bowen St **E14** 127 M8
Bower St **E1** 127 H8
Bowerdean St **SW6** 128 B7
Bowerman Av **SE14** 131 J5
Bowhill Cl **SW9** 129 N6
Bowl Ct **EC2** 126 C6
Bowland Rd **SW4** 129 K10
Bowling Grn La **EC1** 125 N6
Bowling Grn Pl **SE1** 130 B1
Bowling Grn St **SE11** 129 N5
Bowood Rd **SW11** 128 G10
Bowsprit Pt **E14** 131 L2
Bowyer Pl **SE5** 130 B6
Bowyer St **SE5** 130 A6
Boyd St **E1** 126 E8
Boyfield St **SE1** 129 P1
Boyne Rd **SE13** 131 N9
Boyson Rd **SE17** 130 B5
Brabazon St **E14** 127 M8
Brabourn Gro **SE15** 130 G8
Brackley Av **SE15** 130 F9
Bracklyn St **N1** 126 B4
Bradbourne St **SW6** 128 A8
Bradenham Cl **SE17** 130 B5
Bradmead **SW8** 129 H6
Bradstock Rd **E9** 127 H1
Bradwell St **E1** 127 H5
Brady St **E1** 126 F6
Braes St **N1** 125 P2
Braganza St **SE17** 129 P4
Braham St **E1** 126 D8
Braintree St **E2** 126 G5
Braithwaite Twr **W2** 124 D7
Bramah Grn **SW9** 129 N7
Bramcote Gro **SE16** 130 G4
Bramerton St **SW3** 128 E5
Bramford Rd **SW18** 128 C10
Bramham Gdns **SW5** 128 B4
Bramlands Cl **SW11** 128 E9
Bramshaw Rd **E9** 127 H1
Bramwell Ms **N1** 125 M3
Branch Pl **N1** 126 B3
Branch Rd **E14** 127 J9
Branch St **SE15** 130 C6
Brand St **SE10** 131 N6
Brandon Est **SE17** 129 P5
Brandon Rd **N7** 125 L2
Brandon St **SE17** 130 A3
Brangton Rd **SE11** 129 M4
Branscombe St **SE13** 131 M9
Brassey Sq **SW11** 128 G9
Braxfield Rd **SE4** 131 J10
Bray **NW3** 124 E2
Bray Pl **SW3** 128 F3
Brayards Rd **SE15** 130 F8
Brayburne Av **SW4** 129 J8
Bread St **EC4** 126 A9
Breakspears Rd **SE4** 131 K9
Bream St **E3** 127 L2
Bream's Bldgs **EC4** 125 N8
Breer St **SW6** 128 B9
Bremner Rd **SW7** 128 C1
Brendon St **W1** 124 E8
Brenthouse Rd **E9** 126 F2
Brenton St **E14** 127 J8
Bressenden Pl **SW1** 129 H2
Brewer St **W1** 125 J9
Brewery Rd **N7** 125 L2
Brewhouse La **E1** 126 F10
Brewhouse Wk **SE16** 127 J10
Brewster Ho **E14** 127 K9
Briant St **SE14** 131 H7
Brick La **E1** 126 D7
Brick La **E2** 126 D5
Brick St **W1** 125 H10
Bricklayer's Arms Distribution Cen **SE1** 130 C3
Bride St **N7** 125 M1
Bridewain St **SE1** 130 D2
Bridge App **NW1** 124 G2
Bridge La **SW11** 128 E7
Bridge Meadows **SE14** 131 H5
Bridge Pl **SW1** 129 H3
Bridge Rd **E15** 127 P2
Bridge St **SW1** 129 L1
Bridgefoot **SE1** 129 L4
Bridgeman Rd **N1** 125 M2
Bridgeman St **NW8** 124 E4
Bridgend Rd **SW18** 128 C10
Bridges Ct **SW11** 128 D9
Bridgeway St **NW1** 125 J4
Bridgwater Rd **E15** 127 N3
Bridport Pl **N1** 126 B4
Brief St **SE5** 129 P7
Bright St **E14** 127 M8
Brightlingsea Pl **E14** 127 K9
Brighton Ter **SW9** 129 M10
Brill Pl **NW1** 125 K4
Brindley St **SE14** 131 K7
Brinklow Ho **W2** 124 B7
Brinkworth Way **E9** 127 K1
Brion Pl **E14** 127 N7
Brisbane St **SE5** 130 B6
Bristol Gdns **W9** 124 B6
Britannia Rd **E14** 131 L3
Britannia Rd **SW6** 128 B6
Britannia Row **N1** 125 P3
Britannia St **WC1** 125 M5
Britannia Wk **N1** 126 B5
British St **E3** 127 K5
Britten St **SW3** 128 E4
Britton St **EC1** 125 P6
Brixton Oval **SW2** 129 N10
Brixton Rd **SW9** 129 N8
Brixton Sta Rd **SW9** 129 N10
Broad La **EC2** 126 C7
Broad Sanctuary **SW1** 129 K1
Broad Wk **NW1** 125 H5
Broad Wk **W1** 124 G10
Broad Wk, The **W8** 124 B10
Broadfield La **NW1** 125 L2
Broadhinton Rd **SW4** 129 H9
Broadhurst Gdns **NW6** 124 B1
Broadley St **NW8** 124 E7
Broadley Ter **NW1** 124 E6
Broadwalk Ct **W8** 124 A10
Broadwall **SE1** 125 N10
Broadway **E15** 127 P2
Broadway **SW1** 129 K2
Broadway Mkt **E8** 126 F3
Broadwick St **W1** 125 J8
Brock Pl **E3** 127 M6
Brockham St **SE1** 130 A2
Brockill Cres **SE4** 131 J10
Brocklehurst St **SE14** 131 H6
Brockley Footpath **SE15** 130 G10
Brockley Gdns **SE4** 131 K8
Brockley Rd **SE4** 131 K9
Brodlove La **E1** 127 H9
Broke Wk **E8** 126 E3
Brokesley St **E3** 127 K6
Bromar Rd **SE5** 130 C9
Bromell's Rd **SW4** 129 J10
Bromfelde Rd **SW4** 129 K8
Bromfelde Wk **SW4** 129 K8
Bromfield St **N1** 125 N4
Bromley Hall Rd **E14** 127 N7
Bromley High St **E3** 127 M5
Bromley St **E1** 127 H7
Brompton Pk Cres **SW6** 128 B5
Brompton Pl **SW3** 128 E2
Brompton Rd **SW1** 128 E2
Brompton Rd **SW3** 128 E2
Brompton Rd **SW7** 128 E2
Brompton Sq **SW3** 128 E2
Bromyard Ho **SE15** 130 F6
Bronte Ho **NW6** 124 B5
Bronti Cl **SE17** 130 A4
Bronze St **SE8** 131 L6
Brook Dr **SE11** 129 N3
Brook Gate **W1** 124 F9
Brook St **W1** 125 H8
Brook St **W2** 124 D9
Brookbank Rd **SE13** 131 L9
Brooke St **EC1** 125 N7
Brookfield Rd **E9** 127 J1
Brookmill Rd **SE8** 131 L7
Brook's Ms **W1** 125 H9
Brooksbank St **E9** 126 G1
Brooksby St **N1** 125 N2
Broome Way **SE5** 130 B6
Broomfield St **E14** 127 L7
Broomgrove Rd **SW9** 129 M8
Broomhouse La **SW6** 128 A8
Broomhouse Rd **SW6** 128 A8
Brougham Rd **E8** 126 E3
Brougham St **SW11** 128 F8
Broughton Dr **SW9** 129 N10
Broughton Rd **SW6** 128 B8

Bro - Cla


Broughton St **SW8** 128 G8
Brown Hart Gdns **W1** 124 G9
Brown St **W1** 124 F8
Brownfield St **E14** 127 M8
Browning St **SE17** 130 A4
Brownlow Ms **WC1** 125 M6
Brownlow Rd **E8** 126 D3
Brown's Bldgs **EC3** 126 C8
Broxwood Way **NW8** 124 E3
Bruce Rd **E3** 127 M5
Bruford Ct **SE8** 131 L5
Brune St **E1** 126 D7
Brunel Est **W2** 124 A7
Brunel Rd **SE16** 130 E2
Brunswick Ct **SE1** 130 C1
Brunswick Gdns **W8** 124 A10
Brunswick Pk **SE5** 130 B7
Brunswick Pl **N1** 126 B5
Brunswick Pl **NW1** 124 G6
Brunswick Quay **SE16** 131 H2
Brunswick Sq **WC1** 125 L6
Brunswick Vil **SE5** 130 C7
Brunton Pl **E14** 127 J8
Brushfield St **E1** 126 C7
Brussels Rd **SW11** 128 D10
Bruton La **W1** 125 H9
Bruton Pl **W1** 125 H9
Bruton St **W1** 125 H9
Bryan Rd **SE16** 131 K1
Bryanston Pl **W1** 124 F7
Bryanston Sq **W1** 124 F7
Bryanston St **W1** 124 F8
Bryant Ct **E2** 126 D4
Bryant St **E15** 127 P2
Brymay Cl **E3** 127 L4
Brynmaer Rd **SW11** 128 F7
Buchan Rd **SE15** 130 G9
Buck St **NW1** 125 H2
Buckfast St **E2** 126 E5
Buckhurst St **E1** 126 F6
Buckingham Gate **SW1** 129 J2
Buckingham Palace Rd **SW1** 129 H3
Buckingham Rd **N1** 126 C1
Buckland Cres **NW3** 124 D2
Buckland St **N1** 126 B4
Bucklersbury **EC4** 126 B8
Buckmaster Rd **SW11** 128 E10
Bucknall St **WC2** 125 K8
Bucknell Cl **SW2** 129 M10
Buckner Rd **SW2** 129 M10
Buckters Rents **SE16** 127 J10
Budge's Wk **W2** 124 C9
Bulinga St **SW1** 129 K3
Bullace Row **SE5** 130 B6
Bullards Pl **E2** 127 H5
Bullen St **SW11** 128 E8
Buller Cl **SE15** 130 E6
Bullivant St **E14** 127 N9
Bulmer Pl **W11** 124 A10
Bulstrode St **W1** 124 G8
Bunhill Row **EC1** 126 B6
Bunhouse Pl **SW1** 128 G4
Bunning Way **N7** 125 L2
Burbage Cl **SE1** 130 B2
Burcham St **E14** 127 M8
Burchell Rd **SE15** 130 F7
Burder Cl **N1** 126 C1
Burdett Rd **E3** 127 K6
Burdett Rd **E14** 127 K6
Burford Rd **E15** 127 P2
Burge St **SE1** 130 B2
Burgess Business Pk **SE5** 130 B6
Burgess St **E14** 127 L7
Burgh St **N1** 125 P4
Burgos Gro **SE10** 131 M7
Burgoyne Rd **SW9** 129 M9
Burlington Arc **W1** 125 J9
Burlington Gdns **W1** 125 J9
Burnaby St **SW10** 128 C6
Burne St **NW1** 124 E7
Burney St **SE10** 131 N6
Burnham **NW3** 124 E2
Burnham St **E2** 126 G5
Burnley Rd **SW9** 129 M8
Burns Rd **SW11** 128 F8
Burnsall St **SW3** 128 E4
Burnside Cl **SE16** 127 H10
Burnthwaite Rd **SW6** 128 A6
Burr Cl **E1** 126 E10
Burrell St **SE1** 125 P10
Burrells Wf Sq **E14** 131 M4
Burrow Rd **SE22** 130 C10
Burslem St **E1** 126 E8
Burton La **SW9** 129 N8
Burton Rd **SW9** 129 P8
Burton St **WC1** 125 K5
Burwell Wk **E3** 127 L6
Burwood Pl **W2** 124 E8
Bury Pl **WC1** 125 L7
Bury St **EC3** 126 C8
Bury St **SW1** 125 J10
Bury Wk **SW3** 128 E4
Busby Pl **NW5** 125 K1
Bush Rd **E8** 126 F3
Bush Rd **SE8** 131 H3
Bushberry Rd **E9** 127 J1
Bushey Hill Rd **SE5** 130 C7
Bushwood Dr **SE1** 130 D3
Butcher Row **E1** 127 H9
Butcher Row **E14** 127 H9
Bute St **SW7** 128 D3
Butlers Wf **SE1** 126 D10
Buttermere Wk **E8** 126 D1
Buttesland St **N1** 126 B5
Buxhall Cres **E9** 127 K1
Buxted Rd **E8** 126 D2
Buxted Rd **SE22** 130 C10
Buxton Ms **SW4** 129 K8
Buxton St **E1** 126 D6
Byam St **SW6** 128 C8
Byfield Cl **SE16** 131 J1
Bygrove St **E14** 127 M8
Byng Pl **WC1** 125 K6
Byng St **E14** 131 L1
Byron Cl **E8** 126 E3
Bythorn St **SW9** 129 M9
Byward St **EC3** 126 C9
Bywater Pl **SE16** 127 J10
Bywater St **SW3** 128 F4

**C**

Cabbell St **NW1** 124 E7
Cable St **E1** 126 E9
Cabot Pl **E14** 127 L10
Cabot Sq **E14** 127 L10
Cabul Rd **SW11** 128 E8
Cade Rd **SE10** 131 P7
Cadet Dr **SE1** 130 E3
Cadiz St **SE17** 130 A4
Cadogan Gdns **SW3** 128 F3
Cadogan Gate **SW1** 128 F3
Cadogan La **SW1** 128 G2
Cadogan Pl **SW1** 128 F2
Cadogan Sq **SW1** 128 F2
Cadogan St **SW3** 128 F3
Cadogan Ter **E9** 127 K1
Cahir St **E14** 131 M3
Calabria Rd **N5** 125 P1
Calais St **SE5** 129 P7
Caldecot Rd **SE5** 130 A8
Caldwell St **SW9** 129 M6
Cale St **SW3** 128 E4
Caledonia St **N1** 125 L4
Caledonian Rd **N1** 125 M4
Caledonian Wf **E14** 131 P3
Callendar Rd **SW7** 128 D2
Callow St **SW3** 128 D5
Calshot St **N1** 125 M4
Calthorpe St **WC1** 125 M6
Calvert Av **E2** 126 C5
Calverton **SE5** 130 C5
Calvin St **E1** 126 D6
Calypso Cres **SE15** 130 D6
Calypso Way **SE16** 131 K2
Cam Rd **E15** 127 P3
Camberwell Ch St **SE5** 130 B7
Camberwell Glebe **SE5** 130 B7
Camberwell Grn **SE5** 130 B7
Camberwell Gro **SE5** 130 B7
Camberwell New Rd **SE5** 129 N6
Camberwell Rd **SE5** 130 A5
Camberwell Sta Rd **SE5** 130 A7
Cambria Rd **SE5** 130 A9
Cambria St **SW6** 128 B6
Cambridge Av **NW6** 124 A4
Cambridge Circ **WC2** 125 K8
Cambridge Cres **E2** 126 F4
Cambridge Gdns **NW6** 124 A4
Cambridge Heath Rd **E1** 126 F4
Cambridge Heath Rd **E2** 126 F4
Cambridge Pl **W8** 128 B1
Cambridge Rd **NW6** 124 A5
Cambridge Rd **SW11** 128 F7
Cambridge Sq **W2** 124 E8
Cambridge St **SW1** 129 H4
Camden High St **NW1** 125 H3
Camden Ms **NW1** 125 K1
Camden Pk Rd **NW1** 125 K1
Camden Pas **N1** 125 P3
Camden Rd **NW1** 125 J3
Camden Sq **NW1** 125 K1
Camden St **NW1** 125 H2
Camden Wk **N1** 125 P3
Camdenhurst St **E14** 127 J8
Camera Pl **SW10** 128 D5
Camilla Rd **SE16** 130 F3
Camlet St **E2** 126 D6
Camley St **NW1** 125 K2
Camomile St **EC3** 126 C8
Campana Rd **SW6** 128 A7
Campbell Rd **E3** 127 L5
Campden Gro **W8** 128 A1
Campden Hill **W8** 128 A1
Campden Hill Gdns **W8** 124 A10
Campden Hill Rd **W8** 124 A10
Campden St **W8** 124 A10
Camplin St **SE14** 131 H6
Canada Est **SE16** 130 G2
Canada Sq **E14** 127 M10
Canada St **SE16** 131 H1
Canal App **SE8** 131 J5
Canal Boul **NW1** 125 K1
Canal Cl **E1** 127 J6
Canal Gro **SE15** 130 E5
Canal Path **E2** 126 D3
Canal St **SE5** 130 B5
Canal Wk **N1** 126 B3
Cancell Rd **SW9** 129 N7
Candahar Rd **SW11** 128 E8
Candle Gro **SE15** 130 F9
Candy St **E3** 127 K3
Canfield Gdns **NW6** 124 C2
Canning Cross **SE5** 130 C8
Canning Pas **W8** 128 C2
Canning Pl **W8** 128 C2
Cannon Dr **E14** 127 L9
Cannon St **EC4** 126 A8
Cannon St Rd **E1** 126 F8
Cannon Wf Business Cen **SE8** 131 J3
Canon Beck Rd **SE16** 130 G1
Canon Row **SW1** 129 L1
Canon St **N1** 126 A3
Canonbury Cres **N1** 126 A2
Canonbury Gro **N1** 126 A2
Canonbury La **N1** 125 P2
Canonbury Pk N **N1** 126 A1
Canonbury Pk S **N1** 126 A1
Canonbury Pl **N1** 125 P1
Canonbury Rd **N1** 125 P1
Canonbury Sq **N1** 125 P2
Canonbury St **N1** 126 A2
Canonbury Vil **N1** 125 P2
Canrobert St **E2** 126 F5
Cantelowes Rd **NW1** 125 K1
Canterbury Cres **SW9** 129 N9
Canterbury Pl **SE17** 129 P3
Canterbury Rd **NW6** 124 A4
Canterbury Ter **NW6** 124 A4
Cantium Retail Pk **SE1** 130 E5
Canton St **E14** 127 L8
Cantrell Rd **E3** 127 K6
Canute Gdns **SE16** 131 H3
Capland St **NW8** 124 D6
Capper St **WC1** 125 J6
Capstan Rd **SE8** 131 K3
Capstan Sq **E14** 131 N1
Capstan Way **SE16** 127 J10
Caradoc Cl **W2** 124 A8
Carbis Rd **E14** 127 K8
Carburton St **W1** 125 H7
Carden Rd **SE15** 130 F9
Cardigan Rd **E3** 127 K4
Cardigan St **SE11** 129 N4
Cardinal Bourne St **SE1** 130 B2
Cardine Ms **SE15** 130 F6
Cardington St **NW1** 125 J5
Carew St **SE5** 130 A8
Carey Gdns **SW8** 129 J7
Carey St **WC2** 125 M8
Carlile Cl **E3** 127 K4
Carlisle La **SE1** 129 M2
Carlisle Ms **NW8** 124 D7
Carlisle Pl **SW1** 129 J2
Carlos Pl **W1** 124 G9
Carlton Ct **SW9** 129 P7
Carlton Gdns **SW1** 125 K10
Carlton Gro **SE15** 130 F7
Carlton Hill **NW8** 124 B4
Carlton Ho Ter **SW1** 125 K10
Carlton Twr Pl **SW1** 128 F2
Carlton Vale **NW6** 124 B4
Carlyle Sq **SW3** 128 D4
Carmelite St **EC4** 125 N9
Carmen St **E14** 127 M8
Carnaby St **W1** 125 J8
Carnegie St **N1** 125 M3
Carnoustie Dr **N1** 125 M2
Carnwath Rd **SW6** 128 A9
Carol St **NW1** 125 J3
Caroline Gdns **SE15** 130 F6
Caroline Pl **SW11** 128 G8
Caroline Pl **W2** 124 B9
Caroline St **E1** 127 H8
Caroline Ter **SW1** 128 G3
Carpenters Pl **SW4** 129 K10
Carpenters Rd **E15** 127 M1
Carr St **E14** 127 J7
Carriage Dr E **SW11** 128 G6
Carriage Dr N **SW11** 128 G5
Carriage Dr S **SW11** 128 F7
Carriage Dr W **SW11** 128 F6
Carron Cl **E14** 127 M8
Carroun Rd **SW8** 129 M6
Carter La **EC4** 125 P8
Carter Pl **SE17** 130 A4
Carter St **SE17** 130 A5
Carteret St **SW1** 129 K1
Carteret Way **SE8** 131 J3
Cartier Circle **E14** 127 M10
Carting La **WC2** 125 L9
Cartwright Gdns **WC1** 125 L5
Cartwright St **E1** 126 D9
Casella Rd **SE14** 131 H6
Casey Cl **NW8** 124 E5
Caspian St **SE5** 130 B6
Cassidy Rd **SW6** 128 A6
Cassilis Rd **E14** 131 L1
Cassland Rd **E9** 126 G2
Casson St **E1** 126 E7
Castellain Rd **W9** 124 B6
Casterbridge **NW6** 124 B3
Castle La **SW1** 129 J2
Castle Pl **NW1** 125 H1
Castle Rd **NW1** 125 H1
Castlebrook Cl **SE11** 129 P3
Castlehaven Rd **NW1** 125 H2
Castlemain St **E1** 126 F7
Castlemaine Twr **SW11** 128 F7
Castor La **E14** 127 M9
Caterham Rd **SE13** 131 N9
Catesby St **SE17** 130 B3
Cathay St **SE16** 130 F1
Cathcart Rd **SW10** 128 C5
Cathcart St **NW5** 125 H1
Cathedral St **SE1** 126 B10
Catherine Gro **SE10** 131 M7
Catherine Pl **SW1** 129 J2
Catherine St **WC2** 125 M9
Catlin St **SE16** 130 E4
Cato Rd **SW4** 129 K9
Cato St **W1** 124 E7
Cator St **SE15** 130 D5
Catton St **WC1** 125 M7
Caulfield Rd **SE15** 130 F8
Causeway, The **SW18** 128 B10
Causton St **SW1** 129 K3
Cavell St **E1** 126 F7
Cavendish Av **NW8** 124 D4
Cavendish Cl **NW8** 124 D5
Cavendish Pl **W1** 125 H8
Cavendish Sq **W1** 125 H8
Cavendish St **N1** 126 B4
Caversham Rd **NW5** 125 J1
Caversham St **SW3** 128 F5
Caxton Gro **E3** 127 L5
Caxton St **SW1** 129 J2
Cedar Cl **E3** 127 K3
Cedar Way **NW1** 125 K2
Cedarne Rd **SW6** 128 B6
Cedars Cl **SE13** 131 P9
Cedars Rd **SW4** 129 H9
Celandine Cl **E14** 127 L7
Celandine Dr **E8** 126 D2
Celestial Gdns **SE13** 131 P10
Celtic St **E14** 127 M7
Centaur St **SE1** 129 M2
Central Av **SW11** 128 F6
Central Mkts **EC1** 125 P7
Central St **EC1** 126 A5
Centre St **E2** 126 F4
Centrepoint **WC1** 125 K8
Centurion Cl **N7** 125 M2
Cephas Av **E1** 126 G6
Cephas St **E1** 126 G6
Cerise Rd **SE15** 130 E7
Chabot Dr **SE15** 130 F9
Chadbourn St **E14** 127 M7
Chadwell St **EC1** 125 N5
Chadwick Rd **SE15** 130 D8
Chadwick St **SW1** 129 K2
Chagford St **NW1** 124 F6
Chalbury Wk **N1** 125 M4
Chalcot Cres **NW1** 124 F3
Chalcot Gdns **NW3** 124 F1
Chalcot Rd **NW1** 124 G2
Chalcot Sq **NW1** 124 G2
Chalk Fm Rd **NW1** 124 G2
Chalsey Rd **SE4** 131 K10
Chalton St **NW1** 125 K4
Chamber St **E1** 126 D9
Chambers St **SE16** 130 E1
Chambord St **E2** 126 D5
Champion Gro **SE5** 130 B9
Champion Hill **SE5** 130 B9
Champion Hill Est **SE5** 130 C9
Champion Pk **SE5** 130 B8
Chance St **E1** 126 D6
Chance St **E2** 126 D6
Chancel St **SE1** 125 P10
Chancery La **WC2** 125 N7
Chandler Way **SE15** 130 D6
Chandlers Ms **E14** 131 L1
Chandos Pl **WC2** 125 L9
Chandos St **W1** 125 H7
Channelsea Rd **E15** 127 P3
Chant Sq **E15** 127 P2
Chant St **E15** 127 P2
Chantrey Rd **SW9** 129 M9
Chantry St **N1** 125 P3
Chapel Ho St **E14** 131 M4
Chapel Mkt **N1** 125 N4
Chapel Pl **W1** 125 H8
Chapel Side **W2** 124 B9
Chapel St **NW1** 124 E7
Chapel St **SW1** 128 G2
Chaplin Cl **SE1** 129 N1
Chapman Rd **E9** 127 K1
Chapman St **E1** 126 F9
Chapter Rd **SE17** 129 P4
Chapter St **SW1** 129 K3
Charing Cross Rd **WC2** 125 K8
Charlbert St **NW8** 124 E4
Charles Barry Cl **SW4** 129 J9
Charles Coveney Rd **SE15** 130 D7
Charles Dickens Ho **E2** 126 F5
Charles II St **SW1** 125 K10
Charles Sq **N1** 126 B5
Charles St **W1** 125 H10
Charleston St **SE17** 130 A3
Charlotte Despard Av **SW11** 128 G7
Charlotte Rd **EC2** 126 C6
Charlotte Row **SW4** 129 J9
Charlotte St **W1** 125 J7
Charlotte Ter **N1** 125 M3
Charlton Pl **N1** 125 P4
Charlwood Pl **SW1** 129 J3
Charlwood St **SW1** 129 J4
Charnwood Gdns **E14** 131 L3
Charrington St **NW1** 125 K4
Chart St **N1** 126 B5
Charterhouse Sq **EC1** 125 P7
Charterhouse St **EC1** 125 P7
Chase, The **SW4** 129 H9
Chaseley St **E14** 127 J8
Chatfield Rd **SW11** 128 C9
Chatham Pl **E9** 126 G1
Chatham St **SE17** 130 B3
Chatsworth Ct **W8** 128 A3
Chaucer Dr **SE1** 130 D3
Cheapside **EC2** 126 A8
Chelsea Br **SW1** 129 H5
Chelsea Br **SW8** 129 H5
Chelsea Br Rd **SW1** 128 G4
Chelsea Embk **SW3** 128 E5
Chelsea Harbour **SW10** 128 C7
Chelsea Harbour Dr **SW10** 128 C7
Chelsea Manor Gdns **SW3** 128 E5
Chelsea Manor St **SW3** 128 E4
Chelsea Pk Gdns **SW3** 128 D5
Chelsea Sq **SW3** 128 D4
Chelsea Wf **SW10** 128 D6
Chelsham Rd **SW4** 129 K9
Cheltenham Rd **SE15** 130 G10
Cheltenham Ter **SW3** 128 F4
Chelwood Wk **SE4** 131 J10
Chenies Pl **NW1** 125 K4
Chenies St **WC1** 125 K7
Cheniston Gdns **W8** 128 B2
Chepstow Cres **W11** 124 A9
Chepstow Pl **W2** 124 A8
Chepstow Rd **W2** 124 A8
Cherbury St **N1** 126 B4
Cherry Gdn St **SE16** 130 F1
Cherrywood Cl **E3** 127 J5
Cheryls Cl **SW6** 128 B7
Chesham Ms **SW1** 128 G2
Chesham Pl **SW1** 128 G2
Chesham St **SW1** 128 G2
Cheshire Cl **SE4** 131 K8
Cheshire St **E2** 126 D6
Chesil Ct **E2** 126 G4
Chesney St **SW11** 128 G7
Chester Cl **SW1** 128 G1
Chester Ct **SE5** 130 B6
Chester Gate **NW1** 125 H5
Chester Ms **SW1** 129 H2
Chester Rd **NW1** 124 G5
Chester Row **SW1** 128 G3
Chester Sq **SW1** 129 H2
Chester St **E2** 126 E6
Chester St **SW1** 128 G2
Chester Way **SE11** 129 N3
Chesterfield Gdns **W1** 125 H10
Chesterfield Hill **W1** 125 H9
Chesterfield St **W1** 125 H10
Chesterfield Wk **SE10** 131 P7
Chesterfield Way **SE15** 130 G6
Chestnut Cl **SE14** 131 K7
Cheval Pl **SW7** 128 E2
Cheval St **E14** 131 L2
Cheyne Gdns **SW3** 128 E5
Cheyne Ms **SW3** 128 E5
Cheyne Pl **SW3** 128 F5
Cheyne Row **SW3** 128 E5
Cheyne Wk **SW3** 128 E5
Cheyne Wk **SW10** 128 D6
Chicheley St **SE1** 129 M1
Chichester Rd **NW6** 124 A4
Chichester Rd **W2** 124 B7
Chichester St **SW1** 129 J4
Chichester Way **E14** 131 P3
Chicksand St **E1** 126 D7
Chiddingstone St **SW6** 128 A8
Childeric Rd **SE14** 131 J6
Childers St **SE8** 131 J5
Child's Pl **SW5** 128 A3
Child's St **SW5** 128 A3
Chillington Dr **SW11** 128 C10
Chiltern Rd **E3** 127 L6
Chiltern St **W1** 124 G7
Chilton Gro **SE8** 131 H3
Chilton St **E2** 126 D6
Chilworth Ms **W2** 124 C8
Chilworth St **W2** 124 C8
Chip St **SW4** 129 K9
Chipka St **E14** 131 N1
Chipley St **SE14** 131 J5
Chippenham Gdns **NW6** 124 A5
Chippenham Ms **W9** 124 A6
Chippenham Rd **W9** 124 A6
Chipstead St **SW6** 128 A7
Chisenhale Rd **E3** 127 J4
Chiswell St **EC1** 126 A7
Chitty St **W1** 125 J7
Choumert Gro **SE15** 130 E8
Choumert Ms **SE15** 130 E8
Choumert Rd **SE15** 130 D9
Choumert Sq **SE15** 130 E8
Chrisp St **E14** 127 M7
Christchurch St **SW3** 128 F5
Christian Ct **SE16** 127 K10
Christian St **E1** 126 E8
Christie Rd **E9** 127 J1
Christopher Cl **SE16** 131 H1
Christopher St **EC2** 126 B6
Chryssell Rd **SW9** 129 N6
Chubworthy St **SE14** 131 J5
Chudleigh St **E1** 127 H8
Chumleigh St **SE5** 130 C5
Church Cres **E9** 127 H2
Church Gro **SE13** 131 M10
Church Rd **N1** 126 A1
Church St **NW8** 124 D7
Church St **W2** 124 D7
Church St Est **NW8** 124 D6
Church Ter **SW8** 129 K8
Churchill Gdns **SW1** 129 J4
Churchill Gdns Rd **SW1** 129 H4
Churchill Pl **E14** 127 M10
Churchway **NW1** 125 K5
Churton Pl **SW1** 129 J3
Churton St **SW1** 129 J3
Cicely Rd **SE15** 130 E7
Cinnabar Wf **E1** 126 E10
Cinnamon Row **SW11** 128 C9
Cinnamon St **E1** 126 F10
Circus Rd **NW8** 124 D5
Circus St **SE10** 131 N6
Cirencester St **W2** 124 B7
City Gdn Row **N1** 125 P4
City Mill River Towpath **E15** 127 M2
City Rd **EC1** 125 P4
Clabon Ms **SW1** 128 F2
Clack St **SE16** 130 G1
Claire Pl **E14** 131 L2
Clancarty Rd **SW6** 128 A8
Clandon St **SE8** 131 L8
Clanricarde Gdns **W2** 124 A9
Clapham Common N Side **SW4** 129 H10
Clapham Common W Side **SW4** 128 G10
Clapham Cres **SW4** 129 K10
Clapham Est **SW11** 128 E10
Clapham High St **SW4** 129 K10
Clapham Junct Sta **SW11** 128 D10
Clapham Manor St **SW4** 129 J9
Clapham Pk Rd **SW4** 129 K10
Clapham Rd **SW9** 129 L9
Clapham Rd Est **SW4** 129 K9
Clare Ho **E3** 127 K3
Clare La **N1** 126 A2
Clare Rd **SE14** 131 K7
Clare St **E2** 126 F4
Claredale St **E2** 126 E4
Claremont Cl **N1** 125 N4
Claremont Sq **N1** 125 N4
Claremont St **SE10** 131 M5
Clarence Gdns **NW1** 125 H5
Clarence Ms **SE16** 127 H10
Clarence Rd **SE8** 131 M5
Clarence Wk **SW4** 129 L8
Clarence Way **NW1** 125 H2
Clarence Way Est **NW1** 125 H2
Clarendon Cl **E9** 126 G2
Clarendon Gdns **W9** 124 C6
Clarendon Pl **W2** 124 E9
Clarendon Ri **SE13** 131 N9
Clarendon St **SW1** 129 H4
Clareville Gro **SW7** 128 C3
Clareville St **SW7** 128 C3
Clarewood Wk **SW9** 129 P10
Clarges Ms **W1** 125 H10
Clarges St **W1** 125 H10
Claribel Rd **SW9** 129 P8
Clarissa St **E8** 126 D3
Clark St **E1** 126 F7
Clarkson Row **NW1** 125 J4
Clarkson St **E2** 126 F5
Claude Rd **SE15** 130 F8
Claude St **E14** 131 L3
Clavell St **SE10** 131 N5

Cla - Dom


Claverton St SW1 129 J4
Claylands Pl SW8 129 N6
Claylands Rd SW8 129 M5
Claypole Rd E15 127 N4
Clayton Cres N1 125 L3
Clayton Ms SE10 131 P7
Clayton Rd SE15 130 E7
Clayton St SE11 129 N5
Clearwell Dr W9 124 B6
Cleaver Sq SE11 129 N4
Cleaver St SE11 129 N4
Clemence St E14 127 K7
Clement Av SW4 129 K10
Clement's Inn WC2 125 M8
Clements La EC4 126 B9
Clements Rd SE16 130 E2
Clephane Rd N1 126 A1
Clerkenwell Cl EC1 125 N6
Clerkenwell Grn EC1 125 P6
Clerkenwell Rd EC1 125 N7
Clermont Rd E9 126 G3
Cleve Rd NW6 124 A2
Cleveland Gdns W2 124 C8
Cleveland Rd N1 126 B2
Cleveland Row SW1 125 J10
Cleveland Sq W2 124 C8
Cleveland St W1 125 H6
Cleveland Ter W2 124 C8
Cleveland Way E1 126 G6
Clichy Est E1 126 G7
Cliff Rd NW1 125 K1
Cliff Ter SE8 131 L8
Cliff Vil NW1 125 K1
Clifford Dr SW9 129 P10
Clifford St W1 125 J9
Cliffview Rd SE13 131 L9
Clifton Cres SE15 130 F6
Clifton Gdns W9 124 C6
Clifton Gro E8 126 E1
Clifton Hill NW8 124 B4
Clifton Pl W2 124 D9
Clifton Ri SE14 131 J6
Clifton Rd N1 126 A1
Clifton Rd W9 124 C6
Clifton St EC2 126 C7
Clifton Vil W9 124 B7
Clifton Way SE15 130 F6
Clink St SE1 126 A10
Clinton Rd E3 127 J5
Clipper Way SE13 131 N10
Clipstone Ms W1 125 J6
Clipstone St W1 125 J7
Clitheroe Rd SW9 129 L8
Cliveden Pl SW1 128 G3
Cloak La EC4 126 A9
Clock Twr Pl N7 125 L1
Cloth Fair EC1 125 P7
Cloudesley Pl N1 125 N3
Cloudesley Rd N1 125 N3
Cloudesley Sq N1 125 N3
Cloudesley St N1 125 N3
Clove Cres E14 127 P9
Clove Hitch Quay SW11 128 C9
Cloysters Grn E1 126 E10
Club Row E1 126 D6
Club Row E2 126 D6
Cluny Ms SW5 128 A3
Clutton St E14 127 M7
Clyde St SE8 131 K5
Clyston St SW8 129 J8
Coate St E2 126 E4
Cobb St E1 126 D7
Cobbett St SW8 129 M6
Coborn Rd E3 127 K5
Coborn St E3 127 K5
Cobourg Rd SE5 130 D5
Cobourg St NW1 125 J5
Cochrane St NW8 124 D4
Cock La EC1 125 P7
Cockayne Way SE8 131 J4
Cockspur St SW1 125 K10
Code St E1 126 D6
Cody Rd E16 127 P6
Cody Rd Business Cen
E16 127 P6
Coin St SE1 125 N10
Coity Rd NW5 124 G1
Coke St E1 126 E8
Colbeck Ms SW7 128 B3
Cold Blow La SE14 131 H6
Cold Harbour E14 131 N1
Coldbath St SE13 131 M7
Coldharbour La SE5 129 N10
Coldharbour La SW9 129 N10
Cole St SE1 130 A1
Colebeck Ms N1 125 P1
Colebert Av E1 126 G6
Colebrooke Row N1 125 P4
Colegrove Rd SE15 130 D6
Coleherne Ct SW5 128 B4
Coleherne Ms SW10 128 B4
Coleherne Rd SW10 128 B4
Coleman Flds N1 126 A3
Coleman Rd SE5 130 C6
Coleman St EC2 126 B8
Coleridge Cl SW8 129 H8
Coleridge Gdns SW10 128 B6
Coleridge Sq SW10 128 C6
Colestown St SW11 128 E8
Coley St WC1 125 M6
College App SE10 131 N5
College Cres NW3 124 D1
College Cross N1 125 N2
College Pk Cl SE13 131 P10
College Pl NW1 125 J3
College Ter E3 127 K5
Collent St E9 126 G1
Collett Rd SE16 130 E2
Collier St N1 125 M4
Collingham Gdns SW5 128 B3
Collingham Pl SW5 128 B3
Collingham Rd SW5 128 B3
Collingwood St E1 126 F6
Colls Rd SE15 130 G7
Colmore Ms SE15 130 F7
Colnbrook St SE1 129 P2
Cologne Rd SW11 128 D10
Colombo St SE1 125 P10
Colonnade WC1 125 L6
Colonnade Wk SW1 129 H3
Colonnades, The W2 124 B8
Columbia Rd E2 126 D5
Columbine Way SE13 131 N8
Colville Est N1 126 B3
Colyer Cl N1 125 M4
Comber Gro SE5 130 A7
Combermere Rd SW9 129 M9
Comerford Rd SE4 131 J10
Comet Pl SE8 131 L6
Comet St SE8 131 L6
Comfort St SE15 130 C5
Commercial Rd E1 126 E8
Commercial Rd E14 126 G8
Commercial St E1 126 D6
Commercial Way SE15 130 D6
Commodore St E1 127 J6
Compayne Gdns NW6 124 B2
Compton Av N1 125 P1
Compton Cl E3 127 L7
Compton Rd N1 125 P1
Compton St EC1 125 P6
Compton Ter N1 125 P1
Comus Pl SE17 130 C3
Comyn Rd SW11 128 E10
Concanon Rd SW2 129 M10
Concert Hall App SE1 125 M10
Concorde Way SE16 131 H3
Condell Rd SW8 129 J7
Condray Pl SW11 128 E6
Conduit Ms W2 124 D8
Conduit Pl W2 124 D8
Conduit St W1 125 H9
Coney Way SW8 129 M5
Congreve St SE17 130 C3
Coniger Rd SW6 128 A8
Conington Rd SE13 131 M8
Coniston Ho SE5 130 A6
Conistone Way N7 125 L2
Connaught Pl W2 124 F9
Connaught Sq W2 124 F8
Connaught St W2 124 E8
Consort Rd SE15 130 F7
Constitution Hill SW1 129 H1
Content St SE17 130 B3
Conway St W1 125 J6
Conyer St E3 127 J4
Cook's Rd E15 127 M4
Cooks Rd SE17 129 P5
Coombs St N1 125 P4
Coopers Cl E1 126 G6
Coopers La NW1 125 K4
Coopers Rd SE1 130 D4
Cope Pl W8 128 A2
Cope St SE16 131 H3
Copeland Dr E14 131 L3
Copeland Rd SE15 130 E8
Copenhagen Pl E14 127 K8
Copenhagen St N1 125 L3
Copleston Pas SE15 130 D9
Copleston Rd SE15 130 D9
Copley St E1 127 H7
Copper Row SE1 126 D10
Copperas St SE8 131 M5
Copperfield Rd E3 127 J6
Copperfield St SE1 129 P1
Coppock Cl SW11 128 E8
Copthall Av EC2 126 B8
Copthall Ct EC2 126 B8
Coptic St WC1 125 L7
Coral St SE1 129 N1
Coram St WC1 125 L6
Corbden Cl SE15 130 D7
Corbiere Ho N1 126 C3
Corbridge Cres E2 126 F4
Cordelia Cl SE24 129 P10
Cordelia St E14 127 M8
Corfield St E2 126 F5
Coriander Av E14 127 P8
Cork St W1 125 J9
Corlett St NW1 124 E7
Cormont Rd SE5 129 P7
Cornelia St N7 125 M1
Cornhill EC3 126 B8
Cornmill La SE13 131 M9
Cornwall Av E2 126 G5
Cornwall Gdns SW7 128 B2
Cornwall Ms S SW7 128 C2
Cornwall Rd SE1 125 N10
Cornwall Sq SE11 129 P4
Cornwood Dr E1 126 G8
Coronet St N1 126 C5
Corporation Row EC1 125 N6
Corrance Rd SW2 129 L10
Corry Dr SW9 129 P10
Corsham St N1 126 B5
Corsica St N5 125 P1
Corunna Rd SW8 129 J7
Corunna Ter SW8 129 J7
Cossall Wk SE15 130 F7
Cosser St SE1 129 N2
Costa St SE15 130 E8
Cosway St NW1 124 E7
Cotall St E14 127 L8
Cotleigh Rd NW6 124 A2
Cottage Grn SE5 130 B6
Cottage Gro SW9 129 L9
Cottage Pl SW3 128 E2
Cottage St E14 127 M9
Cottesmore Gdns W8 128 B2
Cottingham Rd SW8 129 M6
Cotton Row SW11 128 C9
Cotton St E14 127 N9
Coulgate St SE4 131 J9
Coulson St SW3 128 F3
Councillor St SE5 130 A6
County Gro SE5 130 A7
County St SE1 130 A2
Courland Gro SW8 129 K7
Courland Gro Hall SW8 129 K8
Courland St SW8 129 K7
Court Gdns N7 125 N1
Courtenay St SE11 129 N4
Courtfield Gdns SW5 128 B3
Courtfield Rd SW7 128 B3
Courthill Rd SE13 131 N10
Courtnell St W2 124 A8
Courtyard, The N1 125 M2
Covent Gdn WC2 125 L9
Coventry Rd E1 126 F6
Coventry Rd E2 126 F6
Coventry St W1 125 K9
Coverley Cl E1 126 E7
Cowcross St EC1 125 P7
Cowdenbeath Path N1 125 M3
Cowley Rd SW9 129 N7
Cowper St EC2 126 B6
Cowthorpe Rd SW8 129 K7
Crabtree Cl E2 126 D4
Crampton St SE17 129 P3
Cranbourn St WC2 125 K9
Cranbrook Rd SE8 131 L7
Cranbury Rd SW6 128 B8
Crane Gro N7 125 N1
Crane St SE10 131 P4
Crane St SE15 130 D7
Cranfield Rd SE4 131 K9
Cranford St E1 127 H9
Cranleigh Ms SW11 128 E8
Cranleigh St NW1 125 J4
Cranley Gdns SW7 128 C4
Cranley Ms SW7 128 C4
Cranley Pl SW7 128 D3
Cranmer Ct SW4 129 K9
Cranmer Rd SW9 129 N6
Cranston Est N1 126 B4
Cranswick Rd SE16 130 F4
Cranwell Cl E3 127 M6
Cranwood St EC1 126 B5
Cranworth Gdns SW9 129 N7
Craven Hill W2 124 C9
Craven Hill Gdns W2 124 C9
Craven Hill Ms W2 124 C9
Craven Pas WC2 125 L10
Craven Rd W2 124 C9
Craven St WC2 125 L10
Craven Ter W2 124 C9
Crawford Est SE5 130 A8
Crawford Pl W1 124 E8
Crawford Rd SE5 130 A7
Crawford St W1 124 F7
Crawthew Gro SE22 130 D10
Creasy Est SE1 130 C2
Credon Rd SE16 130 F4
Creechurch La EC3 126 C8
Creek Rd SE8 131 L5
Creek Rd SE10 131 L5
Creekside SE8 131 M6
Cremer St E2 126 D4
Cremorne Rd SW10 128 C6
Crescent Gro SW4 129 J10
Crescent Pl SW3 128 E3
Crescent St N1 125 M2
Crescent Way SE4 131 L9
Cresford Rd SW6 128 B7
Cresset Rd E9 126 G1
Cresset St SW4 129 K9
Cressingham Rd SE13 131 N9
Cresswell Gdns SW5 128 C4
Cresswell Pl SW10 128 C4
Cressy Pl E1 126 G7
Crestfield St WC1 125 L5
Crewdson Rd SW9 129 N6
Crews St E14 131 L3
Crewys Rd SE15 130 F8
Cricketers Ct SE11 129 P3
Crimscott St SE1 130 C2
Crimsworth Rd SW8 129 K7
Crinan St N1 125 L4
Cringle St SW8 129 J6
Crispin St E1 126 D7
Croft St SE8 131 J3
Crofters Way NW1 125 K3
Crofton Rd SE5 130 C7
Crofts St E1 126 E9
Crogsland Rd NW1 124 G2
Cromer St WC1 125 L5
Crompton St W2 124 D6
Cromwell Cres SW5 128 A3
Cromwell Gdns SW7 128 D2
Cromwell Ms SW7 128 D3
Cromwell Pl SW7 128 D3
Cromwell Rd SW5 128 B3
Cromwell Rd SW7 128 B3
Cromwell Rd SW9 129 P7
Cromwell Twr EC2 126 A7
Crondace Rd SW6 128 A7
Crondall St N1 126 B4
Cronin St SE15 130 D6
Crooke Rd SE8 131 J4
Crooms Hill SE10 131 P6
Crooms Hill Gro SE10 131 N6
Cropley St N1 126 B4
Cropthorne Ct W9 124 C5
Crosby Row SE1 130 B1
Cross Av SE10 131 P5
Cross Rd SE5 130 C8
Cross St N1 125 P3
Crossfield Rd NW3 124 D2
Crossfield St SE8 131 L6
Crossford St SW9 129 M8
Crosslet Vale SE10 131 M7
Crossley St N7 125 N1
Crossmount Ho SE5 130 A6
Crossthwaite Av SE5 130 B10
Crosswall EC3 126 D9
Croston St E8 126 E3
Crowder St E1 126 F9
Crowhurst Cl SW9 129 N8
Crowland Ter N1 126 B2
Crown Cl E3 127 L3
Crown Cl NW6 124 B1
Crown Pas SW1 125 J10
Crown Pl EC2 126 C7
Crown St SE5 130 A6
Crowndale Rd NW1 125 J4
Crows Rd E15 127 P5
Crucifix La SE1 130 C1
Cruden St N1 125 P3
Cruikshank St WC1 125 N5
Crutched Friars EC3 126 C9
Crystal Palace Rd SE22 130 E10
Cuba St E14 131 L1
Cubitt St WC1 125 M5
Cubitt Ter SW4 129 J9
Cudworth St E1 126 F6
Cuff Pt E2 126 D5
Culford Gdns SW3 128 F3
Culford Gro N1 126 C1
Culford Rd N1 126 C2
Culloden Cl SE16 130 E4
Culloden St E14 127 N8
Culmore Rd SE15 130 F6
Culross St W1 124 G9
Culvert Pl SW11 128 G8
Culvert Rd SW11 128 F8
Cumberland Cl E8 126 D1
Cumberland Gate W1 124 F9
Cumberland Mkt NW1 125 H5
Cumberland St SW1 129 H4
Cumming St N1 125 M4
Cunard Wk SE16 131 J3
Cundy St SW1 128 G3
Cunningham Pl NW8 124 D6
Cupar Rd SW11 128 G7
Cureton St SW1 129 K3
Curlew St SE1 130 D1
Curness St SE13 131 N10
Cursitor St EC4 125 N8
Curtain Rd EC2 126 C6
Curtis St SE1 130 D3
Curtis Way SE1 130 D3
Curzon Gate W1 124 G10
Curzon St W1 124 G10
Custom Ho Reach SE16 131 K1
Custom Ho Wk EC3 126 C9
Cut, The SE1 129 N1
Cutcombe Rd SE5 130 A8
Cuthbert St W2 124 D6
Cuthill Wk SE5 130 B7
Cutler St E1 126 C8
Cyclops Ms E14 131 L3
Cynthia St N1 125 M4
Cyntra Pl E8 126 F2
Cyprus Pl E2 126 G4
Cyprus St E2 126 G4
Cyril Mans SW11 128 F7
Cyrus St EC1 125 P6
Czar St SE8 131 L5


## D


Dabin Cres SE10 131 N7
Dacca St SE8 131 K5
Dace Rd E3 127 L2
Dacre St SW1 129 K2
Dagmar Rd SE5 130 C7
Dagmar Ter N1 125 P3
Dagnall St SW11 128 F8
Dairy Ms SW9 129 L9
Daisy La SW6 128 A9
Dalberg Rd SW2 129 N10
Dalby Rd SW18 128 C10
Dalby St NW5 125 H1
Dale Rd SE17 129 P5
Daleham Ms NW3 124 D1
Dalehead NW1 125 J4
Daley St E9 127 H1
Daley Thompson Way
SW8 129 H8
Dalgleish St E14 127 J8
Daling Way E3 127 J3
Dallington St EC1 125 P6
Dalrymple Rd SE4 131 J10
Dalston La E8 126 D1
Dalwood St SE5 130 C7
Dalyell Rd SW9 129 M9
Dame St N1 126 A4
Damien St E1 126 F8
Danbury St N1 125 P4
Danby St SE15 130 D9
Danesdale Rd E9 127 J1
Danesfield SE5 130 C5
Daneville Rd SE5 130 B7
Daniel Gdns SE15 130 D6
Daniels Rd SE15 130 G9
Dante Rd SE11 129 P3
Danvers St SW3 128 D5
D'Arblay St W1 125 J8
Darien Rd SW11 128 D9
Darling Rd SE4 131 L9
Darling Row E1 126 F6
Darnley Ho E14 127 J8
Darnley Rd E9 126 F1
Darsley Dr SW8 129 K7
Dartford St SE17 130 A5
Dartmouth Gro SE10 131 N7
Dartmouth Hill SE10 131 N7
Dartmouth Row SE10 131 N8
Dartmouth St SW1 129 K1
Dartmouth Ter SE10 131 P7
Darwin St SE17 130 B3
Datchelor Pl SE5 130 B7
Date St SE17 130 A4
Daubeney Twr SE8 131 K4
Davenant St E1 126 E7
Daventry St NW1 124 E7
Davey Cl N7 125 M1
Davey Rd E9 127 L2
Davey St SE15 130 D5
David St E15 127 P1
Davidge St SE1 129 P1
Davidson Gdns SW8 129 L6
Davies St W1 125 H9
Dawes St SE17 130 B4
Dawson Pl W2 124 A9
Dawson St E2 126 D4
Dayton Gro SE15 130 G7
De Beauvoir Cres N1 126 C3
De Beauvoir Est N1 126 B3
De Beauvoir Rd N1 126 C3
De Beauvoir Sq N1 126 C2
De Crespigny Pk SE5 130 B8
De Laune St SE17 129 P4
De Morgan Rd SW6 128 B9
De Vere Gdns W8 128 C1
Deacon Ms N1 126 B2
Deacon Way SE17 130 A3
Deal Porters Way SE16 130 G2
Deal St E1 126 E7
Deals Gateway SE13 131 L7
Dean Bradley St SW1 129 L2
Dean Farrar St SW1 129 K2
Dean Ryle St SW1 129 L3
Dean Stanley St SW1 129 L2
Dean St W1 125 K8
Dean Trench St SW1 129 L2
Deancross St E1 126 G8
Deanery St W1 124 G10
Deans Bldgs SE17 130 B3
Decima St SE1 130 C2
Dee St E14 127 N8
Deeley Rd SW8 129 K7
Deepdene Rd SE5 130 B10
Deerdale Rd SE24 130 A10
Delaford Rd SE16 130 F4
Delamere Ter W2 124 B7
Delancey St NW1 125 H3
Delaware Rd W9 124 B6
Delhi St N1 125 L3
Delius Gro E15 127 P4
Dell Cl E15 127 P3
Dellow St E1 126 F9
Deloraine St SE8 131 L7
Delverton Rd SE17 129 P4
Delvino Rd SW6 128 A7
Denbigh Pl SW1 129 J4
Denbigh St SW1 129 J3
Dene Cl SE4 131 J9
Denman Rd SE15 130 D7
Denmark Gro N1 125 N4
Denmark Hill SE5 130 B7
Denmark Hill Est SE5 130 B10
Denmark Rd SE5 130 A7
Denmark St WC2 125 K8
Denne Ter E8 126 D3
Dennetts Rd SE14 130 G7
Denning Cl NW8 124 C5
Dennington Pk Rd NW6 124 A1
Dennison Pt E15 127 N2
Denny St SE11 129 N4
Denyer St SW3 128 E3
Deptford Br SE8 131 L7
Deptford Bdy SE8 131 L7
Deptford Ch St SE8 131 L5
Deptford Ferry Rd E14 131 L3
Deptford Grn SE8 131 L5
Deptford High St SE8 131 L5
Deptford Strand SE8 131 K3
Deptford Wf SE8 131 K3
Derby Rd E9 127 H3
Derbyshire St E2 126 E5
Dericote St E8 126 E3
Dering St W1 125 H8
Derry St W8 128 B1
Derwent Gro SE22 130 D10
Desborough Cl W2 124 B7
Desmond St SE14 131 J5
Devas St E3 127 M6
Deverell St SE1 130 B2
Devon St SE15 130 F5
Devonia Rd N1 125 P4
Devonport St E1 126 G8
Devons Est E3 127 M5
Devons Rd E3 127 L7
Devonshire Cl W1 125 H7
Devonshire Dr SE10 131 M6
Devonshire Gro SE15 130 F5
Devonshire Ms S W1 125 H7
Devonshire Ms W W1 125 H7
Devonshire Pl W1 124 G6
Devonshire St W1 125 H7
Devonshire Ter W2 124 C8
Dewar St SE15 130 E9
Dewberry St E14 127 N7
Dewey Rd N1 125 N4
D'Eynsford Rd SE5 130 B7
Dial Wk, The W8 128 B1
Diamond St SE15 130 C6
Diamond Ter SE10 131 N7
Dibden St N1 125 P3
Dickens Est SE1 130 D1
Dickens Est SE16 130 D1
Dickens Ho NW6 124 A5
Dickens Sq SE1 130 A2
Dickens St SW8 129 H8
Digby Rd E9 127 H1
Digby St E2 126 G5
Dighton Ct SE5 130 A5
Dilke St SW3 128 F5
Dimson Cres E3 127 L6
Dingle Gdns E14 127 L9
Dingley Pl EC1 126 A5
Dingley Rd EC1 126 A5
Discovery Wk E1 126 F10
Diss St E2 126 D5
Distaff La EC4 126 A9
Distin St SE11 129 N3
Ditch All SE10 131 M7
Ditchburn St E14 127 N9
Dixon Rd SE14 131 J7
Dixon's All SE16 130 F1
Dobson Cl NW6 124 D2
Dock Hill Av SE16 131 H1
Dock St E1 126 E9
Dockers Tanner Rd E14 131 L2
Dockhead SE1 130 D1
Dockley Rd SE16 130 E2
Docwra's Bldgs N1 126 C1
Dod St E14 127 K8
Doddington Gro SE17 129 P5
Doddington Pl SE17 129 P5
Dodson St SE1 129 N1
Dog Kennel Hill SE22 130 C9
Dog Kennel Hill Est SE22 130 C9
Dolben St SE1 125 P10
Dolland St SE11 129 M4
Dolman St SW4 129 M10
Dolphin La E14 127 M9
Dolphin Sq SW1 129 J4
Dombey St WC1 125 M7

Dom - Fri


Domett Cl **SE5** 130 B10
Don Phelan Cl **SE5** 130 B7
Donegal St **N1** 125 M4
Dongola Rd **E1** 127 J7
Donne Pl **SW3** 128 E3
Dora St **E14** 127 K8
Dora Way **SW9** 129 N8
Doran Wk **E15** 127 N2
Doric Way **NW1** 125 K5
Dorking Cl **SE8** 131 K5
Dorman Way **NW8** 124 D3
Dorney **NW3** 124 E2
Dorothy Rd **SW11** 128 F9
Dorrington St **EC1** 125 N7
Dorset Est **E2** 126 D5
Dorset Pl **E15** 127 P1
Dorset Ri **EC4** 125 P8
Dorset Rd **SW8** 129 M6
Dorset Sq **NW1** 124 F6
Dorset St **W1** 124 G7
Doughty Ms **WC1** 125 M6
Doughty St **WC1** 125 M6
Douglas Rd **N1** 126 A2
Douglas St **SW1** 129 K3
Douglas Way **SE8** 131 K6
Douro Pl **W8** 128 B2
Douro St **E3** 127 L4
Dove Ms **SW5** 128 C3
Dove Rd **N1** 126 B1
Dove Row **E2** 126 E3
Dovehouse St **SW3** 128 D4
Dover St **W1** 125 H9
Dovercourt Est **N1** 126 B1
Doves Yd **N1** 125 N3
Dowgate Hill **EC4** 126 B9
Dowlas St **SE5** 130 C6
Down St **W1** 125 H10
Downfield Cl **W9** 124 B6
Downham Rd **N1** 126 B2
Downing St **SW1** 129 L1
Downtown Rd **SE16** 131 J1
Dowson Cl **SE5** 130 B10
D'Oyley St **SW1** 128 G3
Draco St **SE17** 130 A5
Dragon Rd **SE15** 130 C5
Dragoon Rd **SE8** 131 K4
Drake Rd **SE4** 131 L9
Drakefell Rd **SE4** 131 H8
Drakefell Rd **SE14** 131 H8
Draper Ho **SE1** 129 P3
Drawdock Rd **SE10** 127 P10
Draycott Av **SW3** 128 E3
Draycott Pl **SW3** 128 F3
Draycott Ter **SW3** 128 F3
Drayson Ms **W8** 128 A1
Drayton Gdns **SW10** 128 C4
Dresden Cl **NW6** 124 B1
Driffield Rd **E3** 127 J4
Drovers Pl **SE15** 130 F6
Druid St **SE1** 130 C1
Drummond Cres **NW1** 125 K5
Drummond Gate **SW1** 129 K4
Drummond Rd **SE16** 130 F2
Drummond St **NW1** 125 J6
Drury La **WC2** 125 L8
Dryden Ct **SE11** 129 N3
Drysdale St **N1** 126 C5
Dublin Av **E8** 126 E3
Duchess of Bedford's Wk **W8** 128 A1
Duchess St **W1** 125 H7
Duchy St **SE1** 125 N10
Ducie St **SW4** 129 M10
Duckett St **E1** 127 H6
Dudley St **W2** 124 D7
Duff St **E14** 127 M8
Dufferin St **EC1** 126 A6
Dugard Way **SE11** 129 P3
Duke of Wellington Pl **SW1** 128 G1
Duke of York Sq **SW3** 128 F3
Duke of York St **SW1** 125 J10
Duke St **SW1** 125 J10
Duke St **W1** 124 G8
Dukes La **W8** 128 A1
Dukes Pl **EC3** 126 C8
Duke's Rd **WC1** 125 K5
Dunbridge St **E2** 126 E6
Duncan Rd **E8** 126 F3
Duncan St **N1** 125 P4
Duncan Ter **N1** 125 P4
Duncannon St **WC2** 125 L9
Dundalk Rd **SE4** 131 J9
Dundas Rd **SE15** 130 G8
Dundee St **E1** 126 F10
Dunelm St **E1** 127 H8
Dunloe St **E2** 126 D4
Dunston Rd **E8** 126 D3
Dunston Rd **SW11** 128 G8
Dunston St **E8** 126 D3
Dunton Rd **SE1** 130 D4
Durand Gdns **SW9** 129 M7
Durands Wk **SE16** 131 K1
Durant St **E2** 126 E4
Durham Row **E1** 127 J7
Durham St **SE11** 129 M4
Durham Ter **W2** 124 B8
Durward St **E1** 126 F7
Durweston St **W1** 124 F7
Dutton St **SE10** 131 N7
Dye Ho La **E3** 127 L3
Dylan Rd **SE24** 129 P10
Dylways **SE5** 130 B10
Dymock St **SW6** 128 B9
Dynham Rd **NW6** 124 A2
Dyott St **WC1** 125 K8

## E

Eagle Ct **EC1** 125 P7
Eagle St **WC1** 125 M7
Eagle Wf Rd **N1** 126 A4
Eamont St **NW8** 124 E4
Eardley Cres **SW5** 128 A4
Earl St **EC2** 126 B7
Earlham St **WC2** 125 K8
Earls Ct Gdns **SW5** 128 B3
Earls Ct Rd **SW5** 128 A3
Earls Ct Rd **W8** 128 A3
Earls Ct Sq **SW5** 128 B4
Earls Wk **W8** 128 A2
Earlsferry Way **N1** 125 M2
Earlston Gro **E9** 126 F3
Earnshaw St **WC2** 125 K8
East Arbour St **E1** 127 H8
East Cross Cen **E15** 127 L1
East Cross Route **E3** 127 K2
East Cross Route **E9** 127 K2
East Dulwich Rd **SE15** 130 D10
East Dulwich Rd **SE22** 130 D10
East Ferry Rd **E14** 131 M2
East India Dock Rd **E14** 127 L8
East La **SE16** 130 E1
East Mt St **E1** 126 F7
East Rd **N1** 126 B5
East Smithfield **E1** 126 D9
East St **SE17** 130 A4
East Surrey Gro **SE15** 130 D6
East Tenter St **E1** 126 D8
Eastbourne Ms **W2** 124 C8
Eastbourne Ter **W2** 124 C8
Eastbury Ter **E1** 127 H6
Eastcastle St **W1** 125 J8
Eastcheap **EC3** 126 B9
Eastcote St **SW9** 129 M8
Eastdown Pk **SE13** 131 P10
Eastern Rd **SE4** 131 L10
Eastfield St **E14** 127 J7
Eastfields Av **SW18** 128 A10
Eastlake Rd **SE5** 129 P8
Eastney St **SE10** 131 P4
Eastway **E9** 127 K1
Eaton Cl **SW1** 128 G3
Eaton Dr **SW9** 129 P10
Eaton Gate **SW1** 128 G3
Eaton La **SW1** 129 H2
Eaton Ms N **SW1** 128 G2
Eaton Ms S **SW1** 129 H2
Eaton Ms W **SW1** 128 G3
Eaton Pl **SW1** 128 G2
Eaton Row **SW1** 129 H2
Eaton Sq **SW1** 128 G3
Eaton Ter **SW1** 128 G3
Ebbisham Dr **SW8** 129 M5
Ebenezer St **N1** 126 B5
Ebley Cl **SE15** 130 D5
Ebor St **E1** 126 D6
Ebury Br **SW1** 129 H4
Ebury Br Est **SW1** 129 H4
Ebury Br Rd **SW1** 128 G4
Ebury Ms **SW1** 129 H3
Ebury Sq **SW1** 128 G3
Ebury St **SW1** 128 G3
Eccles Rd **SW11** 128 F10
Ecclesbourne Rd **N1** 126 A2
Eccleston Br **SW1** 129 H3
Eccleston Ms **SW1** 128 G2
Eccleston Pl **SW1** 129 H3
Eccleston Sq **SW1** 129 H3
Eccleston Sq Ms **SW1** 129 H3
Eccleston St **SW1** 128 G2
Eckford St **N1** 125 N4
Eckstein Rd **SW11** 128 E10
Edbrooke Rd **W9** 124 A6
Eddystone Twr **SE8** 131 J3
Edenbridge Rd **E9** 127 H2
Edenvale St **SW6** 128 B8
Edgar Kail Way **SE22** 130 C10
Edgar Rd **E3** 127 M5
Edgeley Rd **SW4** 129 K9
Edgware Rd **W2** 124 E8
Edinburgh Gate **SW1** 128 F1
Edinburgh Ho **W9** 124 C5
Edis St **NW1** 124 G3
Edith Gro **SW10** 128 C5
Edith Row **SW6** 128 B7
Edith St **E2** 126 E4
Edith Ter **SW10** 128 C6
Edithna St **SW9** 129 L9
Edmeston Cl **E9** 127 J1
Edmund St **SE5** 130 B6
Edna St **SW11** 128 E7
Edric Rd **SE14** 131 H6
Edrich Ho **SW4** 129 L7
Edward Pl **SE8** 131 K5
Edward St **SE8** 131 K5
Edward St **SE14** 131 J6
Edwardes Sq **W8** 128 A2
Edwards Ms **N1** 125 N2
Edwards Ms **W1** 124 G8
Edwin St **E1** 126 G6
Effie Pl **SW6** 128 A6
Effie Rd **SW6** 128 A6
Effra Rd **SW2** 129 N10
Egbert St **NW1** 124 G3
Egeremont Rd **SE13** 131 M8
Egerton Cres **SW3** 128 E3
Egerton Dr **SE10** 131 M7
Egerton Gdns **SW3** 128 E2
Egerton Gdns Ms **SW3** 128 E2
Egerton Pl **SW3** 128 E2
Egerton Ter **SW3** 128 E2
Egmont St **SE14** 131 H6
Elam Cl **SE5** 129 P8
Elam St **SE5** 129 P8
Eland Rd **SW11** 128 F9
Elbe St **SW6** 128 C8
Elcho St **SW11** 128 E6
Elcot Av **SE15** 130 F6
Elder St **E1** 126 D7
Eldon Rd **W8** 128 B2
Eldon St **EC2** 126 B7
Eleanor Cl **SE16** 131 H1
Eleanor Rd **E8** 126 F2
Eleanor St **E3** 127 L5
Electra Business Pk **E16** 127 P7
Electric Av **SW9** 129 N10
Electric La **SW9** 129 N10
Elephant & Castle **SE1** 129 P3
Elephant La **SE16** 130 G1
Elephant Rd **SE17** 130 A3
Elf Row **E1** 126 G9
Elgar St **SE16** 131 J2
Elgin Av **W9** 124 B5
Elia Ms **N1** 125 P4
Elia St **N1** 125 P4
Elias Pl **SW8** 129 N5
Elim Est **SE1** 130 B2
Eliot Hill **SE13** 131 N8
Eliot Ms **NW8** 124 C4
Eliot Pk **SE13** 131 N9
Eliot Vale **SE3** 131 P8
Elizabeth Av **N1** 126 A2
Elizabeth Br **SW1** 129 H3
Elizabeth Est **SE17** 130 B5
Elizabeth Ms **NW3** 124 E1
Elizabeth St **SW1** 128 G3
Elland Rd **SE15** 130 G10
Ellen St **E1** 126 E8
Ellerdale St **SE13** 131 M10
Ellery St **SE15** 130 F8
Ellesmere Rd **E3** 127 J4
Ellesmere St **E14** 127 M8
Ellingfort Rd **E8** 126 F2
Ellington St **N7** 125 N1
Elliott Rd **SW9** 129 P6
Elliott Sq **NW3** 124 E2
Elliotts Row **SE11** 129 P3
Ellis St **SW1** 128 F3
Ellsworth St **E2** 126 F5
Elm Friars Wk **NW1** 125 K2
Elm Gro **SE15** 130 D8
Elm Pk Gdns **SW10** 128 D4
Elm Pk La **SW3** 128 D4
Elm Pk Rd **SW3** 128 D5
Elm Pl **SW7** 128 D4
Elm Quay Ct **SW8** 129 K5
Elm St **WC1** 125 M6
Elm Tree Cl **NW8** 124 D5
Elm Tree Rd **NW8** 124 D5
Elmfield Way **W9** 124 A7
Elmhurst St **SW4** 129 K9
Elmington Est **SE5** 130 B6
Elmington Rd **SE5** 130 B7
Elmira St **SE13** 131 M9
Elmore St **N1** 126 A2
Elms Ms **W2** 124 D9
Elmslie Pt **E3** 127 K7
Elmstone Rd **SW6** 128 A7
Elmwood Ct **SW11** 129 H7
Elrington Rd **E8** 126 E1
Elsa St **E1** 127 J7
Elsdale St **E9** 126 G1
Elsie Rd **SE22** 130 D10
Elsley Rd **SW11** 128 F9
Elspeth Rd **SW11** 128 F10
Elsted St **SE17** 130 B3
Elswick Rd **SE13** 131 M8
Elswick St **SW6** 128 C8
Elsworthy Ri **NW3** 124 E2
Elsworthy Rd **NW3** 124 E3
Elsworthy Ter **NW3** 124 E2
Elthiron Rd **SW6** 128 A7
Elton Ho **E3** 127 K3
Eltringham St **SW18** 128 C10
Elvaston Ms **SW7** 128 C2
Elvaston Pl **SW7** 128 C2
Elverson Ms **SE8** 131 M8
Elverson Rd **SE8** 131 M8
Elverton St **SW1** 129 K3
Elwin St **E2** 126 E5
Elystan Pl **SW3** 128 E4
Elystan St **SW3** 128 E3
Emba St **SE16** 130 E1
Embankment Gdns **SW3** 128 F5
Embankment Pl **WC2** 125 L10
Emberton **SE5** 130 C5
Embleton Rd **SE13** 131 M9
Emden St **SW6** 128 B7
Emerald St **WC1** 125 M7
Emerson St **SE1** 126 A10
Emery Hill St **SW1** 129 J2
Emma St **E2** 126 F4
Emmott Cl **E1** 127 J6
Emperor's Gate **SW7** 128 B2
Empire Wf Rd **E14** 131 P3
Empress Ms **SE5** 130 A8
Empress Pl **SW6** 128 A4
Empress St **SE17** 130 A5
Empson St **E3** 127 M6
Emu Rd **SW8** 129 H8
Endell St **WC2** 125 L8
Endsleigh Gdns **WC1** 125 K6
Endsleigh Pl **WC1** 125 K6
Endsleigh St **WC1** 125 K6
Endwell Rd **SE4** 131 J8
Enfield Rd **N1** 126 C2
Enford St **W1** 124 F7
Engate St **SE13** 131 N10
Englands La **NW3** 124 F1
Englefield Rd **N1** 126 B1
English St **E3** 127 K6
Enid St **SE16** 130 D2
Ennerdale Ho **E3** 127 K6
Ennismore Gdns **SW7** 128 E1
Ennismore Gdns Ms **SW7** 128 E2
Ennismore Ms **SW7** 128 E1
Ennismore St **SW7** 128 E2
Ensign St **E1** 126 E9
Enterprise Way **SW18** 128 A10
Enterprize Way **SE8** 131 K3
Epirus Ms **SW6** 128 A6
Epping Cl **E14** 131 L3
Epworth St **EC2** 126 B6
Erasmus St **SW1** 129 K3
Eresby Pl **NW6** 124 A2
Eric St **E3** 127 K6
Erlanger Rd **SE14** 131 H7
Ermine Rd **SE13** 131 M9
Ernest St **E1** 127 H6
Errol St **EC1** 126 A6
Erskine Rd **NW3** 124 F2
Esmeralda Rd **SE1** 130 E3
Essendine Rd **W9** 124 A6
Essex Rd **N1** 125 P3
Essex Vil **W8** 128 A1
Essian St **E1** 127 J7
Este Rd **SW11** 128 E9
Esterbrooke St **SW1** 129 K3
Ethelburga St **SW11** 128 E7
Ethnard Rd **SE15** 130 F5
Eton Av **NW3** 124 D2
Eton Coll Rd **NW3** 124 F1
Eton Rd **NW3** 124 F2
Eton Vil **NW3** 124 F1
Etta St **SE8** 131 J5
Ettrick St **E14** 127 N8
Eugenia Rd **SE16** 130 G3
Eustace Rd **SW6** 128 A6
Euston Gro **NW1** 125 K5
Euston Rd **N1** 125 K6
Euston Rd **NW1** 125 H6
Euston Sq **NW1** 125 K5
Euston Sta **NW1** 125 J5
Euston St **NW1** 125 J5
Euston Twr **NW1** 125 J6
Evandale Rd **SW9** 129 N8
Evelina Rd **SE15** 130 G9
Eveline Lowe Est **SE16** 130 E2
Evelyn Gdns **SW7** 128 D4
Evelyn St **SE8** 131 J4
Evelyn Wk **N1** 126 B4
Everest Pl **E14** 127 N7
Evergreen Sq **E8** 126 D2
Everilda St **N1** 125 M3
Eversholt St **NW1** 125 J4
Eversleigh Rd **SW11** 128 F9
Everthorpe Rd **SE15** 130 D9
Evesham Wk **SW9** 129 N8
Evesham Way **SW11** 128 G9
Ewe Cl **N7** 125 L1
Ewer St **SE1** 126 A10
Ewhurst Cl **E1** 126 G7
Excelsior Gdns **SE13** 131 N8
Exchange Sq **EC2** 126 C7
Exeter St **WC2** 125 L9
Exeter Way **SE14** 131 K6
Exhibition Rd **SW7** 128 D2
Exmouth Mkt **EC1** 125 N6
Exmouth Pl **E8** 126 F2
Exon St **SE17** 130 C4
Exton St **SE1** 125 N10
Eythorne Rd **SW9** 129 N7
Ezra St **E2** 126 D5

## F

Fairbairn Grn **SW9** 129 N7
Faircharm Trd Est **SE8** 131 M6
Fairclough St **E1** 126 E8
Fairfax Pl **NW6** 124 C2
Fairfax Rd **NW6** 124 C2
Fairfield Rd **E3** 127 L4
Fairfoot Rd **E3** 127 L6
Fairhazel Gdns **NW6** 124 B1
Fairmont Av **E14** 127 P10
Fakruddin St **E1** 126 E6
Falcon Ct **EC4** 125 N8
Falcon Gro **SW11** 128 E9
Falcon La **SW11** 128 E9
Falcon Rd **SW11** 128 E8
Falcon Ter **SW11** 128 E9
Falcon Way **E14** 131 M3
Falkirk Ho **W9** 124 B5
Falkirk St **N1** 126 C4
Falmouth Rd **SE1** 130 A2
Fann St **EC1** 126 A6
Fann St **EC2** 126 A6
Fanshaw St **N1** 126 C5
Farm La **SW6** 128 A5
Farm St **W1** 125 H9
Farmers Rd **SE5** 129 P6
Farncombe St **SE16** 130 E1
Farrance St **E14** 127 K8
Farrell Ho **E1** 126 G8
Farrier St **NW1** 125 H2
Farrier Wk **SW10** 128 C5
Farringdon La **EC1** 125 N6
Farringdon Rd **EC1** 125 N6
Farringdon St **EC4** 125 P7
Farrins Rents **SE16** 127 J10
Farrow La **SE14** 130 G6
Farthingale Wk **E15** 127 P2
Fashion St **E1** 126 D7
Fassett Rd **E8** 126 E1
Fassett Sq **E8** 126 E1
Faulkner St **SE14** 130 G7
Favart Rd **SW6** 128 A7
Fawcett Cl **SW11** 128 D8
Fawcett St **SW10** 128 C5
Fawe St **E14** 127 M7
Feathers Pl **SE10** 131 P5
Featherstone St **EC1** 126 B6
Featley Rd **SW9** 129 P9
Fellows Ct **E2** 126 D4
Fellows Rd **NW3** 124 D2
Felstead St **E9** 127 K1
Felton St **N1** 126 B3
Fenchurch Av **EC3** 126 C8
Fenchurch St **EC3** 126 C9
Fendall St **SE1** 130 C2
Fenham Rd **SE15** 130 E6
Fentiman Rd **SW8** 129 L5
Fenton Cl **SW9** 129 M8
Fenwick Gro **SE15** 130 E9
Fenwick Pl **SW9** 129 L9
Fenwick Rd **SE15** 130 E9
Ferdinand St **NW1** 124 G1
Ferguson Cl **E14** 131 L3
Fern St **E3** 127 L6
Ferndale Rd **SW4** 129 L10
Ferndale Rd **SW9** 129 M9
Ferndene Rd **SE24** 130 A10
Fernshaw Rd **SW10** 128 C5
Ferrey Ms **SW9** 129 N8
Ferrier St **SW18** 128 B10
Ferris Rd **SE22** 130 E10
Ferry St **E14** 131 N4
Ferryman's Quay **SW6** 128 C8
Fetter La **EC4** 125 N8
Ffinch St **SE8** 131 L6
Field St **WC1** 125 M5
Fieldgate St **E1** 126 E7
Fielding Ho **NW6** 124 A5
Fielding St **SE17** 130 A5
Fields Est **E8** 126 E2
Fife Ter **N1** 125 M4
Finborough Rd **SW10** 128 B4
Finch Ms **SE15** 130 D6
Finchley Pl **NW8** 124 D4
Finchley Rd **NW3** 124 C1
Finchley Rd **NW8** 124 D3
Findhorn St **E14** 127 N8
Finland Rd **SE4** 131 J9
Finland St **SE16** 131 J2
Finnis St **E2** 126 F5
Finsbury Circ **EC2** 126 B7
Finsbury Est **EC1** 125 N5
Finsbury Mkt **EC2** 126 C6
Finsbury Pavement **EC2** 126 B7
Finsbury Sq **EC2** 126 B7
Finsbury St **EC2** 126 B7
Finsen Rd **SE5** 130 A9
Fir Trees Cl **SE16** 127 J10
Firbank Rd **SE15** 130 F8
First St **SW3** 128 E3
Fish St Hill **EC3** 126 B9
Fisher St **WC1** 125 M7
Fishermans Dr **SE16** 131 H1
Fisherman's Wk **E14** 127 L10
Fisherton St **NW8** 124 D6
Fitzalan St **SE11** 129 M3
Fitzgerald Ho **E14** 127 M8
Fitzhardinge St **W1** 124 G8
Fitzmaurice Pl **W1** 125 H9
Fitzroy Rd **NW1** 124 G3
Fitzroy Sq **W1** 125 J6
Fitzroy St **W1** 125 J6
Fitzwilliam Rd **SW4** 129 J9
Fiveways Rd **SW9** 129 N8
Flamborough St **E14** 127 J8
Flanders Way **E9** 127 H1
Flaxman Rd **SE5** 129 P8
Flaxman Ter **WC1** 125 K5
Fleet St **EC4** 125 N8
Fleming Rd **SE17** 129 P5
Fleur de Lis St **E1** 126 C6
Flint St **SE17** 130 B3
Flinton St **SE17** 130 C4
Flodden Rd **SE5** 130 A7
Flood St **SW3** 128 E4
Flood Wk **SW3** 128 E5
Flora Cl **E14** 127 M8
Floral St **WC2** 125 L9
Florence Rd **SE14** 131 K7
Florence St **N1** 125 P2
Florence Ter **SE14** 131 K7
Florida St **E2** 126 E5
Flower Wk, The **SW7** 128 C1
Foley St **W1** 125 J7
Folgate St **E1** 126 C7
Follett St **E14** 127 N8
Folly Wall **E14** 131 N1
Fontarabia Rd **SW11** 128 G10
Ford Rd **E3** 127 J3
Ford Sq **E1** 126 F7
Ford St **E3** 127 J3
Fordham St **E1** 126 E8
Fore St **EC2** 126 A7
Foreign St **SE5** 129 P8
Foreshore **SE8** 131 K3
Forest Gro **E8** 126 D1
Forest Rd **E8** 126 D1
Forester Rd **SE15** 130 F10
Forfar Rd **SW11** 128 G7
Formosa St **W9** 124 B7
Forset St **W1** 124 E8
Forsyth Gdns **SE17** 129 P5
Fort Rd **SE1** 130 D3
Forthbridge Rd **SW11** 128 G10
Fortune St **EC1** 126 A6
Fossil Rd **SE13** 131 L9
Foster La **EC2** 126 A8
Foubert's Pl **W1** 125 J8
Foulis Ter **SW7** 128 D4
Foundry Cl **SE16** 127 J10
Fount St **SW8** 129 K6
Fountain Ms **NW3** 124 F1
Fountain Pl **SW9** 129 N7
Fountain Sq **SW1** 129 H3
Four Seasons Cl **E3** 127 L4
Fournier St **E1** 126 D7
Fowler Cl **SW11** 128 D9
Fownes St **SW11** 128 E9
Fox Cl **E1** 126 G6
Foxberry Rd **SE4** 131 J9
Foxcote **SE5** 130 C4
Foxley Rd **SW9** 129 N6
Foxmore St **SW11** 128 F7
Foxwell St **SE4** 131 J9
Frampton Pk Rd **E9** 126 G1
Frampton St **NW8** 124 D6
Francis Chichester Way **SW11** 128 G7
Francis St **SW1** 129 J3
Frankham St **SE8** 131 L6
Frankland Cl **SE16** 130 F2
Franklin Cl **SE13** 131 M7
Franklin Pl **SE13** 131 M7
Franklin St **E3** 127 M5
Franklin's Row **SW3** 128 F4
Frazier St **SE1** 129 N1
Frean St **SE16** 130 E2
Frederick Cl **W2** 124 E9
Frederick Cres **SW9** 129 P6
Frederick St **WC1** 125 M5
Freedom St **SW11** 128 F8
Freemantle St **SE17** 130 C4
Freke Rd **SW11** 128 G9
Fremont St **E9** 126 G3
Frendsbury Rd **SE4** 131 J10
Frensham St **SE15** 130 E5
Frere St **SW11** 128 E8
Freshfield Av **E8** 126 D2
Friars Mead **E14** 131 N2
Friary Est **SE15** 130 E5
Friary Rd **SE15** 130 E6
Friday St **EC4** 126 A8
Friend St **EC1** 125 P5

Fri - Hen


Friendly St **SE8** 131 L7
Frimley Way **E1** 127 H6
Friston St **SW6** 128 B8
Frith St **W1** 125 K8
Frogley Rd **SE22** 130 D10
Frognal Ct **NW3** 124 C1
Frome St **N1** 126 A4
Frostic Wk **E1** 126 D7
Froude St **SW8** 129 H8
Fulford St **SE16** 130 F1
Fulham Bdy **SW6** 128 A6
Fulham Rd **SW3** 128 C5
Fulham Rd **SW10** 128 B6
Fulmead St **SW6** 128 B7
Fulwood Pl **WC1** 125 M7
Furley Rd **SE15** 130 E6
Furlong Rd **N7** 125 N1
Furness Rd **SW6** 128 B8
Furnival St **EC4** 125 N8
Furze St **E3** 127 L7
Fyfield Rd **SW9** 129 N9
Fynes St **SW1** 129 K3

## G

Gables Cl **SE5** 130 C7
Gabrielle Ct **NW3** 124 D1
Gainsford St **SE1** 130 D1
Gairloch Rd **SE5** 130 C8
Gaisford St **NW5** 125 J1
Gaitskell Ct **SW11** 128 E8
Galbraith St **E14** 131 N2
Gale St **E3** 127 L7
Gales Gdns **E2** 126 F5
Galleywall Rd **SE16** 130 F3
Galsworthy Av **E14** 127 J7
Galway St **EC1** 126 A5
Gambetta St **SW8** 129 H8
Garden Rd **NW8** 124 C5
Garden Row **SE1** 129 P2
Garden St **E1** 127 H7
Gardens, The **SE22** 130 E10
Garfield Rd **SW11** 128 G9
Garford St **E14** 127 L9
Garlick Hill **EC4** 126 A9
Garnet St **E1** 126 G9
Garnies Cl **SE15** 130 D6
Garrick Cl **SW18** 128 C10
Garrick St **WC2** 125 L9
Garsington Ms **SE4** 131 K9
Gartons Way **SW11** 128 C9
Garway Rd **W2** 124 B8
Gascoigne Pl **E2** 126 D5
Gascony Av **NW6** 124 A2
Gascoyne Rd **E9** 127 H2
Gaselee St **E14** 127 N9
Gaskell St **SW4** 129 L8
Gaskin St **N1** 125 P3
Gataker St **SE16** 130 F2
Gate Ms **SW7** 128 E1
Gateforth St **NW8** 124 E6
Gateley Rd **SW9** 129 M9
Gateway **SE17** 130 A5
Gateways, The **SW3** 128 F3
Gatliff Rd **SW1** 128 G4
Gatonby St **SE15** 130 D7
Gauden Cl **SW4** 129 K9
Gauden Rd **SW4** 129 K8
Gautrey Rd **SE15** 130 G8
Gawber St **E2** 126 G5
Gay Rd **E15** 127 P4
Gaydon Ho **W2** 124 B7
Gayfere St **SW1** 129 L2
Gayhurst Rd **E8** 126 E2
Gayton Ho **E3** 127 L6
Gaywood Est **SE1** 129 P2
Gedling Pl **SE1** 130 D1
Gee St **EC1** 126 A6
Geffrye St **E2** 126 D4
Geldart Rd **SE15** 130 F6
Gellatly Rd **SE14** 130 G8
General Wolfe Rd **SE10** 131 P7
Geneva Dr **SW9** 129 N10
Geoffrey Cl **SE5** 130 A8
Geoffrey Rd **SE4** 131 K9
George Beard Rd **SE8** 131 K3
George Mathers Rd **SE11** 129 P3
George Row **SE16** 130 E1
George St **W1** 124 G8
George Yd **W1** 124 G9
Georgiana St **NW1** 125 J3
Gerald Rd **SW1** 128 G3
Geraldine St **SE11** 129 P2
Gerards Cl **SE16** 130 G4
Gernon Rd **E3** 127 J4
Gerrard Rd **N1** 125 P4
Gerrard St **W1** 125 K9
Gerridge St **SE1** 129 N2
Gertrude St **SW10** 128 C5
Gervase St **SE15** 130 F6
Gibbins Rd **E15** 127 N2
Gibbon Rd **SE15** 130 G8
Gibraltar Wk **E2** 126 D5
Gibson Rd **SE11** 129 M3
Gibson Sq **N1** 125 N3
Gideon Rd **SW11** 128 G9
Giffin St **SE8** 131 L6
Gifford St **N1** 125 L2
Gilbert Rd **SE11** 129 N3
Gilbert St **W1** 124 G8
Gilbeys Yd **NW1** 124 G2
Gill St **E14** 127 K8
Gillender St **E3** 127 N6
Gillender St **E14** 127 N6
Gillfoot **NW1** 125 J4
Gilling Ct **NW3** 124 E1
Gillingham St **SW1** 129 H3
Gilmore Rd **SE13** 131 P10
Gilstead Rd **SW6** 128 B8
Gilston Rd **SW10** 128 C4
Giltspur St **EC1** 125 P8
Giraud St **E14** 127 M8
Gladstone St **SE1** 129 P2
Gladys Rd **NW6** 124 A2
Glaisher St **SE8** 131 L5
Glamis Pl **E1** 126 G9
Glamis Rd **E1** 126 G9
Glasgow Ho **W9** 124 B4
Glasgow Ter **SW1** 129 J4
Glasshill St **SE1** 129 P1
Glasshouse Flds **E1** 127 H9
Glasshouse St **W1** 125 J9
Glasshouse Wk **SE11** 129 L4
Glaucus St **E3** 127 M7
Glebe Pl **SW3** 128 E5
Gledhow Gdns **SW5** 128 C3
Glenaffric Av **E14** 131 P3
Glendall St **SW9** 129 M10
Glendower Pl **SW7** 128 D3
Glenfinlas Way **SE5** 129 P6
Glengall Causeway **E14** 131 L2
Glengall Gro **E14** 131 M2
Glengall Rd **SE15** 130 D5
Glengall Ter **SE15** 130 D5
Glengarnock Av **E14** 131 N3
Glenilla Rd **NW3** 124 E1
Glenloch Rd **NW3** 124 E1
Glenmore Rd **NW3** 124 E1
Glenrosa St **SW6** 128 C8
Glensdale Rd **SE4** 131 K9
Glentworth St **NW1** 124 F6
Glenville Gro **SE8** 131 K6
Glenworth Av **E14** 131 P3
Globe Pond Rd **SE16** 127 J10
Globe Rd **E1** 126 G5
Globe Rd **E2** 126 G5
Globe Rope Wk **E14** 131 N3
Globe St **SE1** 130 A2
Gloucester Av **NW1** 124 G2
Gloucester Circ **SE10** 131 N6
Gloucester Cres **NW1** 125 H3
Gloucester Gate **NW1** 125 H4
Gloucester Ho **NW6** 124 A4
Gloucester Ms **W2** 124 C8
Gloucester Pl **NW1** 124 F6
Gloucester Pl **W1** 124 F7
Gloucester Rd **SW7** 128 C2
Gloucester Sq **W2** 124 D8
Gloucester St **SW1** 129 J4
Gloucester Ter **W2** 124 D9
Gloucester Wk **W8** 128 A1
Gloucester Way **EC1** 125 N5
Glycena Rd **SW11** 128 F9
Godalming Rd **E14** 127 M7
Godfrey St **E15** 127 N4
Godfrey St **SW3** 128 E4
Goding St **SE11** 129 L4
Godliman St **EC4** 126 A8
Godman Rd **SE15** 130 F8
Godson St **N1** 125 N4
Goffers Rd **SE3** 131 P7
Golden Jubilee Br **SE1** 125 L10
Golden Jubilee Br **WC2** 125 L10
Golden La **EC1** 126 A6
Golden Sq **W1** 125 J9
Goldhurst Ter **NW6** 124 B2
Golding St **E1** 126 E8
Goldington Cres **NW1** 125 K4
Goldington St **NW1** 125 K4
Goldman Cl **E2** 126 E6
Goldney Rd **W9** 124 A6
Goldsboro Rd **SW8** 129 K7
Goldsmith Rd **SE15** 130 E7
Goldsmith's Row **E2** 126 E4
Goldsmith's Sq **E2** 126 E4
Goldsworthy Gdns **SE16** 130 G3
Goldwin Cl **SE14** 130 G7
Gomm Rd **SE16** 130 G2
Gonson St **SE8** 131 M5
Goodge St **W1** 125 J7
Goodhart Pl **E14** 127 J9
Goodinge Cl **N7** 125 L1
Goodman's Stile **E1** 126 E8
Goodmans Yd **E1** 126 D9
Goods Way **NW1** 125 L4
Goodway Gdns **E14** 127 P8
Goodwin Cl **SE16** 130 E2
Goodwood Rd **SE14** 131 J6
Gopsall St **N1** 126 B3
Gordon Gro **SE5** 129 P8
Gordon Pl **W8** 128 A1
Gordon Rd **SE15** 130 F8
Gordon Sq **WC1** 125 K6
Gordon St **WC1** 125 K6
Gore Rd **E9** 126 G3
Gore St **SW7** 128 C2
Gorefield Pl **NW6** 124 A4
Goring St **EC3** 126 C8
Gorsuch St **E2** 126 D5
Gosfield St **W1** 125 J7
Gosling Way **SW9** 129 N7
Gosset St **E2** 126 D5
Gosterwood St **SE8** 131 J5
Goswell Rd **EC1** 125 P5
Gough Sq **EC4** 125 N8
Gough St **WC1** 125 M6
Goulden Ho App **SW11** 128 E8
Goulston St **E1** 126 D8
Gower Ms **WC1** 125 K7
Gower Pl **WC1** 125 J6
Gower St **WC1** 125 J6
Gower's Wk **E1** 126 E8
Gowlett Rd **SE15** 130 E9
Gowrie Rd **SW11** 128 G9
Grace St **E3** 127 M5
Gracechurch St **EC3** 126 B9
Grace's All **E1** 126 E9
Graces Ms **SE5** 130 C8
Graces Rd **SE5** 130 C8
Grafton Cres **NW1** 125 H1
Grafton Ho **E3** 127 L5
Grafton Pl **NW1** 125 K5
Grafton Sq **SW4** 129 J9
Grafton St **W1** 125 H9
Grafton Way **W1** 125 J6
Grafton Way **WC1** 125 J6
Graham Rd **E8** 126 D1
Graham St **N1** 125 P4
Graham Ter **SW1** 128 G3
Granary Rd **E1** 126 F6
Granary St **NW1** 125 K3
Granby St **E2** 126 D6
Granby Ter **NW1** 125 J4
Grand Junct Wf **N1** 126 A4
Grand Union Cres **E8** 126 E2
Grand Union Wk **NW1** 125 H2
Granfield St **SW11** 128 D7
Grange, The **SE1** 130 D2
Grange Gro **N1** 125 P1
Grange Pl **NW6** 124 A2
Grange Rd **SE1** 130 C2
Grange St **N1** 126 B3
Grange Wk **SE1** 130 C2
Grange Yd **SE1** 130 D2
Gransden Av **E8** 126 F2
Grant Rd **SW11** 128 D10
Grantbridge St **N1** 125 P4
Grantham Rd **SW9** 129 L8
Grantley St **E1** 127 H5
Grantully Rd **W9** 124 B5
Granville Ct **N1** 126 B3
Granville Gro **SE13** 131 N9
Granville Pk **SE13** 131 N9
Granville Pl **W1** 124 G8
Granville Rd **NW6** 124 A4
Granville Sq **SE15** 130 C6
Granville Sq **WC1** 125 M5
Grayling Sq **E2** 126 E5
Gray's Inn **WC1** 125 M7
Gray's Inn Rd **WC1** 125 M5
Grayshott Rd **SW11** 128 G8
Great Castle St **W1** 125 J8
Great Cen St **NW1** 124 F7
Great Chapel St **W1** 125 K8
Great Chart St **SW11** 128 D10
Great Coll St **SW1** 129 L2
Great Cumberland Pl
**W1** 124 F8
Great Dover St **SE1** 130 A1
Great Eastern
Enterprise Cen **E14** 131 M1
Great Eastern Rd **E15** 127 P2
Great Eastern St **EC2** 126 C5
Great George St **SW1** 129 K1
Great Guildford St **SE1** 126 A10
Great James St **WC1** 125 M7
Great Marlborough St
**W1** 125 J8
Great Maze Pond **SE1** 130 B1
Great Ormond St **WC1** 125 L7
Great Percy St **WC1** 125 M5
Great Peter St **SW1** 129 K2
Great Portland St **W1** 125 H6
Great Pulteney St **W1** 125 J9
Great Queen St **WC2** 125 L8
Great Russell St **WC1** 125 L7
Great St. Helens **EC3** 126 C8
Great Scotland Yd **SW1** 125 L10
Great Smith St **SW1** 129 K2
Great Suffolk St **SE1** 125 P10
Great Sutton St **EC1** 125 P6
Great Titchfield St **W1** 125 J8
Great Twr St **EC3** 126 C9
Great Winchester St **EC2** 126 B8
Great Windmill St **W1** 125 K9
Greatfield Cl **SE4** 131 L10
Greatorex St **E1** 126 E7
Greek St **W1** 125 K8
Green Bk **E1** 126 F10
Green Dale **SE5** 130 B10
Green Hundred Rd **SE15** 130 E5
Green St **W1** 124 G9
Greenberry St **NW8** 124 E4
Greencoat Pl **SW1** 129 J3
Greencroft Gdns **NW6** 124 B2
Greenfield Rd **E1** 126 E7
Greenham Cl **SE1** 129 N1
Greenland Quay **SE16** 131 H3
Greenland Rd **NW1** 125 J3
Greenman St **N1** 126 A2
Greenwell St **W1** 125 H6
Greenwich Ch St **SE10** 131 N5
Greenwich Foot Tunnel
**E14** 131 N4
Greenwich Foot Tunnel
**SE10** 131 N4
Greenwich High Rd **SE10** 131 M7
Greenwich Pk St **SE10** 131 P4
Greenwich Quay **SE8** 131 M5
Greenwich S St **SE10** 131 M7
Greenwich Vw Pl **E14** 131 M2
Greenwood Ct **SW1** 129 J4
Greenwood Rd **E8** 126 E1
Greet St **SE1** 125 N10
Gregory Pl **W8** 128 B1
Grenade St **E14** 127 K9
Grenard Cl **SE15** 130 E6
Grendon St **NW8** 124 E6
Grenville Ms **SW7** 128 C3
Grenville Pl **SW7** 128 C2
Grenville St **WC1** 125 L6
Gresham Rd **SW9** 129 N9
Gresham St **EC2** 126 A8
Gresse St **W1** 125 K7
Greville Pl **NW6** 124 B4
Greville Rd **NW6** 124 B3
Greville St **EC1** 125 N7
Grey Eagle St **E1** 126 D7
Greycoat Pl **SW1** 129 K2
Greycoat St **SW1** 129 K2
Grimwade Cl **SE15** 130 G9
Grinling Pl **SE8** 131 L5
Grinstead Rd **SE8** 131 J4
Grittleton Rd **W9** 124 A6
Groom Pl **SW1** 128 G2
Groombridge Rd **E9** 127 H2
Grosvenor Cres **SW1** 128 G1
Grosvenor Cres Ms **SW1** 128 G1
Grosvenor Est **SW1** 129 K3
Grosvenor Gdns **SW1** 129 H2
Grosvenor Gate **W1** 124 F9
Grosvenor Hill **W1** 125 H9
Grosvenor Pk **SE5** 130 A5
Grosvenor Pl **SW1** 128 G1
Grosvenor Rd **SW1** 129 H5
Grosvenor Sq **W1** 124 G9
Grosvenor St **W1** 125 H9
Grosvenor Ter **SE5** 129 P6
Grosvenor Wf Rd **E14** 131 P3
Grove Cotts **SW3** 128 E5
Grove Cres Rd **E15** 127 P1
Grove End Rd **NW8** 124 D5
Grove Hill Rd **SE5** 130 C9
Grove La **SE5** 130 B7
Grove Pk **SE5** 130 C8
Grove Pas **E2** 126 F4
Grove Rd **E3** 127 H3
Grove St **SE8** 131 K3
Grove Vale **SE22** 130 C10
Grove Vil **E14** 127 M9
Grovelands Cl **SE5** 130 C8
Groveway **SW9** 129 M7
Grummant Rd **SE15** 130 D7
Grundy St **E14** 127 M8
Guerin Sq **E3** 127 K5
Guildford Gro **SE10** 131 M7
Guildford Rd **SW8** 129 L7
Guildhouse St **SW1** 129 J3
Guilford Pl **WC1** 125 M6
Guilford St **WC1** 125 L6
Guinness Cl **E9** 127 J2
Guinness Trust Bldgs
**SE11** 129 P4
Guinness Trust Bldgs
**SW9** 129 P10
Gulliver St **SE16** 131 K2
Gun St **E1** 126 D7
Gunmakers La **E3** 127 J3
Gunter Gro **SW10** 128 C5
Gunthorpe St **E1** 126 D7
Gunwhale Cl **SE16** 127 H10
Gurney Rd **SW6** 128 C9
Gutter La **EC2** 126 A8
Guy St **SE1** 130 B1
Gwyn Cl **SW6** 128 C6
Gwynne Rd **SW11** 128 D8
Gylcote Cl **SE5** 130 B10

## H

Haberdasher St **N1** 126 B5
Hackford Rd **SW9** 129 M7
Hackford Wk **SW9** 129 M7
Hackney Rd **E2** 126 D5
Haddo St **SE10** 131 M5
Haddonfield **SE8** 131 H3
Hadleigh St **E2** 126 G6
Hadley St **NW1** 125 H1
Hadrian Est **E2** 126 E4
Hafer Rd **SW11** 128 F10
Haggerston Rd **E8** 126 D2
Hainford Cl **SE4** 131 H10
Hainton Cl **E1** 126 F8
Halcomb St **N1** 126 C3
Hale St **E14** 127 M9
Halesworth Rd **SE13** 131 M9
Half Moon Cres **N1** 125 M4
Half Moon St **W1** 125 H10
Halford Rd **SW6** 128 A5
Halkin Arc **SW1** 128 F2
Halkin Pl **SW1** 128 G2
Halkin St **SW1** 128 G1
Hall Pl **W2** 124 D6
Hall Rd **NW8** 124 C5
Hall St **EC1** 125 P5
Hall Twr **W2** 124 D7
Hallam St **W1** 125 H7
Halley Gdns **SE13** 131 P10
Halley St **E14** 127 J7
Hallfield Est **W2** 124 C8
Halliford St **N1** 126 A2
Halsey St **SW3** 128 F3
Halsmere Rd **SE5** 129 P7
Halton Cross St **N1** 125 P3
Halton Rd **N1** 125 P2
Hamble St **SW6** 128 B9
Hamilton Cl **NW8** 124 D5
Hamilton Gdns **NW8** 124 C5
Hamilton Pl **W1** 124 G10
Hamilton Ter **NW8** 124 B4
Hamlet, The **SE5** 130 B9
Hamlets Way **E3** 127 K6
Hammond St **NW5** 125 J1
Hampson Way **SW8** 129 M7
Hampstead Rd **NW1** 125 J4
Hampton Cl **NW6** 124 A5
Hampton St **SE1** 129 P3
Hampton St **SE17** 129 P3
Hanbury St **E1** 126 D7
Hancock Rd **E3** 127 N5
Hand Ct **WC1** 125 M7
Handel St **WC1** 125 L6
Handforth Rd **SW9** 129 N6
Handley Rd **E9** 126 G2
Hankey Pl **SE1** 130 B1
Hannibal Rd **E1** 126 G7
Hannington Rd **SW4** 129 H9
Hanover Gdns **SE11** 129 N5
Hanover Gate **NW1** 124 E5
Hanover Pk **SE15** 130 E7
Hanover Sq **W1** 125 H8
Hanover St **W1** 125 H8
Hanover Ter **NW1** 124 E5
Hans Cres **SW1** 128 F2
Hans Pl **SW1** 128 F2
Hans Rd **SW3** 128 F2
Hanson St **W1** 125 J7
Hanway St **W1** 125 K8
Harben Rd **NW6** 124 C2
Harbet Rd **W2** 124 D7
Harbinger Rd **E14** 131 M3
Harbledown Rd **SW6** 128 A7
Harbour Av **SW10** 128 C7
Harbour Ex Sq **E14** 131 M1
Harbour Rd **SE5** 130 A9
Harbut Rd **SW11** 128 D10
Harcourt Rd **SE4** 131 J10
Harcourt St **W1** 124 E7
Harcourt Ter **SW10** 128 B4
Harders Rd **SE15** 130 F8
Hardinge St **E1** 126 G8
Hardwick St **EC1** 125 N5
Hare & Billet Rd **SE3** 131 P7
Hare Row **E2** 126 F4
Hare Wk **N1** 126 C4
Harecourt Rd **N1** 126 A1
Haredale Rd **SE24** 130 A10
Harefield Ms **SE4** 131 K9
Harefield Rd **SE4** 131 K9
Harewood Av **NW1** 124 E6
Harfield Gdns **SE5** 130 C9
Harford St **E1** 127 J6
Hargwyne St **SW9** 129 M9
Harlescott Rd **SE15** 131 H10
Harley Gdns **SW10** 128 C4
Harley Gro **E3** 127 K5
Harley Pl **W1** 125 H7
Harley Rd **NW3** 124 D2
Harley St **W1** 125 H6
Harleyford Rd **SE11** 129 M5
Harleyford St **SE11** 129 N5
Harmood St **NW1** 125 H2
Harmsworth St **SE17** 129 P4
Harold Est **SE1** 130 C2
Harold Pl **SE11** 129 N4
Harper Rd **SE1** 130 A2
Harpley Sq **E1** 126 G5
Harpsden St **SW11** 128 G7
Harpur St **WC1** 125 M7
Harrap St **E14** 127 N9
Harriet Cl **E8** 126 E3
Harriet Wk **SW1** 128 F1
Harrington Gdns **SW7** 128 B3
Harrington Rd **SW7** 128 D3
Harrington Sq **NW1** 125 J4
Harrington St **NW1** 125 J5
Harris St **SE5** 130 B6
Harrison St **WC1** 125 L5
Harrow La **E14** 127 N9
Harrow Pl **E1** 126 C8
Harroway Rd **SW11** 128 D8
Harrowby St **W1** 124 E8
Harrowgate Rd **E9** 127 J1
Hartfield Ter **E3** 127 L4
Hartington Rd **SW8** 129 L7
Hartlake Rd **E9** 127 H1
Hartland Rd **NW1** 125 H2
Hartley St **E2** 126 G5
Harton St **SE8** 131 L7
Harts La **SE14** 131 J6
Harvey Rd **SE5** 130 B7
Harvey St **N1** 126 B3
Harwood Rd **SW6** 128 A6
Harwood Ter **SW6** 128 B7
Haselrigge Rd **SW4** 129 K10
Hasker St **SW3** 128 E3
Haslam Cl **N1** 125 N2
Haslam St **SE15** 130 D6
Hassett Rd **E9** 127 H1
Hastings Cl **SE15** 130 E6
Hastings St **WC1** 125 L5
Hatcham Pk Rd **SE14** 131 H7
Hatcham Rd **SE15** 130 G5
Hatfields **SE1** 125 P10
Hatherley Gro **W2** 124 B8
Hathorne Cl **SE15** 130 F8
Hatton Gdn **EC1** 125 N7
Hatton Pl **EC1** 125 N6
Hatton Wall **EC1** 125 N7
Haul Rd **NW1** 125 L4
Havannah St **E14** 131 L1
Havelock St **N1** 125 L3
Havelock Ter **SW8** 129 H6
Haverfield Rd **E3** 127 J5
Haverstock St **N1** 125 P4
Havil St **SE5** 130 C6
Hawes St **N1** 125 P2
Hawgood St **E3** 127 L7
Hawkstone Est **SE16** 130 G3
Hawkstone Rd **SE16** 130 G3
Hawley Cres **NW1** 125 H2
Hawley Rd **NW1** 125 H2
Hawley St **NW1** 125 H2
Hawthorn Av **E3** 127 K3
Hawthorne Cl **N1** 126 C1
Hawtrey Rd **NW3** 124 E2
Hay Currie St **E14** 127 M8
Hay Hill **W1** 125 H9
Hay St **E2** 126 E3
Haydon Way **SW11** 128 D10
Hayes Gro **SE22** 130 D10
Hayles St **SE11** 129 P3
Haymarket **SW1** 125 K9
Haymerle Rd **SE15** 130 E5
Hay's Galleria **SE1** 126 C10
Hay's Ms **W1** 125 H9
Hazel Cl **SE15** 130 E8
Hazelmere Rd **NW6** 124 A3
Hazlebury Rd **SW6** 128 B8
Head St **E1** 127 H8
Headfort Pl **SW1** 128 G1
Headlam St **E1** 126 F6
Heald St **SE14** 131 K7
Healey St **NW1** 125 H1
Hearn St **EC2** 126 C6
Heath La **SE3** 131 P8
Heath Rd **SW8** 129 H8
Heathcote St **WC1** 125 M6
Heather Cl **SW8** 129 H9
Heathwall St **SW11** 128 F9
Heaton Rd **SE15** 130 E9
Heddon St **W1** 125 J9
Hedgers Gro **E9** 127 J1
Heiron St **SE17** 129 P5
Helmet Row **EC1** 126 A6
Helmsley Pl **E8** 126 F2
Helsinki Sq **SE16** 131 J2
Hemans St **SW8** 129 K6
Hemberton Rd **SW9** 129 L9
Hemingford Rd **N1** 125 M3
Hemming St **E1** 126 E6
Hemp Wk **SE17** 130 B3
Hemstal Rd **NW6** 124 A2
Hemsworth St **N1** 126 C4
Heneage St **E1** 126 D7
Henley Dr **SE1** 130 D3
Henley St **SW11** 128 G8
Henning St **SW11** 128 E7
Henrietta Cl **SE8** 131 L5
Henrietta Pl **W1** 125 H8

Hen - Lau


Henrietta St **WC2** 125 L9
Henriques St **E1** 126 E8
Henry Dent Cl **SE5** 130 B9
Henshall St **N1** 126 B1
Henshaw St **SE17** 130 B3
Henstridge Pl **NW8** 124 E4
Henty Cl **SW11** 128 E6
Hepscott Rd **E9** 127 L2
Herbal Hill **EC1** 125 N6
Herbert St **NW5** 124 G1
Herbrand St **WC1** 125 L6
Hercules Rd **SE1** 129 M2
Hereford Ho **NW6** 124 A4
Hereford Rd **W2** 124 A8
Hereford Sq **SW7** 128 C3
Hereford St **E2** 126 E6
Heritage Cl **SW9** 129 P9
Hermit St **EC1** 125 P5
Hermitage St **W2** 124 D7
Hermitage Wall **E1** 126 E10
Herne Hill Rd **SE24** 130 A9
Heron Pl **SE16** 127 J10
Heron Quay **E14** 127 L10
Heron Rd **SE24** 130 A10
Herrick St **SW1** 129 K3
Hertford Rd **N1** 126 C3
Hertford St **W1** 125 H10
Hertsmere Rd **E14** 127 L9
Hesper Ms **SW5** 128 B4
Hesperus Cres **E14** 131 M3
Hessel St **E1** 126 F8
Hester Rd **SW11** 128 E6
Heston St **SE14** 131 K7
Hetherington Rd **SW4** 129 L10
Hewison St **E3** 127 K4
Hewlett Rd **E3** 127 J4
Heyford Av **SW8** 129 L6
Heygate St **SE17** 130 A3
Hibbert St **SW11** 128 C9
Hickmore Wk **SW4** 129 J9
Hicks Cl **SW11** 128 E9
Hicks St **SE8** 131 J4
Hide Pl **SW1** 129 K3
Hide Twr **SW1** 129 K3
High Br **SE10** 131 P4
High Br Wf **SE10** 131 P4
High Holborn **WC1** 125 L8
High St **E15** 127 N4
High Timber St **EC4** 126 A9
Highbury Cor **N5** 125 N1
Highbury Gro **N5** 125 P1
Highbury Pl **N5** 125 P1
Highbury Sta Rd **N1** 125 N1
Highshore Rd **SE15** 130 D8
Highway, The **E1** 126 F9
Highway, The **E14** 126 F9
Hilary Cl **SW6** 128 B6
Hilda Ter **SW9** 129 N8
Hildyard Rd **SW6** 128 A5
Hilgrove Rd **NW6** 124 C2
Hill Rd **NW8** 124 C4
Hill St **W1** 125 H10
Hillbeck Cl **SE15** 130 G6
Hillgate Pl **W8** 124 A10
Hillgate St **W8** 124 A10
Hillingdon St **SE17** 129 P6
Hillman St **E8** 126 F1
Hillmead Dr **SW9** 129 P10
Hillside Cl **NW8** 124 B4
Hilltop Rd **NW6** 124 A2
Hilly Flds Cres **SE4** 131 L9
Hillyard St **SW9** 129 N7
Hinckley Rd **SE15** 130 E10
Hind Gro **E14** 127 L8
Hinde St **W1** 124 G8
Hinton Rd **SE24** 129 P9
Hitchin Sq **E3** 127 J4
Hobart Pl **SW1** 129 H2
Hobday St **E14** 127 M7
Hobury St **SW10** 128 C5
Hodnet Gro **SE16** 131 H3
Hogarth Rd **SW5** 128 B3
Holbeck Row **SE15** 130 E6
Holbein Ms **SW1** 128 G4
Holbein Pl **SW1** 128 G3
Holborn **EC1** 125 N7
Holborn Viaduct **EC1** 125 N7
Holcroft Rd **E9** 126 G2
Holden St **SW11** 128 G8
Holford St **WC1** 125 N5
Holgate Av **SW11** 128 D9
Holland Gro **SW9** 129 N6
Holland St **SE1** 125 P10
Holland St **W8** 128 A1
Hollen St **W1** 125 J8
Holles St **W1** 125 H8
Holly Gro **SE15** 130 D8
Holly St **E8** 126 D1
Hollybush Gdns **E2** 126 F5
Hollydale Rd **SE15** 130 G7
Hollydene **SE15** 130 F7
Hollymount Cl **SE10** 131 N7
Hollywood Rd **SW10** 128 C5
Holman Rd **SW11** 128 D8
Holmead Rd **SW6** 128 B6
Holmefield Ct **NW3** 124 E1
Holmes Cl **SE22** 130 E10
Holmes Ter **SE1** 129 N1
Holms St **E2** 126 E4
Holton St **E1** 127 H6
Holwood Pl **SW4** 129 K10
Holyhead Cl **E3** 127 L5
Holywell La **EC2** 126 C6
Holywell Row **EC2** 126 C6
Home Rd **SW11** 128 E8
Homefield St **N1** 126 C4
Homer Dr **E14** 131 L3
Homer Rd **E9** 127 J1
Homer Row **W1** 124 E7
Homer St **W1** 124 E7
Hooper St **E1** 126 E8
Hope St **SW11** 128 D9
Hopewell St **SE5** 130 B6
Hopton Gdns **SE1** 125 P10
Hopton St **SE1** 125 P10
Hopwood Rd **SE17** 130 B5
Horatio St **E2** 126 D4
Horbury Cres **W11** 124 A9
Horle Wk **SE5** 129 P8
Hornby Cl **NW3** 124 D2
Hornshay St **SE15** 130 G5
Hornton Pl **W8** 128 A1
Hornton St **W8** 124 A10
Horse Guards Av **SW1** 125 L10
Horse Guards Rd **SW1** 125 K10
Horse Ride **SW1** 125 J10
Horseferry Pl **SE10** 131 N5
Horseferry Rd **E14** 127 J9
Horseferry Rd **SW1** 129 K3
Horselydown La **SE1** 130 D1
Horseshoe Cl **E14** 131 N4
Horsley St **SE17** 130 B5
Hortensia Rd **SW10** 128 C6
Horton Rd **E8** 126 F1
Horton St **SE13** 131 M9
Hosier La **EC1** 125 P7
Hoskins St **SE10** 131 P4
Hotspur St **SE11** 129 N4
Houndsditch **EC3** 126 C8
Howard Bldg **SW8** 129 H5
Howbury Rd **SE15** 130 G9
Howden St **SE15** 130 E9
Howick Pl **SW1** 129 J2
Howie St **SW11** 128 E6
Howitt Rd **NW3** 124 E1
Howland Est **SE16** 130 G2
Howland St **W1** 125 J7
Howland Way **SE16** 131 J1
Howley Pl **W2** 124 C7
Hows St **E2** 126 D4
Howson Rd **SE4** 131 J10
Hoxton Sq **N1** 126 C5
Hoxton St **N1** 126 C3
Hubert Gro **SW9** 129 L9
Huddart St **E3** 127 K7
Huddleston Cl **E2** 126 G4
Hugh St **SW1** 129 H3
Hugon Rd **SW6** 128 B9
Huguenot Pl **E1** 126 D7
Hull Cl **SE16** 131 H1
Humphrey St **SE1** 130 D4
Hungerford Br **SE1** 125 L10
Hungerford Br **WC2** 125 L10
Hunsdon Rd **SE14** 131 H5
Hunter St **WC1** 125 L6
Huntingdon St **N1** 125 M2
Huntley St **WC1** 125 J6
Hunton St **E1** 126 E6
Hunts La **E15** 127 N4
Huntsman St **SE17** 130 B3
Hurlingham Business Pk **SW6** 128 A9
Hurlingham Sq **SW6** 128 A9
Huson Cl **NW3** 124 E2
Hutchings St **E14** 131 L1
Hyde Pk **SW7** 124 E10
Hyde Pk **W1** 124 E10
Hyde Pk **W2** 124 E10
Hyde Pk Cor **W1** 128 G1
Hyde Pk Cres **W2** 124 E8
Hyde Pk Gdns **W2** 124 D9
Hyde Pk Gate **SW7** 128 C1
Hyde Pk Pl **W2** 124 E9
Hyde Pk Sq **W2** 124 E8
Hyde Pk St **W2** 124 E8
Hyde Rd **N1** 126 B3
Hyde Vale **SE10** 131 N6
Hyndman St **SE15** 130 F5


## I


Iceland Rd **E3** 127 L3
Ida St **E14** 127 N8
Idonia St **SE8** 131 K6
Ifield Rd **SW10** 128 B5
Ilchester Gdns **W2** 124 B9
Ilderton Rd **SE15** 130 G6
Ilderton Rd **SE16** 130 F4
Iliffe St **SE17** 129 P4
Ilminster Gdns **SW11** 128 E10
Imber St **N1** 126 B3
Imperial Coll **SW7** 128 D2
Imperial Coll Rd **SW7** 128 D2
Imperial Cres **SW6** 128 C8
Imperial Rd **SW6** 128 B7
Imperial Sq **SW6** 128 B7
Imperial St **E3** 127 N5
Imperial Wf **SW6** 128 C8
Indescon Ct **E14** 131 L1
Ingate Pl **SW8** 129 H7
Ingelow Rd **SW8** 129 H8
Ingleborough St **SW9** 129 N8
Inglesham Wk **E9** 127 K1
Ingleton St **SW9** 129 N8
Inglewood Cl **E14** 131 L3
Inglis St **SE5** 129 P7
Ingrave St **SW11** 128 D9
Inkerman Rd **NW5** 125 H1
Inner Circle **NW1** 124 G5
Innes St **SE15** 130 C6
Inverness Pl **W2** 124 B9
Inverness St **NW1** 125 H3
Inverness Ter **W2** 124 B9
Inverton Rd **SE15** 131 H10
Inville Rd **SE17** 130 B4
Inwen Ct **SE8** 131 J4
Inworth St **SW11** 128 E8
Ireland Yd **EC4** 125 P8
Irene Rd **SW6** 128 A7
Ironmonger Row **EC1** 126 A5
Irving Gro **SW9** 129 M8
Irving St **WC2** 125 K9
Isabel St **SW9** 129 M7
Isabella St **SE1** 125 P10
Isambard Ms **E14** 131 N2
Island Rd **SE16** 131 H3
Island Row **E14** 127 K8
Islington Grn **N1** 125 P3
Islington High St **N1** 125 P4
Islington Pk St **N1** 125 N2
Ivanhoe Rd **SE5** 130 D9
Iveagh Cl **E9** 127 H3
Iveley Rd **SW4** 129 J8
Iverna Ct **W8** 128 A2
Iverna Gdns **W8** 128 A2
Ives St **SW3** 128 E3
Ivimey St **E2** 126 E5
Ivor Pl **NW1** 124 F6
Ivor St **NW1** 125 J2
Ivy Rd **SE4** 131 K10
Ivy St **N1** 126 C4
Ivydale Rd **SE15** 131 H9
Ixworth Pl **SW3** 128 E4


## J


Jacaranda Gro **E8** 126 D2
Jackman St **E8** 126 F3
Jackson Cl **E9** 126 G2
Jacob St **SE1** 130 D1
Jago Wk **SE5** 130 B6
Jamaica Rd **SE1** 130 D1
Jamaica Rd **SE16** 130 D1
Jamaica St **E1** 126 G8
James St **W1** 124 G8
Jameson Ct **E2** 126 G4
Jameson St **W8** 124 A10
Jamestown Rd **NW1** 125 H3
Jamestown Way **E14** 127 P9
Jamuna Cl **E14** 127 J7
Janet St **E14** 131 L2
Janeway St **SE16** 130 E1
Jardine Rd **E1** 127 H9
Jarrow Rd **SE16** 130 G3
Jay Ms **SW7** 128 C1
Jebb St **E3** 127 L4
Jedburgh St **SW11** 128 G10
Jeffreys Rd **SW4** 129 L8
Jeffreys St **NW1** 125 H2
Jeffreys Wk **SW4** 129 L8
Jeger Av **E2** 126 D3
Jerdan Pl **SW6** 128 A6
Jeremiah St **E14** 127 M8
Jermyn St **SW1** 125 K9
Jerningham Rd **SE14** 131 J8
Jerome Cres **NW8** 124 E6
Jerrard St **SE13** 131 M9
Jewry St **EC3** 126 D8
Jew's Row **SW18** 128 B10
Joan St **SE1** 125 P10
Jocelyn St **SE15** 130 E7
Jockey's Flds **WC1** 125 M7
Jodane St **SE8** 131 K3
Jodrell Rd **E3** 127 K3
John Adam St **WC2** 125 L9
John Aird Ct **W2** 124 C7
John Carpenter St **EC4** 125 P9
John Felton Rd **SE16** 130 E1
John Fisher St **E1** 126 E9
John Islip St **SW1** 129 L3
John Maurice Cl **SE17** 130 B3
John Penn St **SE13** 131 M7
John Princes St **W1** 125 H8
John Roll Way **SE16** 130 E2
John Ruskin St **SE5** 129 P6
John Silkin La **SE8** 131 H4
John Spencer Sq **N1** 125 P1
John St **WC1** 125 M6
John Williams Cl **SE14** 131 H5
John's Ms **WC1** 125 M6
Johnson Cl **E8** 126 E3
Johnson's Pl **SW1** 129 J4
Jonathan St **SE11** 129 M4
Joseph Hardcastle Cl **SE14** 131 H6
Joseph St **E3** 127 K6
Joubert St **SW11** 128 F8
Jowett St **SE15** 130 D6
Jubilee Cres **E14** 131 N2
Jubilee Pl **SW3** 128 E4
Jubilee St **E1** 126 G8
Judd St **WC1** 125 L5
Juer St **SW11** 128 E6
Julian Pl **E14** 131 M4
Junction App **SE13** 131 N9
Junction App **SW11** 128 E9
Juniper Cres **NW1** 124 G2
Juniper St **E1** 126 G9
Juno Way **SE14** 131 H5
Jupiter Way **N7** 125 M1
Jupp Rd **E15** 127 P2
Jupp Rd W **E15** 127 N3
Juxon St **SE11** 129 M3


## K


Kambala Rd **SW11** 128 D8
Kassala Rd **SW11** 128 F7
Kathleen Rd **SW11** 128 F9
Kay Rd **SW9** 129 L8
Kay St **E2** 126 E4
Kean St **WC2** 125 M8
Keel Cl **SE16** 127 H10
Keeley St **WC2** 125 M8
Keetons Rd **SE16** 130 F2
Keildon Rd **SW11** 128 F10
Kellett Rd **SW2** 129 N10
Kelly Av **SE15** 130 D6
Kelly St **NW1** 125 H1
Kelman Cl **SW4** 129 K8
Kelmore Gro **SE22** 130 E10
Kelsey St **E2** 126 F6
Kelso Pl **W8** 128 B2
Kelson Ho **E14** 131 N2
Kelvedon Ho **SW8** 129 L7
Kemble St **WC2** 125 M8
Kemerton Rd **SE5** 130 A9
Kempsford Gdns **SW5** 128 A4
Kempsford Rd **SE11** 129 N3
Kempson Rd **SW6** 128 A7
Kempthorne Rd **SE8** 131 J3
Kenbury St **SE5** 130 A8
Kenchester Cl **SW8** 129 L6
Kendal Cl **SW9** 129 P6
Kendal St **W2** 124 E8
Kender St **SE14** 130 G6
Kendoa Rd **SW4** 129 K10
Kendrick Pl **SW7** 128 D3
Kenilworth Rd **E3** 127 J4
Kennard Rd **E15** 127 P2
Kennard St **SW11** 128 G8
Kennet St **E1** 126 E10
Kenning Ter **N1** 126 C3
Kennings Way **SE11** 129 N4
Kennington La **SE11** 129 M4
Kennington Oval **SE11** 129 M5
Kennington Pk **SW9** 129 N6
Kennington Pk Gdns **SE11** 129 P5
Kennington Pk Pl **SE11** 129 N5
Kennington Pk Rd **SE11** 129 N5
Kennington Rd **SE1** 129 N2
Kennington Rd **SE11** 129 N3
Kensington Ch Ct **W8** 128 B1
Kensington Ch St **W8** 124 A10
Kensington Ch Wk **W8** 128 B1
Kensington Ct **W8** 128 B1
Kensington Ct Pl **W8** 128 B2
Kensington Gdns **W2** 124 C10
Kensington Gdns Sq **W2** 124 B8
Kensington Gate **W8** 128 C2
Kensington Gore **SW7** 128 D1
Kensington High St **W8** 128 A2
Kensington Mall **W8** 124 A10
Kensington Palace Gdns **W8** 124 B10
Kensington Pl **W8** 124 A10
Kensington Rd **SW7** 128 D1
Kensington Rd **W8** 128 B1
Kensington Sq **W8** 128 B1
Kent Pas **NW1** 124 F5
Kent St **E2** 126 D4
Kent Ter **NW1** 124 E5
Kentish Town Rd **NW1** 125 H2
Kentish Town Rd **NW5** 125 H2
Kenton Rd **E9** 127 H1
Kenton St **WC1** 125 L6
Kentwell Cl **SE4** 131 J10
Kenway Rd **SW5** 128 B3
Kenwyn Rd **SW4** 129 K10
Kepler Rd **SW4** 129 L10
Keppel St **WC1** 125 K7
Kerbey St **E14** 127 M8
Kerfield Cres **SE5** 130 B7
Kerfield Pl **SE5** 130 B7
Kerridge Ct **N1** 126 C1
Kerrison Rd **E15** 127 P3
Kerrison Rd **SW11** 128 E9
Kerry Path **SE14** 131 K5
Kerry Rd **SE14** 131 K5
Kersley Ms **SW11** 128 F8
Kersley St **SW11** 128 F8
Keston Rd **SE15** 130 E9
Kestrel Ho **EC1** 125 P5
Kevan Ho **SE5** 130 A6
Key Cl **E1** 126 F6
Keybridge Ho **SW8** 129 L5
Keyworth St **SE1** 129 P2
Khyber Rd **SW11** 128 E8
Kibworth St **SW8** 129 M6
Kilburn Pk Rd **NW6** 124 A5
Kilburn Pl **NW6** 124 A3
Kilburn Priory **NW6** 124 B3
Kilburn Sq **NW6** 124 A3
Kildare Gdns **W2** 124 A8
Kildare Ter **W2** 124 A8
Kilkie St **SW6** 128 C8
Killick St **N1** 125 M4
Killowen Rd **E9** 127 H1
Killyon Rd **SW8** 129 J8
Killyon Ter **SW8** 129 J8
Kilner St **E14** 127 L7
Kimberley Av **SE15** 130 F8
Kimberley Rd **SW9** 129 L8
Kimpton Rd **SE5** 130 B7
Kinburn St **SE16** 131 H1
Kincaid Rd **SE15** 130 F6
King & Queen St **SE17** 130 A4
King Arthur Cl **SE15** 130 G6
King Charles St **SW1** 129 K1
King David La **E1** 126 G9
King Edward St **EC1** 126 A8
King Edward Wk **SE1** 129 N2
King Edwards Rd **E9** 126 F3
King Frederik IX Twr **SE16** 131 K2
King George St **SE10** 131 N6
King Henry's Rd **NW3** 124 E2
King Henry's Wk **N1** 126 C1
King James St **SE1** 129 P1
King John St **E1** 127 H7
King St **EC2** 126 A8
King St **SW1** 125 J10
King St **WC2** 125 L9
King William St **EC4** 126 B9
King William Wk **SE10** 131 N5
Kingdon Rd **NW6** 124 A1
Kingfield St **E14** 131 N3
Kingfisher Ms **SE13** 131 M10
Kingfisher Sq **SE8** 131 K5
Kinglake St **SE17** 130 C4
Kingly St **W1** 125 J8
Kings Coll Rd **NW3** 124 E2
King's Cross Rd **WC1** 125 M5
King's Cross Sta **N1** 125 L4
Kings Gro **SE15** 130 F6
King's Ms **WC1** 125 M7
King's Reach Twr **SE1** 125 N10
King's Rd **SW1** 128 F4
King's Rd **SW3** 128 F4
King's Rd **SW6** 128 B7
King's Rd **SW10** 128 B7
Kingsbury Rd **N1** 126 C1
Kingsbury Ter **N1** 126 C1
Kingsgate Pl **NW6** 124 A2
Kingsgate Rd **NW6** 124 A2
Kingshold Rd **E9** 126 G2
Kingsland Grn **E8** 126 C1
Kingsland Rd **E2** 126 C4
Kingsland Rd **E8** 126 C4
Kingsland Shop Cen **E8** 126 D1
Kingsley St **SW11** 128 F9
Kingsmill Ter **NW8** 124 D4
Kingstown St **NW1** 124 G3
Kingsway **WC2** 125 M8
Kingswood Cl **SW8** 129 L6
Kinnerton St **SW1** 128 G1
Kinsale Rd **SE15** 130 E9
Kipling Est **SE1** 130 B1
Kipling St **SE1** 130 B1
Kirby Est **SE16** 130 F2
Kirby Gro **SE1** 130 C1
Kirkland Wk **E8** 126 D1
Kirkwall Pl **E2** 126 G5
Kirkwood Rd **SE15** 130 F8
Kirtling St **SW8** 129 J6
Kirwyn Way **SE5** 129 P6
Kitcat Ter **E3** 127 L5
Kitson Rd **SE5** 130 A6
Kitto Rd **SE14** 131 H8
Knapp Rd **E3** 127 L6
Knaresborough Pl **SW5** 128 B3
Knatchbull Rd **SE5** 130 A7
Kneller Rd **SE4** 131 J10
Knighten St **E1** 126 E10
Knighthead Pt **E14** 131 L2
Knightsbridge **SW1** 128 F1
Knightsbridge **SW7** 128 E1
Knivet Rd **SW6** 128 A5
Knobs Hill Rd **E15** 127 M3
Knottisford St **E2** 126 G5
Knowle Cl **SW9** 129 N9
Knowles Wk **SW4** 129 J9
Knowsley Rd **SW11** 128 F8
Knox St **W1** 124 F7
Knoyle St **SE14** 131 J5
Kylemore Rd **NW6** 124 A2
Kynance Ms **SW7** 128 B2
Kynance Pl **SW7** 128 C2


## L


Laburnum St **E2** 126 D3
Lacey Wk **E3** 127 L4
Lackington St **EC2** 126 B7
Lacon Rd **SE22** 130 E10
Ladycroft Rd **SE13** 131 M9
Lafone St **SE1** 130 D1
Lagado Ms **SE16** 127 H10
Laird Ho **SE5** 130 A6
Lamb La **E8** 126 F2
Lamb St **E1** 126 D7
Lambert St **N1** 125 N2
Lambeth Br **SE1** 129 L3
Lambeth Br **SW1** 129 L3
Lambeth High St **SE1** 129 M3
Lambeth Hill **EC4** 126 A9
Lambeth Palace Rd **SE1** 129 M2
Lambeth Rd **SE1** 129 M3
Lambeth Rd **SE11** 129 M3
Lambeth Wk **SE1** 129 M3
Lambeth Wk **SE11** 129 M3
Lambolle Pl **NW3** 124 E1
Lambolle Rd **NW3** 124 E1
Lambourn Rd **SW4** 129 H9
Lambourne Gro **SE16** 131 H3
Lamb's Conduit St **WC1** 125 M6
Lamb's Pas **EC1** 126 B7
Lamerton St **SE8** 131 L5
Lammas Rd **E9** 127 H2
Lamont Rd **SW10** 128 C5
Lanark Pl **W9** 124 C6
Lanark Rd **W9** 124 B4
Lanark Sq **E14** 131 M2
Lanbury Rd **SE15** 131 H10
Lancaster Dr **NW3** 124 E1
Lancaster Gate **W2** 124 C9
Lancaster Gro **NW3** 124 D1
Lancaster Ms **W2** 124 C9
Lancaster Pl **WC2** 125 M9
Lancaster St **SE1** 129 P1
Lancaster Ter **W2** 124 D9
Lancaster Wk **W2** 124 C10
Lancelot Pl **SW7** 128 F1
Lanchester Way **SE14** 130 G7
Lancresse Ct **N1** 126 C3
Landmann Way **SE14** 131 H5
Landon Pl **SW1** 128 F2
Landons Cl **E14** 127 N10
Landor Rd **SW9** 129 L9
Lanfranc Rd **E3** 127 J4
Lang St **E1** 126 G6
Langbourne Pl **E14** 131 M4
Langdale Cl **SE17** 130 A5
Langdale Rd **SE10** 131 N6
Langford Ct **NW8** 124 C4
Langford Grn **SE5** 130 C9
Langford Pl **NW8** 124 C4
Langford Rd **SW6** 128 B8
Langham Pl **W1** 125 H7
Langham St **W1** 125 H7
Langley La **SW8** 129 M5
Langley St **WC2** 125 L8
Langton Rd **SW9** 129 P6
Langton St **SW10** 128 C5
Langtry Rd **NW8** 124 B3
Lanhill Rd **W9** 124 A6
Lanrick Rd **E14** 127 P8
Lansbury Est **E14** 127 M8
Lansbury Gdns **E14** 127 P8
Lanscombe Wk **SW8** 129 L7
Lansdowne Dr **E8** 126 E1
Lansdowne Gdns **SW8** 129 L7
Lansdowne Ter **WC1** 125 L6
Lansdowne Way **SW8** 129 K7
Lant St **SE1** 130 A1
Lanterns Ct **E14** 131 L1
Lanvanor Rd **SE15** 130 G8
Larcom St **SE17** 130 A3
Lark Row **E2** 126 G3
Larkhall La **SW4** 129 K8
Larkhall Ri **SW4** 129 J9
Lassell St **SE10** 131 P4
Latchmere Rd **SW11** 128 F8
Latchmere St **SW11** 128 F8
Latham Ho **E1** 127 H8
Latona Rd **SE15** 130 E5
Lauderdale Rd **W9** 124 B5
Lauderdale Twr **EC2** 126 A7
Launceston Pl **W8** 128 C2

Lau - Mil


Launch St **E14** 131 N2
Laurel St **E8** 126 D1
Laurie Gro **SE14** 131 J7
Lauriston Rd **E9** 127 H3
Lausanne Rd **SE15** 130 G7
Lavender Gdns **SW11** 128 F10
Lavender Gro **E8** 126 D2
Lavender Hill **SW11** 128 E10
Lavender Rd **SE16** 127 J10
Lavender Rd **SW11** 128 D9
Lavender Sweep **SW11** 128 F10
Lavender Wk **SW11** 128 F10
Laverton Pl **SW5** 128 B3
Lavington St **SE1** 125 P10
Law St **SE1** 130 B2
Lawford Rd **N1** 126 C2
Lawford Rd **NW5** 125 J1
Lawless St **E14** 127 M9
Lawn Ho Cl **E14** 131 N1
Lawn La **SW8** 129 L5
Lawrence Cl **E3** 127 L4
Lawrence St **SW3** 128 E5
Lawson Est **SE1** 130 B2
Lawton Rd **E3** 127 J5
Laxley Cl **SE5** 129 P6
Layard Rd **SE16** 130 F3
Layard Sq **SE16** 130 F3
Laycock St **N1** 125 N1
Laystall St **EC1** 125 N6
Lea Valley Wk **E3** 127 N6
Lea Valley Wk **E14** 127 M7
Lea Valley Wk **E15** 127 N5
Leabank Sq **E9** 127 L1
Leadenhall St **EC3** 126 C8
Leake St **SE1** 129 M1
Leamouth Rd **E14** 127 P8
Leander Ct **SE8** 131 L7
Leather La **EC1** 125 N7
Leather Rd **SE16** 131 H3
Leathermarket Ct **SE1** 130 C1
Leathermarket St **SE1** 130 C1
Leathwaite Rd **SW11** 128 F10
Leathwell Rd **SE8** 131 M8
Lecky St **SW7** 128 D4
Ledbury Est **SE15** 130 F6
Ledbury St **SE15** 130 E6
Lee Br **SE13** 131 N9
Lee High Rd **SE12** 131 P9
Lee High Rd **SE13** 131 P9
Lee St **E8** 126 D3
Leeke St **WC1** 125 M5
Leerdam Dr **E14** 131 N2
Lees Pl **W1** 124 G9
Leeson Rd **SE24** 129 N10
Leeway **SE8** 131 K4
Lefevre Wk **E3** 127 K3
Leggatt Rd **E15** 127 N4
Legion Cl **N1** 125 N1
Leicester Sq **WC2** 125 K9
Leigh St **WC1** 125 L6
Leinster Gdns **W2** 124 C8
Leinster Ms **W2** 124 C9
Leinster Pl **W2** 124 C8
Leinster Sq **W2** 124 A8
Leinster Ter **W2** 124 C9
Leman St **E1** 126 D8
Lendal Ter **SW4** 129 K9
Lennox Gdns **SW1** 128 F2
Lennox Gdns Ms **SW1** 128 F2
Lenthall Rd **E8** 126 E2
Leo St **SE15** 130 F6
Leonard St **EC2** 126 B6
Leontine Cl **SE15** 130 E6
Leopold St **E3** 127 K7
Leroy St **SE1** 130 C3
Lethbridge Cl **SE13** 131 N7
Lett Rd **E15** 127 P2
Lettsom St **SE5** 130 C8
Levehurst Way **SW4** 129 L8
Leven Rd **E14** 127 N7
Lever St **EC1** 125 P5
Lewey Ho **E3** 127 K6
Lewis Gro **SE13** 131 N9
Lewis St **NW1** 125 H1
Lewisham Cen **SE13** 131 N9
Lewisham High St **SE13** 131 N9
Lewisham Hill **SE13** 131 N8
Lewisham Rd **SE13** 131 M7
Lewisham Way **SE4** 131 K7
Lewisham Way **SE14** 131 K7
Lexham Gdns **W8** 128 B2
Lexham Gdns Ms **W8** 128 B2
Lexham Ms **W8** 128 A3
Lexington St **W1** 125 J8
Leybourne Rd **NW1** 125 H2
Leyland Rd **SE14** 131 H6
Liardet St **SE14** 131 J5
Liberia Rd **N5** 125 P1
Liberty St **SW9** 129 M7
Libra Rd **E3** 127 K3
Library St **SE1** 129 P1
Lichfield Rd **E3** 127 J5
Lidcote Gdns **SW9** 129 N8
Liddell Rd **NW6** 124 A1
Lidlington Pl **NW1** 125 J4
Lighter Cl **SE16** 131 J3
Lighterman Ms **E1** 127 H8
Lightermans Rd **E14** 131 L1
Lilac Pl **SE11** 129 M3
Lilestone St **NW8** 124 E6
Lilford Rd **SE5** 129 P8
Lillie Yd **SW6** 128 A5
Lillieshall Rd **SW4** 129 H9
Lily Pl **EC1** 125 N7
Limburg Rd **SW11** 128 F10
Lime Cl **E1** 126 E10
Lime St **EC3** 126 C9
Limeburner La **EC4** 125 P8
Limeharbour **E14** 131 M2
Limehouse Causeway **E14** 127 K9
Limehouse Flds Est **E14** 127 J7
Limehouse Link **E14** 127 J9
Limerston St **SW10** 128 C5
Limes Gro **SE13** 131 N10
Limes Wk **SE15** 130 F10
Limesford Rd **SE15** 131 H10
Linacre Cl **SE15** 130 F9
Linberry Wk **SE8** 131 K3
Lincoln St **SW3** 128 F3
Lincoln's Inn **WC2** 125 N8
Lincoln's Inn Flds **WC2** 125 M8
Lind St **SE8** 131 M8
Linden Gdns **W2** 124 A9
Linden Gro **SE15** 130 F9
Lindfield St **E14** 127 L8
Lindley St **E1** 126 G7
Lindore Rd **SW11** 128 F10
Lindrop St **SW6** 128 C8
Lindsay Sq **SW1** 129 K4
Lindsell St **SE10** 131 N7
Lindsey Ms **N1** 126 A2
Lindsey St **EC1** 125 P7
Linford St **SW8** 129 J7
Lingards Rd **SE13** 131 N10
Lingham St **SW9** 129 L8
Linhope St **NW1** 124 F6
Link St **E9** 126 G1
Linnell Rd **SE5** 130 C8
Linom Rd **SW4** 129 L10
Linsey St **SE16** 130 E3
Linstead St **NW6** 124 A2
Linton St **N1** 126 A3
Linver Rd **SW6** 128 A8
Linwood Cl **SE5** 130 D8
Lisford St **SE15** 130 D7
Lisle St **WC2** 125 K9
Lisson Grn Est **NW8** 124 E6
Lisson Gro **NW1** 124 E6
Lisson Gro **NW8** 124 D5
Lisson St **NW1** 124 E7
Liston Rd **SW4** 129 J9
Litchfield St **WC2** 125 K9
Lithos Rd **NW3** 124 B1
Little Boltons, The **SW5** 128 B4
Little Boltons, The **SW10** 128 B4
Little Britain **EC1** 125 P7
Little Chester St **SW1** 129 H2
Little Dorrit Ct **SE1** 130 A1
Little Newport St **WC2** 125 K9
Little Portland St **W1** 125 H8
Little Russell St **WC1** 125 L7
Little St. James's St **SW1** 125 J10
Littlebury Rd **SW4** 129 K9
Livermere Rd **E8** 126 D3
Liverpool Gro **SE17** 130 B4
Liverpool Rd **N1** 125 N4
Liverpool St **EC2** 126 C7
Livingstone Rd **E15** 127 N3
Livingstone Wk **SW11** 128 D9
Lizard St **EC1** 126 A5
Lloyd Baker St **WC1** 125 M5
Lloyd Sq **WC1** 125 N5
Lloyd St **WC1** 125 N5
Lloyd's Av **EC3** 126 C8
Loampit Hill **SE13** 131 L8
Loampit Vale **SE13** 131 M9
Lochnagar St **E14** 127 N7
Lockesfield Pl **E14** 131 M4
Lockhart Cl **N7** 125 M1
Lockhart St **E3** 127 K6
Lockington Rd **SW8** 129 H7
Lockmead Rd **SE13** 131 N9
Locksley Est **E14** 127 K8
Locksley St **E14** 127 K7
Lockwood Sq **SE16** 130 F2
Loddiges Rd **E9** 126 G2
Loder St **SE15** 130 G7
Lodge Rd **NW8** 124 D5
Lodore St **E14** 127 N8
Loftie St **SE16** 130 E1
Lofting Rd **N1** 125 M2
Logan Ms **W8** 128 A3
Logan Pl **W8** 128 A3
Lollard St **SE11** 129 M3
Loman St **SE1** 129 P1
Lomas Dr **E8** 126 D2
Lomas St **E1** 126 E7
Lombard Rd **SW11** 128 D8
Lombard St **EC3** 126 B8
Lomond Gro **SE5** 130 B6
Loncroft Rd **SE5** 130 C5
London Br **EC4** 126 B10
London Br **SE1** 126 B10
London Br St **SE1** 126 B10
London Br Wk **SE1** 126 B10
London Flds **E8** 126 F2
London Flds E Side **E8** 126 F2
London Flds W Side **E8** 126 E2
London La **E8** 126 F2
London Rd **SE1** 129 P2
London Silver Vaults **WC2** 125 N7
London St **W2** 124 D8
London Trocadero, The **W1** 125 K9
London Wall **EC2** 126 A7
Long Acre **WC2** 125 L9
Long La **EC1** 125 P7
Long La **SE1** 130 B1
Long Rd **SW4** 129 H10
Long St **E2** 126 D5
Long Yd **WC1** 125 M6
Longbeach Rd **SW11** 128 F9
Longfield Est **SE1** 130 D3
Longford St **NW1** 125 H6
Longhedge St **SW11** 128 G8
Longhope Cl **SE15** 130 C5
Longley St **SE1** 130 E3
Longmoore St **SW1** 129 J3
Longnor Rd **E1** 127 H5
Longridge Rd **SW5** 128 A3
Long's Ct **WC2** 125 K9
Longshore **SE8** 131 K3
Lonsdale Sq **N1** 125 N2
Lord Amory Way **E14** 131 N1
Lord Hills Rd **W2** 124 B7
Lord N St **SW1** 129 L2
Lorden Wk **E2** 126 E5
Lorenzo St **WC1** 125 M5
Loring Rd **SE14** 131 J7
Lorn Ct **SW9** 129 N8
Lorn Rd **SW9** 129 M8
Lorrimore Rd **SE17** 129 P5
Lorrimore Sq **SE17** 129 P5
Lothbury **EC2** 126 B8
Lothian Rd **SW9** 129 P7
Lots Rd **SW10** 128 C6
Loudoun Rd **NW8** 124 C3
Lough Rd **N7** 125 M1
Loughborough Pk **SW9** 129 P10
Loughborough Rd **SW9** 129 N8
Loughborough St **SE11** 129 M4
Louisa St **E1** 127 H6
Louvaine Rd **SW11** 128 D10
Love La **EC2** 126 A8
Love Wk **SE5** 130 B8
Lovegrove St **SE1** 130 E4
Lovegrove Wk **E14** 127 N10
Lovelinch Cl **SE15** 130 G5
Lovell Ho **E8** 126 E3
Lover's Wk **W1** 124 G10
Lowden Rd **SE24** 129 P10
Lowell St **E14** 127 J8
Lower Belgrave St **SW1** 129 H2
Lower Grosvenor Pl **SW1** 129 H2
Lower Marsh **SE1** 129 N1
Lower Merton Ri **NW3** 124 E2
Lower Rd **SE8** 130 G2
Lower Rd **SE16** 130 G2
Lower Sloane St **SW1** 128 G3
Lower Thames St **EC3** 126 B9
Lowfield Rd **NW6** 124 A2
Lowndes Cl **SW1** 128 G2
Lowndes Pl **SW1** 128 G2
Lowndes Sq **SW1** 128 F1
Lowndes St **SW1** 128 F2
Lowth Rd **SE5** 130 A8
Lowther Gdns **SW7** 128 D1
Lubbock St **SE14** 130 G6
Lucan Pl **SW3** 128 E3
Lucas St **SE8** 131 L7
Lucey Rd **SE16** 130 E2
Lucey Way **SE16** 130 E2
Ludgate Hill **EC4** 125 P8
Ludgate Sq **EC4** 125 P8
Ludwick Ms **SE14** 131 J6
Lugard Rd **SE15** 130 F8
Luke Ho **E1** 126 F8
Luke St **EC2** 126 C6
Lukin St **E1** 126 G8
Lulworth Rd **SE15** 130 F8
Lupus St **SW1** 129 H5
Lurline Gdns **SW11** 128 G7
Luscombe Way **SW8** 129 L6
Luton Pl **SE10** 131 N6
Luton St **NW8** 124 D6
Luxborough St **W1** 124 G6
Luxford St **SE16** 131 H3
Luxmore St **SE4** 131 K7
Luxor St **SE5** 129 P8
Lyal Rd **E3** 127 J4
Lyall Ms **SW1** 128 G2
Lyall St **SW1** 128 G2
Lydon Rd **SW4** 129 J9
Lyme St **NW1** 125 J2
Lymington Rd **NW6** 124 B1
Lympstone Gdns **SE15** 130 E6
Lynbrook Gro **SE15** 130 C6
Lyncott Cres **SW4** 129 H10
Lyndhurst Gro **SE15** 130 C8
Lyndhurst Sq **SE15** 130 D7
Lyndhurst Way **SE15** 130 D7
Lynton Rd **SE1** 130 D3
Lyons Pl **NW8** 124 D6
Lytham St **SE17** 130 B4
Lyttelton Cl **NW3** 124 E2


## M


Mabledon Pl **WC1** 125 K5
Mabley St **E9** 127 J1
Macaulay Ct **SW4** 129 H9
Macaulay Rd **SW4** 129 H9
Macaulay Sq **SW4** 129 H10
Macauley Ms **SE13** 131 N8
Macclesfield Br **NW1** 124 E4
Macclesfield Rd **EC1** 126 A5
Macclesfield St **W1** 125 K9
Macduff Rd **SW11** 128 G7
Mace St **E2** 127 H4
Macfarland Gro **SE15** 130 C6
Machell Rd **SE15** 130 G9
Mackay Rd **SW4** 129 H9
Mackennal St **NW8** 124 E4
Mackenzie Rd **N7** 125 M1
Mackenzie Wk **E14** 127 L10
Macklin St **WC2** 125 L8
Macks Rd **SE16** 130 E3
Mackworth St **NW1** 125 J5
Macleod St **SE17** 130 A4
Maconochies Rd **E14** 131 M4
Macquarie Way **E14** 131 M3
Maddams St **E3** 127 M6
Maddock Way **SE17** 129 P5
Maddox St **W1** 125 H9
Madinah Rd **E8** 126 E1
Madras Pl **N7** 125 N1
Madrigal La **SE5** 129 P6
Madron St **SE17** 130 C4
Magdalen St **SE1** 126 C10
Magee St **SE11** 129 N5
Maguire St **SE1** 130 D1
Mahogany Cl **SE16** 127 J10
Maida Av **W2** 124 C7
Maida Vale **W9** 124 B4
Maiden La **NW1** 125 K2
Maiden La **WC2** 125 L9
Maidenstone Hill **SE10** 131 N7
Maitland Pk Est **NW3** 124 F1
Maitland Pk Rd **NW3** 124 F1
Maitland Pk Vil **NW3** 124 F1
Major Cl **SW9** 129 P9
Makins St **SW3** 128 E3
Malabar St **E14** 131 L1
Malcolm Pl **E2** 126 G6
Malcolm Rd **E1** 126 G6
Malden Cres **NW1** 124 G1
Maldon Cl **SE5** 130 C9
Malet Pl **WC1** 125 K6
Malet St **WC1** 125 K6
Malfort Rd **SE5** 130 C9
Mall, The **SW1** 129 J1
Mallard Cl **NW6** 124 A4
Mallord St **SW3** 128 D5
Mallory Cl **SE4** 131 J10
Mallory St **NW8** 124 E6
Malmesbury Rd **E3** 127 K5
Malpas Rd **E8** 126 F1
Malpas Rd **SE4** 131 K8
Malt St **SE1** 130 E5
Maltby St **SE1** 130 D1
Malting Ho **E14** 127 K9
Maltings Pl **SW6** 128 B7
Malvern Ct **SW7** 128 D3
Malvern Rd **E8** 126 E2
Malvern Rd **NW6** 124 A5
Malvern Ter **N1** 125 N3
Manaton Cl **SE15** 130 F9
Manchester Gro **E14** 131 N4
Manchester Rd **E14** 131 N4
Manchester Sq **W1** 124 G8
Manchester St **W1** 124 G7
Manciple St **SE1** 130 B2
Mandela St **NW1** 125 J3
Mandela St **SW9** 129 N6
Mandela Way **SE1** 130 C3
Mandeville Pl **W1** 124 G8
Manette St **W1** 125 K8
Manger Rd **N7** 125 L1
Manilla St **E14** 131 L1
Manley St **NW1** 124 G3
Manor Av **SE4** 131 K8
Manor Est **SE16** 130 F3
Manor Gro **SE15** 130 G5
Manor Ms **SE4** 131 K8
Manor Pk **SE13** 131 P10
Manor Pl **SE17** 129 P4
Manresa Rd **SW3** 128 E4
Mansell St **E1** 126 D8
Mansfield St **W1** 125 H7
Mansford St **E2** 126 E4
Mansion Ho **EC4** 126 B8
Manson Ms **SW7** 128 C3
Manson Pl **SW7** 128 D3
Mantle Rd **SE4** 131 J9
Mantua St **SW11** 128 D9
Mantus Rd **E1** 126 G6
Mape St **E2** 126 F6
Maple St **E2** 126 E4
Maple St **W1** 125 J7
Mapledene Rd **E8** 126 D2
Maplin St **E3** 127 K5
Marble Arch **W1** 124 F9
Marble Quay **E1** 126 E10
Marcella Rd **SW9** 129 N8
Marchant St **SE14** 131 J5
Marchmont St **WC1** 125 L6
Marchwood Cl **SE5** 130 C6
Marcia Rd **SE1** 130 C3
Marcon Pl **E8** 126 F1
Marcus Garvey Way **SE24** 129 N10
Marden Sq **SE16** 130 F2
Mare St **E8** 126 F3
Margaret St **W1** 125 H8
Margaretta Ter **SW3** 128 E5
Margery St **WC1** 125 N5
Maria Ter **E1** 127 H7
Marian Pl **E2** 126 F4
Marigold St **SE16** 130 F1
Marinefield Rd **SW6** 128 B8
Mariners Ms **E14** 131 P3
Marischal Rd **SE13** 131 P9
Maritime Quay **E14** 131 L4
Maritime St **E3** 127 K6
Marjorie Gro **SW11** 128 F10
Mark La **EC3** 126 C9
Market Est **N7** 125 L1
Market Ms **W1** 125 H10
Market Pl **W1** 125 J8
Market Rd **N7** 125 L1
Markham Sq **SW3** 128 F4
Markham St **SW3** 128 E4
Marl Rd **SW18** 128 B10
Marlborough Av **E8** 126 E3
Marlborough Ct **W8** 128 A3
Marlborough Gro **SE1** 130 E4
Marlborough Hill **NW8** 124 C3
Marlborough Pl **NW8** 124 C4
Marlborough Rd **SW1** 125 J10
Marlborough St **SW3** 128 E3
Marloes Rd **W8** 128 B2
Marlow Way **SE16** 131 H1
Marlowes, The **NW8** 124 D3
Marmion Rd **SW11** 128 G10
Marmont Rd **SE15** 130 E7
Marney Rd **SW11** 128 G10
Maroon St **E14** 127 J7
Marquess Rd **N1** 126 B1
Marquis Rd **NW1** 125 K1
Marsala Rd **SE13** 131 M10
Marsden Rd **SE15** 130 D9
Marsden St **NW5** 124 G1
Marsh Wall **E14** 127 L10
Marshall St **W1** 125 J8
Marshalsea Rd **SE1** 130 A1
Marsham St **SW1** 129 K2
Marshfield St **E14** 131 N2
Marshgate La **E15** 127 M3
Marshgate Sidings **E15** 127 M3
Marsland Cl **SE17** 129 P4
Marston Cl **NW6** 124 C2
Martello St **E8** 126 F2
Martello Ter **E8** 126 F2
Martha Ct **E2** 126 F4
Martha St **E1** 126 F8
Martineau St **E1** 126 G9
Mary Ann Gdns **SE8** 131 L5
Mary Datchelor Cl **SE5** 130 B7
Mary Grn **NW8** 124 B3
Mary St **N1** 126 A3
Mary Ter **NW1** 125 H3
Marylands Rd **W9** 124 A6
Marylebone High St **W1** 124 G7
Marylebone La **W1** 124 G8
Marylebone Ms **W1** 125 H7
Marylebone Rd **NW1** 124 E7
Marylebone St **W1** 124 G7
Marylee Way **SE11** 129 M3
Maskelyne Cl **SW11** 128 E7
Mason St **SE17** 130 B3
Mason's Pl **EC1** 125 P5
Massingham St **E1** 127 H6
Mast Leisure Pk **SE16** 131 H2
Masterman Ho **SE5** 130 A6
Masters Dr **SE16** 130 F4
Masters St **E1** 127 H7
Masthouse Ter **E14** 131 L3
Mastmaker Rd **E14** 131 L1
Matham Gro **SE22** 130 D10
Matilda St **N1** 125 M3
Matlock Cl **SE24** 130 A10
Matlock St **E14** 127 J8
Matrimony Pl **SW8** 129 J8
Matthew Parker St **SW1** 129 K1
Matthews St **SW11** 128 F8
Maude Rd **SE5** 130 C7
Maunsel St **SW1** 129 K3
Maverton Rd **E3** 127 L3
Mawbey Est **SE1** 130 D4
Mawbey Pl **SE1** 130 D4
Mawbey St **SW8** 129 L6
Maxted Rd **SE15** 130 D9
Maxwell Rd **SW6** 128 B6
Maya Cl **SE15** 130 F8
Maydew Ho **SE16** 130 G3
Mayfair Pl **W1** 125 H10
Mayfield Rd **E8** 126 D2
Mayflower Rd **SW9** 129 L9
Mayflower St **SE16** 130 G1
Maygood St **N1** 125 M4
Maysoule Rd **SW11** 128 D10
Mazenod Av **NW6** 124 A2
McAuley Cl **SE1** 129 N2
McCullum Rd **E3** 127 K3
McDermott Cl **SW11** 128 E9
McDermott Rd **SE15** 130 E9
McDowall Rd **SE5** 130 A7
McEwen Way **E15** 127 P3
McKerrell Rd **SE15** 130 E7
McMillan St **SE8** 131 L5
McNeil Rd **SE5** 130 C8
Mead Pl **E9** 126 G1
Meadcroft Rd **SE11** 129 P5
Meadow Ms **SW8** 129 M5
Meadow Pl **SW8** 129 L6
Meadow Rd **SW8** 129 M5
Meadow Row **SE1** 130 A2
Meadowbank **NW3** 124 F2
Meakin Est **SE1** 130 C2
Meard St **W1** 125 K8
Meath St **SW11** 129 H7
Mecklenburgh Pl **WC1** 125 M6
Mecklenburgh Sq **WC1** 125 M6
Medburn St **NW1** 125 K4
Medlar St **SE5** 130 A7
Medley Rd **NW6** 124 A1
Medway Rd **E3** 127 J4
Medway St **SW1** 129 K2
Medwin St **SW4** 129 M10
Meeting Ho La **SE15** 130 F7
Mehetabel Rd **E9** 126 G1
Melba Way **SE13** 131 M7
Melbourne Gro **SE22** 130 C10
Melbourne Ms **SW9** 129 N7
Melbourne Pl **WC2** 125 M9
Melcombe Pl **NW1** 124 F7
Melcombe St **NW1** 124 F6
Melina Pl **NW8** 124 D5
Melior St **SE1** 130 B1
Mellish St **E14** 131 L2
Melon Rd **SE15** 130 E7
Melton St **NW1** 125 K5
Mendip Rd **SW11** 128 C9
Mentmore Ter **E8** 126 F2
Mepham St **SE1** 125 M10
Mercator Rd **SE13** 131 P10
Mercer St **WC2** 125 L8
Merceron St **E1** 126 F6
Merchant St **E3** 127 K5
Mercia Gro **SE13** 131 N10
Mercury Way **SE14** 131 H5
Mercy Ter **SE13** 131 M10
Meredith Ms **SE4** 131 K10
Meretone Cl **SE4** 131 J10
Meridian Gate **E14** 131 N1
Meridian Pl **E14** 131 M1
Meridian Sq **E15** 127 P2
Mermaid Ct **SE1** 130 B1
Mermaid Ct **SE16** 127 K10
Merriam Av **E9** 127 K1
Merrick Sq **SE1** 130 A2
Merrington Rd **SW6** 128 A5
Merrow St **SE17** 130 A5
Merton Ri **NW3** 124 E2
Mervan Rd **SW2** 129 N10
Messina Av **NW6** 124 A2
Meteor St **SW11** 128 G10
Methley St **SE11** 129 N4
Mews St **E1** 126 E10
Meymott St **SE1** 125 P10
Meynell Cres **E9** 127 H2
Meynell Gdns **E9** 127 H2
Meynell Rd **E9** 127 H2
Meyrick Rd **SW11** 128 D9
Micawber St **N1** 126 A5
Michael Rd **SW6** 128 B7
Micklethwaite Rd **SW6** 128 A5
Middle Fld **NW8** 124 D3
Middle Temple La **EC4** 125 N8
Middlesex St **E1** 126 C7
Middleton Dr **SE16** 131 H1
Middleton Rd **E8** 126 D2
Middleton St **E2** 126 F5
Middleton Way **SE13** 131 P10
Midland Rd **NW1** 125 K4
Midship Pt **E14** 131 L1
Milborne Gro **SW10** 128 C4
Milborne St **E9** 126 G1

## Mil - Par


Milcote St **SE1** 129 P1
Mildmay Av **N1** 126 B1
Mildmay St **N1** 126 B1
Mile End Pl **E1** 127 H6
Mile End Rd **E1** 126 G7
Mile End Rd **E3** 126 G7
Miles St **SW8** 129 L5
Milford La **WC2** 125 M9
Milk Yd **E1** 126 G9
Milkwell Yd **SE5** 130 A7
Mill Row **N1** 126 C3
Mill St **SE1** 130 D1
Mill St **W1** 125 J9
Millbank **SW1** 129 L2
Millbank Twr **SW1** 129 L3
Millbrook Rd **SW9** 129 P9
Millender Wk **SE16** 130 G3
Millennium Br **EC4** 126 A9
Millennium Br **SE1** 126 A9
Millennium Dr **E14** 131 P3
Millennium Harbour **E14** 131 K1
Millennium Pl **E2** 126 F4
Miller St **NW1** 125 J4
Miller Wk **SE1** 125 N10
Millgrove St **SW11** 128 G8
Millharbour **E14** 131 M2
Milligan St **E14** 127 K9
Millman Ms **WC1** 125 M6
Millman St **WC1** 125 M6
Millmark Gro **SE14** 131 J8
Millstream Rd **SE1** 130 D1
Millwall Dock Rd **E14** 131 L2
Milman's St **SW10** 128 D5
Milner Pl **N1** 125 N3
Milner Sq **N1** 125 P2
Milner St **SW3** 128 F3
Milton Cl **SE1** 130 D3
Milton Ct Rd **SE14** 131 J5
Milton St **EC2** 126 B7
Milverton St **SE11** 129 N4
Mina Rd **SE17** 130 C4
Mincing La **EC3** 126 C9
Minera Ms **SW1** 128 G3
Minerva Cl **SW9** 129 N6
Minerva St **E2** 126 F4
Minet Rd **SW9** 129 P8
Ming St **E14** 127 L9
Minories **EC3** 126 D8
Minson Rd **E9** 127 H3
Mintern St **N1** 126 B4
Mission Pl **SE15** 130 E7
Mitchell St **EC1** 126 A6
Mitchison Rd **N1** 126 B1
Mitre Rd **SE1** 129 N1
Mitre St **EC3** 126 C8
Moat Pl **SW9** 129 M9
Modling Ho **E2** 126 G4
Molesford Rd **SW6** 128 A7
Molesworth St **SE13** 131 N9
Molyneux St **W1** 124 E7
Mona Rd **SE15** 130 G8
Monck St **SW1** 129 K2
Monclar Rd **SE5** 130 B10
Moncrieff St **SE15** 130 E8
Monier Rd **E3** 127 L2
Monkton St **SE11** 129 N3
Monmouth Rd **W2** 124 B8
Monmouth St **WC2** 125 L9
Monnow Rd **SE1** 130 E3
Monson Rd **SE14** 131 H6
Montagu Ms N **W1** 124 F7
Montagu Pl **W1** 124 F7
Montagu Sq **W1** 124 F7
Montagu St **W1** 124 F8
Montague Av **SE4** 131 K10
Montague Cl **SE1** 126 B10
Montague Pl **WC1** 125 K7
Montague St **EC1** 126 A8
Montague St **WC1** 125 L7
Monteagle Way **SE15** 130 F9
Montefiore St **SW8** 129 H8
Montevetro **SW11** 128 D7
Montford Pl **SE11** 129 N4
Montgomery St **E14** 127 M10
Montpelier Pl **E1** 126 G8
Montpelier Pl **SW7** 128 E2
Montpelier Rd **SE15** 130 F7
Montpelier Sq **SW7** 128 E1
Montpelier St **SW7** 128 E1
Montpelier Wk **SW7** 128 E2
Montrose Ct **SW7** 128 D1
Montrose Pl **SW1** 128 G1
Monument St **EC3** 126 B9
Monza St **E1** 126 G9
Moodkee St **SE16** 130 G2
Moody Rd **SE15** 130 D6
Moody St **E1** 127 H5
Moon St **N1** 125 P3
Moor La **EC2** 126 B7
Moore Pk Rd **SW6** 128 B6
Moore St **SW3** 128 F3
Moorfields **EC2** 126 B7
Moorgate **EC2** 126 B8
Moorhouse Rd **W2** 124 A8
Moorland Rd **SW9** 129 P10
Moorlands Est **SW9** 129 N10
Mora St **EC1** 126 A5
Morant St **E14** 127 L9
Morat St **SW9** 129 M7
Moravian St **E2** 126 G5
Mordaunt St **SW9** 129 M9
Morden Hill **SE13** 131 N8
Morden La **SE13** 131 N7
Morden St **SE13** 131 M7
More London Pl **SE1** 126 C10
Morecambe Cl **E1** 127 H7
Morecambe St **SE17** 130 A3
Moreland St **EC1** 125 P5
Moresby Wk **SW8** 129 H8
Moreton Pl **SW1** 129 J4
Moreton St **SW1** 129 K4
Moreton Ter **SW1** 129 J4
Morgan St **E3** 127 J5
Morgans La **SE1** 126 C10
Morley Rd **SE13** 131 N10
Morley St **SE1** 129 N1
Morna Rd **SE5** 130 A8
Morning La **E9** 126 G1
Mornington Cres **NW1** 125 J4
Mornington Gro **E3** 127 L5
Mornington Ms **SE5** 130 A7
Mornington Rd **SE8** 131 K6
Mornington St **NW1** 125 H4
Mornington Ter **NW1** 125 H3
Morocco St **SE1** 130 C1
Morpeth Gro **E9** 127 H3
Morpeth Rd **E9** 126 G3
Morpeth St **E2** 127 H5
Morpeth Ter **SW1** 129 J2
Morris Rd **E14** 127 M7
Morris St **E1** 126 F8
Morrison St **SW11** 128 G9
Morshead Rd **W9** 124 A5
Mortham St **E15** 127 P3
Mortimer Cres **NW6** 124 B3
Mortimer Est **NW6** 124 B3
Mortimer Pl **NW6** 124 B3
Mortimer Rd **N1** 126 C2
Mortimer St **W1** 125 H8
Morton Rd **N1** 126 A2
Morville St **E3** 127 L4
Moscow Rd **W2** 124 A9
Mossbury Rd **SW11** 128 E9
Mossford St **E3** 127 K6
Mossop St **SW3** 128 E3
Mostyn Gro **E3** 127 K4
Mostyn Rd **SW9** 129 N7
Motcomb St **SW1** 128 G2
Moulins Rd **E9** 126 G3
Mount Pleasant **WC1** 125 N6
Mount Row **W1** 125 H9
Mount St **W1** 124 G9
Mountague Pl **E14** 127 N9
Mounts Pond Rd **SE3** 131 P8
Mowlem St **E2** 126 F4
Mowll St **SW9** 129 N6
Moxon St **W1** 124 G7
Mozart Ter **SW1** 128 G3
Mulberry Rd **E8** 126 D2
Mulberry Wk **SW3** 128 D5
Mulvaney Way **SE1** 130 B1
Mundy St **N1** 126 C5
Munro Ter **SW10** 128 D6
Munster Sq **NW1** 125 H5
Munton Rd **SE17** 130 A3
Murdock St **SE15** 130 F5
Muriel St **N1** 125 M4
Murillo Rd **SE13** 131 P10
Murphy St **SE1** 129 N1
Murray Gro **N1** 126 A4
Murray Ms **NW1** 125 K2
Murray St **NW1** 125 K2
Mursell Est **SW8** 129 M7
Musbury St **E1** 126 G8
Muschamp Rd **SE15** 130 D9
Museum St **WC1** 125 L8
Musgrave Cres **SW6** 128 A7
Musgrove Rd **SE14** 131 H7
Mutrix Rd **NW6** 124 A3
Myatt Rd **SW9** 129 P7
Myddelton Sq **EC1** 125 N5
Myddelton St **EC1** 125 N5
Myers La **SE14** 131 H5
Mylne St **EC1** 125 N5
Myrdle St **E1** 126 E7
Myron Pl **SE13** 131 N9
Myrtle Wk **N1** 126 C4
Mysore Rd **SW11** 128 F9

### N

N1 Shop Cen **N1** 125 N4
Nairn St **E14** 127 N7
Nankin St **E14** 127 L8
Nansen Rd **SW11** 128 G10
Nantes Cl **SW18** 128 C10
Napier Av **E14** 131 L4
Napier Gro **N1** 126 A4
Napier Ter **N1** 125 P2
Narborough St **SW6** 128 B8
Narrow St **E14** 127 J9
Naseby Cl **NW6** 124 C2
Nash Rd **SE4** 131 H10
Nassau St **W1** 125 J7
Naval Row **E14** 127 N9
Navarino Gro **E8** 126 E1
Navarino Rd **E8** 126 E1
Navarre St **E2** 126 D6
Navy St **SW4** 129 K9
Naylor Rd **SE15** 130 F6
Nazareth Gdns **SE15** 130 F8
Nazrul St **E2** 126 D5
Neal St **WC2** 125 L8
Nealden St **SW9** 129 M9
Neate St **SE5** 130 D5
Nebraska St **SE1** 130 B1
Neckinger **SE16** 130 D2
Neckinger Est **SE16** 130 D2
Neckinger St **SE1** 130 D1
Nectarine Way **SE13** 131 M8
Needleman St **SE16** 131 H1
Nelldale Rd **SE16** 130 G3
Nelson Cl **NW6** 124 A5
Nelson Gdns **E2** 126 E5
Nelson Pl **N1** 125 P4
Nelson Rd **SE10** 131 N5
Nelson Sq **SE1** 129 P1
Nelson St **E1** 126 F8
Nelson Ter **N1** 125 P4
Nelson's Row **SW4** 129 K10
Nepaul Rd **SW11** 128 E8
Neptune St **SE16** 130 G2
Nesham St **E1** 126 E10
Netherford Rd **SW4** 129 J8
Netherhall Gdns **NW3** 124 C1
Netherton Gro **SW10** 128 C5
Nettleton Rd **SE14** 131 H7
Nevada St **SE10** 131 N5
Nevern Pl **SW5** 128 A3
Nevern Rd **SW5** 128 A3
Nevern Sq **SW5** 128 A3
Neville Cl **SE15** 130 E6
Neville St **SW7** 128 D4
Neville Ter **SW7** 128 D4
New Bond St **W1** 125 H9
New Br St **EC4** 125 P8
New Broad St **EC2** 126 C7
New Burlington St **W1** 125 J9
New Butt La **SE8** 131 L6
New Caledonian Wf **SE16** 131 K2
New Cavendish St **W1** 124 G7
New Change **EC4** 126 A8
New Ch Rd **SE5** 130 A6
New Compton St **WC2** 125 K8
New Covent Gdn Mkt **SW8** 129 K6
New Cross Rd **SE14** 130 G6
New Fetter La **EC4** 125 N8
New Globe Wk **SE1** 126 A10
New Inn Yd **EC2** 126 C6
New Kent Rd **SE1** 130 A2
New King St **SE8** 131 L5
New Mt St **E15** 127 P2
New N Rd **N1** 126 B4
New N St **WC1** 125 M7
New Oxford St **WC1** 125 K8
New Pl Sq **SE16** 130 F2
New Quebec St **W1** 124 F8
New Ride **SW7** 128 E1
New River Wk **N1** 126 A1
New Rd **E1** 126 F7
New Row **WC2** 125 L9
New Sq **WC2** 125 M8
New St **EC2** 126 C7
New Union Cl **E14** 131 N2
New Union St **EC2** 126 B7
New Wf Rd **N1** 125 L4
Newark St **E1** 126 F7
Newburgh St **W1** 125 J8
Newburn St **SE11** 129 M4
Newby Pl **E14** 127 N9
Newby St **SW8** 129 H9
Newcastle Pl **W2** 124 D7
Newcomen Rd **SW11** 128 D9
Newcomen St **SE1** 130 B1
Newcourt St **NW8** 124 E4
Newell St **E14** 127 K8
Newent Cl **SE15** 130 C6
Newgate St **EC1** 125 P8
Newington Butts **SE1** 129 P3
Newington Butts **SE11** 129 P3
Newington Causeway **SE1** 129 P2
Newington Grn Rd **N1** 126 B1
Newlands Quay **E1** 126 G9
Newman St **W1** 125 J7
Newport Av **E14** 127 P9
Newport Pl **WC2** 125 K9
Newport St **SE11** 129 M3
Newton Pl **E14** 131 L3
Newton Rd **W2** 124 A8
Newton St **WC2** 125 L8
Nicholas Rd **E1** 126 G6
Nicholl St **E2** 126 E3
Nicholson St **SE1** 125 P10
Nigel Rd **SE15** 130 E9
Nightingale Rd **N1** 126 A1
Nile St **N1** 126 B5
Nile Ter **SE15** 130 D4
Nine Elms La **SW8** 129 J6
Noble St **EC2** 126 A8
Noel Rd **N1** 125 P4
Noel St **W1** 125 J8
Norbiton Rd **E14** 127 K8
Norfolk Cres **W2** 124 E8
Norfolk Pl **W2** 124 D8
Norfolk Rd **NW8** 124 D3
Norfolk Sq **W2** 124 D8
Norman Gro **E3** 127 J4
Norman Rd **SE10** 131 M6
Normandy Rd **SW9** 129 N7
North Audley St **W1** 124 G8
North Bk **NW8** 124 E5
North Carriage Dr **W2** 124 E9
North Colonnade **E14** 127 L10
North Cres **E16** 127 P6
North Cres **WC1** 125 K7
North Gower St **NW1** 125 J5
North Ms **WC1** 125 M6
North Pas **SW18** 128 A10
North Ride **W2** 124 E9
North Rd **N7** 125 L1
North Row **W1** 124 F9
North St **SW4** 129 J9
North Tenter St **E1** 126 D8
North Ter **SW3** 128 E2
North Vil **NW1** 125 K1
North Wf Rd **W2** 124 D7
Northampton Pk **N1** 126 A1
Northampton Rd **EC1** 125 N6
Northampton Sq **EC1** 125 P5
Northampton St **N1** 126 A2
Northbourne Rd **SW4** 129 K10
Northburgh St **EC1** 125 P6
Northchurch Rd **N1** 126 B2
Northchurch Ter **N1** 126 C2
Northcote Rd **SW11** 128 E10
Northdown St **N1** 125 M4
Northey St **E14** 127 J9
Northfields **SW18** 128 A10
Northiam St **E9** 126 F3
Northington St **WC1** 125 M6
Northlands St **SE5** 130 A8
Northpoint Sq **NW1** 125 K1
Northport St **N1** 126 B3
Northumberland All **EC3** 126 C8
Northumberland Av **WC2** 125 L10
Northumberland Pl **W2** 124 A8
Northumberland St **WC2** 125 L10
Northumbria St **E14** 127 L8
Northway Rd **SE5** 130 A9
Northwick Ter **NW8** 124 D6
Norton Folgate **E1** 126 C7
Norway Gate **SE16** 131 J2
Norway St **SE10** 131 M5
Norwich St **EC4** 125 N8
Notley St **SE5** 130 B6
Notre Dame Est **SW4** 129 J10
Notting Hill Gate **W11** 124 A10
Nottingham Pl **W1** 124 G6
Nottingham St **W1** 124 G7
Novello St **SW6** 128 A7
Nuding Cl **SE13** 131 L9
Nugent Ter **NW8** 124 C4
Nunhead Cres **SE15** 130 F9
Nunhead Est **SE15** 130 F10
Nunhead Grn **SE15** 130 F9
Nunhead Gro **SE15** 130 F9
Nunhead La **SE15** 130 F9
Nursery Cl **SE4** 131 K8
Nursery La **E2** 126 D3
Nursery Rd **SW9** 129 M10
Nutbrook St **SE15** 130 E9
Nutcroft Rd **SE15** 130 F6
Nutford Pl **W1** 124 F8
Nutley Ter **NW3** 124 C1
Nutmeg La **E14** 127 P8
Nutt St **SE15** 130 D6
Nuttall St **N1** 126 C4
Nynehead St **SE14** 131 J6

### O

Oak La **E14** 127 K9
Oak Tree Rd **NW8** 124 E5
Oakbank Gro **SE24** 130 A10
Oakbury Rd **SW6** 128 B8
Oakcroft Rd **SE13** 131 P8
Oakdale Rd **SE15** 130 G9
Oakden St **SE11** 129 N3
Oakey La **SE1** 129 N2
Oakfield St **SW10** 128 C5
Oakhurst Gro **SE22** 130 E10
Oakington Rd **W9** 124 A6
Oakley Gdns **SW3** 128 E5
Oakley Pl **SE1** 130 D4
Oakley Rd **N1** 126 B2
Oakley Sq **NW1** 125 J4
Oakley St **SW3** 128 E5
Oat La **EC2** 126 A8
Oban St **E14** 127 P8
Oberstein Rd **SW11** 128 D10
Observatory Gdns **W8** 128 A1
Occupation Rd **SE17** 130 A4
Ocean Est **E1** 127 H6
Ocean St **E1** 127 H7
Ocean Wf **E14** 131 K1
Ockendon Rd **N1** 126 B1
Octavia St **SW11** 128 E7
Octavius St **SE8** 131 L6
Odessa St **SE16** 131 K1
Odger St **SW11** 128 F8
Offenbach Ho **E2** 127 H4
Offerton Rd **SW4** 129 J9
Offley Rd **SW9** 129 N6
Offord Rd **N1** 125 M2
Offord St **N1** 125 M2
Oglander Rd **SE15** 130 D10
Ogle St **W1** 125 J7
Old Bailey **EC4** 125 P8
Old Bellgate Pl **E14** 131 L2
Old Bethnal Grn Rd **E2** 126 E5
Old Bond St **W1** 125 J9
Old Broad St **EC2** 126 B8
Old Brompton Rd **SW5** 128 A4
Old Brompton Rd **SW7** 128 A4
Old Burlington St **W1** 125 J9
Old Castle St **E1** 126 D7
Old Cavendish St **W1** 125 H8
Old Ch Rd **E1** 127 H8
Old Ch St **SW3** 128 D4
Old Compton St **W1** 125 K9
Old Ct Pl **W8** 128 B1
Old Ford Rd **E2** 126 G4
Old Ford Rd **E3** 127 J4
Old Gloucester St **WC1** 125 L7
Old Jamaica Rd **SE16** 130 E2
Old James St **SE15** 130 F9
Old Jewry **EC2** 126 B8
Old Kent Rd **SE1** 130 C3
Old Kent Rd **SE15** 130 C3
Old Marylebone Rd **NW1** 124 E7
Old Montague St **E1** 126 E7
Old Nichol St **E2** 126 D6
Old Palace Yd **SW1** 129 L2
Old Paradise St **SE11** 129 M3
Old Pk La **W1** 124 G10
Old Pye St **SW1** 129 K2
Old Quebec St **W1** 124 F8
Old Queen St **SW1** 129 K1
Old Royal Free Sq **N1** 125 N3
Old S Lambeth Rd **SW8** 129 L6
Old Spitalfields Mkt **E1** 126 D7
Old Sq **WC2** 125 N8
Old St **EC1** 126 A6
Old Town **SW4** 129 J9
Old Woolwich Rd **SE10** 131 P5
Oldbury Pl **W1** 124 G6
Oldfield Gro **SE16** 131 H3
O'Leary Sq **E1** 126 G7
Olga St **E3** 127 J4
Oliver Ms **SE15** 130 E8
Oliver-Goldsmith Est **SE15** 130 E7
Ollerton Grn **E3** 127 K3
Olliffe St **E14** 131 N2
Olmar St **SE1** 130 E5
Olney Rd **SE17** 129 P5
O'Meara St **SE1** 126 A10
Omega St **SE14** 131 L7
Ommaney Rd **SE14** 131 H7
Ondine Rd **SE15** 130 D10
Onega Gate **SE16** 131 J2
Ongar Rd **SW6** 128 A5
Onslow Cres **SW7** 128 D3
Onslow Gdns **SW7** 128 D4
Onslow Sq **SW7** 128 D3
Ontario St **SE1** 129 P2
Ontario Way **E14** 127 L9
Opal St **SE11** 129 P3
Ophir Ter **SE15** 130 E7
Oppenheim Rd **SE13** 131 N8
Oppidans Rd **NW3** 124 F2
Orange St **WC2** 125 K9
Oransay Rd **N1** 126 A1
Orb St **SE17** 130 B3
Orbel St **SW11** 128 E7
Orchard, The **SE3** 131 P8
Orchard Cl **N1** 126 A2
Orchard St **W1** 124 G8
Orchardson St **NW8** 124 D6
Orde Hall St **WC1** 125 M6
Ordell Rd **E3** 127 K4
Ordnance Cres **SE10** 131 P1
Ordnance Hill **NW8** 124 D3
Oregano Dr **E14** 127 P8
Oriel Rd **E9** 127 H1
Orkney St **SW11** 128 G8
Orlando Rd **SW4** 129 J9
Orleston Ms **N7** 125 N1
Orleston Rd **N7** 125 N1
Orme Ct **W2** 124 B9
Orme La **W2** 124 B9
Ormonde Gate **SW3** 128 F4
Ormonde Ter **NW8** 124 F3
Ormsby St **E2** 126 D4
Ormside St **SE15** 130 G5
Orpheus St **SE5** 130 B7
Orsett St **SE11** 129 M4
Orsett Ter **W2** 124 C8
Orsman Rd **N1** 126 C3
Orville Rd **SW11** 128 D8
Osborn Cl **E8** 126 E3
Osborn St **E1** 126 D7
Osborne Rd **E9** 127 K1
Oscar St **SE8** 131 L7
Oseney Cres **NW5** 125 J1
Osier St **E1** 126 G6
Osiers Rd **SW18** 128 A10
Oslo Sq **SE16** 131 J2
Osnaburgh St **NW1** 125 H6
Osnaburgh St (north section) **NW1** 125 H5
Osric Path **N1** 126 C4
Ossington St **W2** 124 A9
Ossory Rd **SE1** 130 E4
Ossulston St **NW1** 125 K5
Oswell Ho **E1** 126 F10
Oswin St **SE11** 129 P3
Oswyth Rd **SE5** 130 C8
Otis St **E3** 127 N5
Otter Cl **E15** 127 N3
Otterburn Ho **SE5** 130 A6
Otto St **SE17** 129 P5
Outer Circle **NW1** 125 H4
Outram Pl **N1** 125 L3
Oval, The **E2** 126 F4
Oval Pl **SW8** 129 M6
Oval Rd **NW1** 125 H3
Oval Way **SE11** 129 M4
Overcliff Rd **SE13** 131 L9
Oversley Ho **W2** 124 A7
Overton Rd **SW9** 129 N8
Ovex Cl **E14** 131 N1
Ovington Gdns **SW3** 128 E2
Ovington Ms **SW3** 128 E2
Ovington Sq **SW3** 128 E2
Ovington St **SW3** 128 E2
Oxendon St **SW1** 125 K9
Oxenford St **SE15** 130 D9
Oxenholme **NW1** 125 J4
Oxestalls Rd **SE8** 131 J4
Oxford Rd **E15** 127 P1
Oxford Rd **NW6** 124 A4
Oxford Sq **W2** 124 E8
Oxford St **W1** 125 H8
Oxley Cl **SE1** 130 D4
Oxo Twr Wf **SE1** 125 N9
Oxonian St **SE22** 130 D10
Oyster Wf **SW11** 128 D8

### P

Packington Sq **N1** 126 A3
Packington St **N1** 125 P3
Padbury **SE17** 130 C4
Padbury Ct **E2** 126 D5
Paddington Grn **W2** 124 D7
Paddington Sta **W2** 124 C8
Paddington St **W1** 124 G7
Paddington Underground Sta **W2** 124 C8
Padfield Rd **SE5** 130 A9
Padfield Rd **SW9** 130 A9
Pagden St **SW8** 129 H7
Page St **SW1** 129 K3
Pages Wk **SE1** 130 C3
Pagnell St **SE14** 131 K6
Pagoda Gdns **SE3** 131 P8
Pakenham St **WC1** 125 M5
Palace Av **W8** 124 B10
Palace Ct **W2** 124 B9
Palace Gdns Ms **W8** 124 A10
Palace Gdns Ter **W8** 124 A10
Palace Gate **W8** 128 C1
Palace Grn **W8** 128 B1
Palace St **SW1** 129 J2
Palfrey Pl **SW8** 129 M6
Palgrave Gdns **NW1** 124 E6
Pall Mall **SW1** 125 J10
Pall Mall E **SW1** 125 K10
Palmer St **SW1** 129 K2
Palmers Rd **E2** 127 H4
Palmerston Rd **NW6** 124 A2
Pancras Rd **NW1** 125 K4
Pandora Rd **NW6** 124 A1
Parade, The **SW11** 128 F6
Paradise Rd **SW4** 129 L8
Paradise St **SE16** 130 F1
Paradise Wk **SW3** 128 F5
Paragon Rd **E9** 126 G1
Pardoner St **SE1** 130 B2
Parfett St **E1** 126 E7
Paris Gdn **SE1** 125 P10
Park Cl **E9** 126 G3
Park Cl **SW1** 128 F1
Park Cres **W1** 125 H6
Park La **W1** 124 G9
Park Pl **E14** 127 L10

Par - Roc


Park Pl N1 126 B3
Park Pl SW1 125 J10
Park Pl Vil W2 124 C7
Park Rd NW1 124 E5
Park Rd NW8 124 E5
Park Row SE10 131 P5
Park Sq E NW1 125 H6
Park Sq Ms NW1 125 H6
Park Sq W NW1 125 H6
Park St SE1 126 A10
Park St W1 124 G9
Park Vw Est E2 127 H4
Park Vw Ms SW9 129 M8
Park Village E NW1 125 H4
Park Village W NW1 125 H4
Park Vista SE10 131 P5
Park Wk SW10 128 C5
Parker St WC2 125 L8
Parkfield Rd SE14 131 K7
Parkgate Rd SW11 128 E6
Parkham St SW11 128 E7
Parkholme Rd E8 126 D1
Parkhouse St SE5 130 B6
Parkside Rd SW11 128 G7
Parkway NW1 125 H3
Parliament Sq SW1 129 L1
Parliament St SW1 129 L1
Parliament Vw Apts SE1 129 M3
Parma Cres SW11 128 F10
Parmiter St E2 126 F4
Parnell Rd E3 127 K3
Parr St N1 126 B4
Parry St SW8 129 L5
Parsonage St E14 131 N3
Parsons Grn SW6 128 A7
Parsons Grn La SW6 128 A7
Parson's Ho W2 124 D6
Parthenia Rd SW6 128 A7
Parvin St SW8 129 K7
Pascal St SW8 129 K6
Passmore St SW1 128 G3
Pastor St SE11 129 P3
Patcham Ter SW8 129 H7
Pater St W8 128 A2
Patience Rd SW11 128 E8
Patmore Est SW8 129 J7
Patmore St SW8 129 J7
Patmos Rd SW9 129 P6
Paton Cl E3 127 L5
Patriot Sq E2 126 F4
Patshull Rd NW5 125 J1
Patterdale Rd SE15 130 G6
Pattina Wk SE16 127 K10
Paul Julius Cl E14 127 P9
Paul St E15 127 P3
Paul St EC2 126 B6
Paulet Rd SE5 129 P8
Paul's Wk EC4 126 A9
Paultons Sq SW3 128 D5
Paultons St SW3 128 D5
Paveley Dr SW11 128 E6
Paveley St NW8 124 E6
Pavement, The SW4 129 J10
Pavilion Rd SW1 128 F1
Paxton Ter SW1 129 H5
Payne Rd E3 127 M4
Payne St SE8 131 K5
Peabody Est SW1 129 J3
Peabody Sq SE1 129 P1
Peabody Trust SE1 126 A10
Pear Tree Cl E2 126 D3
Pear Tree Ct EC1 125 N6
Pear Tree St EC1 125 P6
Peardon St SW8 129 H8
Pearman St SE1 129 N1
Pearscroft Ct SW6 128 B7
Pearscroft Rd SW6 128 B7
Pearson St E2 126 C4
Peckford Pl SW9 129 N8
Peckham Gro SE15 130 C6
Peckham High St SE15 130 E7
Peckham Hill St SE15 130 E6
Peckham Pk Rd SE15 130 E6
Peckham Rd SE5 130 C7
Peckham Rd SE15 130 C7
Peckham Rye SE15 130 E9
Peckham Rye SE22 130 E10
Pedlars Wk N7 125 L1
Pedley St E1 126 D6
Peel Gro E2 126 G4
Peel Prec NW6 124 A4
Peel St W8 124 A10
Peerless St EC1 126 B5
Pekin St E14 127 L8
Pelham Cl SE5 130 C8
Pelham Cres SW7 128 E3
Pelham Pl SW7 128 E3
Pelham St SW7 128 E3
Pelican Est SE15 130 D7
Pelling St E14 127 L8
Pelter St E2 126 D5
Pembridge Cres W11 124 A9
Pembridge Gdns W2 124 A9
Pembridge Ms W11 124 A9
Pembridge Pl W2 124 A9
Pembridge Rd W11 124 A9
Pembridge Sq W2 124 A9
Pembridge Vil W2 124 A9
Pembridge Vil W11 124 A9
Pembroke Av N1 125 L3
Pembroke Cl SW1 128 G1
Pembroke Gdns Cl W8 128 A2
Pembroke Pl W8 128 A2
Pembroke Rd W8 128 A3
Pembroke Sq W8 128 A2
Pembroke St N1 125 L2
Pembroke Vil W8 128 A3
Pembroke Wk W8 128 A3
Pembry Cl SW9 129 N7
Penang St E1 126 F10
Penarth St SE15 130 G5
Pencraig Way SE15 130 F5
Pendrell Rd SE4 131 J8
Penfold Pl NW1 124 E7
Penfold St NW1 124 D6
Penfold St NW8 124 D6
Penford St SE5 129 P8
Penn St N1 126 B3
Pennack Rd SE15 130 D5
Pennant Ms W8 128 B3
Pennethorne Rd SE15 130 F6
Pennington St E1 126 E9
Pennyfields E14 127 L9
Penpoll Rd E8 126 F1
Penrose Gro SE17 130 A4
Penrose Ho SE17 130 A4
Penrose St SE17 130 A4
Penryn St NW1 125 K4
Pensbury Pl SW8 129 J8
Pensbury St SW8 129 J8
Penshurst Rd E9 127 H2
Pentland Rd NW6 124 A5
Penton Pl SE17 129 P4
Penton Ri WC1 125 M5
Penton St N1 125 N4
Pentonville Rd N1 125 M4
Pentridge St SE15 130 D6
Penywern Rd SW5 128 A4
Pepper St E14 131 M2
Pepys Rd SE14 131 H7
Pepys St EC3 126 C9
Percival St EC1 125 P6
Percy Circ WC1 125 M5
Percy St W1 125 K7
Peregrine Ho EC1 125 P5
Perkin's Rents SW1 129 K2
Perrymead St SW6 128 A7
Perseverance Pl SW9 129 N6
Peter St W1 125 K9
Peterborough Ms SW6 128 A8
Peterborough Rd SW6 128 A8
Peterborough Vil SW6 128 B7
Petergate SW11 128 C10
Petersham La SW7 128 C2
Petersham Ms SW7 128 C2
Petersham Pl SW7 128 C2
Peto Pl NW1 125 H6
Petticoat La E1 126 C7
Petticoat Sq E1 126 D8
Petty France SW1 129 J2
Petty Wales EC3 126 C9
Petworth St SW11 128 E7
Petyward SW3 128 E3
Peyton Pl SE10 131 N6
Phelp St SE17 130 B5
Phene St SW3 128 E5
Philbeach Gdns SW5 128 A4
Philip Wk SE15 130 E9
Phillimore Gdns W8 128 A1
Phillimore Pl W8 128 A1
Phillimore Wk W8 128 A2
Phillipp St N1 126 C3
Philpot St E1 126 F8
Phipp St EC2 126 C6
Phoenix Pl WC1 125 M6
Phoenix Rd NW1 125 K5
Piccadilly W1 125 H10
Piccadilly Circ W1 125 K9
Pickfords Wf N1 126 A4
Picton St SE5 130 B6
Pier St E14 131 N3
Pigott St E14 127 L8
Pilgrimage St SE1 130 B1
Pilkington Rd SE15 130 F8
Pilot Cl SE8 131 K5
Pilton Pl SE17 130 A4
Pimlico Rd SW1 128 G4
Pinchin St E1 126 E9
Pincott Pl SE4 131 H10
Pindar St EC2 126 C7
Pine St EC1 125 N6
Pinefield Cl E14 127 L9
Pioneer St SE15 130 E7
Piper Cl N7 125 M1
Pitchford St E15 127 P2
Pitfield Est N1 126 B5
Pitfield St N1 126 C5
Pitman St SE5 130 A6
Pitsea St E1 127 H8
Pitt St W8 128 A1
Pitt's Head Ms W1 124 G10
Pixley St E14 127 K8
Plantation Wf SW11 128 C9
Plato Rd SW2 129 L10
Platt St NW1 125 K4
Plaza Shop Cen, The W1 125 J8
Pleasant Pl N1 125 P2
Pleasant Row NW1 125 H3
Plender St NW1 125 J3
Plevna St E14 131 N2
Plough Rd SW11 128 D9
Plough Ter SW11 128 D10
Plough Way SE16 131 H3
Plough Yd EC2 126 C6
Plover Way SE16 131 J2
Plumbers Row E1 126 E7
Plymouth Wf E14 131 P3
Plympton St NW8 124 E6
Pocock St SE1 129 P1
Podmore Rd SW18 128 C10
Point Hill SE10 131 N6
Point Pleasant SW18 128 A10
Pointers Cl E14 131 M4
Poland Ho E15 127 P3
Poland St W1 125 J8
Polesworth Ho W2 124 A7
Pollard Row E2 126 E5
Pollard St E2 126 E5
Polygon Rd NW1 125 K4
Pomeroy St SE14 130 G7
Pond Pl SW3 128 E3
Ponler St E1 126 F8
Ponsford St E9 126 G1
Ponsonby Pl SW1 129 K4
Ponsonby Ter SW1 129 K4
Pont St SW1 128 F2
Pont St Ms SW1 128 F2
Ponton Rd SW8 129 K5
Poole Rd E9 127 H1
Poole St N1 126 B3
Poolmans St SE16 131 H1
Pope St SE1 130 C1
Popes Rd SW9 129 N9
Popham Rd N1 126 A3
Popham St N1 125 P3
Poplar Business Pk E14 127 N9
Poplar High St E14 127 L9
Poplar Pl W2 124 B9
Poplar Rd SE24 130 A10
Poplar Wk SE24 130 A10
Porchester Cl SE5 130 A10
Porchester Gdns W2 124 B9
Porchester Ms W2 124 B8
Porchester Pl W2 124 E8
Porchester Rd W2 124 B7
Porchester Sq W2 124 B8
Porchester Ter W2 124 C9
Porchester Ter N W2 124 B8
Porden Rd SW2 129 M10
Porlock St SE1 130 B1
Portelet Rd E1 127 H5
Porteus Rd W2 124 C7
Portia Way E3 127 K6
Portland Gro SW8 129 M7
Portland Pl W1 125 H7
Portland St SE17 130 B4
Portman Cl W1 124 F8
Portman Ms S W1 124 G8
Portman Pl E2 126 G5
Portman Sq W1 124 F8
Portman St W1 124 G8
Portpool La EC1 125 N7
Portree St E14 127 P8
Portslade Rd SW8 129 J8
Portsoken St E1 126 D9
Portugal St WC2 125 M8
Post Office Way SW8 129 K6
Potier St SE1 130 B2
Pott St E2 126 F5
Potters Rd SW6 128 C8
Pottery St SE16 130 F1
Poultry EC2 126 B8
Pountney Rd SW11 128 G9
Powis Pl WC1 125 L6
Powis Rd E3 127 M5
Pownall Rd E8 126 D3
Poyntz Rd SW11 128 F8
Poyser St E2 126 F4
Praed St W2 124 D8
Prairie St SW8 128 G8
Pratt St NW1 125 J3
Pratt Wk SE11 129 M3
Prebend St N1 126 A3
Prescot St E1 126 D9
Prescott Pl SW4 129 K9
Prestage Way E14 127 N9
Prestons Rd E14 131 N1
Price's Ct SW11 128 D9
Prices Ms N1 125 M3
Price's St SE1 125 P10
Prideaux Pl WC1 125 M5
Prideaux Rd SW9 129 L9
Prima Rd SW9 129 N6
Primrose Cl E3 127 L4
Primrose Gdns NW3 124 E1
Primrose Hill Ct NW3 124 F2
Primrose Hill Rd NW3 124 E2
Primrose Sq E9 126 G2
Primrose St EC2 126 C7
Prince Albert Rd NW1 124 E4
Prince Albert Rd NW8 124 E4
Prince Consort Rd SW7 128 C2
Prince Edwards Rd E9 127 K1
Prince of Wales Dr SW8 129 H6
Prince of Wales Dr SW11 128 F7
Prince of Wales Gate SW7 128 E1
Prince of Wales Rd NW5 124 G1
Prince St SE8 131 K5
Princelet St E1 126 D7
Princes Ct SE16 131 K2
Princes Ct Business Cen E1 126 F9
Princes Gdns SW7 128 D2
Princes Gate SW7 128 E1
Princes Gate Ms SW7 128 D2
Princes Ri SE13 131 N8
Princes Riverside Rd SE16 127 H10
Princes Sq W2 124 B9
Princes St EC2 126 B8
Princes St W1 125 H8
Princess Rd NW1 124 G3
Princess Rd NW6 124 A4
Princess St SE1 129 P2
Princethorpe Ho W2 124 A7
Princeton St WC1 125 M7
Printers Ms E3 127 J3
Prior Bolton St N1 125 P1
Prior St SE10 131 N6
Prioress St SE1 130 B2
Priory Ct SW8 129 K7
Priory Grn Est N1 125 M4
Priory Gro SW8 129 L7
Priory Ms SW8 129 K7
Priory Rd NW6 124 B3
Priory St E3 127 M5
Priory Ter NW6 124 B3
Priory Wk SW10 128 C4
Pritchard's Rd E2 126 E3
Priter Rd SE16 130 E2
Procter St WC1 125 M7
Prospect Pl E1 126 G10
Prospect Quay SW18 128 A10
Providence Ct W1 124 G9
Provost Est N1 126 B4
Provost Rd NW3 124 F2
Provost St N1 126 B5
Prusom St E1 126 F10
Pudding La EC3 126 B9
Pudding Mill La E15 127 M3
Pulross Rd SW9 129 M9
Pulteney Cl E3 127 K3
Pulteney Ter N1 125 M3
Pulton Pl SW6 128 A6
Pump La SE14 130 G6
Pundersons Gdns E2 126 F5
Purbrook St SE1 130 C2
Purcell St N1 126 C4
Purchese St NW1 125 K4
Purdy St E3 127 M6
Purelake Ms SE13 131 P9
Puteaux Ho E2 127 H4
Pytchley Rd SE22 130 C9

Q

Quaker St E1 126 D6
Quality Ct WC2 125 N8
Quarrendon St SW6 128 A8
Quarterdeck, The E14 131 L1
Quebec Way SE16 131 H1
Queen Anne Rd E9 127 H1
Queen Anne St W1 125 H8
Queen Anne's Gate SW1 129 K1
Queen Elizabeth St SE1 130 D1
Queen of Denmark Ct SE16 131 K2
Queen Sq WC1 125 L6
Queen St EC4 126 A9
Queen St W1 125 H10
Queen Victoria St EC4 125 P9
Queenhithe EC4 126 A9
Queen's Cres NW5 124 G1
Queens Gdns W2 124 C9
Queen's Gate SW7 128 D3
Queen's Gate Gdns SW7 128 C2
Queen's Gate Ms SW7 128 C1
Queen's Gate Pl SW7 128 C2
Queen's Gate Pl Ms SW7 128 C2
Queen's Gate Ter SW7 128 C2
Queen's Gro NW8 124 D3
Queen's Gro Ms NW8 124 D3
Queen's Head St N1 125 P3
Queens Ms W2 124 B9
Queens Rd SE14 130 F7
Queens Rd SE15 130 F7
Queen's Row SE17 130 B5
Queen's Ter NW8 124 D4
Queen's Wk SE1 126 C10
Queen's Wk SW1 125 J10
Queensberry Pl SW7 128 D3
Queensborough Ter W2 124 B9
Queensbridge Rd E2 126 D3
Queensbridge Rd E8 126 D2
Queensbury St N1 126 A2
Queensgate Pl NW6 124 A2
Queensmead NW8 124 D3
Queenstown Rd SW8 129 H5
Queensway W2 124 B8
Querrin St SW6 128 C8
Quex Rd NW6 124 A3
Quick St N1 125 P4
Quilter St E2 126 E5
Quince Rd SE13 131 M8
Quixley St E14 127 P9
Quorn Rd SE22 130 C10

R

Racton Rd SW6 128 A5
Radcot St SE11 129 N4
Radlett Pl NW8 124 E3
Radley Ms W8 128 A2
Radnor Pl W2 124 E8
Radnor Rd SE15 130 E6
Radnor St EC1 126 A5
Radnor Wk SW3 128 E4
Radstock St SW11 128 E6
Raeburn St SW2 129 L10
Raglan St NW5 125 H1
Railton Rd SE24 129 N10
Railway App SE1 126 B10
Railway Av SE16 130 G1
Railway St N1 125 L4
Rainbow Av E14 131 M4
Rainbow Quay SE16 131 J2
Rainbow St SE5 130 C6
Raine St E1 126 F10
Rainhill Way E3 127 L5
Rainsborough Av SE8 131 J3
Raleana Rd E14 127 N10
Raleigh St N1 125 P3
Ramillies Pl W1 125 J8
Rampayne St SW1 129 K4
Ramsey St E2 126 E6
Ramsey Wk N1 126 B1
Randall Cl SW11 128 E7
Randall Pl SE10 131 N6
Randall Rd SE11 129 M3
Randell's Rd N1 125 L3
Randolph Av W9 124 C6
Randolph Cres W9 124 C6
Randolph Gdns NW6 124 B4
Randolph Ms W9 124 C6
Randolph Rd W9 124 C6
Randolph St NW1 125 J2
Ranelagh Gdns SW3 128 G4
Ranelagh Gro SW1 128 G4
Rangers Sq SE10 131 P7
Ranwell St E3 127 K3
Raphael St SW7 128 F1
Ratcliffe Cross St E1 127 H8
Ratcliffe La E14 127 J8
Ratcliffe Orchard E1 127 H9
Rathbone Pl W1 125 K8
Rathbone St W1 125 J7
Rattray Rd SW2 129 N10
Raul Rd SE15 130 E7
Raven Row E1 126 F7
Ravensbourne Pl SE13 131 M8
Ravenscroft St E2 126 D4
Ravensdon St SE11 129 N4
Ravenstone SE17 130 C4
Rawlings St SW3 128 F3
Rawstorne St EC1 125 P5
Ray St EC1 125 N6
Raymouth Rd SE16 130 F3
Reading La E8 126 F1
Reardon Path E1 126 F10
Reardon St E1 126 F10
Reaston St SE14 130 G6
Record St SE15 130 G5
Rector St N1 126 A3
Rectory Gro SW4 129 J9
Rectory Sq E1 127 H7
Reculver Rd SE16 131 H4
Red Lion Row SE17 130 A5
Red Lion Sq WC1 125 M7
Red Lion St WC1 125 M7
Red Path E9 127 K1
Red Post Hill SE24 130 B10
Redan Pl W2 124 B8
Redbridge Gdns SE5 130 C6
Redburn St SW3 128 F5
Redcar St SE5 130 A6
Redcastle Cl E1 126 G9
Redchurch St E2 126 D6
Redcliffe Gdns SW5 128 B4
Redcliffe Gdns SW10 128 B4
Redcliffe Ms SW10 128 B4
Redcliffe Pl SW10 128 C5
Redcliffe Rd SW10 128 C4
Redcliffe Sq SW10 128 B4
Redcliffe St SW10 128 B5
Redcross Way SE1 130 A1
Reddins Rd SE15 130 E5
Redesdale St SW3 128 F5
Redfield La SW5 128 A3
Redhill St NW1 125 H4
Redman's Rd E1 126 G7
Redriff Est SE16 131 K2
Redriff Rd SE16 131 H3
Redruth Rd E9 127 H3
Redwood Cl E3 127 L4
Redwood Cl SE16 127 J10
Reece Ms SW7 128 D3
Reed Pl SW4 129 K10
Reedham St SE15 130 E8
Reedworth St SE11 129 N3
Rees St N1 126 A3
Reeves Ms W1 124 G9
Reeves Rd E3 127 M6
Reform St SW11 128 F8
Regan Way N1 126 C4
Regency St SW1 129 K3
Regeneration Rd SE16 131 H3
Regent Sq E3 127 M5
Regent Sq WC1 125 L5
Regent St SW1 125 K9
Regent St W1 125 H8
Regents Br Gdns SW8 129 L6
Regent's Pk, The NW1 124 G4
Regents Pk Rd NW1 124 F3
Regents Row E8 126 E3
Reginald Rd SE8 131 L6
Reginald Sq SE8 131 L6
Regis Pl SW2 129 M10
Relf Rd SE15 130 E9
Rembrandt Cl E14 131 P2
Remington St N1 125 P4
Renforth St SE16 130 G1
Renfrew Rd SE11 129 P3
Rennell St SE13 131 N9
Rennie Est SE16 130 F3
Rennie St SE1 125 P10
Repton St E14 127 J8
Reservoir Rd SE4 131 J8
Retreat Pl E9 126 G1
Revelon Rd SE4 131 J10
Reverdy Rd SE1 130 E3
Rheidol Ter N1 125 P4
Rhodesia Rd SW9 129 L8
Rhodeswell Rd E14 127 J7
Rhondda Gro E3 127 J5
Rhyl St NW5 124 G1
Ricardo St E14 127 M8
Rich St E14 127 K9
Richborne Ter SW8 129 M6
Richmond Av N1 125 M3
Richmond Cres N1 125 M3
Richmond Gro N1 125 P2
Richmond Rd E8 126 D2
Richmond Ter SW1 129 L1
Rick Roberts Way E15 127 N3
Rickett St SW6 128 A5
Ridgdale St E3 127 M4
Ridgeway Rd SW9 129 P9
Riding Ho St W1 125 H7
Rifle Ct SE11 129 N5
Rifle St E14 127 M7
Rigden St E14 127 M8
Rigge Pl SW4 129 K10
Riley Rd SE1 130 D2
Riley St SW10 128 D5
Ring, The W2 124 D9
Ripplevale Gro N1 125 M2
Risdon St SE16 130 G1
Risinghill St N1 125 M4
Rita Rd SW8 129 M6
Ritchie St N1 125 N4
Ritson Rd E8 126 E1
Rivaz Pl E9 126 G1
River Pl N1 126 A2
River St EC1 125 N5
Riverside Ct SW8 129 K5
Riverside Rd E15 127 N4
Riverside Twr SW6 128 C8
Rivington St EC2 126 C5
Roach Rd E3 127 L2
Roan St SE10 131 N5
Robert Adam St W1 124 G8
Robert Dashwood Way SE17 130 A3
Robert Lowe Cl SE14 131 H6
Robert St NW1 125 H5
Roberta St E2 126 E5
Roberts Cl SE16 131 H1
Robertson Rd E15 127 N3
Robertson St SW8 129 H9
Robin Ct SE16 130 E3
Robin Hood La E14 127 N9
Robinson Rd E2 126 G4
Robsart St SW9 129 M8
Rochelle Cl SW11 128 D10
Rochester Ms NW1 125 J2
Rochester Pl NW1 125 J1
Rochester Rd NW1 125 J1
Rochester Row SW1 129 J3
Rochester Sq NW1 125 J2

Roc - Spe


Rochester St **SW1** 129 K2
Rochester Ter **NW1** 125 J1
Rockingham Est **SE1** 130 A2
Rockingham St **SE1** 130 A2
Rodmarton St **W1** 124 F7
Rodney Pl **SE17** 130 A3
Rodney Rd **SE17** 130 A3
Rodney St **N1** 125 M4
Roffey St **E14** 131 N1
Roger Dowley Ct **E2** 126 G4
Roger St **WC1** 125 M6
Rokeby Rd **SE4** 131 K8
Roland Gdns **SW7** 128 C4
Roland Way **SE17** 130 B4
Rollins St **SE15** 130 G5
Rolls Rd **SE1** 130 D4
Rolt St **SE8** 131 J5
Roman Rd **E2** 126 G5
Roman Rd **E3** 127 J4
Roman Way **N7** 125 M1
Romford St **E1** 126 E7
Romilly St **W1** 125 K9
Romney Rd **SE10** 131 N5
Romney St **SW1** 129 K2
Rood La **EC3** 126 C9
Rookery Rd **SW4** 129 J10
Rope St **SE16** 131 J3
Ropemaker Rd **SE16** 131 J2
Ropemaker St **EC2** 126 B7
Ropery St **E3** 127 K6
Ropley St **E2** 126 E4
Rosary Gdns **SW7** 128 C3
Rose All **SE1** 126 A10
Rose Sq **SW3** 128 D4
Rosebank Gdns **E3** 127 K4
Roseberry Pl **E8** 126 D1
Roseberry St **SE16** 130 F3
Rosebery Av **EC1** 125 N6
Rosebury Rd **SW6** 128 B8
Rosefield Gdns **E14** 127 L9
Rosemary Dr **E14** 127 P8
Rosemary Rd **SE15** 130 D6
Rosemont Rd **NW3** 124 C1
Rosemoor St **SW3** 128 F3
Rosenau Cres **SW11** 128 E7
Rosenau Rd **SW11** 128 E7
Roserton St **E14** 131 N1
Rosetta Cl **SW8** 129 L6
Rosher Cl **E15** 127 P2
Rosoman St **EC1** 125 N5
Rossendale Way **NW1** 125 J2
Rossetti Rd **SE16** 130 F4
Rossmore Rd **NW1** 124 E6
Rothbury Rd **E9** 127 K2
Rotherfield St **N1** 126 A2
Rotherhithe New Rd **SE16** 130 E4
Rotherhithe Old Rd **SE16** 131 H3
Rotherhithe St **SE16** 130 G1
Rotherhithe Tunnel **E1** 126 G10
Rotherhithe Tunnel App **E14** 127 J9
Rotherhithe Tunnel App **SE16** 130 G1
Rothery Ter **SW9** 129 P6
Rothsay St **SE1** 130 C2
Rothwell St **NW1** 124 F3
Rotten Row **SW1** 128 F1
Rotten Row **SW7** 128 E1
Rotterdam Dr **E14** 131 N2
Rouel Rd **SE16** 130 E2
Rounton Rd **E3** 127 L6
Roupell St **SE1** 125 N10
Rousden St **NW1** 125 J2
Rowcross St **SE1** 130 D4
Rowditch La **SW11** 128 G8
Rowena Cres **SW11** 128 E8
Rowington Cl **W2** 124 B7
Rowley Way **NW8** 124 B3
Rowse Cl **E15** 127 N3
Roxby Pl **SW6** 128 A5
Royal Av **SW3** 128 F4
Royal Cl **SE8** 131 K5
Royal Coll St **NW1** 125 J2
Royal Ct **SE16** 131 K2
Royal Ex **EC3** 126 B8
Royal Hill **SE10** 131 N6
Royal Hosp Rd **SW3** 128 F5
Royal Ms, The **SW1** 129 H2
Royal Mint Ct **EC3** 126 D9
Royal Mint St **E1** 126 D9
Royal Naval Pl **SE14** 131 K6
Royal Oak Rd **E8** 126 F1
Royal Oak Yd **SE1** 130 C1
Royal Opera Arc **SW1** 125 K10
Royal Pl **SE10** 131 N6
Royal Rd **SE17** 129 P5
Royal St **SE1** 129 M2
Royal Victor Pl **E3** 127 H4
Royston St **E2** 126 G4
Rozel Ct **N1** 126 C3
Rozel Rd **SW4** 129 J8
Ruby St **SE15** 130 F5
Rudolph Rd **NW6** 124 A4
Rufford St **N1** 125 L3
Rugby St **WC1** 125 M6
Rugg St **E14** 127 L9
Rum Cl **E1** 126 G9
Rumbold Rd **SW6** 128 B6
Rumsey Rd **SW9** 129 M9
Rupert Gdns **SW9** 129 P8
Rupert St **W1** 125 K9
Rush Hill Rd **SW11** 128 G9
Rushcroft Rd **SW2** 129 N10
Rushton St **N1** 126 B4
Rushworth St **SE1** 129 P1
Ruskin Pk Ho **SE5** 130 B9
Russell Gro **SW9** 129 N6
Russell Sq **WC1** 125 L7
Russell St **WC2** 125 M8
Russia Dock Rd **SE16** 127 J10
Russia La **E2** 126 G4
Russia Wk **SE16** 131 J1
Rust Sq **SE5** 130 B6
Ruston St **E3** 127 K3
Rutherford St **SW1** 129 K3
Rutland Gdns **SW7** 128 E1
Rutland Gate **SW7** 128 E1
Rutland Rd **E9** 126 G3
Rutland St **SW7** 128 E2
Rutts Ter **SE14** 131 H7
Ryder Dr **SE16** 130 F4
Ryder St **SW1** 125 J10
Rye Hill Pk **SE15** 130 G10
Rye La **SE15** 130 E7
Rye Pas **SE15** 130 E9
Rye Rd **SE15** 131 H10
Ryecroft St **SW6** 128 B7
Ryland Rd **NW5** 125 H1
Rysbrack St **SW3** 128 F2

**S**

Sabella Ct **E3** 127 K4
Sabine Rd **SW11** 128 F9
Sable St **N1** 125 P2
Sackville St **W1** 125 J9
Saffron Av **E14** 127 P9
Saffron Hill **EC1** 125 N6
Sail St **SE11** 129 M3
St. Agnes Pl **SE11** 129 N5
St. Albans Gro **W8** 128 B2
St. Alban's Pl **N1** 125 P3
St. Alfege Pas **SE10** 131 N5
St. Alphonsus Rd **SW4** 129 J10
St. Andrew St **EC4** 125 N7
St. Andrew's Hill **EC4** 125 P9
St. Andrews Pl **NW1** 125 H6
St. Andrews Way **E3** 127 M6
St. Ann's St **SW1** 129 K2
St. Ann's Ter **NW8** 124 D4
St. Anthonys Cl **E1** 126 E10
St. Asaph Rd **SE4** 131 H9
St. Augustines Rd **NW1** 125 K2
St. Austell Rd **SE13** 131 N8
St. Barnabas St **SW1** 128 G4
St. Barnabas Vil **SW8** 129 L7
St. Botolph St **EC3** 126 D8
St. Bride St **EC4** 125 P8
St. Chad's Pl **WC1** 125 L5
St. Chad's St **WC1** 125 L5
St. Clements St **N7** 125 N1
St. Cross St **EC1** 125 N7
St. Davids Sq **E14** 131 M4
St. Donatts Rd **SE14** 131 K7
St. Dunstan's Hill **EC3** 126 C9
St. Edmunds Ter **NW8** 124 E3
St. Elmos Rd **SE16** 131 H1
St. Francis Rd **SE22** 130 C10
St. George St **W1** 125 H8
St. George Wf **SW8** 129 L4
St. Georges Circ **SE1** 129 P2
St. George's Dr **SW1** 129 H3
St. Georges Flds **W2** 124 E8
St. Georges Rd **SE1** 129 N2
St. Georges Sq **SE8** 131 K3
St. George's Sq **SW1** 129 K4
St. George's Sq Ms **SW1** 129 K4
St. Georges Way **SE15** 130 C5
St. Giles High St **WC2** 125 K8
St. Giles Rd **SE5** 130 C6
St. Gilles Ho **E2** 127 H4
St. Helena Rd **SE16** 131 H3
St. James Ms **E14** 131 N2
St. James's **SE14** 131 J7
St. James's Av **E2** 126 G4
St. James's Ct **SW1** 129 J2
St. James's Cres **SW9** 129 N9
St. James's Palace **SW1** 125 J10
St. James's Pk **SW1** 129 K1
St. James's Pl **SW1** 125 J10
St. James's Rd **SE1** 130 E4
St. James's Rd **SE16** 130 E2
St. James's Sq **SW1** 125 J10
St. James's St **SW1** 125 J10
St. James's Ter Ms **NW8** 124 F3
St. James's Wk **EC1** 125 P6
St. John St **EC1** 125 P6
St. John's Cres **SW9** 129 N9
St. John's Est **N1** 126 B4
St. John's Hill **SW11** 128 D10
St. John's Hill Gro **SW11** 128 D10
St. John's La **EC1** 125 P6
St. John's Rd **SW11** 128 E10
St. Johns Vale **SE8** 131 L8
St. John's Wd High St **NW8** 124 D4
St. John's Wd Pk **NW8** 124 D3
St. John's Wd Rd **NW8** 124 D6
St. John's Wd Ter **NW8** 124 D4
St. Joseph's Vale **SE3** 131 P8
St. Jude's Rd **E2** 126 F4
St. Katharine's Way **E1** 126 D10
St. Lawrence St **E14** 127 N10
St. Lawrence Way **SW9** 129 N7
St. Leonards Ct **N1** 126 B5
St. Leonards Rd **E14** 127 M7
St. Leonards Sq **NW5** 124 G1
St. Leonards St **E3** 127 M5
St. Leonard's Ter **SW3** 128 F4
St. Loo Av **SW3** 128 E5
St. Luke's Av **SW4** 129 K10
St. Luke's Cl **EC1** 126 A6
St. Luke's Est **EC1** 126 B5
St. Luke's St **SW3** 128 E4
St. Margarets La **W8** 128 B2
St. Margarets Rd **SE4** 131 K10
St. Margaret's St **SW1** 129 L1
St. Mark St **E1** 126 D8
St. Marks Cres **NW1** 124 G3
St. Mark's Gro **SW10** 128 B5
St. Marks Sq **NW1** 124 G3
St. Martins Cl **NW1** 125 J3
St. Martin's La **WC2** 125 L9
St. Martin's Pl **WC2** 125 L9
St. Martin's Rd **SW9** 129 M8
St. Martin's-le-Grand **EC1** 126 A8
St. Mary at Hill **EC3** 126 C9
St. Mary Axe **EC3** 126 C8
St. Marychurch St **SE16** 130 G1
St. Mary's Gdns **SE11** 129 N3
St. Mary's Gate **W8** 128 B2
St. Mary's Gro **N1** 125 P1
St. Marys Mans **W2** 124 C7
St. Marys Path **N1** 125 P3
St. Mary's Pl **W8** 128 B2
St. Mary's Rd **SE15** 130 G7
St. Marys Sq **W2** 124 D7
St. Marys Ter **W2** 124 D7
St. Mary's Wk **SE11** 129 N3
St. Matthew's Rd **SW2** 129 M10
St. Matthew's Row **E2** 126 E5
St. Michael's Rd **SW9** 129 M8
St. Michaels St **W2** 124 D8
St. Norbert Grn **SE4** 131 J10
St. Norbert Rd **SE4** 131 J10
St. Olav's Sq **SE16** 130 G2
St. Oswald's Pl **SE11** 129 M4
St. Pancras Way **NW1** 125 J2
St. Paul St **N1** 126 A3
St. Paul's Av **SE16** 127 H10
St. Paul's Chyd **EC4** 125 P8
St. Paul's Cres **NW1** 125 K2
St. Paul's Ms **NW1** 125 K2
St. Paul's Pl **N1** 126 B1
St. Paul's Rd **N1** 125 P1
St. Paul's Shrubbery **N1** 126 B1
St. Pauls Way **E3** 127 K7
St. Pauls Way **E14** 127 K7
St. Peter's Cl **E2** 126 E4
St. Peters St **N1** 125 P3
St. Peter's Way **N1** 126 C2
St. Petersburgh Ms **W2** 124 B9
St. Petersburgh Pl **W2** 124 B9
St. Philip Sq **SW8** 129 H8
St. Philip St **SW8** 129 H8
St. Philip's Rd **E8** 126 E1
St. Rule St **SW8** 129 J8
St. Saviour's Est **SE1** 130 D2
St. Silas Pl **NW5** 124 G1
St. Silas St Est **NW5** 124 G1
St. Stephens Cres **W2** 124 A8
St. Stephens Gdns **W2** 124 A8
St. Stephens Gro **SE13** 131 N9
St. Stephen's Rd **E3** 127 K4
St. Stephens Ter **SW8** 129 M6
St. Stephen's Wk **SW7** 128 C3
St. Swithin's La **EC4** 126 B9
St. Thomas St **SE1** 126 B10
St. Thomas's Pl **E9** 126 G2
St. Thomas's Sq **E9** 126 F2
Salamanca St **SE1** 129 L3
Sale Pl **W2** 124 E7
Salem Rd **W2** 124 B9
Salisbury Ct **EC4** 125 P8
Salisbury Pl **SW9** 129 P6
Salisbury Pl **W1** 124 F7
Salisbury St **NW8** 124 E6
Salisbury Ter **SE15** 130 G9
Salmon La **E14** 127 J8
Salter Rd **SE16** 127 H10
Salter St **E14** 127 L9
Saltoun Rd **SW2** 129 N10
Saltwell St **E14** 127 L9
Samford St **NW8** 124 E6
Sampson St **E1** 126 E10
Samuel Cl **SE14** 131 H5
Samuel Lewis Trust Dws **SW6** 128 A6
Samuel St **SE15** 130 D6
Sancroft St **SE11** 129 M4
Sandall Rd **NW5** 125 J1
Sandbourne Rd **SE4** 131 J8
Sandgate St **SE15** 130 F5
Sandilands Rd **SW6** 128 B7
Sandison St **SE15** 130 D9
Sandland St **WC1** 125 M7
Sandmere Rd **SW4** 129 L10
Sandpiper Cl **SE16** 131 K1
Sandrock Rd **SE13** 131 L9
Sand's End La **SW6** 128 B7
Sandwell Cres **NW6** 124 A1
Sandwich St **WC1** 125 L5
Sandy's Row **E1** 126 C7
Sanford St **SE14** 131 J5
Sangora Rd **SW11** 128 D10
Sans Wk **EC1** 125 N6
Sansom St **SE5** 130 B6
Santley St **SW4** 129 M10
Saperton Wk **SE11** 129 M3
Sapphire Rd **SE8** 131 J3
Saracen St **E14** 127 L8
Sartor Rd **SE15** 131 H10
Satchwell Rd **E2** 126 E5
Saunders Ness Rd **E14** 131 N4
Saunders St **SE11** 129 N3
Savile Row **W1** 125 J9
Savona Est **SW8** 129 J6
Savona St **SW8** 129 J6
Savoy Ms **SW9** 129 L9
Savoy Pl **WC2** 125 L9
Savoy St **WC2** 125 M9
Sawmill Yd **E3** 127 J3
Sawyer St **SE1** 130 A1
Saxon Rd **E3** 127 K4
Saxton Cl **SE13** 131 P9
Sayes Ct St **SE8** 131 K5
Scala St **W1** 125 J7
Scandrett St **E1** 126 F10
Scarsdale Vil **W8** 128 A2
Scawen Rd **SE8** 131 J4
Scawfell St **E2** 126 D4
Sceaux Est **SE5** 130 C7
Sceptre Rd **E2** 126 G5
Schoolhouse La **E1** 127 H9
Schooner Cl **E14** 131 P2
Sclater St **E1** 126 D6
Scoresby St **SE1** 125 P10
Scott Ellis Gdns **NW8** 124 D5
Scott Lidgett Cres **SE16** 130 E1
Scott St **E1** 126 F6
Scriven St **E8** 126 D3
Scrutton St **EC2** 126 C6
Scylla Rd **SE15** 130 F9
Seacon Twr **E14** 131 K1
Seaford St **WC1** 125 M5
Seagrave Rd **SW6** 128 A5
Searles Cl **SW11** 128 E6
Searles Rd **SE1** 130 B3
Sears St **SE5** 130 B6
Sebastian St **EC1** 125 P5
Sebbon St **N1** 125 P2
Sedding St **SW1** 128 G3
Sedgmoor Pl **SE5** 130 C6
Seething La **EC3** 126 C9
Sekforde St **EC1** 125 P6
Selby St **E1** 126 E6
Selden Rd **SE15** 130 G8
Selsdon Way **E14** 131 M2
Selsey St **E14** 127 L7
Selwood Pl **SW7** 128 D4
Selworthy Ho **SW11** 128 D7
Selwyn Rd **E3** 127 K4
Semley Pl **SW1** 128 G3
Senate St **SE15** 130 G8
Sendall Ct **SW11** 128 D9
Senior St **W2** 124 B7
Senrab St **E1** 127 H8
Serenaders Rd **SW9** 129 N8
Serle St **WC2** 125 M8
Serpentine Rd **W2** 124 F10
Settles St **E1** 126 E7
Settrington Rd **SW6** 128 B8
Severnake Cl **E14** 131 L3
Severus Rd **SW11** 128 E10
Seville Ms **N1** 126 C2
Seville St **SW1** 128 F1
Sevington St **W9** 124 B6
Seward St **EC1** 126 A5
Sewardstone Rd **E2** 126 G4
Sextant Av **E14** 131 P3
Seymour Gdns **SE4** 131 J9
Seymour Ms **W1** 124 G8
Seymour Pl **W1** 124 E7
Seymour St **W1** 124 F8
Seymour St **W2** 124 F8
Seymour Wk **SW10** 128 C5
Seyssel St **E14** 131 N3
Shacklewell St **E2** 126 D6
Shad Thames **SE1** 126 D10
Shaftesbury Av **W1** 125 K9
Shaftesbury Av **WC2** 125 K9
Shaftesbury St **N1** 126 A4
Shafton Rd **E9** 127 H3
Shalbourne Sq **E9** 127 K1
Shalcomb St **SW10** 128 C5
Shamrock St **SW4** 129 K9
Shand St **SE1** 130 C1
Shandy St **E1** 127 H7
Shannon Gro **SW9** 129 M10
Shardeloes Rd **SE4** 131 K9
Shardeloes Rd **SE14** 131 K9
Sharon Gdns **E9** 126 G3
Sharpleshall St **NW1** 124 F2
Sharratt St **SE15** 130 G5
Sharsted St **SE17** 129 P4
Shaw Ct **SW11** 128 D9
Shaw Rd **SE22** 130 C10
Shawfield St **SW3** 128 E4
Shearling Way **N7** 125 L1
Sheep La **E8** 126 F3
Sheepcote La **SW11** 128 F8
Sheffield Ter **W8** 124 A10
Sheldon Pl **E2** 126 E4
Sheldon Sq **W2** 124 C7
Shell Rd **SE13** 131 M9
Shelley Cl **SE15** 130 F8
Shellwood Rd **SW11** 128 F8
Shelmerdine Cl **E3** 127 L7
Shelton St **WC2** 125 L8
Shenfield St **N1** 126 C4
Shenley Rd **SE5** 130 C7
Shepherdess Wk **N1** 126 A4
Sheppard Dr **SE16** 130 F4
Shepperton Rd **N1** 126 A3
Sherborne St **N1** 126 B3
Sheringham Rd **N7** 125 M1
Sherriff Rd **NW6** 124 A1
Sherwin Rd **SE14** 131 H7
Sherwood Gdns **E14** 131 L3
Sherwood Gdns **SE16** 130 E4
Shetland Rd **E3** 127 K4
Ship St **SE8** 131 L7
Shipton St **E2** 126 D5
Shipwright Rd **SE16** 131 J1
Shirbutt St **E14** 127 M9
Shirland Rd **W9** 124 A5
Shirley Gro **SW11** 128 G9
Shoe La **EC4** 125 N8
Shooters Hill Rd **SE10** 131 P7
Shore Pl **E9** 126 G2
Shore Rd **E9** 126 G2
Shoreditch High St **E1** 126 C6
Shorncliffe Rd **SE1** 130 D4
Short Wall **E15** 127 N5
Shorter St **E1** 126 D9
Shorts Gdns **WC2** 125 L8
Shottendane Rd **SW6** 128 A7
Shouldham St **W1** 124 E7
Shrewsbury Rd **W2** 124 A8
Shroton St **NW1** 124 E7
Shrubland Rd **E8** 126 E3
Shuttleworth Rd **SW11** 128 E8
Sibella Rd **SW4** 129 K8
Sidmouth St **WC1** 125 L5
Sidney Rd **SW9** 129 M8
Sidney Sq **E1** 126 G8
Sidney St **E1** 126 F7
Sidworth St **E8** 126 F2
Silex St **SE1** 129 P1
Silk Mills Sq **E9** 127 K1
Silk St **EC2** 126 A7
Silver Rd **SE13** 131 M9
Silver Wk **SE16** 127 K10
Silverthorne Rd **SW8** 129 H8
Silvocea Way **E14** 127 P8
Silwood St **SE16** 130 G3
Simms Rd **SE1** 130 E3
Simpson St **SW11** 128 E8
Simpsons Rd **E14** 127 M9
Sirinham Pt **SW8** 129 M5
Sisters Av **SW11** 128 F10
Sisulu Pl **SW9** 129 N9
Sivill Ho **E2** 126 D5
Six Bridges Trd Est **SE1** 130 E4
Sketchley Gdns **SE16** 131 H4
Skinner St **EC1** 125 N5
Skipworth Rd **E9** 126 G3
Skylines Village **E14** 131 N1
Slaidburn St **SW10** 128 C5
Slaithwaite Rd **SE13** 131 N10
Sleaford Ho **E3** 127 L6
Sleaford St **SW8** 129 J6
Slippers Pl **SE16** 130 F2
Sloane Av **SW3** 128 E3
Sloane Ct W **SW3** 128 G4
Sloane Gdns **SW1** 128 G3
Sloane Sq **SW1** 128 F3
Sloane St **SW1** 128 F1
Sloane Ter **SW1** 128 F3
Smart St **E2** 127 H5
Smeaton St **E1** 126 F10
Smedley St **SW4** 129 K8
Smedley St **SW8** 129 K8
Smeed Rd **E3** 127 L2
Smiles Pl **SE13** 131 N8
Smith Cl **SE16** 127 H10
Smith Sq **SW1** 129 L2
Smith St **SW3** 128 F4
Smith Ter **SW3** 128 F4
Smithy St **E1** 126 G7
Smokehouse Yd **EC1** 125 P7
Smugglers Way **SW18** 128 B10
Smyrks Rd **SE17** 130 C4
Smyrna Rd **NW6** 124 A2
Smythe St **E14** 127 M9
Snow Hill **EC1** 125 P7
Snowbury Rd **SW6** 128 B8
Snowden St **EC2** 126 C6
Snowman Ho **NW6** 124 B3
Snowsfields **SE1** 130 B1
Soames St **SE15** 130 D9
Soho Sq **W1** 125 K8
Solebay St **E1** 127 J6
Solomon's Pas **SE15** 130 F10
Solon New Rd **SW4** 129 L10
Solon Rd **SW2** 129 L10
Solway Rd **SE22** 130 E10
Somerfield St **SE16** 131 H4
Somerford St **E1** 126 F6
Somerford Way **SE16** 131 J1
Somerleyton Pas **SW9** 129 P10
Somerleyton Rd **SW9** 129 N10
Somers Cres **W2** 124 E8
Somerset Est **SW11** 128 D7
Somerset Gdns **SE13** 131 M8
Somerton Rd **SE15** 130 F10
Sondes St **SE17** 130 B5
Sopwith Way **SW8** 129 H6
Sorrel La **E14** 127 P8
Sotheran Cl **E8** 126 E3
Sotheron Rd **SW6** 128 B6
Soudan Rd **SW11** 128 F7
South Audley St **W1** 124 G9
South Bolton Gdns **SW5** 128 B4
South Carriage Dr **SW1** 128 E1
South Carriage Dr **SW7** 128 E1
South Colonnade **E14** 127 L10
South Cres **E16** 127 P6
South Cres **WC1** 125 K7
South Eaton Pl **SW1** 128 G3
South End Row **W8** 128 B2
South Island Pl **SW9** 129 M6
South Kensington Underground Sta **SW7** 128 D3
South Lambeth Pl **SW8** 129 L5
South Lambeth Rd **SW8** 129 L5
South Molton La **W1** 125 H8
South Molton St **W1** 125 H8
South Par **SW3** 128 D4
South Pk **SW6** 128 A8
South Pk Ms **SW6** 128 B9
South Pl **EC2** 126 B7
South Quay Plaza **E14** 131 M1
South Sea St **SE16** 131 K2
South St **W1** 124 G10
South Tenter St **E1** 126 D9
South Ter **SW7** 128 E3
South Vil **NW1** 125 K1
South Wf Rd **W2** 124 D8
Southall Pl **SE1** 130 B1
Southampton Pl **WC1** 125 L7
Southampton Row **WC1** 125 L7
Southampton St **WC2** 125 L9
Southampton Way **SE5** 130 B6
Southbank Business Cen **SW8** 129 K5
Southborough Rd **E9** 126 G3
Southern Gro **E3** 127 K5
Southern St **N1** 125 M4
Southerngate Way **SE14** 131 J6
Southey Rd **SW9** 129 N7
Southgate Gro **N1** 126 B2
Southgate Rd **N1** 126 B3
Southmoor Way **E9** 127 K1
Southolm St **SW11** 129 H7
Southville **SW8** 129 K7
Southwark Br **EC4** 126 A10
Southwark Br **SE1** 126 A10
Southwark Br Rd **SE1** 129 P2
Southwark Pk **SE16** 130 G3
Southwark Pk Est **SE16** 130 F3
Southwark Pk Rd **SE16** 130 D3
Southwark St **SE1** 125 P10
Southwater Cl **E14** 127 K8
Southwell Gdns **SW7** 128 C3
Southwell Rd **SE5** 130 A9
Southwick Pl **W2** 124 E8
Southwick St **W2** 124 E8
Sovereign Cl **E1** 126 F9
Spa Grn Est **EC1** 125 N5
Spa Rd **SE16** 130 D2
Spanby Rd **E3** 127 L6
Spanish Pl **W1** 124 G8
Sparkford Ho **SW11** 128 D7
Sparta St **SE10** 131 M7
Spear Ms **SW5** 128 A3
Speke Ho **SE5** 130 A6
Speldhurst Rd **E9** 127 H2

Spe - Van

Spelman St **E1** 126 E7
Spencer Rd **SW18** 128 D10
Spencer St **EC1** 125 P5
Spenser St **SW1** 129 J2
Spert St **E14** 127 J9
Spey St **E14** 127 N7
Spicer Cl **SW9** 129 P8
Spindrift Av **E14** 131 M3
Spital Sq **E1** 126 C7
Spital St **E1** 126 E6
Sporle Ct **SW11** 128 D9
Sprimont Pl **SW3** 128 F4
Spring St **W2** 124 D8
Springall St **SE15** 130 F6
Springfield La **NW6** 124 B3
Springfield Rd **NW8** 124 C3
Springfield Wk **NW6** 124 B3
Springhill Cl **SE5** 130 B9
Springwood Cl **E3** 127 L4
Sprules Rd **SE4** 131 J8
Spur Rd **SE1** 129 N1
Spur Rd **SW1** 129 J1
Spurgeon St **SE1** 130 B2
Spurling Rd **SE22** 130 D10
Squirries St **E2** 126 E5
Stable Yd Rd **SW1** 125 J10
Stables Way **SE11** 129 N4
Stacey St **WC2** 125 K8
Stadium St **SW10** 128 C6
Stafford Cl **NW6** 124 A5
Stafford Ct **W8** 128 A2
Stafford Pl **SW1** 129 J2
Stafford Rd **E3** 127 K4
Stafford Rd **NW6** 124 A5
Stafford St **W1** 125 J10
Stafford Ter **W8** 128 A2
Staffordshire St **SE15** 130 E7
Stag Pl **SW1** 129 J2
Stainer St **SE1** 126 B10
Staining La **EC2** 126 A8
Stainsby Rd **E14** 127 L8
Stalham St **SE16** 130 F2
Stamford Rd **N1** 126 C2
Stamford St **SE1** 125 N10
Stamp Pl **E2** 126 D5
Stanbury Rd **SE15** 130 F7
Stanfield Rd **E3** 127 J4
Stanford Rd **W8** 128 B2
Stanhope Gdns **SW7** 128 C3
Stanhope Gate **W1** 124 G10
Stanhope Ms E **SW7** 128 C3
Stanhope Ms W **SW7** 128 C3
Stanhope Pl **W2** 124 F8
Stanhope St **NW1** 125 J5
Stanhope Ter **W2** 124 D9
Stanley Cl **SW8** 129 M5
Stanley Gro **SW8** 128 G8
Stanley Rd **E15** 127 P3
Stanley St **SE8** 131 K6
Stanmer St **SW11** 128 E7
Stannard Ms **E8** 126 E1
Stannard Rd **E8** 126 E1
Stannary Pl **SE11** 129 N4
Stannary St **SE11** 129 N5
Stansfield Rd **SW9** 129 M9
Stanswood Gdns **SE5** 130 C6
Stanway St **N1** 126 C4
Stanworth St **SE1** 130 D1
Staple Inn Bldgs **WC1** 125 N7
Staple St **SE1** 130 B1
Staples Cl **SE16** 127 J10
Star St **W2** 124 E7
Starboard Way **E14** 131 L2
Starcross St **NW1** 125 J5
Station App **SE1** 129 N1
Station Ct **SW6** 128 C7
Station Pas **SE15** 130 G7
Station Rd **SE13** 131 N9
Station St **E15** 127 P2
Station Ter **SE5** 130 A7
Staunton St **SE8** 131 K5
Stave Yd Rd **SE16** 127 J10
Stayner's Rd **E1** 127 H6
Stead St **SE17** 130 B3
Stean St **E8** 126 D3
Stebondale St **E14** 131 N4
Steeles Rd **NW3** 124 F1
Steers Way **SE16** 131 J1
Stephan Cl **E8** 126 E3
Stephen St **W1** 125 K7
Stephendale Rd **SW6** 128 B8
Stephenson Way **NW1** 125 J6
Stepney Causeway **E1** 127 H8
Stepney Grn **E1** 126 G7
Stepney High St **E1** 127 H7
Stepney Way **E1** 126 F7
Sterling Gdns **SE14** 131 J5
Sternhall La **SE15** 130 E9
Sterry St **SE1** 130 B1
Stevens Av **E9** 126 G1
Stevenson Cres **SE16** 130 E4
Steward St **E1** 126 C7
Stewart St **E14** 131 N1
Stewart's Gro **SW3** 128 D3
Stewart's Rd **SW8** 129 J6
Stillington St **SW1** 129 J3
Stirling Rd **SW9** 129 L8
Stockholm Ho **E1** 126 E9
Stockholm Rd **SE16** 130 G4
Stockholm Way **E1** 126 E10
Stockwell Av **SW9** 129 M9
Stockwell Gdns **SW9** 129 M8
Stockwell Gdns Est **SW9** 129 L8
Stockwell Grn **SW9** 129 M8
Stockwell La **SW9** 129 M8
Stockwell Pk Cres **SW9** 129 M8
Stockwell Pk Est **SW9** 129 M8
Stockwell Pk Rd **SW9** 129 M7
Stockwell Pk Wk **SW9** 129 M9
Stockwell Rd **SW9** 129 M8
Stockwell St **SE10** 131 N5
Stockwell Ter **SW9** 129 M7
Stokenchurch St **SW6** 128 B7
Stone Bldgs **WC2** 125 M7
Stonecutter St **EC4** 125 P8
Stonefield St **N1** 125 N3
Stones End St **SE1** 130 A1
Stoney St **SE1** 126 B10
Stonhouse St **SW4** 129 K9
Stopes St **SE15** 130 D6
Stopford Rd **SE17** 129 P4
Store St **WC1** 125 K7
Storers Quay **E14** 131 P3
Storey's Gate **SW1** 129 K1
Stories Ms **SE5** 130 C8
Stories Rd **SE5** 130 C9
Storks Rd **SE16** 130 E2
Stormont Rd **SW11** 128 G9
Stour Rd **E3** 127 L2
Stourcliffe St **W1** 124 F8
Stowage **SE8** 131 L5
Strafford St **E14** 131 L1
Strahan Rd **E3** 127 J5
Straightsmouth **SE10** 131 N6
Straker's Rd **SE15** 130 F10
Strand **WC2** 125 L9
Stranraer Way **N1** 125 L2
Strasburg Rd **SW11** 129 H7
Stratford Cen, The **E15** 127 P2
Stratford Pl **W1** 125 H8
Stratford Rd **W8** 128 A2
Stratford Vil **NW1** 125 J2
Strath Ter **SW11** 128 E10
Strathblaine Rd **SW11** 128 D10
Strathearn Pl **W2** 124 E9
Strathnairn St **SE1** 130 E3
Strathray Gdns **NW3** 124 E1
Stratton St **W1** 125 H10
Strattondale St **E14** 131 N2
Streatham St **WC1** 125 K8
Streimer Rd **E15** 127 N4
Strickland St **SE8** 131 L8
Stroudley Wk **E3** 127 M5
Strutton Grd **SW1** 129 K2
Stuart Rd **NW6** 124 A5
Stuart Rd **SE15** 130 G10
Stuart Twr **W9** 124 C6
Stubbs Dr **SE16** 130 F4
Studd St **N1** 125 P3
Studdridge St **SW6** 128 A8
Studholme St **SE15** 130 F6
Studley Est **SW4** 129 L7
Studley Rd **SW4** 129 L7
Stukeley St **WC1** 125 L8
Stukeley St **WC2** 125 L8
Sturdy Rd **SE15** 130 F8
Sturgeon Rd **SE17** 130 A4
Sturry St **E14** 127 M8
Sturt St **N1** 126 A4
Stutfield St **E1** 126 E8
Styles Gdns **SW9** 129 P9
Sudeley St **N1** 125 P4
Sudlow Rd **SW18** 128 A10
Sugar Ho La **E15** 127 N4
Sugar Quay Wk **EC3** 126 C9
Sugden Rd **SW11** 128 G9
Sulivan Ct **SW6** 128 A9
Sulivan Rd **SW6** 128 A9
Sullivan Cl **SW11** 128 E9
Sullivan Rd **SE11** 129 N3
Sultan St **SE5** 130 A6
Summercourt Rd **E1** 126 G8
Sumner Pl **SW7** 128 D3
Sumner Rd **SE15** 130 D6
Sumner St **SE1** 126 A10
Sumpter Cl **NW3** 124 C1
Sun St **EC2** 126 B7
Sunbury La **SW11** 128 D7
Sunderland Ter **W2** 124 B8
Sunlight Sq **E2** 126 F5
Sunninghill Rd **SE13** 131 M8
Sunray Av **SE24** 130 B10
Sunset Rd **SE5** 130 A10
Surma Cl **E1** 126 F6
Surrendale Pl **W9** 124 A6
Surrey Canal Rd **SE14** 130 G5
Surrey Canal Rd **SE15** 130 G5
Surrey La **SW11** 128 E7
Surrey La Est **SW11** 128 E7
Surrey Quays Retail Cen **SE16** 131 H2
Surrey Quays Rd **SE16** 130 G2
Surrey Row **SE1** 129 P1
Surrey Sq **SE17** 130 C4
Surrey St **WC2** 125 M9
Surrey Ter **SE17** 130 C4
Surrey Water Rd **SE16** 127 H10
Susannah St **E14** 127 M8
Sussex Gdns **W2** 124 D8
Sussex Pl **NW1** 124 F5
Sussex Pl **W2** 124 D8
Sussex Sq **W2** 124 D9
Sussex St **SW1** 129 H4
Sutherland Av **W9** 124 C5
Sutherland Pl **W2** 124 A8
Sutherland Row **SW1** 129 H4
Sutherland Sq **SE17** 130 A4
Sutherland St **SW1** 129 H4
Sutherland Wk **SE17** 130 A4
Sutterton St **N7** 125 M1
Sutton Est **SW3** 128 E4
Sutton Est, The **N1** 125 P2
Sutton Row **W1** 125 K8
Sutton St **E1** 126 G8
Swain St **NW8** 124 E6
Swallow Cl **SE14** 130 G7
Swan Mead **SE1** 130 C2
Swan Rd **SE16** 130 G1
Swan St **SE1** 130 A2
Swan Wk **SW3** 128 F5
Swandon Way **SW18** 128 B10
Swanfield St **E2** 126 D5
Swaton Rd **E3** 127 L6
Sweden Gate **SE16** 131 J2
Swedenborg Gdns **E1** 126 E9
Sweeney Cres **SE1** 130 D1
Swinford Gdns **SW9** 129 P9
Swinton Pl **WC1** 125 M5
Swinton St **WC1** 125 M5
Swiss Ter **NW6** 124 D2
Sybil Phoenix Cl **SE8** 131 H4
Sycamore Av **E3** 127 K3
Sycamore Ms **SW4** 129 J9
Sydney Cl **SW3** 128 D3
Sydney Ms **SW3** 128 D3
Sydney Pl **SW7** 128 D3
Sydney St **SW3** 128 E3
Sylvan Gro **SE15** 130 F6
Sylvester Rd **E8** 126 F1
Symons St **SW3** 128 F3

## T

Tabard Gdn Est **SE1** 130 B1
Tabard St **SE1** 130 B1
Tabernacle St **EC2** 126 B6
Tachbrook Est **SW1** 129 K4
Tachbrook St **SW1** 129 J3
Tack Ms **SE4** 131 L9
Tadema Rd **SW10** 128 C6
Taeping St **E14** 131 M3
Talacre Rd **NW5** 124 G1
Talbot Rd **SE22** 130 C10
Talbot Rd **W2** 124 A8
Talbot Sq **W2** 124 D8
Talfourd Pl **SE15** 130 D7
Talfourd Rd **SE15** 130 D7
Tallis St **EC4** 125 N9
Talma Rd **SW2** 129 N10
Talwin St **E3** 127 M5
Tamworth St **SW6** 128 A5
Tanner St **SE1** 130 C1
Tanners Hill **SE8** 131 K7
Taplow **NW3** 124 D2
Taplow St **N1** 126 A4
Tapp St **E1** 126 F6
Tappesfield Rd **SE15** 130 G9
Tariff Cres **SE8** 131 K3
Tarling St **E1** 126 F8
Tarling St Est **E1** 126 G8
Tarragon Cl **SE14** 131 J6
Tarrant Pl **W1** 124 F7
Tarver Rd **SE17** 129 P4
Tarves Way **SE10** 131 M6
Tasman Rd **SW9** 129 L9
Tatham Pl **NW8** 124 D4
Tatum St **SE17** 130 B3
Taunton Pl **NW1** 124 F6
Tavern La **SW9** 129 N8
Tavistock Pl **WC1** 125 L6
Tavistock Sq **WC1** 125 K6
Tavistock St **WC2** 125 L9
Taviton St **WC1** 125 K6
Tavy Cl **SE11** 129 N4
Tawny Way **SE16** 131 H3
Taybridge Rd **SW11** 128 G9
Tayburn Cl **E14** 127 N8
Taylor Cl **SE8** 131 K5
Tayport Cl **N1** 125 L2
Teak Cl **SE16** 127 J10
Teale St **E2** 126 E4
Tedworth Sq **SW3** 128 F4
Teesdale Cl **E2** 126 F4
Teesdale St **E2** 126 F4
Teignmouth Cl **SW4** 129 K10
Telegraph Pl **E14** 131 M3
Telford Ter **SW1** 129 J5
Tell Gro **SE22** 130 D10
Templar St **SE5** 129 P8
Temple, The **EC4** 125 N9
Temple Av **EC4** 125 N9
Temple Pl **WC2** 125 M9
Temple St **E2** 126 F4
Temple W Ms **SE11** 129 P2
Templecombe Rd **E9** 126 G3
Templeton Pl **SW5** 128 A3
Tench St **E1** 126 F10
Tenison Way **SE1** 125 M10
Tennis St **SE1** 130 B1
Tennyson St **SW8** 129 H8
Tent St **E1** 126 F6
Tenterden St **W1** 125 H8
Teredo St **SE16** 131 H2
Terminus Pl **SW1** 129 H2
Terrace, The **NW6** 124 A3
Terrace Rd **E9** 126 G2
Tessa Sanderson Pl **SW8** 129 H9
Tetcott Rd **SW10** 128 C6
Teversham La **SW8** 129 L7
Teviot St **E14** 127 N7
Thackeray Rd **SW8** 129 H8
Thackeray St **W8** 128 B1
Thalia Cl **SE10** 131 P5
Thame Rd **SE16** 131 H1
Thames Av **SW10** 128 C7
Thames St **SE10** 131 M5
Thanet St **WC1** 125 L5
Thayer St **W1** 124 G7
Theatre St **SW11** 128 F9
Theberton St **N1** 125 N3
Theed St **SE1** 125 N10
Theobald's Rd **WC1** 125 M7
Thermopylae Gate **E14** 131 M3
Thessaly Rd **SW8** 129 J6
Thirleby Rd **SW1** 129 J2
Thirsk Rd **SW11** 128 G9
Thistle Gro **SW10** 128 C4
Thomas Baines Rd **SW11** 128 D9
Thomas Doyle St **SE1** 129 P2
Thomas More St **E1** 126 E9
Thomas Rd **E14** 127 K8
Thompson's Av **SE5** 130 A6
Thorburn Sq **SE1** 130 E3
Thoresby St **N1** 126 A5
Thorncroft St **SW8** 129 L6
Thorndike Cl **SW10** 128 C6
Thorndike Rd **N1** 126 A1
Thorndike St **SW1** 129 J3
Thorne Rd **SW8** 129 L6
Thorney Cres **SW11** 128 D6
Thorney St **SW1** 129 L3
Thorngate Rd **W9** 124 A6
Thornham St **SE10** 131 M5
Thornhaugh St **WC1** 125 K6
Thornhill Cres **N1** 125 M2
Thornhill Rd **N1** 125 N2
Thornhill Sq **N1** 125 M2
Thornton Pl **W1** 124 F7
Thornton St **SW9** 129 N8
Thornville St **SE8** 131 L7
Thorparch Rd **SW8** 129 K7
Thoydon Rd **E3** 127 J4
Thrale St **SE1** 126 A10
Thrawl St **E1** 126 D7
Threadneedle St **EC2** 126 B8
Three Colt St **E14** 127 K9
Three Colts La **E2** 126 F6
Three Kings Yd **W1** 125 H9
Three Mill La **E3** 127 N5
Three Quays Wk **EC3** 126 C9
Throgmorton Av **EC2** 126 B8
Throgmorton St **EC2** 126 B8
Thurland Rd **SE16** 130 E2
Thurloe Cl **SW7** 128 E2
Thurloe Pl **SW7** 128 D3
Thurloe Sq **SW7** 128 E3
Thurloe St **SW7** 128 D3
Thurlow St **SE17** 130 B4
Thurston Rd **SE13** 131 M8
Thurtle Rd **E2** 126 D3
Tibbatts Rd **E3** 127 M6
Tideway Ind Est **SW8** 129 J5
Tidey St **E3** 127 L7
Tidworth Rd **E3** 127 L6
Tileyard Rd **N7** 125 L2
Tiller Rd **E14** 131 L2
Tilney Gdns **N1** 126 B1
Tilney St **W1** 124 G10
Timber Mill Way **SW4** 129 K9
Timber Pond Rd **SE16** 131 H1
Timberland Rd **E1** 126 F8
Timothy Rd **E3** 127 K7
Tindal St **SW9** 129 P7
Tinsley Rd **E1** 126 G7
Tintagel Cres **SE22** 130 D10
Tintern St **SW4** 129 L10
Tinworth St **SE11** 129 M4
Tipthorpe Rd **SW11** 128 G9
Tisdall Pl **SE17** 130 B3
Titchfield Rd **NW8** 124 F3
Tite St **SW3** 128 F4
Tiverton St **SE1** 130 A2
Tivoli Ct **SE16** 131 K1
Tobacco Dock **E1** 126 F9
Tobin Cl **NW3** 124 E2
Toby La **E1** 127 J6
Tollet St **E1** 127 H6
Tollgate Gdns **NW6** 124 B4
Tolpuddle St **N1** 125 N4
Tomlins Gro **E3** 127 L5
Tomlinson Cl **E2** 126 D5
Tonbridge St **WC1** 125 L5
Tooley St **SE1** 126 B10
Topmast Pt **E14** 131 L1
Tor Gdns **W8** 128 A1
Torrens St **EC1** 125 N4
Torridge Gdns **SE15** 130 G10
Torrington Pl **E1** 126 E10
Torrington Pl **WC1** 125 K7
Torrington Sq **WC1** 125 K6
Tothill St **SW1** 129 K1
Tottan Ter **E1** 127 H8
Tottenham Ct Rd **W1** 125 J6
Tottenham Rd **N1** 126 C1
Tottenham St **W1** 125 J7
Totteridge Ho **SW11** 128 D8
Toulmin St **SE1** 130 A1
Toulon St **SE5** 130 A6
Tours Pas **SW11** 128 D10
Towcester Rd **E3** 127 M6
Tower 42 **EC2** 126 C8
Tower Br **E1** 126 D10
Tower Br **SE1** 126 D10
Tower Br App **E1** 126 D10
Tower Br Rd **SE1** 130 C2
Tower Br Wf **E1** 126 E10
Tower Mill Rd **SE15** 130 C6
Tower Millennium Pier **EC3** 126 C10
Tower St **WC2** 125 K8
Town Hall Rd **SW11** 128 F9
Townmead Rd **SW6** 128 C8
Townsend St **SE17** 130 B3
Townshend Est **NW8** 124 E4
Townshend Rd **NW8** 124 E3
Toynbee St **E1** 126 D7
Tradescant Rd **SW8** 129 L6
Trafalgar Av **SE15** 130 D4
Trafalgar Gdns **E1** 127 H7
Trafalgar Gro **SE10** 131 P5
Trafalgar Ms **E9** 127 K1
Trafalgar Rd **SE10** 131 P5
Trafalgar Sq **SW1** 125 K10
Trafalgar Sq **WC2** 125 K10
Trafalgar St **SE17** 130 B4
Trafalgar Way **E14** 127 N10
Trahorn Cl **E1** 126 E6
Transept St **NW1** 124 E7
Transom Sq **E14** 131 M3
Tranton Rd **SE16** 130 E2
Treadway St **E2** 126 F4
Treaty St **N1** 125 M3
Trebovir Rd **SW5** 128 A4
Treby St **E3** 127 K6
Tredegar Rd **E3** 127 K4
Tredegar Sq **E3** 127 K5
Tredegar Ter **E3** 127 K5
Trederwen Rd **E8** 126 E3
Tregarvon Rd **SW11** 128 G10
Trego Rd **E9** 127 L2
Tregothnan Rd **SW9** 129 L9
Tregunter Rd **SW10** 128 C5
Trelawney Est **E9** 126 G1
Tremadoc Rd **SW4** 129 K10
Tremaine Cl **SE4** 131 L8
Trenchard St **SE10** 131 P4
Trenchold St **SW8** 129 L5
Tresco Rd **SE15** 130 F10
Tresham Cres **NW8** 124 E6
Tressillian Cres **SE4** 131 L9
Tressillian Rd **SE4** 131 K10
Trevithick St **SE8** 131 L4
Trevor Pl **SW7** 128 E1
Trevor Sq **SW7** 128 F1
Trevor St **SW7** 128 E1
Triangle Pl **SW4** 129 K10
Triangle Rd **E8** 126 F3
Trident St **SE16** 131 H3
Trigon Rd **SW8** 129 M6
Trim St **SE14** 131 K5
Trinidad St **E14** 127 K9
Trinity Ch Sq **SE1** 130 A2
Trinity Cl **E8** 126 D1
Trinity Cl **SE13** 131 P10
Trinity Gdns **SW9** 129 M10
Trinity Gro **SE10** 131 N7
Trinity Sq **EC3** 126 C9
Trinity St **SE1** 130 A1
Trinity Wk **NW3** 124 C1
Triton Sq **NW1** 125 J6
Trott St **SW11** 128 E7
Troutbeck Rd **SE14** 131 J7
Trowbridge Rd **E9** 127 K1
Troy Town **SE15** 130 E9
Trundleys Rd **SE8** 131 H4
Trundleys Ter **SE8** 131 H3
Truro St **NW5** 124 G1
Tryon Cres **E9** 126 G3
Tryon St **SW3** 128 F4
Tudor Gro **E9** 126 G2
Tudor Rd **E9** 126 F3
Tudor St **EC4** 125 N9
Tufton St **SW1** 129 K2
Tuilerie St **E2** 126 E4
Tunnel Av **SE10** 131 P1
Tunstall Rd **SW9** 129 M10
Turenne Cl **SW18** 128 C10
Turin St **E2** 126 E5
Turks Row **SW3** 128 F4
Turner Cl **SW9** 129 P7
Turner St **E1** 126 F7
Turners Rd **E3** 127 K7
Turnmill St **EC1** 125 N6
Turnpike Ho **EC1** 125 P5
Turnpin La **SE10** 131 N5
Turret Gro **SW4** 129 J9
Tustin Est **SE15** 130 G5
Twelvetrees Cres **E3** 127 N6
Twine Ct **E1** 126 G9
Twyford St **N1** 125 M3
Tyburn Way **W1** 124 F9
Tyers Est **SE1** 130 C1
Tyers St **SE11** 129 M4
Tyers Ter **SE11** 129 M4
Tyler Cl **E2** 126 D4
Tyndale Ct **E14** 131 M4
Tyneham Rd **SW11** 128 G8
Tynemouth St **SW6** 128 C8
Type St **E2** 127 H4
Tyrawley Rd **SW6** 128 B7
Tyrrell Rd **SE22** 130 E10
Tyrwhitt Rd **SE4** 131 L9
Tyssen Pas **E8** 126 D1
Tyssen St **E8** 126 D1

## U

Uamvar St **E14** 127 M7
Ufford St **SE1** 129 N1
Ufton Gro **N1** 126 B2
Ufton Rd **N1** 126 B2
Undercliff Rd **SE13** 131 L9
Undershaft **EC3** 126 C8
Underwood Rd **E1** 126 E6
Underwood Row **N1** 126 A5
Underwood St **N1** 126 A5
Undine Rd **E14** 131 M3
Union Gro **SW8** 129 K8
Union Rd **SW4** 129 K8
Union Rd **SW8** 129 K8
Union Sq **N1** 126 A3
Union St **E15** 127 N3
Union St **SE1** 125 P10
University St **WC1** 125 J6
Unwin Cl **SE15** 130 E5
Upcerne Rd **SW10** 128 C6
Upper Bk St **E14** 127 M10
Upper Belgrave St **SW1** 128 G2
Upper Berkeley St **W1** 124 F8
Upper Brockley Rd **SE4** 131 K8
Upper Brook St **W1** 124 G9
Upper Cheyne Row **SW3** 128 E5
Upper Grosvenor St **W1** 124 G9
Upper Grd **SE1** 125 N10
Upper Marsh **SE1** 129 M2
Upper Montagu St **W1** 124 F7
Upper N St **E14** 127 L7
Upper Phillimore Gdns **W8** 128 A1
Upper St **N1** 125 N4
Upper Tachbrook St **SW1** 129 J3
Upper Thames St **EC4** 126 A9
Upper Wimpole St **W1** 124 G7
Upper Woburn Pl **WC1** 125 K5
Upstall St **SE5** 129 P7
Urlwin St **SE5** 130 A5
Urlwin Wk **SW9** 129 N8
Ursula St **SW11** 128 E7
Usborne Ms **SW8** 129 M6
Usher Rd **E3** 127 K4
Usk Rd **SW11** 128 C10
Usk St **E2** 127 H5
Uverdale Rd **SW10** 128 C6
Uxbridge St **W8** 124 A10

## V

Vale, The **SW3** 128 D5
Vale Ct **W9** 124 C5
Vale Royal **N7** 125 L2
Valentine Pl **SE1** 129 P1
Valentine Rd **E9** 127 H1
Valentine Row **SE1** 129 P1
Valette St **E9** 126 F1
Vallance Rd **E1** 126 E6
Vallance Rd **E2** 126 E5
Valmar Rd **SE5** 130 A7
Vandon St **SW1** 129 J2
Vanguard St **SE8** 131 L7
Vansittart St **SE14** 131 J6

Van - Zet

Vanston Pl **SW6** 128 A6
Varcoe Rd **SE16** 130 F4
Varden St **E1** 126 F8
Vardens Rd **SW11** 128 D10
Varndell St **NW1** 125 J5
Vassall Rd **SW9** 129 N6
Vauban Est **SE16** 130 D2
Vauban St **SE16** 130 D2
Vaughan Rd **SE5** 130 A8
Vaughan St **SE16** 131 K1
Vaughan Way **E1** 126 E9
Vauxhall Br **SE1** 129 L4
Vauxhall Br **SW1** 129 L4
Vauxhall Br Rd **SW1** 129 J3
Vauxhall Gdns Est **SE11** 129 M4
Vauxhall Gro **SW8** 129 L5
Vauxhall St **SE11** 129 M4
Vauxhall Wk **SE11** 129 M4
Vawdrey Cl **E1** 126 G6
Veda Rd **SE13** 131 L10
Velletri Ho **E2** 127 H4
Venables St **NW8** 124 D6
Venetian Rd **SE5** 130 A8
Venn St **SW4** 129 J10
Ventnor Rd **SE14** 131 H6
Venue St **E14** 127 N7
Vere St **W1** 125 H8
Verney Rd **SE16** 130 E5
Verney Way **SE16** 130 F4
Vernon Pl **WC1** 125 L7
Vernon Ri **WC1** 125 M5
Vernon Rd **E3** 127 K4
Vesta Rd **SE4** 131 J8
Vestry Ms **SE5** 130 C7
Vestry Rd **SE5** 130 C7
Vestry St **N1** 126 B5
Viaduct St **E2** 126 F5
Vian St **SE13** 131 M9
Vicarage Cres **SW11** 128 D7
Vicarage Gdns **W8** 124 A10
Vicarage Gate **W8** 128 B1
Vicarage Gro **SE5** 130 B7
Vicars Hill **SE13** 131 M10
Viceroy Rd **SW8** 129 L7
Victoria Embk **EC4** 125 M9
Victoria Embk **SW1** 129 L1
Victoria Embk **WC2** 129 L1
Victoria Gdns **W11** 124 A10
Victoria Gro **W8** 128 C2
Victoria Ms **NW6** 124 A3
Victoria Pk **E9** 127 J2
Victoria Pk Rd **E9** 126 G3
Victoria Pk Sq **E2** 126 G5
Victoria Pl **SW1** 129 H3
Victoria Ri **SW4** 129 H9
Victoria Rd **W8** 128 C2
Victoria Sta **SW1** 129 H3
Victoria St **SW1** 129 J2
Victoria Wf **E14** 127 J9
Victory Pl **SE17** 130 A3
Victory Way **SE16** 131 J1
Vigo St **W1** 125 J9
Viking Ct **SW6** 128 A5
Villa Rd **SW9** 129 N9
Villa St **SE17** 130 B4
Villiers St **WC2** 125 L9
Vince St **EC1** 126 B5
Vincent Cl **SE16** 131 J1
Vincent Sq **SW1** 129 J3
Vincent St **SW1** 129 K3
Vincent Ter **N1** 125 P4
Vine St Br **EC1** 125 N6
Viney Rd **SE13** 131 M9
Vineyard Wk **EC1** 125 N6
Vining St **SW9** 129 N10
Violet Hill **NW8** 124 C4
Violet Rd **E3** 127 M6
Virgil St **SE1** 129 M2
Virginia Rd **E2** 126 D5
Virginia St **E1** 126 E9
Vivian Rd **E3** 127 J4
Voltaire Rd **SW4** 129 K9
Voss St **E2** 126 E5
Vulcan Rd **SE4** 131 K8
Vulcan Ter **SE4** 131 K8
Vulcan Way **N7** 125 M1
Vyner St **E2** 126 F3

## W

Wadding St **SE17** 130 B3
Waddington St **E15** 127 P1
Wades Pl **E14** 127 M9
Wadeson St **E2** 126 F4
Wadham Gdns **NW3** 124 E3
Wadhurst Rd **SW8** 129 J7
Wager St **E3** 127 K6
Waghorn St **SE15** 130 E9
Wagner St **SE15** 130 G6
Waite St **SE15** 130 D5
Wakefield St **WC1** 125 L5
Wakeham St **N1** 126 B1
Wakeling St **E14** 127 J8
Wakley St **EC1** 125 P5
Walberswick St **SW8** 129 L6
Walbrook **EC4** 126 B9
Walcot Sq **SE11** 129 N3
Walden St **E1** 126 F8
Walerand Rd **SE13** 131 N8
Wales Cl **SE15** 130 F6
Waley St **E1** 127 H7
Walham Gro **SW6** 128 A6
Wall St **N1** 126 B1
Wallace Rd **N1** 126 A1
Wallbutton Rd **SE4** 131 J8
Waller Rd **SE14** 131 H7
Wallgrave Rd **SW5** 128 B3
Wallis Cl **SW11** 128 D9
Wallis Rd **E9** 127 K1
Wallwood St **E14** 127 K7
Walnut Tree Wk **SE11** 129 N3
Walpole St **SW3** 128 F4
Walsham Rd **SE14** 131 H8
Walter St **E2** 127 H5
Walter Ter **E1** 127 H8
Walton Cl **SW8** 129 L6
Walton Pl **SW3** 128 F2
Walton St **SW3** 128 E3
Walworth Pl **SE17** 130 A4
Walworth Rd **SE1** 130 A3
Walworth Rd **SE17** 130 A3
Wandon Rd **SW6** 128 B6
Wandsworth Br **SW6** 128 B9
Wandsworth Br **SW18** 128 B9
Wandsworth Br Rd **SW6** 128 B7
Wandsworth Rd **SW8** 129 K6
Wanless Rd **SE24** 130 A9
Wanley Rd **SE5** 130 B10
Wansbeck Rd **E3** 127 K2
Wansbeck Rd **E9** 127 K2
Wansey St **SE17** 130 A3
Wapping High St **E1** 126 E10
Wapping La **E1** 126 F9
Wapping Wall **E1** 126 G10
Warburton Rd **E8** 126 F2
Ward Rd **E15** 127 P3
Wardalls Gro **SE14** 130 G6
Warden Rd **NW5** 124 G1
Wardour St **W1** 125 K9
Warham St **SE5** 129 P6
Warley St **E2** 127 H5
Warlock Rd **W9** 124 A6
Warndon St **SE16** 131 H3
Warneford St **E9** 126 F3
Warner Pl **E2** 126 E4
Warner Rd **SE5** 130 A7
Warner St **EC1** 125 N6
Warren St **W1** 125 J6
Warriner Gdns **SW11** 128 F7
Warrington Cres **W9** 124 C6
Warton Rd **E15** 127 N2
Warwick Av **W2** 124 C6
Warwick Av **W9** 124 C6
Warwick Bldg **SW8** 129 H5
Warwick Ct **SE15** 130 E8
Warwick Cres **W2** 124 C7
Warwick Est **W2** 124 B7
Warwick Ho St **SW1** 125 K10
Warwick La **EC4** 125 P8
Warwick Pl **W9** 124 C7
Warwick Pl N **SW1** 129 J3
Warwick Row **SW1** 129 H2
Warwick Sq **SW1** 129 J4
Warwick Sq Ms **SW1** 129 J3
Warwick St **W1** 125 J9
Warwick Way **SW1** 129 J3
Warwickshire Path **SE8** 131 K6
Washington Cl **E3** 127 M5
Wat Tyler Rd **SE3** 131 N8
Wat Tyler Rd **SE10** 131 N8
Water Gdns, The **W2** 124 E8
Water La **SE14** 130 G6
Water Ms **SE15** 130 G10
Waterford Rd **SW6** 128 B7
Watergate St **SE8** 131 L5
Waterloo Br **SE1** 125 M9
Waterloo Br **WC2** 125 M9
Waterloo Est **E2** 126 G4
Waterloo Gdns **E2** 126 G4
Waterloo Pl **SW1** 125 K10
Waterloo Rd **SE1** 129 N1
Waterloo Sta **SE1** 129 N1
Waterloo Ter **N1** 125 P2
Waterman Way **E1** 126 F10
Watermans Wk **SE16** 131 J2
Watermeadow La **SW6** 128 C8
Waterside Cl **E3** 127 K3
Waterside Pt **SW11** 128 E6
Waterside Twr **SW6** 128 C7
Waterson St **E2** 126 C5
Waterview Ho **E14** 127 J7
Watkinson Rd **N7** 125 M1
Watling St **EC4** 126 A8
Watney St **E1** 126 F8
Watson's St **SE8** 131 L6
Watts Gro **E3** 127 M7
Watts St **E1** 126 F10
Watts St **SE15** 130 D7
Waveney Av **SE15** 130 F10
Waverley Pl **NW8** 124 D4
Waverley Wk **W2** 124 A7
Waverton Ho **E3** 127 K3
Waverton St **W1** 124 G10
Wayford St **SW11** 128 E8
Wayman Ct **E8** 126 F1
Wear Pl **E2** 126 F5
Weardale Rd **SE13** 131 P10
Wearside Rd **SE13** 131 M10
Weatherley Cl **E3** 127 K7
Weaver St **E1** 126 E6
Weavers Ter **SW6** 128 A5
Weavers Way **NW1** 125 K3
Webb St **SE1** 130 C2
Webber Row **SE1** 129 P1
Webber St **SE1** 129 N1
Webster Rd **SE16** 130 E2
Weighhouse St **W1** 124 G8
Weir's Pas **NW1** 125 K5
Welbeck St **W1** 124 G7
Welbeck Way **W1** 125 H8
Welby St **SE5** 129 P7
Well St **E9** 126 F2
Welland St **SE10** 131 N5
Wellclose Sq **E1** 126 E9
Wellesley Ct **W9** 124 C5
Wellesley St **E1** 127 H7
Wellesley Ter **N1** 126 A5
Wellington Pl **NW8** 124 E4
Wellington Rd **NW8** 124 D4
Wellington Row **E2** 126 D5
Wellington Sq **SW3** 128 F4
Wellington St **WC2** 125 L9
Wellington Ter **E1** 126 F10
Wellington Way **E3** 127 L5
Wells Ri **NW8** 124 F3
Wells St **W1** 125 J8
Wells Way **SE5** 130 B5
Wells Way **SW7** 128 D2
Welmar Ms **SW4** 129 K10
Welsford St **SE1** 130 E4
Wendle Ct **SW8** 129 L5
Wendon St **E3** 127 K3
Wendover **SE17** 130 C4
Wenlock Rd **N1** 126 A4
Wenlock St **N1** 126 A4
Wennington Rd **E3** 127 H4
Wentworth Cres **SE15** 130 E6
Wentworth St **E1** 126 D8
Werrington St **NW1** 125 J4
Wesley Cl **SE17** 129 P3
Wessex St **E2** 126 G5
West Arbour St **E1** 127 H8
West Carriage Dr **W2** 124 D9
West Eaton Pl **SW1** 128 G3
West End La **NW6** 124 A2
West Gdns **E1** 126 F9
West Gro **SE10** 131 N7
West Halkin St **SW1** 128 G2
West Hampstead Ms **NW6** 124 B1
West India Av **E14** 127 L10
West India Dock Rd **E14** 127 K8
West La **SE16** 130 F1
West One Shop Cen **W1** 125 H8
West Rd **SW3** 128 F5
West Smithfield **EC1** 125 P7
West Sq **SE11** 129 P2
West St **E2** 126 F4
West Tenter St **E1** 126 D8
Westbourne Br **W2** 124 C7
Westbourne Cres **W2** 124 D9
Westbourne Gdns **W2** 124 B8
Westbourne Gro **W2** 124 A8
Westbourne Gro **W11** 124 A8
Westbourne Gro Ter **W2** 124 B8
Westbourne Pk Rd **W2** 124 A7
Westbourne Pk Vil **W2** 124 A7
Westbourne Rd **N7** 125 N1
Westbourne St **W2** 124 D9
Westbourne Ter **W2** 124 D8
Westbourne Ter Ms **W2** 124 C8
Westbourne Ter Rd **W2** 124 C7
Westbridge Rd **SW11** 128 D7
Westbury St **SW8** 129 J8
Westcott Rd **SE17** 129 P5
Western Rd **SW9** 129 N9
Westferry Circ **E14** 127 K10
Westferry Rd **E14** 127 L10
Westfield Cl **SW10** 128 C6
Westfield Way **E1** 127 J5
Westgate St **E8** 126 F3
Westgate Ter **SW10** 128 B4
Westgrove La **SE10** 131 N7
Westminster Br **SE1** 129 L1
Westminster Br **SW1** 129 L1
Westminster Br Rd **SE1** 129 N2
Westminster Gdns **SW1** 129 K3
Westmoreland Pl **SW1** 129 H4
Westmoreland Rd **SE17** 130 A5
Westmoreland St **W1** 124 G7
Westmoreland Ter **SW1** 129 H4
Westmoreland Wk **SE17** 130 B5
Weston Ri **WC1** 125 M4
Weston St **SE1** 130 B2
Westport St **E1** 127 H8
Westway **W2** 124 A7
Westway **W9** 124 A7
Wetherby Gdns **SW5** 128 C3
Wetherby Pl **SW7** 128 C3
Wetherell Rd **E9** 127 H3
Weybridge Pt **SW11** 128 G8
Weymouth Ms **W1** 125 H7
Weymouth St **W1** 125 H7
Weymouth Ter **E2** 126 D4
Wharf Pl **E2** 126 E3
Wharf Rd **N1** 126 A4
Wharf Rd (King's Cross) **N1** 125 L4
Wharfdale Rd **N1** 125 L4
Wharfedale St **SW10** 128 B4
Wharton St **WC1** 125 M5
Wheat Sheaf Cl **E14** 131 M3
Wheatsheaf La **SW8** 129 L6
Wheelwright St **N7** 125 M2
Wheler St **E1** 126 D6
Whidborne St **WC1** 125 L5
Whiskin St **EC1** 125 P5
Whistlers Av **SW11** 128 D6
Whiston Rd **E2** 126 D4
Whitbread Rd **SE4** 131 J10
Whitburn Rd **SE13** 131 M10
Whitcher Cl **SE14** 131 J5
Whitcomb St **WC2** 125 K9
White Ch La **E1** 126 E8
White Hart St **SE11** 129 N4
White Horse La **E1** 127 H6
White Horse Rd **E1** 127 J8
White Horse St **W1** 125 H10
White Lion Hill **EC4** 125 P9
White Lion St **N1** 125 N4
White Post La **E9** 127 K2
White Post La **SE13** 131 L9
White Post St **SE15** 130 G6
Whiteadder Way **E14** 131 M3
Whitear Wk **E15** 127 P1
Whitechapel High St **E1** 126 D8
Whitechapel Rd **E1** 126 E8
Whitecross St **EC1** 126 A6
Whitefriars St **EC4** 125 N8
Whitehall **SW1** 125 L10
Whitehall Ct **SW1** 125 L10
Whitehall Pl **SW1** 125 L10
Whitehead's Gro **SW3** 128 E4
Whiteleys Shop Cen **W2** 124 B8
Whites Grds **SE1** 130 C1
White's Row **E1** 126 D7
Whitethorn St **E3** 127 L6
Whitfield Rd **SE3** 131 P7
Whitfield St **W1** 125 K7
Whitgift St **SE11** 129 M3
Whitmore Est **N1** 126 C3
Whitmore Rd **N1** 126 C3
Whittaker St **SW1** 128 G3
Whitton Wk **E3** 127 L4
Whorlton Rd **SE15** 130 F9
Wick La **E3** 127 L4
Wick Rd **E9** 127 H1
Wickersley Rd **SW11** 128 G8
Wickford St **E1** 126 G6
Wickham Cl **E1** 126 G7
Wickham Gdns **SE4** 131 K9
Wickham Ms **SE4** 131 K8
Wickham Rd **SE4** 131 K10
Wickham St **SE11** 129 M4
Wicklow St **WC1** 125 M5
Wickwood St **SE5** 129 P8
Widdin St **E15** 127 P2
Widley Rd **W9** 124 A5
Wigmore Pl **W1** 125 H8
Wigmore St **W1** 124 G8
Wilbraham Pl **SW1** 128 F3
Wilcox Cl **SW8** 129 L6
Wilcox Rd **SW8** 129 L6
Wild Ct **WC2** 125 M8
Wild Goose Dr **SE14** 130 G7
Wild St **WC2** 125 L8
Wilde Cl **E8** 126 E3
Wild's Rents **SE1** 130 C2
Wilfred St **SW1** 129 J2
Wilkes St **E1** 126 D7
Wilkin St **NW5** 125 H1
Wilkinson St **SW8** 129 M6
Willard St **SW8** 129 H9
Willes Rd **NW5** 125 H1
William Bonney Est **SW4** 129 K10
William Cl **SE13** 131 N8
William IV St **WC2** 125 L9
William Morris Way **SW6** 128 C9
William Rd **NW1** 125 H5
William St **SW1** 128 F1
Williams Bldgs **E2** 126 G6
Willington Rd **SW9** 129 L9
Willis St **E14** 127 M8
Willoughby Pas **E14** 127 L10
Willow Br Rd **N1** 126 A1
Willow Pl **SW1** 129 J3
Willow St **EC2** 126 C6
Willow Wk **SE1** 130 C3
Willowbrook Rd **SE15** 130 D5
Wilman Gro **E8** 126 E2
Wilmcote Ho **W2** 124 A7
Wilmer Gdns **N1** 126 C3
Wilmer Lea Cl **E15** 127 N2
Wilmington Sq **WC1** 125 N5
Wilmington St **WC1** 125 N5
Wilmot Cl **SE15** 130 E6
Wilmot Pl **NW1** 125 J2
Wilmot St **E2** 126 F6
Wilshaw St **SE14** 131 L7
Wilson Gro **SE16** 130 F1
Wilson Rd **SE5** 130 C7
Wilson St **EC2** 126 B7
Wilton Cres **SW1** 128 G1
Wilton Ms **SW1** 128 G2
Wilton Pl **SW1** 128 G1
Wilton Rd **SW1** 129 H2
Wilton Row **SW1** 128 G1
Wilton Sq **N1** 126 B3
Wilton St **SW1** 129 H2
Wilton Ter **SW1** 128 G2
Wilton Vil **N1** 126 B3
Wilton Way **E8** 126 E1
Wiltshire Rd **SW9** 129 N9
Wiltshire Row **N1** 126 B3
Wimbolt St **E2** 126 E5
Wimbourne St **N1** 126 B4
Wimpole Ms **W1** 125 H7
Wimpole St **W1** 125 H8
Winans Wk **SW9** 129 N8
Winchester Cl **SE17** 129 P3
Winchester Rd **NW3** 124 D2
Winchester Sq **SE1** 126 B10
Winchester St **SW1** 129 H4
Winchester Wk **SE1** 126 B10
Wincott St **SE11** 129 N3
Winders Rd **SW11** 128 E8
Windlass Pl **SE8** 131 J3
Windmill Cl **SE13** 131 N8
Windmill La **E15** 127 P1
Windmill Row **SE11** 129 N4
Windmill St **W1** 125 K7
Windmill Wk **SE1** 125 N10
Windrose Cl **SE16** 131 H1
Windsock Cl **SE16** 131 K3
Windsor Gdns **W9** 124 A7
Windsor St **N1** 125 P3
Windsor Ter **N1** 126 A5
Windsor Wk **SE5** 130 B8
Wine Cl **E1** 126 G9
Winford Ho **E3** 127 K2
Winforton St **SE10** 131 N7
Wingfield St **SE15** 130 E9
Wingmore Rd **SE24** 130 A9
Winifred Gro **SW11** 128 F10
Winkley St **E2** 126 F4
Winsland St **W2** 124 D8
Winsley St **W1** 125 J8
Winslow **SE17** 130 C4
Winstanley Est **SW11** 128 D9
Winstanley Rd **SW11** 128 D9
Winterton Ho **E1** 126 F8
Winthrop St **E1** 126 F7
Wise Rd **E15** 127 P3
Wisteria Rd **SE13** 131 P10
Witan St **E2** 126 F5
Wivenhoe Cl **SE15** 130 F9
Wixs La **SW4** 129 H10
Woburn Pl **WC1** 125 K6
Woburn Sq **WC1** 125 K6
Woburn Wk **WC1** 125 K5
Wodeham Gdns **E1** 126 E7
Wodehouse Av **SE5** 130 D7
Wolfe Cres **SE16** 131 H1
Wolftencroft Cl **SW11** 128 D9
Wolseley St **SE1** 130 D1
Wolsey Ms **NW5** 125 J1
Wood Cl **E2** 126 E6
Wood St **EC2** 126 A8
Wood Wf **SE10** 131 M5
Woodbridge St **EC1** 125 P6
Woodchester Sq **W2** 124 B7
Woodchurch Rd **NW6** 124 A2
Woodfall St **SW3** 128 F4
Woodfarrs **SE5** 130 B10
Woodhouse Cl **SE22** 130 E10
Woodland Cres **SE16** 131 H1
Woodpecker Rd **SE14** 131 J5
Woods Ms **W1** 124 F9
Woods Rd **SE15** 130 F7
Woodseer St **E1** 126 D7
Woodstock Ter **E14** 127 M9
Wooler St **SE17** 130 B4
Woolmore St **E14** 127 N9
Woolneigh St **SW6** 128 B9
Woolstaplers Way **SE16** 130 E3
Wooster Gdns **E14** 127 P8
Wootton St **SE1** 125 N10
Worfield St **SW11** 128 E6
Worgan St **SE11** 129 M4
Worgan St **SE16** 131 H2
World's End Est **SW10** 128 C6
Worlingham Rd **SE22** 130 D10
Wormwood St **EC2** 126 C8
Woronzow Rd **NW8** 124 D3
Worship St **EC2** 126 B6
Wotton Rd **SE8** 131 K5
Wren Rd **SE5** 130 B7
Wren St **WC1** 125 M6
Wrexham Rd **E3** 127 L4
Wrigglesworth St **SE14** 131 H6
Wrights Cl **SE13** 131 P10
Wrights La **W8** 128 B1
Wrights Rd **E3** 127 K4
Wroxton Rd **SE15** 130 F8
Wyatt Cl **SE16** 131 K1
Wycliffe Rd **SW11** 128 G8
Wye St **SW11** 128 D8
Wyke Rd **E3** 127 L2
Wyllen Cl **E1** 126 G6
Wymering Rd **W9** 124 A5
Wynan Rd **E14** 131 M4
Wyndham Est **SE5** 130 A6
Wyndham Pl **W1** 124 F7
Wyndham Rd **SE5** 129 P6
Wyndham St **W1** 124 F7
Wynford Rd **N1** 125 M4
Wynne Rd **SW9** 129 N8
Wynnstay Gdns **W8** 128 A2
Wynter St **SW11** 128 C10
Wynyard Ter **SE11** 129 M4
Wyvil Rd **SW8** 129 L5
Wyvis St **E14** 127 M7

## Y

Yabsley St **E14** 127 N10
Yalding Rd **SE16** 130 E2
Yardley St **WC1** 125 N5
Yeate St **N1** 126 B2
Yelverton Rd **SW11** 128 D8
Yeo St **E3** 127 M7
Yeoman St **SE8** 131 J3
Yeoman's Row **SW3** 128 E2
York Br **NW1** 124 G6
York Gate **NW1** 124 G6
York Gro **SE15** 130 G7
York Ho Pl **W8** 128 B1
York Pl **SW11** 128 D9
York Rd **SE1** 129 M1
York Rd **SW11** 128 C10
York Rd **SW18** 128 C10
York Sq **E14** 127 J8
York St **W1** 124 F7
York Ter E **NW1** 124 G6
York Ter W **NW1** 124 G6
York Way **N1** 125 L3
York Way **N7** 125 K1
York Way Ct **N1** 125 L3
Yorkshire Rd **E14** 127 J8
Yorkton St **E2** 126 E4
Young St **W8** 128 B1

## Z

Zampa Rd **SE16** 130 G4
Zealand Rd **E3** 127 J4
Zenoria St **SE22** 130 D10
Zetland St **E14** 127 M7

# INDEX TO GREAT BRITAIN

## Administrative area abbreviations

| Abbreviation | Area |
|---|---|
| *Aber.* | Aberdeenshire |
| *Arg. & B.* | Argyll & Bute |
| *B'burn.* | Blackburn with Darwen |
| *B'pool* | Blackpool |
| *B. & H.* | Brighton & Hove |
| *B. & N.E.Som.* | Bath & North East Somerset |
| *B.Gwent* | Blaenau Gwent |
| *Bed.* | Bedford |
| *Bourne.* | Bournemouth |
| *Brack.F.* | Bracknell Forest |
| *Bucks.* | Buckinghamshire |
| *Caerp.* | Caerphilly |
| *Cambs.* | Cambridgeshire |
| *Carmar.* | Carmarthenshire |
| *Cen.Beds.* | Central Bedfordshire |
| *Cere.* | Ceredigion |
| *Chan.I.* | Channel Islands |
| *Ches.E.* | Cheshire East |
| *Ches.W. & C.* | Cheshire West & Chester |
| *Cornw.* | Cornwall |
| *Cumb.* | Cumbria |
| *D. & G.* | Dumfries & Galloway |
| *Darl.* | Darlington |
| *Denb.* | Denbighshire |
| *Derbys.* | Derbyshire |
| *Dur.* | Durham |
| *E.Ayr.* | East Ayrshire |
| *E.Dun.* | East Dunbartonshire |
| *E.Loth.* | East Lothian |
| *E.Renf.* | East Renfrewshire |
| *E.Riding* | East Riding of Yorkshire |
| *E.Suss.* | East Sussex |
| *Edin.* | Edinburgh |
| *Falk.* | Falkirk |
| *Flints.* | Flintshire |
| *Glas.* | Glasgow |
| *Glos.* | Gloucestershire |
| *Gt.Lon.* | Greater London |
| *Gt.Man.* | Greater Manchester |
| *Gwyn.* | Gwynedd |
| *Hants.* | Hampshire |
| *Hart.* | Hartlepool |
| *Here.* | Herefordshire |
| *Herts.* | Hertfordshire |
| *High.* | Highland |
| *Hull* | Kingston upon Hull |
| *I.o.A.* | Isle of Anglesey |
| *I.o.M.* | Isle of Man |
| *I.o.S.* | Isles of Scilly |
| *I.o.W.* | Isle of Wight |
| *Inclyde* | Inverclyde |
| *Lancs.* | Lancashire |
| *Leic.* | Leicester |
| *Leics.* | Leicestershire |
| *Lincs.* | Lincolnshire |
| *M.K.* | Milton Keynes |
| *M.Tyd.* | Merthyr Tydfil |
| *Med.* | Medway |
| *Mersey.* | Merseyside |
| *Middbro.* | Middlesbrough |
| *Midloth.* | Midlothian |
| *Mon.* | Monmouthshire |
| *N.Ayr.* | North Ayrshire |
| *N.E.Lincs.* | North East Lincolnshire |
| *N.Lan.* | North Lanarkshire |
| *N.Lincs.* | North Lincolnshire |
| *N.P.T.* | Neath Port Talbot |
| *N.Som.* | North Somerset |
| *N.Yorks.* | North Yorkshire |
| *Norf.* | Norfolk |
| *Northants.* | Northamptonshire |
| *Northumb.* | Northumberland |
| *Nott.* | Nottingham |
| *Notts.* | Nottinghamshire |
| *Ork.* | Orkney |
| *Oxon.* | Oxfordshire |
| *P. & K.* | Perth & Kinross |
| *Pembs.* | Pembrokeshire |
| *Peter.* | Peterborough |
| *Plym.* | Plymouth |
| *Ports.* | Portsmouth |
| *R. & C.* | Redcar & Cleveland |
| *R.C.T.* | Rhondda Cynon Taff |
| *Read.* | Reading |
| *Renf.* | Renfrewshire |
| *Rut.* | Rutland |
| *S'end* | Southend |
| *S'ham.* | Southampton |
| *S.Ayr.* | South Ayrshire |
| *S.Glos.* | South Gloucestershire |
| *S.Lan.* | South Lanarkshire |
| *S.Yorks.* | South Yorkshire |
| *Sc.Bord.* | Scottish Borders |
| *Shet.* | Shetland |
| *Shrop.* | Shropshire |
| *Slo.* | Slough |
| *Som.* | Somerset |
| *Staffs.* | Staffordshire |
| *Stir.* | Stirling |
| *Stock.* | Stockton-on-Tees |
| *Stoke* | Stoke-on-Trent |
| *Suff.* | Suffolk |
| *Surr.* | Surrey |
| *Swan.* | Swansea |
| *Swin.* | Swindon |
| *T. & W.* | Tyne & Wear |
| *Tel. & W.* | Telford & Wrekin |
| *Thur.* | Thurrock |
| *V. of Glam.* | Vale of Glamorgan |
| *W'ham* | Wokingham |
| *W. & M.* | Windsor & Maidenhead |
| *W.Berks.* | West Berkshire |
| *W.Dun.* | West Dunbartonshire |
| *W.Isles* | Western Isles (Na h-Eileanan an Iar) |
| *W.Loth.* | West Lothian |
| *W.Mid.* | West Midlands |
| *W.Suss.* | West Sussex |
| *W.Yorks.* | West Yorkshire |
| *Warks.* | Warwickshire |
| *Warr.* | Warrington |
| *Wilts.* | Wiltshire |
| *Worcs.* | Worcestershire |
| *Wrex.* | Wrexham |

## Notes

This index reads in the sequence: Place Name / Postal District / Map Page Number / Grid Reference.

Example: Bishop's Cleeve **GL52** **29** J6

Where there is more than one place with the same name, the index reads in the sequence: Place Name / Administrative Area / Postal District / Map Page Number / Grid Reference.

Example: Prestbury, *Ches.* **SK10** **49** H5
Prestbury, *Glos.* **GL52** **29** J6

Entries in the index shown in **BOLD CAPITALS** indicate the principal post town within a postcode area.
Entries in the index shown in **bold** indicate other post towns.

Example: **GLOUCESTER GL** **29 H7**
Example: **Cheltenham GL50** **29 J6**

## A


Ab Kettleby **LE14** 42 A3
Ab Lench **WR10** 30 B3
Abbas Combe **BA8** 9 G2
Abberley **WR6** 29 G2
Abberley Common **WR6** 29 G2
Abberton *Essex* **CO5** 34 E7
Abberton *Worcs.* **WR10** 29 J3
Abberwick **NE66** 71 G2
Abbess Roding **CM5** 33 J7
Abbey Dore **HR2** 28 C5
Abbey Hulton **ST2** 40 B1
Abbey St. Bathans **TD11** 77 F4
Abbey Town **CA7** 60 C1
Abbey Village **PR6** 56 B7
Abbey Wood **SE2** 23 H4
Abbeycwmhir **LD1** 27 K1
Abbeydale **S7** 51 F4
Abbeystead **LA2** 55 J4
Abbotrule **TD9** 70 B2
Abbots Bickington **EX22** 6 B4
Abbots Bromley **WS15** 40 C3
**Abbots Langley WD5 22 D1**
Abbots Leigh **BS8** 19 J4
Abbots Morton **WR7** 30 B3
Abbots Ripton **PE28** 33 F1
Abbot's Salford **WR11** 30 B3
Abbots Worthy **SO21** 11 F1
Abbotsbury **DT3** 8 E6
Abbotsfield Farm **WA9** 48 E3
Abbotsham **EX39** 6 C3
Abbotskerswell **TQ12** 5 J4
Abbotsley **PE19** 33 F3
Abbotstone **SO24** 11 G1
Abbotts Ann **SP11** 21 G7
Abbott's Barton **SO23** 11 F1
Abbottswood **SO51** 10 E2
Abdon **SY7** 38 E7
Abdy **S62** 51 G3
Abenhall **GL17** 29 F7
Aber **SA40** 17 H1
Aber Village **LD3** 28 A6
**Aberaeron SA46 26 D2**
Aberaman **CF44** 18 D1
Aberangell **SY20** 37 H5
Aber-Arad **SA38** 17 G1
Aberarder **PH20** 88 B6
Aberarder House **IV2** 88 D2
Aberargie **PH2** 82 C6
Aberarth **SA46** 26 D2
Aberavon **SA12** 18 A3
Aber-banc **SA44** 17 G1
Aberbargoed **CF81** 18 E1
Aberbeeg **NP13** 19 F1
Aberbowlan **SA19** 17 K2
Aberbran **LD3** 27 J6
Abercanaid **CF48** 18 D1
Abercarn **NP11** 19 F2
Abercastle **SA62** 16 B2
Abercegir **SY20** 37 H5
Aberchalder **PH35** 87 K4
Aberchirder **AB54** 98 E5
Abercorn **EH30** 75 J3
Abercraf **SA9** 27 H7
Abercregan **SA13** 18 B2
Abercrombie **KY10** 83 G7
Abercrychan **SA20** 27 G5
Abercwmboi **CF44** 18 D1
Abercych **SA37** 17 F1
Abercynafon **LD3** 27 K7
Abercynon **CF45** 18 D2
Abercywarch **SY20** 37 H4
Aberdalgie **PH2** 82 B5
**Aberdare CF44 18 C1**
Aberdaron **LL53** 36 A3
**Aberdaugleddau (Milford Haven) SA73 16 B5**
**ABERDEEN AB 91 H4**
Aberdeen Airport **AB21** 91 G3
Aberdesach **LL54** 46 C7
Aberdour **KY3** 75 K2
**Aberdovey (Aberdyfi) LL35 37 F6**
Aberduhonw **LD2** 27 K3
Aberdulais **SA10** 18 A2
**Aberdyfi (Aberdovey) LL35 37 F6**
Aberedw **LD2** 27 K4
Abereiddy **SA62** 16 A2
Abererch **LL53** 36 C2
Aberfan **CF48** 18 D1
**Aberfeldy PH15 81 K3**
Aberffraw **LL63** 46 B6
Aberffrwd **SY23** 27 F1
Aberford **LS25** 57 K6
Aberfoyle **FK8** 81 G7
**Abergavenny (Y Fenni) NP7 28 B7**
**Abergele LL22 47 H5**
Aber-Giâr **SA40** 17 J1
Abergorlech **SA32** 17 J2
**Abergwaun (Fishguard) SA65 16 C2**
Abergwesyn **LD5** 27 H3
Abergwili **SA31** 17 H3
Abergwydol **SY20** 37 G5
Abergwynant **LL40** 37 F4
Abergwynfi **SA13** 18 B2
Abergwyngregyn **LL33** 46 E5
Abergynolwyn **LL36** 37 F5
Aberhafesp **SY16** 37 K6
**Aberhonddu (Brecon) LD3 27 K6**
Aberhosan **SY20** 37 H6
Aberkenfig **CF32** 18 B3
Aberlady **EH32** 76 C2
Aberlemno **DD8** 83 G2
Aberllefenni **SY20** 37 G5
Aber-Ilia **CF44** 27 J7
Aberllynfi (Three Cocks) **LD3** 28 A5
**Aberlour (Charlestown of Aberlour) AB38 97 K7**
Abermad **SY23** 26 E1
**Abermaw (Barmouth) LL42 37 F4**
Abermeurig **SA48** 26 E3
Aber-miwl (Abermule) **SY15** 38 A6
Abermule (Aber-miwl) **SY15** 38 A6
Abernaint **SY22** 38 A3
Abernant *Carmar.* **SA33** 17 G3
Aber-nant *R.C.T.* **CF44** 18 D1
Abernethy **PH2** 82 C6
Abernyte **PH14** 82 D4
**Aberpennar (Mountain Ash) CF45 18 D2**
Aberporth **SA43** 26 B3
Aberriw (Berriew) **SY21** 38 A5
Aberscross **KW10** 96 E2
Abersky **IV2** 88 C2
Abersoch **LL53** 36 C3
Abersychan **NP4** 19 F1
**ABERTAWE (SWANSEA) SA 17 K6**
**Aberteifi (Cardigan) SA43 16 E1**
Aberthin **CF71** 18 D4
**Abertillery NP13 19 F1**
Abertridwr *Caerp.* **CF83** 18 E3
Abertridwr *Powys* **SY10** 37 K4
Abertysswg **NP22** 18 E1
Aberuthven **PH3** 82 A6
Aberyscir **LD3** 27 J6
**Aberystwyth SY23 36 E7**
Abhainnsuidhe **HS3** 100 C7
**Abingdon OX14 21 H2**
Abinger Common **RH5** 22 E7
Abinger Hammer **RH5** 22 D7
Abington **ML12** 68 E1
Abington Pigotts **SG8** 33 G4
Abingworth **RH20** 12 E5
Ablington *Glos.* **GL7** 20 E1
Ablington *Wilts.* **SP4** 20 E7
Abney **S32** 50 D5
Above Church **ST10** 50 C7
**Aboyne AB34 90 D5**
Abram **WN2** 49 F2
Abriachan **IV3** 88 C1
Abridge **RM4** 23 H2
Abronhill **G67** 75 F3
Abson **BS30** 20 A4
Abthorpe **NN12** 31 H4
Abune-the-Hill **KW17** 106 B5
Aby **LN13** 53 H5
Acaster Malbis **YO23** 58 B5
Acaster Selby **YO23** 58 B5
**Accrington BB5 56 C7**
Accurrach **PA33** 80 C5
Acha **PA78** 78 C2
Achacha **PA37** 80 A3
Achadacaie **PA29** 73 G4
Achadh Mòr **HS2** 101 F5
Achadh-chaorrunn **PA29** 73 F5
Achadunan **PA26** 80 D6
Achagavel **PH33** 79 J2
Achaglass **PA29** 73 F6
Achahoish **PA31** 73 F3
Achalader **PH10** 82 C3
Achallader **PA36** 80 E3
Achamore **PA60** 72 D3
Achandunie **IV17** 96 D4
Achany **IV27** 96 C1
Achaphubuil **PH33** 87 G7
**Acharacle PH36 79 H1**
Achargary **KW11** 104 C3
Acharn *Arg. & B.* **PA35** 80 C4
Acharn *P. & K.* **PH15** 81 J3
Acharonich **PA73** 79 F4
Acharosson **PA21** 73 H3
Achateny **PH36** 86 B7
Achath **AB32** 91 F3
Achavanich **KW5** 105 G4
Achddu **SA16** 17 H5
Achduart **IV26** 95 G1
Achentoul **KW11** 104 D5
Achfary **IV27** 102 E5
Achgarve **IV22** 94 E2
Achiemore *High.* **IV27** 103 F2
Achiemore *High.* **KW13** 104 D3
Achies **KW12** 105 G3
A'Chill **PH44** 85 H4
Achiltibuie **IV26** 95 G1
Achina **KW14** 104 C2
Achindown **IV12** 97 F7
Achinduich **IV27** 96 C2
Achingills **KW12** 105 G2
Achintee **IV54** 95 F7
Achintee House **PH33** 87 H7
Achintraid **IV54** 86 E1
Achlean **PH21** 89 F5
Achleanan **PA34** 79 G2
Achleek **PH33** 79 J2
Achlian **PA33** 80 C5
Achlyness **IV27** 102 E3
Achmelvich **IV27** 102 C6
Achmony **IV63** 88 C1
Achmore *High.* **IV53** 86 E1
Achmore *High.* **IV23** 95 G2
Achmore *Stir.* **FK21** 81 G4
Achnaba **PA31** 73 H2
Achnabat **IV2** 88 C1
Achnabourin **KW14** 104 C3
Achnacairn **PA37** 80 A4
Achnacarnin **IV27** 102 C5
Achnacarry **PH34** 87 H6
Achnaclerach **IV23** 96 B5
Achnacloich *Arg. & B.* **PA37** 80 A4
Achnacloich *High.* **IV46** 86 B4
Achnaclyth **KW6** 105 F5
Achnacraig **PA73** 79 F3
Achnacroish **PA34** 79 K3
Achnadrish **PA75** 79 F2
Achnafalnich **PA33** 80 D5
Achnafauld **PH8** 81 K4
Achnagairn **IV5** 96 C7
Achnagarron **IV18** 96 D4
Achnaha *High.* **PA34** 79 H3
Achnaha *High.* **PH36** 79 F1
Achnahanat **IV24** 96 C2
Achnahannet **PH26** 89 G2
Achnairn **IV27** 103 H7
Achnalea **PH33** 79 K1
Achnamara **PA31** 73 F2
Achnanellan **PH37** 79 J1
Achnasaul **PH34** 87 H6
**Achnasheen IV22 95 H6**
Achnashelloch **PA31** 73 G1
Achnastank **AB55** 89 K1
Achorn **KW6** 105 G5
Achosnich *High.* **IV25** 96 E2
Achosnich *High.* **PH36** 79 F1
Achreamie **KW14** 105 F2
Achriabhach **PH33** 80 C1
Achriesgill **IV27** 102 E3
Achtoty **KW14** 103 J2
Achurch **PE8** 42 D7
Achuvoldrach **IV27** 103 H3
Achvaich **IV25** 96 E2
Achvarasdal **KW14** 104 E2
Achvlair **PA38** 80 A2
Achvraie **IV26** 95 G1
Ackenthwaite **LA7** 55 J1
Ackergill **KW1** 105 J3
Acklam *Middbro.* **TS5** 63 F5
Acklam *N.Yorks.* **YO17** 58 D3
Ackleton **WV6** 39 G6
Acklington **NE65** 71 H3
Ackton **WF7** 57 K7
Ackworth Moor Top **WF7** 51 G1
Acle **NR13** 45 J4
Acock's Green **B27** 40 D7
Acol **CT7** 25 K5
Acomb *Northumb.* **NE46** 70 E7
Acomb *York* **YO24** 58 B4
Aconbury **HR2** 28 E5
Acre **BB5** 56 C7
Acrefair **LL14** 38 B1
Acrise Place **CT18** 15 G3
Acton *Ches.E.* **CW5** 49 F7
Acton *Dorset* **BH19** 9 J7
Acton *Gt.Lon.* **W3** 22 E3
Acton *Shrop.* **SY9** 38 C7
Acton *Staffs.* **ST5** 40 A1
Acton *Suff.* **CO10** 34 C4
Acton *Worcs.* **DY13** 29 H2
Acton *Wrex.* **LL12** 48 C7
Acton Beauchamp **WR6** 29 F3
Acton Bridge **CW8** 48 E5
Acton Burnell **SY5** 38 E5
Acton Green **WR6** 29 F3
Acton Pigott **SY5** 38 E5
Acton Round **WV16** 39 F6
Acton Scott **SY6** 38 D7
Acton Trussell **ST17** 40 B4
Acton Turville **GL9** 20 B3
Adamhill **KA1** 74 C7
Adbaston **ST20** 39 G3
Adber **DT9** 8 E2
Adderbury **OX17** 31 F5
Adderley **TF9** 39 F2
Adderstone **NE70** 77 K7
Addiewell **EH55** 75 H4
Addingham **LS29** 57 F5
Addington *Bucks.* **MK18** 31 J6
Addington *Gt.Lon.* **CR0** 23 G5
Addington *Kent* **ME19** 23 K6
Addiscombe **CR0** 23 G5
**Addlestone KT15 22 D5**
Addlethorpe **PE24** 53 J6
Adel **LS16** 57 H6
Adeney **TF10** 39 G4
Adeyfield **HP2** 22 D1
Adfa **SY16** 37 K5
Adforton **SY7** 28 D1
Adisham **CT3** 15 H2
Adlestrop **GL56** 30 D6
Adlingfleet **DN14** 58 E7
Adlington *Ches.E.* **SK10** 49 J4
Adlington *Lancs.* **PR7** 48 E1
Admaston *Staffs.* **WS15** 40 C3
Admaston *Tel. & W.* **TF5** 39 F4
Admington **CV36** 30 D4
Adsborough **TA2** 8 B2
Adscombe **TA5** 7 K2
Adstock **MK18** 31 J5
Adstone **NN12** 31 G3
Adversane **RH14** 12 D4
Advie **PH26** 89 J1
Adwalton **BD11** 57 H7
Adwell **OX9** 21 K2

## Adw - Ard



| | | |
|---|---|---|
| Adwick le Street **DN6** | 51 | H2 |
| Adwick upon Dearne **S64** | 51 | G2 |
| Adziel **AB43** | 99 | H5 |
| Ae Village **DG1** | 68 | E5 |
| Affetside **BL8** | 49 | G1 |
| Affleck **AB21** | 91 | G2 |
| Affpuddle **DT2** | 9 | H5 |
| Afon Wen **LL53** | 36 | D2 |
| Afon-wen **CH7** | 47 | K5 |
| Afton **PO40** | 10 | E6 |
| Afton Bridgend **KA18** | 68 | B2 |
| Agglethorpe **DL8** | 57 | F1 |
| Aigburth **L17** | 48 | C4 |
| Aiginis **HS2** | 101 | G4 |
| Aike **YO25** | 59 | G5 |
| Aikerness **KW17** | 106 | D2 |
| Aikers **KW17** | 106 | D8 |
| Aiketgate **CA4** | 61 | F2 |
| Aikshaw **CA7** | 60 | C2 |
| Aikton **CA7** | 60 | D1 |
| Aikwood Tower **TD7** | 69 | K1 |
| Ailby **LN13** | 53 | H5 |
| Ailey **HR3** | 28 | C4 |
| Ailsworth **PE5** | 42 | E6 |
| Aimes Green **EN9** | 23 | H1 |
| Aimster **KW14** | 105 | G2 |
| Ainderby Quernhow **YO7** | 57 | J1 |
| Ainderby Steeple **DL7** | 62 | E7 |
| Aingers Green **CO7** | 35 | F6 |
| Ainsdale **PR8** | 48 | C1 |
| Ainsdale-on-Sea **PR8** | 48 | C1 |
| Ainstable **CA4** | 61 | G2 |
| Ainsworth **BL2** | 49 | G1 |
| Ainthorpe **YO21** | 63 | J6 |
| Aintree **L10** | 48 | C3 |
| Aird *W.Isles* **HS7** | 92 | C6 |
| Aird *W.Isles* **HS2** | 101 | H4 |
| Aird a' Mhachair **HS8** | 92 | C7 |
| Aird a' Mhulaidh **HS3** | 100 | D6 |
| Aird Asaig **HS3** | 100 | D7 |
| Aird Dhail **HS2** | 101 | G1 |
| Aird Leimhe **HS3** | 93 | G3 |
| Aird Mhige **HS3** | 93 | G2 |
| Aird Mhighe **HS3** | 93 | F3 |
| Aird of Sleat **IV45** | 86 | B4 |
| Aird Thunga **HS2** | 101 | G4 |
| Aird Uig **HS2** | 100 | C4 |
| Airdrie *Fife* **KY10** | 83 | G7 |
| **Airdrie *N.Lan.* ML6** | **75** | **F4** |
| Aire View **BD20** | 56 | E5 |
| Airidh a' Bhruaich **HS2** | 100 | E6 |
| Airieland **DG7** | 65 | H5 |
| Airies **DG9** | 66 | D7 |
| Airigh-drishaig **IV54** | 86 | D1 |
| Airmyn **DN14** | 58 | D7 |
| Airntully **PH1** | 82 | B4 |
| Airor **PH41** | 86 | D4 |
| Airth **FK2** | 75 | G2 |
| Airton **BD23** | 56 | E4 |
| Airyhassen **DG8** | 64 | D6 |
| Aisby *Lincs.* **DN21** | 52 | B3 |
| Aisby *Lincs.* **NG32** | 42 | D2 |
| Aisgernis (Askernish) **HS8** | 84 | C2 |
| Aisgill **CA17** | 61 | J7 |
| Aish *Devon* **TQ10** | 5 | G4 |
| Aish *Devon* **TQ9** | 5 | J5 |
| Aisholt **TA5** | 7 | K2 |
| Aiskew **DL8** | 57 | H1 |
| Aislaby *N.Yorks.* **YO21** | 63 | K6 |
| Aislaby *N.Yorks.* **YO18** | 58 | D1 |
| Aislaby *Stock.* **TS16** | 63 | F5 |
| Aisthorpe **LN1** | 52 | C4 |
| Aith *Ork.* **KW16** | 106 | B6 |
| Aith *Ork.* **KW17** | 106 | F5 |
| Aith *Shet.* **ZE2** | 107 | M7 |
| Aith *Shet.* **ZE2** | 107 | Q3 |
| Aithsetter **ZE2** | 107 | N9 |
| Aitnoch **PH26** | 89 | G1 |
| Akeld **NE71** | 70 | E1 |
| Akeley **MK18** | 31 | J5 |
| Akenham **IP1** | 35 | F4 |
| Albaston **PL18** | 4 | E3 |
| Albecq **GY5** | 3 | H5 |
| Alberbury **SY5** | 38 | C4 |
| Albert Town **SA61** | 16 | C4 |
| Albourne **BN6** | 13 | F5 |
| Albourne Green **BN6** | 13 | F5 |
| Albrighton *Shrop.* **WV7** | 40 | A5 |
| Albrighton *Shrop.* **SY4** | 38 | D4 |
| Alburgh **IP20** | 45 | G7 |
| Albury *Herts.* **SG11** | 33 | H6 |
| Albury *Oxon.* **OX9** | 21 | K1 |
| Albury *Surr.* **GU5** | 22 | D7 |
| Albury End **SG11** | 33 | H6 |
| Albury Heath **GU5** | 22 | D7 |
| Albyfield **CA8** | 61 | G1 |
| Alcaig **IV7** | 96 | C6 |
| Alcaston **SY6** | 38 | D7 |
| **Alcester B49** | **30** | **B3** |
| Alciston **BN26** | 13 | J6 |
| Alcombe **TA24** | 7 | H1 |
| Alconbury **PE28** | 32 | E1 |
| Alconbury Hill **PE28** | 32 | E1 |
| Alconbury Weston **PE28** | 32 | E1 |
| Aldborough *N.Yorks.* **YO51** | 57 | K3 |
| Aldborough *Norf.* **NR11** | 45 | F2 |
| Aldbourne **SN8** | 21 | F4 |
| Aldbrough **HU11** | 59 | J6 |
| Aldbrough St. John **DL11** | 62 | D5 |
| Aldbury **HP23** | 32 | C7 |
| Aldclune **PH16** | 82 | A1 |
| **Aldeburgh IP15** | **35** | **J3** |
| Aldeby **NR34** | 45 | J6 |
| Aldenham **WD25** | 22 | E2 |
| Alderbury **SP5** | 10 | C2 |
| Alderford **NR9** | 45 | F4 |
| Alderholt **SP6** | 10 | C3 |
| Alderley **GL12** | 20 | A2 |
| **Alderley Edge SK9** | **49** | **H5** |
| Aldermaston **RG7** | 21 | J5 |
| Aldermaston Wharf **RG7** | 21 | K5 |
| Alderminster **CV37** | 30 | D4 |
| Alderney **GY9** | 3 | K4 |
| Alderney Airport **GY9** | 3 | J4 |
| Alder's End **HR1** | 29 | F5 |
| Aldersey Green **CH3** | 48 | D7 |
| **Aldershot GU11** | **22** | **B6** |
| Alderton *Glos.* **GL20** | 29 | J5 |
| Alderton *Northants.* **NN12** | 31 | J4 |
| Alderton *Suff.* **IP12** | 35 | H4 |
| Alderton *Wilts.* **SN14** | 20 | B3 |
| Alderwasley **DE56** | 51 | F7 |
| Aldfield **HG4** | 57 | H3 |
| Aldford **CH3** | 48 | D7 |
| Aldham *Essex* **CO6** | 34 | D6 |
| Aldham *Suff.* **IP7** | 34 | E4 |
| Aldie *Aber.* **AB42** | 99 | J6 |
| Aldie *High.* **IV19** | 96 | E3 |
| Aldingbourne **PO20** | 12 | C6 |
| Aldingham **LA12** | 55 | F2 |
| Aldington *Kent* **TN25** | 15 | F4 |
| Aldington *Worcs.* **WR11** | 30 | B4 |
| Aldivalloch **AB54** | 90 | B2 |
| Aldochlay **G83** | 74 | B1 |
| Aldons **KA26** | 67 | F5 |
| Aldous's Corner **IP19** | 45 | H7 |
| Aldreth **CB6** | 33 | H1 |
| Aldridge **WS9** | 40 | C5 |
| Aldringham **IP16** | 35 | J2 |
| Aldsworth *Glos.* **GL54** | 20 | E1 |
| Aldsworth *W.Suss.* **PO10** | 11 | J4 |
| Aldunie **AB54** | 90 | B2 |
| Aldville **PH8** | 82 | A4 |
| Aldwark *Derbys.* **DE4** | 50 | E7 |
| Aldwark *N.Yorks.* **YO61** | 57 | K3 |
| Aldwick **PO21** | 12 | C7 |
| Aldwincle **NN14** | 42 | D7 |
| Aldworth **RG8** | 21 | J4 |
| **Alexandria G83** | **74** | **B3** |
| Aley **TA5** | 7 | K2 |
| Aley Green **LU1** | 32 | D7 |
| Alfardisworthy **EX22** | 6 | A4 |
| Alfington **EX11** | 7 | K6 |
| Alfold **GU6** | 12 | D3 |
| Alfold Crossways **GU6** | 12 | D3 |
| **Alford *Aber.* AB33** | **90** | **D3** |
| **Alford *Lincs.* LN13** | **53** | **H5** |
| Alford *Som.* **BA7** | 9 | F1 |
| **Alfreton DE55** | **51** | **G7** |
| Alfrick **WR6** | 29 | G3 |
| Alfrick Pound **WR6** | 29 | G3 |
| Alfriston **BN26** | 13 | J6 |
| Algarkirk **PE20** | 43 | F2 |
| Alhampton **BA4** | 9 | F1 |
| Alkborough **DN15** | 58 | E7 |
| Alkerton **OX15** | 30 | E4 |
| Alkham **CT15** | 15 | H3 |
| Alkington **SY13** | 38 | E2 |
| Alkmonton **DE6** | 40 | D2 |
| All Cannings **SN10** | 20 | D5 |
| All Saints South Elmham **IP19** | 45 | H7 |
| All Stretton **SY6** | 38 | D6 |
| Allaleigh **TQ9** | 5 | J5 |
| Allanaquoich **AB35** | 89 | J5 |
| Allancreich **AB34** | 90 | D5 |
| Allanfearn **IV2** | 96 | E7 |
| Allangillfoot **DG13** | 69 | H4 |
| Allanton *D. & G.* **DG2** | 68 | E5 |
| Allanton *E.Ayr.* **KA17** | 74 | E7 |
| Allanton *N.Lan.* **ML7** | 75 | G5 |
| Allanton *S.Lan.* **ML3** | 75 | F5 |
| Allanton *Sc.Bord.* **TD11** | 77 | G5 |
| Allardice **DD10** | 91 | G7 |
| Allathasdal **HS9** | 84 | B4 |
| Allbrook **SO50** | 11 | F2 |
| Allendale Town **NE47** | 61 | K1 |
| Allenheads **NE47** | 61 | K2 |
| Allen's Green **CM21** | 33 | H7 |
| Allensford **DH8** | 62 | B1 |
| Allensmore **HR2** | 28 | D5 |
| Allenton **DE24** | 41 | F2 |
| Aller **TA10** | 8 | D2 |
| Allerby **CA7** | 60 | B3 |
| Allercombe **EX5** | 7 | J6 |
| Allerford *Devon* **EX20** | 6 | C7 |
| Allerford *Som.* **TA24** | 7 | H1 |
| Allerston **YO18** | 58 | E1 |
| Allerthorpe **YO42** | 58 | D5 |
| Allerton *Mersey.* **L18** | 48 | D4 |
| Allerton *W.Yorks.* **BD15** | 57 | G6 |
| Allerton Bywater **WF10** | 57 | K7 |
| Allerton Mauleverer **HG5** | 57 | K4 |
| Allesley **CV5** | 40 | E7 |
| Allestree **DE22** | 41 | F2 |
| Allet Common **TR4** | 2 | E4 |
| Allexton **LE15** | 42 | B5 |
| Allgreave **SK11** | 49 | J6 |
| Allhallows **ME3** | 24 | E4 |
| Allhallows-on-Sea **ME3** | 24 | E4 |
| Alligin Shuas **IV22** | 94 | E6 |
| Allimore Green **ST18** | 40 | A4 |
| Allington *Dorset* **DT6** | 8 | D5 |
| Allington *Lincs.* **NG32** | 42 | B1 |
| Allington *Wilts.* **SP4** | 10 | D1 |
| Allington *Wilts.* **SN10** | 20 | D5 |
| Allington *Wilts.* **SN14** | 20 | B4 |
| Allithwaite **LA11** | 55 | G2 |
| Allnabad **IV27** | 103 | G4 |
| **Alloa FK10** | **75** | **G1** |
| Allonby **CA15** | 60 | B2 |
| Allostock **WA16** | 49 | G5 |
| Alloway **KA7** | 67 | H2 |
| Allowenshay **TA17** | 8 | C3 |
| Allscot **WV15** | 39 | G6 |
| Allscott **TF6** | 39 | F4 |
| Allt na h-Airbhe **IV26** | 95 | H2 |
| Alltachonaich **PA34** | 79 | J2 |
| Alltbeithe **IV4** | 87 | G2 |
| Alltforgan **SY10** | 37 | J3 |
| Alltmawr **LD2** | 27 | K4 |
| Alltnacaillich **IV27** | 103 | G4 |
| Allt-na-subh **IV40** | 87 | F1 |
| Alltsigh **IV63** | 88 | B3 |
| Alltwalis **SA32** | 17 | H2 |
| Alltwen **SA8** | 18 | A1 |
| Alltyblaca **SA40** | 17 | J1 |
| Allwood Green **IP22** | 34 | E1 |
| Almeley **HR3** | 28 | C3 |
| Almeley Wootton **HR3** | 28 | C3 |
| Almer **DT11** | 9 | J5 |
| Almington **TF9** | 39 | G2 |
| Almiston Cross **EX39** | 6 | B3 |
| Almondbank **PH1** | 82 | B5 |
| Almondbury **HD4** | 50 | D1 |
| Almondsbury **BS32** | 19 | K3 |
| Alne **YO61** | 57 | K3 |
| **Alness IV17** | **96** | **D5** |
| Alnham **NE66** | 70 | E2 |
| Alnmouth **NE66** | 71 | H2 |
| **Alnwick NE66** | **71** | **G2** |
| Alperton **HA0** | 22 | E3 |
| Alphamstone **CO8** | 34 | C5 |
| Alpheton **CO10** | 34 | C3 |
| Alphington **EX2** | 7 | H6 |
| Alport **DE45** | 50 | E6 |
| Alpraham **CW6** | 48 | E7 |
| Alresford **CO7** | 34 | E6 |
| Alrewas **DE13** | 40 | D4 |
| Alrick **PH11** | 82 | C1 |
| Alsager **ST7** | 49 | G7 |
| Alsagers Bank **ST7** | 40 | A1 |
| Alsop en le Dale **DE6** | 50 | D7 |
| **Alston *Cumb.* CA9** | **61** | **J2** |
| Alston *Devon* **EX13** | 8 | C4 |
| Alston Sutton **BS26** | 19 | H6 |
| Alstone *Glos.* **GL20** | 29 | J5 |
| Alstone *Som.* **TA9** | 19 | G7 |
| Alstone *Staffs.* **ST18** | 40 | A4 |
| Alstonefield **DE6** | 50 | D7 |
| Alswear **EX36** | 7 | F3 |
| Alt **OL8** | 49 | J2 |
| Altandhu **IV26** | 102 | B7 |
| Altanduin **KW11** | 104 | D6 |
| Altarnun **PL15** | 4 | C2 |
| Altass **IV27** | 96 | C1 |
| Altens **AB12** | 91 | H4 |
| Alterwall **KW1** | 105 | H2 |
| Altham **BB5** | 56 | C6 |
| Althorne **CM3** | 25 | F2 |
| Althorpe **DN17** | 52 | B2 |
| Alticry **DG8** | 64 | C5 |
| Altnafeadh **PH49** | 80 | D2 |
| Altnaharra **IV27** | 103 | H5 |
| Altofts **WF6** | 57 | J7 |
| Alton *Derbys.* **S42** | 51 | F6 |
| **Alton *Hants.* GU34** | **11** | **J1** |
| Alton *Staffs.* **ST10** | 40 | C1 |
| Alton Barnes **SN8** | 20 | E5 |
| Alton Pancras **DT2** | 9 | G4 |
| Alton Priors **SN8** | 20 | E5 |
| Altonside **IV30** | 97 | K6 |
| **Altrincham WA14** | **49** | **G4** |
| Altura **PH34** | 87 | J5 |
| **Alva FK12** | **75** | **G1** |
| Alvanley **WA6** | 48 | D5 |
| Alvaston **DE24** | 41 | F2 |
| Alvechurch **B48** | 30 | B1 |
| Alvecote **B79** | 40 | E5 |
| Alvediston **SP5** | 9 | J2 |
| Alveley **WV15** | 39 | G7 |
| Alverdiscott **EX31** | 6 | D3 |
| Alverstoke **PO12** | 11 | H5 |
| Alverstone **PO36** | 11 | G6 |
| Alverthorpe **WF2** | 57 | J7 |
| Alverton **NG13** | 42 | A1 |
| Alves **IV30** | 97 | J5 |
| Alvescot **OX18** | 21 | F1 |
| Alveston *S.Glos.* **BS35** | 19 | K3 |
| Alveston *Warks.* **CV37** | 30 | D3 |
| Alvie **PH21** | 89 | F4 |
| Alvingham **LN11** | 53 | G3 |
| Alvington **GL15** | 19 | K1 |
| Alwalton **PE2** | 42 | E6 |
| Alweston **DT9** | 9 | F3 |
| Alwington **EX39** | 6 | C3 |
| Alwinton **NE65** | 70 | E3 |
| Alwoodley **LS17** | 57 | J5 |
| Alwoodley Gates **LS17** | 57 | J5 |
| Alyth **PH11** | 82 | D3 |
| Amalebra **TR20** | 2 | B5 |
| Ambaston **DE72** | 41 | G2 |
| Amber Hill **PE20** | 43 | F1 |
| Ambergate **DE56** | 51 | F7 |
| Amberley *Glos.* **GL5** | 20 | B1 |
| Amberley *W.Suss.* **BN18** | 12 | D5 |
| Amble **NE65** | 71 | H3 |
| Amblecote **DY8** | 40 | A7 |
| **Ambleside LA22** | **60** | **E6** |
| Ambleston **SA62** | 16 | D3 |
| Ambrismore **PA20** | 73 | J5 |
| Ambrosden **OX25** | 31 | H7 |
| Amcotts **DN17** | 52 | B1 |
| **Amersham HP6** | **22** | **C2** |
| Amerton **ST18** | 40 | B3 |
| Amesbury **SP4** | 20 | E7 |
| Ameysford **BH22** | 10 | B4 |
| Amington **B77** | 40 | E5 |
| Amisfield Town **DG1** | 69 | F5 |
| **Amlwch LL68** | **46** | **C3** |
| Amlwch Port **LL68** | 46 | C3 |
| **Ammanford (Rhydaman) SA18** | **17** | **K4** |
| Amotherby **YO17** | 58 | D2 |
| Ampfield **SO51** | 10 | E2 |
| Ampleforth **YO62** | 58 | B2 |
| Ampleforth College **YO62** | 58 | B2 |
| Ampney Crucis **GL7** | 20 | D1 |
| Ampney St. Mary **GL7** | 20 | D1 |
| Ampney St. Peter **GL7** | 20 | D1 |
| Amport **SP11** | 21 | G7 |
| Ampthill **MK45** | 32 | D5 |
| Ampton **IP31** | 34 | C1 |
| Amroth **SA67** | 16 | E5 |
| Amulree **PH8** | 81 | K4 |
| An T-Òb (Leverburgh) **HS5** | 93 | F3 |
| Anaboard **PH26** | 89 | H1 |
| Anaheilt **PH36** | 79 | K1 |
| Ancaster **NG32** | 42 | C1 |
| Anchor **SY7** | 38 | A7 |
| Anchor Corner **NR17** | 44 | E6 |
| Ancroft **TD15** | 77 | H6 |
| Ancrum **TD8** | 70 | B1 |
| Ancton **PO22** | 12 | C6 |
| Anderby **PE24** | 53 | J5 |
| Anderby Creek **PE24** | 53 | J5 |
| Andersea **TA7** | 8 | C1 |
| Andersfield **TA5** | 8 | B1 |
| Anderson **DT11** | 9 | H5 |
| Anderton **CW9** | 49 | F5 |
| **Andover SP10** | **21** | **G7** |
| Andover Down **SP11** | 21 | G7 |
| Andoversford **GL54** | 30 | B7 |
| Andreas **IM7** | 54 | D4 |
| Anelog **LL53** | 36 | A3 |
| Anfield **L4** | 48 | C3 |
| Angarrack **TR27** | 2 | C5 |
| Angarrick **TR3** | 2 | E5 |
| Angelbank **SY8** | 28 | E1 |
| Angerton **CA7** | 60 | D1 |
| Angle **SA71** | 16 | B5 |
| Angler's Retreat **SY20** | 37 | G6 |
| Anglesey (Ynys Môn) **LL** | 46 | B4 |
| Angmering **BN16** | 12 | D6 |
| Angmering-on-Sea **BN16** | 12 | D6 |
| Angram *N.Yorks.* **YO23** | 58 | B5 |
| Angram *N.Yorks.* **DL11** | 61 | K7 |
| Anick **NE46** | 70 | E7 |
| Anie **FK17** | 81 | G6 |
| Ankerville **IV19** | 97 | F4 |
| Anlaby **HU10** | 59 | G7 |
| Anmer **PE31** | 44 | B3 |
| Anmore **PO7** | 11 | H3 |
| Anna Valley **SP11** | 21 | G7 |
| **Annan DG12** | **69** | **G7** |
| Annaside **LA19** | 54 | D1 |
| Annat *Arg. & B.* **PA35** | 80 | B5 |
| Annat *High.* **IV22** | 94 | E6 |
| Annbank **KA6** | 67 | J1 |
| Annesley **NG15** | 51 | H7 |
| Annesley Woodhouse **NG17** | 51 | G7 |
| Annfield Plain **DH9** | 62 | C1 |
| Anniesland **G13** | 74 | D4 |
| Annscroft **SY5** | 38 | D5 |
| Ansdell **FY8** | 55 | G7 |
| Ansford **BA7** | 9 | F1 |
| Ansley **CV10** | 40 | E6 |
| Anslow **DE13** | 40 | E3 |
| Anslow Gate **DE13** | 40 | D3 |
| Ansteadbrook **GU27** | 12 | C3 |
| Anstey *Herts.* **SG9** | 33 | H5 |
| Anstey *Leics.* **LE7** | 41 | H5 |
| **Anstruther KY10** | **83** | **G7** |
| Ansty *W.Suss.* **RH17** | 13 | F4 |
| Ansty *Warks.* **CV7** | 41 | F7 |
| Ansty *Wilts.* **SP3** | 9 | J2 |
| Ansty Coombe **SP3** | 9 | J2 |
| Ansty Cross **DT2** | 9 | G4 |
| Anthill Common **PO7** | 11 | H3 |
| Anthorn **CA7** | 60 | C1 |
| Antingham **NR28** | 45 | G2 |
| Anton's Gowt **PE22** | 43 | F1 |
| Antony **PL11** | 4 | D5 |
| Antrobus **CW9** | 49 | F5 |
| Anvil Corner **EX22** | 6 | B5 |
| Anvil Green **CT4** | 15 | G3 |
| Anwick **NG34** | 52 | E7 |
| Anwoth **DG7** | 65 | F5 |
| Aoradh **PA44** | 72 | A4 |
| Apethorpe **PE8** | 42 | D6 |
| Apeton **ST20** | 40 | A4 |
| Apley **LN8** | 52 | E5 |
| Apperknowle **S18** | 51 | F5 |
| Apperley **GL19** | 29 | H6 |
| Apperley Bridge **BD10** | 57 | G6 |
| Appersett **DL8** | 61 | K7 |
| **Appin PA38** | **80** | **A3** |
| Appin House **PA38** | 80 | A3 |
| Appleby **DN15** | 52 | C1 |
| Appleby Magna **DE12** | 41 | F4 |
| Appleby Parva **DE12** | 41 | F5 |
| **Appleby-in-Westmorland CA16** | **61** | **H4** |
| Applecross **IV54** | 94 | D7 |
| Appledore *Devon* **EX39** | 6 | C2 |
| Appledore *Devon* **EX16** | 7 | J4 |
| Appledore *Kent* **TN26** | 14 | E5 |
| Appledore Heath **TN26** | 14 | E4 |
| Appleford **OX14** | 21 | J2 |
| Appleshaw **SP11** | 21 | G7 |
| Applethwaite **CA12** | 60 | D4 |
| Appleton *Halton* **WA8** | 48 | E4 |
| Appleton *Oxon.* **OX13** | 21 | H1 |
| Appleton Roebuck **YO23** | 58 | B5 |
| Appleton Thorn **WA4** | 49 | F4 |
| Appleton Wiske **DL6** | 62 | E6 |
| Appleton-le-Moors **YO62** | 58 | D1 |
| Appleton-le-Street **YO17** | 58 | D2 |
| Appletreehall **TD9** | 70 | A2 |
| Appletreewick **BD23** | 57 | F3 |
| Appley **TA21** | 7 | J3 |
| Appley Bridge **WN6** | 48 | E2 |
| Apse Heath **PO36** | 11 | G6 |
| Apsey Green **IP13** | 35 | G2 |
| Apsley **HP3** | 22 | D1 |
| Apsley End **SG5** | 32 | E5 |
| Apuldram **PO20** | 12 | B6 |
| **Arberth (Narberth) SA67** | **16** | **E4** |
| Arbirlot **DD11** | 83 | G3 |
| Arborfield **RG2** | 22 | A5 |
| Arborfield Cross **RG2** | 22 | A5 |
| Arborfield Garrison **RG2** | 22 | A5 |
| Arbourthorne **S2** | 51 | F4 |
| **Arbroath DD11** | **83** | **H3** |
| Arbuthnott **AB30** | 91 | F7 |
| Archdeacon Newton **DL2** | 62 | D5 |
| Archiestown **AB38** | 97 | K7 |
| Arclid **CW11** | 49 | G6 |
| Ard a' Chapuill **PA22** | 73 | J2 |
| Ardachearanbeg **PA22** | 73 | J2 |
| Ardacheranmor **PA22** | 73 | J2 |
| Ardachoil **PA65** | 79 | J4 |
| Ardachu **IV28** | 96 | D1 |
| Ardailly **PA41** | 72 | E5 |
| Ardalanish **PA67** | 78 | E6 |
| Ardallie **AB42** | 91 | J1 |
| Ardanaiseig **PA35** | 80 | B5 |
| Ardaneaskan **IV54** | 86 | E1 |
| Ardanstur **PA34** | 79 | K6 |
| Ardantiobairt **PA34** | 79 | H2 |
| Ardantrive **PA34** | 79 | K5 |
| Ardarroch **IV54** | 94 | E7 |
| Ardbeg *Arg. & B.* **PA20** | 73 | J4 |
| Ardbeg *Arg. & B.* **PA42** | 72 | C6 |
| Ardbeg *Arg. & B.* **PA23** | 73 | K2 |
| Ardblair **IV4** | 88 | C1 |
| Ardbrecknish **PA33** | 80 | B5 |
| Ardcharnich **IV23** | 95 | H3 |
| Ardchiavaig **PA67** | 78 | E6 |
| Ardchonnel **PA37** | 80 | A4 |
| Ardchonnell **PA33** | 80 | A6 |
| Ardchrishnish **PA70** | 79 | F5 |
| Ardchronie **IV24** | 96 | D3 |
| Ardchuilk **IV4** | 87 | J1 |
| Ardchullarie More **FK18** | 81 | G6 |
| Ardchyle **FK21** | 81 | G5 |
| Arddlin **SY22** | 38 | B4 |
| Ardechvie **PH34** | 87 | H5 |
| Ardeley **SG2** | 33 | G6 |
| Ardelve **IV40** | 86 | E2 |
| Arden **G83** | 74 | B2 |
| Ardencaple House **PA34** | 79 | J6 |
| Ardens Grafton **B49** | 30 | C3 |
| Ardentallan **PA34** | 79 | K5 |
| Ardentinny **PA23** | 73 | K2 |
| Ardeonaig **FK21** | 81 | H4 |
| Ardersier **IV2** | 96 | E6 |
| Ardery **PH36** | 79 | J1 |
| Ardessie **IV23** | 95 | G3 |
| Ardfad **PA34** | 79 | J6 |
| Ardfern **PA31** | 79 | K7 |
| Ardfin **PA60** | 72 | C4 |
| Ardgartan **G83** | 80 | D7 |
| **Ardgay IV24** | **96** | **D2** |
| Ardgenavan **PA26** | 80 | C6 |
| Ardgour (Corran) **PH33** | 80 | B1 |
| Ardgowan **PA16** | 74 | A3 |
| Ardgowse **AB33** | 90 | E3 |
| Ardgye **IV30** | 97 | J5 |
| Ardhallow **PA23** | 73 | K3 |
| Ardheslaig **IV54** | 94 | D6 |
| Ardiecow **AB45** | 98 | D4 |
| Ardinamar **PA34** | 79 | J6 |
| Ardindrean **IV23** | 95 | H3 |
| Ardingly **RH17** | 13 | G4 |
| Ardington **OX12** | 21 | H3 |
| Ardington Wick **OX12** | 21 | H3 |
| Ardintoul **IV40** | 86 | E2 |
| Ardkinglas House **PA26** | 80 | C6 |
| Ardlair **AB52** | 90 | D2 |
| Ardlamont **PA21** | 73 | H4 |
| Ardleigh **CO7** | 34 | E6 |
| Ardleigh Green **RM2** | 23 | J3 |
| Ardleigh Heath **CO7** | 34 | E5 |
| Ardleish **G83** | 80 | E6 |
| Ardler **PH12** | 82 | D3 |
| Ardley **OX27** | 31 | G6 |
| Ardley End **CM22** | 33 | J7 |
| Ardlui **G83** | 80 | E6 |
| Ardlussa **PA60** | 72 | E2 |
| Ardmaddy **PA35** | 80 | B4 |
| Ardmair **IV26** | 95 | H2 |
| Ardmaleish **PA20** | 73 | J4 |
| Ardmay **G83** | 80 | D7 |
| Ardmenish **PA60** | 72 | D3 |
| Ardmhòr **HS9** | 84 | C4 |
| Ardminish **PA41** | 72 | E6 |
| Ardmolich **PH36** | 86 | D7 |
| Ardmore *Arg. & B.* **PA42** | 72 | C5 |
| Ardmore *Arg. & B.* **PA34** | 79 | J5 |
| Ardmore *Arg. & B.* **G82** | 74 | B3 |
| Ardmore *High.* **IV19** | 96 | E3 |
| Ardnackaig **PA31** | 73 | F1 |
| Ardnacross **PA72** | 79 | G3 |
| Ardnadam **PA23** | 73 | K2 |
| Ardnadrochit **PA64** | 79 | J4 |
| Ardnagoine **IV26** | 95 | F1 |
| Ardnagowan **PA25** | 80 | C7 |
| Ardnahein **PA24** | 73 | K1 |
| Ardnahoe **PA46** | 72 | C3 |
| Ardnarff **IV53** | 86 | E1 |
| Ardnastang **PH36** | 79 | K1 |
| Ardnave **PA44** | 72 | A3 |
| Ardno **PA26** | 80 | C7 |
| Ardo **AB41** | 91 | G1 |
| Ardoch *D. & G.* **DG3** | 68 | D3 |
| Ardoch *Moray* **IV36** | 97 | J6 |
| Ardoch *P. & K.* **PH1** | 82 | B4 |
| Ardochrig **G75** | 74 | E6 |
| Ardoyne **AB52** | 90 | E2 |
| Ardpatrick **PA29** | 73 | F4 |
| Ardpeaton **G84** | 74 | A2 |
| Ardradnaig **PH15** | 81 | J3 |
| Ardrishaig **PA30** | 73 | G2 |
| Ardroe **IV27** | 102 | C6 |
| Ardross **IV17** | 96 | D4 |
| **Ardrossan KA22** | **74** | **A6** |
| Ardscalpsie **PA20** | 73 | J5 |

Ard - Bab

Ardshave IV25 96 E2
Ardshealach PH36 79 H1
Ardshellach PA34 79 J6
Ardsley S71 51 F2
Ardslignish PH36 79 G1
Ardtalla PA42 72 C5
Ardtalnaig PH15 81 J4
Ardtaraig PA23 73 J2
Ardteatle PA33 80 C5
Ardtoe PH36 86 C7
Ardtornish PA34 79 J3
Ardtrostan PH6 81 H5
Ardtur PA38 80 A3
Arduaine PA34 79 K6
Ardullie IV15 96 C5
Ardura PA65 79 H4
Ardvar IV27 102 D5
Ardvasar IV45 86 C4
Ardveenish HS9 84 C4
Ardveich FK19 81 H5
Ardverikie PH20 88 C6
Ardvorlich *Arg. & B.* G83 80 E6
Ardvorlich *P. & K.* FK19 81 H5
Ardwall DG7 65 F5
Ardwell *D. & G.* DG9 64 B6
Ardwell *Moray* AB54 90 B1
Ardwell *S.Ayr.* KA26 67 F4
Ardwick M12 49 H3
Areley Kings DY13 29 H1
Arford GU35 12 B3
Argaty FK16 81 J7
Argoed NP12 18 E2
Argoed Mill LD1 27 J2
Argos Hill TN20 13 J4
Argrennan House DG7 65 H5
Arichamish PA31 80 A7
Arichastlich PA33 80 D4
Arichonan PA31 73 F1
Aridhglas PA66 78 E5
Arienskill PH38 86 D6
Arileod PA78 78 C2
Arinacrinachd IV54 94 D6
Arinafad Beg PA31 73 F2
Arinagour PA78 78 D2
Arinambane HS8 84 C2
**Arisaig** PH39 86 C6
Arivegaig PH36 79 H1
Arkendale HG5 57 J3
Arkesden CB11 33 H5
Arkholme LA6 55 J2
Arkle Town DL11 62 B6
Arkleby CA7 60 C3
Arkleside DL8 57 F1
Arkleton DG13 69 J4
Arkley EN5 23 F2
Arksey DN5 51 H2
Arkwright Town S44 51 G5
Arlary KY13 82 C7
Arle GL51 29 J6
Arlecdon CA26 60 B5
**Arlesey** SG15 32 E5
Arleston TF1 39 F4
Arley CW9 49 F4
Arlingham GL2 29 G7
Arlington *Devon* EX31 6 E1
Arlington *E.Suss.* BN26 13 J6
Arlington *Glos.* GL7 20 E1
Arlington Beccott EX31 6 E1
Armadale *High.* KW14 104 C2
Armadale *High.* IV45 86 C4
Armadale *W.Loth.* EH48 75 H4
Armathwaite CA4 61 G2
Arminghall NR14 45 G5
Armitage WS15 40 C4
Armitage Bridge HD4 50 D1
Armley LS12 57 H6
Armscote CV37 30 D4
Armshead ST9 40 B1
Armston PE8 42 D7
Armthorpe DN3 51 J2
Arnabost PA78 78 D1
Arnaby LA18 54 E1
Arncliffe BD23 56 E2
Arncliffe Cote BD23 56 E2
Arncroach KY10 83 G7
Arne BH20 9 J6
Arnesby LE8 41 J6
Arngask PH2 82 C6
Arngibbon FK8 74 E1
Arngomery FK8 74 E1
Arnhall DD9 83 H1
Arnicle PA29 73 F7
Arnipol PH38 86 D6
Arnisdale IV40 86 E3
Arnish IV40 94 B7
Arniston Engine EH23 76 B4
Arnol HS2 101 F3
Arnold *E.Riding* HU11 59 H5
Arnold *Notts.* NG5 41 H1
Arnprior FK8 74 E1
Arnside LA5 55 H2
Arowry SY13 38 D2
Arrad Foot LA12 55 G1
Arradoul AB56 98 C4
Arram HU17 59 G5
**Arran** KA27 73 H7
Arras YO43 59 F5
Arrat DD9 83 H2
Arrathorne DL8 62 D7
Arreton PO30 11 G6
Arrington SG8 33 G3
Arrivain FK20 80 D4
**Arrochar** G83 80 E7
Arrow B49 30 B3
Arscaig IV27 103 H7
Arscott SY5 38 D5
Arthington LS21 57 H5
Arthingworth LE16 42 A7
**Arthog** LL39 37 F4
Arthrath AB41 91 H1
Arthurstone PH12 82 D3
Artrochie AB41 91 J1
Aruadh PA49 72 A4
**Arundel** BN18 12 D6
Aryhoulan PH33 80 B1
Asby CA14 60 B4
Ascog PA20 73 K4
**Ascot** SL5 22 C5
Ascott CV36 30 E5
Ascott d'Oyley OX7 30 E7
Ascott Earl OX7 30 D7
Ascott-under-Wychwood
OX7 30 E7
Ascreavie DD8 82 E2
Asenby YO7 57 K2
Asfordby LE14 42 A4
Asfordby Hill LE14 42 A4
Asgarby *Lincs.* PE23 53 G6
Asgarby *Lincs.* NG34 42 E1
Ash *Dorset* DT11 9 H3
Ash *Kent* CT3 15 H2
Ash *Kent* TN15 24 C5
Ash *Som.* TA12 8 D2
Ash *Surr.* GU12 22 B6
Ash Barton EX20 6 D5
Ash Bullayne EX17 7 F5
Ash Green *Surr.* GU12 22 C7
Ash Green *Warks.* CV7 41 F7
Ash Magna SY13 38 E2
Ash Mill EX36 7 F3
Ash Parva SY13 38 E2
Ash Priors TA4 7 K3
Ash Street IP7 34 E4
Ash Thomas EX16 7 J4
Ash Vale GU12 22 B6
Ashampstead RG8 21 J4
Ashbocking IP6 35 F3
**Ashbourne** DE6 40 D1
Ashbrittle TA21 7 J3
Ashburnham Place TN33 13 K5
Ashburton TQ13 5 H4
Ashbury *Devon* EX20 6 D6
Ashbury *Oxon.* SN6 21 F3
Ashby DN16 52 B2
Ashby by Partney PE23 53 H6
Ashby cum Fenby DN37 53 F2
Ashby de la Launde LN4 52 D7
**Ashby de la Zouch** LE65 41 F4
Ashby Dell NR32 45 J6
Ashby Folville LE14 42 A4
Ashby Hill DN37 53 F2
Ashby Magna LE17 41 H6
Ashby Parva LE17 41 H7
Ashby Puerorum LN9 53 G5
Ashby St. Ledgers CV23 31 G2
Ashby St. Mary NR14 45 H5
Ashchurch GL20 29 J5
Ashcombe *Devon* EX7 5 K3
Ashcombe *N.Som.* BS22 19 G5
Ashcott TA7 8 D1
Ashdon CB10 33 J4
Ashe RG25 21 J7
Asheldham CM0 25 F1
Ashen CO10 34 B4
Ashenden TN30 14 D4
Ashendon HP18 31 J7
Ashens PA29 73 G3
Ashfield *Arg. & B.* PA31 73 F2
Ashfield *Here.* HR9 28 E6
Ashfield *Stir.* FK15 81 J7
Ashfield *Suff.* IP14 35 G2
Ashfield Green *Suff.* IP21 35 G1
Ashfield Green *Suff.* CB8 34 B3
Ashfold Crossways RH13 13 F4
Ashford *Devon* TQ7 5 G6
Ashford *Devon* EX31 6 D2
Ashford *Hants.* SP6 10 C3
**Ashford** *Kent* TN23 15 F3
**Ashford** *Surr.* TW15 22 D4
Ashford Bowdler SY8 28 E1
Ashford Carbonel SY8 28 E1
Ashford Hill RG19 21 J5
Ashford in the Water DE45 50 D5
Ashgill ML9 75 F5
Ashiestiel TD1 76 C7
Ashill *Devon* EX15 7 J4
Ashill *Norf.* IP25 44 C5
Ashill *Som.* TA19 8 C3
Ashingdon SS4 24 E2
**Ashington** *Northumb.*
NE63 71 H5
Ashington *Som.* BA22 8 E2
Ashington *W.Suss.* RH20 12 E5
Ashkirk TD7 69 K1
Ashlett SO45 11 F4
Ashleworth GL19 29 H6
Ashleworth Quay GL19 29 H6
Ashley *Cambs.* CB8 33 K2
Ashley *Ches.E.* WA15 49 G4
Ashley *Devon* EX18 6 E4
Ashley *Glos.* GL8 20 C2
Ashley *Hants.* SO20 10 E1
Ashley *Hants.* BH25 10 D5
Ashley *Kent* CT15 15 J3
Ashley *Northants.* LE16 42 A6
Ashley *Staffs.* TF9 39 G2
Ashley *Wilts.* SN13 20 B5
Ashley Down BS7 19 J4
Ashley Green HP5 22 C1
Ashley Heath *Dorset* BH24 10 C4
Ashley Heath *Staffs.* TF9 39 G2
Ashmanhaugh NR12 45 H3
Ashmansworth RG20 21 H6
Ashmansworthy EX39 6 B4
Ashmore *Dorset* SP5 9 J3
Ashmore *P. & K.* PH10 82 C2
Ashmore Green RG18 21 J5
Ashorne CV35 30 E3
Ashover S45 51 F6
Ashover Hay S45 51 F6
Ashow CV8 30 E1
Ashperton HR8 29 F4
Ashprington TQ9 5 J5
Ashreigney EX18 6 E4
**Ashtead** KT21 22 E6
Ashton *Ches.W. & C.* CH3 48 E6
Ashton *Cornw.* TR13 2 D6
Ashton *Cornw.* PL17 4 D4
Ashton *Hants.* SO32 11 G3
Ashton *Here.* HR6 28 E2
Ashton *Inclyde* PA19 74 A3
Ashton *Northants.* PE8 42 D7
Ashton *Northants.* NN7 31 J4
Ashton *Peter.* PE9 42 E5
Ashton Common BA14 20 B6
Ashton Keynes SN6 20 D2
Ashton under Hill WR11 29 J5
Ashton upon Mersey
M33 49 G3
Ashton-in-Makerfield
WN4 48 E3
**Ashton-under-Lyne** OL7 49 J3
Ashurst *Hants.* SO40 10 E3
Ashurst *Kent* TN3 13 J3
Ashurst *W.Suss.* BN44 12 E5
Ashurst Bridge SO40 10 E3
Ashurstwood RH18 13 H3
Ashwater EX21 6 B6
Ashwell *Herts.* SG7 33 F5
Ashwell *Rut.* LE15 42 B4
Ashwell End SG7 33 F4
Ashwellthorpe NR16 45 F6
Ashwick BA3 19 K7
Ashwicken PE32 44 B4
Ashybank TD9 70 A2
**Askam in Furness** LA16 55 F2
Askern DN6 51 H1
Askernish (Aisgernis) HS8 84 C2
Askerswell DT2 8 E5
Askett HP27 22 B1
Askham *Cumb.* CA10 61 G4
Askham *Notts.* NG22 51 K5
Askham Bryan YO23 58 B5
Askham Richard YO23 58 B5
Asknish PA31 73 H1
Askrigg DL8 62 A7
Askwith LS21 57 G5
Aslackby NG34 42 D2
Aslacton NR15 45 F6
Aslockton NG13 42 A1
Asloun AB33 90 D3
Aspall IP14 35 F2
Aspatria CA7 60 C2
Aspenden SG9 33 G6
Asperton PE20 43 F2
Aspley Guise MK17 32 C5
Aspley Heath MK17 32 C5
Aspull WN2 49 F2
Asselby DN14 58 D7
Asserby LN13 53 H5
Assington CO10 34 D5
Assington Green CO10 34 B3
Astbury CW12 49 H6
Astcote NN12 31 H3
Asterby LN11 53 F5
Asterley SY5 38 C5
Asterton SY7 38 D6
Asthall OX18 30 D7
Asthall Leigh OX29 30 E7
Astle SK10 49 H5
Astley *Gt.Man.* M29 49 G2
Astley *Shrop.* SY4 38 E4
Astley *Warks.* CV10 41 F7
Astley *Worcs.* DY13 29 G2
Astley Abbotts WV16 39 G6
Astley Bridge BL1 49 G1
Astley Cross DY13 29 H2
Astley Green M29 49 G3
Astley Lodge SY4 38 E4
Aston *Ches.E.* CW5 39 F1
Aston *Ches.W. & C.* WA7 48 E5
Aston *Derbys.* S33 50 D4
Aston *Derbys.* DE6 40 D2
Aston *Flints.* CH5 48 C6
Aston *Here.* SY8 28 D1
Aston *Here.* HR6 28 D2
Aston *Herts.* SG2 33 F6
Aston *Oxon.* OX18 21 G1
Aston *S.Yorks.* S26 51 G4
Aston *Shrop.* SY4 38 E3
Aston *Shrop.* WV5 40 A6
Aston *Staffs.* TF9 39 G1
Aston *Tel. & W.* TF6 39 F5
Aston *W'ham* RG9 22 A3
Aston *W.Mid.* B6 40 C7
Aston Abbotts HP22 32 B6
Aston Botterell WV16 39 F7
Aston Cantlow B95 30 C3
Aston Clinton HP22 32 B7
Aston Crews HR9 29 F6
Aston Cross GL20 29 J5
Aston End SG2 33 F6
Aston Eyre WV16 39 F6
Aston Fields B60 29 J2
Aston Flamville LE10 41 G6
Aston Heath WA7 48 E5
Aston Ingham HR9 29 F6
Aston juxta Mondrum
CW5 49 F7
Aston le Walls NN11 31 F3
Aston Magna GL56 30 C5
Aston Munslow SY7 38 E7
Aston on Carrant GL20 29 J5
Aston on Clun SY7 38 C7
Aston Pigott SY5 38 C5
Aston Rogers SY5 38 C5
Aston Rowant OX49 22 A2
Aston Sandford HP17 22 A1
Aston Somerville WR12 30 B5
Aston Subedge GL55 30 C4
Aston Tirrold OX11 21 J3
Aston Upthorpe OX11 21 J3
Aston-by-Stone ST15 40 B2
Aston-on-Trent DE72 41 G3
Astwick SG5 33 F5
Astwood MK16 32 C4
Astwood Bank B96 30 B2
Aswarby NG34 42 D1
Aswardby PE23 53 G5
Aswick Grange PE12 43 G4
Atch Lench WR11 30 B3
Atcham SY5 38 E5
Ath Linne HS2 100 D6
Athelhampton DT2 9 G5
Athelington IP21 35 G1
Athelney TA7 8 C2
Athelstaneford EH39 76 D3
Atherington *Devon* EX37 6 D3
Atherington *W.Suss.* BN17 12 D6
Athersley North S71 51 F2
**Atherstone** CV9 41 F6
Atherstone on Stour CV37 30 D3
Atherton M46 49 F2
Atlow DE6 40 E1
Attadale IV54 87 F1
Attenborough NG9 41 H2
Atterby LN8 52 C3
Attercliffe S9 51 F4
Atterley TF13 39 F6
Atterton CV13 41 F6
**Attleborough** *Norf.* NR17 44 E6
Attleborough *Warks.* CV11 41 F6
Attlebridge NR9 45 F4
Attleton Green CB8 34 B3
Atwick YO25 59 H4
Atworth SN12 20 B5
Auberrow HR4 28 D4
Aubourn LN5 52 C6
Auch PA36 80 E4
Auchairne KA26 67 F5
Auchallater AB35 89 J6
Auchameanach PA29 73 G5
Auchamore KA27 73 G6
Aucharnie AB54 98 E6
Aucharrigill IV27 96 B1
Auchattie AB31 90 E5
Auchavan PH11 82 C1
Auchbraad PA30 73 G2
Auchbreck AB37 89 K2
Auchenback G78 74 D5
Auchenblae AB30 91 F7
Auchenbothie PA13 74 B3
Auchenbrack DG3 68 C4
Auchenbreck PA22 73 J2
Auchencairn DG7 65 H5
Auchencrow TD14 77 G4
Auchendinny EH26 76 A4
Auchendolly DG7 65 H4
Auchenfoyle PA13 74 B3
Auchengillan G63 74 D2
Auchengray ML11 75 H5
Auchenhalrig IV32 98 B4
Auchenheath ML11 75 G6
Auchenhessnane DG3 68 D4
Auchenlochan PA21 73 H3
Auchenmalg DG8 64 C5
Auchenrivock DG14 69 J5
Auchentiber KA13 74 B6
Auchenvennel G84 74 A2
Auchessan FK20 81 F5
Auchgourish PH24 89 G3
Auchinafaud PA29 73 F5
Auchincruive KA6 67 H1
Auchindarrach PA31 73 G2
Auchindarroch PA38 80 B2
Auchindrain PA32 80 B7
Auchindrean IV23 95 H3
Auchininna AB53 98 E6
Auchinleck KA18 67 K1
Auchinloch G66 74 E3
Auchinner PH6 81 H6
Auchinroath AB38 97 K6
Auchintoul *Aber.* AB33 90 D3
Auchintoul *Aber.* AB54 98 E5
Auchintoul *High.* IV27 96 C2
Auchiries AB42 91 J1
Auchleven AB52 90 E2
Auchlochan ML11 75 G7
Auchlunachan IV23 95 H3
Auchlunies AB12 91 G5
Auchlunkart AB55 98 B6
Auchlyne FK21 81 G5
Auchmacoy AB41 91 H1
Auchmair AB54 90 B2
Auchmantle DG8 64 B4
Auchmithie DD11 83 H3
Auchmuirbridge KY6 82 D7
Auchmull DD9 90 D7
Auchnabony DG6 65 H6
Auchnabreac PA32 80 B7
Auchnacloich PH8 81 K4
Auchnacraig PA64 79 J4
Auchnacree DD8 83 F1
Auchnafree PH8 81 K4
Auchnagallin PH26 89 H1
Auchnagatt AB41 99 H6
Auchnaha PA21 73 H2
Auchnangoul PA32 80 B7
Aucholzie AB35 90 B5
Auchorrie AB51 90 E4
Auchrannie PH11 82 D2
Auchraw FK19 81 G5
Auchreoch FK20 80 E5
Auchronie DD9 90 C6
**Auchterarder** PH3 82 A6
Auchtercairn IV21 94 E4
Auchterderran KY5 76 A1
Auchterhouse DD3 82 E4
Auchtermuchty KY14 82 D6
Auchterneed IV14 96 B6
Auchtertool KY2 76 A1
Auchtertyre *Angus* PH12 82 D3
Auchtertyre *High.* IV40 86 E2
Auchtertyre *Moray* IV30 97 J6
Auchtertyre *Stir.* FK20 80 E5
Auchtubh FK19 81 G5
Auckengill KW1 105 J2
Auckley DN9 51 J2
Audenshaw M34 49 J3
Audlem CW3 39 F1
Audley ST7 49 G7
Audley End *Essex* CB11 33 J5
Audley End *Essex* CO9 34 C5
Audley End *Suff.* IP29 34 C3
Audmore ST20 40 A3
Auds AB45 98 E4
Aughton *E.Riding* YO42 58 D6
Aughton *Lancs.* L39 48 C2
Aughton *Lancs.* LA2 55 J3
Aughton *S.Yorks.* S26 51 G4
Aughton *Wilts.* SN8 21 F6
Aughton Park L39 48 D2
Auldearn IV12 97 G6
Aulden HR6 28 D3
Auldgirth DG2 68 E5
Auldhame EH39 76 D2
Auldhouse G75 74 E5
Aulich PH17 81 H2
Ault a'chruinn IV40 87 F2
Ault Hucknall S44 51 G6
Aultanrynie IV27 103 F5
Aultbea IV22 94 E3
Aultgrishan IV21 94 D3
Aultguish Inn IV23 95 K4
Aultibea KW7 105 F6
Aultiphurst KW14 104 D2
Aultmore AB55 98 C5
Ault-na-goire IV2 88 C2
Aultnamain Inn IV19 96 D3
Aultnapaddock AB55 98 B6
Aulton AB52 90 E2
Aultvaich IV4 96 C7
Aultvoulin PH41 86 D4
Aunby PE9 42 D4
Aundorach PH25 89 G3
Aunk EX15 7 J5
Aunsby NG34 42 D2
Auquhorthies AB51 91 G2
Aust BS35 19 J3
Austerfield DN10 51 J3
Austrey CV9 40 E5
Austwick LA2 56 C3
Authorpe LN11 53 H4
Authorpe Row PE24 53 J5
Avebury SN8 20 E4
Avebury Trusloe SN8 20 D5
Aveley RM15 23 J3
Avening GL8 20 B2
Averham NG23 51 K7
Avery Hill SE9 23 H4
Aveton Gifford TQ7 5 G6
Avielochan PH22 89 G3
**Aviemore** PH22 89 F3
Avington *Hants.* SO21 11 G1
Avington *W.Berks.* RG17 21 G5
**Avoch** IV9 96 D6
Avon BH23 10 C5
Avon Dassett CV47 31 F3
Avonbridge FK1 75 H3
Avoncliff BA15 20 B6
Avonmouth BS11 19 J4
Avonwick TQ10 5 H5
Awbridge SO51 10 E2
Awhirk DG9 64 A5
Awkley BS35 19 J3
Awliscombe EX14 7 K5
Awre GL14 20 A1
Awsworth NG16 41 G1
**Axbridge** BS26 19 H6
Axford *Hants.* RG25 21 K7
Axford *Wilts.* SN8 21 F4
**Axminster** EX13 8 B5
Axmouth EX12 8 B5
Axton CH8 47 K4
Axtown PL20 5 F4
Aycliffe DL5 62 D4
Aydon NE45 71 F7
Aylburton GL15 19 K1
Ayle CA9 61 J2
Aylesbeare EX5 7 J6
**Aylesbury** HP20 32 B7
Aylesby DN37 53 F2
**Aylesford** ME20 14 C2
Aylesham CT3 15 H2
Aylestone LE2 41 H5
Aylmerton NR11 45 F2
Aylsham NR11 45 F3
Aylton HR8 29 F5
Aymestrey HR6 28 D2
Aynho OX17 31 G5
Ayot Green AL6 33 F7
Ayot St. Lawrence AL6 32 E7
Ayot St. Peter AL6 33 F7
**Ayr** KA7 67 H1
Aysgarth DL8 57 F1
Ayshford EX16 7 J4
Ayside LA11 55 G1
Ayston LE15 42 B5
Aythorpe Roding CM6 33 J7
Ayton *P. & K.* PH2 82 C6
Ayton *Sc.Bord.* TD14 77 H4
Aywick ZE2 107 P4
Azerley HG4 57 H2

## B

Babbacombe TQ1 5 K4
Babbinswood SY11 38 C2
Babb's Green SG12 33 G7
Babcary TA11 8 E2

# Bab - Bar



Babel SA20 27 H5
Babell CH8 47 K5
Babeny TQ13 5 G3
Bablock Hythe OX29 21 H1
Babraham CB22 33 J3
Babworth DN22 51 J4
Baby's Hill AB37 89 K1
Bac HS2 101 G3
Bachau LL71 46 C4
Back of Keppoch PH39 86 C6
Back Street CB8 34 B3
Backaland KW17 106 E4
Backaskaill KW17 106 D2
Backbarrow LA12 55 G1
Backburn AB54 90 D1
Backe SA33 17 F4
Backfolds AB42 99 J5
Backford CH2 48 D5
Backhill AB53 91 F1
Backhill of Clackriach AB42 99 H6
Backhill of Trustach AB31 90 E5
Backies *High.* KW10 97 F1
Backies *Moray* AB56 98 D5
Backlass KW1 105 H3
Backside AB54 90 C1
Backwell BS48 19 H5
Backworth NE23 71 H6
Bacon End CM6 33 J7
Baconend Green CM6 33 J7
Baconsthorpe NR25 45 F2
Bacton *Here.* HR2 28 C5
Bacton *Norf.* NR12 45 H2
Bacton *Suff.* IP14 34 E2
Bacton Green IP14 34 E2
**Bacup OL13 56 D7**
Badachro IV21 94 D4
Badanloch Lodge KW11 104 C5
Badavanich IV22 95 H6
Badbea KW7 105 F7
Badbury SN4 20 E3
Badbury Wick SN4 20 E3
Badby NN11 31 G3
Badcall *High.* IV27 102 D4
Badcall *High.* IV27 102 E3
Badcaul IV23 95 G2
Baddeley Green ST2 49 J7
Badden PA31 73 G2
Baddesley Clinton B93 30 C1
Baddesley Ensor CV9 40 E6
Baddidarach IV27 102 C6
Badenscoth AB51 91 F1
Badenyon AB36 90 B3
Badgall PL15 4 C2
Badger WV6 39 G6
Badgerbank SK11 49 H5
Badgers Mount TN14 23 H5
Badgeworth GL51 29 J7
Badgworth BS26 19 G6
Badicaul IV40 86 D2
Badingham IP13 35 H2
Badintagairt IV27 103 G7
Badlesmere ME13 15 F2
Badley IP6 34 E3
Badlipster KW1 105 H4
Badluarach IV23 95 F2
**Badminton GL9 20 B3**
Badnaban IV27 102 C6
Badnabay IV27 102 E4
Badnafrave AB37 89 K3
Badnagie KW6 105 G5
Badnambiast PH18 88 E7
Badninish IV25 96 E2
Badrallach IV23 95 G2
Badsey WR11 30 B4
Badshot Lea GU9 22 B7
Badsworth WF9 51 G1
Badwell Ash IP31 34 D2
Badworthy TQ10 5 G4
Badyo PH16 82 A1
Bae Cinmel (Kinmel Bay) LL18 47 H4
**Bae Colwyn (Colwyn Bay) LL29 47 G5**
Bae Penrhyn (Penrhyn Bay) LL30 47 G4
Bag Enderby PE23 53 G5
Bagber DT10 9 G3
Bagby YO7 57 K1
Bagendon GL7 20 D1
Bagginswood DY14 39 F7
Baggrave Hall LE7 41 J5
Baggrow CA7 60 C2
Bàgh a'Chaisteil (Castlebay) HS9 84 B5
Bàgh Mòr HS6 92 D6
Baghasdal HS8 84 C3
**Bagillt CH6 48 B5**
Baginton CV8 30 E1
Baglan SA12 18 A2
Bagley *Shrop.* SY12 38 D3
Bagley *Som.* BS28 19 H7
Bagmore RG25 21 K7
Bagnall ST9 49 J7
Bagnor RG20 21 H5
Bagpath GL8 20 B2
**Bagshot *Surr.* GU19 22 C5**
Bagshot *Wilts.* RG17 21 G5
Bagstone GL12 19 K3
Bagthorpe *Norf.* PE31 44 B2
Bagthorpe *Notts.* NG16 51 G7
Baguley M23 49 H4
Bagworth LE67 41 G5
Bagwyllydiart HR2 28 D6
Baildon BD17 57 G6
Baile Ailein (Balallan) HS2 100 E5
Baile a'Mhanaich (Balivanich) HS7 92 C6
Baile an Truiseil HS2 101 F2
Baile Boidheach PA31 73 F3
Baile Gharbhaidh HS8 92 C7
Baile Glas HS6 92 D6
Baile Lion (Balelone) HS6 92 C4
Baile Mhartainn HS6 92 C4
Baile Mhic Phail HS6 92 D4
Baile Mòr *Arg. & B.* PA76 78 D5
Baile Mòr (Balemore) *W.Isles* HS6 92 C5
Baile nan Cailleach HS7 92 C6
Baile Raghaill HS6 92 C5
Bailebeag IV2 88 C3
Baileguish PH21 89 F5
Baile-na-Cille HS6 92 D3
Bailetonach PH36 86 C7
Bailiesward AB54 90 C1
Bailiff Bridge HD6 57 G7
Baillieston G69 74 E4
Bainbridge DL8 62 A7
Bainsford FK2 75 G2
Bainshole AB54 90 E1
Bainton *E.Riding* YO25 59 F4
Bainton *Oxon.* OX27 31 G6
Bainton *Peter.* PE9 42 D5
Bairnkine TD8 70 B2
Bakebare AB55 90 B1
Baker Street RM16 24 C3
Baker's End SG12 33 G7
**Bakewell DE45 50 E6**
**Bala (Y Bala) LL23 37 J2**
Balachuirn IV40 94 B7
Balado KY13 82 B7
Balafark G63 74 E1
Balaldie IV20 97 F4
**Balallan (Baile Ailein) HS2 100 E5**
Balavil PH21 88 E4
Balbeg *High.* IV63 88 B1
Balbeg *High.* IV63 88 B2
Balbeggie PH2 82 C5
Balbirnie KY7 82 D7
Balbithan AB51 91 F3
Balblair *High.* IV7 96 E5
Balblair *High.* IV24 96 C2
Balblair *High.* IV19 96 E3
Balby DN4 51 H2
Balcharn IV27 96 C1
Balcherry IV19 97 F3
Balchers AB45 99 F5
Balchladich IV27 102 C5
Balchraggan *High.* IV5 96 C7
Balchraggan *High.* IV3 88 C1
Balchrick IV27 102 D3
Balcombe RH17 13 G3
Balcurvie KY8 82 E7
Baldernock G62 74 D3
Baldersby YO7 57 J2
Baldersby St. James YO7 57 J2
Balderstone *Gt.Man.* OL16 49 J1
Balderstone *Lancs.* BB2 56 B6
Balderton *Ches.W. & C.* CH4 48 C6
Balderton *Notts.* NG24 52 B7
Baldhu TR3 2 E4
Baldinnie KY15 83 F6
**Baldock SG7 33 F5**
Baldon Row OX44 21 J1
Baldovan DD3 82 E4
Baldovie *Angus* DD8 82 E2
Baldovie *Dundee* DD5 83 F4
Baldrine IM4 54 D5
Baldslow TN37 14 C6
Baldwin IM4 54 C5
Baldwinholme CA5 60 E1
Baldwin's Gate ST5 39 G1
Baldwins Hill RH19 13 G3
Bale NR21 44 E2
Balelone (Baile Lion) HS6 92 C4
Balemartine PA77 78 A3
Balemore (Baile Mòr) HS6 92 C5
Balendoch PH12 82 D3
Balephuil PA77 78 A3
**Balerno EH14 75 K4**
Balernock G84 74 A2
Baleromindubh PA61 72 B1
Balerominmore PA61 72 B1
Baleshare (Bhaleshear) HS6 92 C5
Balevulin PA69 79 F5
Balfield DD9 83 G1
Balfour *Aber.* AB34 90 D5
Balfour *Ork.* KW17 106 D6
Balfron G63 74 D2
Balfron Station G63 74 D2
Balgonar KY12 75 J1
Balgove AB51 91 G1
Balgowan *D. & G.* DG9 64 B6
Balgowan *High.* PH20 88 D5
Balgown IV51 93 J5
Balgreen AB45 99 F5
Balgreggan DG9 64 A5
Balgy IV54 94 E6
Balhaldie FK15 81 K7
Balhalgardy AB51 91 F2
Balham SW12 23 F4
Balhary PH11 82 D3
Balhelvie KY14 82 E5
Balhousie KY8 83 F7
Baliasta ZE2 107 Q2
Baligill KW14 104 D2
Baligrundle PA34 79 K3
Balindore PA35 80 A4
Balintore *Angus* DD8 82 D2
Balintore *High.* IV20 97 F4
Balintraid IV18 96 E4
Balintyre PH15 81 H3
Balivanich (Baile a'Mhanaich) HS7 92 C6
Balkeerie DD8 82 E3
Balkholme DN14 58 D7
Balkissock KA26 67 F5
Ball SY10 38 C3
Ball Haye Green ST13 49 J7
Ball Hill RG20 21 H5
Balla HS8 84 C3
Ballabeg IM9 54 B6
Ballacannell IM4 54 D5
Ballacarnane Beg IM6 54 B5
**Ballachulish PH49 80 B2**
Balladoole IM9 54 B7
Ballafesson IM9 54 B6
Ballagyr IM5 54 B5
Ballajora IM7 54 D4
Ballakilpheric IM9 54 B6
Ballamodha IM9 54 B6
Ballantrae KA26 66 E5
Ballards Gore SS4 25 F2
Ballasalla *I.o.M.* IM9 54 B6
Ballasalla *I.o.M.* IM7 54 C4
**Ballater AB35 90 B5**
Ballaterach AB34 90 C5
Ballaugh IM7 54 C4
Ballaveare IM4 54 C6
Ballchraggan IV18 96 E4
Ballechin PH9 82 A2
Balleich FK8 81 G7
Ballencrieff EH32 76 C3
Ballidon DE6 50 E7
Balliekine KA27 73 G6
Balliemeanoch PA27 80 C7
Balliemore *Arg. & B.* PA27 73 K1
Balliemore *Arg. & B.* PA34 79 K5
Ballig IM4 54 B5
Ballimeanoch PA33 80 B6
Ballimore *Arg. & B.* PA21 73 H2
Ballimore *Stir.* FK19 81 G6
Ballinaby PA44 72 A4
Ballindean PH14 82 D5
Ballingdon CO10 34 C4
Ballinger Common HP16 22 C1
Ballingham HR2 28 E5
Ballingry KY5 75 K1
Ballinlick PH8 82 A3
Ballinluig *P. & K.* PH9 82 A2
Ballinluig *P. & K.* PH10 82 B2
Ballintuim PH10 82 C2
Balloch *Angus* DD8 82 E2
Balloch *High.* IV2 96 E7
Balloch *N.Lan.* G68 75 F3
Balloch *W.Dun.* G83 74 B2
Ballochan AB31 90 D5
Ballochandrain PA22 73 H2
Ballochford AB54 90 B1
Ballochgair PA28 66 B1
Ballochmartin KA28 73 K5
Ballochmorrie KA26 67 G5
Ballochmyle KA5 67 K1
Ballochroy PA29 73 F5
Ballogie AB34 90 D5
Balls Cross GU28 12 C4
Balls Green *Essex* CO7 34 E6
Ball's Green *Glos.* GL6 20 B2
Balls Hill B71 40 B6
Ballyaurgan PA31 73 F3
Ballygown PA73 79 F3
Ballygrant PA45 72 B4
Ballyhaugh PA78 78 C2
Ballymeanoch PA31 73 G1
Ballymichael KA27 73 H7
Balmacara IV40 86 E2
Balmaclellan DG7 65 G3
Balmacneil PH8 82 A2
Balmadies DD8 83 G3
Balmae DG6 65 G6
Balmaha G63 74 C1
Balmalcolm KY15 82 E7
Balmaqueen IV51 93 K4
Balmeanach *Arg. & B.* PA65 79 H3
Balmeanach *Arg. & B.* PA68 79 F4
Balmedie AB23 91 H3
Balmer Heath SY12 38 D2
Balmerino DD6 82 E5
Balmerlawn SO42 10 E4
Balminnoch DG8 64 C4
Balmore *E.Dun.* G64 74 E3
Balmore *High.* IV12 97 F7
Balmore *High.* IV4 87 K1
Balmore *High.* IV55 93 H7
Balmore *P. & K.* PH16 81 J2
Balmullo KY16 83 F5
Balmungie IV10 96 E6
Balmyle PH10 82 B2
Balnaboth DD8 82 E1
Balnabruaich IV19 96 E4
Balnacra IV54 95 F7
Balnafoich IV2 88 D1
Balnagall IV20 97 F3
Balnagown Castle IV18 96 E4
Balnaguard PH9 82 A2
Balnaguisich IV18 96 D4
Balnahard *Arg. & B.* PA61 72 C1
Balnahard *Arg. & B.* PA68 79 F4
Balnain IV63 88 B1
Balnakeil IV27 103 F2
Balnaknock IV51 93 K5
Balnamoon DD9 83 G1
Balnapaling IV19 96 E5
Balnespick PH21 89 F4
Balquhidder FK19 81 G5
Balsall CV7 30 D1
Balsall Common CV7 30 D1
Balsall Heath B12 40 C7
Balscote OX15 30 E4
Balsham CB21 33 J3
Baltasound ZE2 107 Q2
Balterley CW2 49 G7
Balterley Heath CW2 49 G7
Baltersan DG8 64 E4
Balthangie AB53 99 G5
Balthayock PH2 82 C5
Baltonsborough BA6 8 E1
Baluachraig PA31 73 G1
Balulive PA45 72 C4
Balure *Arg. & B.* PA35 80 B4
Balure *Arg. & B.* PA37 79 K4
Balvaird IV6 96 C6
Balvarran PH10 82 B1
Balvicar PA34 79 J6
Balvraid *High.* IV40 86 E3
Balvraid *High.* IV13 89 F1
Bamber Bridge PR5 55 J7
Bamber's Green CM22 33 J6
**Bamburgh NE69 77 K7**
Bamff PH11 82 D2
Bamford *Derbys.* S33 50 E4
Bamford *Gt.Man.* OL11 49 H1
Bampton *Cumb.* CA10 61 G5
Bampton *Devon* EX16 7 H3
**Bampton *Oxon.* OX18 21 G1**
Bampton Grange CA10 61 G5
Banavie PH33 87 H7
**Banbury OX16 31 F4**
Bancffosfelen SA15 17 H4
Banchor IV12 97 G7
**Banchory AB31 91 F5**
Banchory-Devenick AB12 91 H4
Bancycapel SA32 17 H4
Bancyfelin SA33 17 G4
Bancyffordd SA44 17 H2
Bandon KY7 82 D7
Bandrake Head LA12 55 G1
**Banff AB45 98 E4**
**Bangor LL57 46 D5**
Bangor-is-y-coed LL13 38 C1
Bangor's Green L39 48 C2
Banham NR16 44 E7
Bank SO43 10 D4
Bank End LA20 54 E1
Bank Newton BD23 56 E4
Bank Street WR15 29 F2
Bank Top *Lancs.* WN8 48 E2
Bank Top *W.Yorks.* HX3 57 G7
Bankend DG1 69 F7
Bankfoot PH1 82 B4
Bankglen KA18 67 K2
Bankhead *Aber.* AB33 90 E3
Bankhead *Aber.* AB51 90 E4
Bankhead *Aberdeen* AB21 91 G3
Bankhead *D. & G.* DG6 65 H6
Bankland TA7 8 C2
Banknock FK4 75 F3
Banks *Cumb.* CA8 70 A7
Banks *Lancs.* PR9 55 G7
Bankshill DG11 69 G5
Banningham NR11 45 G3
Bannister Green CM6 33 K6
Bannockburn FK7 75 G1
**Banstead SM7 23 F6**
Bantam Grove LS27 57 H7
Bantham TQ7 5 G6
Banton G65 75 F3
**Banwell BS29 19 G6**
Banwen Pyrddin SA10 18 B1
Banyard's Green IP13 35 H1
Bapchild ME9 25 F5
Baptiston G63 74 D2
Bapton BA12 9 J1
Bar End SO23 11 F2
Bar Hill CB23 33 G2
Barabhas (Barvas) HS2 101 F3
Barachander PA35 80 B5
Barassie KA10 74 B7
Barbaraville IV18 96 E4
Barber Booth S33 50 D4
Barber Green LA11 55 G1
Barber's Moor PR26 48 D1
Barbon LA6 56 B1
Barbridge CW5 49 F7
Barbrook EX35 7 F1
Barby CV23 31 G1
Barcaldine PA37 80 A3
Barcaple DG7 65 G5
Barcheston CV36 30 D5
Barclose CA6 69 K7
Barcombe BN8 13 H5
Barcombe Cross BN8 13 H5
Barden DL8 62 C7
Barden Park TN9 23 J7
Bardennoch DG7 67 K4
Bardfield End Green CM6 33 K5
Bardfield Saling CM7 33 K6
Bardister ZE2 107 M5
Bardney LN3 52 E6
Bardon *Leics.* LE67 41 G4
Bardon *Moray* IV30 97 K6
Bardon Mill NE47 70 C7
Bardowie G62 74 D3
Bardsea LA12 55 F2
Bardsey LS17 57 J5
Bardsey Island (Ynys Enlli) LL53 36 A3
Bardwell IP31 34 D1
Bare LA4 55 H3
Barewood HR6 28 C3
Barfad PA29 73 G4
Barford *Norf.* NR9 45 F5
Barford *Warks.* CV35 30 D2
Barford St. John OX15 31 F5
Barford St. Martin SP3 10 B1
Barford St. Michael OX15 31 F5
Barfrestone CT15 15 H2
Bargaly DG8 64 E4
Bargany Mains KA26 67 G3
Bargeddie G69 74 E4
**Bargoed CF81 18 E2**
Bargrennan DG8 64 D3
Barham *Cambs.* PE28 32 E1
Barham *Kent* CT4 15 H2
Barham *Suff.* IP6 35 F3
Barharrow DG7 65 G5
Barholm PE9 42 D4
Barholm Mains DG8 64 E5
Barkby LE7 41 J5
Barkby Thorpe LE7 41 J5
Barkers Green SY4 38 E3
Barkestone-le-Vale NG13 42 A2
Barkham RG41 22 A5
**Barking *Gt.Lon.* IG11 23 H3**
Barking *Suff.* IP6 34 E3
Barking Tye IP6 34 E3
Barkisland HX4 57 F7
Barkston NG32 42 C1
Barkston Ash LS24 57 K6
Barkway SG8 33 G5
Barlae DG8 64 C4
Barland LD8 28 B2
Barlaston ST12 40 A2
Barlavington GU28 12 C5
Barlborough S43 51 G5
Barlby YO8 58 C6
Barlestone CV13 41 G5
Barley *Herts.* SG8 33 G5
Barley *Lancs.* BB12 56 D5
Barley Green IP21 35 G1
Barleycroft End SG9 33 H6
Barleyhill NE44 62 B1
Barleythorpe LE15 42 B5
Barling SS3 25 F3
Barlings LN3 52 D5
Barlow *Derbys.* S18 51 F5
Barlow *N.Yorks.* YO8 58 C7
Barlow *T. & W.* NE21 71 G7
Barmby Moor YO42 58 D5
Barmby on the Marsh DN14 58 C7
Barmer PE31 44 C2
Barmolloch PA31 73 G1
Barmoor Lane End TD15 77 J7
**Barmouth (Abermaw) LL42 37 F4**
Barmpton DL1 62 E5
Barmston YO25 59 H4
Barnaby Green NR34 35 J1
Barnacabber PA23 73 K2
Barnacarry PA27 73 H1
Barnack PE9 42 D5
Barnacle CV7 41 F7
Barnamuc PA38 80 B3
**Barnard Castle DL12 62 B5**
Barnard Gate OX29 31 F7
Barnardiston CB9 34 B4
Barnard's Green WR14 29 G4
Barnbarroch *D. & G.* DG8 64 D5
Barnbarroch *D. & G.* DG5 65 J5
Barnburgh DN5 51 G2
Barnby NR34 45 J7
Barnby Dun DN3 51 J2
Barnby in the Willows NG24 52 B7
Barnby Moor DN22 51 J4
Barndennoch DG2 68 D5
Barne Barton PL5 4 E5
Barnehurst DA7 23 J4
Barnes SW13 23 F4
Barnes Street TN11 23 K7
**Barnet EN5 23 F2**
Barnet Gate EN5 23 F2
**Barnetby le Wold DN38 52 D2**
Barney NR21 44 D2
Barnham *Suff.* IP24 34 C1
Barnham *W.Suss.* PO22 12 C6
Barnham Broom NR9 44 E5
Barnhead DD10 83 H2
Barnhill *Ches.W. & C.* CH3 48 D7
Barnhill *Dundee* DD5 83 F4
Barnhill *Moray* IV30 97 J6
Barnhills DG9 66 D6
Barningham *Dur.* DL11 62 B5
Barningham *Suff.* IP31 34 D1
Barningham Green NR11 45 F2
Barnoldby le Beck DN37 53 F2
**Barnoldswick BB18 56 D5**
Barns Green RH13 12 E4
Barnsdale Bar WF8 51 H1
Barnsley *Glos.* GL7 20 D1
**Barnsley *S.Yorks.* S70 51 F2**
Barnsole CT3 15 H2
**Barnstaple EX31 6 D2**
Barnston *Essex* CM6 33 K7
Barnston *Mersey.* CH61 48 B4
Barnstone NG13 42 A2
Barnt Green B45 30 B1
Barnton *Ches.W. & C.* CW8 49 F5
Barnton *Edin.* EH4 75 K3
Barnwell All Saints PE8 42 D7
Barnwell St. Andrew PE8 42 D7
Barnwood GL4 29 H7
Barons' Cross HR6 28 D3
Barr *Arg. & B.* PA44 72 B4
Barr *High.* PA34 79 H2
Barr *S.Ayr.* KA26 67 G4
Barr *Som.* TA4 7 K3
Barr Hall CO9 34 B5
**Barra (Barraigh) HS9 84 B4**
Barra (Tràigh Mhòr) Airport HS9 84 B4
Barrachan DG8 64 D6
Barrackan PA31 79 J7
Barraer DG8 64 D4
Barraglom HS2 100 D4
Barrahormid PA31 73 F2
**Barraigh (Barra) HS9 84 B4**
Barran PA33 80 C5
Barrapoll PA77 78 A3
Barrasford NE48 70 E6
Barravullin PA31 79 K7
Barregarrow IM6 54 C5

Bar - Bet

Barrets Green CW6 48 E7
Barrhead G78 74 C5
Barrhill KA26 67 G5
Barrington Cambs. CB22 33 G4
Barrington Som. TA19 8 C3
Barripper TR14 2 D5
Barrisdale PH35 86 E4
Barrmill KA15 74 B5
Barrnacarry PA34 79 K5
Barrock KW14 105 H1
Barrow Glos. GL51 29 H6
Barrow Lancs. BB7 56 C6
Barrow Rut. LE15 42 B4
Barrow Shrop. TF12 39 F5
Barrow Som. BA9 9 G1
Barrow Som. BA4 19 J7
Barrow Suff. IP29 34 B2
Barrow Gurney BS48 19 J5
Barrow Hann DN19 59 G7
Barrow Haven DN19 59 G7
Barrow Hill S43 51 G5
Barrow Nook L39 48 D2
Barrow Street BA12 9 H1
Barrow upon Humber DN19 59 G7
Barrow upon Soar LE12 41 H4
Barrow upon Trent DE73 41 F3
Barroway Drove PE38 43 J5
Barrowby NG32 42 B2
Barrowcliff YO12 59 G1
Barrowden LE15 42 C5
Barrowford BB9 56 D6
Barrow-in-Furness LA14 55 F3
Barrows Green LA8 55 J1
Barry Angus DD7 83 G4
Barry V. of Glam. CF62 18 E5
Barsby LE7 41 J4
Barsham NR34 45 H7
Barskimming KA5 67 J1
Barsloisnoch PA31 73 G1
Barston B92 30 D1
Bartestree HR1 28 E4
Barthol Chapel AB51 91 G1
Bartholomew Green CM77 34 B6
Barthomley CW2 49 G7
Bartley SO40 10 E3
Bartley Green B32 40 C7
Bartlow CB21 33 J4
Barton Cambs. CB23 33 H3
Barton Ches.W. & C. SY14 48 D7
Barton Cumb. CA10 61 F4
Barton Glos. GL54 30 B6
Barton Lancs. PR3 55 J6
Barton Lancs. L39 48 C2
Barton N.Yorks. DL10 62 D6
Barton Oxon. OX3 21 J1
Barton Torbay TQ2 5 K4
Barton Warks. B50 30 C3
Barton Bendish PE33 44 B5
Barton End GL6 20 B2
Barton Green DE13 40 D4
Barton Hartshorn MK18 31 H5
Barton Hill YO60 58 D3
Barton in Fabis NG11 41 H2
Barton in the Beans CV13 41 F5
Barton Mills IP28 34 B1
Barton on Sea BH25 10 D5
Barton St. David TA11 8 E1
Barton Seagrave NN15 32 B1
Barton Stacey SO21 21 H7
Barton Town EX31 6 E1
Barton Turf NR12 45 H3
Bartongate OX7 31 F6
Barton-le-Clay MK45 32 D5
Barton-le-Street YO17 58 D2
Barton-le-Willows YO60 58 D3
Barton-on-the-Heath GL56 30 D5
Barton-under-Needwood DE13 40 D4
Barton-upon-Humber DN18 59 G7
Barvas (Barabhas) HS2 101 F3
Barway CB7 33 J1
Barwell LE9 41 G6
Barwhinnock DG6 65 G5
Barwick Herts. SG11 33 G7
Barwick Som. BA22 8 E3
Barwick in Elmet LS15 57 J6
Barwinnock DG8 64 D6
Baschurch SY4 38 D3
Bascote CV47 31 F2
Base Green IP14 34 E2
Basford Green ST13 49 J7
Bashall Eaves BB7 56 B5
Bashall Town BB7 56 C5
Bashley BH25 10 D5
Basildon Essex SS14 24 D3
Basildon W.Berks. RG8 21 K4
Basingstoke RG21 21 K6
Baslow DE45 50 E5
Bason Bridge TA9 19 G7
Bassaleg NP10 19 F3
Bassenthwaite CA12 60 D3
Basset's Cross EX20 6 D5
Bassett SO16 11 F3
Bassingbourn SG8 33 G4
Bassingfield NG12 41 J2
Bassingham LN5 52 C7
Bassingthorpe NG33 42 C3
Basta ZE2 107 P3
Baston PE6 42 E4
Bastonford WR2 29 H3
Bastwick NR29 45 J4
Batavaime FK21 81 F4
Batch BS24 19 G6
Batchley B97 30 B2
Batchworth WD3 22 D2
Batchworth Heath WD3 22 D2
Batcombe Dorset DT2 9 F4
Batcombe Som. BA4 9 F1
Bate Heath CW9 49 F5
BATH BA 20 A5
Bathampton BA2 20 A5
Bathealton TA4 7 J3
Batheaston BA1 20 A5
Bathford BA1 20 A5
Bathgate EH48 75 H4
Bathley NG23 51 K7
Bathpool Cornw. PL15 4 C3
Bathpool Som. TA2 8 B2
Bathway BA3 19 J6
Batley WF17 57 H7
Batsford GL56 30 C5
Batson TQ8 5 H7
Battersby TS9 63 G6
Battersea SW11 23 F4
Battisborough Cross PL8 5 G6
Battisford IP14 34 E3
Battisford Tye IP14 34 E3
Battle E.Suss. TN33 14 C6
Battle Powys LD3 27 K5
Battledown GL52 29 J6
Battlefield SY1 38 E4
Battlesbridge SS11 24 D2
Battlesden MK17 32 C6
Battlesea Green IP21 35 G1
Battleton TA22 7 H3
Battlies Green IP30 34 D2
Battramsley SO41 10 E5
Batt's Corner GU10 22 B7
Bauds of Cullen AB56 98 C4
Baugh PA77 78 B3
Baughton WR8 29 H4
Baughurst RG26 21 J5
Baulds AB31 90 E5
Baulking SN7 21 G2
Baumber LN9 53 F5
Baunton GL7 20 D1
Baveney Wood DY14 29 F1
Baverstock SP3 10 B1
Bawburgh NR9 45 F5
Bawdeswell NR20 44 E3
Bawdrip TA7 8 C1
Bawdsey IP12 35 H4
Bawdsey Manor IP12 35 H5
Bawsey PE32 44 A4
Bawtry DN10 51 J3
Baxenden BB5 56 C7
Baxterley CV9 40 E6
Baxter's Green CB8 34 B3
Bay SP8 9 H2
Baybridge DH8 62 A2
Baycliff LA12 55 F2
Baydon SN8 21 F4
Bayford Herts. SG13 23 G1
Bayford Som. BA9 9 G2
Bayfordbury SG13 33 G7
Bayham Abbey TN3 13 K3
Bayles CA9 61 J2
Baylham IP6 35 F3
Baynards Green OX27 31 G6
Baysham HR9 28 E6
Bayston Hill SY3 38 D5
Bayswater W2 23 F3
Baythorn End CO9 34 B4
Bayton DY14 29 F1
Bayworth OX13 21 J1
Beach High. PA34 79 J2
Beach S.Glos. BS30 20 A4
Beachampton MK19 31 J5
Beachamwell PE37 44 B5
Beacharr PA29 72 E6
Beachley NP16 19 J2
Beacon Devon EX14 7 K5
Beacon Devon EX14 8 B4
Beacon Hill Dorset BH16 9 J5
Beacon Hill Essex CM8 34 C7
Beacon Hill Surr. GU26 12 B3
Beacon's Bottom HP14 22 A2
Beaconsfield HP9 22 C2
Beacravik HS3 93 G2
Beadlam YO62 58 C1
Beadlow SG17 32 E5
Beadnell NE67 71 H1
Beaford EX19 6 D4
Beal N.Yorks. DN14 58 B7
Beal Northumb. TD15 77 J6
Bealach PA38 80 A2
Bealsmill PL17 4 D3
Beambridge CW5 49 F7
Beamhurst ST14 40 C2
Beaminster DT8 8 D4
Beamish DH9 62 D1
Beamsley BD23 57 F4
Bean DA2 23 J4
Beanacre SN12 20 C5
Beanley NE66 71 F2
Beaquoy KW17 106 C5
Beardon EX20 6 D7
Beardwood BB2 56 B7
Beare EX5 7 H5
Beare Green RH5 22 E7
Bearley CV37 30 C2
Bearnie AB41 91 H1
Bearnock IV63 88 B1
Bearnus PA73 78 E3
Bearpark DH7 62 D2
Bearsbridge NE47 61 J1
Bearsden G61 74 D3
Bearsted ME14 14 C2
Bearstone TF9 39 G2
Bearwood Poole BH11 10 B5
Bearwood W.Mid. B66 40 C7
Beattock DG10 69 F3
Beauchamp Roding CM5 33 J7
Beauchief S8 51 F4
Beaudesert B95 30 C2
Beaufort NP23 28 A7
Beaulieu SO42 10 E4
Beauly IV4 96 C7
Beaumaris (Biwmares) LL58 46 E5
Beaumont Chan.I. JE3 3 J7
Beaumont Cumb. CA5 60 E1
Beaumont Essex CO16 35 F6
Beaumont Hill DL1 62 D5
Beaumont Leys LE4 41 H5
Beausale CV35 30 D1
Beauvale NG16 41 G1
Beauworth SO24 11 G2
Beaver Green TN23 14 E3
Beaworthy EX21 6 C6
Beazley End CM7 34 B6
Bebington CH63 48 C4
Bebside NE24 71 H5
Beccles NR34 45 J6
Beccles Heliport NR34 45 J7
Becconsall PR4 55 H7
Beck Foot LA8 61 H7
Beck Hole YO22 63 K6
Beck Row IP28 33 K1
Beck Side Cumb. LA17 55 F1
Beck Side Cumb. LA11 55 G1
Beckbury TF11 39 G5
Beckenham BR3 23 G5
Beckering LN8 52 E4
Beckermet CA21 60 B6
Beckermonds BD23 56 D1
Beckett End IP26 44 B6
Beckfoot Cumb. CA19 60 C6
Beckfoot Cumb. CA7 60 B2
Beckford GL20 29 J5
Beckhampton SN8 20 D5
Beckingham Lincs. LN5 52 B7
Beckingham Notts. DN10 51 K4
Beckington BA11 20 B6
Beckley E.Suss. TN31 14 D5
Beckley Oxon. OX3 31 G7
Beck's Green NR34 45 H7
Beckside LA6 56 B1
Beckton E6 23 H3
Beckwithshaw HG3 57 H4
Becontree RM8 23 H3
Bedale DL8 57 H1
Bedburn DL13 62 B3
Bedchester SP7 9 H3
Beddau CF38 18 D3
Beddgelert LL55 36 E1
Beddingham BN8 13 H6
Beddington SM6 23 F5
Beddington Corner CR4 23 F5
Bedfield IP13 35 G2
Bedfield Little Green IP13 35 G2
Bedford MK40 32 D4
Bedgebury Cross TN17 14 C4
Bedgrove HP21 32 B7
Bedham RH20 12 D4
Bedhampton PO9 11 J4
Bedingfield IP23 35 F2
Bedingfield Green IP23 35 F2
Bedingfield Street IP23 35 F2
Bedingham Green NR35 45 G6
Bedlam Lancs. BB5 56 C7
Bedlam N.Yorks. HG3 57 H3
Bedlar's Green CM22 33 J6
Bedlington NE22 71 H5
Bedlinog CF46 18 D1
Bedminster BS3 19 J4
Bedmond WD5 22 D1
Bednall ST17 40 B4
Bedol CH6 48 B5
Bedrule TD9 70 B2
Bedstone SY7 28 C1
Bedwas CF83 18 E3
Bedwell SG1 33 F6
Bedwellty NP12 18 E1
Bedworth CV12 41 F7
Bedworth Woodlands CV12 41 F7
Beeby LE7 41 J5
Beech Hants. GU34 11 H1
Beech Staffs. ST4 40 A2
Beech Hill RG7 21 K5
Beechingstoke SN9 20 D6
Beechwood WA7 48 E4
Beedon RG20 21 H4
Beeford YO25 59 H4
Beeley DE4 50 E6
Beelsby DN37 53 F2
Beenham RG7 21 J5
Beeny PL35 4 B1
Beer EX12 8 B6
Beer Hackett DT9 9 F3
Beercrocombe TA3 8 C2
Beesands TQ7 5 J6
Beesby Lincs. LN13 53 H4
Beesby N.E.Lincs. DN36 53 F3
Beeson TQ7 5 J6
Beeston Cen.Beds. SG19 32 E4
Beeston Ches.W. & C. CW6 48 E7
Beeston Norf. PE32 44 D4
Beeston Notts. NG9 41 H2
Beeston W.Yorks. LS11 57 H6
Beeston Regis NR26 45 F1
Beeston St. Lawrence NR12 45 H3
Beeswing DG2 65 J4
Beetham Cumb. LA7 55 H2
Beetham Som. TA20 8 B3
Beetley NR20 44 D4
Beffcote ST20 40 A4
Began CF3 19 F3
Begbroke OX5 31 F7
Begdale PE14 43 H5
Begelly SA68 16 E5
Beggar's Bush LD8 28 B2
Beggearn Huish TA23 7 J2
Beggshill AB54 90 D1
Beguildy (Bugeildy) LD7 28 A1
Beighton Norf. NR13 45 H5
Beighton S.Yorks. S20 51 G4
Beili-glas NP7 19 G1
Beinn na Faoghla (Benbecula) HS7 92 D6
Beith KA15 74 B5
Bekesbourne CT4 15 G2
Belaugh NR12 45 G4
Belbroughton DY9 29 J1
Belchalwell DT11 9 G4
Belchalwell Street DT11 9 G4
Belchamp Otten CO10 34 C4
Belchamp St. Paul CO10 34 B4
Belchamp Walter CO10 34 C4
Belchford LN9 53 F5
Belfield OL16 49 J1
Belford NE70 77 K7
Belgrave LE4 41 H5
Belhaven EH42 76 E3
Belhelvie AB23 91 H3
Belhinnie AB54 90 C2
Bell Bar AL9 23 F1
Bell Busk BD23 56 E4
Bell End DY9 29 J1
Bell Heath DY9 29 J1
Bell Hill GU32 11 J2
Bell o' th' Hill SY13 38 E1
Bellabeg AB36 90 B3
Belladrum IV4 96 C7
Bellanoch PA31 73 G1
Bellaty PH11 82 D2
Belle Isle LS10 57 J7
Belle Vue CA2 60 E1
Belleau LN13 53 H5
Belleheiglash AB37 89 J1
Bellerby DL8 62 C7
Bellever PL20 5 G3
Bellfields GU1 22 C6
Belliehill DD9 83 G1
Bellingdon HP5 22 C1
Bellingham Gt.Lon. SE6 23 G4
Bellingham Northumb. NE48 70 D5
Belloch PA29 72 E7
Bellochantuy PA28 72 E7
Bell's Cross IP6 35 F3
Bells Yew Green TN3 13 K3
Bellsbank KA6 67 J3
Bellshill N.Lan. ML4 75 F4
Bellshill Northumb. NE70 77 K7
Bellside ML1 75 G5
Bellsmyre G82 74 C3
Bellsquarry EH54 75 J4
Belluton BS39 19 K5
Belmaduthy IV8 96 D6
Belmesthorpe PE9 42 D4
Belmont B'burn. BL7 49 F1
Belmont Gt.Lon. SM2 23 F5
Belmont Gt.Lon. HA7 22 E2
Belmont Shet. ZE2 107 P2
Belnie PE11 43 F2
Belowda PL26 3 G2
Belper DE56 41 F1
Belper Lane End DE56 41 F1
Belsay NE20 71 G6
Belsford TQ9 5 H5
Belsize WD3 22 D1
Belstead IP8 35 F4
Belston KA6 67 H1
Belstone EX20 6 E6
Belstone Corner EX20 6 E6
Belsyde EH49 75 H3
Belthorn BB1 56 C7
Beltinge CT6 25 H5
Beltingham NE47 70 C7
Beltoft DN9 52 B2
Belton Leics. LE12 41 G3
Belton Lincs. NG32 42 C2
Belton N.Lincs. DN9 51 K2
Belton Norf. NR31 45 J5
Belton Rut. LE15 42 B5
Beltring TN12 23 K7
Belvedere DA17 23 H4
Belvoir NG32 42 B2
Bembridge PO35 11 H6
Bemersyde TD6 76 D7
Bemerton SP2 10 C1
Bempton YO15 59 H2
Ben Alder Cottage PH17 81 F1
Ben Alder Lodge PH19 88 C7
Ben Rhydding LS29 57 G5
Benacre NR34 45 K7
Benbecula (Beinn na Faoghla) HS7 92 D6
Benbecula (Balivanich) Airport HS7 92 C6
Benbuie DG3 68 C4
Benderloch PA37 80 A4
Bendish SG4 32 E6
Benenden TN17 14 D4
Benfield DG8 64 D4
Benfieldside DH8 62 B1
Bengate NR28 45 H3
Bengeo SG14 33 G7
Bengeworth WR11 30 B4
Benhall GL51 29 J6
Benhall Green IP17 35 H2
Benhall Street IP17 35 H2
Benholm DD10 83 K1
Beningbrough YO30 58 B4
Benington Herts. SG2 33 F6
Benington Lincs. PE22 43 G1
Benington Sea End PE22 43 H1
Benllech LL74 46 D4
Benmore Arg. & B. PA23 73 K2
Benmore Stir. FK20 81 F5
Bennacott PL15 4 C1
Bennan Cottage DG7 65 G3
Bennett End HP14 22 A2
Bennetts End HP3 22 D1
Benniworth LN8 53 F4
Benover ME18 14 C3
Benson OX10 21 K2
Benston ZE2 107 N7
Benthall Northumb. NE67 71 H1
Benthall Shrop. TF12 39 F5
Bentham GL51 29 J7
Benthoul AB14 91 G4
Bentlawnt SY5 38 C5
Bentley E.Riding HU17 59 G6
Bentley Essex CM15 23 J2
Bentley Hants. GU10 22 A7
Bentley S.Yorks. DN5 51 H2
Bentley Suff. IP9 35 F5
Bentley W.Mid. WS2 40 B6
Bentley W.Yorks. LS6 57 H6
Bentley Warks. CV9 40 E6
Bentley Heath Herts. EN5 23 F2
Bentley Heath W.Mid. B93 30 C1
Bentley Rise DN5 51 H2
Benton EX32 6 E2
Benton Square NE12 71 J6
Bentpath DG13 69 J4
Bentworth GU34 21 K7
Benvie DD2 82 E4
Benville Lane DT2 8 E4
Benwell NE15 71 H7
Benwick PE15 43 G6
Beoley B98 30 B2
Beoraidbeg PH40 86 C5
Bepton GU29 12 B5
Berden CM23 33 H6
Bere Alston PL20 4 E4
Bere Ferrers PL20 4 E4
Bere Regis BH20 9 H5
Berea SA62 16 A2
Berepper TR12 2 D6
Bergh Apton NR15 45 H5
Berinsfield OX10 21 J2
Berkeley GL13 19 K2
Berkhamsted HP4 22 C1
Berkley BA11 20 B7
Berkswell CV7 30 D1
Bermondsey SE16 23 G4
Bernera IV40 86 E2
Berneray (Eilean Bhearnaraigh) HS6 92 E3
Berners Roding CM5 24 C1
Bernice PA23 73 K1
Bernisdale IV51 93 K6
Berrick Prior OX10 21 K2
Berrick Salome OX10 21 K2
Berriedale KW7 105 G6
Berriew (Aberriw) SY21 38 A5
Berrington Northumb. TD15 77 J6
Berrington Shrop. SY5 38 E5
Berrington Worcs. WR15 28 E2
Berrington Green WR15 28 E2
Berriowbridge PL15 4 C3
Berrow Som. TA8 19 F6
Berrow Worcs. WR13 29 G5
Berrow Green WR6 29 G3
Berry Cross EX38 6 C4
Berry Down Cross EX34 6 D1
Berry Hill Glos. GL16 28 E7
Berry Hill Pembs. SA42 16 D1
Berry Pomeroy TQ9 5 J4
Berryhillock AB56 98 D4
Berrynarbor EX34 6 D1
Berry's Green TN16 23 H6
Bersham LL14 38 C1
Berstane KW15 106 D6
Berthlŵyd SA4 17 J6
Berwick BN26 13 J6
Berwick Bassett SN4 20 E4
Berwick Hill NE20 71 G6
Berwick St. James SP3 10 B1
Berwick St. John SP7 9 J2
Berwick St. Leonard SP3 9 J1
Berwick-upon-Tweed TD15 77 H5
Bescar L40 48 C1
Bescot WS2 40 C6
Besford Shrop. SY4 38 E3
Besford Worcs. WR8 29 J4
Bessacarr DN4 51 J2
Bessels Leigh OX13 21 H1
Besses o' th' Barn M45 49 H2
Bessingby YO16 59 H3
Bessingham NR11 45 F2
Best Beech Hill TN5 13 K3
Besthorpe Norf. NR17 44 E6
Besthorpe Notts. NG23 52 B6
Bestwood Village NG5 41 H1
Beswick E.Riding YO25 59 G5
Beswick Gt.Man. M11 49 H3
Betchworth RH3 23 F6
Bethania Cere. SY23 26 E2
Bethania Gwyn. LL41 37 G1
Bethel Gwyn. LL55 46 D6
Bethel Gwyn. LL23 37 J2
Bethel I.o.A. LL62 46 B5
Bethersden TN26 14 E4
Bethesda Gwyn. LL57 46 E6
Bethesda Pembs. SA67 16 D4
Bethlehem SA19 17 K3
Bethnal Green E2 23 G3
Betley CW3 39 G1
Betley Common CW3 39 G1
Betsham DA13 24 C4
Betteshanger CT14 15 J2
Bettiscombe DT6 8 C5
Bettisfield SY13 38 D2
Betton Shrop. SY5 38 C5
Betton Shrop. TF9 39 F2
Betton Strange SY5 38 E5
Bettws Bridgend CF32 18 C3
Bettws Newport NP20 19 F2
Bettws Bledrws SA48 26 E3
Bettws Cedewain SY16 38 A6

## Bet - Bli



Bettws Gwerfil Goch LL21 37 K1
Bettws Newydd NP15 19 G1
Bettws-y-crwyn SY7 38 B7
Bettyhill KW14 104 C2
Betws SA18 17 K4
Betws Disserth LD1 28 A3
Betws Garmon LL54 46 D7
Betws Ifan SA38 17 G1
**Betws-y-coed LL24 47 F7**
Betws-yn-Rhos LL22 47 H5
Beulah *Cere.* SA38 17 F1
Beulah *Powys* LD5 27 J3
Bevendean BN2 13 G6
Bevercotes NG22 51 J5
**Beverley HU17 59 G6**
Beverstone GL8 20 B2
Bevington GL13 19 K2
Bewaldeth CA13 60 D3
Bewcastle CA6 70 A6
**Bewdley DY12 29 G1**
Bewerley HG3 57 G3
Bewholme YO25 59 H4
Bewley Common SN15 20 C5
**Bexhill TN40 14 C7**
**Bexley DA5 23 H4**
**Bexleyheath DA6 23 H4**
Bexwell PE38 44 A5
Beyton IP30 34 D2
Beyton Green IP30 34 D2
Bhalamus HS2 100 E7
Bhaleshear (Baleshare) HS6 92 C5
Bhaltos HS2 100 C4
Bhatarsaigh (Vatersay) HS9 84 B5
Biallaid PH20 88 E5
Bibury GL7 20 E1
**Bicester OX26 31 G6**
Bickenhall TA3 8 B3
Bickenhill B92 40 D7
Bicker PE20 43 F2
Bickershaw WN2 49 F2
Bickerstaffe L39 48 D2
Bickerton *Ches.W. & C.* SY14 48 E7
Bickerton *Devon* TQ7 5 J7
Bickerton *N.Yorks.* LS22 57 K4
Bickerton *Northumb.* NE65 70 E3
Bickford ST19 40 A4
Bickham TA24 7 H1
Bickham Bridge TQ9 5 H5
Bickham House EX6 7 H7
Bickington *Devon* EX31 6 D2
Bickington *Devon* TQ12 5 H3
Bickleigh *Devon* PL6 5 F4
Bickleigh *Devon* EX16 7 H5
Bickleton EX31 6 D2
Bickley BR1 23 H5
Bickley Moss SY13 38 E1
Bickley Town SY14 38 E1
Bicknacre CM3 24 D1
Bicknoller TA4 7 K2
Bicknor ME9 14 D2
Bickton SP6 10 C3
Bicton *Here.* HR6 28 D2
Bicton *Shrop.* SY3 38 D4
Bicton *Shrop.* SY7 38 B7
Bicton Heath SY3 38 D4
Bidborough TN4 23 J7
Biddenden TN27 14 D4
Biddenden Green TN27 14 D3
Biddenham MK40 32 D4
Biddestone SN14 20 B4
Biddick NE38 62 E1
Biddisham BS26 19 G6
Biddlesden NN13 31 H4
Biddlestone NE65 70 E3
Biddulph ST8 49 H7
Biddulph Moor ST8 49 J7
**Bideford EX39 6 C3**
Bidford-on-Avon B50 30 C3
Bidham Dock ME9 25 F5
Bidlake EX20 6 C7
Bidston CH43 48 B3
Bidwell LU5 32 D6
Bielby YO42 58 D5
Bieldside AB15 91 G4
Bierley *I.o.W.* PO38 11 G7
Bierley *W.Yorks.* BD4 57 G6
Bierton HP22 32 B7
Big Sand IV21 94 D4
Bigbury TQ7 5 G6
Bigbury-on-Sea TQ7 5 G6
Bigby DN38 52 D2
Bigert Mire LA20 60 C7
Biggar *Cumb.* LA14 54 E3
**Biggar *S.Lan.* ML12 75 J7**
Biggin *Derbys.* DE6 40 E1
Biggin *Derbys.* SK17 50 D7
Biggin *N.Yorks.* LS25 58 B6
Biggin Hill TN16 23 H6
Biggings ZE2 107 K6
**Biggleswade SG18 32 E4**
Bigholms DG13 69 J5
Bighouse KW14 104 D2
Bighton SO24 11 H1
Biglands CA7 60 D1
Bignor RH20 12 C5
Bigrigg CA24 60 B5
Bigton ZE2 107 M10
Bilberry PL26 4 A5
Bilborough NG8 41 H1
Bilbrook *Som.* TA24 7 J1
Bilbrook *Staffs.* WV8 40 A5
Bilbrough YO23 58 B5
Bilbster KW1 105 H3
Bilby DN22 51 J4
Bildershaw DL14 62 C4
Bildeston IP7 34 D4
**Billericay CM12 24 C2**
Billesdon LE7 42 A5
Billesley B49 30 C3
Billholm DG13 69 H4
Billingborough NG34 42 E2
Billinge WN5 48 E3
Billingford *Norf.* IP21 35 F1
Billingford *Norf.* NR20 44 E3
**Billingham TS23 63 F4**
Billinghay LN4 52 E7
Billingley S72 51 G2
**Billingshurst RH14 12 D4**
Billingsley WV16 39 G7
Billington *Cen.Beds.* LU7 32 C6
Billington *Lancs.* BB7 56 C6
Billington *Staffs.* ST18 40 A3
Billister ZE2 107 N6
Billockby NR29 45 J4
Billy Row DL15 62 C3
Bilsborrow PR3 55 J6
Bilsby LN13 53 H5
Bilsby Field LN13 53 H5
Bilsdean TD13 77 F3
Bilsham BN18 12 C6
Bilsington TN25 15 F4
Bilson Green GL14 29 F7
Bilsthorpe NG22 51 J6
Bilsthorpe Moor NG22 51 J7
Bilston *Midloth.* EH25 76 A4
**Bilston *W.Mid.* WV14 40 B6**
Bilstone CV13 41 F5
Bilting TN25 15 F3
Bilton *E.Riding* HU11 59 H6
Bilton *N.Yorks.* HG1 57 J4
Bilton *Northumb.* NE66 71 H2
Bilton *Warks.* CV22 31 F1
Bilton-in-Ainsty YO26 57 K5
Bimbister KW17 106 C6
Binbrook LN8 53 F3
Bincombe DT3 9 F6
Bindal IV20 97 G3
Bindon TA21 7 K3
Binegar BA3 19 K7
Bines Green RH13 12 E5
Binfield RG42 22 B4
Binfield Heath RG9 22 A4
Bingfield NE19 70 E6
Bingham NG13 42 A2
Bingham's Melcombe DT2 9 G4
**Bingley BD16 57 G6**
Bings Heath SY4 38 E4
Binham NR21 44 D2
Binley *Hants.* SP11 21 H6
Binley *W.Mid.* CV3 30 E1
Binniehill FK1 75 G3
Binsoe HG4 57 H2
Binstead PO33 11 G5
Binsted *Hants.* GU34 22 A7
Binsted *W.Suss.* BN18 12 C6
Binton CV37 30 C3
Bintree NR20 44 E3
Binweston SY5 38 C5
Birch *Essex* CO2 34 D6
Birch *Gt.Man.* M24 49 H2
Birch Cross ST14 40 D2
Birch Green *Essex* CO2 34 D7
Birch Green *Herts.* SG14 33 F7
Birch Grove RH17 13 H4
Birch Heath CW6 48 E6
Birch Vale SK22 50 C4
Birch Wood TA20 8 B3
Bircham Newton PE31 44 B2
Bircham Tofts PE31 44 B2
Birchanger CM23 33 J6
Bircher HR6 28 D2
Bircher Common HR6 28 D2
Birchfield IV24 96 B2
Birchgrove *Cardiff* CF14 18 E3
Birchgrove *Swan.* SA7 18 A2
**Birchington CT7 25 K5**
Birchmoor B78 40 E5
Birchover DE4 50 E6
Birchwood *Lincs.* LN6 52 C6
Birchwood *Warr.* WA3 49 F3
Bircotes DN11 51 J3
Bird Street IP7 34 E3
Birdbrook CO9 34 B4
Birdbush SP7 9 J2
Birdfield PA32 73 H1
Birdforth YO7 57 K2
Birdham PO20 12 B6
Birdingbury CV23 31 F2
Birdlip GL4 29 J7
Birdoswald CA8 70 B7
Birds Green CM5 23 J1
Birdsall YO17 58 E3
Birdsgreen WV15 39 G7
Birdsmoor Gate DT6 8 C4
Birdston G66 74 E3
Birdwell S70 51 F2
Birdwood GL19 29 G7
Birgham TD12 77 F7
Birichen IV25 96 E2
Birkby *Cumb.* CA15 60 B3
Birkby *N.Yorks.* DL7 62 E6
Birkdale *Mersey.* PR8 48 C1
Birkdale *N.Yorks.* DL11 61 K6
**Birkenhead CH41 48 C4**
Birkenhills AB53 99 F6
Birkenshaw BD11 57 H7
Birkhall AB35 90 B5
Birkhill *Angus* DD2 82 E4
Birkhill *Sc.Bord.* TD4 76 D6
Birkhill *Sc.Bord.* TD7 69 H2
Birkholme NG33 42 C3
Birkin WF11 58 B7
Birks LS27 57 H7
Birkwood ML11 75 G7
Birley HR4 28 D3
Birley Carr S6 51 F3
Birling *Kent* ME19 24 C5
Birling *Northumb.* NE65 71 H3
Birling Gap BN20 13 J7
Birlingham WR10 29 J4
**BIRMINGHAM B 40 C7**
Birmingham International Airport B26 40 D7
Birnam PH8 82 B3
Birsay KW17 106 B5
Birse AB34 90 D5
Birsemore AB34 90 D5
Birstall LE4 41 H5
Birstall Smithies WF17 57 H7
Birstwith HG3 57 H4
Birthorpe NG34 42 E2
Birtle OL11 49 H1
Birtley *Here.* SY7 28 C2
Birtley *Northumb.* NE48 70 D6
Birtley *T. & W.* DH3 62 D1
Birts Street WR13 29 G5
Birtsmorton WR13 29 H5
Bisbrooke LE15 42 B6
Biscathorpe LN11 53 F4
Bish Mill EX36 7 F3
Bisham SL7 22 B3
Bishampton WR10 29 J3
**Bishop Auckland DL14 62 D4**
Bishop Burton HU17 59 F5
Bishop Middleham DL17 62 E3
Bishop Monkton HG3 57 J3
Bishop Norton LN8 52 C3
Bishop Sutton BS39 19 J6
Bishop Thornton HG3 57 H3
Bishop Wilton YO42 58 D4
Bishopbridge LN8 52 D3
Bishopbriggs G64 74 E3
Bishopmill IV30 97 K5
Bishops Cannings SN10 20 D5
**Bishop's Castle SY9 38 C7**
Bishop's Caundle DT9 9 F3
Bishop's Cleeve GL52 29 J6
Bishop's Frome WR6 29 F4
Bishops Gate TW20 22 C4
Bishop's Green *Essex* CM6 33 K7
Bishop's Green *Hants.* RG19 21 J5
Bishop's Hull TA1 8 B2
Bishop's Itchington CV47 30 E3
Bishop's Lydeard TA4 7 K3
Bishop's Norton GL2 29 H6
Bishops Nympton EX36 7 F3
Bishop's Offley ST21 39 G3
**Bishop's Stortford CM23 33 H6**
Bishop's Sutton SO24 11 H1
Bishop's Tachbrook CV33 30 E2
Bishop's Tawton EX32 6 D2
Bishop's Waltham SO32 11 G3
Bishop's Wood ST19 40 A5
Bishopsbourne CT4 15 G2
Bishopsteignton TQ14 5 K3
Bishopstoke SO50 11 F3
Bishopston *Bristol* BS6 19 J4
Bishopston *Swan.* SA3 17 J7
Bishopstone *Bucks.* HP17 32 B7
Bishopstone *E.Suss.* BN25 13 H6
Bishopstone *Here.* HR4 28 D4
Bishopstone *Swin.* SN6 21 F3
Bishopstone *Wilts.* SP5 10 B2
Bishopstrow BA12 20 B7
Bishopswood TA20 8 B3
Bishopsworth BS13 19 J5
Bishopthorpe YO23 58 B5
Bishopton *Darl.* TS21 62 E4
Bishopton *N.Yorks.* HG4 57 H2
**Bishopton *Renf.* PA7 74 C3**
Bishopton *Warks.* CV37 30 C3
Bishton NP18 19 G3
Bisley *Glos.* GL6 20 C1
Bisley *Surr.* GU24 22 C6
Bispham FY2 55 G6
Bispham Green L40 48 D1
Bissoe TR4 2 E4
Bisterne BH24 10 C4
Bisterne Close BH24 10 D4
Bitchet Green TN15 23 J6
Bitchfield NG33 42 C3
Bittadon EX31 6 D1
Bittaford PL21 5 G5
Bittering NR19 44 D4
Bitterley SY8 28 E1
Bitterne SO18 11 F3
Bitteswell LE17 41 H7
Bitton BS30 19 K5
**Biwmares (Beaumaris) LL58 46 E5**
Bix RG9 22 A3
Bixter ZE2 107 M7
Blaby LE8 41 H6
Black Bourton OX18 21 F1
Black Bridge SA73 16 C5
Black Callerton NE5 71 G7
Black Carr NR17 44 E6
Black Clauchrie KA26 67 G5
Black Corries Lodge PH49 80 D2
Black Crofts PA37 80 A4
Black Cross TR8 3 G2
Black Dog EX17 7 G5
Black Heddon NE20 71 F6
Black Hill CV37 30 D3
Black Marsh SY5 38 C6
Black Moor LS17 57 H5
Black Mount PA36 80 D3
Black Notley CM77 34 B6
Black Pill SA3 17 K6
Black Street NR33 45 K7
Black Torrington EX21 6 C5
Blackaburn NE48 70 C6
Blackacre DG11 69 F4
Blackadder TD11 77 G5
Blackawton TQ9 5 J5
Blackborough *Devon* EX15 7 J5
Blackborough *Norf.* PE32 44 A4
Blackborough End PE32 44 A4
Blackboys TN22 13 J4
Blackbraes *Aber.* AB21 91 G3
Blackbraes *Falk.* FK1 75 H3
Blackbrook *Derbys.* DE56 41 F1
Blackbrook *Leics.* LE12 41 G4
Blackbrook *Mersey.* WA11 48 E3
Blackbrook *Staffs.* ST5 39 G2
Blackburn *Aber.* AB21 91 G3
**BLACKBURN *B'burn.* BB 56 B7**
Blackburn *W.Loth.* EH47 75 H4
Blackbushe GU17 22 A6
Blackcastle IV2 97 F6
Blackchambers AB32 91 F3
Blackcraig *D. & G.* DG8 64 E4
Blackcraig *D. & G.* DG7 68 C5
Blackden Heath CW4 49 G5
Blackdog AB23 91 H3
Blackdown *Devon* PL19 5 F3
Blackdown *Dorset* DT8 8 C4
Blackdown *Warks.* CV32 30 E2
Blacker Hill S74 51 F2
Blackfen DA15 23 H4
Blackfield SO45 11 F4
Blackford *Aber.* AB51 91 F1
Blackford *Cumb.* CA6 69 J7
Blackford *P. & K.* PH4 81 K7
Blackford *Som.* BA22 9 F2
Blackford *Som.* BS28 19 H7
Blackford Bridge BL9 49 H2
Blackfordby DE11 41 F4
Blackgang PO38 11 F7
Blackhall *Edin.* EH4 76 A3
Blackhall *Renf.* PA1 74 C4
Blackhall Colliery TS27 63 F3
Blackhall Mill NE17 62 C1
Blackhall Rocks TS27 63 F3
Blackham TN3 13 J3
Blackhaugh TD1 76 C7
Blackheath *Essex* CO2 34 E6
Blackheath *Gt.Lon.* SE3 23 G4
Blackheath *Suff.* IP19 35 J1
Blackheath *Surr.* GU4 22 D7
Blackheath *W.Mid.* B65 40 B7
Blackhill *Aber.* AB42 99 J5
Blackhill *Aber.* AB42 99 J6
Blackhillock AB55 98 C6
Blackhills IV30 97 K6
Blackland SN11 20 D5
Blacklands TA24 7 G2
Blackleach PR4 55 H6
Blackley M9 49 H2
Blacklunans PH10 82 C1
Blackmill CF35 18 C3
Blackmoor *Hants.* GU33 11 J1
Blackmoor *Som.* TA21 7 K4
Blackmoor Gate EX31 6 E1
Blackmoorfoot HD7 50 C1
Blackmore CM4 24 C1
Blackmore End *Essex* CM7 34 B5
Blackmore End *Herts.* AL4 32 E7
Blackness *Aber.* AB31 90 E5
Blackness *Falk.* EH49 75 J3
Blackness *High.* KW3 105 H5
Blacknest GU34 22 A7
Blackney DT6 8 D5
Blacko BB9 56 D5
Blackpole WR3 29 H3
**BLACKPOOL *B'pool* FY 55 G6**
Blackpool *Devon* TQ6 5 J6
Blackpool Bridge SA67 16 D4
Blackpool Gate CA6 70 A6
Blackpool International Airport FY4 55 G6
Blackridge EH48 75 G4
Blackrock *Arg. & B.* PA44 72 B4
Blackrock *Mon.* NP7 28 B7
Blackrod BL6 49 F1
Blackshaw DG1 69 F7
Blackshaw Head HX7 56 E7
Blacksmith's Green IP14 35 F2
Blacksnape BB3 56 C7
Blackstone BN5 13 F5
Blackthorn OX25 31 H7
Blackthorpe IP30 34 D2
Blacktoft DN14 58 E7
Blacktop AB15 91 G4
Blacktown CF3 19 F3
Blackwater *Cornw.* TR4 2 E4
Blackwater *Hants.* GU17 22 B6
Blackwater *I.o.W.* PO30 11 G6
Blackwater *Norf.* NR9 44 E3
Blackwater *Som.* TA20 8 B3
Blackwaterfoot KA27 66 D1
Blackwell *Darl.* DL3 62 D5
Blackwell *Derbys.* SK17 50 D5
Blackwell *Derbys.* DE55 51 G7
Blackwell *W.Suss.* RH19 13 G3
Blackwell *Warks.* CV36 30 D4
Blackwell *Worcs.* B60 29 J1
Blackwells End GL19 29 G6
**Blackwood (Coed-duon) *Caerp.* NP12 18 E2**
Blackwood *D. & G.* DG2 68 E5
Blackwood *S.Lan.* ML11 75 F6
Blackwood Hill ST9 49 J7
Blacon CH1 48 C6
Bladbean CT4 15 G3
Bladnoch DG8 64 E5
Bladon OX20 31 F7
Blaen Clydach CF40 18 C2
Blaenannerch SA43 17 F1
Blaenau Dolwyddelan LL25 46 E7
**Blaenau Ffestiniog LL41 37 F1**
Blaenavon NP4 19 F1
Blaenawey NP7 28 B7
Blaencelyn SA44 26 C3
Blaencwm CF42 18 C1
Blaendyryn LD3 27 J5
Blaenffos SA37 16 E2
Blaengarw CF32 18 C2
Blaengeuffordd SY23 37 F7
Blaengweche SA18 17 K4
Blaengwrach SA11 18 B1
Blaengwynfi SA13 18 B2
Blaenllechau CF43 18 D2
Blaenos SA20 27 G5
Blaenpennal SY23 27 F2
Blaenplwyf SY23 26 E1
Blaenporth SA43 17 F1
Blaenrhondda CF42 18 C1
Blaenwaun SA34 17 F3
Blaen-y-coed SA33 17 G3
Blagdon *N.Som.* BS40 19 H6
Blagdon *Torbay* TQ3 5 J4
Blagdon Hill TA3 8 B3
Blaguegate WN8 48 D2
Blaich PH33 87 G7
Blaina NP13 18 E1
Blair KA24 74 B6
Blair Atholl PH18 81 K1
Blair Drummond FK9 75 F1
Blairannaich G83 80 E7
Blairbuie PA23 73 K3
**Blairgowrie PH10 82 C3**
Blairhall KY12 75 J2
Blairhoyle FK8 81 H7
Blairhullichan FK8 81 F7
Blairingone FK14 75 H1
Blairkip KA5 74 D7
Blairlogie FK9 75 G1
Blairmore *Arg. & B.* PA23 73 K2
Blairmore *High.* IV28 96 E1
Blairmore *High.* IV27 102 D3
Blairnairn G84 74 A2
Blairnamarrow AB37 89 K3
Blairpark KA24 74 A5
Blairquhan KA19 67 H3
Blairquhosh G63 74 D2
Blair's Ferry PA21 73 H4
Blairshinnoch AB45 98 E4
Blairuskinmore FK8 81 F7
Blairvadach G84 74 A2
Blairydryne AB31 91 F5
Blairythan Cottage AB41 91 H2
Blaisdon GL17 29 G7
Blake End CM77 34 B6
Blakebrook DY11 29 H1
Blakedown DY10 29 H1
Blakelaw *Sc.Bord.* TD5 77 F7
Blakelaw *T. & W.* NE5 71 H7
Blakeley WV5 40 A6
Blakelow CW5 49 F7
Blakemere HR2 28 C4
**Blakeney *Glos.* GL15 19 K1**
Blakeney *Norf.* NR25 44 E1
Blakenhall *Ches.E.* CW5 39 G1
Blakenhall *W.Mid.* WV2 40 B6
Blakeshall DY11 40 A7
Blakesley NN12 31 H3
Blanchland DH8 62 A1
Bland Hill HG3 57 H4
Blandford Camp DT11 9 J4
**Blandford Forum DT11 9 H4**
Blandford St. Mary DT11 9 H4
Blanefield G63 74 D3
Blanerne TD11 77 G5
Blankney LN4 52 D6
Blantyre G72 74 E5
Blar a' Chaorainn PH33 80 C1
Blargie PH20 88 D5
Blarglas G83 74 B2
Blarmachfoldach PH33 80 B1
Blarnalearoch IV23 95 H2
Blashford BH24 10 C4
Blaston LE16 42 B6
Blathaisbhal HS6 92 D4
Blatherwycke PE8 42 C6
Blawith LA12 55 F1
Blaxhall IP12 35 H3
Blaxton DN9 51 J2
**Blaydon NE21 71 G7**
Bleadney BA5 19 H7
Bleadon BS24 19 G6
Bleak Hey Nook OL3 50 C2
Blean CT2 25 H5
Bleasby *Lincs.* LN8 52 E4
Bleasby *Notts.* NG14 42 A1
Bleasby Moor LN8 52 E4
Bleatarn CA16 61 J5
Bleathwood Common SY8 28 E2
Blebocraigs KY15 83 F6
Bleddfa LD7 28 B2
Bledington OX7 30 D6
Bledlow HP27 22 A1
Bledlow Ridge HP14 22 A2
Blencarn CA10 61 H3
Blencogo CA7 60 C2
Blencow CA11 61 F3
Blendworth PO8 11 J3
Blennerhasset CA7 60 C2
Blervie Castle IV36 97 H6
Bletchingdon OX5 31 G7
Bletchingley RH1 23 G6
Bletchley *M.K.* MK3 32 B5
Bletchley *Shrop.* TF9 39 F2
Bletherston SA63 16 D3
Bletsoe MK44 32 D3
Blewbury OX11 21 J3
Blickling NR11 45 F3
Blidworth NG21 51 H7
Blidworth Bottoms NG21 51 H7
Blindburn *Aber.* AB41 91 H1
Blindburn *Northumb.* NE65 70 D2
Blindcrake CA13 60 C3

Bli - Bra


Blindley Heath **RH7** 23 G7
Blisland **PL30** 4 A3
Bliss Gate **DY14** 29 G1
Blissford **SP6** 10 C3
Blisworth **NN7** 31 J3
Blithbury **WS15** 40 C3
Blitterlees **CA7** 60 C1
Blo' Norton **IP22** 34 E1
Blockley **GL56** 30 C5
Blofield **NR13** 45 H5
Blofield Heath **NR13** 45 H4
Blore **DE6** 40 D1
Blossomfield **B91** 30 C1
Blount's Green **ST14** 40 C2
Blowick **PR9** 48 C1
Bloxham **OX15** 31 F5
Bloxholm **LN4** 52 D7
Bloxwich **WS3** 40 B5
Bloxworth **BH20** 9 H5
Blubberhouses **LS21** 57 G4
Blue Anchor *Cornw.* **TR9** 3 G3
Blue Anchor *Som.* **TA24** 7 J1
Blue Bell Hill **ME5** 24 D5
Bluewater **DA9** 23 J4
Blundellsands **L23** 48 C3
Blundeston **NR32** 45 K6
Blunham **MK44** 32 E3
Blunsdon St. Andrew **SN26** 20 E3
Bluntington **DY10** 29 H1
Bluntisham **PE28** 33 G1
Blunts **PL12** 4 D4
Blurton **ST3** 40 A1
Blyborough **DN21** 52 C3
Blyford **IP19** 35 J1
Blymhill **TF11** 40 A4
Blymhill Common **TF11** 39 G4
Blymhill Lawn **TF11** 40 A4
**Blyth *Northumb.* NE24 71 J5**
Blyth *Notts.* **S81** 51 J4
Blyth Bridge **EH46** 75 K6
Blyth End **B46** 40 E6
Blythburgh **IP19** 35 J1
Blythe Bridge **ST11** 40 B1
Blythe Marsh **ST11** 40 B1
Blyton **DN21** 52 B3
Boarhills **KY16** 83 G6
Boarhunt **PO17** 11 H4
Boars Hill **OX1** 21 H1
Boarsgreave **BB4** 56 D7
Boarshead **TN6** 13 J3
Boarstall **HP18** 31 H7
Boarzell **TN19** 14 C5
Boasley Cross **EX20** 6 D6
Boat o' Brig **IV32** 98 B5
**Boat of Garten PH24 89 G3**
Boath **IV17** 96 C4
Bobbing **ME9** 24 E5
Bobbington **DY7** 40 A6
Bobbingworth **CM5** 23 J1
Bocaddon **PL13** 4 B5
Bochastle **FK17** 81 H7
Bockhampton **RG17** 21 G4
Bocking **CM7** 34 B6
Bocking Churchstreet **CM7** 34 B6
Bockleton **WR15** 28 E2
Boconnoc **PL22** 4 B4
Boddam *Aber.* **AB42** 99 K6
Boddam *Shet.* **ZE2** 107 M11
Bodden **BA4** 19 K7
Boddington **GL51** 29 H6
Bodedern **LL65** 46 B4
Bodelwyddan **LL18** 47 J5
Bodenham *Here.* **HR1** 28 E3
Bodenham *Wilts.* **SP5** 10 C2
Bodenham Moor **HR1** 28 E3
Bodesbeck **DG10** 69 G3
Bodewryd **LL66** 46 B3
Bodfari **LL16** 47 J5
Bodffordd **LL77** 46 C5
Bodfuan **LL53** 36 C2
Bodham **NR25** 45 F1
Bodiam **TN32** 14 C5
Bodicote **OX15** 31 F5
Bodieve **PL27** 3 G1
Bodinnick **PL23** 4 B5
Bodior **LL65** 46 A5
Bodle Street Green **BN27** 13 K5
**Bodmin PL31 4 A4**
Bodney **IP26** 44 C6
**Bodorgan LL62 46 B6**
Bodrane **PL14** 4 C4
Bodsham Green **TN25** 15 G3
Bodwen **PL26** 4 A4
Bodymoor Heath **B76** 40 D6
Bogallan **IV1** 96 D6
Bogbain **IV2** 96 E7
Bogbrae **AB42** 91 J1
Bogbuie **IV7** 96 C6
Bogend **KA1** 74 B7
Bogfern **AB33** 90 D4
Bogfields **AB33** 90 D4
Bogfold **AB43** 99 G5
Boghead *Aber.* **AB45** 98 E5
Boghead *E.Ayr.* **KA18** 68 B1
Boghead *S.Lan.* **ML11** 75 F6
Boghole Farm **IV12** 97 G6
Bogmoor **IV32** 98 B4
Bogniebrae **AB54** 98 D6
**Bognor Regis PO21 12 C7**
Bograxie **AB51** 91 F3
Bogroy **PH23** 89 G2
Bogside **FK10** 75 H1
Bogston **AB36** 90 B4
Bogton **AB53** 98 E5
Bogue **DG7** 68 B5
Bohemia **SP5** 10 D3
Bohenie **PH31** 87 J6
Bohetherick **PL12** 4 E4
Bohortha **TR2** 3 F5
Bohuntine **PH31** 87 J6
Boirseam **HS3** 93 F3
Bojewyan **TR19** 2 A5
Bokiddick **PL30** 4 A4
Bolam *Dur.* **DL2** 62 C4
Bolam *Northumb.* **NE61** 71 F5
Bolberry **TQ7** 5 G7
Bold Heath **WA8** 48 E4
Bolderwood **SO43** 10 D4
Boldon **NE36** 71 J7
**Boldon Colliery NE35 71 J7**
Boldre **SO41** 10 E5
Boldron **DL12** 62 B5
Bole **DN22** 51 K4
Bolehill **DE4** 50 E7
Boleigh **TR19** 2 B6
Bolenowe **TR14** 2 D5
Boleside **TD1** 76 C7
Bolfracks **PH15** 81 K3
Bolgoed **SA4** 17 K5
Bolham *Devon* **EX16** 7 H4
Bolham *Notts.* **DN22** 51 K4
Bolham Water **EX15** 7 K4
Bolingey **TR6** 2 E3
Bollington **SK10** 49 J5
Bolney **RH17** 13 F4
Bolnhurst **MK44** 32 D3
Bolshan **DD11** 83 H2
Bolsover **S44** 51 G5
Bolsterstone **S36** 50 E3
Bolstone **HR2** 28 E5
Boltby **YO7** 57 K1
Bolter End **HP14** 22 A2
Bolton *Cumb.* **CA16** 61 H4
Bolton *E.Loth.* **EH41** 76 D3
Bolton *E.Riding* **YO42** 58 D4
**BOLTON *Gt.Man.* BL 49 G2**
Bolton *Northumb.* **NE66** 71 G2
Bolton Abbey **BD23** 57 F4
Bolton Bridge **BD23** 57 F4
Bolton by Bowland **BB7** 56 C5
Bolton Houses **PR4** 55 H6
Bolton Low Houses **CA7** 60 D2
Bolton Percy **YO23** 58 B5
Bolton upon Dearne **S63** 51 G2
Bolton Wood Lane **CA7** 60 D2
Boltonfellend **CA6** 69 K7
Boltongate **CA7** 60 D2
Bolton-le-Sands **LA5** 55 H3
Bolton-on-Swale **DL10** 62 D7
Bolventor **PL15** 4 B3
Bombie **DG6** 65 H6
Bomere Heath **SY4** 38 D4
Bonar Bridge **IV24** 96 D2
Bonawe **PA37** 80 B4
Bonby **DN20** 52 D1
**Boncath SA37 17 F2**
Bonchester Bridge **TD9** 70 A2
Bonchurch **PO38** 11 G7
Bondleigh **EX20** 6 E5
Bonds **PR3** 55 H5
Bonehill **B78** 40 D5
**Bo'ness EH51 75 H2**
Bonhill **G83** 74 B3
Boningale **WV7** 40 A5
Bonjedward **TD8** 70 B1
Bonkle **ML2** 75 G5
Bonning Gate **LA8** 61 F7
Bonnington *Edin.* **EH27** 75 K4
Bonnington *Kent* **TN25** 15 F4
Bonnybank **KY8** 82 E7
**Bonnybridge FK4 75 G2**
Bonnykelly **AB53** 99 G5
**Bonnyrigg EH19 76 B4**
Bonnyton *Aber.* **AB52** 90 E1
Bonnyton *Angus* **DD11** 83 G4
Bonnyton *Angus* **DD10** 83 H2
Bonnyton *Angus* **DD3** 82 E4
Bonsall **DE4** 50 E7
Bont **NP7** 28 C7
Bont Dolgadfan **SY19** 37 H5
Bont Newydd **LL40** 37 G3
Bontddu **LL40** 37 F4
Bont-goch (Elerch) **SY24** 37 F7
Bonthorpe **LN13** 53 H5
Bont-newydd *Conwy* **LL17** 47 J5
Bontnewydd *Gwyn.* **LL55** 46 C6
Bontuchel **LL15** 47 J7
Bonvilston **CF5** 18 D4
Bon-y-maen **SA1** 17 K6
Boode **EX33** 6 D2
Boohay **TQ6** 5 K5
Booker **HP12** 22 B2
Booley **SY4** 38 E3
Boor **IV22** 94 E3
Boorley Green **SO32** 11 G3
Boosbeck **TS12** 63 H5
Boose's Green **CO6** 34 C5
Boot **CA19** 60 C6
Boot Street **IP6** 35 G4
Booth **HX2** 57 F7
Booth Bank **HD7** 50 C1
Booth Green **SK10** 49 J4
Booth Wood **HX6** 50 C1
Boothby Graffoe **LN5** 52 C7
Boothby Pagnell **NG33** 42 C2
Boothstown **M28** 49 G2
Boothville **NN3** 31 J2
Bootle *Cumb.* **LA19** 54 E1
**Bootle *Mersey.* L20 48 C3**
Booton **NR10** 45 F3
Boots Green **WA16** 49 G5
Booze **DL11** 62 B6
Boquhan **G63** 74 D2
Boraston **WR15** 29 F1
Bordeaux **GY3** 3 J5
Borden *Kent* **ME9** 24 E5
Borden *W.Suss.* **GU30** 12 B4
Bordley **BD23** 56 E3
**Bordon GU35 11 J1**
Boreham *Essex* **CM3** 24 D1
Boreham *Wilts.* **BA12** 20 B7
Boreham Street **BN27** 13 K5
**Borehamwood WD6 22 E2**
Boreland *D. & G.* **DG11** 69 G4
Boreland *D. & G.* **DG8** 64 D4
Boreland *Stir.* **FK21** 81 G4
Boreley **WR9** 29 H2
Boreraig **IV55** 93 G6
Borgh *W.Isles* **HS6** 92 E3
Borgh *W.Isles* **HS9** 84 B4
Borgh (Borve) *W.Isles* **HS2** 101 G2
Borghastan **HS2** 100 D3
Borgie **KW14** 103 J3
Borgue *D. & G.* **DG6** 65 G6
Borgue *High.* **KW7** 105 G6
Borley **CO10** 34 C4
Borley Green *Essex* **CO10** 34 C4
Borley Green *Suff.* **IP30** 34 D2
Bornais **HS8** 84 C2
Borness **DG6** 65 G6
Bornisketaig **IV51** 93 J4
Borough Green **TN15** 23 K6
Boroughbridge **YO51** 57 J3
Borras Head **LL13** 48 C7
Borrowash **DE72** 41 G2
Borrowby *N.Yorks.* **TS13** 63 J5
Borrowby *N.Yorks.* **YO7** 57 K1
Borrowdale **CA12** 60 D5
Borrowfield **AB39** 91 G5
Borstal **ME1** 24 D5
**Borth SY24 37 F7**
Borthwick **EH23** 76 B5
Borthwickbrae **TD9** 69 K2
Borthwickshiels **TD9** 69 K2
Borth-y-Gest **LL49** 36 E2
Borve *High.* **IV51** 93 K7
Borve (Borgh) *W.Isles* **HS2** 101 G2
Borwick **LA6** 55 J2
Borwick Rails **LA18** 54 E2
Bosavern **TR19** 2 A5
Bosbury **HR8** 29 F4
Boscarne **PL30** 4 A4
**Boscastle PL35 4 A1**
Boscombe *Bourne.* **BH5** 10 C5
Boscombe *Wilts.* **SP4** 10 D1
Bosham **PO18** 12 B6
Bosham Hoe **PO18** 12 B6
Bosherston **SA71** 16 C6
Bosley **SK11** 49 J6
Bossall **YO60** 58 D3
Bossiney **PL34** 4 A2
Bossingham **CT4** 15 G3
Bossington *Hants.* **SO20** 10 E1
Bossington *Som.* **TA24** 7 G1
Bostadh **HS2** 100 D4
Bostock Green **CW10** 49 F6
**Boston PE21 43 G1**
Boston Spa **LS23** 57 K5
Boswarthan **TR20** 2 B5
Boswinger **PL26** 3 G4
Botallack **TR19** 2 A5
Botany Bay **EN2** 23 G2
Botcheston **LE9** 41 G5
Botesdale **IP22** 34 E1
Bothal **NE61** 71 H5
Bothamsall **DN22** 51 J5
Bothel **CA7** 60 C3
Bothenhampton **DT6** 8 D5
Bothwell **G71** 75 F5
Botley *Bucks.* **HP5** 22 C1
Botley *Hants.* **SO30** 11 G3
Botley *Oxon.* **OX2** 21 H1
Botloe's Green **GL18** 29 G6
Botolph Claydon **MK18** 31 J6
Botolphs **BN44** 12 E6
Botolph's Bridge **CT21** 15 G4
Bottacks **IV14** 96 B5
Bottesford *Leics.* **NG13** 42 B2
Bottesford *N.Lincs.* **DN16** 52 B2
Bottisham **CB25** 33 J2
Bottlesford **SN9** 20 E6
Bottom Boat **WF3** 57 J7
Bottom of Hutton **PR4** 55 H7
Bottom o'th'Moor **BL6** 49 F1
Bottomcraig **DD6** 82 E5
Bottoms **OL14** 56 E7
Botton Head **LA2** 56 B3
Botusfleming **PL12** 4 E4
Botwnnog **LL53** 36 B2
Bough Beech **TN8** 23 H7
Boughrood **LD3** 28 A5
Boughspring **NP16** 19 J2
Boughton *Norf.* **PE33** 44 B5
Boughton *Northants.* **NN2** 31 J2
Boughton *Notts.* **NG22** 51 J6
Boughton Aluph **TN25** 15 F3
Boughton Green **ME17** 14 C2
Boughton Lees **TN25** 15 F3
Boughton Malherbe **ME17** 14 D3
Boughton Street **ME13** 15 F2
Boulby **TS13** 63 J5
Bouldnor **PO41** 10 E6
Bouldon **SY7** 38 E7
Boulge **IP13** 35 G3
Boulmer **NE66** 71 H2
Boulston **SA62** 16 C4
Boultenstone Hotel **AB36** 90 C3
Boultham **LN6** 52 C6
Boundary *Derbys.* **DE11** 41 F4
Boundary *Staffs.* **ST10** 40 B1
Bourn **CB23** 33 G3
**Bourne PE10 42 D3**
**Bourne End *Bucks.* SL8 22 B3**
Bourne End *Cen.Beds.* **MK43** 32 C4
Bourne End *Herts.* **HP1** 22 D1
Bournebridge **RM4** 23 J2
**BOURNEMOUTH BH 10 B5**
Bournemouth Airport **BH23** 10 C5
Bournheath **B61** 29 J1
Bournmoor **DH4** 62 E1
Bournville **B30** 40 C7
Bourton *Bucks.* **MK18** 31 J5
Bourton *Dorset* **SP8** 9 G1
Bourton *N.Som.* **BS22** 19 G5
Bourton *Oxon.* **SN6** 21 F3
Bourton *Shrop.* **TF13** 38 E6
Bourton *Wilts.* **SN10** 20 D5
Bourton on Dunsmore **CV23** 31 F1
Bourton-on-the-Hill **GL56** 30 C5
Bourton-on-the-Water **GL54** 30 C6
Bousd **PA78** 78 D1
Boustead Hill **CA5** 60 D1
Bouth **LA12** 55 G1
Bouthwaite **HG3** 57 G2
Bovain **FK21** 81 G4
Boveney **SL4** 22 C4
Boveridge **BH21** 10 B3
Boverton **CF61** 18 C5
Bovey Tracey **TQ13** 5 J3
Bovingdon **HP3** 22 D1
Bovinger **CM5** 23 J1
Bovington Camp **BH20** 9 H6
Bow *Cumb.* **CA5** 60 E1
Bow *Devon* **EX17** 7 F5
Bow *Devon* **TQ9** 5 J5
Bow *Ork.* **KW16** 106 C8
Bow Brickhill **MK17** 32 C5
Bow of Fife **KY15** 82 E6
**Bow Street *Cere.* SY24 37 F7**
Bow Street *Norf.* **NR17** 44 E6
Bowbank **DL12** 62 A4
Bowburn **DH6** 62 E3
Bowcombe **PO30** 11 F6
Bowd **EX10** 7 K6
Bowden *Devon* **TQ6** 5 J6
Bowden *Sc.Bord.* **TD6** 76 D7
Bowden Hill **SN15** 20 C5
Bowdon **WA14** 49 G4
Bower **NE48** 70 C5
Bower Hinton **TA12** 8 D3
Bower House Tye **CO6** 34 D4
Bowerchalke **SP5** 10 B2
Bowerhill **SN12** 20 C5
Bowermadden **KW1** 105 H2
Bowers **ST21** 40 A2
Bowers Gifford **SS13** 24 D3
Bowershall **KY12** 75 J1
Bowertower **KW1** 105 H2
Bowes **DL12** 62 A5
Bowgreave **PR3** 55 H5
Bowhousebog **ML7** 75 G5
Bowithick **PL15** 4 B2
Bowker's Green **L39** 48 D2
Bowland Bridge **LA11** 55 H1
Bowley **HR1** 28 E3
Bowley Town **HR1** 28 E3
Bowlhead Green **GU8** 12 C3
Bowling *W.Dun.* **G60** 74 C3
Bowling *W.Yorks.* **BD4** 57 G6
Bowling Bank **LL13** 38 C1
Bowlish **BA4** 19 K7
Bowmanstead **LA21** 60 E7
Bowmore **PA43** 72 B4
Bowness-on-Solway **CA7** 69 H7
Bowness-on-Windermere **LA23** 60 F7
Bowscale **CA11** 60 E3
Bowsden **TD15** 77 H6
Bowside Lodge **KW14** 104 D2
Bowston **LA8** 61 F7
Bowthorpe **NR5** 45 F5
Bowtrees **FK2** 75 H2
Box *Glos.* **GL6** 20 B1
Box *Wilts.* **SN13** 20 B5
Box End **MK43** 32 D4
Boxbush *Glos.* **GL14** 29 G7
Boxbush *Glos.* **GL17** 29 F6
Boxford *Suff.* **CO10** 34 D4
Boxford *W.Berks.* **RG20** 21 H4
Boxgrove **PO18** 12 C6
Boxley **ME14** 14 C2
Boxmoor **HP1** 22 D1
Box's Shop **EX23** 6 A5
Boxted *Essex* **CO4** 34 D5
Boxted *Suff.* **IP29** 34 C3
Boxted Cross **CO4** 34 D5
Boxwell **GL8** 20 B2
Boxworth **CB23** 33 G2
Boxworth End **CB24** 33 G2
Boyden Gate **CT3** 25 J5
Boydston **KA1** 74 C7
Boylestone **DE6** 40 D2
Boyndie **AB45** 98 E4
Boynton **YO16** 59 H3
Boys Hill **DT9** 9 F4
Boysack **DD11** 83 H3
Boyton *Cornw.* **PL15** 6 B6
Boyton *Suff.* **IP12** 35 H4
Boyton *Wilts.* **BA12** 9 J1
Boyton Cross **CM1** 24 C1
Boyton End **CO10** 34 B4
Bozeat **NN29** 32 C3
Braaid **IM4** 54 C6
Braal Castle **KW12** 105 G2
Brabling Green **IP13** 35 G2
Brabourne **TN25** 15 F3
Brabourne Lees **TN25** 15 F3
Brabster **KW1** 105 J2
Bracadale **IV56** 85 J1
Braceborough **PE9** 42 D4
Bracebridge Heath **LN4** 52 C6
Braceby **NG34** 42 D2
Bracewell **BD23** 56 D5
Brachla **IV3** 88 C1
Bracken Hill **WF14** 57 G7
Brackenber **CA16** 61 J5
Brackenbottom **BD24** 56 D2
Brackenfield **DE55** 51 F7
Brackens **AB53** 99 F5
Bracklach **AB54** 90 B2
Bracklamore **AB43** 99 G5
Bracklesham **PO20** 12 B7
Brackletter **PH34** 87 H6
Brackley *Arg. & B.* **PA31** 73 G2
Brackley *High.* **IV2** 97 F6
**Brackley *Northants.* NN13 31 G5**
Brackley Gate **DE7** 41 F1
Brackley Hatch **NN13** 31 H4
**Bracknell RG12 22 B5**
Braco **FK15** 81 K7
Bracobrae **AB55** 98 D5
Bracon Ash **NR14** 45 F6
Bracora **PH40** 86 D5
Bracorina **PH40** 86 D5
Bradbourne **DE6** 50 E7
Bradbury **TS21** 62 E4
Bradda **IM9** 54 A6
Bradden **NN12** 31 H4
Braddock **PL22** 4 B4
Bradenham *Bucks.* **HP14** 22 B2
Bradenham *Norf.* **IP25** 44 D5
Bradenstoke **SN15** 20 D4
Bradfield *Devon* **EX15** 7 J5
Bradfield *Essex* **CO11** 35 F5
Bradfield *Norf.* **NR28** 45 G2
Bradfield *W.Berks.* **RG7** 21 K4
Bradfield Combust **IP30** 34 C3
Bradfield Green **CW1** 49 F7
Bradfield Heath **CO11** 35 F6
Bradfield St. Clare **IP30** 34 D3
Bradfield St. George **IP30** 34 D2
Bradford *Cornw.* **PL30** 4 B3
Bradford *Derbys.* **DE45** 50 E6
Bradford *Devon* **EX22** 6 C5
Bradford *Northumb.* **NE70** 77 K7
Bradford *Northumb.* **NE20** 71 F6
**BRADFORD *W.Yorks.* BD 57 G6**
Bradford Abbas **DT9** 8 E3
Bradford Leigh **BA15** 20 B5
Bradford Peverell **DT2** 9 F5
**Bradford-on-Avon BA15 20 B5**
Bradford-on-Tone **TA4** 7 K3
Bradiford **EX31** 6 D2
Brading **PO36** 11 H6
Bradley *Ches.W. & C.* **WA6** 48 E5
Bradley *Derbys.* **DE6** 40 E1
Bradley *Hants.* **SO24** 21 K7
Bradley *N.E.Lincs.* **DN37** 53 F2
Bradley (Low Bradley) *N.Yorks.* **BD20** 57 F5
Bradley *Staffs.* **ST18** 40 A4
Bradley *W.Mid.* **WV14** 40 B6
Bradley Fold **BL2** 49 G2
Bradley Green *Warks.* **CV9** 40 E5
Bradley Green *Worcs.* **B96** 29 J2
Bradley in the Moors **ST10** 40 C1
Bradley Mills **HD5** 50 D1
Bradley Stoke **BS32** 19 K3
Bradmore *Notts.* **NG11** 41 H2
Bradmore *W.Mid.* **WV3** 40 A6
Bradney **TA7** 8 C1
Bradninch **EX5** 7 J5
Bradnop **ST13** 50 C7
Bradnor Green **HR5** 28 B3
Bradpole **DT6** 8 D5
Bradshaw *Gt.Man.* **BL2** 49 G1
Bradshaw *W.Yorks.* **HX2** 57 F6
Bradstone **PL19** 6 B7
Bradwall Green **CW11** 49 G6
Bradwell *Derbys.* **S33** 50 D4
Bradwell *Devon* **EX34** 6 C1
Bradwell *Essex* **CM77** 34 C6
Bradwell *M.K.* **MK13** 32 B5
Bradwell *Norf.* **NR31** 45 K5
Bradwell Grove **OX18** 21 F1
Bradwell Waterside **CM0** 25 F1
Bradwell-on-Sea **CM0** 25 G1
Bradworthy **EX22** 6 B4
Brae *D. & G.* **DG2** 65 J3
Brae *High.* **IV24** 96 B1
Brae *Shet.* **ZE2** 107 M6
Brae of Achnahaird **IV26** 102 C7
Braeantra **IV17** 96 C4
Braedownie **DD8** 89 K7
Braefoot **AB53** 99 F6
Braegrum **PH1** 82 B5
Braehead *D. & G.* **DG8** 64 E5
Braehead *Glas.* **G51** 74 D4
Braehead *Moray* **AB55** 98 B6
Braehead *Ork.* **KW17** 106 E7
Braehead *Ork.* **KW17** 106 D3
Braehead *S.Lan.* **ML11** 75 G7
Braehead *S.Lan.* **ML11** 75 H5
Braehead of Lunan **DD10** 83 H2
Braehoulland **ZE2** 107 L5
Braeleny **FK17** 81 H6
Braemar **AB35** 89 J5
Braemore *High.* **IV27** 96 C1
Braemore *High.* **KW6** 105 F5
Braemore *High.* **IV23** 95 H4
Braenaloin **AB35** 89 K5
Braes of Enzie **AB56** 98 B5
Braes of Foss **PH16** 81 J2
Braes of Ullapool **IV26** 95 H2
Braeswick **KW17** 106 F4
Braeval **FK8** 81 G7
Braewick **ZE2** 107 M7
Brafferton *Darl.* **DL1** 62 D4
Brafferton *N.Yorks.* **YO61** 57 K2
Brafield-on-the-Green **NN7** 32 B3
Bragar **HS2** 100 E3
Bragbury End **SG2** 33 F6
Bragenham **LU7** 32 C6

Bra - Bro


Bragleenbeg PA34 80 A5
Braichmelyn LL57 46 E6
Braides LA2 55 H4
Braidley DL8 57 F1
Braidwood ML8 75 G6
Braigo PA44 72 A4
Brailsford DE6 40 E1
Brain's Green GL15 19 K1
**Braintree CM7 34 B6**
Braiseworth IP23 35 F1
Braishfield SO51 10 E2
Braithwaite *Cumb.* CA12 60 D4
Braithwaite *S.Yorks.* DN7 51 J1
Braithwaite *W.Yorks.* BD22 57 F5
Braithwell S66 51 H3
Bramber BN44 12 E5
Brambletye RH18 13 H3
Brambridge SO50 11 F2
Bramcote *Notts.* NG9 41 H2
Bramcote *Warks.* CV11 41 G7
Bramdean SO24 11 H2
Bramerton NR14 45 G5
Bramfield *Herts.* SG14 33 F7
Bramfield *Suff.* IP19 35 H1
Bramford IP8 35 F4
Bramhall SK7 49 H4
Bramham LS23 57 K5
Bramhope LS16 57 H5
Bramley *Hants.* RG26 21 K6
Bramley *S.Yorks.* S66 51 G3
Bramley *Surr.* GU5 22 D7
Bramley Corner RG26 21 K6
Bramley Head HG3 57 G4
Bramley Vale S44 51 G6
Bramling CT3 15 H2
Brampford Speke EX5 7 H6
Brampton *Cambs.* PE28 33 F1
**Brampton *Cumb.* CA8 70 A7**
Brampton *Cumb.* CA16 61 H4
Brampton *Derbys.* S40 51 F5
Brampton *Lincs.* LN1 52 B5
Brampton *Norf.* NR10 45 G3
Brampton *S.Yorks.* S73 51 G2
Brampton *Suff.* NR34 45 J7
Brampton Abbotts HR9 29 F6
Brampton Ash LE16 42 A7
Brampton Bryan SY7 28 C1
Brampton en le Morthen S66 51 G4
Brampton Street NR34 45 J7
Bramshall ST14 40 C2
Bramshaw SO43 10 D3
Bramshill RG27 22 A5
Bramshott GU30 12 B3
Bramwell TA10 8 D2
Bran End CM6 33 K6
Branault PH36 79 G1
Brancaster PE31 44 B1
Brancaster Staithe PE31 44 B1
Brancepeth DH7 62 D3
Branchill IV36 97 H6
Brand Green GL19 29 G6
Brandelhow CA12 60 D4
Branderburgh IV31 97 K4
Brandesburton YO25 59 H5
Brandeston IP13 35 G2
Brandis Corner EX22 6 C5
Brandiston NR10 45 F3
Brandon *Dur.* DH7 62 D3
Brandon *Lincs.* NG32 42 C1
Brandon *Northumb.* NE66 71 F2
**Brandon *Suff.* IP27 44 B7**
Brandon *Warks.* CV8 31 F1
Brandon Bank PE38 44 A7
Brandon Creek PE38 44 A6
Brandon Parva NR9 44 E5
Brandsby YO61 58 B2
Brandy Wharf DN21 52 D3
Brane TR20 2 B6
Branksome BH12 10 B5
Branksome Park BH13 10 B5
Bransbury SO21 21 H7
Bransby LN1 52 B5
Branscombe EX12 7 K7
Bransford WR6 29 G3
Bransford Bridge WR6 29 H3
Bransgore BH23 10 C5
Bransholme HU7 59 H6
Branson's Cross B98 30 B1
Branston *Leics.* NG32 42 B3
Branston *Lincs.* LN4 52 D6
Branston *Staffs.* DE14 40 E3
Branston Booths LN4 52 D6
Brant Broughton LN5 52 C7
Brantham CO11 35 F5
Branthwaite *Cumb.* CA7 60 D3
Branthwaite *Cumb.* CA14 60 B4
Brantingham HU15 59 F7
Branton *Northumb.* NE66 71 F2
Branton *S.Yorks.* DN3 51 J2
Brantwood LA21 60 E7
Branxholm Bridgend TD9 69 K2
Branxholme TD9 69 K2
Branxton TD12 77 G7
Brassey Green CW6 48 E6
Brassington DE4 50 E7
Brasted TN16 23 H6
Brasted Chart TN16 23 H6
Brathens AB31 90 E5
Bratoft PE24 53 H6
Brattleby LN1 52 C4
Bratton *Som.* TA24 7 H1
Bratton *Tel. & W.* TF5 39 F4
Bratton *Wilts.* BA13 20 C6
Bratton Clovelly EX20 6 C6
Bratton Fleming EX31 6 E2
Bratton Seymour BA9 9 F2
Braughing SG11 33 G6
Brauncewell NG34 52 D7
Braunston *Northants.* NN11 31 G2
Braunston *Rut.* LE15 42 B5
Braunstone LE3 41 H5
**Braunton EX33 6 C2**
Brawby YO17 58 D2
Brawdy SA62 16 B3
Brawith TS9 63 G6
Brawl KW14 104 D2
Brawlbin KW12 105 F3
Bray SL6 22 C4
Bray Shop PL17 4 D3
Bray Wick SL6 22 B4
Braybrooke LE16 42 A7
Braydon Side SN15 20 D3
Brayford EX32 6 E2
Brayshaw BD23 56 C4
Braythorn LS21 57 H5
Brayton YO8 58 C6
Braywoodside SL6 22 B4
Brazacott PL15 4 C1
Brea TR15 2 D4
Breach *Kent* CT4 15 G3
Breach *Kent* ME9 24 E5
Breachwood Green SG4 32 E6
Breacleit HS2 100 D4
Breaden Heath SY13 38 D2
Breadsall DE21 41 F2
Breadstone GL13 20 A1
Breage TR13 2 D6
Breakon ZE2 107 P2
Bream GL15 19 K1
Breamore SP6 10 C3
Brean TA8 19 F6
Breanais HS2 100 B5
Brearton HG3 57 J3
Breascleit HS2 100 E4
Breaston DE72 41 G2
Brechfa SA32 17 J2
**Brechin DD9 83 H1**
Brecklate PA28 66 A2
Breckles NR17 44 D6
**Brecon (Aberhonddu) LD3 27 K6**
Breconside DG3 68 D3
Bredbury SK6 49 J3
Brede TN31 14 D6
Bredenbury HR7 29 F3
Bredfield IP13 35 G3
Bredgar ME9 24 E5
Bredhurst ME7 24 D5
Bredon GL20 29 J5
Bredon's Hardwick GL20 29 J5
Bredon's Norton GL20 29 J5
Bredwardine HR3 28 C4
Breedon on the Hill DE73 41 G3
Breibhig HS2 101 G4
Breich EH55 75 H4
Breightmet BL2 49 G2
Breighton YO8 58 D6
Breinton HR4 28 D5
Breinton Common HR4 28 D5
Bremhill SN11 20 C4
Bremhill Wick SN11 20 C4
Brenachoille PA32 80 B7
Brenchley TN12 23 K7
Brendon *Devon* EX35 7 F1
Brendon *Devon* EX22 6 B4
Brendon *Devon* EX22 6 B5
Brenkley NE13 71 H6
Brent Eleigh CO10 34 D4
Brent Knoll TA9 19 G6
Brent Pelham SG9 33 H5
**Brentford TW8 22 E4**
Brentingby LE14 42 A4
**Brentwood CM14 23 J2**
Brenzett TN29 15 F5
Brenzett Green TN29 15 F5
Breoch DG7 65 H5
Brereton WS15 40 C4
Brereton Green CW11 49 G6
Brereton Heath CW12 49 H6
Breretonhill WS15 40 C4
Bressay ZE2 107 P8
Bressingham IP22 44 E7
Bressingham Common IP22 44 E7
Bretby DE15 40 E3
Bretford CV23 31 F1
Bretforton WR11 30 B4
Bretherdale Head CA10 61 G6
Bretherton PR26 55 H7
Brettabister ZE2 107 N7
Brettenham *Norf.* IP24 44 D7
Brettenham *Suff.* IP7 34 D3
Bretton *Derbys.* S32 50 D5
Bretton *Flints.* CH4 48 C6
Brevig HS9 84 B5
Brewood ST19 40 A5
Briach IV36 97 H6
Briantspuddle DT2 9 H5
Brick End CM6 33 J6
Brickendon SG13 23 G1
Bricket Wood AL2 22 E1
Brickkiln Green CM7 34 B5
Bricklehampton WR10 29 J4
Bride IM7 54 D3
Bridekirk CA13 60 C3
Bridell SA43 16 F1
Bridestones CW12 49 J6
Bridestowe EX20 6 D7
Brideswell AB54 90 D1
Bridford EX6 7 G7
Bridge *Cornw.* TR16 2 D4
Bridge *Kent* CT4 15 G2
Bridge End *Cumb.* LA20 55 F1
Bridge End *Devon* TQ7 5 G6
Bridge End *Essex* CM7 33 K5
Bridge End *Lincs.* NG34 42 E2
Bridge End *Shet.* ZE2 107 M9
Bridge Hewick HG4 57 J2
Bridge o'Ess AB34 90 D5
Bridge of Alford AB33 90 D3
Bridge of Allan FK9 75 F1
Bridge of Avon AB37 89 J1
Bridge of Balgie PH15 81 G3
Bridge of Bogendreip AB31 90 E5
Bridge of Brewlands PH11 82 C1
Bridge of Brown AB37 89 J2
Bridge of Cally PH10 82 C2
Bridge of Canny AB31 90 E5
Bridge of Craigisla PH11 82 D2
Bridge of Dee *Aber.* AB35 89 J5
Bridge of Dee *Aber.* AB31 90 E5
Bridge of Dee *D. & G.* DG7 65 H4
Bridge of Don AB23 91 H4
Bridge of Dun DD10 83 H2
Bridge of Dye AB31 90 E6
Bridge of Earn PH2 82 C6
Bridge of Ericht PH17 81 G2
Bridge of Feugh AB31 90 E5
Bridge of Forss KW14 105 F2
Bridge of Gairn AB35 90 B5
Bridge of Gaur PH17 81 G2
Bridge of Muchalls AB39 91 G5
Bridge of Muick AB35 90 B5
**Bridge of Orchy PA36 80 D4**
Bridge of Tynet AB56 98 B4
Bridge of Walls ZE2 107 L7
**Bridge of Weir PA11 74 B4**
Bridge Reeve EX18 6 E4
Bridge Sollers HR4 28 D4
Bridge Street CO10 34 C4
Bridge Trafford CH2 48 D5
Bridgefoot *Angus* DD3 82 E4
Bridgefoot *Cambs.* SG8 33 H4
Bridgefoot *Cumb.* CA14 60 B4
Bridgehampton BA22 8 E2
Bridgehaugh AB55 90 B1
Bridgehill DH8 62 B1
Bridgemary PO13 11 G4
Bridgemere CW5 39 G1
Bridgend *Aber.* AB54 90 D1
Bridgend *Aber.* AB53 99 F6
Bridgend *Angus* DD9 83 G1
Bridgend *Arg. & B.* PA44 72 B4
Bridgend *Arg. & B.* PA31 73 G1
**Bridgend (Pen-y-bont ar Ogwr) *Bridgend* CF31 18 C4**
Bridgend *Cornw.* PL22 4 B5
Bridgend *Cumb.* CA11 60 F5
Bridgend *Fife* KY15 82 E6
Bridgend *Moray* AB54 90 B1
Bridgend *P. & K.* PH2 82 C5
Bridgend *W.Loth.* EH49 75 J3
Bridgend of Lintrathen DD8 82 D2
Bridgerule EX22 6 A5
Bridges SY5 38 C6
Bridgeton *Aber.* AB33 90 D3
Bridgeton *Glas.* G40 74 E4
Bridgetown *Cornw.* PL15 6 B7
Bridgetown *Som.* TA22 7 H2
Bridgeyate BS30 19 K4
Bridgham NR16 44 D7
**Bridgnorth WV16 39 G6**
Bridgtown WS11 40 B5
**Bridgwater TA6 8 B1**
**Bridlington YO16 59 H3**
**Bridport DT6 8 D5**
Bridstow HR9 28 E6
Brierfield BB9 56 D6
Brierley *Glos.* GL17 29 F7
Brierley *Here.* HR6 28 D3
Brierley *S.Yorks.* S72 51 G1
**Brierley Hill DY5 40 B7**
Brierton TS22 63 F4
Briestfield WF12 50 E1
Brig o'Turk FK17 81 G7
**Brigg DN20 52 D2**
Briggate NR28 45 H3
Briggswath YO21 63 K6
Brigham *Cumb.* CA13 60 B3
Brigham *E.Riding* YO25 59 G4
**Brighouse HD6 57 G7**
Brighstone PO30 11 F6
Brightgate DE4 50 E7
Brighthampton OX29 21 G1
Brightholmlee S35 50 E3
Brightling TN32 13 K4
Brightlingsea CO7 34 E7
**BRIGHTON *B. & H.* BN 13 G6**
Brighton *Cornw.* TR2 3 G3
Brightons FK2 75 H3
Brightwalton RG20 21 H4
Brightwalton Green RG20 21 H4
Brightwell IP10 35 G4
Brightwell Baldwin OX49 21 K2
Brightwell Upperton OX49 21 K2
Brightwell-cum-Sotwell OX10 21 J2
Brignall DL12 62 B5
Brigsley DN37 53 F2
Brigsteer LA8 55 H1
Brigstock NN14 42 C7
Brill *Bucks.* HP18 31 H7
Brill *Cornw.* TR11 2 E6
Brilley HR3 28 B4
Brilley Mountain HR3 28 B3
Brimaston SA62 16 C3
Brimfield SY8 28 E2
Brimington S43 51 G5
Brimington Common S43 51 G5
Brimley TQ13 5 J3
Brimpsfield GL4 29 J7
Brimpton RG7 21 J5
Brims KW16 106 B9
Brimscombe GL5 20 B1
Brimstage CH63 48 C4
Brinacory PH41 86 D5
Brindham BA6 19 J7
Brindister *Shet.* ZE2 107 N9
Brindister *Shet.* ZE2 107 L7
Brindle PR6 55 J7
Brindley Ford ST8 49 H7
Brineton TF11 40 A4
Bringhurst LE16 42 B6
Brington PE28 32 D1
Brinian KW17 106 D5
Briningham NR24 44 E2
Brinkhill LN11 53 G5
Brinkley *Cambs.* CB8 33 K3
Brinkley *Notts.* NG25 51 K7
Brinklow CV23 31 F1
Brinkworth SN15 20 D3
Brinmore IV2 88 D2
Brinscall PR6 56 B7
Brinsea BS49 19 H5
Brinsley NG16 41 G1
Brinsop HR4 28 D4
Brinsworth S60 51 G3
Brinton NR24 44 E2
Brisco CA4 60 F1
Brisley NR20 44 D3
Brislington BS4 19 K4
Brissenden Green TN26 14 E4
**BRISTOL BS 19 J4**
Bristol Filton Airport BS10 19 J3
Bristol International Airport BS48 19 J5
Briston NR24 44 E2
Britannia OL13 56 D7
Britford SP5 10 C2
Brithdir *Caerp.* NP24 18 E1
Brithdir *Gwyn.* LL40 37 G4
Brithem Bottom EX15 7 J4
Briton Ferry (Llansawel) SA11 18 A2
Britwell SL2 22 C3
Britwell Salome OX49 21 K2
**Brixham TQ5 5 K5**
Brixton *Devon* PL8 5 F5
Brixton *Gt.Lon.* SW2 23 G4
Brixton Deverill BA12 9 H1
Brixworth NN6 31 J1
Brize Norton OX18 21 F1
Broad Alley WR9 29 H2
Broad Blunsdon SN26 20 E2
Broad Campden GL55 30 C5
Broad Carr HX4 50 C1
Broad Chalke SP5 10 B2
Broad Ford TN12 14 C4
Broad Green *Cambs.* CB8 33 K3
Broad Green *Cen.Beds.* MK43 32 C4
Broad Green *Essex* CO6 34 C6
Broad Green *Essex* SG8 33 H5
Broad Green *Mersey.* L14 48 D3
Broad Green *Suff.* IP6 34 E3
Broad Green *Worcs.* WR6 29 G3
Broad Haven SA62 16 B4
Broad Hill CB7 33 J1
Broad Hinton SN4 20 E4
Broad Laying RG20 21 H5
Broad Marston CV37 30 C4
Broad Oak *Carmar.* SA32 17 J3
Broad Oak *Cumb.* CA18 60 C7
Broad Oak *E.Suss.* TN31 14 D6
Broad Oak *E.Suss.* TN21 13 K4
Broad Oak *Here.* HR2 28 D6
Broad Road IP21 35 G1
Broad Street *E.Suss.* TN36 14 D6
Broad Street *Kent* ME17 14 D2
Broad Street *Kent* TN25 15 G4
Broad Street *Wilts.* SN9 20 E6
Broad Street Green CM9 24 E1
Broad Town SN4 20 D4
Broadbottom SK14 49 J3
Broadbridge PO18 12 B6
Broadbridge Heath RH12 12 E3
Broadclyst EX5 7 H6
Broadfield *Lancs.* BB5 56 C7
Broadfield *Lancs.* PR25 55 J7
Broadford IV49 86 C2
Broadford Bridge RH14 12 D4
Broadgate LA18 54 E1
Broadhaugh TD9 69 K3
Broadhaven KW1 105 J3
Broadheath *Gt.Man.* WA14 49 G4
Broadheath *Worcs.* WR15 29 F2
Broadhembury EX14 7 K5
Broadhempston TQ9 5 J4
Broadholme LN1 52 B5
Broadland Row TN31 14 D6
Broadlay SA17 17 G5
Broadley *Lancs.* OL12 49 H1
Broadley *Moray* AB56 98 B4
Broadley Common EN9 23 H1
Broadmayne DT2 9 G6
Broadmeadows TD7 76 C7
Broadmere RG25 21 K7
Broadmoor SA68 16 D5
Broadnymett EX17 7 F5
Broadoak *Dorset* DT6 8 D5
Broadoak *Glos.* GL14 29 F7
Broadoak *Kent* CT2 25 H5
Broadoak End SG14 33 G7
Broadrashes AB55 98 C5
Broad's Green CM3 33 K7
Broadsea AB43 99 H4
**Broadstairs CT10 25 K5**
**Broadstone *Poole* BH18 10 B5**
Broadstone *Shrop.* SY7 38 E7
Broadstreet Common NP18 19 G3
Broadwas WR6 29 G3
Broadwater *Herts.* SG2 33 F6
Broadwater *W.Suss.* BN14 12 E6
Broadwater Down TN2 13 J3
Broadwaters DY10 29 H1
Broadway *Carmar.* SA17 17 G5
Broadway *Carmar.* SA33 17 F4
Broadway *Pembs.* SA62 16 B4
Broadway *Som.* TA19 8 C3
Broadway *Suff.* IP19 35 H1
**Broadway *Worcs.* WR12 30 C5**
Broadwell *Glos.* GL56 30 D6
Broadwell *Oxon.* GL7 21 F1
Broadwell *Warks.* CV23 31 F2
Broadwell House NE47 62 A1
Broadwey DT3 9 F6
Broadwindsor DT8 8 D4
Broadwood Kelly EX19 6 E5
Broadwoodwidger PL16 6 C7
Brobury HR3 28 C4
Brocastle CF35 18 C4
Brochel IV40 94 B7
Brochloch DG7 67 K4
Brock PA77 78 B3
Brockamin WR6 29 G3
Brockbridge SO32 11 H3
Brockdish IP21 35 G1
**Brockenhurst SO42 10 D4**
Brockford Green IP14 35 F2
Brockford Street IP14 35 F2
Brockhall NN7 31 H2
Brockham RH3 22 E7
Brockhampton *Glos.* GL54 30 B6
Brockhampton *Glos.* GL51 29 J6
Brockhampton *Here.* HR1 28 E5
Brockhampton *Here.* WR6 29 F3
Brockhampton Green DT2 9 G4
Brockholes HD9 50 D1
Brockhurst *Hants.* PO12 11 G4
Brockhurst *W.Suss.* RH19 13 H3
Brocklebank CA7 60 E2
Brocklesby DN41 52 E1
Brockley *N.Som.* BS48 19 H5
Brockley *Suff.* IP29 34 C3
Brockley Green CO10 34 B4
Brock's Green RG20 21 H5
Brockton *Shrop.* TF13 38 E6
Brockton *Shrop.* TF11 39 G5
Brockton *Shrop.* SY5 38 C5
Brockton *Shrop.* SY7 38 C7
Brockton *Tel. & W.* TF10 39 G4
Brockweir NP16 19 J1
Brockwood Park SO24 11 H2
Brockworth GL3 29 H7
Brocton ST17 40 B4
Brodick KA27 73 J7
Brodsworth DN5 51 H2
Brogborough MK43 32 C5
Brogden BB18 56 D5
Brogyntyn SY10 38 B2
Broken Cross *Ches.E.* SK11 49 H5
Broken Cross *Ches.W. & C.* CW9 49 F5
Brokenborough SN16 20 C3
Brokes DL11 62 C7
Bromborough CH62 48 C4
Brome IP23 35 F1
Brome Street IP23 35 F1
Bromeswell IP12 35 H3
Bromfield *Cumb.* CA7 60 C2
Bromfield *Shrop.* SY8 28 D1
Bromham *Bed.* MK43 32 D3
Bromham *Wilts.* SN15 20 C5
**BROMLEY *Gt.Lon.* BR 23 H5**
Bromley *S.Yorks.* S35 51 F3
Bromley Cross BL7 49 G1
Bromley Green TN26 14 E4
Brompton *Med.* ME7 24 D5
Brompton *N.Yorks.* DL6 62 E7
Brompton *N.Yorks.* YO13 59 F1
Brompton *Shrop.* SY5 38 E5
Brompton on Swale DL10 62 D7
Brompton Ralph TA4 7 J2
Brompton Regis TA22 7 H2
Bromsash HR9 29 F6
Bromsberrow HR8 29 G5
Bromsberrow Heath HR8 29 G5
**Bromsgrove B61 29 J1**
Bromstead Heath TF10 40 A4
**Bromyard HR7 29 F3**
Bromyard Downs HR7 29 F3
Bronaber LL41 37 G2
Brondesbury NW6 23 F3
Brongest SA38 17 G1
Bronington SY13 38 D2
Bronllys LD3 28 A5
Bronnant SY23 27 F2
Bronwydd Arms SA33 17 H3
Bronydd HR3 28 B4
Bron-y-gaer SA33 17 G4
Bronygarth SY10 38 B2
Brook *Carmar.* SA33 17 F5
Brook *Hants.* SO43 10 D3
Brook *Hants.* SO20 10 E2
Brook *I.o.W.* PO30 10 E6
Brook *Kent* TN25 15 F3
Brook *Surr.* GU8 12 C3
Brook *Surr.* GU5 22 D7
Brook Bottom OL5 49 J2
Brook End *Bed.* MK44 32 D2
Brook End *Herts.* SG9 33 G6
Brook End *M.K.* MK16 32 C4
Brook End *Worcs.* WR5 29 H4
Brook Hill SO43 10 D3
Brook Street *Essex* CM14 23 J2
Brook Street *Kent* TN26 14 E4
Brook Street *Suff.* CO10 34 C4
Brook Street *W.Suss.* RH17 13 G4
Brooke *Norf.* NR15 45 G6
Brooke *Rut.* LE15 42 B5
Brookend *Glos.* GL15 19 J2

Bro - Bus


Brookend *Glos.* GL13 19 K1
Brookfield SK14 50 C3
Brookhampton OX44 21 K2
Brookhouse *Ches.E.* SK10 49 J5
Brookhouse *Denb.* LL16 47 J6
Brookhouse *Lancs.* LA2 55 J3
Brookhouse *S.Yorks.* S25 51 H4
Brookhouse Green CW11 49 H6
Brookhouses ST10 40 B1
Brookland TN29 14 E5
Brooklands *D. & G.* DG2 65 J3
Brooklands *Shrop.* SY13 38 E1
Brookmans Park AL9 23 F1
Brooks SY21 38 A6
Brooks Green RH13 12 E4
Brooksby LE14 41 J4
Brookthorpe GL4 29 H7
Brookwood GU24 22 C6
Broom *Cen.Beds.* SG18 32 E4
Broom *Fife* KY8 82 E7
Broom *Warks.* B50 30 B3
Broom Green NR20 44 D3
Broom Hill *Dorset* BH21 10 B4
Broom Hill *Worcs.* DY9 29 J1
Broom of Dalreach PH3 82 B6
Broomcroft SY5 38 E5
Broome *Norf.* NR35 45 H6
Broome *Shrop.* SY7 38 D7
Broome *Worcs.* DY9 29 J1
Broome Wood NE66 71 G2
Broomedge WA13 49 G4
Broomer's Corner RH13 12 E4
Broomfield *Aber.* AB41 91 H1
Broomfield *Essex* CM1 34 B7
Broomfield *Kent* CT6 25 H5
Broomfield *Kent* ME17 14 D2
Broomfield *Som.* TA5 8 B1
Broomfleet HU15 58 E7
Broomhall Green CW5 39 F1
Broomhaugh NE44 71 F7
Broomhead AB43 99 H4
Broomhill *Bristol* BS16 19 K4
Broomhill *Northumb.* NE65 71 H3
Broomielaw DL12 62 B5
Broomley NE43 71 F7
Broompark DH7 62 D2
Broom's Green GL18 29 G5
**Brora** KW9 97 G1
**Broseley** TF12 39 F5
Brotherlee DL13 62 A3
Brothertoft PE20 43 F1
Brotherton WF11 57 K7
Brotton TS12 63 H5
Broubster KW14 105 F2
Brough *Cumb.* CA17 61 J5
Brough *Derbys.* S33 50 D4
**Brough** *E.Riding* HU15 59 F7
Brough *High.* KW14 105 H1
Brough *Notts.* NG23 52 B7
Brough *Ork.* KW17 106 C6
Brough *Shet.* ZE2 107 P8
Brough *Shet.* ZE2 107 N5
Brough *Shet.* ZE2 107 P6
Brough *Shet.* ZE2 107 P5
Brough Lodge ZE2 107 P3
Brough Sowerby CA17 61 J5
Broughall SY13 38 E1
Brougham CA10 61 G4
Broughton *Bucks.* HP20 32 B7
Broughton *Cambs.* PE28 33 F1
Broughton *Flints.* CH4 48 C6
Broughton *Hants.* SO20 10 E1
Broughton *Lancs.* PR3 55 J6
Broughton *M.K.* MK16 32 B4
Broughton *N.Lincs.* DN20 52 C2
Broughton *N.Yorks.* YO17 58 D2
Broughton *N.Yorks.* BD23 56 E4
Broughton *Northants.* NN14 32 B1
Broughton *Ork.* KW17 106 D3
Broughton *Oxon.* OX15 31 F5
Broughton *Sc.Bord.* ML12 75 K7
Broughton *V. of Glam.* CF71 18 C4
Broughton Astley LE9 41 H6
Broughton Beck LA12 55 F1
Broughton Gifford SN12 20 B5
Broughton Green WR9 29 J2
Broughton Hackett WR7 29 J3
**Broughton in Furness** LA20 55 F1
Broughton Mills LA20 60 D7
Broughton Moor CA15 60 B3
Broughton Poggs GL7 21 F1
Broughtown KW17 106 F3
Broughty Ferry DD5 83 F4
Browland ZE2 107 L7
Brown Candover SO24 11 G1
Brown Edge *Lancs.* PR8 48 C1
Brown Edge *Staffs.* ST6 49 J7
Brown Heath CH3 48 D6
Brown Lees ST8 49 H7
Brown Street IP14 34 E2
Brownber CA17 61 J6
Browndown PO13 11 G5
Brownheath SY12 38 D3
Brownhill AB41 99 G6
Brownhills *Fife* KY16 83 G6
Brownhills *W.Mid.* WS8 40 C5
Brownieside NE67 71 G1
Brownlow CW12 49 H6
Brownlow Heath CW12 49 H6
Brown's Bank CW3 39 F1
Brownsea Island BH15 10 B6
Brownshill GL6 20 B1
Brownshill Green CV5 41 F7
Brownsover CV21 31 G1
Brownston PL21 5 G5
Browston Green NR31 45 J5
Broxa YO13 63 J3
**Broxbourne** EN10 23 G1
Broxburn *E.Loth.* EH42 76 E3
**Broxburn** *W.Loth.* EH52 75 J3
Broxholme LN1 52 C5
Broxted CM6 33 J6
Broxton CH3 48 D7
Broxwood HR6 28 C3
Broyle Side BN8 13 H5
Bru (Brue) HS2 101 F3
Bruachmary IV12 97 F7
Bruan KW2 105 J5
Brue (Bru) HS2 101 F3
Bruera CH3 48 D6
Bruern OX7 30 D6
Bruernish HS9 84 C4
Bruichladdich PA49 72 A4
Bruisyard IP17 35 H2
Bruisyard Street IP17 35 H2
Brumby DN16 52 C1
Brund SK17 50 D6
Brundall NR13 45 H5
Brundish *Norf.* NR14 45 H6
Brundish *Suff.* IP13 35 G2
Brundish Street IP13 35 G1
Brunstock CA6 60 F1
Brunswick Village NE13 71 H6
Bruntingthorpe LE17 41 J6
Bruntland AB54 90 C2
Brunton *Fife* KY15 82 E5
Brunton *Northumb.* NE66 71 H1
Brunton *Wilts.* SN8 21 F6
Brushfield SK17 50 D5
Brushford *Devon* EX18 6 E5
Brushford *Som.* TA22 7 H3
**Bruton** BA10 9 F1
Bryanston DT11 9 H4
Bryant's Bottom HP16 22 B2
Brydekirk DG12 69 G6
Brymbo LL11 48 B7
Brympton BA22 8 E3
Bryn *Caerp.* NP12 18 E2
Bryn *Carmar.* SA14 17 J5
Bryn *Ches.W. & C.* CW8 49 F5
Bryn *Gt.Man.* WN4 48 E2
Bryn *N.P.T.* SA13 18 B2
Bryn *Shrop.* SY9 38 B7
Bryn Bwbach LL47 37 F2
Bryn Gates WN2 48 E2
Bryn Pen-y-lan LL14 38 C1
Brynamman SA18 27 G7
Brynberian SA41 16 E2
**Brynbuga (Usk)** NP15 19 G1
Bryncae CF72 18 C3
Bryncethin CF32 18 C3
Bryncir LL51 36 D1
Bryncoch *Bridgend* CF32 18 C3
Bryn-côch *N.P.T.* SA10 18 A2
Bryncroes LL53 36 B2
Bryncrug LL36 37 F5
Bryneglwys LL21 38 A1
Brynford CH8 47 K5
Bryngwran LL65 46 B5
Bryngwyn *Mon.* NP15 19 G1
Bryngwyn *Powys* HR5 28 A4
Bryn-henllan SA42 16 D2
Brynhoffnant SA44 26 C3
Bryning PR4 55 H6
Brynithel NP13 19 F1
Brynmawr *B.Gwent* NP23 28 A7
Bryn-mawr *Gwyn.* LL53 36 B2
Brynmelyn LD1 28 A1
Brynmenyn CF32 18 C3
Brynna CF72 18 C3
Brynnau Gwynion CF72 18 C3
Brynog SA48 26 E3
Bryn-penarth SY21 38 A5
Brynrefail *Gwyn.* LL55 46 D6
Brynrefail *I.o.A.* LL70 46 C4
Brynsadler CF72 18 D3
Brynsaithmarchog LL21 47 J7
Brynsiencyn LL61 46 C6
Bryn-teg *I.o.A.* LL78 46 C4
**Brynteg** *Wrex.* LL11 48 C7
Bryn-y-cochin SY12 38 C2
Brynygwenin NP7 28 C7
Bryn-y-maen LL28 47 G5
Buaile nam Bodach HS9 84 C4
Bualadubh HS8 92 C7
Bualintur IV47 85 K2
Bualnaluib IV22 94 E2
Bubbenhall CV8 30 E1
Bubnell DE45 50 E5
Bubwith YO8 58 D6
Buccleuch TD9 69 J2
Buchan DG7 65 H4
Buchanan Castle G63 74 C2
Buchanhaven AB42 99 K6
Buchanty PH1 82 A5
Buchlyvie FK8 74 D1
Buckabank CA5 60 E2
Buckby Wharf NN11 31 H2
Buckden *Cambs.* PE19 32 E2
Buckden *N.Yorks.* BD23 56 E2
Buckenham NR13 45 H5
Buckerell EX14 7 K5
Buckfast TQ11 5 H4
**Buckfastleigh** TQ11 5 H4
Buckhaven KY8 76 B1
Buckholm TD1 76 C7
Buckholt NP25 28 E7
Buckhorn Weston SP8 9 G2
**Buckhurst Hill** IG9 23 H2
**Buckie** AB56 98 C4
Buckies KW14 105 G2
**Buckingham** MK18 31 H5
Buckland *Bucks.* HP22 32 B7
Buckland *Devon* TQ7 5 G6
Buckland *Glos.* WR12 30 B5
Buckland *Hants.* SO41 10 E5
Buckland *Here.* HR6 28 E3
Buckland *Herts.* SG9 33 G5
Buckland *Kent* CT16 15 J3
Buckland *Oxon.* SN7 21 G2
Buckland *Surr.* RH3 23 F6
Buckland Brewer EX39 6 C3
Buckland Common HP23 22 C1
Buckland Dinham BA11 20 A6
Buckland Filleigh EX21 6 C5
Buckland in the Moor TQ13 5 H3
Buckland Monachorum PL20 4 E4
Buckland Newton DT2 9 F4
Buckland Ripers DT3 9 F6
Buckland St. Mary TA20 8 B3
Buckland-tout-Saints TQ7 5 H6
Bucklebury RG7 21 J4
Bucklerheads DD5 83 F4
Bucklers Hard SO42 11 F5
Bucklesham IP10 35 G4
**Buckley (Bwcle)** CH7 48 B6
Buckley Green B95 30 C2
Bucklow Hill WA16 49 G4
Buckman Corner RH14 12 E4
Buckminster NG33 42 B3
Bucknall *Lincs.* LN10 52 E6
Bucknall *Stoke* ST2 40 B1
Bucknell *Oxon.* OX27 31 G6
**Bucknell** *Shrop.* SY7 28 C1
Buckridge DY14 29 G1
Buck's Cross EX39 6 B3
Bucks Green RH12 12 D3
Bucks Hill WD4 22 D1
Bucks Horn Oak GU10 22 B7
Buck's Mills EX39 6 B3
Bucksburn AB21 91 G4
Buckspool SA71 16 C6
Buckton *E.Riding* YO15 59 H2
Buckton *Here.* SY7 28 C1
Buckton *Northumb.* NE70 77 J7
Buckton Vale SK15 49 J2
Buckworth PE28 32 E1
Budbrooke CV35 30 D2
Budby NG22 51 J5
Buddon DD7 83 G4
**Bude** EX23 6 A5
Budge's Shop PL12 4 D5
Budlake EX5 7 H5
Budle NE69 77 K7
**Budleigh Salterton** EX9 7 J7
Budock Water TR11 2 E5
Budworth Heath CW9 49 F5
Buerton CW3 39 F1
Bugbrooke NN7 31 H3
Bugeildy (Beguildy) LD7 28 A1
Buglawton CW12 49 H6
Bugle PL26 4 A5
Bugthorpe YO41 58 D4
Building End SG8 33 H5
Buildwas TF8 39 F5
Builth Road LD2 27 K3
**Builth Wells (Llanfair-ym-Muallt)** LD2 27 K3
Bulby PE10 42 D3
Bulcote NG14 41 J1
Buldoo KW14 104 E2
Bulford SP4 20 E7
Bulford Camp SP4 20 E7
Bulkeley SY14 48 E7
Bulkington *Warks.* CV12 41 F7
Bulkington *Wilts.* SN10 20 C6
Bulkworthy EX22 6 B4
Bull Bay (Porth Llechog) LL68 46 C3
Bull Green TN26 14 E4
Bullbridge DE56 51 F7
Bullbrook RG12 22 B5
Bullen's Green AL4 23 F1
Bulley GL2 29 G7
Bullington LN3 52 D5
Bullpot Farm LA6 56 B1
Bulls Cross EN2 23 G2
Bull's Green *Herts.* SG3 33 F7
Bull's Green *Norf.* NR34 45 J6
Bullwood PA23 73 K3
Bulmer *Essex* CO10 34 C4
Bulmer *N.Yorks.* YO60 58 C3
Bulmer Tye CO10 34 C5
Bulphan RM14 24 C3
Bulstone EX12 7 K7
Bulverhythe TN38 14 C7
Bulwark AB42 99 H6
Bulwell NG6 41 H1
Bulwick NN17 42 C6
Bumble's Green EN9 23 H1
Bun Abhainn Eadarra HS3 100 D7
Bun Loyne IV63 87 J4
Bunarkaig PH34 87 H6
Bunbury CW6 48 E7
Bunbury Heath CW6 48 E7
Bunchrew IV3 96 D7
Bundalloch IV40 86 E2
Buness ZE2 107 Q2
Bunessan PA67 78 E5
**Bungay** NR35 45 H7
Bunker's Hill LN4 53 F7
Bunlarie PA28 73 F7
Bunloit IV63 88 C2
Bunmhullin HS8 84 C3
Bunnahabhain PA46 72 C3
Bunny NG11 41 H3
Buntait IV63 87 K1
**Buntingford** SG9 33 G6
Bunwell NR16 45 F6
Bunwell Street NR16 45 F6
Burbage *Derbys.* SK17 50 C5
Burbage *Leics.* LE10 41 G6
Burbage *Wilts.* SN8 21 F5
Burchett's Green SL6 22 B3
Burcombe SP2 10 B1
Burcot *Oxon.* OX14 21 J2
Burcot *Worcs.* B60 29 J1
Burcott LU7 32 B6
Burdale YO17 58 E3
Burdocks RH14 12 D4
Burdon SR3 62 E1
Burdrop OX15 30 E5
**Bures** CO8 34 D5
Bures Green CO8 34 D5
Burfa LD8 28 B2
**Burford** *Oxon.* OX18 30 D7
Burford *Shrop.* WR15 28 E2
Burg PA74 78 E3
Burgate IP22 34 E1
Burgates GU33 11 J2
Burge End SG5 32 E5
**Burgess Hill** RH15 13 G5
Burgh IP13 35 G3
Burgh by Sands CA5 60 E1
Burgh Castle NR31 45 J5
Burgh Heath KT20 23 F6
Burgh le Marsh PE24 53 H6
Burgh next Aylsham NR11 45 G3
Burgh on Bain LN8 53 F4
Burgh St. Margaret (Fleggburgh) NR29 45 J4
Burgh St. Peter NR34 45 J6
Burghclere RG20 21 H5
Burghead IV30 97 J5
Burghfield RG30 21 K5
Burghfield Common RG7 21 K5
Burghfield Hill RG7 21 K5
Burghill HR4 28 D4
Burghwallis DN6 51 H1
Burham ME1 24 D5
Buriton GU31 11 J2
Burland CW5 49 F7
Burlawn PL27 3 G2
Burleigh SL5 22 C5
Burlescombe EX16 7 J4
Burleston DT2 9 G5
Burley *Hants.* BH24 10 D4
Burley *Rut.* LE15 42 B4
Burley *W.Yorks.* LS6 57 H6
Burley Gate HR1 28 E4
Burley in Wharfedale LS29 57 G5
Burley Street BH24 10 D4
Burley Woodhead LS29 57 G5
Burleydam SY13 39 F1
Burlingjobb LD8 28 B3
Burlow TN21 13 J5
Burlton SY4 38 D3
Burmarsh TN29 15 G4
Burmington CV36 30 D5
Burn YO8 58 B7
Burn Farm DD9 90 E7
Burn Naze FY5 55 G5
Burn of Cambus FK16 81 J7
Burnage M19 49 H3
Burnaston DE65 40 E2
Burnby YO42 58 E5
Burncross S35 51 F3
Burndell BN18 12 C6
Burnden BL3 49 G2
Burnedge OL2 49 J1
Burnend AB41 99 G6
Burneside LA9 61 G7
Burness KW17 106 F3
Burneston DL8 57 J1
Burnett BS31 19 K5
Burnfoot *High.* KW11 104 D6
Burnfoot *P. & K.* FK14 82 A7
Burnfoot *Sc.Bord.* TD9 70 A2
Burnfoot *Sc.Bord.* TD9 69 K2
Burnham *Bucks.* SL1 22 C3
Burnham *N.Lincs.* DN18 52 D1
Burnham Deepdale PE31 44 C1
Burnham Green AL6 33 F7
Burnham Market PE31 44 C1
Burnham Norton PE31 44 C1
Burnham Overy Staithe PE31 44 C1
Burnham Overy Town PE31 44 C1
Burnham Thorpe PE31 44 C1
**Burnham-on-Crouch** CM0 25 F2
**Burnham-on-Sea** TA8 19 G7
Burnhaven AB42 99 K6
Burnhead *D. & G.* DG7 67 K5
Burnhead *D. & G.* DG3 68 D4
Burnhervie AB51 91 F3
Burnhill Green WV6 39 G5
Burnhope DH7 62 C2
Burnhouse KA15 74 B5
Burniston YO13 63 K3
**Burnley** BB11 56 D6
Burnmouth TD14 77 H4
Burnopfield NE16 62 C1
Burn's Green SG2 33 G6
Burnsall BD23 57 F3
Burnside *Aber.* AB32 91 F3
Burnside *Angus* DD8 83 G2
Burnside *E.Ayr.* KA18 67 K2
Burnside *Fife* KY13 82 C7
Burnside *Shet.* ZE2 107 L5
Burnside *W.Loth.* EH52 75 J3
Burnside of Duntrune DD4 83 F4
Burnstones CA8 61 H1
Burnswark DG11 69 G6
Burnt Hill RG18 21 J4
Burnt Houses DL13 62 C4
Burnt Oak HA8 23 F2
Burnt Yates HG3 57 H3
Burntcliff Top SK11 49 J6
**Burntisland** KY3 76 A2
Burnton *E.Ayr.* KA18 67 J2
Burnton *E.Ayr.* KA6 67 J3
**Burntwood** WS7 40 C5
Burntwood Green WS7 40 C5
Burnworthy TA3 7 K4
Burpham *Surr.* GU1 22 D6
Burpham *W.Suss.* BN18 12 D6
Burra ZE2 107 M9
Burradon *Northumb.* NE65 70 E3
Burradon *T. & W.* NE23 71 H6
Burrafirth ZE2 107 Q1
Burraland ZE2 107 M5
Burras TR13 2 D5
Burraton *Cornw.* PL12 4 E4
Burraton *Cornw.* PL12 4 E5
Burravoe *Shet.* ZE2 107 P5
Burravoe *Shet.* ZE2 107 M6
Burray KW17 106 D8
Burrells CA16 61 H5
Burrelton PH13 82 D4
Burridge *Devon* EX13 8 C4
Burridge *Hants.* SO31 11 G3
Burrill DL8 57 H1
Burringham DN17 52 B2
Burrington *Devon* EX37 6 E4
Burrington *Here.* SY8 28 D1
Burrington *N.Som.* BS40 19 H6
Burrough Green CB8 33 K3
Burrough on the Hill LE14 42 A4
Burrow *Som.* TA24 7 H1
Burrow *Som.* TA12 8 D3
Burrow Bridge TA7 8 C1
Burrowhill GU24 22 C5
Burrows Cross GU5 22 D7
Burry SA3 17 H6
Burry Green SA3 17 H6
**Burry Port** SA16 17 H5
Burscough L40 48 D1
Burscough Bridge L40 48 D1
Bursea YO43 58 E6
Burshill YO25 59 G5
Bursledon SO31 11 F4
Burslem ST6 40 A1
Burstall IP8 35 F4
Burstock DT8 8 D4
Burston *Norf.* IP22 45 F7
Burston *Staffs.* ST18 40 B2
Burstow RH6 23 G7
Burstwick HU12 59 J7
Burtersett DL8 56 D1
Burthorpe IP29 34 B2
Burthwaite CA4 60 F2
Burtle TA7 19 H7
Burtle Hill TA7 19 G7
Burton *Ches.W. & C.* CH64 48 C5
Burton *Ches.W. & C.* CW6 48 E6
Burton *Dorset* BH23 10 C5
Burton *Lincs.* LN1 52 C5
Burton *Northumb.* NE69 77 K7
Burton *Pembs.* SA73 16 C5
Burton *Som.* TA5 7 K1
Burton *Wilts.* SN14 20 B4
Burton *Wilts.* BA12 9 H1
Burton Agnes YO25 59 H3
Burton Bradstock DT6 8 D6
Burton Coggles NG33 42 C3
Burton End CM24 33 J6
Burton Ferry SA73 16 C5
Burton Fleming YO25 59 G2
Burton Green *Warks.* CV8 30 D1
Burton Green *Wrex.* LL12 48 C7
Burton Hastings CV11 41 G7
Burton in Lonsdale LA6 56 B2
Burton Joyce NG14 41 J1
Burton Latimer NN15 32 C1
Burton Lazars LE14 42 A4
Burton Leonard HG3 57 J3
Burton on the Wolds LE12 41 H3
Burton Overy LE8 41 J6
Burton Pedwardine NG34 42 E1
Burton Pidsea HU12 59 J6
Burton Salmon LS25 57 K7
Burton Stather DN15 52 B1
Burton upon Stather DN15 52 B1
**Burton upon Trent** DE14 40 E3
Burton-in-Kendal LA6 55 J2
Burton's Green CM77 34 C6
Burtonwood WA5 48 E3
Burwardsley CH3 48 E7
Burwarton WV16 39 F7
Burwash TN19 13 K4
Burwash Common TN19 13 K4
Burwash Weald TN19 13 K4
Burwell *Cambs.* CB25 33 J2
Burwell *Lincs.* LN11 53 G5
Burwen LL68 46 C3
Burwick *Ork.* KW17 106 D9
Burwick *Shet.* ZE1 107 M8
Bury *Cambs.* PE26 43 F7
**Bury** *Gt.Man.* BL9 49 H1
Bury *Som.* TA22 7 H3
Bury *W.Suss.* RH20 12 D5
Bury End WR12 30 B5
Bury Green SG11 33 H6
**Bury St. Edmunds** IP33 34 C2
Buryas Bridge TR19 2 B6
Burythorpe YO17 58 D3
Busbridge GU7 22 C7
Busby *E.Renf.* G76 74 D5
Busby *P. & K.* PH1 82 B5
Buscot SN7 21 F2
Bush EX23 6 A5
Bush Bank HR4 28 D3
Bush Crathie AB35 89 K5
Bush Green IP21 45 G7
Bushbury WV10 40 B5
Bushby LE7 41 J5
**Bushey** WD23 22 E2
Bushey Heath WD23 22 E2
Bushley GL20 29 H5
Bushley Green GL20 29 H5
Bushton SN4 20 D4
Bushy Common NR19 44 D4
Busk CA10 61 H2
Buslingthorpe LN8 52 D4

Bus - Car


Bussage **GL6** 20 B1
Busta **ZE2** 107 M6
Butcher's Common **NR12** 45 H3
Butcher's Cross **TN20** 13 J4
Butcher's Pasture **CM6** 33 K6
Butcombe **BS40** 19 J5
**Bute PA20** 73 J4
Bute Town **NP22** 18 E1
Buthill **IV30** 97 J5
Butleigh **BA6** 8 E1
Butleigh Wootton **BA6** 8 E1
Butler's Cross **HP17** 22 B1
Butler's Hill **NG15** 41 H1
Butlers Marston **CV35** 30 E4
Butlersbank **SY4** 38 E3
Butley **IP12** 35 H3
Butley Abbey **IP12** 35 H4
Butley Low Corner **IP12** 35 H4
Butley Mills **IP12** 35 H3
Butley Town **SK10** 49 J5
Butt Green **CW5** 49 F7
Butt Lane **ST7** 49 H7
Butterburn **CA8** 70 B6
Buttercrambe **YO41** 58 D4
Butterknowle **DL13** 62 C4
Butterleigh **EX15** 7 H5
Butterley **DE5** 51 G7
Buttermere *Cumb.* **CA13** 60 C5
Buttermere *Wilts.* **SN8** 21 G5
Butters Green **ST7** 49 H7
Buttershaw **BD6** 57 G6
Butterstone **PH8** 82 B3
Butterton *Staffs.* **ST13** 50 C7
Butterton *Staffs.* **ST5** 40 A1
Butterwick *Dur.* **TS21** 62 E4
Butterwick *Lincs.* **PE22** 43 G1
Butterwick *N.Yorks.* **YO17** 59 F2
Butterwick *N.Yorks.* **YO17** 58 D2
Buttington **SY21** 38 B5
Buttonbridge **DY12** 29 G1
Buttonoak **DY12** 29 G1
Buttons' Green **IP30** 34 D3
Butts **EX6** 7 G7
Butt's Green *Essex* **CM2** 24 D1
Butt's Green *Hants.* **SO51** 10 D2
Buttsash **SO45** 11 F4
Buxhall **IP14** 34 E3
Buxted **TN22** 13 H4
**Buxton *Derbys.* SK17** 50 C5
Buxton *Norf.* **NR10** 45 G3
Buxton Heath **NR10** 45 F3
Buxworth **SK23** 50 C4
**Bwcle (Buckley) CH7** 48 B6
Bwlch **LD3** 28 A6
Bwlch-clawdd **SA44** 17 G2
Bwlch-derwin **LL51** 36 D1
Bwlchgwyn **LL11** 48 B7
Bwlch-llan **SA48** 26 E3
Bwlchnewydd **SA33** 17 G3
Bwlchtocyn **LL53** 36 C3
Bwlch-y-cibau **SY22** 38 A4
Bwlch-y-ddar **SY10** 38 A3
Bwlchyfadfa **SA44** 17 H1
Bwlch-y-ffridd **SY16** 37 K6
Bwlch-y-groes **SA35** 17 F2
Bwlchyllyn **LL54** 46 D7
Bwlchymynydd **SA4** 17 J6
Bwlch-y-sarnau **LD6** 27 K1
Byers Green **DL16** 62 D3
Byfield **NN11** 31 G3
Byfleet **KT14** 22 D5
Byford **HR4** 28 C4
Bygrave **SG7** 33 F5
Byker **NE6** 71 H7
Byland Abbey **YO61** 58 B2
Bylane End **PL14** 4 C5
Bylchau **LL16** 47 H6
Byley **CW10** 49 G6
Bynea **SA14** 17 J6
Byrness **NE19** 70 C3
Bystock **EX8** 7 J7
Bythorn **PE28** 32 D1
Byton **LD8** 28 C2
Bywell **NE43** 71 F7
Byworth **GU28** 12 C4

## C

Cabharstadh **HS2** 101 F5
Cabourne **LN7** 52 E2
Cabourne Parva **LN7** 52 E2
Cabrach *Arg. & B.* **PA60** 72 C4
Cabrach *Moray* **AB54** 90 B2
Cabus **PR3** 55 H5
Cackle Street *E.Suss.* **TN31** 14 D6
Cackle Street *E.Suss.* **TN22** 13 H4
Cacrabank **TD7** 69 J2
Cadboll **IV20** 97 F4
Cadbury **EX5** 7 H5
Cadbury Barton **EX18** 6 E4
Cadbury Heath **BS30** 19 K4
Cadder **G64** 74 E3
Cadderlie **PA35** 80 B4
Caddington **LU1** 32 D7
Caddleton **PA34** 79 J6
Caddonfoot **TD1** 76 C7
Cade Street **TN21** 13 K4
Cadeby *Leics.* **CV13** 41 G5
Cadeby *S.Yorks.* **DN5** 51 H2
Cadeleigh **EX16** 7 H5
Cader **LL16** 47 J6
Cadgwith **TR12** 2 E7
Cadham **KY7** 82 D7
Cadishead **M44** 49 G3
Cadle **SA5** 17 K6
Cadley *Lancs.* **PR2** 55 J6
Cadley *Wilts.* **SN8** 21 F5
Cadmore End **HP14** 22 A2
Cadnam **SO40** 10 D3
Cadney **DN20** 52 D2
Cadole **CH7** 48 B6
Cadover Bridge **PL7** 5 F4
Cadoxton **CF63** 18 E5
Cadoxton-Juxta-Neath **SA10** 18 A2
Cadwell **SG5** 32 E5
Cadwst **LL21** 37 K2
Cadzow **ML3** 75 F5
Cae Ddafydd **LL48** 37 F1
Caeathro **LL55** 46 D6
Caehopkin **SA9** 27 H7
Caen **KW8** 105 F7
Caenby **LN8** 52 D4
Caenby Corner **LN8** 52 C4
Caer Llan **NP25** 19 H1
Caerau *Bridgend* **CF34** 18 B2
Caerau *Cardiff* **CF5** 18 E4
Caerdeon **LL42** 37 F4
**CAERDYDD (CARDIFF) CF** 18 E4
Caerfarchell **SA62** 16 A3
**Caerfyrddin (Carmarthen) SA31** 17 H3
Caergeiliog **LL65** 46 B5
Caergwrle **LL12** 48 C7
**Caergybi (Holyhead) LL65** 46 A4
Caerhun **LL32** 47 F5
Caer-Lan **SA9** 27 H7
Caerleon **NP18** 19 G2
**Caernarfon LL55** 46 C6
**Caerphilly CF83** 18 E3
**Caersws SY17** 37 K6
Caerwedros **SA44** 26 C3
Caerwent **NP26** 19 H2
Caerwys **CH7** 47 K5
Caethle Farm **LL36** 37 F6
Caggan **PH22** 89 F3
Caggle Street **NP7** 28 C7
Caim *High.* **PH36** 79 G1
Caim *I.o.A.* **LL58** 46 E4
Caio **SA19** 17 K2
Cairinis (Carinish) **HS6** 92 D5
Cairisiadar **HS2** 100 C4
Cairminis **HS5** 93 F3
Cairnargat **AB54** 90 C1
Cairnbaan **PA31** 73 G1
Cairnbeathie **AB31** 90 D4
Cairnbrogie **AB51** 91 G2
Cairnbulg **AB43** 99 J4
Cairncross *Angus* **DD9** 90 D7
Cairncross *Sc.Bord.* **TD14** 77 G4
Cairncurran **PA13** 74 B4
Cairndoon **DG8** 64 D7
**Cairndow PA26** 80 C6
Cairness **AB43** 99 J4
Cairney Lodge **KY15** 82 E6
Cairneyhill **KY12** 75 J2
Cairnhill *Aber.* **AB41** 91 H2
Cairnhill *Aber.* **AB52** 90 E1
Cairnie *Aber.* **AB32** 91 G4
Cairnie *Aber.* **AB54** 98 C6
Cairnorrie **AB41** 99 G6
Cairnryan **DG9** 64 A4
Cairnsmore **DG8** 64 E4
Caister-on-Sea **NR30** 45 K4
Caistor **LN7** 52 E2
Caistor St. Edmund **NR14** 45 G5
Caistron **NE65** 70 E3
Cake Street **NR17** 44 E6
Cakebole **DY10** 29 H1
Calanais (Callanish) **HS2** 100 E4
Calbost **HS2** 101 G6
Calbourne **PO30** 11 F6
Calceby **LN13** 53 G5
Calcoed **CH8** 47 K5
Calcot **RG31** 21 K4
Calcott *Kent* **CT3** 25 H5
Calcott *Shrop.* **SY3** 38 D4
Calcotts Green **GL2** 29 G7
Calcutt **SN6** 20 E2
Caldarvan **G83** 74 C2
Caldback **ZE2** 107 Q2
Caldbeck **CA7** 60 E3
Caldbergh **DL8** 57 F1
Caldecote *Cambs.* **CB23** 33 G3
Caldecote *Cambs.* **PE7** 42 E7
Caldecote *Herts.* **SG7** 33 F5
Caldecote *Northants.* **NN12** 31 H3
Caldecote *Warks.* **CV10** 41 F6
Caldecott *Northants.* **NN9** 32 C2
Caldecott *Oxon.* **OX14** 21 H2
Caldecott *Rut.* **LE16** 42 B6
Calder Bridge **CA20** 60 B6
Calder Grove **WF4** 51 F1
Calder Mains **KW12** 105 F3
Calder Vale **PR3** 55 J5
Calderbank **ML6** 75 F4
Calderbrook **OL15** 49 J1
Caldercruix **ML6** 75 G4
Calderglen **G72** 74 E5
Caldermill **ML10** 74 E6
Caldey Island **SA70** 16 E6
Caldhame **DD8** 83 F3
**Caldicot NP26** 19 H3
Caldwell *Derbys.* **DE12** 40 E4
Caldwell *E.Renf.* **G78** 74 C5
Caldwell *N.Yorks.* **DL11** 62 C5
Caldy **CH48** 48 B4
Calebreck **CA7** 60 E3
Caledrhydiau **SA48** 26 D3
Calford Green **CB9** 33 K4
Calfsound **KW17** 106 E4
Calgary **PA75** 78 E2
Califer **IV36** 97 H6
California *Falk.* **FK1** 75 H3
California *Norf.* **NR29** 45 K4
California *Suff.* **IP4** 35 G4
Calke **DE73** 41 F3
Callakille **IV54** 94 C6
Callaly **NE66** 71 F3
**Callander FK17** 81 H7
Callanish (Calanais) **HS2** 100 E4
Callaughton **TF13** 39 F6
Callerton Lane End **NE5** 71 G7
Calliburn **PA28** 66 B1
Calligarry **IV45** 86 C4
**Callington PL17** 4 D4
Callingwood **DE13** 40 D3
Callisterhall **DG11** 69 H5
Callow **HR2** 28 D5
Callow End **WR2** 29 H4
Callow Hill *Wilts.* **SN15** 20 D3
Callow Hill *Worcs.* **DY14** 29 G1
Callow Hill *Worcs.* **B97** 30 B2
Callows Grave **WR15** 28 E2
Calmore **SO40** 10 E3
Calmsden **GL7** 20 D1
**Calne SN11** 20 C4
Calow **S44** 51 G5
Calrossie **IV19** 96 E4
Calshot **SO45** 11 F4
**Calstock PL18** 4 E4
Calstone Wellington **SN11** 20 D5
Calthorpe **NR11** 45 F2
Calthwaite **CA11** 61 F2
Calton *N.Yorks.* **BD23** 56 E4
Calton *Staffs.* **ST10** 50 D7
Calveley **CW6** 48 E7
Calver **S32** 50 E5
Calver Hill **HR4** 28 C4
Calverhall **SY13** 39 F2
Calverleigh **EX16** 7 H4
Calverley **LS28** 57 H6
Calvert **MK18** 31 H6
Calverton *M.K.* **MK19** 31 J5
Calverton *Notts.* **NG14** 41 J1
Calvine **PH18** 81 J1
Calvo **CA7** 60 C1
Cam **GL11** 20 A2
Camasnacroise **PH33** 79 K2
Camastianavaig **IV51** 86 B1
Camasunary **IV49** 86 B3
Camault Muir **IV4** 96 C7
Camb **ZE2** 107 P3
Camber **TN31** 14 E6
**Camberley GU15** 22 B5
Camberwell **SE15** 23 G4
Camblesforth **YO8** 58 C7
Cambo **NE61** 71 F5
Cambois **NE24** 71 J5
**Camborne TR14** 2 D5
**CAMBRIDGE *Cambs.* CB** 33 H3
Cambridge *Glos.* **GL2** 20 A1
Cambridge City Airport **CB5** 33 H3
Cambus **FK10** 75 G1
Cambus o'May **AB35** 90 C5
Cambusbarron **FK7** 75 F1
Cambuskenneth **FK9** 75 G1
Cambuslang **G72** 74 E4
Cambusnethan **ML2** 75 G5
Camden Town **NW1** 23 F3
Camel Hill **BA22** 8 E2
Cameley **BS39** 19 K6
**Camelford PL32** 4 B2
Camelon **FK1** 75 G2
Camelsdale **GU27** 12 B3
Camer **DA13** 24 C5
Cameron House **G83** 74 B2
Camerory **PH26** 89 H1
Camer's Green **WR13** 29 G5
Camerton *B. & N.E.Som.* **BA2** 19 K6
Camerton *Cumb.* **CA14** 60 B3
Camerton *E.Riding* **HU12** 59 J7
Camghouran **PH17** 81 G2
Camis Eskan **G84** 74 B2
Cammachmore **AB39** 91 H5
Cammeringham **LN1** 52 C4
Camore **IV25** 96 E2
Camp Hill *Pembs.* **SA67** 16 E4
Camp Hill *Warks.* **CV10** 41 F6
**Campbeltown PA28** 66 B1
Campbeltown Airport **PA28** 66 A1
Camperdown **NE12** 71 H6
Campmuir **PH13** 82 D4
Camps **EH27** 75 K4
Camps End **CB21** 33 K4
Camps Heath **NR32** 45 K6
Campsall **DN6** 51 H1
Campsea Ashe **IP13** 35 H3
Campton **SG17** 32 E5
Camptown **TD8** 70 B2
Camquhart **PA22** 73 H2
Camrose **SA62** 16 C3
Camserney **PH15** 81 K3
Camstraddan House **G83** 74 B1
Camus Croise **IV43** 86 C3
Camus-luinie **IV40** 87 F2
Camusnagaul *High.* **PH33** 87 G7
Camusnagaul *High.* **IV23** 95 G3
Camusrory **PH41** 86 E5
Camusteel **IV54** 94 D7
Camusterrach **IV54** 94 D7
Camusurich **FK21** 81 H4
Camusvrachan **PH15** 81 H3
Canada **SO51** 10 D3
Canaston Bridge **SA67** 16 D4
Candacraig **AB35** 90 B5
Candlesby **PE23** 53 H6
Candy Mill **ML12** 75 J6
Cane End **RG4** 21 K4
Canewdon **SS4** 24 E2
Canfield End **CM6** 33 J6
Canford Bottom **BH21** 10 B4
Canford Cliffs **BH13** 10 B6
Canford Magna **BH21** 10 B5
Canham's Green **IP14** 34 E2
Canisbay **KW1** 105 J1
Canley **CV4** 30 E1
Cann **SP7** 9 H2
Cann Common **SP7** 9 H2
**Canna PH44** 85 H4
Cannard's Grave **BA4** 19 K7
Cannich **IV4** 87 K1
Canning Town **E16** 23 H3
Cannington **TA5** 8 B1
**Cannock WS11** 40 B5
Cannock Wood **WS15** 40 C4
Cannop **GL16** 29 F7
Canon Bridge **HR2** 28 D4
Canon Frome **HR8** 29 F4
Canon Pyon **HR4** 28 D4
**Canonbie DG14** 69 J6
Canons Ashby **NN11** 31 G3
Canon's Town **TR27** 2 C5
Canterbury *Aber.* **AB45** 98 D5
**CANTERBURY *Kent* CT** 15 G2
Cantley *Norf.* **NR13** 45 H5
Cantley *S.Yorks.* **DN3** 51 J2
Cantlop **SY5** 38 E5
Canton **CF11** 18 E4
Cantray **IV2** 96 E7
Cantraydoune **IV12** 96 E7
Cantraywood **IV2** 96 E7
Cantsfield **LA6** 56 B2
**Canvey Island SS8** 24 D3
Canwell Hall **B75** 40 D5
Canwick **LN4** 52 C6
Canworthy Water **PL15** 4 C1
Caol **PH33** 87 H7
Caolas *Arg. & B.* **PA77** 78 B3
Caolas *W.Isles* **HS9** 84 B5
Caolas Scalpaigh (Kyles Scalpay) **HS3** 93 H2
Caolasnacon **PH50** 80 C1
Capel *Kent* **TN12** 23 K7
Capel *Surr.* **RH5** 22 E7
Capel Bangor **SY23** 37 F7
Capel Betws Lleucu **SY25** 27 F3
Capel Carmel **LL53** 36 A3
Capel Celyn **LL23** 37 H1
Capel Coch **LL77** 46 C4
Capel Curig **LL24** 47 F7
Capel Cynon **SA44** 17 G1
Capel Dewi *Carmar.* **SA32** 17 H3
Capel Dewi *Cere.* **SY23** 37 F7
Capel Dewi *Cere.* **SA44** 17 H1
Capel Garmon **LL26** 47 G7
Capel Gwyn *Carmar.* **SA32** 17 H3
Capel Gwyn *I.o.A.* **LL65** 46 B5
Capel Gwynfe **SA19** 27 G6
Capel Hendre **SA18** 17 J4
Capel Isaac **SA19** 17 J3
Capel Iwan **SA38** 17 F2
Capel le Ferne **CT18** 15 H4
Capel Llanilltern **CF5** 18 D3
Capel Mawr **LL62** 46 C5
Capel Parc **LL71** 46 C4
Capel St. Andrew **IP12** 35 H4
Capel St. Mary **IP9** 34 E5
Capel St. Silin **SA48** 26 E3
Capel Seion **SY23** 27 F1
Capel Tygwydd **SA38** 17 F1
Capeluchaf **LL54** 36 D1
Capelulo **LL34** 47 F5
Capel-y-ffin **NP7** 28 B5
Capel-y-graig **LL57** 46 D6
Capenhurst **CH1** 48 C5
Capernwray **LA6** 55 J2
Capheaton **NE19** 71 F5
Caplaw **G78** 74 C5
Capon's Green **IP13** 35 G2
Cappercleuch **TD7** 69 H1
Capplegill **DG10** 69 G3
Capstone **ME7** 24 D5
Capton *Devon* **TQ6** 5 J5
Capton *Som.* **TA4** 7 J2
Caputh **PH1** 82 B3
Car Colston **NG13** 42 A1
Caradon Town **PL14** 4 C3
Carbellow **KA18** 68 B1
Carbeth **G63** 74 D3
Carbis Bay **TR26** 2 C5
Carbost *High.* **IV51** 93 K7
Carbost *High.* **IV47** 85 J1
Carbrain **G67** 75 F3
Carbrooke **IP25** 44 D5
Carburton **S80** 51 J5
Carcary **DD9** 83 H2
Carco **DG4** 68 C2
Carcroft **DN6** 51 H1
Cardenden **KY5** 76 A1
Cardeston **SY5** 38 C4
Cardew **CA5** 60 E2
**CARDIFF (CAERDYDD) CF** 18 E4
Cardiff International Airport **CF62** 18 D5
**Cardigan (Aberteifi) SA43** 16 E1
Cardinal's Green **CB21** 33 K4
Cardington *Bed.* **MK44** 32 D4
Cardington *Shrop.* **SY6** 38 E6
Cardinham **PL30** 4 B4
Cardno **AB43** 99 H4
Cardonald **G52** 74 D4
Cardoness **DG7** 65 F5
Cardow **AB38** 97 J7
Cardrona **EH45** 76 A7
Cardross **G82** 74 B3
Cardurnock **CA7** 60 C1
Careby **PE9** 42 D4
Careston **DD9** 83 G2
Carew **SA70** 16 D5
Carew Cheriton **SA70** 16 D5
Carew Newton **SA68** 16 D5
Carey **HR2** 28 E5
Carfin **ML1** 75 F5
Carfrae **EH41** 76 D4
Carfraemill **TD2** 76 D5
Cargate Green **NR13** 45 H4
Cargen **DG2** 65 K3
Cargenbridge **DG2** 65 K3
Cargill **PH2** 82 C4
Cargo **CA6** 60 E1
Cargreen **PL12** 4 E4
Carham **TD12** 77 F7
Carhampton **TA24** 7 J1
Carharrack **TR16** 2 E4
Carie *P. & K.* **PH17** 81 H2
Carie *P. & K.* **PH15** 81 H4
Carines **TR8** 2 E3
Carinish (Cairinis) **HS6** 92 D5
Carisbrooke **PO30** 11 F6
Cark **LA11** 55 G2
Carkeel **PL12** 4 E4
Carlabhagh (Carloway) **HS2** 100 E3
Carland Cross **TR8** 3 F3
Carlatton **CA8** 61 G1
Carlby **PE9** 42 D4
Carlecotes **S36** 50 D2
Carleen **TR13** 2 D6
Carleton *Cumb.* **CA1** 60 F1
Carleton *Cumb.* **CA11** 61 G4
Carleton *Lancs.* **FY6** 55 G5
Carleton *N.Yorks.* **BD23** 56 E5
Carleton *W.Yorks.* **WF8** 57 K7
Carleton Fishery **KA26** 67 F5
Carleton Forehoe **NR9** 44 E5
Carleton Rode **NR16** 45 F6
Carleton St. Peter **NR14** 45 H5
Carlin How **TS13** 63 J5
**CARLISLE CA** 60 F1
Carloggas **TR8** 3 F2
Carlops **EH26** 75 K5
Carloway (Carlabhagh) **HS2** 100 E3
Carlton *Bed.* **MK43** 32 C3
Carlton *Cambs.* **CB8** 33 K3
Carlton *Leics.* **CV13** 41 F5
Carlton *N.Yorks.* **DN14** 58 C7
Carlton *N.Yorks.* **DL8** 57 F1
Carlton *N.Yorks.* **YO62** 58 C1
Carlton *Notts.* **NG4** 41 J1
Carlton *S.Yorks.* **S71** 51 F1
Carlton *Stock.* **TS21** 62 E4
Carlton *Suff.* **IP17** 35 H2
Carlton *W.Yorks.* **WF3** 57 J7
Carlton Colville **NR33** 45 K6
Carlton Curlieu **LE8** 41 J6
Carlton Green **CB8** 33 K3
Carlton Husthwaite **YO7** 57 K2
Carlton in Lindrick **S81** 51 H4
Carlton Miniott **YO7** 57 J1
Carlton Scroop **NG32** 42 C1
Carlton-in-Cleveland **TS9** 63 G6
Carlton-le-Moorland **LN5** 52 C7
Carlton-on-Trent **NG23** 52 B6
**Carluke ML8** 75 G5
Carlyon Bay **PL25** 4 A5
Carmacoup **ML11** 68 C1
**Carmarthen (Caerfyrddin) SA31** 17 H3
Carmel *Carmar.* **SA14** 17 J4
Carmel *Flints.* **CH8** 47 K5
Carmel *Gwyn.* **LL54** 46 C7
Carmel *I.o.A.* **LL71** 46 B4
Carmichael **ML12** 75 H7
Carmont **AB39** 91 G6
Carmunnock **G76** 74 D5
Carmyle **G32** 74 E4
Carmyllie **DD11** 83 G3
Carn **PA48** 72 A5
Carn Brea Village **TR15** 2 D4
Carn Dearg **IV21** 94 D4
Carnaby **YO16** 59 H3
Carnach *High.* **IV40** 87 G2
Carnach *High.* **IV23** 95 G2
Carnach *W.Isles* **HS6** 92 D5
Carnan **HS8** 92 C7
Carnassarie **PA31** 79 K7
Carnbee **KY10** 83 G7
Carnbo **KY13** 82 B7
Carndu **IV40** 86 E2
Carnduncan **PA44** 72 A4
**Carnforth LA5** 55 H2
Carnhedryn **SA62** 16 B3
Carnhell Green **TR14** 2 D5
Carnichal **AB42** 99 H5
Carnkie *Cornw.* **TR16** 2 D5
Carnkie *Cornw.* **TR13** 2 E5
Carnmore **PA42** 72 B6
Carno **SY17** 37 J6
Carnoch *High.* **IV4** 87 K1
Carnoch *High.* **IV6** 95 J6
Carnoch *High.* **IV12** 97 F7
Carnock **KY12** 75 J2
Carnon Downs **TR3** 3 F4
Carnousie **AB53** 98 E5
**Carnoustie DD7** 83 G4
Carntyne **G32** 74 E4
Carnwath **ML11** 75 H6
Carnyorth **TR19** 2 A5
Carol Green **CV7** 30 D1
Carperby **DL8** 57 F1
Carr **S66** 51 H3
Carr Hill **DN10** 51 J3
Carr Houses **L38** 48 C2
Carr Shield **NE47** 61 K2
Carr Vale **S44** 51 G5
Carradale **PA28** 73 F7
Carradale East **PA28** 73 G7
Carragrich **HS3** 93 G2
**Carrbridge PH23** 89 G2
Carrefour Selous **JE3** 3 J7
Carreg-lefn **LL68** 46 B4
Carreg-wen **SA37** 17 F1
Carrhouse **DN9** 51 K2
Carrick **PA31** 73 H2
Carrick Castle **PA24** 73 K1

Car - Che


Carriden EH51 75 J2
Carrine PA28 66 A3
Carrington Gt.Man. M31 49 G3
Carrington Lincs. PE22 53 G7
Carrington Midloth. EH23 76 B4
Carroch DG7 68 B4
Carrog Conwy LL24 37 G1
Carrog Denb. LL21 38 A1
Carroglen PH6 81 J5
Carrol KW9 97 F1
Carron Arg. & B. PA31 73 H1
Carron Falk. FK2 75 G2
Carron Moray AB38 97 K7
Carron Bridge FK6 75 F2
Carronbridge DG3 68 D4
Carronshore FK2 75 G2
Carrot DD8 83 F3
Carrow Hill NP26 19 H2
Carrutherstown DG1 69 G6
Carruthmuir PA10 74 B4
Carrville DH1 62 E2
Carry PA21 73 H4
Carsaig PA70 79 G5
Carscreugh DG8 64 C4
Carse PA29 73 F4
Carse of Ardersier IV2 97 F6
Carsegowan DG8 64 E5
Carseriggan DG8 64 D4
Carsethorn DG2 65 K5
Carsgoe KW12 105 G2
**Carshalton SM5 23 F5**
Carshalton Beeches SM5 23 F5
Carsie PH10 82 C3
Carsington DE4 50 E7
Carsluith DG8 64 E5
Carsphairn DG7 67 K4
Carstairs ML11 75 H6
Carstairs Junction ML11 75 H6
Carswell Marsh SN7 21 G2
Carter's Clay SO51 10 E2
**Carterton OX18 21 F1**
Carterway Heads DH8 62 B1
Carthew PL26 4 A5
Carthorpe DL8 57 J1
Cartington NE65 71 F3
Cartland ML11 75 G6
Cartmel LA11 55 G2
Cartmel Fell LA11 55 H1
Cartworth HD9 50 D2
Carway SA17 17 H5
Cascob LD8 28 B2
**Cas-gwent (Chepstow) NP16 19 J2**
Cashel Farm G63 74 C1
Cashes Green GL5 20 B1
Cashlie PH15 81 F3
Cashmoor DT11 9 J3
Caskieberran KY6 82 D7
**CASNEWYDD (NEWPORT) NP 19 G3**
Cassencarie DG8 64 E5
Cassington OX29 31 F7
Cassop DH6 62 E3
Castell LL32 47 F6
Castell Gorfod SA33 17 F3
Castell Howell SA44 17 H1
**Castell Newydd Emlyn (Newcastle Emlyn) SA38 17 G1**
Castellau CF38 18 D3
**Castell-nedd (Neath) SA11 18 A2**
Castell-y-bwch NP44 19 F2
Casterton LA6 56 B2
Castle Acre PE32 44 C4
Castle Ashby NN7 32 B3
Castle Bolton DL8 62 B7
Castle Bromwich B36 40 D7
Castle Bytham NG33 42 C4
Castle Caereinion SY21 38 A5
Castle Camps CB21 33 K4
Castle Carrock CA8 61 G1
**Castle Cary BA7 9 F1**
Castle Combe SN14 20 B4
Castle Donington DE74 41 G3
**Castle Douglas DG7 65 H4**
Castle Eaton SN6 20 E2
Castle Eden TS27 63 F3
Castle End CV8 30 D1
Castle Frome HR8 29 F4
Castle Gate TR20 2 B5
Castle Goring BN13 12 E6
Castle Green GU24 22 C5
Castle Gresley DE11 40 E4
Castle Heaton TD12 77 H6
Castle Hedingham CO9 34 B5
Castle Hill Kent TN12 23 K7
Castle Hill Suff. IP1 35 F4
Castle Kennedy DG9 64 B5
Castle Leod IV14 96 B6
Castle Levan PA19 74 A3
Castle Madoc LD3 27 K5
Castle Morris SA62 16 C2
Castle O'er DG13 69 H4
Castle Rising PE31 44 A3
Castle Stuart IV2 96 E7
Castlebay (Bàgh a'Chaisteil) HS9 84 B5
Castlebythe SA62 16 D3
Castlecary G68 75 F3
Castlecraig High. IV19 97 F5
Castlecraig Sc.Bord. EH46 75 K6
Castlefairn DG3 68 C5
**Castleford WF10 57 K7**
Castlemartin SA71 16 C6
Castlemilk D. & G. DG11 69 G6
Castlemilk Glas. G45 74 E5
Castlemorton WR13 29 G5
Castlerigg CA12 60 D4
Castleside DH8 62 B2
Castlesteads CA8 70 A7
Castlethorpe MK19 31 J4
Castleton Aber. AB45 99 F5
Castleton Angus DD8 82 E3
Castleton Arg. & B. PA31 73 G2
Castleton Derbys. S33 50 D4
Castleton Gt.Man. OL11 49 H1
Castleton N.Yorks. YO21 63 H6
Castleton Newport CF3 19 F3
Castleton Sc.Bord. TD9 70 A4
Castletown Dorset DT5 9 F7
Castletown High. KW14 105 G2
Castletown High. IV2 96 E7
Castletown I.o.M. IM9 54 B7
Castletown T. & W. SR5 62 E1
Castleweary TD9 69 K3
Castlewigg DG8 64 E6
Castley LS21 57 H5
Caston NR17 44 D6
Castor PE5 42 E6
Castramont DG7 65 F4
Caswell SA3 17 J7
Cat & Fiddle Inn SK11 50 C5
Catacol KA27 73 H6
Catbrain BS10 19 J3
Catbrook NP16 19 J1
Catchall TR19 2 B6
Catcleugh NE19 70 C3
Catcliffe S60 51 G4
Catcott TA7 8 C1
**Caterham CR3 23 G6**
Catfield NR29 45 H3
Catfirth ZE2 107 N7
Catford SE6 23 G4
Catforth PR4 55 H6
Cathays CF24 18 E4
Cathcart G44 74 D4
Cathedine LD3 28 A6
Catherine-de-Barnes B91 40 D7
Catherington PO8 11 H3
Catherston Leweston DT6 8 C5
Catherton DY14 29 F1
Cathkin G73 74 E5
Catisfield PO15 11 G4
Catlodge PH20 88 D5
Catlowdy CA6 69 K6
Catmere End CB11 33 H5
Catmore RG20 21 H3
Caton Devon TQ13 5 H3
Caton Lancs. LA2 55 J3
Caton Green LA2 55 J3
Cator Court TQ13 5 G3
Catrine KA5 67 K1
Catsfield TN33 14 C6
Catsfield Stream TN33 14 C6
Catshaw S36 50 E2
Catshill B61 29 J1
Cattadale PA44 72 B4
Cattal YO26 57 K4
Cattawade CO11 34 E5
Catterall PR3 55 J5
Catterick DL10 62 D7
Catterick Bridge DL10 62 D7
**Catterick Garrison DL9 62 C7**
Catterlen CA11 61 F3
Catterline AB39 91 G7
Catterton LS24 58 B5
Catteshall GU7 22 C7
Catthorpe LE17 31 G1
Cattishall IP31 34 C2
Cattistock DT2 8 E4
Catton N.Yorks. YO7 57 J2
Catton Norf. NR6 45 G4
Catton Northumb. NE47 61 K1
Catton Hall DE12 40 E4
Catwick HU17 59 H5
Catworth PE28 32 D1
Caudle Green GL53 29 J7
Caulcott Cen.Beds. MK43 32 D4
Caulcott Oxon. OX25 31 G6
Cauldcots DD11 83 H3
Cauldhame Stir. FK8 74 E1
Cauldhame Stir. FK15 81 K7
Cauldon ST10 40 C1
Caulkerbush DG2 65 K5
Caulside DG14 69 K5
Caundle Marsh DT9 9 F3
Caunsall DY11 40 A7
Caunton NG23 51 K6
Causeway End D. & G. DG8 64 E4
Causeway End Essex CM6 33 K7
Causeway End Lancs. L40 48 D1
Causewayhead Cumb. CA7 60 C1
Causewayhead Stir. FK9 75 G1
Causey DH9 62 D1
Causey Park NE61 71 G4
Causeyend AB23 91 H3
Cautley LA10 61 H7
Cavendish CO10 34 C4
Cavendish Bridge DE72 41 G3
Cavenham IP28 34 B2
Cavens DG2 65 K5
Cavers TD9 70 A2
Caversfield OX27 31 G6
Caversham RG4 22 A4
Caverswall ST11 40 B1
Cawdor IV12 97 F6
Cawkeld YO25 59 F4
Cawkwell LN11 53 F4
Cawood YO8 58 B6
Cawsand PL10 4 E6
Cawston Norf. NR10 45 F3
Cawston Warks. CV22 31 F1
Cawthorn YO18 58 D1
Cawthorne S75 50 E2
Cawthorpe PE10 42 D3
Cawton YO62 58 C2
Caxton CB23 33 G3
Caxton Gibbet CB23 33 F2
Caynham SY8 28 E1
Caythorpe Lincs. NG32 42 C1
Caythorpe Notts. NG14 41 J1
Cayton YO11 59 G1
Ceallan HS6 92 D6
Ceann a' Bhàigh W.Isles HS6 92 C5
Ceann a' Bhàigh W.Isles HS3 93 F3
Ceann Loch Shiphoirt HS2 100 E6
Ceann Lochroag (Kinlochroag) HS2 100 D5
Ceannaridh HS6 92 D6
Cearsiadar HS2 101 F6
Ceathramh Meadhanach (Middlequarter) HS6 92 D4
Cedig SY10 37 J3
Cefn Berain LL16 47 H6
Cefn Bychan (Newbridge) NP11 19 F2
Cefn Canol SY10 38 B2
Cefn Cantref LD3 27 K6
Cefn Coch LL15 47 K7
Cefn Cribwr CF32 18 B3
Cefn Cross CF32 18 B3
Cefn Einion SY9 38 B7
Cefn Hengoed CF82 18 E2
Cefn Llwyd SY23 37 F7
Cefn Rhigos CF44 18 C1
Cefn-brith LL21 47 H7
Cefn-caer-Ferch LL53 36 D1
Cefn-coch SY10 38 A3
Cefn-coed-y-cymmer CF48 18 D1
Cefn-ddwysarn LL23 37 J2
Cefndeuddwr LL40 37 G3
Cefneithin SA14 17 J4
Cefn-gorwydd LD4 27 J4
Cefn-gwyn SY16 38 A7
Cefn-mawr LL14 38 B1
Cefnpennar CF45 18 D1
Cefn-y-bedd LL12 48 C7
Cefn-y-pant SA34 16 E3
Cegidfa (Guilsfield) SY21 38 B4
Ceidio LL71 46 C4
Ceidio Fawr LL53 36 B2
**Ceinewydd (New Quay) SA45 26 C2**
Ceint LL77 46 C5
Cellan SA48 17 K1
Cellardyke KY10 83 G7
Cellarhead ST9 40 B1
**Cemaes LL67 46 B3**
Cemmaes SY20 37 H5
Cemmaes Road (Glantwymyn) SY20 37 H5
Cenarth SA38 17 F1
Cennin LL51 36 D1
Ceos (Keose) HS2 101 F5
Ceres KY15 83 F6
Ceri (Kerry) SY16 38 A6
Cerist SY17 37 J7
Cerne Abbas DT2 9 F4
Cerney Wick GL7 20 D2
Cerrigceinwen LL62 46 C5
Cerrigydrudion LL21 37 J1
Cessford TD5 70 C1
Ceunant LL55 46 D6
Chaceley GL19 29 H5
Chacewater TR4 2 E4
Chackmore MK18 31 H5
Chacombe OX17 31 F4
Chad Valley B15 40 C7
Chadderton OL9 49 J2
Chadderton Fold OL9 49 H2
Chaddesden DE21 41 F2
Chaddesley Corbett DY10 29 H1
Chaddleworth RG20 21 H4
Chadlington OX7 30 E6
Chadshunt CV35 30 E3
Chadstone NN7 32 B3
Chadwell Leics. LE14 42 A3
Chadwell Shrop. TF10 39 G4
Chadwell St. Mary RM16 24 C4
Chadwick End B93 30 D1
Chaffcombe TA20 8 C3
Chafford Hundred RM16 24 C4
Chagford TQ13 7 F7
Chailey BN8 13 G5
Chainhurst TN12 14 C3
Chalbury BH21 10 B4
Chalbury Common BH21 10 B4
Chaldon CR3 23 G6
Chaldon Herring (East Chaldon) DT2 9 G6
Chale PO38 11 F7
Chale Green PO38 11 F6
Chalfont Common SL9 22 D2
**Chalfont St. Giles HP8 22 C2**
Chalfont St. Peter SL9 22 D2
Chalford Glos. GL6 20 B1
Chalford Wilts. BA13 20 B7
Chalgrove OX44 21 K2
Chalk DA12 24 C4
Chalk End CM1 33 K7
Challacombe EX31 6 E1
Challister ZE2 107 P6
Challoch DG8 64 D4
Challock TN25 15 F2
Chalmington DT2 8 E4
Chalton Cen.Beds. LU4 32 D6
Chalton Hants. PO8 11 J3
Chalvey SL1 22 C4
Chalvington BN27 13 J6
Champany EH49 75 J3
Chancery SY23 26 E1
Chandler's Cross WD3 22 D2
Chandler's Ford SO53 11 F2
Channel Islands GYJE 3 G7
Channel's End MK44 32 E3
Channerwick ZE2 107 N10
Chantry Som. BA11 20 A7
Chantry Suff. IP2 35 F4
Chapel KY2 76 A1
Chapel Allerton Som. BS26 19 H6
Chapel Allerton W.Yorks. LS7 57 J6
Chapel Amble PL27 3 G1
Chapel Brampton NN6 31 J2
Chapel Chorlton ST5 40 A2
Chapel Cleeve TA24 7 J1
Chapel Cross TN21 13 K4
Chapel End MK45 32 D4
Chapel Green Warks. CV7 40 E7
Chapel Green Warks. CV47 31 F2
Chapel Haddlesey YO8 58 B7
Chapel Hill Aber. AB42 91 J1
Chapel Hill Lincs. LN4 53 F7
Chapel Hill Mon. NP16 19 J1
Chapel Hill N.Yorks. LS22 57 J5
Chapel Knapp SN13 20 B5
Chapel Lawn SY7 28 C1
Chapel Leigh TA4 7 K3
Chapel Milton SK23 50 C4
Chapel of Garioch AB51 91 F2
Chapel Rossan DG9 64 B6
Chapel Row Essex CM3 24 D1
Chapel Row W.Berks. RG7 21 J5
Chapel St. Leonards PE24 53 J5
Chapel Stile LA22 60 E6
Chapel Town TR8 3 F3
Chapelbank PH3 82 B6
Chapeldonan KA26 67 F3
Chapelend Way CO9 34 B5
Chapel-en-le-Frith SK23 50 C4
Chapelgate PE12 43 H3
Chapelhall ML6 75 F4
Chapelhill High. IV20 97 F4
Chapelhill P. & K. PH2 82 D5
Chapelhill P. & K. PH1 82 B4
Chapelknowe DG14 69 J6
Chapel-le-Dale LA6 56 C2
Chapelthorpe WF2 51 F1
Chapelton Aber. AB39 91 G6
Chapelton Angus DD11 83 H3
Chapelton Devon EX37 6 D3
Chapelton S.Lan. ML10 74 E6
Chapeltown B'burn. BL7 49 G1
Chapeltown Cumb. CA6 69 K6
Chapeltown Moray AB37 89 K2
Chapeltown S.Yorks. S35 51 F3
Chapmans Well PL15 6 B6
Chapmanslade BA13 20 B7
Chapmore End SG12 33 G7
Chappel CO6 34 C6
Chard TA20 8 C4
Chard Junction TA20 8 C4
Chardleigh Green TA20 8 C3
Chardstock EX13 8 C4
Charfield GL12 20 A2
Charing TN27 14 E3
Charing Cross SP6 10 C3
Charing Heath TN27 14 E3
Charingworth GL55 30 C5
Charlbury OX7 30 E7
Charlcombe BA1 20 A5
Charlecote CV35 30 D3
Charles EX32 6 E2
Charles Tye IP14 34 E3
Charlesfield TD6 70 A1
Charleshill GU10 22 B7
Charleston DD8 82 E3
Charlestown Aber. AB43 99 J4
Charlestown Aberdeen AB12 91 H4
Charlestown Cornw. PL25 4 A5
Charlestown Derbys. SK13 50 C3
Charlestown Dorset DT3 9 F7
Charlestown Fife KY11 75 J2
Charlestown Gt.Man. M7 49 H2
Charlestown High. IV21 94 E4
Charlestown High. IV1 96 D7
Charlestown W.Yorks. BD17 57 G6
Charlestown W.Yorks. HX7 56 E7
**Charlestown of Aberlour (Aberlour) AB38 97 K7**
Charlesworth SK13 50 C3
Charleton KY9 83 F7
Charlinch TA5 8 B1
Charlotteville GU1 22 D7
Charlton Gt.Lon. SE7 23 H4
Charlton Hants. SP10 21 G7
Charlton Herts. SG5 32 E6
Charlton Northants. OX17 31 G5
Charlton Northumb. NE48 70 D5
Charlton Oxon. OX12 21 H3
Charlton Som. BA3 19 K6
Charlton Som. BA4 19 K7
Charlton Som. TA3 8 B2
Charlton Tel. & W. TF6 38 E4
Charlton W.Suss. PO18 12 B5
Charlton Wilts. SP7 9 J2
Charlton Wilts. SN16 20 C3
Charlton Wilts. SN9 20 E6
Charlton Worcs. WR10 30 B4
Charlton Abbots GL54 30 B6
Charlton Adam TA11 8 E2
Charlton Down DT2 9 F5
Charlton Horethorne DT9 9 F2
Charlton Kings GL52 29 J6
Charlton Mackrell TA11 8 E2
Charlton Marshall DT11 9 H4
Charlton Musgrove BA9 9 G2
Charlton on the Hill DT11 9 H4
Charlton-All-Saints SP5 10 C2
Charlton-on-Otmoor OX5 31 G7
Charltons TS12 63 H5
Charlwood RH6 23 F7
Charminster DT2 9 F5
Charmouth DT6 8 C5
Charndon OX27 31 H6
Charney Bassett OX12 21 G2
Charnock Richard PR7 48 E1
Charsfield IP13 35 G3
Chart Corner ME17 14 C3
Chart Sutton ME17 14 D3
Charter Alley RG26 21 J6
Charterhouse BS40 19 H6
Charterville Allotments OX29 21 G1
Chartham CT4 15 G2
Chartham Hatch CT4 15 G2
Chartridge HP5 22 C1
Charvil RG10 22 A4
Charwelton NN11 31 G3
Chase End Street HR8 29 G5
Chase Terrace WS7 40 C5
Chasetown WS7 40 C5
Chastleton GL56 30 D6
Chasty EX22 6 B5
Chatburn BB7 56 C5
Chatcull ST21 39 G2
**Chatham ME4 24 D5**
Chatham Green CM3 34 B7
**Chathill NE67 71 G1**
Chattenden ME3 24 D4
**Chatteris PE16 43 G7**
Chattisham IP8 34 E4
Chatto TD5 70 C2
Chatton NE66 71 F1
Chaul End LU1 32 D6
Chavey Down SL5 22 B5
Chawleigh EX18 7 F4
Chawley OX2 21 H1
Chawston MK44 32 E3
Chawton GU34 11 J1
Chazey Heath RG4 21 K4
**Cheadle Gt.Man. SK8 49 H4**
Cheadle Staffs. ST10 40 C1
Cheadle Heath SK3 49 H4
Cheadle Hulme SK8 49 H4
Cheam SM3 23 F5
Cheapside SL5 22 C5
Chearsley HP18 31 J7
Chebsey ST21 40 A3
Checkendon RG8 21 K3
Checkley Ches.E. CW5 39 G1
Checkley Here. HR1 28 E5
Checkley Staffs. ST10 40 C2
Checkley Green CW5 39 G1
Chedburgh IP29 34 B3
**Cheddar BS27 19 H6**
Cheddington LU7 32 C7
Cheddleton ST13 49 J7
Cheddon Fitzpaine TA2 8 B2
Chedglow SN16 20 C2
Chedgrave NR14 45 H6
Chedington DT8 8 D4
Chediston IP19 35 H1
Chediston Green IP19 35 H1
Chedworth GL54 30 B7
Chedzoy TA7 8 C1
Cheesden OL12 49 H1
Cheeseman's Green TN24 15 F4
Cheetham Hill M8 49 H2
Cheglinch EX34 6 D1
Cheldon EX18 7 F4
Chelford SK11 49 H5
Chellaston DE73 41 F2
Chells SG2 33 F6
Chelmarsh WV16 39 G7
Chelmondiston IP9 35 G5
Chelmorton SK17 50 D6
**CHELMSFORD CM 24 D1**
Chelmsley Wood B37 40 D7
Chelsea SW3 23 F4
Chelsfield BR6 23 H5
Chelsham CR6 23 G6
Chelston Heath TA21 7 K3
Chelsworth IP7 34 D4
**Cheltenham GL50 29 J6**
Chelveston NN9 32 C2
Chelvey BS48 19 H5
Chelwood BS39 19 K5
Chelwood Common RH17 13 H4
Chelwood Gate RH17 13 H4
Chelworth SN16 20 C2
Cheney Longville SY7 38 D7
Chenies WD3 22 D2
**Chepstow (Cas-gwent) NP16 19 J2**
Cherhill SN11 20 D4
Cherington Glos. GL8 20 C2
Cherington Warks. CV36 30 D5
Cheriton Devon EX35 7 F1
Cheriton Hants. SO24 11 G2
Cheriton Kent CT19 15 G4
Cheriton Pembs. SA71 16 C6
Cheriton Swan. SA3 17 H6
Cheriton Bishop EX6 7 F6
Cheriton Cross EX6 7 F6
Cheriton Fitzpaine EX17 7 G5
Cherrington TF6 39 F3
Cherry Burton HU17 59 F5
Cherry Green CM6 33 J6
Cherry Hinton CB1 33 H3
Cherry Willingham LN3 52 D5
**Chertsey KT16 22 D5**
Cheselbourne DT2 9 G5
**Chesham HP5 22 C1**
Chesham Bois HP6 22 C1
Cheshunt EN8 23 G1
Cheslyn Hay WS6 40 B5
**Chessington KT9 22 E5**
Chestall WS15 40 C4

Che - Clo

CHESTER CH 48 D6
Chester Moor DH2 62 D2
Chesterblade BA4 19 K7
Chesterfield Derbys. S40 51 F5
Chesterfield Staffs. WS14 40 D5
Chester-le-Street DH3 62 D1
Chesters Sc.Bord. TD9 70 B2
Chesters Sc.Bord. TD8 70 B1
Chesterton Cambs. CB4 33 H2
Chesterton Cambs. PE7 42 E6
Chesterton Oxon. OX26 31 G6
Chesterton Shrop. WV15 39 G6
Chesterton Staffs. ST5 40 A1
Chesterton Warks. CV33 30 E3
Chesterton Green CV33 30 E3
Chestfield CT5 25 H5
Cheston TQ10 5 G5
Cheswardine TF9 39 G3
Cheswick TD15 77 J6
Cheswick Buildings TD15 77 J6
Cheswick Green B90 30 C1
Chetnole DT9 9 F4
Chettiscombe EX16 7 H4
Chettisham CB6 43 J7
Chettle DT11 9 J3
Chetton WV16 39 F6
Chetwode MK18 31 H6
Chetwynd Aston TF10 39 G4
Chetwynd Park TF10 39 G3
Cheveley CB8 33 K2
Chevening TN14 23 H6
Cheverell's Green AL3 32 D7
Chevington IP29 34 B3
Chevington Drift NE61 71 H4
Chevithorne EX16 7 H4
Chew Magna BS40 19 J5
Chew Moor BL6 49 F2
Chew Stoke BS40 19 J5
Chewton Keynsham BS31 19 K5
Chewton Mendip BA3 19 J6
Chichacott EX20 6 E6
Chicheley MK16 32 C4
Chichester PO19 12 B6
Chickerell DT3 9 F6
Chickering IP21 35 G1
Chicklade SP3 9 J1
Chickney CM6 33 J6
Chicksands SG17 32 E5
Chidden PO7 11 H3
Chidden Holt PO7 11 H3
Chiddingfold GU8 12 C3
Chiddingly BN8 13 J5
Chiddingstone TN8 23 H7
Chiddingstone Causeway TN11 23 J7
Chiddingstone Hoath TN8 23 H7
Chideock DT6 8 D5
Chidham PO18 11 J4
Chidswell WF12 57 H7
Chieveley RG20 21 H4
Chignall St. James CM1 24 C1
Chignall Smealy CM1 33 K7
Chigwell IG7 23 H2
Chigwell Row IG7 23 H2
Chilbolton SO20 21 G7
Chilcomb SO21 11 G2
Chilcombe DT6 8 E5
Chilcompton BA3 19 K6
Chilcote DE12 40 E4
Child Okeford DT11 9 H3
Childer Thornton CH66 48 C5
Childerditch CM13 24 C3
Childrey OX12 21 G3
Child's Ercall TF9 39 F3
Childs Hill NW3 23 F3
Childswickham WR12 30 B5
Childwall L16 48 D4
Childwick Green AL3 32 E7
Chilfrome DT2 8 E5
Chilgrove PO18 12 B5
Chilham CT4 15 F2
Chilhampton SP2 10 B1
Chilla EX21 6 C5
Chillaton PL16 6 C7
Chillenden CT3 15 H2
Chillerton PO30 11 F6
Chillesford IP12 35 H3
Chilley TQ9 5 H5
Chillingham NE66 71 F1
Chillington Devon TQ7 5 H6
Chillington Som. TA19 8 C3
Chilmark SP3 9 J1
Chilson Oxon. OX7 30 E7
Chilson Som. TA20 8 C4
Chilsworthy Cornw. PL18 4 E3
Chilsworthy Devon EX22 6 B5
Chilthorne Domer BA22 8 E3
Chilton Bucks. HP18 31 H7
Chilton Devon EX17 7 G5
Chilton Dur. DL17 62 D4
Chilton Oxon. OX11 21 H3
Chilton Suff. CO10 34 C4
Chilton Candover SO24 11 G1
Chilton Cantelo BA22 8 E2
Chilton Foliat RG17 21 G4
Chilton Polden TA7 8 C1
Chilton Street CO10 34 B4
Chilton Trinity TA5 8 B1
Chilvers Coton CV10 41 F6
Chilwell NG9 41 H2
Chilworth Hants. SO16 11 F3
Chilworth Surr. GU4 22 D7
Chimney OX18 21 G1
Chimney Street CO10 34 B4
Chineham RG24 21 K6
Chingford E4 23 G2
Chinley SK23 50 C4
Chinley Head SK23 50 C4
Chinnor OX39 22 A1
Chipchase Castle NE48 70 D6
Chipley TA21 7 K3
Chipnall TF9 39 G2
Chippenham Cambs. CB7 33 K2
Chippenham Wilts. SN15 20 C4
Chipperfield WD4 22 D1
Chipping Herts. SG9 33 G5
Chipping Lancs. PR3 56 B5
Chipping Campden GL55 30 C5
Chipping Hill CM8 34 C7
Chipping Norton OX7 30 E6
Chipping Ongar CM5 23 J1
Chipping Sodbury BS37 20 A3
Chipping Warden OX17 31 F4
Chipstable TA4 7 J3
Chipstead Kent TN13 23 H6
Chipstead Surr. CR5 23 F6
Chirbury SY15 38 B6
Chirk (Y Waun) LL14 38 B2
Chirk Green LL14 38 B2
Chirmorrie KA26 64 C3
Chirnside TD11 77 G5
Chirnsidebridge TD11 77 G5
Chirton T. & W. NE29 71 J7
Chirton Wilts. SN10 20 D6
Chisbury SN8 21 F5
Chiscan PA28 66 A2
Chiselborough TA14 8 D3
Chiseldon SN4 20 E4
Chiserley HX7 57 F7
Chislehampton OX44 21 J2
Chislehurst BR7 23 H4
Chislet CT3 25 J5
Chiswell Green AL2 22 E1
Chiswick W4 23 F4
Chiswick End SG8 33 G4
Chisworth SK13 49 J3
Chithurst GU31 12 B4
Chittering CB25 33 H1
Chitterne BA12 20 C7
Chittlehamholt EX37 6 E3
Chittlehampton EX37 6 E3
Chittoe SN15 20 C5
Chivelstone TQ7 5 H7
Chivenor EX31 6 D2
Chobham GU24 22 C5
Choicelee TD11 77 F5
Cholderton SP4 21 F7
Cholesbury HP23 22 C1
Chollerford NE46 70 E6
Chollerton NE46 70 E6
Cholsey OX10 21 J3
Cholstrey HR6 28 D3
Cholwell B. & N.E.Som. BS39 19 K6
Cholwell Devon PL19 4 E3
Chop Gate TS9 63 G7
Choppington NE62 71 H5
Chopwell NE17 62 C1
Chorley Ches.E. CW5 48 E7
Chorley Lancs. PR7 48 E1
Chorley Shrop. WV16 39 F7
Chorley Staffs. WS13 40 C4
Chorleywood WD3 22 D2
Chorlton CW2 49 G7
Chorlton Lane SY14 38 D1
Chorlton-cum-Hardy M21 49 H3
Chowley CH3 48 D7
Chrishall SG8 33 H5
Chrishall Grange SG8 33 H4
Chrisswell PA16 74 A3
Christchurch Cambs. PE14 43 H6
Christchurch Dorset BH23 10 C5
Christchurch Glos. GL16 28 E7
Christchurch Newport NP18 19 G3
Christian Malford SN15 20 C4
Christleton CH3 48 D6
Christmas Common OX49 22 A2
Christon BS26 19 G6
Christon Bank NE66 71 H1
Christow EX6 7 G7
Christskirk AB52 90 E2
Chryston G69 74 E3
Chudleigh TQ13 5 J3
Chudleigh Knighton TQ13 5 J3
Chulmleigh EX18 6 E4
Chunal SK13 50 C3
Church BB5 56 C7
Church Aston TF10 39 G4
Church Brampton NN6 31 J2
Church Brough CA17 61 J5
Church Broughton DE65 40 E2
Church Charwelton NN11 31 G3
Church Common IP17 35 H3
Church Crookham GU52 22 B6
Church Eaton ST20 40 A4
Church End Cambs. PE13 43 G5
Church End Cambs. CB24 33 G1
Church End Cambs. PE28 43 F7
Church End Cen.Beds. SG15 32 E5
Church End Cen.Beds. MK17 32 C5
Church End Cen.Beds. LU6 32 C6
Church End Cen.Beds. SG19 32 E3
Church End Cen.Beds. MK43 32 C5
Church End E.Riding YO25 59 G4
Church End Essex CB10 33 J4
Church End Essex CM7 34 B6
Church End Glos. GL20 29 H5
Church End Hants. RG27 21 K6
Church End Herts. AL3 32 E7
Church End Herts. SG11 33 H6
Church End Lincs. PE11 43 F2
Church End Lincs. LN11 53 H3
Church End Warks. CV10 40 E6
Church End Wilts. SN15 20 D4
Church Enstone OX7 30 E6
Church Fenton LS24 58 B6
Church Green EX24 7 K6
Church Gresley DE11 40 E4
Church Hanborough OX29 31 F7
Church Hill Ches.W. & C. CW7 49 F6
Church Hill Derbys. S42 51 G6
Church Houses YO62 63 H7
Church Knowle BH20 9 J6
Church Laneham DN22 52 B5
Church Langley CM17 23 H1
Church Langton LE16 42 A6
Church Lawford CV23 31 F1
Church Lawton ST7 49 H7
Church Leigh ST10 40 C2
Church Lench WR11 30 B3
Church Mayfield DE6 40 D1
Church Minshull CW5 49 F6
Church Norton PO20 12 B7
Church Preen SY6 38 E6
Church Pulverbatch SY5 38 D5
Church Stoke SY15 38 B6
Church Stowe NN7 31 H3
Church Street Essex CO10 34 B4
Church Street Kent ME3 24 D4
Church Stretton SY6 38 D6
Church Town Leics. LE67 41 F4
Church Town Surr. RH9 23 G6
Church Village CF38 18 D3
Church Warsop NG20 51 H6
Church Westcote OX7 30 D6
Church Wilne DE72 41 G2
Churcham GL2 29 G7
Churchdown GL3 29 H7
Churchend Essex SS3 25 G2
Churchend Essex CM6 33 K6
Churchend S.Glos. GL12 20 A2
Churchfield B71 40 C6
Churchgate EN7 23 G1
Churchgate Street CM17 33 H7
Churchill Devon EX31 6 D1
Churchill Devon EX13 8 B4
Churchill N.Som. BS25 19 H6
Churchill Oxon. OX7 30 D6
Churchill Worcs. WR7 29 J3
Churchill Worcs. DY10 29 H1
Churchingford TA3 8 B3
Churchover CV23 41 H7
Churchstanton TA3 7 K4
Churchstow TQ7 5 H6
Churchtown Devon EX31 6 E1
Churchtown I.o.M. IM7 54 D4
Churchtown Lancs. PR3 55 H5
Churchtown Mersey. PR9 48 C1
Churnsike Lodge NE48 70 B6
Churston Ferrers TQ5 5 K5
Churt GU10 12 B3
Churton CH3 48 D7
Churwell LS27 57 H7
Chute Cadley SP11 21 G6
Chute Standen SP11 21 G6
Chwilog LL53 36 D2
Chwitffordd (Whitford) CH8 47 K5
Chyandour TR18 2 B5
Chysauster TR20 2 B5
Cilan Uchaf LL53 36 B3
Cilcain CH7 47 K6
Cilcennin SA48 26 E2
Cilcewydd SY21 38 B5
Cilfrew SA10 18 A1
Cilfynydd CF37 18 D2
Cilgerran SA43 16 E1
Cilgwyn Carmar. SA20 27 G5
Cilgwyn Pembs. SA42 16 D2
Ciliau Aeron SA48 26 E3
Cilldonnain (Kildonan) HS8 84 C2
Cille Bhrighde HS8 84 C3
Cille Pheadair HS8 84 C3
Cilmaengwyn SA8 18 A1
Cilmery LD2 27 K3
Cilrhedyn SA35 17 F2
Cilrhedyn Bridge SA65 16 D2
Cilsan SA19 17 J3
Ciltalgarth LL23 37 H1
Cilwendeg SA37 17 F2
Cilybebyll SA8 18 A1
Cilycwm SA20 27 G4
Cimla SA11 18 A2
Cinderford GL14 29 F7
Cippenham SL1 22 C3
Cippyn SA43 16 E1
Cirbhig HS2 100 D3
Circebost (Kirkibost) HS2 100 D4
Cirencester GL7 20 D1
City Gt.Lon. EC3M 23 G3
City V. of Glam. CF71 18 C4
City Airport E16 23 H3
City Dulas LL70 46 C4
Clabhach PA78 78 C2
Clachaig PA23 73 K2
Clachan Arg. & B. PA26 80 C6
Clachan Arg. & B. PA34 79 K3
Clachan Arg. & B. PA29 73 F5
Clachan High. IV40 86 B1
Clachan W.Isles HS8 92 C7
Clachan Mòr PA77 78 A3
Clachan of Campsie G66 74 E3
Clachan of Glendaruel PA22 73 H2
Clachan Strachur (Strachur) PA27 80 B7
Clachan-a-Luib HS6 92 D5
Clachandhu PA68 79 F4
Clachaneasy DG8 64 D3
Clachanmore DG9 64 A6
Clachan-Seil PA34 79 J6
Clachanturn AB35 89 K5
Clachbreck PA31 73 F3
Clachnabrain DD8 82 E1
Clachnaharry IV3 96 D7
Clachtoll IV27 102 C6
Clackmannan FK10 75 H1
Clackmarras IV30 97 K6
Clacton-on-Sea CO15 35 F7
Cladach a Bhale Shear HS6 92 D5
Cladach a' Chaolais HS6 92 C5
Cladach Chircebost HS6 92 C5
Cladach Chnoc a Lin HS6 92 C5
Cladich PA33 80 B5
Cladswell B49 30 B3
Claggan High. PH33 87 H7
Claggan High. PA34 79 J3
Claigan IV55 93 H6
Claines WR3 29 H3
Clandown BA3 19 K6
Clanfield Hants. PO8 11 J3
Clanfield Oxon. OX18 21 F1
Clannaborough Barton EX17 7 F5
Clanville SP11 21 G7
Claonaig PA29 73 G5
Claonairigh PA32 80 B7
Claonel IV27 96 C1
Clapgate SG11 33 H6
Clapham Bed. MK41 32 D3
Clapham Devon EX2 7 G7
Clapham Gt.Lon. SW4 23 F4
Clapham N.Yorks. LA2 56 C3
Clapham W.Suss. BN13 12 D6
Clapham Green MK41 32 D3
Clapham Hill CT5 25 H5
Clappers TD15 77 H5
Clappersgate LA22 60 E6
Clapton Som. TA18 8 D4
Clapton Som. BA3 19 K6
Clapton-in-Gordano BS20 19 H4
Clapton-on-the-Hill GL54 30 C7
Clapworthy EX36 6 E3
Clara Vale NE40 71 G7
Clarach SY23 37 F7
Clarbeston SA63 16 D3
Clarbeston Road SA63 16 D3
Clarborough DN22 51 K4
Clardon KW14 105 G2
Clare CO10 34 B4
Clarebrand DG7 65 H4
Clarencefield DG1 69 F7
Clarilaw TD9 70 A2
Clark's Green RH5 12 E3
Clarkston G76 74 D5
Clashban IV24 96 D2
Clashcoig IV24 96 D2
Clashdorran IV4 96 C7
Clashgour PA36 80 D3
Clashindarroch AB54 90 C1
Clashmore High. IV25 96 E3
Clashmore High. IV27 102 C5
Clashnessie IV27 102 C5
Clashnoir AB37 89 K2
Clatford SN8 20 E5
Clathy PH7 82 A5
Clatt AB54 90 D2
Clatter SY17 37 J6
Clattercote OX17 31 F4
Clatterford PO30 11 F6
Clatterford End CM5 23 J1
Clatterin Brig AB30 90 E7
Clatteringshaws DG7 65 F3
Clatworthy TA4 7 J2
Claughton Lancs. LA2 55 J3
Claughton Lancs. PR3 55 J5
Clavelshay TA6 8 B1
Claverdon CV35 30 C2
Claverham BS49 19 H5
Clavering CB11 33 H5
Claverley WV5 39 G6
Claverton BA2 20 A5
Claverton Down BA2 20 A5
Clawdd-côch CF71 18 D4
Clawdd-newydd LL15 47 J7
Clawfin KA6 67 K3
Clawthorpe LA6 55 J2
Clawton EX22 6 B6
Claxby LN8 52 E3
Claxby Pluckacre LN9 53 G6
Claxby St. Andrew LN13 53 H5
Claxton N.Yorks. YO60 58 C3
Claxton Norf. NR14 45 H5
Claxton Grange TS22 63 F4
Clay Common NR34 45 J7
Clay Coton NN6 31 G1
Clay Cross S45 51 F6
Clay End SG2 33 G6
Clay Hill BS16 19 K4
Clay of Allan IV20 97 F4
Claybrooke Magna LE17 41 G7
Claybrooke Parva LE17 41 G7
Claydene TN8 23 H7
Claydon Oxon. OX17 31 F3
Claydon Suff. IP6 35 F4
Claygate Kent TN12 14 C3
Claygate Surr. KT10 22 E5
Claygate Cross TN15 23 K6
Clayhanger Devon EX16 7 J3
Clayhanger W.Mid. WS8 40 C5
Clayhidon EX15 7 K4
Clayhill E.Suss. TN31 14 D5
Clayhill Hants. SO43 10 E4
Clayhithe CB25 33 J2
Clayock KW12 105 G3
Claypit Hill CB23 33 G3
Claypits GL10 20 A1
Claypole NG23 42 B1
Claythorpe LN13 53 H5
Clayton S.Yorks. DN5 51 G2
Clayton Staffs. ST5 40 A1
Clayton W.Suss. BN6 13 F5
Clayton W.Yorks. BD14 57 G6
Clayton Green PR6 55 J7
Clayton West HD8 50 E1
Clayton-le-Moors BB5 56 C6
Clayton-le-Woods PR25 55 J7
Clayworth DN22 51 K4
Cleadale PH42 85 K6
Cleadon SR6 71 J7
Clearbrook PL20 5 F4
Clearwell GL16 19 J1
Cleasby DL2 62 D5
Cleat Ork. KW17 106 D9
Cleat W.Isles HS9 84 B4
Cleatlam DL2 62 C5
Cleatop BD24 56 D3
Cleator CA23 60 B5
Cleator Moor CA25 60 B5
Cleckheaton BD19 57 G7
Clee St. Margaret SY7 38 E7
Cleedownton SY8 38 E7
Cleehill SY8 28 E1
Cleestanton SY8 28 E1
Cleethorpes DN35 53 G2
Cleeton St. Mary DY14 29 F1
Cleeve N.Som. BS49 19 H5
Cleeve Oxon. RG8 21 K3
Cleeve Hill GL52 29 J6
Cleeve Prior WR11 30 B4
Cleghorn ML11 75 G6
Clehonger HR2 28 D5
Cleigh PA34 79 K5
Cleish KY13 75 J1
Cleland ML1 75 F5
Clement's End LU6 32 D7
Clench Common SN8 20 E5
Clenchwarton PE34 43 J3
Clennell NE65 70 E3
Clent DY9 29 J1
Cleobury Mortimer DY14 29 F1
Cleobury North WV16 39 F7
Clephanton IV2 97 F6
Clerklands TD6 70 A1
Clermiston EH4 75 K3
Clestrain KW17 106 C7
Cleuch Head TD9 70 A2
Cleughbrae DG1 69 F6
Clevancy SN11 20 D4
Clevedon BS21 19 H4
Cleveland Tontine Inn DL6 63 F7
Cleveley OX7 30 E6
Cleveleys FY5 55 G5
Clevelode WR13 29 H4
Cleverton SN15 20 C3
Clewer BS28 19 H6
Clewer Green SL4 22 C4
Clewer Village SL4 22 C4
Cley next the Sea NR25 44 E1
Cliburn CA10 61 G4
Cliddesden RG25 21 K7
Cliff Carmar. SA17 17 G5
Cliff High. PH36 79 H1
Cliff End TN35 14 D6
Cliff Grange TF9 39 F2
Cliffe Lancs. BB6 56 C6
Cliffe Med. ME3 24 D4
Cliffe N.Yorks. YO8 58 C6
Cliffe Woods ME3 24 D4
Clifford Here. HR3 28 B4
Clifford W.Yorks. LS23 57 K5
Clifford Chambers CV37 30 C3
Clifford's Mesne GL18 29 F6
Cliffs End CT12 25 K5
Clifton Bristol BS8 19 J4
Clifton Cen.Beds. SG17 32 E5
Clifton Cumb. CA10 61 G4
Clifton Derbys. DE6 40 D1
Clifton Devon EX31 6 D1
Clifton Lancs. PR4 55 H6
Clifton N.Yorks. LS21 57 G5
Clifton Northumb. NE61 71 H5
Clifton Nott. NG11 41 H2
Clifton Oxon. OX15 31 F5
Clifton S.Yorks. S66 51 H3
Clifton Stir. FK20 80 E4
Clifton W.Yorks. HD6 57 G7
Clifton Worcs. WR8 29 H4
Clifton York YO30 58 B4
Clifton Campville B79 40 E4
Clifton Hampden OX14 21 J2
Clifton Maybank BA22 8 E3
Clifton Reynes MK46 32 C3
Clifton upon Dunsmore CV23 31 G1
Clifton upon Teme WR6 29 G2
Cliftonville CT9 25 K4
Climping BN17 12 D6
Climpy ML11 75 H5
Clink BA11 20 A7
Clint HG3 57 H4
Clint Green NR19 44 E4
Clinterty AB21 91 G3
Clintmains TD6 76 E7
Clippesby NR29 45 J4
Clippings Green NR20 44 E4
Clipsham LE15 42 C4
Clipston Northants. LE16 42 A7
Clipston Notts. NG12 41 J2
Clipstone NG21 51 H6
Clitheroe BB7 56 C5
Cliuthar (Cluer) HS3 93 G2
Clive SY4 38 E3
Clivocast ZE2 107 Q2
Clixby DN38 52 E2
Clocaenog LL15 47 J7
Clochan AB56 98 C4
Clochtow AB41 91 J1
Clock Face WA9 48 E3
Clockhill AB42 99 G6

Clo - Cor

Cloddach IV30 97 J6
Cloddiau SY21 38 A5
Clodock HR2 28 C6
Cloford BA11 20 A7
Cloichran FK21 81 H4
Clola AB42 99 J6
Clonrae DG3 68 D4
Clophill MK45 32 D5
Clopton NN14 42 D7
Clopton Corner IP13 35 G3
Clopton Green *Suff.* CB8 34 B3
Clopton Green *Suff.* IP13 35 G3
Close Clark IM9 54 B6
Closeburn DG3 68 D4
Closworth BA22 8 E3
Clothall SG7 33 F5
Clothan ZE2 107 N4
Clotton CW6 48 E6
Clough *Cumb.* LA10 61 J7
Clough *Gt.Man.* OL15 49 J1
Clough *Gt.Man.* OL2 49 J2
Clough *W.Yorks.* HD7 50 C1
Clough Foot OL14 56 E7
Clough Head HX6 57 F7
Cloughfold BB4 56 D7
Cloughton YO13 63 K3
Cloughton Newlands YO13 63 K3
Clounlaid PA34 79 J2
Clousta ZE2 107 M7
Clouston KW16 106 C6
Clova *Aber.* AB54 90 C2
Clova *Angus* DD8 90 B7
Clove Lodge DL12 62 A5
Clovelly EX39 6 B3
Clovelly Cross EX39 6 B3
Clovenfords TD1 76 C7
Clovenstone AB51 91 F3
Cloverhill AB23 91 H3
Cloves IV36 97 J5
Clovullin PH33 80 B1
Clow Bridge BB11 56 D7
Clowne S43 51 G5
Clows Top DY14 29 G1
Cloyntie KA19 67 H3
Cluanach PA43 72 B5
Clubworthy PL15 4 C1
Cluddley TF6 39 F4
Cluer (Cliuthar) HS3 93 G2
Clun SY7 38 B7
Clunas IV12 97 F7
Clunbury SY7 38 C7
Clune *High.* IV13 88 E2
Clune *Moray* AB56 98 D4
Clunes PH34 87 J6
Clungunford SY7 28 C1
Clunie *Aber.* AB53 98 E5
Clunie *P.& K.* PH10 82 C3
Clunton SY7 38 C7
Cluny KY2 76 A1
Clutton *B.& N.E.Som.* BS39 19 K6
Clutton *Ches.W.& C.* CH3 48 D7
Clwt-y-bont LL55 46 D6
Clwydyfagwyr CF48 18 D1
Clydach *Mon.* NP7 28 B7
Clydach *Swan.* SA6 17 K5
Clydach Terrace NP23 28 A7
Clydach Vale CF40 18 C2
**Clydebank G81 74 C3**
Clydey SA35 17 F2
Clyffe Pypard SN4 20 D4
Clynder G84 74 A2
**Clynderwen SA66 16 E4**
Clyne SA11 18 B1
Clynelish KW9 97 F1
Clynfyw SA37 17 F2
Clynnog-fawr LL54 36 D1
Clyro HR3 28 B4
Clyst Honiton EX5 7 H6
Clyst Hydon EX15 7 J5
Clyst St. George EX3 7 H7
Clyst St. Lawrence EX15 7 J5
Clyst St. Mary EX5 7 H6
Clyst William EX15 7 J5
Cnewr LD3 27 H6
Cnoc HS2 101 G4
Cnoc an Torrain (Knockintorran) HS6 92 C5
Cnwch Coch SY23 27 F1
Coachford AB54 98 C6
Coad's Green PL15 4 C3
Coal Aston S18 51 F5
Coalbrookdale TF8 39 F5
Coalbrookvale NP13 18 E1
Coalburn ML11 75 G7
Coalburns NE40 71 G7
Coalcleugh NE47 61 K2
Coaley GL11 20 A1
Coalmoor TF6 39 F5
Coalpit Heath BS36 19 K3
Coalpit Hill ST7 49 H7
Coalport TF8 39 G5
Coalsnaughton FK13 75 H1
Coaltown of Balgonie KY7 76 B1
Coaltown of Wemyss KY1 76 B1
**Coalville LE67 41 G4**
Coalway GL16 28 E7
Coanwood NE49 61 H1
Coast IV22 95 F2
Coat TA12 8 D2
**Coatbridge ML5 75 F4**
Coate *Swin.* SN3 20 E3
Coate *Wilts.* SN10 20 D5
Coates *Cambs.* PE7 43 G6
Coates *Glos.* GL7 20 C1
Coates *Lincs.* LN1 52 C4
Coates *Notts.* DN22 52 B4
Coates *W.Suss.* RH20 12 C5
Coatham TS10 63 G4
Coatham Mundeville DL3 62 D4
Cobairdy AB54 98 D6
Cobbaton EX37 6 E3
Cobbler's Plain NP16 19 H1
Cobby Syke HG3 57 G4
Cobden EX5 7 J6
Coberley GL53 29 J7
Cobhall Common HR2 28 D5
Cobham *Kent* DA12 24 C5
**Cobham *Surr.* KT11 22 E5**
Cobleland FK8 74 D1
Cobley Hill B60 30 B1
Cobnash HR6 28 D2
Coburty AB43 99 H4
Cochno G81 74 C3
Cock Alley S44 51 G6
Cock Bank LL13 38 C1
Cock Bevington WR11 30 B3
Cock Bridge AB36 89 K4
Cock Clarks CM3 24 E1
Cock Green CM6 34 B7
Cock Marling TN31 14 D6
Cockayne YO62 63 H7
Cockayne Hatley SG19 33 F4
**Cockburnspath TD13 77 F3**
Cockenzie & Port Seton EH32 76 C3
Cocker Bar PR26 55 J7
Cockerham LA2 55 H4
**Cockermouth CA13 60 C3**
Cockernhoe LU2 32 E6
Cockerton DL3 62 D5
Cockett SA2 17 K6
Cockfield *Dur.* DL13 62 C4
Cockfield *Suff.* IP30 34 D3
Cockfosters EN4 23 F2
Cocking GU29 12 B5
Cockington TQ2 5 J4
Cocklake BS28 19 H7
Cocklaw NE46 70 E6
Cockle Park NE61 71 H4
Cockleford GL53 29 J7
Cockley Beck LA20 60 D6
Cockley Cley PE37 44 B5
Cockpen EH19 76 B4
Cockpole Green RG10 22 A3
Cockshutt SY12 38 D3
Cockthorpe NR23 44 D1
Cockwood *Devon* EX6 7 H7
Cockwood *Som.* TA5 19 F7
Cockyard SK23 50 C4
Codda PL15 4 B3
Coddenham IP6 35 F3
Coddington *Ches.W.& C.* CH3 48 D7
Coddington *Here.* HR8 29 G4
Coddington *Notts.* NG24 52 B7
Codford St. Mary BA12 9 J1
Codford St. Peter BA12 9 J1
Codicote SG4 33 F7
Codmore Hill RH20 12 D5
Codnor DE5 41 G1
Codnor Park NG16 51 G7
Codrington BS37 20 A4
Codsall WV8 40 A5
Codsall Wood WV8 40 A5
Coed Morgan NP7 28 C7
Coed Ystumgwern LL44 36 E3
Coedcae NP4 19 F1
**Coed-duon (Blackwood) NP12 18 E2**
Coedely CF39 18 D3
Coedkernew NP10 19 F3
Coedpoeth LL11 48 B7
Coedway SY5 38 C4
Coed-y-bryn SA44 17 G1
Coed-y-caerau NP18 19 G2
Coed-y-paen NP4 19 G2
Coed-y-parc LL57 46 E6
Coed-yr-ynys NP8 28 A6
Coelbren SA10 27 H7
Coffinswell TQ12 5 J4
Cofton EX6 7 H7
Cofton Hackett B45 30 B1
Cogan CF64 18 E4
Cogenhoe NN7 32 B2
Cogges OX28 21 G1
Coggeshall CO6 34 C6
Coggeshall Hamlet CO6 34 C6
Coggins Mill TN20 13 J4
Cóig Peighinnean HS2 101 H1
Coilantogle FK17 81 G7
Coilcitir PH49 80 C3
Coilessan G83 80 D7
Coillaig PA35 80 B5
Coille Mhorgil PH35 87 G4
Coille-righ IV40 87 F2
Coillore IV56 85 J1
Coity CF35 18 C3
Col HS2 101 G4
Col Uarach HS2 101 G4
Colaboll IV27 103 H7
Colan TR8 3 F2
Colaton Raleigh EX10 7 J7
Colbost IV55 93 H7
Colburn DL9 62 D7
Colbury SO40 10 E3
Colby *Cumb.* CA16 61 H4
Colby *I.o.M.* IM9 54 B6
Colby *Norf.* NR11 45 G2
**COLCHESTER CO 34 D6**
Colchester Green IP30 34 D3
Colcot CF62 18 E5
Cold Ash RG18 21 J5
Cold Ashby NN6 31 H1
Cold Ashton SN14 20 A4
Cold Aston GL54 30 C7
Cold Blow SA67 16 E4
Cold Brayfield MK46 32 C3
Cold Chapel ML12 68 E1
Cold Cotes LA2 56 C2
Cold Hanworth LN8 52 D4
Cold Harbour RG8 21 K3
Cold Hatton TF6 39 F3
Cold Hatton Heath TF6 39 F3
Cold Hesledon SR7 63 F2
Cold Higham NN12 31 H3
Cold Inn SA68 16 E5
Cold Kirby YO7 58 B1
Cold Newton LE7 42 A5
Cold Northcott PL15 4 C2
Cold Norton CM3 24 E1
Cold Overton LE15 42 B5
Cold Row FY6 55 G5
Coldbackie IV27 103 J2
Coldblow DA5 23 J4
Coldean BN1 13 G6
Coldeast TQ12 5 J3
Coldeaton DE6 50 D7
Colden Common SO21 11 F2
Coldfair Green IP17 35 J2
Coldham PE14 43 H5
Coldharbour *Glos.* GL15 19 J1
Coldharbour *Surr.* RH5 22 E7
Coldingham TD14 77 H4
Coldrain KY13 82 B7
Coldred CT15 15 H3
Coldrey GU34 22 A7
Coldridge EX17 6 E5
Coldrife NE61 71 F4
**Coldstream TD12 77 G7**
Coldvreath PL26 3 G3
Coldwaltham RH20 12 D5
Coldwells AB42 99 K6
Cole BA10 9 F1
Cole End B46 40 D7
Cole Green SG14 33 F7
Cole Henley RG28 21 H6
Colebatch SY9 38 C7
Colebrook EX15 7 J5
Colebrooke EX17 7 F5
Coleburn IV30 97 K6
Coleby *Lincs.* LN5 52 C6
Coleby *N.Lincs.* DN15 52 B1
Coleford *Devon* EX17 7 F5
**Coleford *Glos.* GL16 28 E7**
Coleford *Som.* BA3 19 K7
Colegate End IP21 45 F7
Colehill BH21 10 B4
Coleman Green AL4 32 E7
Coleman's Hatch TN7 13 H3
Colemere SY12 38 D2
Colemore GU34 11 J1
Colemore Green WV16 39 G6
Colenden PH2 82 C5
Coleorton LE67 41 G4
Colerne SN14 20 B4
Cole's Common IP21 45 G7
Cole's Cross TQ9 5 H6
Cole's Green IP13 35 G2
Colesbourne GL53 30 B7
Colesden MK44 32 E3
Coleshill *Bucks.* HP7 22 C2
Coleshill *Oxon.* SN6 21 F2
Coleshill *Warks.* B46 40 E7
Colestocks EX14 7 J5
Coley *B.& N.E.Som.* BS40 19 J6
Coley *Staffs.* ST18 40 C3
Colfin DG9 64 A5
Colgate RH12 13 F3
Colgrain G82 74 B3
Colindale NW9 23 F3
Colinsburgh KY9 83 F7
Colinton EH13 76 A4
**Colintraive PA22 73 J3**
Colkirk NR21 44 D3
**Coll PA78 78 C2**
Collace PH2 82 D4
Collafirth ZE2 107 N6
Collamoor Head PL32 4 B1
Collaton St. Mary TQ3 5 J4
Collessie KY15 82 D6
Colleton Mills EX37 6 E4
Collett's Green WR2 29 H3
Collier Row RM5 23 J2
Collier Street TN12 14 C3
Collier's End SG11 33 G6
Collier's Wood SW19 23 F4
Colliery Row DH4 62 E2
Collieston AB41 91 J2
Collin DG1 69 F6
Collingbourne Ducis SN8 21 F6
Collingbourne Kingston SN8 21 F6
Collingham *Notts.* NG23 52 B6
Collingham *W.Yorks.* LS22 57 J5
Collington HR7 29 F2
Collingtree NN4 31 J3
Collins End RG8 21 K4
Collins Green *Warr.* WA5 48 E3
Collins Green *Worcs.* WR6 29 G3
Colliston DD11 83 H3
Colliton EX14 7 J5
Collmuir AB31 90 D4
Collycroft CV12 41 F7
Collyhurst M8 49 H2
Collynie AB41 91 G1
Collyweston PE9 42 C5
Colmonell KA26 67 F5
Colmworth MK44 32 E3
Coln Rogers GL54 20 D1
Coln St. Aldwyns GL7 20 E1
Coln St. Dennis GL54 30 B7
Colnabaichin AB36 89 K4
Colnbrook SL3 22 D4
Colne *Cambs.* PE28 33 G1
**Colne *Lancs.* BB8 56 D6**
Colne Engaine CO6 34 C5
Colney NR4 45 F5
Colney Heath AL4 23 F1
Colney Street AL2 22 E1
**Colonsay PA61 72 B1**
Colonsay House PA61 72 B1
Colpy AB52 90 E1
Colquhar EH44 76 B6
Colsterdale HG4 57 G1
Colsterworth NG33 42 C3
Colston Bassett NG12 42 A2
Coltfield IV36 97 J5
Colthouse LA22 60 E7
Coltishall NR12 45 G4
Coltness ML2 75 G5
Colton *Cumb.* LA12 55 G1
Colton *N.Yorks.* LS24 58 B5
Colton *Norf.* NR9 45 F5
Colton *Staffs.* WS15 40 C3
Colton *W.Yorks.* LS15 57 J6
Colva HR5 28 B3
Colvend DG5 65 J5
Colvister ZE2 107 P3
Colwall WR13 29 G4
Colwall Green WR13 29 G4
Colwall Stone WR13 29 G4
Colwell NE46 70 E6
Colwich ST18 40 C3
Colwick NG4 41 J2
Colwinston CF71 18 C4
Colworth PO20 12 C6
**Colwyn Bay (Bae Colwyn) LL29 47 G5**
Colyford EX24 8 B5
**Colyton EX24 8 B5**
Combe *Here.* LD8 28 C2
Combe *Oxon.* OX29 31 F7
Combe *Som.* TA10 8 D2
Combe *W.Berks.* RG17 21 G5
Combe Common GU8 12 C3
Combe Cross TQ13 5 H3
Combe Down BA2 20 A5
Combe Florey TA4 7 K2
Combe Hay BA2 20 A6
Combe Martin EX34 6 D1
Combe Pafford TQ1 5 K4
Combe Raleigh EX14 7 K5
Combe St. Nicholas TA20 8 C3
Combeinteignhead TQ12 5 J3
Comberbach CW9 49 F5
Comberford B79 40 D5
Comberton *Cambs.* CB23 33 G3
Comberton *Here.* SY8 28 D2
Combpyne EX13 8 B5
Combridge ST14 40 C2
Combrook CV35 30 E3
Combs *Derbys.* SK23 50 C5
Combs *Suff.* IP14 34 E3
Combs Ford IP14 34 E3
Combwich TA5 19 F7
Comer FK8 80 E7
Comers AB51 90 E4
Comhampton DY13 29 H2
Comins Coch SY23 37 F7
Commercial End CB25 33 J2
Commins Coch SY20 37 H5
Common Edge FY4 55 G6
Common Moor PL14 4 C3
Common Platt SN5 20 E3
Common Side S18 51 F5
Common Square LN4 52 D5
Commondale YO21 63 H5
Commonside DE6 40 E1
Compstall SK6 49 J3
Compton *Devon* TQ3 5 J4
Compton *Hants.* SO21 11 F2
Compton *Plym.* PL3 4 E5
Compton *Staffs.* DY7 40 A7
Compton *Surr.* GU3 22 C7
Compton *W.Berks.* RG20 21 J4
Compton *W.Suss.* PO18 11 J3
Compton *W.Yorks.* LS22 57 K5
Compton *Wilts.* SN9 20 E6
Compton Abbas SP7 9 H3
Compton Abdale GL54 30 B7
Compton Bassett SN11 20 D4
Compton Beauchamp SN6 21 F3
Compton Bishop BS26 19 G6
Compton Chamberlayne SP3 10 B2
Compton Dando BS39 19 K5
Compton Dundon TA11 8 D1
Compton Martin BS40 19 J6
Compton Pauncefoot BA22 9 F2
Compton Valence DT2 8 E5
Compton Verney CV35 30 E3
Compton Wynyates CV35 30 E4
Comra PH20 88 C5
Comrie *Fife* KY12 75 J2
Comrie *P.& K.* PH6 81 J5
Conchra *Arg.& B.* PA22 73 J2
Conchra *High.* IV40 86 E2
Concraigie PH10 82 C3
Conder Green LA2 55 H4
Conderton GL20 29 J5
Condicote GL54 30 C6
Condorrat G67 75 F3
Condover SY5 38 D5
Coney Weston IP31 34 D1
Coneyhurst RH14 12 E4
Coneysthorpe YO60 58 D2
Coneythorpe HG5 57 J4
Conford GU30 12 B3
Congash PH26 89 H2
Congdon's Shop PL15 4 C3
Congerstone CV13 41 F5
Congham PE32 44 B3
**Congleton CW12 49 H6**
Congresbury BS49 19 H5
Congreve ST19 40 B4
Conicavel IV36 97 G6
Coningsby LN4 53 F7
Conington *Cambs.* PE7 42 E7
Conington *Cambs.* CB23 33 G2
Conisbrough DN12 51 H3
Conisby PA49 72 A4
Conisholme LN11 53 H3
**Coniston *Cumb.* LA21 60 E7**
Coniston *E.Riding* HU11 59 H6
Coniston Cold BD23 56 E4
Conistone BD23 56 E3
Conland AB54 98 E6
Connah's Quay CH5 48 B6
Connel PA37 80 A4
Connel Park KA18 68 B2
Connor Downs TR27 2 C5
Conock SN10 20 D6
Conon Bridge IV7 96 C6
Cononish FK20 80 E5
Cononley BD20 56 E5
Cononsyth DD11 83 G3
Consall ST9 40 B1
**Consett DH8 62 C1**
Constable Burton DL8 62 C7
Constantine TR11 2 E6
Constantine Bay PL28 3 F1
Contin IV14 96 B6
Contlaw AB13 91 G4
Contullich IV17 96 D4
**Conwy LL32 47 F5**
Conyer ME9 25 F5
Conyer's Green IP31 34 C2
Cooden TN39 14 C7
Coodham KA1 74 C7
Cooil IM4 54 C6
Cookbury EX22 6 C5
Cookbury Wick EX22 6 B5
Cookham SL6 22 B3
Cookham Dean SL6 22 B3
Cookham Rise SL6 22 B3
Cookhill B49 30 B3
Cookley *Suff.* IP19 35 H1
Cookley *Worcs.* DY10 40 A7
Cookley Green *Oxon.* RG9 21 K2
Cookley Green *Suff.* IP19 35 H1
Cookney AB39 91 G5
Cook's Green IP7 34 D3
Cooksbridge BN7 13 G5
Cooksey Green B61 29 J2
Cookshill ST11 40 B1
Cooksmill Green CM1 24 C1
Cookston AB41 91 H1
Coolham RH13 12 E4
Cooling ME3 24 D4
Cooling Street ME3 24 D4
Coombe *Cornw.* PL26 3 G3
Coombe *Cornw.* EX23 6 A4
Coombe *Cornw.* TR14 2 D4
Coombe *Cornw.* TR3 3 F4
Coombe *Devon* TQ9 5 H6
Coombe *Devon* EX6 7 G7
Coombe *Devon* EX10 7 K6
Coombe *Som.* TA2 8 B2
Coombe *Som.* TA18 8 D4
Coombe *Wilts.* SN9 20 E6
Coombe Bissett SP5 10 C2
Coombe End TA4 7 J3
Coombe Hill GL19 29 H6
Coombe Keynes BH20 9 H6
Coombes BN15 12 E6
Coombes Moor LD8 28 C2
Cooper's Corner *E.Suss.* TN19 14 C5
Cooper's Corner *Kent* TN14 23 H7
Cooper's Green AL4 22 E1
Coopersale CM16 23 H1
Coopersale Street CM16 23 H1
Cootham RH20 12 D5
Cop Street CT3 15 H2
Copdock IP8 35 F4
Copford Green CO6 34 D6
Copgrove HG3 57 J3
Copister ZE2 107 N5
Cople MK44 32 E4
Copley *Dur.* DL13 62 B4
Copley *W.Yorks.* HX4 57 F7
Coplow Dale SK17 50 D5
Copmanthorpe YO23 58 B5
Copmere End ST21 40 A3
Copp PR3 55 H6
Coppathorne EX23 6 A5
Coppenhall ST18 40 B4
Coppenhall Moss CW1 49 G7
Copperhouse TR27 2 C5
Coppicegate DY12 39 G7
Coppingford PE28 42 E7
Coppleridge SP7 9 H2
Copplestone EX17 7 F5
Coppull PR7 48 E1
Coppull Moor PR7 48 E1
Copsale RH13 12 E4
Copse Hill SW20 23 F5
Copster Green BB1 56 B6
Copston Magna LE10 41 G7
Copt Heath B93 30 C1
Copt Hewick HG4 57 J2
Copt Oak LE67 41 G4
Copthall Green EN9 23 H1
Copthorne RH10 13 G3
Copy Lake EX18 6 E4
Copythorne SO40 10 E3
Coralhill AB43 99 J4
Corbets Tey RM14 23 J3
Corbiegoe KW1 105 J4
**Corbridge NE45 70 E7**
**Corby NN17 42 B7**
Corby Glen NG33 42 D3
Cordach AB34 90 E5
Cordorcan DG8 64 D3
Coreley SY8 29 F1
Corfcott Green EX22 6 B6
Corfe TA3 8 B3
Corfe Castle BH20 9 J6

Cor - Cro


Corfe Mullen BH21 9 J5
Corfton SY7 38 D7
Corgarff AB36 89 K4
Corhampton SO32 11 H2
Corley CV7 40 E7
Corley Ash CV7 40 E7
Corley Moor CV7 40 E7
Cornabus PA42 72 B6
Cornard Tye CO10 34 D4
Corndon TQ13 6 E7
Corney LA19 60 C7
Cornforth DL17 62 E3
Cornhill AB45 98 D5
Cornhill on Tweed TD12 77 G7
Cornholme OL14 56 E7
Cornish Hall End CM7 33 K5
Cornquoy KW17 106 E7
Cornriggs DL13 61 K2
Cornsay DH7 62 C2
Cornsay Colliery DH7 62 C2
Corntown High. IV7 96 C6
Corntown V. of Glam. CF35 18 C4
Cornwell OX7 30 D6
Cornwood PL21 5 G5
Cornworthy TQ9 5 J5
Corpach PH33 87 H7
Corpusty NR11 45 F3
Corrachree AB34 90 C4
Corran Arg. & B. PA24 74 A1
Corran High. IV40 86 E4
Corran (Ardgour) High. PH33 80 B1
Corranbuie PA29 73 G4
Corranmore PA31 79 J7
Corrany IM7 54 D5
Corribeg PH33 87 F7
Corrie KA27 73 J6
Corrie Common DG11 69 H5
Corriechrevie PA29 73 F5
Corriecravie KA27 66 D1
Corriedoo DG7 68 B5
Corriekinloch IV27 103 F6
Corrielorne PA34 79 K6
Corrievorrie IV13 88 E2
Corrimony IV63 87 K1
Corringham Lincs. DN21 52 B3
Corringham Thur. SS17 24 D3
Corris SY20 37 G5
Corris Uchaf SY20 37 G5
Corrlarach PH33 87 F7
Corrour Shooting Lodge PH30 81 F1
Corrow PA24 80 C7
Corry IV49 86 C2
Corrychurrachan PH33 80 B1
Corrylach PA28 73 F7
Corrymuckloch PH8 81 K4
Corsback KW1 105 H2
Corscombe DT2 8 E4
Corse Aber. AB54 98 E6
Corse Glos. GL19 29 G6
Corse Lawn GL19 29 H5
Corse of Kinnoir AB54 98 D6
Corsebank DG4 68 D2
Corsegight AB53 99 G5
Corsehill DG11 69 G5
Corsewall DG9 64 A4
Corsham SN13 20 B4
Corsindae AB51 90 E4
Corsley BA12 20 B7
Corsley Heath BA12 20 B7
Corsock DG7 65 H3
Corston B. & N.E.Som. BA2 19 K5
Corston Wilts. SN16 20 C3
Corstorphine EH12 75 K3
Cortachy DD8 82 E2
Corton Suff. NR32 45 K6
Corton Wilts. BA12 20 C7
Corton Denham DT9 9 F2
Corwar House KA26 67 G5
Corwen LL21 37 K1
Coryton Devon EX20 6 C7
Coryton Thur. SS17 24 D3
Cosby LE9 41 H6
Coscote OX11 21 J3
Coseley WV14 40 B6
Cosford Shrop. WV7 39 G5
Cosford Warks. CV21 31 G1
Cosgrove MK19 31 J4
Cosham PO6 11 H4
Cosheston SA72 16 D5
Coshieville PH15 81 J3
Coskills DN38 52 D2
Cosmeston CF64 18 E5
Cossall NG16 41 G1
Cossington Leics. LE7 41 J4
Cossington Som. TA7 19 G7
Costa KW17 106 C5
Costessey NR8 45 F4
Costock LE12 41 H3
Coston Leics. LE14 42 B3
Coston Norf. NR9 44 E5
Cote Oxon. OX18 21 G1
Cote Som. TA9 19 G7
Cotebrook CW6 48 E6
Cotehill CA4 61 F1
Cotes Cumb. LA8 55 H1
Cotes Leics. LE12 41 H3
Cotes Staffs. ST15 40 A2
Cotesbach LE17 41 H7
Cotgrave NG12 41 J2
Cothall AB21 91 G3
Cotham NG23 42 A1
Cothelstone TA4 7 K2
Cotheridge WR6 29 G3
Cotherstone DL12 62 B5
Cothill OX13 21 H2
Cotleigh EX14 8 B4
Cotmanhay DE7 41 G1
Coton Cambs. CB23 33 H3
Coton Northants. NN6 31 H1
Coton Staffs. ST18 40 B2
Coton Staffs. B79 40 D5
Coton Staffs. ST20 40 A3
Coton Clanford ST18 40 A3
Coton Hill ST18 40 B2
Coton in the Clay DE6 40 D3
Coton in the Elms DE12 40 E4
Cotonwood Shrop. SY13 38 E2
Cotonwood Staffs. ST20 40 A3
Cott TQ9 5 H4
Cottam Lancs. PR4 55 H6
Cottam Notts. DN22 52 B4
Cottartown PH26 89 H1
Cottenham CB24 33 H2
Cotterdale DL8 61 K7
Cottered SG9 33 G6
Cotteridge B30 30 B1
Cotterstock PE8 42 D6
Cottesbrooke NN6 31 J1
Cottesmore LE15 42 C4
Cottingham E.Riding HU16 59 G6
Cottingham Northants. LE16 42 B6
Cottingley BD16 57 G6
Cottisford NN13 31 G5
Cotton Staffs. ST10 40 C1
Cotton Suff. IP14 34 E2
Cotton End MK45 32 D4
Cottonworth SP11 10 E1
Cottown Aber. AB54 90 D2
Cottown Aber. AB53 99 G6
Cottown Aber. AB51 91 F3
Cotts PL20 4 E4
Cottwood EX18 6 E4
Cotwall TF6 39 F4
Cotwalton ST15 40 B2
Couch's Mill PL22 4 B5
Coughton Here. HR9 28 E6
Coughton Warks. B49 30 B2
Cougie IV4 87 J2
Coulaghailtro PA29 73 F4
Coulags IV54 95 F7
Coulby Newham TS8 63 G5
Coulderton CA22 60 A6
Coull AB34 90 D4
Coulport G84 74 A2
Coulsdon CR5 23 F6
Coulston BA13 20 C6
Coulter ML12 75 J7
Coultershaw Bridge GU28 12 C5
Coultings TA5 19 F7
Coulton YO62 58 C2
Coultra KY15 82 E5
Cound SY5 38 E5
Coundlane SY5 38 E5
Coundon Dur. DL14 62 D4
Coundon W.Mid. CV6 41 F7
Countersett DL8 56 E1
Countess Wear EX2 7 H6
Countesthorpe LE8 41 H6
Countisbury EX35 7 F1
Coup Green PR5 55 J7
Coupar Angus PH13 82 D3
Coupland Cumb. CA16 61 J5
Coupland Northumb. NE71 77 H7
Cour PA28 73 G6
Court Colman CF32 18 B3
Court Henry SA32 17 J3
Court House Green CV6 41 F7
Court-at-Street CT21 15 F4
Courteenhall NN7 31 J3
Courtsend SS3 25 G2
Courtway TA5 8 B1
Cousland EH22 76 B4
Cousley Wood TN5 13 K3
Coustonn PA22 73 J3
Cove Arg. & B. G84 74 A2
Cove Devon EX16 7 H4
Cove Hants. GU14 22 B6
Cove High. IV22 94 E2
Cove Sc.Bord. TD13 77 F3
Cove Bay AB12 91 H4
Cove Bottom NR34 45 J7
Covehithe NR34 45 K7
Coven WV9 40 B5
Coveney CB6 43 H7
Covenham St. Bartholomew LN11 53 G3
Covenham St. Mary LN11 53 G3
COVENTRY CV 30 E1
Coventry Airport CV3 30 E1
Coverack TR12 2 E7
Coverham DL8 57 G1
Covesea IV30 97 J4
Covingham SN3 20 E3
Covington Cambs. PE28 32 D1
Covington S.Lan. ML12 75 H7
Cowan Bridge LA6 56 B2
Cowbeech BN27 13 K5
Cowbit PE12 43 F4
Cowbridge Som. TA24 7 H1
Cowbridge V. of Glam. CF71 18 C4
Cowden TN8 23 H7
Cowden Pound TN8 23 H7
Cowdenbeath KY4 75 K1
Cowdenburn EH46 76 A5
Cowers Lane DE56 41 F1
Cowes PO31 11 F5
Cowesby YO7 57 K1
Cowesfield Green SP5 10 D2
Cowey Green CO7 34 E6
Cowfold RH13 13 F4
Cowgill LA10 56 C1
Cowie Aber. AB39 91 G6
Cowie Stir. FK7 75 G2
Cowlam Manor YO25 59 F3
Cowley Devon EX4 7 H6
Cowley Glos. GL53 29 J7
Cowley Gt.Lon. UB8 22 D3
Cowley Oxon. OX4 21 J1
Cowling Lancs. PR7 48 E1
Cowling N.Yorks. BD22 56 E5
Cowling N.Yorks. DL8 57 H1
Cowlinge CB8 34 B3
Cowmes HD8 50 D1
Cowpe BB4 56 D7
Cowpen NE24 71 H5
Cowpen Bewley TS23 63 F4
Cowplain PO8 11 H3
Cowsden WR7 29 J3
Cowshill DL13 61 K2
Cowthorpe LS22 57 K4
Cox Common IP19 45 H7
Coxbank CW3 39 F1
Coxbench DE21 41 F1
Coxbridge BA6 8 E1
Coxford PE31 44 C3
Coxheath ME17 14 C2
Coxhoe DH6 62 E3
Coxley BA5 19 J7
Coxley Wick BA5 19 J7
Coxpark PL18 4 E3
Coxtie Green CM14 23 J2
Coxwold YO61 58 B2
Coychurch CF35 18 C4
Coylet PA23 73 K2
Coylton KA6 67 J2
Coylumbridge PH22 89 G3
Coynach AB34 90 C4
Coynachie AB54 90 C1
Coytrahen CF32 18 B3
Crabbet Park RH10 13 G3
Crabgate NR11 44 E3
Crabtree Plym. PL3 5 F5
Crabtree S.Yorks. S4 51 F4
Crabtree W.Suss. RH13 13 F4
Crabtree Green LL13 38 C1
Crackaig PA60 72 D4
Crackenthorpe CA16 61 H4
Crackington EX23 4 B1
Crackington Haven EX23 4 B1
Crackley ST5 40 A1
Crackleybank TF11 39 G4
Crackpot DL11 62 A7
Crackthorn Corner IP22 34 E1
Cracoe BD23 56 E3
Craddock EX15 7 J4
Cradhlastadh HS2 100 C4
Cradley Here. WR13 29 G4
Cradley W.Mid. B63 40 B7
Cradley Heath B64 40 B7
Crafthole PL11 4 D5
Crafton LU7 32 B7
Cragg HX7 57 F7
Cragg Hill LS18 57 H6
Craggan Moray AB37 89 J1
Craggan P. & K. PH5 81 K6
Cragganruar PH15 81 H3
Craggie High. IV2 88 E1
Craggie High. KW8 104 D7
Craghead DH9 62 D1
Craibstone Aberdeen AB21 91 G3
Craibstone Moray AB56 98 C5
Craichie DD8 83 G3
Craig Arg. & B. PA35 80 B4
Craig Arg. & B. PA70 79 G4
Craig D. & G. DG7 65 G4
Craig High. IV22 94 D5
Craig High. IV54 95 G7
Craig S.Ayr. KA19 67 H3
Craig Berthlŵyd CF46 18 D2
Craigans PA31 73 G1
Craigbeg PH31 88 B6
Craig-cefn-parc SA6 17 K5
Craigcleuch DG13 69 J5
Craigculter AB43 99 H5
Craigdallie PH14 82 D5
Craigdam AB41 91 G1
Craigdarroch D. & G. DG3 68 C4
Craigdarroch E.Ayr. KA18 68 B3
Craigdhu D. & G. DG8 64 D6
Craigdhu High. IV4 96 B7
Craigearn AB51 91 F3
Craigellachie AB38 97 K7
Craigellie AB43 99 J4
Craigencallie DG7 65 F3
Craigend Moray IV36 97 J6
Craigend P. & K. PH2 82 C5
Craigendive PA23 73 J2
Craigendoran G84 74 B2
Craigengillan KA6 67 J3
Craigenputtock DG2 68 C5
Craigens PA44 72 A4
Craigglas PA31 73 G1
Craighall KY15 83 F6
Craighat G63 74 C2
Craighead Fife KY10 83 H6
Craighead High. IV11 96 E5
Craighlaw DG8 64 D4
Craighouse PA60 72 D4
Craigie Aber. AB23 91 H3
Craigie Dundee DD4 83 F4
Craigie P. & K. PH10 82 C3
Craigie S.Ayr. KA1 74 C7
Craigie Brae AB41 91 G1
Craigieburn DG10 69 G3
Craigieholm PH13 82 C4
Craigielaw EH32 76 C3
Craiglockhart EH14 76 A3
Craiglug AB31 91 G5
Craigmaud AB43 99 G5
Craigmillar EH16 76 A3
Craigmore PA20 73 K4
Craigmyle House AB31 90 E4
Craignafeoch PA21 73 H3
Craignant SY10 38 B2
Craignavie FK21 81 G4
Craigneil KA26 67 F5
Craigneuk ML1 75 F5
Craignure PA65 79 J4
Craigo DD10 83 H1
Craigoch KA19 67 G3
Craigow KY13 82 B7
Craigrothie KY15 82 E6
Craigroy IV36 97 J6
Craigroy Farm AB37 89 J1
Craigruie FK19 81 F5
Craigsanquhar KY15 82 E6
Craigton Aberdeen AB14 91 G4
Craigton Angus DD5 83 G4
Craigton Angus DD8 82 E2
Craigton High. IV1 96 D7
Craigton Stir. G63 74 E2
Craigtown KW13 104 D3
Craig-y-nos SA9 27 H7
Craik Aber. AB54 90 C2
Craik Sc.Bord. TD9 69 J3
Crail KY10 83 H7
Crailing TD8 70 B1
Crailinghall TD8 70 B1
Crakehill YO7 57 K2
Crakemarsh ST14 40 C2
Crambe YO60 58 D3
Cramlington NE23 71 H6
Cramond EH4 75 K3
Cranage CW4 49 G6
Cranberry ST21 40 A2
Cranborne BH21 10 B3
Cranbourne SL4 22 C4
Cranbrook Gt.Lon. IG1 23 H3
Cranbrook Kent TN17 14 C4
Cranbrook Common TN17 14 C4
Crane Moor S35 51 F2
Cranfield MK43 32 C4
Cranford Devon EX39 6 B3
Cranford Gt.Lon. TW5 22 E4
Cranford St. Andrew NN14 32 C1
Cranford St. John NN14 32 C1
Cranham Glos. GL4 29 H7
Cranham Gt.Lon. RM14 23 J3
Crank WA11 48 E3
Cranleigh GU6 12 D3
Cranmer Green IP31 34 E1
Cranmore I.o.W. PO41 10 E6
Cranmore Som. BA4 19 K7
Cranna AB54 98 E5
Crannoch AB55 98 C5
Cranoe LE16 42 A6
Cransford IP13 35 H2
Cranshaws TD11 76 E4
Cranstal IM7 54 D3
Crantock TR8 2 E2
Cranwell NG34 42 D1
Cranwich IP26 44 B6
Cranworth IP25 44 D5
Craobh Haven PA31 79 J7
Crapstone PL20 5 F4
Crarae PA32 73 H1
Crask Inn IV27 103 H6
Crask of Aigas IV4 96 B7
Craskins AB34 90 D4
Craster NE66 71 H2
Craswall HR2 28 B5
Crateford ST19 40 B5
Cratfield IP19 35 H1
Crathes AB31 91 F5
Crathie Aber. AB35 89 K5
Crathie High. PH20 88 C5
Crathorne TS15 63 F6
Craven Arms SY7 38 D7
Craw KA27 73 G6
Crawcrook NE40 71 G7
Crawford Lancs. WN8 48 D2
Crawford S.Lan. ML12 68 E1
Crawfordjohn ML12 68 D1
Crawfordton DG3 68 C4
Crawick DG4 68 C2
Crawley Devon EX14 8 B4
Crawley Hants. SO21 11 F1
Crawley Oxon. OX29 30 E7
Crawley W.Suss. RH11 13 F3
Crawley Down RH10 13 G3
Crawleyside DL13 62 A2
Crawshawbooth BB4 56 D7
Crawton AB39 91 G7
Crawyn IM7 54 C4
Cray N.Yorks. BD23 56 E2
Cray P. & K. PH10 82 C1
Cray Powys LD3 27 H6
Crayford DA1 23 J4
Crayke YO61 58 B2
Crays Hill CM11 24 D2
Cray's Pond RG8 21 K3
Crazies Hill RG10 22 A3
Creacombe EX16 7 G4
Creag Ghoraidh (Creagorry) HS7 92 C7
Creagan PA38 80 A3
Creagbheitheachain PH33 80 A1
Creagorry (Creag Ghoraidh) HS7 92 C7
Creamore Bank SY4 38 E2
Creaton NN6 31 J1
Creca DG12 69 H6
Credenhill HR4 28 D4
Crediton EX17 7 G5
Creebridge DG8 64 E4
Creech Heathfield TA3 8 B2
Creech St. Michael TA3 8 B2
Creed TR2 3 G4
Creedy Park EX17 7 G5
Creekmouth IG11 23 H3
Creeting St. Mary IP6 34 E3
Creeton NG33 42 D3
Creetown DG8 64 E5
Creggans PA27 80 B7
Cregneash IM9 54 A7
Cregrina LD1 28 A3
Creich KY15 82 E5
Creigau NP16 19 H2
Creigiau CF15 18 D3
Crelevan IV4 87 K1
Crelly TR13 2 D5
Cremyll PL10 4 E5
Crendell SP6 10 B3
Cressage SY5 38 E5
Cressbrook SK17 50 D5
Cresselly SA68 16 D5
Cressing CM77 34 B6
Cresswell Northumb. NE61 71 H4
Cresswell Staffs. ST11 40 B2
Cresswell Quay SA68 16 D5
Creswell S80 51 H5
Cretingham IP13 35 G3
Cretshengan PA29 73 F4
CREWE Ches.E. CW 49 G7
Crewe Ches.W. & C. CH3 48 D7
Crewe Green CW1 49 G7
Crewgreen SY5 38 C4
Crewkerne TA18 8 D4
Crew's Hole BS5 19 K4
Crewton DE24 41 F2
Crianlarich FK20 80 E5
Cribbs Causeway BS34 19 J3
Cribyn SA48 26 E3
Criccieth LL52 36 D2
Crich DE4 51 F7
Crich Carr DE4 51 F7
Crich Common DE4 51 F7
Crichie AB42 99 H6
Crichton EH37 76 B4
Crick Mon. NP26 19 H2
Crick Northants. NN6 31 G1
Crickadarn LD2 27 K4
Cricket Hill GU46 22 B5
Cricket St. Thomas TA20 8 C4
Crickham BS28 19 H7
Crickheath SY10 38 B3
Crickhowell NP8 28 B7
Cricklade SN6 20 E2
Cricklewood NW2 23 F3
Crick's Green HR7 29 F3
Criddlestyle SP6 10 C3
Cridling Stubbs WF11 58 B7
Crieff PH7 81 K5
Criftins (Dudleston Heath) SY12 38 C2
Criggan PL26 4 A4
Criggion SY5 38 B4
Crigglestone WF4 51 F1
Crimble OL11 49 H1
Crimchard TA20 8 C4
Crimdon Park TS27 63 F3
Crimond AB43 99 J5
Crimonmogate AB43 99 J5
Crimplesham PE33 44 A5
Crinan PA31 73 F1
Crinan Ferry PA31 73 F1
Cringleford NR4 45 F5
Cringletie EH45 76 A6
Crinow SA67 16 E4
Cripplestyle SP6 10 B3
Cripp's Corner TN32 14 C5
Crix CM3 34 B7
Crizeley HR2 28 D5
Croalchapel DG3 68 E4
Croasdale CA23 60 B5
Crock Street TA19 8 C3
Crockenhill BR8 23 J5
Crocker End RG9 22 A3
Crockerhill PO17 11 G4
Crockernwell EX6 7 F6
Crockerton BA12 20 B7
Crockerton Green BA12 20 B7
Crocketford (Ninemile Bar) DG2 65 J3
Crockey Hill YO19 58 C5
Crockham Hill TN8 23 H6
Crockhurst Street TN11 23 K7
Crockleford Heath CO7 34 E6
Croes Hywel NP7 28 C7
Croes y pant NP4 19 G1
Croesau Bach SY10 38 B3
Croeserw SA13 18 B2
Croesgoch SA62 16 B2
Croes-lan SA44 17 G1
Croesor LL48 37 F1
Croespenmaen NP11 18 E2
Croesyceiliog Carmar. SA32 17 H4
Croesyceiliog Torfaen NP44 19 G2
Croes-y-mwyalch NP44 19 G2
Croesywaun LL55 46 D7
Croford TA4 7 K3
Croft Here. HR6 28 D2
Croft Leics. LE9 41 H6
Croft Lincs. PE24 53 J6
Croft Warr. WA3 49 F3
Croftamie G63 74 C2
Crofthead CA6 69 J6
Croftmore PH18 81 K1
Crofton W.Yorks. WF4 51 F1
Crofton Wilts. SN8 21 F5
Croft-on-Tees DL2 62 D6
Crofts DG7 65 H3
Crofts of Benachielt KW5 105 G5
Crofts of Buinach IV30 97 J6
Crofts of Haddo AB41 91 G1
Crofty SA4 17 J6
Crogen LL21 37 K2
Croggan PA63 79 J5

Cro - Dal


Croglin CA4 61 G2
Croick High. IV24 96 B2
Croick High. KW13 104 D3
Croig PA75 79 F2
Crois Dughaill HS8 84 C3
Croit e Caley IM9 54 B7
Cromarty IV11 96 E5
Crombie KY12 75 J2
Crombie Mill DD7 83 G4
Cromblet AB51 91 F1
Cromdale PH26 89 H2
Cromer Herts. SG2 33 F6
Cromer Norf. NR27 45 G1
Cromford DE4 50 E7
Cromhall GL12 19 K2
Cromhall Common GL12 19 K3
Cromore HS2 101 G5
Crompton Fold OL2 49 J1
Cromwell NG23 51 K6
Cronberry KA18 68 B1
Crondall GU10 22 A7
Cronk-y-Voddy IM6 54 C5
Cronton WA8 48 D4
Crook Cumb. LA8 61 F7
Crook Dur. DL15 62 C3
Crook of Devon KY13 82 B7
Crooked Soley RG17 21 G4
Crookedholm KA3 74 C7
Crookham Northumb. TD12 77 H7
Crookham W.Berks. RG19 21 J5
Crookham Eastfield TD12 77 H7
Crookham Village GU51 22 A6
Crooklands LA7 55 J1
Cropredy OX17 31 F4
Cropston LE7 41 H4
Cropthorne WR10 29 J4
Cropton YO18 58 D1
Cropwell Bishop NG12 41 J2
Cropwell Butler NG12 41 J2
Cros (Cross) HS2 101 H1
Crosbie KA23 74 A6
Crosbost HS2 101 F5
Crosby Cumb. CA15 60 B3
Crosby I.o.M. IM4 54 C6
Crosby Mersey. L23 48 C3
Crosby N.Lincs. DN15 52 B1
Crosby Court DL6 62 E7
Crosby Garrett CA17 61 J6
Crosby Ravensworth CA10 61 H5
Crosby Villa CA15 60 B3
Crosby-on-Eden CA6 60 F1
Croscombe BA5 19 J7
Crosemere SY12 38 D3
Crosland Hill HD4 50 D1
Cross Som. BS26 19 H6
Cross (Cros) W.Isles HS2 101 H1
Cross Ash NP7 28 D7
Cross Bank DY12 29 G1
Cross End Bed. MK44 32 D3
Cross End Essex CO9 34 C5
Cross Foxes Inn LL40 37 G4
Cross Gates LS15 57 J6
Cross Green Devon PL15 6 B7
Cross Green Staffs. WV10 40 B5
Cross Green Suff. IP7 34 D3
Cross Green Suff. IP30 34 C3
Cross Green Suff. IP29 34 C3
Cross Hands Carmar. SA14 17 J4
Cross Hands Pembs. SA67 16 D4
Cross Hill DE5 41 G1
Cross Hills BD20 57 F5
Cross Houses SY5 38 E5
Cross in Hand TN21 13 J4
Cross Inn Cere. SA44 26 C3
Cross Inn Cere. SY23 26 E2
Cross Inn R.C.T. CF72 18 D3
Cross Keys SN13 20 B4
Cross Lane PO30 11 G6
Cross Lane Head WV16 39 G6
Cross Lanes Cornw. TR4 2 E4
Cross Lanes Cornw. TR12 2 D6
Cross Lanes N.Yorks. YO61 58 B3
Cross Lanes Wrex. LL13 38 C1
Cross of Jackston AB51 91 F1
Cross o'th'hands DE56 40 E1
Cross Street IP21 35 F1
Crossaig PA29 73 G6
Crossapol PA78 78 C2
Crossapoll PA77 78 A3
Cross-at-Hand TN12 14 C3
Crossbush BN18 12 D6
Crosscanonby CA15 60 B3
Crossdale Street NR27 45 G2
Crossens PR9 48 C1
Crossflatts BD16 57 G5
Crossford D. & G. DG3 68 D5
Crossford Fife KY12 75 J2
Crossford S.Lan. ML8 75 G6
Crossgate Lincs. PE11 43 F3
Crossgate Staffs. ST11 40 B2
Crossgatehall EH22 76 B4
Crossgates Fife KY4 75 K2
Crossgates N.Yorks. YO12 59 G1
Crossgates P. & K. PH2 82 B5
Crossgates Powys LD1 27 K2
Crossgill LA2 55 J3
Crosshands KA5 74 C7
Crosshill Fife KY5 75 K1
Crosshill S.Ayr. KA19 67 H3
Crosshouse KA2 74 B7
Crosskeys NP11 19 F2
Crosskirk KW14 105 F1
Crosslanes SY10 38 C4
Crosslee Renf. PA6 74 C4
Crosslee Sc.Bord. TD7 69 J2
Crossmichael DG7 65 H4
Crossmoor PR4 55 H6
Crossroads Aber. AB31 91 F5
Crossroads E.Ayr. KA1 74 C7
Crossway Mon. NP25 28 D7
Crossway Powys LD1 27 K3
Crossway Green Mon. NP16 19 J2
Crossway Green Worcs. DY13 29 H2
Crossways Dorset DT2 9 G6
Crossways Glos. GL16 28 E7
Crosswell SA41 16 E2
Crosswood SY23 27 F1
Crosthwaite LA8 60 F7
Croston PR26 48 D1
Crostwick NR12 45 G4
Crostwight NR28 45 H3
Crothair HS2 100 D4
Crouch TN15 23 K6
Crouch End N8 23 F3
Crouch Hill DT9 9 G3
Croucheston SP5 10 B2
Croughton NN13 31 G5
Crovie AB45 99 G4
Crow BH24 10 C4
Crow Edge S36 50 D2
Crow Green CM15 23 J2
Crow Hill HR9 29 F6
Crowan TR14 2 D5
Crowborough TN6 13 J3
Crowborough Warren TN6 13 J3
Crowcombe TA4 7 K2
Crowdecote SK17 50 D6
Crowden SK13 50 C3
Crowdhill SO50 11 F2
Crowell OX39 22 A2
Crowfield Northants. NN13 31 H4
Crowfield Suff. IP6 35 F3
Crowhurst E.Suss. TN33 14 C6
Crowhurst Surr. RH7 23 G7
Crowhurst Lane End RH7 23 G7
Crowland Lincs. PE6 43 F4
Crowland Suff. IP31 34 E1
Crowlas TR20 2 C5
Crowle N.Lincs. DN17 51 K1
Crowle Worcs. WR7 29 J3
Crowle Green WR7 29 J3
Crowmarsh Gifford OX10 21 K3
Crown Corner IP13 35 G1
Crownhill PL6 4 E5
Crownthorpe NR18 44 E5
Crowntown TR13 2 D5
Crow's Nest PL14 4 C4
Crows-an-wra TR19 2 A6
Crowsnest SY5 38 C5
Crowthorne RG45 22 B5
Crowton CW8 48 E5
Croxall WS13 40 E4
Croxby LN7 52 E3
Croxdale DH6 62 D3
Croxden ST14 40 C2
Croxley Green WD3 22 D2
Croxton Cambs. PE19 33 F3
Croxton N.Lincs. DN39 52 D1
Croxton Norf. IP24 44 C7
Croxton Staffs. ST21 39 G2
Croxton Green SY14 48 E7
Croxton Kerrial NG32 42 B3
Croxtonbank ST21 39 G2
Croy High. IV2 96 E7
Croy N.Lan. G65 75 F3
Croyde EX33 6 C2
Croyde Bay EX33 6 C2
Croydon Cambs. SG8 33 G4
CROYDON Gt.Lon. CR 23 G5
Cruach PA43 72 B5
Cruchie AB54 98 D6
Cruckmeole SY5 38 D5
Cruckton SY5 38 D4
Cruden Bay AB42 91 J1
Crudgington TF6 39 F4
Crudwell SN16 20 C2
Crug LD1 28 A1
Crugmeer PL28 3 G1
Crugybar SA19 17 K2
Crùlabhig HS2 100 D4
Crumlin NP11 19 F2
Crumpsall M8 49 H2
Crumpsbrook DY14 29 F1
Crundale Kent CT4 15 F3
Crundale Pembs. SA62 16 C4
Crunwere Farm SA67 16 E4
Crutherland Farm G75 74 E5
Cruwys Morchard EX16 7 G4
Crux Easton RG20 21 H6
Crwbin SA17 17 H4
Cryers Hill HP15 22 B2
Crymlyn LL33 46 E5
Crymych SA41 16 E2
Crynant SA10 18 A1
Crystal Palace SE26 23 G4
Cuaig IV54 94 D6
Cubbington CV32 30 E2
Cubert TR8 2 E3
Cubley S36 50 E2
Cublington Bucks. LU7 32 B6
Cublington Here. HR2 28 D5
Cuckfield RH17 13 G4
Cucklington BA9 9 G2
Cuckney NG20 51 H5
Cuckold's Green NR34 45 J7
Cuckoo Bridge PE11 43 F3
Cuckoo's Corner GU34 22 A7
Cuckoo's Nest CH4 48 C6
Cuddesdon OX44 21 J1
Cuddington Bucks. HP18 31 J7
Cuddington Ches.W. & C. CW8 48 E5
Cuddington Heath SY14 38 D1
Cuddy Hill PR4 55 H6
Cudham TN14 23 H6
Cudlipptown PL19 5 F3
Cudworth S.Yorks. S72 51 F2
Cudworth Som. TA19 8 C3
Cuerdley Cross WA5 48 E4
Cuffley EN6 23 G1
Cuidhaseadair HS2 101 H2
Cuidhir HS9 84 B4
Cuidhtinis (Quidinish) HS3 93 F3
Cuidrach IV51 93 J6
Cuilmuich PA24 73 K1
Cuil-uaine PA37 80 A4
Culag G83 74 B1
Culbo IV7 96 D5
Culbokie IV7 96 D6
Culbone TA24 7 G1
Culburnie IV4 96 B7
Culcabock IV2 96 D7
Culcharan PA37 80 A4
Culcharry IV12 97 F6
Culcheth WA3 49 F3
Culdrain AB54 90 D1
Culduie IV54 94 D7
Culford IP28 34 C2
Culfordheath IP31 34 C1
Culgaith CA10 61 H4
Culgower KW8 104 E7
Culham OX14 21 J2
Culindrach PA29 73 H5
Culkein IV27 102 C5
Culkerton GL8 20 C2
Cullachie PH24 89 G2
Cullen AB56 98 D4
Cullercoats NE30 71 J6
Cullicudden IV7 96 D5
Culligran IV4 95 K7
Cullingworth BD13 57 F6
Cullipool PA34 79 J6
Cullivoe ZE2 107 P2
Culloch PH6 81 J6
Culloden IV2 96 E7
Cullompton EX15 7 J5
Culmaily KW10 97 F2
Culmalzie DG8 64 D5
Culmington SY8 38 D7
Culmstock EX15 7 K4
Culnacraig IV26 95 G1
Culnadalloch PA37 80 A4
Culnaknock IV51 94 B5
Culnamean IV47 85 K2
Culpho IP6 35 G4
Culquhirk DG8 64 E5
Culrain IV24 96 C2
Culross KY12 75 H2
Culroy KA19 67 H2
Culsh AB35 90 B5
Culshabbin DG8 64 D5
Culswick ZE2 107 L8
Culter Allers Farm ML12 75 J7
Cultercullen AB41 91 H2
Cults Aber. AB54 90 D1
Cults Aberdeen AB15 91 G4
Cults D. & G. DG8 64 E6
Cultybraggan Camp PH6 81 J6
Culverhouse Cross CF5 18 E4
Culverstone Green DA13 24 C5
Culverthorpe NG32 42 D1
Culvie AB54 98 D5
Culworth OX17 31 G4
Cumberhead ML11 75 F7
Cumberlow Green SG9 33 G5
Cumbernauld G67 75 F3
Cumberworth LN13 53 J5
Cuminestown AB53 99 G6
Cumloden DG8 64 E4
Cummersdale CA2 60 E1
Cummertrees DG12 69 G7
Cummingstown IV30 97 J5
Cumnock KA18 67 K1
Cumnor OX2 21 H1
Cumrew CA8 61 G1
Cumrue DG11 69 F5
Cumstoun DG6 65 G5
Cumwhinton CA4 61 F1
Cumwhitton CA8 61 G1
Cundall YO61 57 K2
Cunninghamhead KA3 74 B6
Cunningsburgh ZE2 107 N10
Cunnister ZE2 107 P3
Cunnoquhie KY15 82 E6
Cupar KY15 82 E6
Cupar Muir KY15 82 E6
Curbar S32 50 E5
Curborough WS13 40 D4
Curbridge Hants. SO30 11 G3
Curbridge Oxon. OX29 21 G1
Curdridge SO32 11 G3
Curdworth B76 40 D6
Curland TA3 8 B3
Curlew Green IP17 35 H2
Curling Tye Green CM9 24 E1
Curload TA3 8 C2
Curridge RG18 21 H4
Currie EH14 75 K4
Curry Mallet TA3 8 C2
Curry Rivel TA10 8 C2
Curteis' Corner TN27 14 D4
Curtisden Green TN17 14 C3
Curtisknowle TQ9 5 H5
Cury TR12 2 D6
Cusgarne TR4 2 E4
Cushnie AB45 99 F4
Cushuish TA2 7 K2
Cusop HR3 28 B4
Cusworth DN5 51 H2
Cutcloy DG8 64 E7
Cutcombe TA24 7 H2
Cutgate OL11 49 H1
Cuthill IV25 96 E3
Cutiau LL42 37 F4
Cutlers Green CM6 33 J5
Cutnall Green WR9 29 H2
Cutsdean GL54 30 B5
Cutsyke WF10 57 K7
Cutthorpe S42 51 F5
Cutts ZE1 107 N9
Cuttyhill AB42 99 J5
Cuxham OX49 21 K2
Cuxton ME2 24 D5
Cuxwold LN7 52 E2
Cwm B.Gwent NP23 18 E1
Cwm Denb. LL18 47 J5
Cwm Ffrwd-oer NP4 19 F1
Cwm Gwaun SA65 16 D2
Cwm Head SY6 38 D7
Cwm Irfon LD5 27 H4
Cwm Penmachno LL24 37 G1
Cwm Plysgog SA43 16 E1
Cwmafan SA12 18 A2
Cwmaman CF44 18 D2
Cwmann SA48 17 J1
Cwmbach Carmar. SA34 17 F3
Cwmbach Carmar. SA15 17 H5
Cwmbach Powys HR3 28 A5
Cwmbach Powys LD2 27 K3
Cwmbach R.C.T. CF44 18 D1
Cwmbelan SY18 37 J7
Cwmbrân NP44 19 F2
Cwmbrwyno SY23 37 G7
Cwmcarn NP11 19 F2
Cwmcarvan NP25 19 H1
Cwm-Cewydd SY20 37 H4
Cwm-cou SA38 17 F1
Cwmcrawnon LD3 28 A7
Cwmdare CF44 18 C1
Cwmdu Carmar. SA19 17 K2
Cwmdu Powys NP8 28 A6
Cwmduad SA33 17 G2
Cwmerfyn SY23 37 G7
Cwmfelin CF46 18 D1
Cwmfelin Boeth SA34 16 E4
Cwmfelin Mynach SA34 17 F3
Cwmfelinfach NP11 18 E2
Cwmffrwd SA31 17 H4
Cwmgiedd SA9 27 G7
Cwmgors SA18 27 G7
Cwmgwili SA14 17 J4
Cwmgwrach SA11 18 B1
Cwmgwyn SA2 17 K6
Cwmhiraeth SA44 17 G2
Cwmifor SA19 17 K3
Cwmisfael SA32 17 H4
Cwm-Llinau SY20 37 H5
Cwmllyfri SA33 17 G4
Cwmllynfell SA9 27 G7
Cwm-mawr SA14 17 J4
Cwm-miles SA34 16 E3
Cwm-Morgan SA38 17 F2
Cwm-parc CF42 18 C2
Cwmpengraig SA44 17 G2
Cwmpennar CF45 18 D1
Cwmsychbant SA40 17 H1
Cwmsymlog SY23 37 F7
Cwmtillery NP13 19 F1
Cwm-twrch Isaf SA9 27 G7
Cwm-twrch Uchaf SA9 27 G7
Cwm-y-glo LL55 46 D6
Cwmyoy NP7 28 C6
Cwm-yr-Eglwys SA42 16 D1
Cwmyrhaiadr SY20 37 G6
Cwmystwyth SY23 27 G1
Cwrt SY20 37 F5
Cwrt-newydd SA40 17 H1
Cwrt-y-cadno SA19 17 K1
Cwrt-y-gollen NP8 28 B7
Cydweli (Kidwelly) SA17 17 H5
Cyffylliog LL15 47 J7
Cyfronydd SY21 38 A5
Cymau LL11 48 B7
Cymmer N.P.T. SA13 18 B2
Cymmer R.C.T. CF39 18 D2
Cyncoed CF23 18 E3
Cynghordy SA20 27 H5
Cynheidre SA15 17 H5
Cynwyd LL21 37 K1
Cynwyl Elfed SA33 17 G3


## D


Dabton DG3 68 D4
Daccombe TQ12 5 K4
Dacre Cumb. CA11 61 F4
Dacre N.Yorks. HG3 57 G3
Dacre Banks HG3 57 G3
Daddry Shield DL13 61 K3
Dadford MK18 31 H5
Dadlington CV13 41 G6
Dafen SA14 17 J5
Daffy Green IP25 44 D5
Dagdale ST14 40 C2
Dagenham RM10 23 H3
Daggons SP6 10 C3
Daglingworth GL7 20 C1
Dagnall HP4 32 C7
Dail PA35 80 B4
Dail Beag HS2 100 E3
Dail Bho Dheas (South Dell) HS2 101 G1
Dail Bho Thuath (North Dell) HS2 101 G1
Dail Mòr HS2 100 E3
Dailly KA26 67 G3
Dailnamac PA35 80 A4
Dainton TQ12 5 J4
Dairsie (Osnaburgh) KY15 83 F6
Dairy House HU12 59 J7
Daisy Bank WS5 40 C6
Daisy Green IP31 34 E2
Dalabrog HS8 84 C2
Dalavich PA35 80 A6
Dalballoch PH20 88 D5
Dalbeattie DG5 65 J4
Dalblair KA18 68 B2
Dalbog DD9 90 D7
Dalbreck IV28 104 C7
Dalbury DE6 40 E2
Dalby I.o.M. IM5 54 B6
Dalby Lincs. PE23 53 H6
Dalby N.Yorks. YO60 58 C2
Dalcairnie KA6 67 J3
Dalchalloch PH18 81 J1
Dalchalm KW9 97 G1
Dalchenna PA32 80 B7
Dalchirach AB37 89 J1
Dalchork IV27 103 H7
Dalchreichart IV63 87 J3
Dalchruin PH6 81 J6
Dalcross IV2 96 E7
Dalderby LN9 53 F6
Dalditch EX9 7 J7
Daldownie AB35 89 K4
Dale Cumb. CA4 61 G2
Dale Gt.Man. OL3 49 J2
Dale Pembs. SA62 16 B5
Dale Abbey DE7 41 G2
Dale End Derbys. DE45 50 E6
Dale End N.Yorks. BD20 56 E5
Dale Head CA10 60 F5
Dale of Walls ZE2 107 K7
Dale Park BN18 12 C5
Dalehouse TS13 63 J5
Dalelia PH36 79 J1
Daless IV12 89 F1
Dalestie AB37 89 J3
Dalfad AB35 90 B4
Dalganachan KW12 105 F4
Dalgarven KA13 74 A6
Dalgety Bay KY11 75 K2
Dalgig KA18 67 K2
Dalginross PH6 81 J5
Dalgonar DG3 68 C3
Dalguise PH8 82 A3
Dalhalvaig KW13 104 D3
Dalham CB8 34 B2
Daligan G84 74 B2
Dalinlongart PA23 73 K2
Dalivaddy PA28 66 A1
Daljarrock KA26 67 F5
Dalkeith EH22 76 B4
Dallachulish PA37 80 A3
Dallas IV36 97 J6
Dallaschyle IV12 97 F7
Dallash DG8 64 E4
Dalleagles KA18 67 K2
Dallinghoo IP13 35 G3
Dallington E.Suss. TN21 13 K5
Dallington Northants. NN5 31 J2
Dallow HG4 57 G2
Dalmadilly AB51 91 F3
Dalmally PA33 80 C5
Dalmarnock PH8 82 B3
Dalmary FK8 74 D1
Dalmellington KA6 67 J3
Dalmeny EH30 75 K3
Dalmichy IV27 103 H7
Dalmigavie IV13 88 E3
Dalmore IV17 96 D5
Dalmuir G81 74 C3
Dalmunzie House Hotel PH10 89 H7
Dalnabreck PH36 79 J1
Dalnacarn PH10 82 B1
Dalnaglar Castle PH10 82 C1
Dalnaha PA63 79 H5
Dalnahaitnach PH23 89 F3
Dalnamain IV25 96 E2
Dalnatrat PA38 80 A2
Dalnavert PH21 89 F4
Dalnavie IV17 96 D4
Dalness PH49 80 C2
Dalnessie IV27 103 J7
Dalnigap DG8 64 B3
Dalqueich KY13 82 B7
Dalreoch KA26 67 F5
Dalriech PH8 81 J4
Dalroy IV2 96 E7
Dalrulzian PH10 82 C2
Dalry KA24 74 A6
Dalrymple KA6 67 H2
Dalscote NN12 31 H3
Dalserf ML9 75 F5
Dalsetter ZE2 107 P3
Dalshangan DG7 67 K5
Dalskairth DG2 65 K3
Dalston CA5 60 E1
Dalswinton DG2 68 E5
Daltomach IV13 88 E2
Dalton Cumb. LA6 55 J2
Dalton D. & G. DG11 69 G6
Dalton Lancs. WN8 48 D2
Dalton N.Yorks. YO7 57 K2
Dalton N.Yorks. DL11 62 C6
Dalton Northumb. NE18 71 G6
Dalton Northumb. NE46 62 A1
Dalton S.Yorks. S65 51 G3
Dalton Magna S65 51 G3
Dalton Piercy TS27 63 F3
Dalton-in-Furness LA15 55 F2
Dalton-le-Dale SR7 63 F2
Dalton-on-Tees DL2 62 D6
Daltote PA31 73 F2
Daltra IV12 97 G7
Dalveich FK19 81 H5
Dalvennan KA19 67 H2
Dalvourn IV2 88 D1
Dalwhinnie PH19 88 D6
Dalwood EX13 8 B4

Dam - Dra


Dam Green NR16 44 E7
Damask Green SG4 33 F6
Damerham SP6 10 C3
Damgate NR13 45 J5
Damnaglaur DG9 64 B7
Damside PH3 82 A6
Danaway ME9 24 E5
Danbury CM3 24 D1
Danby YO21 63 J6
Danby Wiske DL7 62 E7
Dancers Hill EN5 23 F2
Dandaleith AB38 97 K7
Danderhall EH22 76 B4
Dane Bank M34 49 J3
Dane End SG12 33 G6
Dane Hills LE3 41 H5
Danebridge SK11 49 J6
Danehill RH17 13 H4
Danesmoor S45 51 G6
Danestone AB22 91 H3
Daniel's Water TN26 14 E3
Danskine EH41 76 D4
Danthorpe HU12 59 J6
Danzey Green B94 30 C2
Darby End B64 40 B7
Darby Green GU46 22 B5
Darenth DA2 23 J4
Daresbury WA4 48 E4
Darfield S73 51 G2
Dargate ME13 25 G5
Dargues NE19 70 D4
Darite PL14 4 C4
Darland ME7 24 D5
Darlaston WS10 40 B6
Darley HG3 57 H4
Darley Bridge DE4 50 E6
Darley Dale DE4 50 E6
Darley Head HG3 57 G4
Darley Hillside DE4 50 E6
Darlingscott CV36 30 D4
**DARLINGTON DL 62 D5**
Darliston SY13 38 E2
Darlton NG22 51 K5
Darnabo AB53 99 F6
Darnall S9 51 F4
Darnconner KA18 67 K1
Darnford AB31 91 F5
Darngarroch DG7 65 G4
Darnick TD6 76 D7
Darowen SY20 37 H5
Darra AB53 99 F6
Darracott EX39 6 A4
Darras Hall NE20 71 G6
Darrington WF8 51 G1
Darrow Green IP20 45 G7
Darsham IP17 35 J2
Dartfield AB43 99 J5
**DARTFORD DA 23 J4**
Dartington TQ9 5 H4
Dartmeet TQ13 5 G3
**Dartmouth TQ6 5 J5**
Darton S75 51 F1
**Darvel KA17 74 D7**
Darvell TN32 14 C5
Darwell Hole TN33 13 K5
**Darwen BB3 56 B7**
Datchet SL3 22 C4
Datchworth SG3 33 F7
Datchworth Green SG3 33 F7
Daubhill BL3 49 F2
Daugh of Kinermony AB38 97 K7
Dauntsey SN15 20 C3
Dauntsey Green SN15 20 C3
Dauntsey Lock SN15 20 C3
Dava PH26 89 H1
Davaar PA28 66 B2
Davan AB34 90 C4
Davenham CW9 49 F5
Davenport Green WA15 49 H4
**Daventry NN11 31 G2**
Davidstow PL32 4 B2
Davington DG13 69 H3
Daviot *Aber.* AB51 91 F2
Daviot *High.* IV2 88 E1
Davoch of Grange AB55 98 C5
Davyhulme M41 49 G3
Dawley TF4 39 F5
**Dawlish EX7 5 K3**
Dawn LL22 47 G5
Daws Heath SS7 24 E3
Daw's House PL15 6 B7
Dawsmere PE12 43 H2
Day Green CW11 49 G7
Dayhills ST15 40 B2
Dayhouse Bank B62 29 J1
Daylesford GL56 30 D6
Ddôl CH7 47 K5
Deadman's Cross MK45 32 E4
Deadwaters ML11 75 F6
**Deal CT14 15 J2**
Deal Hall CM0 25 G2
Dean *Cumb.* CA14 60 B4
Dean *Devon* TQ11 5 H4
Dean *Dorset* SP5 9 J3
Dean *Hants.* SO32 11 G3
Dean *Oxon.* OX7 30 E6
Dean *Som.* BA4 19 K7
Dean Bank DL17 62 D3
Dean Cross EX34 6 D1
Dean Head S35 50 E2
Dean Prior TQ11 5 H4
Dean Row SK9 49 H4
Dean Street ME15 14 C2
Deanburnhaugh TD9 69 J2
Deane *Gt.Man.* BL3 49 F2
Deane *Hants.* RG25 21 J6
Deanland SP5 9 J3
Deanlane End PO9 11 J3
Deans Bottom ME9 24 E5
Deanscales CA13 60 B4
Deansgreen WA13 49 F4
Deanshanger MK19 31 J5
Deanston FK16 81 J7
Dearham CA15 60 B3
Debach IP13 35 G3
Debate DG11 69 H5
Debden CB11 33 J5
Debden Cross CB11 33 J5
Debden Green *Essex* CB11 33 J5
Debden Green *Essex* IG10 23 H2
Debenham IP14 35 F2
Deblin's Green WR2 29 H4
Dechmont EH52 75 J3
Decker Hill TF11 39 G4
Deddington OX15 31 F5
Dedham CO7 34 E5
Dedham Heath CO7 34 E5
Dedworth SL4 22 C4
Deecastle AB34 90 C5
Deene NN17 42 C6
Deenethorpe NN17 42 C6
Deepcar S36 50 E3
Deepcut GU16 22 C6
Deepdale *Cumb.* LA10 56 C1
Deepdale *N.Yorks.* BD23 56 D2
Deeping Gate PE6 42 E5
Deeping St. James PE6 42 E5
Deeping St. Nicholas PE11 43 F4
Deepweir NP26 19 H3
Deerhill AB55 98 C5
Deerhurst GL19 29 H6
Deerhurst Walton GL19 29 H6
Deerton Street ME9 25 F5
Defford WR8 29 J4
Defynnog LD3 27 J6
Deganwy LL31 47 F5
Degnish PA34 79 J6
Deighton *N.Yorks.* DL6 62 E6
Deighton *W.Yorks.* HD2 50 D1
Deighton *York* YO19 58 C5
Deiniolen LL55 46 D6
**Delabole PL33 4 A2**
Delamere CW8 48 E6
Delavorar AB37 89 J3
Delfrigs AB23 91 H2
Dell Lodge PH25 89 H3
Dell Quay PO20 12 B6
Delliefure PH26 89 H1
Delly End OX29 30 E7
Delnabo AB37 89 J3
Delny IV18 96 E4
Delph OL3 49 J2
Delphorrie AB33 90 C3
Delves DH8 62 C2
Delvine PH1 82 C3
Dembleby NG34 42 D2
Denaby DN12 51 G3
Denaby Main DN12 51 G3
**Denbigh (Dinbych) LL16 47 J6**
Denbury TQ12 5 J4
Denby DE5 41 F1
Denby Dale HD8 50 E2
Denchworth OX12 21 G2
Dendron LA12 55 F2
Denend AB54 90 E1
Denford NN14 32 C1
Dengie CM0 25 F1
Denham *Bucks.* UB9 22 D3
Denham *Suff.* IP21 35 F1
Denham *Suff.* IP29 34 B2
Denham Green UB9 22 D3
Denham Street IP23 35 F1
Denhead *Aber.* AB51 91 F3
Denhead *Aber.* AB42 99 J5
Denhead *Fife* KY16 83 F6
Denhead of Arbirlot DD11 83 G3
Denhead of Gray DD2 82 E4
Denholm TD9 70 A2
Denholme BD13 57 F6
Denholme Clough BD13 57 F6
Denio LL53 36 C2
Denmead PO7 11 H3
Denmill AB51 91 G3
Denmoss AB54 98 E6
Dennington IP13 35 G2
**Denny FK6 75 G2**
Dennyloanhead FK4 75 G2
Denshaw OL3 49 J1
Denside AB31 91 G5
Densole CT18 15 H3
Denston CB8 34 B3
Denstone ST14 40 C1
Dent LA10 56 C1
Denton *Cambs.* PE7 42 E7
Denton *Darl.* DL2 62 D5
Denton *E.Suss.* BN9 13 H6
Denton *Gt.Man.* M34 49 J3
Denton *Kent* CT4 15 H3
Denton *Kent* DA12 24 C4
Denton *Lincs.* NG32 42 B2
Denton *N.Yorks.* LS29 57 G5
Denton *Norf.* IP20 45 G7
Denton *Northants.* NN7 32 B3
Denton *Oxon.* OX44 21 J1
Denton's Green WA10 48 D3
Denver PE38 44 A5
Denvilles PO9 11 J4
Denwick NE66 71 H2
Deopham NR18 44 E5
Deopham Green NR18 44 E6
Depden IP29 34 B3
Depden Green IP29 34 B3
Deptford *Gt.Lon.* SE8 23 G4
Deptford *Wilts.* BA12 10 B1
**DERBY DE 41 F2**
Derbyhaven IM9 54 B7
**Dereham (East Dereham) NR19 44 D4**
Dererach PA70 79 G5
Deri CF81 18 E1
Derril EX22 6 B5
Derringstone CT4 15 H3
Derrington ST18 40 A3
Derriton EX22 6 B5
Derry FK19 81 H5
Derry Hill SN11 20 C4
Derrythorpe DN17 52 B2
Dersingham PE31 44 A2
Dervaig PA75 79 F2
Derwen LL21 47 J7
Derwenlas SY20 37 G6
Derwydd SA18 17 K4
Derybruich PA21 73 H3
Desborough NN14 42 B7
Desford LE9 41 G5
Detchant NE70 77 J7
Dethick DE4 51 F7
Detling ME14 14 C2
Deuddwr SY22 38 B4
Deunant LL16 47 H6
Deuxhill WV16 39 F7
Devauden NP16 19 H2
Devil's Bridge (Pontarfynach) SY23 27 G1
Devitts Green CV7 40 E6
**Devizes SN10 20 D5**
Devonport PL1 4 E5
Devonside FK13 75 H1
Devoran TR3 2 E5
Dewar EH38 76 B6
Dewlish DT2 9 G5
Dewsall Court HR2 28 D5
**Dewsbury WF12 57 H7**
Dewsbury Moor WF15 57 H7
Dhiseig PA68 79 F4
Dhoon IM7 54 D5
Dhoor IM7 54 D4
Dhowin IM7 54 D3
Dhuhallow IV2 88 C2
Dial Green GU28 12 C4
Dial Post RH13 12 E5
Dibden SO45 11 F4
Dibden Hill HP8 22 C2
Dibden Purlieu SO45 11 F4
Dickleburgh IP21 45 F7
Dickleburgh Moor IP21 45 F7
Didbrook GL54 30 B5
**Didcot OX11 21 J2**
Diddington PE19 32 E2
Diddlebury SY7 38 E7
Didley HR2 28 D5
Didling GU29 12 B5
Didmarton GL9 20 B3
Didsbury M20 49 H3
Didworthy TQ10 5 G4
Digby LN4 52 D7
Digg IV51 93 K5
Diggle OL3 50 C2
Digmoor WN8 48 D2
Digswell AL6 33 F7
Dihewyd SA48 26 D3
Dildawn DG7 65 H5
Dilham NR28 45 H3
Dilhorne ST10 40 B1
Dillington PE19 32 E2
Dilston NE45 70 E7
Dilton Marsh BA13 20 B7
Dilwyn HR4 28 D3
Dilwyn Common HR4 28 D3
Dimple BL7 49 G1
Dinas *Carmar.* SA33 17 F2
Dinas *Gwyn.* LL54 46 C7
Dinas *Gwyn.* LL53 36 B2
Dinas Cross SA42 16 D2
Dinas Dinlle LL54 46 C7
**Dinas Powys CF64 18 E4**
Dinas-Mawddwy SY20 37 H4
**Dinbych (Denbigh) LL16 47 J6**
**Dinbych-y-pysgod (Tenby) SA70 16 E5**
Dinckley BB6 56 B6
Dinder BA5 19 J7
Dinedor HR2 28 E5
Dingestow NP25 28 D7
Dingley LE16 42 A7
**Dingwall IV15 96 C6**
Dinlabyre TD9 70 A4
Dinnet AB34 90 C5
Dinnington *S.Yorks.* S25 51 H4
Dinnington *Som.* TA17 8 D3
Dinnington *T.& W.* NE13 71 H6
Dinorwig LL55 46 D6
Dinton *Bucks.* HP17 31 J7
Dinton *Wilts.* SP3 10 B1
Dinvin DG9 64 A5
Dinwoodie Mains DG11 69 G4
Dinworthy EX22 6 B4
Dipford TA3 8 B2
Dippen *Arg. & B.* PA28 73 F7
Dippen *N.Ayr.* KA27 66 E1
Dippenhall GU10 22 B7
Dipple *Moray* IV32 98 B5
Dipple *S.Ayr.* KA26 67 G3
Diptford TQ9 5 H5
Dipton DH9 62 C1
Dirdhu PH26 89 H2
Dirleton EH39 76 D2
Discoed LD8 28 B2
Diseworth DE74 41 G3
Dishes KW17 106 F5
Dishforth YO7 57 J2
Dishley LE11 41 H3
Disley SK12 49 J4
**Diss IP22 45 F7**
Disserth LD1 27 K3
Distington CA14 60 B4
Ditcheat BA4 9 F1
Ditchingham NR35 45 H6
Ditchley OX29 30 E6
Ditchling BN6 13 G5
Ditteridge SN13 20 B5
Dittisham TQ6 5 J5
Ditton *Halton* WA8 48 D4
Ditton *Kent* ME20 14 C2
Ditton Green CB8 33 K3
Ditton Priors WV16 39 F7
Dixton *Glos.* GL20 29 J5
Dixton *Mon.* NP25 28 E7
Dobcross OL3 49 J2
Dobwalls PL14 4 C4
**Doc Penfro (Pembroke Dock) SA72 16 C5**
Doccombe TQ13 7 F7
Dochgarroch IV3 88 D1
Dockenfield GU10 22 B7
Docker *Cumb.* LA8 61 G7
Docker *Lancs.* LA6 55 J2
Docking PE31 44 B2
Docklow HR6 28 E3
Dockray *Cumb.* CA11 60 E4
Dockray *Cumb.* CA7 60 D1
Dodbrooke TQ7 5 H6
Doddenham WR6 29 G3
Doddinghurst CM15 23 J2
Doddington *Cambs.* PE15 43 H6
Doddington *Kent* ME9 14 E2
Doddington *Lincs.* LN6 52 C5
Doddington *Northumb.* NE71 77 H7
Doddington *Shrop.* DY14 29 F1
Doddiscombsleigh EX6 7 G7
Doddycross PL14 4 D4
Dodford *Northants.* NN7 31 H2
Dodford *Worcs.* B61 29 J1
Dodington *S.Glos.* BS37 20 A3
Dodington *Som.* TA5 7 K1
Dodington Ash BS37 20 A4
Dodleston CH4 48 C6
Dods Leigh ST10 40 C2
Dodscott EX38 6 D4
Dodworth S75 51 F2
Doehole DE55 51 F7
Doffcocker BL1 49 F1
Dog Village EX5 7 H6
Dogdyke LN4 53 F7
Dogmersfield RG27 22 A6
Dogsthorpe PE1 43 F5
Dol Fawr SY19 37 H5
Dolanog SY21 37 K4
Dolau *Powys* LD1 28 A2
Dolau *R.C.T.* CF72 18 D3
Dolbenmaen LL51 36 E1
Doley ST20 39 G3
Dolfach SY18 27 J1
Dolfor SY16 38 A7
Dolgarreg SA20 27 G5
Dolgarrog LL32 47 F6
**Dolgellau LL40 37 G4**
Dolgoch LL36 37 F5
Dolgran SA39 17 H2
Doll KW9 97 F1
**Dollar FK14 75 H1**
Dollarbeg FK14 75 H1
Dolphin CH8 47 K5
Dolphinholme LA2 55 J4
Dolphinton EH46 75 K6
Dolton EX19 6 D4
Dolwen *Conwy* LL22 47 G5
Dolwen *Powys* SY21 37 J5
**Dolwyddelan LL25 47 F7**
Dôl-y-bont SY24 37 F7
Dol-y-cannau HR5 28 A4
Dolyhir LD8 28 B3
Dolywern LL20 38 B2
Domgay SY22 38 B4
**DONCASTER DN 51 H2**
Donhead St. Andrew SP7 9 J2
Donhead St. Mary SP7 9 J2
Donibristle KY4 75 K2
Doniford TA23 7 J1
Donington *Lincs.* PE11 43 F2
Donington *Shrop.* WV7 40 A5
Donington le Heath LE67 41 G4
Donington on Bain LN11 53 F4
Donisthorpe DE12 41 F4
Donna Nook LN11 53 H3
Donnington *Glos.* GL56 30 C6
Donnington *Here.* HR8 29 G5
Donnington *Shrop.* SY5 38 E5
Donnington *Tel. & W.* TF2 39 G4
Donnington *W.Berks.* RG14 21 H5
Donnington *W.Suss.* PO20 12 B6
Donyatt TA19 8 C3
**DORCHESTER *Dorset* DT 9 F5**
Dorchester *Oxon.* OX10 21 J2
Dordon B78 40 E5
Dore S17 51 F4
Dores IV2 88 C1
Dorket Head NG5 41 H1
**Dorking RH4 22 E7**
Dorley's Corner IP17 35 H2
Dormans Park RH19 23 G7
Dormansland RH7 23 H7
Dormanstown TS10 63 G4
Dormer's Wells UB1 22 E3
Dormington HR1 28 E4
Dormston WR7 29 J3
Dorn GL56 30 D5
Dorney SL4 22 C4
Dorney Reach SL6 22 C4
Dornie IV40 86 E2
**Dornoch IV25 96 E3**
Dornock DG12 69 H7
Dorrery KW12 105 F3
Dorridge B93 30 C1
Dorrington *Lincs.* LN4 52 D7
Dorrington *Shrop.* SY5 38 D5
Dorsell AB33 90 D3
Dorsington CV37 30 C4
Dorstone HR3 28 C4
Dorton HP18 31 H7
Dorusduain IV40 87 F2
Dosthill B77 40 E6
Dotland NE46 62 A1
Dottery DT6 8 D5
Doublebois PL14 4 B4
Dougalston G62 74 D3
Dougarie KA27 73 G7
Doughton GL8 20 B2
Douglas *I.o.M.* IM1 54 C6
Douglas *S.Lan.* ML11 75 G7
Douglas & Angus DD5 83 F4
Douglas Water ML11 75 G7
Douglastown DD8 83 F3
Doulting BA4 19 K7
Dounby KW17 106 B5
Doune *Arg. & B.* G83 74 B1
Doune *Arg. & B.* FK17 80 E6
Doune *High.* PH22 89 F3
Doune *High.* IV24 96 B1
**Doune *Stir.* FK16 81 J7**
Dounepark AB45 99 F4
Douneside AB34 90 C4
Dounie *High.* IV19 96 D3
Dounie *High.* IV24 96 C2
Dounreay KW14 104 E2
Dousland PL20 5 F4
Dovaston SY10 38 C3
Dove Holes SK17 50 C5
Dovenby CA13 60 B3
Dovendale LN11 53 G4
**Dover CT16 15 J3**
Dovercourt CO12 35 G5
Doverdale WR9 29 H2
Doveridge DE6 40 D2
Doversgreen RH2 23 F7
Dowally PH9 82 B3
Dowdeswell GL54 30 B6
Dowhill KA26 67 G3
Dowlais CF48 18 D1
Dowland EX19 6 D4
Dowlands DT7 8 B5
Dowlish Ford TA19 8 C3
Dowlish Wake TA19 8 C3
Down Ampney GL7 20 E2
Down End TA6 19 G7
Down Hatherley GL2 29 H6
Down St. Mary EX17 7 F5
Down Thomas PL9 5 F6
Downderry PL11 4 D5
Downe BR6 23 H5
Downend *I.o.W.* PO30 11 G6
Downend *S.Glos.* BS16 19 K4
Downend *W.Berks.* RG20 21 H4
Downfield DD3 82 E4
Downfields CB7 33 K1
Downgate PL17 4 D3
Downham *Essex* CM11 24 D2
Downham *Lancs.* BB7 56 C5
Downham *Northumb.* TD12 77 G7
**Downham Market PE38 44 A5**
Downhead *Cornw.* PL15 4 C2
Downhead *Som.* BA4 19 K7
Downhead *Som.* BA22 8 E2
Downholland Cross L39 48 C2
Downholme DL11 62 C7
Downies AB12 91 H5
Downley HP13 22 B2
Downs CF5 18 E4
Downside *N.Som.* BS48 19 H5
Downside *Som.* BA4 19 K7
Downside *Som.* BA3 19 K6
Downside *Surr.* KT11 22 E6
Downton *Devon* EX20 6 D7
Downton *Devon* TQ6 5 J5
Downton *Hants.* SO41 10 D5
Downton *Wilts.* SP5 10 C2
Downton on the Rock SY8 28 D1
Dowsby PE10 42 E3
Dowthwaitehead CA11 60 E4
Doxey ST16 40 B3
Doynton BS30 20 A4
Drabblegate NR11 45 G3
Draethen NP10 19 F3
Draffan ML11 75 F6
Dragley Beck LA12 55 F2
Drakeland Corner PL7 5 F5
Drakelow DY11 40 A7
Drakemyre KA24 74 A5
Drakes Broughton WR10 29 J4
Drakes Cross B47 30 B1
Draughton *N.Yorks.* BD23 57 F4
Draughton *Northants.* NN6 31 J1
Drax YO8 58 C7
Draycot Foliat SN4 20 E4
Draycote CV23 31 F2
Draycott *Derbys.* DE72 41 G2
Draycott *Glos.* GL56 30 C5
Draycott *Shrop.* WV5 40 A6
Draycott *Som.* BS27 19 H6
Draycott *Worcs.* WR5 29 H4
Draycott in the Clay DE6 40 D3
Draycott in the Moors ST10 40 B2
Drayford EX17 7 F4
Draynes PL14 4 C4
Drayton *Leics.* LE16 42 B6
Drayton *Lincs.* PE20 43 F2
Drayton *Norf.* NR8 45 F4
Drayton *Oxon.* OX15 31 F4
Drayton *Oxon.* OX14 21 H2
Drayton *Ports.* PO6 11 H4
Drayton *Som.* TA10 8 D2
Drayton *Warks.* CV37 30 C3
Drayton *Worcs.* DY9 29 J1
Drayton Bassett B78 40 D5

Dra - Eas


Drayton Beauchamp HP22 32 C7
Drayton Parslow MK17 32 B6
Drayton St. Leonard OX10 21 J2
Drebley BD23 57 F4
Dreemskerry IM7 54 D4
Dreenhill SA62 16 C4
Drefach *Carmar.* SA44 17 G2
Drefach *Carmar.* SA14 17 J4
Dre-fach *Cere.* SA40 17 J1
Drefelin SA44 17 G2
Dreghorn KA11 74 B7
Drem EH39 76 D3
Dreumasdal (Drimsdale) HS8 84 C1
Drewsteignton EX6 7 F6
Driby LN13 53 G5
Driffield *E.Riding* YO25 59 G4
Driffield *Glos.* GL7 20 D2
Drigg CA19 60 B7
Drighlington BD11 57 H7
Drimfern PA32 80 B6
Drimlee PA32 80 C6
Drimnin PA34 79 G2
Drimore HS8 92 C7
Drimpton DT8 8 D4
Drimsdale (Dreumasdal) HS8 84 C1
Drimsynie PA24 80 C7
Drimvore PA31 73 G1
Drinan IV49 86 B3
Dringhouses YO24 58 B4
Drinisiader HS3 93 G2
Drinkstone IP30 34 D2
Drinkstone Green IP30 34 D2
Drishaig PA32 80 C6
Drissaig PA35 80 A6
Drointon ST18 40 C3
Droitwich Spa WR9 29 H2
Dron PH2 82 C6
Dronfield S18 51 F5
Dronfield Woodhouse S18 51 F5
Drongan KA6 67 J2
Dronley DD3 82 E4
Droop DT10 9 G4
Dropmore SL1 22 C3
Droxford SO32 11 H3
Droylsden M43 49 J3
Druid LL21 37 K1
Druidston SA62 16 B4
Druimarbin PH33 87 G7
Druimavuic PA38 80 B3
Druimdrishaig PA31 73 F3
Druimindarroch PH39 86 C6
Druimkinnerras IV4 88 B1
Drum *Arg. & B.* PA21 73 H3
Drum *P. & K.* KY13 82 B7
Drumachloy PA20 73 J4
Drumbeg IV27 102 D5
Drumblade AB54 98 D6
Drumblair AB54 98 E6
Drumbuie *D. & G.* DG4 68 C2
Drumbuie *High.* IV40 86 D1
Drumburgh CA7 60 D1
Drumchapel G15 74 D3
Drumchardine IV5 96 C7
Drumchork IV22 94 E3
Drumclog ML10 74 E7
Drumdelgie AB54 98 C6
Drumderfit IV1 96 D6
Drumeldrie KY8 83 F7
Drumelzier ML12 75 K7
Drumfearn IV43 86 C3
Drumfern PH33 87 F7
Drumgarve PA28 66 B1
Drumgley DD8 83 F2
Drumguish PH21 88 E5
Drumhead AB31 90 E5
Drumin AB37 89 J1
Drumine IV2 96 E6
Drumjohn DG7 67 K4
Drumlamford House KA26 64 C3
Drumlasie AB31 90 E4
Drumlemble PA28 66 A2
Drumlithie AB39 91 F6
Drummond *High.* IV16 96 D5
Drummond *Stir.* FK17 81 H7
Drummore DG9 64 B7
Drummuir Castle AB55 98 B6
Drumnadrochit IV63 88 C2
Drumnagorrach AB54 98 D5
Drumnatorran PH36 79 K1
Drumoak AB31 91 F5
Drumore PA28 66 B1
Drumour PH8 82 A4
Drumrash DG7 65 G3
Drumrunie IV26 95 H1
Drums AB41 91 H2
Drumsturdy DD5 83 F4
Drumuie IV51 93 K7
Drumuillie PH24 89 G2
Drumvaich FK17 81 H7
Drumwhindle AB41 91 H1
Drumwhirn DG7 68 C5
Drunkendub DD11 83 H3
Druridge NE61 71 H4
Drury CH7 48 B6
Drws-y-nant LL40 37 H3
Dry Doddington NG23 42 B1
Dry Drayton CB23 33 G2
Dry Harbour IV40 94 C6
Dry Sandford OX13 21 H1
Dry Street SS16 24 C3
Drybeck CA16 61 H5
Drybridge *Moray* AB56 98 C4
Drybridge *N.Ayr.* KA11 74 B7
Drybrook GL17 29 F7
Dryburgh TD6 76 D7
Drygrange TD6 76 D7
Dryhope TD7 69 H1
Drymen G63 74 C2
Drymuir AB42 99 H6
Drynoch IV47 85 K1
Dryslwyn SA32 17 J3
Dryton SY5 38 E5
Duachy PA34 79 K5
Dubford AB45 99 F4
Dubhchladach PA29 73 G4
Dubheads PH7 82 A5
Dublin IP23 35 F2
Dubton DD8 83 G2
Duchal PA13 74 B4
Duchally IV27 103 F7
Duchray FK8 81 F7
Duck Bay G83 74 B2
Duck End *Bed.* MK45 32 D4
Duck End *Cambs.* PE19 33 F2
Duck End *Essex* CM6 33 K6
Duck Street HG3 57 G3
Duckington SY14 48 D7
Ducklington OX29 21 G1
Duckmanton S44 51 G5
Duck's Cross MK44 32 E3
Ducks Island EN5 23 F2
Duddenhoe End CB11 33 H5
Duddingston EH15 76 A3
Duddington PE9 42 C5
Duddlestone TA3 8 B2
Duddleswell TN22 13 H4
Duddo TD15 77 H6
Duddon CW6 48 E6
Duddon Bridge LA18 54 E1
Dudleston SY12 38 C2
Dudleston Heath (Criftins) SY12 38 C2
Dudley *T. & W.* NE23 71 H6
DUDLEY *W.Mid.* DY 40 B6
Dudley Port DY4 40 B6
Dudlow's Green WA4 49 F4
Dudsbury BH22 10 B5
Duffield DE56 41 F1
Duffryn SA13 18 B2
Dufftown AB55 90 B1
Duffus IV30 97 J5
Dufton CA16 61 H4
Duggleby YO17 58 E3
Duiar PH26 89 J1
Duible KW8 104 E6
Duiletter PA33 80 C5
Duinish PH17 81 H1
Duirinish IV40 86 D1
Duisdealmor IV43 86 D3
Duisky PH33 87 G7
Duke End B46 40 E7
Dukestown NP22 28 A7
Dukinfield SK16 49 J3
Dulas LL70 46 C4
Dulax AB36 90 B3
Dulcote BA5 19 J7
Dulford EX15 7 J5
Dull PH15 81 K3
Dullatur G68 75 F3
Dullingham CB8 33 K3
Dullingham Ley CB8 33 K3
Dulnain Bridge PH26 89 G2
Duloe *Bed.* PE19 32 E2
Duloe *Cornw.* PL14 4 C5
Dulsie IV12 97 G7
Dulverton TA22 7 H3
Dulwich SE21 23 G4
Dumbarton G82 74 B3
Dumbleton WR11 30 B5
Dumcrieff DG10 69 G3
Dumeath AB54 90 C1
Dumfin G84 74 B2
DUMFRIES DG 65 K3
Dumgoyne G63 74 D2
Dummer RG25 21 J7
Dun DD10 83 H2
Dunach PA34 79 K5
Dunalastair PH16 81 J2
Dunan *Arg. & B.* PA23 73 K3
Dunan *High.* IV49 86 B2
Dunans PA22 73 J1
Dunball TA6 19 G7
Dunbar EH42 76 E3
Dunbeath KW6 105 G5
Dunbeg PA37 79 K4
Dunblane FK15 81 J7
Dunbog KY14 82 D6
Dunbridge SO51 10 E2
Duncanston *Aber.* AB52 90 D2
Duncanston *High.* IV7 96 C6
Dunchideock EX2 7 G7
Dunchurch CV22 31 F1
Duncote NN12 31 H3
Duncow DG1 68 E5
Duncraggan FK17 81 G7
Duncrievie PH2 82 C7
Duncroist FK21 81 G4
Duncrub PH2 82 B6
Duncryne G83 74 C2
Duncton GU28 12 C5
DUNDEE DD 83 F4
Dundee Airport DD2 82 E5
Dundon TA11 8 D1
Dundon Hayes TA11 8 D1
Dundonald KA2 74 B7
Dundonnell IV23 95 G3
Dundraw CA7 60 D2
Dundreggan IV63 87 K3
Dundrennan DG6 65 H6
Dundridge SO32 11 G3
Dundry BS41 19 J5
Dunearn KY3 76 A2
Dunecht AB32 91 F4
Dunfermline KY12 75 J2
Dunfield GL7 20 E2
Dunford Bridge S36 50 D2
Dungate ME9 14 E2
Dungavel ML10 74 E7
Dungworth S6 50 E3
Dunham NG22 52 B5
Dunham Town WA14 49 G4
Dunham Woodhouses WA14 49 G4
Dunham-on-the-Hill WA6 48 D5
Dunhampton DY13 29 H2
Dunholme LN2 52 D5
Dunino KY16 83 G6
Dunipace FK6 75 G2
Dunira PH6 81 J5
Dunkeld PH8 82 B3
Dunkerton BA2 20 A6
Dunkeswell EX14 7 K5
Dunkeswick LS17 57 J5
Dunkirk *Ches.W. & C.* CH1 48 C5
Dunkirk *Kent* ME13 15 F2
Dunk's Green TN11 23 K6
Dunlappie DD9 83 G1
Dunley *Hants.* RG28 21 H6
Dunley *Worcs.* DY13 29 G2
Dunlop KA3 74 C6
Dunloskin PA23 73 K3
Dunmere PL31 4 A4
Dunmore *Arg. & B.* PA29 73 F4
Dunmore *Falk.* FK2 75 G2
Dunn KW1 105 G3
Dunn Street ME7 24 D5
Dunnabie DG11 69 H5
Dunnet KW14 105 H1
Dunnichen DD8 83 G3
Dunning PH2 82 B6
Dunnington *E.Riding* YO25 59 H4
Dunnington *Warks.* B49 30 B3
Dunnington *York* YO19 58 C4
Dunnockshaw BB11 56 D7
Dunoon PA23 73 K3
Dunragit DG9 64 B5
Dunrostan PA31 73 F2
Duns TD11 77 F5
Duns Tew OX25 31 F6
Dunsa DE45 50 E5
Dunsby PE10 42 E3
Dunscore DG2 68 D5
Dunscroft DN7 51 J2
Dunsdale TS14 63 H5
Dunsden Green RG4 22 A4
Dunsfold GU8 12 D3
Dunsford EX6 7 G7
Dunshalt KY14 82 D6
Dunshill GL19 29 H5
Dunsinnan PH2 82 C4
Dunsland Cross EX22 6 C5
Dunsley *N.Yorks.* YO21 63 K5
Dunsley *Staffs.* DY7 40 A7
Dunsmore HP22 22 B1
Dunsop Bridge BB7 56 B4
Dunstable LU6 32 D6
Dunstall DE13 40 D3
Dunstall Green CB8 34 B2
Dunstan NE66 71 H2
Dunstan Steads NE66 71 H1
Dunster TA24 7 H1
Dunston *Lincs.* LN4 52 D6
Dunston *Norf.* NR14 45 G5
Dunston *Staffs.* ST18 40 B4
Dunston Heath ST18 40 B4
Dunston Hill NE11 71 H7
Dunstone *Devon* TQ13 5 H3
Dunstone *Devon* PL8 5 F5
Dunsville DN7 51 J2
Dunswell HU6 59 G6
Dunsyre ML11 75 J6
Dunterton PL19 4 D3
Duntisbourne Abbots GL7 20 C1
Duntisbourne Leer GL7 20 C1
Duntisbourne Rouse GL7 20 C1
Duntish DT2 9 F4
Duntocher G81 74 C3
Dunton *Bucks.* MK18 32 B6
Dunton *Cen.Beds.* SG18 33 F4
Dunton *Norf.* NR21 44 C2
Dunton Bassett LE17 41 H6
Dunton Green TN13 23 J6
Dunton Wayletts CM13 24 C2
Duntulm IV51 93 K4
Dunure KA7 67 G2
Dunure Mains KA7 67 G2
Dunvant SA2 17 J6
Dunvegan IV55 93 H7
Dunwich IP17 35 J1
Dura KY15 83 F6
Durdar CA2 60 F1
Durgan TR11 2 E6
Durgates TN5 13 K3
DURHAM DH 62 D2
Durham Tees Valley Airport DL2 62 E5
Durinemast PA34 79 H2
Durisdeer DG3 68 D3
Durleigh TA5 8 B1
Durley *Hants.* SO32 11 G3
Durley *Wilts.* SN8 21 F5
Durley Street SO32 11 G3
Durlow Common HR8 29 F5
Durnamuck IV23 95 G2
Durness IV27 103 G2
Durno AB51 91 F2
Duror PA38 80 A2
Durran *Arg. & B.* PA33 80 A7
Durran *High.* KW14 105 G2
Durrants PO9 11 J4
Durrington *W.Suss.* BN13 12 E6
Durrington *Wilts.* SP4 20 E7
Dursley GL11 20 A2
Dursley Cross GL17 29 F7
Durston TA3 8 B2
Durweston DT11 9 H4
Dury ZE2 107 N6
Duston NN5 31 J2
Duthil PH23 89 G2
Dutlas LD7 28 B1
Duton Hill CM6 33 K6
Dutson PL15 6 B7
Dutton WA4 48 E5
Duxford CB22 33 H4
Dwygyfylchi LL34 47 F5
Dwyran LL61 46 C6
Dyce AB21 91 G3
Dyfatty SA16 17 H5
Dyffryn *Bridgend* CF34 18 B2
Dyffryn *Pembs.* SA64 16 C2
Dyffryn *V. of Glam.* CF5 18 D4
Dyffryn Ardudwy LL44 36 E3
Dyffryn Castell SY23 37 G7
Dyffryn Ceidrych SA19 27 G6
Dyffryn Cellwen SA10 27 H7
Dyke *Devon* EX39 6 B3
Dyke *Lincs.* PE10 42 E3
Dyke *Moray* IV36 97 G6
Dykehead *Angus* DD8 82 E1
Dykehead *N.Lan.* ML7 75 G5
Dykehead *Stir.* FK8 74 D1
Dykelands AB30 83 J1
Dykends PH11 82 D2
Dykeside AB53 99 F6
Dylife SY19 37 H6
Dymchurch TN29 15 G5
Dymock GL18 29 G5
Dyrham SN14 20 A4
Dysart KY1 76 B1
Dyserth LL18 47 J5


## E


Eachwick NE18 71 G6
Eadar dha Fhadhail HS2 100 C4
Eagland Hill PR3 55 H5
Eagle LN6 52 B6
Eagle Barnsdale LN6 52 B6
Eagle Moor LN6 52 B6
Eaglescliffe TS16 63 F5
Eaglesfield *Cumb.* CA13 60 B4
Eaglesfield *D. & G.* DG11 69 H6
Eaglesham G76 74 D5
Eaglethorpe PE8 42 D6
Eagley BL1 49 G1
Eairy IM4 54 B6
Eakley MK16 32 B3
Eakring NG22 51 J6
Ealand DN17 51 K1
Ealing W5 22 E3
Eamont Bridge CA10 61 G4
Earby BB18 56 E5
Earcroft BB2 56 B7
Eardington WV16 39 G6
Eardisland HR6 28 D3
Eardisley HR3 28 C4
Eardiston *Shrop.* SY11 38 C3
Eardiston *Worcs.* WR15 29 F2
Earith PE28 33 G1
Earl Shilton LE9 41 G6
Earl Soham IP13 35 G2
Earl Sterndale SK17 50 C6
Earl Stonham IP14 35 F3
Earle NE71 70 E1
Earlestown WA12 48 E3
Earley RG6 22 A4
Earlham NR4 45 F5
Earlish IV51 93 J5
Earls Barton NN6 32 B2
Earls Colne CO6 34 C6
Earl's Common WR9 29 J3
Earl's Court SW5 23 F4
Earl's Croome WR8 29 H4
Earl's Green IP14 34 E2
Earlsdon CV5 30 E1
Earlsferry KY9 83 F7
Earlsford AB51 91 G1
Earlsheaton WF12 57 H7
Earlston TD4 76 D7
Earlswood *Mon.* NP16 19 H2
Earlswood *Surr.* RH1 23 F7
Earlswood *Warks.* B94 30 C1
Earnley PO20 12 B7
Earnshaw Bridge PR26 55 J7
Earsairidh HS9 84 C5
Earsdon NE25 71 J6
Earsdon Moor NE61 71 G4
Earsham NR35 45 H7
Earsham Street IP21 35 G1
Earswick YO32 58 C4
Eartham PO18 12 C6
Earthcott Green BS35 19 K3
Easby TS9 63 G6
Easdale PA34 79 J6
Easebourne GU29 12 B4
Easenhall CV23 31 F1
Eashing GU7 22 C7
Easington *Bucks.* HP18 31 H7
Easington *Dur.* SR8 63 F2
Easington *E.Riding* HU12 53 G1
Easington *Northumb.* NE70 77 K7
Easington *Oxon.* OX49 21 K2
Easington *R. & C.* TS13 63 J5
Easington Colliery SR8 63 F2
Easington Lane DH5 62 E2
Easingwold YO61 58 B3
Easole Street CT15 15 H2
Eassie DD8 82 E3
East Aberthaw CF62 18 D5
East Acton W3 23 F3
East Allington TQ9 5 H6
East Anstey EX16 7 G3
East Anton SP11 21 G7
East Appleton DL10 62 D7
East Ardsley WF3 57 J7
East Ashey PO33 11 G6
East Ashling PO18 12 B6
East Auchronie AB32 91 G4
East Ayton YO12 59 F1
East Barkwith LN8 52 E4
East Barming ME16 14 C2
East Barnby YO21 63 K5
East Barnet EN4 23 F2
East Barsham NR22 44 D2
East Beckham NR11 45 F2
East Bedfont TW14 22 D4
East Bergholt CO7 34 E5
East Bierley BD4 57 G7
East Bilney NR20 44 D4
East Blatchington BN25 13 H7
East Boldon NE36 71 J7
East Boldre SO42 10 E4
East Bolton NE66 71 G2
East Bower TA6 8 C1
East Brent TA9 19 G6
East Bridge IP16 35 J2
East Bridgford NG13 41 J1
East Brora KW9 97 G1
East Buckland EX32 6 E2
East Budleigh EX9 7 J7
East Burnham SL2 22 C3
East Burra ZE2 107 M9
East Burrafirth ZE2 107 M7
East Burton BH20 9 H6
East Butsfield DL13 62 C2
East Butterleigh EX15 7 H5
East Butterwick DN17 52 B2
East Cairnbeg AB30 91 F7
East Calder EH53 75 J4
East Carleton NR14 45 F5
East Carlton *Northants.* LE16 42 B7
East Carlton *W.Yorks.* LS19 57 H5
East Chaldon (Chaldon Herring) DT2 9 G6
East Challow OX12 21 G3
East Charleton TQ7 5 H6
East Chelborough DT2 8 E4
East Chiltington BN7 13 G5
East Chinnock BA22 8 D3
East Chisenbury SN9 20 E6
East Clandon GU4 22 D6
East Claydon MK18 31 J6
East Clyne KW9 97 G1
East Clyth KW3 105 H5
East Coker BA22 8 E3
East Compton *Dorset* SP7 9 H3
East Compton *Som.* BA4 19 K7
East Coombe EX17 7 G5
East Cornworthy TQ9 5 J5
East Cottingwith YO42 58 D5
East Cowes PO32 11 G5
East Cowick DN14 58 C7
East Cowton DL7 62 E6
East Cramlington NE23 71 H6
East Cranmore BA4 19 K7
East Creech BH20 9 J6
East Croachy IV2 88 D2
East Darlochan PA28 66 A1
East Davoch AB34 90 C4
East Dean *E.Suss.* BN20 13 J7
East Dean *Hants.* SP5 10 D2
East Dean *W.Suss.* PO18 12 C5
East Dereham (Dereham) NR19 44 D4
East Down EX31 6 D1
East Drayton DN22 51 K5
East Dundry BS41 19 J5
East Ella HU5 59 G7
East End *E.Riding* HU12 59 H6
East End *E.Riding* HU12 59 J7
East End *Essex* CM0 25 G1
East End *Hants.* RG20 21 H5
East End *Hants.* SO41 10 E5
East End *Herts.* SG9 33 H6
East End *Kent* TN17 14 D4
East End *Kent* ME12 25 F4
East End *M.K.* MK16 32 C4
East End *N.Som.* BS48 19 H4
East End *Oxon.* OX29 30 E7
East End *Poole* BH21 9 J5
East End *Som.* BA3 19 J6
East End *Suff.* CO7 35 F5
East End *Suff.* IP14 35 F3
East Farleigh ME15 14 C2
East Farndon LE16 42 A7
East Ferry DN21 52 B3
East Firsby LN8 52 D4
East Fleetham NE68 71 H1
East Fortune EH39 76 D3
East Garston RG17 21 G4
East Ginge OX12 21 H3
East Goscote LE7 41 J4
East Grafton SN8 21 F5
East Green *Suff.* IP17 35 J2
East Green *Suff.* CB8 33 K3
East Grimstead SP5 10 D2
East Grinstead RH19 13 G3
East Guldeford TN31 14 E5
East Haddon NN6 31 H2
East Hagbourne OX11 21 J3
East Halton DN40 52 E1
East Ham E6 23 H3
East Hanney OX12 21 H2
East Hanningfield CM3 24 D1
East Hardwick WF8 51 G1
East Harling NR16 44 D7
East Harlsey DL6 63 F7
East Harnham SP2 10 C2
East Harptree BS40 19 J6
East Hartford NE23 71 H6
East Harting GU31 11 J3
East Hatch SP3 9 J2
East Hatley SG19 33 F3
East Hauxwell DL8 62 C7
East Haven DD7 83 G4

Eas - Elt

East Heckington PE20 42 E1
East Hedleyhope DL13 62 C2
East Helmsdale KW8 105 F7
East Hendred OX12 21 H3
East Herrington SR3 62 E1
East Heslerton YO17 59 F2
East Hewish BS24 19 H5
East Hoathly BN8 13 J5
East Holme BH20 9 H6
East Horndon CM13 24 C3
East Horrington BA5 19 J7
East Horsley KT24 22 D6
East Horton NE71 77 J7
East Howe BH10 10 B5
East Huntspill TA9 19 G7
East Hyde LU2 32 E7
East Ilsley RG20 21 H3
East Keal PE23 53 G6
East Kennett SN8 20 E5
East Keswick LS17 57 J5
East Kilbride G74 74 E5
East Kimber EX20 6 C6
East Kirkby PE23 53 G6
East Knapton YO17 58 E2
East Knighton DT2 9 H6
East Knowstone EX36 7 G3
East Knoyle SP3 9 H1
East Kyloe NE70 77 J7
East Lambrook TA13 8 D3
East Langdon CT15 15 J3
East Langton LE16 42 A6
East Langwell IV28 96 E1
East Lavant PO18 12 B6
East Lavington GU28 12 C5
East Layton DL11 62 C5
East Leake LE12 41 H3
East Learmouth TD12 77 G7
East Learney AB31 90 E4
East Leigh Devon EX17 7 F5
East Leigh Devon EX18 7 F4
East Leigh Devon TQ9 5 H5
East Leigh Devon PL21 5 G5
East Lexham PE32 44 C4
East Lilburn NE66 71 F1
East Linton EH40 76 D3
East Liss GU33 11 J2
East Lockinge OX12 21 H3
East Looe PL13 4 C5
East Lound DN9 51 K2
East Lulworth BH20 9 H6
East Lutton YO17 59 F3
East Lydford TA11 8 E1
East Lyn EX35 7 F1
East Lyng TA3 8 C2
East Mains AB31 90 E5
East Malling ME19 14 C2
East Malling Heath ME19 23 K6
East March DD4 83 F4
East Marden PO18 12 B5
East Markham NG22 51 K5
East Martin SP6 10 B3
East Marton BD23 56 E4
East Meon GU32 11 H2
East Mere EX16 7 H4
East Mersea CO5 34 E7
East Mey KW14 105 J1
East Molesey KT8 22 E5
East Moor WF1 57 J7
East Morden BH20 9 J5
East Morriston TD4 76 E6
East Morton BD20 57 G5
East Ness YO62 58 C2
East Newton HU11 59 J6
East Norton LE7 42 A5
East Oakley RG23 21 J6
East Ogwell TQ12 5 J3
East Orchard SP7 9 H3
East Ord TD15 77 H5
East Panson PL15 6 B6
East Parley BH23 10 C5
East Peckham TN12 23 K7
East Pennard BA4 8 E1
East Portlemouth TQ8 5 H7
East Prawle TQ7 5 H7
East Preston BN16 12 D6
East Pulham DT2 9 G4
East Putford EX22 6 B4
East Quantoxhead TA5 7 K1
East Rainton DH5 62 E2
East Ravendale DN37 53 F3
East Raynham NR21 44 C3
East Retford (Retford) DN22 51 K4
East Rigton LS17 57 J5
East Rolstone BS24 19 G5
East Rounton DL6 63 F6
East Row YO21 63 K5
East Rudham PE31 44 C3
East Runton NR27 45 G1
East Ruston NR12 45 H3
East Saltoun EH34 76 C4
East Shefford RG17 21 G4
East Sleekburn NE22 71 H5
East Somerton NR29 45 J4
East Stockwith DN21 51 K3
East Stoke Dorset BH20 9 H6
East Stoke Notts. NG23 42 A1
East Stour SP8 9 H2
East Stourmouth CT3 25 J5
East Stratton SO21 21 J7
East Street BA6 8 E1
East Studdal CT15 15 J3
East Suisnish IV40 86 B1
East Taphouse PL14 4 B4
East Thirston NE65 71 G4
East Tilbury RM18 24 C4
East Tisted GU34 11 J1
East Torrington LN8 52 E4
East Town BA4 19 K7
East Tuddenham NR20 44 E4
East Tytherley SP5 10 D2
East Tytherton SN15 20 C4
East Village EX17 7 G5
East Wall TF13 38 E6
East Walton PE32 44 B4
East Wellow SO51 10 E2
East Wemyss KY1 76 B1
East Whitburn EH47 75 H4
East Wickham DA16 23 H4
East Williamston SA70 16 D5
East Winch PE32 44 A4
East Winterslow SP5 10 D1
East Wittering PO20 11 J5
East Witton DL8 57 G1
East Woodburn NE48 70 E5
East Woodhay RG20 21 H5
East Woodlands BA11 20 A7
East Worldham GU34 11 J1
East Worlington EX17 7 F4
East Youlstone EX23 6 A4
Eastacott EX37 6 E3
Eastbourne BN21 13 K7
Eastbrook CF64 18 E4
Eastburn E.Riding YO25 59 F4
Eastburn W.Yorks. BD20 57 F5
Eastbury Herts. HA6 22 E2
Eastbury W.Berks. RG17 21 G4
Eastby BD23 57 F4
Eastchurch ME12 25 F4
Eastcombe Glos. GL6 20 B1
Eastcombe Som. TA4 7 K2
Eastcote Gt.Lon. HA5 22 E3
Eastcote Northants. NN12 31 H3
Eastcote W.Mid. B92 30 C1
Eastcott Cornw. EX23 6 A4
Eastcott Wilts. SN10 20 D6
Eastcourt SN16 20 C2
Eastdown TQ6 5 J6
Eastend OX7 30 E6
Easter Ardross IV17 96 D4
Easter Balgedie KY13 82 C7
Easter Balmoral AB35 89 K5
Easter Boleskine IV2 88 C2
Easter Borland FK8 81 H7
Easter Brae IV7 96 D5
Easter Buckieburn FK6 75 F2
Easter Compton BS35 19 J3
Easter Drummond IV2 88 B3
Easter Dullater FK17 81 H7
Easter Ellister PA48 72 A5
Easter Fearn IV24 96 D3
Easter Galcantray IV12 97 F7
Easter Howlaws TD10 77 F6
Easter Kinkell IV7 96 C6
Easter Knox DD11 83 G3
Easter Lednathie DD8 82 E1
Easter Moniack IV5 96 C7
Easter Ord AB32 91 G4
Easter Poldar FK8 74 E1
Easter Skeld (Skeld) ZE2 107 M8
Easter Suddie IV8 96 D6
Easter Tulloch AB30 91 F7
Easter Whyntie AB45 98 E4
Eastergate PO20 12 C6
Easterhouse G34 74 E4
Easterton SN10 20 D6
Easterton Sands SN10 20 D6
Eastertown BS24 19 G6
Eastfield Bristol BS9 19 J4
Eastfield N.Lan. ML7 75 G4
Eastfield N.Yorks. YO11 59 G1
Eastfield Hall NE65 71 H3
Eastgate Dur. DL13 62 A3
Eastgate Lincs. PE10 42 E4
Eastgate Norf. NR10 45 F3
Easthall SG4 33 F6
Eastham Mersey. CH62 48 C4
Eastham Worcs. WR15 29 F2
Easthampstead RG12 22 B5
Easthampton HR6 28 D2
Easthaugh NR9 44 E4
Eastheath RG41 22 B5
Easthope TF13 38 E6
Easthorpe Essex CO6 34 D6
Easthorpe Leics. NG13 42 B2
Easthorpe Notts. NG25 51 K7
Easthouses EH22 76 B4
Eastington Devon EX17 7 F5
Eastington Glos. GL54 30 C7
Eastington Glos. GL10 20 A1
Eastleach Martin GL7 21 F1
Eastleach Turville GL7 21 F1
Eastleigh Devon EX39 6 C3
Eastleigh Hants. SO50 11 F3
Eastling ME13 14 E2
Eastmoor Derbys. S42 51 F5
Eastmoor Norf. PE33 44 B5
Eastnor HR8 29 G5
Eastoft DN17 52 B1
Eastoke PO11 11 J5
Easton Cambs. PE28 32 E1
Easton Cumb. CA6 69 K6
Easton Cumb. CA7 60 D1
Easton Devon TQ13 7 F7
Easton Dorset DT5 9 F7
Easton Hants. SO21 11 G1
Easton I.o.W. PO40 10 E6
Easton Lincs. NG33 42 C3
Easton Norf. NR9 45 F4
Easton Som. BA5 19 J7
Easton Suff. IP13 35 G3
Easton Wilts. SN13 20 B4
Easton Grey SN16 20 B3
Easton Maudit NN29 32 B3
Easton on the Hill PE9 42 D5
Easton Royal SN9 21 F5
Easton-in-Gordano BS20 19 J4
Eastrea PE7 43 F6
Eastriggs DG12 69 H7
Eastrington DN14 58 D6
Eastry CT13 15 J2
Eastside KW17 106 D8
East-the-Water EX39 6 C3
Eastville BS16 19 K4
Eastwell LE14 42 A3
Eastwick CM20 33 H7
Eastwood Notts. NG16 41 G1
Eastwood S'end SS9 24 E3
Eastwood S.Yorks. S65 51 G3
Eastwood W.Yorks. OL14 56 E7
Eastwood End PE15 43 H6
Eathorpe CV33 30 E2
Eaton Ches.E. CW12 49 H6
Eaton Ches.W. & C. CW6 48 E6
Eaton Leics. NG32 42 A3
Eaton Norf. NR2 45 G5
Eaton Norf. PE36 44 A2
Eaton Notts. DN22 51 K5
Eaton Oxon. OX13 21 H1
Eaton Shrop. SY6 38 E6
Eaton Shrop. SY9 38 C7
Eaton Bishop HR2 28 D5
Eaton Bray LU6 32 C6
Eaton Constantine SY5 39 F5
Eaton Ford PE19 32 E3
Eaton Hall CH4 48 D6
Eaton Hastings SN7 21 F2
Eaton Socon PE19 32 E3
Eaton upon Tern TF9 39 F3
Eaves Green CV7 40 E7
Eavestone HG4 57 H3
Ebberston YO13 58 E1
Ebbesborne Wake SP5 9 J2
Ebbw Vale (Glynebwy) NP23 18 E1
Ebchester DH8 62 C1
Ebdon BS22 19 G5
Ebford EX3 7 H7
Ebley GL5 20 B1
Ebnal SY14 38 D1
Ebost IV56 85 J1
Ebrington GL55 30 C4
Ebsworthy Town EX20 6 D6
Ecchinswell RG20 21 H6
Ecclaw TD13 77 F4
Ecclefechan DG11 69 G6
Eccles Gt.Man. M30 49 G3
Eccles Kent ME20 24 D5
Eccles Sc.Bord. TD5 77 F6
Eccles Green HR4 28 C4
Eccles Road NR16 44 E6
Ecclesfield S35 51 F3
Ecclesgreig DD10 83 J1
Eccleshall ST21 40 A3
Eccleshill BD10 57 G6
Ecclesmachan EH52 75 J3
Eccles-on-Sea NR12 45 J3
Eccleston Ches.W. & C. CH4 48 D6
Eccleston Lancs. PR7 48 E1
Eccleston Mersey. WA10 48 D3
Eccup LS16 57 H5
Echt AB32 91 F4
Eckford TD5 70 C1
Eckington Derbys. S21 51 G5
Eckington Worcs. WR10 29 J4
Ecton Northants. NN6 32 B2
Ecton Staffs. SK17 50 C7
Edale S33 50 D4
Eday KW17 106 E4
Eday Airfield KW17 106 E4
Edburton BN5 13 F5
Edderside CA15 60 C2
Edderton IV19 96 E3
Eddington RG17 21 G5
Eddleston EH45 76 A6
Eden Park BR3 23 G5
Eden Vale TS27 63 F3
Edenbridge TN8 23 H7
Edendonich PA33 80 C5
Edenfield BL0 49 G1
Edenhall CA11 61 G3
Edenham PE10 42 D3
Edensor DE45 50 E5
Edentaggart G83 74 B1
Edenthorpe DN3 51 J2
Edern LL53 36 B2
Edgarley BA6 8 E1
Edgbaston B15 40 C7
Edgcote OX17 31 G4
Edgcott Bucks. HP18 31 H6
Edgcott Som. TA24 7 G2
Edgcumbe TR10 2 E5
Edge Glos. GL6 20 B1
Edge Shrop. SY5 38 C5
Edge End GL16 28 E7
Edge Green Ches.W. & C. SY14 48 D7
Edge Green Gt.Man. WA3 48 E3
Edge Green Norf. NR16 44 E7
Edgebolton SY4 38 E3
Edgefield NR24 44 E2
Edgehead EH37 76 B4
Edgeley SY13 38 E1
Edgerley SY10 38 C4
Edgerton HD2 50 D1
Edgeworth GL6 20 C1
Edginswell TQ2 5 J4
Edgmond TF10 39 G4
Edgmond Marsh TF10 39 G3
Edgton SY7 38 C7
Edgware HA8 23 F2
Edgworth BL7 49 G1
Edinample FK19 81 H5
Edinbanchory AB33 90 C3
Edinbane IV51 93 J6
Edinbarnet G81 74 D3
EDINBURGH EH 76 A3
Edinburgh Airport EH12 75 K3
Edinchip FK19 81 G5
Edingale B79 40 E4
Edingley NG22 51 J7
Edingthorpe NR28 45 H2
Edingthorpe Green NR28 45 H2
Edington Som. TA7 8 C1
Edington Wilts. BA13 20 C6
Edintore AB55 98 C6
Edinvale IV36 97 J6
Edistone EX39 6 A3
Edith Weston LE15 42 C5
Edithmead TA9 19 G7
Edlaston DE6 40 D1
Edlesborough LU6 32 C7
Edlingham NE66 71 G3
Edlington LN9 53 F5
Edmondsham BH21 10 B3
Edmondsley DH7 62 D2
Edmondstown CF40 18 D2
Edmondthorpe LE14 42 B4
Edmonstone KW17 106 E5
Edmonton Cornw. PL27 3 G1
Edmonton Gt.Lon. N18 23 G2
Edmundbyers DH8 62 B1
Ednam TD5 77 F7
Ednaston DE6 40 E1
Edney Common CM1 24 C1
Edra FK17 81 F6
Edradynate PH15 81 K2
Edrom TD11 77 G5
Edstaston SY4 38 E2
Edstone B95 30 C2
Edvin Loach HR7 29 F3
Edwalton NG12 41 H2
Edwardstone CO10 34 D4
Edwardsville CF46 18 D2
Edwinsford SA19 17 K2
Edwinstowe NG21 51 J6
Edworth SG18 33 F4
Edwyn Ralph HR7 29 F3
Edzell DD9 83 H1
Efail Isaf CF38 18 D3
Efail-fâch SA12 18 A2
Efailnewydd LL53 36 C2
Efailwen SA66 16 E3
Efenechtyd LL15 47 K7
Effingham KT24 22 E6
Effirth ZE2 107 M7
Efflinch DE13 40 D4
Efford EX17 7 G5
Egbury SP11 21 H6
Egdean RH20 12 C4
Egdon WR7 29 J3
Egerton Gt.Man. BL7 49 G1
Egerton Kent TN27 14 E3
Egerton Forstal TN27 14 D3
Egerton Green SY14 48 E7
Egg Buckland PL6 4 E5
Eggborough DN14 58 B7
Eggerness DG8 64 E6
Eggesford Barton EX18 6 E4
Eggington LU7 32 C6
Egginton DE65 40 E3
Egglescliffe TS16 63 F5
Eggleston DL12 62 A4
Egham TW20 22 D4
Egham Wick TW20 22 C4
Egilsay KW17 106 D5
Egleton LE15 42 B5
Eglingham NE66 71 G2
Eglinton KA12 74 B6
Egloshayle PL27 4 A3
Egloskerry PL15 4 C2
Eglwys Cross SY13 38 D1
Eglwys Fach SY20 37 F6
Eglwys Nunydd SA13 18 A3
Eglwysbach LL28 47 G5
Eglwys-Brewis CF62 18 D5
Eglwyswrw SA41 16 E2
Egmanton NG22 51 K6
Egmere NR22 44 D2
Egremont CA22 60 B5
Egton YO21 63 K6
Egton Bridge YO21 63 K6
Egypt SO21 21 H7
Eigg PH42 85 K6
Eight Ash Green CO6 34 D6
Eignaig PA34 79 J3
Eil PH22 89 F3
Eilanreach IV40 86 E3
Eildon TD6 76 D7
Eilean Bhearnaraigh (Berneray) HS6 92 E3
Eilean Darach IV23 95 H3
Eilean Iarmain (Isleornsay) IV43 86 C3
Eilean Leodhais (Isle of Lewis) HS 101 F3
Eilean Scalpaigh (Scalpay) HS4 93 H2
Eilean Shona PH36 86 C7
Einacleit HS2 100 D5
Eiriosgaigh (Eriskay) HS8 84 C3
Eisgean HS2 101 F6
Eisingrug LL47 37 F2
Eisteddfa Gurig SY23 37 G7
Elan Village LD6 27 J2
Elberton BS35 19 K3
Elborough BS24 19 G6
Elburton PL9 5 F5
Elcho PH2 82 C5
Elcombe SN4 20 E3
Elder Street CB10 33 J5
Eldernell PE7 43 G6
Eldersfield GL19 29 G5
Elderslie PA5 74 C4
Eldon DL14 62 D4
Eldrick KA26 67 G5
Eldroth LA2 56 C3
Eldwick BD16 57 G5
Elemore Vale DH5 62 E2
Elerch (Bont-goch) SY24 37 F7
Elford Northumb. NE68 77 K7
Elford Staffs. B79 40 D4
Elford Closes CB6 33 J1
Elgin IV30 97 K5
Elgol IV49 86 B3
Elham CT4 15 G3
Elie KY9 83 F7
Elilaw NE65 70 E3
Elim LL65 46 B4
Eling Hants. SO40 10 E3
Eling W.Berks. RG18 21 J4
Eliock DG4 68 D3
Elishader IV51 93 K5
Elishaw NE19 70 D4
Elkesley DN22 51 J5
Elkington NN6 31 H1
Elkstone GL53 29 J7
Elland HX5 57 G7
Elland Upper Edge HX5 57 G7
Ellary PA31 73 F3
Ellastone DE6 40 D1
Ellbridge PL12 4 E4
Ellel LA2 55 H4
Ellemford TD11 77 F4
Ellenborough CA15 60 B3
Ellenhall ST21 40 A3
Ellen's Green RH12 12 D3
Ellerbeck DL6 63 F7
Ellerby TS13 63 J5
Ellerdine TF6 39 F3
Ellerdine Heath TF6 39 F3
Elleric PA38 80 B3
Ellerker HU15 59 F7
Ellerton E.Riding YO42 58 D5
Ellerton N.Yorks. DL10 62 D7
Ellerton Shrop. TF9 39 G3
Ellerton Abbey DL11 62 B7
Ellesborough HP17 22 B1
Ellesmere SY12 38 C2
Ellesmere Park M30 49 G3
Ellesmere Port CH65 48 D5
Ellingham Hants. BH24 10 C4
Ellingham Norf. NR35 45 H6
Ellingham Northumb. NE67 71 G1
Ellingstring HG4 57 G1
Ellington Cambs. PE28 32 E1
Ellington Northumb. NE61 71 H4
Ellington Thorpe PE28 32 E1
Elliot's Green BA11 20 A7
Ellisfield RG25 21 K7
Ellistown LE67 41 G4
Ellon AB41 91 H1
Ellonby CA11 60 F3
Ellough NR34 45 J7
Ellough Moor NR34 45 J7
Elloughton HU15 59 F7
Ellwood GL16 19 J1
Elm PE14 43 H5
Elm Park RM12 23 J3
Elmbridge WR9 29 J2
Elmdon Essex CB11 33 H5
Elmdon W.Mid. B26 40 D7
Elmdon Heath B92 40 D7
Elmers End BR3 23 G5
Elmer's Green WN8 48 D2
Elmesthorpe LE9 41 G6
Elmhurst WS13 40 D4
Elmley Castle WR10 29 J4
Elmley Lovett WR9 29 H2
Elmore GL2 29 G7
Elmore Back GL2 29 G7
Elmscott EX39 6 A3
Elmsett IP7 34 E4
Elmstead Essex CO7 34 E6
Elmstead Gt.Lon. BR7 23 H4
Elmstead Market CO7 34 E6
Elmstone CT3 25 J5
Elmstone Hardwicke GL51 29 J6
Elmswell E.Riding YO25 59 F4
Elmswell Suff. IP30 34 D2
Elmton S80 51 H5
Elphin IV27 102 E7
Elphinstone EH33 76 B3
Elrick Aber. AB32 91 G4
Elrick Moray AB54 90 C2
Elrig DG8 64 D6
Elrigbeag PA32 80 C6
Elsdon NE19 70 E4
Elsecar S74 51 F2
Elsenham CM22 33 J6
Elsfield OX3 31 G7
Elsham DN20 52 D1
Elsing NR20 44 E4
Elslack BD23 56 E5
Elson Hants. PO12 11 H4
Elson Shrop. SY12 38 C2
Elsrickle ML12 75 J6
Elstead GU8 22 C7
Elsted GU29 12 B5
Elsthorpe PE10 42 D3
Elstob TS21 62 E4
Elston Lancs. PR2 55 J6
Elston Notts. NG23 42 A1
Elstone EX18 6 E4
Elstow MK42 32 D4
Elstree WD6 22 E2
Elstronwick HU12 59 J6
Elswick PR4 55 H6
Elsworth CB23 33 G2
Elterwater LA22 60 E6
Eltham SE9 23 H4
Eltisley PE19 33 F3
Elton Cambs. PE8 42 D6
Elton Ches.W. & C. CH2 48 D5
Elton Derbys. DE4 50 E6
Elton Glos. GL14 29 G7
Elton Gt.Man. BL8 49 G1
Elton Here. SY8 28 D1

Elt - Ffy


Elton Notts. NG13 42 A2
Elton Stock. TS21 63 F5
Elton Green CH2 48 D5
Elvanfoot ML12 68 E2
Elvaston DE72 41 G2
Elveden IP24 34 C1
Elvingston EH33 76 C3
Elvington Kent CT15 15 H2
Elvington York YO41 58 D5
Elwick Hart. TS27 63 F3
Elwick Northumb. NE70 77 K7
Elworth CW11 49 G6
Elworthy TA4 7 J2
Ely Cambs. CB7 33 J1
Ely Cardiff CF5 18 E4
Emberton MK46 32 B4
Embleton Cumb. CA13 60 C3
Embleton Hart. TS22 63 F4
Embleton Northumb. NE66 71 H1
Embo IV25 97 F2
Embo Street IV25 97 F2
Emborough BA3 19 K6
Embsay BD23 57 F4
Emerson Park RM11 23 J3
Emery Down SO43 10 D4
Emley HD8 50 E1
Emmington OX39 22 A1
Emneth PE14 43 H5
Emneth Hungate PE14 43 J5
Empingham LE15 42 C5
Empshott GU33 11 J1
Empshott Green GU33 11 J1
Emsworth PO10 11 J4
Enborne RG20 21 H5
Enborne Row RG20 21 H5
Enchmarsh SY6 38 E6
Enderby LE19 41 H6
Endmoor LA8 55 J1
Endon ST9 49 J7
Endon Bank ST9 49 J7
ENFIELD EN 23 G2
Enfield Wash EN3 23 G2
Enford SN9 20 E6
Engine Common BS37 19 K3
Englefield RG7 21 K4
Englefield Green TW20 22 C4
Englesea-brook CW2 49 G7
English Bicknor GL16 28 E7
English Frankton SY12 38 D3
Englishcombe BA2 20 A5
Enham Alamein SP11 21 G7
Enmore TA5 8 B1
Ennerdale Bridge CA23 60 B5
Enniscaven PL26 3 G3
Ennochdhu PH10 82 B1
Ensay PA75 78 E3
Ensdon SY4 38 D4
Ensis EX31 6 D3
Enson ST18 40 B3
Enstone OX7 30 E6
Enterkinfoot DG3 68 D3
Enterpen TS15 63 F6
Enton Green GU8 22 C7
Enville DY7 40 A7
Eolaigearraidh HS9 84 C4
Eorabus PA67 78 E5
Eorodal HS2 101 H1
Eoropaidh HS2 101 H1
Epney GL2 29 G7
Epperstone NG14 41 J1
Epping CM16 23 H1
Epping Green Essex CM16 23 H1
Epping Green Herts. SG13 23 F1
Epping Upland CM16 23 H1
Eppleby DL11 62 C5
Eppleworth HU16 59 G6
Epsom KT17 23 F5
Epwell OX15 30 E4
Epworth DN9 51 K2
Epworth Turbary DN9 51 K2
Erbistock LL13 38 C1
Erbusaig IV40 86 D2
Erchless Castle IV4 96 B7
Erdington B24 40 D6
Eredine PA33 80 A7
Eriboll IV27 103 G3
Ericstane DG10 69 F2
Eridge Green TN3 13 J3
Eriff DG7 67 K3
Erines PA29 73 G3
Erisey Barton TR12 2 E7
Eriskay (Eiriosgaigh) HS8 84 C3
Eriswell IP28 34 B1
Erith DA8 23 J4
Erlestoke SN10 20 C6
Ermington PL21 5 G5
Ernesettle PL5 4 E4
Erpingham NR11 45 F2
Erringden Grange HX7 56 E7
Errogie IV2 88 C2
Errol PH2 82 D5
Errollston AB42 91 J1
Erskine PA8 74 C3
Ervie DG9 66 D7
Erwarton IP9 35 G5
Erwood LD2 27 K4
Eryholme DL2 62 E6
Eryrys CH7 48 B7
Escart PA29 73 G4
Escart Farm PA29 73 G5
Escomb DL14 62 C4
Escrick YO19 58 C5
Esgair SA33 17 G3
Esgairgeiliog SY20 37 G5
Esgyryn LL31 47 G5
Esh DH7 62 C2
Esh Winning DH7 62 C2
Esher KT10 22 E5
Eshott NE65 71 H4
Eshton BD23 56 E4
Eskadale IV4 88 B1
Eskbank EH22 76 B4
Eskdale Green CA19 60 C6
Eskdalemuir DG13 69 H4
Eskham DN36 53 G3
Esknish PA44 72 B4
Esperley Lane Ends DL13 62 C4
Espley Hall NE61 71 G4
Esprick PR4 55 H6
Essendine PE9 42 D4
Essendon AL9 23 F1
Essich IV2 88 D1
Essington WV11 40 B5
Esslemont AB41 91 H2
Eston TS6 63 G5
Eswick ZE2 107 N7
Etal TD12 77 H7
Etchilhampton SN10 20 D5
Etchingham TN19 14 C5
Etchinghill Kent CT18 15 G4
Etchinghill Staffs. WS15 40 C4
Etherdwick Grange HU11 59 J6
Etherley Dene DL14 62 C4
Ethie Mains DD11 83 H3
Eton SL4 22 C4
Eton Wick SL4 22 C4
Etteridge PH20 88 D5
Ettiley Heath CW11 49 G6
Ettington CV37 30 D4
Etton E.Riding HU17 59 F5
Etton Peter. PE6 42 E5
Ettrick TD7 69 H2
Ettrickbridge TD7 69 J1
Ettrickhill TD7 69 H2
Etwall DE65 40 E2
Eudon George WV16 39 F7
Eurach PA31 79 K7
Euston IP24 34 C1
Euxton PR7 48 E1
Evanstown CF39 18 C3
Evanton IV16 96 D5
Evedon NG34 42 D1
Evelix IV25 96 E2
Evenjobb LD8 28 B2
Evenley NN13 31 G5
Evenlode GL56 30 D6
Evenwood DL14 62 C4
Evenwood Gate DL14 62 C4
Everbay KW17 106 F5
Evercreech BA4 9 F1
Everdon NN11 31 G3
Everingham YO42 58 E5
Everleigh SN8 21 F6
Everley High. KW1 105 J2
Everley N.Yorks. YO13 59 F1
Eversholt MK17 32 C5
Evershot DT2 8 E4
Eversley RG27 22 A5
Eversley Cross RG27 22 A5
Everthorpe HU15 59 F6
Everton Cen.Beds. SG19 33 F3
Everton Hants. SO41 10 D5
Everton Mersey. L5 48 C3
Everton Notts. DN10 51 J3
Evertown DG14 69 J6
Eves Corner CM0 25 F2
Evesbatch WR6 29 F4
Evesham WR11 30 B4
Evie KW17 106 C5
Evington LE5 41 J5
Ewart Newtown NE71 77 H7
Ewden Village S36 50 E3
Ewell KT17 23 F5
Ewell Minnis CT15 15 H3
Ewelme OX10 21 K2
Ewen GL7 20 D2
Ewenny CF35 18 C4
Ewerby NG34 42 E1
Ewerby Thorpe NG34 42 E1
Ewhurst GU6 22 D7
Ewhurst Green E.Suss. TN32 14 C5
Ewhurst Green Surr. GU6 12 D3
Ewloe CH5 48 C6
Ewloe Green CH5 48 B6
Ewood BB2 56 B7
Ewood Bridge BB4 56 C7
Eworthy EX21 6 C6
Ewshot GU10 22 B7
Ewyas Harold HR2 28 C6
Exbourne EX20 6 E5
Exbury SO45 11 F4
Exceat BN25 13 J7
Exebridge TA22 7 H3
Exelby DL8 57 H1
EXETER EX 7 H6
Exeter International Airport EX5 7 H6
Exford TA24 7 G2
Exfords Green SY5 38 D5
Exhall Warks. B49 30 C3
Exhall Warks. CV7 41 F7
Exlade Street RG8 21 K3
Exminster EX6 7 H7
Exmouth EX8 7 J7
Exnaboe ZE3 107 M11
Exning CB8 33 K2
Exton Devon EX3 7 H7
Exton Hants. SO32 11 H2
Exton Rut. LE15 42 C4
Exton Som. TA22 7 H2
Exwick EX4 7 H6
Eyam S32 50 E5
Eydon NN11 31 G4
Eye Here. HR6 28 D2
Eye Peter. PE6 43 F5
Eye Suff. IP23 35 F1
Eye Green PE6 43 F5
Eyemouth TD14 77 H4
Eyeworth SG19 33 F4
Eyhorne Street ME17 14 D2
Eyke IP12 35 H3
Eynesbury PE19 32 E3
Eynort IV47 85 J2
Eynsford DA4 23 J5
Eynsham OX29 21 H1
Eype DT6 8 D5
Eyre IV51 93 K6
Eythorne CT15 15 H3
Eyton Here. HR6 28 D2
Eyton Shrop. SY7 38 C7
Eyton on Severn SY5 38 E5
Eyton upon the Weald Moors TF6 39 F4
Eywood HR5 28 C3


## F


Faccombe SP11 21 G6
Faceby TS9 63 F6
Fachwen LL55 46 D6
Facit OL12 49 H1
Faddiley CW5 48 E7
Fadmoor YO62 58 C1
Faebait IV6 96 B6
Faifley G81 74 D3
Fail KA5 67 J1
Failand BS8 19 J4
Failford KA5 67 J1
Failsworth M35 49 H2
Fain IV23 95 H4
Fair Isle ZE2 107 K2
Fair Isle Airstrip ZE2 107 K2
Fair Oak Devon EX16 7 J4
Fair Oak Hants. SO50 11 F3
Fair Oak Hants. RG19 21 J5
Fair Oak Green RG7 21 K5
Fairbourne LL38 37 F4
Fairburn WF11 57 K7
Fairfield Derbys. SK17 50 C5
Fairfield Gt.Man. M43 49 J3
Fairfield Kent TN29 14 E5
Fairfield Mersey. CH63 48 B4
Fairfield Stock. TS19 63 F5
Fairfield Worcs. B61 29 J1
Fairford GL7 20 E1
Fairgirth DG5 65 J5
Fairhaven FY8 55 G7
Fairhill ML3 75 F5
Fairholm ML9 75 F5
Fairley AB15 91 G4
Fairlie KA29 74 A5
Fairlight TN35 14 D6
Fairlight Cove TN35 14 D6
Fairmile Devon EX11 7 J6
Fairmile Surr. KT11 22 E5
Fairmilehead EH10 76 A4
Fairnington TD5 70 B1
Fairoak ST21 39 G2
Fairseat TN15 24 C5
Fairstead CM3 34 B7
Fairwarp TN22 13 H4
Fairwater CF5 18 E4
Fairy Cross EX39 6 C3
Fairyhill SA3 17 H6
Fakenham NR21 44 D3
Fala EH37 76 C4
Fala Dam EH37 76 C4
Falahill EH38 76 B5
Faldingworth LN8 52 D4
Falfield Fife KY15 83 F7
Falfield S.Glos. GL12 19 K2
Falin-Wnda SA44 17 G1
Falkenham IP10 35 G5
FALKIRK FK 75 G3
Falkland KY15 82 D7
Falla TD8 70 C2
Fallgate S45 51 F6
Fallin FK7 75 G1
Falmer BN1 13 G6
Falmouth TR11 3 F5
Falsgrave YO12 59 G1
Falstone NE48 70 C5
Fanagmore IV27 102 D4
Fanans PA35 80 B5
Fancott LU5 32 D6
Fangdale Beck TS9 63 G7
Fangfoss YO41 58 D4
Fankerton FK6 75 F2
Fanmore PA73 79 F3
Fanner's Green CM3 33 K7
Fans TD4 76 E6
Far Cotton NN4 31 J3
Far Forest DY14 29 G1
Far Gearstones LA6 56 C1
Far Green GL11 20 A1
Far Moor WN5 48 E2
Far Oakridge GL6 20 C1
Far Royds LS12 57 H6
Far Sawrey LA22 60 E7
Farcet PE7 43 F6
Farden SY8 28 E1
Fareham PO16 11 G4
Farewell WS13 40 C4
Farforth LN11 53 G5
Faringdon SN7 21 F2
Farington PR25 55 J7
Farlam CA8 61 G1
Farlary IV28 96 E1
Farleigh N.Som. BS48 19 J5
Farleigh Surr. CR6 23 G5
Farleigh Hungerford BA2 20 B6
Farleigh Wallop RG25 21 K7
Farlesthorpe LN13 53 H5
Farleton Cumb. LA6 55 J1
Farleton Lancs. LA2 55 J3
Farley Derbys. DE4 50 E6
Farley Shrop. SY5 38 C5
Farley Staffs. ST10 40 C1
Farley Wilts. SP5 10 D2
Farley Green Suff. CB8 34 B3
Farley Green Surr. GU5 22 D7
Farley Hill RG7 22 A5
Farleys End GL2 29 G7
Farlington YO61 58 C3
Farlow DY14 39 F7
Farm Town LE67 41 F4
Farmborough BA2 19 K5
Farmcote GL54 30 B6
Farmington GL54 30 C7
Farmoor OX2 21 H1
Farmtown AB55 98 D5
Farnborough Gt.Lon. BR6 23 H5
Farnborough Hants. GU14 22 B6
Farnborough W.Berks. OX12 21 H3
Farnborough Warks. OX17 31 F4
Farnborough Street GU14 22 B6
Farncombe GU7 22 C7
Farndish NN29 32 C2
Farndon Ches.W. & C. CH3 48 D7
Farndon Notts. NG24 51 K7
Farnell DD9 83 H2
Farnham Dorset DT11 9 J3
Farnham Essex CM23 33 H6
Farnham N.Yorks. HG5 57 J3
Farnham Suff. IP17 35 H2
Farnham Surr. GU9 22 B7
Farnham Common SL2 22 C3
Farnham Green CM23 33 H6
Farnham Royal SL2 22 C3
Farningham DA4 23 J5
Farnley N.Yorks. LS21 57 H5
Farnley W.Yorks. LS12 57 H6
Farnley Tyas HD4 50 D1
Farnsfield NG22 51 J7
Farnworth Gt.Man. BL4 49 G2
Farnworth Halton WA8 48 E4
Farr High. KW14 104 C2
Farr High. IV2 88 D1
Farr High. PH21 89 F4
Farr House IV2 88 D1
Farraline IV2 88 C2
Farringdon EX5 7 J6
Farrington Gurney BS39 19 K6
Farsley LS28 57 H6
Farthing Corner ME8 24 E5
Farthing Green TN12 14 D3
Farthinghoe NN13 31 G5
Farthingstone NN12 31 H3
Farthorpe LN9 53 F5
Fartown HD2 50 D1
Farway EX24 7 K6
Fasag IV22 94 E6
Fasagrianach IV23 95 H3
Fascadale PH36 86 B7
Faslane G84 74 A2
Fasnacloich PA38 80 B3
Fasnakyle IV4 87 K2
Fassfern PH33 87 G7
Fatfield NE38 62 E1
Fattahead AB45 98 E5
Faugh CA8 61 G1
Fauldhouse EH47 75 H4
Faulkbourne CM8 34 B7
Faulkland BA3 20 A6
Fauls SY13 38 E2
Faulston SP5 10 B2
Faversham ME13 25 G5
Favillar AB55 89 K1
Fawdington YO61 57 K2
Fawdon NE3 71 H7
Fawfieldhead SK17 50 C6
Fawkham Green DA3 23 J5
Fawler OX7 30 E7
Fawley Bucks. RG9 22 A3
Fawley Hants. SO45 11 F4
Fawley W.Berks. OX12 21 G3
Fawley Chapel HR1 28 E6
Fawsyde DD10 91 G7
Faxfleet DN14 58 E7
Faxton NN6 31 J1
Faygate RH12 13 F3
Fazakerley L9 48 C3
Fazeley B78 40 E5
Fearby HG4 57 G1
Fearn IV20 97 F4
Fearnan PH15 81 J3
Fearnbeg IV54 94 D6
Fearnhead WA2 49 F3
Fearnmore IV54 94 D5
Fearnoch Arg. & B. PA22 73 J3
Fearnoch Arg. & B. PA21 73 H2
Featherstone Staffs. WV10 40 B5
Featherstone W.Yorks. WF7 57 K7
Featherstone Castle NE49 70 B7
Feckenham B96 30 B2
Feering CO5 34 C6
Feetham DL11 62 A7
Feith-hill AB53 98 E6
Feizor LA2 56 C3
Felbridge RH19 13 G3
Felbrigg NR11 45 G2
Felcourt RH19 23 G7
Felden HP3 22 D1
Felhampton SY6 38 D7
Felindre Carmar. SA19 27 G6
Felindre Carmar. SA32 17 J3
Felindre Carmar. SA44 17 G2
Felindre Carmar. SA19 17 K2
Felindre Cere. SA48 26 E3
Felindre Powys LD7 38 A7
Felindre Powys NP8 28 A6
Felindre Swan. SA5 17 K5
Felinfach Cere. SA48 26 E3
Felinfach Powys LD3 27 K5
Felinfoel SA14 17 J5
Felingwmisaf SA32 17 J3
Felingwmuchaf SA32 17 J3
Felixkirk YO7 57 K1
Felixstowe IP11 35 H5
Felixstowe Ferry IP11 35 H5
Felkington TD15 77 H6
Felldownhead PL19 6 B7
Felling NE10 71 H7
Fellonmore PA65 79 H5
Felmersham MK43 32 C3
Felmingham NR28 45 G3
Felpham PO22 12 C7
Felsham IP30 34 D3
Felsted CM6 33 K6
Feltham TW13 22 E4
Felthamhill TW16 22 E4
Felthorpe NR10 45 F4
Felton Here. HR1 28 E4
Felton N.Som. BS40 19 J5
Felton Northumb. NE65 71 G3
Felton Butler SY4 38 C4
Feltwell IP26 44 B6
Fen Ditton CB5 33 H2
Fen Drayton CB24 33 G2
Fen End CV8 30 D1
Fen Street Norf. NR17 44 D6
Fen Street Norf. IP22 34 E1
Fen Street Suff. IP22 34 D1
Fen Street Suff. IP14 35 F2
Fenay Bridge HD8 50 D1
Fence BB12 56 D6
Fence Houses DH4 62 E1
Fencott OX5 31 G7
Fendike Corner PE24 53 H6
Fenham TD15 77 J6
Fenhouses PE20 43 F1
Feniscowles BB2 56 B7
Feniton EX14 7 K6
Fenn Street ME3 24 D4
Fenni-fach LD3 27 K6
Fenny Bentley DE6 50 D7
Fenny Bridges EX14 7 K6
Fenny Compton CV47 31 F3
Fenny Drayton CV13 41 F6
Fenny Stratford MK2 32 B5
Fenrother NE61 71 G4
Fenstanton PE28 33 G2
Fenton Cambs. PE28 33 G1
Fenton Lincs. LN1 52 B5
Fenton Lincs. NG23 52 B7
Fenton Northumb. NE71 77 H7
Fenton Notts. DN22 51 K4
Fenton Stoke ST4 40 A1
Fenton Barns EH39 76 D2
Fenwick E.Ayr. KA3 74 C6
Fenwick Northumb. NE18 71 F6
Fenwick Northumb. TD15 77 J6
Fenwick S.Yorks. DN6 51 H1
Feochaig PA28 66 B2
Feock TR3 3 F5
Feolin PA60 72 D4
Feolin Ferry PA60 72 C4
Feorlan PA28 66 A3
Feorlin PA32 73 H1
Ferguslie Park PA3 74 C4
Feriniquarrie IV55 93 G6
Fern DD8 83 F1
Ferndale CF43 18 C2
Ferndown BH22 10 B4
Ferness IV12 97 G7
Fernham SN7 21 F2
Fernhill Heath WR3 29 H3
Fernhurst GU27 12 B4
Fernie KY15 82 E6
Fernilea IV47 85 J1
Fernilee SK23 50 C5
Fernybank DD9 90 D7
Ferrensby HG5 57 J3
Ferrindonald IV44 86 C4
Ferring BN12 12 D6
Ferry Hill PE16 43 G7
Ferrybridge WF11 57 K7
Ferryden DD10 83 J2
Ferryhill DL17 62 D3
Ferryside (Glanyferi) SA17 17 G4
Fersfield IP22 44 E7
Fersit PH31 87 K7
Ferwig SA43 16 E1
Feshiebridge PH21 89 F4
Fetcham KT22 22 E6
Fetlar ZE2 107 Q3
Fetterangus AB42 99 H5
Fettercairn AB30 90 E7
Fetternear House AB51 91 F3
Feus of Caldhame AB30 83 H1
Fewcott OX27 31 G6
Fewston HG3 57 G4
Ffairfach SA19 17 K3
Ffair-Rhos SY25 27 G2
Ffaldybrenin SA19 17 K1
Ffarmers SA19 17 K1
Ffawyddog NP8 28 B7
Ffestiniog (Llan Ffestiniog) LL41 37 G1
Ffordd-las Denb. LL16 47 K6
Fforddlas Powys HR3 28 B5
Fforest SA4 17 J5
Fforest-fach SA5 17 K6
Ffostrasol SA44 17 G1
Ffos-y-ffin SA46 26 D2
Ffridd Uchaf LL54 46 D7
Ffrith Denb. LL19 47 J4
Ffrith Flints. LL11 48 B7
Ffrwdgrech LD3 27 K6
Ffynnon SA33 17 G4
Ffynnon Taf (Taff's Well) CF15 18 E3
Ffynnongroyw CH8 47 K4

## Fib - Fro


Fibhig **HS2** 100 E3
Fichlie **AB33** 90 C3
Fidden **PA66** 78 E5
Fiddington *Glos.* **GL20** 29 J5
Fiddington *Som.* **TA5** 19 F7
Fiddleford **DT10** 9 H3
Fiddler's Green *Glos.* **GL51** 29 J6
Fiddler's Green *Here.* **HR1** 28 E5
Fiddler's Green *Norf.* **PE32** 44 C4
Fiddler's Green *Norf.* **NR17** 44 E6
Fiddlers Hamlet **CM16** 23 H1
Field **ST14** 40 C2
Field Broughton **LA11** 55 G1
Field Dalling **NR25** 44 E2
Field Head **LE67** 41 G5
Fife Keith **AB55** 98 C5
Fifehead Magdalen **SP8** 9 G2
Fifehead Neville **DT10** 9 G3
Fifehead St. Quintin **DT10** 9 G3
Fifield *Oxon.* **OX7** 30 D7
Fifield *W. & M.* **SL6** 22 C4
Fifield Bavant **SP5** 10 B2
Figheldean **SP4** 20 E7
Filby **NR29** 45 J4
**Filey YO14 59 H1**
Filgrave **MK16** 32 B4
Filham **PL21** 5 G5
Filkins **GL7** 21 F1
Filleigh *Devon* **EX32** 6 E3
Filleigh *Devon* **EX17** 7 F4
Fillingham **DN21** 52 C4
Fillongley **CV7** 40 E7
Filmore Hill **GU34** 11 H2
Filton **BS34** 19 K4
Fimber **YO25** 58 E3
Finavon **DD8** 83 F2
Fincham **PE33** 44 A5
Finchampstead **RG40** 22 A5
Finchdean **PO8** 11 J3
Finchingfield **CM7** 33 K5
Finchley **N3** 23 F2
Findern **DE65** 41 F2
Findhorn **IV36** 97 H5
Findhorn Bridge **IV13** 89 F2
Findhuglen **PH6** 81 J6
Findo Gask **PH1** 82 B5
Findochty **AB56** 98 C4
Findon *Aber.* **AB12** 91 H5
Findon *W.Suss.* **BN14** 12 E6
Findon Mains **IV7** 96 D5
Findon Valley **BN14** 12 E6
Findrassie **IV30** 97 J5
Findron **AB37** 89 J3
Finedon **NN9** 32 C1
Finegand **PH10** 82 C1
Fingal Street **IP13** 35 G1
Fingask **AB51** 91 F2
Fingerpost **DY14** 29 G1
Fingest **RG9** 22 A2
Finghall **DL8** 57 G1
Fingland *Cumb.* **CA7** 60 D1
Fingland *D. & G.* **DG13** 69 H3
Fingland *D. & G.* **DG4** 68 C2
Finglesham **CT14** 15 J2
Fingringhoe **CO5** 34 E6
Finkle Street **S35** 51 F3
Finlarig **FK21** 81 G4
Finmere **MK18** 31 H5
Finnart *Arg. & B.* **G84** 74 A1
Finnart *P. & K.* **PH17** 81 G2
Finney Hill **LE12** 41 G4
Finningham **IP14** 34 E2
Finningley **DN9** 51 J3
Finnygaud **AB54** 98 E5
Finsbay (Fionnsbhagh) **HS3** 93 F3
Finsbury **EC1R** 23 G3
Finstall **B60** 29 J1
Finsthwaite **LA12** 55 G1
Finstock **OX7** 30 E7
Finstown **KW17** 106 C6
Fintry *Aber.* **AB53** 99 F5
Fintry *Stir.* **G63** 74 E2
Finwood **CV35** 30 C2
Finzean **AB31** 90 D5
Fionnphort **PA66** 78 D5
Fionnsbhagh (Finsbay) **HS3** 93 F3
Fir Tree **DL15** 62 C3
Firbank **LA10** 61 H7
Firbeck **S81** 51 H4
Firby *N.Yorks.* **DL8** 57 H1
Firby *N.Yorks.* **YO60** 58 D3
Firgrove **OL16** 49 J1
Firs Lane **WN7** 49 F2
Firsby **PE23** 53 H6
Firsdown **SP5** 10 D1
Firth **ZE2** 107 N5
Fishbourne *I.o.W.* **PO33** 11 G5
Fishbourne *W.Suss.* **PO18** 12 B6
Fishburn **TS21** 62 E3
Fishcross **FK10** 75 H1
Fisherford **AB51** 90 E1
Fisher's Pond **SO50** 11 F2
Fisher's Row **PR3** 55 H5
Fishersgate **BN41** 13 F6
Fisherstreet **GU8** 12 C3
Fisherton *High.* **IV2** 96 E6
Fisherton *S.Ayr.* **KA7** 67 G2
Fisherton de la Mere **BA12** 9 J1
**Fishguard (Abergwaun) SA65 16 C2**
Fishlake **DN7** 51 J1
Fishleigh Barton **EX37** 6 D3
Fishley **NR13** 45 J4
Fishnish **PA65** 79 H3
Fishpond Bottom **DT6** 8 C5
Fishponds **BS16** 19 K4
Fishpool **BL9** 49 H2
Fishtoft **PE21** 43 G1
Fishtoft Drove **PE22** 43 G1
Fishtown of Usan **DD10** 83 J2
Fishwick **TD15** 77 H5
Fiskerton *Lincs.* **LN3** 52 D5
Fiskerton *Notts.* **NG25** 51 K7
Fitling **HU11** 59 J6
Fittleton **SP4** 20 E7
Fittleworth **RH20** 12 D5
Fitton End **PE13** 43 H4
Fitz **SY4** 38 D4
Fitzhead **TA4** 7 K3
Fitzroy **TA2** 7 K3
Fitzwilliam **WF9** 51 G1
Fiunary **PA34** 79 H3
Five Acres **GL16** 28 E7
Five Ash Down **TN22** 13 H4
Five Ashes **TN20** 13 J4
Five Bridges **WR6** 29 F4
Five Houses **PO30** 11 F6
Five Lanes **NP26** 19 H2
Five Oak Green **TN12** 23 K7
Five Oaks *Chan.I.* **JE2** 3 K7
Five Oaks *W.Suss.* **RH14** 12 D4
Five Roads **SA15** 17 H5
Five Turnings **LD7** 28 B1
Five Wents **ME17** 14 D2
Fivehead **TA3** 8 C2
Fivelanes **PL15** 4 C2
Flack's Green **CM3** 34 B7
Flackwell Heath **HP10** 22 B3
Fladbury **WR10** 29 J4
Fladdabister **ZE2** 107 N9
Flagg **SK17** 50 D6
Flamborough **YO15** 59 J2
Flamstead **AL3** 32 D7
Flamstead End **EN7** 23 G1
Flansham **PO22** 12 C6
Flanshaw **WF2** 57 J7
Flasby **BD23** 56 E4
Flash **SK17** 50 C6
Flashader **IV51** 93 J6
Flask Inn **YO22** 63 J2
Flaunden **HP3** 22 D1
Flawborough **NG13** 42 A1
Flawith **YO61** 57 K3
Flax Bourton **BS48** 19 J5
Flax Moss **BB4** 56 C7
Flaxby **HG5** 57 J4
Flaxholme **DE56** 41 F1
Flaxlands **NR16** 45 F6
Flaxley **GL14** 29 F7
Flaxpool **TA4** 7 K2
Flaxton **YO60** 58 C3
Fleckney **LE8** 41 J6
Flecknoe **CV23** 31 G2
Fledborough **NG22** 52 B5
**Fleet *Hants.* GU51 22 B6**
Fleet *Hants.* **PO11** 11 J4
Fleet *Lincs.* **PE12** 43 G3
Fleet Hargate **PE12** 43 G3
Fleetville **AL1** 22 E1
**Fleetwood FY7 55 G5**
Fleggburgh (Burgh St. Margaret) **NR29** 45 J4
Flemingston **CF62** 18 D4
Flemington **G72** 74 E5
Flempton **IP28** 34 C2
Fleoideabhagh **HS3** 93 F3
Flesherin **HS2** 101 H4
Fletchersbridge **PL30** 4 B4
Fletchertown **CA7** 60 D2
Fletching **TN22** 13 H4
Fleuchats **AB36** 90 B4
Fleur-de-lis **NP12** 18 E2
Flexbury **EX23** 6 A5
Flexford **GU3** 22 C6
Flimby **CA15** 60 B3
Flimwell **TN5** 14 C4
**Flint (Y Fflint) CH6 48 B5**
Flint Cross **SG8** 33 H4
Flint Mountain **CH6** 48 B5
Flintham **NG23** 42 A1
Flinton **HU11** 59 J6
Flint's Green **CV7** 30 D1
Flishinghurst **TN17** 14 C4
Flitcham **PE31** 44 B3
Flitholme **CA16** 61 J5
Flitton **MK45** 32 D5
Flitwick **MK45** 32 D5
Flixborough **DN15** 52 B1
Flixton *Gt.Man.* **M41** 49 G3
Flixton *N.Yorks.* **YO11** 59 G2
Flixton *Suff.* **NR35** 45 H7
Flockton **WF4** 50 E1
Flockton Green **WF4** 50 E1
Flodden **NE71** 77 H7
Flodigarry **IV51** 93 K4
Flood's Ferry **PE15** 43 G6
Flookburgh **LA11** 55 G2
Floors **AB55** 98 C5
Flordon **NR15** 45 F6
Flore **NN7** 31 H2
Flotta **KW16** 106 C8
Flotterton **NE65** 71 F3
Flowton **IP8** 34 E4
Flushdyke **WF5** 57 H7
Flushing *Aber.* **AB42** 99 J6
Flushing *Cornw.* **TR11** 3 F5
Flushing *Cornw.* **TR12** 2 E6
Fluxton **EX11** 7 J6
Flyford Flavell **WR7** 29 J3
Foals Green **IP21** 35 G1
Fobbing **SS17** 24 D3
**Fochabers IV32 98 B5**
Fochriw **CF81** 18 E1
Fockerby **DN17** 52 B1
Fodderletter **AB37** 89 J2
Fodderty **IV15** 96 C6
Foddington **TA11** 8 E2
Foel **SY21** 37 J4
Foelgastell **SA14** 17 J4
Foggathorpe **YO8** 58 D6
Fogo **TD11** 77 F6
Fogorig **TD11** 77 F6
Fogwatt **IV30** 97 K6
Foindle **IV27** 102 D4
Folda **PH11** 82 C1
Fole **ST14** 40 C2
Foleshill **CV6** 41 F7
Folke **DT9** 9 F3
**Folkestone CT20 15 H4**
Folkingham **NG34** 42 D2
Folkington **BN26** 13 J6
Folksworth **PE7** 42 E7
Folkton **YO11** 59 G2
Folla Rule **AB51** 91 F1
Follifoot **HG3** 57 J4
Folly *Dorset* **DT2** 9 G4
Folly *Pembs.* **SA62** 16 C3
Folly Gate **EX20** 6 D6
Fonmon **CF62** 18 D5
Fonthill Bishop **SP3** 9 J1
Fonthill Gifford **SP3** 9 J1
Fontmell Magna **SP7** 9 H3
Fontmell Parva **DT11** 9 H3
Fontwell **BN18** 12 C6
Font-y-gary **CF62** 18 D5
Foolow **S32** 50 D5
Footherley **WS14** 40 D5
Foots Cray **DA14** 23 H4
Forbestown **AB36** 90 B3
Force Forge **LA12** 60 E7
Force Green **TN16** 23 H6
Forcett **DL11** 62 C5
Forches Cross **EX17** 7 F5
Ford *Arg. & B.* **PA31** 79 K7
Ford *Bucks.* **HP17** 22 A1
Ford *Devon* **PL8** 5 G5
Ford *Devon* **EX39** 6 C3
Ford *Devon* **TQ7** 5 H6
Ford *Glos.* **GL54** 30 B6
Ford *Mersey.* **L30** 48 C3
Ford *Midloth.* **EH37** 76 B4
Ford *Northumb.* **TD15** 77 H7
Ford *Pembs.* **SA62** 16 C3
Ford *Plym.* **PL2** 4 E5
Ford *Shrop.* **SY5** 38 D4
Ford *Som.* **TA4** 7 J3
Ford *Staffs.* **ST13** 50 C7
Ford *W.Suss.* **BN18** 12 C6
Ford *Wilts.* **SN14** 20 B4
Ford End **CM3** 33 K7
Ford Green **PR3** 55 H5
Ford Heath **SY5** 38 D4
Ford Street **TA21** 7 K4
Forda **EX20** 6 D6
Fordbridge **B37** 40 D7
Fordcombe **TN3** 23 J7
Forddun (Forden) **SY21** 38 B5
Fordell **KY4** 75 K2
Forden (Forddun) **SY21** 38 B5
Forder Green **TQ13** 5 H4
Fordgate **TA7** 8 C1
Fordham *Cambs.* **CB7** 33 K1
Fordham *Essex* **CO6** 34 D6
Fordham *Norf.* **PE38** 44 A6
Fordham Abbey **CB7** 33 K2
Fordham Heath **CO3** 34 D6
Fordhouses **WV10** 40 B5
**Fordingbridge SP6 10 C3**
Fordon **YO25** 59 G2
Fordoun **AB30** 91 F7
Ford's Green **IP14** 34 E2
Fordstreet **CO6** 34 D6
Fordwells **OX29** 30 E7
Fordwich **CT2** 15 G2
Fordyce **AB45** 98 D4
Forebrae **PH1** 82 A5
Forebridge **ST17** 40 B3
Foredale **BD24** 56 D3
Foreland **PA49** 72 A4
Foremark **DE65** 41 F3
Forest **DL10** 62 D6
Forest Coal Pit **NP7** 28 B6
Forest Gate **E7** 23 H3
Forest Green **RH5** 22 E7
Forest Hall *Cumb.* **LA8** 61 G6
Forest Hall *T. & W.* **NE12** 71 H7
Forest Head **CA8** 61 G1
Forest Hill *Gt.Lon.* **SE23** 23 G4
Forest Hill *Oxon.* **OX33** 21 J1
Forest Lane Head **HG2** 57 J4
Forest Lodge *Arg. & B.* **PA36** 80 D3
Forest Lodge *P. & K.* **PH18** 89 G7
**Forest Row RH18 13 H3**
Forest Side **PO30** 11 F6
Forest Town **NG19** 51 H6
Forestburn Gate **NE61** 71 F4
Forest-in-Teesdale **DL12** 61 K4
Forestmill **FK10** 75 H1
Forestside **PO9** 11 J3
**Forfar DD8 83 F2**
Forgandenny **PH2** 82 B6
Forge **SY20** 37 G6
Forgie **AB55** 98 B5
Forhill **B38** 30 B1
Formby **L37** 48 B2
Forncett End **NR16** 45 F6
Forncett St. Mary **NR16** 45 F6
Forncett St. Peter **NR16** 45 F6
Forneth **PH10** 82 B3
Fornham All Saints **IP28** 34 C2
Fornham St. Martin **IP31** 34 C2
Fornighty **IV12** 97 G6
**Forres IV36 97 H6**
Forrest **ML6** 75 G4
Forrest Lodge **DG7** 67 K5
Forsbrook **ST11** 40 B1
Forse **KW5** 105 H5
Forsie **KW14** 105 F2
Forsinain **KW13** 104 E4
**Forsinard KW13 104 D4**
Forston **DT2** 9 F5
**Fort Augustus PH32 87 K4**
Fort George **IV2** 96 E6
**Fort William PH33 87 H7**
Forter **PH11** 82 C1
Forteviot **PH2** 82 B6
Forth **ML11** 75 H5
Forthampton **GL19** 29 H5
Fortingall **PH15** 81 J3
Fortis Green **N2** 23 F3
Forton *Hants.* **SP11** 21 H7
Forton *Lancs.* **PR3** 55 H4
Forton *Shrop.* **SY4** 38 D4
Forton *Som.* **TA20** 8 C4
Forton *Staffs.* **TF10** 39 G3
Fortrie **AB53** 98 E6
**Fortrose IV10 96 E6**
Fortuneswell **DT5** 9 F7
Forty Green **HP9** 22 C2
Forty Hill **EN2** 23 G2
Forward Green **IP14** 34 E3
Fosbury **SN8** 21 G6
Foscot **OX7** 30 D6
Fosdyke **PE20** 43 G2
Foss **PH16** 81 J2
Foss Cross **GL54** 20 D1
Fossdale **DL8** 61 K7
Fossebridge **GL54** 30 B7
Foster Street **CM17** 23 H1
Fosterhouses **DN14** 51 J1
Foster's Booth **NN12** 31 H3
Foston *Derbys.* **DE65** 40 D2
Foston *Leics.* **LE8** 41 J6
Foston *Lincs.* **NG32** 42 B1
Foston *N.Yorks.* **YO60** 58 C3
Foston on the Wolds **YO25** 59 H4
Fotherby **LN11** 53 G3
Fotheringhay **PE8** 42 D6
Foubister **KW17** 106 E7
Foul Mile **BN27** 13 K5
Foula **ZE2** 107 L2
Foula Airstrip **ZE2** 107 L2
Foulbog **DG13** 69 H3
Foulden *Norf.* **IP26** 44 B6
Foulden *Sc.Bord.* **TD15** 77 H5
Foulness Island **SS3** 25 G2
Foulridge **BB8** 56 D5
Foulsham **NR20** 44 E3
Foulstone **LA6** 55 J1
Foulzie **AB45** 99 F4
Fountainhall **TD1** 76 C6
Four Ashes *Staffs.* **WV10** 40 B5
Four Ashes *Staffs.* **DY7** 40 A7
Four Ashes *Suff.* **IP31** 34 D1
Four Crosses *Denb.* **LL21** 37 K1
Four Crosses *Powys* **SY22** 38 B4
Four Crosses *Powys* **SY21** 37 K5
Four Crosses *Staffs.* **WS11** 40 B5
Four Elms **TN8** 23 H7
Four Forks **TA5** 8 B1
Four Gotes **PE13** 43 H4
Four Lane Ends *B'burn.* **BB1** 56 B7
Four Lane Ends *Ches.W. & C.* **CW6** 48 E6
Four Lane Ends *York* **YO19** 58 C4
Four Lanes **TR16** 2 D5
Four Marks **GU34** 11 H1
Four Mile Bridge **LL65** 46 A5
Four Oaks *E.Suss.* **TN31** 14 D5
Four Oaks *Glos.* **GL18** 29 F6
Four Oaks *W.Mid.* **CV7** 40 E7
Four Oaks *W.Mid.* **B74** 40 D6
Four Oaks Park **B74** 40 D6
Four Roads **SA17** 17 H5
Four Throws **TN18** 14 C5
Fourlane Ends **DE55** 51 F7
Fourlanes End **CW11** 49 H7
Fourpenny **IV25** 97 F2
Fourstones **NE47** 70 D7
Fovant **SP3** 10 B2
Foveran House **AB41** 91 H2
**Fowey PL23 4 B5**
Fowlis **DD2** 82 E4
Fowlis Wester **PH7** 82 A5
Fowlmere **SG8** 33 H4
Fownhope **HR1** 28 E5
Fox Hatch **CM15** 23 J2
Fox Lane **GU14** 22 B6
Fox Street **CO7** 34 E6
Foxbar **PA2** 74 C4
Foxcombe Hill **OX1** 21 H1
Foxcote *Glos.* **GL54** 30 B7
Foxcote *Som.* **BA3** 20 A6
Foxdale **IM4** 54 B6
Foxearth **CO10** 34 C4
Foxfield **LA20** 55 F1
Foxham **SN15** 20 C4
Foxhole *Cornw.* **PL26** 3 G3
Foxhole *High.* **IV4** 88 C1
Foxholes **YO25** 59 G2
Foxhunt Green **TN21** 13 J5
Foxley *Here.* **HR4** 28 D4
Foxley *Norf.* **NR20** 44 E3
Foxley *Northants.* **NN12** 31 H3
Foxley *Wilts.* **SN16** 20 B3
Foxt **ST10** 40 C1
Foxton *Cambs.* **CB22** 33 H4
Foxton *Dur.* **TS21** 62 E4
Foxton *Leics.* **LE16** 41 J6
Foxup **BD23** 56 D2
Foxwist Green **CW8** 49 F6
Foy **HR9** 28 E6
Foyers **IV2** 88 B2
Frachadil **PA75** 78 E2
Fraddam **TR27** 2 C5
Fraddon **TR9** 3 G3
Fradley **WS13** 40 D4
Fradswell **ST18** 40 B2
Fraisthorpe **YO15** 59 H3
Framfield **TN22** 13 H4
Framingham Earl **NR14** 45 G5
Framingham Pigot **NR14** 45 G5
Framlingham **IP13** 35 G2
Frampton *Dorset* **DT2** 9 F5
Frampton *Lincs.* **PE20** 43 G2
Frampton Cotterell **BS36** 19 K3
Frampton Mansell **GL6** 20 C1
Frampton on Severn **GL2** 20 A1
Frampton West End **PE20** 43 F1
Framsden **IP14** 35 G3
Framwellgate Moor **DH1** 62 D2
France Lynch **GL6** 20 C1
Frances Green **PR3** 56 B6
Franche **DY11** 29 H1
Frandley **CW9** 49 F5
Frankby **CH48** 48 B4
Frankfort **NR12** 45 H3
Frankley **B32** 40 B7
Franksbridge **LD1** 28 A3
Frankton **CV23** 31 F1
Frant **TN3** 13 J3
**Fraserburgh AB43 99 H4**
Frating **CO7** 34 E6
Fratton **PO1** 11 H4
Freasley **B78** 40 E6
Freathy **PL10** 4 D5
Freckenham **IP28** 33 K1
Freckleton **PR4** 55 H7
Freeby **LE14** 42 B3
Freefolk **RG28** 21 H7
Freehay **ST10** 40 C1
Freeland **OX29** 31 F7
Freester **ZE2** 107 N7
Freethorpe **NR13** 45 J5
Freethorpe Common **NR13** 45 J5
Freiston **PE22** 43 G1
Freiston Shore **PE22** 43 G1
Fremington *Devon* **EX31** 6 D2
Fremington *N.Yorks.* **DL11** 62 B7
Frenchay **BS16** 19 K4
Frenchbeer **TQ13** 6 E7
Frendraught **AB54** 98 E6
Frenich **FK8** 81 F7
Frensham **GU10** 22 B7
Fresgoe **KW14** 104 E2
Freshbrook **SN5** 20 E3
Freshfield **L37** 48 B2
Freshford **BA2** 20 A6
**Freshwater PO40 10 E6**
Freshwater Bay **PO40** 10 E6
Freshwater East **SA71** 16 D6
Fressingfield **IP21** 35 G1
Freston **IP9** 35 F5
Freswick **KW1** 105 J2
Fretherne **GL2** 20 A1
Frettenham **NR12** 45 G4
Freuchie **KY15** 82 D7
Freystrop Cross **SA62** 16 C4
Friars Carse **DG2** 68 E5
Friar's Gate **TN6** 13 H3
Friarton **PH2** 82 C5
Friday Bridge **PE14** 43 H5
Friday Street *E.Suss.* **BN23** 13 K6
Friday Street *Suff.* **IP13** 35 G3
Friday Street *Suff.* **IP12** 35 H3
Friday Street *Surr.* **RH5** 22 E7
Fridaythorpe **YO25** 58 E4
Friern Barnet **N11** 23 F2
Friesthorpe **LN3** 52 D4
Frieston **NG32** 42 C1
Frieth **RG9** 22 A2
Frilford **OX13** 21 H2
Frilsham **RG18** 21 J4
Frimley **GU16** 22 B6
Frimley Green **GU16** 22 B6
Frindsbury **ME2** 24 D5
Fring **PE31** 44 B2
Fringford **OX27** 31 H6
Frinningham **ME14** 14 D2
Frinsted **ME9** 14 D2
**Frinton-on-Sea CO13 35 G7**
Friockheim **DD11** 83 G3
Friog **LL38** 37 F4
Frisby on the Wreake **LE14** 41 J4
Friskney **PE22** 53 H7
Friskney Eaudyke **PE22** 53 H7
Friston *E.Suss.* **BN20** 13 J7
Friston *Suff.* **IP17** 35 J2
Fritchley **DE56** 51 F7
Frith **ME13** 14 E2
Frith Bank **PE22** 43 G1
Frith Common **WR15** 29 F2
Fritham **SO43** 10 D3
Frithelstock **EX38** 6 C4
Frithelstock Stone **EX38** 6 C4
Frithville **PE22** 53 G7
Frittenden **TN17** 14 D3
Frittiscombe **TQ7** 5 J6
Fritton *Norf.* **NR15** 45 G6
Fritton *Norf.* **NR31** 45 J5
Fritwell **OX27** 31 G6
Frizinghall **BD9** 57 G6
**Frizington CA26 60 B5**
Frocester **GL10** 20 A1
Frochas **SY21** 38 B5
Frodesley **SY5** 38 E5
Frodesley Lane **SY5** 38 E5
Frodingham **DN15** 52 B1
**Frodsham WA6 48 E5**
Frog End **CB23** 33 H3
Frog Pool **WR6** 29 G2
Frogden **TD5** 70 C1
Froggatt **S32** 50 E5
Froghall **ST10** 40 C1

Fro - Gle


Frogham SP6 10 C3
Frogland Cross BS36 19 K3
Frogmore *Devon* TQ7 5 H6
Frogmore *Hants.* GU17 22 B6
Frogmore *Herts.* AL2 22 E1
Frogwell PL17 4 D4
Frolesworth LE17 41 H6
**Frome BA11** 20 **A7**
Frome Market BA11 20 B6
Frome St. Quintin DT2 8 E4
Frome Whitfield DT2 9 F5
Fromes Hill HR8 29 F4
Fron *Gwyn.* LL53 36 C2
Fron *Powys* SY21 38 B5
Fron *Powys* LD1 27 K2
Fron *Powys* SY15 38 A6
Fron Isaf LL14 38 B2
Froncysyllte LL20 38 B1
Fron-goch LL23 37 J2
Frostenden NR34 45 J7
Frosterley DL13 62 B3
Froxfield SN8 21 G5
Froxfield Green GU32 11 J2
Fryerning CM4 24 C1
Fugglestone St. Peter SP2 10 C1
Fulbeck NG32 52 C7
Fulbourn CB21 33 J3
Fulbrook OX18 30 D7
Fulflood SO22 11 F2
Fulford *Som.* TA2 8 B2
Fulford *Staffs.* ST11 40 B2
Fulford *York* YO10 58 C5
Fulham SW6 23 F4
Fulking BN5 13 F5
Full Sutton YO41 58 D4
Fullaford EX31 6 E2
Fuller Street CM3 34 B7
Fuller's Moor CH3 48 D7
Fullerton SP11 10 E1
Fulletby LN9 53 F5
Fullwood KA3 74 C5
Fulmer SL3 22 D3
Fulmodeston NR21 44 D2
Fulnetby LN8 52 E5
Fulready CV37 30 D4
Fulstone HD9 50 D2
Fulstow LN11 53 G3
Fulwell *Oxon.* OX7 30 E6
Fulwell *T. & W.* SR5 62 E1
Fulwood *Lancs.* PR2 55 J6
Fulwood *S.Yorks.* S10 51 F4
Fundenhall NR16 45 F6
Fundenhall Street NR16 45 F6
Funtington PO18 12 B6
Funtley PO16 11 G4
Funzie ZE2 107 Q3
Furley EX13 8 B4
Furnace *Arg. & B.* PA32 80 B7
Furnace *Carmar.* SA15 17 J5
Furnace *Cere.* SY20 37 F6
Furnace *High.* IV22 95 F4
Furnace End B46 40 E6
Furner's Green TN22 13 H4
Furness Vale SK23 50 C4
Furneux Pelham SG9 33 H6
Furnham TA20 8 C4
Further Quarter TN26 14 D4
Furtho MK19 31 J4
Furze Green IP21 45 G7
Furze Platt SL6 22 B3
Furzehill *Devon* EX35 7 F1
Furzehill *Dorset* BH21 10 B4
Furzeley Corner PO7 11 H3
Furzey Lodge SO42 10 E4
Furzley SO43 10 D3
Fyfett TA20 8 B3
Fyfield *Essex* CM5 23 J1
Fyfield *Glos.* GL7 21 F1
Fyfield *Hants.* SP11 21 F7
Fyfield *Oxon.* OX13 21 H2
Fyfield *Wilts.* SN8 20 E5
Fyfield *Wilts.* SN9 20 E5
Fylingthorpe YO22 63 J2
Fyning GU31 12 B4
Fyvie AB53 91 F1

## G

Gabalfa CF14 18 E4
Gabhsunn Bho Dheas HS2 101 G2
Gabhsunn Bho Thuath HS2 101 G2
Gablon IV25 96 E2
Gabroc Hill KA3 74 C5
Gaddesby LE7 41 J4
Gaddesden Row HP2 32 D7
Gadebridge HP1 22 D1
Gadshill ME3 24 D4
Gaer *Newport* NP20 19 F3
Gaer *Powys* NP8 28 A6
Gaer-fawr NP15 19 H2
Gaerllwyd NP16 19 H2
**Gaerwen LL60** 46 **C5**
Gagingwell OX7 31 F6
Gaich *High.* PH26 89 H2
Gaich *High.* IV2 88 D1
Gaick Lodge PH21 88 E6
Gailes KA11 74 B7
Gailey ST19 40 B4
Gainford DL2 62 C5
**Gainsborough DN21** 52 **B3**
Gainsford End CO9 34 B5
**Gairloch IV21** 94 **D4**
Gairlochy PH34 87 H6
Gairney Bank KY13 75 K1
Gairnshiel Lodge AB35 89 K4
Gaitsgill CA5 60 E2
Galabank TD1 76 C6
**GALASHIELS TD** 76 **C7**
Galdenoch DG8 64 B4
Gale OL15 49 J1
Galgate LA2 55 H4
Galhampton BA22 9 F2
Gallanach PA34 79 K5
Gallantry Bank SY14 48 E7
Gallatown KY1 76 A1
Gallchoille PA31 73 F1
Gallery AB30 83 H1
Galley Common CV10 41 F6
Galleyend CM2 24 D1
Galleywood CM2 24 D1
Gallowfauld DD8 83 F3
Gallowhill PA3 74 C4
Gallows Green ST10 40 C1
Gallowstree Common RG4 21 K3
Gallowstree Elm DY7 40 A7
Gallt Melyd (Meliden) LL19 47 J4
Galltair IV40 86 E2
Gallt-y-foel LL55 46 D6
Gallypot Street TN7 13 H3
Galmington TA1 8 B2
Galmisdale PH42 85 K6
Galmpton *Devon* TQ7 5 G6
Galmpton *Torbay* TQ5 5 J5
Galmpton Warborough TQ4 5 J5
Galphay HG4 57 H2
**Galston KA4** 74 **C7**
Galtrigill IV55 93 G6
Gamble's Green CM3 34 B7
Gamblesby CA10 61 H3
Gamelsby CA7 60 D1
Gamesley SK13 50 C3
Gamlingay SG19 33 F3
Gamlingay Cinques SG19 33 F3
Gamlingay Great Heath SG19 33 F3
Gammaton EX39 6 C3
Gammaton Moor EX39 6 C3
Gammersgill DL8 57 F1
Gamrie AB45 99 F4
Gamston *Notts.* DN22 51 K5
Gamston *Notts.* NG2 41 J2
Ganarew NP25 28 E7
Gang PL14 4 D4
Ganllwyd LL40 37 G3
Gannochy DD9 90 E7
Ganstead HU11 59 H6
Ganthorpe YO60 58 C2
Ganton YO12 59 F2
Ganwick Corner EN5 23 F2
Gaodhail PA72 79 H4
Gappah TQ13 5 J3
Gara Bridge TQ9 5 H5
Garabal G83 80 E6
Garadheancal IV26 95 F1
Garbat IV23 96 B5
Garbhallt PA27 73 J1
Garboldisham IP22 44 E7
Garden FK8 74 D1
Garden City CH5 48 C6
Garden Village S36 50 E3
Gardeners Green RG40 22 B5
Gardenstown AB45 99 F4
Garderhouse ZE2 107 M8
Gardham HU17 59 F5
Gare Hill BA11 20 A7
Garelochhead G84 74 A1
Garford OX13 21 H2
Garforth LS25 57 K6
Gargrave BD23 56 E4
Gargunnock FK8 75 F1
Gariob PA31 73 F2
Garlic Street IP20 45 G7
Garlies Castle DG8 64 E4
Garlieston DG8 64 E6
Garlinge Green CT4 15 G2
Garlogie AB32 91 F4
Garmelow ST21 40 A3
Garmond AB53 99 G5
Garmony PA65 79 H3
Garmouth IV32 98 B4
Garmston SY5 39 F5
Garnant SA18 17 K4
**Garndolbenmaen LL51** 36 **D1**
Garneddwen SY20 37 G5
Garnett Bridge LA8 61 G7
Garnfadryn LL53 36 B2
Garnswllt SA18 17 K5
Garrabost HS2 101 H4
Garrachra PA23 73 J2
Garralburn AB55 98 C5
Garras TR12 2 E6
Garreg LL48 37 F1
Garreg Bank SY21 38 B4
Garrett's Green B33 40 D7
Garrick FK15 81 K6
Garrigill CA9 61 J2
Garriston DL8 62 C7
Garroch DG7 67 K5
Garrochty PA20 73 J5
Garros IV51 93 K5
Garrow PH8 81 K4
Garryhorn DG7 67 K4
Garrynahine (Gearraidh na h-Aibhne) HS2 100 E4
Garsdale LA10 56 C1
Garsdale Head LA10 61 J7
Garsdon SN16 20 C3
Garshall Green ST18 40 B2
Garsington OX44 21 J1
Garstang PR3 55 H5
Garston L19 48 D4
Garswood WN4 48 E3
Gartachoil G63 74 D1
Gartally IV63 88 B1
Gartavaich PA29 73 G5
Gartbreck PA43 72 A5
Gartcosh G69 74 E4
Garth *Bridgend* CF34 18 B2
Garth *Cere.* SY23 37 F7
Garth *Gwyn.* LL57 46 D5
Garth *I.o.M.* IM4 54 C6
Garth *Powys* LD4 27 J4
Garth *Shet.* ZE2 107 L7
Garth *Wrex.* LL20 38 B1
Garth Row LA8 61 G7
Garthbrengy LD3 27 K5
Garthdee AB15 91 H4
Gartheli SA48 26 E3
Garthmyl SY21 38 A6
Garthorpe *Leics.* LE14 42 B3
Garthorpe *N.Lincs.* DN17 52 B1
Garths LA8 61 G7
Garthynty SA20 27 G4
Gartincaber FK16 81 H7
Gartly AB54 90 D1
Gartmore FK8 74 D1
Gartnagrenach PA29 73 F5
Gartnatra PA43 72 B4
Gartness G63 74 D2
Gartocharn G83 74 C2
Garton HU11 59 J6
Garton-on-the-Wolds YO25 59 F3
Gartymore KW8 105 F7
Garvald EH41 76 D3
Garvamore PH20 88 C5
Garvan PH33 87 F7
Garvard PA61 72 B1
**Garve IV23** 95 **K5**
Garveld PA28 66 A3
Garvestone NR9 44 E5
Garvie PA22 73 J2
Garvock *Aber.* AB30 91 F7
Garvock *Inclyde* PA16 74 A3
Garvock *P. & K.* PH2 82 B6
Garwald DG13 69 H3
Garwaldwaterfoot DG13 69 H3
Garway HR2 28 D6
Garway Hill HR2 28 D6
Gask *Aber.* AB42 99 J6
Gask *Aber.* AB53 99 F6
Gask *P. & K.* PH3 82 A6
Gaskan PH37 86 E7
Gass KA19 67 J3
Gastard SN13 20 B5
Gasthorpe IP22 44 D7
Gaston Green CM22 33 J7
Gatcombe PO30 11 F6
Gate Burton DN21 52 B4
Gate Helmsley YO41 58 C4
Gate House PA60 72 D3
Gateacre L25 48 D4
Gateford S81 51 H4
Gateforth YO8 58 B7
Gatehead KA2 74 B7
Gatehouse PH15 81 K3
Gatehouse of Fleet DG7 65 G5
Gatelawbridge DG3 68 E4
Gateley NR20 44 D3
Gatenby DL7 57 J1
Gatesgarth CA13 60 C5
Gateshaw TD5 70 C1
**Gateshead NE8** 71 **H7**
Gatesheath CH3 48 D6
Gateside *Aber.* AB33 90 E3
Gateside *Angus* DD8 83 F3
Gateside *Fife* KY14 82 C7
Gateside *N.Ayr.* KA15 74 B5
Gateslack DG3 68 D3
Gathurst WN5 48 E2
Gatley SK8 49 H4
Gattonside TD6 76 D7
Gatwick Airport (London Gatwick Airport) RH6 23 F7
Gaufron LD6 27 J2
Gaulby LE7 41 J5
Gauldry DD6 82 E5
Gauntons Bank SY13 38 E1
Gaunt's Common BH21 10 B4
Gaunt's Earthcott BS32 19 K3
Gautby LN8 52 E5
Gavinton TD11 77 F5
Gawber S75 51 F2
Gawcott MK18 31 H5
Gawsworth SK11 49 H5
Gawthrop LA10 56 B1
Gawthwaite LA12 55 F1
Gay Bowers CM3 24 D1
Gay Street RH20 12 D4
Gaydon CV35 30 E3
Gayhurst MK16 32 B4
Gayle DL8 56 D1
Gayles DL11 62 C6
Gayton *Mersey.* CH60 48 B4
Gayton *Norf.* PE32 44 B4
Gayton *Northants.* NN7 31 J3
Gayton *Staffs.* ST18 40 B3
Gayton le Marsh LN13 53 H4
Gayton le Wold LN11 53 F4
Gayton Thorpe PE32 44 B4
Gaywood PE30 44 A3
Gazeley CB8 34 B2
Geanies House IV20 97 F4
Gearach PA48 72 A5
Gearnsary KW11 104 C5
Gearradh PH33 80 A1
Gearraidh Bhailteas HS8 84 C2
Gearraidh Bhaird HS2 101 F5
Gearraidh na h-Aibhne (Garrynahine) HS2 100 E4
Gearraidh na Monadh HS8 84 C3
Gearrannan HS2 100 D3
Geary IV55 93 H5
Gedding IP30 34 D3
Geddington NN14 42 B7
Gedgrave Hall IP12 35 J4
Gedintailor IV51 86 B1
Gedling NG4 41 J1
Gedney PE12 43 H3
Gedney Broadgate PE12 43 H3
Gedney Drove End PE12 43 H3
Gedney Dyke PE12 43 H3
Gedney Hill PE12 43 G4
Gee Cross SK14 49 J3
Geilston G82 74 B3
Geirinis HS8 92 C7
Geisiadar HS2 100 D4
Geldeston NR34 45 H6
Gell *Conwy* LL22 47 G6
Gell *Gwyn.* LL52 36 D2
Gelli CF41 18 C2
Gelli Gynan CH7 47 K7
Gellideg CF48 18 D1
Gellifor LL15 47 K6
Gelligaer CF82 18 E2
Gellilydan LL41 37 F2
Gellioedd LL21 37 J1
Gelly SA66 16 D4
Gellyburn PH1 82 B4
Gellywen SA33 17 F3
Gelston *D. & G.* DG7 65 H5
Gelston *Lincs.* NG32 42 C1
Gembling YO25 59 H4
Gemmil PA31 79 J7
Genoch DG9 64 B5
Genoch Square DG9 64 B5
Gentleshaw WS15 40 C4
Geocrab HS3 93 G2
George Green SL3 22 D3
George Nympton EX36 7 F3
Georgeham EX33 6 C2
Georgetown PA6 74 C4
Gerlan LL57 46 E6
Germansweek EX21 6 C6
Germoe TR20 2 C6
Gerrans TR2 3 F5
**Gerrards Cross SL9** 22 **D3**
Gerston KW12 105 G3
Gestingthorpe CO9 34 C5
Geuffordd SY22 38 B4
Geufron SY18 37 H7
Gibbet Hill BA11 20 A7
Gibbshill DG7 65 H3
Gibraltar *Lincs.* PE24 53 J7
Gibraltar *Suff.* IP6 35 F3
Giddeahall SN14 20 B4
Giddy Green BH20 9 H6
Gidea Park RM2 23 J3
Gidleigh TQ13 6 E7
Giffnock G46 74 D5
Gifford EH41 76 D4
Giffordland KA24 74 A6
Giffordtown KY15 82 D6
Giggleswick BD24 56 D3
**Gigha PA41** 72 **E6**
Gilberdyke HU15 58 E7
Gilbert's End WR8 29 H4
Gilchriston EH36 76 C4
Gilcrux CA7 60 C3
Gildersome LS27 57 H7
Gildingwells S81 51 H4
Gilesgate Moor DH1 62 D2
Gileston CF62 18 D5
Gilfach CF81 18 E2
Gilfach Goch CF39 18 C3
Gilfachrheda SA45 26 D3
Gilgarran CA14 60 B4
Gill CA11 60 F4
Gillamoor YO62 58 C1
Gillen IV55 93 H5
Gillenbie DG11 69 G5
Gillfoot DG2 65 K3
Gilling East YO62 58 C2
Gilling West DL10 62 C6
**Gillingham *Dorset* SP8** 9 **H2**
**Gillingham *Med.* ME7** 24 **D5**
Gillingham *Norf.* NR34 45 J6
Gillivoan KW5 105 G5
Gillock KW1 105 H3
Gillow Heath ST8 49 H7
Gills KW1 105 J1
Gill's Green TN18 14 C4
Gilmanscleuch TD7 69 J1
Gilmerton *Edin.* EH17 76 A4
Gilmerton *P. & K.* PH7 81 K5
Gilmilnscroft KA5 67 K1
Gilmonby DL12 62 A5
Gilmorton LE17 41 H7
Gilsland CA8 70 B7
Gilsland Spa CA8 70 B7
Gilson B46 40 D7
Gilstead BD16 57 G6
Gilston EH38 76 C5
Gilston Park CM20 33 H7
Giltbrook NG16 41 G1
Gilwern NP7 28 B7
Gimingham NR11 45 G2
Gin Pit M29 49 F2
Ginclough SK10 49 J5
Ginger's Green BN27 13 K5
Giosla HS2 100 D5
Gipping IP14 34 E2
Gipsey Bridge PE22 43 F1
Girlsta ZE2 107 N7
Girsby DL2 62 E6
Girtford SG19 32 E4
Girthon DG7 65 G5
Girton *Cambs.* CB3 33 H2
Girton *Notts.* NG23 52 B6
**Girvan KA26** 67 **F4**
Gisburn BB7 56 D5
Gisburn Cotes BB7 56 D5
Gisleham NR33 45 K7
Gislingham IP23 34 E1
Gissing IP22 45 F7
Gittisham EX14 7 K6
Givons Grove KT22 22 E6
Glackour IV23 95 H3
Gladestry HR5 28 B3
Gladsmuir EH33 76 C3
Glaic PA22 73 J3
Glais SA7 18 A1
Glaisdale YO21 63 J6
Glaister KA27 73 H7
Glame IV40 94 B7
Glamis DD8 82 E3
Glan Conwy LL24 47 G7
Glanaber Terrace LL24 37 G1
Glanaman SA18 17 K4
Glanbran SA20 27 H5
Glan-Denys SA48 26 E3
Glanderston AB52 90 D2
Glandford NR25 44 E1
Glan-Duar SA40 17 J1
Glandwr SA34 16 E3
Glan-Dwyfach LL51 36 D1
Glangrwyney NP8 28 B7
Glanllynfi CF34 18 B2
Glanmule SY16 38 A6
Glan-rhyd *N.P.T.* SA9 18 A1
Glanrhyd *Pembs.* SA43 16 E1
Glanton NE66 71 F2
Glanton Pyke NE66 71 F2
Glantwymyn (Cemmaes Road) SY20 37 H5
Glanvilles Wootton DT9 9 F4
Glanwern SY24 37 F7
Glanwydden LL31 47 G4
Glan-y-don CH8 47 K5
**Glanyferi (Ferryside) SA17** 17 **G4**
Glan-y-llyn CF15 18 E3
Glan-y-nant SY18 37 J7
Glan-yr-afon *Gwyn.* LL23 37 J1
Glan-yr-afon *Gwyn.* LL21 37 K1
Glan-yr-afon *I.o.A.* LL58 46 E4
Glan-y-Wern LL47 37 F2
Glapthorn PE8 42 D6
Glapwell S44 51 G6
Glasahoile FK8 81 F7
Glasbury HR3 28 A5
Glaschoil PH26 89 H1
Glascoed *Mon.* NP4 19 G1
Glascoed *Wrex.* LL11 48 B7
Glascorrie AB35 90 C5
Glascote B77 40 E5
Glascwm LD1 28 A3
Glasdrum PA38 80 B3
Glasfryn LL21 47 H7
**GLASGOW G** 74 **D4**
Glasgow Airport PA3 74 C4
Glasgow Prestwick Airport KA9 67 H1
Glashmore AB31 91 F4
Glasinfryn LL57 46 D6
Glasnacardoch PH41 86 C5
Glasnakille IV49 86 B3
Glaspant SA38 17 F2
Glaspwll SY20 37 G6
Glassburn IV4 87 K1
Glassel AB31 90 E5
Glassenbury TN17 14 C4
Glasserton DG8 64 E7
Glassford ML10 75 F6
Glasshouse GL17 29 G6
Glasshouses HG3 57 G3
Glassingall FK15 81 J7
Glasslie KY6 82 D7
Glasson *Cumb.* CA7 69 H7
Glasson *Lancs.* LA2 55 H4
Glassonby CA10 61 G3
Glasterlaw DD11 83 G2
Glaston LE15 42 B5
**Glastonbury BA6** 8 **D1**
Glatton PE28 42 E7
Glazebrook WA3 49 F3
Glazebury WA3 49 F3
Glazeley WV16 39 G7
Gleadless S12 51 F4
Gleadsmoss SK11 49 H6
Gleann Tholastaidh HS2 101 H3
Gleaston LA12 55 F2
Glecknabae PA20 73 J4
Gledhow LS8 57 J6
Gledrid LL14 38 B2
Glemsford CO10 34 C4
Glen *D. & G.* DG2 65 J3
Glen *D. & G.* DG7 65 F5
Glen Auldyn IM7 54 D4
Glen Mona IM7 54 D5
Glen Parva LE2 41 H6
Glen Trool Lodge DG8 67 J5
Glen Village FK1 75 G3
Glen Vine IM4 54 C6
Glenae DG1 68 E5
Glenaladale PH37 86 E7
Glenald G84 74 A1
Glenamachrie PA34 80 A5
Glenapp Castle KA26 66 E5
Glenarm DD8 82 E1
Glenbarr PA29 72 E7
Glenbatrick PA60 72 D3
Glenbeg *High.* IV24 95 K3
Glenbeg *High.* PH26 89 H2
Glenbeg *High.* PH36 79 G1
Glenbeich FK19 81 H5
Glenbervie *Aber.* AB39 91 F6
Glenbervie *Falk.* FK5 75 G2
Glenboig ML5 75 F4
Glenborrodale PH36 79 H1
Glenbranter PA27 73 K1
Glenbreck ML12 69 F1
Glenbrittle IV47 85 K2
Glenburn PA2 74 C4
Glenbyre PA62 79 G5
Glencaple DG1 65 K4
Glencarse PH2 82 C5
Glencat AB34 90 D5
Glenceitlein PH49 80 C3
Glencloy KA27 73 J7

Gle - Gre


Glencoe PH49 80 C2
Glenconglass AB37 89 J2
Glencraig KY5 75 K1
Glencripesdale PH36 79 H2
Glencrosh DG3 68 C5
Glencruitten PA34 79 K5
Glencuie AB33 90 C3
Glendearg D. & G. DG13 69 H3
Glendearg Sc.Bord. TD1 76 D7
Glendessary PH34 87 F5
Glendevon FK14 82 A7
Glendoebeg PH32 88 B4
Glendoick PH2 82 D5
Glendoll Lodge DD8 89 K7
Glendoune KA26 67 F4
Glendrissaig KA26 67 F4
Glenduckie KY14 82 D6
Glenduisk KA26 67 G5
Glendye Lodge AB31 90 E6
Gleneagles Hotel PH3 82 A6
Gleneagles House PH3 82 A7
Glenearn PH2 82 C6
Glenegedale PA42 72 B5
Glenelg IV40 86 E3
Glenfarg PH2 82 C6
Glenfeochan PA34 79 K5
Glenfield LE3 41 H5
Glenfinnan PH37 87 F6
Glenfoot PH2 82 C6
Glengalmadale PH33 79 K2
Glengap DG6 65 G5
Glengarnock KA14 74 B5
Glengarrisdale PA60 72 E1
Glengennet KA26 67 G4
Glengolly KW14 105 G2
Glengrasco IV51 93 K7
Glengyle FK8 80 E6
Glenhead DG2 68 D5
Glenhead Farm PH11 82 D1
Glenhurich PH37 79 K1
Glenkerry TD7 69 H2
Glenkiln KA27 73 J7
Glenkin PA23 73 K2
Glenkindie AB33 90 C3
Glenlair DG7 65 H3
Glenlatterach IV30 97 K6
Glenlean PA23 73 J2
Glenlee Angus DD9 90 C7
Glenlee D. & G. DG7 68 B5
Glenlichorn FK15 81 J6
Glenlivet AB37 89 J2
Glenlochar DG7 65 H4
Glenluce DG8 64 B5
Glenmallan G84 74 A1
Glenmanna DG3 68 C3
Glenmavis ML6 75 F4
Glenmaye IM5 54 B6
Glenmeanie IV6 95 J6
Glenmore Arg. & B. PA20 73 J4
Glenmore High. IV51 93 K7
Glenmore High. PH22 89 G4
Glenmore Lodge PH22 89 G4
Glenmoy DD8 83 F1
Glenmuick IV27 103 F7
Glennoe PA35 80 B4
Glenochar ML12 68 E2
Glenogil DD8 83 F1
Glenprosen Village DD8 82 E1
Glenquiech DD8 83 F1
Glenramskill PA28 66 B2
Glenrazie DG8 64 D4
Glenridding CA11 60 E5
Glenrisdell PA29 73 G5
Glenrossal IV27 96 B1
Glenrothes KY7 82 D7
Glensanda PA34 79 K3
Glensaugh AB30 90 E7
Glensgaich IV14 96 B5
Glenshalg AB31 90 D4
Glenshellish PA27 73 K1
Glensluain PA27 73 J1
Glentaggart ML11 68 D1
Glentham LN8 52 D3
Glenton AB51 90 E2
Glentress EH45 76 A7
Glentrool DG8 64 D3
Glentruan IM7 54 D3
Glentworth DN21 52 C4
Glenuachdarach IV51 93 K6
Glenuig PH38 86 C7
Glenure PA38 80 B3
Glenurquhart IV11 96 E5
Glenwhilly DG8 64 B3
Glespin ML11 68 D1
Gletness ZE2 107 N7
Glewstone HR9 28 E6
Glinton PE6 42 E5
Glooston LE16 42 A6
Glororum NE69 77 K7
Glossop SK13 50 C3
Gloster Hill NE65 71 H3
GLOUCESTER GL 29 H7
Gloup ZE2 107 P2
Gloweth TR1 2 E4
Glusburn BD20 57 F5
Gluss ZE2 107 M5
Glympton OX20 31 F6
Glyn LL24 47 F7
Glyn Ceiriog LL20 38 B2
Glynarthen SA44 17 G1
Glyncoch CF37 18 D2
Glyncorrwg SA13 18 B2
Glyn-Cywarch LL47 37 F2
Glynde BN8 13 H6
Glyndebourne BN8 13 H5
Glyndyfrdwy LL21 38 A1
Glynebwy (Ebbw Vale) NP23 18 E1
Glynneath (Glyn-Nedd) SA11 18 B1
Glyn-Nedd (Glynneath) SA11 18 B1
Glynogwr CF35 18 C3
Glyntaff CF37 18 D3
Gnosall ST20 40 A3
Gnosall Heath ST20 40 A3
Goadby LE7 42 A6
Goadby Marwood LE14 42 A3
Goatacre SN11 20 D4
Goatfield PA32 80 B7
Goathill DT9 9 F3
Goathland YO22 63 K6
Goathurst TA5 8 B1
Gobernuisgeach KW12 104 E5
Gobhaig HS3 100 C7
Gobowen SY11 38 C2
Godalming GU7 22 C7
Goddard's Corner IP13 35 G2
Goddards Green BN6 13 F4
Godden Green TN15 23 J6
Goddington BR6 23 H5
Godford Cross EX14 7 K5
Godington OX27 31 H6
Godleybrook ST10 40 B1
Godmanchester PE29 33 F1
Godmanstone DT2 9 F5
Godmersham CT4 15 F2
Godney BA5 19 H7
Godolphin Cross TR13 2 D5
Godor SY22 38 B4
Godre'r-graig SA9 18 A1
Godshill Hants. SP6 10 C3
Godshill I.o.W. PO38 11 G6
Godstone RH9 23 G6
Godwick PE32 44 D3
Goetre NP4 19 G1
Goff's Oak EN7 23 G1
Gogar EH12 75 K3
Gogarth LL30 47 F4
Goginan SY23 37 F7
Goirtean a' Chladaich PH33 87 G7
Goirtein PA27 73 H2
Golan LL51 36 E1
Golant PL23 4 B5
Golberdon PL17 4 D3
Golborne WA3 49 F3
Golcar HD7 50 D1
Gold Hill Cambs. PE14 43 J6
Gold Hill Dorset DT11 9 H3
Goldcliff NP18 19 G3
Golden Cross BN27 13 J5
Golden Green TN11 23 K7
Golden Grove SA32 17 J4
Golden Pot GU34 22 A7
Golden Valley Derbys. DE55 51 G7
Golden Valley Glos. GL51 29 J6
Goldenhill ST6 49 H7
Golders Green NW11 23 F3
Goldhanger CM9 25 F1
Goldielea DG2 65 K3
Golding SY5 38 E5
Goldington MK41 32 D3
Goldsborough N.Yorks. YO21 63 K5
Goldsborough N.Yorks. HG5 57 J4
Goldsithney TR20 2 C5
Goldstone TF9 39 G3
Goldthorn Park WV2 40 B6
Goldthorpe S63 51 G2
Goldworthy EX39 6 B3
Golford TN17 14 C4
Gollanfield IV2 97 F6
Gollinglith Foot HG4 57 G1
Golspie KW10 97 F2
Golval KW13 104 D2
Gomeldon SP4 10 C1
Gomersal BD19 57 H7
Gometra PA73 78 E3
Gometra House PA73 78 E3
Gomshall GU5 22 D7
Gonachan Cottage G63 74 E2
Gonalston NG14 41 J1
Gonerby Hill Foot NG31 42 C2
Gonfirth ZE2 107 M6
Good Easter CM1 33 K7
Gooderstone PE33 44 B5
Goodleigh EX32 6 E2
Goodmanham YO43 58 E5
Goodmayes IG3 23 H3
Goodnestone Kent CT3 15 H2
Goodnestone Kent ME13 25 G5
Goodrich HR9 28 E7
Goodrington TQ4 5 J5
Goodshaw BB4 56 D7
Goodshaw Fold BB4 56 D7
Goodwick (Wdig) SA64 16 C2
Goodworth Clatford SP11 21 G7
Goodyers End CV12 41 F7
Goole DN14 58 D7
Goom's Hill WR7 30 B3
Goonbell TR5 2 E4
Goonhavern TR4 2 E3
Goonvrea TR5 2 E4
Goose Green Essex CO11 35 F6
Goose Green Essex CO16 35 F6
Goose Green Gt.Man. WN3 48 E2
Goose Green Kent TN11 23 K6
Goose Green S.Glos. BS30 19 K4
Goose Pool HR2 28 D5
Gooseham EX23 6 A4
Goosehill Green WR9 29 J2
Goosewell PL9 5 F5
Goosey SN7 21 G2
Goosnargh PR3 55 J6
Goostrey CW4 49 G5
Gorcott Hill B98 30 B2
Gorddinog LL33 46 E5
Gordon TD3 76 E6
Gordonbush KW9 97 F1
Gordonstoun IV30 97 J5
Gordonstown Aber. AB45 98 D5
Gordonstown Aber. AB51 91 F1
Gore Cross SN10 20 D6
Gore End RG20 21 H5
Gore Pit CO5 34 C7
Gore Street CT12 25 J5
Gorebridge EH23 76 B4
Gorefield PE13 43 H4
Gorey JE3 3 K7
Gorgie EH11 76 A3
Goring RG8 21 K3
Goring Heath RG8 21 K4
Goring-by-Sea BN12 12 E6
Gorleston-on-Sea NR31 45 K5
Gorllwyn SA33 17 G2
Gornalwood DY3 40 B6
Gorrachie AB45 99 F5
Gorran Churchtown PL26 3 G4
Gorran Haven PL26 4 A6
Gors SY23 27 F1
Gorsedd CH8 47 K5
Gorseinon SA4 17 J6
Gorseness KW17 106 D6
Gorseybank DE4 50 E7
Gorsgoch SA40 26 D3
Gorslas SA14 17 J4
Gorsley HR9 29 F6
Gorsley Common HR9 29 F6
Gorstage CW8 49 F5
Gorstan IV23 95 K5
Gorstanvorran PH37 86 E7
Gorsty Hill ST14 40 D3
Gorten PA64 79 J4
Gortenbuie PA70 79 G4
Gorteneorn PH36 79 H1
Gorton Arg. & B. PA78 78 C2
Gorton Gt.Man. M18 49 H3
Gosbeck IP6 35 F3
Gosberton PE11 43 F2
Gosberton Clough PE11 42 E3
Goseley Dale DE11 41 F3
Gosfield CO9 34 B6
Gosford Here. SY8 28 E2
Gosford Oxon. OX5 31 G7
Gosforth Cumb. CA20 60 B6
Gosforth T. & W. NE3 71 H7
Gosland Green CW6 48 E7
Gosmore SG4 32 E6
Gospel End DY3 40 B6
Gosport PO12 11 H5
Gossabrough ZE2 107 P4
Gossington GL2 20 A1
Gossops Green RH11 13 F3
Goswick TD15 77 J6
Gotham NG11 41 H2
Gotherington GL52 29 J6
Gothers PL26 3 G3
Gott ZE2 107 N8
Gotton TA2 8 B2
Goudhurst TN17 14 C4
Goulceby LN11 53 F5
Gourdas AB53 99 F6
Gourdon DD10 91 G7
Gourock PA19 74 A3
Govan G51 74 D4
Goverton NG14 51 K7
Goveton TQ7 5 H6
Govilon NP7 28 B7
Gowanhill AB43 99 J4
Gowdall DN14 58 C7
Gowerton SA4 17 J6
Gowkhall KY12 75 J2
Gowkthrapple ML2 75 F5
Gowthorpe YO41 58 D4
Goxhill E.Riding HU11 59 H5
Goxhill N.Lincs. DN19 59 H7
Goytre SA13 18 A3
Gozzard's Ford OX13 21 H2
Grabhair HS2 101 F6
Graby NG34 42 D3
Gradbach SK17 49 J6
Grade TR12 2 E7
Gradeley Green CW5 48 E7
Graffham GU28 12 C5
Grafham Cambs. PE28 32 E2
Grafham Surr. GU5 22 D7
Grafton Here. HR2 28 D5
Grafton N.Yorks. YO51 57 K3
Grafton Oxon. OX18 21 F1
Grafton Shrop. SY4 38 D4
Grafton Worcs. HR6 28 E2
Grafton Worcs. GL20 29 J5
Grafton Flyford WR7 29 J3
Grafton Regis NN12 31 J4
Grafton Underwood NN14 42 C7
Grafty Green ME17 14 D3
Graianrhyd CH7 48 B7
Graig Carmar. SA16 17 H5
Graig Conwy LL28 47 G5
Graig Denb. LL17 47 J5
Graig-fechan LL15 47 K7
Grain ME3 24 E4
Grainel PA44 72 A4
Grainhow AB53 99 G6
Grains Bar OL4 49 J2
Grainsby DN36 53 F3
Grainthorpe LN11 53 G3
Graiselound DN9 51 K3
Gramisdale (Gramsdal) HS7 92 D6
Grampound TR2 3 G4
Grampound Road TR2 3 G3
Gramsdal (Gramisdale) HS7 92 D6
Granborough MK18 31 J6
Granby NG13 42 A2
Grandborough CV23 31 F2
Grandes Rocques GY5 3 J5
Grandtully PH9 82 A2
Grange Cumb. CA12 60 D5
Grange E.Ayr. KA1 74 C7
Grange High. IV63 87 K1
Grange Med. ME7 24 D5
Grange Mersey. CH48 48 B4
Grange P. & K. PH2 82 D5
Grange Crossroads AB55 98 C5
Grange de Lings LN2 52 C5
Grange Hall IV36 97 H5
Grange Hill IG7 23 H2
Grange Moor WF4 50 E1
Grange of Lindores KY14 82 D6
Grange Villa DH2 62 D1
Grangemill DE4 50 E7
Grangemouth FK3 75 H2
Grangemuir KY10 83 G7
Grange-over-Sands LA11 55 H2
Grangeston KA26 67 G4
Grangetown Cardiff CF11 18 E4
Grangetown R. & C. TS6 63 G4
Granish PH22 89 G3
Gransmoor YO25 59 H4
Granston SA62 16 B2
Grantchester CB3 33 H3
Grantham NG31 42 C2
Grantley HG4 57 H2
Grantlodge AB51 91 F3
Granton EH5 76 A3
Granton House DG10 69 F3
Grantown-on-Spey PH26 89 H2
Grantsfield HR6 28 E2
Grantshouse TD11 77 G4
Grappenhall WA4 49 F4
Grasby DN38 52 D2
Grasmere LA22 60 E6
Grass Green CO9 34 B5
Grasscroft OL4 49 J2
Grassendale L19 48 C4
Grassgarth LA8 60 F7
Grassholme DL12 62 A4
Grassington BD23 57 F3
Grassmoor S42 51 G6
Grassthorpe NG23 51 K6
Grateley SP11 21 F7
Gratwich ST14 40 C2
Gravel Hill SL9 22 D2
Graveley Cambs. PE19 33 F2
Graveley Herts. SG4 33 F6
Gravelly Hill B23 40 D6
Gravels SY5 38 C5
Graven ZE2 107 N5
Graveney ME13 25 G5
Gravesend DA11 24 C4
Grayingham DN21 52 C3
Grayrigg LA8 61 G7
Grays RM17 24 C4
Grayshott GU26 12 B3
Grayswood GU27 12 C3
Grazeley RG7 21 K5
Greasbrough S61 51 G3
Greasby CH49 48 B4
Great Abington CB21 33 J4
Great Addington NN14 32 C1
Great Alne B49 30 C3
Great Altcar L37 48 C2
Great Amwell SG12 33 G7
Great Asby CA16 61 H5
Great Ashfield IP31 34 D2
Great Ayton TS9 63 G5
Great Baddow CM2 24 D1
Great Bardfield CM7 33 K5
Great Barford MK44 32 E3
Great Barr B43 40 C6
Great Barrington OX18 30 D7
Great Barrow CH3 48 D6
Great Barton IP31 34 C2
Great Barugh YO17 58 D2
Great Bavington NE19 70 E5
Great Bealings IP13 35 G4
Great Bedwyn SN8 21 F5
Great Bentley CO7 35 F6
Great Bernera HS2 100 D4
Great Billing NN3 32 B2
Great Bircham PE31 44 B2
Great Blakenham IP6 35 F3
Great Bolas TF6 39 F3
Great Bookham KT23 22 E6
Great Bourton OX17 31 F4
Great Bowden LE16 42 A7
Great Bradley CB8 33 K3
Great Braxted CM8 34 C7
Great Bricett IP7 34 E3
Great Brickhill MK17 32 C5
Great Bridgeford ST18 40 A3
Great Brington NN7 31 H2
Great Bromley CO7 34 E6
Great Broughton Cumb. CA13 60 B3
Great Broughton N.Yorks. TS9 63 G6
Great Buckland DA13 24 C5
Great Budworth CW9 49 F5
Great Burdon DL1 62 E5
Great Burstead CM12 24 C2
Great Busby TS9 63 G6
Great Cambourne CB23 33 G3
Great Canfield CM6 33 J7
Great Canney CM3 24 E1
Great Carlton LN11 53 H4
Great Casterton PE9 42 D5
Great Chalfield SN12 20 B5
Great Chart TN23 14 E3
Great Chatwell TF10 39 G4
Great Chell ST6 49 H7
Great Chesterford CB10 33 J4
Great Cheverell SN10 20 C6
Great Chishill SG8 33 H5
Great Clacton CO15 35 F7
Great Clifton CA14 60 B4
Great Coates DN37 53 F2
Great Comberton WR10 29 J4
Great Corby CA4 61 F1
Great Cornard CO10 34 C4
Great Cowden HU11 59 J5
Great Coxwell SN7 21 F2
Great Crakehall DL8 57 H1
Great Cransley NN14 32 B1
Great Cressingham IP25 44 C5
Great Crosby L23 48 C2
Great Crosthwaite CA12 60 D4
Great Cubley DE6 40 D2
Great Cumbrae KA28 73 K5
Great Dalby LE14 42 A4
Great Doddington NN29 32 B2
Great Doward HR9 28 E7
Great Dunham PE32 44 C4
Great Dunmow CM6 33 K6
Great Durnford SP4 10 C1
Great Easton Essex CM6 33 K6
Great Easton Leics. LE16 42 B6
Great Eccleston PR3 55 H5
Great Edstone YO62 58 D1
Great Ellingham NR17 44 E6
Great Elm BA11 20 A7
Great Eversden CB23 33 G3
Great Fencote DL7 62 D7
Great Finborough IP14 34 E3
Great Fransham NR19 44 C4
Great Gaddesden HP1 32 D7
Great Gidding PE28 42 E7
Great Givendale YO42 58 E4
Great Glemham IP17 35 H2
Great Glen LE8 41 J6
Great Gonerby NG31 42 B2
Great Gransden SG19 33 F3
Great Green Cambs. SG8 33 F4
Great Green Norf. IP20 45 G7
Great Green Suff. IP30 34 D3
Great Green Suff. IP21 35 F1
Great Green Suff. IP22 34 E1
Great Habton YO17 58 D2
Great Hale NG34 42 E1
Great Hallingbury CM22 33 J7
Great Hampden HP16 22 B1
Great Harrowden NN9 32 B1
Great Harwood BB6 56 C6
Great Haseley OX44 21 K1
Great Hatfield HU11 59 H5
Great Haywood ST18 40 C3
Great Heath CV6 41 F7
Great Heck DN14 58 B7
Great Henny CO10 34 C5
Great Hinton BA14 20 C6
Great Hockham IP24 44 D6
Great Holland CO13 35 G7
Great Horkesley CO6 34 D5
Great Hormead SG9 33 H5
Great Horton BD7 57 G6
Great Horwood MK17 31 J5
Great Houghton Northants. NN4 31 J3
Great Houghton S.Yorks. S72 51 G2
Great Hucklow SK17 50 D5
Great Kelk YO25 59 H4
Great Kimble HP17 22 B1
Great Kingshill HP15 22 B2
Great Langton DL7 62 D7
Great Leighs CM3 34 B7
Great Limber DN37 52 E2
Great Linford MK14 32 B4
Great Livermere IP31 34 C1
Great Longstone DE45 50 E5
Great Lumley DH3 62 D2
Great Lyth SY3 38 D5
Great Malvern WR14 29 G4
Great Maplestead CO9 34 C5
Great Marton FY4 55 G6
Great Massingham PE32 44 B3
Great Melton NR9 45 F5
Great Milton OX44 21 K1
Great Missenden HP16 22 B1
Great Mitton BB7 56 C6
Great Mongeham CT14 15 J2
Great Moulton NR15 45 F6
Great Munden SG11 33 G6
Great Musgrave CA17 61 J5
Great Ness SY4 38 D4
Great Notley CM77 34 B6
Great Nurcot TA24 7 H2
Great Oak NP15 19 G1
Great Oakley Essex CO12 35 F6
Great Oakley Northants. NN18 42 B7
Great Offley SG5 32 E6
Great Ormside CA16 61 J5
Great Orton CA5 60 E1
Great Ouseburn YO26 57 K3
Great Oxendon LE16 42 A7
Great Oxney Green CM1 24 C1
Great Palgrave PE32 44 C4
Great Parndon CM19 23 H1
Great Paxton PE19 33 F2
Great Plumpton PR4 55 G6
Great Plumstead NR13 45 H5
Great Ponton NG33 42 C2
Great Potheridge EX20 6 D4
Great Preston LS26 57 J7
Great Purston NN13 31 G5
Great Raveley PE28 43 F7
Great Rissington GL54 30 C7
Great Rollright OX7 30 E5
Great Ryburgh NR21 44 D3
Great Ryle NE66 71 F2
Great Ryton SY5 38 D5
Great Saling CM7 34 B6

Gre - Hal


Great Salkeld **CA11** 61 G3
Great Sampford **CB10** 33 K5
Great Sankey **WA5** 48 E4
Great Saredon **WV10** 40 B5
Great Saxham **IP29** 34 B2
Great Shefford **RG17** 21 G4
Great Shelford **CB22** 33 H3
Great Smeaton **DL6** 62 E6
Great Snoring **NR21** 44 D2
Great Somerford **SN15** 20 C3
Great Stainton **TS21** 62 E4
Great Stambridge **SS4** 25 F2
Great Staughton **PE19** 32 E2
Great Steeping **PE23** 53 H6
Great Stonar **CT13** 15 J2
Great Strickland **CA10** 61 G4
Great Stukeley **PE28** 33 F1
Great Sturton **LN9** 53 F5
Great Sutton *Ches.W. & C.* **CH66** 48 C5
Great Sutton *Shrop.* **SY8** 38 E7
Great Swinburne **NE48** 70 E6
Great Tew **OX7** 30 E6
Great Tey **CO6** 34 C6
Great Thorness **PO30** 11 F5
Great Thurlow **CB9** 33 K4
Great Torr **TQ7** 5 G6
**Great Torrington EX38** **6 C4**
Great Tosson **NE65** 71 F3
Great Totham *Essex* **CM9** 34 C7
Great Totham *Essex* **CM9** 34 C7
Great Tows **LN8** 53 F3
Great Urswick **LA12** 55 F2
Great Wakering **SS3** 25 F3
Great Waldingfield **CO10** 34 D4
**Great Walsingham NR22** **44 D2**
Great Waltham **CM3** 33 K7
Great Warley **CM13** 23 J2
Great Washbourne **GL20** 29 J5
Great Weeke **TQ13** 7 F7
Great Welnetham **IP30** 34 C3
Great Wenham **CO7** 34 E5
Great Whittington **NE19** 71 F6
Great Wigborough **CO5** 34 D7
Great Wigsell **TN32** 14 C5
Great Wilbraham **CB21** 33 J3
Great Wilne **DE72** 41 G2
Great Wishford **SP2** 10 B1
Great Witcombe **GL3** 29 J7
Great Witley **WR6** 29 G2
Great Wolford **CV36** 30 D5
Great Wratting **CB9** 33 K4
Great Wymondley **SG4** 33 F6
Great Wyrley **WS6** 40 B5
Great Wytheford **SY4** 38 E4
**Great Yarmouth NR30** **45 K5**
Great Yeldham **CO9** 34 B5
Greatford **PE9** 42 D4
Greatgate **ST10** 40 C1
Greatham *Hants.* **GU33** 11 J1
Greatham *Hart.* **TS25** 63 F4
Greatham *W.Suss.* **RH20** 12 D5
Greatness **TN14** 23 J6
Greatstone-on-Sea **TN28** 15 F5
Greatworth **OX17** 31 G4
Green **LL16** 47 J6
Green Cross **GU10** 12 B3
Green End *Bed.* **MK44** 32 E3
Green End *Bucks.* **MK17** 32 C5
Green End *Cambs.* **PE29** 33 F1
Green End *Cambs.* **PE27** 33 G1
Green End *Herts.* **SG12** 33 G6
Green End *Herts.* **SG9** 33 G5
Green End *Warks.* **CV7** 40 E7
Green Hammerton **YO26** 57 K4
Green Hill **SN4** 20 D3
Green Lane **B80** 30 B2
Green Moor **S35** 50 E3
Green Ore **BA5** 19 J6
Green Quarter **LA8** 61 F6
Green Street *E.Suss.* **TN38** 14 C6
Green Street *Herts.* **WD6** 22 E2
Green Street *Herts.* **SG11** 33 H6
Green Street *W.Suss.* **RH13** 12 E4
Green Street *Worcs.* **WR5** 29 H4
Green Street Green *Gt.Lon.* **BR6** 23 H5
Green Street Green *Kent* **DA2** 23 J4
Green Tye **SG10** 33 H7
Greenburn **DD5** 83 F3
Greencroft **DH7** 62 C2
Greendams **AB31** 90 E6
Greendykes **NE66** 71 F1
Greenend **OX7** 30 E6
Greenfaulds **G67** 75 F3
Greenfield *Cen.Beds.* **MK45** 32 D5
Greenfield (Maes-Glas) *Flints.* **CH8** 47 K5
Greenfield *Gt.Man.* **OL3** 50 C2
Greenfield *High.* **PH35** 87 J4
Greenfield *Lincs.* **LN13** 53 H5
Greenfield *Oxon.* **OX49** 22 A2
**Greenford UB6** **22 E3**
Greengairs **ML6** 75 F3
Greengates **BD10** 57 G6
Greengill **CA7** 60 C3
Greenhalgh **PR4** 55 H6
Greenhall **AB52** 90 E2
Greenham **RG14** 21 H5
Greenhaugh **NE48** 70 C5
Greenhead **CA8** 70 B7
Greenheads **AB42** 91 J1
Greenheys **BL5** 49 G2
Greenhill *Gt.Lon.* **HA1** 22 E3
Greenhill *High.* **KW9** 97 G1
Greenhill *S.Yorks.* **S8** 51 F4
**Greenhithe DA9** **23 J4**
Greenholm **KA16** 74 D7
Greenholme **CA10** 61 G6
Greenhow Hill **HG3** 57 G3
Greenigo **KW15** 106 D7
Greenland **KW14** 105 H2
Greenlands **RG9** 22 A3
Greenlaw *Aber.* **AB45** 98 E5
Greenlaw *Sc.Bord.* **TD10** 77 F6
Greenloaning **FK15** 81 K7
Greenmeadow **NP44** 19 F2
Greenmoor Hill **RG8** 21 K3
Greenmount **BL8** 49 G1
Greenmyre **AB53** 91 G1
**Greenock PA16** **74 A3**
Greenodd **LA12** 55 G1
Greens Norton **NN12** 31 H4
Greenscares **FK15** 81 J6
Greenside *T. & W.* **NE40** 71 G7
Greenside *W.Yorks.* **HD5** 50 D1
Greenstead **CO4** 34 E6
Greenstead Green **CO9** 34 C6
Greensted **CM5** 23 J1
Greensted Green **CM5** 23 J1
Greenway *Pembs.* **SA66** 16 D2
Greenway *Som.* **TA3** 8 C2
Greenwell **CA8** 61 G1
Greenwich **SE10** 23 G4
Greet **GL54** 30 B5
Greete **SY8** 28 E1
Greetham *Lincs.* **LN9** 53 G5
Greetham *Rut.* **LE15** 42 C4
Greetland **HX4** 57 F7
Gregson Lane **PR5** 55 J7
Greinetobht (Grenitote) **HS6** 92 D4
Greinton **TA7** 8 D1
Grenaby **IM9** 54 B6
Grendon *Northants.* **NN7** 32 B2
Grendon *Warks.* **CV9** 40 E6
Grendon Common **CV9** 40 E6
Grendon Green **HR6** 28 E3
Grendon Underwood **HP18** 31 H6
Grenitote (Greinetobht) **HS6** 92 D4
Grenofen **PL19** 4 E3
Grenoside **S35** 51 F3
Greosabhagh **HS3** 93 G2
Gresford **LL12** 48 C7
Gresham **NR11** 45 F2
Greshornish **IV51** 93 J6
Gress (Griais) **HS2** 101 G3
Gressenhall **NR20** 44 D4
Gressingham **LA2** 55 J3
Greta Bridge **DL12** 62 B5
**Gretna DG16** **69 J7**
Gretna Green **DG16** 69 J7
Gretton *Glos.* **GL54** 30 B5
Gretton *Northants.* **NN17** 42 C6
Gretton *Shrop.* **SY6** 38 E6
Grewelthorpe **HG4** 57 H2
Greygarth **HG4** 57 G2
Greylake **TA7** 8 C1
Greys Green **RG9** 22 A3
Greysouthen **CA13** 60 B4
Greystead **NE48** 70 C5
Greystoke **CA11** 60 F3
Greystone *Aber.* **AB35** 89 K5
Greystone *Angus* **DD11** 83 G3
Greystone *Lancs.* **BB9** 56 D5
Greystones **S11** 51 F4
Greywell **RG29** 22 A6
Griais (Gress) **HS2** 101 G3
Gribthorpe **DN14** 58 D6
Gribton **DG2** 68 E5
Griff **CV10** 41 F7
Griffithstown **NP4** 19 F2
Grigadale **PH36** 79 F1
Grigghall **LA8** 61 F7
Grimeford Village **PR6** 49 F1
Grimesthorpe **S4** 51 F3
Grimethorpe **S72** 51 G2
Griminis (Griminish) **HS7** 92 C6
Griminish (Griminis) **HS7** 92 C6
Grimister **ZE2** 107 N3
Grimley **WR2** 29 H2
Grimmet **KA19** 67 H2
Grimness **KW17** 106 D8
Grimoldby **LN11** 53 G4
Grimpo **SY11** 38 C3
Grimsargh **PR2** 55 J6
Grimsay (Griomsaigh) **HS6** 92 D6
Grimsbury **OX16** 31 F4
**Grimsby DN32** **53 F2**
Grimscote **NN12** 31 H3
Grimscott **EX23** 6 A5
Grimshader (Griomsiadar) **HS2** 101 G5
Grimsthorpe **PE10** 42 D3
Grimston *E.Riding* **HU11** 59 J6
Grimston *Leics.* **LE14** 41 J3
Grimston *Norf.* **PE32** 44 B3
Grimstone **DT2** 9 F5
Grimstone End **IP31** 34 D2
Grindale **YO16** 59 H2
Grindiscol **ZE2** 107 N9
Grindle **TF11** 39 G5
Grindleford **S32** 50 E5
Grindleton **BB7** 56 C5
Grindley **ST14** 40 C3
Grindley Brook **SY13** 38 E1
Grindlow **SK17** 50 D5
Grindon *Northumb.* **TD15** 77 H6
Grindon *Staffs.* **ST13** 50 C7
Grindon *Stock.* **TS21** 62 E4
Grindon *T. & W.* **SR4** 62 E1
Gringley on the Hill **DN10** 51 K3
Grinsdale **CA5** 60 E1
Grinshill **SY4** 38 E3
Grinton **DL11** 62 B7
Griomarstaidh **HS2** 100 E4
Griomsaigh (Grimsay) **HS6** 92 D6
Griomsiadar (Grimshader) **HS2** 101 G5
Grisdale **LA10** 61 J7
Grishipoll **PA78** 78 C2
Gristhorpe **YO14** 59 G1
Griston **IP25** 44 D6
Gritley **KW17** 106 E7
Grittenham **SN15** 20 D3
Grittleton **SN14** 20 B4
Grizebeck **LA17** 55 F1
Grizedale **LA22** 60 E7
Grobister **KW17** 106 F5
Groby **LE6** 41 H5
Groes **LL16** 47 J6
Groes-faen **CF72** 18 D3
Groesffordd **LL53** 36 B2
Groesffordd Marli **LL22** 47 J5
Groeslon *Gwyn.* **LL54** 46 C7
Groeslon *Gwyn.* **LL55** 46 D6
Groes-lwyd **SY21** 38 B4
Groes-wen **CF15** 18 E3
Grogport **PA28** 73 G6
Groigearraidh **HS8** 84 C1
Gromford **IP17** 35 H3
Gronant **LL19** 47 J4
Groombridge **TN3** 13 J3
Grosmont *Mon.* **NP7** 28 D6
Grosmont *N.Yorks.* **YO22** 63 K6
Grotaig **IV63** 88 B2
Groton **CO10** 34 D4
Groundistone Heights **TD9** 69 K2
Grouville **JE3** 3 K7
Grove *Bucks.* **LU7** 32 C6
Grove *Dorset* **DT5** 9 F7
Grove *Kent* **CT3** 25 J5
Grove *Notts.* **DN22** 51 K5
Grove *Oxon.* **OX12** 21 H2
Grove End **ME9** 24 E5
Grove Green **ME14** 14 C2
Grove Park **SE12** 23 H4
Grove Town **WF8** 57 K7
Grovehill **HP2** 22 D1
Grovesend *S.Glos.* **BS35** 19 K3
Grovesend *Swan.* **SA4** 17 J5
Gruids **IV27** 96 C1
Grula **IV47** 85 J2
Gruline **PA71** 79 G3
Grumbla **TR20** 2 B6
Grundcruie **PH1** 82 B5
Grundisburgh **IP13** 35 G3
Gruting **ZE2** 107 L8
Grutness **ZE3** 107 N11
Gualachulain **PH49** 80 C3
Guardbridge **KY16** 83 F6
Guarlford **WR13** 29 H4
Guay **PH9** 82 B3
Gubbergill **CA19** 60 B7
Gubblecote **HP23** 32 C7
**GUERNSEY GY** **3 J5**
Guernsey Airport **GY8** 3 H5
Guestling Green **TN35** 14 D6
Guestling Thorn **TN35** 14 D6
Guestwick **NR20** 44 E3
Guestwick Green **NR20** 44 E3
Guide **BB1** 56 C7
Guide Post **NE62** 71 H5
Guilden Down **SY7** 38 C7
Guilden Morden **SG8** 33 F4
Guilden Sutton **CH3** 48 D6
**GUILDFORD GU** **22 C7**
Guildtown **PH2** 82 C4
Guilsborough **NN6** 31 H1
Guilsfield (Cegidfa) **SY21** 38 B4
Guilthwaite **S60** 51 G4
**Guisborough TS14** **63 H5**
Guiseley **LS20** 57 G5
Guist **NR20** 44 E3
Guith **KW17** 106 E4
Guiting Power **GL54** 30 B6
Gulberwick **ZE2** 107 N9
**Gullane EH31** **76 C2**
Gulval **TR18** 2 B5
Gulworthy **PL19** 4 E3
Gumfreston **SA70** 16 E5
Gumley **LE16** 41 J6
Gunby *Lincs.* **NG33** 42 C3
Gunby *Lincs.* **PE23** 53 H6
Gundleton **SO24** 11 H1
Gunn **EX32** 6 E2
Gunnersbury **W4** 22 E4
Gunnerside **DL11** 62 A7
Gunnerton **NE48** 70 E6
Gunness **DN15** 52 B1
**Gunnislake PL18** **4 E3**
Gunnista **ZE2** 107 P8
Gunnister **ZE2** 107 M5
Gunstone **WV8** 40 A5
Gunter's Bridge **GU28** 12 C4
Gunthorpe *Norf.* **NR24** 44 E2
Gunthorpe *Notts.* **NG14** 41 J1
Gunthorpe *Rut.* **LE15** 42 B5
Gunville **PO30** 11 F6
Gunwalloe **TR12** 2 D6
Gupworthy **TA24** 7 H2
Gurnard **PO31** 11 F5
Gurnett **SK11** 49 J5
Gurney Slade **BA3** 19 K7
Gurnos *M.Tyd.* **CF47** 18 D1
Gurnos *Powys* **SA9** 18 A1
Gushmere **ME13** 15 F2
Gussage All Saints **BH21** 10 B3
Gussage St. Andrew **DT11** 9 J3
Gussage St. Michael **BH21** 9 J3
Guston **CT15** 15 J3
Gutcher **ZE2** 107 P3
Guthram Gowt **PE11** 42 E3
Guthrie **DD8** 83 G2
Guyhirn **PE13** 43 G5
Guynd **DD11** 83 G3
Guy's Head **PE12** 43 H3
Guy's Marsh **SP7** 9 H2
Guyzance **NE65** 71 H3
Gwaelod-y-garth **CF15** 18 E3
Gwaenysgor **LL18** 47 J4
Gwaithla **HR5** 28 B3
Gwalchmai **LL65** 46 B5
Gwastad **SA63** 16 D3
Gwastadnant **LL55** 46 E7
Gwaun-Cae-Gurwen **SA18** 27 G7
Gwaynynog **LL16** 47 J6
Gwbert **SA43** 16 E1
Gweek **TR12** 2 E6
Gwehelog **NP15** 19 G1
Gwenddwr **LD2** 27 K4
Gwendreath **TR12** 2 E7
Gwennap **TR16** 2 E4
Gwenter **TR12** 2 E7
Gwernaffield **CH7** 48 B6
Gwernesney **NP15** 19 H1
Gwernogle **SA32** 17 J2
Gwernymynydd **CH7** 48 B6
Gwern-y-Steeple **CF5** 18 D4
Gwersyllt **LL11** 48 C7
Gwespyr **CH8** 47 K4
Gwinear **TR27** 2 C5
Gwithian **TR27** 2 C4
Gwredog **LL71** 46 C4
Gwrhay **NP12** 18 E2
Gwyddelwern **LL21** 37 K1
Gwyddgrug **SA39** 17 H2
Gwynfryn **LL11** 48 B7
Gwystre **LD1** 27 K2
Gwytherin **LL22** 47 G6
Gyfelia **LL13** 38 C1
Gyre **KW17** 106 C7
Gyrn Goch **LL54** 36 C1


## H


Habberley **SY5** 38 C5
Habin **GU31** 12 B4
Habrough **DN40** 52 E1
Haccombe **TQ12** 5 J3
Hacconby **PE10** 42 E3
Haceby **NG34** 42 D2
Hacheston **IP13** 35 H3
Hackbridge **SM6** 23 F5
Hackenthorpe **S12** 51 G4
Hackford **NR18** 44 E5
Hackforth **DL8** 62 D7
Hackland **KW17** 106 C5
Hacklet (Haclait) **HS7** 92 D7
Hacklete (Tacleit) **HS2** 100 D4
Hackleton **NN7** 32 B3
Hacklinge **CT14** 15 J2
Hackness *N.Yorks.* **YO13** 63 J3
Hackness *Ork.* **KW16** 106 C8
Hackney **E9** 23 G3
Hackthorn **LN2** 52 C4
Hackthorpe **CA10** 61 G4
Haclait (Hacklet) **HS7** 92 D7
Hacton **RM14** 23 J3
Hadden **TD5** 77 F7
Haddenham *Bucks.* **HP17** 22 A1
Haddenham *Cambs.* **CB6** 33 H1
**Haddington *E.Loth.* EH41** **76 D3**
Haddington *Lincs.* **LN5** 52 C6
Haddiscoe **NR14** 45 J6
Haddon **PE7** 42 E6
Hade Edge **HD9** 50 D2
Hademore **WS14** 40 D5
Hadfield **SK13** 50 C3
Hadham Cross **SG10** 33 H7
Hadham Ford **SG11** 33 H6
Hadleigh *Essex* **SS7** 24 E3
Hadleigh *Suff.* **IP7** 34 E4
Hadleigh Heath **IP7** 34 D4
Hadley *Tel. & W.* **TF1** 39 F4
Hadley *Worcs.* **WR9** 29 H2
Hadley End **DE13** 40 D3
Hadley Wood **EN4** 23 F2
Hadlow **TN11** 23 K7
Hadlow Down **TN22** 13 J4
Hadnall **SY4** 38 E3
Hadspen **BA7** 9 F1
Hadstock **CB21** 33 J4
Hadston **NE65** 71 H4
Hadzor **WR9** 29 J2
Haffenden Quarter **TN27** 14 D3
Hafod Bridge **SA19** 17 K2
Hafod-Dinbych **LL24** 47 G7
Hafodunos **LL22** 47 G6
Hafodyrynys **NP11** 19 F2
Haggate **BB10** 56 D6
Haggbeck **CA6** 69 K6
Haggersta **ZE2** 107 M8
Haggerston *Gt.Lon.* **E2** 23 G3
Haggerston *Northumb.* **TD15** 77 J6
Haggrister **ZE2** 107 M5
Haggs **FK4** 75 F3
Hagley *Here.* **HR1** 28 E4
Hagley *Worcs.* **DY9** 40 B7
Hagnaby *Lincs.* **PE23** 53 G6
Hagnaby *Lincs.* **LN13** 53 H5
Hague Bar **SK22** 49 J4
Hagworthingham **PE23** 53 G6
Haigh **WN2** 49 F2
Haighton Green **PR2** 55 J6
Hail Weston **PE19** 32 E2
Haile **CA22** 60 B6
Hailes **GL54** 30 B5
Hailey *Herts.* **SG13** 33 G7
Hailey *Oxon.* **OX10** 21 K3
Hailey *Oxon.* **OX29** 30 E7
**Hailsham BN27** **13 J6**
Haimer **KW14** 105 G2
Hainault **IG6** 23 H2
Haine **CT12** 25 K5
Hainford **NR10** 45 G4
Hainton **LN8** 52 E4
Haisthorpe **YO25** 59 H3
Hakin **SA73** 16 B5
Halam **NG22** 51 J7
Halbeath **KY11** 75 K2
Halberton **EX16** 7 J4
Halcro **KW1** 105 H2
Hale *Cumb.* **LA7** 55 J2
Hale *Gt.Man.* **WA15** 49 G4
Hale *Halton* **L24** 48 D4
Hale *Hants.* **SP6** 10 C3
Hale *Surr.* **GU9** 22 B7
Hale Bank **WA8** 48 D4
Hale Barns **WA15** 49 G4
Hale Nook **PR3** 55 G5
Hale Street **TN12** 23 K7
Hales *Norf.* **NR14** 45 H6
Hales *Staffs.* **TF9** 39 G2
Hales Green **DE6** 40 D1
Hales Place **CT2** 15 G2
Halesgate **PE12** 43 G3
**Halesowen B63** **40 B7**
**Halesworth IP19** **35 H1**
Halewood **L26** 48 D4
Half Way Inn **EX5** 7 J6
Halford *Devon* **TQ12** 5 J3
Halford *Shrop.* **SY7** 38 D7
Halford *Warks.* **CV36** 30 D4
Halfpenny **LA8** 55 J1
Halfpenny Green **DY7** 40 A6
Halfway *Carmar.* **SA19** 17 K2
Halfway *Carmar.* **SA15** 17 J5
Halfway *Powys* **SA20** 27 H5
Halfway *S.Yorks.* **S20** 51 G4
Halfway *W.Berks.* **RG20** 21 H5
Halfway Bridge **GU28** 12 C4
Halfway House **SY5** 38 C4
Halfway Houses *Kent* **ME12** 25 F4
Halfway Houses *Lincs.* **LN6** 52 B6
Halghton Mill **LL13** 38 D1
**HALIFAX HX** **57 F7**
Halistra **IV55** 93 H6
Halket **KA3** 74 C5
**Halkirk KW12** **105 G3**
Halkyn **CH8** 48 B5
Hall **G78** 74 C5
Hall Cross **PR4** 55 H7
Hall Dunnerdale **LA20** 60 D7
Hall Green *Ches.E.* **ST7** 49 H7
Hall Green *Lancs.* **PR4** 55 H7
Hall Green *W.Mid.* **B28** 40 D7
Hall Grove **AL7** 33 F7
Hall of the Forest **SY7** 38 B7
Halland **BN8** 13 J5
Hallaton **LE16** 42 A6
Hallatrow **BS39** 19 K6
Hallbankgate **CA8** 61 G1
Hallen **BS10** 19 J3
Hallfield Gate **DE55** 51 F7
Hallglen **FK1** 75 G3
Hallin **IV55** 93 H6
Halling **ME2** 24 D5
Hallington *Lincs.* **LN11** 53 G4
Hallington *Northumb.* **NE19** 70 E6
Halliwell **BL1** 49 F1
Halloughton **NG25** 51 J7
Hallow **WR2** 29 H3
Hallow Heath **WR2** 29 H3
Hallrule **TD9** 70 A2
Halls **EH42** 76 E3
Halls Green *Essex* **CM19** 23 H1
Hall's Green *Herts.* **SG4** 33 F6
Hallsands **TQ7** 5 J7
Hallthwaites **LA18** 54 E1
Hallwood Green **GL18** 29 F5
Hallworthy **PL32** 4 B2
Hallyne **EH45** 75 K6
Halmer End **ST7** 39 G1
Halmond's Frome **WR6** 29 F4
Halmore **GL13** 19 K1
Halmyre Mains **EH46** 75 K6
Halnaker **PO18** 12 C6
Halsall **L39** 48 C1
Halse *Northants.* **NN13** 31 G4
Halse *Som.* **TA4** 7 K3
Halsetown **TR26** 2 C5
Halsham **HU12** 59 J7
Halsinger **EX33** 6 D2
**Halstead *Essex* CO9** **34 C5**
Halstead *Kent* **TN14** 23 H5
Halstead *Leics.* **LE7** 42 A5
Halstock **BA22** 8 E4
Halsway **TA4** 7 K2
Haltemprice Farm **HU10** 59 G6
Haltham **LN9** 53 F6
Haltoft End **PE22** 43 G1
Halton *Bucks.* **HP22** 32 B7
Halton *Halton* **WA7** 48 E4
Halton *Lancs.* **LA2** 55 J3
Halton *Northumb.* **NE45** 70 E7
Halton *Wrex.* **LL14** 38 C2
Halton East **BD23** 57 F4
Halton Gill **BD23** 56 D2
Halton Green **LA2** 55 J3
Halton Holegate **PE23** 53 H6
Halton Lea Gate **CA8** 61 H1
Halton Park **LA2** 55 J3
Halton West **BD23** 56 D4
**Haltwhistle NE49** **70 C7**
Halvergate **NR13** 45 J5
Halwell **TQ9** 5 H5
Halwill **EX21** 6 C6
Halwill Junction **EX21** 6 C6

Ham - Hea


Ham Devon EX13 8 B4
Ham Glos. GL13 19 K2
Ham Glos. GL52 29 J6
Ham Gt.Lon. TW10 22 E4
Ham High. KW14 105 H1
Ham Kent CT14 15 J2
Ham Plym. PL2 4 E5
Ham Shet. ZE2 107 L2
Ham Som. TA3 8 B2
Ham Som. TA20 8 B3
Ham Wilts. SN8 21 G5
Ham Common SP8 9 H2
Ham Green Here. WR13 29 G4
Ham Green Kent ME9 24 E5
Ham Green Kent TN30 14 D5
Ham Green N.Som. BS20 19 J4
Ham Green Worcs. B97 30 B2
Ham Hill ME6 24 C5
Ham Street BA6 8 E1
Hambleden RG9 22 A3
Hambledon Hants. PO7 11 H3
Hambledon Surr. GU8 12 C3
Hamble-le-Rice SO31 11 F4
Hambleton Lancs. FY6 55 G5
Hambleton N.Yorks. YO8 58 B6
Hambridge TA10 8 C2
Hambrook S.Glos. BS16 19 K4
Hambrook W.Suss. PO18 11 J4
Hameringham LN9 53 G6
Hamerton PE28 32 E1
Hamilton ML3 75 F5
Hamlet Devon EX14 7 K6
Hamlet Dorset DT9 8 E4
Hammer GU27 12 B3
Hammerpot BN16 12 D6
Hammersmith W6 23 F4
Hammerwich WS7 40 C5
Hammerwood RH19 13 H3
Hammond Street EN7 23 G1
Hammoon DT10 9 H3
Hamnavoe Shet. ZE2 107 M9
Hamnavoe Shet. ZE2 107 N4
Hamnavoe Shet. ZE2 107 L4
Hamnavoe Shet. ZE2 107 N5
Hamnish Clifford HR6 28 E3
Hamp TA6 8 B1
Hampden Park BN22 13 K6
Hamperden End CB11 33 J5
Hampnett GL54 30 C7
Hampole DN6 51 H2
Hampreston BH21 10 B5
Hampstead NW3 23 F3
Hampstead Norreys RG18 21 J4
Hampsthwaite HG3 57 H4
Hampton Devon EX13 8 B5
Hampton Gt.Lon. TW12 22 E5
Hampton Kent CT6 25 H5
Hampton Peter. PE7 42 E6
Hampton Shrop. WV16 39 G7
Hampton Swin. SN6 20 E2
Hampton Worcs. WR11 30 B4
Hampton Bishop HR1 28 E5
Hampton Fields GL6 20 B2
Hampton Heath SY14 38 D1
Hampton in Arden B92 40 E7
Hampton Loade WV15 39 G7
Hampton Lovett WR9 29 H2
Hampton Lucy CV35 30 D3
Hampton on the Hill CV35 30 D2
Hampton Poyle OX5 31 G7
Hampton Wick KT1 22 E5
Hamptworth SP5 10 D3
Hamsey BN8 13 H5
Hamstall Ridware WS15 40 D4
Hamstead PO41 10 E5
Hamstead Marshall RG20 21 H5
Hamsteels DH7 62 C2
Hamsterley Dur. DL13 62 C3
Hamsterley Dur. NE17 62 C1
Hamstreet TN26 15 F4
Hamworthy BH15 9 J5
Hanbury Staffs. DE13 40 D3
Hanbury Worcs. B60 29 J2
Hanbury Woodend DE13 40 D3
Hanby NG33 42 D2
Hanchurch ST4 40 A1
Handa Island IV27 102 D4
Handale TS13 63 J5
Handbridge CH4 48 D6
Handcross RH17 13 F3
Handforth SK9 49 H4
Handley Ches.W. & C. CH3 48 D7
Handley Derbys. DE55 51 F6
Handley Green CM4 24 C1
Handsacre WS15 40 C4
Handside AL8 33 F7
Handsworth S.Yorks. S13 51 G4
Handsworth W.Mid. B21 40 C6
Handwoodbank SY5 38 D4
Handy Cross SL7 22 B2
Hanford Dorset DT11 9 H3
Hanford Stoke ST4 40 A1
Hanging Bridge DE6 40 D1
Hanging Houghton NN6 31 J1
Hanging Langford SP3 10 B1
Hangingshaw DG11 69 G5
Hanham BS15 19 K4
Hankelow CW3 39 F1
Hankerton SN16 20 C2
Hankham BN24 13 K6
Hanley ST1 40 A1
Hanley Castle WR8 29 H4
Hanley Child WR15 29 F2
Hanley Swan WR8 29 H4
Hanley William WR15 29 F2
Hanlith BD23 56 E3
Hanmer SY13 38 D2
Hannah LN13 53 H5
Hannington Hants. RG26 21 J6
Hannington Northants. NN6 32 B1
Hannington Swin. SN6 20 E2
Hannington Wick SN6 20 E2
Hanslope MK19 32 B4
Hanthorpe PE10 42 D3
Hanwell Gt.Lon. W7 22 E3
Hanwell Oxon. OX17 31 F4
Hanwood SY5 38 D5
Hanworth Gt.Lon. TW13 22 E4
Hanworth Norf. NR11 45 F2
Happisburgh NR12 45 H2
Happisburgh Common NR12 45 H3
Hapsford WA6 48 D5
Hapton Lancs. BB11 56 C6
Hapton Norf. NR15 45 F6
Harberton TQ9 5 H5
Harbertonford TQ9 5 H5
Harbledown CT2 15 G2
Harborne B17 40 C7
Harborough Magna CV23 31 F1
Harbost (Tabost) HS2 101 H1
Harbottle NE65 70 E3
Harbourneford TQ10 5 H4
Harbridge BH24 10 C3
Harbridge Green BH24 10 C3
Harburn EH55 75 J4
Harbury CV33 30 E3
Harby Leics. LE14 42 A2
Harby Notts. NG23 52 B5
Harcombe EX10 7 K6
Harcombe Bottom DT7 8 C5
Harden W.Mid. WS3 40 C5
Harden W.Yorks. BD16 57 F6
Hardendale CA10 61 G5
Hardenhuish SN14 20 C4
Hardgate Aber. AB31 91 F4
Hardgate N.Yorks. HG3 57 H3
Hardham RH20 12 D5
Hardhorn FY6 55 G6
Hardingham NR9 44 E5
Hardingstone NN4 31 J3
Hardington BA11 20 A6
Hardington Mandeville BA22 8 E3
Hardington Marsh BA22 8 E4
Hardington Moor BA22 8 E3
Hardley SO45 11 F4
Hardley Street NR14 45 H5
Hardmead MK16 32 C4
Hardraw DL8 61 K7
Hardstoft S45 51 G6
Hardway Hants. PO12 11 H4
Hardway Som. BA10 9 G1
Hardwick Bucks. HP22 32 B7
Hardwick Cambs. CB23 33 G3
Hardwick Lincs. LN1 52 B5
Hardwick Norf. NR15 45 G6
Hardwick Northants. NN9 32 B2
Hardwick Oxon. OX29 21 G1
Hardwick Oxon. OX27 31 G6
Hardwick S.Yorks. S26 51 G4
Hardwick W.Mid. B74 40 C6
Hardwick Village S80 51 J5
Hardwicke Glos. GL51 29 J6
Hardwicke Glos. GL2 29 G7
Hardwicke Here. HR3 28 B4
Hardy's Green CO2 34 D6
Hare Green CO7 34 E6
Hare Hatch RG10 22 B4
Hare Street Herts. SG2 33 G6
Hare Street Herts. SG9 33 G6
Hareby PE23 53 G6
Harecroft BD15 57 F6
Hareden BB7 56 B4
Harefield UB9 22 D2
Harehill DE6 40 D2
Harehills LS9 57 J6
Harehope NE66 71 F1
Harelaw ML11 75 H6
Hareplain TN27 14 D4
Harescough CA10 61 H2
Harescombe GL4 29 H7
Haresfield GL10 29 H7
Hareshaw N.Lan. ML1 75 G4
Hareshaw S.Lan. ML10 74 E6
Harestock SO22 11 F1
Harewood LS17 57 J5
Harewood End HR2 28 E6
Harford Devon PL21 5 G5
Harford Devon EX6 7 G6
Hargate NR16 45 F6
Hargatewall SK17 50 D5
Hargrave Ches.W. & C. CH3 48 D6
Hargrave Northants. NN9 32 D1
Hargrave Suff. IP29 34 B3
Hargrave Green IP29 34 B3
Harker CA6 69 J7
Harkstead IP9 35 F5
Harlaston B79 40 E4
Harlaxton NG32 42 B2
Harle Syke BB10 56 D6
Harlech LL46 36 E2
Harlequin NG12 41 J2
Harlescott SY1 38 E4
Harlesden NW10 23 F3
Harleston Devon TQ7 5 H6
Harleston Norf. IP20 45 G7
Harleston Suff. IP14 34 E2
Harlestone NN7 31 J2
Harley S.Yorks. S62 51 F3
Harley Shrop. SY5 38 E5
Harleyholm ML12 75 H7
Harlington Cen.Beds. LU5 32 D5
Harlington Gt.Lon. UB3 22 D4
Harlosh IV55 93 H7
Harlow CM17 33 H7
Harlow Hill NE15 71 F7
Harlthorpe YO8 58 D6
Harlton CB23 33 G3
Harlyn PL28 3 F1
Harman's Cross BH19 9 J6
Harmby DL8 57 G1
Harmer Green AL6 33 F7
Harmer Hill SY4 38 D3
Harmondsworth UB7 22 D4
Harmston LN5 52 C6
Harnage SY5 38 E5
Harnham SP2 10 C2
Harnhill GL7 20 D1
Harold Hill RM3 23 J2
Harold Park RM3 23 J2
Harold Wood RM3 23 J2
Haroldston West SA62 16 B4
Haroldswick ZE2 107 Q1
Harome YO62 58 C1
Harpenden AL5 32 E7
Harpford EX10 7 J6
Harpham YO25 59 G3
Harpley Norf. PE31 44 B3
Harpley Worcs. WR6 29 F2
Harpole NN7 31 H2
Harprigg LA6 56 B1
Harpsdale KW12 105 G3
Harpsden RG9 22 A3
Harpswell DN21 52 C4
Harpur Hill SK17 50 C5
Harpurhey M9 49 H2
Harracott EX31 6 D3
Harrapool IV49 86 C2
Harrietfield PH1 82 A5
Harrietsham ME17 14 D2
Harringay N8 23 G3
Harrington Cumb. CA14 60 A4
Harrington Lincs. PE23 53 G5
Harrington Northants. NN6 31 J1
Harringworth NN17 42 C6
Harris PH43 85 J5
Harris Green NR15 45 G6
Harriseahead ST7 49 H7
Harriston CA7 60 C2
HARROGATE HG 57 J4
Harrold MK43 32 C3
Harrop Fold BB7 56 C5
HARROW Gt.Lon. HA 22 E3
Harrow High. KW14 105 H1
Harrow Green IP29 34 C3
Harrow on the Hill HA1 22 E3
Harrow Weald HA3 22 E2
Harrowbarrow PL17 4 E3
Harrowden MK42 32 D4
Harrowgate Hill DL3 62 D5
Harry Stoke BS34 19 K4
Harston Cambs. CB22 33 H3
Harston Leics. NG32 42 B2
Harswell YO42 58 E5
Hart TS27 63 F3
Hartburn NE61 71 F5
Hartest IP29 34 C3
Hartfield E.Suss. TN7 13 H3
Hartfield High. IV54 94 D7
Hartford Cambs. PE29 33 F1
Hartford Ches.W. & C. CW8 49 F5
Hartford Som. TA22 7 H3
Hartford End CM3 33 K7
Hartfordbridge RG27 22 A6
Hartforth DL10 62 C6
Hartgrove SP7 9 H3
Harthill Ches.W. & C. CH3 48 E7
Harthill N.Lan. ML7 75 H4
Harthill S.Yorks. S26 51 G4
Hartington SK17 50 D6
Hartington Hall NE61 71 F5
Hartland EX39 6 A3
Hartland Quay EX39 6 A3
Hartlebury DY11 29 H1
Hartlepool TS24 63 G3
Hartley Cumb. CA17 61 J6
Hartley Kent DA3 24 C5
Hartley Kent TN17 14 C4
Hartley Northumb. NE26 71 J6
Hartley Green ST18 40 B3
Hartley Mauditt GU34 11 J1
Hartley Wespall RG27 21 K6
Hartley Wintney RG27 22 A6
Hartlington BD23 57 F3
Hartlip ME9 24 E5
Hartoft End YO18 63 J7
Harton N.Yorks. YO60 58 D3
Harton Shrop. SY6 38 D7
Harton T. & W. NE34 71 J7
Hartpury GL19 29 H6
Hartrigge TD8 70 B1
Hartshead WF15 57 G7
Hartshill CV10 41 F6
Hartshorne DE11 41 F3
Hartsop CA10 60 F5
Hartwell Bucks. HP17 31 J7
Hartwell E.Suss. TN7 13 H3
Hartwell Northants. NN7 31 J3
Hartwith HG3 57 H3
Hartwood ML7 75 G5
Harvel DA13 24 C5
Harvington Worcs. WR11 30 B4
Harvington Worcs. DY10 29 H1
Harwell Notts. DN10 51 J3
Harwell Oxon. OX11 21 H3
Harwich CO12 35 G5
Harwood Dur. DL12 61 K3
Harwood Gt.Man. BL2 49 G1
Harwood Northumb. NE61 71 F4
Harwood Dale YO13 63 J3
Harwood on Teviot TD9 69 K3
Harworth DN11 51 J3
Hasbury B63 40 B7
Hascombe GU8 22 D7
Haselbech NN6 31 J1
Haselbury Plucknett TA18 8 D3
Haseley CV35 30 D2
Haseley Knob CV35 30 D1
Haselor B49 30 C3
Hasfield GL19 29 H6
Hasguard SA62 16 B5
Haskayne L39 48 C2
Hasketon IP13 35 G3
Hasland S41 51 F6
Hasland Green S41 51 F6
Haslemere GU27 12 C3
Haslingden BB4 56 C7
Haslingden Grane BB4 56 C7
Haslingfield CB23 33 H3
Haslington CW1 49 G7
Hassall CW11 49 G7
Hassall Green CW11 49 G7
Hassell Street TN25 15 F3
Hassendean TD9 70 A1
Hassingham NR13 45 H5
Hassocks BN6 13 G5
Hassop DE45 50 E5
Haster KW1 105 J3
Hasthorpe LN13 53 H6
Hastigrow KW1 105 H2
Hastingleigh TN25 15 F3
Hastings E.Suss. TN34 14 D7
Hastings Som. TA19 8 C3
Hastingwood CM17 23 H1
Hastoe HP23 22 C1
Haswell DH6 62 E2
Haswell Plough DH6 62 E2
Hatch Cen.Beds. SG19 32 E4
Hatch Hants. RG24 21 K6
Hatch Beauchamp TA3 8 C2
Hatch End HA5 22 E2
Hatch Green TA3 8 C3
Hatching Green AL5 32 E7
Hatchmere WA6 48 E5
Hatcliffe DN37 53 F2
Hatfield Here. HR6 28 E3
Hatfield Herts. AL10 23 F1
Hatfield S.Yorks. DN7 51 J2
Hatfield Broad Oak CM22 33 J7
Hatfield Heath CM22 33 J7
Hatfield Peverel CM3 34 B7
Hatfield Woodhouse DN7 51 J2
Hatford SN7 21 G2
Hatherden SP11 21 G6
Hatherleigh EX20 6 D5
Hathern LE12 41 G3
Hatherop GL7 20 E1
Hathersage S32 50 E4
Hathersage Booths S32 50 E4
Hathershaw OL8 49 J2
Hatherton Ches.E. CW5 39 F1
Hatherton Staffs. WS11 40 B4
Hatley St. George SG19 33 F3
Hatt PL12 4 D4
Hattingley GU34 11 H1
Hatton Aber. AB42 91 J1
Hatton Derbys. DE65 40 E3
Hatton Gt.Lon. TW14 22 E4
Hatton Lincs. LN8 52 E5
Hatton Shrop. SY6 38 D6
Hatton Warks. CV35 30 D2
Hatton Warr. WA4 48 E4
Hatton Castle AB53 99 F6
Hatton Heath CH3 48 D6
Hatton of Fintray AB21 91 G3
Hattoncrook AB21 91 G2
Haugh LN13 53 H5
Haugh Head NE71 71 F1
Haugh of Glass AB54 90 C1
Haugh of Urr DG7 65 J4
Haugham LN11 53 G4
Haughhead G66 74 E3
Haughley IP14 34 E2
Haughley Green IP14 34 E2
Haughley New Street IP14 34 E2
Haughs AB54 98 D6
Haughton Ches.E. CW6 48 E7
Haughton Notts. DN22 51 J5
Haughton Powys SY22 38 C4
Haughton Shrop. WV16 39 F6
Haughton Shrop. SY4 38 E4
Haughton Shrop. SY11 38 C3
Haughton Staffs. ST18 40 A3
Haughton Green M34 49 J3
Haughton Le Skerne DL1 62 E5
Haultwick SG11 33 G6
Haunn HS8 84 C3
Haunton B79 40 E4
Hauxton CB22 33 H3
Havannah CW12 49 H6
Havant PO9 11 J4
Haven HR4 28 D3
Havenstreet PO33 11 G5
Havercroft WF4 51 F1
Haverfordwest (Hwlffordd) SA61 16 C4
Haverhill CB9 33 K4
Haverigg LA18 54 E2
Havering Park RM5 23 H2
Havering-atte-Bower RM4 23 J2
Haversham MK19 32 B4
Haverthwaite LA12 55 G1
Haverton Hill TS23 63 F4
Haviker Street TN12 14 C3
Havyat BA6 8 E1
Hawarden (Penarlâg) CH5 48 C6
Hawbridge WR8 29 J4
Hawbush Green CM77 34 B6
Hawcoat LA14 55 F2
Hawes DL8 56 D1
Hawe's Green NR15 45 G6
Hawick TD9 70 A2
Hawkchurch EX13 8 C4
Hawkedon IP29 34 B3
Hawkenbury Kent TN2 13 J3
Hawkenbury Kent TN12 14 D3
Hawkeridge BA13 20 B6
Hawkerland EX10 7 J7
Hawkes End CV5 40 E7
Hawkesbury GL9 20 A3
Hawkesbury Upton GL9 20 A3
Hawkhill NE66 71 H2
Hawkhurst TN18 14 C4
Hawkinge CT18 15 H3
Hawkley GU33 11 J2
Hawkridge TA22 7 G2
Hawkshead LA22 60 E7
Hawkshead Hill LA22 60 E7
Hawksheads LA5 55 H3
Hawksland ML11 75 G6
Hawkswick BD23 56 E2
Hawksworth Notts. NG13 42 A1
Hawksworth W.Yorks. LS20 57 G5
Hawksworth W.Yorks. LS18 57 H6
Hawkwell Essex SS5 24 E2
Hawkwell Northumb. NE18 71 F6
Hawley Hants. GU17 22 B6
Hawley Kent DA2 23 J4
Hawley's Corner TN16 23 H6
Hawling GL54 30 B6
Hawnby YO62 58 B1
Haworth BD22 57 F6
Hawstead IP29 34 C3
Hawstead Green IP29 34 C3
Hawthorn Dur. SR7 63 F2
Hawthorn Hants. GU34 11 H1
Hawthorn R.C.T. CF37 18 D3
Hawthorn Wilts. SN13 20 B5
Hawthorn Hill Brack.F. RG42 22 B4
Hawthorn Hill Lincs. LN4 53 F7
Hawthorpe PE10 42 D3
Hawton NG24 51 K7
Haxby YO32 58 C4
Haxey DN9 51 K2
Haxted TN8 23 H7
Haxton SP4 20 E7
Hay Green PE34 43 J4
Hay Mills B25 40 D7
Hay Street SG11 33 G6
Haydock WA11 48 E3
Haydon Dorset DT9 9 F3
Haydon Swin. SN25 20 E3
Haydon Bridge NE47 70 D7
Haydon Wick SN25 20 E3
Hayes Gt.Lon. UB3 22 D3
Hayes Gt.Lon. BR2 23 H5
Hayes End UB4 22 D3
Hayfield Arg. & B. PA35 80 B5
Hayfield Derbys. SK22 50 C4
Hayfield Fife KY2 76 A1
Hayfield High. KW14 105 G2
Haygrove TA6 8 B1
Hayhillock DD11 83 G3
Hayle TR27 2 C5
Hayling Island PO11 11 J4
Haymoor Green CW5 49 F7
Hayne EX16 7 H4
Haynes MK45 32 E4
Haynes Church End MK45 32 D4
Haynes West End MK45 32 D4
Hay-on-Wye (Y Gelli Gandryll) HR3 28 B4
Hayscastle SA62 16 B3
Hayscastle Cross SA62 16 C3
Hayton Cumb. CA8 61 G1
Hayton Cumb. CA7 60 C2
Hayton E.Riding YO42 58 E5
Hayton Notts. DN22 51 K4
Hayton's Bent SY8 38 E7
Haytor Vale TQ13 5 H3
Haytown EX22 6 B4
Haywards Heath RH16 13 G4
Haywood Oaks NG21 51 J7
Hazel End CM23 33 H6
Hazel Grove SK7 49 J4
Hazel Street TN12 13 K3
Hazelbank Arg. & B. PA25 80 B7
Hazelbank S.Lan. ML11 75 G6
Hazelbury Bryan DT10 9 G4
Hazeleigh CM3 24 E1
Hazeley RG27 22 A6
Hazelhurst BL8 49 G1
Hazelside ML11 68 D1
Hazelslack LA7 55 H2
Hazelslade WS12 40 C4
Hazelton Walls KY15 82 E5
Hazelwood Derbys. DE56 41 F1
Hazelwood Gt.Lon. TN14 23 H5
Hazlefield DG7 65 H6
Hazlehead Aberdeen AB15 91 G4
Hazlehead S.Yorks. S36 50 D2
Hazlemere HP15 22 B2
Hazlerigg NE13 71 H6
Hazleton GL54 30 B7
Hazon NE65 71 G3
Heacham PE31 44 A2
Head Bridge EX37 6 E4
Headbourne Worthy SO23 11 F1
Headcorn TN27 14 D3
Headingley LS6 57 H6
Headington OX3 21 J1
Headlam DL2 62 C5
Headless Cross B97 30 B2
Headley Hants. GU35 12 B3
Headley Hants. RG19 21 J5
Headley Surr. KT18 23 F6
Headley Down GU35 12 B3
Headley Heath B38 30 B1

Hea - Hil


Headon DN22 51 K5
Heads Nook CA8 61 F1
Heady Hill OL10 49 H1
Heage DE56 51 F7
Healaugh N.Yorks. DL11 62 B7
Healaugh N.Yorks. LS24 58 B5
Heald Green SK8 49 H4
Heale Devon EX31 6 E1
Heale Som. TA10 8 C2
Healey Lancs. OL12 49 H1
Healey N.Yorks. HG4 57 G1
Healey Northumb. NE44 62 B1
Healey W.Yorks. WF17 57 H7
Healeyfield DH8 62 B2
Healing DN41 53 F1
Heamoor TR18 2 B5
Heaning LA23 60 F7
Heanish PA77 78 B3
**Heanor DE75 41 G1**
Heanton Punchardon EX31 6 D2
Heanton Satchville EX20 6 D4
Heap Bridge BL9 49 H1
Heapey PR6 56 B7
Heapham DN21 52 B4
Hearn GU35 12 B3
Hearthstane ML12 69 G1
Heasley Mill EX36 7 F2
Heast IV49 86 C3
Heath Cardiff CF14 18 E3
Heath Derbys. S44 51 G6
Heath W.Yorks. WF1 51 F1
Heath & Reach LU7 32 C6
Heath End Derbys. LE65 41 F3
Heath End Hants. RG26 21 J5
Heath End Hants. RG20 21 H5
Heath End Surr. GU9 22 B7
Heath Hayes WS12 40 C4
Heath Hill TF11 39 G4
Heath House BS28 19 H7
Heath Town WV10 40 B6
Heathbrook TF9 39 F3
Heathcot AB12 91 G4
Heathcote Derbys. SK17 50 D6
Heathcote Shrop. TF9 39 F3
Heathencote NN12 31 J4
Heather LE67 41 F4
Heathfield Devon TQ12 5 J3
**Heathfield E.Suss. TN21 13 J4**
Heathfield N.Yorks. HG3 57 G3
Heathfield Som. TA4 7 K3
Heathrow Airport TW6 22 D4
Heathton WV5 40 A6
Heatley WA13 49 G4
Heaton Lancs. LA3 55 H3
Heaton Staffs. SK11 49 J6
Heaton T.& W. NE6 71 H7
Heaton W.Yorks. BD9 57 G6
Heaton Moor SK4 49 H3
Heaton's Bridge L40 48 D1
Heaverham TN15 23 J6
Heaviley SK2 49 J4
Heavitree EX1 7 H6
**Hebburn NE31 71 J7**
Hebden BD23 57 F3
**Hebden Bridge HX7 56 E7**
Hebden Green CW7 49 F6
Hebing End SG2 33 G6
Hebron Carmar. SA34 16 E3
Hebron Northumb. NE61 71 G5
Heck DG11 69 F5
Heckfield RG27 22 A5
Heckfield Green IP21 35 F1
Heckfordbridge CO3 34 D6
Heckingham NR14 45 H6
Heckington NG34 42 E1
**Heckmondwike WF16 57 H7**
Heddington SN11 20 C5
Heddle KW17 106 C6
Heddon-on-the-Wall NE15 71 G7
Hedenham NR35 45 H6
Hedge End SO30 11 F3
Hedgerley SL2 22 C3
Hedging TA7 8 C2
Hedley on the Hill NE43 62 B1
Hednesford WS12 40 C4
Hedon HU12 59 H7
Hedsor HP10 22 C3
Heeley S8 51 F4
Heglibister ZE2 107 M7
Heighington Darl. DL5 62 D4
Heighington Lincs. LN4 52 D6
Heightington DY12 29 G1
Heights of Brae IV14 96 C5
Heilam IV27 103 G3
Heisker Islands
(Monach Islands) HS6 92 B5
Heithat DG11 69 G5
Heiton TD5 77 F7
Hele Devon EX34 6 D1
Hele Devon EX5 7 H5
Hele Devon PL15 6 B6
Hele Devon TQ13 5 H3
Hele Som. TA4 7 K3
Hele Torbay TQ1 5 K4
Hele Bridge EX20 6 D5
Hele Lane EX17 7 F4
Helebridge EX23 6 A5
**Helensburgh G84 74 A2**
Helford TR12 2 E6
Helhoughton NR21 44 C3
Helions Bumpstead CB9 33 K4
Hell Corner RG17 21 G5
Hellaby S66 51 H3
Helland Cornw. PL30 4 A3
Helland Som. TA3 8 C2
Hellandbridge PL30 4 A3
Hellesdon NR6 45 G4
Hellidon NN11 31 G3
Hellifield BD23 56 D4
Hellingly BN27 13 J5
Hellington NR14 45 H5
Hellister ZE2 107 M8
Helmdon NN13 31 G4
Helmingham IP14 35 F3
Helmington Row DL15 62 C3
**Helmsdale KW8 105 F7**
Helmshore BB4 56 C7
Helmsley YO62 58 C1
Helperby YO61 57 K3
Helperthorpe YO17 59 F2
Helpringham NG34 42 E1
Helpston PE6 42 E5
Helsby WA6 48 D5
Helsey PE24 53 J5
**Helston TR13 2 D6**
Helstone PL32 4 A2
Helton CA10 61 G4
Helwith DL11 62 B6
Helwith Bridge BD24 56 D3
Hem SY21 38 B5
Hemborough Post TQ9 5 J5
**HEMEL HEMPSTEAD HP 22 D1**
Hemerdon PL7 5 F5
Hemingbrough YO8 58 C6
Hemingby LN9 53 F5
Hemingfield S73 51 F2
Hemingford Abbots PE28 33 F1
Hemingford Grey PE28 33 F1
Hemingstone IP6 35 F3
Hemington Leics. DE74 41 G3
Hemington Northants.
PE8 42 D7
Hemington Som. BA3 20 A6
Hemley IP12 35 G4
Hemlington TS8 63 F5
Hemp Green IP17 35 H2
Hempholme YO25 59 G4
Hempnall NR15 45 G6
Hempnall Green NR15 45 G6
Hempriggs IV36 97 J5
Hempriggs House KW1 105 J4
Hempstead Essex CB10 33 K5
Hempstead Med. ME7 24 D5
Hempstead Norf. NR12 45 J3
Hempstead Norf. NR25 45 F2
Hempsted GL2 29 H7
Hempton Norf. NR21 44 D3
Hempton Oxon. OX15 31 F5
Hemsby NR29 45 J4
Hemswell DN21 52 C3
Hemswell Cliff DN21 52 C4
Hemsworth WF9 51 G1
Hemyock EX15 7 K4
Henbury Bristol BS10 19 J4
Henbury Ches.E. SK10 49 H5
Henderland DG2 65 J3
Hendersyde Park TD5 77 F7
Hendham TQ7 5 H5
Hendon Gt.Lon. NW4 23 F3
Hendon T.& W. SR2 62 E1
Hendraburnick PL32 4 B2
Hendre Bridgend CF35 18 C3
Hendre Gwyn. LL53 36 C2
Hendreforgan CF39 18 C3
Hendy SA4 17 J5
**Hendy-Gwyn (Whitland)**
**SA34 17 F4**
Heneglwys LL77 46 C5
Henfield S.Glos. BS36 19 K4
**Henfield W.Suss. BN5 13 F5**
Henford EX21 6 B6
Hengherst TN26 14 E4
**Hengoed Caerp. CF82 18 E2**
Hengoed Powys HR5 28 B3
Hengoed Shrop. SY10 38 B2
Hengrave IP28 34 C2
Henham CM22 33 J6
Heniarth SY21 38 A5
Henlade TA3 8 B2
Henley Dorset DT2 9 F4
Henley Shrop. SY8 28 E1
Henley Som. TA10 8 D1
Henley Som. TA18 8 D4
Henley Suff. IP6 35 F3
Henley W.Suss. GU27 12 B4
Henley Corner TA10 8 D1
Henley Park GU3 22 C6
**Henley-in-Arden B95 30 C2**
**Henley-on-Thames RG9 22 A3**
Henley's Down TN33 14 C6
Henllan Carmar. SA44 17 G1
Henllan Denb. LL16 47 J6
Henllan Amgoed SA34 16 E3
Henllys NP44 19 F2
**Henlow SG16 32 E5**
Hennock TQ13 7 G7
Henny Street CO10 34 C5
Henryd LL32 47 F5
Henry's Moat SA63 16 D3
Hensall DN14 58 B7
Henshaw NE47 70 C7
Hensingham CA28 60 A5
Henstead NR34 45 J7
Hensting SO21 11 F2
Henstridge BA8 9 G3
Henstridge Ash BA8 9 G3
Henstridge Bowden BA8 9 F2
Henstridge Marsh BA8 9 G2
Henton Oxon. OX39 22 A1
Henton Som. BA5 19 H7
Henwood PL14 4 C3
Heogan ZE2 107 N8
Heol Senni LD3 27 J6
Heolgerrig CF48 18 D1
Heol-y-Cyw CF35 18 C3
Hepburn NE66 71 F1
Hepburn Bell NE66 71 F1
Hepple NE65 70 E3
Hepscott NE61 71 H5
Hepthorne Lane S42 51 G6
Heptonstall HX7 56 E7
Hepworth Suff. IP22 34 D1
Hepworth W.Yorks. HD9 50 D2
Hepworth South Common
IP22 34 D1
Herbrandston SA73 16 B5
**HEREFORD HR 28 E4**
**Heriot EH38 76 B5**
Herm GY1 3 J5
Hermiston EH14 75 K3
Hermitage D.& G. DG7 65 H4
Hermitage Dorset DT2 9 F4
Hermitage Sc.Bord. TD9 70 A4
Hermitage W.Berks. RG18 21 J4
Hermitage W.Suss. PO10 11 J4
Hermitage Green WA2 49 F3
Hermon Carmar. SA33 17 G2
Hermon I.o.A. LL62 46 B6
Hermon Pembs. SA36 17 F2
Herne CT6 25 H5
**Herne Bay CT6 25 H5**
Herne Common CT6 25 H5
Herne Pound ME18 23 K6
Herner EX32 6 D3
Hernhill ME13 25 G5
Herodsfoot PL14 4 C4
Herongate CM13 24 C2
Heron's Ghyll TN22 13 H4
Heronsgate WD3 22 D2
Herriard RG25 21 K7
Herringfleet NR32 45 J6
Herring's Green MK45 32 D4
Herringswell IP28 34 B2
Herringthorpe S65 51 G3
Hersden CT3 25 H5
Hersham Cornw. EX23 6 A5
Hersham Surr. KT12 22 E5
Herstmonceux BN27 13 K5
Herston KW17 106 D8
**Hertford SG14 33 G7**
Hertford Heath SG13 33 G7
Hertingfordbury SG14 33 G7
Hesket Newmarket CA7 60 E3
Hesketh Bank PR4 55 H7
Hesketh Lane PR3 56 B5
Heskin Green PR7 48 E1
Hesleden TS27 63 F3
Hesleyside NE48 70 D5
Heslington YO10 58 C4
Hessay YO26 58 B4
Hessenford PL11 4 D5
Hessett IP30 34 D2
**Hessle HU13 59 G7**
Hest Bank LA2 55 H3
Hester's Way GL51 29 J6
Hestley Green IP23 35 F2
Heston TW5 22 E4
Heswall CH60 48 B4
Hethe OX27 31 G6
Hethelpit Cross GL19 29 G6
Hetherington NE48 70 D6
Hethersett NR9 45 F5
Hethersgill CA6 69 K7
Hethpool NE71 70 D1
Hett DH6 62 D3
Hetton BD23 56 E4
Hetton-le-Hole DH5 62 E2
Heugh NE18 71 F6
Heugh-head Aber. AB36 90 B3
Heugh-head Aber. AB34 90 D5
Heveningham IP19 35 H1
Hever TN8 23 H7
Heversham LA7 55 H1
Hevingham NR10 45 F3
Hewas Water PL26 3 G4
Hewell Grange B97 30 B2
Hewell Lane B60 30 B2
Hewelsfield GL15 19 J1
Hewelsfield Common GL15 19 J1
Hewish N.Som. BS24 19 H5
Hewish Som. TA18 8 D4
Hewood TA20 8 C4
Heworth YO31 58 C4
Hewton EX20 6 D6
**Hexham NE46 70 E7**
Hextable BR8 23 J4
Hexthorpe DN4 51 H2
Hexton SG5 32 E5
Hexworthy PL20 5 G3
Hey BB8 56 D5
Hey Houses FY8 55 G7
Heybridge Essex CM4 24 C2
Heybridge Essex CM9 24 E1
Heybridge Basin CM9 24 E1
Heybrook Bay PL9 4 E6
Heydon Cambs. SG8 33 H4
Heydon Norf. NR11 45 F3
Heydour NG32 42 D2
Heylipoll PA77 78 A3
Heylor ZE2 107 L4
Heyop LD7 28 B1
Heysham LA3 55 H3
Heyshaw HG3 57 G3
Heyshott GU29 12 B5
Heyside OL2 49 J2
Heytesbury BA12 20 C7
Heythrop OX7 30 E6
**Heywood Gt.Man. OL10 49 H1**
Heywood Wilts. BA13 20 B6
Hibaldstow DN20 52 C2
Hibb's Green IP29 34 C3
Hickleton DN5 51 G2
Hickling Norf. NR12 45 J3
Hickling Notts. LE14 41 J3
Hickling Green NR12 45 J3
Hickling Heath NR12 45 J3
Hickstead RH17 13 F4
Hidcote Bartrim GL55 30 C4
Hidcote Boyce GL55 30 C4
High Ackworth WF7 51 G1
High Angerton NE61 71 F5
High Balantyre PA32 80 B6
High Bankhill CA10 61 G2
High Beach IG10 23 H2
High Bentham (Higher
Bentham) LA2 56 B3
High Bickington EX37 6 D3
High Birkwith BD24 56 C2
High Blantyre G72 74 E5
High Bonnybridge FK4 75 G3
High Borgue DG6 65 G5
High Borve HS2 101 G2
High Bradfield S6 50 E3
High Bradley BD20 57 F5
High Bransholme HU7 59 H6
High Bray EX32 6 E2
High Bridge CA5 60 E2
High Brooms TN4 23 J7
High Bullen EX38 6 D3
High Burton HG4 57 H1
High Buston NE66 71 H3
High Callerton NE20 71 G6
High Casterton LA6 56 B2
High Catton YO41 58 D4
High Close DL11 62 C5
High Cogges OX29 21 G1
High Common IP21 45 F7
High Coniscliffe DL2 62 D5
High Crompton OL2 49 J2
High Cross Hants. GU32 11 J2
High Cross Herts. SG11 33 G7
High Cross W.Suss. BN6 13 F5
High Easter CM1 33 K7
High Ellington HG4 57 G1
High Entercommon DL6 62 E6
High Ercall TF6 38 E4
High Etherley DL14 62 C4
High Ferry PE22 43 G1
High Flatts HD8 50 E2
High Garrett CM7 34 B6
High Gate HX7 56 E7
High Grange DL15 62 C3
High Green Norf. NR9 45 F5
High Green Norf. NR19 44 D4
High Green Norf. IP25 44 D5
High Green S.Yorks. S35 51 F3
High Green Suff. IP29 34 C2
High Green Worcs. WR8 29 H4
High Halden TN26 14 D4
High Halstow ME3 24 D4
High Ham TA10 8 D1
High Harrington CA14 60 B4
High Harrogate HG2 57 J4
High Hatton SY4 39 F3
High Hauxley NE65 71 H3
High Hawsker YO22 63 J2
High Heath Shrop. TF9 39 F3
High Heath W.Mid. WS4 40 C5
High Hesket CA4 61 F2
High Hesleden TS27 63 F3
High Hoyland S75 50 E1
High Hunsley YO43 59 F6
High Hurstwood TN22 13 H4
High Hutton YO60 58 D3
High Ireby CA7 60 D3
High Kelling NR25 44 E2
High Kilburn YO61 58 B2
High Kingthorpe YO18 58 E1
High Knipe CA10 61 G5
High Lane Derbys. DE7 41 G1
High Lane Gt.Man. SK6 49 J4
High Lane Worcs. WR6 29 F2
High Laver CM5 23 J1
High Legh WA16 49 G4
High Leven TS15 63 F5
High Littleton BS39 19 K6
High Lorton CA13 60 C4
High Marishes YO17 58 E2
High Marnham NG23 52 B5
High Melton DN5 51 H2
High Moor S21 51 G4
High Newton LA11 55 H1
High Newton-by-the-Sea
NE66 71 H1
High Nibthwaite LA12 60 D7
High Offley ST20 39 G3
High Ongar CM5 23 J1
High Onn ST20 40 A4
High Park Corner CO5 34 E6
High Roding CM6 33 K7
High Shaw DL8 61 K7
High Spen NE39 71 G7
High Stoop DL13 62 C2
High Street Cornw. PL26 3 G3
High Street Kent TN18 14 C4
High Street Suff. IP12 35 J3
High Street Suff. NR35 45 H7
High Street Suff. IP17 35 J1
High Street Suff. CO10 34 C4
High Street Green IP14 34 E3
High Throston TS26 63 F3
High Town WS11 40 B4
High Toynton LN9 53 F6
High Trewhitt NE65 71 F3
High Wham DL13 62 C4
High Wigsell TN32 14 C5
High Woolaston GL15 19 J2
High Worsall TS15 62 E6
High Wray LA22 60 E7
High Wych CM21 33 H7
**High Wycombe HP13 22 B2**
Higham Derbys. DE55 51 F7
Higham Kent ME3 24 D4
Higham Lancs. BB12 56 D6
Higham S.Yorks. S75 51 F2
Higham Suff. IP28 34 B2
Higham Suff. CO7 34 E5
Higham Dykes NE20 71 G6
Higham Ferrers NN10 32 C2
Higham Gobion SG5 32 E5
Higham on the Hill CV13 41 F6
Higham Wood TN10 23 K7
Highampton EX21 6 C5
Highams Park E4 23 G2
Highbridge Hants. SO50 11 F2
**Highbridge Som. TA9 19 G7**
Highbrook RH17 13 G3
Highburton HD8 50 D1
Highbury BA3 19 K7
Highclere RG20 21 H5
Highcliffe BH23 10 D5
Higher Alham BA4 19 K7
Higher Ansty DT2 9 G4
Higher Ashton EX6 7 G7
Higher Ballam FY8 55 G6
Higher Bentham
(High Bentham) LA2 56 B3
Higher Blackley M9 49 H2
Higher Brixham TQ5 5 K5
Higher Cheriton EX14 7 K5
Higher Combe TA22 7 H2
Higher Folds WN7 49 F2
Higher Gabwell TQ1 5 K4
Higher Green M29 49 G3
Higher Halstock Leigh BA22 8 E4
Higher Kingcombe DT2 8 E5
Higher Kinnerton CH4 48 C6
Higher Muddiford EX31 6 D2
Higher Nyland SP8 9 G2
Higher Prestacott EX21 6 B6
Higher Standen BB7 56 C5
Higher Tale EX14 7 J5
Higher Thrushgill LA2 56 B3
Higher Town Cornw. PL26 4 A4
Higher Town I.o.S. TR25 2 C1
Higher Walreddon PL19 4 E3
Higher Walton Lancs. PR5 55 J7
Higher Walton Warr. WA4 48 E4
Higher Wambrook TA20 8 B4
Higher Whatcombe DT11 9 H4
Higher Wheelton PR6 56 B7
Higher Whiteleigh EX22 4 C1
Higher Whitley WA4 49 F4
Higher Wincham CW9 49 F5
Higher Woodhill BL8 49 G1
Higher Woodsford DT2 9 G6
Higher Wraxall DT2 8 E4
Higher Wych SY14 38 D1
Highfield E.Riding YO8 58 D6
Highfield N.Ayr. KA24 74 B5
Highfield Oxon. OX26 31 G6
Highfield S.Yorks. S2 51 F4
Highfield T.& W. NE39 62 C1
Highfields Cambs. CB23 33 G3
Highfields Northumb.
TD15 77 H5
Highgate E.Suss. RH18 13 H3
Highgate Gt.Lon. N6 23 F3
Highgreen Manor NE48 70 D4
Highlane Ches.E. SK11 49 H6
Highlane Derbys. S12 51 G4
Highlaws CA7 60 C2
Highleadon GL18 29 G6
Highleigh Devon TA22 7 H3
Highleigh W.Suss. PO20 12 B7
Highley WV16 39 G7
Highmead SA40 17 J1
Highmoor Cross RG9 21 K3
Highmoor Hill NP26 19 H3
Highnam GL2 29 G7
Highstead CT3 25 J5
Highsted ME9 25 F5
Highstreet ME13 25 G5
Highstreet Green Essex
CO9 34 B5
Highstreet Green Surr.
GU8 12 C3
Hightae DG11 69 F6
Highter's Heath B14 30 B1
Hightown Hants. BH24 10 C4
Hightown Mersey. L38 48 B2
Hightown Green IP30 34 D3
Highway SN11 20 D4
Highweek TQ12 5 J3
Highwood WR15 29 F2
Highwood Hill NW7 23 F2
Highworth SN6 21 F2
Hilborough IP26 44 C5
Hilcote DE55 51 G7
Hilcott SN9 20 E6
Hilden Park TN11 23 J7
Hildenborough TN11 23 J7
Hildenley YO17 58 D2
Hildersham CB21 33 J4
Hilderstone ST15 40 B2
Hilderthorpe YO15 59 H3
Hilfield DT2 9 F4
Hilgay PE38 44 A6
Hill S.Glos. GL13 19 K2
Hill Warks. CV23 31 F2
Hill Worcs. WR10 29 J4
Hill Brow GU33 11 J2
Hill Chorlton ST5 39 G2
Hill Common NR12 45 J3
Hill Cottages YO18 63 J7
Hill Croome WR8 29 H4
Hill Deverill BA12 20 B7
Hill Dyke PE22 43 G1
Hill End Dur. DL13 62 B3
Hill End Fife KY12 75 J1
Hill End Glos. GL20 29 H5
Hill End Gt.Lon. UB9 22 D2
Hill End N.Yorks. BD23 57 F4
Hill Green CB11 33 H5
Hill Head PO14 11 G4
Hill Houses DY14 29 F1
Hill Mountain SA62 16 C5
Hill of Beath KY4 75 K2
Hill of Fearn IV20 97 F4
Hill Ridware WS15 40 C4

Hil - Hou


Hill Row **CB6** 33 H1
Hill Side **HD5** 50 D1
Hill Street **SO40** 10 E3
Hill Top *Hants.* **SO42** 11 F4
Hill Top *S.Yorks.* **DN12** 51 G3
Hill Top *S.Yorks.* **S6** 50 E4
Hill View **BH21** 9 J5
Hill Wootton **CV35** 30 E2
Hillam **LS25** 58 B7
Hillbeck **CA17** 61 J5
Hillberry **IM4** 54 C6
Hillborough **CT6** 25 J5
Hillbrae *Aber.* **AB54** 98 E6
Hillbrae *Aber.* **AB51** 91 F2
Hillbrae *Aber.* **AB51** 91 G1
Hillbutts **BH21** 9 J4
Hillclifflane **DE56** 40 E1
Hillend *Aber.* **AB55** 98 C6
Hillend *Fife* **KY11** 75 K2
Hillend *Midloth.* **EH10** 76 A4
Hillend *N.Lan.* **ML6** 75 G4
Hillend *Swan.* **SA3** 17 H6
Hillend Green **GL18** 29 G6
Hillersland **GL16** 28 E7
Hillesden **MK18** 31 H6
Hillesley **GL12** 20 A3
Hillfarrance **TA4** 7 K3
Hillfoot End **SG5** 32 E5
Hillhead *Devon* **TQ5** 5 K5
Hillhead *S.Ayr.* **KA6** 67 J1
Hillhead of Auchentumb **AB43** 99 H5
Hillhead of Cocklaw **AB42** 99 J6
Hilliard's Cross **WS13** 40 D4
Hilliclay **KW14** 105 G2
Hillingdon **UB10** 22 D3
Hillington *Glas.* **G52** 74 D4
Hillington *Norf.* **PE31** 44 B3
Hillmorton **CV21** 31 G1
Hillockhead *Aber.* **AB36** 90 B4
Hillockhead *Aber.* **AB33** 90 C3
Hillowton **DG7** 65 H4
Hillpound **SO32** 11 G3
Hill's End **MK17** 32 C5
Hills Town **S44** 51 G6
Hillsborough **S6** 51 F3
Hillsford Bridge **EX35** 7 F1
Hillside *Aber.* **AB12** 91 H5
Hillside *Angus* **DD10** 83 J1
Hillside *Moray* **IV30** 97 J5
Hillside *Shet.* **ZE2** 107 N6
Hillside *Worcs.* **WR6** 29 G2
Hillswick **ZE2** 107 L5
Hillway **PO35** 11 H6
Hillwell **ZE2** 107 M11
Hillyfields **SO16** 10 E3
Hilmarton **SN11** 20 D4
Hilperton **BA14** 20 B6
Hilsea **PO3** 11 H4
Hilston **HU11** 59 J6
Hilton *Cambs.* **PE28** 33 F2
Hilton *Cumb.* **CA16** 61 J4
Hilton *Derbys.* **DE65** 40 E2
Hilton *Dorset* **DT11** 9 G4
Hilton *Dur.* **DL2** 62 C4
Hilton *High.* **IV20** 97 G3
Hilton *Shrop.* **WV15** 39 G6
Hilton *Staffs.* **WS14** 40 C5
Hilton *Stock.* **TS15** 63 F5
Hilton Croft **AB41** 91 H1
Hilton of Cadboll **IV20** 97 F4
Hilton of Delnies **IV12** 97 F6
Himbleton **WR9** 29 J3
Himley **DY3** 40 A6
Hincaster **LA7** 55 J1
Hinchley Wood **KT10** 22 E5
**Hinckley LE10** 41 **G6**
Hinderclay **IP22** 34 E1
Hinderton **CH64** 48 C5
Hinderwell **TS13** 63 J5
Hindford **SY11** 38 C2
**Hindhead GU26** 12 **B3**
Hindley *Gt.Man.* **WN2** 49 F2
Hindley *Northumb.* **NE43** 62 B1
Hindley Green **WN2** 49 F2
Hindlip **WR3** 29 H3
Hindolveston **NR20** 44 E3
Hindon *Som.* **TA24** 7 H1
Hindon *Wilts.* **SP3** 9 J1
Hindringham **NR21** 44 D2
Hingham **NR9** 44 E5
Hinksford **DY3** 40 A7
Hinstock **TF9** 39 F3
Hintlesham **IP8** 34 E4
Hinton *Glos.* **GL13** 19 K1
Hinton *Hants.* **BH23** 10 D5
Hinton *Here.* **HR2** 28 C5
Hinton *Northants.* **NN11** 31 G3
Hinton *S.Glos.* **SN14** 20 A4
Hinton *Shrop.* **SY5** 38 D5
Hinton Admiral **BH23** 10 D5
Hinton Ampner **SO24** 11 G2
Hinton Blewett **BS39** 19 J6
Hinton Charterhouse **BA2** 20 A6
Hinton Martell **BH21** 10 B4
Hinton on the Green **WR11** 30 B4
Hinton Parva *Dorset* **BH21** 9 J4
Hinton Parva *Swin.* **SN4** 21 F3
**Hinton St. George TA17** 8 **D3**
Hinton St. Mary **DT10** 9 G3
Hinton Waldrist **SN7** 21 G2
Hinton-in-the-Hedges **NN13** 31 G5
Hints *Shrop.* **SY8** 29 F1
Hints *Staffs.* **B78** 40 D5
Hinwick **NN29** 32 C2
Hinxhill **TN25** 15 F3
Hinxton **CB10** 33 H4
Hinxworth **SG7** 33 F4
Hipperholme **HX3** 57 G7
Hipsburn **NE66** 71 H2
Hipswell **DL9** 62 C7
Hirn **AB31** 91 F4
Hirnant **SY10** 37 K3
Hirst **NE63** 71 H5
Hirst Courtney **YO8** 58 C7
Hirwaen **LL15** 47 K6
Hirwaun **CF44** 18 C1
Hiscott **EX31** 6 D3
Histon **CB24** 33 H2
Hitcham *Bucks.* **SL1** 22 C3
Hitcham *Suff.* **IP7** 34 D3
**Hitchin SG5** 32 **E6**
Hither Green **SE13** 23 G4
Hittisleigh **EX6** 7 F6
Hittisleigh Barton **EX6** 7 F6
Hive **HU15** 58 E6
Hixon **ST18** 40 C3
Hoaden **CT3** 15 H2
Hoaldalbert **NP7** 28 C6
Hoar Cross **DE13** 40 D3
Hoarwithy **HR2** 28 E6
Hoath **CT3** 25 J5
Hobarris **SY7** 28 C1
Hobbister **KW17** 106 C7
Hobbles Green **CB8** 34 B3
Hobbs Cross **CM16** 23 H2
Hobbs Lots Bridge **PE15** 43 G5
Hobkirk **TD9** 70 A2
Hobland Hall **NR31** 45 K5
Hobson **NE16** 62 C1
Hoby **LE14** 41 J4
Hockerill **CM23** 33 H6
Hockering **NR20** 44 E4
Hockerton **NG25** 51 K7
**Hockley SS5** 24 **E2**
Hockley Heath **B94** 30 C1
Hockliffe **LU7** 32 C6
Hockwold cum Wilton **IP26** 44 B7
Hockworthy **TA21** 7 J4
**Hoddesdon EN11** 23 **G1**
Hoddlesden **BB3** 56 C7
Hodgehill **SK11** 49 H6
Hodgeston **SA71** 16 D6
Hodnet **TF9** 39 F3
Hodnetheath **TF9** 39 F3
Hodsoll Street **TN15** 24 C5
Hodson **SN4** 20 E3
Hodthorpe **S80** 51 H5
Hoe **NR20** 44 D4
Hoe Gate **PO7** 11 H3
Hoff **CA16** 61 H5
Hoffleet Stow **PE20** 43 F2
Hoggard's Green **IP29** 34 C3
Hoggeston **MK18** 32 B6
Hoggie **AB56** 98 D5
Hoggrill's End **B46** 40 E6
Hogha Gearraidh **HS6** 92 C4
Hoghton **PR5** 56 B7
Hognaston **DE6** 50 E7
Hogsthorpe **PE24** 53 J5
Holbeach **PE12** 43 G3
Holbeach Bank **PE12** 43 G3
Holbeach Clough **PE12** 43 G3
Holbeach Drove **PE12** 43 G4
Holbeach Hurn **PE12** 43 G3
Holbeach St. Johns **PE12** 43 G4
Holbeach St. Marks **PE12** 43 G2
Holbeach St. Matthew **PE12** 43 H2
Holbeck **S80** 51 H5
Holbeck Woodhouse **S80** 51 H5
Holberrow Green **B96** 30 B3
Holbeton **PL8** 5 G5
Holborough **ME2** 24 D5
Holbrook *Derbys.* **DE56** 41 F1
Holbrook *Suff.* **IP9** 35 F5
Holbrooks **CV6** 41 F7
Holburn **TD15** 77 J7
Holbury **SO45** 11 F4
Holcombe *Devon* **EX7** 5 K3
Holcombe *Gt.Man.* **BL8** 49 G1
Holcombe *Som.* **BA3** 19 K7
Holcombe Burnell Barton **EX6** 7 G6
Holcombe Rogus **TA21** 7 J4
Holcot **NN6** 31 J2
Holden **BB7** 56 C5
Holden Gate **OL14** 56 D7
Holdenby **NN6** 31 H2
Holdenhurst **BH8** 10 C5
Holder's Green **CM6** 33 K6
Holders Hill **NW4** 23 F3
Holdgate **TF13** 38 E7
Holdingham **NG34** 42 D1
Holditch **TA20** 8 C4
Hole **EX15** 7 K4
Hole Park **TN17** 14 D4
Hole Street **BN44** 12 E5
Holehouse **SK13** 50 C3
Hole-in-the-Wall **HR9** 29 F6
Holford **TA5** 7 K1
Holgate **YO26** 58 B4
Holker **LA11** 55 G2
Holkham **NR23** 44 C1
Hollacombe *Devon* **EX22** 6 B5
Hollacombe *Devon* **EX17** 7 G5
Hollacombe Town **EX18** 6 E4
Holland *Ork.* **KW17** 106 D2
Holland *Ork.* **KW17** 106 F5
Holland *Surr.* **RH8** 23 H6
Holland Fen **LN4** 43 F1
Holland-on-Sea **CO15** 35 F7
Hollandstoun **KW17** 106 G2
Hollee **DG11** 69 H7
Hollesley **IP12** 35 H4
Hollicombe **TQ2** 5 K4
Hollingbourne **ME17** 14 D2
Hollingbury **BN1** 13 G6
Hollingrove **TN32** 13 K4
Hollington *Derbys.* **DE6** 40 E2
Hollington *E.Suss.* **TN38** 14 C6
Hollington *Staffs.* **ST10** 40 C2
Hollingworth **SK14** 50 C3
Hollins **S42** 51 F5
Hollins Green **WA3** 49 F3
Hollins Lane **PR3** 55 H4
Hollinsclough **SK17** 50 C6
Hollinwood *Gt.Man.* **OL9** 49 J2
Hollinwood *Shrop.* **SY13** 38 E2
Hollocombe **EX18** 6 E4
Hollow Meadows **S6** 50 E4
Holloway **DE4** 51 F7
Hollowell **NN6** 31 H1
Holly Bush **LL13** 38 D1
Holly End **PE14** 43 H5
Holly Green **HP27** 22 A1
Hollybush *Caerp.* **NP12** 18 E1
Hollybush *E.Ayr.* **KA6** 67 H2
Hollybush *Worcs.* **HR8** 29 G5
Hollyhurst **SY13** 38 E1
Hollym **HU19** 59 K7
Hollywater **GU35** 12 B3
Hollywood **B47** 30 B1
Holm *D. & G.* **DG13** 69 H4
Holm (Tolm) *W.Isles* **HS2** 101 G4
Holm of Drumlanrig **DG3** 68 D4
Holmbridge **HD9** 50 D2
Holmbury St. Mary **RH5** 22 E7
Holmbush **RH12** 13 F3
Holme *Cambs.* **PE7** 42 E7
Holme *Cumb.* **LA6** 55 J2
Holme *N.Lincs.* **DN16** 52 C2
Holme *N.Yorks.* **YO7** 57 J1
Holme *Notts.* **NG23** 52 B7
Holme *W.Yorks.* **HD9** 50 D2
Holme Chapel **BB10** 56 D7
Holme Hale **IP25** 44 C5
Holme Lacy **HR2** 28 E5
Holme Marsh **HR5** 28 C3
Holme next the Sea **PE36** 44 B1
Holme on the Wolds **HU17** 59 F5
Holme Pierrepont **NG12** 41 J2
Holme St. Cuthbert **CA15** 60 C2
Holme-on-Spalding-Moor **YO43** 58 E6
Holmer **HR1** 28 E4
Holmer Green **HP15** 22 C2
Holmes **PR4** 48 D1
Holmes Chapel **CW4** 49 G6
Holme's Hill **BN8** 13 J5
Holmesfield **S18** 51 F5
Holmeswood **L40** 48 D1
Holmewood **S42** 51 G6
Holmfield **HX2** 57 F7
**Holmfirth HD9** 50 **D2**
Holmhead *D. & G.* **DG7** 68 C5
Holmhead *E.Ayr.* **KA18** 67 K1
Holmpton **HU19** 59 K7
**Holmrook CA19** 60 **B6**
Holmsgarth **ZE1** 107 N8
Holmside **DH7** 62 D2
Holmsleigh Green **EX14** 8 B4
Holmston **KA7** 67 H1
Holmwrangle **CA4** 61 G2
Holne **TQ13** 5 H4
Holnest **DT9** 9 F4
Holnicote **TA24** 7 H1
**Holsworthy EX22** 6 **B5**
Holsworthy Beacon **EX22** 6 B5
Holt *Dorset* **BH21** 10 B4
**Holt *Norf.* NR25** 44 **E2**
Holt *Wilts.* **BA14** 20 B5
Holt *Worcs.* **WR6** 29 H2
Holt *Wrex.* **LL13** 48 D7
Holt End *Hants.* **GU34** 11 H1
Holt End *Worcs.* **B98** 30 B2
Holt Fleet **WR6** 29 H2
Holt Heath *Dorset* **BH21** 10 B4
Holt Heath *Worcs.* **WR6** 29 H2
Holt Wood **BH21** 10 B4
Holtby **YO19** 58 C4
Holton *Oxon.* **OX33** 21 K1
Holton *Som.* **BA9** 9 F2
Holton *Suff.* **IP19** 35 J1
Holton cum Beckering **LN8** 52 E4
Holton Heath **BH16** 9 J5
Holton le Clay **DN36** 53 F2
Holton le Moor **LN7** 52 D3
Holton St. Mary **CO7** 34 E5
Holtspur **HP9** 22 C3
Holtye **TN8** 13 H3
Holtye Common **TN8** 13 H3
Holway **TA1** 8 B2
Holwell *Dorset* **DT9** 9 F3
Holwell *Herts.* **SG5** 32 E5
Holwell *Leics.* **LE14** 42 A3
Holwell *Oxon.* **OX18** 21 F1
Holwell *Som.* **BA11** 20 A7
Holwick **DL12** 62 A4
Holworth **DT2** 9 G6
Holy Cross **DY9** 29 J1
Holy Island *I.o.A.* **LL65** 46 A5
Holy Island *Northumb.* **TD15** 77 K6
Holybourne **GU34** 22 A7
Holyfield **EN9** 23 G1
**Holyhead (Caergybi) LL65** 46 **A4**
Holymoorside **S42** 51 F6
Holyport **SL6** 22 B4
Holystone **NE65** 70 E3
Holytown **ML1** 75 F4
Holywell *Cambs.* **PE27** 33 G1
Holywell *Cornw.* **TR8** 2 E3
Holywell *Dorset* **DT2** 8 E4
Holywell *E.Suss.* **BN20** 13 K7
**Holywell (Treffynnon) *Flints.* CH8** 47 **K5**
Holywell *Northumb.* **NE25** 71 J6
Holywell Green **HX4** 50 C1
Holywell Lake **TA21** 7 K3
Holywell Row **IP28** 34 B1
Holywood **DG2** 68 E5
Hom Green **HR9** 28 E6
Homer **TF13** 39 F5
Homersfield **IP20** 45 G7
Homington **SP5** 10 C2
Homore (Tobha Mòr) **HS8** 84 C1
Honey Hill **CT2** 25 H5
Honey Street **SN9** 20 E5
Honey Tye **CO6** 34 D5
Honeyborough **SA73** 16 C5
Honeybourne **WR11** 30 C4
Honeychurch **EX20** 6 E5
Honicknowle **PL5** 4 E5
Honiley **CV8** 30 D1
Honing **NR28** 45 H3
Honingham **NR9** 45 F4
Honington *Lincs.* **NG32** 42 C1
Honington *Suff.* **IP31** 34 D1
Honington *Warks.* **CV36** 30 D4
**Honiton EX14** 7 **K5**
Honkley **LL12** 48 C7
Honley **HD9** 50 D1
Hoo *Med.* **ME3** 24 D4
Hoo *Suff.* **IP13** 35 G3
Hoo Green **WA16** 49 G4
Hoo Meavy **PL20** 5 F4
Hood Green **S75** 51 F2
Hood Hill **S35** 51 F3
Hooe *E.Suss.* **TN33** 13 K6
Hooe *Plym.* **PL9** 5 F5
Hooe Common **TN33** 13 K5
Hook *Cambs.* **PE15** 43 H6
Hook *E.Riding* **DN14** 58 D7
Hook *Gt.Lon.* **KT9** 22 E5
**Hook *Hants.* RG27** 22 **A6**
Hook *Hants.* **SO31** 11 G4
Hook *Pembs.* **SA62** 16 C4
Hook *Wilts.* **SN4** 20 D3
Hook Green *Kent* **TN3** 13 K3
Hook Green *Kent* **DA13** 24 C5
Hook Green *Kent* **DA13** 24 C4
Hook Green *Kent* **DA2** 23 J4
Hook Norton **OX15** 30 E5
Hook-a-Gate **SY5** 38 D5
Hooke **DT8** 8 E4
Hookgate **TF9** 39 G2
Hookway **EX17** 7 G6
Hookwood **RH6** 23 F7
Hoole **CH3** 48 D6
Hooley **CR5** 23 F6
Hoop **NP25** 19 J1
Hooton **CH66** 48 C5
Hooton Levitt **S66** 51 H3
Hooton Pagnell **DN5** 51 G2
Hooton Roberts **S65** 51 G3
Hop Pole **PE11** 42 E4
Hopcrofts Holt **OX25** 31 F6
Hope *Derbys.* **S33** 50 D4
Hope *Devon* **TQ7** 5 G7
Hope *Flints.* **LL12** 48 C7
Hope *Powys* **SY21** 38 B5
Hope *Shrop.* **SY5** 38 C5
Hope *Staffs.* **DE6** 50 D7
Hope Bagot **SY8** 28 E1
Hope Bowdler **SY6** 38 D6
Hope End Green **CM22** 33 J6
Hope Mansell **HR9** 29 F7
Hope under Dinmore **HR6** 28 E3
Hopehouse **TD7** 69 H2
Hopeman **IV30** 97 J5
Hope's Green **SS7** 24 D3
Hopesay **SY7** 38 C7
Hopkinstown **CF37** 18 D2
Hopley's Green **HR3** 28 C3
Hopperton **HG5** 57 K4
Hopsford **CV7** 41 G7
Hopstone **WV5** 39 G6
Hopton *Derbys.* **DE4** 50 E7
Hopton *Norf.* **NR31** 45 K6
Hopton *Shrop.* **TF9** 38 E3
Hopton *Shrop.* **SY4** 38 C3
Hopton *Staffs.* **ST18** 40 B3
Hopton *Suff.* **IP22** 34 D1
Hopton Cangeford **SY8** 38 E7
Hopton Castle **SY7** 28 C1
Hopton Wafers **DY14** 29 F1
Hoptonheath **SY7** 28 C1
Hopwas **B78** 40 D5
Hopwood **B48** 30 B1
Horam **TN21** 13 J5
Horbling **NG34** 42 E2
Horbury **WF4** 50 E1
Horden **SR8** 63 F2
Horderley **SY7** 38 D7
Hordle **SO41** 10 D5
Hordley **SY12** 38 C2
Horeb *Carmar.* **SA15** 17 H5
Horeb *Cere.* **SA44** 17 G1
Horeb *Flints.* **LL12** 48 B7
Horfield **BS7** 19 J4
Horham **IP21** 35 G1
Horkesley Heath **CO6** 34 D6
Horkstow **DN18** 52 C1
Horley *Oxon.* **OX15** 31 F4
**Horley *Surr.* RH6** 23 **F7**
Horn Hill **SL9** 22 D2
Hornblotton **BA4** 8 E1
Hornblotton Green **BA4** 8 E1
Hornby *Lancs.* **LA2** 55 J3
Hornby *N.Yorks.* **DL8** 62 D7
Hornby *N.Yorks.* **DL6** 62 E6
**Horncastle LN9** 53 **F6**
**Hornchurch RM11** 23 **J3**
Horncliffe **TD15** 77 H6
Horndean *Hants.* **PO8** 11 J3
Horndean *Sc.Bord.* **TD15** 77 H6
Horndon **PL19** 6 D7
Horndon on the Hill **SS17** 24 C3
Horne **RH6** 23 G7
Horne Row **CM3** 24 D1
Horner **TA24** 7 G1
Horniehaugh **DD8** 83 F1
Horning **NR12** 45 H4
Horninghold **LE16** 42 B6
Horninglow **DE13** 40 E3
Horningsea **CB25** 33 H2
Horningsham **BA12** 20 B7
Horningtoft **NR20** 44 D3
Horningtops **PL14** 4 C4
Horns Cross *Devon* **EX39** 6 B3
Horns Cross *E.Suss.* **TN31** 14 D5
Horns Green **TN14** 23 H6
Hornsbury **TA20** 8 C3
Hornsby **CA8** 61 G2
Hornsby Gate **CA8** 61 G1
**Hornsea HU18** 59 **J5**
Hornsey **N8** 23 G3
Hornton **OX15** 30 E4
Horrabridge **PL20** 5 F4
Horridge **TQ13** 5 H3
Horringer **IP29** 34 C2
Horrocks Fold **BL1** 49 G1
Horse Bridge **ST9** 49 J7
Horsebridge *Devon* **PL19** 4 E3
Horsebridge *Hants.* **SO20** 10 E1
Horsebrook **ST19** 40 A4
Horsecastle **BS49** 19 H5
Horsehay **TF4** 39 F5
Horseheath **CB21** 33 K4
Horsehouse **DL8** 57 F1
Horsell **GU21** 22 C6
Horseman's Green **SY13** 38 D1
Horsenden **HP27** 22 A1
Horseshoe Green **TN8** 23 H7
Horseway **PE16** 43 H7
Horsey **NR29** 45 J3
Horsey Corner **NR29** 45 J3
Horsford **NR10** 45 F4
Horsforth **LS18** 57 H6
**Horsham *W.Suss.* RH12** 12 **E3**
Horsham *Worcs.* **WR6** 29 G3
Horsham St. Faith **NR10** 45 G4
Horsington *Lincs.* **LN10** 52 E6
Horsington *Som.* **BA8** 9 G2
Horsington Marsh **BA8** 9 G2
Horsley *Derbys.* **DE21** 41 F1
Horsley *Glos.* **GL6** 20 B2
Horsley *Northumb.* **NE15** 71 F7
Horsley *Northumb.* **NE19** 70 D4
Horsley Cross **CO11** 35 F6
Horsley Woodhouse **DE7** 41 F1
Horsleycross Street **CO11** 35 F6
Horsleygate **S18** 51 F5
Horsleyhill **TD9** 70 A2
Horsmonden **TN12** 23 K7
Horspath **OX33** 21 J1
Horstead **NR12** 45 G4
Horsted Keynes **RH17** 13 G4
Horton *Bucks.* **LU7** 32 C7
Horton *Dorset* **BH21** 10 B4
Horton *Lancs.* **BD23** 56 D4
Horton *Northants.* **NN7** 32 B3
Horton *S.Glos.* **BS37** 20 A3
Horton *Shrop.* **SY4** 38 D3
Horton *Som.* **TA19** 8 C3
Horton *Staffs.* **ST13** 49 J7
Horton *Swan.* **SA3** 17 H7
Horton *Tel. & W.* **TF6** 39 F4
Horton *W. & M.* **SL3** 22 D4
Horton *Wilts.* **SN10** 20 D5
Horton Cross **TA19** 8 C3
Horton Grange **NE13** 71 H6
Horton Green **SY14** 38 D1
Horton Heath **SO50** 11 F3
Horton in Ribblesdale **BD24** 56 D2
Horton Inn **BH21** 10 B4
Horton Kirby **DA4** 23 J5
Horton-cum-Studley **OX33** 31 H7
Horwich **BL6** 49 F1
Horwich End **SK23** 50 C4
Horwood **EX39** 6 D3
Hoscar **L40** 48 D1
Hose **LE14** 42 A3
Hoses **LA20** 60 D7
Hosh **PH7** 81 K5
Hosta **HS6** 92 C4
Hoswick **ZE2** 107 N10
Hotham **YO43** 58 E6
Hothfield **TN26** 14 E3
Hoton **LE12** 41 H3
Houbie **ZE2** 107 Q3
Houdston **KA26** 67 F4
Hough **CW2** 49 G7
Hough Green **WA8** 48 D4
Hougham **NG32** 42 B1
Hough-on-the-Hill **NG32** 42 C1
Houghton *Cambs.* **PE28** 33 F1
Houghton *Cumb.* **CA3** 60 F1
Houghton *Devon* **TQ7** 5 G6
Houghton *Hants.* **SO20** 10 E1
Houghton *Pembs.* **SA73** 16 C5
Houghton *W.Suss.* **BN18** 12 D5
Houghton Bank **DL2** 62 D4
Houghton Conquest **MK45** 32 D4
**Houghton le Spring DH4** 62 **E2**
Houghton on the Hill **LE7** 41 J5
Houghton Regis **LU5** 32 D6
Houghton St. Giles **NR22** 44 D2
Houghton-le-Side **DL2** 62 D4
Houlsyke **YO21** 63 J6
Hound **SO31** 11 F4
Hound Green **RG27** 22 A6
Houndslow **TD3** 76 E6
Houndsmoor **TA4** 7 K3
Houndwood **TD14** 77 G4
Hounsdown **SO40** 10 E3
**Hounslow TW3** 22 **E4**

Hou - Itt

Housebay **KW17** 106 F5
Househill **IV12** 97 F6
Houses Hill **HD5** 50 D1
Housetter **ZE2** 107 M4
Housham Tye **CM17** 33 J7
Houss **ZE2** 107 M9
Houston **PA6** 74 C4
Houstry **KW6** 105 G5
Houstry of Dunn **KW1** 105 H3
Houton **KW17** 106 C7
**Hove BN3** 13 **F6**
Hove Edge **HD6** 57 G7
Hoveringham **NG14** 41 J1
Hoveton **NR12** 45 H4
Hovingham **YO62** 58 C2
How **CA8** 61 G1
How Caple **HR1** 29 F5
How End **MK45** 32 D4
How Green **TN8** 23 H7
How Man **CA22** 60 A5
Howbrook **S35** 51 F3
Howden **DN14** 58 D7
Howden Clough **WF17** 57 H7
Howden-le-Wear **DL15** 62 C3
Howe *Cumb.* **LA8** 55 H1
Howe *High.* **KW1** 105 J2
Howe *N.Yorks.* **YO7** 57 J1
Howe *Norf.* **NR15** 45 G6
Howe Green **CM2** 24 D1
Howe of Teuchar **AB53** 99 F6
Howe Street *Essex* **CM3** 33 K7
Howe Street *Essex* **CM7** 33 K5
Howegreen **CM3** 24 E1
Howell **NG34** 42 E1
Howey **LD1** 27 K3
Howgate *Cumb.* **CA28** 60 A4
Howgate *Midloth.* **EH26** 76 A5
Howgill *Lancs.* **BB7** 56 D5
Howgill *N.Yorks.* **BD23** 57 F4
Howick **NE66** 71 H2
Howle **TF10** 39 F3
Howle Hill **HR9** 29 F6
Howlett End **CB10** 33 J5
Howley **TA20** 8 B4
Hownam **TD5** 70 C2
Hownam Mains **TD5** 70 C1
Howpasley **TD9** 69 J3
Howsham *N.Lincs.* **LN7** 52 D2
Howsham *N.Yorks.* **YO60** 58 D3
Howt Green **ME9** 24 E5
Howtel **TD12** 77 G7
Howton **HR2** 28 D6
Howwood **PA9** 74 C4
Hoxa **KW17** 106 D8
Hoxne **IP21** 35 F1
Hoy *High.* **KW14** 105 H2
Hoy *Ork.* **KW16** 106 B8
Hoylake **CH47** 48 B4
Hoyland **S74** 51 F2
Hoylandswaine **S36** 50 E2
Hoyle **GU29** 12 C5
Hubberholme **BD23** 56 E2
Hubberston **SA73** 16 B5
Hubbert's Bridge **PE20** 43 F1
Huby *N.Yorks.* **YO61** 58 B3
Huby *N.Yorks.* **LS17** 57 H5
Hucclecote **GL3** 29 H7
Hucking **ME17** 14 D2
Hucknall **NG15** 41 H1
**HUDDERSFIELD HD** 50 **D1**
Huddington **WR9** 29 J3
Huddlesford **WS13** 40 D5
Hudnall **HP4** 32 D7
Hudscott **EX37** 6 E3
Hudswell **DL11** 62 C7
Huggate **YO42** 58 E4
Hugglescote **LE67** 41 G4
Hugh Town **TR21** 2 C1
Hughenden Valley **HP14** 22 B2
Hughley **SY5** 38 E6
Hugmore **LL13** 48 C7
Hugus **TR3** 2 E4
Huish *Devon* **EX20** 6 D4
Huish *Wilts.* **SN8** 20 E5
Huish Champflower **TA4** 7 J3
Huish Episcopi **TA10** 8 D2
Huisinis **HS3** 100 B6
Hulcote **MK17** 32 C5
Hulcott **HP22** 32 B7
**HULL HU** 59 **H7**
Hulland **DE6** 40 E1
Hulland Ward **DE6** 40 E1
Hullavington **SN14** 20 B3
Hullbridge **SS5** 24 E2
Hulme **ST3** 40 B1
Hulme End **SK17** 50 D7
Hulme Walfield **CW12** 49 H6
Hulver Street **NR34** 45 J7
Hulverstone **PO30** 10 E6
Humber *Devon* **TQ14** 5 J3
Humber *Here.* **HR6** 28 E3
Humberside Airport **DN39** 52 D1
Humberston **DN36** 53 G2
Humberstone **LE5** 41 J5
Humberton **YO61** 57 K3
**Humbie EH36** 76 **C4**
Humbleton *Dur.* **DL2** 62 B5
Humbleton *E.Riding* **HU11** 59 J6
Humbleton *Northumb.* **NE71** 70 E1
Humby **NG33** 42 D2
Hume **TD5** 77 F6
Humehall **TD5** 77 F6
Hummer **DT9** 8 E3
Humshaugh **NE46** 70 E6
Huna **KW1** 105 J1
Huncoat **BB5** 56 C6
Huncote **LE9** 41 H6
Hundalee **TD8** 70 B2
Hundall **S18** 51 F5
Hunderthwaite **DL12** 62 A4
Hundleby **PE23** 53 G6
Hundleton **SA71** 16 C5
Hundon **CO10** 34 B4
Hundred Acres **PO17** 11 G3
Hundred End **PR4** 55 H7
Hundred House **LD1** 28 A3
Hungarton **LE7** 41 J5
Hungate End **MK19** 31 J4
Hungerford *Hants.* **SP6** 10 C3
Hungerford *Shrop.* **SY7** 38 E7
**Hungerford *W.Berks.* RG17** 21 **G5**
Hungerford Newtown **RG17** 21 G4
Hungerton **NG32** 42 B3
Hunglader **IV51** 93 J4
Hunmanby **YO14** 59 G2
Hunningham **CV33** 30 E2
Hunningham Hill **CV33** 30 E2
Hunny Hill **PO30** 11 F6
Hunsdon **SG12** 33 H7
Hunsingore **LS22** 57 K4
Hunslet **LS10** 57 J6
Hunsonby **CA10** 61 G3
Hunspow **KW14** 105 H1
**Hunstanton PE36** 44 **A1**
Hunstanworth **DH8** 62 A2
Hunston *Suff.* **IP31** 34 D2
Hunston *W.Suss.* **PO20** 12 B6
Hunsworth **BD19** 57 G7
Hunt End **B97** 30 B2
Hunt House **YO22** 63 K7
Huntercombe End **RG9** 21 K3
Hunters Forstal **CT6** 25 H5
Hunter's Inn **EX31** 6 E1
Hunter's Quay **PA23** 73 K3
Hunterston **KA23** 73 K5
Huntford **TD8** 70 B3
Huntham **TA3** 8 C2
**Huntingdon PE29** 33 **F1**
Huntingfield **IP19** 35 H1
Huntingford **SP8** 9 H1
Huntington *Here.* **HR5** 28 B3
Huntington *Here.* **HR4** 28 D4
Huntington *Staffs.* **WS12** 40 B4
Huntington *Tel. & W.* **TF6** 39 F5
Huntington *York* **YO32** 58 C4
Huntingtower **PH1** 82 B5
Huntley **GL19** 29 G7
**Huntly AB54** 90 **D1**
Huntlywood **TD4** 76 E6
Hunton *Hants.* **SO21** 21 H7
Hunton *Kent* **ME15** 14 C3
Hunton *N.Yorks.* **DL8** 62 C7
Hunton Bridge **WD4** 22 D1
Hunt's Cross **L25** 48 D4
Huntscott **TA24** 7 H1
Huntsham **EX16** 7 J3
Huntshaw **EX38** 6 D3
Huntshaw Cross **EX31** 6 D3
Huntshaw Water **EX38** 6 D3
Huntspill **TA9** 19 G7
Huntworth **TA7** 8 C1
Hunwick **DL15** 62 C3
Hunworth **NR24** 44 E2
Hurcott *Som.* **TA11** 8 E2
Hurcott *Som.* **TA19** 8 C3
Hurdley **SY15** 38 B6
Hurdsfield **SK10** 49 J5
Hurley *W. & M.* **SL6** 22 B3
Hurley *Warks.* **CV9** 40 E6
Hurley Bottom **SL6** 22 B3
Hurlford **KA1** 74 C7
Hurliness **KW16** 106 B9
Hurlston Green **L40** 48 C1
Hurn **BH23** 10 C5
Hursley **SO21** 11 F2
Hurst *N.Yorks.* **DL11** 62 B6
Hurst *W'ham* **RG10** 22 A4
Hurst Green *E.Suss.* **TN19** 14 C5
Hurst Green *Essex* **CO7** 34 E7
Hurst Green *Lancs.* **BB7** 56 B6
Hurst Green *Surr.* **RH8** 23 G6
Hurst Wickham **BN6** 13 F5
Hurstbourne Priors **RG28** 21 H7
Hurstbourne Tarrant **SP11** 21 G6
Hurstpierpoint **BN6** 13 F5
Hurstwood **BB10** 56 D6
Hurtmore **GU7** 22 C7
Hurworth-on-Tees **DL2** 62 E5
Hury **DL12** 62 A4
Husabost **IV55** 93 G6
Husbands Bosworth **LE17** 41 J7
Husborne Crawley **MK43** 32 C5
Husthwaite **YO61** 58 B2
Hutcherleigh **TQ9** 5 H5
Huthwaite **NG17** 51 G7
Huttoft **LN13** 53 J5
Hutton *Cumb.* **CA11** 60 F4
Hutton *Essex* **CM13** 24 C2
Hutton *Lancs.* **PR4** 55 H7
Hutton *N.Som.* **BS24** 19 G6
Hutton *Sc.Bord.* **TD15** 77 H5
Hutton Bonville **DL7** 62 E6
Hutton Buscel **YO13** 59 F1
Hutton Conyers **HG4** 57 J2
Hutton Cranswick **YO25** 59 G4
Hutton End **CA11** 60 F3
Hutton Hang **DL8** 57 G1
Hutton Henry **TS27** 63 F3
Hutton Magna **DL11** 62 C5
Hutton Mount **CM13** 24 C2
Hutton Mulgrave **YO21** 63 K6
Hutton Roof *Cumb.* **LA6** 55 J2
Hutton Roof *Cumb.* **CA11** 60 E3
Hutton Rudby **TS15** 63 F6
Hutton Sessay **YO7** 57 K2
Hutton Wandesley **YO26** 58 B4
Hutton-le-Hole **YO62** 63 J7
Huxham **EX5** 7 H6
Huxham Green **BA4** 8 E1
Huxley **CH3** 48 E6
Huxter *Shet.* **ZE2** 107 M7
Huxter *Shet.* **ZE2** 107 P6
Huyton **L36** 48 D3
**Hwlffordd (Haverfordwest) SA61** 16 **C4**
Hycemoor **LA19** 54 D1
Hyde *Glos.* **GL6** 20 B1
**Hyde *Gt.Man.* SK14** 49 **J3**
Hyde End *W'ham* **RG7** 22 A5
Hyde End *W.Berks.* **RG7** 21 J5
Hyde Heath **HP6** 22 C1
Hyde Lea **ST18** 40 B4
Hydestile **GU8** 22 C7
Hyndford Bridge **ML11** 75 H6
Hyndlee **TD9** 70 A3
Hynish **PA77** 78 A4
Hyssington **SY15** 38 C6
Hythe *Hants.* **SO45** 11 F4
**Hythe *Kent* CT21** 15 **G4**
Hythe End **TW19** 22 D4
Hythie **AB42** 99 J5
Hyton **LA19** 54 D1

**I**

Ianstown **AB56** 98 C4
Iarsiadar **HS2** 100 D4
Ibberton **DT11** 9 G4
Ible **DE4** 50 E7
Ibsley **BH24** 10 C4
**Ibstock LE67** 41 **G4**
Ibstone **HP14** 22 A2
Ibthorpe **SP11** 21 G6
Ibworth **RG26** 21 J6
Icelton **BS22** 19 G5
Ickburgh **IP26** 44 C6
Ickenham **UB10** 22 D3
Ickford **HP18** 21 K1
Ickham **CT3** 15 H2
Ickleford **SG5** 32 E5
Icklesham **TN36** 14 D6
Ickleton **CB10** 33 H4
Icklingham **IP28** 34 B1
Ickwell Green **SG18** 32 E4
Icomb **GL54** 30 D6
Idbury **OX7** 30 D6
Iddesleigh **EX19** 6 D5
Ide **EX2** 7 H6
Ide Hill **TN14** 23 H6
Ideford **TQ13** 5 J3
Iden **TN31** 14 E5
Iden Green *Kent* **TN17** 14 C4
Iden Green *Kent* **TN17** 14 D4
Idle **BD10** 57 G6
Idless **TR4** 3 F4
Idlicote **CV36** 30 D4
Idmiston **SP4** 10 C1
Idridgehay **DE56** 40 E1
Idridgehay Green **DE56** 40 E1
Idrigil **IV51** 93 J5
Idstone **SN6** 21 F3
Idvies **DD8** 83 G3
Iffley **OX4** 21 J1
Ifield **RH11** 13 F3
Ifieldwood **RH11** 13 F3
Ifold **RH14** 12 D3
Iford *Bourne.* **BH7** 10 C5
Iford *E.Suss.* **BN7** 13 H6
Ifton **NP26** 19 H3
Ifton Heath **SY11** 38 C2
Ightfield **SY13** 38 E2
Ightham **TN15** 23 J6
Iken **IP12** 35 J3
Ilam **DE6** 50 D7
Ilchester **BA22** 8 E2
Ilderton **NE66** 71 F1
**ILFORD IG** 23 **H3**
**Ilfracombe EX34** 6 **D1**
**Ilkeston DE7** 41 **G1**
Ilketshall St. Andrew **NR34** 45 H7
Ilketshall St. Lawrence **NR34** 45 H7
Ilketshall St. Margaret **NR35** 45 H7
**Ilkley LS29** 57 **G5**
Illey **B62** 40 B7
Illidge Green **CW11** 49 G6
Illington **IP24** 44 D7
Illingworth **HX2** 57 F7
Illogan **TR16** 2 D4
Illston on the Hill **LE7** 42 A6
Ilmer **HP27** 22 A1
Ilmington **CV36** 30 D4
**Ilminster TA19** 8 **C3**
Ilsington *Devon* **TQ13** 5 H3
Ilsington *Dorset* **DT2** 9 G5
Ilston **SA2** 17 J6
Ilton *N.Yorks.* **HG4** 57 G2
Ilton *Som.* **TA19** 8 C3
Imachar **KA27** 73 G6
Imber **BA12** 20 C7
Immeroin **FK19** 81 G6
**Immingham DN40** 52 **E1**
Immingham Dock **DN40** 53 F1
Impington **CB24** 33 H2
Ince **CH2** 48 D5
Ince Blundell **L38** 48 C2
Ince-in-Makerfield **WN3** 48 E2
Inch Kenneth **PA68** 79 F4
Inch of Arnhall **DD9** 90 E7
Inchbae Lodge **IV23** 96 B5
Inchbare **DD9** 83 H1
Inchberry **IV32** 98 B5
Inchbraoch **DD10** 83 J2
Inchgrundle **DD9** 90 C7
Inchindown **IV18** 96 D4
Inchinnan **PA4** 74 C4
Inchkinloch **IV27** 103 J4
Inchlaggan **PH35** 87 H4
Inchlumpie **IV17** 96 C4
Inchmarlo **AB31** 90 E5
Inchmarnock **PA20** 73 J5
Inchnabobart **AB35** 90 B6
Inchnacardoch Hotel **PH32** 87 K3
Inchnadamph **IV27** 102 E6
Inchock **DD11** 83 H3
Inchrory **AB37** 89 J4
Inchture **PH14** 82 D5
Inchvuilt **IV4** 87 J1
Inchyra **PH2** 82 C5
Indian Queens **TR9** 3 G3
Inerval **PA42** 72 B6
**Ingatestone CM4** 24 **C2**
Ingbirchworth **S36** 50 E2
Ingerthorpe **HG3** 57 H3
Ingestre **ST18** 40 B3
Ingham *Lincs.* **LN1** 52 C4
Ingham *Norf.* **NR12** 45 H3
Ingham *Suff.* **IP31** 34 C1
Ingham Corner **NR12** 45 H3
Ingleborough **PE14** 43 H4
Ingleby *Derbys.* **DE73** 41 F3
Ingleby *Lincs.* **LN1** 52 B5
Ingleby Arncliffe **DL6** 63 F6
Ingleby Barwick **TS17** 63 F5
Ingleby Cross **DL6** 63 F6
Ingleby Greenhow **TS9** 63 G6
Ingleigh Green **EX19** 6 E5
Inglesbatch **BA2** 20 A5
Inglesham **SN6** 21 F2
Ingleton *Dur.* **DL2** 62 C4
Ingleton *N.Yorks.* **LA6** 56 B2
Inglewhite **PR3** 55 J6
Ingliston **EH28** 75 K3
Ingmire Hall **LA10** 61 H7
Ingoe **NE20** 71 F6
Ingoldisthorpe **PE31** 44 A2
Ingoldmells **PE25** 53 J6
Ingoldsby **NG33** 42 D2
Ingon **CV37** 30 D3
Ingram **NE66** 71 F2
Ingrave **CM13** 24 C2
Ingrow **BD21** 57 F6
Ings **LA8** 60 F7
Ingst **BS35** 19 J3
Ingworth **NR11** 45 F3
Inhurst **RG26** 21 J5
Inistrynich **PA33** 80 C5
Injebreck **IM4** 54 C5
Inkberrow **WR7** 30 B3
Inkersall **S43** 51 G5
Inkersall Green **S43** 51 G5
Inkhorn **AB41** 91 H1
Inkpen **RG17** 21 G5
Inkstack **KW14** 105 H1
Inmarsh **SN12** 20 C5
Innellan **PA23** 73 K4
Innergellie **KY10** 83 G7
Innerhadden **PH16** 81 H2
**Innerleithen EH44** 76 **B7**
Innerleven **KY8** 82 E7
Innermessan **DG9** 64 A4
Innerwick *E.Loth.* **EH42** 77 F3
Innerwick *P. & K.* **PH15** 81 G3
Inninbeg **PA34** 79 H3
Innsworth **GL3** 29 H6
**Insch AB52** 90 **E2**
Insh **PH21** 89 F4
Inshore **IV27** 103 F2
Inskip **PR4** 55 H6
Instow **EX39** 6 C2
Intake **DN2** 51 H2
Intwood **NR4** 45 F5
Inver *Aber.* **AB35** 89 K5
Inver *Arg. & B.* **PA38** 80 A3
Inver *High.* **IV20** 97 F3
Inver *High.* **KW6** 105 G5
Inver *P. & K.* **PH8** 82 B3
Inver Mallie **PH34** 87 H6
Inverailort **PH38** 86 D6
Inveralligin **IV22** 94 E6
Inverallochy **AB43** 99 J4
Inveran **IV27** 96 C2
**Inveraray PA32** 80 **B7**
Inverardoch Mains **FK15** 81 J7
Inverardran **FK20** 80 E5
Inverarish **IV40** 86 B1
Inverarity **DD8** 83 F3
Inverarnan **G83** 80 E6
Inverasdale **IV22** 94 E3
Inverbain **IV54** 94 D6
Inverbeg **G83** 74 B1
Inverbervie **DD10** 91 G7
Inverbroom **IV23** 95 H3
Inverbrough **IV13** 89 F2
Invercassley **IV27** 96 B1
Inverchaolain **PA23** 73 J3
Invercharnan **PH49** 80 C3
Inverchorachan **PA26** 80 D6
Inverchoran **IV6** 95 J6
Invercreran **PA38** 80 B3
Inverdruie **PH22** 89 G3
Inverebrie **AB41** 91 H1
Invereen **IV13** 88 E1
Invererne **IV36** 97 H5
Inveresk **EH21** 76 B3
Inverey **AB35** 89 H6
Inverfarigaig **IV2** 88 C2
**Invergarry PH35** 87 **K4**
Invergelder **AB35** 89 K5
Invergeldie **PH6** 81 J5
Invergloy **PH34** 87 J6
**Invergordon IV18** 96 **E5**
Invergowrie **DD2** 82 E4
Inverguseran **PH41** 86 D4
Inverharroch Farm **AB54** 90 B1
Inverherive **FK20** 80 E5
Inverhope **IV27** 103 G2
Inverie **PH41** 86 D4
Inverinan **PA35** 80 A6
Inverinate **IV40** 87 F2
Inverkeilor **DD11** 83 H3
**Inverkeithing KY11** 75 **K2**
Inverkeithny **AB54** 98 E6
Inverkip **PA16** 74 A3
Inverkirkaig **IV27** 102 C7
Inverlael **IV23** 95 H3
Inverlauren **G84** 74 B2
Inverliever **PA31** 79 K7
Inverliver **PA35** 80 B4
Inverlochlarig **FK19** 81 F6
Inverlochy **PA33** 80 C5
Inverlussa **PA60** 72 E2
Invermay **PH2** 82 B6
Invermoriston **IV63** 88 B3
Invernaver **KW14** 104 C2
Inverneil **PA30** 73 G2
**INVERNESS IV** 96 **D7**
Inverness Airport **IV2** 96 E6
Invernettie **AB42** 99 K6
Invernoaden **PA27** 73 K1
Inveroran Hotel **PA36** 80 D3
Inverquharity **DD8** 83 F2
Inverquhomery **AB42** 99 J6
Inverroy **PH31** 87 J6
Inversanda **PH33** 80 A2
Invershiel **IV40** 87 F3
Invershore **KW3** 105 H5
Inversnaid Hotel **FK8** 80 E7
Invertrossachs **FK17** 81 G7
Inverugie **AB42** 99 K6
Inveruglas **G83** 80 E7
Inveruglass **PH21** 89 F4
**Inverurie AB51** 91 **F2**
Invervar **PH15** 81 H3
Invervegain **PA23** 73 J3
Invery House **AB31** 90 E5
Inverythan **AB53** 99 F6
Inwardleigh **EX20** 6 D6
Inworth **CO5** 34 C7
Iochdar **HS8** 92 C7
**Iona PA76** 78 **D5**
Iping **GU29** 12 B4
Ipplepen **TQ12** 5 J4
Ipsden **OX10** 21 K3
Ipstones **ST10** 40 C1
**IPSWICH IP** 35 **F4**
Irby **CH61** 48 B4
Irby Hill **CH61** 48 B4
Irby in the Marsh **PE24** 53 H6
Irby upon Humber **DN37** 52 E2
Irchester **NN29** 32 C2
Ireby *Cumb.* **CA7** 60 D3
Ireby *Lancs.* **LA6** 56 B2
Ireland *Ork.* **KW16** 106 C7
Ireland *Shet.* **ZE2** 107 M10
Ireland's Cross **CW3** 39 G1
Ireleth **LA16** 55 F2
Ireshopeburn **DL13** 61 K3
Irlam **M44** 49 G3
Irnham **NG33** 42 D3
Iron Acton **BS37** 19 K3
Iron Cross **WR11** 30 B3
Ironbridge **TF8** 39 F5
Irons Bottom **RH2** 23 F7
Ironside **AB53** 99 G5
Ironville **NG16** 51 G7
Irstead **NR12** 45 H3
Irthington **CA6** 69 K7
Irthlingborough **NN9** 32 C1
Irton **YO12** 59 G1
**Irvine KA12** 74 **B7**
Isauld **KW14** 104 E2
Isbister *Ork.* **KW17** 106 C6
Isbister *Ork.* **KW17** 106 B5
Isbister *Shet.* **ZE2** 107 P6
Isbister *Shet.* **ZE2** 107 M3
Isfield **TN22** 13 H5
Isham **NN14** 32 B1
Ishriff **PA65** 79 H4
Isington **GU34** 22 A7
Island of Stroma **KW1** 105 J1
Islawr-dref **LL40** 37 F4
**Islay PA** 72 **A4**
Islay Airport **PA42** 72 B5
Islay House **PA44** 72 B4
Isle Abbotts **TA3** 8 C2
Isle Brewers **TA3** 8 C2
**Isle of Lewis (Eilean Leodhais) HS** 101 **F3**
**ISLE OF MAN IM** 54 **C5**
Isle of Man Airport **IM9** 54 B7
Isle of May **KY10** 76 E1
Isle of Noss **ZE2** 107 P8
Isle of Sheppey **ME12** 25 F4
Isle of Walney **LA14** 54 E3
Isle of Whithorn **DG8** 64 E7
Isle of Wight **PO** 11 F6
Isleham **CB7** 33 K1
Isleornsay (Eilean Iarmain) **IV43** 86 C3
**Isles of Scilly (Scilly Isles) TR** 2 **C1**
Islesburgh **ZE2** 107 M6
**Isleworth TW7** 22 **E4**
Isley Walton **DE74** 41 G3
Islibhig **HS2** 100 B5
Islip *Northants.* **NN14** 32 C1
Islip *Oxon.* **OX5** 31 G7
Isombridge **TF6** 39 F4
Istead Rise **DA13** 24 C5
Itchen **SO19** 11 F3
Itchen Abbas **SO21** 11 G1
Itchen Stoke **SO24** 11 G1
Itchingfield **RH13** 12 E4
Itchington **BS35** 19 K3
Itteringham **NR11** 45 F2

Itt - Kin


Itton Devon EX20 6 E6
Itton Mon. NP16 19 H2
Itton Common NP16 19 H2
Ivegill CA4 60 F2
Ivelet DL11 62 A7
Iver SL0 22 D3
Iver Heath SL0 22 D3
Iveston DH8 62 C1
Ivetsey Bank ST19 40 A4
Ivinghoe LU7 32 C7
Ivinghoe Aston LU7 32 C7
Ivington HR6 28 D3
Ivington Green HR6 28 D3
Ivy Hatch TN15 23 J6
Ivy Todd PE37 44 C5
Ivybridge PL21 5 G5
Ivychurch TN29 15 F5
Iwade ME9 25 F5
Iwerne Courtney (Shroton) DT11 9 H3
Iwerne Minster DT11 9 H3
Ixworth IP31 34 D1
Ixworth Thorpe IP31 34 D1

## J

Jack Hill LS21 57 G4
Jackfield TF8 39 F5
Jacksdale NG16 51 G7
Jackstown AB51 91 F1
Jackton G75 74 D5
Jacobstow EX23 4 B1
Jacobstowe EX20 6 D5
Jacobswell GU4 22 C6
Jameston SA70 16 D6
Jamestown D. & G. DG13 69 J4
Jamestown High. IV14 96 B6
Jamestown W.Dun. G83 74 B2
Janefield IV10 96 E6
Janetstown High. KW14 105 F2
Janetstown High. KW1 105 J3
Jarrow NE32 71 J7
Jarvis Brook TN6 13 J3
Jasper's Green CM7 34 B6
Jawcraig FK1 75 G3
Jayes Park RH5 22 E7
Jaywick CO15 35 F7
Jealott's Hill RG42 22 B4
Jeater Houses DL6 63 F7
Jedburgh TD8 70 B1
Jeffreyston SA68 16 D5
Jemimaville IV7 96 E5
Jericho BL9 49 H1
Jersay ML7 75 G4
JERSEY JE 3 J7
Jersey Airport JE3 3 J7
Jersey Marine SA1 18 A2
Jerviswood ML11 75 G6
Jesmond NE2 71 H7
Jevington BN26 13 J6
Jockey End HP2 32 D7
Jodrell Bank SK11 49 G5
John o' Groats KW1 105 J1
Johnby CA11 60 F3
John's Cross TN32 14 C5
Johnshaven DD10 83 J1
Johnson Street NR29 45 H4
Johnston SA62 16 C4
Johnston Mains AB30 91 F7
Johnstone PA5 74 C4
Johnstone Castle PA5 74 C4
Johnstonebridge DG11 69 F4
Johnstown Carmar. SA31 17 G4
Johnstown Wrex. LL14 38 C1
Joppa KA6 67 J2
Jordans HP9 22 C2
Jordanston SA62 16 C2
Jordanstone PH11 82 D3
Joy's Green GL17 29 F7
Jumpers Common BH23 10 C5
Juniper Hill NN13 31 G5
Jura PA60 72 D2
Jura House PA60 72 C4
Jurby East IM7 54 C4
Jurby West IM7 54 C4

## K

Kaber CA17 61 J5
Kaimes EH17 76 A4
Kames Arg. & B. PA21 73 H3
Kames Arg. & B. PA34 79 K6
Kames E.Ayr. KA18 68 B1
Kea TR3 3 F4
Keadby DN17 52 B1
Keal Cotes PE23 53 G6
Kearsley BL4 49 G2
Kearstwick LA6 56 B2
Kearton DL11 62 B7
Kearvaig IV27 102 E1
Keasden LA2 56 C3
Kebholes AB45 98 E5
Keckwick WA4 48 E4
Keddington LN11 53 G4
Keddington Corner LN11 53 G4
Kedington CB9 34 B4
Kedleston DE22 40 E1
Keelby DN41 52 E1
Keele ST5 40 A1
Keeley Green MK43 32 D4
Keelham BD13 57 F6
Keeres Green CM6 33 J7
Keeston SA62 16 B4
Keevil BA14 20 C6
Kegworth DE74 41 G3
Kehelland TR14 2 D4
Keig AB33 90 E3
Keighley BD21 57 F5
Keil Arg. & B. PA28 66 A3
Keil High. PA38 80 A2
Keilhill AB45 99 F5
Keillmore PA31 72 E2
Keillor PH13 82 D3
Keillour PH1 82 A5
Keills PA46 72 C4
Keils PA60 72 D4
Keinton Mandeville TA11 8 E1
Keir House FK15 75 F1
Keir Mill DG3 68 D4
Keisby PE10 42 D3
Keisley CA16 61 J4
Keiss KW1 105 J2
Keith AB55 98 C5
Keithick PH13 82 D4
Keithmore AB55 90 B1
Keithock DD9 83 H1
Kelbrook BB18 56 E5
Kelby NG32 42 D1
Keld Cumb. CA10 61 G5
Keld N.Yorks. DL11 61 K6
Keldholme YO62 58 D1
Keldy Castle YO18 63 J7
Kelfield N.Lincs. DN9 52 B2
Kelfield N.Yorks. YO19 58 B6
Kelham NG23 51 K7
Kella IM7 54 C4
Kellacott PL15 6 C7
Kellan PA72 79 G3
Kellas Angus DD5 83 F4
Kellas Moray IV30 97 J6
Kellaton TQ7 5 H7
Kellaways SN15 20 C4
Kelleth CA10 61 H6
Kelleythorpe YO25 59 G4
Kelling NR25 44 E1
Kellington DN14 58 B7
Kelloe DH6 62 E3
Kelloholm DG4 68 C2
Kelly Cornw. PL27 4 A3
Kelly Devon PL16 6 B7
Kelly Bray PL17 4 D3
Kelmarsh NN6 31 J1
Kelmscott GL7 21 F2
Kelsale IP17 35 H2
Kelsall CW6 48 E6
Kelsay PA47 72 A5
Kelshall SG8 33 G5
Kelsick CA7 60 D1
Kelso TD5 77 F7
Kelstedge S45 51 F6
Kelstern LN11 53 F3
Kelston BA1 20 A5
Keltneyburn PH15 81 J3
Kelton DG1 65 K3
Kelton Hill (Rhonehouse) DG7 65 H5
Kelty KY4 75 K1
Kelvedon CO5 34 C7
Kelvedon Hatch CM15 23 J2
Kelvinside G12 74 D4
Kelynack TR19 2 A6
Kemacott EX31 6 E1
Kemback KY15 83 F6
Kemberton TF11 39 G5
Kemble GL7 20 C2
Kemerton GL20 29 J5
Kemeys Commander NP15 19 G1
Kemeys Inferior NP18 19 G2
Kemnay AB51 91 F3
Kemp Town BN2 13 G6
Kempe's Corner TN25 15 F3
Kempley GL18 29 F6
Kempley Green GL18 29 F6
Kemps Green B94 30 C1
Kempsey WR5 29 H4
Kempsford GL7 20 E2
Kempshott RG22 21 J7
Kempston MK42 32 D4
Kempston Hardwick MK45 32 D4
Kempston West End MK43 32 C4
Kempton SY7 38 C7
Kemsing TN15 23 J6
Kemsley ME10 25 F5
Kenardington TN26 14 E4
Kenchester HR4 28 D4
Kencot GL7 21 F1
Kendal LA9 61 G7
Kenderchurch HR2 28 D6
Kendleshire BS36 19 K4
Kenfig CF33 18 A3
Kenfig Hill CF33 18 B3
Kenidjack TR19 2 A5
Kenilworth CV8 30 D1
Kenknock P. & K. PH15 81 G3
Kenknock Stir. FK21 81 F4
Kenley Gt.Lon. CR8 23 G5
Kenley Shrop. SY5 38 E5
Kenmore Arg. & B. PA32 80 B7
Kenmore High. IV54 94 D6
Kenmore P. & K. PH15 81 J3
Kenmore W.Isles HS2 100 E7
Kenn Devon EX6 7 H7
Kenn N.Som. BS21 19 H5
Kennacley HS3 93 G2
Kennacraig PA29 73 G4
Kennards House PL15 4 C2
Kennavay HS4 93 H2
Kenneggy Downs TR20 2 C6
Kennerleigh EX17 7 G5
Kennerty AB31 90 E5
Kennet FK10 75 H1
Kennethmont AB54 90 D2
Kennett CB8 33 K2
Kennford EX6 7 H7
Kenninghall NR16 44 E7
Kennington Kent TN24 15 F3
Kennington Oxon. OX1 21 J1
Kennoway KY8 82 E7
Kenny TA19 8 C3
Kennyhill IP28 33 K1
Kennythorpe YO17 58 D3
Kenovay PA77 78 A3
Kensaleyre IV51 93 K6
Kensington W8 23 F3
Kenstone TF9 38 E3
Kensworth LU6 32 D7
Kent International Airport CT12 25 K5
Kent Street E.Suss. TN33 14 C6
Kent Street Kent ME18 23 K6
Kentallen PA38 80 B2
Kentchurch HR2 28 D6
Kentford CB8 34 B2
Kentisbeare EX15 7 J5
Kentisbury EX31 6 E1
Kentisbury Ford EX31 6 E1
Kentish Town NW5 23 F3
Kentmere LA8 61 F6
Kenton Devon EX6 7 H7
Kenton Suff. IP14 35 F2
Kenton T. & W. NE3 71 H7
Kenton Corner IP14 35 G2
Kentra PH36 79 H1
Kents Bank LA11 55 G2
Kent's Green GL18 29 G6
Kent's Oak SO51 10 E2
Kenwick SY12 38 D2
Kenwyn TR1 3 F4
Kenyon WA3 49 F3
Keoldale IV27 103 F2
Keose (Ceos) HS2 101 F5
Keppanach PH33 80 B1
Keppoch Arg. & B. G82 74 B3
Keppoch High. IV40 86 E2
Keprigan PA28 66 A2
Kepwick YO7 63 F7
Keresley CV6 41 F7
Kernborough TQ7 5 H6
Kerrera PA34 79 K5
Kerridge SK10 49 J5
Kerris TR19 2 B6
Kerry (Ceri) SY16 38 A6
Kerrycroy PA20 73 K4
Kerry's Gate HR2 28 C5
Kerrysdale IV21 94 E4
Kersall NG22 51 K6
Kersey IP7 34 E4
Kersey Vale IP7 34 E4
Kershopefoot TD9 69 K5
Kerswell EX15 7 J5
Kerswell Green WR5 29 H4
Kerthen Wood TR27 2 C5
Kesgrave IP5 35 G4
Kessingland NR33 45 K7
Kessingland Beach NR33 45 K7
Kestle PL26 3 G4
Kestle Mill TR8 3 F3
Keston BR2 23 H5
Keswick Cumb. CA12 60 D4
Keswick Norf. NR4 45 G5
Keswick Norf. NR12 45 H2
Ketley Bank TF2 39 F4
Ketsby LN11 53 G5
Kettering NN16 32 B1
Ketteringham NR18 45 F5
Kettins PH13 82 D4
Kettle Corner ME15 14 C2
Kettlebaston IP7 34 D3
Kettlebridge KY15 82 E7
Kettlebrook B77 40 E5
Kettleburgh IP13 35 G2
Kettlehill KY15 82 E7
Kettleholm DG11 69 G6
Kettleness YO21 63 K5
Kettleshulme SK23 49 J5
Kettlesing HG3 57 H4
Kettlesing Bottom HG3 57 H4
Kettlesing Head HG3 57 H4
Kettlestone NR21 44 D2
Kettlethorpe LN1 52 B5
Kettletoft KW17 106 F4
Kettlewell BD23 56 E2
Ketton PE9 42 C5
Kevingtown BR5 23 H5
Kew TW9 22 E4
Kewstoke BS22 19 G5
Kexbrough S75 51 F2
Kexby Lincs. DN21 52 B4
Kexby York YO41 58 D4
Key Green CW12 49 H6
Keyham LE7 41 J5
Keyhaven SO41 10 E5
Keyingham HU12 59 J7
Keymer BN6 13 G5
Keynsham BS31 19 K5
Key's Toft PE24 53 H7
Keysoe MK44 32 D2
Keysoe Row MK44 32 D2
Keyston PE28 32 D1
Keyworth NG12 41 J2
Kibblesworth NE11 62 D1
Kibworth Beauchamp LE8 41 J6
Kibworth Harcourt LE8 41 J6
Kidbrooke SE3 23 H4
Kiddemore Green ST19 40 A5
Kidderminster DY10 29 H1
Kiddington OX20 31 F6
Kidlington OX5 31 F7
Kidmore End RG4 21 K4
Kidnal SY14 38 D1
Kidsdale DG8 64 E7
Kidsgrove ST7 49 H7
Kidstones DL8 56 E1
Kidwelly (Cydweli) SA17 17 H5
Kiel Crofts PA37 79 K4
Kielder NE48 70 B4
Kilbarchan PA10 74 C4
Kilbeg IV44 86 C4
Kilberry PA29 73 F4
Kilbirnie KA25 74 B5
Kilblaan PA32 80 C6
Kilbraur KW9 104 D7
Kilbrennan PA73 79 F3
Kilbride Arg. & B. PA34 79 K5
Kilbride Arg. & B. PA20 73 J4
Kilbride High. IV49 86 B2
Kilbride Farm PA21 73 H4
Kilbridemore PA22 73 J1
Kilburn Derbys. DE56 41 F1
Kilburn Gt.Lon. NW6 23 F3
Kilburn N.Yorks. YO61 58 B2
Kilby LE18 41 J6
Kilchattan Bay PA20 73 K5
Kilchenzie PA28 66 A1
Kilcheran PA34 79 K4
Kilchiaran PA48 72 A4
Kilchoan Arg. & B. PA34 79 J6
Kilchoan High. PH36 79 F1
Kilchoman PA49 72 A4
Kilchrenan PA35 80 B5
Kilchrist PA28 66 A2
Kilconquhar KY9 83 F7
Kilcot GL18 29 F6
Kilcoy IV6 96 C6
Kilcreggan G84 74 A2
Kildale YO21 63 H6
Kildary IV18 96 E4
Kildavie PA28 66 B2
Kildermorie Lodge IV17 96 C4
Kildonan N.Ayr. KA27 66 E1
Kildonan (Cilldonnain) W.Isles HS8 84 C2
Kildonan Lodge KW8 104 E6
Kildonnan PH42 85 K6
Kildrochet House DG9 64 A5
Kildrummy AB33 90 C3
Kildwick BD20 57 F5
Kilfinan PA21 73 H3
Kilfinnan PH34 87 J5
Kilgetty SA68 16 E5
Kilgwrrwg Common NP16 19 H2
Kilham E.Riding YO25 59 G3
Kilham Northumb. TD12 77 G7
Kilkenneth PA77 78 A3
Kilkenny GL54 30 B7
Kilkerran Arg. & B. PA28 66 B2
Kilkerran S.Ayr. KA19 67 H3
Kilkhampton EX23 6 A4
Killamarsh S21 51 G4
Killay SA2 17 K6
Killbeg PA72 79 H3
Killean Arg. & B. PA29 72 E6
Killean Arg. & B. PA32 80 B7
Killearn G63 74 D2
Killellan PA28 66 A2
Killen IV9 96 D6
Killerby DL2 62 C4
Killerton EX5 7 H5
Killichonan PH17 81 G2
Killiechonate PH34 87 J6
Killiechronan PA72 79 G3
Killiecrankie PH16 82 A1
Killiehuntly PH21 88 E5
Killiemor PA72 79 F4
Killilan IV40 87 F1
Killimster KW1 105 J3
Killin High. KW9 97 F1
Killin Stir. FK21 81 G4
Killinallan PA44 72 B3
Killinghall HG3 57 H4
Killington Cumb. LA6 56 B1
Killington Devon EX31 6 E1
Killingworth NE12 71 H6
Killochyett TD1 76 C6
Killocraw PA28 72 E7
Killunaig PA70 79 F5
Killundine PA34 79 G3
Kilmacolm PA13 74 B4
Kilmaha PA35 80 A7
Kilmahog FK17 81 H7
Kilmalieu PH33 79 K2
Kilmaluag IV51 93 K4
Kilmany KY15 82 E5
Kilmarie IV49 86 B3
KILMARNOCK KA 74 C7
Kilmartin PA31 73 G1
Kilmaurs KA3 74 C6
Kilmelford PA34 79 K6
Kilmeny PA45 72 B4
Kilmersdon BA3 19 K6
Kilmeston SO24 11 G2
Kilmichael PA28 66 A1
Kilmichael Glassary PA31 73 G1
Kilmichael of Inverlussa PA31 73 F2
Kilmington Devon EX13 8 B5
Kilmington Wilts. BA12 9 G1
Kilmington Common BA12 9 G1
Kilmorack IV4 96 B7
Kilmore Arg. & B. PA34 79 K5
Kilmore High. IV44 86 C4
Kilmory Arg. & B. PA31 73 F2
Kilmory Arg. & B. PA31 73 F3
Kilmory High. PH43 85 J4
Kilmory High. PH36 86 B7
Kilmory N.Ayr. KA27 66 D1
Kilmote KW8 104 E7
Kilmuir High. IV55 93 H7
Kilmuir High. IV1 96 D7
Kilmuir High. IV18 96 E4
Kilmuir High. IV51 93 J4
Kilmun PA23 73 K2
Kilmux KY8 82 E7
Kiln Green Here. HR9 29 F7
Kiln Green W'ham RG10 22 B4
Kiln Pit Hill DH8 62 B1
Kilnave PA44 72 A3
Kilncadzow ML8 75 G6
Kilndown TN17 14 C4
Kilnhurst S64 51 G3
Kilninian PA74 79 F3
Kilninver PA34 79 K5
Kilnsea HU12 53 H1
Kilnsey BD23 56 E3
Kilnwick YO25 59 F5
Kilnwick Percy YO42 58 E4
Kiloran PA61 72 B1
Kilpatrick KA27 66 D1
Kilpeck HR2 28 D5
Kilphedir KW8 104 E7
Kilpin DN14 58 D7
Kilpin Pike DN14 58 D7
Kilrenny KY10 83 G7
Kilsby CV23 31 G1
Kilspindie PH2 82 D5
Kilstay DG9 64 B7
Kilsyth G65 75 F3
Kiltarlity IV4 96 C7
Kilton Notts. S81 51 H5
Kilton R. & C. TS13 63 H5
Kilton Som. TA5 7 K1
Kilton Thorpe TS12 63 H5
Kiltyrie FK21 81 H4
Kilvaxter IV51 93 J5
Kilve TA5 7 K1
Kilverstone IP24 44 C7
Kilvington NG13 42 B1
Kilwinning KA13 74 B6
Kimberley Norf. NR18 44 E5
Kimberley Notts. NG16 41 H1
Kimberworth S61 51 G3
Kimble Wick HP17 22 B1
Kimblesworth DH2 62 D2
Kimbolton Cambs. PE28 32 D2
Kimbolton Here. HR6 28 E2
Kimbridge SO51 10 E2
Kimcote LE17 41 H7
Kimmeridge BH20 9 J7
Kimmerston NE71 77 H7
Kimpton Hants. SP11 21 F7
Kimpton Herts. SG4 32 E7
Kinaldy KY16 83 G6
Kinblethmont DD11 83 H3
Kinbrace KW11 104 D5
Kinbreack PH34 87 G5
Kinbuck FK15 81 J7
Kincaldrum DD8 83 F3
Kincaple KY16 83 F6
Kincardine Fife FK10 75 H2
Kincardine High. IV24 96 D3
Kincardine O'Neil AB34 90 D5
Kinclaven PH1 82 C4
Kincorth AB12 91 H4
Kincraig Aber. AB41 91 H2
Kincraig High. PH21 89 F4
Kincraigie PH8 82 A3
Kindallachan PH9 82 A2
Kindrogan Field Centre PH10 82 B1
Kinellar AB21 91 G3
Kineton Glos. GL54 30 B6
Kineton Warks. CV35 30 E3
Kineton Green B92 40 D7
Kinfauns PH2 82 C5
King Sterndale SK17 50 C5
Kingarth PA20 73 J5
Kingcoed NP15 19 H1
Kingerby LN8 52 D3
Kingham OX7 30 D6
Kingholm Quay DG1 65 K3
Kinghorn KY3 76 A2
Kinglassie KY5 76 A1
Kingoodie DD2 82 E5
King's Acre HR4 28 D4
King's Bank TN31 14 D5
King's Bromley DE13 40 D4
Kings Caple HR1 28 E6
King's Cliffe PE8 42 D6
King's Coughton B49 30 B3
King's Green WR13 29 G5
King's Heath B14 40 C7
Kings Hill Kent ME19 23 K6
King's Hill W.Mid. WS10 40 B6
Kings Hill Warks. CV3 30 E1
Kings Langley WD4 22 D1
King's Lynn PE30 44 A3
King's Meaburn CA10 61 H4
Kings Mills GY5 3 H5
King's Moss WA11 48 E2
Kings Muir EH45 76 A7
King's Newnham CV23 31 F1
King's Newton DE73 41 F3
King's Norton Leics. LE7 41 J5
King's Norton W.Mid. B30 30 B1
Kings Nympton EX37 6 E4
King's Pyon HR4 28 D3
Kings Ripton PE28 33 F1
King's Somborne SO20 10 E1
King's Stag DT10 9 G3
King's Stanley GL10 20 B1
King's Sutton OX17 31 F5
King's Tamerton PL5 4 E5
King's Walden SG4 32 E6
Kings Worthy SO23 11 F1
Kingsand PL10 4 E5
Kingsbarns KY16 83 G6
Kingsbridge Devon TQ7 5 H6
Kingsbridge Som. TA23 7 H2
Kingsburgh IV51 93 J6
Kingsbury Gt.Lon. HA3 22 E3
Kingsbury Warks. B78 40 E6
Kingsbury Episcopi TA12 8 D2
Kingscavil EH49 75 J3
Kingsclere RG20 21 J6
Kingscote GL8 20 B2
Kingscott EX38 6 D4
Kingscross KA27 66 E1
Kingsdale KY8 82 E7
Kingsdon TA11 8 E2
Kingsdown Kent CT14 15 J3

Kin - Lai

Kingsdown Swin. SN2 20 E3
Kingsdown Wilts. SN13 20 B5
Kingseat KY12 75 K1
Kingsey HP17 22 A1
Kingsfold Pembs. SA71 16 C6
Kingsfold W.Suss. RH12 12 E3
Kingsford Aber. AB53 99 F6
Kingsford Aber. AB33 90 D3
Kingsford Aberdeen AB15 91 G4
Kingsford E.Ayr. KA3 74 C6
Kingsford Worcs. DY11 40 A7
Kingsgate CT10 25 K4
Kingshall Street IP30 34 D2
Kingsheanton EX31 6 D2
Kingshouse FK19 81 G5
Kingshouse Hotel PH49 80 D2
Kingshurst B37 40 D7
Kingskerswell TQ12 5 J4
Kingskettle KY15 82 E7
Kingsland Here. HR6 28 D2
Kingsland I.o.A. LL65 46 A4
Kingsley Ches.W. & C. WA6 48 E5
Kingsley Hants. GU35 11 J1
Kingsley Staffs. ST10 40 C1
Kingsley Green GU27 12 B3
Kingsley Holt ST10 40 C1
Kingslow WV6 39 G6
Kingsmoor CM19 23 H1
Kingsmuir Angus DD8 83 F3
Kingsmuir Fife KY16 83 G7
Kingsnorth TN23 15 F4
Kingsnorth Power Station ME3 24 E4
Kingstanding B44 40 C6
Kingsteignton TQ12 5 J3
Kingsteps IV12 97 G6
Kingsthorne HR2 28 D5
Kingsthorpe NN2 31 J2
Kingston Cambs. CB23 33 G3
Kingston Cornw. PL17 4 D3
Kingston Devon TQ7 5 G6
Kingston Devon EX10 7 J7
Kingston Dorset DT10 9 G4
Kingston Dorset BH20 9 J7
Kingston E.Loth. EH39 76 D2
Kingston Gt.Man. SK14 49 J3
Kingston Hants. BH24 10 C4
Kingston I.o.W. PO38 11 F6
Kingston Kent CT4 15 G2
Kingston M.K. MK10 32 C5
Kingston Moray IV32 98 B4
Kingston W.Suss. BN16 12 D6
Kingston Bagpuize OX13 21 G2
Kingston Blount OX39 22 A2
Kingston by Sea BN43 13 F6
Kingston Deverill BA12 9 H1
Kingston Gorse BN16 12 D6
Kingston Lisle OX12 21 G3
Kingston Maurward DT2 9 G5
Kingston near Lewes BN7 13 G6
Kingston on Soar NG11 41 H3
Kingston Russell DT2 8 E5
Kingston St. Mary TA2 8 B2
Kingston Seymour BS21 19 H5
Kingston Stert OX39 22 A1
KINGSTON UPON HULL HU 59 H7
KINGSTON UPON THAMES KT 22 E5
Kingston Warren OX12 21 G3
Kingstone Here. HR2 28 D5
Kingstone Here. HR9 29 F6
Kingstone Som. TA19 8 C3
Kingstone Staffs. ST14 40 C3
Kingstone Winslow SN6 21 F3
Kingstown CA3 60 E1
Kingswear TQ6 5 J5
Kingswell KA3 74 D6
Kingswells AB15 91 G4
Kingswinford DY6 40 A7
Kingswood Bucks. HP18 31 H7
Kingswood Glos. GL12 20 A2
Kingswood Here. HR5 28 B3
Kingswood Kent ME17 14 D2
Kingswood Powys SY21 38 B5
Kingswood S.Glos. BS15 19 K4
Kingswood Som. TA4 7 K2
Kingswood Surr. KT20 23 F6
Kingswood Warks. B94 30 C1
Kingthorpe LN8 52 E5
Kington Here. HR5 28 B3
Kington Worcs. WR7 29 J3
Kington Langley SN15 20 C4
Kington Magna SP8 9 G2
Kington St. Michael SN14 20 C4
Kingussie PH21 88 E4
Kingweston TA11 8 E1
Kinharrachie AB41 91 H1
Kinharvie DG2 65 K4
Kinkell G66 74 E3
Kinkell Bridge PH3 82 A6
Kinknockie AB42 99 J6
Kinlet DY12 39 G7
Kinloch Fife KY15 82 D6
Kinloch High. IV27 103 F5
Kinloch High. PA34 79 H2
Kinloch High. PH43 85 K5
Kinloch High. IV16 96 C4
Kinloch P. & K. PH12 82 D3
Kinloch P. & K. PH10 82 C3
Kinloch Hourn PH35 87 F4
Kinloch Laggan PH20 88 C6
Kinloch Rannoch PH16 81 H2
Kinlochan PH37 79 K1
Kinlochard FK8 81 F7
Kinlocharkaig PH34 87 F5
Kinlochbeoraid PH38 86 E6
Kinlochbervie IV27 102 E3
Kinlocheil PH33 87 F7
Kinlochetive PH49 80 C3
Kinlochewe IV22 95 G5
Kinlochlaich PA38 80 A3
Kinlochleven PH50 80 C1
Kinlochmoidart PH38 86 D7
Kinlochmorar PH41 86 E5
Kinlochmore PH50 80 C1
Kinlochroag (Ceann Lochroag) HS2 100 D5
Kinlochspelve PA63 79 H5
Kinloss IV36 97 H5
Kinmel Bay (Bae Cinmel) LL18 47 H4
Kinmuck AB51 91 G3
Kinnaber DD10 83 J1
Kinnadie AB41 99 H6
Kinnaird PH14 82 D5
Kinneff DD10 91 G7
Kinnelhead DG10 69 F3
Kinnell Angus DD11 83 H2
Kinnell Stir. FK21 81 G4
Kinnerley SY10 38 C3
Kinnersley Here. HR3 28 C4
Kinnersley Worcs. WR8 29 H4
Kinnerton LD8 28 B2
Kinnerton Green CH4 48 C6
Kinnesswood KY13 82 C7
Kinnettles DD8 83 F3
Kinninvie DL12 62 B4
Kinnordy DD8 82 E2
Kinoulton NG12 41 J2
Kinrara PH22 89 F4
Kinross KY13 82 C7
Kinrossie PH2 82 C4
Kinsbourne Green AL5 32 E7
Kinsham Here. LD8 28 C2
Kinsham Worcs. GL20 29 J5
Kinsley WF9 51 G1
Kinson BH10 10 B5
Kintarvie HS2 100 E6
Kintbury RG17 21 G5
Kintessack IV36 97 G5
Kintillo PH2 82 C6
Kintocher AB33 90 D4
Kinton Here. SY7 28 D1
Kinton Shrop. SY4 38 C4
Kintore AB51 91 F3
Kintour PA42 72 C5
Kintra Arg. & B. PA42 72 B6
Kintra Arg. & B. PA66 78 E5
Kintradwell KW9 97 G1
Kintraw PA31 79 K7
Kinuachdrachd PA60 73 F1
Kinveachy PH24 89 G3
Kinver DY7 40 A7
Kinwarton B49 30 C3
Kiplaw Croft AB42 91 J1
Kipp FK18 81 G6
Kippax LS25 57 K6
Kippen P. & K. PH2 82 B6
Kippen Stir. FK8 74 E1
Kippenross House FK15 81 J7
Kippford (Scaur) DG5 65 J5
Kipping's Cross TN12 23 K7
Kippington TN13 23 J6
Kirbister Ork. KW17 106 C7
Kirbister Ork. KW17 106 F5
Kirbuster KW17 106 B5
Kirby Bedon NR14 45 G5
Kirby Bellars LE14 42 A4
Kirby Cane NR35 45 H6
Kirby Corner CV4 30 D1
Kirby Cross CO13 35 G6
Kirby Fields LE9 41 H5
Kirby Green NR35 45 H6
Kirby Grindalythe YO17 59 F3
Kirby Hill N.Yorks. DL11 62 C6
Kirby Hill N.Yorks. YO51 57 J3
Kirby Knowle YO7 57 K1
Kirby le Soken CO13 35 G6
Kirby Misperton YO17 58 D2
Kirby Muxloe LE9 41 H5
Kirby Row NR35 45 H6
Kirby Sigston DL6 63 F7
Kirby Underdale YO41 58 E4
Kirby Wiske YO7 57 J1
Kirdford RH14 12 D4
Kirk KW1 105 H3
Kirk Bramwith DN7 51 J1
Kirk Deighton LS22 57 J4
Kirk Ella HU10 59 G7
Kirk Hallam DE7 41 G1
Kirk Hammerton YO26 57 K4
Kirk Ireton DE6 50 E7
Kirk Langley DE6 40 E2
Kirk Merrington DL16 62 D3
Kirk Michael IM6 54 C4
Kirk of Shotts ML7 75 G4
Kirk Sandall DN3 51 J2
Kirk Smeaton WF8 51 H1
Kirk Yetholm TD5 70 D1
Kirkabister ZE2 107 N9
Kirkandrews DG6 65 G6
Kirkandrews-upon-Eden CA5 60 E1
Kirkbampton CA5 60 E1
Kirkbean DG2 65 K5
Kirkbride CA7 60 D1
Kirkbuddo DD8 83 G3
Kirkburn E.Riding YO25 59 F4
Kirkburn Sc.Bord. EH45 76 A7
Kirkburton HD8 50 D1
Kirkby Lincs. LN8 52 D3
Kirkby Mersey. L32 48 D3
Kirkby N.Yorks. TS9 63 G6
Kirkby Fleetham DL7 62 D7
Kirkby Green LN4 52 D7
Kirkby in Ashfield NG17 51 G7
Kirkby la Thorpe NG34 42 D1
Kirkby Lonsdale LA6 56 B2
Kirkby Malham BD23 56 D3
Kirkby Mallory LE9 41 G5
Kirkby Malzeard HG4 57 H2
Kirkby on Bain LN10 53 F6
Kirkby Overblow HG3 57 J5
Kirkby Stephen CA17 61 J6
Kirkby Thore CA10 61 H4
Kirkby Underwood PE10 42 D3
Kirkby Wharfe LS24 58 B5
Kirkby Woodhouse NG17 51 G7
Kirkby-in-Furness LA17 55 F1
Kirkbymoorside YO62 58 C1
KIRKCALDY KY 76 A1
Kirkcambeck CA8 70 A7
Kirkcolm DG9 64 A4
Kirkconnel DG4 68 C2
Kirkconnell DG2 65 K4
Kirkcowan DG8 64 D4
Kirkcudbright DG6 65 G5
Kirkdale House DG8 65 F5
Kirkdean EH46 75 K6
Kirkfieldbank ML11 75 G6
Kirkgunzeon DG2 65 J4
Kirkham Lancs. PR4 55 H6
Kirkham N.Yorks. YO60 58 D3
Kirkhamgate WF2 57 J7
Kirkharle NE19 71 F5
Kirkhaugh CA9 61 H2
Kirkheaton Northumb. NE19 71 F6
Kirkheaton W.Yorks. HD5 50 D1
Kirkhill Angus DD10 83 H1
Kirkhill High. IV5 96 C7
Kirkhill Moray AB38 98 B5
Kirkhope TD7 69 J1
Kirkibost High. IV49 86 B3
Kirkibost (Circebost) W.Isles HS2 100 D4
Kirkinch PH12 82 E3
Kirkinner DG8 64 E5
Kirkintilloch G66 74 E3
Kirkland Cumb. CA10 61 H3
Kirkland Cumb. CA26 60 B5
Kirkland D. & G. DG3 68 D4
Kirkland D. & G. DG4 68 C2
Kirkland D. & G. DG11 69 F5
Kirkland of Longcastle DG8 64 D6
Kirkleatham TS10 63 G4
Kirklevington TS15 63 F5
Kirkley NR33 45 K6
Kirklington N.Yorks. DL8 57 J1
Kirklington Notts. NG22 51 J7
Kirklinton CA6 69 K7
Kirkliston EH29 75 K3
Kirkmaiden DG9 64 B7
Kirkmichael P. & K. PH10 82 B1
Kirkmichael S.Ayr. KA19 67 H3
Kirkmuirhill ML11 75 F6
Kirknewton Northumb. NE71 77 H7
Kirknewton W.Loth. EH27 75 K4
Kirkney AB54 90 D1
Kirkoswald Cumb. CA10 61 G2
Kirkoswald S.Ayr. KA19 67 G3
Kirkpatrick Durham DG7 65 H3
Kirkpatrick-Fleming DG11 69 H6
Kirksanton LA18 54 E1
Kirkstall LS5 57 H6
Kirkstead LN10 52 E6
Kirkstile Aber. AB54 90 D1
Kirkstile D. & G. DG13 69 J4
Kirkstyle KW1 105 J1
Kirkthorpe WF1 57 J7
Kirkton Aber. AB52 90 E2
Kirkton Aber. AB53 98 E5
Kirkton Aber. AB33 90 E3
Kirkton Angus DD8 83 F3
Kirkton Arg. & B. PA31 79 J7
Kirkton D. & G. DG1 68 E5
Kirkton Fife DD6 82 E5
Kirkton High. IV3 88 D1
Kirkton High. KW10 96 E2
Kirkton High. IV2 96 E6
Kirkton High. KW13 104 D2
Kirkton High. IV40 86 E2
Kirkton P. & K. PH3 82 A6
Kirkton Sc.Bord. TD9 70 A2
Kirkton Manor EH45 76 A7
Kirkton of Airlie DD8 82 E2
Kirkton of Auchterhouse DD3 82 E4
Kirkton of Barevan IV12 97 F7
Kirkton of Bourtie AB51 91 G2
Kirkton of Collace PH2 82 C4
Kirkton of Craig DD10 83 J2
Kirkton of Culsalmond AB52 90 E1
Kirkton of Durris AB31 91 F5
Kirkton of Glenbuchat AB36 90 B3
Kirkton of Glenisla PH11 82 D1
Kirkton of Kingoldrum DD8 82 E2
Kirkton of Lethendy PH2 82 C3
Kirkton of Logie Buchan AB41 91 H2
Kirkton of Maryculter AB12 91 G5
Kirkton of Menmuir DD9 83 G1
Kirkton of Monikie DD5 83 G4
Kirkton of Rayne AB51 90 E1
Kirkton of Skene AB32 91 G4
Kirkton of Tealing DD4 83 F4
Kirktonhill Aber. AB30 83 H1
Kirktonhill W.Dun. G82 74 B3
Kirktown AB42 99 J5
Kirktown of Alvah AB45 98 E4
Kirktown of Auchterless AB53 99 F6
Kirktown of Deskford AB56 98 D4
Kirktown of Fetteresso AB39 91 G6
Kirktown of Slains AB41 91 J2
KIRKWALL KW 106 D6
Kirkwall Airport KW15 106 D7
Kirkwhelpington NE19 70 E5
Kirmington DN39 52 E1
Kirmond le Mire LN8 52 E3
Kirn PA23 73 K3
Kirriemuir DD8 82 E2
Kirstead Green NR15 45 G6
Kirtlebridge DG11 69 H6
Kirtleton DG11 69 H5
Kirtling CB8 33 K3
Kirtling Green CB8 33 K3
Kirtlington OX5 31 G7
Kirtomy KW14 104 C2
Kirton Lincs. PE20 43 G2
Kirton Notts. NG22 51 J6
Kirton Suff. IP10 35 G5
Kirton End PE20 43 F1
Kirton Holme PE20 43 F1
Kirton in Lindsey DN21 52 C3
Kiscadale KA27 66 E1
Kislingbury NN7 31 H3
Kismeldon Bridge EX22 6 B4
Kites Hardwick CV23 31 F2
Kitley PL8 5 F5
Kittisford TA21 7 J3
Kittisford Barton TA21 7 J3
Kittle SA3 17 J7
Kitt's End EN5 23 F2
Kitt's Green B33 40 D7
Kitwood SO24 11 H1
Kivernoll HR2 28 D5
Kiveton Park S26 51 G4
Klibreck IV27 103 H5
Knabbygates AB54 98 D5
Knaith DN21 52 B4
Knaith Park DN21 52 B4
Knap Corner SP8 9 H2
Knaphill GU21 22 C6
Knaplock TA22 7 G2
Knapp P. & K. PH14 82 D4
Knapp Som. TA3 8 C2
Knapthorpe NG23 51 K7
Knaptoft LE17 41 J7
Knapton Norf. NR28 45 H2
Knapton York YO26 58 B4
Knapton Green HR4 28 D3
Knapwell CB23 33 G2
Knaresborough HG5 57 J4
Knarsdale CA8 61 H1
Knarston KW17 106 C5
Knaven AB42 99 G6
Knayton YO7 57 K1
Knebworth SG3 33 F6
Knedlington DN14 58 D7
Kneesall NG22 51 K6
Kneesworth SG8 33 G4
Kneeton NG13 42 A1
Knelston SA3 17 H7
Knenhall ST15 40 B2
Knettishall IP22 44 D7
Knightacott EX31 6 E2
Knightcote CV47 31 F3
Knightley ST20 40 A3
Knightley Dale ST20 40 A3
Knighton Devon PL9 5 F6
Knighton Dorset DT9 9 F3
Knighton Leic. LE2 41 J5
Knighton Poole BH21 10 B5
Knighton (Tref-y-clawdd) Powys LD7 28 B1
Knighton Som. TA5 7 K1
Knighton Staffs. ST20 39 G3
Knighton Staffs. TF9 39 G1
Knighton Wilts. SN8 21 F4
Knighton on Teme WR15 29 F1
Knightswood G15 74 D4
Knightwick WR6 29 G3
Knill LD8 28 B2
Knipoch PA34 79 K5
Knipton NG32 42 B2
Knitsley DH8 62 C2
Kniveton DE6 50 E7
Knock Arg. & B. PA71 79 G4
Knock Cumb. CA16 61 H4
Knock High. IV44 86 C4
Knock Moray AB54 98 D5
Knock of Auchnahannet PH26 89 H1
Knockalava PA31 73 H1
Knockally KW6 105 G6
Knockaloe Moar IM5 54 B5
Knockan IV27 102 E7
Knockandhu AB37 89 K2
Knockando AB38 97 J7
Knockarthur IV28 96 E1
Knockbain IV8 96 D6
Knockban IV23 95 J5
Knockbreck IV19 96 E3
Knockbrex DG6 65 F6
Knockdamph IV26 95 J2
Knockdee KW12 105 G2
Knockdow PA23 73 K3
Knockdown GL8 20 B3
Knockenkelly KA27 66 E1
Knockentiber KA2 74 B7
Knockfin IV4 87 K2
Knockgray DG7 67 K4
Knockholt TN14 23 H6
Knockholt Pound TN14 23 H6
Knockin SY10 38 C3
Knockinlaw KA3 74 C7
Knockintorran (Cnoc an Torrain) HS6 92 C5
Knocklearn DG7 65 H3
Knockmill TN15 23 J5
Knocknaha PA28 66 A2
Knocknain DG9 66 D7
Knocknalling DG7 67 K5
Knockrome PA60 72 D3
Knocksharry IM5 54 B5
Knockville DG8 64 D3
Knockvologan PA66 78 E6
Knodishall IP17 35 J2
Knodishall Common IP17 35 J2
Knodishall Green IP17 35 J2
Knole TA10 8 D2
Knolls Green WA16 49 H5
Knolton LL13 38 C2
Knook BA12 20 C7
Knossington LE15 42 B5
Knott End-on-Sea FY6 55 G5
Knotting MK44 32 D2
Knotting Green MK44 32 D2
Knottingley WF11 58 B7
Knotts BD23 56 C4
Knotty Green HP9 22 C2
Knowbury SY8 28 E1
Knowe DG8 64 D3
Knowes of Elrick AB54 98 E5
Knowesgate NE19 70 E5
Knoweside KA19 67 G2
Knowetownhead TD9 70 A2
Knowhead AB43 99 H5
Knowl Green CO10 34 B4
Knowl Hill RG10 22 B4
Knowl Wall ST4 40 A2
Knowle Bristol BS4 19 K4
Knowle Devon EX17 7 F5
Knowle Devon EX33 6 C2
Knowle Devon EX9 7 J7
Knowle Shrop. SY8 28 E1
Knowle Som. TA24 7 H1
Knowle W.Mid. B93 30 C1
Knowle Cross EX5 7 J6
Knowle Green PR3 56 B6
Knowle Hall TA7 19 G7
Knowle St. Giles TA20 8 C3
Knowlton Dorset BH21 10 B3
Knowlton Kent CT3 15 H2
Knowsley L34 48 D3
Knowstone EX36 7 G3
Knox Bridge TN17 14 C3
Knucklas LD7 28 B1
Knutsford WA16 49 G5
Knypersley ST8 49 H7
Krumlin HX4 50 C1
Kuggar TR12 2 E7
Kyle of Lochalsh IV40 86 D2
Kyleakin IV41 86 D2
Kylerhea IV40 86 D2
Kyles Scalpay (Caolas Scalpaigh) HS3 93 H2
Kylesbeg PH38 86 C7
Kylesknoydart PH41 86 E5
Kylesku IV27 102 E5
Kylesmorar PH41 86 E5
Kylestrome IV27 102 E5
Kyloag IV24 96 D2
Kynaston SY10 38 C3
Kynnersley TF6 39 F4
Kyre Park WR15 29 F2

## L

Labost HS2 100 E3
Lacasaigh HS2 101 F5
Lacasdal (Laxdale) HS2 101 G4
Laceby DN37 53 F2
Lacey Green HP27 22 B1
Lach Dennis CW9 49 G5
Lacharn (Laugharne) SA33 17 G4
Lackford IP28 34 B1
Lacklee (Leac a' Li) HS3 93 G2
Lacock SN15 20 C5
Ladbroke CV47 31 F3
Laddingford ME18 23 K7
Lade Bank PE22 53 G7
Ladies Hill PR3 55 H5
Ladock TR2 3 F3
Lady Hall LA18 54 E1
Ladybank KY15 82 E6
Ladycross PL15 6 B7
Ladyfield PA32 80 B6
Ladykirk TD15 77 G6
Ladysford AB43 99 H4
Ladywood WR9 29 H2
Laga PH36 79 H1
Lagalochan PA35 79 K6
Lagavulin PA42 72 C6
Lagg Arg. & B. PA60 72 D3
Lagg N.Ayr. KA27 66 D1
Lagg S.Ayr. KA7 67 G2
Laggan Arg. & B. PA43 72 A5
Laggan High. PH34 87 J5
Laggan High. PH20 88 D5
Laggan Moray AB55 90 B1
Laggan Stir. FK18 81 G6
Lagganulva PA73 79 F3
Lagganvoulin AB37 89 J3
Laglingarten PA25 80 C7
Lagnalean IV3 96 D7
Lagrae DG4 68 C2
Laguna PH1 82 C4
Laid IV27 103 G3
Laide IV22 95 F2
Laig PH42 85 K6
Laight KA18 68 B2
Lainchoil PH25 89 H3
Laindon SS15 24 C3
Lair PH10 82 C1
Lairg IV27 96 C1
Lairg Lodge IV27 96 C1
Lairigmor PH33 80 C1
Laisterdyke BD4 57 G6

Lai - Lev


Laithers AB53 98 E6
Laithes CA11 61 F3
Lake Devon EX31 6 D2
Lake Devon PL20 5 F4
Lake I.o.W. PO36 11 G6
Lake Wilts. SP4 10 C1
Lakenham NR1 45 G5
Lakenheath IP27 44 B7
Lakesend PE14 43 J6
Lakeside Cumb. LA12 55 G1
Lakeside S.Yorks. DN4 51 H2
Lakeside Thur. RM20 23 J4
Laleham TW18 22 D5
Laleston CF32 18 B4
Lamancha EH46 76 A5
Lamarsh CO8 34 C5
Lamas NR10 45 G3
Lamb Corner CO7 34 E5
Lamb Roe BB7 56 C6
Lambden TD10 77 F6
Lamberhurst TN3 13 K3
Lamberhurst Quarter TN3 13 K3
Lamberton TD15 77 H5
Lambfell Moar IM4 54 B5
Lambley Northumb. CA8 61 H1
Lambley Notts. NG4 41 J1
Lambourn RG17 21 G4
Lambourn Woodlands RG17 21 G4
Lambourne End RM4 23 H2
Lambs Green RH12 13 F3
Lambston SA62 16 C4
Lambton NE38 62 D1
Lamellion PL14 4 C4
Lamerton PL19 4 E3
Lamesley NE11 62 D1
Lamington High. IV18 96 E4
Lamington S.Lan. ML12 75 H7
Lamlash KA27 73 J7
Lamloch DG7 67 K4
Lamonby CA11 60 F3
Lamorna TR19 2 B6
Lamorran TR2 3 F4
Lampert NE48 70 B6
Lampeter (Llanbedr Pont Steffan) SA48 17 J1
Lampeter Velfrey SA67 16 E4
Lamphey SA71 16 D5
Lamplugh CA14 60 B4
Lamport NN6 31 J1
Lamyatt BA4 9 F1
Lana Devon EX22 6 B6
Lana Devon EX22 6 B5
Lanark ML11 75 G6
Lanarth TR12 2 E6
LANCASTER LA 55 H3
Lanchester DH7 62 C2
Lancing BN15 12 E6
Landbeach CB25 33 H2
Landcross EX39 6 C3
Landerberry AB32 91 F4
Landewednack TR12 2 E7
Landford SP5 10 D3
Landhallow KW5 105 G5
Landican CH49 48 B4
Landimore SA3 17 H6
Landkey EX32 6 D2
Landmoth DL6 63 F7
Landore SA1 17 K6
Landrake PL12 4 D4
Landscove TQ13 5 H4
Landshipping SA67 16 D4
Landulph PL12 4 E4
Landwade CB8 33 K2
Landywood WS6 40 B5
Lane Bottom BB10 56 D6
Lane End Bucks. HP14 22 B2
Lane End Cumb. LA19 60 C7
Lane End Derbys. DE55 51 G6
Lane End Dorset BH20 9 H5
Lane End Hants. SO21 11 G2
Lane End Here. HR9 29 F7
Lane End Kent DA2 23 J4
Lane End Wilts. BA12 20 B7
Lane Ends Derbys. DE6 40 E2
Lane Ends Gt.Man. SK6 49 J3
Lane Ends Lancs. BB11 56 C6
Lane Ends N.Yorks. BD22 56 E5
Lane Green WV8 40 A5
Lane Head Dur. DL11 62 C5
Lane Head Dur. DL13 62 B4
Lane Head Gt.Man. WA3 49 F3
Lane Head W.Yorks. HD8 50 D2
Lane Heads PR3 55 H6
Lane Side BB4 56 C7
Laneast PL15 4 C2
Lane-end PL30 4 A4
Laneham DN22 52 B5
Lanehead Dur. DL13 61 K2
Lanehead Northumb. NE48 70 C5
Lanesend SA68 16 D5
Lanesfield WV4 40 B6
Laneshawbridge BB8 56 E5
Langais HS6 92 D5
Langamull PA75 78 E2
Langar NG13 42 A2
Langbank PA14 74 B3
Langbar LS29 57 F4
Langbaurgh TS9 63 G5
Langcliffe BD24 56 D3
Langdale End YO13 63 J3
Langdon Cornw. EX23 4 C1
Langdon Cornw. PL15 6 B7
Langdon Beck DL12 61 K3
Langdon Hills SS16 24 C3
Langdon House EX7 5 K3
Langdyke KY8 82 E7
Langford Cen.Beds. SG18 32 E4
Langford Essex CM9 24 E1
Langford Notts. NG23 52 B7
Langford Oxon. GL7 21 F1
Langford Budville TA21 7 K3
Langham Essex CO4 34 E5
Langham Norf. NR25 44 E1
Langham Rut. LE15 42 B4
Langham Suff. IP31 34 D2
Langham Moor CO4 34 E5
Langho BB6 56 B6
Langholm DG13 69 J5
Langland SA3 17 K7
Langlands DG6 65 G5
Langlee TD8 70 B2
Langleeford NE71 70 E1
Langley Ches.E. SK11 49 J5
Langley Derbys. NG16 41 G1
Langley Essex CB11 33 H5
Langley Glos. GL54 30 B6
Langley Gt.Man. M24 49 H2
Langley Hants. SO45 11 F4
Langley Herts. SG4 33 F6
Langley Kent ME17 14 C2
Langley Northumb. NE47 70 D7
Langley Oxon. OX29 30 E7
Langley Slo. SL3 22 D4
Langley Som. TA4 7 J3
Langley W.Suss. GU33 12 B4
Langley Warks. CV37 30 C2
Langley Burrell SN15 20 C4
Langley Corner SL3 22 D3
Langley Green Derbys. DE6 40 E2
Langley Green W.Suss. RH11 13 F3
Langley Green Warks. CV35 30 D2
Langley Heath ME17 14 D2
Langley Marsh TA4 7 J3
Langley Mill NG16 41 G1
Langley Moor DH7 62 D2
Langley Park DH7 62 D2
Langley Street NR14 45 H5
Langney BN23 13 K6
Langold S81 51 H4
Langore PL15 4 C2
Langport TA10 8 D2
Langrick PE22 43 F1
Langrick Bridge PE22 43 F1
Langridge B. & N.E.Som. BA1 20 A5
Langridge Devon EX37 6 D3
Langridgeford EX37 6 D3
Langrigg CA7 60 C2
Langrish GU32 11 J2
Langsett S36 50 E2
Langshaw TD1 76 D7
Langshawburn DG13 69 H3
Langside Glas. G43 74 D4
Langside P. & K. PH6 81 J6
Langskaill KW17 106 D3
Langstone Hants. PO9 11 J4
Langstone Newport NP18 19 G2
Langthorne DL8 62 D7
Langthorpe YO51 57 J3
Langthwaite DL11 62 B6
Langtoft E.Riding YO25 59 G3
Langtoft Lincs. PE6 42 E4
Langton Dur. DL2 62 C5
Langton Lincs. PE23 53 G5
Langton Lincs. LN9 53 F6
Langton N.Yorks. YO17 58 D3
Langton by Wragby LN8 52 E5
Langton Green Kent TN3 13 J3
Langton Green Suff. IP23 35 F1
Langton Herring DT3 9 F6
Langton Long Blandford DT11 9 H4
Langton Matravers BH19 9 J7
Langtree EX38 6 C4
Langtree Week EX38 6 C4
Langwathby CA10 61 G3
Langwell IV27 96 B1
Langwell House KW7 105 G6
Langwith NG20 51 H5
Langworth LN3 52 D5
Lanivet PL30 4 A4
Lank PL30 4 A3
Lanlivery PL30 4 A5
Lanner TR16 2 E4
Lanoy PL15 4 C3
Lanreath PL13 4 B5
Lansallos PL13 4 B5
Lansdown BA1 20 A5
Lanteglos PL32 4 A2
Lanteglos Highway PL23 4 B5
Lanton Northumb. NE71 77 H7
Lanton Sc.Bord. TD8 70 B1
Lanvean TR8 3 F2
Lapford EX17 7 F5
Laphroaig PA42 72 B6
Lapley ST19 40 A4
Lapworth B94 30 C1
Larach na Gaibhre PA31 73 F3
Larachbeg PA34 79 H3
Larbert FK5 75 G2
Larbreck PR3 55 H5
Larden Green CW5 48 E7
Larg DG8 64 D3
Largie AB52 90 E1
Largiemore PA21 73 H2
Largoward KY9 83 F7
Largs KA30 74 A5
Largue AB54 98 E6
Largybaan PA28 66 A2
Largybeg KA27 66 E1
Largymore KA27 66 E1
Lark Hall CB8 33 J3
Larkfield PA16 74 A3
Larkhall ML9 75 F5
Larkhill SP4 20 E7
Larklands DE7 41 G1
Larling NR16 44 D7
Larriston TD9 70 A4
Lartington DL12 62 B5
Lary AB35 90 B4
Lasborough GL8 20 B2
Lasham GU34 21 K7
Lashbrook EX22 6 C5
Lashenden TN27 14 D3
Lassington GL2 29 G6
Lassintullich PH16 81 J2
Lassodie KY12 75 K1
Lasswade EH18 76 B4
Lastingham YO62 63 J7
Latchford WA4 49 F4
Latchingdon CM3 24 E1
Latchley PL18 4 E3
Lately Common WN7 49 F3
Lathallan Mill KY9 83 F7
Lathbury MK16 32 B4
Latheron KW5 105 G5
Latheronwheel KW5 105 G5
Lathockar KY16 83 F6
Lathones KY15 83 F7
Lathrisk KY15 82 D7
Latimer HP5 22 D2
Latteridge BS37 19 K3
Lattiford BA9 9 F2
Latton SN6 20 D2
Lauchentyre DG7 65 F5
Lauchintilly AB51 91 F3
Lauder TD2 76 D6
Laugharne (Lacharn) SA33 17 G4
Laughterton LN1 52 B5
Laughton E.Suss. BN8 13 J5
Laughton Leics. LE17 41 J7
Laughton Lincs. NG34 42 D2
Laughton Lincs. DN21 52 B3
Laughton en le Morthen S25 51 H4
Launcells EX23 6 A5
Launcells Cross EX23 6 A5
Launceston PL15 6 B7
Launde Abbey LE7 42 A5
Launton OX26 31 H6
Laurencekirk AB30 91 F7
Laurieston D. & G. DG7 65 G4
Laurieston Falk. FK2 75 H3
Lavendon MK46 32 C3
Lavenham CO10 34 D4
Laverhay DG10 69 G4
Lavernock CF64 18 E5
Laversdale CA6 69 K7
Laverstock SP1 10 C1
Laverstoke RG28 21 H7
Laverton Glos. WR12 30 B5
Laverton N.Yorks. HG4 57 H2
Laverton Som. BA2 20 A6
Lavister LL12 48 C7
Law ML8 75 G5
Lawers P. & K. PH6 81 J5
Lawers P. & K. PH15 81 H4
Lawford Essex CO11 34 E5
Lawford Som. TA4 7 K2
Lawhitton PL15 6 B7
Lawkland LA2 56 C3
Lawkland Green LA2 56 C3
Lawley TF4 39 F5
Lawnhead ST20 40 A3
Lawrence Weston BS11 19 J4
Lawrenny SA68 16 D5
Laws DD5 83 F4
Lawshall IP29 34 C3
Lawshall Green IP30 34 C3
Lawton HR6 28 D3
Laxdale (Lacasdal) HS2 101 G4
Laxey IM4 54 D5
Laxfield IP13 35 G1
Laxfirth Shet. ZE2 107 N7
Laxfirth Shet. ZE2 107 N8
Laxford Bridge IV27 102 E4
Laxo ZE2 107 N6
Laxton E.Riding DN14 58 D7
Laxton Northants. NN17 42 C6
Laxton Notts. NG22 51 K6
Laycock BD22 57 F5
Layer Breton CO2 34 D7
Layer de la Haye CO2 34 D7
Layer Marney CO5 34 D7
Layham IP7 34 E4
Laymore TA20 8 C4
Layter's Green SL9 22 C2
Laytham YO42 58 D6
Layton FY3 55 G6
Lazenby TS6 63 G4
Lazonby CA10 61 G3
Lea Derbys. DE4 51 F7
Lea Here. HR9 29 F6
Lea Lincs. DN21 52 B4
Lea Shrop. SY9 38 C7
Lea Shrop. SY5 38 D5
Lea Wilts. SN16 20 C3
Lea Bridge DE4 51 F7
Lea Green WR6 29 F2
Lea Marston B76 40 E6
Lea Town PR4 55 H6
Lea Yeat LA10 56 C1
Leac a' Li (Lacklee) HS3 93 G2
Leachd PA27 73 J1
Leachkin IV3 96 D7
Leadburn EH46 76 A5
Leaden Roding CM6 33 J7
Leadenham LN5 52 C7
Leaderfoot TD6 76 D7
Leadgate Cumb. CA9 61 J2
Leadgate Dur. DH8 62 C1
Leadgate Northumb. NE17 62 C1
Leadhills ML12 68 D2
Leadingcross Green ME17 14 D2
Leafield OX29 30 E7
Leagrave LU4 32 D6
Leake Commonside PE22 53 G7
Leake Hurn's End PE22 43 H1
Lealands BN27 13 J5
Lealholm YO21 63 J6
Lealt Arg. & B. PA60 72 E1
Lealt High. IV51 94 B5
Leam S32 50 E5
Leamington Hastings CV23 31 F2
Leamington Spa CV32 30 E2
Leamoor Common SY7 38 D7
Leanach Arg. & B. PA27 73 J1
Leanach High. IV2 96 E7
Leanaig IV7 96 C6
Leanoch IV30 97 J6
Leargybreck PA60 72 D3
Leasgill LA7 55 H1
Leasingham NG34 42 D1
Leask AB41 91 J1
Leason SA3 17 H6
Leasowe CH46 48 B3
Leat PL15 6 B7
Leatherhead KT22 22 E6
Leathley LS21 57 H5
Leaton Shrop. SY4 38 D4
Leaton Tel. & W. TF6 39 F4
Leaveland ME13 15 F2
Leavenheath CO6 34 D5
Leavening YO17 58 D3
Leaves Green BR2 23 H5
Leavesden Green WD25 22 E1
Lebberston YO11 59 G1
Lechlade GL7 21 F2
Leck LA6 56 B2
Leckford SO20 10 E1
Leckfurin KW14 104 C3
Leckgruinart PA44 72 A4
Leckhampstead Bucks. MK18 31 J5
Leckhampstead W.Berks. RG20 21 H4
Leckhampstead Thicket RG20 21 H4
Leckhampton GL53 29 J7
Leckie High. IV22 95 G5
Leckie Stir. FK8 74 E1
Leckmelm IV23 95 H3
Leckroy PH31 87 K5
Leckuary PA31 73 G1
Leckwith CF11 18 E4
Leconfield HU17 59 G5
Ledaig PA37 80 A4
Ledard FK8 81 F7
Ledbeg IV27 102 E7
Ledburn LU7 32 B6
Ledbury HR8 29 G5
Ledcharrie FK20 81 G5
Ledgemoor HR4 28 D3
Ledicot HR6 28 D2
Ledmore Arg. & B. PA72 79 G3
Ledmore High. IV27 102 E7
Lednagullin KW14 104 D2
Ledsham Ches.W. & C. CH66 48 C5
Ledsham W.Yorks. LS25 57 K7
Ledston WF10 57 K7
Ledstone TQ7 5 H6
Ledwell OX7 31 F6
Lee Arg. & B. PA67 79 F5
Lee Devon EX34 6 C1
Lee Hants. SO51 10 E3
Lee Lancs. LA2 55 J4
Lee Shrop. SY12 38 D2
Lee Brockhurst SY4 38 E3
Lee Chapel SS15 24 C3
Lee Clump HP16 22 C1
Lee Mill Bridge PL21 5 F5
Lee Moor PL7 5 F4
Leebotten ZE2 107 N10
Leebotwood SY6 38 D6
Leece LA12 55 F3
Leeds Kent ME17 14 D2
LEEDS W.Yorks. LS 57 H6
Leeds Bradford International Airport LS19 57 H5
Leedstown TR27 2 D5
Leegomery TF1 39 F4
Leek ST13 49 J7
Leek Wootton CV35 30 D2
Leekbrook ST13 49 J7
Leeming N.Yorks. DL7 57 H1
Leeming W.Yorks. BD22 57 F6
Leeming Bar DL7 57 H1
Lee-on-the-Solent PO13 11 G4
Lees Derbys. DE6 40 E2
Lees Gt.Man. OL4 49 J2
Leeswood CH7 48 B7
Leftwich CW9 49 F5
Legars TD5 77 F6
Legbourne LN11 53 G4
Legerwood TD4 76 D6
Legsby LN8 52 E4
LEICESTER LE 41 H5
Leicester Forest East LE3 41 H5
Leideag HS9 84 B5
Leigh Dorset DT9 9 F4
Leigh Dorset BH21 10 B5
Leigh Gt.Man. WN7 49 F2
Leigh Kent TN11 23 J7
Leigh Shrop. SY5 38 C5
Leigh Surr. RH2 23 F7
Leigh Wilts. SN6 20 D2
Leigh Worcs. WR6 29 G3
Leigh Beck SS8 24 E3
Leigh Common BA9 9 G2
Leigh Delamere SN14 20 B4
Leigh Green TN30 14 E4
Leigh Park PO9 11 J4
Leigh Sinton WR13 29 G3
Leigh upon Mendip BA3 19 K7
Leigh Woods BS8 19 J4
Leigham PL6 5 F5
Leighland Chapel TA23 7 J2
Leigh-on-Sea SS9 24 E3
Leighterton GL8 20 B2
Leighton N.Yorks. HG4 57 G2
Leighton (Tre'r Llai) Powys SY21 38 B5
Leighton Shrop. SY5 39 F5
Leighton Som. BA11 20 A7
Leighton Bromswold PE28 32 E1
Leighton Buzzard LU7 32 C6
Leinthall Earls HR6 28 D2
Leinthall Starkes SY8 28 D2
Leintwardine SY7 28 D1
Leire LE17 41 H7
Leirinmore IV27 103 G2
Leiston IP16 35 J2
Leitfie PH11 82 D3
Leith EH6 76 A3
Leitholm TD12 77 F6
Lelant TR26 2 C5
Lelley HU12 59 J6
Lemington NE15 71 G7
Lemnas AB43 99 G4
Lempitlaw TD5 77 F7
Lemsford AL8 33 F7
Lenchwick WR11 30 B4
Lendalfoot KA26 67 F4
Lendrick Lodge FK17 81 G7
Lenham ME17 14 D2
Lenham Heath ME17 14 E3
Lenie IV63 88 C2
Lenimore KA27 73 G6
Lennel TD12 77 G6
Lennox Plunton DG6 65 G5
Lennoxtown G66 74 E3
Lent Rise SL6 22 C3
Lenton Lincs. NG33 42 D2
Lenton Nott. NG7 41 H2
Lenton Abbey NG7 41 H2
Lenwade NR9 44 E4
Lenzie G66 74 E3
Leoch DD3 82 E4
Leochel-Cushnie AB33 90 D3
Leominster HR6 28 D3
Leonard Stanley GL10 20 B1
Leorin PA42 72 B6
Lepe SO45 11 F5
Lephin IV55 93 G7
Lephinchapel PA27 73 H1
Lephinmore PA27 73 H1
Leppington YO17 58 D3
Lepton HD8 50 E1
Lerags PA34 79 K5
Lerryn PL22 4 B5
Lerwick ZE1 107 N8
Lesbury NE66 71 H2
Leschangie AB51 91 F3
Leslie Aber. AB52 90 D2
Leslie Fife KY6 82 D7
Lesmahagow ML11 75 G7
Lesnewth PL35 4 B1
Lessendrum AB54 98 D6
Lessingham NR12 45 H3
Lessness Heath DA8 23 H4
Lessonhall CA7 60 D1
Leswalt DG9 64 A4
Letchmore Heath WD25 22 E2
Letchworth Garden City SG6 33 F5
Letcombe Bassett OX12 21 G3
Letcombe Regis OX12 21 G3
Leth Meadhanach HS8 84 C3
Letham Angus DD8 83 G3
Letham Falk. FK2 75 G2
Letham Fife KY15 82 E6
Lethanhill KA6 67 J2
Lethenty AB53 99 G6
Letheringham IP13 35 G3
Letheringsett NR25 44 E2
Lettaford TQ13 7 F7
Letter Finlay PH34 87 J5
Letterewe IV22 95 F4
Letterfearn IV40 86 E2
Lettermorar PH40 86 D6
Lettermore Arg. & B. PA72 79 F3
Lettermore High. IV27 103 J4
Letters IV23 95 H3
Lettershaws ML12 68 D1
Letterston SA62 16 C3
Lettoch High. PH25 89 H3
Lettoch High. PH26 89 J1
Letton Here. SY7 28 C1
Letton Here. HR3 28 C4
Letty Green SG14 33 F7
Letwell S81 51 H4
Leuchars KY16 83 F5
Leumrabhagh HS2 101 F6
Leurbost (Liurbost) HS2 101 F5
Leusdon TQ13 5 H3
Levedale ST18 40 A4
Level's Green CM23 33 H6
Leven E.Riding HU17 59 H5
Leven Fife KY8 82 E7
Levencorroch KA27 66 E1
Levenhall EH21 76 B3
Levens LA8 55 H1
Levens Green SG11 33 G6
Levenshulme M12 49 H3
Levenwick ZE2 107 N10
Leverburgh (An T-Òb) HS5 93 F3
Leverington PE13 43 H4
Leverstock Green HP3 22 D1
Leverton PE22 43 G1
Leverton Lucasgate PE22 43 H1
Leverton Outgate PE22 43 H1
Levington IP10 35 G5

Lev - Lla


Levisham YO18 63 K7
Levishie IV63 88 B3
Lew OX18 21 G1
Lewannick PL15 4 C2
Lewcombe DT2 8 E4
Lewdown EX20 6 C7
Lewes BN7 13 H5
Leweston SA62 16 C3
Lewisham SE13 23 G4
Lewiston IV63 88 C2
Lewistown CF32 18 C3
Lewknor OX49 22 A2
Leworthy EX32 6 E2
Lewson Street ME9 25 F5
Lewth PR4 55 H6
Lewtrenchard EX20 6 C7
Ley Aber. AB33 90 D3
Ley Cornw. PL14 4 B4
Ley Green SG4 32 E6
Leybourne ME19 23 K6
Leyburn DL8 62 C7
Leyland PR25 55 J7
Leylodge AB51 91 F3
Leymoor HD3 50 D1
Leys Aber. AB42 99 J5
Leys Aber. AB34 90 C4
Leys P. & K. PH13 82 D4
Leys of Cossans DD8 82 E3
Leysdown-on-Sea ME12 25 G4
Leysmill DD11 83 H3
Leysters HR6 28 E2
Leyton E10 23 G3
Leytonstone E11 23 G3
Lezant PL15 4 D3
Lezerea TR13 2 D5
Lhanbryde IV30 97 K5
Liatrie IV4 87 J1
Libanus LD3 27 J6
Libberton ML11 75 H6
Libbery WR7 29 J3
Liberton EH16 76 A4
Liceasto HS3 93 G2
Lichfield WS13 40 D5
Lickey B45 29 J1
Lickey End B60 29 J1
Lickfold GU28 12 C4
Liddaton Green EX20 6 C7
Liddel KW17 106 D9
Liddesdale PH33 79 J2
Liddington SN4 21 F3
Lidgate Derbys. S18 51 F5
Lidgate Suff. CB8 34 B3
Lidgett NG21 51 J6
Lidlington MK43 32 C5
Lidsey PO22 12 C6
Lidsing ME7 24 D5
Lidstone OX7 30 E6
Lienassie IV40 87 F2
Lieurary KW14 105 F2
Liff DD2 82 E4
Lifton PL16 6 B7
Liftondown PL15 6 B7
Lightcliffe HX3 57 G7
Lighthorne CV35 30 E3
Lighthorne Heath CV33 30 E3
Lightwater GU18 22 C5
Lightwood ST3 40 B1
Lightwood Green Ches.E. CW3 39 F1
Lightwood Green Wrex. LL13 38 C1
Lilbourne CV23 31 G1
Lilburn Tower NE66 71 F1
Lillesdon TA3 8 C2
Lilleshall TF10 39 G4
Lilley Herts. LU2 32 E6
Lilley W.Berks. RG20 21 H4
Lilliesleaf TD6 70 A1
Lilling Green YO32 58 C3
Lillingstone Dayrell MK18 31 J5
Lillingstone Lovell MK18 31 J4
Lillington Dorset DT9 9 F3
Lillington Warks. CV32 30 E2
Lilliput BH14 10 B6
Lilly EX32 6 D2
Lilstock TA5 7 K1
Lilyhurst TF11 39 G4
Limbury LU3 32 D6
Lime Side OL8 49 J2
Limefield BL9 49 H1
Limehillock AB54 98 D5
Limehurst OL8 49 J2
Limekilnburn ML3 75 F5
Limekilns KY11 75 J2
Limerigg FK1 75 G3
Limerstone PO30 11 F6
Limington BA22 8 E2
Limpenhoe NR13 45 H5
Limpley Stoke BA2 20 A5
Limpsfield RH8 23 H6
Limpsfield Chart TN8 23 H6
Linaclate (Lionacleit) HS7 92 C7
Linbriggs NE65 70 D3
Linby NG15 51 H7
Linchmere GU27 12 B3
Lincluden DG2 65 K3
LINCOLN LN 52 C5
Lincomb DY13 29 H2
Lincombe Devon TQ9 5 H5
Lincombe Devon TQ7 5 H6
Lindal in Furness LA12 55 F2
Lindale LA11 55 H1
Lindean TD7 76 C7
Lindertis DD8 82 E2
Lindfield RH16 13 G4
Lindford GU35 12 B3
Lindifferon KY15 82 E6
Lindisfarne (Holy Island) TD15 77 K6
Lindley LS21 57 H5
Lindores KY14 82 D6
Lindow End WA16 49 H5
Lindridge WR15 29 F2
Lindsaig PA21 73 H3
Lindsell CM6 33 K6
Lindsey IP7 34 D4
Lindsey Tye IP7 34 D4
Linfitts OL3 49 J2
Linford Hants. BH24 10 C4
Linford Thur. SS17 24 C4
Linford Wood MK13 32 B4
Lingague IM9 54 B6
Lingards Wood HD7 50 C1
Lingdale TS12 63 H5
Lingen SY7 28 C2
Lingfield RH7 23 G7
Lingley Green WA5 48 E4
Lingwood NR13 45 H5
Linhead AB45 98 E5
Linhope TD9 69 K3
Linicro IV51 93 J5
Linkend GL19 29 H5
Linkenholt SP11 21 G6
Linkhill TN18 14 D5
Linkinhorne PL17 4 D3
Linklater KW17 106 D9
Linksness Ork. KW16 106 B7
Linksness Ork. KW17 106 E6
Linktown KY1 76 A1
Linley Shrop. SY9 38 C6
Linley Shrop. TF12 39 F6
Linley Green WR6 29 F3
Linlithgow EH49 75 J3
Linlithgow Bridge EH49 75 H3
Linn of Muick Cottage AB35 90 B6
Linnels NE46 70 E7
Linney SA71 16 B6
Linshiels NE65 70 D3
Linsiadar HS2 100 E4
Linsidemore IV27 96 C2
Linslade LU7 32 C6
Linstead Parva IP19 35 H1
Linstock CA6 60 F1
Linthwaite HD7 50 D1
Lintlaw TD11 77 G5
Lintmill AB56 98 D4
Linton Cambs. CB21 33 J4
Linton Derbys. DE12 40 E4
Linton Here. HR9 29 F6
Linton Kent ME17 14 C2
Linton N.Yorks. BD23 56 E3
Linton Sc.Bord. TD5 70 C1
Linton W.Yorks. LS22 57 J5
Linton-on-Ouse YO30 57 K3
Lintzford NE39 62 C1
Linwood Hants. BH24 10 C4
Linwood Lincs. LN8 52 E4
Linwood Renf. PA3 74 C4
Lionacleit (Linaclate) HS7 92 C7
Lional (Lionel) HS2 101 H1
Lionel (Lional) HS2 101 H1
Liphook GU30 12 B3
Lipley TF9 39 G2
Liscard CH45 48 C3
Liscombe TA22 7 G2
Liskeard PL14 4 C4
L'Islet GY2 3 J5
Lismore PA34 79 K4
Liss GU33 11 J2
Liss Forest GU33 11 J2
Lissett YO25 59 H4
Lissington LN3 52 E4
Liston CO10 34 C4
Lisvane CF14 18 E3
Liswerry NP19 19 G3
Litcham PE32 44 C4
Litchborough NN12 31 H3
Litchfield RG28 21 H6
Litherland L21 48 C3
Litlington Cambs. SG8 33 G4
Litlington E.Suss. BN26 13 J6
Little Abington CB21 33 J4
Little Addington NN14 32 C1
Little Alne B95 30 C2
Little Altcar L37 48 C2
Little Amwell SG13 33 G7
Little Ann SP11 21 G7
Little Asby CA16 61 H6
Little Assynt IV27 102 D6
Little Aston B74 40 C6
Little Atherfield PO38 11 F7
Little Ayton TS9 63 G5
Little Baddow CM3 24 D1
Little Badminton GL9 20 B3
Little Ballinluig PH15 82 A2
Little Bampton CA7 60 D1
Little Bardfield CM7 33 K5
Little Barford PE19 32 E3
Little Barningham NR11 45 F2
Little Barrington OX18 30 D7
Little Barrow CH3 48 D6
Little Barugh YO17 58 D2
Little Bavington NE19 70 E6
Little Bealings IP13 35 G4
Little Bedwyn SN8 21 F5
Little Beeby LE7 41 J5
Little Bentley CO7 35 F6
Little Berkhamsted SG13 23 F1
Little Billing NN3 32 B2
Little Birch HR2 28 E5
Little Bispham FY5 55 G5
Little Blakenham IP8 35 F4
Little Bloxwich WS3 40 C5
Little Bollington WA14 49 G4
Little Bookham KT23 22 E6
Little Bourton OX17 31 F4
Little Bowden LE16 42 A7
Little Bradley CB9 33 K3
Little Brampton SY7 38 C7
Little Braxted CM8 34 C7
Little Brechin DD9 83 G1
Little Brickhill MK17 32 C5
Little Bridgeford ST18 40 A3
Little Brington NN7 31 H2
Little Bromley CO11 34 E6
Little Broughton CA13 60 B3
Little Budworth CW6 48 E6
Little Burdon DL1 62 E5
Little Burstead CM12 24 C2
Little Burton YO25 59 H5
Little Bytham NG33 42 D4
Little Canford BH21 10 B5
Little Carlton Lincs. LN11 53 G4
Little Carlton Notts. NG23 51 K7
Little Casterton PE9 42 D4
Little Catwick HU17 59 H5
Little Catworth PE28 32 D1
Little Cawthorpe LN11 53 G4
Little Chalfield SN12 20 B5
Little Chalfont HP6 22 C2
Little Chart TN27 14 E3
Little Chesterford CB10 33 J4
Little Chesterton OX26 31 G6
Little Cheverell SN10 20 C6
Little Clacton CO16 35 F7
Little Clanfield OX18 21 F1
Little Clifton CA14 60 B4
Little Coates DN34 53 F2
Little Comberton WR10 29 J4
Little Common TN39 14 C7
Little Compton GL56 30 D5
Little Corby CA4 61 F1
Little Cornard CO10 34 C5
Little Cowarne HR7 29 F3
Little Coxwell SN7 21 F2
Little Crakehall DL8 62 D7
Little Cransley NN14 32 B1
Little Crawley MK16 32 C4
Little Creaton NN6 31 J1
Little Creich IV24 96 D3
Little Cressingham IP25 44 C6
Little Crosby L23 48 C2
Little Crosthwaite CA12 60 D4
Little Cubley DE6 40 D2
Little Dalby LE14 42 A4
Little Dens AB42 99 J6
Little Dewchurch HR2 28 E5
Little Ditton CB8 33 K3
Little Doward HR9 28 E7
Little Down SP11 21 G6
Little Downham CB6 43 J7
Little Drayton TF9 39 F2
Little Driffield YO25 59 G4
Little Dunham PE32 44 C4
Little Dunkeld PH8 82 B3
Little Dunmow CM6 33 K6
Little Durnford SP4 10 C1
Little Easton CM6 33 K6
Little Eaton DE21 41 F1
Little Eccleston PR3 55 H5
Little Ellingham NR17 44 E6
Little End CM5 23 J1
Little Everdon NN11 31 G3
Little Eversden CB23 33 G3
Little Fakenham IP24 34 D1
Little Faringdon GL7 21 F1
Little Fencote DL7 62 D7
Little Fenton LS25 58 B6
Little Finborough IP14 34 E3
Little Fransham NR19 44 D4
Little Gaddesden HP4 32 C7
Little Garway HR2 28 D6
Little Gidding PE28 42 E7
Little Glemham IP13 35 H3
Little Glenshee PH1 82 A4
Little Gorsley HR9 29 F6
Little Gransden SG19 33 F3
Little Green Cambs. SG8 33 F4
Little Green Notts. NG13 42 A1
Little Green Suff. IP23 34 E1
Little Green Suff. IP22 34 E1
Little Green Wrex. SY13 38 D1
Little Grimsby LN11 53 G3
Little Gringley DN22 51 K4
Little Gruinard IV22 95 F3
Little Habton YO17 58 D2
Little Hadham SG11 33 H6
Little Hale NG34 42 E1
Little Hallingbury CM22 33 H7
Little Hampden HP16 22 B1
Little Haresfield GL10 20 B1
Little Harrowden NN9 32 B1
Little Haseley OX44 21 K1
Little Hatfield HU11 59 H5
Little Hautbois NR12 45 G3
Little Haven Pembs. SA62 16 B4
Little Haven W.Suss. RH12 12 E3
Little Hay WS14 40 D5
Little Hayfield SK22 50 C4
Little Haywood ST18 40 C3
Little Heath CV6 41 F7
Little Hereford SY8 28 E2
Little Hockham IP24 44 D6
Little Horkesley CO6 34 D5
Little Hormead SG9 33 H6
Little Horsted TN22 13 H5
Little Horton SN10 20 D5
Little Horwood MK17 31 J5
Little Houghton NN7 32 B3
Little Hucklow SK17 50 D5
Little Hulton M38 49 G2
Little Hungerford RG18 21 J4
Little Hutton YO7 57 K2
Little Irchester NN8 32 C2
Little Keyford BA11 20 A7
Little Kimble HP17 22 B1
Little Kineton CV35 30 E3
Little Kingshill HP16 22 B2
Little Langdale LA22 60 E6
Little Langford SP3 10 B1
Little Laver CM5 23 J1
Little Lawford CV23 31 F1
Little Leigh CW8 49 F5
Little Leighs CM3 34 B7
Little Lever BL3 49 G2
Little Ley AB51 90 E3
Little Linford MK19 32 B4
Little Linton CB21 33 J4
Little London Bucks. HP18 31 H7
Little London E.Suss. TN21 13 J5
Little London Essex CM23 33 H6
Little London Hants. SP11 21 G7
Little London Hants. RG26 21 K6
Little London I.o.M. IM6 54 C5
Little London Lincs. PE12 43 H3
Little London Lincs. PE11 43 F3
Little London Lincs. LN9 53 G5
Little London Lincs. LN8 52 E4
Little London Norf. PE34 43 J3
Little London Norf. IP26 44 B6
Little London Oxon. OX14 21 J1
Little London Powys SY17 37 K7
Little London Suff. IP14 34 E3
Little London W.Yorks. LS19 57 H6
Little Longstone DE45 50 D5
Little Lyth SY3 38 D5
Little Malvern WR14 29 G4
Little Maplestead CO9 34 C5
Little Marcle HR8 29 F5
Little Marland EX20 6 D4
Little Marlow SL7 22 B3
Little Marsden BB9 56 D6
Little Massingham PE32 44 B3
Little Melton NR9 45 F5
Little Milford SA62 16 C4
Little Mill NP4 19 G1
Little Milton OX44 21 K1
Little Missenden HP7 22 C2
Little Musgrave CA17 61 J5
Little Ness SY4 38 D4
Little Neston CH64 48 B5
Little Newcastle SA62 16 C3
Little Newsham DL2 62 C5
Little Oakley Essex CO12 35 G6
Little Oakley Northants. NN18 42 B7
Little Odell MK43 32 C3
Little Offley SG5 32 E6
Little Onn ST20 40 A4
Little Orton Cumb. CA5 60 E1
Little Orton Leics. CV9 41 F5
Little Ouse CB7 44 A7
Little Ouseburn YO26 57 K3
Little Overton LL13 38 C1
Little Packington CV7 40 E7
Little Parndon CM20 33 H7
Little Paxton PE19 32 E2
Little Petherick PL27 3 G1
Little Plumpton PR4 55 G6
Little Plumstead NR13 45 H4
Little Ponton NG33 42 C2
Little Posbrook PO14 11 G4
Little Potheridge EX20 6 D4
Little Preston NN11 31 G3
Little Raveley PE28 43 F7
Little Ribston LS22 57 J4
Little Rissington GL54 30 C7
Little Rogart IV28 96 E1
Little Rollright OX7 30 D5
Little Ryburgh NR21 44 D3
Little Ryle NE66 71 F2
Little Ryton SY5 38 D5
Little Salkeld CA10 61 G3
Little Sampford CB10 33 K5
Little Saxham IP29 34 C2
Little Scatwell IV14 95 K6
Little Shelford CB22 33 H3
Little Shrawardine SY5 38 C4
Little Silver EX16 7 H5
Little Singleton FY6 55 G6
Little Smeaton N.Yorks. WF8 51 H1
Little Smeaton N.Yorks. DL6 62 E6
Little Snoring NR21 44 D2
Little Sodbury BS37 20 A3
Little Sodbury End BS37 20 A3
Little Somborne SO20 10 E1
Little Somerford SN15 20 C3
Little Soudley TF9 39 G3
Little Stainforth BD24 56 D3
Little Stainton TS21 62 E5
Little Stanney CH2 48 D5
Little Staughton MK44 32 E2
Little Steeping PE23 53 H6
Little Stoke ST15 40 B2
Little Stonham IP14 35 F3
Little Street CB6 43 J7
Little Stretton Leics. LE2 41 J6
Little Stretton Shrop. SY6 38 D6
Little Strickland CA10 61 G5
Little Stukeley PE28 33 F1
Little Sugnall ST21 40 A2
Little Sutton CH66 48 C5
Little Swinburne NE46 70 E6
Little Tarrington HR1 29 F4
Little Tew OX7 30 E6
Little Tey CO6 34 C6
Little Thetford CB6 33 J1
Little Thornage NR25 44 E2
Little Thornton FY5 55 G5
Little Thorpe SR8 63 F2
Little Thurlow CB9 33 K3
Little Thurlow Green CB9 33 K3
Little Thurrock RM17 24 C4
Little Torboll IV25 96 E2
Little Torrington EX38 6 C4
Little Tosson NE65 71 F3
Little Totham CM9 34 C7
Little Town Cumb. CA12 60 D5
Little Town Lancs. PR3 56 B6
Little Town Warr. WA3 49 F3
Little Twycross CV9 41 F5
Little Urswick LA12 55 F2
Little Wakering SS3 25 F3
Little Walden CB10 33 J4
Little Waldingfield CO10 34 D4
Little Walsingham NR22 44 D2
Little Waltham CM3 34 B7
Little Warley CM13 24 C2
Little Washbourne GL20 29 J5
Little Weighton HU20 59 F6
Little Welland WR13 29 H5
Little Welnetham IP30 34 C2
Little Wenham CO7 34 E5
Little Wenlock TF6 39 F5
Little Whittington NE19 70 E7
Little Wilbraham CB21 33 J3
Little Wishford SP2 10 B1
Little Witcombe GL3 29 J7
Little Witley WR6 29 G2
Little Wittenham OX14 21 J2
Little Wittingham Green IP21 35 G1
Little Wolford CV36 30 D5
Little Woodcote SM5 23 F5
Little Wratting CB9 33 K4
Little Wymington NN10 32 C2
Little Wymondley SG4 33 F6
Little Wyrley WS3 40 C5
Little Wytheford SY4 38 E4
Little Yeldham CO9 34 B5
Littlebeck YO22 63 K6
Littleborough Devon EX17 7 G4
Littleborough Gt.Man. OL15 49 J1
Littleborough Notts. DN22 52 B4
Littlebourne CT3 15 H2
Littlebredy DT2 8 E6
Littlebury CB11 33 J5
Littlebury Green CB11 33 H5
Littledean GL14 29 F7
Littleferry KW10 97 F2
Littleham Devon EX39 6 C3
Littleham Devon EX8 7 J7
Littlehampton BN17 12 D6
Littlehempston TQ9 5 J4
Littlehoughton NE66 71 H2
Littlemill E.Ayr. KA6 67 J2
Littlemill High. IV12 97 G6
Littlemoor Derbys. S45 51 F6
Littlemoor Dorset DT3 9 F6
Littlemore OX4 21 J1
Littlemoss M43 49 J3
Littleover DE23 41 F2
Littleport CB6 43 J7
Littlestead Green RG4 22 A4
Littlestone-on-Sea TN28 15 F5
Littlethorpe HG4 57 J3
Littleton Ches.W. & C. CH3 48 D6
Littleton Hants. SO22 11 F1
Littleton P. & K. PH14 82 D4
Littleton Som. TA11 8 D1
Littleton Surr. TW17 22 D5
Littleton Drew SN14 20 B3
Littleton Panell SN10 20 D6
Littleton-on-Severn BS35 19 J2
Littletown Dur. DH6 62 E2
Littletown I.o.W. PO33 11 G5
Littlewick Green SL6 22 B4
Littlewindsor DT8 8 D4
Littleworth Glos. GL55 30 C5
Littleworth Oxon. SN7 21 G2
Littleworth S.Yorks. DN11 51 J3
Littleworth Staffs. WS12 40 C4
Littleworth Worcs. WR5 29 H4
Littley Green CM3 33 K7
Litton Derbys. SK17 50 D5
Litton N.Yorks. BD23 56 E2
Litton Som. BA3 19 J6
Litton Cheney DT2 8 E5
Liurbost (Leurbost) HS2 101 F5
LIVERPOOL L 48 C3
Liverpool John Lennon Airport L24 48 D4
Liversedge WF15 57 H7
Liverton Devon TQ12 5 J3
Liverton R. & C. TS13 63 J5
Liverton Street ME17 14 D3
Livingston EH54 75 J4
Livingston Village EH54 75 J4
Lixwm CH8 47 K5
Lizard TR12 2 E7
Llaingarreglwyd SA47 26 D3
Llaingoch LL65 46 A4
Llaithddu LD1 37 K7
Llampha CF35 18 C4
Llan SY19 37 H5
Llan Ffestiniog (Ffestiniog) LL41 37 G1
Llanaber LL42 37 F4
Llanaelhaearn LL54 36 C1
Llanaeron SA48 26 D2
Llanafan SY23 27 F1
Llanafan-fawr LD2 27 J3
Llanafan-fechan LD4 27 J3
Llanallgo LL72 46 D4
Llanandras (Presteigne) LD8 28 C2
Llanarmon LL53 36 D2
Llanarmon Dyffryn Ceiriog LL20 38 A2
Llanarmon-yn-Ial CH7 47 K7
Llanarth Cere. SA47 26 D3
Llanarth Mon. NP15 28 C7
Llanarthney SA32 17 J3
Llanasa CH8 47 K4
Llanbabo LL68 46 B4

# Lla - Lon



Llanbadarn Fawr **SY23** 36 E7
Llanbadarn Fynydd **LD1** 27 K1
Llanbadarn-y-garreg **LD2** 28 A4
Llanbadoc **NP15** 19 G1
Llanbadrig **LL67** 46 B3
Llanbeder **NP18** 19 G2
**Llanbedr *Gwyn.* LL45 36 E3**
Llanbedr *Powys* **NP8** 28 B6
Llanbedr *Powys* **LD2** 28 A4
**Llanbedr Pont Steffan (Lampeter) SA48 17 J1**
Llanbedr-Dyffryn-Clwyd **LL15** 47 K7
**Llanbedrgoch LL76 46 D4**
Llanbedrog **LL53** 36 C2
Llanbedr-y-cennin **LL32** 47 F6
Llanberis **LL55** 46 D7
Llanbethery **CF62** 18 D5
Llanbister **LD1** 28 A1
Llanblethian **CF71** 18 C4
Llanboidy **SA34** 17 F3
Llanbradach **CF83** 18 E2
**Llanbryn-mair SY19 37 H5**
Llancadle **CF62** 18 D5
Llancarfan **CF62** 18 D4
Llancayo **NP15** 19 G1
Llancynfelyn **SY20** 37 F6
Llandafal **NP13** 18 E1
Llandaff **CF5** 18 E4
Llandaff North **CF14** 18 E4
Llandanwg **LL46** 36 E3
Llandawke **SA33** 17 F4
Llanddaniel Fab **LL60** 46 C5
Llanddarog **SA32** 17 H4
Llanddeiniol **SY23** 26 E1
Llanddeiniolen **LL55** 46 D6
Llandderfel **LL23** 37 J2
Llanddeusant *Carmar.* **SA19** 27 G6
Llanddeusant *I.o.A.* **LL65** 46 B4
Llanddew **LD3** 27 K5
Llanddewi **SA3** 17 H7
Llanddewi Rhydderch **NP7** 28 C7
Llanddewi Skirrid **NP7** 28 C7
Llanddewi Velfrey **SA67** 16 E4
Llanddewi Ystradenni **LD1** 28 A2
Llanddewi-Brefi **SY25** 27 F3
Llanddewi'r Cwm **LD2** 27 K4
Llanddoged **LL26** 47 G6
Llanddona **LL58** 46 D5
Llanddowror **SA33** 17 F4
Llanddulas **LL22** 47 H5
Llanddwywe **LL44** 36 E3
Llanddyfnan **LL78** 46 D5
Llandefaelog Fach **LD3** 27 K5
Llandefaelog-tre'r-graig **LD3** 28 A6
Llandefalle **LD3** 28 A5
Llandegfan **LL59** 46 D5
Llandegla **LL11** 47 K7
Llandegley **LD1** 28 A2
Llandegveth **NP18** 19 G2
Llandegwning **LL53** 36 B2
**Llandeilo SA19 17 K3**
Llandeilo Abercywyn **SA33** 17 G4
Llandeilo Graban **LD2** 27 K4
Llandeilo'r-Fan **LD3** 27 H5
Llandeloy **SA62** 16 B3
Llandenny **NP15** 19 H1
Llandevaud **NP18** 19 H2
Llandevenny **NP26** 19 H3
Llandinabo **HR2** 28 E6
**Llandinam SY17 37 K7**
Llandissilio **SA66** 16 E3
Llandogo **NP25** 19 J1
Llandough *V. of Glam.* **CF11** 18 E4
Llandough *V. of Glam.* **CF71** 18 C4
**Llandovery (Llanymddyfri) SA20 27 G5**
Llandow **CF71** 18 C4
Llandre *Carmar.* **SA19** 17 K1
Llandre *Carmar.* **SA34** 16 E3
Llandre *Cere.* **SY24** 37 F7
Llandrillo **LL21** 37 K2
**LLANDRINDOD WELLS LD 27 K2**
Llandrinio **SY22** 38 B4
**LLANDUDNO LL 47 F4**
**Llandudno Junction LL31 47 F5**
Llandudoch (St. Dogmaels) **SA43** 16 E1
Llandwrog **LL54** 46 C7
Llandybie **SA18** 17 K4
Llandyfaelog **SA17** 17 H4
Llandyfan **SA18** 17 K4
Llandyfriog **SA38** 17 G1
Llandyfrydog **LL71** 46 C4
Llandygai **LL57** 46 D5
Llandygwydd **SA43** 17 F1
Llandyrnog **LL16** 47 K6
Llandyry **SA17** 17 H5
Llandysilio **SY22** 38 B4
Llandyssil **SY15** 38 A6
**Llandysul SA44 17 H1**
Llanedeyrn **CF23** 19 F3
Llanedy **SA4** 17 J5
Llaneglwys **LD2** 27 K5
Llanegryn **LL36** 37 F5
Llanegwad **SA32** 17 J3
Llaneilian **LL68** 46 C3
Llanelian-yn-Rhos **LL29** 47 G5
Llanelidan **LL15** 47 K7
Llanelieu **LD3** 28 A5
Llanellen **NP7** 28 C7
**Llanelli SA15 17 J5**
Llanelltyd **LL40** 37 G4
Llanelly **NP7** 28 B7
Llanelly Hill **NP7** 28 B7
Llanelwedd **LD2** 27 K3
**Llanelwy (St. Asaph) LL17 47 J5**
Llanenddwyn **LL44** 36 E3
Llanengan **LL53** 36 B3
Llanerfyl **SY21** 37 K5
Llaneuddog **LL70** 46 C4
Llaneurgain (Northop) **CH7** 48 B6
Llanfachraeth **LL65** 46 B4
Llanfachreth **LL40** 37 G3
Llanfaelog **LL63** 46 B5
Llanfaelrhys **LL53** 36 B3
Llanfaenor **NP25** 28 D7
Llan-faes *I.o.A.* **LL58** 46 E5
Llanfaes *Powys* **LD3** 27 K6
Llanfaethlu **LL65** 46 B4
Llanfaglan **LL54** 46 C6
Llanfair **LL46** 36 E3
Llanfair Caereinion **SY21** 38 A5
Llanfair Clydogau **SA48** 27 F3
Llanfair Dyffryn Clwyd **LL15** 47 K7
Llanfair Talhaiarn **LL22** 47 H5
Llanfair Waterdine **LD7** 28 B1
**Llanfairfechan LL33 46 E5**
Llanfair-Nant-Gwyn **SA37** 16 E2
Llanfair-Orllwyn **SA44** 17 G1
**Llanfairpwllgwyngyll LL61 46 D5**
**Llanfair-ym-Muallt (Builth Wells) LD2 27 K3**
Llanfairynghornwy **LL65** 46 B3
Llanfair-yn-neubwll **LL65** 46 B5
Llanfallteg **SA34** 16 E4
Llanfaredd **LD2** 27 K3
Llanfarian **SY23** 26 E1
**Llanfechain SY22 38 A3**
Llanfechell **LL68** 46 B3
Llanfendigaid **LL36** 36 E5
Llanferres **CH7** 47 K6
Llanfflewyn **LL68** 46 B4
Llanfigael **LL65** 46 B4
Llanfihangel Crucornau (Llanvihangel Crucorney) **NP7** 28 C6
Llanfihangel Glyn Myfyr **LL21** 37 J1
Llanfihangel Nant Bran **LD3** 27 J5
Llanfihangel Rhydithon **LD1** 28 A2
Llanfihangel Rogiet **NP26** 19 H3
Llanfihangel Tal-y-llyn **LD3** 28 A6
Llanfihangel-ar-arth **SA39** 17 H1
Llanfihangel-nant-Melan **LD8** 28 A3
Llanfihangel-uwch-Gwili **SA32** 17 H3
Llanfihangel-y-Creuddyn **SY23** 27 F1
Llanfihangel-yng-Ngwynfa **SY22** 37 K4
Llanfihangel-yn-Nhywyn **LL65** 46 B5
Llanfihangel-y-pennant *Gwyn.* **LL51** 36 E1
Llanfihangel-y-pennant *Gwyn.* **LL36** 37 F5
Llanfilo **LD3** 28 A5
Llanfoist **NP7** 28 B7
Llanfor **LL23** 37 J2
Llanfrechfa **NP44** 19 G2
Llanfrothen **LL48** 37 F1
Llanfrynach **LD3** 27 K6
Llanfwrog *Denb.* **LL15** 47 K7
Llanfwrog *I.o.A.* **LL65** 46 A4
**Llanfyllin SY22 38 A4**
Llanfynydd *Carmar.* **SA32** 17 J3
Llanfynydd *Flints.* **LL11** 48 B7
**Llanfyrnach SA35 17 F2**
Llangadfan **SY21** 37 K4
**Llangadog SA19 27 G6**
Llangadwaladr *I.o.A.* **LL62** 46 B6
Llangadwaladr *Powys* **SY10** 38 A2
Llangaffo **LL60** 46 C6
Llangain **SA33** 17 G4
**Llangammarch Wells LD4 27 J4**
Llangan **CF35** 18 C4
Llangarron **HR9** 28 E6
Llangasty-Talyllyn **LD3** 28 A6
Llangathen **SA32** 17 J3
Llangattock **NP8** 28 B7
Llangattock Lingoed **NP7** 28 C7
Llangattock-Vibon-Avel **NP25** 28 D7
Llangedwyn **SY10** 38 A3
**Llangefni LL77 46 C5**
Llangeinor **CF32** 18 C3
Llangeitho **SY25** 27 F3
Llangeler **SA44** 17 G2
Llangelynin **LL36** 36 E5
Llangendeirne **SA17** 17 H4
Llangennech **SA14** 17 J5
Llangennith **SA3** 17 H6
Llangenny **NP8** 28 B7
Llangernyw **LL22** 47 G6
Llangian **LL53** 36 B3
Llangiwg **SA8** 18 A1
Llangloffan **SA62** 16 C2
Llanglydwen **SA34** 16 E3
Llangoed **LL58** 46 E5
Llangoedmor **SA43** 16 E1
**Llangollen LL20 38 B1**
Llangolman **SA66** 16 E3
Llangorse **LD3** 28 A6
Llangorwen **SY23** 37 F7
Llangovan **NP25** 19 H1
Llangower **LL23** 37 J2
Llangrannog **SA44** 26 C3
Llangristiolus **LL62** 46 C5
Llangrove **HR9** 28 E7
Llangua **NP7** 28 C6
Llangunllo **LD7** 28 B1
Llangunnor **SA31** 17 H3
Llangurig **SY18** 27 J1
Llangwm *Conwy* **LL21** 37 J1
Llangwm *Mon.* **NP15** 19 H1
Llangwm *Pembs.* **SA62** 16 C5
Llangwnnadl **LL53** 36 B2
Llangwyfan **LL16** 47 K6
Llangwyllog **LL77** 46 C5
Llangwyryfon **SY23** 27 F1
Llangybi *Cere.* **SA48** 27 F3
Llangybi *Gwyn.* **LL53** 36 D1
Llangybi *Mon.* **NP15** 19 G2
Llangyfelach **SA5** 17 K6
Llangynhafal **LL16** 47 K6
Llangynidr **NP8** 28 A7
Llangyniew **SY21** 38 A5
Llangynin **SA33** 17 F4
Llangynllo **SA44** 17 G1
Llangynog *Carmar.* **SA33** 17 G4
Llangynog *Powys* **SY10** 37 K3
Llangynwyd **CF34** 18 B3
Llanhamlach **LD3** 27 K6
Llanharan **CF72** 18 D3
Llanharry **CF72** 18 D3
Llanhennock **NP18** 19 G2
Llanhilleth **NP13** 19 F1
**Llanidloes SY18 37 J7**
Llaniestyn **LL53** 36 B2
Llanigon **HR3** 28 B5
Llanilar **SY23** 27 F1
Llanilid **CF35** 18 C3
Llanishen *Cardiff* **CF14** 18 E3
Llanishen *Mon.* **NP16** 19 H1
Llanllawddog **SA32** 17 H3
Llanllechid **LL57** 46 E6
Llanlleonfel **LD4** 27 J3
Llanllugan **SY21** 37 K5
Llanllwch **SA31** 17 G4
Llanllwchaiarn **SY16** 38 A6
Llanllwni **SA39** 17 H1
Llanllyfni **LL54** 46 C7
Llanllywel **NP15** 19 G2
Llanmadoc **SA3** 17 H6
Llanmaes **CF61** 18 C5
Llanmartin **NP18** 19 G3
Llanmerewig **SY15** 38 A6
Llanmihangel **CF71** 18 C4
Llan-mill **SA67** 16 E4
Llanmiloe **SA33** 17 F5
Llanmorlais **SA4** 17 J6
Llannefydd **LL16** 47 H5
Llannerch Hall **LL17** 47 J5
**Llannerch-y-medd LL71 46 C4**
Llannerch-y-Môr **CH8** 47 K5
Llannon *Carmar.* **SA14** 17 J5
**Llan-non *Cere.* SY23 26 E2**
Llannor **LL53** 36 C2
Llanover **NP7** 19 G1
Llanpumsaint **SA33** 17 H3
Llanreithan **SA62** 16 B3
Llanrhaeadr **LL16** 47 J6
Llanrhaeadr-ym-Mochnant **SY10** 38 A3
Llanrhian **SA62** 16 B2
Llanrhidian **SA3** 17 H6
Llanrhyddlad **LL65** 46 B4
**Llanrhystud SY23 26 E2**
Llanrothal **NP25** 28 D7
Llanrug **LL55** 46 D6
Llanrumney **CF3** 19 F3
**Llanrwst LL26 47 F6**
Llansadurnen **SA33** 17 F4
Llansadwrn *Carmar.* **SA19** 17 K2
Llansadwrn *I.o.A.* **LL59** 46 D5
Llansaint **SA17** 17 G5
Llansamlet **SA7** 17 K6
Llansanffraid **SY23** 26 E2
Llansanffraid Glan Conwy **LL28** 47 G5
Llansannan **LL16** 47 H6
Llansannor **CF71** 18 C4
Llansantffraed **LD3** 28 A6
Llansantffraed-Cwmdeuddwr **LD6** 27 J2
Llansantffraed-in-Elwel **LD1** 27 K3
**Llansantffraid-ym-Mechain SY22 38 B3**
Llansawel *Carmar.* **SA19** 17 K2
Llansawel (Briton Ferry) *N.P.T.* **SA11** 18 A2
Llansilin **SY10** 38 B3
Llansoy **NP15** 19 H1
Llanspyddid **LD3** 27 K6
Llanstadwell **SA73** 16 C5
Llansteffan **SA33** 17 G4
Llanstephan **LD3** 28 A4
Llantarnam **NP44** 19 G2
Llanteg **SA67** 16 E4
Llanthony **NP7** 28 B6
Llantilio Crossenny **NP7** 28 C7
Llantilio Pertholey **NP7** 28 C7
Llantood **SA43** 16 E1
Llantrisant *I.o.A.* **LL65** 46 B4
Llantrisant *Mon.* **NP15** 19 G2
Llantrisant *R.C.T.* **CF72** 18 D3
Llantrithyd **CF71** 18 D4
Llantwit Fardre **CF38** 18 D3
**Llantwit Major CF61 18 C5**
Llantysilio **LL20** 38 A1
Llanuwchllyn **LL23** 37 H3
Llanvaches **NP26** 19 H2
Llanvair-Discoed **NP16** 19 H2
Llanvapley **NP7** 28 C7
Llanvetherine **NP7** 28 C7
Llanveynoe **HR2** 28 C5
Llanvihangel Crucorney (Llanfihangel Crucornau) **NP7** 28 C6
Llanvihangel Gobion **NP7** 19 G1
Llanvihangel-Ystern-Llewern **NP25** 28 D7
Llanvithyn **CF62** 18 D4
Llanwarne **HR2** 28 E6
Llanwddyn **SY10** 37 K4
Llanwenog **SA40** 17 H1
Llanwern **NP18** 19 G3
Llanwinio **SA34** 17 F3
Llanwnda *Gwyn.* **LL54** 46 C7
Llanwnda *Pembs.* **SA64** 16 C2
Llanwnnen **SA48** 17 J1
Llanwnog **SY17** 37 K6
Llanwonno **CF37** 18 D2
**Llanwrda SA19 27 G5**
Llanwrin **SY20** 37 G5
Llanwrthwl **LD1** 27 J2
Llanwrtyd **LD5** 27 H4
**Llanwrtyd Wells LD5 27 H4**
Llanwyddelan **SY16** 37 K5
Llanyblodwel **SY10** 38 B3
Llanybri **SA33** 17 G4
**Llanybydder SA40 17 J1**
Llanycefn **SA66** 16 E3
Llanychaer Bridge **SA65** 16 C2
Llanycil **LL23** 37 J2
Llanycrwys **SA19** 17 K1
Llanymawddwy **SY20** 37 H4
**Llanymddyfri (Llandovery) SA20 27 G5**
**Llanymynech SY22 38 B3**
Llanynghenedl **LL65** 46 B4
Llanynys **LL16** 47 K6
Llan-y-pwll **LL13** 48 C7
Llanyre **LD1** 27 K2
Llanystumdwy **LL52** 36 D2
Llanywern **LD3** 28 A6
Llawhaden **SA67** 16 D4
Llawndy **CH8** 47 K4
Llawnt **SY10** 38 B2
Llawr-y-dref **LL53** 36 B3
Llawryglyn **SY17** 37 J6
Llay **LL12** 48 C7
Llechcynfarwy **LL71** 46 B4
Llecheiddior **LL51** 36 D1
Llechfaen **LD3** 27 K6
Llechryd *Caerp.* **NP22** 18 E1
Llechryd *Cere.* **SA43** 17 F1
Llechrydau **SY10** 38 B2
Lledrod *Cere.* **SY23** 27 F1
Lledrod *Powys* **SY10** 38 B3
Llethrid **SA2** 17 J6
Llidiad-Nenog **SA32** 17 J2
Llidiardau **LL23** 37 H2
Llithfaen **LL53** 36 C1
Lloc **CH8** 47 K5
Llong **CH7** 48 B6
Llowes **HR3** 28 A4
Lloyney **LD7** 28 B1
Llundain-fach **SA48** 26 E3
Llwydcoed **CF44** 18 C1
Llwydiarth **SY21** 37 K4
Llwyn *M.Tyd.* **CF48** 27 K7
Llwyn *Shrop.* **SY7** 38 B7
Llwyncelyn **SA46** 26 D3
Llwyn-croes **SA33** 17 H3
Llwyndafydd **SA44** 26 C3
Llwynderw **SY21** 38 B5
Llwyndyrys **LL53** 36 C1
Llwyneinion **LL14** 38 B1
**Llwyngwril LL37 36 E5**
Llwynhendy **SA14** 17 J6
Llwyn-Madoc **LD5** 27 J3
Llwynmawr **LL20** 38 B2
Llwyn-onn **SA45** 26 D3
Llwyn-y-brain *Carmar.* **SA34** 16 E4
Llwyn-y-brain *Carmar.* **SA20** 27 G5
Llwyn-y-groes **SY25** 26 E3
Llwynypia **CF40** 18 C2
Llyn Penmaen (Penmaenpool) **LL40** 37 F4
Llynclys **SY10** 38 B3
Llynfaes **LL65** 46 C5
Llysfaen **LL29** 47 G5
Llyswen **LD3** 28 A5
Llysworney **CF71** 18 C4
Llys-y-frân **SA63** 16 D3
Llywel **LD3** 27 H5
Load Brook **S6** 50 E4
Loandhu **IV20** 97 F4
Loanhead *Aber.* **AB41** 91 H1
**Loanhead *Midloth.* EH20 76 A4**
Loans **KA10** 74 B7
Lobb **EX33** 6 C2
Lobhillcross **EX20** 6 C7
Loch a Charnain **HS8** 92 D7
Loch Baghasdail (Lochboisdale) **HS8** 84 C3
Loch Choire Lodge **KW11** 103 J5
Loch Eil Outward Bound **PH33** 87 G7
Loch Head *D. & G.* **DG8** 64 D6
Loch Head *D. & G.* **KA6** 67 J4
Loch na Madadh (Lochmaddy) **HS6** 92 E5
Loch Sgioport **HS8** 84 D1
**Lochailort PH38 86 D6**
Lochaline **PA34** 79 H3
Lochans **DG9** 64 A5
Locharbriggs **DG1** 68 E5
Lochawe **PA33** 80 C5
Lochboisdale (Loch Baghasdail) **HS8** 84 C3
Lochbuie **PA62** 79 H5
Lochcarron **IV54** 94 E7
Lochdhu Hotel **KW12** 105 F4
Lochdon **PA64** 79 J4
Lochdrum **IV23** 95 J4
**Lochearnhead FK19 81 G5**
Lochee **DD2** 82 E4
Lochend *High.* **KW14** 105 H2
Lochend *High.* **IV3** 88 C1
Locheport (Locheuphort) **HS6** 92 D5
Locheuphort (Locheport) **HS6** 92 D5
Lochfoot **DG2** 65 K3
Lochgair **PA31** 73 H1
Lochgarthside **IV2** 88 C3
**Lochgelly KY5 75 K1**
**Lochgilphead PA31 73 G2**
Lochgoilhead **PA24** 80 D7
Lochgoyn **KA3** 74 D6
Lochhill *E.Ayr.* **KA18** 67 K2
Lochhill *Moray* **IV30** 97 K5
Lochinch Castle **DG9** 64 B4
Lochinver **IV27** 102 C6
Lochlair **DD8** 83 G3
Lochlane **PH7** 81 K5
Lochlea **KA1** 74 C7
Lochluichart **IV23** 95 K5
Lochmaben **DG11** 69 F5
Lochmaddy (Loch na Madadh) **HS6** 92 E5
Lochore **KY5** 75 K1
Lochportain **HS6** 92 E4
Lochranza **KA27** 73 H5
Lochside *Aber.* **DD10** 83 J1
Lochside *High.* **IV27** 103 G3
Lochside *High.* **KW11** 104 D5
Lochside *High.* **KW14** 105 H2
Lochslin **IV20** 97 F3
Lochton **KA26** 67 G5
Lochty **KY10** 83 G7
Lochuisge **PH33** 79 J2
Lochurr **DG3** 68 C5
Lochussie **IV7** 95 B6
**Lochwinnoch PA12 74 B5**
Lockengate **PL26** 4 A4
**Lockerbie DG11 69 G5**
Lockeridge **SN8** 20 E5
Lockerley **SO51** 10 D2
Lockhills **CA4** 61 G2
Locking **BS24** 19 G6
Lockington *E.Riding* **YO25** 59 F5
Lockington *Leics.* **DE74** 41 G3
Lockleywood **TF9** 39 F3
Locks Heath **SO31** 11 G4
Locksbottom **BR6** 23 H5
Locksgreen **PO30** 11 F5
Lockton **YO18** 58 E1
Loddington *Leics.* **LE7** 42 A5
Loddington *Northants.* **NN14** 32 B1
Loddiswell **TQ7** 5 H6
Loddon **NR14** 45 H6
Lode **CB25** 33 J2
Loders **DT6** 8 D5
Lodsworth **GU28** 12 C4
Lofthouse *N.Yorks.* **HG3** 57 G2
Lofthouse *W.Yorks.* **WF3** 57 J7
Loftus **TS13** 63 J5
Logan *D. & G.* **DG9** 64 A6
Logan *E.Ayr.* **KA18** 67 K1
Loganlea **EH55** 75 H4
Loggerheads **TF9** 39 G2
Loggie **IV23** 95 H2
Logie *Angus* **DD10** 83 H1
Logie *Angus* **DD8** 82 E2
Logie *Fife* **KY15** 83 F5
Logie *Moray* **IV36** 97 H6
Logie Coldstone **AB34** 90 C4
Logie Hill **IV18** 96 E4
Logie Newton **AB54** 90 E1
Logie Pert **DD10** 83 H1
Logierait **PH9** 82 A2
Login **SA34** 16 E3
Lolworth **CB23** 33 G2
Lonbain **IV54** 94 C6
Londesborough **YO43** 58 E5
**LONDON E, EC, N, NW, SE, SW, W, WC 23 G3**
London Apprentice **PL26** 4 A6
London Ashford Airport **TN29** 15 F5
London Beach **TN30** 14 D4
London City Airport **E16** 23 H3
London Colney **AL2** 22 E1
London Gatwick Airport (Gatwick Airport) **RH6** 23 F7
London Heathrow Airport **TW6** 22 D4
London Luton Airport (Luton Airport) **LU2** 32 E6
London Minstead **SO43** 10 D3
London Southend Airport **SS2** 24 E3
London Stansted Airport (Stansted Airport) **CM24** 33 J6
Londonderry **DL7** 57 H1
Londonthorpe **NG31** 42 C2
Londubh **IV22** 94 E3
Lonemore **IV25** 96 E3
Long Ashton **BS41** 19 J4
Long Bank **DY12** 29 G1
Long Bennington **NG23** 42 B1
Long Bredy **DT2** 8 E5
Long Buckby **NN6** 31 H2
Long Clawson **LE14** 42 A3
Long Compton *Staffs.* **ST18** 40 A3
Long Compton *Warks.* **CV36** 30 D5
Long Crendon **HP18** 21 K1
Long Crichel **BH21** 9 J3

Lon - Lym

Long Dean SN14 20 B4
Long Downs TR10 2 E5
Long Drax YO8 58 C7
Long Duckmanton S44 51 G5
Long Eaton NG10 41 G2
Long Gill BD23 56 C4
Long Green Ches.W. & C. CH3 48 D5
Long Green Essex CO6 34 D6
Long Green Worcs. GL19 29 H5
Long Hanborough OX29 31 F7
Long Itchington CV47 31 F2
Long Lane TF6 39 F4
Long Lawford CV23 31 F1
Long Load TA10 8 D2
Long Marston Herts. HP23 32 B7
Long Marston N.Yorks. YO26 58 B4
Long Marston Warks. CV37 30 C4
Long Marton CA16 61 H4
Long Meadowend SY7 38 D7
Long Melford CO10 34 C4
Long Newnton GL8 20 C2
Long Preston BD23 56 D4
Long Riston HU11 59 H5
Long Stratton NR15 45 F6
Long Street MK19 31 J4
Long Sutton Hants. RG29 22 A7
Long Sutton Lincs. PE12 43 H3
Long Sutton Som. TA10 8 D2
Long Thurlow IP31 34 E2
Long Whatton LE12 41 G3
Long Wittenham OX14 21 J2
Longbenton NE7 71 H7
Longborough GL56 30 C6
Longbridge Plym. PL6 5 F5
Longbridge W.Mid. B31 30 B1
Longbridge Warks. CV34 30 D2
Longbridge Deverill BA12 20 B7
Longburgh CA5 60 E1
Longburton DT9 9 F3
Longcliffe DE4 50 E7
Longcombe TQ9 5 J5
Longcot SN7 21 F2
Longcroft FK4 75 F3
Longcross Devon PL19 4 E3
Longcross Surr. KT16 22 C5
Longden SY5 38 D5
Longdon Staffs. WS15 40 C4
Longdon Worcs. GL20 29 H5
Longdon Green WS15 40 C4
Longdon upon Tern TF6 39 F4
Longdown EX6 7 G6
Longdrum AB23 91 H3
Longfield DA3 24 C5
Longfield Hill DA3 24 C5
Longfleet BH15 10 B5
Longford Derbys. DE6 40 E2
Longford Glos. GL2 29 H6
Longford Gt.Lon. UB7 22 D4
Longford Shrop. TF9 39 F2
Longford Tel. & W. TF10 39 G4
Longford W.Mid. CV6 41 F7
Longforgan DD2 82 E5
Longformacus TD11 76 E5
Longframlington NE65 71 G3
Longham Dorset BH22 10 B5
Longham Norf. NR19 44 D4
Longhill AB42 99 H5
Longhirst NE61 71 H5
Longhope Glos. GL17 29 F7
Longhope Ork. KW16 106 C8
Longhorsley NE65 71 G4
Longhoughton NE66 71 H2
Longlands Aber. AB54 90 C2
Longlands Cumb. CA7 60 D3
Longlands Gt.Lon. SE9 23 H4
Longlane Derbys. DE6 40 E2
Longlane W.Berks. RG18 21 H4
Longlevens GL2 29 H7
Longley HD9 50 D2
Longley Green WR6 29 G3
Longmanhill AB45 99 F4
Longmoor Camp GU33 11 J1
Longmorn IV30 97 K6
Longnewton Sc.Bord. TD6 70 A1
Longnewton Stock. TS21 62 E5
Longney GL2 29 G7
Longniddry EH32 76 C3
Longnor Shrop. SY5 38 D5
Longnor Staffs. SK17 50 C6
Longparish SP11 21 H7
Longridge Lancs. PR3 56 B6
Longridge Staffs. ST18 40 B4
Longridge W.Loth. EH47 75 H4
Longridge End GL19 29 H6
Longridge Towers TD15 77 H5
Longriggend ML6 75 G3
Longrock TR20 2 C5
Longsdon ST9 49 J7
Longshaw WN5 48 E2
Longside AB42 99 J6
Longslow TF9 39 F2
Longsowerby CA2 60 E1
Longstanton CB24 33 H2
Longstock SO20 10 E1
Longstone TR26 2 C5
Longstowe CB23 33 G3
Longstreet SN9 20 E6
Longthorpe PE3 42 E6
Longton Lancs. PR4 55 H7
Longton Stoke ST3 40 B1
Longtown Cumb. CA6 69 J7
Longtown Here. HR2 28 C6
Longville in the Dale TF13 38 E6
Longwell Green BS30 19 K4
Longwick HP27 22 A1
Longwitton NE61 71 F5
Longworth OX13 21 G2
Longyester EH41 76 D4
Lonmay AB43 99 J5
Lonmore IV55 93 H7
Looe PL13 4 C5
Loose ME15 14 C2
Loosebeare EX17 7 F5
Loosegate PE12 43 G3
Loosley Row HP27 22 B1
Lopcombe Corner SP5 10 D1
Lopen TA13 8 D3
Loppington SY4 38 D3
Lorbottle NE65 71 F3
Lorbottle Hall NE66 71 F3
Lordington PO18 11 J4
Lord's Hill SO16 10 E3
Lorgill IV55 93 G7
Lorn G83 74 B2
Lornty PH10 82 C3
Loscoe DE75 41 G1
Loscombe DT6 8 D5
Losgaintir HS3 93 F2
Lossiemouth IV31 97 K4
Lossit PA47 72 A5
Lostock Gralam CW9 49 F5
Lostock Green CW9 49 F5
Lostock Junction BL6 49 F2
Lostwithiel PL22 4 B5
Loth KW17 106 F4
Lothbeg KW8 104 E7
Lothersdale BD20 56 E5
Lothmore KW8 104 E7
Loudwater HP10 22 C2
Loughborough LE11 41 H4
Loughor SA4 17 J6
Loughton Essex IG10 23 H2
Loughton M.K. MK5 32 B5
Loughton Shrop. WV16 39 F7
Lound Lincs. PE10 42 D4
Lound Notts. DN22 51 J4
Lound Suff. NR32 45 K6
Lount LE65 41 F4
Lour DD8 83 F3
Louth LN11 53 G4
Love Clough BB4 56 D7
Lovedean PO8 11 H3
Lover SP5 10 D3
Loversall DN11 51 H3
Loves Green CM1 24 C1
Lovesome Hill DL6 62 E7
Loveston SA68 16 D5
Lovington BA7 8 E1
Low Ackworth WF7 51 G1
Low Angerton NE61 71 F5
Low Ballevain PA28 66 A1
Low Barlay DG7 65 F5
Low Barlings LN3 52 D5
Low Bentham (Lower Bentham) LA2 56 B3
Low Bolton DL8 62 B7
Low Bradfield S6 50 E3
Low Bradley (Bradley) BD20 57 F5
Low Braithwaite CA4 60 F2
Low Brunton NE46 70 E6
Low Burnham DN9 51 K2
Low Burton HG4 57 H1
Low Buston NE65 71 H3
Low Catton YO41 58 D4
Low Coniscliffe DL2 62 D5
Low Craighead KA26 67 G3
Low Dinsdale DL2 62 E5
Low Ellington HG4 57 H1
Low Entercommon DL6 62 E6
Low Etherley DL14 62 C4
Low Fell NE11 62 D1
Low Gate NE46 70 E7
Low Grantley HG4 57 H2
Low Green IP29 34 C2
Low Habberley DY11 29 H1
Low Ham TA10 8 D2
Low Hawsker YO22 63 J2
Low Haygarth LA10 61 H7
Low Hesket CA4 61 F2
Low Hesleyhurst NE65 71 F4
Low Hutton YO60 58 D3
Low Kingthorpe YO18 58 E1
Low Laithe HG3 57 G3
Low Langton LN8 52 E5
Low Leighton SK22 50 C4
Low Lorton CA13 60 C4
Low Marishes YO17 58 E2
Low Marnham NG23 52 B6
Low Middleton NE70 77 K7
Low Mill YO62 63 H7
Low Moor Lancs. BB7 56 C5
Low Moor W.Yorks. BD12 57 G7
Low Moorsley DH5 62 E2
Low Moresby CA28 60 A4
Low Newton-by-the-Sea NE66 71 H1
Low Row Cumb. CA8 70 A7
Low Row N.Yorks. DL11 62 A7
Low Stillaig PA21 73 H4
Low Street NR9 44 E5
Low Tharston NR15 45 F6
Low Torry KY12 75 J2
Low Town NE65 71 G3
Low Toynton LN9 53 F5
Low Wood LA12 55 G1
Low Worsall TS15 62 E6
Lowbands GL19 29 G5
Lowdham NG14 41 J1
Lowe SY4 38 E2
Lowe Hill ST13 49 J7
Lower Achachenna PA35 80 B5
Lower Aisholt TA5 8 B1
Lower Apperley GL19 29 H6
Lower Arncott OX25 31 H7
Lower Ashtead KT21 22 E6
Lower Ashton EX6 7 G7
Lower Assendon RG9 22 A3
Lower Auchalick PA21 73 H3
Lower Ballam PR4 55 G6
Lower Barewood HR6 28 C3
Lower Bartle PR4 55 H6
Lower Bayble (Pabail Iarach) HS2 101 H4
Lower Beeding RH13 13 F4
Lower Benefield PE8 42 C7
Lower Bentham (Low Bentham) LA2 56 B3
Lower Bentley B60 29 J2
Lower Berry Hill GL16 28 E7
Lower Birchwood DE55 51 G7
Lower Boddington NN11 31 F3
Lower Boscaswell TR19 2 A5
Lower Bourne GU10 22 B7
Lower Brailes OX15 30 E5
Lower Breakish IV42 86 C2
Lower Bredbury SK6 49 J3
Lower Broadheath WR2 29 H3
Lower Brynamman SA18 27 G7
Lower Bullingham HR2 28 E5
Lower Bullington SO21 21 H7
Lower Burgate SP6 10 C3
Lower Burrow TA12 8 D2
Lower Burton HR6 28 D3
Lower Caldecote SG18 32 E4
Lower Cam GL11 20 A1
Lower Cambourne CB23 33 G3
Lower Camster KW3 105 H4
Lower Chapel LD3 27 K5
Lower Cheriton EX14 7 K5
Lower Chicksgrove SP3 9 J1
Lower Chute SP11 21 G6
Lower Clent DY9 40 B7
Lower Creedy EX17 7 G5
Lower Cumberworth HD8 50 E2
Lower Darwen BB3 56 B7
Lower Dean PE28 32 D2
Lower Diabaig IV22 94 D5
Lower Dicker BN27 13 J5
Lower Dinchope SY7 38 D7
Lower Down SY7 38 C7
Lower Drift TR19 2 B6
Lower Dunsforth YO26 57 K3
Lower Earley RG6 22 A4
Lower Edmonton N9 23 G2
Lower Elkstone SK17 50 C7
Lower End Bucks. HP18 21 K1
Lower End M.K. MK17 32 C5
Lower End Northants. NN7 32 B2
Lower Everleigh SN8 20 E6
Lower Eythorne CT15 15 H3
Lower Failand BS8 19 J4
Lower Farringdon GU34 11 J1
Lower Fittleworth RH20 12 D5
Lower Foxdale IM4 54 B6
Lower Freystrop SA62 16 C4
Lower Froyle GU34 22 A7
Lower Gabwell TQ12 5 K4
Lower Gledfield IV24 96 C2
Lower Godney BA5 19 H7
Lower Gravenhurst MK45 32 E5
Lower Green Essex CB11 33 H5
Lower Green Herts. SG5 32 E5
Lower Green Kent TN2 23 K7
Lower Green Norf. NR21 44 D2
Lower Green Staffs. WV9 40 B5
Lower Green Bank LA2 55 J4
Lower Halstock Leigh BA22 8 E4
Lower Halstow ME9 24 E5
Lower Hardres CT4 15 G2
Lower Harpton LD8 28 B2
Lower Hartshay DE5 51 F7
Lower Hartwell HP17 31 J7
Lower Hawthwaite LA20 55 F1
Lower Haysden TN11 23 J7
Lower Hayton SY8 38 E7
Lower Heath CW12 49 H6
Lower Hergest HR5 28 B3
Lower Heyford OX25 31 F6
Lower Higham ME3 24 D4
Lower Holbrook IP9 35 F5
Lower Hopton WF14 50 D1
Lower Hordley SY12 38 C3
Lower Horncroft RH20 12 D5
Lower Horsebridge BN27 13 J5
Lower Houses HD5 50 D1
Lower Howsell WR14 29 G4
Lower Kersal M25 49 H2
Lower Kilchattan PA61 72 B1
Lower Kilcott GL12 20 A3
Lower Killeyan PA42 72 A6
Lower Kingcombe DT2 8 E5
Lower Kingswood KT20 23 F6
Lower Kinnerton CH4 48 C6
Lower Langford BS40 19 H5
Lower Largo KY8 83 F7
Lower Leigh ST10 40 C2
Lower Lemington GL56 30 D5
Lower Lovacott EX31 6 D3
Lower Loxhore EX31 6 E2
Lower Lydbrook GL17 28 E7
Lower Lye HR6 28 D2
Lower Machen NP10 19 F3
Lower Maes-coed HR2 28 C5
Lower Mannington BH21 10 B4
Lower Middleton Cheney OX17 31 G4
Lower Milton BA5 19 J7
Lower Moor WR10 29 J4
Lower Morton BS35 19 K2
Lower Nash SA72 16 D5
Lower Nazeing EN9 23 G1
Lower Netchwood WV16 39 F6
Lower Nyland SP8 9 G2
Lower Oddington GL56 30 D6
Lower Ollach IV51 86 B1
Lower Penarth CF64 18 E4
Lower Penn WV4 40 A6
Lower Pennington SO41 10 E5
Lower Peover WA16 49 G5
Lower Pollicott HP18 31 J7
Lower Quinton CV37 30 C4
Lower Race NP4 19 F1
Lower Rainham ME8 24 E5
Lower Roadwater TA23 7 J2
Lower Sapey WR6 29 F2
Lower Seagry SN15 20 C3
Lower Shelton MK43 32 C4
Lower Shiplake RG9 22 A4
Lower Shuckburgh NN11 31 F2
Lower Slaughter GL54 30 C6
Lower Soothill WF17 57 H7
Lower Stanton St. Quintin SN14 20 C3
Lower Stoke ME3 24 E4
Lower Stondon SG16 32 E5
Lower Stone GL13 19 K2
Lower Stonnall WS9 40 C5
Lower Stow Bedon NR17 44 D6
Lower Street Dorset DT11 9 H5
Lower Street E.Suss. TN33 14 C6
Lower Street Norf. NR11 45 G2
Lower Street Norf. NR11 45 F2
Lower Street Suff. IP6 35 F3
Lower Stretton WA4 49 F4
Lower Sundon LU3 32 D6
Lower Swanwick SO31 11 F4
Lower Swell GL54 30 C6
Lower Tadmarton OX15 31 F5
Lower Tale EX14 7 J5
Lower Tean ST10 40 C2
Lower Thurlton NR14 45 J6
Lower Thurnham LA2 55 H4
Lower Town Cornw. TR13 2 D6
Lower Town Devon TQ13 5 H3
Lower Town I.o.S. TR25 2 C1
Lower Town Pembs. SA65 16 C2
Lower Trebullett PL15 4 D3
Lower Tysoe CV35 30 E4
Lower Upcott TQ13 7 G7
Lower Upham SO32 11 G3
Lower Upnor ME2 24 D4
Lower Vexford TA4 7 K2
Lower Wallop SY5 38 C5
Lower Walton WA4 49 F4
Lower Waterhay SN6 20 D2
Lower Weald MK19 31 J5
Lower Wear EX2 7 H7
Lower Weare BS26 19 H6
Lower Welson HR3 28 B3
Lower Whatley BA11 20 A7
Lower Whitley WA4 49 F5
Lower Wick WR2 29 H3
Lower Wield SO24 21 K7
Lower Winchendon (Nether Winchendon) HP18 31 J7
Lower Withington SK11 49 H6
Lower Woodend SL7 22 B3
Lower Woodford SP4 10 C1
Lower Wyche WR14 29 G4
Lowerhouse BB12 56 D6
Lowertown KW17 106 D8
Lowesby LE7 42 A5
Lowestoft NR32 45 K6
Loweswater CA13 60 C4
Lowfield Heath RH11 23 F7
Lowgill Cumb. LA8 61 H7
Lowgill Lancs. LA2 56 B3
Lowick Cumb. LA12 55 F1
Lowick Northants. NN14 42 C7
Lowick Northumb. TD15 77 J7
Lowick Bridge LA12 55 F1
Lowick Green LA12 55 F1
Lownie Moor DD8 83 F3
Lowsonford B95 30 C2
Lowther CA10 61 G4
Lowther Castle CA10 61 G4
Lowthorpe YO25 59 G3
Lowton Devon EX20 6 E5
Lowton Gt.Man. WA3 49 F3
Lowton Som. TA3 7 K4
Lowton Common WA3 49 F3
Loxbeare EX16 7 H4
Loxhill GU8 12 D3
Loxhore EX31 6 E2
Loxley CV35 30 D3
Loxley Green ST14 40 C2
Loxton BS26 19 G6
Loxwood RH14 12 D3
Lubachoinnich IV24 96 B2
Lubcroy IV27 95 K1
Lubenham LE16 42 A7
Lubfearn IV23 95 K4
Lubmore IV22 95 G6
Lubreoch PH15 81 F3
Luccombe TA24 7 H1
Luccombe Village PO37 11 G6
Lucker NE70 77 K7
Luckett PL17 4 D3
Luckington SN14 20 B3
Lucklawhill KY16 83 F5
Luckwell Bridge TA24 7 H2
Lucton HR6 28 D2
Lucy Cross DL11 62 D5
Ludag HS8 84 C3
Ludborough DN36 53 F3
Ludbrook PL21 5 G5
Ludchurch SA67 16 E4
Luddenden HX2 57 F7
Luddenden Foot HX2 57 F7
Luddenham Court ME13 25 F5
Luddesdown DA13 24 C5
Luddington N.Lincs. DN17 52 B1
Luddington Warks. CV37 30 C3
Luddington in the Brook PE8 42 E7
Ludford Lincs. LN8 52 E4
Ludford Shrop. SY8 28 E1
Ludgershall Bucks. HP18 31 H7
Ludgershall Wilts. SP11 21 F6
Ludgvan TR20 2 C5
Ludham NR29 45 H4
Ludlow SY8 28 E1
Ludney LN11 53 G3
Ludstock HR8 29 F5
Ludstone WV5 40 A6
Ludwell SP7 9 J2
Ludworth DH6 62 E2
Luffincott EX22 6 B6
Luffness EH32 76 C2
Lufton BA22 8 E3
Lugar KA18 67 K1
Luggate EH41 76 D3
Luggate Burn EH41 76 E3
Luggiebank G67 75 F3
Lugton KA3 74 C5
Lugwardine HR1 28 E4
Luib IV49 86 B2
Luibeilt PH30 80 D1
Luing PA34 79 J6
Lulham HR2 28 D4
Lullington Derbys. DE12 40 E4
Lullington Som. BA11 20 A6
Lulsgate Bottom BS40 19 J5
Lulsley WR6 29 G3
Lulworth Camp BH20 9 H6
Lumb Lancs. BB4 56 D7
Lumb W.Yorks. HX6 57 F7
Lumbutts OL14 56 E7
Lumby LS25 57 K6
Lumphanan AB31 90 D4
Lumphinnans KY4 75 K1
Lumsdaine TD14 77 G4
Lumsdale DE4 51 F6
Lumsden AB54 90 C2
Lunan DD11 83 H2
Lunanhead DD8 83 F2
Luncarty PH1 82 B5
Lund E.Riding YO25 59 F5
Lund N.Yorks. YO8 58 C6
Lund Shet. ZE2 107 P2
Lundale HS2 100 D4
Lundavra PH33 80 B1
Lunderton AB42 99 K6
Lundie Angus DD2 82 D4
Lundie High. IV63 87 H3
Lundin Links KY8 83 F7
Lundwood S71 51 F2
Lundy EX34 6 A1
Lunga PA31 79 K7
Lunna ZE2 107 N6
Lunning ZE2 107 P6
Lunnon SA3 17 J7
Lunsford's Cross TN39 14 C6
Lunt L29 48 C2
Luntley HR6 28 C3
Luppitt EX14 7 K5
Lupset WF2 51 F1
Lupton LA6 55 J1
Lurgashall GU28 12 C4
Lurignich PA38 80 A2
Lusby PE23 53 G6
Luss G83 74 B1
Lussagiven PA60 72 E2
Lusta IV55 93 H6
Lustleigh TQ13 7 F7
Luston HR6 28 D2
Luthermuir AB30 83 H1
Luthrie KY15 82 E6
Luton Devon EX14 7 J5
Luton Devon TQ13 5 K3
LUTON Luton LU 32 D6
Luton Med. ME5 24 D5
Luton Airport (London Luton Airport) LU2 32 E6
Lutterworth LE17 41 H7
Lutton Devon PL21 5 F5
Lutton Dorset BH20 9 J6
Lutton Lincs. PE12 43 H3
Lutton Northants. PE8 42 E7
Luxborough TA23 7 H2
Luxulyan PL30 4 A5
Lybster High. KW14 105 F2
Lybster High. KW3 105 H5
Lydacott EX21 6 C5
Lydbury North SY7 38 C7
Lydcott EX32 6 E2
Lydd TN29 15 F5
Lydden CT15 15 H3
Lyddington LE15 42 B6
Lydd-on-Sea TN29 15 F5
Lyde Green BS16 19 K4
Lydeard St. Lawrence TA4 7 K2
Lydford EX20 6 D7
Lydford-on-Fosse TA11 8 E1
Lydgate Gt.Man. OL15 49 J1
Lydgate Gt.Man. OL4 49 J2
Lydgate W.Yorks. OL14 56 E7
Lydham SY9 38 C6
Lydiard Millicent SN5 20 D3
Lydiard Tregoze SN5 20 E3
Lydiate L31 48 C2
Lydlinch DT10 9 G3
Lydney GL15 19 K1
Lydstep SA70 16 D6
Lye DY9 40 B7
Lye Cross BS40 19 H5
Lye Green Bucks. HP5 22 C1
Lye Green E.Suss. TN6 13 J3
Lye Green Warks. CV35 30 C2
Lye's Green BA12 20 B7
Lyford OX12 21 G2
Lymbridge Green TN25 15 G3
Lyme Regis DT7 8 C5
Lymekilns G74 74 E5
Lyminge CT18 15 G3
Lymington SO41 10 E5

## Lym - Mea


Lyminster **BN17** 12 D6
**Lymm WA13** 49 **F4**
Lymore **SO41** 10 D5
Lympne **CT21** 15 G4
Lympsham **BS24** 19 G6
Lympstone **EX8** 7 H7
Lynaberack **PH21** 88 E5
Lynch **TA24** 7 G1
Lynch Green **NR9** 45 F5
Lynchat **PH21** 88 E4
Lyndale House **IV51** 93 J6
**Lyndhurst SO43** 10 **D4**
Lyndon **LE15** 42 C5
Lyne *Aber.* **AB51** 91 F4
Lyne *Sc.Bord.* **EH45** 76 A6
Lyne *Surr.* **KT16** 22 D5
Lyne Down **HR8** 29 F5
Lyne of Gorthleck **IV2** 88 C2
Lyne of Skene **AB32** 91 F3
Lyne Station **EH45** 76 A6
Lyneal **SY12** 38 D2
Lynegar **KW1** 105 H3
Lyneham *Oxon.* **OX7** 30 D6
Lyneham *Wilts.* **SN15** 20 D4
Lyneholmeford **CA6** 70 A6
Lynemore *High.* **PH26** 89 H2
Lynemore *Moray* **AB37** 89 J1
Lynemouth **NE61** 71 H4
Lyness **KW16** 106 C8
Lynford **IP26** 44 C6
Lyng *Norf.* **NR9** 44 E4
Lyng *Som.* **TA3** 8 C2
Lyngate **NR28** 45 H3
**Lynmouth EX35** 7 **F1**
Lynn **TF10** 39 G4
Lynsted **ME9** 25 F5
Lynstone **EX23** 6 A5
**Lynton EX35** 7 **F1**
Lyon's Gate **DT2** 9 F4
Lyonshall **HR5** 28 C3
Lyrabus **PA44** 72 A4
Lytchett Matravers **BH16** 9 J5
Lytchett Minster **BH16** 9 J5
Lyth **KW1** 105 H2
Lytham **FY8** 55 G7
**Lytham St. Anne's FY8** 55 **G7**
Lythe **YO21** 63 K5
Lythe Hill **GU27** 12 C3
Lythes **KW17** 106 D9
Lythmore **KW14** 105 F2

### M

Maaruig (Maraig) **HS3** 100 E7
Mabe Burnthouse **TR10** 2 E5
Mabie **DG2** 65 K3
**Mablethorpe LN12** 53 **J4**
**Macclesfield SK11** 49 **J5**
Macclesfield Forest **SK11** 49 J5
**Macduff AB44** 99 **F4**
Macedonia **KY6** 82 D7
Machan **ML9** 75 F5
Machany **PH3** 81 K6
Macharioch **PA28** 66 B3
Machen **CF83** 19 F3
Machrie *Arg. & B.* **PA49** 72 A4
Machrie *Arg. & B.* **PA42** 72 B6
Machrie *N.Ayr.* **KA27** 73 G7
Machrihanish **PA28** 66 A1
Machrins **PA61** 72 B1
**Machynlleth SY20** 37 **G5**
McInroy's Point **PA19** 74 A3
Mackerye End **AL4** 32 E7
Mackworth **DE22** 41 F2
Macmerry **EH33** 76 C3
Macterry **AB53** 99 F6
Madderty **PH7** 82 A5
Maddiston **FK2** 75 H3
Madehurst **BN18** 12 C5
Madeley *Staffs.* **CW3** 39 G1
Madeley *Tel. & W.* **TF7** 39 G5
Madeley Heath **CW3** 39 G1
Maders **PL17** 4 D3
Madford **EX15** 7 K4
Madingley **CB23** 33 G2
Madjeston **SP8** 9 H2
Madley **HR2** 28 D5
Madresfield **WR13** 29 H4
Madron **TR20** 2 B5
Maenaddwyn **LL71** 46 C4
Maenclochog **SA66** 16 D3
Maendy *Cardiff* **CF14** 18 E4
Maendy *V. of Glam.* **CF71** 18 D4
Maenporth **TR11** 2 E6
Maentwrog **LL41** 37 F1
Maen-y-groes **SA45** 26 C3
Maer *Cornw.* **EX23** 6 A5
Maer *Staffs.* **ST5** 39 G2
Maerdy *Carmar.* **SA19** 17 K3
Maerdy *Carmar.* **SA19** 17 K3
Maerdy *Conwy* **LL21** 37 K1
Maerdy *R.C.T.* **CF43** 18 C2
Maesbrook **SY10** 38 B3
Maesbury Marsh **SY10** 38 C3
Maes-Glas (Greenfield) *Flints.* **CH8** 47 K5
Maes-glas *Newport* **NP20** 19 F3
Maesgwynne **SA34** 17 F3
Maeshafn **CH7** 48 B6
Maesllyn **SA44** 17 G1
Maesmynis **LD2** 27 K4
**Maesteg CF34** 18 **B2**
Maes-Treylow **LD8** 28 B2
Maesybont **SA14** 17 J4
Maesycrugiau **SA39** 17 H1
Maesycwmmer **CF82** 18 E2
Maesyfed (New Radnor) **LD8** 28 B2
Magdalen Laver **CM5** 23 J1
Maggieknockater **AB38** 98 B6
Maggots End **CM23** 33 H6
Magham Down **BN27** 13 K5
Maghull **L31** 48 C2
Magna Park **LE17** 41 H7
Magor **NP26** 19 H3
Magpie Green **IP22** 34 E1
Maiden Bradley **BA12** 9 G1
Maiden Head **BS41** 19 J5
Maiden Law **DH7** 62 C2
Maiden Newton **DT2** 8 E5
Maiden Wells **SA71** 16 C6
Maidencombe **TQ1** 5 K4
Maidenhayne **EX13** 8 B5
**Maidenhead SL6** 22 **B3**
Maidens **KA26** 67 G3
Maiden's Green **RG42** 22 B4
Maidensgrove **RG9** 22 A3
Maidenwell *Cornw.* **PL30** 4 B3
Maidenwell *Lincs.* **LN11** 53 G5
Maidford **NN12** 31 H3
Maids' Moreton **MK18** 31 J5
**Maidstone ME14** 14 **C2**
Maidwell **NN6** 31 J1
Mail **ZE2** 107 N10
Maindee **NP19** 19 G3
Mainland *Ork.* **KW** 106 B6
Mainland *Shet.* **ZE** 107 M7
Mains of Ardestie **DD5** 83 G4
Mains of Balgavies **DD8** 83 G2
Mains of Balhall **DD9** 83 G1
Mains of Ballindarg **DD8** 83 F2
Mains of Burgie **IV36** 97 H6
Mains of Culsh **AB53** 99 G6
Mains of Dillavaird **AB30** 91 F6
Mains of Drum **AB31** 91 G4
Mains of Dudwick **AB41** 91 H1
Mains of Faillie **IV2** 88 E1
Mains of Fedderate **AB42** 99 G6
Mains of Glack **AB51** 91 F2
Mains of Glassaugh **AB45** 98 D4
Mains of Glenbuchat **AB36** 90 B3
Mains of Linton **AB51** 91 F3
Mains of Melgund **DD9** 83 G2
Mains of Pitfour **AB42** 99 H6
Mains of Pittrichie **AB21** 91 G2
Mains of Sluie **IV36** 97 H6
Mains of Tannachy **AB56** 98 B4
Mains of Thornton **AB30** 90 E7
Mains of Tig **KA26** 67 F5
Mains of Watten **KW1** 105 H3
Mainsforth **DL17** 62 E3
Mainsriddle **DG2** 65 K5
Mainstone **SY9** 38 B7
Maisemore **GL2** 29 H6
Major's Green **B90** 30 C1
Makendon **NE65** 70 D3
Makeney **DE56** 41 F1
Makerstoun **TD5** 76 E7
Malacleit **HS6** 92 C4
Malborough **TQ7** 5 H7
Malden Rushett **KT9** 22 E5
**Maldon CM9** 24 **E1**
Malham **BD23** 56 E3
Maligar **IV51** 93 K5
Malinbridge **S6** 51 F4
**Mallaig PH41** 86 **C5**
Mallaigmore **PH41** 86 C5
Mallaigvaig **PH41** 86 C5
Malleny Mills **EH14** 75 K4
Malletsheugh **G77** 74 D5
Malling **FK8** 81 G7
Mallows Green **CM23** 33 H6
Malltraeth **LL62** 46 C6
Mallwyd **SY20** 37 H4
**Malmesbury SN16** 20 **C3**
Malmsmead **EX35** 7 F1
**Malpas** ***Ches.W. & C.*** **SY14** 38 **D1**
Malpas *Cornw.* **TR1** 3 F4
Malpas *Newport* **NP20** 19 G2
Maltby *Lincs.* **LN11** 53 G4
Maltby *S.Yorks.* **S66** 51 H3
Maltby *Stock.* **TS8** 63 F5
Maltby le Marsh **LN13** 53 H4
Malting End **CB8** 34 B3
Malting Green **CO2** 34 D7
Maltman's Hill **TN27** 14 D3
**Malton YO17** 58 **D2**
Malvern Link **WR14** 29 G4
Malvern Wells **WR14** 29 G4
Mambeg **G84** 74 A2
Mamble **DY14** 29 F1
Mamhead **EX6** 7 H7
Mamhilad **NP4** 19 G1
Manaccan **TR12** 2 E6
Manadon **PL5** 4 E5
Manafon **SY21** 38 A5
Manais (Manish) **HS3** 93 G3
Manaton **TQ13** 7 F7
Manby **LN11** 53 G4
Mancetter **CV9** 41 F6
**MANCHESTER M** 49 **H3**
Manchester Airport **M90** 49 H4
Mancot Royal **CH5** 48 C6
Mandally **PH35** 87 J4
Manea **PE15** 43 H7
Maneight **KA18** 67 K3
Manfield **DL2** 62 D5
Mangaster **ZE2** 107 M5
Mangerton **DT6** 8 D5
Mangotsfield **BS16** 19 K4
Mangrove Green **LU2** 32 E6
Mangurstadh **HS2** 100 C4
Manish (Manais) **HS3** 93 G3
Mankinholes **OL14** 56 E7
Manley **WA6** 48 E5
Manmoel **NP12** 18 E1
Mannal **PA77** 78 A3
Manningford Abbots **SN9** 20 E6
Manningford Bohune **SN9** 20 E6
Manningford Bruce **SN9** 20 E6
Manningham **BD8** 57 G6
Mannings Heath **RH13** 13 F4
Mannington **BH21** 10 B4
**Manningtree CO11** 35 **F5**
Mannofield **AB15** 91 H4
Manor Park **SL2** 22 C3
Manorbier **SA70** 16 D6
Manorbier Newton **SA70** 16 D5
Manordeifi **SA43** 17 F1
Manordeilo **SA19** 17 K3
Manorowen **SA65** 16 C2
Mansell Gamage **HR4** 28 C4
Mansell Lacy **HR4** 28 D4
Mansergh **LA6** 56 B1
**Mansfield NG18** 51 **H6**
Mansfield Woodhouse **NG19** 51 H6
Manson Green **NR9** 44 E5
Mansriggs **LA12** 55 F1
Manston *Dorset* **DT10** 9 H3
Manston *Kent* **CT12** 25 K5
Manston *W.Yorks.* **LS15** 57 J6
Manswood **BH21** 9 J4
Manthorpe *Lincs.* **PE10** 42 D4
Manthorpe *Lincs.* **NG31** 42 C2
Manton *N.Lincs.* **DN21** 52 C2
Manton *Notts.* **S80** 51 H5
Manton *Rut.* **LE15** 42 B5
Manton *Wilts.* **SN8** 20 E5
Manuden **CM23** 33 H6
Manwood Green **CM5** 33 J7
Maolachy **PA35** 79 K6
Maperton **BA9** 9 F2
Maple Cross **WD3** 22 D2
Maplebeck **NG22** 51 K6
Mapledurham **RG4** 21 K4
Mapledurwell **RG25** 21 K6
Maplehurst **RH13** 12 E4
Maplescombe **DA4** 23 J5
Mapleton **DE6** 40 D1
Mapperley *Derbys.* **DE7** 41 G1
Mapperley *Notts.* **NG5** 41 H1
Mapperton *Dorset* **DT8** 8 E5
Mapperton *Dorset* **DT11** 9 J5
Mappleborough Green **B80** 30 B2
Mappleton **HU18** 59 J5
Mapplewell **S75** 51 F2
Mappowder **DT10** 9 G4
Mar Lodge **AB35** 89 H5
Maraig (Maaruig) **HS3** 100 E7
**Marazion TR17** 2 **C5**
Marbhig **HS2** 101 G6
Marbury **SY13** 38 E1
**March PE15** 43 **H6**
Marcham **OX13** 21 H2
Marchamley **SY4** 38 E3
Marchamley Wood **SY4** 38 E2
Marchington **ST14** 40 D2
Marchington Woodlands **ST14** 40 D3
Marchwiel **LL13** 38 C1
Marchwood **SO40** 10 E3
Marcross **CF61** 18 C5
Marcus **DD8** 83 G2
Marden *Here.* **HR1** 28 E4
Marden *Kent* **TN12** 14 C3
Marden *T. & W.* **NE30** 71 J6
Marden *Wilts.* **SN10** 20 D6
Marden Ash **CM5** 23 J1
Marden Beech **TN12** 14 C3
Marden Thorn **TN12** 14 C3
Marden's Hill **TN6** 13 H3
Mardon **TD12** 77 H7
Mardy **NP7** 28 C7
Mare Green **TA3** 8 C2
Marefield **LE7** 42 A5
Mareham le Fen **PE22** 53 F6
Mareham on the Hill **LN9** 53 F6
Maresfield **TN22** 13 H4
Marfleet **HU9** 59 H6
Marford **LL12** 48 C7
Margam **SA13** 18 A3
Margaret Marsh **SP7** 9 H3
Margaret Roding **CM6** 33 J7
Margaretting **CM4** 24 C1
Margaretting Tye **CM4** 24 C1
**Margate CT9** 25 **K4**
Margnaheglish **KA27** 73 J7
Margreig **DG2** 65 J3
Margrove Park **TS12** 63 H5
Marham **PE33** 44 B5
Marhamchurch **EX23** 6 A5
Marholm **PE6** 42 E5
Marian Cwm **LL18** 47 J5
Mariandyrys **LL58** 46 E4
**Marian-glas LL73** 46 **D4**
Mariansleigh **EX36** 7 F3
Marine Town **ME12** 25 F4
Marishader **IV51** 93 K5
Maristow House **PL6** 4 E4
Mark **TA9** 19 G7
Mark Causeway **TA9** 19 G7
Mark Cross **TN6** 13 J3
Markbeech **TN8** 23 H7
Markby **LN13** 53 H5
Markdhu **DG8** 64 B3
Markeaton **DE22** 41 F2
Market Bosworth **CV13** 41 G5
Market Deeping **PE6** 42 E4
**Market Drayton TF9** 39 **F2**
**Market Harborough LE16** 42 **A7**
Market Lavington **SN10** 20 D6
Market Overton **LE15** 42 B4
**Market Rasen LN8** 52 **E4**
Market Stainton **LN8** 53 F5
Market Street **NR12** 45 G3
Market Warsop **NG20** 51 H6
Market Weighton **YO43** 58 E5
Market Weston **IP22** 34 D1
Markethill **PH13** 82 D4
**Markfield LE67** 41 **G4**
Markham **NP12** 18 E1
Markham Moor **DN22** 51 K5
Markinch **KY7** 82 D7
Markington **HG3** 57 H3
Marks Gate **RM6** 23 H2
Marks Tey **CO6** 34 D6
Marksbury **BA2** 19 K5
Markwell **PL12** 4 D5
Markyate **AL3** 32 D7
Marl Bank **WR14** 29 G4
Marland **OL11** 49 H1
**Marlborough SN8** 20 **E5**
Marlbrook **B60** 29 J1
Marlcliff **B50** 30 B3
Marldon **TQ3** 5 J4
Marle Green **TN21** 13 J5
Marlesford **IP13** 35 H3
Marley Green **SY13** 38 E1
Marley Hill **NE16** 62 D1
Marlingford **NR9** 45 F5
Marloes **SA62** 16 A5
**Marlow** ***Bucks.*** **SL7** 22 **B3**
Marlow *Here.* **SY7** 28 D1
Marlpit Hill **TN8** 23 H7
Marlpool **DE75** 41 G1
Marnhull **DT10** 9 G3
Marnoch **AB54** 98 D5
Marple **SK6** 49 J4
Marple Bridge **SK6** 49 J4
Marr **DN5** 51 H2
Marrel **KW8** 105 F7
Marrick **DL11** 62 B7
Marrister **ZE2** 107 P6
Marros **SA33** 17 F5
Marsden *T. & W.* **NE34** 71 J7
Marsden *W.Yorks.* **HD7** 50 C1
Marsett **DL8** 56 E1
Marsh **EX14** 8 B3
Marsh Baldon **OX44** 21 J2
Marsh Benham **RG20** 21 H5
Marsh Gibbon **OX27** 31 H6
Marsh Green *Devon* **EX5** 7 J6
Marsh Green *Gt.Man.* **WN5** 48 E2
Marsh Green *Kent* **TN8** 23 H7
Marsh Green *Tel. & W.* **TF6** 39 F4
Marsh Lane **S21** 51 G5
Marsh Street **TA24** 7 H1
Marshall Meadows **TD15** 77 H5
Marshalsea **DT6** 8 C4
Marshalswick **AL1** 22 E1
Marsham **NR10** 45 F3
Marshaw **LA2** 55 J4
Marshborough **CT13** 15 J2
Marshbrook **SY6** 38 D7
Marshchapel **DN36** 53 G3
Marshfield *Newport* **CF3** 19 F3
Marshfield *S.Glos.* **SN14** 20 A4
Marshgate **PL32** 4 B1
Marshland St. James **PE14** 43 J5
Marshside **PR9** 48 C1
Marshwood **DT6** 8 C5
Marske **DL11** 62 C6
Marske-by-the-Sea **TS11** 63 H4
Marsland Green **M29** 49 F3
Marston *Ches.W. & C.* **CW9** 49 F5
Marston *Here.* **HR6** 28 C3
Marston *Lincs.* **NG32** 42 B1
Marston *Oxon.* **OX3** 21 J1
Marston *Staffs.* **ST18** 40 B3
Marston *Staffs.* **ST20** 40 A4
Marston *Warks.* **B76** 40 E6
Marston *Wilts.* **SN10** 20 C6
Marston Doles **CV47** 31 F3
Marston Green **B37** 40 D7
Marston Magna **BA22** 8 E2
Marston Meysey **SN6** 20 E2
Marston Montgomery **DE6** 40 D2
Marston Moretaine **MK43** 32 C4
Marston on Dove **DE65** 40 E3
Marston St. Lawrence **OX17** 31 G4
Marston Stannett **HR6** 28 E3
Marston Trussell **LE16** 41 J7
Marstow **HR9** 28 E7
Marsworth **HP23** 32 C7
Marten **SN8** 21 F5
Marthall **WA16** 49 G5
Martham **NR29** 45 J4
Martin *Hants.* **SP6** 10 B3
Martin *Lincs.* **LN4** 52 E7
Martin *Lincs.* **LN9** 53 F6
Martin Drove End **SP6** 10 B2
Martin Hussingtree **WR3** 29 H2
Martinhoe **EX31** 6 E1
Martinscroft **WA1** 49 F4
Martinstown **DT2** 9 F6
Martlesham **IP12** 35 G4
Martlesham Heath **IP5** 35 G4
Martletwy **SA67** 16 D4
Martley **WR6** 29 G2
**Martock TA12** 8 **D3**
Marton *Ches.E.* **SK11** 49 H6
Marton *Cumb.* **LA12** 55 F2
Marton *E.Riding* **HU11** 59 H6
Marton *E.Riding* **YO15** 59 J3
Marton *Lincs.* **DN21** 52 B4
Marton *Middbro.* **TS7** 63 G5
Marton *N.Yorks.* **YO51** 57 K3
Marton *N.Yorks.* **YO62** 58 D1
Marton *Shrop.* **SY21** 38 B5
Marton *Shrop.* **SY4** 38 D3
Marton *Warks.* **CV23** 31 F2
Marton Abbey **YO61** 58 B3
Marton-in-the-Forest **YO61** 58 B3
Marton-le-Moor **HG4** 57 J2
Martyr Worthy **SO21** 11 G1
Martyr's Green **KT11** 22 D6
Marwick **KW17** 106 B5
Marwood **EX31** 6 D2
Mary Tavy **PL19** 5 F3
Marybank *High.* **IV6** 96 B6
Marybank *W.Isles* **HS2** 101 G4
Maryburgh **IV7** 96 C6
Maryfield *Cornw.* **PL11** 4 E5
Maryfield *Shet.* **ZE2** 107 N8
Marygold **TD11** 77 G5
Maryhill *Aber.* **AB53** 99 G6
Maryhill *Glas.* **G20** 74 D4
Marykirk **AB30** 83 H1
Marylebone *Gt.Lon.* **W1G** 23 F3
Marylebone *Gt.Man.* **WN1** 48 E2
Marypark **AB37** 89 J1
**Maryport** ***Cumb.*** **CA15** 60 **B3**
Maryport *D. & G.* **DG9** 64 B7
Marystow **PL16** 6 C7
Maryton **DD10** 83 H2
Marywell *Aber.* **AB12** 91 H5
Marywell *Aber.* **AB34** 90 D5
Marywell *Angus* **DD11** 83 H3
Masham **HG4** 57 H1
Mashbury **CM1** 33 K7
Masongill **LA6** 56 B2
Mastin Moor **S43** 51 G5
Mastrick **AB16** 91 H4
Matchborough **B98** 30 B2
Matching **CM17** 33 J7
Matching Green **CM17** 33 J7
Matching Tye **CM17** 33 J7
Matfen **NE20** 71 F6
Matfield **TN12** 23 K7
Mathern **NP16** 19 J2
Mathon **WR13** 29 G4
Mathry **SA62** 16 B2
Matlaske **NR11** 45 F2
**Matlock DE4** 51 **F6**
Matlock Bank **DE4** 51 F6
Matlock Bath **DE4** 50 E7
Matson **GL4** 29 H7
Matterdale End **CA11** 60 E4
Mattersey **DN10** 51 J4
Mattersey Thorpe **DN10** 51 J4
Mattingley **RG27** 22 A6
Mattishall **NR20** 44 E4
Mattishall Burgh **NR20** 44 E4
**Mauchline KA5** 67 **J1**
Maud **AB42** 99 H6
Maufant **JE2** 3 K7
Maugersbury **GL54** 30 C6
Maughold **IM7** 54 D4
Mauld **IV4** 87 K1
Maulden **MK45** 32 D5
Maulds Meaburn **CA10** 61 H5
Maunby **YO7** 57 J1
Maund Bryan **HR1** 28 E3
Maundown **TA4** 7 J3
Mautby **NR29** 45 J4
Mavesyn Ridware **WS15** 40 C4
Mavis Enderby **PE23** 53 G6
Maw Green **CW1** 49 G7
Mawbray **CA15** 60 B2
Mawdesley **L40** 48 D1
Mawdlam **CF33** 18 B3
Mawgan **TR12** 2 E6
Mawgan Porth **TR8** 3 F2
Mawla **TR16** 2 E4
Mawnan **TR11** 2 E6
Mawnan Smith **TR11** 2 E6
Mawsley **NN14** 32 B1
Mawthorpe **LN13** 53 H5
Maxey **PE6** 42 E5
Maxstoke **B46** 40 E7
Maxted Street **CT4** 15 G3
Maxton *Kent* **CT17** 15 J3
Maxton *Sc.Bord.* **TD6** 76 E7
Maxwellheugh **TD5** 77 F7
Maxwelltown **DG2** 65 K3
Maxworthy **PL15** 4 C1
May Hill **GL17** 29 G6
Mayals **SA3** 17 K6
**Maybole KA19** 67 **H3**
Maybury **GU22** 22 D6
Mayen **AB54** 98 D6
Mayfair **W1J** 23 F3
**Mayfield** ***E.Suss.*** **TN20** 13 **J4**
Mayfield *Midloth.* **EH22** 76 B4
Mayfield *Staffs.* **DE6** 40 D1
Mayford **GU22** 22 C6
Mayland **CM3** 25 F1
Maylandsea **CM3** 25 F1
Maynard's Green **TN21** 13 J5
Maypole *I.o.S.* **TR21** 2 C1
Maypole *Kent* **CT3** 25 H5
Maypole *Mon.* **NP25** 28 D7
Maypole Green *Essex* **CO2** 34 D6
Maypole Green *Norf.* **NR14** 45 J6
Maypole Green *Suff.* **IP13** 35 G2
Maypole Green *Suff.* **IP30** 34 D3
May's Green *N.Som.* **BS24** 19 G5
Mays Green *Oxon.* **RG9** 22 A3
Maywick **ZE2** 107 M10
Mead **EX39** 6 A4
Mead End **SP5** 10 B2
Meadgate **BA2** 19 K6
Meadle **HP17** 22 B1
Meadow Green **WR6** 29 G3
Meadowhall **S9** 51 F3
Meadowmill **EH33** 76 C3
Meadowtown **SY5** 38 C5
Meadwell **PL16** 6 C7
Meaford **ST15** 40 A2
Meal Bank **LA9** 61 G7

Mea - Min

Mealabost (Melbost Borve) HS2 101 G2
Mealasta HS2 100 B5
Meals LN11 53 H3
Mealsgate CA7 60 D2
Meanley BB7 56 C5
Meanwood LS6 57 H6
Mearbeck BD23 56 D3
Meare BA6 19 H7
Meare Green TA3 8 B2
Mearns G77 74 D5
Mears Ashby NN6 32 B2
Measham DE12 41 F4
Meathop LA11 55 H1
Meavy PL20 5 F4
Medbourne LE16 42 B6
Meddon EX39 6 A4
Meden Vale NG20 51 H6
Medlar PR4 55 H6
Medmenham SL7 22 B3
Medomsley DH8 62 C1
Medstead GU34 11 H1
Meer Common HR3 28 C3
Meer End CV8 30 D1
Meerbrook ST13 49 J6
Meesden SG9 33 H5
Meeson TF6 39 F3
Meeth EX20 6 D5
Meeting House Hill NR28 45 H3
Meggethead TD7 69 G1
Meidrim SA33 17 F3
Meifod Denb. LL16 47 J7
Meifod Powys SY22 38 A4
Meigle PH12 82 D3
Meikle Earnock ML3 75 F5
Meikle Grenach PA20 73 J4
Meikle Kilmory PA20 73 J4
Meikle Rahane G84 74 A2
Meikle Strath AB30 90 E7
Meikle Tarty AB41 91 H2
Meikle Wartle AB51 91 F1
Meikleour PH2 82 C4
Meikleyard KA4 74 D7
Meinciau SA17 17 H4
Meir ST3 40 B1
Meirheath ST3 40 B2
Melbost HS2 101 G4
Melbost Borve (Mealabost) HS2 101 G2
Melbourn SG8 33 G4
Melbourne Derbys. DE73 41 F3
Melbourne E.Riding YO42 58 D5
Melbury EX39 6 B4
Melbury Abbas SP7 9 H3
Melbury Bubb DT2 8 E4
Melbury Osmond DT2 8 E4
Melbury Sampford DT2 8 E4
Melby ZE2 107 K7
Melchbourne MK44 32 D2
Melcombe Bingham DT2 9 G4
Melcombe Regis DT4 9 F6
Meldon Devon EX20 6 D6
Meldon Northumb. NE61 71 G5
Meldreth SG8 33 G4
Meledor PL26 3 G3
Melfort PA34 79 K6
Melgarve PH20 88 B5
Melgum AB34 90 C4
Meliden (Gallt Melyd) LL19 47 J4
Melincourt SA11 18 B1
Melin-y-coed LL26 47 G6
Melin-y-ddol SY21 37 K5
Melin-y-grug SY21 37 K5
Melin-y-Wig LL21 37 K1
Melkinthorpe CA10 61 G4
Melkridge NE49 70 C7
Melksham SN12 20 C5
Melksham Forest SN12 20 C5
Melldalloch PA21 73 H3
Melling Lancs. LA6 55 J2
Melling Mersey. L31 48 C2
Melling Mount L31 48 D2
Mellis IP23 34 E1
Mellon Charles IV22 94 E2
Mellon Udrigle IV22 94 E2
Mellor Gt.Man. SK6 49 J4
Mellor Lancs. BB2 56 B6
Mellor Brook BB2 56 B6
Mells BA11 20 A7
Melmerby Cumb. CA10 61 H3
Melmerby N.Yorks. DL8 57 F1
Melmerby N.Yorks. HG4 57 J2
Melplash DT6 8 D5
Melrose Aber. AB45 99 F4
Melrose Sc.Bord. TD6 76 D7
Melsetter KW16 106 B9
Melsonby DL10 62 C6
Meltham HD9 50 C1
Melton E.Riding HU14 59 F7
Melton Suff. IP12 35 G3
Melton Constable NR24 44 E2
Melton Mowbray LE13 42 A4
Melton Ross DN38 52 D1
Meltonby YO42 58 D4
Melvaig IV21 94 D3
Melverley SY10 38 C4
Melverley Green SY10 38 C4
Melvich KW14 104 D2
Membury EX13 8 B4
Memsie AB43 99 H4
Memus DD8 83 F2
Menabilly PL24 4 A5
Menai Bridge (Porthaethwy) LL59 46 D5
Mendham IP20 45 G7
Mendlesham IP14 35 F2
Mendlesham Green IP14 34 E2
Menethorpe YO17 58 D3
Menheniot PL14 4 C4
Menie House AB23 91 H2
Menithwood WR6 29 G2
Mennock DG4 68 D3
Menston LS29 57 G5
Menstrie FK11 75 G1
Mentmore LU7 32 C7
Meoble PH40 86 D6
Meole Brace SY3 38 D4
Meon PO14 11 G4
Meonstoke SO32 11 H3
Meopham DA13 24 C5
Meopham Green DA13 24 C5
Mepal CB6 43 H7
Meppershall SG17 32 E5
Merbach HR3 28 C4
Mercaston DE6 40 E1
Mere Ches.E. WA16 49 G4
Mere Wilts. BA12 9 H1
Mere Brow PR9 48 D1
Mere Green B75 40 D6
Mere Heath CW9 49 F5
Mereclough BB10 56 D6
Mereside FY4 55 G6
Meretown TF10 39 G3
Mereworth ME18 23 K6
Mergie AB39 91 F6
Meriden CV7 40 E7
Merkadale IV47 85 J1
Merkinch IV3 96 D7
Merkland DG7 65 H3
Merley BH21 10 B5
Merlin's Bridge SA61 16 C4
Merridge TA5 8 B1
Merrifield TQ7 5 J6
Merrington SY4 38 D3
Merrion SA71 16 C6
Merriott TA16 8 D3
Merrivale PL19 5 F3
Merrow GU1 22 D6
Merry Hill Herts. WD23 22 E2
Merry Hill W.Mid. DY5 40 B7
Merry Hill W.Mid. WV3 40 A6
Merrymeet PL14 4 C4
Mersea Island CO5 34 E7
Mersham TN25 15 F4
Merstham RH1 23 F6
Merston PO20 12 B6
Merstone PO30 11 G6
Merther TR2 3 F4
Merthyr SA33 17 G3
Merthyr Cynog LD3 27 J5
Merthyr Dyfan CF62 18 E5
Merthyr Mawr CF32 18 B4
Merthyr Tydfil CF47 18 D1
Merthyr Vale CF48 18 D2
Merton Devon EX20 6 D4
Merton Norf. IP25 44 D6
Merton Oxon. OX25 31 G7
Mervinslaw TD8 70 B2
Meshaw EX36 7 F4
Messing CO5 34 D7
Messingham DN17 52 B2
Metcombe EX11 7 J6
Metfield IP20 45 G7
Metheringham LN4 52 D6
Metherwell PL17 4 E4
Methil KY8 76 B1
Methlem LL53 36 A2
Methley LS26 57 J7
Methley Junction LS26 57 J7
Methlick AB41 91 G1
Methven PH1 82 B5
Methwold IP26 44 B6
Methwold Hythe IP26 44 B6
MetroCentre NE11 71 H7
Mettingham NR35 45 H7
Metton NR11 45 F2
Mevagissey PL26 4 A6
Mewith Head LA2 56 C3
Mexborough S64 51 G3
Mey KW14 105 H1
Meysey Hampton GL7 20 E1
Miabhag W.Isles HS3 93 G2
Miabhag W.Isles HS3 100 C7
Miabhaig (Miavaig) HS2 100 C4
Mial IV21 94 D4
Miavaig (Miabhaig) HS2 100 C4
Michaelchurch HR2 28 E6
Michaelchurch Escley HR2 28 C5
Michaelchurch-on-Arrow HR5 28 B3
Michaelston-le-Pit CF64 18 E4
Michaelston-super-Ely CF5 18 E4
Michaelston-y-Fedw CF3 19 F3
Michaelstow PL30 4 A3
Michelcombe TQ13 5 G4
Micheldever SO21 11 G1
Michelmersh SO51 10 E2
Mickfield IP14 35 F2
Mickle Trafford CH2 48 D6
Micklebring S66 51 H3
Mickleby TS13 63 K5
Micklefield LS25 57 K6
Micklefield Green WD3 22 D2
Mickleham RH5 22 E6
Micklehurst OL5 49 J2
Mickleover DE3 41 F2
Micklethwaite Cumb. CA7 60 D1
Micklethwaite W.Yorks. BD20 57 F5
Mickleton Dur. DL12 62 A4
Mickleton Glos. GL55 30 C4
Mickletown LS26 57 J7
Mickley Derbys. S18 51 F5
Mickley N.Yorks. HG4 57 H2
Mickley Green IP29 34 C3
Mickley Square NE43 71 F7
Mid Ardlaw AB43 99 H4
Mid Beltie AB31 90 E4
Mid Calder EH53 75 J4
Mid Clyth KW3 105 H5
Mid Lambrook TA13 8 D3
Mid Lavant PO18 12 B6
Mid Letter PA27 80 B7
Mid Lix FK21 81 G4
Mid Mossdale DL8 61 K7
Mid Yell ZE2 107 P3
Midbea KW17 106 D3
Middle Assendon RG9 22 A3
Middle Aston OX25 31 F6
Middle Barton OX7 31 F6
Middle Bickenhill B92 40 E7
Middle Bockhampton BH23 10 C5
Middle Claydon MK18 31 J6
Middle Drift PL14 4 B4
Middle Drums DD9 83 G2
Middle Duntisbourne GL7 20 C1
Middle Handley S21 51 G5
Middle Harling NR16 44 D7
Middle Kames PA31 73 H2
Middle Littleton WR11 30 B4
Middle Maes-coed HR2 28 C5
Middle Marwood EX31 6 D2
Middle Mill SA62 16 B3
Middle Quarter TN26 14 D4
Middle Rasen LN8 52 D4
Middle Rigg PH2 82 B7
Middle Salter LA2 56 B3
Middle Sontley LL13 38 C1
Middle Stoford TA21 7 K3
Middle Taphouse PL14 4 B4
Middle Town TR25 2 C1
Middle Tysoe CV35 30 E4
Middle Wallop SO20 10 D1
Middle Winterslow SP5 10 D1
Middle Woodford SP4 10 C1
Middlebie DG11 69 H6
Middlecliff S72 51 G2
Middlecott EX22 6 C5
Middleham DL8 57 G1
Middlehill Aber. AB53 99 G6
Middlehill Cornw. PL14 4 C4
Middlehope SY7 38 E7
Middlemarsh DT9 9 F4
Middlemoor PL19 4 E3
Middlequarter (Ceathramh Meadhanach) HS6 92 D4
Middlesbrough TS1 63 F4
Middlesceugh CA4 60 F2
Middleshaw LA8 55 J1
Middlesmoor HG3 57 F2
Middlestone DL16 62 D3
Middlestone Moor DL16 62 D3
Middlestown WF4 50 E1
Middleton Aber. AB21 91 G3
Middleton Angus DD11 83 G3
Middleton Cumb. LA6 56 B1
Middleton Derbys. DE4 50 E7
Middleton Derbys. DE45 50 D6
Middleton Essex CO10 34 C4
Middleton Gt.Man. M24 49 H2
Middleton Hants. SP11 21 H7
Middleton Here. SY8 28 E2
Middleton Lancs. LA3 55 H4
Middleton Midloth. EH23 76 B5
Middleton N.Yorks. YO18 58 D1
Middleton Norf. PE32 44 A4
Middleton Northants. LE16 42 B7
Middleton Northumb. NE61 71 F5
Middleton Northumb. NE70 77 J7
Middleton P.& K. KY13 82 C7
Middleton P.& K. PH10 82 C3
Middleton Shrop. SY15 38 B6
Middleton Shrop. SY8 28 E1
Middleton Shrop. SY11 38 C3
Middleton Suff. IP17 35 J2
Middleton Swan. SA3 17 H7
Middleton W.Yorks. LS29 57 G5
Middleton W.Yorks. LS10 57 J7
Middleton Warks. B78 40 D6
Middleton Baggot WV16 39 F6
Middleton Bank Top NE61 71 F5
Middleton Cheney OX17 31 F4
Middleton Green ST10 40 B2
Middleton Hall NE71 70 E1
Middleton Moor IP17 35 J2
Middleton of Potterton AB23 91 H3
Middleton on the Hill SY8 28 E2
Middleton One Row DL2 62 E5
Middleton Park AB22 91 H3
Middleton Priors WV16 39 F7
Middleton Quernhow HG4 57 J2
Middleton St. George DL2 62 E5
Middleton Scriven WV16 39 F7
Middleton Stoney OX25 31 G6
Middleton Tyas DL10 62 D6
Middleton-in-Teesdale DL12 62 A4
Middleton-on-Leven TS15 63 F5
Middleton-on-Sea PO22 12 C6
Middleton-on-the-Wolds YO25 59 F5
Middletown Cumb. CA22 60 A6
Middletown Powys SY21 38 C4
Middlewich CW10 49 G6
Middlewood Ches.E. SK12 49 J4
Middlewood S.Yorks. S6 51 F3
Middlewood Green IP14 34 E2
Middlezoy TA7 8 C1
Middridge DL4 62 D4
Midfield IV27 103 H2
Midford BA2 20 A5
Midge Hall PR26 55 J7
Midgeholme CA8 61 H1
Midgham RG7 21 J5
Midgley W.Yorks. WF4 50 E1
Midgley W.Yorks. HX2 57 F7
Midhopestones S36 50 E3
Midhurst GU29 12 B4
Midlem TD7 70 A1
Midloe Grange PE19 32 E2
Midpark PA20 73 J5
Midsomer Norton BA3 19 K6
Midthorpe LN9 53 F5
Midtown High. IV27 103 H2
Midtown High. IV22 94 E3
Midtown of Barras AB39 91 G6
Midville PE22 53 G7
Midway DE11 41 F3
Migdale IV24 96 D2
Migvie AB34 90 C4
Milarrochy G63 74 C1
Milber TQ12 5 J3
Milbethill AB54 98 E5
Milborne Port DT9 9 F3
Milborne St. Andrew DT11 9 G5
Milborne Wick DT9 9 F2
Milbourne Northumb. NE20 71 G6
Milbourne Wilts. SN16 20 C3
Milburn CA10 61 H4
Milbury Heath GL12 19 K2
Milcombe OX15 31 F5
Milden IP7 34 D4
Mildenhall Suff. IP28 34 B1
Mildenhall Wilts. SN8 21 F5
Mile Elm SN11 20 C5
Mile End Essex CO4 34 D6
Mile End Glos. GL16 28 E7
Mile Oak TN12 23 K7
Mile Town ME12 25 F4
Milebrook LD7 28 C1
Milebush TN12 14 C3
Mileham PE32 44 D4
Miles Green ST7 40 A1
Miles Hope WR15 28 E2
Milesmark KY12 75 J2
Miles's Green RG7 21 J5
Milfield NE71 77 H7
Milford Derbys. DE56 41 F1
Milford Devon EX39 6 A3
Milford Shrop. SY4 38 D3
Milford Staffs. ST17 40 B3
Milford Surr. GU8 22 C7
Milford Haven (Aberdaugleddau) SA73 16 B5
Milford on Sea SO41 10 D5
Milkwall GL16 19 J1
Mill Bank HX6 57 F7
Mill Brow SK6 49 J4
Mill End Bucks. RG9 22 A3
Mill End Cambs. CB8 33 K3
Mill End Herts. SG9 33 G5
Mill End Green CM6 33 K6
Mill Green Cambs. CB21 33 K4
Mill Green Essex CM4 24 C1
Mill Green Herts. AL9 23 F1
Mill Green Norf. IP22 45 F7
Mill Green Shrop. TF9 39 F3
Mill Green Staffs. WS15 40 C3
Mill Green Suff. IP13 35 H2
Mill Green Suff. IP14 35 F3
Mill Green Suff. IP14 34 D3
Mill Green W.Mid. WS9 40 C5
Mill Hill B'burn. BB2 56 B7
Mill Hill Cambs. SG19 33 F3
Mill Hill Gt.Lon. NW7 23 F2
Mill Houses LA2 56 B3
Mill Lane GU10 22 A6
Mill of Camsail G84 74 A2
Mill of Colp AB53 99 F6
Mill of Elrick AB41 99 H6
Mill of Fortune PH6 81 J5
Mill of Kingoodie AB21 91 G2
Mill of Monquich AB39 91 G5
Mill of Uras AB39 91 G6
Mill Side LA11 55 H1
Mill Street Kent ME19 23 K6
Mill Street Norf. NR20 44 E4
Milland GU30 12 B4
Millbank AB42 99 J6
Millbeck CA12 60 D4
Millbounds KW17 106 E4
Millbreck AB42 99 J6
Millbridge GU10 22 B7
Millbrook Cen.Beds. MK45 32 D5
Millbrook Cornw. PL10 4 E5
Millbrook Devon EX13 8 C5
Millbrook S'ham. SO15 10 E3
Millburn Aber. AB33 90 D2
Millburn Aber. AB54 90 E1
Millcombe TQ9 5 J6
Millcorner TN31 14 D5
Milldale DE6 50 D7
Millden AB23 91 H3
Milldens DD8 83 G2
Millearne PH7 82 A6
Millend OX7 30 E6
Millenheath SY13 38 E2
Millerhill EH22 76 B4
Miller's Dale SK17 50 D5
Millers Green Derbys. DE4 50 E7
Miller's Green Essex CM5 23 J1
Millgate OL12 56 D7
Millhalf HR3 28 B4
Millhayes Devon EX15 7 K4
Millhayes Devon EX14 8 B4
Millholme LA8 61 G7
Millhouse Arg. & B. PA21 73 H3
Millhouse Cumb. CA7 60 E3
Millhouse Green S36 50 E2
Millhousebridge DG11 69 G5
Millikenpark PA10 74 C4
Millin Cross SA62 16 C4
Millington YO42 58 E4
Millington Green DE6 40 E1
Millmeece ST21 40 A2
Millness IV63 87 K1
Millom LA18 54 E1
Millow SG18 33 F4
Millpool PL30 4 B3
Millport KA28 73 K5
Millthorpe S18 51 F5
Millthrop LA10 61 H7
Milltimber AB13 91 G4
Milltown Aber. AB36 89 K4
Milltown Cornw. PL22 4 B5
Milltown D. & G. DG14 69 J6
Milltown Derbys. S45 51 F6
Milltown Devon EX31 6 D2
Milltown High. IV12 97 G7
Milltown of Aberdalgie PH2 82 B5
Milltown of Auchindoun AB55 90 B1
Milltown of Craigston AB53 99 F5
Milltown of Edinvillie AB38 97 K7
Milltown of Kildrummy AB33 90 C3
Milltown of Rothiemay AB54 98 D6
Milltown of Towie AB33 90 C3
Milnathort KY13 82 C7
Milners Heath CH3 48 D6
Milngavie G62 74 D3
Milnrow OL16 49 J1
Milnsbridge HD3 50 D1
Milnthorpe LA7 55 H1
Milovaig IV55 93 G6
Milrig KA4 74 D7
Milson DY14 29 F1
Milstead ME9 14 E2
Milston SP4 20 E7
Milton Angus DD8 82 E3
Milton Cambs. CB24 33 H2
Milton Cumb. CA8 70 A7
Milton D. & G. DG2 68 D5
Milton D. & G. DG2 65 J3
Milton D. & G. DG8 64 C5
Milton Derbys. DE65 41 F3
Milton High. IV6 95 K6
Milton High. IV18 96 E4
Milton High. IV12 97 G6
Milton High. IV54 94 D7
Milton High. IV6 96 C7
Milton High. KW1 105 J3
Milton High. IV63 88 B1
Milton Moray AB56 98 D4
Milton N.Som. BS22 19 G5
Milton Newport NP19 19 G3
Milton Notts. NG22 51 K5
Milton Oxon. OX15 31 F5
Milton Oxon. OX14 21 H2
Milton P. & K. PH8 82 A4
Milton Pembs. SA70 16 D5
Milton Ports. PO4 11 H5
Milton Som. TA12 8 D2
Milton Stir. FK8 81 G7
Milton Stoke ST2 49 J7
Milton W.Dun. G82 74 C3
Milton Abbas DT11 9 H4
Milton Abbot PL19 4 E3
Milton Bridge EH26 76 A4
Milton Bryan MK17 32 C5
Milton Clevedon BA4 9 F1
Milton Combe PL20 4 E4
Milton Damerel EX22 6 B4
Milton End GL2 29 G7
Milton Ernest MK44 32 D3
Milton Green CH3 48 D7
Milton Hill OX13 21 H2
MILTON KEYNES MK 32 B5
Milton Keynes Village MK10 32 B5
Milton Lilbourne SN9 20 E5
Milton Malsor NN7 31 J3
Milton Morenish FK21 81 H4
Milton of Auchinhove AB31 90 D4
Milton of Balgonie KY7 82 E7
Milton of Buchanan G63 74 C1
Milton of Cairnborrow AB54 98 C6
Milton of Callander FK17 81 G7
Milton of Campfield AB31 90 E4
Milton of Campsie G66 74 E3
Milton of Coldwells AB41 91 H1
Milton of Cullerlie AB32 91 F4
Milton of Cushnie AB33 90 D3
Milton of Dalcapon PH9 82 A2
Milton of Inveramsay AB51 91 F2
Milton of Noth AB54 90 D2
Milton of Tullich AB35 90 B5
Milton on Stour SP8 9 G2
Milton Regis ME10 24 E5
Milton Street BN26 13 J6
Miltonduff IV30 97 J5
Miltonhill IV36 97 H5
Miltonise DG8 64 B3
Milton-Lockhart ML8 75 G6
Milton-under-Wychwood OX7 30 D7
Milverton Som. TA4 7 K3
Milverton Warks. CV32 30 E2
Milwich ST18 40 B2
Mimbridge GU24 22 C5
Minard PA32 73 H1
Minard Castle PA32 73 H1
Minchington DT11 9 J3
Minchinhampton GL6 20 B1
Mindrum TD12 77 G7
Mindrummill TD12 77 G7
Minehead TA24 7 H1
Minera LL11 48 B7
Minety SN16 20 D2
Minety Lower Moor SN16 20 D2

## Min - Nai

Minffordd *Gwyn.* **LL40** **37** G4
Minffordd *Gwyn.* **LL48** **36** E2
Minffordd *Gwyn.* **LL57** **46** D5
Miningsby **PE22** **53** G6
Minions **PL14** **4** C3
Minishant **KA19** **67** H2
Minley Manor **GU17** **22** B6
Minllyn **SY20** **37** H4
Minnes **AB41** **91** H2
Minngearraidh **HS8** **84** C2
Minnigaff **DG8** **64** E4
Minnonie **AB45** **99** F4
Minskip **YO51** **57** J3
Minstead **SO43** **10** D3
Minsted **GU29** **12** B4
Minster *Kent* **ME12** **25** F4
Minster *Kent* **CT12** **25** K5
Minster Lovell **OX29** **30** E7
Minsteracres **NE44** **62** B1
Minsterley **SY5** **38** C5
Minsterworth **GL2** **29** G7
Minterne Magna **DT2** **9** F4
Minterne Parva **DT2** **9** F4
Minting **LN9** **52** E5
Mintlaw **AB42** **99** J6
Minto **TD9** **70** A1
Minton **SY6** **38** D6
Minwear **SA67** **16** D4
Minworth **B76** **40** D6
Miodar **PA77** **78** B2
Mirbister **KW17** **106** C6
Mirehouse **CA28** **60** A5
Mireland **KW1** **105** J2
**Mirfield WF14 57 H7**
Miserden **GL6** **20** C1
Miskin *R.C.T.* **CF72** **18** D3
Miskin *R.C.T.* **CF45** **18** D2
Misselfore **SP5** **10** B2
Misson **DN10** **51** J3
Misterton *Leics.* **LE17** **41** H7
Misterton *Notts.* **DN10** **51** K3
Misterton *Som.* **TA18** **8** D4
Mistley **CO11** **35** F5
**Mitcham CR4 23 F5**
Mitchel Troy **NP25** **28** D7
**Mitcheldean GL17 29 F7**
Mitchell **TR8** **3** F3
Mitchelland **LA8** **60** F7
Mitcheltroy Common **NP25** **19** H1
Mitford **NE61** **71** G5
Mithian **TR5** **2** E3
Mitton **ST19** **40** A4
Mixbury **NN13** **31** H5
Mixenden **HX2** **57** F7
Moar **PH15** **81** G3
Moat **CA6** **69** K6
Moats Tye **IP14** **34** E3
Mobberley *Ches.E.* **WA16** **49** G5
Mobberley *Staffs.* **ST10** **40** C1
Moccas **HR2** **28** C4
Mochdre *Conwy* **LL28** **47** G5
Mochdre *Powys* **SY16** **37** K7
Mochrum **DG8** **64** D6
Mockbeggar *Hants.* **BH24** **10** C4
Mockbeggar *Kent* **TN12** **14** C3
Mockerkin **CA13** **60** B4
Modbury **PL21** **5** G5
Moddershall **ST15** **40** B2
Modsarie **KW14** **103** J2
**Moelfre *I.o.A.* LL72 46 D4**
Moelfre *Powys* **SY10** **38** A3
**Moffat DG10 69 F3**
Mogerhanger **MK44** **32** E4
Moin'a'choire **PA44** **72** B4
Moine House **IV27** **103** H3
Moira **DE12** **41** F4
Molash **CT4** **15** F2
Mol-chlach **PH41** **85** K3
**Mold (Yr Wyddgrug) CH7 48 B6**
Molehill Green *Essex* **CM6** **33** J6
Molehill Green *Essex* **CM6** **34** B6
Molescroft **HU17** **59** G5
Molesden **NE61** **71** G5
Molesworth **PE28** **32** D1
Mollance **DG7** **65** H4
Molland **EX36** **7** G3
Mollington *Ches.W. & C.* **CH1** **48** C5
Mollington *Oxon.* **OX17** **31** F4
Mollinsburn **G67** **75** F3
Monach Islands (Heisker Islands) **HS6** **92** B5
Monachty **SY23** **26** E2
Monachyle **FK19** **81** F6
Monevechadan **PA24** **80** C7
Monewden **IP13** **35** G3
Moneydie **PH1** **82** B5
Moneyrow Green **SL6** **22** B4
Moniaive **DG3** **68** C4
Monifieth **DD5** **83** G4
Monikie **DD5** **83** G4
Monimail **KY15** **82** D6
Monington **SA43** **16** E1
Monk Bretton **S71** **51** F2
Monk Fryston **LS25** **58** B7
Monk Hesleden **TS27** **63** F3
Monk Sherborne **RG26** **21** K6
Monk Soham **IP13** **35** G2
Monk Soham Green **IP13** **35** G2
Monk Street **CM6** **33** K6
Monken Hadley **EN5** **23** F2
Monkerton **EX1** **7** H6
Monkhide **HR8** **29** F4
Monkhill **CA5** **60** E1
Monkhopton **WV16** **39** F6
Monkland **HR6** **28** D3
Monkleigh **EX39** **6** C3
Monknash **CF71** **18** C4
Monkokehampton **EX19** **6** D5
Monks Eleigh **IP7** **34** D4
Monks Eleigh Tye **IP7** **34** D4
Monk's Gate **RH13** **13** F4
Monks' Heath **SK10** **49** H5
Monk's Hill **TN27** **14** D3
Monks Kirby **CV23** **41** G7
Monks Risborough **HP27** **22** B1
Monkscross **PL17** **4** D3
Monkseaton **NE25** **71** J6
Monkshill **AB53** **99** F6
Monksilver **TA4** **7** J2
Monkstadt **IV51** **93** J5
Monkswood **NP15** **19** G1
Monkton *Devon* **EX14** **7** K5
Monkton *Kent* **CT12** **25** J5
Monkton *Pembs.* **SA71** **16** C5
Monkton *S.Ayr.* **KA9** **67** H1
Monkton *T. & W.* **NE32** **71** J7
Monkton *V. of Glam.* **CF71** **18** C4
Monkton Combe **BA2** **20** A5
Monkton Deverill **BA12** **9** H1
Monkton Farleigh **BA15** **20** B5
Monkton Heathfield **TA2** **8** B2
Monkton Up Wimborne **BH21** **10** B3
Monkton Wyld **DT6** **8** C5
Monkwearmouth **SR6** **62** E1
Monkwood **SO24** **11** H1
**Monmouth (Trefynwy) NP25 28 E7**
Monnington Court **HR2** **28** C5
Monnington on Wye **HR4** **28** C4
Monreith **DG8** **64** D6
**Montacute TA15 8 E3**
Monteach **AB41** **99** G6
Montford **SY4** **38** D4
Montford Bridge **SY4** **38** D4
Montgarrie **AB33** **90** D3
**Montgomery (Trefaldwyn) SY15 38 B6**
Montgreenan **KA13** **74** B6
Montrave **KY8** **82** E7
**Montrose DD10 83 J2**
Monxton **SP11** **21** G7
Monyash **DE45** **50** D6
Monymusk **AB51** **90** E3
Monzie **PH7** **81** K5
Moodiesburn **G69** **74** E3
Moons Moat North **B98** **30** B2
Moonzie **KY15** **82** E6
Moor Allerton **LS17** **57** J6
Moor Cock **LA2** **56** B3
Moor Crichel **BH21** **9** J4
Moor End *Bed.* **MK43** **32** D3
Moor End *Cen.Beds.* **LU6** **32** C6
Moor End *Cumb.* **LA6** **55** J2
Moor End *E.Riding* **YO43** **58** E6
Moor End *Lancs.* **FY6** **55** G5
Moor End *N.Yorks.* **YO19** **58** B6
Moor End *W.Yorks.* **HX2** **57** F7
Moor Green *W.Mid.* **B13** **40** C7
Moor Green *Wilts.* **SN13** **20** B5
Moor Head **BD18** **57** G6
Moor Monkton **YO26** **58** B4
**Moor Row CA24 60 B5**
Moor Side *Cumb.* **LA16** **55** F2
Moor Side *Lancs.* **PR4** **55** H6
Moor Side *Lancs.* **PR4** **55** H6
Moor Side *Lincs.* **PE22** **53** F7
Moor Street **ME8** **24** E5
Moorby **PE22** **53** F6
Moorcot **HR5** **28** C3
Moordown **BH9** **10** B5
Moore **WA4** **48** E4
Moorend **CA5** **60** E1
Moorends **DN8** **51** J1
Moorfield **SK13** **50** C3
Moorgreen *Hants.* **SO30** **11** F3
Moorgreen *Notts.* **NG16** **41** G1
Moorhall **S18** **51** F5
Moorhampton **HR4** **28** C4
Moorhouse *Cumb.* **CA5** **60** E1
Moorhouse *Notts.* **NG23** **51** K6
Moorland (Northmoor Green) **TA7** **8** C1
Moorlinch **TA7** **8** C1
Moorsholm **TS12** **63** H5
Moorside *Dorset* **DT10** **9** G3
Moorside *Gt.Man.* **OL1** **49** J2
Moorside *W.Yorks.* **LS13** **57** H6
Moorthorpe **WF9** **51** G1
Moortown *I.o.W.* **PO30** **11** F6
Moortown *Lincs.* **LN7** **52** D3
Moortown *Tel. & W.* **TF6** **39** F4
Morangie **IV19** **96** E3
Morar **PH40** **86** C5
Morborne **PE7** **42** E6
Morchard Bishop **EX17** **7** F5
Morcombelake **DT6** **8** D5
Morcott **LE15** **42** C5
Morda **SY10** **38** B3
Morden *Dorset* **BH20** **9** J5
**Morden *Gt.Lon.* SM4 23 F5**
Morden Park **SM4** **23** F5
Mordiford **HR1** **28** E5
Mordington Holdings **TD15** **77** H5
Mordon **TS21** **62** E4
More **SY9** **38** C6
Morebath **EX16** **7** H3
Morebattle **TD5** **70** C1
**Morecambe LA4 55 H3**
Morefield **IV26** **95** H2
Moreleigh **TQ9** **5** H5
Morenish **FK21** **81** H4
Moresby Parks **CA28** **60** A5
Morestead **SO21** **11** G2
Moreton *Dorset* **DT2** **9** H6
Moreton *Essex* **CM5** **23** J1
Moreton *Here.* **HR6** **28** E2
Moreton *Mersey.* **CH46** **48** B4
Moreton *Oxon.* **OX9** **21** K1
Moreton *Staffs.* **DE6** **40** D2
Moreton *Staffs.* **TF10** **39** G4
Moreton Corbet **SY4** **38** E3
Moreton Jeffries **HR1** **29** F4
Moreton Mill **SY4** **38** E3
Moreton Morrell **CV35** **30** E3
Moreton on Lugg **HR4** **28** E4
Moreton Paddox **CV35** **30** E3
Moreton Pinkney **NN11** **31** G4
Moreton Say **TF9** **39** F2
Moreton Valence **GL2** **20** A1
Moretonhampstead **TQ13** **7** F7
**Moreton-in-Marsh GL56 30 D5**
Morfa *Carmar.* **SA14** **17** J4
Morfa *Cere.* **SA44** **26** C3
Morfa Bychan **LL49** **36** E2
Morfa Glas **SA11** **18** B1
Morfa Nefyn **LL53** **36** B1
Morgan's Vale **SP5** **10** C2
Morganstown **CF15** **18** E3
Mork **GL15** **19** J1
Morland **CA10** **61** G4
Morley *Derbys.* **DE7** **41** F1
Morley *Dur.* **DL14** **62** C4
Morley *W.Yorks.* **LS27** **57** H7
Morley Green **SK9** **49** H4
Morley St. Botolph **NR18** **44** E6
Mornick **PL17** **4** D3
Morningside *Edin.* **EH10** **76** A3
Morningside *N.Lan.* **ML2** **75** G5
Morningthorpe **NR15** **45** G6
**Morpeth NE61 71 H5**
Morphie **DD10** **83** J1
Morrey **DE13** **40** D4
Morridge Side **ST13** **50** C7
Morrilow Heath **ST10** **40** B2
Morriston *S.Ayr.* **KA19** **67** G3
Morriston *Swan.* **SA6** **17** K6
Morristown **CF64** **18** E4
Morroch **PH39** **86** C6
Morston **NR25** **44** E1
Mortehoe **EX34** **6** C1
Morthen **S66** **51** G4
Mortimer **RG7** **21** K5
Mortimer West End **RG7** **21** K5
Mortimer's Cross **HR6** **28** D2
Mortlake **SW14** **23** F4
Morton *Derbys.* **DE55** **51** G6
Morton *Lincs.* **PE10** **42** D3
Morton *Lincs.* **DN21** **52** B3
Morton *Lincs.* **LN6** **52** B6
Morton *Notts.* **NG25** **51** K7
Morton *S.Glos.* **BS35** **19** K2
Morton *Shrop.* **SY10** **38** B3
Morton Bagot **B80** **30** C2
Morton on the Hill **NR9** **45** F4
Morton Tinmouth **DL2** **62** C4
Morton-on-Swale **DL7** **62** E7
Morvah **TR20** **2** B5
Morval **PL13** **4** C5
Morvich *High.* **IV40** **87** F2
Morvich *High.* **IV28** **96** E1
Morvil **SA66** **16** D2
Morville **WV16** **39** F6
Morwellham **PL19** **4** E4
Morwenstow **EX23** **6** A4
Morwick Hall **NE65** **71** H3
Mosborough **S20** **51** G4
Moscow **KA4** **74** C6
Mosedale **CA11** **60** E3
Moselden Height **HD3** **50** C1
Moseley *W.Mid.* **B13** **40** C7
Moseley *W.Mid.* **WV1** **40** B6
Moseley *Worcs.* **WR2** **29** H3
Moses Gate **BL3** **49** G2
Moss *Arg. & B.* **PA77** **78** A3
Moss *S.Yorks.* **DN6** **51** H1
Moss *Wrex.* **LL11** **48** C7
Moss Bank **WA11** **48** E3
Moss Houses **SK11** **49** H5
Moss Nook **M22** **49** H4
Moss of Barmuckity **IV30** **97** K5
Moss Side *Gt.Man.* **M14** **49** H3
Moss Side *Lancs.* **FY8** **55** G6
Moss Side *Mersey.* **L31** **48** C2
Mossat **AB33** **90** C3
Mossbank **ZE2** **107** N5
Mossblown **KA6** **67** J1
Mossburnford **TD8** **70** B2
Mossdale **DG7** **65** G3
Mossend **ML4** **75** F4
Mossgiel **KA5** **67** J1
Mosshead **AB54** **90** D1
Mosside of Ballinshoe **DD8** **83** F2
Mossley *Ches.E.* **CW12** **49** H6
Mossley *Gt.Man.* **OL5** **49** J2
Mossley Hill **L18** **48** C4
Mosspaul Hotel **TD9** **69** J4
Moss-side *High.* **IV12** **97** F6
Moss-side *Moray* **AB54** **98** D5
Mosstodloch **IV32** **98** B4
Mosston **DD11** **83** G3
Mossy Lea **WN6** **48** E1
Mosterton **DT8** **8** D4
Moston *Gt.Man.* **M40** **49** H2
Moston *Shrop.* **SY4** **38** E3
Moston Green **CW11** **49** G6
Mostyn **CH8** **47** K4
Motcombe **SP7** **9** H2
Mothecombe **PL8** **5** G6
Motherby **CA11** **60** F4
**MOTHERWELL ML 75 F5**
Mottingham **SE9** **23** H4
Mottisfont **SO51** **10** E2
Mottistone **PO30** **11** F6
Mottram in Longdendale **SK14** **49** J3
Mottram St. Andrew **SK10** **49** H5
Mouldsworth **WA6** **48** E5
Moulin **PH16** **82** A2
Moulsecoomb **BN2** **13** G6
Moulsford **OX10** **21** J3
Moulsham **CM2** **24** D1
Moulsoe **MK16** **32** C4
Moulton *Ches.W. & C.* **CW9** **49** F6
Moulton *Lincs.* **PE12** **43** G3
Moulton *N.Yorks.* **DL10** **62** D6
Moulton *Northants.* **NN3** **31** J2
Moulton *Suff.* **CB8** **33** K2
Moulton *V. of Glam.* **CF62** **18** D4
Moulton Chapel **PE12** **43** F4
Moulton St. Mary **NR13** **45** J5
Moulton Seas End **PE12** **43** G3
Mounie Castle **AB51** **91** F2
Mount *Cornw.* **TR8** **2** E3
Mount *Cornw.* **PL30** **4** B4
Mount *High.* **IV12** **97** G7
Mount *Kent* **CT4** **15** G3
Mount *W.Yorks.* **HD3** **50** D1
Mount Ambrose **TR16** **2** E4
Mount Bures **CO8** **34** D5
Mount Charles **PL25** **4** A5
Mount Hawke **TR4** **2** E4
Mount Manisty **CH65** **48** C5
Mount Oliphant **KA6** **67** H2
Mount Pleasant *Ches.E.* **ST7** **49** H7
Mount Pleasant *Derbys.* **DE56** **41** F1
Mount Pleasant *Derbys.* **DE11** **40** E4
Mount Pleasant *E.Suss.* **BN8** **13** H5
Mount Pleasant *Flints.* **CH6** **48** B5
Mount Pleasant *Gt.Lon.* **UB9** **22** D2
Mount Pleasant *Hants.* **SO41** **10** E5
Mount Pleasant *Norf.* **NR17** **44** D6
Mount Pleasant *Suff.* **CO10** **34** B4
Mount Sorrel **SP5** **10** B2
Mount Tabor **HX2** **57** F7
Mountain **HX2** **57** F6
**Mountain Ash (Aberpennar) CF45 18 D2**
Mountain Cross **EH46** **75** K6
Mountain Water **SA62** **16** C3
Mountbenger **TD7** **69** J1
Mountblairy **AB53** **98** E5
Mountblow **G60** **74** C3
Mountfield **TN32** **14** C5
Mountgerald **IV15** **96** C5
Mountjoy **TR8** **3** F2
Mountnessing **CM15** **24** C2
Mounton **NP16** **19** J2
Mountsorrel **LE12** **41** H4
Mousa **ZE2** **107** N10
Mousehole **TR19** **2** B6
Mouswald **DG1** **69** F6
Mow Cop **ST7** **49** H7
Mowden **DL3** **62** D5
Mowhaugh **TD5** **70** D1
Mowsley **LE17** **41** J7
Mowtie **AB39** **91** G6
Moxley **WS10** **40** B6
Moy *High.* **PH33** **87** H6
Moy *High.* **PH31** **88** B6
Moy *High.* **IV13** **88** E1
Moy House **IV36** **97** H6
Moylgrove **SA43** **16** E1
Muasdale **PA29** **72** E6
Much Birch **HR2** **28** E5
Much Cowarne **HR7** **29** F4
Much Dewchurch **HR2** **28** D5
**Much Hadham SG10 33 H7**
Much Hoole **PR4** **55** H7
Much Hoole Town **PR4** **55** H7
Much Marcle **HR8** **29** F5
**Much Wenlock TF13 39 F5**
Muchalls **AB39** **91** H5
Muchelney **TA10** **8** D2
Muchelney Ham **TA10** **8** D2
Muchlarnick **PL13** **4** C5
Muchra **TD7** **69** H2
Muchrachd **IV4** **87** J1
Muck **PH41** **85** K7
Mucking **SS17** **24** C3
Muckle Roe **ZE2** **107** M6
Muckleford **DT2** **9** F5
Mucklestone **TF9** **39** G2
Muckleton **TF6** **38** E3
Muckletown **AB33** **90** D2
Muckley **WV16** **39** F6
Muckley Corner **WS14** **40** C5
Muckton **LN11** **53** G4
Mudale **IV27** **103** H5
Muddiford **EX31** **6** D2
Muddles Green **BN8** **13** J5
Muddleswood **BN6** **13** F5
Mudeford **BH23** **10** C5
Mudford **BA21** **8** E3
Mudgley **BS28** **19** H7
Mugdock **G62** **74** D3
Mugeary **IV51** **85** K1
Mugginton **DE6** **40** E1
Muggintonlane End **DE6** **40** E1
Muggleswick **DH8** **62** B2
Mugswell **KT20** **23** F6
Muie **IV28** **96** D1
Muir **AB35** **89** H6
Muir of Fowlis **AB33** **90** D3
Muir of Lochs **IV32** **98** B4
**Muir of Ord IV6 96 C6**
Muirden **AB53** **99** F5
Muirdrum **DD7** **83** G4
Muiredge **KY8** **76** B1
Muirhead *Aber.* **AB33** **90** D3
Muirhead *Angus* **DD2** **82** E4
Muirhead *Fife* **KY15** **82** D7
Muirhead *Moray* **IV36** **97** H5
Muirhead *N.Lan.* **G69** **74** E4
Muirhouses **EH51** **75** J2
Muirkirk **KA18** **68** B1
Muirmill **FK6** **75** F2
Muirtack *Aber.* **AB41** **91** H1
Muirtack *Aber.* **AB53** **99** G6
Muirton *High.* **IV11** **96** E5
Muirton *P. & K.* **PH3** **82** A6
Muirton *P. & K.* **PH1** **82** C5
Muirton of Ardblair **PH10** **82** C3
Muirton of Ballochy **DD10** **83** H1
Muirtown **IV36** **97** G6
Muiryfold **AB53** **99** F5
Muker **DL11** **62** A7
Mulbarton **NR14** **45** F5
Mulben **AB55** **98** B5
Mulhagery **HS2** **101** F7
**Mull PA 79 G4**
Mullach Charlabhaigh **HS2** **100** E3
Mullacott Cross **EX34** **6** D1
Mullion **TR12** **2** D7
Mullion Cove **TR12** **2** D7
Mumby **LN13** **53** J5
Munderfield Row **HR7** **29** F3
Munderfield Stocks **HR7** **29** F3
Mundesley **NR11** **45** H2
Mundford **IP26** **44** C6
Mundham **NR14** **45** H6
Mundon **CM9** **24** E1
Mundurno **AB23** **91** H3
Munerigie **PH35** **87** J4
Mungasdale **IV22** **95** F2
Mungoswells **EH39** **76** C3
Mungrisdale **CA11** **60** E3
**Munlochy IV8 96 D6**
Munnoch **KA22** **74** A6
Munsley **HR8** **29** F4
Munslow **SY7** **38** E7
Murchington **TQ13** **6** E7
Murcott *Oxon.* **OX5** **31** G7
Murcott *Wilts.* **SN16** **20** C2
Murdostoun **ML2** **75** G5
Murieston **EH54** **75** J4
Murkle **KW14** **105** G2
Murlaganmore **FK21** **81** G4
Murlaggan *High.* **PH34** **87** G5
Murlaggan *High.* **PH31** **87** K6
Murra **KW16** **106** B7
Murrell Green **RG27** **22** A6
Murroes **DD5** **83** F4
Murrow **PE13** **43** G5
Mursley **MK17** **32** B6
Murston **ME10** **25** F5
Murthill **DD8** **83** F2
Murthly **PH1** **82** B4
Murton *Cumb.* **CA16** **61** J4
Murton *Dur.* **SR7** **62** E2
Murton *Northumb.* **TD15** **77** H6
Murton *Swan.* **SA3** **17** J7
Murton *York* **YO19** **58** C4
Musbury **EX13** **8** B5
Muscliff **BH9** **10** B5
Musdale **PA34** **80** A5
**Musselburgh EH21 76 B3**
Mustard Hyrn **NR29** **45** J4
Muston *Leics.* **NG13** **42** B2
Muston *N.Yorks.* **YO14** **59** G2
Mustow Green **DY10** **29** H1
Mutford **NR34** **45** J7
Muthill **PH5** **81** K6
Mutley **PL3** **4** E5
Mutterton **EX15** **7** J5
Muxton **TF2** **39** G4
Mybster **KW1** **105** G3
Myddfai **SA20** **27** G5
Myddle **SY4** **38** D3
Myddlewood **SY4** **38** D3
Mydroilyn **SA48** **26** D3
Myerscough College **PR3** **55** H6
Myerscough Smithy **PR5** **56** B6
Mylor **TR11** **3** F5
Mylor Bridge **TR11** **3** F5
Mynachdy **CF14** **18** E4
Mynachlog-ddu **SA66** **16** E2
Myndtown **SY7** **38** C7
Mynydd Llandygai **LL57** **46** E6
Mynydd-bach *Mon.* **NP16** **19** H2
Mynydd-bach *Swan.* **SA5** **17** K6
Mynyddmechell **LL68** **46** B3
Mynyddygarreg **SA17** **17** H5
Mynytho **LL53** **36** C2
Myrebird **AB31** **91** F5
Mytchett **GU16** **22** B6
Mytholm **HX7** **56** E7
Mytholmroyd **HX7** **57** F7
Mythop **FY4** **55** G6
Myton-on-Swale **YO61** **57** K3
Mytton **SY4** **38** D4

## N

Naast **IV22** **94** E3
Nab's Head **PR5** **56** B7
Na-Buirgh **HS3** **93** F2
Naburn **YO19** **58** B5
Nackington **CT4** **15** G2
Nacton **IP10** **35** G4
Nadderwater **EX4** **7** G6
Nafferton **YO25** **59** G4
Nailbridge **GL17** **29** F7
Nailsbourne **TA2** **8** B2
Nailsea **BS48** **19** H4

Nai - New

Nailstone CV13 41 G5
Nailsworth GL6 20 B2
Nairn IV12 97 F6
Nancegollan TR13 2 D5
Nancekuke TR16 2 D4
Nancledra TR20 2 B5
Nanhoron LL53 36 B2
Nannau LL40 37 G3
Nannerch CH7 47 K6
Nanpantan LE11 41 H4
Nanpean PL26 3 G3
Nanstallon PL30 4 A4
Nant Peris LL55 46 E7
Nant-ddu CF48 27 K7
Nanternis SA45 26 C3
Nantgaredig SA32 17 H3
Nantgarw CF15 18 E3
Nant-glas LD1 27 J2
Nantglyn LL16 47 J6
Nantgwyn LD6 27 J1
Nantlle LL54 46 D7
Nantmawr SY10 38 B3
Nantmel LD1 27 K2
Nantmor LL55 37 F1
Nantwich CW5 49 F7
Nantycaws SA32 17 H4
Nant-y-derry NP7 19 G1
Nant-y-dugoed SY21 37 J4
Nantyffyllon CF34 18 B2
Nantyglo NP23 28 A7
Nant-y-Gollen SY10 38 B3
Nant-y-groes LD1 27 K2
Nant-y-moel CF32 18 C2
Nant-y-Pandy LL33 46 E5
Naphill HP14 22 B2
Napley Heath TF9 39 G2
Nappa BD23 56 D4
Napton on the Hill CV47 31 F2
Narberth (Arberth) SA67 16 E4
Narborough Leics. LE19 41 H6
Narborough Norf. PE32 44 B4
Narkurs PL11 4 D5
Narrachan PA35 80 A6
Nasareth LL54 36 D1
Naseby NN6 31 H1
Nash Bucks. MK17 31 J5
Nash Here. LD8 28 C2
Nash Newport NP18 19 G3
Nash Shrop. SY8 29 F1
Nash V. of Glam. CF71 18 C4
Nash Street DA13 24 C5
Nassington PE8 42 D6
Nasty SG11 33 G6
Nateby Cumb. CA17 61 J6
Nateby Lancs. PR3 55 H5
Nately Scures RG27 22 A6
Natland LA9 55 J1
Naughton IP7 34 E4
Naunton Glos. GL54 30 C6
Naunton Worcs. WR8 29 H5
Naunton Beauchamp WR10 29 J3
Navenby LN5 52 C7
Navestock RM4 23 J2
Navestock Side CM14 23 J2
Navidale KW8 105 F7
Navity IV11 96 E5
Nawton YO62 58 C1
Nayland CO6 34 D5
Nazeing EN9 23 H1
Neacroft BH23 10 C5
Neal's Green CV7 41 F7
Neap ZE2 107 P7
Neap House DN15 52 B1
Near Sawrey LA22 60 E7
Nearton End MK17 32 B6
Neasden NW10 23 F3
Neasham DL2 62 E5
Neat Enstone OX7 30 E6
Neath (Castell-nedd) SA11 18 A2
Neatham GU34 22 A7
Neatishead NR12 45 H3
Nebo Cere. SY23 26 E2
Nebo Conwy LL26 47 G7
Nebo Gwyn. LL54 46 C7
Nebo I.o.A. LL68 46 C3
Necton PE37 44 C5
Nedd IV27 102 D5
Nedderton NE22 71 H5
Nedging IP7 34 D4
Nedging Tye IP7 34 E4
Needham IP20 45 G7
Needham Market IP6 34 E3
Needham Street CB8 34 B2
Needingworth PE27 33 G1
Needwood DE13 40 D3
Neen Savage DY14 29 F1
Neen Sollars DY14 29 F1
Neenton WV16 39 F7
Nefyn LL53 36 C1
Neighbourne BA3 19 K7
Neilston G78 74 C5
Neithrop OX16 31 F4
Nelson Caerp. CF46 18 E2
Nelson Lancs. BB9 56 D6
Nelson Village NE23 71 H6
Nemphlar ML11 75 G6
Nempnett Thrubwell BS40 19 J5
Nenthall CA9 61 J2
Nenthead CA9 61 J2
Nenthorn TD5 76 E7
Neopardy EX17 7 F6
Nerabus PA48 72 A5
Nercwys CH7 48 B6
Neriby PA44 72 B4
Nerston G74 74 E5
Nesbit NE71 77 H7
Nesfield LS29 57 F5
Ness CH64 48 C5
Ness of Tenston KW16 106 B6
Nesscliffe SY4 38 C4
Neston Ches.W. & C. CH64 48 B5
Neston Wilts. SN13 20 B5
Nether Alderley SK10 49 H5
Nether Auchendrane KA7 67 H2
Nether Barr DG8 64 E4
Nether Blainslie TD1 76 D6
Nether Broughton LE14 41 J3
Nether Burrow LA6 56 B2
Nether Cerne DT2 9 F5
Nether Compton DT9 8 E3
Nether Crimond AB51 91 G2
Nether Dalgliesh TD7 69 H3
Nether Dallachy IV32 98 B4
Nether Edge S7 51 F4
Nether End DE45 50 E5
Nether Exe EX5 7 H6
Nether Glasslaw AB43 99 G5
Nether Handwick DD8 82 E3
Nether Haugh S62 51 G3
Nether Heage DE56 51 F7
Nether Heselden BD23 56 D2
Nether Heyford NN7 31 H3
Nether Kellet LA6 55 J3
Nether Kinmundy AB42 99 J6
Nether Langwith NG20 51 H5
Nether Lenshie AB51 98 E6
Nether Loads S42 51 F6
Nether Moor S42 51 F6
Nether Padley S32 50 E5
Nether Pitforthie AB30 91 G7
Nether Poppleton YO26 58 B4
Nether Silton YO7 63 F7
Nether Skyborry LD7 28 B1
Nether Stowey TA5 7 K2
Nether Urquhart KY14 82 C7
Nether Wallop SO20 10 E1
Nether Wasdale CA20 60 C6
Nether Wellwood KA18 68 B1
Nether Welton CA5 60 E2
Nether Westcote OX7 30 D6
Nether Whitacre B46 40 E6
Nether Winchendon (Lower Winchendon) HP18 31 J7
Nether Worton OX7 31 F6
Netheravon SP4 20 E7
Netherbrae AB53 99 F5
Netherbrough KW17 106 C6
Netherburn ML9 75 G6
Netherbury DT6 8 D5
Netherby Cumb. CA6 69 J6
Netherby N.Yorks. HG3 57 J5
Nethercott OX5 31 F6
Netherfield E.Suss. TN33 14 C6
Netherfield Notts. NG4 41 J1
Netherfield S.Lan. ML10 75 F6
Netherhall KA30 74 A4
Netherhampton SP2 10 C2
Netherhay DT8 8 D4
Netherland Green ST14 40 D2
Netherley AB39 91 G5
Nethermill DG1 69 F5
Nethermuir AB42 99 H6
Netherseal DE12 40 E4
Nethershield KA5 67 K1
Netherstreet SN15 20 C5
Netherthird D. & G. DG7 65 H5
Netherthird E.Ayr. KA18 67 K2
Netherthong HD9 50 D2
Netherthorpe S80 51 H4
Netherton Angus DD9 83 G2
Netherton Ches.W. & C. WA6 48 E5
Netherton Devon TQ12 5 J3
Netherton Hants. SP11 21 G6
Netherton Mersey. L30 48 C2
Netherton N.Lan. ML2 75 F5
Netherton Northumb. NE65 70 E3
Netherton Oxon. OX13 21 H1
Netherton P. & K. PH10 82 C2
Netherton S.Lan. ML11 75 H5
Netherton W.Mid. DY2 40 B7
Netherton W.Yorks. WF4 50 E1
Netherton W.Yorks. HD4 50 D1
Netherton Worcs. WR10 29 J4
Netherton Burnfoot NE65 70 E3
Netherton Northside NE65 70 E3
Nethertown Cumb. CA22 60 A6
Nethertown Ork. KW1 105 J1
Nethertown Staffs. WS15 40 D4
Netherwitton NE61 71 G4
Netherwood D. & G. DG1 65 K3
Netherwood E.Ayr. KA18 68 B1
Nethy Bridge PH25 89 H2
Netley Abbey SO31 11 F4
Netley Marsh SO40 10 E3
Nettlebed RG9 21 K3
Nettlebridge BA3 19 K7
Nettlecombe Dorset DT6 8 E5
Nettlecombe I.o.W. PO38 11 G7
Nettlecombe Som. TA4 7 J2
Nettleden HP1 32 D7
Nettleham LN2 52 D5
Nettlestead Kent ME18 23 K6
Nettlestead Suff. IP8 34 E4
Nettlestead Green ME18 23 K6
Nettlestone PO34 11 H5
Nettlesworth DH2 62 D2
Nettleton Lincs. LN7 52 E2
Nettleton Wilts. SN14 20 B4
Nettleton Hill HD7 50 C1
Netton Devon PL8 5 F6
Netton Wilts. SP4 10 C1
Neuadd Cere. SA47 26 D3
Neuadd I.o.A. LL67 46 B3
Neuadd Powys LD2 27 J4
Nevendon SS12 24 D2
Nevern SA42 16 D2
Nevill Holt LE16 42 B6
New Abbey DG2 65 K4
New Aberdour AB43 99 G4
New Addington CR0 23 G5
New Alresford SO24 11 G1
New Alyth PH11 82 D3
New Arley CV7 40 E6
New Arram HU17 59 G5
New Ash Green DA3 24 C5
New Balderton NG24 52 B7
New Barn DA3 24 C5
New Belses TD8 70 A1
New Bewick NE66 71 F1
New Bolingbroke PE22 53 G7
New Boultham LN6 52 C5
New Bradwell MK13 32 B4
New Brancepeth DH7 62 D2
New Bridge D. & G. DG2 65 K3
New Bridge Devon TQ13 5 H3
New Brighton Flints. CH7 48 B6
New Brighton Hants. PO10 11 J4
New Brighton Mersey. CH45 48 C3
New Brighton W.Yorks. LS27 57 H7
New Brighton Wrex. LL11 48 B7
New Brinsley NG16 51 G7
New Broughton LL11 48 C7
New Buckenham NR16 44 E6
New Byth AB53 99 G5
New Cheriton SO24 11 G2
New Cross Cere. SY23 27 F1
New Cross Gt.Lon. SE14 23 G4
New Cumnock KA18 68 B2
New Deer AB53 99 G6
New Duston NN5 31 J2
New Earswick YO31 58 C4
New Edlington DN12 51 H3
New Elgin IV30 97 K5
New Ellerby HU11 59 H6
New Eltham SE9 23 H4
New End B96 30 B2
New England PE1 42 E5
New Farnley LS12 57 H6
New Ferry CH62 48 C4
New Galloway DG7 65 G3
New Gilston KY8 83 F7
New Greens AL3 22 E1
New Grimsby TR24 2 B1
New Hartley NE25 71 J6
New Haw KT15 22 D5
New Heaton TD12 77 G7
New Hedges SA70 16 E5
New Herrington DH4 62 E1
New Hinksey OX1 21 J1
New Holland DN19 59 G7
New Houghton Derbys. NG19 51 H6
New Houghton Norf. PE31 44 B3
New Houses BD24 56 D2
New Hunwick DL15 62 C3
New Hutton LA8 61 G7
New Hythe ME20 14 C2
New Inn Carmar. SA39 17 H2
New Inn Fife KY7 82 D7
New Inn Mon. NP16 19 H1
New Inn Torfaen NP4 19 F2
New Invention Shrop. SY7 28 B1
New Invention W.Mid. WV12 40 B5
New Kelso IV54 95 F7
New Lanark ML11 75 G6
New Lane L40 48 D1
New Lane End WA3 49 F3
New Leake PE22 53 H7
New Leeds AB42 99 H5
New Leslie AB52 90 D2
New Lodge S75 51 F2
New Longton PR4 55 J7
New Luce DG8 64 B4
New Mains ML11 75 G7
New Mains of Ury AB39 91 G6
New Malden KT3 23 F5
New Marske TS11 63 H4
New Marton SY11 38 C2
New Mill Cornw. TR20 2 B5
New Mill Herts. HP23 32 C7
New Mill W.Yorks. HD9 50 D2
New Mill End LU1 32 E7
New Mills Cornw. TR2 3 F3
New Mills Derbys. SK22 50 C4
New Mills Glos. GL15 19 K1
New Mills Mon. NP25 19 J1
New Mills (Y Felin Newydd) Powys SY16 37 K5
New Milton BH25 10 D5
New Mistley CO11 35 F5
New Moat SA63 16 D3
New Ollerton NG22 51 J6
New Orleans PA28 66 B2
New Oscott B44 40 C6
New Park Cornw. PL15 4 B2
New Park N.Yorks. HG1 57 H4
New Pitsligo AB43 99 G5
New Polzeath PL27 3 G1
New Quay (Ceinewydd) SA45 26 C2
New Rackheath NR13 45 G4
New Radnor (Maesyfed) LD8 28 B2
New Rent CA11 61 F3
New Ridley NE43 71 F7
New Road Side BD22 56 E5
New Romney TN28 15 F5
New Rossington DN11 51 J3
New Row Cere. SY25 27 G1
New Row Lancs. PR3 56 B6
New Sawley NG10 41 G2
New Shoreston NE69 77 K7
New Silksworth SR3 62 E1
New Stevenston ML1 75 F5
New Swannington LE67 41 G4
New Totley S17 51 F5
New Town Cen.Beds. SG18 32 E4
New Town Cere. SA43 16 E1
New Town Dorset SP5 9 J3
New Town Dorset BH21 9 J4
New Town E.Loth. EH34 76 C3
New Town E.Suss. TN22 13 H4
New Town Glos. GL54 30 B5
New Tredegar NP24 18 E1
New Tupton S42 51 F6
New Ulva PA31 73 F2
New Valley HS2 101 G4
New Village DN5 51 H2
New Walsoken PE13 43 H5
New Waltham DN36 53 F2
New Winton EH33 76 C3
New World PE15 43 G6
New Yatt OX29 30 E7
New York Lincs. LN4 53 F7
New York T. & W. NE27 71 J6
Newall LS21 57 H5
Newark Ork. KW17 106 G3
Newark Peter. PE1 43 F5
Newark-on-Trent NG24 52 B7
Newarthill ML1 75 F5
Newball LN3 52 D5
Newbarn CT18 15 G4
Newbarns LA14 55 F2
Newbattle EH22 76 B4
Newbiggin Cumb. CA11 61 F4
Newbiggin Cumb. CA10 61 H4
Newbiggin Cumb. CA8 61 G2
Newbiggin Cumb. LA12 55 F3
Newbiggin Cumb. LA19 60 B7
Newbiggin Dur. DL12 62 A4
Newbiggin N.Yorks. DL8 57 F1
Newbiggin N.Yorks. DL8 62 A7
Newbiggin Northumb. NE46 70 E7
Newbiggin-by-the-Sea NE64 71 J5
Newbigging Aber. AB39 91 G5
Newbigging Aber. AB35 89 J6
Newbigging Angus DD4 83 F4
Newbigging Angus DD5 83 F4
Newbigging Angus PH12 82 D3
Newbigging S.Lan. ML11 75 J6
Newbiggin-on-Lune CA17 61 J6
Newbold Derbys. S41 51 F5
Newbold Leics. LE67 41 G4
Newbold on Avon CV21 31 F1
Newbold on Stour CV37 30 D4
Newbold Pacey CV35 30 D3
Newbold Verdon LE9 41 G5
Newborough (Niwbwrch) I.o.A. LL61 46 C6
Newborough Peter. PE6 43 F5
Newborough Staffs. DE13 40 D3
Newbottle Northants. OX17 31 G5
Newbottle T. & W. DH4 62 E1
Newbourne IP12 35 G4
Newbridge (Cefn Bychan) Caerp. NP11 19 F2
Newbridge Cornw. TR20 2 B5
Newbridge Cornw. PL17 4 D4
Newbridge E.Suss. TN7 13 H3
Newbridge Edin. EH28 75 K3
Newbridge Hants. SO40 10 D3
Newbridge I.o.W. PO41 11 F6
Newbridge N.Yorks. YO18 58 E1
Newbridge Oxon. OX29 21 H1
Newbridge Pembs. SA62 16 C2
Newbridge Wrex. LL14 38 B1
Newbridge Green WR8 29 H5
Newbridge on Wye LD1 27 K3
Newbridge-on-Usk NP15 19 G2
Newbrough NE47 70 D7
Newbuildings EX17 7 F5
Newburgh Aber. AB43 99 H5
Newburgh Aber. AB41 91 H2
Newburgh Fife KY14 82 D6
Newburgh Lancs. WN8 48 D1
Newburgh Sc.Bord. TD7 69 J1
Newburn NE15 71 G7
Newbury Som. BA11 19 K6
Newbury W.Berks. RG14 21 H5
Newbury Wilts. BA12 20 B7
Newbury Park IG2 23 H3
Newby Cumb. CA10 61 G4
Newby Lancs. BB7 56 D5
Newby N.Yorks. TS8 63 G5
Newby N.Yorks. LA2 56 C3
Newby N.Yorks. YO12 59 G1
Newby Bridge LA12 55 G1
Newby Cote LA2 56 C2
Newby Cross CA5 60 E1
Newby East CA4 61 F1
Newby West CA2 60 E1
Newby Wiske DL7 57 J1
Newcastle Bridgend CF31 18 B4
Newcastle Mon. NP25 28 D7
Newcastle Shrop. SY7 38 B7
Newcastle Emlyn (Castell Newydd Emlyn) SA38 17 G1
Newcastle International Airport NE13 71 G6
NEWCASTLE UPON TYNE NE 71 H7
Newcastleton TD9 69 K5
Newcastle-under-Lyme ST5 40 A1
Newchapel Pembs. SA37 17 F2
Newchapel Staffs. ST7 49 H7
Newchapel Surr. RH7 23 G7
Newchurch Carmar. SA33 17 G3
Newchurch I.o.W. PO36 11 G6
Newchurch Kent TN29 15 F4
Newchurch Lancs. BB4 56 D7
Newchurch Lancs. BB12 56 D6
Newchurch Mon. NP16 19 H2
Newchurch Powys HR5 28 B3
Newchurch Staffs. DE13 40 D3
Newcott EX14 8 B4
Newcraighall EH21 76 B3
Newdigate RH5 22 E7
Newell Green RG42 22 B4
Newenden TN18 14 D5
Newent GL18 29 G6
Newerne GL15 19 K1
Newfield Dur. DL14 62 D3
Newfield Dur. DH2 62 D1
Newfield High. IV19 96 E4
Newfound RG23 21 J6
Newgale SA62 16 B3
Newgate NR25 44 E1
Newgate Street SG13 23 G1
Newgord ZE2 107 P2
Newhall Ches.E. CW5 39 F1
Newhall Derbys. DE11 40 E3
Newham NE67 71 G1
Newham Hall NE67 71 G1
Newhaven BN9 13 H6
Newhey OL16 49 J1
Newholm YO21 63 K5
Newhouse ML1 75 F4
Newick BN8 13 H4
Newingreen CT21 15 G4
Newington Edin. EH9 76 A3
Newington Kent CT18 15 G4
Newington Kent ME9 24 E5
Newington Notts. DN10 51 J3
Newington Oxon. OX10 21 K2
Newington Bagpath GL8 20 B2
Newland Cumb. LA12 55 G2
Newland Glos. GL16 19 J1
Newland Hull HU6 59 G6
Newland N.Yorks. YO8 58 C7
Newland Oxon. OX28 30 E7
Newland Worcs. WR13 29 G4
Newlandrig EH23 76 B4
Newlands Cumb. CA7 60 E3
Newlands Essex SS8 24 E3
Newlands Northumb. DH8 62 B1
Newlands Sc.Bord. TD9 70 A4
Newland's Corner GU4 22 D7
Newlands of Geise KW14 105 F2
Newlands of Tynet IV32 98 B4
Newlyn TR18 2 B6
Newmachar AB21 91 G3
Newmains ML2 75 G5
Newman's End CM22 33 J7
Newman's Green CO10 34 C4
Newmarket Suff. CB8 33 K2
Newmarket W.Isles HS2 101 G4
Newmill Aber. AB39 91 F6
Newmill Aber. AB41 99 G6
Newmill Aber. AB51 91 G2
Newmill Moray AB55 98 C5
Newmill Sc.Bord. TD9 69 K2
Newmill of Inshewan DD8 83 F1
Newmillerdam WF2 51 F1
Newmills IV7 96 D5
Newmiln P. & K. PH2 82 C4
Newmiln P. & K. PH1 82 B5
Newmilns KA16 74 D7
Newney Green CM1 24 C1
Newnham Glos. GL14 29 F7
Newnham Hants. RG27 22 A6
Newnham Herts. SG7 33 F5
Newnham Kent ME9 14 E2
Newnham Northants. NN11 31 G3
Newnham Bridge WR15 29 F2
Newnham Paddox CV23 41 G7
Newnoth AB54 90 D1
Newport Cornw. PL15 6 B7
Newport Devon EX32 6 D2
Newport E.Riding HU15 58 E6
Newport Essex CB11 33 J5
Newport Glos. GL13 19 K2
Newport High. KW7 105 G6
Newport I.o.W. PO30 11 G6
NEWPORT (CASNEWYDD) Newport NP 19 G3
Newport Norf. NR29 45 K4
Newport (Trefdraeth) Pembs. SA42 16 D2
Newport Som. TA3 8 C2
Newport Tel. & W. TF10 39 G4
Newport Pagnell MK16 32 B4
Newport-on-Tay DD6 83 F5
Newpound Common RH14 12 D4
Newquay TR7 3 F2
Newquay Cornwall International Airport TR8 3 F2
Newsbank CW12 49 H6
Newseat AB51 91 F1
Newsells SG8 33 G5
Newsham Lancs. PR3 55 J6
Newsham N.Yorks. DL11 62 C5
Newsham N.Yorks. YO7 57 J1
Newsham Northumb. NE24 71 H6
Newsholme E.Riding DN14 58 D7
Newsholme Lancs. BB7 56 D4
Newsome HD4 50 D1
Newstead Northumb. NE67 71 G1
Newstead Notts. NG15 51 H7
Newstead Sc.Bord. TD6 76 D7
Newthorpe N.Yorks. LS25 57 K6
Newthorpe Notts. NG16 41 G1
Newtoft LN8 52 D4
Newton Aber. AB54 98 C6
Newton Aber. AB42 99 J6
Newton Arg. & B. PA27 73 J1

## New - Nor

Newton Bridgend CF36 18 B4
Newton Cambs. PE13 43 H4
Newton Cambs. CB22 33 H4
Newton Cardiff CF3 19 F4
Newton Ches.W. & C. CH3 48 E7
Newton Ches.W. & C. WA6 48 E5
Newton Cumb. LA13 55 F2
Newton D. & G. DG10 69 G4
Newton Derbys. DE55 51 G7
Newton Gt.Man. SK14 49 J3
Newton Here. SY7 28 C2
Newton Here. HR6 28 E3
Newton Here. HR2 28 C5
Newton High. KW1 105 J3
Newton High. IV2 96 E7
Newton High. KW1 105 H3
Newton High. IV27 102 E5
Newton High. IV6 96 C6
Newton High. IV11 96 E5
Newton Lancs. BB7 56 B4
Newton Lancs. LA6 55 J2
Newton Lancs. FY3 55 G6
Newton Lincs. NG34 42 D2
Newton Moray IV32 98 B4
Newton N.Ayr. KA27 73 H5
Newton Norf. PE32 44 C4
Newton Northants. NN14 42 B7
Newton Northumb. NE43 71 F7
Newton Northumb. NE65 70 E3
Newton Notts. NG13 41 J1
Newton P. & K. PH8 81 K4
Newton Pembs. SA62 16 B3
Newton Pembs. SA71 16 C5
Newton S.Glos. BS35 19 K2
Newton S.Lan. ML12 75 H7
Newton Sc.Bord. TD8 70 B1
Newton Shrop. SY12 38 D2
Newton Som. TA4 7 K2
Newton Staffs. WS15 40 C3
Newton Suff. CO10 34 D4
Newton Swan. SA3 17 K7
Newton W.Loth. EH52 75 J3
Newton W.Yorks. WF10 57 K7
Newton Warks. CV23 31 G1
Newton Wilts. SP5 10 D2
**Newton Abbot TQ12** 5 J3
Newton Arlosh CA7 60 D1
**Newton Aycliffe DL5** 62 D4
Newton Bewley TS22 63 F4
Newton Blossomville MK43 32 C3
Newton Bromswold MK44 32 C2
Newton Burgoland LE67 41 F5
Newton by Toft LN8 52 D4
Newton Ferrers PL8 5 F6
Newton Flotman NR15 45 G6
Newton Green NP16 19 J2
Newton Harcourt LE8 41 J6
Newton Kyme LS24 57 K5
Newton Longville MK17 32 B5
Newton Mearns G77 74 D5
Newton Morrell N.Yorks. DL10 62 D6
Newton Morrell Oxon. OX27 31 H6
Newton Mountain SA73 16 C5
Newton Mulgrave TS13 63 J5
Newton of Affleck DD5 83 F4
Newton of Ardtoe PH36 86 C7
Newton of Balcanquhal PH2 82 C6
Newton of Dalvey IV36 97 H6
Newton of Falkland KY15 82 D7
Newton of Leys IV2 88 D1
Newton on the Hill SY4 38 D3
Newton on Trent LN1 52 B5
Newton Poppleford EX10 7 J7
Newton Purcell MK18 31 H5
Newton Regis B79 40 E5
Newton Reigny CA11 61 F3
Newton St. Cyres EX5 7 G6
Newton St. Faith NR10 45 G4
Newton St. Loe BA2 20 A5
Newton St. Petrock EX22 6 C4
Newton Solney DE15 40 E3
Newton Stacey SO20 21 H7
**Newton Stewart DG8** 64 E4
Newton Tony SP4 21 F7
Newton Tracey EX31 6 D3
Newton under Roseberry TS9 63 G5
Newton Underwood NE61 71 G5
Newton upon Derwent YO41 58 D5
Newton Valence GU34 11 J1
Newton with Scales PR4 55 H6
Newtonairds DG2 68 D5
Newtongrange EH22 76 B4
Newtonhill AB39 91 H5
**Newton-le-Willows Mersey. WA12** 48 E3
Newton-le-Willows N.Yorks. DL8 57 H1
Newtonmill DD9 83 H1
**Newtonmore PH20** 88 E5
Newton-on-Ouse YO30 58 B4
Newton-on-Rawcliffe YO18 63 K7
Newton-on-the-Moor NE65 71 G3
Newtown Bucks. HP5 22 C1
Newtown Ches.W. & C. CH3 48 E7
Newtown Cornw. PL15 4 C3
Newtown Cornw. TR20 2 C6
Newtown Cumb. CA6 70 A7
Newtown Derbys. SK22 49 J4
Newtown Devon EX36 7 F3
Newtown Devon EX5 7 J6
Newtown Dorset DT8 8 D4
Newtown Glos. GL13 19 K1
Newtown Gt.Man. WN5 48 E2
Newtown Gt.Man. M27 49 G2
Newtown Hants. PO17 11 H3
Newtown Hants. RG20 21 H5
Newtown Hants. SO43 10 D3
Newtown Hants. SO51 10 E2
Newtown Hants. SO32 11 G3
Newtown Here. HR8 29 F4
Newtown Here. HR6 28 D3
Newtown High. PH35 87 K4
Newtown I.o.M. IM4 54 C6
Newtown I.o.W. PO30 11 F5
Newtown Northumb. NE65 71 F3
Newtown Northumb. NE66 71 F1
Newtown Oxon. RG9 22 A3
**Newtown (Y Drenewydd) Powys SY16** 38 A6
Newtown R.C.T. CF45 18 D2
Newtown Shrop. SY4 38 D2
Newtown Som. TA6 8 B1
Newtown Som. TA20 8 B3
Newtown Staffs. ST8 49 J6
Newtown Staffs. SK17 50 C6
Newtown Staffs. WS6 40 B5
Newtown Wilts. SP3 9 J2
Newtown Wilts. SN8 21 G5
Newtown Linford LE6 41 H5
Newtown St. Boswells TD6 76 D7
Newtown Unthank LE9 41 G5
Newtown-in-St-Martin TR12 2 E6
Newtyle PH12 82 D3
Newyears Green UB9 22 D3
Neyland SA73 16 C5
Nibley Glos. GL15 19 K1
Nibley S.Glos. BS37 19 K3
Nibley Green GL11 20 A2
Nicholashayne TA21 7 K4
Nicholaston SA3 17 J7
Nidd HG3 57 J3
Nigg Aberdeen AB12 91 H4
Nigg High. IV19 97 F4
Nightcott TA22 7 G3
Nilig LL15 47 J7
Nilston Rigg NE47 70 D7
Nimlet SN14 20 A4
Nine Ashes CM4 23 J1
Nine Elms SN5 20 E3
Nine Mile Burn EH26 75 K5
Ninebanks NE47 61 J1
Ninemile Bar (Crocketford) DG2 65 J3
Nineveh WR15 29 F2
Ninfield TN33 14 C6
Ningwood PO30 11 F6
Nisbet TD8 70 B1
Niton PO38 11 G7
Nitshill G53 74 D4
Niwbwrch (Newborough) LL61 46 C6
Nizels TN11 23 J6
No Man's Heath Ches.W. & C. SY14 38 E1
No Man's Heath Warks. B79 40 E5
No Man's Land PL13 4 C5
Noah's Ark TN15 23 J6
Noak Hill RM4 23 J2
Noblehill DG1 65 K3
Noblethorpe S75 50 E2
Nobottle NN7 31 H2
Nocton LN4 52 D6
Noddsdale KA30 74 A4
Nogdam End NR14 45 H5
Noke OX3 31 G7
Nolton SA62 16 B4
Nolton Haven SA62 16 B4
Nomansland Devon EX16 7 G4
Nomansland Wilts. SP5 10 D3
Noneley SY4 38 D3
Nonington CT15 15 H2
Nook Cumb. CA6 69 K6
Nook Cumb. LA6 55 J1
Noonsbrough ZE2 107 L7
Noranside DD8 83 F1
Norbreck FY5 55 G5
Norbury Ches.E. SY13 38 E1
Norbury Derbys. DE6 40 D1
Norbury Gt.Lon. SW16 23 G4
Norbury Shrop. SY9 38 C6
Norbury Staffs. ST20 39 G3
Norbury Common SY13 38 E1
Norbury Junction ST20 39 G3
Norchard SA70 16 D6
Norcott Brook WA4 49 F4
Nordelph PE38 43 J5
Norden Dorset BH20 9 J6
Norden Gt.Man. OL11 49 H1
Nordley WV16 39 F6
Norham TD15 77 H6
Norland Town HX6 57 F7
Norley WA6 48 E5
Norleywood SO41 10 E5
Norlington BN8 13 H5
Norman Cross PE7 42 E6
Normanby N.Lincs. DN15 52 B1
Normanby N.Yorks. YO62 58 D1
Normanby R. & C. TS6 63 G5
Normanby by Stow DN21 52 B4
Normanby le Wold LN7 52 E3
Normanby-by-Spital LN8 52 D4
Normandy GU3 22 C6
Normann's Ruh PA74 79 F3
Norman's Bay BN24 13 K6
Norman's Green EX15 7 J5
Normanston NR32 45 K6
Normanton Derby DE23 41 F2
Normanton Leics. NG13 42 B1
Normanton Lincs. NG32 42 C1
Normanton Notts. NG25 51 K7
Normanton Rut. LE15 42 C5
**Normanton W.Yorks. WF6** 57 J7
Normanton le Heath LE67 41 F4
Normanton on Soar LE12 41 H3
Normanton on Trent NG23 51 K6
Normanton-on-the-Wolds NG12 41 J2
Normoss FY3 55 G6
Norrington Common SN12 20 B5
Norris Green PL17 4 E4
Norris Hill DE12 41 F4
Norristhorpe WF15 57 H7
North Acton W3 23 F3
North Anston S25 51 H4
North Ascot SL5 22 C5
North Aston OX25 31 F6
North Baddesley SO52 10 E3
North Ballachulish PH33 80 B1
North Balloch KA26 67 H4
North Barrow BA22 9 F2
North Barsham NR22 44 D2
North Benfleet SS12 24 D3
North Bersted PO21 12 C6
**North Berwick EH39** 76 D2
North Boarhunt PO17 11 H3
North Bogbain AB55 98 B5
North Bovey TQ13 7 F7
North Bradley BA14 20 B6
North Brentor PL19 6 C7
North Brewham BA10 9 G1
North Bridge GU8 12 C3
North Buckland EX33 6 C1
North Burlingham NR13 45 H4
North Cadbury BA22 9 F2
North Cairn DG9 66 D6
North Camp GU14 22 B6
North Carlton Lincs. LN1 52 C5
North Carlton Notts. S81 51 H4
North Cave HU15 58 E6
North Cerney GL7 20 D1
North Chailey BN8 13 G4
North Charford SP6 10 C3
North Charlton NE67 71 G1
North Cheriton BA8 9 F2
North Chideock DT6 8 D5
North Cliffe YO43 58 E6
North Clifton NG23 52 B5
North Cockerington LN11 53 G3
North Coker BA22 8 E3
North Collafirth ZE2 107 M4
North Common S.Glos. BS30 19 K4
North Common Suff. IP22 34 D1
North Commonty AB53 99 G6
North Connel PA37 80 A4
North Coombe EX17 7 G5
North Cornelly CF33 18 B3
North Corner BS36 19 K3
North Cotes DN36 53 G2
North Cove NR34 45 J7
North Cowton DL7 62 D6
North Crawley MK16 32 C4
North Cray DA14 23 H4
North Creake NR21 44 C2
North Curry TA3 8 C2
North Dallens PA38 80 A3
North Dalton YO25 59 F4
North Dawn KW17 106 D7
North Deighton LS22 57 J4
North Dell (Dail Bho Thuath) HS2 101 G1
North Duffield YO8 58 C6
North Elkington LN11 53 F3
North Elmham NR20 44 D3
North Elmsall WF9 51 G1
North End Bucks. LU7 32 B6
North End Dorset SP7 9 H2
North End E.Riding YO25 59 H4
North End E.Riding HU11 59 H5
North End E.Riding HU12 59 J6
North End Essex CM6 33 K7
North End Hants. SO24 11 G2
North End Hants. SP6 10 C3
North End Leics. LE12 41 H4
North End N.Som. BS49 19 H5
North End Norf. NR16 44 E6
North End Northumb. NE65 71 G3
North End Ports. PO2 11 H4
North End W.Suss. BN14 12 E5
North End W.Suss. BN18 12 C6
North Erradale IV21 94 D3
North Essie AB42 99 J5
North Fambridge CM3 24 E2
**North Ferriby HU14** 59 F7
North Frodingham YO25 59 H4
North Gorley SP6 10 C3
North Green Norf. IP21 45 G7
North Green Suff. IP19 35 H1
North Green Suff. IP17 35 H2
North Green Suff. IP17 35 H2
North Grimston YO17 58 E3
North Halling ME2 24 D5
North Harby NG23 52 B5
North Hayling PO11 11 J4
North Hazelrigg NE66 77 J7
North Heasley EX36 7 F2
North Heath W.Berks. RG20 21 H4
North Heath W.Suss. RH20 12 D4
North Hill PL15 4 C3
North Hillingdon UB10 22 D3
North Hinksey OX2 21 H1
North Holmwood RH5 22 E7
North Houghton SO20 10 E1
North Huish TQ10 5 H5
North Hykeham LN6 52 C6
North Johnston SA62 16 C4
North Kelsey LN7 52 D2
North Kessock IV1 96 D7
North Killingholme DN40 52 E1
North Kilvington YO7 57 K1
North Kilworth LE17 41 J7
North Kingston BH24 10 C4
North Kyme LN4 52 E7
North Lancing BN15 12 E6
North Lee HP22 22 B1
North Lees HG4 57 J2
North Leigh OX29 30 E7
North Leverton with Habblesthorpe DN22 51 K4
North Littleton WR11 30 B4
North Lopham IP22 44 E7
North Luffenham LE15 42 C5
North Marden PO18 12 B5
North Marston MK18 31 J6
North Middleton Midloth. EH23 76 B5
North Middleton Northumb. NE71 71 F1
North Millbrex AB53 99 G6
North Molton EX36 7 F3
North Moreton OX11 21 J3
North Mundham PO20 12 B6
North Muskham NG23 51 K7
North Newbald YO43 59 F6
North Newington OX15 31 F5
North Newnton SN9 20 E6
North Newton TA7 8 B1
North Nibley GL11 20 A2
North Oakley RG26 21 J6
North Ockendon RM14 23 J3
North Ormesby TS3 63 G5
North Ormsby LN11 53 F3
North Otterington DL7 57 J1
North Owersby LN8 52 D3
North Perrott TA18 8 D4
North Petherton TA6 8 B1
North Petherwin PL15 4 C2
North Pickenham PE37 44 C5
North Piddle WR7 29 J3
North Plain CA7 69 G7
North Pool TQ7 5 H6
North Poorton DT6 8 E5
North Quarme TA24 7 H2
North Queensferry KY11 75 K2
North Radworthy EX36 7 F2
North Rauceby NG34 42 D1
North Reston LN11 53 G4
North Rigton LS17 57 H5
North Rode CW12 49 H6
North Roe ZE2 107 M4
North Ronaldsay KW17 106 G2
North Ronaldsay Airfield KW17 106 G2
North Runcton PE33 44 A4
North Sandwick ZE2 107 P3
North Scale LA14 54 E3
North Scarle LN6 52 B6
North Seaton NE63 71 H5
North Shian PA38 80 A3
**North Shields NE30** 71 J7
North Shoebury SS3 25 F3
North Side PE6 43 F6
North Skelton TS12 63 H5
North Somercotes LN11 53 H3
North Stainley HG4 57 H2
North Stainmore CA17 61 K5
North Stifford RM16 24 C3
North Stoke B. & N.E.Som. BA1 20 A5
North Stoke Oxon. OX10 21 K3
North Stoke W.Suss. BN18 12 D5
North Stoneham SO50 11 F3
North Street Hants. SO24 11 H1
North Street Kent ME13 15 F2
North Street Med. ME3 24 E4
North Street W.Berks. RG7 21 K4
North Sunderland NE68 77 K4
North Tamerton EX22 6 B6
North Tarbothill AB23 91 H3
**North Tawton EX20** 6 E5
North Third FK7 75 F2
North Thoresby DN36 53 F3
North Tidworth SP9 21 F7
North Togston NE65 71 H3
North Town Devon EX20 6 D5
North Town Hants. GU12 22 B6
North Town W. & M. SL6 22 B3
North Tuddenham NR20 44 E4
**North Uist (Uibhist a Tuath) HS6** 92 D4
**North Walsham NR28** 45 G2
North Waltham RG25 21 J7
North Warnborough RG29 22 A6
North Water Bridge AB30 83 H1
North Watten KW1 105 H3
North Weald Bassett CM16 23 H1
North Wembley HA0 22 E3
North Wheatley DN22 51 K4
North Whilborough TQ12 5 J4
North Wick BS41 19 J5
North Widcombe BS40 19 J6
North Willingham LN8 52 E4
North Wingfield S42 51 G6
North Witham NG33 42 C3
North Wootton Dorset DT9 9 F3
North Wootton Norf. PE30 44 A3
North Wootton Som. BA4 19 J7
North Wraxall SN14 20 B4
North Wroughton SN4 20 E3
North Yardhope NE65 70 E3
Northacre NR17 44 D6
Northall LU6 32 C6
Northall Green NR20 44 D4
**Northallerton DL6** 62 E7
Northam Devon EX39 6 C3
Northam S'ham. SO14 11 F3
**NORTHAMPTON NN** 31 J2
Northaw EN6 23 F1
Northay Devon EX13 8 C4
Northay Som. TA20 8 B3
Northbay HS9 84 C4
Northbeck NG34 42 D1
Northborough PE6 42 E5
Northbourne Kent CT14 15 J2
Northbourne Oxon. OX11 21 J3
Northbridge Street TN32 14 C5
Northbrook Hants. SO21 11 G1
Northbrook Oxon. OX5 31 F6
Northburnhill AB53 99 G6
Northchapel GU28 12 C4
Northchurch HP4 22 C1
Northcote Manor EX37 6 E4
Northcott PL15 6 B6
Northcourt OX14 21 J2
Northdyke KW16 106 B5
Northedge S42 51 F6
Northend B. & N.E.Som. BA1 20 A5
Northend Bucks. RG9 22 A2
Northend Warks. CV47 30 E3
Northfield Aber. AB45 99 G4
Northfield Aberdeen AB16 91 H4
Northfield High. KW1 105 J4
Northfield Hull HU4 59 G7
Northfield Sc.Bord. TD14 77 H4
Northfield Som. TA6 8 B1
Northfield W.Mid. B31 30 B1
Northfields PE9 42 D5
Northfleet DA11 24 C4
Northhouse TD9 69 K3
Northiam TN31 14 D5
Northill SG18 32 E4
Northington Glos. GL14 20 A1
Northington Hants. SO24 11 G1
Northlands PE22 53 G7
Northleach GL54 30 C7
Northleigh Devon EX24 7 K6
Northleigh Devon EX32 6 E2
Northlew EX20 6 D6
Northmoor OX29 21 H1
Northmoor Green (Moorland) TA7 8 C1
Northmuir DD8 82 E2
Northney PO11 11 J4
**Northolt UB5** 22 E3
Northop (Llaneurgain) CH7 48 B6
Northop Hall CH7 48 B6
Northorpe Lincs. PE11 43 F2
Northorpe Lincs. DN21 52 B3
Northorpe Lincs. PE10 42 D4
Northover Som. BA22 8 E2
Northover Som. BA6 8 D1
Northowram HX3 57 G7
Northport BH20 9 J6
Northpunds ZE2 107 N10
Northrepps NR27 45 G2
Northton (Taobh Tuath) HS3 92 E3
Northtown KW17 106 D8
Northway Glos. GL20 29 J5
Northway Som. TA4 7 K3
**Northwich CW8** 49 F5
Northwick S.Glos. BS35 19 J3
Northwick Som. TA9 19 G7
Northwick Worcs. WR3 29 H3
Northwold IP26 44 B6
**Northwood Gt.Lon. HA6** 22 D2
Northwood I.o.W. PO31 11 F5
Northwood Kent CT12 25 K5
Northwood Mersey. L33 48 D3
Northwood Shrop. SY4 38 D2
Northwood Green GL14 29 G7
Northwood Hills HA6 22 E2
Norton Glos. GL2 29 H6
Norton Halton WA7 48 E4
Norton Herts. SG6 33 F5
Norton I.o.W. PO41 10 E6
Norton Mon. NP7 28 D6
Norton N.Som. BS22 19 G5
Norton N.Yorks. YO17 58 D2
Norton Northants. NN11 31 H2
Norton Notts. NG20 51 H5
Norton Powys LD8 28 C2
Norton S.Yorks. DN6 51 H1
Norton S.Yorks. S8 51 F4
Norton Shrop. SY4 38 E5
Norton Shrop. TF11 39 G5
Norton Shrop. SY7 38 D7
Norton Stock. TS20 63 F4
Norton Suff. IP31 34 D2
Norton Swan. SA3 17 K7
Norton V. of Glam. CF32 18 B4
Norton W.Mid. DY8 40 A7
Norton W.Suss. PO20 12 C6
Norton W.Suss. PO20 12 B7
Norton Wilts. SN16 20 B3
Norton Worcs. WR5 29 H3
Norton Worcs. WR11 30 B4
Norton Bavant BA12 20 C7
Norton Bridge ST15 40 A2
Norton Canes WS11 40 C5
Norton Canon HR4 28 C4
Norton Disney LN6 52 B7
Norton Ferris BA12 9 G1
Norton Fitzwarren TA2 7 K3
Norton Green Herts. SG1 33 F6
Norton Green I.o.W. PO40 10 E6
Norton Green Stoke ST6 49 J7
Norton Hawkfield BS40 19 J5
Norton Heath CM4 24 C1
Norton in Hales TF9 39 G2
Norton in the Moors ST6 49 H7
Norton Lindsey CV35 30 D2
Norton Little Green IP31 34 D2
Norton Malreward BS39 19 K5
Norton Mandeville CM5 23 J1

Nor - Owt


Norton St. Philip **BA2** 20 A6
Norton Subcourse **NR14** 45 J6
Norton Wood **HR4** 28 C4
Norton Woodseats **S8** 51 F4
Norton-Juxta-Twycross **CV9** 41 F5
Norton-le-Clay **YO61** 57 K2
Norton-sub-Hamdon **TA14** 8 D3
Norwell **NG23** 51 K6
Norwell Woodhouse **NG23** 51 K6
**NORWICH NR** 45 **G5**
Norwich International Airport **NR6** 45 G4
Norwick **ZE2** 107 Q1
Norwood End **CM5** 23 J1
Norwood Green *Gt.Lon.* **UB2** 22 E4
Norwood Green *W.Yorks.* **HX3** 57 G7
Norwood Hill **RH6** 23 F7
Norwood Park **BA6** 8 E1
Noseley **LE7** 42 A6
Noss Mayo **PL8** 5 F6
Nosterfield **DL8** 57 H1
Nosterfield End **CB21** 33 K4
Nostie **IV40** 86 E2
Notgrove **GL54** 30 C6
Nottage **CF36** 18 B4
Notting Hill **W11** 23 F3
Nottingham *High.* **KW5** 105 H5
**NOTTINGHAM *Nott.* NG** 41 **H1**
Nottingham East Midlands Airport **DE74** 41 G3
Nottington **DT3** 9 F6
Notton *W.Yorks.* **WF4** 51 F1
Notton *Wilts.* **SN15** 20 C5
Nottswood Hill **GL17** 29 G7
Nounsley **CM3** 34 B7
Noutard's Green **WR6** 29 G2
Nowton **IP29** 34 C2
Nox **SY5** 38 D4
Noyadd Trefawr **SA43** 17 F1
Nuffield **RG9** 21 K3
Nun Monkton **YO26** 58 B4
Nunburnholme **YO42** 58 E5
**Nuneaton CV11** 41 **F6**
Nuneham Courtenay **OX44** 21 J2
Nunney **BA11** 20 A7
Nunnington *Here.* **HR1** 28 E4
Nunnington *N.Yorks.* **YO62** 58 C2
Nunnington Park **TA4** 7 J3
Nunnykirk **NE61** 71 F4
Nunsthorpe **DN32** 53 F2
Nunthorpe *Middbro.* **TS7** 63 G5
Nunthorpe *York* **YO23** 58 B4
Nunton **SP5** 10 C2
Nunwick *N.Yorks.* **HG4** 57 J2
Nunwick *Northumb.* **NE48** 70 D6
Nup End **SG4** 33 F7
Nupend **GL10** 20 A1
Nursling **SO16** 10 E3
Nursted **GU31** 11 J2
Nurton **WV6** 40 A6
Nutbourne *W.Suss.* **RH20** 12 D5
Nutbourne *W.Suss.* **PO18** 11 J4
Nutfield **RH1** 23 G6
Nuthall **NG16** 41 H1
Nuthampstead **SG8** 33 H5
Nuthurst *W.Suss.* **RH13** 12 E4
Nuthurst *Warks.* **B94** 30 C1
Nutley *E.Suss.* **TN22** 13 H4
Nutley *Hants.* **RG25** 21 K7
Nutwell **DN3** 51 J2
Nyadd **FK9** 75 F1
Nybster **KW1** 105 J2
Nyetimber **PO21** 12 B7
Nyewood **GU31** 11 J2
Nymet Rowland **EX17** 7 F5
Nymet Tracey **EX17** 7 F5
Nympsfield **GL10** 20 B1
Nynehead **TA21** 7 K3
Nythe **TA7** 8 D1
Nyton **PO20** 12 C6

## O

Oad Street **ME9** 24 E5
Oadby **LE2** 41 J5
Oak Cross **EX20** 6 D6
Oak Tree **DL2** 62 E5
Oakamoor **ST10** 40 C1
Oakbank *Arg. & B.* **PA64** 79 J4
Oakbank *W.Loth.* **EH53** 75 J4
Oakdale *Caerp.* **NP12** 18 E2
Oakdale *Poole* **BH15** 10 B5
Oake **TA4** 7 K3
Oaken **WV8** 40 A5
Oakenclough **PR3** 55 J5
Oakengates **TF2** 39 G4
Oakenhead **IV31** 97 K5
Oakenholt **CH6** 48 B5
Oakenshaw *Dur.* **DL15** 62 D3
Oakenshaw *W.Yorks.* **BD12** 57 G7
Oakerthorpe **DE55** 51 F7
Oakes **HD3** 50 D1
Oakfield *I.o.W.* **PO33** 11 G5
Oakfield *Torfaen* **NP44** 19 F2
Oakford *Cere.* **SA47** 26 D3
Oakford *Devon* **EX16** 7 H3
Oakfordbridge **EX16** 7 H3
Oakgrove **SK11** 49 J6
**Oakham LE15** 42 **B5**
Oakhanger **GU35** 11 J1
Oakhill **BA3** 19 K7
Oakington **CB24** 33 H2
Oaklands *Conwy* **LL26** 47 G7
Oaklands *Herts.* **AL6** 33 F7
Oakle Street **GL2** 29 G7
Oakley *Bed.* **MK43** 32 D3
Oakley *Bucks.* **HP18** 31 H7
Oakley *Fife* **KY12** 75 J2
Oakley *Hants.* **RG23** 21 J6
Oakley *Oxon.* **OX39** 22 A1
Oakley *Poole* **BH21** 10 B5
Oakley *Suff.* **IP21** 35 F1
Oakley Green **SL4** 22 C4
Oakley Park **SY17** 37 J7
Oakridge Lynch **GL6** 20 C1
Oaks **SY5** 38 D5
Oaks Green **DE6** 40 D2
Oaksey **SN16** 20 C2
Oakshaw Ford **CA6** 70 A6
Oakshott **GU33** 11 J2
Oakthorpe **DE12** 41 F4
Oaktree Hill **DL6** 62 E7
Oakwoodhill **RH5** 12 E3
Oakworth **BD22** 57 F6
Oare *Kent* **ME13** 25 G5
Oare *Som.* **EX35** 7 G1
Oare *Wilts.* **SN8** 20 E5
Oasby **NG32** 42 D2
Oatfield **PA28** 66 A2
Oath **TA7** 8 C2
Oathlaw **DD8** 83 F2
Oatlands **HG2** 57 J4
**Oban PA34** 79 **K5**
Obley **SY7** 28 C1
Oborne **DT9** 9 F3
Obthorpe **PE10** 42 D4
Occlestone Green **CW10** 49 F6
Occold **IP23** 35 F1
Occumster **KW3** 105 H5
Ochiltree **KA18** 67 K1
Ochr-y-foel **LL18** 47 J5
Ochtermuthill **PH5** 81 K6
Ochtertyre *P. & K.* **PH7** 81 K5
Ochtertyre *Stir.* **FK9** 75 F1
Ockbrook **DE72** 41 G2
Ockeridge **WR6** 29 G2
Ockham **GU23** 22 D6
Ockle **PH36** 86 B7
Ockley **RH5** 12 E3
Ocle Pychard **HR1** 28 E4
Octon **YO25** 59 G2
Odcombe **BA22** 8 E3
Odd Down **BA2** 20 A5
Oddendale **CA10** 61 H5
Oddingley **WR9** 29 J3
Oddington **OX5** 31 G7
Oddsta **ZE2** 107 P3
Odell **MK43** 32 C3
Odham **EX21** 6 C5
Odie **KW17** 106 F5
Odiham **RG29** 22 A6
Odsey **SG7** 33 F5
Odstock **SP5** 10 C2
Odstone **CV13** 41 F5
Offchurch **CV33** 30 E2
Offenham **WR11** 30 B4
Offerton **SK2** 49 J4
Offham *E.Suss.* **BN8** 13 G5
Offham *Kent* **ME19** 23 K6
Offham *W.Suss.* **BN18** 12 D6
Offley Hoo **SG5** 32 E6
Offleymarsh **ST21** 39 G3
Offord Cluny **PE19** 33 F2
Offord D'Arcy **PE19** 33 F2
Offton **IP8** 34 E4
Offwell **EX14** 7 K6
Ogbourne Maizey **SN8** 20 E4
Ogbourne St. Andrew **SN8** 20 E4
Ogbourne St. George **SN8** 20 E4
Ogil **DD8** 83 F1
Ogle **NE20** 71 G6
Oglet **L24** 48 D4
Ogmore **CF32** 18 B4
Ogmore Vale **CF32** 18 C2
Ogmore-by-Sea **CF32** 18 B4
Oil Terminal **KW16** 106 C8
Okeford Fitzpaine **DT11** 9 H3
**Okehampton EX20** 6 **D6**
Okehampton Camp **EX20** 6 D6
Okraquoy **ZE2** 107 N9
Olchard **TQ13** 5 J3
Olchfa **SA2** 17 K6
Old **NN6** 31 J1
Old Aberdeen **AB24** 91 H4
Old Alresford **SO24** 11 G1
Old Arley **CV7** 40 E6
Old Basford **NG6** 41 H1
Old Basing **RG24** 21 K6
Old Belses **TD6** 70 A1
Old Bewick **NE66** 71 F1
Old Blair **PH18** 81 K1
Old Bolingbroke **PE23** 53 G6
Old Bramhope **LS16** 57 H5
Old Brampton **S42** 51 F5
Old Bridge of Urr **DG7** 65 H4
Old Buckenham **NR17** 44 E6
Old Burdon **SR7** 62 E1
Old Burghclere **RG20** 21 H6
Old Byland **YO62** 58 B1
Old Cassop **DH6** 62 E3
Old Church Stoke **SY15** 38 B6
Old Cleeve **TA24** 7 J1
Old Clipstone **NG21** 51 J6
Old Colwyn **LL29** 47 G5
Old Craig **AB41** 91 H2
Old Craighall **EH21** 76 B3
Old Crombie **AB54** 98 D5
Old Dailly **KA26** 67 G4
Old Dalby **LE14** 41 J3
Old Dam **SK17** 50 D5
Old Deer **AB42** 99 H6
Old Dilton **BA13** 20 B7
Old Down *S.Glos.* **BS32** 19 K3
Old Down *Som.* **BA3** 19 K6
Old Edlington **DN12** 51 H3
Old Eldon **DL4** 62 D4
Old Ellerby **HU11** 59 H6
Old Felixstowe **IP11** 35 H5
Old Fletton **PE2** 42 E6
Old Ford **E3** 23 G3
Old Glossop **SK13** 50 C3
Old Goginan **SY23** 37 F7
Old Goole **DN14** 58 D7
Old Gore **HR9** 29 F6
Old Grimsby **TR24** 2 B1
Old Hall **HU12** 53 F1
Old Hall Green **SG11** 33 G6
Old Hall Street **NR28** 45 H2
Old Harlow **CM20** 33 H7
Old Heath **CO2** 34 E6
Old Heathfield **TN21** 13 J4
Old Hill **B64** 40 B7
Old Hurst **PE28** 33 G1
Old Hutton **LA8** 55 J1
Old Kea **TR3** 3 F4
Old Kilpatrick **G60** 74 C3
Old Kinnernie **AB32** 91 F4
Old Knebworth **SG3** 33 F6
Old Leake **PE22** 53 H7
Old Leslie **AB52** 90 D2
Old Malton **YO17** 58 E2
Old Milton **BH25** 10 D5
Old Milverton **CV32** 30 D2
Old Montsale **CM0** 25 G2
Old Netley **SO31** 11 F3
Old Newton **IP14** 34 E2
Old Philpstoun **EH49** 75 J3
Old Poltalloch **PA31** 79 K7
Old Radnor (Pencraig) **LD8** 28 B3
Old Rattray **AB42** 99 J5
Old Rayne **AB52** 90 E2
Old Romney **TN29** 15 F5
Old Scone **PH2** 82 C5
Old Shields **G67** 75 G3
Old Sodbury **BS37** 20 A3
Old Somerby **NG33** 42 C2
Old Stratford **MK19** 31 J4
Old Sunderlandwick **YO25** 59 G4
Old Swarland **NE65** 71 G3
Old Swinford **DY8** 40 B7
Old Thirsk **YO7** 57 K1
Old Town *Cumb.* **LA6** 55 J1
Old Town *I.o.S.* **TR21** 2 C1
Old Town Farm **NE19** 70 D4
Old Tupton **S42** 51 F6
Old Warden **SG18** 32 E4
Old Weston **PE28** 32 D1
Old Windsor **SL4** 22 C4
Old Wives Lees **CT4** 15 F2
Old Woking **GU22** 22 D6
Old Woodhall **LN9** 53 F6
Old Woods **SY4** 38 D3
Oldberrow **B95** 30 C2
Oldborough **EX17** 7 F5
Oldbury *Kent* **TN15** 23 J6
Oldbury *Shrop.* **WV16** 39 G6
**Oldbury *W.Mid.* B69** 40 **B7**
Oldbury *Warks.* **CV10** 41 F6
Oldbury Naite **BS35** 19 K2
Oldbury on the Hill **GL9** 20 B3
Oldbury-on-Severn **BS35** 19 K2
Oldcastle *Bridgend* **CF31** 18 C4
Oldcastle *Mon.* **NP7** 28 C6
Oldcastle Heath **SY14** 38 D1
Oldcotes **S81** 51 H4
Oldcroft **GL15** 19 K1
Oldeamere **PE7** 43 G6
Oldfield **WR9** 29 H2
Oldford **BA11** 20 A6
Oldhall *Aber.* **AB34** 90 C5
Oldhall *High.* **KW1** 105 H3
**OLDHAM OL** 49 **J2**
Oldham Edge **OL1** 49 J2
Oldhamstocks **TD13** 77 F3
Oldland **BS30** 19 K4
Oldmeldrum **AB51** 91 G2
Oldmill **AB31** 90 D4
Oldpark **TF3** 39 F5
Oldridge **EX4** 7 G6
Oldshore Beg **IV27** 102 D3
Oldshoremore **IV27** 102 E3
Oldstead **YO61** 58 B2
Oldtown **IV24** 96 C3
Oldtown of Aigas **IV4** 96 B7
Oldtown of Ord **AB45** 98 E5
Oldwalls **SA3** 17 H6
Oldways End **EX16** 7 G3
Oldwhat **AB53** 99 G5
Oldwich Lane **B93** 30 D1
Olgrinmore **KW12** 105 G3
Oliver **ML12** 69 G1
Oliver's Battery **SO22** 11 F2
Ollaberry **ZE2** 107 M4
Ollerton *Ches.E.* **WA16** 49 G5
Ollerton *Notts.* **NG22** 51 J6
Ollerton *Shrop.* **TF9** 39 F3
Olmstead Green **CB21** 33 K4
**Olney MK46** 32 **B3**
Olrig House **KW14** 105 G2
Olton **B92** 40 D7
Olveston **BS35** 19 K3
Ombersley **WR9** 29 H2
Ompton **NG22** 51 J6
Onchan **IM3** 54 C6
Onecote **ST13** 50 C7
Onehouse **IP14** 34 E3
Ongar Hill **PE34** 43 J3
Ongar Street **HR6** 28 C2
Onibury **SY7** 28 D1
Onich **PH33** 80 B1
Onllwyn **SA10** 27 H7
Onneley **CW3** 39 G1
Onslow Green **CM6** 33 K7
Onslow Village **GU2** 22 C7
Opinan *High.* **IV22** 94 E2
Opinan *High.* **IV21** 94 D4
Orange Lane **TD12** 77 F6
Orasaigh **HS2** 101 F6
Orbliston **IV32** 98 B5
Orbost **IV55** 93 H7
Orby **PE24** 53 H6
Orcadia **PA20** 73 K4
Orchard **PA23** 73 K2
Orchard Portman **TA3** 8 B2
Orcheston **SP3** 20 D7
Orcop **HR2** 28 D6
Orcop Hill **HR2** 28 D6
Ord **IV46** 86 C3
Ordhead **AB51** 90 E3
Ordie **AB34** 90 C4
Ordiequish **IV32** 98 B5
Ordsall **DN22** 51 J5
Ore **TN35** 14 D6
Oreham Common **BN5** 13 F5
Oreston **PL9** 5 F5
Oreton **DY14** 29 F1
Orford *Suff.* **IP12** 35 J4
Orford *Warr.* **WA2** 49 F3
Organford **BH16** 9 J5
Orgreave **DE13** 40 D4
**Orkney Islands KW** 106 **B6**
Orlestone **TN26** 14 E4
Orleton *Here.* **SY8** 28 D2
Orleton *Worcs.* **WR6** 29 F2
Orleton Common **SY8** 28 D2
Orlingbury **NN14** 32 B1
Ormacleit **HS8** 84 C1
Ormesby **TS3** 63 G5
Ormesby St. Margaret **NR29** 45 J4
Ormesby St. Michael **NR29** 45 J4
Ormidale **PA22** 73 J2
Ormiscaig **IV22** 94 E2
Ormiston **EH35** 76 C4
Ormlie **KW14** 105 G2
Ormsaigmore **PH36** 79 F1
Ormsary **PA31** 73 F3
**Ormskirk L39** 48 **D2**
Oronsay **PA61** 72 B2
Orphir **KW17** 106 C7
**Orpington BR6** 23 **H5**
Orrell *Gt.Man.* **WN5** 48 E2
Orrell *Mersey.* **L20** 48 C3
Orrisdale **IM6** 54 C4
Orrok House **AB23** 91 H3
Orroland **DG6** 65 H6
Orsett **RM16** 24 C3
Orsett Heath **RM16** 24 C3
Orslow **TF10** 40 A4
Orston **NG13** 42 A1
Orton *Cumb.* **CA10** 61 H6
Orton *Northants.* **NN14** 32 B1
Orton Longueville **PE2** 42 E6
Orton Rigg **CA5** 60 E1
Orton Waterville **PE2** 42 E6
Orton-on-the-Hill **CV9** 41 F5
Orwell **SG8** 33 G3
Osbaldeston **BB2** 56 B6
Osbaldwick **YO10** 58 C4
Osbaston *Leics.* **CV13** 41 G5
Osbaston *Shrop.* **SY10** 38 C3
Osbaston *Tel. & W.* **TF6** 38 E4
Osbaston Hollow **CV13** 41 G5
Osborne **PO32** 11 G5
Osbournby **NG34** 42 D2
Oscroft **CH3** 48 E6
Ose **IV56** 93 J7
Osgathorpe **LE12** 41 G4
Osgodby *Lincs.* **LN8** 52 D3
Osgodby *N.Yorks.* **YO8** 58 C6
Osgodby *N.Yorks.* **YO11** 59 G1
Oskaig **IV40** 86 B1
Osleston **DE6** 40 E2
Osmaston *Derby* **DE24** 41 F2
Osmaston *Derbys.* **DE6** 40 D1
Osmington **DT3** 9 G6
Osmington Mills **DT3** 9 G6
Osmondthorpe **LS9** 57 J6
Osmotherley **DL6** 63 F7
Osnaburgh (Dairsie) **KY15** 83 F6
Ospringe **ME13** 25 G5
**Ossett WF5** 57 **H7**
Ossett Street Side **WF5** 57 H7
Ossington **NG23** 51 K6
Ostend **CM0** 25 F2
Osterley **TW7** 22 E4
Oswaldkirk **YO62** 58 C2
Oswaldtwistle **BB5** 56 C7
**Oswestry SY11** 38 **B3**
Oteley **SY12** 38 D2
Otford **TN14** 23 J6
Otham **ME15** 14 C2
Otherton **ST19** 40 B4
Othery **TA7** 8 C1
Otley *Suff.* **IP6** 35 G3
**Otley *W.Yorks.* LS21** 57 **H5**
Otter **PA21** 73 H3
Otter Ferry **PA21** 73 H2
Otterbourne **SO21** 11 F2
Otterburn *N.Yorks.* **BD23** 56 D4
Otterburn *Northumb.* **NE19** 70 D4
Otterburn Camp **NE19** 70 D4
Otterden Place **ME13** 14 E2
Otterham **PL32** 4 B1
Otterham Quay **ME8** 24 E5
Otterhampton **TA5** 19 F7
Otternish **HS6** 92 E4
Ottershaw **KT16** 22 D5
Otterswick **ZE2** 107 P4
Otterton **EX9** 7 J7
Otterwood **SO42** 11 F4
**Ottery St. Mary EX11** 7 **J6**
Ottinge **CT4** 15 G3
Ottringham **HU12** 59 J7
Oughterby **CA5** 60 D1
Oughtershaw **BD23** 56 D1
Oughterside **CA7** 60 C2
Oughtibridge **S35** 51 F3
Oulston **YO61** 58 B2
Oulton *Cumb.* **CA7** 60 D1
Oulton *Norf.* **NR11** 45 F3
Oulton *Staffs.* **ST15** 40 B2
Oulton *Staffs.* **ST20** 39 G3
Oulton *Suff.* **NR32** 45 K6
Oulton *W.Yorks.* **LS26** 57 J7
Oulton Broad **NR33** 45 K6
Oulton Grange **ST15** 40 B2
Oulton Street **NR11** 45 F3
Oultoncross **ST15** 40 B2
Oundle **PE8** 42 D7
Ousby **CA10** 61 H3
Ousdale **KW7** 105 F6
Ousden **CB8** 34 B3
Ousefleet **DN14** 58 E7
Ouston *Dur.* **DH2** 62 D1
Ouston *Northumb.* **NE18** 71 F6
Out Newton **HU19** 59 K7
Out Rawcliffe **PR3** 55 H5
Out Skerries Airstrip **ZE2** 107 Q5
Outcast **LA12** 55 G2
Outchester **NE70** 77 K7
Outertown **KW16** 106 B7
Outgate **LA22** 60 E7
Outhgill **CA17** 61 J6
Outlands **ST20** 39 G3
Outlane **HD3** 50 C1
Outwell **PE14** 43 J5
Outwood *Surr.* **RH1** 23 G7
Outwood *W.Yorks.* **WF1** 57 J7
Outwoods **TF10** 39 G4
Ouzlewell Green **WF3** 57 J7
Ovenden **HX3** 57 F7
Over *Cambs.* **CB24** 33 G1
Over *Ches.W. & C.* **CW7** 49 F6
Over *Glos.* **GL2** 29 H7
Over *S.Glos.* **BS32** 19 J3
Over Burrows **DE6** 40 E2
Over Compton **DT9** 8 E3
Over Dinsdale **DL2** 62 E5
Over End **DE45** 50 E5
Over Green **B76** 40 D6
Over Haddon **DE45** 50 E6
Over Hulton **BL5** 49 F2
Over Kellet **LA6** 55 J3
Over Kiddington **OX20** 31 F6
Over Monnow **NP25** 28 D7
Over Norton **OX7** 30 E6
Over Peover **WA16** 49 G5
Over Rankeilour **KY15** 82 E6
Over Silton **YO7** 63 F7
Over Stowey **TA5** 7 K2
Over Stratton **TA13** 8 D3
Over Tabley **WA16** 49 G4
Over Wallop **SO20** 10 D1
Over Whitacre **B46** 40 E6
Over Winchendon (Upper Winchendon) **HP18** 31 J7
Over Worton **OX7** 31 F6
Overbister **KW17** 106 F3
Overbrae **AB53** 99 G5
Overbury **GL20** 29 J5
Overcombe **DT3** 9 F6
Overgreen **S42** 51 F5
Overleigh **BA16** 8 D1
Overpool **CH66** 48 C5
Overscaig Hotel **IV27** 103 G6
Overseal **DE12** 40 E4
Overslade **CV22** 31 F1
Oversland **ME13** 15 F2
Oversley Green **B49** 30 B3
Overstone **NN6** 32 B2
Overstrand **NR27** 45 G1
Overthorpe **OX17** 31 F4
Overton *Aber.* **AB51** 91 F3
Overton *Aberdeen* **AB21** 91 G3
Overton *Ches.W. & C.* **WA6** 48 E5
Overton *Hants.* **RG25** 21 J7
Overton *Lancs.* **LA3** 55 H4
Overton *N.Yorks.* **YO30** 58 B4
Overton *Shrop.* **SY8** 28 E1
Overton *Swan.* **SA3** 17 H7
Overton *W.Yorks.* **WF4** 50 E1
Overton (Owrtyn) *Wrex.* **LL13** 38 C1
Overton Bridge **LL13** 38 C1
Overtown *Lancs.* **LA6** 56 B2
Overtown *N.Lan.* **ML2** 75 G5
Overtown *Swin.* **SN4** 20 E4
Overy **OX10** 21 J2
Oving *Bucks.* **HP22** 31 J6
Oving *W.Suss.* **PO20** 12 C6
Ovingdean **BN2** 13 G6
Ovingham **NE42** 71 F7
Ovington *Dur.* **DL11** 62 C5
Ovington *Essex* **CO10** 34 B4
Ovington *Hants.* **SO24** 11 G1
Ovington *Norf.* **IP25** 44 D5
Ovington *Northumb.* **NE42** 71 F7
Ower *Hants.* **SO51** 10 E3
Ower *Hants.* **SO45** 11 F4
Owermoigne **DT2** 9 G6
Owler Bar **S17** 50 E5
Owlpen **GL11** 20 A2
Owl's Green **IP13** 35 G2
Owlswick **HP27** 22 A1
Owmby **DN38** 52 D2
Owmby-by-Spital **LN8** 52 D4
Owrtyn (Overton) **LL13** 38 C1
Owslebury **SO21** 11 G2
Owston **LE15** 42 A5
Owston Ferry **DN9** 52 B2
Owstwick **HU12** 59 J6
Owthorpe **NG12** 41 J2

# Oxb - Pen



Oxborough **PE33** 44 B5
Oxcliffe Hill **LA3** 55 H3
Oxcombe **LN9** 53 G5
Oxen End **CM7** 33 K6
Oxen Park **LA12** 55 G1
Oxencombe **TQ13** 7 G7
Oxenhall **GL18** 29 G6
Oxenholme **LA9** 61 G7
Oxenhope **BD22** 57 F6
Oxenpill **BA6** 19 H7
Oxenton **GL52** 29 J5
Oxenwood **SN8** 21 G6
**OXFORD OX 21 J1**
Oxhey **WD17** 22 E2
Oxhill **CV35** 30 E4
Oxley **WV10** 40 B5
Oxley Green **CM9** 34 D7
Oxley's Green **TN32** 13 K4
Oxnam **TD8** 70 C2
Oxnead **NR10** 45 G3
Oxnop Ghyll **DL8** 62 A7
Oxshott **KT22** 22 E5
Oxspring **S36** 50 E2
**Oxted RH8 23 G6**
Oxton *Mersey.* **CH43** 48 C4
Oxton *Notts.* **NG25** 51 J7
Oxton *Sc.Bord.* **TD2** 76 C5
Oxwich **SA3** 17 H7
Oxwich Green **SA3** 17 H7
Oxwick **NR21** 44 D3
Oykel Bridge **IV27** 95 K1
Oyne **AB52** 90 E2
Ozleworth **GL12** 20 A2

## P

Pabail Iarach (Lower Bayble) **HS2** 101 H4
Pabail Uarach (Upper Bayble) **HS2** 101 H4
Pabbay **HS6** 92 E3
Packington **LE65** 41 F4
Packwood **B94** 30 C1
Padanaram **DD8** 83 F2
Padbury **MK18** 31 J5
Paddington **W2** 23 F3
Paddlesworth **CT18** 15 G3
Paddock **TN25** 14 E2
Paddock Wood **TN12** 23 K7
Paddockhaugh **IV30** 97 K6
Paddockhole **DG11** 69 H5
Paddolgreen **SY4** 38 E2
Padeswood **CH7** 48 B6
Padfield **SK13** 50 C3
Padiham **BB12** 56 C6
Padside **HG3** 57 G4
**Padstow PL28 3 G1**
Padworth **RG7** 21 K5
Paganhill **GL5** 20 B1
Pagham **PO21** 12 B7
Paglesham Churchend **SS4** 25 F2
Paglesham Eastend **SS4** 25 F2
Paible **HS3** 93 F2
**Paignton TQ3 5 J4**
Pailton **CV23** 41 G7
Paine's Corner **TN21** 13 K4
Painscastle **LD2** 28 A4
Painshawfield **NE43** 71 F7
Painswick **GL6** 20 B1
Pairc **HS2** 100 E3
**PAISLEY PA 74 C4**
Pakefield **NR33** 45 K6
Pakenham **IP31** 34 D2
Pale **LL23** 37 J2
Palehouse Common **TN22** 13 H5
Palestine **SP11** 21 F7
Paley Street **SL6** 22 B4
Palgowan **DG8** 67 H5
Palgrave **IP22** 35 F1
Pallinsburn House **TD12** 77 G7
Palmarsh **CT21** 15 G4
Palmers Cross **GU5** 22 D7
Palmers Green **N13** 23 G2
Palmerscross **IV30** 97 K5
Palmerstown **CF63** 18 E4
Palnackie **DG7** 65 J5
Palnure **DG8** 64 E4
Palterton **S44** 51 G6
Pamber End **RG26** 21 K6
Pamber Green **RG26** 21 K6
Pamber Heath **RG26** 21 K5
Pamington **GL20** 29 J5
Pamphill **BH21** 9 J4
Pampisford **CB22** 33 H4
Pan **KW16** 106 C8
Panborough **BA5** 19 H7
Panbride **DD7** 83 G4
Pancrasweek **EX22** 6 A5
Pancross **CF62** 18 D5
Pandy *Gwyn.* **LL36** 37 F5
Pandy *Mon.* **NP7** 28 C6
Pandy *Powys* **SY19** 37 J5
Pandy *Wrex.* **LL20** 38 A2
Pandy Tudur **LL22** 47 G6
Pandy'r Capel **LL21** 47 J7
Panfield **CM7** 34 B6
Pangbourne **RG8** 21 K4
Pannal **HG3** 57 J4
Pannal Ash **HG3** 57 H4
Panshanger **AL7** 33 F7
Pant **SY10** 38 B3
Pant Glas **LL54** 36 D1
Pant Gwyn **LL40** 37 H3
Pant Mawr **SY18** 37 H7
Pantasaph **CH8** 47 K5
Panteg **NP4** 19 G2
Pantglas **SY20** 37 G6
Pantgwyn *Carmar.* **SA19** 17 J3
Pantgwyn *Cere.* **SA43** 17 F1
Pant-lasau **SA6** 17 K5
Panton **LN8** 52 E5
Pant-pastynog **LL16** 47 J6
Pantperthog **SY20** 37 G5
Pant-y-dwr **LD6** 27 J1
Pantyffordd **CH7** 48 B7
Pant-y-ffridd **SY21** 38 A5
Pantyffynnon **SA18** 17 K4
Pantygasseg **NP4** 19 F2
Pantygelli **NP7** 28 C7
Pantymwyn **CH7** 47 K6
Panxworth **NR13** 45 H4
Papa Stour **ZE2** 107 K6
Papa Stour Airstrip **ZE2** 107 K6
Papa Westray **KW17** 106 D2
Papa Westray Airfield **KW17** 106 D2
Papcastle **CA13** 60 C3
Papil **ZE2** 107 M9
Papple **EH41** 76 D3
Papplewick **NG15** 51 H7
Papworth Everard **CB23** 33 F2
Papworth St. Agnes **CB23** 33 F2
**Par PL24 4 A5**
Parbold **WN8** 48 D1
Parbrook *Som.* **BA6** 8 E1
Parbrook *W.Suss.* **RH14** 12 D4
Parc **LL23** 37 H2
Parcllyn **SA43** 26 B3
Parcrhydderch **SY25** 27 F3
Parc-Seymour **NP26** 19 H2
Parc-y-rhôs **SA48** 17 J1
Pardshaw **CA13** 60 B4
Parham **IP13** 35 H2
Parish Holm **ML11** 68 C1
Park **AB45** 98 D5
Park Close **BB18** 56 D5
Park Corner *E.Suss.* **TN3** 13 J3
Park Corner *Oxon.* **RG9** 21 K3
Park End *Northumb.* **NE48** 70 D6
Park End *Staffs.* **ST7** 49 G7
Park End *Worcs.* **DY12** 29 G1
Park Gate *Hants.* **SO31** 11 G4
Park Gate *W.Yorks.* **LS20** 57 G5
Park Gate *W.Yorks.* **HD8** 50 E1
Park Gate *Worcs.* **B61** 29 J1
Park Green **IP14** 35 F2
Park Hill **S2** 51 F4
Park Lane **LL13** 38 D2
Park Langley **BR4** 23 G5
Park Street **AL2** 22 E1
Parkend *Cumb.* **CA7** 60 E3
Parkend *Glos.* **GL15** 19 K1
Parker's Green **TN10** 23 K7
Parkeston **CO12** 35 G5
Parkfield *Cornw.* **PL14** 4 D4
Parkfield *S.Glos.* **BS16** 19 K4
Parkfield *W.Mid.* **WV4** 40 B6
Parkford **DD8** 83 F2
Parkgate *Ches.W. & C.* **CH64** 48 B5
Parkgate *D. & G.* **DG1** 69 F5
Parkgate *Kent* **TN30** 14 D4
Parkgate *S.Yorks.* **S62** 51 G3
Parkgate *Surr.* **RH5** 23 F7
Parkham **EX39** 6 B3
Parkham Ash **EX39** 6 B3
Parkhead **G31** 74 E4
Parkhill *Angus* **DD11** 83 H3
Parkhill *P. & K.* **PH10** 82 C3
Parkhouse **NP25** 19 H1
Parkhurst **PO30** 11 F5
Parkmill **SA3** 17 J7
Parkmore **AB55** 98 B6
Parkneuk **AB30** 91 F7
Parkside **LL12** 48 C7
Parkstone **BH14** 10 B5
Parkway **BA22** 8 E2
Parley Cross **BH22** 10 B5
Parley Green **BH23** 10 C5
Parlington **LS25** 57 K6
Parracombe **EX31** 6 E1
Parrog **SA42** 16 D2
Parson Cross **S5** 51 F3
Parson Drove **PE13** 43 G5
Parsonage Green **CM1** 33 K7
Parsonby **CA7** 60 C3
Partick **G11** 74 D4
Partington **M31** 49 G3
Partney **PE23** 53 H6
Parton *Cumb.* **CA28** 60 A4
Parton *D. & G.* **DG7** 65 G3
Partridge Green **RH13** 12 E5
Parwich **DE6** 50 D7
Paslow Wood Common **CM4** 23 J1
Passenham **MK19** 31 J5
Passfield **GU30** 12 B3
Passingford Bridge **RM4** 23 J2
Paston **NR28** 45 H2
Paston Street **NR28** 45 H2
Pasturefields **ST18** 40 B3
Patchacott **EX21** 6 C6
Patcham **BN1** 13 G6
Patchetts Green **WD25** 22 E2
Patching **BN13** 12 D6
Patchole **EX31** 6 E1
Patchway **BS34** 19 K3
Pateley Bridge **HG3** 57 G3
Path of Condie **PH2** 82 B6
Pathe **TA7** 8 C1
Pathfinder Village **EX6** 7 G6
Pathhead *Aber.* **DD10** 83 J1
Pathhead *E.Ayr.* **KA18** 68 B2
Pathhead *Fife* **KY1** 76 A1
**Pathhead *Midloth.* EH37 76 B4**
Pathlow **CV37** 30 C3
Patmore Heath **SG11** 33 H6
Patna **KA6** 67 J2
Patney **SN10** 20 D6
Patrick **IM5** 54 B5
Patrick Brompton **DL8** 62 D7
Patrington **HU12** 59 K7
Patrington Haven **HU12** 59 K7
Patrishow **NP7** 28 B6
Patrixbourne **CT4** 15 G2
Patterdale **CA11** 60 E5
Pattingham **WV6** 40 A6
Pattishall **NN12** 31 H3
Pattiswick **CM77** 34 C6
Paul **TR19** 2 B6
Paulerspury **NN12** 31 J4
Paull **HU12** 59 H7
Paull Holme **HU12** 59 H7
Paul's Green **TR27** 2 D5
Paulton **BS39** 19 K6
Pauperhaugh **NE65** 71 F4
Pave Lane **TF10** 39 G4
Pavenham **MK43** 32 C3
Pawlett **TA6** 19 G7
Pawston **TD12** 77 G7
Paxford **GL55** 30 C5
Paxhill Park **RH16** 13 G4
Paxton **TD15** 77 H5
Payden Street **ME17** 14 E2
Payhembury **EX14** 7 J5
Paythorne **BB7** 56 D4
**Peacehaven BN10 13 H6**
Peacemarsh **SP8** 9 H2
Peachley **WR2** 29 H3
Peak Dale **SK17** 50 C5
Peak Forest **SK17** 50 D5
Peakirk **PE6** 42 E5
Pean Hill **CT5** 25 H5
Pear Tree **DE23** 41 F2
Pearsie **DD8** 82 E2
Pearson's Green **TN12** 23 K7
Peartree **AL7** 33 F7
Peartree Green *Essex* **CM15** 23 J2
Peartree Green *Here.* **HR1** 29 F5
Pease Pottage **RH11** 13 F3
Peasedown St. John **BA2** 20 A6
Peasehill **DE5** 41 G1
Peaseland Green **NR20** 44 E4
Peasemore **RG20** 21 H4
Peasenhall **IP17** 35 H2
Peaslake **GU5** 22 D7
Peasley Cross **WA9** 48 E3
Peasmarsh *E.Suss.* **TN31** 14 D5
Peasmarsh *Surr.* **GU3** 22 C7
Peaston **EH35** 76 C4
Peastonbank **EH34** 76 C4
Peat Inn **KY15** 83 F7
Peathill **AB43** 99 H4
Peathrow **DL13** 62 C4
Peatling Magna **LE8** 41 H6
Peatling Parva **LE17** 41 H7
Peaton **SY7** 38 E7
Pebble Coombe **KT20** 23 F6
Pebmarsh **CO9** 34 C5
Pebworth **CV37** 30 C4
Pecket Well **HX7** 56 E7
Peckforton **CW6** 48 E7
Peckham **SE15** 23 G4
Peckleton **LE9** 41 G5
Pedham **NR13** 45 H4
Pedmore **DY9** 40 B7
Pedwell **TA7** 8 D1
**Peebles EH45 76 A6**
Peel *I.o.M.* **IM5** 54 B5
Peel *Lancs.* **FY4** 55 G6
Peening Quarter **TN30** 14 D5
Peggs Green **LE67** 41 G4
Pegsdon **SG5** 32 E5
Pegswood **NE61** 71 H5
Pegwell **CT11** 25 K5
Peighinn nan Aoireann **HS8** 84 C1
Peinchorran **IV51** 86 B1
Peinlich **IV51** 93 K6
Pelaw **NE10** 71 H7
Pelcomb **SA62** 16 C4
Pelcomb Bridge **SA62** 16 C4
Pelcomb Cross **SA62** 16 C4
Peldon **CO5** 34 D7
Pellon **HX2** 57 F7
Pelsall **WS3** 40 C5
Pelton **DH2** 62 D1
Pelutho **CA7** 60 C2
Pelynt **PL13** 4 C5
Pemberton **WN5** 48 E2
Pembrey (Pen-bre) **SA16** 17 H5
Pembridge **HR6** 28 C3
**Pembroke (Penfro) SA71 16 C5**
**Pembroke Dock (Doc Penfro) SA72 16 C5**
Pembury **TN2** 23 K7
Penallt **NP25** 28 E7
Penally **SA70** 16 E6
Penalt **HR1** 28 E6
Penare **PL26** 3 G4
Penarlâg (Hawarden) **CH5** 48 C6
Penarran **SY16** 38 A7
**Penarth CF64 18 E4**
Pen-bont Rhydybeddau **SY23** 37 F7
Penboyr **SA44** 17 G2
Pen-bre (Pembrey) **SA16** 17 H5
Penbryn **SA44** 26 B3
**Pencader SA39 17 H2**
Pen-cae **SA47** 26 D3
Pen-cae-cwm **LL16** 47 H6
Pencaenewydd **LL53** 36 D1
Pencaitland **EH34** 76 C4
Pencarnisiog **LL63** 46 B5
Pencarreg **SA40** 17 J1
Pencarrow **PL32** 4 B2
Pencelli **LD3** 27 K6
Pen-clawdd **SA4** 17 J6
Pencoed **CF35** 18 C3
Pencombe **HR7** 28 E3
Pencoyd **HR2** 28 E6
Pencraig *Here.* **HR9** 28 E6
Pencraig *Powys* **SY10** 37 K3
Pencraig (Old Radnor) *Powys* **LD8** 28 B3
Pendeen **TR19** 2 A5
Penderyn **CF44** 18 C1
Pendine (Pentywyn) **SA33** 17 F5
Pendlebury **M27** 49 G2
Pendleton **BB7** 56 C6
Pendock **GL19** 29 G5
Pendoggett **PL29** 4 A3
Pendomer **BA22** 8 E3
Pendoylan **CF71** 18 D4
Penegoes **SY20** 37 G5
Penelewey **TR3** 3 F4
Pen-ffordd **SA66** 16 D3
Penffordd-las (Staylittle) **SY19** 37 H6
**Penfro (Pembroke) SA71 16 C5**
Pengam **NP12** 18 E2
Penge **SE20** 23 G4
Pengenffordd **LD3** 28 A6
Pengorffwysfa **LL68** 46 C3
Pengover Green **PL14** 4 C4
Pen-groes-oped **NP7** 19 G1
Pengwern **LL18** 47 J5
Penhale **TR12** 2 D7
Penhallow **TR4** 2 E3
Penhalvean **TR16** 2 E5
Penhelig **LL35** 37 F6
Penhill **SN2** 20 E3
Penhow **NP26** 19 H2
Penhurst **TN33** 13 K5
Peniarth **LL36** 37 F5
**Penicuik EH26 76 A4**
Peniel **SA32** 17 H3
Penifiler **IV51** 93 K7
Peninver **PA28** 66 B1
Penisa'r Waun **LL55** 46 D6
Penisarcwm **SY10** 37 K4
Penishawain **LD3** 27 K5
Penistone **S36** 50 E2
Penjerrick **TR11** 2 E5
Penketh **WA5** 48 E4
Penkill **KA26** 67 G4
Penkridge **ST19** 40 B4
Penlean **EX23** 4 C1
Penley **LL13** 38 D2
Penllech **LL53** 36 B2
Penllergaer **SA4** 17 K6
Pen-llyn *I.o.A.* **LL65** 46 B4
Penllyn *V. of Glam.* **CF71** 18 C4
Pen-lôn **LL61** 46 C6
Penmachno **LL24** 47 F7
Penmaen **SA3** 17 J7
Penmaenan **LL34** 47 F5
**Penmaenmawr LL34 47 F5**
Penmaenpool (Llyn Penmaen) **LL40** 37 F4
Penmaen-Rhôs **LL29** 47 G5
Penmark **CF62** 18 D5
Penmon **LL58** 46 E4
Penmorfa **LL49** 36 E1
Penmynydd **LL61** 46 D5
Penn *Bucks.* **HP10** 22 C2
Penn *W.Mid.* **WV4** 40 A6
Penn Street **HP7** 22 C2
Pennal **SY20** 37 F5
Pennal-isaf **SY20** 37 G5
Pennan **AB43** 99 G4
Pennance **TR16** 2 E4
Pennant *Cere.* **SY23** 26 E2
Pennant *Powys* **SY19** 37 H6
Pennant Melangell **SY10** 37 K3
Pennar **SA72** 16 C5
Pennard **SA3** 17 J7
Pennerley **SY5** 38 C6
Penninghame **DG8** 64 D4
Pennington *Cumb.* **LA12** 55 F2
Pennington *Hants.* **SO41** 10 E5
Pennington Green **WN2** 49 F2
Pennorth **LD3** 28 A6
Pennsylvania **SN14** 20 A4
Penny Bridge **LA12** 55 G1
Pennycross **PL5** 4 E5
Pennyfuir **PA34** 79 K4
Pennygate **NR12** 45 H3
Pennyghael **PA70** 79 G5
Pennyglen **KA19** 67 G2
Pennygown **PA72** 79 H3
Pennymoor **EX16** 7 G4
Penny's Green **NR16** 45 F6
Pennyvenie **KA6** 67 J3
Penparc *Cere.* **SA43** 17 F1
Penparc *Pembs.* **SA62** 16 B2
Penparcau **SY23** 36 E7
Penpedairheol **NP15** 19 G1
Penpethy **PL34** 4 A2
Penpillick **PL24** 4 A5
Penpol **TR3** 3 F5
Penpoll **PL22** 4 B5
Penponds **TR14** 2 D5
Penpont *D. & G.* **DG3** 68 D4
Penpont *Powys* **LD3** 27 J6
Penprysg **CF35** 18 C3
Penquit **PL21** 5 G5
Penrherber **SA38** 17 F2
Penrhiw **SA37** 17 F1
Penrhiwceiber **CF45** 18 D2
Penrhiwgoch **SA32** 17 J4
Penrhiw-llan **SA44** 17 G1
Penrhiw-pâl **SA44** 17 G1
Penrhiwtyn **SA11** 18 A2
Penrhos *Gwyn.* **LL53** 36 C2
Penrhos *I.o.A.* **LL65** 46 A4
Penrhos *Mon.* **NP15** 28 D7
Penrhos *Powys* **SA9** 27 H7
Penrhos-garnedd **LL57** 46 D5
Penrhyn Bay (Bae Penrhyn) **LL30** 47 G4
Penrhyn-coch **SY23** 37 F7
**Penrhyndeudraeth LL48 37 F2**
Penrhyn-side **LL30** 47 G4
Penrhys **CF43** 18 D2
Penrice **SA3** 17 H7
**Penrith CA11 61 G4**
Penrose *Cornw.* **PL27** 3 F1
Penrose *Cornw.* **PL15** 4 C2
Penruddock **CA11** 60 F4
**Penryn TR10 2 E5**
Pensarn *Carmar.* **SA31** 17 H4
Pensarn *Conwy* **LL22** 47 H5
Pen-sarn *Gwyn.* **LL45** 36 E3
Pen-sarn *Gwyn.* **LL54** 36 D1
Pensax **WR6** 29 G2
Pensby **CH61** 48 B4
Penselwood **BA9** 9 G1
Pensford **BS39** 19 K5
Pensham **WR10** 29 J4
Penshaw **DH4** 62 E1
Penshurst **TN11** 23 J7
Pensilva **PL14** 4 C4
Pensnett **DY5** 40 B7
Penston **EH33** 76 C3
Pentewan **PL26** 4 A6
Pentir **LL57** 46 D6
Pentire **TR7** 2 E2
Pentireglaze **PL27** 3 G1
Pentlepoir **SA69** 16 E5
Pentlow **CO10** 34 C4
Pentlow Street **CO10** 34 C4
Pentney **PE32** 44 B4
Penton Mewsey **SP11** 21 G7
Pentonville **N1** 23 G3
**Pentraeth LL75 46 D5**
Pentre *Powys* **SY10** 37 K3
Pentre *Powys* **SY16** 37 K7
Pentre *Powys* **LD8** 28 B2
Pentre *Powys* **SY15** 38 B6
Pentre *Powys* **SY16** 38 A7
**Pentre *R.C.T.* CF41 18 C2**
Pentre *Shrop.* **SY4** 38 C4
Pentre *Shrop.* **SY7** 28 C1
Pentre *Wrex.* **LL14** 38 B1
Pentre *Wrex.* **LL14** 38 C1
Pentre Berw **LL60** 46 C5
Pentre Ffwrndan **CH6** 48 B5
Pentre Galar **SA41** 16 E2
Pentre Gwenlais **SA18** 17 K4
Pentre Gwynfryn **LL45** 36 E3
Pentre Halkyn **CH8** 48 B5
Pentre Isaf **LL22** 47 G6
Pentre Llanrhaeadr **LL16** 47 J6
Pentre Maelor **LL13** 38 C1
Pentre Meyrick **CF71** 18 C4
Pentre Poeth **SA6** 17 K6
Pentre Saron **LL16** 47 J6
Pentre-bach *Cere.* **SA48** 17 J1
Pentrebach *M.Tyd.* **CF48** 18 D1
Pentre-bach *Powys* **LD3** 27 J5
Pentrebach *R.C.T.* **CF37** 18 D3
Pentrebach *Swan.* **SA4** 17 J5
Pentre-bont **LL25** 47 F7
Pentre-bwlch **LL11** 38 A1
Pentrecagal **SA38** 17 G1
Pentre-celyn *Denb.* **LL15** 47 K7
Pentre-celyn *Powys* **SY19** 37 H5
Pentre-chwyth **SA1** 17 K6
Pentreclwydau **SA11** 18 B1
Pentre-cwrt **SA44** 17 G2
Pentre-Dolau-Honddu **LD3** 27 J4
Pentredwr *Denb.* **LL20** 38 A1
Pentre-dwr *Swan.* **SA7** 17 K6
Pentrefelin *Carmar.* **SA19** 17 K3
Pentrefelin *Cere.* **SA48** 17 K1
Pentrefelin *Conwy* **LL28** 47 G5
Pentrefelin *Gwyn.* **LL52** 36 E2
Pentrefelin *Powys* **SY10** 38 A3
Pentrefoelas **LL24** 47 G7
Pentregat **SA44** 26 C3
Pentreheyling **SY15** 38 B6
Pentre-llwyn-llŵyd **LD2** 27 J3
Pentre-llyn **SY23** 27 F1
Pentre-llyn-cymmer **LL21** 47 H7
Pentre-piod **LL23** 37 H2
Pentre-poeth **NP10** 19 F3
Pentre'r beirdd **SY21** 38 A4
Pentre'r Felin **LL28** 47 G6
Pentre'r-felin **LD3** 27 J5
Pentre-tafarn-y-fedw **LL26** 47 G6
Pentre-ty-gwyn **SA20** 27 H5
Pentrich **DE5** 51 F7
Pentridge **SP5** 10 B3
Pentwyn *Caerp.* **CF81** 18 E1
Pen-twyn *Caerp.* **NP13** 19 F1
Pentwyn *Cardiff* **CF23** 19 F3
Pen-twyn *Mon.* **NP25** 19 J1
Pentwyn-mawr **NP11** 18 E2
Pentyrch **CF15** 18 E3
Pentywyn (Pendine) **SA33** 17 F5
Penuwch **SY25** 26 E2
Penwithick **PL26** 4 A5
Penwood **RG20** 21 H5
Penwortham **PR1** 55 J7
Penwortham Lane **PR1** 55 J7
Penwyllt **SA9** 27 H7
Pen-y-banc **SA19** 17 K3
Pen-y-bont *Carmar.* **SA20** 27 G5
Pen-y-bont *Carmar.* **SA33** 17 G3
Pen-y-bont *Powys* **SY21** 37 K4
Pen-y-bont *Powys* **SY10** 38 B3
Penybont *Powys* **LD1** 28 A2
**Pen-y-bont ar Ogwr (Bridgend) CF31 18 C4**
Penybontfawr **SY10** 37 K3
Penybryn *Caerp.* **CF82** 18 E2
Pen-y-bryn *Gwyn.* **LL40** 37 F4
Pen-y-bryn *Pembs.* **SA43** 16 E1

Pen - Por


Pen-y-bryn *Wrex.* LL14 38 B1
Pen-y-cae *Powys* SA9 27 H7
Penycae *Wrex.* LL14 38 B1
Pen-y-cae-mawr NP15 19 H2
Pen-y-cefn CH7 47 K5
Pen-y-clawdd NP25 19 H1
Pen-y-coedcae CF37 18 D3
Penycwm SA62 16 B3
Pen-y-Darren CF47 18 D1
Pen-y-fai CF31 18 B3
Penyffordd *Flints.* CH4 48 C6
Pen-y-ffordd *Flints.* CH8 47 K4
Penyffridd LL54 46 D7
Pen-y-gaer NP8 28 A6
Pen-y-garn *Carmar.* SA32 17 J2
Pen-y-garn *Cere.* SY24 37 F7
Penygarn *Torfaen* NP4 19 F1
Penygarnedd SY10 38 A3
Pen-y-garreg LD2 27 K4
Pen-y-Graig *Gwyn.* LL53 36 B2
Penygraig *R.C.T.* CF40 18 D2
Penygroes *Carmar.* SA14 17 J4
Penygroes *Gwyn.* LL54 46 C7
Pen-y-Gwryd Hotel LL55 46 E7
Pen-y-lan CF23 18 E4
Penymynydd CH4 48 C6
Pen-y-parc CH7 48 B6
Pen-y-Park HR3 28 B4
Pen-yr-englyn CF42 18 C2
Pen-yr-heol *Mon.* NP25 28 D7
Penyrheol *Swan.* SA4 17 J6
**Pen-y-sarn LL69 46 C3**
Pen-y-stryt LL11 47 K7
Penywaun CF44 18 C1
**Penzance TR18 2 B5**
Penzance Heliport TR18 2 B5
Peopleton WR10 29 J3
Peover Heath WA16 49 G5
Peper Harow GU8 22 C7
Peplow TF9 39 F3
Pepper Arden DL7 62 D6
Pepper's Green CM1 33 K7
Perceton KA11 74 B6
Percie AB31 90 D5
Percyhorner AB43 99 H4
Perham Down SP11 21 F7
Periton TA24 7 H1
Perivale UB6 22 E3
Perkhill AB31 90 D4
Perkins Beach SY5 38 C5
Perkin's Village EX5 7 J6
Perlethorpe NG22 51 J5
Perran Downs TR20 2 C5
Perranarworthal TR3 2 E5
**Perranporth TR6 2 E3**
Perranuthnoe TR20 2 C6
Perranzabuloe TR4 2 E3
Perrott's Brook GL7 20 D1
Perry Barr B42 40 C6
Perry Crofts B79 40 E5
Perry Green *Essex* CM77 34 C6
Perry Green *Herts.* SG10 33 H7
Perry Green *Wilts.* SN16 20 C3
Perry Street DA11 24 C4
Perrymead BA2 20 A5
Pershall ST21 40 A3
**Pershore WR10 29 J4**
Persie House PH10 82 C2
Pert AB30 83 H1
Pertenhall MK44 32 D2
**PERTH PH 82 C5**
Perthcelyn CF45 18 D2
Perthy SY12 38 C2
Perton WV6 40 A6
Pestalozzi Children's Village TN33 14 C6
Peter Tavy PL19 5 F3
**PETERBOROUGH PE 42 E6**
Peterburn IV21 94 D3
Peterchurch HR2 28 C5
**Peterculter AB14 91 G4**
**Peterhead AB42 99 K6**
**Peterlee SR8 63 F2**
Peter's Green LU2 32 E7
Peters Marland EX38 6 C4
Peters Port (Port Pheadair) HS7 92 D7
**Petersfield GU32 11 J2**
Petersfinger SP5 10 C2
Peterstone Wentlooge CF3 19 F3
Peterston-super-Ely CF5 18 D4
Peterstow HR9 28 E6
Petham CT4 15 G2
Petrockstowe EX20 6 D5
Pett TN35 14 D6
Pettaugh IP14 35 F3
Petteril Green CA11 61 F2
Pettinain ML11 75 H6
Pettistree IP13 35 G3
Petton *Devon* EX16 7 J3
Petton *Shrop.* SY4 38 D3
Petts Wood BR5 23 H5
Petty AB53 91 F1
Pettycur KY3 76 A2
Pettymuick AB41 91 H2
**Petworth GU28 12 C4**
**Pevensey BN24 13 K6**
Pevensey Bay BN24 13 K6
Peverell PL2 4 E5
**Pewsey SN9 20 E5**
Pheasant's Hill RG9 22 A3
Phesdo AB30 90 E7
Philham EX39 6 A3
Philiphaugh TD7 69 K1
Phillack TR27 2 C5
Philleigh TR2 3 F5
Philpstoun EH49 75 J3
Phocle Green HR9 29 F6
Phoenix Green RG27 22 A6
Phones PH20 88 E5
Phorp IV36 97 H6
Pibsbury TA10 8 D2
Pica CA14 60 B4
Piccadilly Corner IP20 45 G7
Pickerells CM5 23 J1
**Pickering YO18 58 D1**
Pickering Nook NE16 62 C1
Picket Piece SP11 21 G7
Picket Post BH24 10 C4
Pickford Green CV5 40 E7
Pickhill YO7 57 J1
Picklescott SY6 38 D6
Pickletillem KY16 83 F5
Pickmere WA16 49 F5
Pickney TA2 7 K3
Pickstock TF10 39 G3
Pickston PH1 82 A5
Pickup Bank BB3 56 C7
Pickwell *Devon* EX33 6 C1
Pickwell *Leics.* LE14 42 A4
Pickworth *Lincs.* NG34 42 D2
Pickworth *Rut.* PE9 42 C4
Picton *Ches.W. & C.* CH2 48 D5
Picton *N.Yorks.* TS15 63 F6
Piddinghoe BN9 13 H6
Piddington *Bucks.* HP14 22 B2
Piddington *Northants.* NN7 32 B3
Piddington *Oxon.* OX25 31 H7
Piddlehinton DT2 9 G5
Piddletrenthide DT2 9 G5
Pidley PE28 33 G1
Piercebridge DL2 62 D5
Pierowall KW17 106 D3
Pigdon NE61 71 G5
Pike Hill BB10 56 D6
Pikehall DE4 50 D7
Pikeshill SO43 10 D4
Pilgrims Hatch CM15 23 J2
Pilham DN21 52 B3
Pill BS20 19 J4
Pillaton *Cornw.* PL12 4 D4
Pillaton *Staffs.* ST19 40 B4
Pillerton Hersey CV35 30 D4
Pillerton Priors CV35 30 D4
Pilleth LD7 28 B2
Pilley *Hants.* SO41 10 E5
Pilley *S.Yorks.* S75 51 F2
Pilling PR3 55 H5
Pilling Lane FY6 55 G5
Pillowell GL15 19 K1
Pilning BS35 19 J3
Pilsbury SK17 50 D6
Pilsdon DT6 8 D5
Pilsgate PE9 42 D5
Pilsley *Derbys.* S45 51 G6
Pilsley *Derbys.* DE45 50 E5
Pilson Green NR13 45 H4
Piltdown TN22 13 H4
Pilton *Devon* EX31 6 D2
Pilton *Northants.* PE8 42 D7
Pilton *Rut.* LE15 42 C5
Pilton *Som.* BA4 19 J7
Pilton *Swan.* SA3 17 H7
Pilton Green SA3 17 H7
Pimhole BL9 49 H1
Pimlico HP3 22 D1
Pimperne DT11 9 J4
Pin Mill IP9 35 G5
Pinchbeck PE11 43 F3
Pinchbeck Bars PE11 43 F3
Pinchbeck West PE11 43 F3
Pincheon Green DN14 51 J1
Pinchinthorpe TS14 63 G5
Pindon End MK19 31 J4
Pinehurst SN25 20 E3
Pinfold L40 48 C1
Pinged SA16 17 H5
Pinhay DT7 8 C5
Pinhoe EX1 7 H6
Pinkneys Green SL6 22 B3
Pinley Green CV35 30 D2
Pinminnoch KA26 67 F4
Pinmore KA26 67 G4
Pinn EX10 7 K7
**Pinner HA5 22 E3**
Pinner Green HA5 22 E2
Pinvin WR10 29 J4
Pinwherry KA26 67 F5
Pinxton NG16 51 G7
Pipe & Lyde HR1 28 E4
Pipe Gate TF9 39 G1
Pipe Ridware WS15 40 C4
Pipehill WS13 40 C5
Piperhall PA20 73 J5
Piperhill IV12 97 F6
Pipers Pool PL15 4 C2
Pipewell NN14 42 B7
Pippacott EX31 6 D2
Pipton LD3 28 A5
Pirbright GU24 22 C6
Pirnmill KA27 73 G6
Pirton *Herts.* SG5 32 E5
Pirton *Worcs.* WR8 29 H4
Pisgah FK15 81 J7
Pishill RG9 22 A3
Pistyll LL53 36 C1
Pitagowan PH18 81 K1
Pitblae AB43 99 H4
Pitcairngreen PH1 82 B5
Pitcairns PH2 82 B6
Pitcaple AB51 91 F2
Pitch Green HP27 22 A1
Pitch Place *Surr.* GU3 22 C6
Pitch Place *Surr.* GU8 12 B3
Pitchcombe GL6 20 B1
Pitchcott HP22 31 J6
Pitchford SY5 38 E5
Pitcombe BA10 9 F1
Pitcot CF32 18 B4
Pitcox EH42 76 E3
Pitcur PH13 82 D4
Pitfichie AB51 90 E3
Pitgrudy IV25 96 E2
Pitinnan AB51 91 F1
Pitkennedy DD8 83 G2
Pitkevy KY6 82 D7
Pitlessie KY15 82 E7
**Pitlochry PH16 82 A2**
Pitman's Corner IP14 35 F2
Pitmedden AB41 91 G2
Pitminster TA3 8 B3
Pitmuies DD8 83 G3
Pitmunie AB51 90 E3
Pitnacree PH9 82 A2
Pitney TA10 8 D2
Pitroddie PH2 82 D5
Pitscottie KY15 83 F6
Pitsea SS13 24 D3
Pitsford NN6 31 J2
Pitsford Hill TA4 7 J2
Pitstone LU7 32 C7
Pitt *Devon* EX16 7 J4
Pitt *Hants.* SO22 11 F2
Pittendreich IV30 97 J5
Pittentrail IV28 96 E1
Pittenweem KY10 83 G7
Pitteuchar KY7 76 A1
Pittington DH6 62 E2
Pittodrie House AB51 90 E2
Pitton *Swan.* SA3 17 H7
Pitton *Wilts.* SP5 10 D1
Pittulie AB43 99 H4
Pittville GL52 29 J6
Pity Me DH1 62 D2
Pityme PL27 3 G1
Pixey Green IP21 35 G1
Pixley HR8 29 F5
Place Newton YO17 58 E2
Plaidy AB53 99 F5
Plain Dealings SA67 16 D4
Plainfield NE65 70 E3
Plains ML6 75 F4
Plainsfield TA5 7 K2
Plaish SY6 38 E6
Plaistow *Gt.Lon.* E13 23 G3
Plaistow *W.Suss.* RH14 12 D3
Plaitford SO51 10 D3
Plaitford Green SO51 10 D2
Plas SA32 17 H3
Plas Gwynant LL55 46 E7
Plas Isaf LL21 37 K1
Plas Llwyd LL18 47 H5
Plas Llwyngwern SY20 37 G5
Plas Llysyn SY17 37 J6
Plas Nantyr LL20 38 A2
Plashett SA33 17 F5
Plasisaf LL16 47 H6
Plas-rhiw-Saeson SY19 37 J5
Plastow Green RG19 21 J5
Plas-yn-Cefn LL17 47 J5
Platt TN15 23 K6
Platt Bridge WN2 49 F2
Platt Lane SY13 38 E2
Platt's Heath ME17 14 D2
Plawsworth DH2 62 D2
Plaxtol TN15 23 K6
Play Hatch RG4 22 A4
Playden TN31 14 E5
Playford IP6 35 G4
Playing Place TR3 3 F4
Playley Green GL19 29 G5
Plealey SY5 38 D5
Plean FK7 75 G2
Pleasance KY14 82 D6
Pleasant Valley CB11 33 J5
Pleasington BB2 56 B7
Pleasley NG19 51 H6
Pleasleyhill NG19 51 H6
Pleck *Dorset* DT9 9 G3
Pleck *W.Mid.* WS2 40 B6
Pledgdon Green CM22 33 J6
Pledwick WF2 51 F1
Plemstall CH2 48 D5
Plenmeller NE49 70 C7
Pleshey CM3 33 K7
**Plockton IV52 86 E1**
Plocropol HS3 93 G2
Plomer's Hill HP13 22 B2
Plot Gate TA11 8 E1
Plough Hill CV10 41 F6
Plowden SY7 38 C7
Ploxgreen SY5 38 C5
Pluckley TN27 14 E3
Pluckley Thorne TN27 14 E3
Plucks Gutter CT3 25 J5
Plumbland CA7 60 C3
Plumbley S20 51 G4
Plumley WA16 49 G5
Plumpton *Cumb.* CA11 61 F3
Plumpton *E.Suss.* BN7 13 G5
Plumpton *Northants.* NN12 31 H4
Plumpton Green BN7 13 G5
Plumpton Head CA11 61 G3
Plumstead *Gt.Lon.* SE18 23 H4
Plumstead *Norf.* NR11 45 F2
Plumtree NG12 41 J2
Plungar NG13 42 A2
Plush DT2 9 G4
Plusha PL15 4 C2
Plushabridge PL14 4 D3
Plwmp SA44 26 C3
Plym Bridge PL7 5 F5
**PLYMOUTH PL 4 E5**
Plymouth City Airport PL6 5 F4
Plympton PL7 5 F5
Plymstock PL9 5 F5
Plymtree EX15 7 J5
Pockley YO62 58 C1
Pocklington YO42 58 E5
Pockthorpe NR20 44 E3
Pocombe Bridge EX2 7 G6
Pode Hole PE11 43 F3
Podimore BA22 8 E2
Podington NN29 32 C2
Podmore ST21 39 G2
Podsmead GL2 29 H7
Poffley End OX29 30 E7
Point Clear CO16 34 E7
Pointon NG34 42 E2
Polanach PA38 80 A2
Polapit Tamar PL15 6 B7
Polbae DG8 64 C3
Polbain IV26 102 B7
Polbathic PL11 4 D5
Polbeth EH55 75 J4
Poldean DG10 69 G4
Pole Moor HD3 50 C1
Polebrook PE8 42 D7
**Polegate BN26 13 J6**
Poles IV25 96 E2
Polesworth B78 40 E5
Polglass IV26 95 G1
Polgooth PL26 3 G3
Polgown DG3 68 C3
Poling BN18 12 D6
Poling Corner BN18 12 D6
Polkerris PL24 4 A5
Poll a' Charra HS8 84 C3
Polla IV27 103 F3
Pollardras TR13 2 D5
Polldubh PH33 80 C1
Pollie IV28 104 C7
Pollington DN14 51 J1
Polloch PH37 79 J1
Pollok G53 74 D4
Pollokshaws G43 74 D4
Pollokshields G41 74 D4
Polmassick PL26 3 G4
Polmont FK2 75 H3
Polnoon G76 74 D5
Polperro PL13 4 C5
Polruan PL23 4 B5
Polsham BA5 19 J7
Polstead CO6 34 D5
Polstead Heath CO6 34 D4
Poltalloch PA31 73 G1
Poltimore EX4 7 H6
Polton EH18 76 A4
Polwarth TD10 77 F5
Polyphant PL15 4 C2
Polzeath PL27 3 G1
Pomphlett PL9 5 F5
Pond Street CB11 33 H5
Ponders End EN3 23 G2
Pondersbridge PE26 43 F6
Ponsanooth TR3 2 E5
Ponsonby CA20 60 B6
Ponsongath TR12 2 E7
Ponsworthy TQ13 5 H3
Pont Aber SA19 27 G6
Pont Aberglaslyn LL55 36 E1
Pont ar Hydfer LD3 27 H6
Pont Crugnant SY19 37 H6
Pont Cyfyng LL24 47 F7
Pont Dolgarrog LL32 47 F6
Pont Pen-y-benglog LL57 46 E6
Pont Rhyd-sarn LL23 37 H3
Pont Rhyd-y-cyff CF34 18 B3
Pont Walby SA11 18 B1
Pont yr Alwen LL21 47 H7
Pontamman SA18 17 K4
Pontantwn SA17 17 H4
Pontardawe SA8 18 A1
Pontarddulais SA4 17 J5
Pontarfynach (Devil's Bridge) SY23 27 G1
Pontargothi SA32 17 J3
Pont-ar-llechau SA19 27 G6
Pontarsais SA32 17 H3
Pontblyddyn CH7 48 B6
Pontbren Llwyd CF44 18 C1
**Pontefract WF8 57 K7**
Ponteland NE20 71 G6
Ponterwyd SY23 37 G7
Pontesbury SY5 38 D5
Pontesbury Hill SY5 38 C5
Pontesford SY5 38 D5
Pontfadog LL20 38 B2
Pontfaen *Pembs.* SA65 16 D2
Pont-faen *Powys* LD3 27 J5
Pontgarreg SA44 26 C3
Pont-Henri SA15 17 H5
Ponthir NP18 19 G2
Ponthirwaun SA43 17 F1
Pont-iets (Pontyates) SA15 17 H5
Pontllanfraith NP12 18 E2
Pontlliw SA4 17 K5
Pontllyfni LL54 46 C7
Pontlottyn CF81 18 E1
Pontneddfechan SA11 18 C1
Pontrhydfendigaid SY25 27 G2
Pontrhydyfen SA12 18 A2
Pont-rhyd-y-groes SY25 27 G1
Pontrhydyrun NP44 19 F2
Pontrilas HR2 28 C6
Pontrobert SY22 38 A4
Pont-rug LL55 46 D6
Ponts Green TN33 13 K5
Pontshill HR9 29 F6
Pont-siân SA44 17 H1
Pontsticill CF48 27 K7
Pontwelly SA44 17 H2
Pontyates (Pont-iets) SA15 17 H5
Pontyberem SA15 17 J4
Pont-y-blew LL14 38 C2
Pontybodkin CH7 48 B7
**Pontyclun CF72 18 D3**
Pontycymer CF32 18 C2
Pontygwaith CF43 18 D2
Pontymister NP11 19 F2
Pontymoel NP4 19 F1
Pont-y-pant LL25 47 F7
**Pontypool NP4 19 F1**
**Pontypridd CF37 18 D2**
Pont-y-rhyl CF32 18 C3
Pontywaun NP11 19 F2
Pooksgreen SO40 10 E3
Pool *Cornw.* TR15 2 D4
Pool *W.Yorks.* LS21 57 H5
Pool Bank LA11 55 H1
Pool Green WS9 40 C5
Pool Head HR1 28 E3
Pool of Muckhart FK14 82 B7
Pool Quay SY21 38 B4
Pool Street CO9 34 B5
**Poole BH15 10 B5**
Poole Keynes GL7 20 C2
Poolend ST13 49 J7
Poolewe IV22 94 E3
Pooley Bridge CA10 61 F4
Pooley Street IP22 44 E7
Poolfold ST8 49 H7
Poolhill GL18 29 G6
Poolsbrook S43 51 G5
Poolthorne Farm DN20 52 D2
Pope Hill SA62 16 C4
Popeswood RG42 22 B5
Popham SO21 21 J7
Poplar E14 23 G3
Porchfield PO30 11 F5
Porin IV6 95 K6
Poringland NR14 45 G5
Porkellis TR13 2 D5
Porlock TA24 7 G1
Porlock Weir TA24 7 G1
Port Allen PH2 82 D5
Port Appin PA38 80 A3
Port Askaig PA46 72 C4
Port Bannatyne PA20 73 J4
Port Carlisle CA7 69 H7
Port Charlotte PA48 72 A5
Port Clarence TS2 63 G4
Port Driseach PA21 73 H3
Port e Vullen IM7 54 D4
Port Ellen PA42 72 B6
Port Elphinstone AB51 91 F3
Port Erin IM9 54 A7
Port Erroll AB42 91 J1
Port Eynon SA3 17 H7
Port Gaverne PL29 4 A2
**Port Glasgow PA14 74 B3**
Port Henderson IV21 94 D4
**Port Isaac PL29 4 A2**
Port Logan DG9 64 A6
Port Mòr PH41 85 K7
Port Mulgrave TS13 63 J5
Port na Craig PH16 82 A2
Port nan Giùran (Portnaguran) HS2 101 H4
Port nan Long HS6 92 D4
Port Nis (Port of Ness) HS2 101 H1
Port of Menteith FK8 81 G7
Port of Ness (Port Nis) HS2 101 H1
Port o'Warren DG5 65 J5
Port Penrhyn LL57 46 D5
Port Pheadair (Peters Port) HS7 92 D7
Port Quin PL29 3 G1
Port Ramsay PA34 79 K3
Port St. Mary IM9 54 B7
Port Solent PO6 11 H4
Port Sunlight CH62 48 C4
**Port Talbot SA12 18 A2**
Port Tennant SA1 17 K6
Port Wemyss PA47 72 A5
Port William DG8 64 D6
Portachoillan PA29 73 F5
Portavadie PA21 73 H4
Portbury BS20 19 J4
Portchester PO16 11 H4
Portencross KA23 73 K6
Portesham DT3 9 F6
Portessie AB56 98 C4
Portfield *Arg. & B.* PA63 79 J5
Portfield *W.Suss.* PO19 12 B6
Portfield Gate SA62 16 C4
Portgate EX20 6 C7
Portgordon AB56 98 B4
Portgower KW8 105 F7
Porth *Cornw.* TR7 3 F2
**Porth *R.C.T.* CF39 18 D2**
Porth Colmon LL53 36 A2
Porth Llechog (Bull Bay) LL68 46 C3
Porth Navas TR11 2 E6
**Porthaethwy (Menai Bridge) LL59 46 D5**
Porthallow *Cornw.* TR12 2 E6
Porthallow *Cornw.* PL13 4 C5
**Porthcawl CF36 18 B4**
Porthcothan PL28 3 F1
Porthcurno TR19 2 A6
Porthgain SA62 16 B2
Porthill ST5 40 A1
Porthkerry CF62 18 D5
Porthleven TR13 2 D6
**Porthmadog LL49 36 E2**
Porthmeor TR20 2 B5
Portholland PL26 3 G4
Porthoustock TR12 3 F6
Porthpean PL26 4 A5
Porthtowan TR4 2 D4
Porthyrhyd *Carmar.* SA19 27 G5
Porthyrhyd *Carmar.* SA32 17 J4
Porth-y-waen SY10 38 B3
Portincaple G84 74 A1

Por - Rea

Portington DN14 58 D6
Portinnisherrich PA33 80 A6
Portinscale CA12 60 D4
Portishead BS20 19 H4
Portknockie AB56 98 C4
Portlethen AB12 91 H5
Portlethen Village AB12 91 H5
Portloe TR2 3 G5
Portlooe PL13 4 C5
Portmahomack IV20 97 G3
Portmeirion LL48 36 E2
Portmellon PL26 4 A6
Portmore SO41 10 E5
Port-na-Con IV27 103 G2
Portnacroish PA38 80 A3
Portnaguran (Port nan Giùran) HS2 101 H4
Portnahaven PA47 72 A5
Portnalong IV47 85 J1
Portnaluchaig PH39 86 C6
Portobello EH15 76 B3
Porton SP4 10 C1
Portpatrick DG9 64 A5
Portreath TR16 2 D4
**Portree IV51 93 K7**
Portscatho TR2 3 F5
Portsea PO1 11 H4
Portskerra KW14 104 D2
Portskewett NP26 19 J3
Portslade BN41 13 F6
Portslade-by-Sea BN41 13 F6
Portslogan DG9 64 A5
**PORTSMOUTH PO 11 H5**
Portsonachan PA33 80 B5
Portsoy AB45 98 D4
Portuairk PH36 79 F1
Portvoller HS2 101 H4
Portway *Here.* HR4 28 C4
Portway *Here.* HR4 28 D4
Portway *Here.* HR2 28 D5
Portway *Worcs.* B48 30 B1
Portwrinkle PL11 4 D5
Portyerrock DG8 64 E7
Posenhall TF12 39 F5
Poslingford CO10 34 B4
Postbridge PL20 5 G3
Postcombe OX9 22 A2
Postling CT21 15 G4
Post-mawr (Synod Inn) SA44 26 D3
Postwick NR13 45 G5
Potarch AB31 90 E5
Potsgrove MK17 32 C6
Pott Row PE32 44 B3
Pott Shrigley SK10 49 J5
Potten End HP4 22 D1
Potter Brompton YO12 59 F2
Potter Heigham NR29 45 J4
Potter Street CM17 23 H1
Pottergate Street NR16 45 F6
Potterhanworth LN4 52 D6
Potterhanworth Booths LN4 52 D6
Potterne SN10 20 C6
Potterne Wick SN10 20 D6
Potternewton LS7 57 J6
**Potters Bar EN6 23 F1**
Potters Crouch AL2 22 E1
Potter's Green CV2 41 F7
Potters Marston LE9 41 G6
Potterspury NN12 31 J4
Potterton *Aber.* AB23 91 H3
Potterton *W.Yorks.* LS15 57 K6
Pottle Street BA12 20 B7
Potto DL6 63 F6
Potton SG19 33 F4
Pott's Green CO6 34 D6
Poughill *Cornw.* EX23 6 A5
Poughill *Devon* EX17 7 G5
Poulshot SN10 20 C6
Poulton GL7 20 E1
**Poulton-le-Fylde FY6 55 G6**
Pound Bank WR14 29 G4
Pound Green *E.Suss.* TN22 13 J4
Pound Green *Suff.* CB8 34 B3
Pound Green *Worcs.* DY12 29 G1
Pound Hill RH10 13 F3
Pound Street RG20 21 H5
Poundbury DT1 9 F5
Poundffald SA4 17 J6
Poundfield TN6 13 J3
Poundgate TN6 13 H4
Poundland KA26 67 F5
Poundon OX27 31 H6
Poundsbridge TN11 23 J7
Poundsgate TQ13 5 H3
Poundstock EX23 4 C1
Povey Cross RH6 23 F7
Pow Green HR8 29 G4
Powburn NE66 71 F2
Powderham EX6 7 H7
Powerstock DT6 8 E5
Powfoot DG12 69 G7
Powick WR2 29 H3
Powler's Piece EX22 6 B4
Powmill FK14 75 J1
Poxwell DT2 9 G6
Poyle SL3 22 D4
Poynings BN45 13 F5
Poyntington DT9 9 F2
Poynton *Ches.E.* SK12 49 J4
Poynton *Tel. & W.* TF6 38 E4
Poynton Green SY4 38 E4
Poyntzfield IV7 96 E5
Poys Street IP17 35 H1
Poyston SA62 16 C4
Poyston Cross SA62 16 C4
Poystreet Green IP30 34 D3
Praa Sands TR13 2 C6
Pratis KY8 82 E7
Pratt's Bottom BR6 23 H5
Praze-an-Beeble TR14 2 D5
Predannack Wollas TR12 2 D7
Prees SY13 38 E2
Prees Green SY13 38 E2
Prees Heath SY13 38 E2
Prees Higher Heath SY13 38 E2
Prees Lower Heath SY13 38 E2
Preesall FY6 55 G5
Preesgweene SY10 38 B2
Prenbrigog CH7 48 B6
Prendergast SA61 16 C4
Prendwick NE66 71 F2
Pren-gwyn SA44 17 H1
Prenteg LL49 36 E1
**Prenton CH42 48 C4**
**Prescot L34 48 D3**
Prescott *Devon* EX15 7 J4
Prescott *Shrop.* SY4 38 D3
Presley IV36 97 H6
Pressen TD12 77 G7
**Prestatyn LL19 47 J4**
Prestbury *Ches.E.* SK10 49 J5
Prestbury *Glos.* GL52 29 J6
**Presteigne (Llanandras) LD8 28 C2**
Presthope TF13 38 E6
Prestleigh BA4 19 K7
Prestolee M26 49 G2
Preston *B. & H.* BN1 13 G6
Preston *Devon* TQ12 5 J3
Preston *Dorset* DT3 9 G6
Preston *E.Loth.* EH40 76 D3
Preston *E.Riding* HU12 59 H6
Preston *Glos.* HR8 29 F5
Preston *Glos.* GL7 20 D1
Preston *Herts.* SG4 32 E6
Preston *Kent* ME13 25 G5
Preston *Kent* CT3 25 J5
**PRESTON *Lancs.* PR 55 J7**
Preston *Northumb.* NE67 71 G1
Preston *Rut.* LE15 42 B5
Preston *Sc.Bord.* TD11 77 F5
Preston *Shrop.* SY4 38 E4
Preston *Som.* TA4 7 J2
Preston *Suff.* CO10 34 D3
Preston *Torbay* TQ3 5 J4
Preston *Wilts.* SN15 20 D4
Preston Bagot B95 30 C2
Preston Bissett MK18 31 H5
Preston Bowyer TA4 7 K3
Preston Brockhurst SY4 38 E3
Preston Brook WA7 48 E4
Preston Candover RG25 21 K7
Preston Capes NN11 31 G3
Preston Deanery NN7 31 J3
Preston Gubbals SY4 38 D4
Preston on Stour CV37 30 D4
Preston on the Hill WA4 48 E4
Preston on Wye HR2 28 C4
Preston Plucknett BA20 8 E3
Preston upon the Weald Moors TF6 39 F4
Preston Wynne HR1 28 E4
Preston-le-Skerne DL5 62 E4
**Prestonpans EH32 76 B3**
Preston-under-Scar DL8 62 B7
Prestwich M25 49 H2
Prestwick *Northumb.* NE20 71 G6
**Prestwick *S.Ayr.* KA9 67 H1**
Prestwold LE12 41 H3
Prestwood *Bucks.* HP16 22 B1
Prestwood *Staffs.* ST14 40 D1
Price Town CF32 18 C2
Prickwillow CB7 43 J7
Priddy BA5 19 J6
Priest Hill PR3 56 B6
Priest Hutton LA6 55 J2
Priest Weston SY15 38 B6
Priestcliffe SK17 50 D5
Priestland KA17 74 D7
Priestwood DA13 24 C5
Primethorpe LE9 41 H6
Primrose Green NR9 44 E4
Primrose Hill NW1 23 F3
Princes End DY4 40 B6
Princes Gate SA67 16 E4
**Princes Risborough HP27 22 B1**
Princethorpe CV23 31 F1
Princetown *Caerp.* NP22 28 A7
Princetown *Devon* PL20 5 F3
Prior Muir KY16 83 G6
Prior's Frome HR1 28 E5
Priors Halton SY8 28 D1
Priors Hardwick CV47 31 F3
Priors Marston CV47 31 F3
Prior's Norton GL2 29 H6
Priors Park GL20 29 H5
Priorslee TF2 39 G4
Priory Wood HR3 28 B4
Priston BA2 19 K5
Pristow Green NR16 45 F7
Prittlewell SS0 24 E3
Privett GU34 11 H2
Prixford EX31 6 D2
Proaig PA44 72 C5
Probus TR2 3 F4
Protstonhill AB45 99 G4
**Prudhoe NE42 71 F7**
Prussia Cove TR20 2 C6
Pubil PH15 81 F3
Publow BS39 19 K5
Puckeridge SG11 33 G6
Puckington TA19 8 C3
Pucklechurch BS16 19 K4
Pucknall SO51 10 E2
Puckrup GL20 29 H5
Puddinglake CW10 49 G6
Puddington *Ches.W. & C.* CH64 48 C5
Puddington *Devon* EX16 7 G4
Puddlebrook GL17 29 F7
Puddledock NR17 44 E6
Puddletown DT2 9 G5
Pudleston HR6 28 E3
**Pudsey LS28 57 H6**
**Pulborough RH20 12 D5**
Puldagon KW1 105 J4
Puleston TF10 39 G3
Pulford CH4 48 C7
Pulham DT2 9 G4
Pulham Market IP21 45 F7
Pulham St. Mary IP21 45 G7
Pulley SY3 38 D5
Pulloxhill MK45 32 D5
Pulrossie IV25 96 E3
Pulverbatch SY5 38 D5
Pumpherston EH53 75 J4
Pumsaint SA19 17 K1
Puncheston SA62 16 D3
Puncknowle DT2 8 E6
Punnett's Town TN21 13 K4
Purbrook PO7 11 H4
Purewell BH23 10 C5
**Purfleet RM19 23 J4**
Puriton TA7 19 G7
Purleigh CM3 24 E1
**Purley CR8 23 G5**
Purley on Thames RG8 21 K4
Purlogue SY7 28 B1
Purlpit SN12 20 B5
Purls Bridge PE15 43 H7
Purse Caundle DT9 9 F3
Purslow SY7 38 C7
Purston Jaglin WF7 51 G1
Purtington TA20 8 C4
Purton *Glos.* GL13 19 K1
Purton *Glos.* GL15 19 K1
Purton *Wilts.* SN5 20 D3
Purton Stoke SN5 20 D2
Purves Hall TD10 77 F6
Pury End NN12 31 J4
Pusey SN7 21 G2
Putley HR8 29 F5
Putley Green HR8 29 F5
Putney SW15 23 F4
Putsborough EX33 6 C1
Puttenham *Herts.* HP23 32 B7
Puttenham *Surr.* GU3 22 C7
Puttock End CO10 34 C4
Putts Corner EX10 7 K6
Puxton BS24 19 H5
Pwll SA15 17 H5
Pwllcrochan SA71 16 C5
Pwlldefaid LL53 36 A3
Pwll-glas LL15 47 K7
Pwllgloyw LD3 27 K5
**Pwllheli LL53 36 C2**
Pwll-Mawr CF3 19 F4
Pwllmeyric NP16 19 J2
Pwll-trap SA33 17 F4
Pwll-y-glaw SA12 18 A2
Pye Corner *Herts.* CM20 33 H7
Pye Corner *Kent* ME17 14 D3
Pye Corner *Newport* NP18 19 G3
Pye Green WS12 40 B4
Pyecombe BN45 13 F5
Pyle *Bridgend* CF33 18 B3
Pyle *I.o.W.* PO38 11 F7
Pyleigh TA4 7 K2
Pylle BA4 9 F1
Pymoor (Pymore) CB6 43 H7
Pymore (Pymoor) *Cambs.* CB6 43 H7
Pymore *Dorset* DT6 8 D5
Pyrford GU22 22 D6
Pyrford Green GU22 22 D6
Pyrton OX49 21 K2
Pytchley NN14 32 B1
Pyworthy EX22 6 B5

## Q

Quabbs LD7 38 B7
Quadring PE11 43 F2
Quadring Eaudike PE11 43 F2
Quainton HP22 31 J6
Quarff ZE2 107 N9
Quarley SP11 21 F7
Quarndon DE22 41 F1
Quarr Hill PO33 11 G5
Quarrier's Village PA11 74 B4
Quarrington NG34 42 D1
Quarrington Hill DH6 62 E3
Quarry Bank DY5 40 B7
Quarrybank CW6 48 E6
Quarrywood IV30 97 J5
Quarter ML3 75 F5
Quatford WV15 39 G6
Quatt WV15 39 G7
Quebec DH7 62 C2
Quedgeley GL2 29 H7
Queen Adelaide CB7 43 J7
Queen Camel BA22 8 E2
Queen Charlton BS31 19 K5
Queen Dart EX16 7 G4
Queen Oak SP8 9 G1
Queen Street TN12 23 K7
**Queenborough ME11 25 F4**
Queen's Bower PO36 11 G6
Queen's Head SY11 38 C3
Queensbury *Gt.Lon.* HA3 22 E3
Queensbury *W.Yorks.* BD13 57 G6
**Queensferry (South Queensferry) *Edin.* EH30 75 K3**
Queensferry *Flints.* CH5 48 C6
Queenzieburn G65 74 E3
Quemerford SN11 20 D5
Quendale ZE2 107 M11
Quendon CB11 33 J5
Queniborough LE7 41 J4
Quenington GL7 20 E1
Quernmore LA2 55 J3
Queslett B43 40 C6
Quethiock PL14 4 D4
Quholm KW16 106 B6
Quick's Green RG8 21 J4
Quidenham NR16 44 E7
Quidhampton RG25 21 J6
Quidinish (Cuidhtinis) HS3 93 F3
Quilquox AB41 91 H1
Quina Brook SY4 38 E2
Quindry KW17 106 D8
Quine's Hill IM4 54 C6
Quinhill PA29 73 F5
Quinton *Northants.* NN7 31 J3
Quinton *W.Mid.* B32 40 B7
Quinton Green NN7 31 J3
Quintrell Downs TR8 3 F2
Quixhill ST14 40 D1
Quoditch EX21 6 C6
Quoig PH7 81 K5
Quoiggs House FK15 81 K7
Quoisley SY13 38 E1
Quorn (Quorndon) LE12 41 H4
Quorndon (Quorn) LE12 41 H4
Quothquan ML12 75 H7
Quoyloo KW16 106 B5
Quoys ZE2 107 Q1
Quoys of Reiss KW1 105 J3

## R

Raasay IV40 94 B7
Raby CH63 48 C5
Rachan ML12 75 K7
Rachub LL57 46 E6
Rackenford EX16 7 G4
Rackham RH20 12 D5
Rackheath NR13 45 G4
Racks DG1 69 F6
Rackwick *Ork.* KW16 106 B8
Rackwick *Ork.* KW17 106 D3
Radbourne DE6 40 E2
Radcliffe *Gt.Man.* M26 49 G2
Radcliffe *Northumb.* NE65 71 H3
Radcliffe on Trent NG12 41 J2
Radclive MK18 31 H5
Radcot OX18 21 F2
Raddington TA4 7 J3
Radernie KY15 83 F7
Radford *B. & N.E.Som.* BA2 19 K6
Radford *Nott.* NG7 41 H1
Radford *Oxon.* OX7 31 F6
Radford *W.Mid.* CV6 41 F7
Radford Semele CV31 30 E2
Radipole DT3 9 F6
**Radlett WD7 22 E1**
Radley OX14 21 J2
Radley Green CM4 24 C1
Radmore Green CW6 48 E7
Radnage HP14 22 A2
**Radstock BA3 19 K6**
Radstone NN13 31 G4
Radway CV35 30 E4
Radway Green CW1 49 G7
Radwell *Bed.* MK43 32 D3
Radwell *Herts.* SG7 33 F5
Radwinter CB10 33 K5
Radyr CF15 18 E3
Raechester NE19 70 E5
Raemoir House AB31 90 E5
Raffin IV27 102 C5
Rafford IV36 97 H6
Ragdale LE14 41 J3
Ragged Appleshaw SP11 21 G7
Raglan NP15 19 H1
Ragnall NG22 52 B5
Rahoy PA34 79 H2
Rain Shore OL12 49 H1
Rainford WA11 48 D2
**Rainham *Gt.Lon.* RM13 23 J3**
Rainham *Med.* ME8 24 E5
Rainhill L35 48 D3
Rainhill Stoops L35 48 E3
Rainow SK10 49 J5
Rainsough M27 49 G2
Rainton YO7 57 J2
Rainworth NG21 51 H7
Raisbeck CA10 61 H6
Raise CA9 61 J2
Rait PH2 82 D5
Raithby *Lincs.* PE23 53 G6
Raithby *Lincs.* LN11 53 G4
Rake GU33 12 B4
Raleigh's Cross TA23 7 J2
Ram SA48 17 J1
Ram Alley SN8 21 F5
Ram Lane TN26 14 E3
Ramasaig IV55 93 G7
Rame *Cornw.* TR10 2 E5
Rame *Cornw.* PL10 4 E6
Rampisham DT2 8 E4
Rampside LA13 55 F3
Rampton *Cambs.* CB24 33 H2
Rampton *Notts.* DN22 52 B5
Ramsbottom BL0 49 G1
Ramsbury SN8 21 F4
Ramscraigs KW6 105 G6
Ramsdean GU32 11 J2
Ramsdell RG26 21 J6
Ramsden OX7 30 E7
Ramsden Bellhouse CM11 24 D2
Ramsden Heath CM11 24 D2
Ramsey *Cambs.* PE26 43 F7
Ramsey *Essex* CO12 35 G5
Ramsey *I.o.M.* IM8 54 D4
Ramsey Forty Foot PE26 43 G7
Ramsey Heights PE26 43 F7
Ramsey Island *Essex* CM0 25 F1
Ramsey Island *Pembs.* SA62 16 A3
Ramsey Mereside PE26 43 F7
Ramsey St. Mary's PE26 43 F7
**Ramsgate CT11 25 K5**
Ramsgate Street NR24 44 E2
Ramsgill HG3 57 G2
Ramsholt IP12 35 H4
Ramshorn ST10 40 C1
Ramsnest Common GU8 12 C3
Ranachan PH36 79 J1
Ranais (Ranish) HS2 101 G5
Ranby *Lincs.* LN8 53 F5
Ranby *Notts.* DN22 51 J4
Rand LN8 52 E5
Randwick GL6 20 B1
Rangemore DE13 40 D3
Rangeworthy BS37 19 K3
Ranish (Ranais) HS2 101 G5
Rankinston KA6 67 J2
Rank's Green CM3 34 B7
Ranmoor S10 51 F4
Rannoch School PH17 81 G2
Ranochan PH38 86 E6
Ranscombe TA24 7 H1
Ranskill DN22 51 J4
Ranton ST18 40 A3
Ranton Green ST18 40 A3
Ranworth NR13 45 H4
Rapness KW17 106 E3
Rapps TA19 8 C3
Rascarrel DG7 65 H6
Rash LA10 56 B1
Rashwood WR9 29 J2
Raskelf YO61 57 K2
Rassau NP23 28 A7
Rastrick HD6 57 G7
Ratagan IV40 87 F3
Ratby LE6 41 H5
Ratcliffe Culey CV9 41 F6
Ratcliffe on Soar NG11 41 G3
Ratcliffe on the Wreake LE7 41 J4
Ratford Bridge SA62 16 B4
Ratfyn SP4 20 E7
Rathen AB43 99 H4
Rathillet KY15 82 E5
Rathliesbeag PH34 87 J6
Rathmell BD24 56 D3
Ratho EH28 75 K3
Ratho Station EH28 75 K3
Rathven AB56 98 C4
Ratley OX15 30 E4
Ratling CT3 15 H2
Ratlinghope SY5 38 D6
Ratsloe EX4 7 H6
Rattar KW14 105 H1
Ratten Row *Cumb.* CA5 60 E2
Ratten Row *Lancs.* PR3 55 H5
Rattery TQ10 5 H4
Rattlesden IP30 34 D3
Rattray PH10 82 C3
Raughton Head CA5 60 E2
Raunds NN9 32 C1
Ravenfield S65 51 G3
**Ravenglass CA18 60 B7**
Raveningham NR14 45 H6
Raven's Green CO7 35 F6
Ravenscar YO13 63 J2
Ravensdale IM7 54 C4
Ravensden MK44 32 D3
Ravenshaw BD23 56 E5
Ravenshayes EX5 7 H5
Ravenshead NG15 51 H7
Ravensmoor CW5 49 F7
Ravensthorpe *Northants.* NN6 31 H1
Ravensthorpe *W.Yorks.* WF13 57 H7
Ravenstone *Leics.* LE67 41 G4
Ravenstone *M.K.* MK46 32 B3
Ravenstonedale CA17 61 J6
Ravenstruther ML11 75 H6
Ravensworth DL11 62 C6
Raw YO22 63 J2
Rawcliffe *E.Riding* DN14 58 C7
Rawcliffe *York* YO30 58 B4
Rawcliffe Bridge DN14 58 C7
Rawdon LS19 57 H6
Rawmarsh S62 51 G3
Rawnsley WS12 40 C4
Rawreth SS11 24 D2
Rawridge EX14 8 B4
Rawson Green DE56 41 F1
Rawtenstall BB4 56 D7
Rawyards ML6 75 F4
Raxton AB41 91 G1
Raydon IP7 34 E5
Raylees NE19 70 E4
**Rayleigh SS6 24 E2**
Raymond's Hill EX13 8 C5
Rayne CM77 34 B6
Rayners Lane HA5 22 E3
Raynes Park SW20 23 F5
Reach CB25 33 J2
Read BB12 56 C6
**READING RG 22 A4**
Reading Green IP21 35 F1
Reading Street TN30 14 E4
Reagill CA10 61 H5
Rearquhar IV25 96 E2
Rearsby LE7 41 J4
Rease Heath CW5 49 F7
Reaster KW1 105 H2
Reaveley NE66 71 F2
Reawick ZE2 107 M8

Rea - Ros


Reay KW14 104 E2
Reculver CT6 25 J5
Red Ball EX16 7 J4
Red Bull ST7 49 H7
Red Dial CA7 60 D2
Red Hill *Hants.* PO9 11 J3
Red Hill *Warks.* B49 30 C3
Red Lodge IP28 33 K1
Red Lumb OL11 49 H1
Red Oaks Hill CB10 33 J5
Red Point IV21 94 D5
Red Post *Cornw.* EX23 6 A5
Red Post *Devon* TQ9 5 J4
Red Rail HR2 28 E6
Red Rock WN2 48 E2
Red Roses SA34 17 F4
Red Row NE61 71 H4
Red Street ST5 49 H7
Red Wharf Bay (Traeth Coch) LL75 46 D4
Redberth SA70 16 D5
Redbourn AL3 32 E7
Redbourne DN21 52 C3
Redbrook *Glos.* NP25 28 E7
Redbrook *Wrex.* SY13 38 E1
Redbrook Street TN26 14 E4
Redburn *High.* IV16 96 C5
Redburn *High.* IV12 97 G7
Redburn *Northumb.* NE47 70 C7
**Redcar TS10 63 H4**
Redcastle *Angus* DD11 83 H2
Redcastle *High.* IV6 96 C7
Redcliff Bay BS20 19 H4
Redcloak AB39 91 G6
Reddingmuirhead FK2 75 H3
Reddish SK5 49 H3
**Redditch B97 30 B2**
Rede IP29 34 C3
Redenhall IP20 45 G7
Redesmouth NE48 70 D5
Redford *Aber.* AB30 91 F7
Redford *Angus* DD11 83 G3
Redford *Dur.* DL13 62 B3
Redford *W.Suss.* GU29 12 B4
Redgrave IP22 34 E1
Redheugh DD8 83 F1
Redhill *Aber.* AB51 90 E1
Redhill *Aber.* AB32 91 F4
Redhill *Moray* AB54 98 D6
Redhill *N.Som.* BS40 19 H5
Redhill *Notts.* NG5 41 H1
**REDHILL *Surr.* RH 23 F6**
Redhill Aerodrome & Heliport RH1 23 F7
Redhouse *Aber.* AB33 90 D2
Redhouse *Arg. & B.* PA29 73 G4
Redhouses PA44 72 B4
Redisham NR34 45 J7
Redland *Bristol* BS6 19 J4
Redland *Ork.* KW17 106 C5
Redlingfield IP23 35 F1
Redlynch *Som.* BA10 9 G1
Redlynch *Wilts.* SP5 10 D2
Redmarley D'Abitot GL19 29 G5
Redmarshall TS21 62 E4
Redmile NG13 42 A2
Redmire DL8 62 B7
Redmoor PL30 4 A4
Rednal SY11 38 C3
Redpath TD4 76 D7
**Redruth TR15 2 D4**
Redscarhead EH45 76 A6
Redshaw ML11 68 D1
Redstone Bank SA67 16 E4
Redwick *Newport* NP26 19 H3
Redwick *S.Glos.* BS35 19 J3
Redworth DL5 62 D4
Reed SG8 33 G5
Reed End SG8 33 G5
Reedham NR13 45 J5
Reedley BB10 56 D6
Reedness DN14 58 D7
Reef (Riof) HS2 100 D4
Reepham *Lincs.* LN3 52 D5
Reepham *Norf.* NR10 44 E3
Reeth DL11 62 B7
Regaby IM7 54 D4
Regil BS40 19 J5
Regoul IV12 97 F6
Reiff IV26 102 B7
**Reigate RH2 23 F6**
Reighton YO14 59 H2
Reinigeadal (Rhenigidale) HS3 100 E7
Reisgill KW3 105 H5
Reiss KW1 105 J3
Rejerrah TR8 3 F3
Releath TR14 2 D5
Relubbus TR20 2 C5
Relugas IV36 97 G7
Remenham RG9 22 A3
Remenham Hill RG9 22 A3
Remony PH15 81 J3
Rempstone LE12 41 H3
Rendcomb GL7 30 B7
Rendham IP17 35 H2
Rendlesham IP12 35 H3
**Renfrew PA4 74 D4**
Renhold MK41 32 D3
Renishaw S21 51 G5
Rennington NE66 71 H2
Renton G82 74 B3
Renwick CA10 61 G2
Repps NR29 45 J4
Repton DE65 41 F3
Rescobie DD8 83 G2
Rescorla PL26 4 A5
Resipole PH36 79 J1
Resolis IV7 96 D5
Resolven SA11 18 B1
Resourie PH37 86 E7
Respryn PL30 4 B4
Reston TD14 77 G4
Restormel PL22 4 B4
Reswallie DD8 83 G2
Reterth TR9 3 G2
Retew PL26 3 G3
**Retford (East Retford) DN22 51 K4**
Rettendon CM3 24 D2
Rettendon Place CM3 24 D2
Retyn TR8 3 F3
Revesby PE22 53 F6
Revesby Bridge PE22 53 G6
Rew TQ13 5 H3
Rew Street PO31 11 F5
Rewe *Devon* EX5 7 H6
Rewe *Devon* EX5 7 G6
Reybridge SN15 20 C5
Reydon IP18 35 J1
Reydon Smear IP18 35 K1
Reymerston NR9 44 E5
Reynalton SA68 16 D5
Reynoldston SA3 17 H7
Rezare PL15 4 D3
Rhadyr NP15 19 G1
**Rhaeadr Gwy (Rhaeadr) LD6 27 J2**
Rhandirmwyn SA20 27 G4
Rhaoine IV28 96 D1
**Rhayader (Rhaeadr Gwy) LD6 27 J2**
Rhedyn LL53 36 B2
Rhegreanoch IV27 102 C7
Rheindown IV4 96 C7
Rhelonie IV24 96 C2
Rhemore PA34 79 G2
Rhenigidale (Reinigeadal) HS3 100 E7
Rheola SA11 18 B1
Rhes-y-cae CH8 47 K6
Rhewl *Denb.* LL20 38 A1
Rhewl *Denb.* LL15 47 K6
Rhewl *Shrop.* SY10 38 C2
Rhian IV27 103 H7
Rhicarn IV27 102 C6
Rhiconich IV27 102 E3
Rhicullen IV18 96 D4
Rhidorroch IV26 95 H2
Rhifail KW11 104 C4
Rhigos CF44 18 C1
Rhilochan IV28 96 E1
Rhinduie IV3 96 C7
Rhireavach IV23 95 G2
Rhiroy IV23 95 H3
Rhiston SY15 38 B6
Rhiw LL53 36 B3
Rhiwabon (Ruabon) LL14 38 C1
Rhiwargor SY10 37 J3
Rhiwbina CF14 18 E3
Rhiwbryfdir LL41 37 F1
Rhiwderin NP10 19 F3
Rhiwinder CF39 18 D3
Rhiwlas *Gwyn.* LL57 46 D6
Rhiwlas *Gwyn.* LL23 37 J2
Rhiwlas *Powys* SY10 38 B2
Rhode TA5 8 B1
Rhodes Minnis CT4 15 G3
Rhodesia S80 51 H5
Rhodiad-y-brenin SA62 16 A3
Rhodmad SY23 26 E1
Rhonadale PA28 73 F7
Rhonehouse (Kelton Hill) DG7 65 H5
Rhoose CF62 18 D5
Rhos *Carmar.* SA44 17 G2
Rhos *N.P.T.* SA8 18 A1
Rhos Common SY22 38 B4
Rhosaman SA18 27 G7
Rhoscolyn LL65 46 A5
Rhoscrowther SA71 16 C5
Rhosesmor CH7 48 B6
Rhos-fawr LL53 36 C2
Rhosgadfan LL54 46 D7
**Rhos-goch *I.o.A.* LL66 46 C4**
Rhosgoch *Powys* LD2 28 A4
Rhos-hill SA43 16 E1
Rhoshirwaun LL53 36 A3
Rhoslan LL52 36 D1
Rhoslefain LL36 36 E5
Rhosllanerchrugog LL14 38 B1
Rhoslligwy LL70 46 C4
Rhosmaen SA19 17 K3
Rhosmeirch LL77 46 C5
**Rhosneigr LL64 46 B5**
Rhosnesni LL13 48 C7
Rhôs-on-Sea LL28 47 G4
Rhossili SA3 17 H7
Rhosson SA62 16 A3
Rhostrehwfa LL77 46 C5
Rhostryfan LL54 46 C7
Rhostyllen LL14 38 C1
Rhos-y-bol LL68 46 C4
Rhos-y-brithdir SY22 38 A3
Rhosycaerau SA64 16 C2
Rhos-y-garth SY23 27 F1
Rhos-y-gwaliau LL23 37 J2
Rhos-y-llan LL53 36 B2
Rhos-y-mawn LL22 47 G6
Rhos-y-Meirch LD7 28 B2
Rhu G84 74 A2
Rhuallt LL17 47 J5
Rhubodach PA20 73 J3
Rhuddall Heath CW6 48 E6
Rhuddlan LL18 47 J5
Rhue IV26 95 H2
Rhulen LD2 28 A4
Rhumach PH39 86 C6
Rhunahaorine PA29 73 F6
**Rhuthun (Ruthin) LL15 47 K7**
Rhyd *Gwyn.* LL48 37 F1
Rhyd *Powys* SY17 37 J5
**Rhydaman (Ammanford) SA18 17 K4**
Rhydargaeau SA32 17 H3
Rhydcymerau SA19 17 J2
Rhyd-Ddu LL54 46 D7
Rhydding SA10 18 A2
Rhydgaled LL16 47 H6
Rhydlanfair LL24 47 G7
Rhydlewis SA44 17 G1
Rhydlios LL53 36 A2
Rhydlydan *Conwy* LL24 47 G7
Rhydlydan *Powys* SY16 37 K6
Rhydolion LL53 36 B3
Rhydowen SA44 17 H1
Rhyd-Rosser SY23 26 E2
Rhydspence HR3 28 B4
Rhydtalog CH7 48 B7
Rhyd-uchaf LL23 37 H2
Rhyd-wen LL23 37 J3
Rhyd-wyn LL65 46 B4
Rhyd-y-ceirw CH7 48 B7
Rhyd-y-clafdy LL53 36 C2
Rhydycroesau SY10 38 B2
Rhydyfelin *Cere.* SY23 26 E1
Rhydyfelin *R.C.T.* CF37 18 D3
Rhyd-y-foel LL22 47 H5
Rhyd-y-fro SA8 18 A1
Rhyd-y-groes LL57 46 D6
Rhydymain LL40 37 H3
Rhydymwyn CH7 48 B6
Rhyd-yr-onnen LL36 37 F5
Rhyd-y-sarn LL41 37 F1
Rhydywrach SA34 16 E4
**Rhyl LL18 47 J4**
Rhymney NP22 18 E1
Rhyn SY11 38 C2
Rhynd PH2 82 C5
Rhynie *Aber.* AB54 90 C2
Rhynie *High.* IV20 97 F4
Ribbesford DY12 29 G1
Ribchester PR3 56 B6
Ribigill IV27 103 H3
Riby DN37 52 E2
Riccall YO19 58 C6
Riccarton KA1 74 C7
Richards Castle SY8 28 D2
Richings Park SL0 22 D4
**Richmond *Gt.Lon.* TW9 22 E4**
**Richmond *N.Yorks.* DL10 62 C6**
Richmond *S.Yorks.* S13 51 G4
Rich's Holford TA4 7 K2
Rickarton AB39 91 G6
Rickerscote ST17 40 B3
Rickford BS40 19 H6
Rickinghall IP22 34 E1
Rickleton NE38 62 D1
Rickling CB11 33 H5
Rickling Green CB11 33 J6
**Rickmansworth WD3 22 D2**
Riddell TD6 70 A1
Riddings DE55 51 G7
Riddlecombe EX18 6 E4
Riddlesden BD20 57 F5
Ridge *Dorset* BH20 9 J6
Ridge *Herts.* EN6 23 F1
Ridge *Wilts.* SP3 9 J1
Ridge Green RH1 23 G7
Ridge Lane CV10 40 E6
Ridgebourne LD1 27 K2
Ridgeway S12 51 G4
Ridgeway Cross WR13 29 G4
Ridgeway Moor S12 51 G4
Ridgewell CO9 34 B4
Ridgewood TN22 13 H4
Ridgmont MK43 32 C5
Riding Gate BA9 9 G2
**Riding Mill NE44 71 F7**
Ridley TN15 24 C5
Ridleywood LL13 48 C7
Ridlington *Norf.* NR28 45 H2
Ridlington *Rut.* LE15 42 B5
Ridsdale NE48 70 E5
Riechip PH8 82 B3
Rievaulx YO62 58 B1
Rift House TS25 63 F3
Rigg *D. & G.* DG16 69 H7
Rigg *High.* IV51 94 B6
Riggend ML6 75 F4
Rigifa KW1 105 J1
Rigmaden Park LA6 56 B1
Rigsby LN13 53 H5
Rigside ML11 75 G7
Riley Green PR5 56 B7
Rileyhill WS13 40 D4
Rilla Mill PL17 4 C3
Rillaton PL17 4 C3
Rillington YO17 58 E2
Rimington BB7 56 D5
Rimpton BA22 9 F2
Rimswell HU19 59 K7
Rinaston SA62 16 C3
Ring o' Bells L40 48 D1
Ringford DG7 65 G5
Ringinglow S11 50 E4
Ringland NR8 45 F4
Ringles Cross TN22 13 H4
Ringmer BN8 13 H5
Ringmore *Devon* TQ7 5 G6
Ringmore *Devon* TQ14 5 K3
Ringorm AB38 97 K7
Ring's End PE13 43 G5
Ringsfield NR34 45 J7
Ringsfield Corner NR34 45 J7
Ringshall *Herts.* HP4 32 C7
Ringshall *Suff.* IP14 34 E3
Ringshall Stocks IP14 34 E3
Ringstead *Norf.* PE36 44 B1
Ringstead *Northants.* NN14 32 C1
**Ringwood BH24 10 C4**
Ringwould CT14 15 J3
Rinloan AB35 89 K4
Rinmore AB33 90 C3
Rinnigill KW16 106 C8
Rinsey TR13 2 C6
Riof (Reef) HS2 100 D4
Ripe BN8 13 J6
**Ripley *Derbys.* DE5 51 F7**
Ripley *Hants.* BH23 10 C5
Ripley *N.Yorks.* HG3 57 H3
Ripley *Surr.* GU23 22 D6
Riplingham HU15 59 F6
**Ripon HG4 57 J2**
Rippingale PE10 42 E3
Ripple *Kent* CT14 15 J3
Ripple *Worcs.* GL20 29 H5
Ripponden HX6 50 C1
Risabus PA42 72 B6
Risbury HR6 28 E3
Risby *E.Riding* HU17 59 G6
Risby *Suff.* IP28 34 B2
Risca NP11 19 F2
Rise HU11 59 H5
Riseden TN17 14 C4
Risegate PE11 43 F3
Riseholme LN2 52 C5
Riseley *Bed.* MK44 32 D2
Riseley *W'ham* RG7 22 A5
Rishangles IP23 35 F2
Rishton BB1 56 C6
Rishworth HX6 50 C1
Risinghurst OX3 21 J1
Risley *Derbys.* DE72 41 G2
Risley *Warr.* WA3 49 F3
Risplith HG4 57 H3
Rispond IV27 103 G2
Rivar SN8 21 G5
Rivenhall CM8 34 C7
Rivenhall End CM8 34 C7
River *Kent* CT17 15 H3
River *W.Suss.* GU28 12 C4
River Bank CB7 33 J2
River Bridge TA7 19 G7
Riverford Bridge TQ9 5 H4
Riverhead TN13 23 J6
Riverside CF11 18 E4
Riverton EX32 6 E2
Riverview Park DA12 24 C4
Rivington BL6 49 F1
Roa Island LA13 55 F3
Roach Bridge PR5 55 J7
Road Green NR15 45 G6
Road Weedon NN7 31 H3
Roade NN7 31 J3
Roadhead CA6 70 A6
Roadside *High.* KW12 105 G2
Roadside *Ork.* KW17 106 F3
Roadside of Kinneff DD10 91 G7
Roadwater TA23 7 J2
Roag IV55 93 H7
Roast Green CB11 33 H5
Roath CF24 18 E4
Roberton *S.Lan.* ML12 68 E1
Roberton *Sc.Bord.* TD9 69 K2
**Robertsbridge TN32 14 C5**
Robertstown *Moray* AB38 97 K7
Robertstown *R.C.T.* CF44 18 D1
Roberttown WF15 57 G7
Robeston Cross SA73 16 B5
Robeston Wathen SA67 16 D4
Robeston West SA73 16 B5
Robin Hood *Derbys.* DE45 50 E5
Robin Hood *Lancs.* WN6 48 E1
Robin Hood *W.Yorks.* LS26 57 J7
Robin Hood Doncaster Sheffield Airport DN10 51 J3
Robin Hood's Bay YO22 63 J2
Robinhood End CO9 34 B5
Robins GU29 12 B4
Roborough *Devon* EX19 6 D4
Roborough *Plym.* PL6 5 F4
Roby L36 48 D3
Roby Mill WN8 48 E2
Rocester ST14 40 D2
Roch SA62 16 B3
Roch Bridge SA62 16 B3
Roch Gate SA62 16 B3
Rochallie PH10 82 C2
**Rochdale OL16 49 H1**
Roche PL26 3 G2
**Rochester *Med.* ME1 24 D5**
Rochester *Northumb.* NE19 70 D4
**Rochford *Essex* SS4 24 E2**
Rochford *Worcs.* WR15 29 F2
Rock *Cornw.* PL27 3 G1
Rock *Northumb.* NE66 71 H2
Rock *Worcs.* DY14 29 G1
Rock Ferry CH42 48 C4
Rockbeare EX5 7 J6
Rockbourne SP6 10 C3
Rockcliffe *Cumb.* CA6 69 J7
Rockcliffe *D. & G.* DG5 65 J5
Rockcliffe Cross CA6 69 J7
Rockfield *Arg. & B.* PA29 73 G5
Rockfield *High.* IV20 97 G3
Rockfield *Mon.* NP25 28 D7
Rockford BH24 10 C4
Rockhampton GL13 19 K2
Rockhead PL33 4 A2
Rockingham LE16 42 B6
Rockland All Saints NR17 44 D6
Rockland St. Mary NR14 45 H5
Rockland St. Peter NR17 44 D6
Rockley SN8 20 E4
Rockside PA49 72 A4
Rockwell End RG9 22 A3
Rockwell Green TA21 7 K4
Rodborough GL5 20 B1
Rodbourne SN16 20 C3
Rodbridge Corner CO10 34 C4
Rodd LD8 28 C2
Roddam NE66 71 F1
Rodden DT3 9 F6
Rode BA11 20 B6
Rode Heath ST7 49 H7
Rodeheath SK11 49 H6
Rodel (Roghadal) HS5 93 F3
Roden TF6 38 E4
Rodhuish TA24 7 J2
Rodington SY4 38 E4
Rodington Heath SY4 38 E4
Rodley GL14 29 G7
Rodmarton GL7 20 C2
Rodmell BN7 13 H6
Rodmersham ME9 25 F5
Rodmersham Green ME9 25 F5
Rodney Stoke BS27 19 H6
Rodsley DE6 40 E1
Rodway TA5 19 F7
Roe Cross SK14 49 J3
Roe Green SG9 33 G5
Roecliffe YO51 57 J3
Roehampton SW15 23 F4
Roesound ZE2 107 M6
Roffey RH12 12 E3
**Rogart IV28 96 E1**
Rogate GU31 12 B4
Rogerstone NP10 19 F3
Roghadal (Rodel) HS5 93 F3
Rogiet NP26 19 H3
Rokemarsh OX10 21 K2
Roker SR6 63 F1
Rollesby NR29 45 J4
Rolleston *Leics.* LE7 42 A5
Rolleston *Notts.* NG23 51 K7
Rollestone SP3 20 D7
Rolleston-on-Dove DE13 40 E3
Rolston HU18 59 J5
Rolstone BS24 19 G5
Rolvenden TN17 14 D4
Rolvenden Layne TN17 14 D4
Romaldkirk DL12 62 A4
Romanby DL7 62 E7
Romannobridge EH46 75 K6
Romansleigh EX36 7 F3
Romesdal IV51 93 K6
Romford *Dorset* BH31 10 B4
**ROMFORD *Gt.Lon.* RM 23 J3**
Romiley SK6 49 J3
Romney Street TN15 23 J5
**Romsey SO51 10 E2**
Romsley *Shrop.* WV15 39 G7
Romsley *Worcs.* B62 29 J1
Rona IV40 94 C6
Ronachan PA29 73 F5
Ronague IM9 54 B6
Ronnachmore PA43 72 B5
Rood End B67 40 C7
Rookhope DL13 62 A2
Rookley PO38 11 G6
Rookley Green PO38 11 G6
Rooks Bridge BS26 19 G6
Rook's Nest TA4 7 J2
Rookwith HG4 57 H1
Roos HU12 59 J6
Roose LA13 55 F3
Roosebeck LA12 55 F3
Roosecote LA13 55 F3
Rootham's Green MK44 32 D3
Rootpark ML11 75 H5
Ropley SO24 11 H1
Ropley Dean SO24 11 H1
Ropley Soke SO24 11 H1
Ropsley NG33 42 C2
Rora AB42 99 J5
Rorandle AB51 90 E3
Rorrington SY15 38 C5
Rosarie AB55 98 B6
Rose TR4 2 E3
Rose Ash EX36 7 F3
Rose Green *Essex* CO6 34 D6
Rose Green *W.Suss.* PO21 12 C7
Rose Hill TN22 13 H5
Roseacre *Kent* ME14 14 C2
Roseacre *Lancs.* PR4 55 H6
Rosebank ML8 75 G6
Rosebrough NE67 71 G1
Rosebush SA66 16 D3
Rosecare EX23 4 B1
Rosecliston TR8 3 F3
Rosedale Abbey YO18 63 J7
Roseden NE66 71 F1
Rosehall IV27 96 B1
Rosehearty AB43 99 H4
Rosehill *Aber.* AB34 90 D5
Rosehill *Shrop.* SY4 38 D4
Roseisle IV30 97 J5
Roselands BN22 13 K6
Rosemarket SA73 16 C5
Rosemarkie IV10 96 E6
Rosemary Lane EX15 7 K4
Rosemount *P. & K.* PH10 82 C3
Rosemount *S.Ayr.* KA9 67 H1
Rosenannon PL30 3 G2
Rosenithon TR12 3 F6
Rosepool SA62 16 B4
Rosevean PL26 4 A5
Roseville WV14 40 B6
**Rosewell EH24 76 A4**
Roseworth TS19 63 F4
Rosgill CA10 61 G5
Roshven PH38 86 D7
Roskhill IV55 93 H7
Roskorwell TR12 2 E6
Rosley CA7 60 E2
**Roslin EH25 76 A4**
Rosliston DE12 40 E4

## Ros - Sal


Rosneath **G84** 74 A2
Ross *D. & G.* **DG6** 65 G6
Ross *Northumb.* **NE70** 77 K7
Ross *P. & K.* **PH6** 81 J5
Ross Priory **G83** 74 C2
Rossdhu House **G83** 74 B2
Rossett **LL12** 48 C7
Rossett Green **HG2** 57 J4
Rosside **LA12** 55 F2
Rossie Farm School **DD10** 83 H2
Rossie Ochill **PH2** 82 B6
Rossie Priory **PH14** 82 D4
Rossington **DN11** 51 J3
Rosskeen **IV18** 96 D5
Rossmore **BH12** 10 B5
**Ross-on-Wye HR9** 29 **F6**
Roster **KW3** 105 H5
Rostherne **WA16** 49 G4
Rosthwaite *Cumb.* **CA12** 60 D5
Rosthwaite *Cumb.* **LA20** 55 F1
Roston **DE6** 40 D1
Rosudgeon **TR20** 2 C6
Rosyth **KY11** 75 K2
Rothbury **NE65** 71 F3
Rotherby **LE14** 41 J4
Rotherfield **TN6** 13 J3
Rotherfield Greys **RG9** 22 A3
Rotherfield Peppard **RG9** 22 A3
**Rotherham S60** 51 **G3**
Rothersthorpe **NN7** 31 J3
Rotherwick **RG27** 22 A6
Rothes **AB38** 97 K7
Rothesay **PA20** 73 J4
Rothiebrisbane **AB53** 91 F1
Rothienorman **AB51** 91 F1
Rothiesholm **KW17** 106 F5
Rothley *Leics.* **LE7** 41 H4
Rothley *Northumb.* **NE61** 71 F5
Rothney **AB52** 90 E2
Rothwell *Lincs.* **LN7** 52 E3
Rothwell *Northants.* **NN14** 42 B7
Rothwell *W.Yorks.* **LS26** 57 J7
Rotsea **YO25** 59 G4
Rottal **DD8** 82 E1
Rotten Row *Bucks.* **RG9** 22 A3
Rotten Row *W.Mid.* **B93** 30 C1
Rottingdean **BN2** 13 G6
Rottington **CA28** 60 A5
Roud **PO38** 11 G6
Roudham **NR16** 44 D7
Rough Close **ST3** 40 B2
Rough Common **CT2** 15 G2
Rougham *Norf.* **PE32** 44 C3
Rougham *Suff.* **IP30** 34 D2
Rougham Green **IP30** 34 D2
Roughburn **PH31** 87 K6
Roughlee **BB9** 56 D5
Roughley **B75** 40 D6
Roughton *Lincs.* **LN10** 53 F6
Roughton *Norf.* **NR11** 45 G2
Roughton *Shrop.* **WV15** 39 G6
Round Bush **WD25** 22 E2
Roundbush Green **CM6** 33 J7
Roundham **TA18** 8 D4
Roundhay **LS8** 57 J6
Roundstreet Common **RH14** 12 D4
Roundway **SN10** 20 D5
Rous Lench **WR11** 30 B3
Rousay **KW17** 106 C4
Rousdon **DT7** 8 B5
Rousham **OX25** 31 F6
Rousham Gap **OX25** 31 F6
Routenburn **KA30** 73 K4
Routh **HU17** 59 G5
Rout's Green **HP14** 22 A2
Row *Cornw.* **PL30** 4 A3
Row *Cumb.* **LA8** 55 H1
Row *Cumb.* **CA10** 61 H3
Row Heath **CO16** 35 F7
Row Town **KT15** 22 D5
Rowanburn **DG14** 69 K6
Rowardennan Lodge **G63** 74 B1
Rowarth **SK22** 50 C4
Rowbarton **TA2** 8 B2
Rowberrow **BS25** 19 H6
Rowchoish **G63** 80 E7
Rowde **SN10** 20 C5
Rowden **EX20** 6 E6
Rowen **LL32** 47 F5
Rowfields **DE6** 40 D1
Rowfoot **NE49** 70 B7
Rowhedge **CO5** 34 E6
Rowhook **RH12** 12 E3
Rowington **CV35** 30 D2
Rowland **DE45** 50 E5
**Rowland's Castle PO9** 11 **J3**
**Rowlands Gill NE39** 62 **C1**
Rowledge **GU10** 22 B7
Rowlestone **HR2** 28 C6
Rowley *Devon* **EX36** 7 F4
Rowley *Dur.* **DH8** 62 B2
Rowley *Shrop.* **SY5** 38 C5
Rowley Park **ST17** 40 B3
**Rowley Regis B65** 40 **B7**
Rowly **GU5** 22 D7
Rowner **PO13** 11 G4
Rowney Green **B48** 30 B1
Rownhams **SO16** 10 E3
Rowrah **CA26** 60 B5
Rowsham **HP22** 32 B7
Rowsley **DE4** 50 E6
Rowstock **OX11** 21 H3
Rowston **LN4** 52 D7
Rowthorne **S44** 51 G6
Rowton *Ches.W. & C.* **CH3** 48 D6
Rowton *Shrop.* **SY5** 38 C4
Rowton *Tel. & W.* **TF6** 39 F4
Roxburgh **TD5** 77 F7
Roxby *N.Lincs.* **DN15** 52 C1
Roxby *N.Yorks.* **TS13** 63 J5
Roxton **MK44** 32 E3
Roxwell **CM1** 24 C1
Royal British Legion Village **ME20** 14 C2
**Royal Leamington Spa CV32** 30 **E2**
Royal Oak **L39** 48 D2
**ROYAL TUNBRIDGE WELLS TN** 13 **J3**
**Roybridge PH31** 87 **J6**
Roydon *Essex* **CM19** 33 H7
Roydon *Norf.* **IP22** 44 E7
Roydon *Norf.* **PE32** 44 B3
Roydon Hamlet **CM19** 23 H1
**Royston *Herts.* SG8** 33 **G4**
Royston *S.Yorks.* **S71** 51 F1
Royton **OL2** 49 J2
Rozel **JE3** 3 K6
Ruabon (Rhiwabon) **LL14** 38 C1
Ruaig **PA77** 78 B3
Ruan Lanihorne **TR2** 3 F4
Ruan Major **TR12** 2 D7
Ruan Minor **TR12** 2 E7
Ruanaich **PA76** 78 D5
**Ruardean GL17** 29 **F7**
Ruardean Hill **GL17** 29 F7
Ruardean Woodside **GL17** 29 F7
Rubery **B45** 29 J1
Ruckcroft **CA4** 61 G2
Ruckinge **TN26** 15 F4
Ruckland **LN11** 53 G5
Rucklers Lane **HP3** 22 D1
Ruckley **SY5** 38 E5
Rudbaxton **SA62** 16 C3
Rudby **TS15** 63 F6
Rudchester **NE15** 71 G7
Ruddington **NG11** 41 H2
Ruddlemoor **PL26** 4 A5
Rudford **GL2** 29 G6
Rudge **BA11** 20 B6
Rudgeway **BS35** 19 K3
Rudgwick **RH12** 12 D3
Rudhall **HR9** 29 F6
Rudheath **CW9** 49 F5
Rudley Green **CM3** 24 E1
Rudloe **SN13** 20 B5
Rudry **CF83** 18 E3
Rudston **YO25** 59 G3
Rudyard **ST13** 49 J7
Rufford **L40** 48 D1
Rufforth **YO23** 58 B4
Ruffside **DH8** 62 A1
**Rugby CV21** 31 **G1**
**Rugeley WS15** 40 **C4**
Ruilick **IV4** 96 C7
Ruishton **TA3** 8 B2
Ruisigearraidh **HS6** 92 E3
**Ruislip HA4** 22 **D3**
Ruislip Gardens **HA4** 22 D3
Ruislip Manor **HA4** 22 E3
**Rum PH43** 85 **J5**
Rumbling Bridge **KY13** 75 J1
Rumburgh **IP19** 45 H7
Rumford **PL27** 3 F1
Rumleigh **PL20** 4 E4
Rumney **CF3** 19 F4
Rumwell **TA4** 7 K3
Runacraig **FK18** 81 G6
**Runcorn WA7** 48 **E4**
Runcton **PO20** 12 B6
Runcton Holme **PE33** 44 A5
Rundlestone **PL20** 5 F3
Runfold **GU10** 22 B7
Runhall **NR9** 44 E5
Runham *Norf.* **NR29** 45 J4
Runham *Norf.* **NR30** 45 K5
Runnington **TA21** 7 K3
Runsell Green **CM3** 24 D1
Runshaw Moor **PR7** 48 E1
Runswick Bay **TS13** 63 K5
Runtaleave **DD8** 82 D1
Runwell **SS11** 24 D2
Ruscombe *Glos.* **GL6** 20 B1
Ruscombe *W'ham* **RG10** 22 A4
Rush Green *Gt.Lon.* **RM7** 23 J3
Rush Green *Herts.* **SG4** 33 F6
Rushall *Here.* **HR8** 29 F5
Rushall *Norf.* **IP21** 45 F7
Rushall *W.Mid.* **WS4** 40 C5
Rushall *Wilts.* **SN9** 20 E6
Rushbrooke **IP30** 34 C2
Rushbury **SY6** 38 E6
Rushden *Herts.* **SG9** 33 G5
**Rushden *Northants.* NN10** 32 **C2**
Rushford *Devon* **PL19** 4 E3
Rushford *Norf.* **IP24** 44 D7
Rushgreen **WA13** 49 F4
Rushlake Green **TN21** 13 K5
Rushmere **NR33** 45 J7
Rushmere St. Andrew **IP5** 35 G4
Rushmoor **GU10** 22 B7
Rushock **WR9** 29 H1
Rusholme **M13** 49 H3
Rushton *Ches.W. & C.* **CW6** 48 E6
Rushton *Northants.* **NN14** 42 B7
Rushton *Shrop.* **TF6** 39 F5
Rushton Spencer **SK11** 49 J6
Rushwick **WR2** 29 H3
Rushy Green **BN8** 13 H5
Rushyford **DL17** 62 D4
Ruskie **FK8** 81 H7
Ruskington **NG34** 52 D7
Rusko **DG7** 65 F5
Rusland **LA12** 55 G1
Rusper **RH12** 13 F3
Ruspidge **GL14** 29 F7
Russ Hill **RH6** 23 F7
Russel **IV54** 94 E7
Russell Green **CM3** 34 B7
Russell's Green **TN33** 14 C6
Russell's Water **RG9** 22 A2
Russel's Green **IP21** 35 G1
Rusthall **TN4** 13 J3
Rustington **BN16** 12 D6
Ruston **YO13** 59 F1
Ruston Parva **YO25** 59 G3
Ruswarp **YO21** 63 K6
Rutherend **ML10** 74 E5
Rutherford **TD5** 76 E7
Rutherglen **G73** 74 E4
Ruthernbridge **PL30** 4 A4
Ruthers of Howe **KW1** 105 J2
**Ruthin (Rhuthun) *Denb.* LL15** 47 **K7**
Ruthin *V. of Glam.* **CF35** 18 C4
Ruthrieston **AB10** 91 H4
Ruthven *Aber.* **AB54** 98 D6
Ruthven *Angus* **PH12** 82 D3
Ruthven *High.* **IV13** 89 F1
Ruthven *High.* **PH21** 88 E5
Ruthvoes **TR9** 3 G2
Ruthwaite **CA7** 60 D3
Ruthwell **DG1** 69 F7
Ruyton-XI-Towns **SY4** 38 C3
Ryal **NE20** 71 F6
Ryal Fold **BB3** 56 B7
Ryall *Dorset* **DT6** 8 D5
Ryall *Worcs.* **WR8** 29 H4
Ryarsh **ME19** 23 K6
Rydal **LA22** 60 E6
**Ryde PO33** 11 **G5**
Rydon **EX22** 6 B5
**Rye TN31** 14 **E5**
Rye Foreign **TN31** 14 D5
Rye Harbour **TN31** 14 E6
Rye Park **EN11** 23 G1
Rye Street **WR13** 29 G5
Ryebank **SY4** 38 E2
Ryeford **HR9** 29 F6
Ryehill *Aber.* **AB52** 90 E2
Ryehill *E.Riding* **HU12** 59 J7
Ryhall **PE9** 42 D4
Ryhill **WF4** 51 F1
Ryhope **SR2** 63 F1
Rylands **NG9** 41 H2
Rylstone **BD23** 56 E4
Ryme Intrinseca **DT9** 8 E3
Ryther **LS24** 58 B6
Ryton *Glos.* **GL18** 29 G5
Ryton *N.Yorks.* **YO17** 58 D2
Ryton *Shrop.* **TF11** 39 G5
**Ryton *T. & W.* NE40** 71 **G7**
Ryton-on-Dunsmore **CV8** 30 E1


### S


Saasaig **IV44** 86 C4
Sabden **BB7** 56 C6
Sabden Fold **BB12** 56 D6
Sackers Green **CO10** 34 D5
Sacombe **SG12** 33 G7
Sacombe Green **SG12** 33 G7
Sacriston **DH7** 62 D2
Sadberge **DL2** 62 E5
Saddell **PA28** 73 F7
Saddington **LE8** 41 J6
Saddle Bow **PE34** 44 A4
Sadgill **LA8** 61 F6
**Saffron Walden CB10** 33 **J5**
Sageston **SA70** 16 D5
Saham Hills **IP25** 44 D5
Saham Toney **IP25** 44 C5
Saighdinis **HS6** 92 D5
Saighton **CH3** 48 D6
St. Abbs **TD14** 77 H4
**St. Agnes TR5** 2 **E3**
**ST. ALBANS AL** 22 **E1**
St. Allen **TR4** 3 F3
**St. Andrews KY16** 83 **G6**
St. Andrews Major **CF64** 18 E4
St. Anne **GY9** 3 K4
St. Anne's **FY8** 55 G7
St. Ann's **DG11** 69 F4
St. Ann's Chapel *Cornw.* **PL18** 4 E3
St. Ann's Chapel *Devon* **TQ7** 5 G6
St. Anthony **TR2** 3 F5
St. Anthony-in-Meneage **TR12** 2 E6
St. Anthony's Hill **BN23** 13 K6
St. Arvans **NP16** 19 J2
**St. Asaph (Llanelwy) LL17** 47 **J5**
St. Athan **CF62** 18 D5
St. Aubin **JE3** 3 J7
St. Audries **TA4** 7 K1
**St. Austell PL25** 4 **A5**
**St. Bees CA27** 60 **A5**
St. Blazey **PL24** 4 A5
St. Blazey Gate **PL24** 4 A5
St. Boswells **TD6** 76 D7
St. Brelade **JE3** 3 J7
St. Breock **PL27** 3 G1
St. Breward **PL30** 4 A3
St. Briavels **GL15** 19 J1
St. Brides **SA62** 16 B4
St. Brides Major **CF32** 18 B4
St. Bride's Netherwent **NP26** 19 H3
St. Brides Wentlooge **NP10** 19 F3
St. Bride's-super-Ely **CF5** 18 D4
St. Budeaux **PL5** 4 E5
St. Buryan **TR19** 2 B6
St. Catherine **BA1** 20 A5
St. Catherines **PA25** 80 C7
St. Clears (Sanclêr) **SA33** 17 F4
St. Cleer **PL14** 4 C4
St. Clement *Chan.I.* **JE2** 3 K7
St. Clement *Cornw.* **TR1** 3 F4
St. Clether **PL15** 4 C2
St. Colmac **PA20** 73 J4
**St. Columb Major TR9** 3 **G2**
St. Columb Minor **TR7** 3 F2
St. Columb Road **TR9** 3 G3
St. Combs **AB43** 99 J4
St. Cross South Elmham **IP20** 45 G7
St. Cyrus **DD10** 83 J1
St. Davids *Fife* **KY11** 75 K2
St. David's *P. & K.* **PH7** 82 A5
St. David's (Tyddewi) *Pembs.* **SA62** 16 A3
St. Day **TR16** 2 E4
St. Decumans **TA23** 7 J1
St. Dennis **PL26** 3 G3
St. Denys **SO17** 11 F3
St. Dogmaels (Llandudoch) **SA43** 16 E1
St. Dogwells **SA62** 16 C3
St. Dominick **PL12** 4 E4
St. Donats **CF61** 18 C5
St. Edith's Marsh **SN15** 20 C5
St. Endellion **PL29** 3 G1
St. Enoder **TR8** 3 F3
St. Erme **TR4** 3 F4
St. Erney **PL12** 4 D5
St. Erth **TR27** 2 C5
St. Erth Praze **TR27** 2 C5
St. Ervan **PL27** 3 F1
St. Eval **PL27** 3 F2
St. Ewe **PL26** 3 G4
St. Fagans **CF5** 18 E4
St. Fergus **AB42** 99 J5
St. Fillans **PH6** 81 H5
St. Florence **SA70** 16 D5
St. Gennys **EX23** 4 B1
St. George *Bristol* **BS5** 19 K4
St. George *Conwy* **LL22** 47 H5
St. Georges *N.Som.* **BS22** 19 G5
St. George's *Tel. & W.* **TF2** 39 G4
St. George's *V. of Glam.* **CF5** 18 D4
St. Germans **PL12** 4 D5
St. Giles in the Wood **EX38** 6 D4
St. Giles on the Heath **PL15** 6 B6
St. Harmon **LD6** 27 J1
St. Helen Auckland **DL14** 62 C4
St. Helena **NR10** 45 F4
St. Helen's *E.Suss.* **TN34** 14 D6
St. Helens *I.o.W.* **PO33** 11 H6
**St. Helens *Mersey.* WA10** 48 **E3**
St. Helier *Chan.I.* **JE2** 3 J7
St. Helier *Gt.Lon.* **SM5** 23 F5
St. Hilary *Cornw.* **TR20** 2 C5
St. Hilary *V. of Glam.* **CF71** 18 D4
St. Hill **RH19** 13 G3
St. Ibbs **SG4** 32 E6
St. Illtyd **NP13** 19 F1
St. Ippollitts **SG4** 32 E6
St. Ishmael **SA17** 17 G5
St. Ishmael's **SA62** 16 B5
St. Issey **PL27** 3 G1
St. Ive **PL14** 4 D4
**St. Ives *Cambs.* PE27** 33 **G1**
**St. Ives *Cornw.* TR26** 2 **C4**
St. Ives *Dorset* **BH24** 10 C4
St. James South Elmham **IP19** 45 H7
St. John *Chan.I.* **JE3** 3 J6
St. John *Cornw.* **PL11** 4 E5
St. John's *Gt.Lon.* **SE4** 23 G4
St. John's *I.o.M.* **IM4** 54 B5
St. John's *Surr.* **GU21** 22 C6
St. John's *Worcs.* **WR2** 29 H3
St. John's Chapel *Devon* **EX31** 6 D3
St. John's Chapel *Dur.* **DL13** 61 K3
St. John's Fen End **PE14** 43 J4
St. John's Hall **DL13** 62 B3
St. John's Highway **PE14** 43 J4
St. John's Kirk **ML12** 75 H7
St. John's Town of Dalry **DG7** 68 B5
St. Judes **IM7** 54 C4
St. Just **TR19** 2 A5
St. Just in Roseland **TR2** 3 F5
St. Katherines **AB51** 91 F1
St. Keverne **TR12** 2 E6
St. Kew **PL30** 4 A3
St. Kew Highway **PL30** 4 A3
St. Keyne **PL14** 4 C4
St. Lawrence *Cornw.* **PL30** 4 A4
St. Lawrence *Essex* **CM0** 25 F1
St. Lawrence *I.o.W.* **PO38** 11 G7
St. Leonards *Bucks.* **HP23** 22 C1
St. Leonards *Dorset* **BH24** 10 C4
**St. Leonards *E.Suss.* TN37** 14 **D7**
St. Leonards Grange **SO42** 11 F5
St. Leonard's Street **ME19** 23 K6
St. Levan **TR19** 2 A6
St. Lythans **CF5** 18 E4
St. Mabyn **PL30** 4 A3
St. Madoes **PH2** 82 C5
St. Margaret South Elmham **IP20** 45 H7
St. Margarets *Here.* **HR2** 28 C5
St. Margarets *Herts.* **SG12** 33 G7
St. Margarets *Wilts.* **SN8** 21 F5
St. Margaret's at Cliffe **CT15** 15 J3
St. Margaret's Hope **KW17** 106 D8
St. Mark's **IM9** 54 B6
St. Martin *Chan.I.* **GY4** 3 J5
St. Martin *Chan.I.* **JE3** 3 K7
St. Martin *Cornw.* **PL13** 4 C5
St. Martin *Cornw.* **TR12** 2 E6
St. Martin's *I.o.S.* **TR25** 2 C1
St. Martins *P. & K.* **PH2** 82 C4
St. Martin's *Shrop.* **SY11** 38 C2
St. Mary **JE3** 3 J6
St. Mary Bourne **SP11** 21 H6
St. Mary Church **CF71** 18 D4
St. Mary Cray **BR5** 23 H5
St. Mary Hill **CF35** 18 C4
St. Mary Hoo **ME3** 24 D4
St. Mary in the Marsh **TN29** 15 F5
St. Marychurch **TQ1** 5 K4
St. Mary's *I.o.S.* **TR21** 2 C1
St. Mary's *Ork.* **KW17** 106 D7
St. Mary's Airport **TR21** 2 C1
St. Mary's Bay **TN29** 15 F5
St. Mary's Croft **DG9** 64 A4
St. Mary's Grove **BS48** 19 H5
St. Maughans Green **NP25** 28 D7
St. Mawes **TR2** 3 F5
St. Mawgan **TR8** 3 F2
St. Mellion **PL12** 4 D4
St. Mellons **CF3** 19 F3
St. Merryn **PL28** 3 F1
St. Mewan **PL26** 3 G3
St. Michael Caerhays **PL26** 3 G4
St. Michael Church **TA7** 8 C1
St. Michael Penkevil **TR2** 3 F4
St. Michael South Elmham **NR35** 45 H7
St. Michaels *Fife* **KY16** 83 F5
St. Michaels *Kent* **TN30** 14 D4
St. Michaels *Worcs.* **WR15** 28 E2
St. Michael's on Wyre **PR3** 55 H5
St. Minver **PL27** 3 G1
St. Monans **KY10** 83 G7
St. Neot **PL14** 4 B4
**St. Neots PE19** 32 **E2**
St. Newlyn East **TR8** 3 F3
St. Nicholas *Pembs.* **SA64** 16 C2
St. Nicholas *V. of Glam.* **CF5** 18 D4
St. Nicholas at Wade **CT7** 25 J5
St. Ninians **FK7** 75 F1
St. Osyth **CO16** 35 F7
St. Ouen **JE3** 3 J6
St. Owen's Cross **HR2** 28 E6
St. Paul's Cray **BR5** 23 H5
St. Paul's Walden **SG4** 32 E6
St. Peter **JE3** 3 J7
St. Peter Port **GY1** 3 J5
St. Peter's **CT10** 25 K5
St. Petrox **SA71** 16 C6
St. Pinnock **PL14** 4 C4
St. Quivox **KA6** 67 H1
St. Ruan **TR12** 2 E7
St. Sampson **GY2** 3 J5
St. Saviour *Chan.I.* **GY7** 3 H5
St. Saviour *Chan.I.* **JE2** 3 K7
St. Stephen **PL26** 3 G3
St. Stephens *Cornw.* **PL12** 4 E5
St. Stephens *Cornw.* **PL15** 6 B7
St. Stephens *Herts.* **AL1** 22 E1
St. Teath **PL30** 4 A2
St. Thomas **EX2** 7 H6
St. Tudy **PL30** 4 A3
St. Twynnells **SA71** 16 C6
St. Veep **PL22** 4 B5
St. Vigeans **DD11** 83 H3
St. Wenn **PL30** 3 G2
St. Weonards **HR2** 28 D6
St. Winnow **PL22** 4 B5
Saintbury **WR12** 30 C5
Salachail **PA38** 80 B2
**Salcombe TQ8** 5 **H7**
Salcombe Regis **EX10** 7 K7
Salcott **CM9** 34 D7
**Sale M33** 49 **G3**
Sale Green **WR9** 29 J3
Saleby **LN13** 53 H5
Salehurst **TN32** 14 C5
Salem *Carmar.* **SA19** 17 K3
Salem *Cere.* **SY23** 37 F7
Salem *Gwyn.* **LL54** 46 D7
Salen *Arg. & B.* **PA72** 79 G3
Salen *High.* **PH36** 79 H1
Salendine Nook **HD3** 50 D1
Salesbury **BB1** 56 B6
Saleway **WR9** 29 J3
Salford *Cen.Beds.* **MK17** 32 C5
**Salford *Gt.Man.* M5** 49 **H3**
Salford *Oxon.* **OX7** 30 D6
Salford Priors **WR11** 30 B3
Salfords **RH1** 23 F7
Salhouse **NR13** 45 H4
Saline **KY12** 75 J1
**SALISBURY SP** 10 **C2**
Salkeld Dykes **CA11** 61 G3
Sallachan **PH33** 80 A1
Sallachry **PA32** 80 B6
Sallachy *High.* **IV27** 96 C1
Sallachy *High.* **IV40** 87 F1
Salle **NR10** 45 F3
Salmonby **LN9** 53 G5
Salmond's Muir **DD11** 83 G4
Salperton **GL54** 30 B6
Salph End **MK41** 32 D3
Salsburgh **ML7** 75 G4
Salt **ST18** 40 B3
Salt Hill **SL1** 22 C3
Salt Holme **TS2** 63 F4
Saltaire **BD18** 57 G6
**Saltash PL12** 4 **E5**
Saltburn **IV18** 96 E4
**Saltburn-by-the-Sea TS12** 63 **H4**
Saltby **LE14** 42 B3
Saltcoats *Cumb.* **CA19** 60 B7
**Saltcoats *N.Ayr.* KA21** 74 **A6**
Saltcotes **FY8** 55 G7
Saltdean **BN2** 13 G6
Salterbeck **CA14** 60 A4

Sal - Sha


Salterforth BB18 56 D5
Saltergate YO18 63 K7
Salterhill IV30 97 K5
Salterswall CW7 49 F6
Saltfleet LN11 53 H3
Saltfleetby All Saints LN11 53 H3
Saltfleetby St. Clements LN11 53 H3
Saltfleetby St. Peter LN11 53 H4
Saltford BS31 19 K5
Salthaugh Grange HU12 59 J7
Salthouse NR25 44 E1
Saltley B8 40 C7
Saltmarshe DN14 58 D7
Saltness KW16 106 B8
Saltney CH4 48 C6
Salton YO62 58 D1
Saltrens EX39 6 C3
Saltwick NE61 71 G6
Saltwood CT21 15 G4
Salum PA77 78 B3
Salvington BN13 12 E6
Salwarpe WR9 29 H2
Salwayash DT6 8 D5
Sambourne B96 30 B2
Sambrook TF10 39 G3
Samhla HS6 92 C5
Samlesbury PR5 56 B6
Sampford Arundel TA21 7 K4
Sampford Brett TA4 7 J1
Sampford Courtenay EX20 6 E5
Sampford Moor TA21 7 K4
Sampford Peverell EX16 7 J4
Sampford Spiney PL20 5 F3
Samuelston EH41 76 C3
Sanaigmore PA44 72 A3
Sanclêr (St. Clears) SA33 17 F4
Sancreed TR20 2 B6
Sancton YO43 59 F6
Sand *Shet.* ZE2 107 M8
Sand *Som.* BS28 19 H7
Sand Hutton YO41 58 C4
Sandaig *Arg. & B.* PA77 78 A3
Sandaig *High.* PH41 86 D4
Sandaig *High.* IV40 86 D3
Sandal Magna WF2 51 F1
Sanday KW17 106 G3
Sanday Airfield KW17 106 F3
**Sandbach CW11 49 G6**
Sandbank PA23 73 K2
Sandbanks BH13 10 B6
Sandend AB45 98 D4
Sanderstead CR2 23 G5
Sandford *Cumb.* CA16 61 J5
Sandford *Devon* EX17 7 G5
Sandford *Dorset* BH20 9 J6
Sandford *I.o.W.* PO38 11 G6
Sandford *N.Som.* BS25 19 H6
Sandford *S.Lan.* ML10 75 F6
Sandford *Shrop.* SY13 38 E2
Sandford *Shrop.* SY11 38 C3
Sandford Orcas DT9 9 F2
Sandford St. Martin OX7 31 F6
Sandfordhill AB42 99 K6
Sandford-on-Thames OX4 21 J1
Sandgarth KW17 106 E6
Sandgate CT20 15 H4
Sandgreen DG7 65 F5
Sandhaven AB43 99 H4
Sandhead DG9 64 A5
Sandhills *Dorset* DT9 9 F3
Sandhills *Dorset* DT2 8 E4
Sandhills *Surr.* GU8 12 C3
Sandhills *W.Yorks.* LS14 57 J6
Sandhoe NE46 70 E7
Sandholme *E.Riding* HU15 58 E6
Sandholme *Lincs.* PE20 43 G2
**Sandhurst *Brack.F.* GU47 22 B5**
Sandhurst *Glos.* GL2 29 H6
Sandhurst *Kent* TN18 14 C5
Sandhurst Cross TN18 14 C5
Sandhutton YO7 57 J1
Sandiacre NG10 41 G2
Sandilands LN12 53 J4
Sandiway CW8 49 F5
Sandleheath SP6 10 C3
Sandleigh OX13 21 H1
Sandling ME14 14 C2
Sandlow Green CW4 49 G6
Sandness ZE2 107 K7
Sandon *Essex* CM2 24 D1
Sandon *Herts.* SG9 33 G5
Sandon *Staffs.* ST18 40 B3
**Sandown PO36 11 H6**
Sandplace PL13 4 C5
Sandquoy KW17 106 G3
Sandridge *Devon* TQ9 5 J5
Sandridge *Herts.* AL4 32 E7
Sandridge *Wilts.* SN12 20 C5
**Sandringham PE35 44 A3**
Sandrocks RH16 13 G4
Sandsend YO21 63 K5
Sandside LA7 55 H1
Sandside House KW14 104 E2
Sandsound ZE2 107 M8
Sandtoft DN8 51 K2
Sanduck TQ13 7 F7
Sandway ME17 14 D2
Sandwell B66 40 C7
**Sandwich CT13 15 J2**
Sandwick *Cumb.* CA10 60 F5
Sandwick *Shet.* ZE2 107 N10
Sandwick (Sanndabhaig) *W.Isles* HS1 101 G4
Sandwith CA28 60 A5
Sandy *Carmar.* SA15 17 H5
**Sandy *Cen.Beds.* SG19 32 E4**
Sandy Bank LN4 53 F7
Sandy Haven SA62 16 B5
Sandy Lane *W.Yorks.* BD15 57 G6
Sandy Lane *Wilts.* SN15 20 C5
Sandy Lane *Wrex.* LL13 38 D1
Sandy Way PO30 11 F6
Sandycroft CH5 48 C6
Sandygate *Devon* TQ12 5 J3
Sandygate *I.o.M.* IM7 54 C4
Sandyhills DG5 65 J5
Sandylands LA3 55 H3
Sandypark TQ13 7 F7
Sandyway HR2 28 D6
Sangobeg IV27 103 G2
Sankyn's Green WR6 29 G2
Sanna PH36 79 F1
Sannaig PA60 72 D4
Sanndabhaig (Sandwick) HS1 101 G4
Sannox KA27 73 J6
**Sanquhar DG4 68 C3**
Santon Bridge CA19 60 C6
Santon Downham IP27 44 C7
Sant-y-Nyll CF5 18 D4
Sapcote LE9 41 G6
Sapey Common WR6 29 G2
Sapiston IP31 34 D1
Sapperton *Derbys.* DE65 40 D2
Sapperton *Glos.* GL7 20 C1
Sapperton *Lincs.* NG34 42 D2
Saracen's Head PE12 43 G3
Sarclet KW1 105 J4
Sardis SA73 16 C5
Sarisbury SO31 11 G4
Sark GY9 3 K6
Sarn *Bridgend* CF32 18 C3
Sarn *Powys* SY16 38 B6
Sarn Bach LL53 36 C3
Sarn Meyllteyrn LL53 36 B2
Sarnau *Carmar.* SA33 17 G4
Sarnau *Cere.* SA44 26 C3
Sarnau *Gwyn.* LL23 37 J2
Sarnau *Powys* SY22 38 B4
Sarnau *Powys* LD3 27 K5
Sarnesfield HR4 28 C3
Saron *Carmar.* SA18 17 K4
Saron *Carmar.* SA44 17 G2
Saron *Gwyn.* LL55 46 D6
Saron *Gwyn.* LL54 46 C7
Sarratt WD3 22 D2
Sarre CT7 25 J5
Sarsden OX7 30 D6
Sarsgrum IV27 103 F2
Sartfield IM7 54 C4
Satley DL13 62 C2
Satron DL11 62 A7
Satterleigh EX37 6 E3
Satterthwaite LA12 60 E7
Sauchen AB51 90 E3
Saucher PH2 82 C4
Sauchie FK10 75 G1
Sauchieburn AB30 83 H1
Sauchrie KA19 67 H2
Saughall CH1 48 C5
Saughall Massie CH46 48 B4
Saughtree TD9 70 A4
Saul GL2 20 A1
Saundby DN22 51 K4
**Saundersfoot SA69 16 E5**
Saunderton HP27 22 A1
Saunton EX33 6 C2
Sausthorpe PE23 53 G6
Saval IV27 96 C1
Savalbeg IV27 96 C1
Saverley Green ST11 40 B2
Savile Town WF12 57 H7
Sawbridge CV23 31 G2
**Sawbridgeworth CM21 33 H7**
Sawdon YO13 59 F1
Sawley *Derbys.* NG10 41 G2
Sawley *Lancs.* BB7 56 C5
Sawley *N.Yorks.* HG4 57 H3
Sawston CB22 33 H4
Sawtry PE28 42 E7
Saxby *Leics.* LE14 42 B4
Saxby *Lincs.* LN8 52 D4
Saxby All Saints DN20 52 C1
Saxelbye LE14 41 J3
Saxham Street IP14 34 E2
Saxilby LN1 52 B5
Saxlingham NR25 44 E2
Saxlingham Green NR15 45 G6
Saxlingham Nethergate NR15 45 G6
Saxlingham Thorpe NR15 45 G6
**Saxmundham IP17 35 H2**
Saxon Street CB8 33 K3
Saxondale NG13 41 J2
Saxtead IP13 35 G2
Saxtead Green IP13 35 G2
Saxtead Little Green IP13 35 G2
Saxthorpe NR11 45 F2
Saxton LS24 57 K6
Sayers Common BN6 13 F5
Scackleton YO62 58 C2
Scadabhagh HS3 93 G2
Scaftworth DN10 51 J3
Scagglethorpe YO17 58 E2
Scaitcliffe BB5 56 C7
Scalasaig PA61 72 B1
Scalby *E.Riding* HU15 58 E7
Scalby *N.Yorks.* YO13 63 K3
Scaldwell NN6 31 J1
Scale Houses CA10 61 G2
Scaleby CA6 69 K7
Scalebyhill CA6 69 K7
Scales *Cumb.* CA12 60 E4
Scales *Cumb.* LA12 55 F2
Scalford LE14 42 A3
Scaling TS13 63 J5
Scallasaig IV40 86 E3
Scallastle PA65 79 J4
Scalloway ZE1 107 M9
**Scalpay (Eilean Scalpaigh) HS4 93 H2**
Scamblesby LN11 53 F5
Scammadale PA34 79 K5
Scamodale PH37 86 E7
Scampston YO17 58 E2
Scampton LN1 52 C5
Scaniport IV2 88 D1
Scapa KW15 106 D7
Scapegoat Hill HD7 50 C1
Scar KW17 106 F3
**Scarborough YO11 59 G1**
Scarcewater TR2 3 G3
Scarcliffe S44 51 G6
Scarcroft LS14 57 J5
Scardroy IV6 95 J6
Scarff ZE2 107 L4
Scarfskerry KW14 105 H1
Scargill DL12 62 B5
Scarinish PA77 78 B3
Scarisbrick L40 48 C1
Scarning NR19 44 D4
Scarrington NG13 42 A1
Scarrowhill CA8 61 G1
Scarth Hill L39 48 D2
Scarthingwell LS24 57 K6
Scartho DN33 53 F2
Scarwell KW16 106 B5
Scatraig IV2 88 E1
Scaur *D. & G.* DG2 65 J3
Scaur (Kippford) *D. & G.* DG5 65 J5
Scawby DN20 52 C2
Scawby Brook DN20 52 C2
Scawton YO7 58 B1
Scayne's Hill RH17 13 G4
Scealascro HS2 100 D5
Scethrog LD3 28 A6
Schaw KA5 67 J1
Scholar Green ST7 49 H7
Scholes *S.Yorks.* S61 51 F3
Scholes *W.Yorks.* LS15 57 J6
Scholes *W.Yorks.* HD9 50 D2
Scholes *W.Yorks.* BD19 57 G7
School Green CW7 49 F6
School House TA20 8 C4
Schoose CA14 60 B4
Sciberscross IV28 96 E1
Scilly Isles (Isles of Scilly) TR 2 C1
Scissett HD8 50 E1
Scleddau SA65 16 C2
Sco Ruston NR12 45 G3
Scofton S81 51 J4
Scole IP21 35 F1
Scolpaig HS6 92 C4
Scone PH2 82 C5
Scones Lethendy PH2 82 C5
Sconser IV48 86 B1
Scoor PA67 79 F6
Scopwick LN4 52 D7
Scoraig IV23 95 G2
Scorborough YO25 59 G5
Scorrier TR16 2 E4
Scorriton TQ11 5 H4
Scorton *Lancs.* PR3 55 J5
Scorton *N.Yorks.* DL10 62 D6
Scot Hay ST5 40 A1
Scotby CA4 60 F1
Scotch Corner DL10 62 D6
Scotforth LA1 55 H4
Scothern LN2 52 D5
Scotland NG33 42 D2
Scotland End OX15 30 E5
Scotland Street CO6 34 D5
Scotlandwell KY13 82 C7
Scotnish PA31 73 F2
Scots' Gap NE61 71 F5
Scotsburn IV18 96 E4
Scotston *Aber.* AB30 91 F7
Scotston *P. & K.* PH8 82 A3
Scotstoun G14 74 D4
Scotstown PH36 79 K1
Scott Willoughby NG34 42 D2
Scotter DN21 52 B2
Scotterthorpe DN21 52 B2
Scottlethorpe PE10 42 D3
Scotton *Lincs.* DN21 52 B3
Scotton *N.Yorks.* DL9 62 C7
Scotton *N.Yorks.* HG5 57 J4
Scottow NR10 45 G3
Scoughall EH39 76 E2
Scoulton NR9 44 D5
Scounslow Green ST14 40 C3
Scourie IV27 102 D4
Scourie More IV27 102 D4
Scousburgh ZE2 107 M11
Scouthead OL4 49 J2
Scrabster KW14 105 G1
Scrafield LN9 53 G6
Scrainwood NE66 70 E3
Scrane End PE22 43 G1
Scraptoft LE7 41 J5
Scratby NR29 45 K4
Scrayingham YO41 58 D4
Scredington NG34 42 D1
Scremby PE23 53 H6
Scremerston TD15 77 J6
Screveton NG13 42 A1
Scriven HG5 57 J4
Scronkey PR3 55 H5
Scrooby DN10 51 J3
Scropton DE65 40 D2
Scrub Hill LN4 53 F7
Scruton DL7 62 E7
Sculthorpe NR21 44 C2
**Scunthorpe DN15 52 B1**
Scurlage SA3 17 H7
Sea TA19 8 C3
Sea Mills BS9 19 J4
Sea Palling NR12 45 J3
Seabank PA37 80 A3
Seaborough DT8 8 D4
Seaburn SR6 71 K7
Seacombe CH41 48 B3
Seacroft *Lincs.* PE25 53 J6
Seacroft *W.Yorks.* LS14 57 J6
Seadyke PE20 43 G2
Seafield *Arg. & B.* PA31 73 F2
Seafield *S.Ayr.* KA7 67 H1
Seafield *W.Loth.* EH47 75 J4
**Seaford BN25 13 H7**
Seaforth L21 48 C3
Seagrave LE12 41 J4
Seagry Heath SN15 20 C3
**Seaham SR7 63 F2**
Seaham Grange SR7 63 F1
**Seahouses NE68 77 K4**
Seal TN15 23 J6
Sealand CH1 48 C6
Seale GU10 22 B7
Sealyham SA62 16 C3
Seamer *N.Yorks.* TS9 63 F5
Seamer *N.Yorks.* YO12 59 G1
Seamill KA23 73 K6
Searby DN38 52 D2
Seasalter CT5 25 G5
**Seascale CA20 60 B6**
Seathorne PE25 53 J6
Seathwaite *Cumb.* CA12 60 D5
Seathwaite *Cumb.* LA20 60 D7
Seatle LA11 55 G1
Seatoller CA12 60 D5
Seaton *Cornw.* PL11 4 D5
Seaton *Cumb.* CA14 60 B3
**Seaton *Devon* EX12 8 B5**
Seaton *Dur.* SR7 62 E1
Seaton *E.Riding* HU11 59 H5
Seaton *Northumb.* NE26 71 J6
Seaton *Rut.* LE15 42 C6
Seaton Burn NE13 71 H6
Seaton Carew TS25 63 G4
Seaton Delaval NE25 71 J6
Seaton Junction EX13 8 B5
Seaton Ross YO42 58 D5
Seaton Sluice NE26 71 J6
Seatown *Aber.* AB42 99 J5
Seatown *Dorset* DT6 8 D5
Seatown *Moray* AB56 98 D4
Seave Green TS9 63 G6
**Seaview PO34 11 H5**
Seaville CA7 60 C1
Seavington St. Mary TA19 8 D3
Seavington St. Michael TA19 8 D3
Seawick CO16 35 F7
Sebastopol NP4 19 F2
Sebergham CA5 60 E2
Seckington B79 40 E5
Second Coast IV22 95 F2
**Sedbergh LA10 61 H7**
Sedbury NP16 19 J2
Sedbusk DL8 61 K7
Seddington SG19 32 E4
Sedgeberrow WR11 30 B5
Sedgebrook NG32 42 B2
Sedgefield TS21 62 E4
Sedgeford PE36 44 B2
Sedgehill SP7 9 H2
Sedgemere CV8 30 D1
Sedgley DY3 40 B6
Sedgwick LA8 55 J1
Sedlescombe TN33 14 C6
Sedlescombe Street TN33 14 C6
Seend SN12 20 C5
Seend Cleeve SN12 20 C5
Seer Green HP9 22 C2
Seething NR15 45 H6
Sefton L29 48 C2
Seghill NE23 71 H6
Seifton SY8 38 D7
Seighford ST18 40 A3
Seil PA34 79 J6
Seilebost HS3 93 F2
Seion LL55 46 D6
Seisdon WV5 40 A6
Seisiadar HS2 101 H4
Selattyn SY10 38 B2
Selborne GU34 11 J1
**Selby YO8 58 C6**
Selham GU28 12 C4
Selhurst SE25 23 G5
**Selkirk TD7 69 K1**
Sellack HR9 28 E6
Sellafield CA20 60 B6
Sellafirth ZE2 107 P3
Sellindge TN25 15 G4
Selling ME13 15 F2
Sells Green SN12 20 C5
Selly Oak B29 40 C7
Selmeston BN26 13 J6
Selsdon CR2 23 G5
Selsey PO20 12 B7
Selsfield Common RH19 13 G3
Selside *Cumb.* LA8 61 G7
Selside *N.Yorks.* BD24 56 C2
Selsley GL5 20 B1
Selstead CT15 15 H3
Selston NG16 51 G7
Selworthy TA24 7 H1
Semblister ZE2 107 M7
Semer IP7 34 D4
Semington BA14 20 B5
Semley SP7 9 H2
Send GU23 22 D6
Send Marsh GU23 22 D6
Senghenydd CF83 18 E2
Sennen TR19 2 A6
Sennen Cove TR19 2 A6
Sennybridge LD3 27 J6
Senwick DG6 65 G6
Sequer's Bridge PL21 5 G5
Serlby DN10 51 J4
Serrington SP3 10 B1
Sessay YO7 57 K2
Setchey PE33 44 A4
Setley SO42 10 E4
Setter *Shet.* ZE2 107 P8
Setter *Shet.* ZE2 107 M7
Settiscarth KW17 106 C6
**Settle BD24 56 D3**
Settrington YO17 58 E2
Seven Ash TA4 7 K2
Seven Bridges SN6 20 E2
Seven Kings IG3 23 H3
Seven Sisters SA10 18 B1
Seven Springs GL53 29 J7
Sevenhampton *Glos.* GL54 30 B6
Sevenhampton *Swin.* SN6 21 F2
**Sevenoaks TN13 23 J6**
Sevenoaks Weald TN14 23 J6
Severn Beach BS35 19 J3
Severn Stoke WR8 29 H4
Sevick End MK44 32 D3
Sevington TN24 15 F3
Sewards End CB10 33 J5
Sewardstone E4 23 G2
Sewerby YO15 59 H3
Seworgan TR11 2 E5
Sewstern NG33 42 B3
Seymour Villas EX34 6 C1
Sezincote GL56 30 C5
Sgarasta Mhòr HS3 93 F2
Sgiogarstaigh HS2 101 H1
Sgodachail IV24 96 B2
Shabbington HP18 21 K1
Shackerley WV7 40 A5
Shackerstone CV13 41 F5
Shackleford GU8 22 C7
Shadfen NE61 71 H5
Shadforth DH6 62 E2
Shadingfield NR34 45 J7
Shadoxhurst TN26 14 E4
Shadsworth BB1 56 C7
Shadwell *Norf.* IP24 44 D7
Shadwell *W.Yorks.* LS17 57 J5
Shaftenhoe End SG8 33 H5
**Shaftesbury SP7 9 H2**
Shafton S72 51 F1
Shalbourne SN8 21 G5
Shalcombe PO41 10 E6
Shalden GU34 21 K7
Shalden Green GU34 22 A7
Shaldon TQ14 5 K3
Shalfleet PO30 11 F6
Shalford *Essex* CM7 34 B6
Shalford *Surr.* GU4 22 D7
Shalford Green CM7 34 B6
Shallowford *Devon* EX31 7 F1
Shallowford *Staffs.* ST15 40 A3
Shalmsford Street CT4 15 F2
Shalmstry KW14 105 G2
Shalstone MK18 31 H5
Shalunt PA20 73 J3
Shambellie DG2 65 K4
Shamley Green GU5 22 D7
Shandon G84 74 A2
Shandwick IV20 97 F4
Shangton LE8 42 A6
Shankend TD9 70 A3
Shankhouse NE23 71 H6
**Shanklin PO37 11 G6**
Shannochie KA27 66 D1
Shantron G83 74 B2
Shantullich IV8 96 D6
Shanzie PH11 82 D2
Shap CA10 61 G5
Shapinsay KW17 106 E6
Shapwick *Dorset* DT11 9 J4
Shapwick *Som.* TA7 8 D1
Sharcott SN9 20 E6
Shard End B34 40 D7
Shardlow DE72 41 G2
Shareshill WV10 40 B5
Sharlston WF4 51 F1
Sharlston Common WF4 51 F1
Sharnal Street ME3 24 D4
Sharnbrook MK44 32 C3
Sharneyford OL13 56 D7
Sharnford LE10 41 G6
Sharnhill Green DT2 9 G4
Sharow HG4 57 J2
Sharp Street NR29 45 H3
Sharpenhoe MK45 32 D5
Sharperton NE65 70 E3
Sharpham House TQ9 5 J5
Sharpness GL13 19 K1
Sharpthorne RH19 13 G3
Sharrington NR24 44 E2
Shatterford DY12 39 G7
Shatterling CT3 15 H2
Shaugh Prior PL7 5 F4
Shave Cross DT6 8 D5
Shavington CW2 49 G7
Shaw *Gt.Man.* OL2 49 J2
Shaw *Swin.* SN5 20 E3
Shaw *W.Berks.* RG14 21 H5
Shaw *Wilts.* SN12 20 B5
Shaw Green *Herts.* SG7 33 F5
Shaw Green *N.Yorks.* HG3 57 H4
Shaw Mills HG3 57 H3
Shaw Side OL2 49 J2
Shawbost (Siabost) HS2 100 E3
Shawbury SY4 38 E3
Shawell LE17 41 H7
Shawfield *Gt.Man.* OL12 49 H1
Shawfield *Staffs.* SK17 50 C6
Shawford SO21 11 F2
Shawforth OL12 56 D7

Sha - Sma

Shawhead DG2 65 J3
Shawtonhill ML10 74 E6
Sheanachie PA28 66 B2
Sheandow AB38 89 K1
Shearington DG1 69 F7
Shearsby LE17 41 J6
Shebbear EX21 6 C5
Shebdon ST20 39 G3
Shebster KW14 105 F2
Shedfield SO32 11 G3
Sheen SK17 50 D6
Sheepridge HD2 50 D1
Sheepscombe GL6 29 H7
Sheepstor PL20 5 F4
Sheepwash *Devon* EX21 6 C5
Sheepwash *Northumb.* NE62 71 H5
Sheepway BS20 19 H4
Sheepy Magna CV9 41 F5
Sheepy Parva CV9 41 F5
Sheering CM22 33 J7
**Sheerness** ME12 25 F4
Sheet GU32 11 J2
**SHEFFIELD** S 51 F4
Sheffield Bottom RG7 21 K5
Sheffield Green TN22 13 H4
**Shefford** SG17 32 E5
Shefford Woodlands RG17 21 G4
Sheigra IV27 102 D2
Sheinton SY5 39 F5
Shelderton SY7 28 D1
Sheldon *Derbys.* DE45 50 D6
Sheldon *Devon* EX14 7 K5
Sheldon *W.Mid.* B26 40 D7
Sheldwich ME13 15 F2
Sheldwich Lees ME13 15 F2
Shelf *Bridgend* CF35 18 C3
Shelf *W.Yorks.* HX3 57 G7
Shelfanger IP22 45 F7
Shelfield *W.Mid.* WS4 40 C5
Shelfield *Warks.* B49 30 C2
Shelfield Green B49 30 C2
Shelford NG12 41 J1
Shellachan *Arg. & B.* PA34 79 K5
Shellachan *Arg. & B.* PA35 80 B5
Shellbrook LE65 41 F4
Shellbrook Hill SY12 38 C1
Shelley *Essex* CM5 23 J1
Shelley *Suff.* IP7 34 E5
Shelley *W.Yorks.* HD8 50 E1
Shellingford SN7 21 G2
Shellow Bowells CM5 24 C1
Shelsley Beauchamp WR6 29 G2
Shelsley Walsh WR6 29 G2
Shelswell MK18 31 H5
Shelthorpe LE11 41 H4
Shelton *Bed.* PE28 32 D2
Shelton *Norf.* NR15 45 G6
Shelton *Notts.* NG23 42 A1
Shelton *Shrop.* SY3 38 D4
Shelve SY5 38 C6
Shelwick HR1 28 E4
Shelwick Green HR1 28 E4
Shenfield CM15 24 C2
Shenington OX15 30 E4
Shenley WD7 22 E1
Shenley Brook End MK5 32 B5
Shenley Church End MK5 32 B5
Shenleybury WD7 22 E1
Shenmore HR2 28 C5
Shennanton DG8 64 D4
Shenstone *Staffs.* WS14 40 D5
Shenstone *Worcs.* DY10 29 H1
Shenstone Woodend WS14 40 D5
Shenton CV13 41 F5
Shenval AB37 89 K2
Shepeau Stow PE12 43 G4
Shephall SG2 33 F6
Shepherd's Bush W12 23 F4
Shepherd's Green RG9 22 A3
Shepherd's Patch GL2 20 A1
Shepherdswell (Sibertswold) CT15 15 H3
Shepley HD8 50 D2
Sheppardstown KW3 105 H5
Shepperdine BS35 19 K2
**Shepperton** TW17 22 D5
Shepreth SG8 33 G4
Shepshed LE12 41 G4
Shepton Beauchamp TA19 8 D3
**Shepton Mallet** BA4 19 K7
Shepton Montague BA9 9 F1
Shepway ME15 14 C2
Sheraton TS27 63 F3
**Sherborne** *Dorset* DT9 9 F3
Sherborne *Glos.* GL54 30 C7
Sherborne St. John RG24 21 K6
Sherbourne CV35 30 D2
Sherbourne Street CO10 34 D4
Sherburn *Dur.* DH6 62 E2
Sherburn *N.Yorks.* YO17 59 F2
Sherburn Hill DH6 62 E2
Sherburn in Elmet LS25 57 K6
Shere GU5 22 D7
Shereford NR21 44 C3
Sherfield English SO51 10 D2
Sherfield on Loddon RG27 21 K6
Sherford *Devon* TQ7 5 H6
Sherford *Som.* TA1 8 B2
Sheriff Hutton YO60 58 C3
Sheriffhales TF11 39 G4
**Sheringham** NR26 45 F1
Sherington MK16 32 B4
Shernal Green WR9 29 J2
Shernborne PE31 44 B2
Sherramore PH20 88 C5
Sherrington BA12 9 J1
Sherston SN16 20 B3
Sherwood NG5 41 H1
Sherwood Green EX31 6 D3
**SHETLAND ISLANDS** ZE 107 M7
Shettleston G32 74 E4
Shevington WN6 48 E2
Shevington Moor WN6 48 E1
Sheviock PL11 4 D5
Shide PO30 11 G6
Shiel Bridge IV40 87 F3
Shieldaig *High.* IV54 94 E6
Shieldaig *High.* IV21 94 E4
Shieldhill FK1 75 G3
Shielfoot PH36 86 C7
Shielhill DD8 83 F2
Shiels AB51 90 E4
Shifford OX29 21 G1
**Shifnal** TF11 39 G5
Shilbottle NE66 71 G3
**Shildon** DL4 62 D4
Shillingford *Devon* EX16 7 H3
Shillingford *Oxon.* OX10 21 J2
Shillingford Abbot EX2 7 H7
Shillingford St. George EX2 7 H7
Shillingstone DT11 9 H3
Shillington SG5 32 E5
Shillmoor NE65 70 D3
Shilstone EX20 6 D5
Shilton *Oxon.* OX18 21 F1
Shilton *Warks.* CV7 41 G7
Shimpling *Norf.* IP21 45 F7
Shimpling *Suff.* IP29 34 C3
Shimpling Street IP29 34 C3
Shincliffe DH1 62 D2
Shiney Row DH4 62 E1
Shinfield RG2 22 A5
Shingay SG8 33 G4
Shingham PE37 44 B5
Shingle Street IP12 35 H4
Shinness Lodge IV27 103 H7
Shipbourne TN11 23 J6
Shipbrookhill CW9 49 F5
Shipdham IP25 44 D5
Shipham BS25 19 H6
Shiphay TQ2 5 J4
Shiplake RG9 22 A4
Shiplake Row RG9 22 A4
Shipley *Northumb.* NE66 71 G2
Shipley *Shrop.* WV6 40 A6
Shipley *W.Suss.* RH13 12 E4
**Shipley** *W.Yorks.* BD18 57 G6
Shipley Bridge *Devon* TQ10 5 G4
Shipley Bridge *Surr.* RH6 23 G7
Shipley Common DE7 41 G1
Shipmeadow NR34 45 H6
Shippea Hill CB7 44 A7
Shippon OX13 21 H2
**Shipston on Stour** CV36 30 D4
Shipton *Glos.* GL54 30 B7
Shipton *N.Yorks.* YO30 58 B4
Shipton *Shrop.* TF13 38 E6
Shipton Bellinger SP9 21 F7
Shipton Gorge DT6 8 D5
Shipton Green PO20 12 B6
Shipton Moyne GL8 20 B3
Shipton Oliffe GL54 30 B7
Shipton Solers GL54 30 B7
Shipton-on-Cherwell OX5 31 F7
Shiptonthorpe YO43 58 E5
Shipton-under-Wychwood OX7 30 D7
Shira PA32 80 C6
Shirburn OX49 21 K2
Shirdley Hill L39 48 C1
Shire Oak WS8 40 C5
Shirebrook NG20 51 H6
Shirecliffe S5 51 F3
Shiregreen S5 51 F3
Shirehampton BS11 19 J4
Shiremoor NE27 71 J6
Shirenewton NP16 19 H2
Shireoaks S81 51 H4
Shirl Heath HR6 28 D3
Shirland DE55 51 F7
Shirley *Derbys.* DE6 40 E1
Shirley *Gt.Lon.* CR0 23 G5
Shirley *Hants.* BH23 10 C5
Shirley *S'ham.* SO15 11 F3
Shirley *W.Mid.* B90 30 C1
Shirley Heath B90 30 C1
Shirley Warren SO16 10 E3
Shirleywich ST18 40 B3
Shirrell Heath SO32 11 G3
Shirwell EX31 6 D2
Shirwell Cross EX31 6 D2
Shiskine KA27 66 D1
Shittlehope DL13 62 B3
Shobdon HR6 28 C2
Shobley BH24 10 C4
Shobrooke EX17 7 G5
Shocklach SY14 38 D1
Shocklach Green SY14 38 D1
Shoeburyness SS3 25 F3
Sholden CT14 15 J2
Sholing SO19 11 F3
Shoot Hill SY5 38 D4
Shooter's Hill DA16 23 H4
Shop *Cornw.* PL28 3 F1
Shop *Cornw.* EX23 6 A4
Shop Corner IP9 35 G5
Shopnoller TA4 7 K2
Shore OL15 49 J1
Shoreditch N1 23 G3
Shoreham TN14 23 J5
**Shoreham Airport** BN15 12 E6
**Shoreham-by-Sea** BN43 13 F6
Shoremill IV11 96 E5
Shoresdean TD15 77 H6
Shoreswood TD15 77 H6
Shoreton IV7 96 D5
Shorley SO24 11 G2
Shorncote GL7 20 D2
Shorne DA12 24 C4
Shorne Ridgeway DA12 24 C4
Short Cross SY21 38 B5
Short Green IP22 44 E7
Short Heath *Derbys.* DE12 41 F4
Short Heath *W.Mid.* B23 40 C6
Shortacombe EX20 6 D7
Shortbridge TN22 13 H4
Shortfield Common GU10 22 B7
Shortgate BN8 13 H5
Shortgrove CB11 33 J5
Shorthampton OX7 30 E6
Shortlands BR2 23 G5
Shortlanesend TR4 3 F4
Shorton TQ3 5 J4
Shorwell PO30 11 F6
Shoscombe BA2 20 A6
Shotatton SY4 38 C3
Shotesham NR15 45 G6
Shotgate SS11 24 D2
Shotley *Northants.* NN17 42 C6
Shotley *Suff.* IP9 35 G5
Shotley Bridge DH8 62 B1
Shotley Gate IP9 35 G5
Shotleyfield DH8 62 B1
Shottenden CT4 15 F2
Shottermill GU27 12 B3
Shottery CV37 30 C3
Shotteswell OX17 31 F4
Shottisham IP12 35 H4
Shottle DE56 41 F1
Shottlegate DE56 41 F1
Shotton *Dur.* SR8 63 F3
Shotton *Dur.* TS21 62 E4
Shotton *Flints.* CH5 48 C6
Shotton *Northumb.* NE13 71 H6
Shotton Colliery DH6 62 E2
**Shotts** ML7 75 G4
Shotwick CH1 48 C5
Shouldham PE33 44 A5
Shouldham Thorpe PE33 44 A5
Shoulton WR2 29 H3
Shover's Green TN5 13 K3
Shrawardine SY4 38 C4
Shrawley WR6 29 H2
Shreding Green SL0 22 D3
Shrewley CV35 30 D2
**SHREWSBURY** SY 38 D4
Shrewton SP3 20 D7
Shripney PO22 12 C6
Shrivenham SN6 21 F3
Shropham NR17 44 D6
Shroton (Iwerne Courtney) DT11 9 H3
Shrub End CO2 34 D6
Shucknall HR1 28 E4
Shudy Camps CB21 33 K4
Shurdington GL51 29 J7
Shurlock Row RG10 22 B4
Shurnock B96 30 B2
Shurrery KW14 105 F3
Shurrery Lodge KW14 105 F3
Shurton TA5 19 F7
Shustoke B46 40 E6
Shut Heath ST18 40 A3
Shute *Devon* EX13 8 B5
Shute *Devon* EX17 7 G5
Shutford OX15 30 E4
Shuthonger GL20 29 H5
Shutlanger NN12 31 J4
Shutt Green ST19 40 A5
Shuttington B79 40 E5
Shuttlewood S44 51 G5
Shuttleworth BL0 49 G1
Siabost (Shawbost) HS2 100 E3
Siabost Bho Dheas HS2 100 E3
Siabost Bho Thuath HS2 100 E3
Siadar Iarach HS2 101 F2
Siadar Uarach HS2 101 F2
Sibbaldbie DG11 69 G5
Sibbertoft LE16 41 J7
Sibdon Carwood SY7 38 D7
Sibertswold (Shepherdswell) CT15 15 H3
Sibford Ferris OX15 30 E5
Sibford Gower OX15 30 E5
Sible Hedingham CO9 34 B5
Sibley's Green CM6 33 K6
Sibsey PE22 53 G7
Sibson *Cambs.* PE8 42 D6
Sibson *Leics.* CV13 41 F5
Sibster KW1 105 J3
Sibthorpe NG23 42 A1
Sibton IP17 35 H2
Sibton Green IP17 35 H1
Sicklesmere IP30 34 C2
Sicklinghall LS22 57 J5
Sidbury *Devon* EX10 7 K6
Sidbury *Shrop.* WV16 39 F7
Sidcot BS25 19 H6
**Sidcup** DA14 23 H4
Siddal HX3 57 G7
Siddington *Ches.E.* SK11 49 H5
Siddington *Glos.* GL7 20 D2
Sidemoor B61 29 J1
Sidestrand NR27 45 G2
Sidford EX10 7 K6
Sidlesham PO20 12 B7
Sidley TN39 14 C7
Sidlow RH2 23 F7
**Sidmouth** EX10 7 K7
Sigford TQ12 5 H3
Sigglesthorne HU11 59 H5
Sigingstone CF71 18 C4
Signet OX18 30 D7
Silchester RG7 21 K5
Sildinis HS2 100 E6
Sileby LE12 41 J4
Silecroft LA18 54 E1
Silfield NR18 45 F6
Silian SA48 26 E3
Silk Willoughby NG34 42 D1
Silkstead SO21 11 F2
Silkstone S75 50 E2
Silkstone Common S75 50 E2
Sill Field LA8 55 J1
Silloth CA7 60 C1
Sills NE19 70 D3
Sillyearn AB55 98 D5
Silpho YO13 63 J3
Silsden BD20 57 F5
Silsoe MK45 32 D5
Silver End *Cen.Beds.* MK45 32 E4
Silver End *Essex* CM8 34 C6
Silver Green NR15 45 G6
Silver Street *Kent* ME9 24 E5
Silver Street *Som.* TA11 8 E1
Silverburn EH26 76 A4
Silvercraigs PA31 73 G2
Silverdale *Lancs.* LA5 55 H2
Silverdale *Staffs.* ST5 40 A1
Silvergate NR11 45 F3
Silverhill TN37 14 C6
Silverlace Green IP13 35 H3
Silverley's Green IP19 35 G1
Silvermoss AB51 91 G1
Silverstone NN12 31 H4
Silverton EX5 7 H5
Silvington DY14 29 F1
Silwick ZE2 107 L8
Simister M25 49 H2
Simmondley SK13 50 C3
Simonburn NE48 70 D6
Simonsbath TA24 7 F2
Simonside NE34 71 J7
Simonstone *Bridgend* CF35 18 C3
Simonstone *Lancs.* BB12 56 C6
Simprim TD12 77 G6
Simpson MK6 32 B5
Sinclair's Hill TD11 77 G5
Sinclairston KA18 67 J2
Sinderby YO7 57 J1
Sinderhope NE47 61 K1
Sindlesham RG41 22 A5
Sinfin DE24 41 F2
Singdean TD9 70 A3
Singleton *Lancs.* FY6 55 G6
Singleton *W.Suss.* PO18 12 B5
Singlewell DA12 24 C4
Singret LL12 48 C7
Sinkhurst Green TN12 14 D3
Sinnahard AB33 90 C3
Sinnington YO62 58 D1
Sinton Green WR2 29 H2
Sipson UB7 22 D4
Sirhowy NP22 28 A7
Sisland NR14 45 H6
Sissinghurst TN17 14 C4
Siston BS16 19 K4
Sithney TR13 2 D6
**Sittingbourne** ME10 25 F5
Siulaisiadar HS2 101 H4
Six Ashes WV15 39 G7
Six Hills LE14 41 J3
Six Mile Bottom CB8 33 J3
Six Roads End DE6 40 D3
Sixhills LN8 52 E4
Sixmile CT4 15 G3
Sixpenny Handley SP5 10 B3
Sizewell IP16 35 J2
Skail KW11 104 C4
Skaill *Ork.* KW16 106 B6
Skaill *Ork.* KW17 106 E7
Skaill *Ork.* KW17 106 D4
Skares *Aber.* AB54 90 E1
Skares *E.Ayr.* KA18 67 K2
Skarpigarth ZE2 107 K7
Skateraw EH42 77 F3
Skaw ZE2 107 P6
Skeabost IV51 93 K7
Skeabrae KW17 106 B5
Skeeby DL10 62 D6
Skeffington LE7 42 A5
Skeffling HU12 53 G1
Skegby NG17 51 H6
**Skegness** PE25 53 J6
Skelberry *Shet.* ZE2 107 M11
Skelberry *Shet.* ZE2 107 N6
Skelbo IV25 96 E2
Skelbo Street IV25 96 E2
Skelbrooke DN6 51 H1
Skeld (Easter Skeld) ZE2 107 M8
Skeldon KA6 67 H2
Skeldyke PE20 43 G2
Skellingthorpe LN6 52 C5
Skellister ZE2 107 N7
Skellow DN6 51 H1
Skelmanthorpe HD8 50 E1
**Skelmersdale** WN8 48 D2
Skelmonae AB41 91 G1
**Skelmorlie** PA17 73 K4
Skelmuir AB42 99 H6
Skelpick KW14 104 C3
Skelton *Cumb.* CA11 60 F3
Skelton *E.Riding* DN14 58 D7
Skelton *N.Yorks.* DL11 62 B6
Skelton (Skelton-in-Cleveland) *R. & C.* TS12 63 H5
Skelton *York* YO30 58 B4
Skelton-in-Cleveland (Skelton) TS12 63 H5
Skelton-on-Ure HG4 57 J3
Skelwick KW17 106 D3
Skelwith Bridge LA22 60 E6
Skendleby PE23 53 H6
Skendleby Psalter LN13 53 H5
Skenfrith NP7 28 D6
Skerne YO25 59 G4
Skeroblingarry PA28 66 B1
Skerray KW14 103 J2
Skerton LA1 55 H3
Sketchley LE10 41 G6
Sketty SA2 17 K6
Skewen SA10 18 A2
Skewsby YO61 58 C2
Skeyton NR10 45 G3
Skeyton Corner NR10 45 G3
Skidbrooke LN11 53 H3
Skidbrooke North End LN11 53 H3
Skidby HU16 59 G6
Skilgate TA4 7 H3
Skillington NG33 42 B3
Skinburness CA7 60 C1
Skinflats FK2 75 H2
Skinidin IV55 93 H7
Skinnet KW12 105 G2
Skinningrove TS13 63 J5
Skipness PA29 73 G5
Skippool FY5 55 G5
Skipsea YO25 59 H4
Skipsea Brough YO25 59 H4
**Skipton** BD23 56 E4
Skipton-on-Swale YO7 57 J2
Skipwith YO8 58 C6
Skirbeck PE21 43 G1
Skirbeck Quarter PE21 43 G1
Skirethorns BD23 56 E3
Skirlaugh HU11 59 H6
Skirling ML12 75 J7
Skirmett RG9 22 A3
Skirpenbeck YO41 58 D4
Skirwith *Cumb.* CA10 61 H3
Skirwith *N.Yorks.* LA6 56 C2
Skirza KW1 105 J2
Skittle Green HP27 22 A1
Skomer Island SA62 16 A5
Skulamus IV42 86 C2
Skullomie IV27 103 J2
Skyborry Green LD7 28 B1
**Skye** IV 85 K1
Skye Green CO5 34 C6
Skye of Curr PH26 89 G2
Skyreholme BD23 57 F3
Slack *Aber.* AB52 90 D1
Slack *Derbys.* S45 51 F6
Slack *W.Yorks.* HX7 56 E7
Slackhall SK23 50 C4
Slackhead AB56 98 C4
Slad GL6 20 B1
Slade *Devon* EX34 6 D1
Slade *Devon* EX14 7 K5
Slade *Pembs.* SA61 16 C4
Slade *Swan.* SA3 17 H7
Slade Green DA8 23 J4
Slade Hooton S25 51 H4
Sladesbridge PL27 4 A3
Slaggyford CA8 61 H1
Slaidburn BB7 56 C4
Slains Park DD10 91 G7
Slaithwaite HD7 50 C1
Slaley NE47 62 A1
Slamannan FK1 75 G3
Slapton *Bucks.* LU7 32 C6
Slapton *Devon* TQ7 5 J6
Slapton *Northants.* NN12 31 H4
Slate Haugh AB56 98 C4
Slatepit Dale S42 51 F6
Slattadale IV22 94 E4
Slaugham RH17 13 F4
Slaughden IP15 35 J3
Slaughterford SN14 20 B4
Slawston LE16 42 A6
Sleaford *Hants.* GU35 12 B3
**Sleaford** *Lincs.* NG34 42 D1
Sleagill CA10 61 G5
Sleap SY4 38 D3
Sledge Green WR13 29 H5
Sledmere YO25 59 F3
Sleights YO22 63 K6
Slepe BH16 9 J5
Slerra EX39 6 B3
Slickly KW1 105 H2
Sliddery KA27 66 D1
Sliemore PH25 89 H2
Sligachan IV47 85 K2
Slimbridge GL2 20 A1
Slindon *Staffs.* ST21 40 A2
Slindon *W.Suss.* BN18 12 C6
Slinfold RH13 12 E3
Sling GL16 19 J1
Slingsby YO62 58 C2
Slioch AB54 90 D1
Slip End *Cen.Beds.* LU1 32 D7
Slip End *Herts.* SG7 33 F5
Slipton NN14 32 C1
Slitting Mill WS15 40 C4
Slochd PH23 89 F2
Slockavullin PA31 73 G1
Slogarie DG7 65 G4
Sloley NR12 45 G3
Slongaber DG2 65 J3
Sloothby LN13 53 H5
**SLOUGH** SL 22 C3
Slough Green *Som.* TA3 8 B2
Slough Green *W.Suss.* RH17 13 F4
Sluggan PH23 89 F2
Slyne LA2 55 H3
Smailholm TD5 76 E7
Small Dole BN5 13 F5
Small Hythe TN30 14 D4
Smallbridge OL16 49 J1
Smallbrook EX5 7 G6
Smallburgh NR12 45 H3
Smallburn *Aber.* AB42 99 J6
Smallburn *E.Ayr.* KA18 68 B1
Smalldale SK17 50 C5

Sma - Sta


Smalley **DE7** 41 G1
Smallfield **RH6** 23 G7
Smallford **AL4** 22 E1
Smallridge **EX13** 8 B4
Smallthorne **ST6** 49 H7
Smallworth **IP22** 44 E7
Smannell **SP11** 21 G7
Smardale **CA17** 61 J6
Smarden **TN27** 14 D3
Smaull **PA44** 72 A4
Smeatharpe **EX14** 7 K4
Smeeth **TN25** 15 F4
Smeeton Westerby **LE8** 41 J6
Smerclet **HS8** 84 C3
Smerral **KW5** 105 G5
Smestow **DY3** 40 A6
**Smethwick B66** 40 **C7**
Smethwick Green **CW11** 49 H6
Smirisary **PH38** 86 C7
Smisby **LE65** 41 F4
Smith End Green **WR13** 29 G3
Smithfield **CA6** 69 K7
Smithies **S71** 51 F2
Smithincott **EX15** 7 J4
Smith's End **SG8** 33 G5
Smith's Green *Essex* **CM22** 33 J6
Smith's Green *Essex* **CB9** 33 K4
Smithstown **IV21** 94 D4
Smithton **IV2** 96 E7
Smithy Green **WA16** 49 G5
Smockington **LE10** 41 G7
Smyrton **KA26** 67 F5
Smythe's Green **CO5** 34 D7
Snailbeach **SY5** 38 C5
Snailwell **CB8** 33 K2
Snainton **YO13** 59 F1
Snaith **DN14** 58 C7
Snape *N.Yorks.* **DL8** 57 H1
Snape *Suff.* **IP17** 35 H3
Snape Green **PR8** 48 C1
Snape Watering **IP17** 35 H3
Snarestone **DE12** 41 F5
Snarford **LN8** 52 D4
Snargate **TN29** 14 E5
Snave **TN29** 15 F5
Sneachill **WR7** 29 J3
Snead **SY15** 38 C6
Snead's Green **DY13** 29 H2
Sneath Common **NR15** 45 F7
Sneaton **YO22** 63 K6
Sneatonthorpe **YO22** 63 J2
Snelland **LN3** 52 D4
Snellings **CA22** 60 A6
Snelston **DE6** 40 D1
Snetterton **NR16** 44 D6
Snettisham **PE31** 44 A2
Snipeshill **ME10** 25 F5
Sniseabhal (Snishival) **HS8** 84 C1
Snishival (Sniseabhal) **HS8** 84 C1
Snitter **NE65** 71 F3
Snitterby **DN21** 52 C3
Snitterfield **CV37** 30 D3
Snitterton **DE4** 50 E6
Snittlegarth **CA7** 60 D3
Snitton **SY8** 28 E1
Snodhill **HR3** 28 C4
**Snodland ME6** 24 **D5**
Snow End **SG9** 33 H5
Snow Street **IP22** 44 E7
Snowden Hill **S35** 50 E2
Snowshill **WR12** 30 B5
Soar *Cardiff* **CF15** 18 D3
Soar *Carmar.* **SA19** 17 K3
Soar *Devon* **TQ7** 5 H7
Soay **PH41** 85 K3
Soberton **SO32** 11 H3
Soberton Heath **SO32** 11 H3
Sockbridge **CA10** 61 G4
Sockburn **DL2** 62 E6
Sodom **LL16** 47 J5
Sodylt Bank **SY12** 38 C2
Softley **DL13** 62 B4
Soham **CB7** 33 J1
Soham Cotes **CB7** 33 J1
Solas (Sollas) **HS6** 92 D4
Soldon **EX22** 6 B4
Soldon Cross **EX22** 6 B4
Soldridge **GU34** 11 H1
Sole Street *Kent* **CT4** 15 F3
Sole Street *Kent* **DA12** 24 C5
Soleburn **DG9** 64 A4
**Solihull B91** 30 **C1**
Solihull Lodge **B90** 30 B1
Sollas (Solas) **HS6** 92 D4
Sollers Dilwyn **HR4** 28 D3
Sollers Hope **HR1** 29 F5
Sollom **PR4** 48 D1
Solomon's Tump **GL19** 29 G7
Solsgirth **FK14** 75 H1
Solva **SA62** 16 A3
Solwaybank **DG14** 69 J6
Somerby *Leics.* **LE14** 42 A4
Somerby *Lincs.* **DN38** 52 D2
Somercotes **DE55** 51 G7
Somerford **ST19** 40 B5
Somerford Keynes **GL7** 20 D2
Somerley **PO20** 12 B7
Somerleyton **NR32** 45 J6
Somersal Herbert **DE6** 40 D2
Somersby **PE23** 53 G5
Somersham *Cambs.* **PE28** 33 G1
Somersham *Suff.* **IP8** 34 E4
Somerton *Newport* **NP19** 19 G3
Somerton *Oxon.* **OX25** 31 F6
**Somerton *Som.* TA11** 8 **D2**
Somerton *Suff.* **IP29** 34 C3
Sompting **BN15** 12 E6
Sompting Abbotts **BN15** 12 E6
Sonning **RG4** 22 A4
Sonning Common **RG4** 22 A3
Sonning Eye **RG4** 22 A4
Sontley **LL13** 38 C1
Sookholme **NG19** 51 H6
Sopley **BH23** 10 C5
Sopworth **SN14** 20 B3
Sorbie **DG8** 64 E6
Sordale **KW12** 105 G2
Sorisdale **PA78** 78 D1
Sorn **KA5** 67 K1
Sornhill **KA4** 74 D7
Soroba **PA34** 79 K5
Sortat **KW1** 105 H2
Sotby **LN8** 53 F5
Sots Hole **LN4** 52 E6
Sotterley **NR34** 45 J7
Soudley **TF9** 39 G3
Soughton **CH7** 48 B6
Soulbury **LU7** 32 B6
Soulby **CA17** 61 J5
Souldern **OX27** 31 G5
Souldrop **MK44** 32 C2
Sound *Ches.E.* **CW5** 39 F1
Sound *Shet.* **ZE1** 107 N8
Sound *Shet.* **ZE2** 107 M7
Sourhope **TD5** 70 D1
Sourin **KW17** 106 D4
Sourton **EX20** 6 D6
Soutergate **LA17** 55 F1
South Acre **PE32** 44 C4
South Acton **W5** 22 E4
South Alkham **CT15** 15 H3
South Allington **TQ7** 5 H7
South Alloa **FK7** 75 G1
South Ambersham **GU29** 12 C4
South Anston **S25** 51 H4
South Ascot **SL5** 22 C5
South Baddesley **SO41** 10 E5
South Ballachulish **PH49** 80 B2
South Balloch **KA26** 67 H4
South Bank **TS6** 63 G4
South Barrow **BA22** 9 F2
South Bellsdyke **FK2** 75 H2
**South Benfleet SS7** 24 **D3**
South Bersted **PO22** 12 C6
South Blackbog **AB51** 91 F1
South Bockhampton **BH23** 10 C5
South Bowood **DT6** 8 D5
**South Brent TQ10** 5 **G4**
South Brentor **PL19** 6 C7
South Brewham **BA10** 9 G1
South Broomhill **NE61** 71 H4
South Burlingham **NR13** 45 H5
South Cadbury **BA22** 9 F2
South Cairn **DG9** 66 D7
South Carlton **LN1** 52 C5
South Cave **HU15** 59 F6
South Cerney **GL7** 20 D2
South Chard **TA20** 8 C4
South Charlton **NE66** 71 G1
South Cheriton **BA8** 9 F2
South Church **DL14** 62 D4
South Cliffe **YO43** 58 E6
South Clifton **NG23** 52 B5
South Cockerington **LN11** 53 G4
South Collafirth **ZE2** 107 M4
South Common **BN8** 13 G5
South Cornelly **CF33** 18 B3
South Corriegills **KA27** 73 J7
South Cove **NR34** 45 J7
South Creagan **PA37** 80 A3
South Creake **NR21** 44 C2
South Crosland **HD4** 50 D1
South Croxton **LE7** 41 J4
South Dalton **HU17** 59 F5
South Darenth **DA4** 23 J4
South Dell (Dail Bho Dheas) **HS2** 101 G1
South Duffield **YO8** 58 C6
South Elkington **LN11** 53 F4
South Elmsall **WF9** 51 G1
South End *Bucks.* **LU7** 32 B6
South End *Cumb.* **LA14** 55 F3
South End *Hants.* **SP6** 10 C3
South End *N.Lincs.* **DN19** 59 H7
South Erradale **IV21** 94 D4
South Fambridge **SS4** 24 E2
South Fawley **OX12** 21 G3
South Ferriby **DN18** 59 F7
South Field **HU13** 59 G7
South Flobbets **AB51** 91 F1
South Garth **ZE2** 107 P3
South Godstone **RH9** 23 G7
South Gorley **SP6** 10 C3
South Green *Essex* **CM11** 24 C2
South Green *Essex* **CO5** 34 E7
South Green *Norf.* **NR20** 44 E4
South Green *Suff.* **IP23** 35 F1
South Gyle **EH12** 75 K3
South Hall **PA22** 73 J3
South Hanningfield **CM3** 24 D2
South Harefield **UB9** 22 D3
South Harting **GU31** 11 J3
South Hayling **PO11** 11 J5
South Hazelrigg **NE66** 77 J7
South Heath **HP16** 22 C1
South Heighton **BN9** 13 H6
South Hetton **DH6** 62 E2
South Hiendley **S72** 51 F1
South Hill **PL17** 4 D3
South Hinksey **OX1** 21 J1
South Hole **EX39** 6 A4
South Holme **YO62** 58 C2
South Holmwood **RH5** 22 E7
South Hornchurch **RM13** 23 J3
South Hourat **KA24** 74 A5
South Huish **TQ7** 5 G6
South Hykeham **LN6** 52 C6
South Hylton **SR4** 62 E1
South Kelsey **LN7** 52 D3
South Kessock **IV3** 96 D7
South Killingholme **DN40** 52 E1
South Kilvington **YO7** 57 K1
South Kilworth **LE17** 41 J7
South Kirkby **WF9** 51 G1
South Kirkton **AB32** 91 F4
South Knighton **TQ12** 5 J3
South Kyme **LN4** 42 E1
South Lancing **BN15** 12 E6
South Ledaig **PA37** 80 A4
South Leigh **OX29** 21 G1
South Leverton **DN22** 51 K4
South Littleton **WR11** 30 B4
South Lopham **IP22** 44 E7
South Luffenham **LE15** 42 C5
South Malling **BN7** 13 H5
South Marston **SN3** 20 E3
South Middleton **NE71** 70 E1
South Milford **LS25** 57 K6
South Milton **TQ7** 5 G6
South Mimms **EN6** 23 F1
**South Molton EX36** 7 **F3**
South Moor **DH9** 62 C1
South Moreton **OX11** 21 J3
South Mundham **PO20** 12 B6
South Muskham **NG23** 51 K7
South Newbald **YO43** 59 F6
South Newington **OX15** 31 F5
South Newton **SP2** 10 B1
South Normanton **DE55** 51 G7
South Norwood **SE25** 23 G5
South Nutfield **RH1** 23 G7
**South Ockendon RM15** 23 **J3**
South Ormsby **LN11** 53 G5
South Ossett **WF5** 50 E1
South Otterington **DL7** 57 J1
South Owersby **LN8** 52 D3
South Oxhey **WD19** 22 E2
South Park **RH2** 23 F7
South Parks **KY6** 82 D7
South Perrott **DT8** 8 D4
**South Petherton TA13** 8 **D3**
South Petherwin **PL15** 6 B7
South Pickenham **PE37** 44 C5
South Pool **TQ7** 5 H6
**South Queensferry (Queensferry) EH30** 75 **K3**
South Radworthy **EX36** 7 F2
South Rauceby **NG34** 42 D1
South Raynham **NR21** 44 C3
South Redbriggs **AB53** 99 F6
South Reston **LN11** 53 H4
South Ronaldsay **KW17** 106 D9
South Ruislip **HA4** 22 E3
South Runcton **PE33** 44 A5
South Scarle **NG23** 52 B6
South Shian **PA37** 80 A3
**South Shields NE33** 71 **J7**
South Somercotes **LN11** 53 H3
South Somercotes Fen Houses **LN11** 53 H3
South Stainley **HG3** 57 J3
South Stoke *Oxon.* **RG8** 21 K3
South Stoke *W.Suss.* **BN18** 12 D6
South Street *E.Suss.* **BN8** 13 G5
South Street *Gt.Lon.* **TN16** 23 H6
South Street *Kent* **DA13** 24 C5
South Street *Kent* **CT5** 25 H5
South Street *Kent* **ME9** 24 E5
South Tawton **EX20** 6 E6
South Thoresby **LN13** 53 H5
South Tidworth **SP9** 21 F7
South Tottenham **N15** 23 G3
South Town *Devon* **EX6** 7 H7
South Town *Hants.* **GU34** 11 H1
**South Uist (Uibhist a Deas) HS8** 84 **C1**
South Upper Barrack **AB41** 99 H6
South View **RG21** 21 K6
South Walsham **NR13** 45 H4
South Warnborough **RG29** 22 A7
South Weald **CM14** 23 J2
South Weston **OX9** 22 A2
South Wheatley *Cornw.* **PL15** 4 C1
South Wheatley *Notts.* **DN22** 51 K4
South Whiteness **ZE2** 107 M8
South Wigston **LE18** 41 H6
South Willingham **LN8** 52 E4
South Wingfield **DE55** 51 F7
South Witham **NG33** 42 C4
South Wonston **SO21** 11 F1
South Woodham Ferrers **CM3** 24 E2
South Wootton **PE30** 44 A3
South Wraxall **BA15** 20 B5
South Yardley **B26** 40 D7
South Zeal **EX20** 6 E6
**SOUTHALL UB** 22 **E3**
Southam *Glos.* **GL52** 29 J6
**Southam *Warks.* CV47** 31 **F2**
**SOUTHAMPTON SO** 11 **F3**
Southampton Airport **SO18** 11 F3
Southbar **PA4** 74 C4
Southborough *Gt.Lon.* **BR2** 23 H5
Southborough *Kent* **TN4** 23 J7
Southbourne *Bourne.* **BH6** 10 C5
Southbourne *W.Suss.* **PO10** 11 J4
Southbrook **EX5** 7 J6
Southburgh **IP25** 44 E5
Southburn **YO25** 59 F4
Southchurch **SS1** 25 F3
Southcott *Devon* **EX20** 6 D6
Southcott *Wilts.* **SN9** 20 E6
Southcourt **HP21** 32 B7
Southdean **TD9** 70 B3
Southdene **L32** 48 D3
Southease **BN7** 13 H6
Southend *Aber.* **AB53** 99 F6
Southend *Arg. & B.* **PA28** 66 A3
Southend *Bucks.* **RG9** 22 A3
Southend *W.Berks.* **RG7** 21 J4
Southend *Wilts.* **SN8** 20 E4
Southend Airport **SS2** 24 E3
**SOUTHEND-ON-SEA SS** 24 **E3**
Southerfield **CA7** 60 C2
Southerly **EX20** 6 D7
Southern Green **SG9** 33 G5
Southerndown **CF32** 18 B4
Southerness **DG2** 65 K5
Southery **PE38** 44 A6
Southfield **KY6** 76 A1
Southfields **SW18** 23 F4
Southfleet **DA13** 24 C4
Southgate *Cere.* **SY23** 36 E7
Southgate *Gt.Lon.* **N14** 23 G2
Southgate *Norf.* **NR10** 45 F3
Southgate *Norf.* **PE31** 44 A2
Southgate *Swan.* **SA3** 17 J7
Southill **SG18** 32 E4
Southington **RG25** 21 J7
Southleigh **EX24** 8 B5
Southmarsh **BA9** 9 G1
**Southminster CM0** 25 **F2**
Southmuir **DD8** 82 E2
Southoe **PE19** 32 E2
Southolt **IP23** 35 F2
Southorpe **PE9** 42 D5
Southowram **HX3** 57 G7
**Southport PR8** 48 **C1**
Southrepps **NR11** 45 G2
Southrey **LN3** 52 E6
Southrop **GL7** 20 E1
Southrope **RG25** 21 K7
**Southsea *Ports.* PO4** 11 **H5**
Southsea *Wrex.* **LL11** 48 B7
Southstoke **BA2** 20 A5
Southtown *Norf.* **NR31** 45 K5
Southtown *Ork.* **KW17** 106 D8
Southwaite *Cumb.* **CA17** 61 J6
Southwaite *Cumb.* **CA4** 61 F2
Southwater **RH13** 12 E4
Southwater Street **RH13** 12 E4
Southway **BA5** 19 J7
Southwell *Dorset* **DT5** 9 F7
**Southwell *Notts.* NG25** 51 **J7**
Southwick *D. & G.* **DG2** 65 K5
Southwick *Hants.* **PO17** 11 H4
Southwick *Northants.* **PE8** 42 D6
Southwick *Som.* **TA9** 19 G7
Southwick *T. & W.* **SR5** 62 E1
Southwick *W.Suss.* **BN42** 13 F6
Southwick *Wilts.* **BA14** 20 B6
**Southwold IP18** 35 **K1**
Southwood **BA6** 8 E1
Sowden **EX8** 7 H7
Sower Carr **FY6** 55 G5
Sowerby *N.Yorks.* **YO7** 57 K1
Sowerby *W.Yorks.* **HX6** 57 F7
**Sowerby Bridge HX6** 57 **F7**
Sowerby Row **CA4** 60 E2
Sowerhill **TA22** 7 G3
Sowley Green **CB9** 34 B3
Sowood **HX4** 50 C1
Sowton **EX5** 7 H6
Soyal **IV24** 96 C2
Spa Common **NR28** 45 G2
Spadeadam **CA8** 70 A6
**Spalding PE11** 43 **F3**
Spaldington **DN14** 58 D6
Spaldwick **PE28** 32 E1
Spalefield **KY10** 83 G7
Spalford **NG23** 52 B6
Spanby **NG34** 42 D2
Sparham **NR9** 44 E4
Spark Bridge **LA12** 55 G1
Sparkford **BA22** 9 F2
Sparkhill **B11** 40 C7
Sparkwell **PL7** 5 F5
Sparrow Green **NR19** 44 D4
Sparrowpit **SK17** 50 C4
Sparrow's Green **TN5** 13 K3
Sparsholt *Hants.* **SO21** 11 F1
Sparsholt *Oxon.* **OX12** 21 G3
Spartylea **NE47** 61 K2
Spath **ST14** 40 C2
Spaunton **YO62** 58 D1
Spaxton **TA5** 8 B1
**Spean Bridge PH34** 87 **J6**
Spear Hill **RH20** 12 E5
Speddoch **DG2** 68 D5
Speedwell **BS16** 19 K4
Speen *Bucks.* **HP27** 22 B1
Speen *W.Berks.* **RG14** 21 H5
Speeton **YO14** 59 H2
Speke **L24** 48 D4
Speldhurst **TN3** 23 J7
Spellbrook **CM23** 33 H7
Spelsbury **OX7** 30 E6
Spen Green **CW11** 49 H6
Spencers Wood **RG7** 22 A5
Spennithorne **DL8** 57 G1
**Spennymoor DL16** 62 **D3**
Spernall **B80** 30 B2
Spetchley **WR5** 29 H3
Spetisbury **DT11** 9 J4
Spexhall **IP19** 45 H7
Spey Bay **IV32** 98 B4
Speybridge **PH26** 89 H2
Speyview **AB38** 97 K7
**Spilsby PE23** 53 **G6**
Spindlestone **NE70** 77 K7
Spinkhill **S21** 51 G5
Spinningdale **IV24** 96 D3
Spirthill **SN11** 20 C4
Spital *High.* **KW1** 105 G3
Spital *W. & M.* **SL4** 22 C4
Spital in the Street **LN8** 52 C3
Spitalbrook **EN11** 23 G1
Spithurst **BN8** 13 H5
Spittal *D. & G.* **DG8** 64 E4
Spittal *D. & G.* **DG8** 64 D5
Spittal *E.Loth.* **EH32** 76 C3
Spittal *Northumb.* **TD15** 77 J5
Spittal *Pembs.* **SA62** 16 C3
Spittal of Glenmuick **AB35** 90 B6
Spittal of Glenshee **PH10** 82 C1
Spittalfield **PH1** 82 C3
Spixworth **NR10** 45 G4
Splayne's Green **TN22** 13 H4
Splott **CF24** 19 F4
Spofforth **HG3** 57 J4
Spondon **DE21** 41 G2
Spooner Row **NR18** 44 E6
Spoonley **TF9** 39 F2
Sporle **PE32** 44 C4
Sportsman's Arms **LL16** 47 H7
Spott **EH42** 76 E3
Spratton **NN6** 31 J1
Spreakley **GU10** 22 B7
Spreyton **EX17** 6 E6
Spriddlestone **PL9** 5 F5
Spridlington **LN8** 52 D4
Spring Grove **TW7** 22 E4
Spring Vale **PO34** 11 H5
Springburn **G21** 74 E4
Springfield *Arg. & B.* **PA22** 73 J3
Springfield *D. & G.* **DG16** 69 J7
Springfield *Fife* **KY15** 82 E6
Springfield *Moray* **IV36** 97 H6
Springfield *P. & K.* **PH13** 82 C4
Springfield *W.Mid.* **B13** 40 C7
Springfields Outlet Village **PE12** 43 F3
Springhill *Staffs.* **WS14** 40 C5
Springhill *Staffs.* **WV11** 40 B5
Springholm **DG7** 65 J4
Springkell **DG11** 69 H6
Springleys **AB51** 91 F1
Springside **KA11** 74 B7
Springthorpe **DN21** 52 B4
Springwell **NE9** 62 D1
Sproatley **HU11** 59 H6
Sproston Green **CW4** 49 G6
Sprotbrough **DN5** 51 H2
Sproughton **IP8** 35 F4
Sprouston **TD5** 77 F7
Sprowston **NR7** 45 G4
Sproxton *Leics.* **LE14** 42 B3
Sproxton *N.Yorks.* **YO62** 58 C1
Sprytown **PL16** 6 C7
Spurlands End **HP15** 22 B2
Spurstow **CW6** 48 E7
Spyway **DT2** 8 E5
Square Point **DG7** 65 H3
Squires Gate **FY4** 55 G6
Sròndoire **PA30** 73 G3
Sronphadruig Lodge **PH18** 88 E7
Stableford *Shrop.* **WV15** 39 G6
Stableford *Staffs.* **ST5** 40 A2
Stacey Bank **S6** 50 E3
Stackhouse **BD24** 56 D3
Stackpole **SA71** 16 C6
Stacksteads **OL13** 56 D7
Staddiscombe **PL9** 5 F5
Staddlethorpe **HU15** 58 E7
Staden **SK17** 50 C5
Stadhampton **OX44** 21 K2
Stadhlaigearraidh (Stilligarry) **HS8** 84 C1
Staffield **CA10** 61 G2
Staffin **IV51** 93 K5
**Stafford ST16** 40 **B3**
Stagden Cross **CM1** 33 K7
Stagsden **MK43** 32 C4
Stagshaw Bank **NE46** 70 E7
Stain **KW1** 105 J2
Stainburn *Cumb.* **CA14** 60 B4
Stainburn *N.Yorks.* **LS21** 57 H5
Stainby **NG33** 42 C3
Staincross **S75** 51 F1
Staindrop **DL2** 62 C4
**Staines TW18** 22 **D4**
Stainfield *Lincs.* **PE10** 42 D3
Stainfield *Lincs.* **LN3** 52 E5
Stainforth *N.Yorks.* **BD24** 56 D3
Stainforth *S.Yorks.* **DN7** 51 J1
Staining **FY3** 55 G6
Stainland **HX4** 50 C1
Stainsacre **YO22** 63 J2
Stainsby *Derbys.* **S44** 51 G6
Stainsby *Lincs.* **LN9** 53 G5
Stainton *Cumb.* **LA8** 55 J1
Stainton *Cumb.* **CA11** 61 F4
Stainton *Dur.* **DL12** 62 B5
Stainton *Middbro.* **TS8** 63 F5
Stainton *N.Yorks.* **DL11** 62 C7
Stainton *S.Yorks.* **S66** 51 H3
Stainton by Langworth **LN3** 52 D5
Stainton le Vale **LN8** 52 E3
Stainton with Adgarley **LA13** 55 F2
Staintondale **YO13** 63 J3
Stair *Cumb.* **CA12** 60 D4
Stair *E.Ayr.* **KA5** 67 J1
Stairfoot **S70** 51 F2
Staithes **TS13** 63 J5
Stake Pool **PR3** 55 H5
Stakeford **NE62** 71 H5
Stakes **PO7** 11 H4
Stalbridge **DT10** 9 G3
Stalbridge Weston **DT10** 9 G3
Stalham **NR12** 45 H3
Stalham Green **NR12** 45 H3
Stalisfield Green **ME13** 14 E2
Stalling Busk **DL8** 56 E1

Sta - Str


Stallingborough DN41 52 E1
Stallington ST11 40 B2
Stalmine FY6 55 G5
**Stalybridge SK15 49 J3**
Stambourne CO9 34 B5
**Stamford Lincs. PE9 42 D5**
Stamford Northumb. NE66 71 H2
Stamford Bridge Ches.W. & C. CH3 48 D6
Stamford Bridge E.Riding YO41 58 D4
Stamfordham NE18 71 F6
Stanah FY5 55 G5
Stanborough AL8 33 F7
Stanbridge Cen.Beds. LU7 32 C6
Stanbridge Dorset BH21 10 B4
Stanbridge Earls SO51 10 E2
Stanbury BD22 57 F6
Stand ML6 75 F4
Standburn FK1 75 H3
Standeford WV10 40 B5
Standen TN27 14 D4
Standen Street TN17 14 D4
Standerwick BA11 20 B6
Standford GU35 12 B3
Standford Bridge TF10 39 G3
Standish Glos. GL10 20 B1
Standish Gt.Man. WN6 48 E1
Standlake OX29 21 G1
Standon Hants. SO21 11 F2
Standon Herts. SG11 33 G6
Standon Staffs. ST21 40 A2
Standon Green End SG11 33 G7
Stane ML7 75 G5
Stanecastle KA11 74 B7
Stanfield NR20 44 D3
Stanford Cen.Beds. SG18 32 E4
Stanford Kent TN25 15 G4
Stanford Shrop. SY5 38 C4
Stanford Bishop WR6 29 F3
Stanford Bridge WR6 29 G2
Stanford Dingley RG7 21 J4
Stanford End RG7 22 A5
Stanford in the Vale SN7 21 G2
Stanford on Avon NN6 31 G1
Stanford on Soar LE12 41 H3
Stanford on Teme WR6 29 G2
Stanford Rivers CM5 23 J1
**Stanford-le-Hope SS17 24 C3**
Stanfree S44 51 G5
Stanghow TS12 63 H5
Stanground PE2 43 F6
Stanhoe PE31 44 C2
Stanhope Dur. DL13 62 A3
Stanhope Sc.Bord. ML12 69 G1
Stanion NN14 42 C7
Stanklyn DY10 29 H1
Stanley Derbys. DE7 41 G1
**Stanley Dur. DH9 62 C1**
Stanley Notts. NG17 51 G6
Stanley P. & K. PH1 82 C4
Stanley Staffs. ST9 49 J7
Stanley W.Yorks. WF3 57 J7
Stanley Wilts. SN15 20 C4
Stanley Common DE7 41 G1
Stanley Crook DL15 62 C3
Stanley Gate L39 48 D2
Stanley Green BH15 10 B5
Stanley Hill HR8 29 F4
Stanleygreen SY13 38 E2
Stanlow Ches.W. & C. CH65 48 D5
Stanlow Shrop. WV6 39 G6
Stanmer BN1 13 G5
**Stanmore Gt.Lon. HA7 22 E2**
Stanmore W.Berks. RG20 21 H4
Stannersburn NE48 70 C5
Stanningfield IP29 34 C3
Stannington Northumb. NE61 71 H6
Stannington S.Yorks. S6 51 F4
Stansbatch HR6 28 C2
Stansfield CO10 34 B3
Stanshope DE6 50 D7
Stanstead CO10 34 C4
Stanstead Abbotts SG12 33 G7
Stansted TN15 24 C5
Stansted Airport (London Stansted Airport) CM24 33 J6
**Stansted Mountfitchet CM24 33 J6**
Stanton Derbys. DE15 40 E4
Stanton Glos. WR12 30 B5
Stanton Northumb. NE65 71 G4
Stanton Staffs. DE6 40 D1
Stanton Suff. IP31 34 D1
Stanton by Bridge DE73 41 F3
Stanton by Dale DE7 41 G2
Stanton Drew BS39 19 J5
Stanton Fitzwarren SN6 20 E2
Stanton Harcourt OX29 21 H1
Stanton Hill NG17 51 G6
Stanton in Peak DE4 50 E6
Stanton Lacy SY8 28 D1
Stanton Lees DE4 50 E6
Stanton Long TF13 38 E6
Stanton Prior BA2 19 K5
Stanton St. Bernard SN8 20 D5
Stanton St. John OX33 21 J1
Stanton St. Quintin SN14 20 C4
Stanton Street IP31 34 D2
Stanton under Bardon LE67 41 G4
Stanton upon Hine Heath SY4 38 E3
Stanton Wick BS39 19 K5
Stanton-on-the-Wolds NG12 41 J2
Stanwardine in the Fields SY4 38 D3
Stanwardine in the Wood SY12 38 D3
Stanway Essex CO3 34 D6
Stanway Glos. GL54 30 B5
Stanway Green Essex CO3 34 D6
Stanway Green Suff. IP13 35 G1
Stanwell TW19 22 D4
Stanwell Moor TW19 22 D4
Stanwick NN9 32 C1
Stanwix CA3 60 F1
Stanydale ZE2 107 L7
Staoinebrig HS8 84 C1
Stapeley CW5 39 F1
Stapenhill DE15 40 E3
Staple Kent CT3 15 H2
Staple Som. TA4 7 K1
Staple Cross TA21 7 J3
Staple Fitzpaine TA3 8 B3
Staplecross TN32 14 C5
Staplefield RH17 13 F4
Stapleford Cambs. CB22 33 H3
Stapleford Herts. SG14 33 G7
Stapleford Leics. LE14 42 B4
Stapleford Lincs. LN6 52 B7
Stapleford Notts. NG9 41 G2
Stapleford Wilts. SP3 10 B1
Stapleford Abbotts RM4 23 H2
Stapleford Tawney RM4 23 J2
Staplegrove TA2 8 B2
Staplehay TA3 8 B2
Staplehurst TN12 14 C3
Staplers PO30 11 G6
Staplestreet ME13 25 G5
Stapleton Cumb. CA6 70 A6
Stapleton Here. LD8 28 C2
Stapleton Leics. LE9 41 G6
Stapleton N.Yorks. DL2 62 D5
Stapleton Shrop. SY5 38 D5
Stapleton Som. TA12 8 D2
Stapley TA3 7 K4
Staploe PE19 32 E2
Staplow HR8 29 F4
Star Fife KY7 82 E7
Star Pembs. SA35 17 F2
Star Som. BS25 19 H6
Starbotton BD23 56 E2
Starcross EX6 7 H7
Stareton CV8 30 E1
Starkholmes DE4 51 F7
Starling BL8 49 G1
Starling's Green CB11 33 H5
Starr KA6 67 J4
Starston IP20 45 G7
Startforth DL12 62 B5
Startley SN15 20 C3
Statham WA13 49 F4
Stathe TA7 8 C2
Stathern LE14 42 A2
Station Town TS28 63 F3
Staughton Green PE19 32 E2
Staughton Highway PE19 32 E2
Staunton Glos. GL16 28 E7
Staunton Glos. GL19 29 G6
Staunton Harold Hall LE65 41 F3
Staunton in the Vale NG13 42 B1
Staunton on Arrow HR6 28 C2
Staunton on Wye HR4 28 C4
Staveley Cumb. LA8 61 F7
Staveley Derbys. S43 51 G5
Staveley N.Yorks. HG5 57 J3
Staveley-in-Cartmel LA12 55 G1
Staverton Devon TQ9 5 H4
Staverton Glos. GL51 29 H6
Staverton Northants. NN11 31 G2
Staverton Wilts. BA14 20 B5
Staverton Bridge GL51 29 H6
Stawell TA7 8 C1
Stawley TA21 7 J3
Staxigoe KW1 105 J3
Staxton YO12 59 G2
Staylittle (Penffordd-las) SY19 37 H6
Staynall FY6 55 G5
Staythorpe NG23 51 K7
Stean HG3 57 F2
Steane NN13 31 G5
Stearsby YO61 58 C2
Steart TA5 19 F7
Stebbing CM6 33 K6
Stebbing Green CM6 33 K6
Stechford B33 40 D7
Stedham GU29 12 B4
Steel Cross TN6 13 J3
Steel Green LA18 54 E2
Steele Road TD9 70 A4
Steen's Bridge HR6 28 E3
Steep GU32 11 J2
Steep Marsh GU32 11 J2
Steeple Dorset BH20 9 J6
Steeple Essex CM0 25 F1
Steeple Ashton BA14 20 C6
Steeple Aston OX25 31 F6
Steeple Barton OX25 31 F6
Steeple Bumpstead CB9 33 K4
Steeple Claydon MK18 31 H6
Steeple Gidding PE28 42 E7
Steeple Langford SP3 10 B1
Steeple Morden SG8 33 F4
Steeraway TF1 39 F5
Steeton BD20 57 F5
Stein IV55 93 H6
Steinmanhill AB53 99 F6
Stella NE21 71 G7
Stelling Minnis CT4 15 G3
Stembridge TA12 8 D2
Stemster High. KW12 105 G2
Stemster High. KW5 105 G4
Stemster House KW12 105 G2
Stenalees PL26 4 A5
Stenhill EX15 7 J4
Stenhousemuir FK5 75 G2
Stenigot LN11 53 F4
Stenis HS1 101 G4
Stenness ZE2 107 L5
Stenscholl IV51 93 K5
Stenson DE73 41 F3
Stenton E.Loth. EH42 76 E3
Stenton P. & K. PH8 82 B3
**Steornabhagh (Stornoway) HS1 101 G4**
Stepaside Pembs. SA67 16 E5
Stepaside Powys SY16 37 K7
Stepney E1 23 G3
Steppingley MK45 32 D5
Stepps G33 74 E4
Sternfield IP17 35 H2
Sterridge EX34 6 D1
Stert SN10 20 D6
Stetchworth CB8 33 K3
**STEVENAGE SG 33 F6**
**Stevenston KA20 74 A6**
Steventon Hants. RG25 21 J7
Steventon Oxon. OX13 21 H2
Steventon End CB10 33 K4
Stevington MK43 32 C3
Stewartby MK43 32 D4
Stewarton D. & G. DG8 64 E6
Stewarton E.Ayr. KA3 74 C6
Stewkley LU7 32 B6
Stewley TA19 8 C3
Stewton LN11 53 G4
**Steyning BN44 12 E5**
Steynton SA73 16 C5
Stibb EX23 6 A4
Stibb Cross EX38 6 C4
Stibb Green SN8 21 F5
Stibbard NR21 44 D3
Stibbington PE8 42 D6
Stichill TD5 77 F7
Sticker PL26 3 G3
Stickford PE22 53 G6
Sticklepath Devon EX20 6 E6
Sticklepath Som. TA20 8 C3
Stickling Green CB11 33 H5
Stickney PE22 53 G7
Stiff Street ME9 24 E5
Stiffkey NR23 44 D1
Stifford's Bridge WR13 29 G4
Stileway BA6 19 H7
Stilligarry (Stadhlaigearraidh) HS8 84 C1
Stillingfleet YO19 58 B5
Stillington N.Yorks. YO61 58 B3
Stillington Stock. TS21 62 E4
Stilton PE7 42 E7
Stinchcombe GL11 20 A2
Stinsford DT2 9 G5
Stirchley Tel. & W. TF3 39 G5
Stirchley W.Mid. B30 40 C7
Stirkoke House KW1 105 J3
Stirling Aber. AB42 99 K6
**Stirling Stir. FK8 75 F1**
Stirton BD23 56 E4
Stisted CM77 34 C6
Stitchcombe SN8 21 F5
Stithians TR3 2 E5
Stittenham IV17 96 D4
Stivichall CV3 30 E1
Stix PH15 81 J3
Stixwould LN10 52 E6
Stoak CH2 48 D5
Stobo EH45 75 K7
Stoborough BH20 9 J6
Stoborough Green BH20 9 J6
Stobwood ML11 75 H5
Stocinis (Stockinish) HS3 93 G2
Stock CM4 24 C2
Stock Green B96 29 J3
Stock Lane SN8 21 F4
Stock Wood B96 30 B3
**Stockbridge Hants. SO20 10 E1**
Stockbridge Stir. FK15 81 J7
Stockbridge W.Suss. PO19 12 B6
Stockbury ME9 24 E5
Stockcross RG20 21 H5
Stockdale TR11 2 E5
Stockdalewath CA5 60 E2
Stockerston LE15 42 B6
Stocking Green Essex CB10 33 J5
Stocking Green M.K. MK19 32 B4
Stocking Pelham SG9 33 H6
Stockingford CV10 41 F6
Stockinish (Stocinis) HS3 93 G2
Stockland Cardiff CF5 18 E4
Stockland Devon EX14 8 B4
Stockland Bristol TA5 19 F7
Stockleigh English EX17 7 G5
Stockleigh Pomeroy EX17 7 G5
Stockley SN11 20 D5
Stocklinch TA19 8 C3
**STOCKPORT SK 49 H3**
Stocksbridge S36 50 E3
**Stocksfield NE43 71 F7**
Stockton Here. HR6 28 E2
Stockton Norf. NR34 45 H6
Stockton Shrop. TF11 39 G6
Stockton Shrop. SY21 38 B5
Stockton Tel. & W. TF10 39 G4
Stockton Warks. CV47 31 F2
Stockton Wilts. BA12 9 J1
Stockton Heath WA4 49 F4
Stockton on Teme WR6 29 G2
Stockton on the Forest YO32 58 C4
**Stockton-on-Tees TS19 63 F5**
Stockwell GL4 29 J7
Stockwell Heath WS15 40 C3
Stockwood Bristol BS14 19 K5
Stockwood Dorset DT2 8 E4
Stodday LA2 55 H4
Stodmarsh CT3 25 J5
Stody NR24 44 E2
Stoer IV27 102 C6
Stoford Som. BA22 8 E3
Stoford Wilts. SP2 10 B1
Stogumber TA4 7 J2
Stogursey TA5 19 F7
Stoke Devon EX39 6 A3
Stoke Hants. SP11 21 H6
Stoke Hants. PO11 11 J4
Stoke Med. ME3 24 E4
Stoke Plym. PL3 4 E5
Stoke W.Mid. CV2 30 E1
Stoke Abbott DT8 8 D4
Stoke Albany LE16 42 B7
Stoke Ash IP23 35 F1
Stoke Bardolph NG14 41 J1
Stoke Bishop BS9 19 J4
Stoke Bliss WR15 29 F2
Stoke Bruerne NN12 31 J3
Stoke by Clare CO10 34 B4
Stoke Canon EX5 7 H6
Stoke Charity SO21 11 F1
Stoke Climsland PL17 4 D3
Stoke D'Abernon KT11 22 E6
Stoke Doyle PE8 42 D7
Stoke Dry LE15 42 B6
Stoke Edith HR1 29 F4
Stoke Farthing SP5 10 B2
Stoke Ferry PE33 44 B6
Stoke Fleming TQ6 5 J6
Stoke Gabriel TQ9 5 J5
Stoke Gifford BS34 19 K4
Stoke Golding CV13 41 F6
Stoke Goldington MK16 32 B4
Stoke Green SL2 22 C3
Stoke Hammond MK17 32 B6
Stoke Heath Shrop. TF9 39 F3
Stoke Heath Worcs. B60 29 J2
Stoke Holy Cross NR14 45 G5
Stoke Lacy HR7 29 F4
Stoke Lyne OX27 31 G6
Stoke Mandeville HP22 32 B7
Stoke Newington N16 23 G3
Stoke on Tern TF9 39 F3
Stoke Orchard GL52 29 J6
Stoke Pero TA24 7 G1
Stoke Poges SL2 22 C3
Stoke Pound B60 29 J2
Stoke Prior Here. HR6 28 E3
Stoke Prior Worcs. B60 29 J2
Stoke Rivers EX32 6 E2
Stoke Rochford NG33 42 C3
Stoke Row RG9 21 K3
Stoke St. Gregory TA3 8 C2
Stoke St. Mary TA3 8 B2
Stoke St. Michael BA3 19 K7
Stoke St. Milborough SY8 38 E7
**Stoke sub Hamdon TA14 8 D3**
Stoke Talmage OX9 21 K2
Stoke Trister BA9 9 G2
Stoke Villice BS40 19 J5
Stoke Wake DT11 9 G4
Stoke-by-Nayland CO6 34 D5
Stokeford BH20 9 H6
Stokeham DN22 51 K5
Stokeinteignhead TQ12 5 K3
Stokenchurch HP14 22 A2
Stokenham TQ7 5 J6
**STOKE-ON-TRENT ST 40 A1**
Stokesay SY7 38 D7
Stokesby NR29 45 J4
Stokesley TS9 63 G6
Stolford TA5 19 F7
Ston Easton BA3 19 K6
Stonar Cut CT13 25 K5
Stondon Massey CM15 23 J1
Stone Bucks. HP17 31 J7
Stone Glos. GL13 19 K2
Stone Kent DA9 23 J4
Stone Kent TN30 14 E5
Stone S.Yorks. S66 51 H4
Stone Som. BA4 8 E1
**Stone Staffs. ST15 40 B2**
Stone Worcs. DY10 29 H1
Stone Allerton BS26 19 H6
Stone Cross Dur. DL12 62 B5
Stone Cross E.Suss. BN24 13 K6
Stone Cross E.Suss. TN6 13 J4
Stone Cross Kent TN25 15 F4
Stone Cross Kent TN3 13 J3
Stone House LA10 56 C1
Stone Street Kent TN15 23 J6
Stone Street Suff. IP19 45 H7
Stone Street Suff. CO10 34 D5
Stonea PE15 43 H6
Stonebridge E.Suss. TN22 13 J4
Stonebridge N.Som. BS29 19 G6
Stonebridge Warks. CV7 40 E7
Stonebroom DE55 51 G7
Stonecross Green IP29 34 C3
Stonefield Arg. & B. PA29 73 G3
Stonefield Staffs. ST15 40 B2
Stonegate E.Suss. TN5 13 K4
Stonegate N.Yorks. YO21 63 J6
Stonegrave YO62 58 C2
Stonehaugh NE48 70 C6
**Stonehaven AB39 91 G6**
Stonehill KT16 22 C5
Stonehouse Ches.W. & C. CH3 48 E5
Stonehouse D. & G. DG2 65 J4
**Stonehouse Glos. GL10 20 B1**
Stonehouse Northumb. NE49 61 H1
Stonehouse Plym. PL1 4 E5
Stonehouse S.Lan. ML9 75 F6
Stoneleigh Surr. KT17 23 F5
Stoneleigh Warks. CV8 30 E1
Stoneley Green CW5 49 F7
Stonely PE19 32 E2
Stoner Hill GU32 11 J2
Stones OL14 56 E7
Stones Green CO12 35 F6
Stonesby LE14 42 B3
Stonesfield OX29 30 E7
Stonestreet Green TN25 15 F4
Stonethwaite CA12 60 D5
Stoney Cross SO43 10 D3
Stoney Middleton S32 50 E5
Stoney Stanton LE9 41 G6
Stoney Stoke BA9 9 G1
Stoney Stratton BA4 9 F1
Stoney Stretton SY5 38 C5
Stoneyburn EH47 75 H4
Stoneyford EX10 7 J7
Stoneygate LE2 41 J5
Stoneyhills CM0 25 F2
Stoneykirk DG9 64 A5
Stoneywood AB21 91 G3
Stonganess ZE2 107 P2
Stonham Aspal IP14 35 F3
Stonnall WS9 40 C5
Stonor RG9 22 A3
Stonton Wyville LE16 42 A6
Stony Houghton NG19 51 G6
Stony Stratford MK11 31 J4
Stonybreck ZE2 107 K2
Stoodleigh Devon EX16 7 H4
Stoodleigh Devon EX32 6 E2
Stopham RH20 12 D5
Stopsley LU2 32 E6
Stoptide PL27 3 G1
Storeton CH63 48 C4
Stormontfield PH2 82 C5
**Stornoway (Steornabhagh) HS1 101 G4**
Stornoway Airport HS2 101 G4
Storridge WR13 29 G4
Storrington RH20 12 D5
Storrs S6 50 E4
Storth LA7 55 H1
Storwood YO42 58 D5
Stotfield IV31 97 K4
Stotfold SG5 33 F5
Stottesdon DY14 39 F7
Stoughton Leics. LE2 41 J5
Stoughton Surr. GU2 22 C6
Stoughton W.Suss. PO18 11 J3
Stoughton Cross BS28 19 H7
Stoul PH41 86 D5
Stoulton WR7 29 J4
Stour Provost SP8 9 G2
Stour Row SP7 9 H2
**Stourbridge DY8 40 A7**
Stourpaine DT11 9 H4
**Stourport-on-Severn DY13 29 H1**
Stourton Staffs. DY7 40 A7
Stourton Warks. CV36 30 D5
Stourton Wilts. BA12 9 G1
Stourton Caundle DT10 9 G3
Stove KW17 106 F4
Stoven NR34 45 J7
Stow Lincs. LN1 52 B4
Stow Sc.Bord. TD1 76 C6
Stow Bardolph PE34 44 A5
Stow Bedon NR17 44 D6
Stow cum Quy CB25 33 J2
Stow Longa PE28 32 E1
Stow Maries CM3 24 E2
Stow Pasture LN1 52 B4
Stowbridge PE34 43 J5
Stowe Glos. GL15 19 J1
Stowe Shrop. LD7 28 C1
Stowe Staffs. WS13 40 D4
Stowe-by-Chartley ST18 40 C3
Stowehill NN7 31 H3
Stowell Glos. GL54 30 B7
Stowell Som. DT9 9 F2
Stowey BS39 19 J6
Stowford Devon EX20 6 C7
Stowford Devon EX37 6 E3
Stowford Devon EX10 7 K7
Stowlangtoft IP31 34 D2
**Stowmarket IP14 34 E3**
Stow-on-the-Wold GL54 30 C6
Stowting TN25 15 G3
Stowupland IP14 34 E3
Straad PA20 73 J4
Stracathro DD9 83 H1
Strachan AB31 90 E5
Strachur (Clachan Strachur) PA27 80 B7
Stradbroke IP21 35 G1
Stradishall CB8 34 B3
Stradsett PE33 44 A5
Stragglethorpe LN5 52 C7
Straight Soley RG17 21 G4
Straiton Edin. EH20 76 A4
Straiton S.Ayr. KA19 67 H3
Straloch Aber. AB21 91 G2
Straloch P. & K. PH10 82 B1
Stramshall ST14 40 C2
Strands LA18 54 E1
Strang IM4 54 C6
Strangford HR9 28 E6
Strannda HS5 93 F3
**Stranraer DG9 64 A4**
Strata Florida SY25 27 G2
Stratfield Mortimer RG7 21 K5
Stratfield Saye RG7 21 K5
Stratfield Turgis RG27 21 K6

Str - Tan


Stratford Cen.Beds. SG19 32 E4
Stratford Glos. GL20 29 H5
Stratford Gt.Lon. E15 23 G3
Stratford St. Andrew IP17 35 H3
Stratford St. Mary CO7 34 E5
Stratford sub Castle SP1 10 C1
Stratford Tony SP5 10 B2
Stratford-upon-Avon CV37 30 D3
Strath KW1 105 H3
Strathan High. IV27 102 C6
Strathan High. PH34 87 F5
Strathaven ML10 75 F6
Strathblane G63 74 D3
Strathcanaird IV26 95 H1
Strathcarron IV54 95 F7
Strathdon AB36 90 B3
Strathgirnock AB35 90 B5
Strathkinness KY16 83 F6
Strathmiglo KY14 82 D6
Strathpeffer IV14 96 B6
Strathrannoch IV23 95 K4
Strathtay PH9 82 A2
Strathwhillan KA27 73 J7
Strathy KW14 104 D2
Strathyre FK18 81 G6
Stratton Cornw. EX23 6 A5
Stratton Dorset DT2 9 F5
Stratton Glos. GL7 20 D1
Stratton Audley OX27 31 H6
Stratton Hall IP10 35 G5
Stratton St. Margaret SN3 20 E3
Stratton St. Michael NR15 45 G6
Stratton Strawless NR10 45 G3
Stratton-on-the-Fosse BA3 19 K6
Stravanan PA20 73 J5
Stravithie KY16 83 G6
Strawberry Hill TW2 22 E4
Stream TA4 7 J2
Streat BN6 13 G5
Streatham SW16 23 F4
Streatham Vale SW16 23 F4
Streatley Cen.Beds. LU3 32 D6
Streatley W.Berks. RG8 21 J3
Street Devon EX12 7 K7
Street Lancs. PR3 55 J4
Street N.Yorks. YO21 63 J6
Street Som. BA16 8 D1
Street Som. TA20 8 C4
Street Ashton CV23 41 G7
Street Dinas SY11 38 C2
Street End PO20 12 B7
Street Gate NE16 62 D1
Street Houses LS24 58 B5
Street Lane DE5 41 F1
Street on the Fosse BA4 9 F1
Streethay WS13 40 D4
Streethouse WF7 57 J7
Streetlam DL7 62 E7
Streetly B74 40 C6
Streetly End CB21 33 K4
Strefford SY7 38 D7
Strelley NG8 41 H1
Strensall YO32 58 C3
Strensham WR8 29 J4
Stretcholt TA6 19 F7
Strete TQ6 5 J6
Stretford Gt.Man. M32 49 G3
Stretford Here. HR6 28 D3
Stretford Here. HR6 28 E3
Strethall CB11 33 H5
Stretham CB6 33 J1
Strettington PO18 12 B6
Stretton Ches.W. & C. SY14 48 D7
Stretton Derbys. DE55 51 F6
Stretton Rut. LE15 42 C4
Stretton Staffs. ST19 40 A4
Stretton Staffs. DE13 40 E3
Stretton Warr. WA4 49 F4
Stretton en le Field DE12 41 F4
Stretton Grandison HR8 29 F4
Stretton Heath SY5 38 C4
Stretton Sugwas HR4 28 D4
Stretton under Fosse CV23 41 G7
Stretton Westwood TF13 38 E6
Stretton-on-Dunsmore CV23 31 F1
Stretton-on-Fosse GL56 30 D5
Stribers LA12 55 G1
Strichen AB43 99 H5
Strines SK6 49 J4
Stringston TA5 7 K1
Strixton NN29 32 C2
Stroat NP16 19 J2
Stromeferry IV53 86 E1
Stromemore IV54 86 E1
Stromness KW16 106 B7
Stronaba PH34 87 J6
Stronachlachar FK8 81 F6
Strone Arg. & B. PA23 73 K2
Strone High. IV63 88 C2
Strone High. PH33 87 H6
Strone Stir. FK17 81 F6
Stronechrubie IV27 102 E7
Stronlonag PA23 73 K2
Stronmilchan PA33 80 C5
Stronsay KW17 106 F5
Stronsay Airfield KW17 106 F5
Strontian PH36 79 K1
Strontoiller PA34 80 A5
Stronvar FK19 81 G5
Strood ME2 24 D5
Strood Green Surr. RH3 23 F7
Strood Green W.Suss. RH14 12 D4
Strood Green W.Suss. RH12 12 E3
Stroquhan DG2 68 D5
Stroud Glos. GL5 20 B1
Stroud Hants. GU32 11 J2
Stroud Common GU5 22 D7
Stroud Green Essex SS4 24 E2
Stroud Green Glos. GL10 20 B1
Stroude GU25 22 D5
Stroul G84 74 A2
Stroxton NG33 42 C2
Struan High. IV56 85 J1
Struan P. & K. PH18 81 J1
Strubby Lincs. LN13 53 H4
Strubby Lincs. LN8 52 E5
Strumpshaw NR13 45 H5
Struthers KY15 82 E7
Struy IV4 88 B1
Stryd y Facsen LL65 46 B4
Stryt-cae-rhedyn CH7 48 B6
Stryt-issa LL14 38 B1
Stuartfield AB42 99 H6
Stub Place LA19 60 B7
Stubber's Green WS9 40 C5
Stubbington PO14 11 G4
Stubbins BL0 49 G1
Stubbs Green NR14 45 H6
Stubhampton DT11 9 J3
Stubley S18 51 F5
Stubshaw Cross WN4 48 E2
Stubton NG23 42 B1
Stuck Arg. & B. PA20 73 J4
Stuck Arg. & B. PA23 73 K1
Stuckbeg PA24 74 A1
Stuckgowan G83 80 E7
Stuckindroin G83 80 E6
Stuckreoch PA27 73 J1
Stuckton SP6 10 C3
Stud Green SL6 22 B4
Studdon NE47 61 K1
Studfold BD24 56 D2
Studham LU6 32 D7
Studholme CA7 60 D1
Studland BH19 10 B6
Studley Warks. B80 30 B2
Studley Wilts. SN11 20 C4
Studley Common B80 30 B2
Studley Green HP14 22 A2
Studley Roger HG4 57 H2
Stuggadhoo IM4 54 C6
Stump Cross Essex CB10 33 J4
Stump Cross Lancs. PR3 55 J6
Stuntney CB7 33 J1
Stunts Green BN27 13 K5
Sturbridge ST21 40 A2
Sturgate DN21 52 B4
Sturmer CB9 33 K4
Sturminster Common DT10 9 G3
Sturminster Marshall BH21 9 J4
Sturminster Newton DT10 9 G3
Sturry CT2 25 H5
Sturton by Stow LN1 52 B4
Sturton le Steeple DN22 51 K4
Stuston IP21 35 F1
Stutton N.Yorks. LS24 57 K5
Stutton Suff. IP9 35 F5
Styal SK9 49 H4
Styrrup DN11 51 J3
Suainebost (Swainbost) HS2 101 H1
Suardail HS2 101 G4
Succoth Aber. AB54 90 C1
Succoth Arg. & B. G83 80 D7
Succothmore PA27 80 C7
Suckley WR6 29 G3
Suckley Green WR6 29 G3
Suckley Knowl WR6 29 G3
Sudborough NN14 42 C7
Sudbourne IP12 35 J3
Sudbrook Lincs. NG32 42 C1
Sudbrook Mon. NP26 19 J3
Sudbrooke LN2 52 D5
Sudbury Derbys. DE6 40 D2
Sudbury Gt.Lon. HA0 22 E3
Sudbury Suff. CO10 34 C4
Sudden OL11 49 H1
Sudgrove GL6 20 C1
Suffield N.Yorks. YO13 63 J3
Suffield Norf. NR11 45 G2
Sugarloaf TN26 14 E4
Sugnall ST21 39 G2
Sugwas Pool HR4 28 D4
Suie Lodge Hotel FK20 81 F5
Suisnish IV49 86 B3
Sulby I.o.M. IM7 54 C4
Sulby I.o.M. IM4 54 C5
Sulgrave OX17 31 G4
Sulham RG8 21 K4
Sulhamstead RG7 21 K5
Sullington RH20 12 D5
Sullom ZE2 107 M5
Sullom Voe Oil Terminal ZE2 107 M5
Sully CF64 18 E5
Sumburgh ZE3 107 M11
Sumburgh Airport ZE3 107 M11
Summer Bridge HG3 57 H3
Summer Isles IV26 95 F1
Summer Lodge DL8 62 A7
Summercourt TR8 3 F3
Summerfield Norf. PE31 44 B2
Summerfield Worcs. DY11 29 H1
Summerhill LL11 48 C7
Summerhouse DL2 62 D5
Summerlands LA8 55 J1
Summerleaze NP26 19 H3
Summertown OX2 21 J1
Summit OL15 49 J1
Sun Green SK15 49 J3
Sunadale PA28 73 G6
Sunbiggin CA10 61 H6
Sunbury TW16 22 E5
Sundaywell DG2 68 D5
Sunderland Cumb. CA13 60 C3
Sunderland Lancs. LA3 55 H4
SUNDERLAND T. & W. SR 62 E1
Sunderland Bridge DH6 62 D3
Sundhope TD7 69 J1
Sundon Park LU3 32 D6
Sundridge TN14 23 H6
Sundrum Mains KA6 67 J1
Sunhill GL7 20 E1
Sunipol PA75 78 E2
Sunk Island HU12 53 F1
Sunningdale SL5 22 C5
Sunninghill SL5 22 C5
Sunningwell OX13 21 H1
Sunniside Dur. DL13 62 C3
Sunniside T. & W. NE16 62 D1
Sunny Bank LA21 60 D7
Sunny Brow DL15 62 C3
Sunnylaw FK9 75 F1
Sunnyside Aber. AB12 91 G5
Sunnyside Northumb. NE46 70 E7
Sunnyside S.Yorks. S65 51 G3
Sunnyside W.Suss. RH19 13 G3
Sunton SN8 21 F6
Sunwick TD15 77 G5
Surbiton KT6 22 E5
Surfleet PE11 43 F3
Surfleet Seas End PE11 43 F3
Surlingham NR14 45 H5
Sustead NR11 45 F2
Susworth DN17 52 B2
Sutcombe EX22 6 B4
Sutcombemill EX22 6 B4
Suton NR18 44 E6
Sutors of Cromarty IV11 97 F5
Sutterby LN13 53 G5
Sutterton PE20 43 F2
Sutton Cambs. CB6 33 H1
Sutton Cen.Beds. SG19 33 F4
Sutton Devon EX17 7 F5
Sutton Devon TQ7 5 H6
SUTTON Gt.Lon. SM 23 F5
Sutton Kent CT15 15 J3
Sutton Lincs. LN5 52 B7
Sutton Norf. NR12 45 H3
Sutton Notts. NG13 42 A2
Sutton Notts. DN22 51 J4
Sutton Oxon. OX29 21 H1
Sutton Pembs. SA62 16 C4
Sutton Peter. PE5 42 D6
Sutton S.Yorks. DN6 51 H1
Sutton Shrop. WV16 39 G7
Sutton Shrop. TF9 39 F2
Sutton Shrop. SY2 38 E4
Sutton Shrop. SY11 38 C3
Sutton Staffs. TF10 39 G3
Sutton Suff. IP12 35 H4
Sutton W.Suss. RH20 12 C5
Sutton Abinger RH5 22 E7
Sutton at Hone DA4 23 J4
Sutton Bassett LE16 42 A7
Sutton Benger SN15 20 C4
Sutton Bingham BA22 8 E3
Sutton Bonington LE12 41 H3
Sutton Bridge PE12 43 H3
Sutton Cheney CV13 41 G5
Sutton Coldfield B74 40 D6
Sutton Courtenay OX14 21 J2
Sutton Crosses PE12 43 H3
Sutton Grange HG4 57 H2
Sutton Green Oxon. OX29 21 H1
Sutton Green Surr. GU4 22 D6
Sutton Green Wrex. LL13 38 D1
Sutton Holms BH21 10 B4
Sutton Howgrave DL8 57 J2
Sutton in Ashfield NG17 51 G7
Sutton in the Elms LE9 41 H6
Sutton Ings HU8 59 H6
Sutton Lane Ends SK11 49 J5
Sutton le Marsh LN12 53 J4
Sutton Leach WA9 48 E3
Sutton Maddock TF11 39 G5
Sutton Mallet TA7 8 C1
Sutton Mandeville SP3 9 J2
Sutton Montis BA22 9 F2
Sutton on Sea LN12 53 J4
Sutton on the Hill DE6 40 E2
Sutton on Trent NG23 51 K6
Sutton Poyntz DT3 9 G6
Sutton St. Edmund PE12 43 G4
Sutton St. James PE12 43 H4
Sutton St. Nicholas HR1 28 E4
Sutton Scarsdale S44 51 G6
Sutton Scotney SO21 11 F1
Sutton upon Derwent YO41 58 D5
Sutton Valence ME17 14 D3
Sutton Veny BA12 20 B7
Sutton Waldron DT11 9 H3
Sutton Weaver WA7 48 E5
Sutton Wick B. & N.E.Som. BS40 19 J6
Sutton Wick Oxon. OX14 21 H2
Sutton-in-Craven BD20 57 F5
Sutton-on-Hull HU7 59 H6
Sutton-on-the-Forest YO61 58 B3
Sutton-under-Brailes CV36 30 E5
Sutton-under-Whitestonecliffe YO7 57 K1
Swaby LN13 53 G5
Swadlincote DE11 41 F4
Swaffham PE37 44 C5
Swaffham Bulbeck CB25 33 J2
Swaffham Prior CB25 33 J2
Swafield NR28 45 G2
Swainbost (Suainebost) HS2 101 H1
Swainby DL6 63 F6
Swainsthorpe NR14 45 G5
Swainswick BA1 20 A5
Swalcliffe OX15 30 E5
Swalecliffe CT5 25 H5
Swallow LN7 52 E2
Swallow Beck LN6 52 C6
Swallowcliffe SP3 9 J2
Swallowfield RG7 22 A5
Swallows Cross CM15 24 C2
Swampton SP11 21 H6
Swan Green Ches.W. & C. WA16 49 G5
Swan Green Suff. IP19 35 G1
Swan Street CO6 34 C6
Swanage BH19 10 B7
Swanbach CW3 39 F1
Swanbourne MK17 32 B6
Swanbridge CF64 18 E5
Swancote WV15 39 G6
Swanland HU14 59 F7
Swanlaws TD8 70 C2
Swanley BR8 23 J5
Swanley Village BR8 23 J5
Swanmore Hants. SO32 11 G3
Swanmore I.o.W. PO33 11 G5
Swannington Leics. LE67 41 G4
Swannington Norf. NR9 45 F4
Swanscombe DA10 24 C4
SWANSEA (ABERTAWE) SA 17 K6
Swanston EH10 76 A4
Swanton Abbot NR10 45 G3
Swanton Morley NR20 44 E4
Swanton Novers NR24 44 E2
Swanton Street ME9 14 D2
Swanwick Derbys. DE55 51 G7
Swanwick Hants. SO31 11 G4
Swanwick Green SY13 38 E1
Swarby NG34 42 D1
Swardeston NR14 45 G5
Swarkestone DE73 41 F3
Swarland NE65 71 G3
Swarraton SO24 11 G1
Swarthmoor LA12 55 F2
Swaton NG34 42 E2
Swavesey CB24 33 G2
Sway SO41 10 D5
Swayfield NG33 42 C3
Swaythling SO18 11 F3
Swaythorpe YO25 59 G3
Sweetham EX5 7 G6
Sweethay TA3 8 B2
Sweetshouse PL30 4 A4
Swefling IP17 35 H2
Swell TA3 8 C2
Swepstone LE67 41 F4
Swerford OX7 30 E5
Swettenham CW12 49 H6
Swffryd NP11 19 F2
Swift's Green TN27 14 D3
Swiftsden TN19 14 C5
Swilland IP6 35 F3
Swillington LS26 57 J6
Swimbridge EX32 6 E3
Swimbridge Newland EX32 6 D2
Swinbrook OX18 30 D7
Swincliffe HG3 57 H4
Swincombe EX31 6 E1
Swinden BD23 56 D4
Swinderby LN6 52 B6
Swindon Staffs. DY3 40 A6
SWINDON Swin. SN 20 E3
Swindon Village GL51 29 J6
Swine HU11 59 H6
Swinefleet DN14 58 D7
Swineford BS30 19 K5
Swineshead Bed. MK44 32 D2
Swineshead Lincs. PE20 43 F1
Swineshead Bridge PE20 43 F1
Swineside DL8 57 F1
Swiney KW3 105 H5
Swinford Leics. LE17 31 G1
Swinford Oxon. OX29 21 H1
Swingate NG16 41 H1
Swingfield Minnis CT15 15 H3
Swingleton Green IP7 34 D4
Swinhoe NE67 71 H1
Swinhope LN8 53 F3
Swining ZE2 107 N6
Swinithwaite DL8 57 F1
Swinscoe DE6 40 D1
Swinside Hall TD8 70 C2
Swinstead NG33 42 D3
Swinton Gt.Man. M27 49 G2
Swinton N.Yorks. YO17 58 D2
Swinton N.Yorks. HG4 57 H2
Swinton S.Yorks. S64 51 G3
Swinton Sc.Bord. TD11 77 G6
Swinton Quarter TD11 77 G6
Swintonmill TD12 77 G6
Swithland LE12 41 H4
Swordale IV16 96 C5
Swordland PH41 86 D5
Swordle PH36 86 B7
Swordly KW14 104 C2
Sworton Heath WA16 49 F4
Swyddffynnon SY25 27 F2
Swyncombe RG9 21 K2
Swynnerton ST15 40 A2
Swyre DT2 8 E6
Sychnant LD6 27 J1
Syde GL53 29 J7
Sydenham Gt.Lon. SE26 23 G4
Sydenham Oxon. OX39 22 A1
Sydenham Damerel PL19 4 E3
Syderstone PE31 44 C2
Sydling St. Nicholas DT2 9 F5
Sydmonton RG20 21 H6
Sydney CW1 49 G7
Syerston NG23 42 A1
Sykehouse DN14 51 J1
Sykes BB7 56 B4
Sylen SA15 17 J5
Symbister ZE2 107 P6
Symington S.Ayr. KA1 74 B7
Symington S.Lan. ML12 75 H7
Symonds Yat HR9 28 E7
Symondsbury DT6 8 D5
Synod Inn (Post-mawr) SA44 26 D3
Syre KW11 103 J4
Syreford GL54 30 B6
Syresham NN13 31 H4
Syston Leics. LE7 41 J4
Syston Lincs. NG32 42 C1
Sytchampton DY13 29 H2
Sywell NN6 32 B2


## T


Taagan IV22 95 G5
Tableyhill WA16 49 G5
Tabost W.Isles HS2 101 F6
Tabost (Harbost) W.Isles HS2 101 H1
Tachbrook Mallory CV33 30 E2
Tacher KW5 105 G4
Tackley OX5 31 F6
Tacleit (Hacklete) HS2 100 D4
Tacolneston NR16 45 F6
Tadcaster LS24 57 K5
Tadden BH21 9 J4
Taddington Derbys. SK17 50 D5
Taddington Glos. GL54 30 B5
Taddiport EX38 6 C4
Tadley RG26 21 K5
Tadlow SG8 33 F4
Tadmarton OX15 30 E5
Tadpole Bridge SN7 21 G1
Tadworth KT20 23 F6
Tafarnaubach NP22 28 A7
Tafarn-y-bwlch SA41 16 D2
Tafarn-y-Gelyn CH7 47 K6
Taff Merthyr Garden Village CF46 18 E2
Taff's Well (Ffynnon Taf) CF15 18 E3
Tafolwern SY19 37 H5
Taibach N.P.T. SA13 18 A3
Tai-bach Powys SY10 38 A3
Taicynhaeaf LL40 37 F4
Tain High. KW14 105 H2
Tain High. IV19 96 E3
Tai'n Lôn LL54 46 C7
Tai'r Bull LD3 27 J6
Tairbeart (Tarbert) HS3 100 D7
Tairgwaith SA18 27 G7
Tai'r-heol CF46 18 E2
Tairlaw KA19 67 J3
Tai'r-ysgol SA7 17 K6
Takeley CM22 33 J6
Takeley Street CM22 33 J6
Talachddu LD3 27 K5
Talacre CH8 47 K4
Talardd LL23 37 H3
Talaton EX5 7 J6
Talbenny SA62 16 B4
Talbot Green CF72 18 D3
Talbot Village BH10 10 B5
Talerddig SY19 37 J5
Talgarreg SA44 26 D3
Talgarth LD3 28 A5
Taliesin SY20 37 F6
Talisker IV47 85 J1
Talke Pits ST7 49 H7
Talkin CA8 61 G1
Talla Linnfoots ML12 69 G1
Talladale IV22 95 F4
Talladh-a-Bheithe PH17 81 G2
Talland PL13 4 C5
Tallarn Green SY14 38 D1
Tallentire CA13 60 C3
Talley (Talyllychau) SA19 17 K2
Tallington PE9 42 D5
Talmine IV27 103 H2
Talog SA33 17 G3
Tal-sarn SA48 26 E3
Talsarnau LL47 37 F2
Talskiddy TR9 3 G2
Talwrn I.o.A. LL77 46 C5
Talwrn Wrex. LL14 38 B1
Talwrn Wrex. LL13 38 C1
Talybont Cere. SY24 37 F7
Tal-y-bont Conwy LL32 47 F6
Tal-y-bont Gwyn. LL43 36 E3
Tal-y-bont Gwyn. LL57 46 E5
Talybont-on-Usk LD3 28 A6
Tal-y-Cae LL57 46 E6
Tal-y-cafn LL28 47 F5
Tal-y-coed NP7 28 D7
Talygarn CF72 18 D3
Talyllychau (Talley) SA19 17 K2
Tal-y-llyn Gwyn. LL36 37 G5
Talyllyn Powys LD3 28 A6
Talysarn LL54 46 C7
Tal-y-wern SY20 37 H5
Tamavoid FK8 74 D1
Tamerton Foliot PL5 4 E4
Tamworth B79 40 E5
Tamworth Green PE22 43 G1
Tan Office Green IP29 34 B3
Tandem HD5 50 D1
Tandridge RH8 23 G6
Tanerdy SA31 17 H3
Tanfield DH9 62 C1
Tanfield Lea DH9 62 C1
Tang HG3 57 H4
Tang Hall YO10 58 C4
Tangiers SA62 16 C4

Tan - Thu


Tanglandford AB41 91 G1
Tangley SP11 21 G6
Tangmere PO20 12 C6
Tangwick ZE2 107 L5
Tangy PA28 66 A1
Tankerness KW17 106 E7
Tankersley S75 51 F2
Tankerton CT5 25 H5
Tan-lan LL48 37 F1
Tannach KW1 105 J4
Tannachie AB39 91 F6
Tannachy IV28 96 E1
Tannadice DD8 83 F2
Tannington IP13 35 G2
Tannochside G71 74 E4
Tansley DE4 51 F7
Tansley Knoll DE4 51 F7
Tansor PE8 42 D6
Tantobie DH9 62 C1
Tanton TS9 63 G5
Tanworth in Arden B94 30 C1
Tan-y-fron LL16 47 H6
Tan-y-graig LL53 36 C2
Tanygrisiau LL41 37 F1
Tan-y-groes SA43 17 F1
Tan-y-pistyll SY10 37 K3
Tan-yr-allt LL19 47 J4
Taobh a' Deas Loch Baghasdail HS8 84 C3
Taobh Siar HS3 100 D7
Taobh Tuath (Northton) HS3 92 E3
Tapeley EX39 6 C3
Taplow SL6 22 C3
Tapton Grove S43 51 G5
Taransay (Tarasaigh) HS3 100 C7
Taraphocain PA38 80 B3
Tarasaigh (Taransay) HS3 100 C7
Tarbat House IV18 96 E4
**Tarbert** *Arg. & B.* PA29 73 G4
Tarbert *Arg. & B.* PA41 72 E5
Tarbert *Arg. & B.* PA60 72 E2
Tarbert *High.* PH36 79 H1
Tarbert (Tairbeart) *W.Isles* HS3 100 D7
Tarbet *Arg. & B.* G83 80 E7
Tarbet *High.* PH41 86 D5
Tarbet *High.* IV27 102 D4
Tarbock Green L35 48 D4
Tarbolton KA5 67 J1
Tarbrax EH55 75 J5
Tardebigge B60 29 J2
Tardy Gate PR5 55 J7
Tarfside DD9 90 C7
Tarland AB34 90 C4
Tarleton PR4 55 H7
Tarlscough L40 48 D1
Tarlton GL7 20 C2
Tarnbrook LA2 55 J4
Tarnock BS26 19 G6
**Tarporley** CW6 48 E6
Tarr TA4 7 K2
Tarrant Crawford DT11 9 J4
Tarrant Gunville DT11 9 J3
Tarrant Hinton DT11 9 J3
Tarrant Keyneston DT11 9 J4
Tarrant Launceston DT11 9 J4
Tarrant Monkton DT11 9 J4
Tarrant Rawston DT11 9 J4
Tarrant Rushton DT11 9 J4
Tarrel IV20 97 F3
Tarring Neville BN9 13 H6
Tarrington HR1 29 F4
Tarrnacraig KA27 73 H7
Tarsappie PH2 82 C5
Tarskavaig IV46 86 B4
Tarves AB41 91 G1
Tarvie *High.* IV14 96 B6
Tarvie *P. & K.* PH10 82 B1
Tarvin CH3 48 D6
Tarvin Sands CH3 48 D6
Tasburgh NR15 45 G6
Tasley WV16 39 F6
Taston OX7 30 E6
Tatenhill DE13 40 E3
Tathall End MK19 32 B4
Tatham LA2 56 B3
Tathwell LN11 53 G4
Tatsfield TN16 23 H6
Tattenhall CH3 48 D7
Tattenhoe MK4 32 B5
Tatterford NR21 44 C3
Tattersett PE31 44 C2
Tattershall LN4 53 F7
Tattershall Bridge LN4 52 E7
Tattershall Thorpe LN4 53 F7
Tattingstone IP9 35 F5
Tatworth TA20 8 C4
Tauchers AB55 98 B6
**TAUNTON** TA 8 B2
Tavelty AB51 91 F3
Taverham NR8 45 F4
Tavernspite SA34 16 E4
**Tavistock** PL19 4 E3
Taw Bridge EX18 6 E5
Taw Green EX20 6 E6
Tawstock EX31 6 D3
Taxal SK23 50 C5
Tayburn KA3 74 D6
Taychreggan PA35 80 B5
Tayinloan PA29 72 E6
Taylors Cross EX23 6 A4
Taynafead PA33 80 B6
Taynish PA31 73 F2
Taynton *Glos.* GL19 29 G6
Taynton *Oxon.* OX18 30 D7
**Taynuilt** PA35 80 B4
Tayock DD10 83 H2
Tayovullin PA44 72 A3
**Tayport** DD6 83 F5
Tayvallich PA31 73 F2
Tea Green LU2 32 E6
Tealby LN8 52 E3
Tealing DD4 83 F4
Team Valley NE11 71 H7
Teanamachar HS6 92 C5
Teangue IV44 86 C4
Teasses KY8 83 F7
Tebay CA10 61 H6
Tebworth LU7 32 C6
Tedburn St. Mary EX6 7 G6
Teddington *Glos.* GL20 29 J5
**Teddington** *Gt.Lon.* TW11 22 E4
Tedstone Delamere HR7 29 F3
Tedstone Wafre HR7 29 F3
Teeton NN6 31 H1
Teffont Evias SP3 9 J1
Teffont Magna SP3 9 J1
Tegryn SA35 17 F2
Teigh LE15 42 B4
Teign Village TQ13 7 G7
Teigngrace TQ12 5 J3
**Teignmouth** TQ14 5 K3
**TELFORD** TF 39 F5
Telham TN33 14 C6
Tellisford BA2 20 B6
Telscombe BN7 13 H6
Telscombe Cliffs BN10 13 H6
Tempar PH16 81 H2
Templand DG11 69 F5
Temple *Cornw.* PL30 4 B3
Temple *Midloth.* EH23 76 B5
Temple Balsall B93 30 D1
Temple Bar SA48 26 E3
Temple Cloud BS39 19 K6
Temple End CB9 33 K3
Temple Ewell CT16 15 H3
Temple Grafton B49 30 C3
Temple Guiting GL54 30 B6
Temple Herdewyke CV47 30 E3
Temple Hirst YO8 58 C7
Temple Normanton S42 51 G6
Temple Sowerby CA10 61 H4
**Templecombe** BA8 9 G2
Templeton *Devon* EX16 7 G4
Templeton *Pembs.* SA67 16 E4
Templeton Bridge EX16 7 G4
Templewood DD9 83 H1
Tempsford SG19 32 E3
Ten Mile Bank PE38 44 A6
**Tenbury Wells** WR15 28 E2
**Tenby (Dinbych-y-pysgod)** SA70 16 E5
Tendring CO16 35 F6
Tendring Green CO16 35 F6
Tenga PA72 79 G3
**Tenterden** TN30 14 D4
Tepersie Castle AB33 90 D2
Terally DG9 64 B6
Terling CM3 34 B7
Tern TF6 39 F4
Ternhill TF9 39 F2
Terregles DG2 65 K3
Terriers HP13 22 B2
Terrington YO60 58 C2
Terrington St. Clement PE34 43 J3
Terrington St. John PE14 43 J4
Terry's Green B94 30 C1
Tervieside AB37 89 K1
Teston ME18 14 C2
Testwood SO40 10 E3
**Tetbury** GL8 20 B2
Tetbury Upton GL8 20 B2
Tetchill SY12 38 C2
Tetcott EX22 6 B6
Tetford LN9 53 G5
Tetney DN36 53 G2
Tetney Lock DN36 53 G2
Tetsworth OX9 21 K1
Tettenhall WV6 40 A5
Tettenhall Wood WV6 40 A6
Tetworth SG19 33 F3
Teuchan AB42 91 J1
Teversal NG17 51 G6
Teversham CB1 33 H3
Teviothead TD9 69 K3
Tewel AB39 91 G6
Tewin AL6 33 F7
**Tewkesbury** GL20 29 H5
Teynham ME9 25 F5
Thackley BD10 57 G6
Thainston AB30 90 E7
Thainstone AB51 91 F3
Thakeham RH20 12 E5
**Thame** OX9 22 A1
**Thames Ditton** KT7 22 E5
Thames Haven SS17 24 D3
Thamesmead SE28 23 H3
Thanington CT1 15 G2
Thankerton ML12 75 H7
Tharston NR15 45 F6
**Thatcham** RG18 21 J5
Thatto Heath WA9 48 E3
Thaxted CM6 33 K5
The Apes Hall CB6 43 J6
The Bage HR3 28 B4
The Balloch PH7 81 K6
The Banking AB51 91 F1
The Bar RH13 12 E4
The Birks AB32 91 F4
The Bog SY5 38 C6
The Bourne GU9 22 B7
The Bratch WV5 40 A6
The Broad HR6 28 D2
The Bryn NP7 19 G1
The Burf DY13 29 H2
The Burn DD9 90 D7
The Butts BA11 20 A7
The Camp GL6 20 C1
The Chequer SY13 38 D1
The City *Bucks.* HP14 22 A2
The City *Suff.* NR34 45 H7
The Common *Wilts.* SP5 10 D1
The Common *Wilts.* SN15 20 D3
The Craigs IV24 96 B2
The Cronk IM7 54 C4
The Delves WS5 40 C6
The Den KA24 74 B5
The Dicker BN27 13 J6
The Down WV16 39 F6
The Drums DD8 82 E1
The Eaves GL15 19 K1
The Flatt CA6 70 A6
The Folly AL4 32 E7
The Forge HR5 28 C3
The Forstal *E.Suss.* TN3 13 J3
The Forstal *Kent* TN25 15 F4
The Grange *Lincs.* LN13 53 J5
The Grange *Shrop.* SY12 38 C2
The Grange *Surr.* RH9 23 G7
The Green *Arg. & B.* PA77 78 A3
The Green *Cumb.* LA18 54 E1
The Green *Essex* CM8 34 B7
The Green *Flints.* CH7 48 B6
The Green *Wilts.* SP3 9 H1
The Grove WR8 29 H4
The Haven RH14 12 D3
The Headland TS24 63 G3
The Heath ST14 40 C2
The Herberts CF71 18 C4
The Hermitage KT20 23 F6
The Hill LA18 54 E1
The Holme HG3 57 H4
The Howe IM9 54 A7
The Isle SY3 38 D4
The Laurels NR14 45 H6
The Leacon TN26 14 E4
The Lee HP16 22 B1
The Leigh GL19 29 H6
The Lhen IM7 54 C3
The Lodge PA24 73 K1
The Marsh SY5 38 C6
The Moor *E.Suss.* TN35 14 D6
The Moor *Kent* TN18 14 C5
The Mumbles SA3 17 K7
The Murray G75 74 E5
The Mythe GL20 29 H5
The Narth NP25 19 J1
The Neuk AB31 91 F5
The Node SG4 33 F7
The Oval BA2 20 A5
The Polchar PH22 89 G4
The Quarter TN27 14 D3
The Reddings GL51 29 J6
The Rhos SA62 16 D4
The Rookery ST7 49 H7
The Rowe ST5 40 A2
The Sale DE13 40 D4
The Sands GU10 22 B7
The Shoe SN14 20 B4
The Slade RG7 21 J4
The Smithies WV16 39 F6
The Stocks TN30 14 E5
The Swillett WD3 22 D2
The Thrift SG8 33 G5
The Vauld HR1 28 E4
The Wern LL14 48 B7
The Wyke TF11 39 G5
Theakston DL8 57 J1
Thealby DN15 52 B1
Theale *Som.* BS28 19 H7
Theale *W.Berks.* RG7 21 K4
Thearne HU17 59 G6
Theberton IP16 35 J2
Thedden Grange GU34 11 H1
Theddingworth LE17 41 J7
Theddlethorpe All Saints LN12 53 H4
Theddlethorpe St. Helen LN12 53 H4
Thelbridge Barton EX17 7 F4
Thelbridge Cross EX17 7 F4
Thelnetham IP22 34 E1
Thelveton IP21 45 F7
Thelwall WA4 49 F4
Themelthorpe NR20 44 E3
Thenford OX17 31 G4
Therfield SG8 33 G5
Thetford *Lincs.* PE6 42 E4
**Thetford** *Norf.* IP24 44 C7
Thethwaite CA5 60 E2
Theydon Bois CM16 23 H2
Theydon Garnon CM16 23 H2
Theydon Mount CM16 23 H2
Thickwood SN14 20 B4
Thimbleby *Lincs.* LN9 53 F6
Thimbleby *N.Yorks.* DL6 63 F7
Thingley SN13 20 B5
Thirkleby YO7 57 K2
Thirlby YO7 57 K1
Thirlestane TD2 76 D6
Thirn HG4 57 H1
**Thirsk** YO7 57 K1
Thirston New Houses NE65 71 G4
Thirtleby HU11 59 H6
Thistleton *Lancs.* PR4 55 H6
Thistleton *Rut.* LE15 42 C4
Thistley Green IP28 33 K1
Thixendale YO17 58 E3
Thockrington NE48 70 E6
Tholomas Drove PE13 43 G5
Tholthorpe YO61 57 K3
Thomas Chapel SA68 16 E5
Thomas Close CA11 60 F2
Thomastown AB54 90 D1
Thompson IP24 44 D6
Thomshill IV30 97 K6
Thong DA12 24 C4
Thongsbridge HD9 50 D2
Thoralby DL8 57 F1
Thoresby NG22 51 J5
Thoresthorpe LN13 53 H5
Thoresway LN8 52 E3
Thorganby *Lincs.* DN37 53 F3
Thorganby *N.Yorks.* YO19 58 C5
Thorgill YO18 63 J7
Thorington IP19 35 J1
Thorington Street CO6 34 E5
Thorley CM23 33 H7
Thorley Houses CM23 33 H6
Thorley Street *Herts.* CM23 33 H7
Thorley Street *I.o.W.* PO41 10 E6
Thormanby YO61 57 K2
Thornaby-on-Tees TS17 63 F5
Thornage NR25 44 E2
Thornborough *Bucks.* MK18 31 J5
Thornborough *N.Yorks.* DL8 57 H2
Thornbury *Devon* EX22 6 B5
Thornbury *Here.* HR7 29 F3
Thornbury *S.Glos.* BS35 19 K2
Thornbury *W.Yorks.* BD3 57 G6
Thornby NN6 31 H1
Thorncliff HD8 50 E1
Thorncliffe ST13 50 C7
Thorncombe TA20 8 C4
Thorncombe Street GU5 22 D7
Thorncote Green SG19 32 E4
Thorncross PO30 11 F6
Thorndon IP23 35 F2
Thorndon Cross EX20 6 D6
Thorne DN8 51 J1
Thorne St. Margaret TA21 7 J3
Thorner LS14 57 J6
Thorney *Bucks.* SL0 22 D4
Thorney *Notts.* NG23 52 B5
Thorney *Peter.* PE6 43 F5
Thorney *Som.* TA10 8 D2
Thorney Close SR4 62 E1
Thorney Hill BH23 10 D5
Thornfalcon TA3 8 B2
Thornford DT9 9 F3
Thorngrafton NE47 70 C7
Thorngrove TA7 8 C1
Thorngumbald HU12 59 J7
Thornham PE36 44 B1
Thornham Magna IP23 35 F1
Thornham Parva IP23 35 F1
Thornhaugh PE8 42 D5
Thornhill *Cardiff* CF83 18 E3
Thornhill *Cumb.* CA22 60 B6
**Thornhill** *D. & G.* DG3 68 D4
Thornhill *Derbys.* S33 50 D4
Thornhill *S'ham.* SO19 11 F3
Thornhill *Stir.* FK8 81 H7
Thornhill *W.Yorks.* WF12 50 E1
Thornhill Lees WF12 50 E1
Thornholme YO25 59 H3
Thornicombe DT11 9 H4
Thornley *Dur.* DH6 62 E3
Thornley *Dur.* DL13 62 C3
Thornley Gate NE47 61 K1
Thornliebank G46 74 D5
Thornroan AB41 91 G1
Thorns CB8 34 B3
Thorns Green WA15 49 G4
Thornsett SK22 50 C4
Thornthwaite *Cumb.* CA12 60 D4
Thornthwaite *N.Yorks.* HG3 57 G4
Thornton *Angus* DD8 82 E3
Thornton *Bucks.* MK17 31 J5
Thornton *E.Riding* YO42 58 D5
Thornton *Fife* KY1 76 A1
**Thornton** *Lancs.* FY5 55 G5
Thornton *Leics.* LE67 41 G5
Thornton *Lincs.* LN9 53 F6
Thornton *Mersey.* L23 48 C2
Thornton *Middbro.* TS8 63 F5
Thornton *Northumb.* TD15 77 H6
Thornton *P. & K.* PH8 82 B3
Thornton *Pembs.* SA73 16 C5
Thornton *W.Yorks.* BD13 57 G6
Thornton Bridge YO61 57 K2
Thornton Curtis DN39 52 D1
**Thornton Heath** CR7 23 G5
Thornton Hough CH63 48 C4
Thornton in Lonsdale LA6 56 B2
Thornton le Moor LN7 52 D3
Thornton Park TD15 77 H6
Thornton Rust DL8 56 E1
Thornton Steward HG4 57 G1
Thornton Watlass HG4 57 H1
Thorntonhall G74 74 D5
Thornton-in-Craven BD23 56 E5
Thornton-le-Beans DL6 63 F7
Thornton-le-Clay YO60 58 C3
Thornton-le-Dale YO18 58 E1
Thornton-le-Moor DL7 57 J1
Thornton-le-Moors CH2 48 D5
Thornton-le-Street YO7 57 K1
Thorntonloch EH42 77 F3
Thornwood CM16 23 H1
Thornyhill AB30 90 E7
Thornylee TD1 76 C7
Thoroton NG13 42 A1
Thorp Arch LS23 57 K5
Thorpe *Derbys.* DE6 50 D7
Thorpe *E.Riding* YO25 59 F5
Thorpe *Lincs.* LN12 53 H4
Thorpe *N.Yorks.* BD23 57 F3
Thorpe *Norf.* NR14 45 J6
Thorpe *Notts.* NG23 51 K7
Thorpe *Surr.* TW20 22 D5
Thorpe Abbotts IP21 45 F7
Thorpe Acre LE11 41 H4
Thorpe Arnold LE14 42 A3
Thorpe Audlin WF8 51 G1
Thorpe Bassett YO17 58 E2
Thorpe Bay SS1 25 F3
Thorpe by Water LE15 42 B6
Thorpe Constantine B79 40 E5
Thorpe Culvert PE24 53 H6
Thorpe End NR13 45 G4
Thorpe Green *Essex* CO16 35 F6
Thorpe Green *Lancs.* PR6 55 J7
Thorpe Green *Suff.* IP30 34 D3
Thorpe Hall YO62 58 B2
Thorpe Hesley S61 51 F3
Thorpe in Balne DN6 51 H1
Thorpe in the Fallows LN1 52 C4
Thorpe Langton LE16 42 A6
Thorpe Larches TS21 62 E4
Thorpe le Street YO42 58 E5
Thorpe Malsor NN14 32 B1
Thorpe Mandeville OX17 31 G4
Thorpe Market NR11 45 G2
Thorpe Morieux IP30 34 D3
Thorpe on the Hill *Lincs.* LN6 52 C6
Thorpe on the Hill *W.Yorks.* WF3 57 J7
Thorpe Row IP25 44 D5
Thorpe St. Andrew NR7 45 G5
Thorpe St. Peter PE24 53 H6
Thorpe Salvin S80 51 H4
Thorpe Satchville LE14 42 A4
Thorpe Street IP22 34 E1
Thorpe Thewles TS21 63 F4
Thorpe Tilney Dales LN4 52 E7
Thorpe Underwood *N.Yorks.* YO26 57 K4
Thorpe Underwood *Northants.* NN6 42 A7
Thorpe Waterville NN14 42 D7
Thorpe Willoughby YO8 58 B6
Thorpefield YO7 57 K2
Thorpe-le-Soken CO16 35 F6
Thorpeness IP16 35 J2
Thorpland PE33 44 A5
Thorrington CO7 34 E6
Thorverton EX5 7 H5
Thrandeston IP21 35 F1
Thrapston NN14 32 C1
Threapland BD23 56 E3
Threapwood SY14 38 D1
Threapwood Head ST10 40 C1
Three Ashes BA3 19 K7
Three Bridges RH10 13 F3
Three Burrows TR4 2 E4
Three Chimneys TN27 14 D4
Three Cocks (Aberllynfi) LD3 28 A5
Three Crosses SA4 17 J6
Three Cups Corner TN21 13 K4
Three Hammers PL15 4 C2
Three Holes PE14 43 J5
Three Leg Cross TN5 13 K3
Three Legged Cross BH21 10 B4
Three Mile Cross RG7 22 A5
Three Oaks TN35 14 D6
Threehammer Common NR12 45 H4
Threekingham NG34 42 D2
Threemilestone TR3 2 E4
Threlkeld CA12 60 E4
Threshfield BD23 56 E3
Threxton Hill IP25 44 C5
Thriepley DD2 82 E4
Thrigby NR29 45 J4
Thringarth DL12 62 A4
Thringstone LE67 41 G4
Thrintoft DL7 62 E7
Thriplow SG8 33 H4
Throapham S25 51 H4
Throckenholt PE12 43 G5
Throcking SG9 33 G5
Throckley NE15 71 G7
Throckmorton WR10 29 J4
Throop DT2 9 H5
Throphill NE61 71 G5
Thropton NE65 71 F3
Througham GL6 20 C1
Throwleigh EX20 6 E6
Throwley ME13 14 E2
Throws CM6 33 K6
Thrumpton *Notts.* NG11 41 H2
Thrumpton *Notts.* DN22 51 K5
Thrumster KW1 105 J4
Thrunton NE66 71 F2
Thrupp *Glos.* GL5 20 B1
Thrupp *Oxon.* OX5 31 F7
Thrupp *Oxon.* SN7 21 F2
Thruscross HG3 57 G4
Thrushelton EX20 6 C7
Thrussington LE7 41 J4
Thruxton *Hants.* SP11 21 F7
Thruxton *Here.* HR2 28 D5
Thrybergh S65 51 G3
Thulston DE72 41 G2
Thunder Bridge HD8 50 D1
Thundergay KA27 73 G6
Thundersley SS7 24 E3
Thunderton AB42 99 J6
Thundridge SG12 33 G7
Thurcaston LE7 41 H4
Thurcroft S66 51 G4
Thurdistoft KW14 105 H2
Thurdon EX23 6 A4
Thurgarton *Norf.* NR11 45 F2
Thurgarton *Notts.* NG14 41 J1
Thurgoland S35 50 E2
Thurlaston *Leics.* LE9 41 H6
Thurlaston *Warks.* CV23 31 F1
Thurlbear TA3 8 B2
Thurlby *Lincs.* PE10 42 E4
Thurlby *Lincs.* LN5 52 C6

Thu - Tre

Thurlby *Lincs.* **LN13** 53 H5
Thurleigh **MK44** 32 D3
Thurlestone **TQ7** 5 G6
Thurloxton **TA2** 8 B1
Thurlstone **S36** 50 E2
Thurlton **NR14** 45 J6
Thurlwood **ST7** 49 H7
Thurmaston **LE4** 41 J5
Thurnby **LE7** 41 J5
Thurne **NR29** 45 J4
Thurnham **ME14** 14 D2
Thurning *Norf.* **NR20** 44 E3
Thurning *Northants.* **PE8** 42 D7
Thurnscoe **S63** 51 G2
Thursby **CA5** 60 E1
Thursden **BB10** 56 E6
Thursford **NR21** 44 D2
Thursley **GU8** 12 C3
**Thurso KW14 105 G2**
Thurstaston **CH61** 48 B4
Thurston **IP31** 34 D2
Thurston Clough **OL3** 49 J2
Thurstonfield **CA5** 60 E1
Thurstonland **HD4** 50 D1
Thurton **NR14** 45 H5
Thurvaston *Derbys.* **DE6** 40 E2
Thurvaston *Derbys.* **DE6** 40 D2
Thuster **KW1** 105 H3
Thuxton **NR9** 44 E5
Thwaite *N.Yorks.* **DL11** 61 K7
Thwaite *Suff.* **IP23** 35 F2
Thwaite Head **LA12** 60 E7
Thwaite St. Mary **NR35** 45 H6
Thwaites **BD21** 57 F5
Thwaites Brow **BD21** 57 F5
Thwing **YO25** 59 G2
Tibbermore **PH1** 82 B5
Tibberton *Glos.* **GL19** 29 G6
Tibberton *Tel. & W.* **TF10** 39 F3
Tibberton *Worcs.* **WR9** 29 J3
Tibbie Shiels Inn **TD7** 69 H1
Tibenham **NR16** 45 F6
Tibertich **PA31** 79 K7
Tibshelf **DE55** 51 G6
Tibthorpe **YO25** 59 F4
Ticehurst **TN5** 13 K3
Tichborne **SO24** 11 G1
Tickencote **PE9** 42 C5
Tickenham **BS21** 19 H4
Tickford End **MK16** 32 B4
Tickhill **DN11** 51 H3
Ticklerton **SY6** 38 D6
Ticknall **DE73** 41 F3
Tickton **HU17** 59 G5
Tidbury Green **B90** 30 C1
Tidcombe **SN8** 21 F6
Tiddington *Oxon.* **OX9** 21 K1
Tiddington *Warks.* **CV37** 30 D3
Tiddleywink **SN14** 20 B4
Tidebrook **TN5** 13 K4
Tideford **PL12** 4 D5
Tideford Cross **PL12** 4 D4
Tidenham **NP16** 19 J2
Tidenham Chase **NP16** 19 J2
Tideswell **SK17** 50 D5
Tidmarsh **RG8** 21 K4
Tidmington **CV36** 30 D5
Tidpit **SP6** 10 B3
**Tidworth SP9 21 F7**
Tiers Cross **SA62** 16 C4
Tiffield **NN12** 31 H3
Tifty **AB53** 99 F6
Tigerton **DD9** 83 G1
Tigh a' Gearraidh **HS6** 92 C4
Tighachnoic **PA34** 79 H3
Tighnablair **PH6** 81 J6
**Tighnabruaich PA21 73 H3**
Tighnacomaire **PH33** 80 A1
Tigley **TQ9** 5 H4
Tilbrook **PE28** 32 D2
**Tilbury RM18 24 C4**
Tilbury Green **CO9** 34 B4
Tile Hill **CV4** 30 D1
Tilehurst **RG31** 21 K4
Tilford **GU10** 22 B7
Tilgate **RH10** 13 F3
Tilgate Forest Row **RH10** 13 F3
Tillathrowie **AB54** 90 C1
Tillers' Green **GL18** 29 F5
Tillery **AB41** 91 H2
Tilley **SY4** 38 E3
**Tillicoultry FK13 75 H1**
Tillingham **CM0** 25 F1
Tillington *Here.* **HR4** 28 D4
Tillington *W.Suss.* **GU28** 12 C4
Tillington Common **HR4** 28 D4
Tillyarblet **DD9** 83 G1
Tillybirloch **AB51** 90 E4
Tillycairn Castle **AB51** 90 E3
Tillycorthie **AB41** 91 H2
Tillydrine **AB34** 90 E5
Tillyfar **AB53** 99 G6
Tillyfour **AB33** 90 D3
Tillyfourie **AB51** 90 E3
Tillygreig **AB41** 91 G2
Tillypronie **AB34** 90 C4
Tilmanstone **CT14** 15 J2
Tiln **DN22** 51 K4
Tilney All Saints **PE34** 43 J4
Tilney Fen End **PE14** 43 J4
Tilney High End **PE34** 43 J4
Tilney St. Lawrence **PE34** 43 J4
Tilshead **SP3** 20 D7
Tilstock **SY13** 38 E2
Tilston **SY14** 48 D7
Tilstone Fearnall **CW6** 48 E6
Tilsworth **LU7** 32 C6
Tilton on the Hill **LE7** 42 A5
Tiltups End **GL6** 20 B2
Timberland **LN4** 52 E7
Timberland Dales **LN10** 52 E6
Timbersbrook **CW12** 49 H6
Timberscombe **TA24** 7 H1
Timble **LS21** 57 G4
Timewell **EX16** 7 H3
Timperley **WA15** 49 G4
Timsbury *B. & N.E.Som.* **BA2** 19 K6
Timsbury *Hants.* **SO51** 10 E2
Timsgearraidh **HS2** 100 C4
Timworth **IP31** 34 C2
Timworth Green **IP31** 34 C2
Tincleton **DT2** 9 G5
Tindale **CA8** 61 H1
Tindon End **CB10** 33 K5
Tingewick **MK18** 31 H5
Tingley **WF3** 57 H7
Tingrith **MK17** 32 D5
Tingwall **KW17** 106 D5
Tingwall (Lerwick) Airport **ZE2** 107 N8
Tinhay **PL16** 6 B7
Tinney **EX22** 4 C1
Tinshill **LS16** 57 H6
Tinsley **S9** 51 G3
Tinsley Green **RH10** 13 F3
**Tintagel PL34 4 A2**
Tintern Parva **NP16** 19 J1
Tintinhull **BA22** 8 D3
Tintwistle **SK13** 50 C3
Tinwald **DG1** 69 F5
Tinwell **PE9** 42 D5
Tippacott **EX35** 7 F1
Tipperty *Aber.* **AB30** 91 F6
Tipperty *Aber.* **AB41** 91 H2
Tipps End **PE14** 43 H6
Tiptoe **SO41** 10 D5
**Tipton DY4 40 B6**
Tipton St. John **EX10** 7 J6
Tiptree **CO5** 34 C7
Tiptree Heath **CO5** 34 C7
Tirabad **LD4** 27 H4
**Tiree PA77 78 A3**
Tiree Airport **PA77** 78 B3
Tirindrish **PH34** 87 J6
Tirley **GL19** 29 H6
Tirphil **NP24** 18 E1
Tirril **CA10** 61 G4
Tir-y-dail **SA18** 17 K4
Tisbury **SP3** 9 J2
Tisman's Common **RH12** 12 D3
Tissington **DE6** 50 D7
Tister **KW12** 105 G2
Titchberry **EX39** 6 A3
Titchfield **PO14** 11 G4
Titchmarsh **NN14** 32 D1
Titchwell **PE31** 44 B1
Tithby **NG13** 41 J2
Titley **HR5** 28 C2
Titlington **NE66** 71 G2
Titmore Green **SG4** 33 F6
Titsey **RH8** 23 H6
Titson **EX23** 6 A5
Tittensor **ST12** 40 A2
Tittleshall **PE32** 44 C3
Tiverton *Ches.W. & C.* **CW6** 48 E6
**Tiverton *Devon* EX16 7 H4**
Tivetshall St. Margaret **NR15** 45 F7
Tivetshall St. Mary **NR15** 45 F7
Tivington **TA24** 7 H1
Tixall **ST18** 40 B3
Tixover **PE9** 42 C5
Toab *Ork.* **KW17** 106 E7
Toab *Shet.* **ZE3** 107 M11
Tobermory **PA75** 79 G2
Toberonochy **PA34** 79 J7
Tobha Mòr (Homore) **HS8** 84 C1
Tobson **HS2** 100 D4
Tocher **AB51** 90 E1
Tockenham **SN4** 20 D4
Tockenham Wick **SN4** 20 D3
Tockholes **BB3** 56 B7
Tockington **BS32** 19 K3
Tockwith **YO26** 57 K4
Todber **DT10** 9 G2
Toddington *Cen.Beds.* **LU5** 32 D6
Toddington *Glos.* **GL54** 30 B5
Todenham **GL56** 30 D5
Todhills *Angus* **DD4** 83 F4
Todhills *Cumb.* **CA6** 69 J7
Todlachie **AB51** 90 E3
**Todmorden OL14 56 E7**
Todwick **S26** 51 G4
Toft *Cambs.* **CB23** 33 G3
Toft *Lincs.* **PE10** 42 D4
Toft *Shet.* **ZE2** 107 N5
Toft Hill **DL14** 62 C4
Toft Monks **NR34** 45 J6
Toft next Newton **LN8** 52 D4
Toftcarl **KW1** 105 J4
Toftrees **NR21** 44 C3
Tofts **KW1** 105 J2
Toftwood **NR19** 44 D4
Togston **NE65** 71 H3
Tokavaig **IV46** 86 C3
Tokers Green **RG4** 21 K4
Tolastadh **HS2** 101 H3
Tolastadh a' Chaolais **HS2** 100 D4
Tolastadh =r **HS2** 101 H3
Toll Bar **DN5** 51 H2
Toll of Birness **AB41** 91 J1
Tolland **TA4** 7 K2
Tollard Farnham **DT11** 9 J3
Tollard Royal **SP5** 9 J3
Tollcross **G32** 74 E4
Toller Down Gate **DT2** 8 E4
Toller Fratrum **DT2** 8 E5
Toller Porcorum **DT2** 8 E5
Toller Whelme **DT8** 8 E4
Tollerton *N.Yorks.* **YO61** 58 B3
Tollerton *Notts.* **NG12** 41 J2
Tollesbury **CM9** 34 D7
Tollesby **TS4** 63 G5
Tolleshunt D'Arcy **CM9** 34 D7
Tolleshunt Knights **CM9** 34 D7
Tolleshunt Major **CM9** 34 C7
Tolm (Holm) **HS2** 101 G4
Tolmachan **HS3** 100 C7
Tolpuddle **DT2** 9 G5
Tolvah **PH21** 89 F5
Tolworth **KT6** 22 E5
Tom an Fhuadain **HS2** 101 F6
Tomatin **IV13** 89 F2
Tombreck **IV2** 88 D1
Tomchrasky **IV63** 87 J3
Tomdoun **PH35** 87 H4
Tomdow **IV36** 97 H7
Tomich *High.* **IV4** 87 K2
Tomich *High.* **IV18** 96 E4
Tomich *High.* **IV27** 96 D1
Tomintoul **AB37** 89 J3
Tomnacross **IV4** 96 C7
Tomnamoon **IV36** 97 H6
Tomnaven **AB54** 90 C1
Tomnavoulin **AB37** 89 K2
Tomvaich **PH26** 89 H1
Ton Pentre **CF41** 18 C2
**Tonbridge TN9 23 J7**
Tondu **CF32** 18 B3
Tonedale **TA21** 7 K3
Tonfanau **LL36** 36 E5
Tong *Kent* **TN27** 14 D3
Tong *Shrop.* **TF11** 39 G5
Tong *W.Yorks.* **BD4** 57 H6
Tong Norton **TF11** 39 G5
Tong Street **BD4** 57 G6
Tonge **DE73** 41 G3
Tongham **GU10** 22 B7
Tongland **DG6** 65 G5
Tongue **IV27** 103 H3
Tongue House **IV27** 103 H3
Tongwynlais **CF15** 18 E3
Tonmawr **SA12** 18 B2
Tonna **SA11** 18 A2
Tonwell **SG12** 33 G7
**Tonypandy CF40 18 C2**
Tonyrefail **CF39** 18 D3
Toot Baldon **OX44** 21 J1
Toot Hill **CM5** 23 J1
Toothill *Hants.* **SO51** 10 E3
Toothill *Swin.* **SN5** 20 E3
Tooting Graveney **SW17** 23 F4
Top End **MK44** 32 D2
Top of Hebers **M24** 49 H2
Topcliffe **YO7** 57 K2
Topcroft **NR35** 45 G6
Topcroft Street **NR35** 45 G6
Toppesfield **CO9** 34 B5
Toppings **BL7** 49 G1
Toprow **NR16** 45 F6
Topsham **EX3** 7 H7
Topsham Bridge **TQ7** 5 H5
Torastan **PA78** 78 D1
Torbain **AB37** 89 J3
Torbeg *Aber.* **AB35** 90 B5
Torbeg *N.Ayr.* **KA27** 66 D1
Torbothie **ML7** 75 G5
Torbryan **TQ12** 5 J4
Torcastle **PH33** 87 H7
Torcross **TQ7** 5 J6
Tordarroch **IV2** 88 D1
Tore **IV6** 96 D6
Toreduff **IV36** 97 J5
Toremore *High.* **PH26** 89 J1
Toremore *High.* **KW6** 105 G5
Torfrey **PL23** 4 B5
Torgyle **IV63** 87 K3
Torksey **LN1** 52 B5
Torlum **HS7** 92 C6
Torlundy **PH33** 87 H7
Tormarton **GL9** 20 A4
Tormisdale **PA47** 72 A5
Tormore **KA27** 73 G7
Tormsdale **KW12** 105 G3
Tornagrain **IV2** 96 E6
Tornahaish **AB36** 89 K4
Tornaveen **AB31** 90 E4
Torness **IV2** 88 C2
Toronto **DL14** 62 C3
Torpenhow **CA7** 60 D3
Torphichen **EH48** 75 H3
Torphins **AB31** 90 E4
**Torpoint PL11 4 E5**
**TORQUAY TQ 5 K4**
Torquhan **TD1** 76 C6
Torr **PL8** 5 F5
Torran *Arg. & B.* **PA31** 79 K7
Torran *High.* **IV18** 96 E4
Torran *High.* **IV40** 94 B7
Torrance **G64** 74 E3
Torrance House **G75** 74 E5
Torrancroy **AB36** 90 B3
Torre *Som.* **TA23** 7 J1
Torre *Torbay* **TQ1** 5 K4
Torrich **IV12** 97 F6
Torridon **IV22** 94 E6
Torrin **IV49** 86 B2
Torrisdale *Arg. & B.* **PA28** 73 F7
Torrisdale *High.* **KW14** 103 J2
Torrish **KW8** 104 E7
Torrisholme **LA4** 55 H3
Torroble **IV27** 96 C1
Torry *Aber.* **AB54** 98 C6
Torry *Aberdeen* **AB11** 91 H4
Torryburn **KY12** 75 J2
Torsonce **TD1** 76 C6
Torterston **AB42** 99 J6
Torthorwald **DG1** 69 F6
Tortington **BN18** 12 C6
Torton **DY10** 29 H1
Tortworth **GL12** 20 A2
Torvaig **IV51** 93 K7
Torver **LA21** 60 D7
Torwood **FK5** 75 G2
Torworth **DN22** 51 J4
Tosberry **EX39** 6 A3
Toscaig **IV54** 86 D1
Toseland **PE19** 33 F2
Tosside **BD23** 56 C4
Tostarie **PA74** 78 E3
Tostock **IP30** 34 D2
Totaig **IV55** 93 G6
Totamore **PA78** 78 C2
Tote **IV51** 93 K7
Tote Hill **GU29** 12 B4
Totegan **KW14** 104 D2
Totford **SO24** 11 G1
Totham Hill **CM9** 34 C7
Tothill **LN13** 53 H4
**Totland PO39 10 E6**
Totley **S17** 51 F5
**Totnes TQ9 5 J4**
Toton **NG9** 41 H2
Totronald **PA78** 78 C2
Totscore **IV51** 93 J5
Tottenham **N17** 23 G2
Tottenhill **PE33** 44 A4
Tottenhill Row **PE33** 44 A4
Totteridge *Bucks.* **HP13** 22 B2
Totteridge *Gt.Lon.* **N20** 23 F2
Totternhoe **LU6** 32 C6
Tottington *Gt.Man.* **BL8** 49 G1
Tottington *Norf.* **IP24** 44 C6
Totton **SO40** 10 E3
Toulton **TA4** 7 K2
Tournaig **IV22** 94 E3
Toux **AB42** 99 H5
Tovil **ME15** 14 C2
Tow Law **DL13** 62 C3
Towan Cross **TR4** 2 E4
Toward **PA23** 73 K4
**Towcester NN12 31 H4**
Towednack **TR26** 2 B5
Tower End **PE32** 44 A4
Towersey **OX9** 22 A1
Towie *Aber.* **AB43** 99 G4
Towie *Aber.* **AB54** 90 D2
Towie *Aber.* **AB33** 90 C3
Towiemore **AB55** 98 B6
Town End *Cambs.* **PE15** 43 H6
Town End *Cumb.* **LA11** 55 H1
Town End *Mersey.* **WA8** 48 D4
Town Green *Lancs.* **L39** 48 D2
Town Green *Norf.* **NR13** 45 H4
Town of Lowton **WA3** 49 F3
Town Row **TN6** 13 J3
Town Street **IP27** 44 B7
Town Yetholm **TD5** 70 D1
Townfield **DH8** 62 A2
Townhead *D. & G.* **DG6** 65 G6
Townhead *S.Yorks.* **S36** 50 D2
Townhead of Greenlaw **DG7** 65 H4
Townhill *Fife* **KY12** 75 K2
Townhill *Swan.* **SA1** 17 K6
Towns End **RG26** 21 J6
Towns Green **CW6** 49 F6
Townshend **TR27** 2 C5
Towthorpe *E.Riding* **YO25** 59 F3
Towthorpe *York* **YO32** 58 C4
Towton **LS24** 57 K6
Towyn **LL22** 47 H5
Toynton All Saints **PE23** 53 G6
Toynton Fen Side **PE23** 53 G6
Toynton St. Peter **PE23** 53 H6
Toy's Hill **TN16** 23 H6
Trabboch **KA5** 67 J1
Traboe **TR12** 2 E6
Tradespark *High.* **IV12** 97 F6
Tradespark *Ork.* **KW15** 106 D7
Traeth Coch (Red Wharf Bay) **LL75** 46 D4
Trafford Centre **M17** 49 G3
Trafford Park **M17** 49 G3
Trallong **LD3** 27 J6
Trallwn **SA7** 17 K6
Tram Inn **HR2** 28 D5
**Tranent EH33 76 C3**
Tranmere **CH42** 48 C4
Trantlebeg **KW13** 104 D3
Trantlemore **KW13** 104 D3
Tranwell **NE61** 71 G5
Trap **SA19** 17 K4
Trap Street **SK11** 49 H6
Traprain **EH41** 76 D3
Trap's Green **B94** 30 C2
Traquair **EH44** 76 B7
Trawden **BB8** 56 E6
Trawsfynydd **LL41** 37 G2
Trealaw **CF40** 18 D2
Treales **PR4** 55 H6
Trearddur **LL65** 46 A5
Treaslane **IV51** 93 J6
Tre-Aubrey **CF71** 18 D4
Trebanog **CF39** 18 D2
Trebanos **SA8** 18 A1
Trebarrow **EX22** 4 C1
Trebartha **PL15** 4 C3
Trebarvah **TR11** 2 E5
Trebarwith **PL33** 4 A2
Trebeath **PL15** 4 C2
Trebetherick **PL27** 3 G1
Trebister **ZE1** 107 N9
Tre-boeth **SA5** 17 K6
Treborough **TA23** 7 J2
Trebudannon **TR8** 3 F2
Trebullett **PL15** 4 D3
Treburley **PL15** 4 D3
Treburrick **PL27** 3 F1
Trebyan **PL30** 4 A4
Trecastle **LD3** 27 H6
Trecott **EX20** 6 E5
Trecrogo **PL15** 6 B7
Trecwn **SA62** 16 C2
Trecynon **CF44** 18 C1
Tredaule **PL15** 4 C2
Tredavoe **TR20** 2 B6
Treddiog **SA62** 16 B3
**Tredegar NP22 18 E1**
Tredington *Glos.* **GL20** 29 J6
Tredington *Warks.* **CV36** 30 D4
Tredinnick *Cornw.* **PL27** 3 G2
Tredinnick *Cornw.* **PL14** 4 C5
Tredogan **CF62** 18 D5
Tredomen **LD3** 28 A5
Tredrissi **SA42** 16 D1
Tredunnock **NP15** 19 G2
Tredustan **LD3** 28 A5
Tredworth **GL1** 29 H7
Treen *Cornw.* **TR19** 2 A6
Treen *Cornw.* **TR20** 2 B5
Treesmill **PL24** 4 A5
Treeton **S60** 51 G4
**Trefaldwyn (Montgomery) SY15 38 B6**
Trefasser **SA64** 16 B2
Trefdraeth *I.o.A.* **LL62** 46 C5
**Trefdraeth (Newport) *Pembs.* SA42 16 D2**
Trefecca **LD3** 28 A5
Trefechan **CF48** 18 D1
Trefeglwys **SY17** 37 J6
Trefenter **SY23** 27 F2
Treffgarne **SA62** 16 C3
**Treffynnon (Holywell) *Flints.* CH8 47 K5**
Treffynnon *Pembs.* **SA62** 16 B3
Trefgarn Owen **SA62** 16 B3
Trefil **NP22** 28 A7
Trefilan **SA48** 26 E3
Trefin **SA62** 16 B2
Treflach **SY10** 38 B3
Trefnanney **SY22** 38 B4
Trefnant **LL16** 47 J5
Trefonen **SY10** 38 B3
Trefor *Gwyn.* **LL54** 36 C1
Trefor *I.o.A.* **LL65** 46 B4
Treforest **CF37** 18 D3
Treforest Industrial Estate **CF37** 18 E3
**Trefriw LL27 47 F6**
**Tref-y-clawdd (Knighton) LD7 28 B1**
**Trefynwy (Monmouth) NP25 28 E7**
Tregadillett **PL15** 4 C2
Tregaian **LL77** 46 C5
Tregare **NP15** 28 D7
Tregarland **PL13** 4 C5
Tregarne **TR12** 2 E6
**Tregaron SY25 27 F3**
Tregarth **LL57** 46 E6
Tregaswith **TR8** 3 F2
Tregavethan **TR4** 2 E4
Tregear **TR2** 3 F3
Tregeare **PL15** 4 C2
Tregeiriog **LL20** 38 A2
Tregele **LL67** 46 B3
Tregidden **TR12** 2 E6
Tregiskey **PL26** 4 A6
Treglemais **SA62** 16 B3
Tregolds **PL28** 3 F1
Tregole **EX23** 4 B1
Tregonetha **TR9** 3 G2
Tregony **TR2** 3 G4
Tregoodwell **PL32** 4 B2
Tregoss **PL26** 3 G2
Tregowris **TR12** 2 E6
Tregoyd **LD3** 28 A5
Tregrehan Mills **PL25** 4 A5
Tre-groes **SA44** 17 H1
Treguff **CF71** 18 D4
Tregullon **PL30** 4 A4
Tregunnon **PL15** 4 C2
Tregurrian **TR8** 3 F2
Tregynon **SY16** 37 K6
Trehafod **CF37** 18 D2
Trehan **PL12** 4 E5
**Treharris CF46 18 D2**
Treherbert **CF42** 18 C2
Tre-hill **CF5** 18 D4
Trekenner **PL15** 4 D3
Treknow **PL34** 4 A2
Trelan **TR12** 2 E7
Trelash **PL15** 4 B1
Trelassick **TR2** 3 F3
Trelawnyd **LL18** 47 J5
Trelech **SA33** 17 F2
Treleddyd-fawr **SA62** 16 A3
Trelewis **CF46** 18 E2
Treligga **PL33** 4 A2
Trelights **PL29** 3 G1
Trelill **PL30** 4 A3
Trelissick **TR3** 3 F5
Trelleck **NP25** 19 J1
Trelleck Grange **NP16** 19 H1
Trelogan **CH8** 47 K4
Trelowla **PL13** 4 C5
Trelystan **SY21** 38 B5
Tremadog **LL49** 36 E1
Tremail **PL32** 4 B2
Tremain **SA43** 17 F1
Tremaine **PL15** 4 C2
Tremar **PL14** 4 C4
Trematon **PL12** 4 D5
Tremeirchion **LL17** 47 J5
Tremethick Cross **TR20** 2 B5
Tremore **PL30** 4 A4

Tre - Upp


Trenance *Cornw.* **TR8** 3 F2
Trenance *Cornw.* **PL27** 3 G1
Trenarren **PL26** 4 A6
Trench *Tel. & W.* **TF2** 39 F4
Trench *Wrex.* **LL13** 38 C2
Trencreek **TR7** 3 F2
Trenear **TR13** 2 D5
Treneglos **PL15** 4 C2
Trenewan **PL13** 4 B5
Trengune **EX23** 4 B1
Trent **DT9** 8 E3
Trent Port **DN21** 52 B4
Trent Vale **ST4** 40 A1
Trentham **ST4** 40 A1
Trentishoe **EX31** 6 E1
Trenwheal **TR27** 2 D5
Treoes **CF35** 18 C4
**Treorchy CF42 18 C2**
Treowen **NP11** 19 F2
Trequite **PL30** 4 A3
Tre'r Llai (Leighton) **SY21** 38 B5
Tre'r-ddol **SY20** 37 F6
Trerhyngyll **CF71** 18 D4
Tre-Rhys **SA43** 16 E1
Trerulefoot **PL12** 4 D5
Tresaith **SA43** 26 B3
Tresco **TR24** 2 B1
Trescott **WV6** 40 A6
Trescowe **TR20** 2 C5
Tresean **TR8** 2 E3
Tresham **GL12** 20 A2
Treshnish **PA75** 78 E3
Tresillian **TR2** 3 F4
Tresinney **PL32** 4 B2
Tresinwen **SA64** 16 B1
Treskinnick Cross **EX23** 4 C1
Treslea **PL30** 4 B4
Tresmeer **PL15** 4 C2
Tresowes Green **TR13** 2 D6
Tresparrett **PL32** 4 B1
Tresparrett Posts **PL32** 4 B1
Tressait **PH16** 81 K1
Tresta *Shet.* **ZE2** 107 Q3
Tresta *Shet.* **ZE2** 107 M7
Treswell **DN22** 51 K5
Trethewey **TR19** 2 A6
Trethomas **CF83** 18 E3
Trethurgy **PL26** 4 A5
Tretio **SA62** 16 A3
Tretire **HR2** 28 E6
Tretower **NP8** 28 A6
Treuddyn **CH7** 48 B7
Trevadlock **PL15** 4 C3
Trevalga **PL35** 4 A1
Trevalyn **LL12** 48 C7
Trevanson **PL27** 3 G1
Trevarnon **TR27** 2 C5
Trevarrack **TR18** 2 B5
Trevarren **TR9** 3 G2
Trevarrian **TR8** 3 F2
Trevarrick **PL26** 3 G4
Tre-vaughan *Carmar.* **SA31** 17 G3
Trevaughan *Carmar.* **SA34** 16 E4
Treveighan **PL30** 4 A3
Trevellas **TR5** 2 E3
Trevelmond **PL14** 4 C4
Trevenen **TR13** 2 D6
Treverva **TR10** 2 E5
Trevescan **TR19** 2 A6
Trevethin **NP4** 19 F1
Trevigro **PL17** 4 D4
Trevine **PA35** 80 B5
Treviscoe **PL26** 3 G3
Trevivian **PL32** 4 B2
Trevone **PL28** 3 F1
Trevor **LL20** 38 B1
Trewalder **PL33** 4 A2
Trewarmett **PL34** 4 A2
Trewarthenick **TR2** 3 G4
Trewassa **PL32** 4 B2
Trewellard **TR19** 2 A5
Trewen *Cornw.* **PL15** 4 C2
Trewen *Here.* **HR9** 28 E7
Trewennack **TR13** 2 D6
Trewent **SA71** 16 D6
Trewern **SY21** 38 B4
Trewethern **PL27** 4 A3
Trewidland **PL14** 4 C5
Trewilym **SA41** 16 E1
Trewint *Cornw.* **EX23** 4 B1
Trewint *Cornw.* **PL15** 4 C2
Trewithian **TR2** 3 F5
Trewoon **PL25** 3 G3
Treworga **TR2** 3 F4
Treworlas **TR2** 3 F5
Trewornan **PL27** 3 G1
Treworthal **TR2** 3 F5
Tre-wyn **NP7** 28 C6
Treyarnon **PL28** 3 F1
Treyford **GU29** 12 B5
Trezaise **PL26** 3 G3
Triangle **HX6** 57 F7
Trickett's Cross **BH22** 10 B4
Triermain **CA8** 70 A7
**Trimdon TS29 62 E3**
Trimdon Colliery **TS29** 62 E3
Trimdon Grange **TS29** 62 E3
Trimingham **NR11** 45 G2
Trimley Lower Street **IP11** 35 G5
Trimley St. Martin **IP11** 35 G5
Trimley St. Mary **IP11** 35 G5
Trimpley **DY12** 29 G1
Trimsaran **SA17** 17 H5
Trimstone **EX34** 6 C1
Trinafour **PH18** 81 J1
Trinant **NP11** 19 F2
**Tring HP23 32 C7**
Trinity *Angus* **DD9** 83 H1
Trinity *Chan.I.* **JE3** 3 K6
Trinity *Edin.* **EH5** 76 A3
Trisant **SY23** 27 G1
Triscombe *Som.* **TA24** 7 H2
Triscombe *Som.* **TA4** 7 K2
Trislaig **PH33** 87 G7
Trispen **TR4** 3 F3
Tritlington **NE61** 71 H4
Trochry **PH8** 82 A4
Troedyraur **SA38** 17 G1
Troedyrhiw **CF48** 18 D1
Trofarth **LL22** 47 G5
Trondavoe **ZE2** 107 M5
Troon *Cornw.* **TR14** 2 D5
**Troon *S.Ayr.* KA10 74 B7**
Trosairidh **HS8** 84 C3
Troston **IP31** 34 C1
Troswell **PL15** 4 C1
Trottick **DD4** 83 F4
Trottiscliffe **ME19** 24 C5
Trotton **GU31** 12 B4
Trough Gate **OL13** 56 D7
Troughend **NE19** 70 D4
Troustan **PA22** 73 J3
Troutbeck *Cumb.* **LA23** 60 F6
Troutbeck *Cumb.* **CA11** 60 E4
Troutbeck Bridge **LA23** 60 F6
Trow Green **GL15** 19 J1
Troway **S21** 51 F5
Trowbridge *Cardiff* **CF3** 19 F3
**Trowbridge *Wilts.* BA14 20 B6**
Trowell **NG9** 41 G2
Trowle Common **BA14** 20 B6
Trowley Bottom **AL3** 32 D7
Trows **TD5** 76 E7
Trowse Newton **NR14** 45 G5
Troy **LS18** 57 H6
Trudernish **PA42** 72 C5
Trudoxhill **BA11** 20 A7
Trull **TA3** 8 B2
Trumaisgearraidh **HS6** 92 D4
Trumpan **IV55** 93 H5
Trumpet **HR8** 29 F5
Trumpington **CB2** 33 H3
Trumps Green **GU25** 22 C5
Trunch **NR28** 45 G2
Trunnah **FY5** 55 G5
**TRURO TR 3 F4**
Truscott **PL15** 6 B7
Trusham **TQ13** 7 G7
Trusley **DE6** 40 E2
Trusthorpe **LN12** 53 J4
Truthan **TR4** 3 F3
Trysull **WV5** 40 A6
Tubney **OX13** 21 H2
Tuckenhay **TQ9** 5 J5
Tuckhill **WV15** 39 G7
Tuckingmill **TR14** 2 D4
Tuddenham *Suff.* **IP6** 35 F4
Tuddenham *Suff.* **IP28** 34 B1
Tudeley **TN11** 23 K7
Tudeley Hale **TN11** 23 K7
Tudhoe **DL16** 62 D3
Tudweiliog **LL53** 36 B2
Tuesley **GU7** 22 C7
Tuffley **GL4** 29 H7
Tufton *Hants.* **RG28** 21 H7
Tufton *Pembs.* **SA63** 16 D3
Tugby **LE7** 42 A5
Tugford **SY7** 38 E7
Tughall **NE67** 71 H1
Tulchan **PH1** 82 A5
Tullibody **FK10** 75 G1
Tullich *Arg. & B.* **PA32** 80 B6
Tullich *Arg. & B.* **PA34** 79 K6
Tullich *High.* **IV20** 97 F4
Tullich *High.* **IV2** 88 D2
Tullich *Moray* **AB55** 98 B6
Tullich *Stir.* **FK21** 81 G4
Tullich Muir **IV18** 96 E4
Tulliemet **PH9** 82 B2
Tulloch *Aber.* **AB51** 91 G1
Tulloch *High.* **IV24** 96 D2
Tulloch *Moray* **IV36** 97 H6
Tullochgorm **PA32** 73 H1
Tullochgribban High **PH26** 89 G2
Tullochvenus **AB31** 90 D4
Tulloes **DD8** 83 G3
Tullybannocher **PH6** 81 J5
Tullybelton **PH1** 82 B4
Tullyfergus **PH11** 82 D3
Tullymurdoch **PH11** 82 C2
Tullynessle **AB33** 90 D3
Tulse Hill **SE21** 23 G4
Tumble (Y Tymbl) **SA14** 17 J4
Tumby **PE22** 53 F7
Tumby Woodside **PE22** 53 F7
Tummel Bridge **PH16** 81 J2
**TUNBRIDGE WELLS TN 13 J3**
Tundergarth Mains **DG11** 69 G5
Tunga **HS2** 101 G4
Tungate **NR28** 45 G3
Tunley **BA2** 19 K6
Tunstall *E.Riding* **HU12** 59 K6
Tunstall *Kent* **ME10** 24 E5
Tunstall *Lancs.* **LA6** 56 B2
Tunstall *N.Yorks.* **DL10** 62 D7
Tunstall *Norf.* **NR13** 45 J5
Tunstall *Stoke* **ST6** 49 H7
Tunstall *Suff.* **IP12** 35 H3
Tunstall *T. & W.* **SR2** 62 E1
Tunstead *Gt.Man.* **OL3** 50 C2
Tunstead *Norf.* **NR12** 45 H3
Tunstead Milton **SK23** 50 C4
Tunworth **RG25** 21 K7
Tupholme **LN3** 52 E6
Tupsley **HR1** 28 E5
Tupton **S42** 51 F6
Tur Langton **LE8** 42 A6
Turbiskill **PA31** 73 F2
Turclossie **AB43** 99 G5
Turgis Green **RG27** 21 K6
Turin **DD8** 83 G2
Turkdean **GL54** 30 C7
Turleigh **BA15** 20 B5
Turn **BL0** 49 H1
Turnastone **HR2** 28 C5
Turnberry **KA26** 67 G3
Turnchapel **PL9** 4 E5
Turnditch **DE56** 40 E1
Turner's Green **CV35** 30 C2
Turners Hill **RH10** 13 G3
Turners Puddle **DT2** 9 H5
Turnford **EN10** 23 G1
Turnworth **DT11** 9 H4
Turret Bridge **PH31** 87 K5
**Turriff AB53 99 F6**
Turton Bottoms **BL7** 49 G1
Turvey **MK43** 32 C3
Turville **RG9** 22 A2
Turville Heath **RG9** 22 A2
Turweston **NN13** 31 H5
Tutbury **DE13** 40 E3
Tutnall **B60** 29 J1
Tutshill **NP16** 19 J2
Tuttington **NR11** 45 G3
Tutts Clump **RG7** 21 J4
Tutwell **PL17** 4 D3
Tuxford **NG22** 51 K5
Twatt *Ork.* **KW17** 106 B5
Twatt *Shet.* **ZE2** 107 M7
Twechar **G65** 75 F3
Tweedmouth **TD15** 77 H5
Tweedsmuir **ML12** 69 F1
Twelve Oaks **TN32** 13 K4
Twelveheads **TR4** 2 E4
Twemlow Green **CW4** 49 G6
Twenty **PE10** 42 E3
**TWICKENHAM TW 22 E4**
Twigworth **GL2** 29 H6
Twineham **RH17** 13 F4
Twineham Green **RH17** 13 F4
Twinhoe **BA2** 20 A6
Twinstead **CO10** 34 C5
Twiss Green **WA3** 49 F3
Twiston **BB7** 56 D5
Twitchen *Devon* **EX36** 7 F2
Twitchen *Shrop.* **SY7** 28 C1
Twitton **TN14** 23 J6
Twizell House **NE70** 71 G1
Two Bridges *Devon* **PL20** 5 G3
Two Bridges *Glos.* **GL14** 19 K1
Two Dales **DE4** 50 E6
Two Gates **B77** 40 E5
Two Mills **CH1** 48 C5
Twycross **CV9** 41 F5
Twyford *Bucks.* **MK18** 31 H6
Twyford *Derbys.* **DE73** 41 F3
Twyford *Dorset* **SP7** 9 H3
Twyford *Hants.* **SO21** 11 F2
Twyford *Leics.* **LE14** 42 A4
Twyford *Norf.* **NR20** 44 E3
Twyford *Oxon.* **OX17** 31 F5
Twyford *W'ham* **RG10** 22 A4
Twyford Common **HR2** 28 E5
Twyn Shôn-Ifan **CF82** 18 E2
Twynholm **DG6** 65 G5
Twyning **GL20** 29 H5
Twynllanan **SA19** 27 G6
Twyn-yr-odyn **CF5** 18 E4
Twyn-y-Sheriff **NP15** 19 H1
Twywell **NN14** 32 C1
Tyberton **HR2** 28 C5
Tycroes **SA18** 17 K4
Tycrwyn **SY22** 38 A4
Tydd Gote **PE13** 43 H4
Tydd St. Giles **PE13** 43 H4
Tydd St. Mary **PE13** 43 H4
Tyddewi (St. David's) **SA62** 16 A3
Tye Common **CM12** 24 C2
Tye Green *Essex* **CM77** 34 B6
Tye Green *Essex* **CM22** 33 J6
Tye Green *Essex* **CM1** 33 K7
Tye Green *Essex* **CM18** 23 H1
Tyersal **BD4** 57 G6
Ty-hen **LL53** 36 A2
Tyldesley **M29** 49 F2
Tyle-garw **CF72** 18 D3
Tyler Hill **CT2** 25 H5
Tylers Green *Bucks.* **HP10** 22 C2
Tyler's Green *Essex* **CM16** 23 J1
Tylorstown **CF43** 18 D2
Tylwch **LD6** 27 J1
Ty-Mawr *Conwy* **LL21** 37 J1
Ty-mawr *Denb.* **LL21** 38 A1
Ty-nant *Conwy* **LL21** 37 J1
Ty-nant *Gwyn.* **LL23** 37 J3
Tyndrum **FK20** 80 E4
Tyneham **BH20** 9 H6
Tynehead **EH37** 76 B5
Tynemouth **NE30** 71 J7
Tynewydd **CF42** 18 C2
Tyninghame **EH42** 76 E3
Tynron **DG3** 68 D4
Tyntesfield **BS48** 19 J4
Tyn-y-cefn **LL21** 37 K1
Ty'n-y-coedcae **CF83** 18 E3
Tyn-y-cwm **SY18** 37 H7
Tyn-y-ffridd **SY10** 38 A2
Ty'n-y-garn **CF31** 18 D3
**Tyn-y-gongl LL74 46 D4**
Tynygraig *Cere.* **SY25** 27 F2
Tyn-y-graig *Powys* **LD2** 27 K4
Ty'n-y-groes **LL32** 47 F5
Tyrie **AB43** 99 H4
Tyringham **MK16** 32 B4
Tyseley **B11** 40 D7
Tythegston **CF32** 18 B4
Tytherington *Ches.E.* **SK10** 49 J5
Tytherington *S.Glos.* **GL12** 19 K3
Tytherington *Som.* **BA11** 20 A7
Tytherington *Wilts.* **BA12** 20 C7
Tytherton Lucas **SN15** 20 C4
Tyttenhanger **AL4** 22 E1
Ty-uchaf **SY10** 37 J3
Tywardreath **PL24** 4 A5
Tywardreath Highway **PL24** 4 A5
**Tywyn LL36 36 E5**


## U


Uachdar **HS7** 92 D6
Uags **IV54** 86 D1
Ubberley **ST2** 40 B1
Ubbeston Green **IP19** 35 H1
Ubley **BS40** 19 J6
Uckerby **DL10** 62 D6
**Uckfield TN22 13 H4**
Uckinghall **GL20** 29 H5
Uckington **GL51** 29 J6
Uddingston **G71** 74 E4
Uddington **ML11** 75 G7
Udimore **TN31** 14 D6
Udley **BS40** 19 H5
Udny Green **AB41** 91 G2
Udny Station **AB41** 91 H2
Udston **ML3** 75 F5
Udstonhead **ML10** 75 F6
Uffcott **SN4** 20 E4
Uffculme **EX15** 7 J4
Uffington *Lincs.* **PE9** 42 D5
Uffington *Oxon.* **SN7** 21 G3
Uffington *Shrop.* **SY4** 38 E4
Ufford *Peter.* **PE9** 42 D5
Ufford *Suff.* **IP13** 35 G3
Ufton **CV33** 30 E2
Ufton Green **RG7** 21 K5
Ufton Nervet **RG7** 21 K5
Ugborough **PL21** 5 G5
Ugford **SP2** 10 B1
Uggeshall **NR34** 45 J7
Ugglebarnby **YO22** 63 K6
Ugley **CM22** 33 J6
Ugley Green **CM22** 33 J6
Ugthorpe **YO21** 63 J5
**Uibhist a Deas (South Uist) HS8 84 C1**
**Uibhist a Tuath (North Uist) HS6 92 D4**
Uidh **HS9** 84 B5
Uig *Arg. & B.* **PA78** 78 C2
Uig *Arg. & B.* **PA23** 73 K2
Uig *High.* **IV51** 93 J5
Uig *High.* **IV55** 93 G6
Uigen **HS2** 100 C4
Uiginish **IV55** 93 H7
Uigshader **IV51** 93 K7
Uisgebhagh (Uiskevagh) **HS7** 92 D6
Uisken **PA67** 78 E6
Uiskevagh (Uisgebhagh) **HS7** 92 D6
Ulbster **KW2** 105 J4
Ulcat Row **CA11** 60 F4
Ulceby *Lincs.* **LN13** 53 H5
**Ulceby *N.Lincs.* DN39 52 E1**
Ulceby Cross **LN13** 53 H5
Ulceby Skitter **DN39** 52 E1
Ulcombe **ME17** 14 D3
Uldale **CA7** 60 D3
Uldale House **CA17** 61 J7
Uley **GL11** 20 A2
Ulgham **NE61** 71 H4
**Ullapool IV26 95 H2**
Ullenhall **B95** 30 C2
Ullenwood **GL53** 29 J7
Ulleskelf **LS24** 58 B6
Ullesthorpe **LE17** 41 H7
Ulley **S26** 51 G4
Ullingswick **HR1** 28 E4
Ullinish **IV56** 85 J1
Ullock **CA14** 60 B4
Ulpha *Cumb.* **LA20** 60 C7
Ulpha *Cumb.* **LA11** 55 H1
Ulrome **YO25** 59 H4
Ulsta **ZE2** 107 N4
Ulting **CM9** 24 E1
Uluvalt **PA70** 79 G4
Ulva **PA73** 79 F4
**Ulverston LA12 55 F2**
Ulwell **BH19** 10 B6
Ulzieside **DG4** 68 C3
**Umberleigh EX37 6 E3**
Unapool **IV27** 102 E5
Underbarrow **LA8** 61 F7
Undercliffe **BD2** 57 G6
Underhill **EN5** 23 F2
Underhoull **ZE2** 107 P2
Underling Green **TN12** 14 C3
Underriver **TN15** 23 J6
Underwood *Newport* **NP18** 19 G3
Underwood *Notts.* **NG16** 51 G7
Underwood *Plym.* **PL7** 5 F5
Undley **IP27** 44 A7
Undy **NP26** 19 H3
Ungisiadar **HS2** 100 D5
Unifirth **ZE2** 107 L7
Union Croft **AB39** 91 G5
Union Mills **IM4** 54 C6
Union Street **TN5** 14 C4
Unst **ZE2** 107 Q1
Unst Airport **ZE2** 107 Q2
Unstone **S18** 51 F5
Unstone Green **S18** 51 F5
Unsworth **BL9** 49 H2
Unthank *Cumb.* **CA11** 61 F3
Unthank *Derbys.* **S18** 51 F5
Up Cerne **DT2** 9 F4
Up Exe **EX5** 7 H5
Up Hatherley **GL51** 29 J6
Up Holland **WN8** 48 E2
Up Marden **PO18** 11 J3
Up Mudford **BA21** 8 E3
Up Nately **RG27** 21 K6
Up Somborne **SO20** 10 E1
Up Sydling **DT2** 9 F4
Upavon **SN9** 20 E6
Upchurch **ME9** 24 E5
Upcott *Devon* **EX21** 6 C6
Upcott *Devon* **EX31** 6 D2
Upcott *Here.* **HR3** 28 C3
Upcott *Som.* **TA22** 7 H3
Upend **CB8** 33 K3
Upgate **NR9** 45 F4
Upgate Street *Norf.* **NR16** 44 E6
Upgate Street *Norf.* **NR35** 45 G6
Uphall *Dorset* **DT2** 8 E4
Uphall *W.Loth.* **EH52** 75 J3
Uphall Station **EH54** 75 J4
Upham *Devon* **EX17** 7 G5
Upham *Hants.* **SO32** 11 G2
Uphampton *Here.* **HR6** 28 C2
Uphampton *Worcs.* **WR9** 29 H2
Uphempston **TQ9** 5 J4
Uphill **BS23** 19 G6
Uplands *Glos.* **GL5** 20 B1
Uplands *Swan.* **SA2** 17 K6
Uplawmoor **G78** 74 C5
Upleadon **GL18** 29 G6
Upleatham **TS11** 63 H5
Uplees **ME13** 25 G5
Uploders **DT6** 8 E5
Uplowman **EX16** 7 J4
Uplyme **DT7** 8 C5
**Upminster RM14 23 J3**
Upottery **EX14** 8 B4
Upper Affcot **SY6** 38 D7
Upper Ardroscadale **PA20** 73 J4
Upper Arley **DY12** 39 G7
Upper Arncott **OX25** 31 H7
Upper Astley **SY4** 38 E4
Upper Aston **WV5** 40 A6
Upper Astrop **OX17** 31 G5
Upper Barvas **HS2** 101 F2
Upper Basildon **RG8** 21 K4
Upper Bayble (Pabail Uarach) **HS2** 101 H4
Upper Beeding **BN44** 12 E5
Upper Benefield **PE8** 42 C7
Upper Bentley **B97** 29 J2
Upper Berwick **SY4** 38 D4
Upper Bighouse **KW13** 104 D3
Upper Boat **CF37** 18 E3
Upper Boddam **AB52** 90 E1
Upper Boddington **NN11** 31 F3
Upper Borth **SY24** 37 F7
Upper Boyndlie **AB43** 99 H4
Upper Brailes **OX15** 30 E5
Upper Breakish **IV42** 86 C2
Upper Breinton **HR4** 28 D4
Upper Broadheath **WR2** 29 H3
Upper Broughton **LE14** 41 J3
Upper Brynamman **SA18** 27 G7
Upper Bucklebury **RG7** 21 J5
Upper Burgate **SP6** 10 C3
Upper Burnhaugh **AB39** 91 G5
Upper Caldecote **SG18** 32 E4
Upper Camster **KW3** 105 H4
Upper Canada **BS24** 19 G6
Upper Catesby **NN11** 31 G3
Upper Catshill **B61** 29 J1
Upper Chapel **LD3** 27 K4
Upper Cheddon **TA2** 8 B2
Upper Chicksgrove **SP3** 9 J1
Upper Chute **SP11** 21 F6
Upper Clatford **SP11** 21 G7
Upper Coberley **GL53** 29 J7
Upper Colwall **WR13** 29 G4
Upper Cotton **ST10** 40 C1
Upper Cound **SY5** 38 E5
Upper Cumberworth **HD8** 50 E2
Upper Cwmbran **NP44** 19 F2
Upper Dallachy **IV32** 98 B4
Upper Dean **PE28** 32 D2
Upper Denby **HD8** 50 E2
Upper Denton **CA8** 70 B7
Upper Derraid **PH26** 89 H1
Upper Diabaig **IV22** 94 E5
Upper Dicker **BN27** 13 J5
Upper Dovercourt **CO12** 35 G5
Upper Dunsforth **YO26** 57 K3
Upper Dunsley **HP23** 32 C7
Upper Eastern Green **CV5** 40 E7
Upper Eathie **IV11** 96 E5
Upper Egleton **HR8** 29 F4
Upper Elkstone **SK17** 50 C7
Upper End **SK17** 50 C5
Upper Enham **SP11** 21 G7
Upper Farringdon **GU34** 11 J1
Upper Framilode **GL2** 29 G7
Upper Froyle **GU34** 22 A7
Upper Gills **KW1** 105 J1
Upper Glendessarry **PH34** 87 F5
Upper Godney **BA5** 19 H7
Upper Gornal **DY3** 40 B6
Upper Gravenhurst **MK45** 32 E5
Upper Green *Essex* **CB11** 33 H5
Upper Green *Essex* **CB10** 33 J5
Upper Green *Mon.* **NP7** 28 C7
Upper Green *W.Berks.* **RG17** 21 G5
Upper Grove Common **HR9** 28 E6
Upper Gylen **PA34** 79 K5
Upper Hackney **DE4** 50 E6
Upper Halliford **TW17** 22 D5
Upper Halling **ME2** 24 C5
Upper Hambleton **LE15** 42 C5
Upper Harbledown **CT2** 15 G2
Upper Hardres Court **CT4** 15 G2
Upper Hartfield **TN7** 13 H3
Upper Hatton **ST21** 40 A2

Upper Hawkhillock AB42 91 J1
Upper Hayesden TN11 23 J7
Upper Hayton SY8 38 E7
Upper Heath SY7 38 E7
Upper Heaton HD5 50 D1
Upper Hellesdon NR3 45 G4
Upper Helmsley YO41 58 C4
Upper Hengoed SY10 38 B2
Upper Hergest HR5 28 B3
Upper Heyford Northants. NN7 31 H3
Upper Heyford Oxon. OX25 31 F6
Upper Hill Here. HR6 28 D3
Upper Hill S.Glos. GL13 19 K2
Upper Horsebridge BN27 13 J5
Upper Howsell WR14 29 G4
Upper Hulme ST13 50 C6
Upper Inglesham SN6 21 F2
Upper Kilchattan PA61 72 B1
Upper Killay SA2 17 J6
Upper Knockando AB38 97 J7
Upper Lambourn RG17 21 G3
Upper Langford BS40 19 H6
Upper Langwith NG20 51 H6
Upper Largo KY8 83 F7
Upper Leigh ST10 40 C2
Upper Ley GL14 29 G7
Upper Llandwrog (Y Fron) LL54 46 D7
Upper Loads S42 51 F6
Upper Lochton AB31 90 E5
Upper Longdon WS15 40 C4
Upper Longwood SY5 39 F5
Upper Ludstone WV5 40 A6
Upper Lybster KW3 105 H5
Upper Lydbrook GL17 29 F7
Upper Lyde HR4 28 D4
Upper Lye HR6 28 C2
Upper Maes-coed HR2 28 C5
Upper Midhope S36 50 E3
Upper Milovaig IV55 93 G7
Upper Milton OX7 30 D7
Upper Minety SN16 20 D2
Upper Moor WR10 29 J4
Upper Morton BS35 19 K2
Upper Muirskie AB12 91 G5
Upper Nash SA71 16 D5
Upper Newbold S41 51 F5
Upper North Dean HP14 22 B2
Upper Norwood SE19 23 G4
Upper Obney PH1 82 B4
Upper Oddington GL56 30 D6
Upper Ollach IV51 86 B1
Upper Padley S32 50 E5
Upper Pennington SO41 10 D5
Upper Pollicott HP18 31 J7
Upper Poppleton YO26 58 B4
Upper Quinton CV37 30 C4
Upper Ratley SO51 10 E2
Upper Ridinghill AB43 99 J5
Upper Rissington GL54 30 D6
Upper Rochford WR15 29 F2
Upper Sanday KW17 106 E7
Upper Sapey WR6 29 F2
Upper Scolton SA62 16 C3
Upper Seagry SN15 20 C3
Upper Shelton MK43 32 C4
Upper Sheringham NR26 45 F1
Upper Shuckburgh NN11 31 F2
Upper Siddington GL7 20 D2
Upper Skelmorlie PA17 74 A4
Upper Slaughter GL54 30 C6
Upper Sonachan PA33 80 B5
Upper Soudley GL14 29 F7
Upper Staploe PE19 32 E3
Upper Stoke NR14 45 G5
Upper Stondon SG16 32 E5
Upper Stowe NN7 31 H3
Upper Street Hants. SP6 10 C3
Upper Street Norf. NR12 45 H4
Upper Street Norf. IP21 35 F1
Upper Street Suff. IP9 35 F5
Upper Street Suff. IP6 35 F3
Upper Strensham WR8 29 J5
Upper Sundon LU5 32 D6
Upper Swanmore SO32 11 G3
Upper Swell GL54 30 C6
Upper Tean ST10 40 C2
Upper Thurnham LA2 55 H4
Upper Tillyrie KY13 82 C7
Upper Tooting SW17 23 F4
Upper Town Derbys. DE4 50 E6
Upper Town Derbys. DE4 50 E7
Upper Town Derbys. DE6 50 E7
Upper Town Here. HR1 28 E4
Upper Town N.Som. BS40 19 J5
Upper Tysoe CV35 30 E4
Upper Upham SN8 21 F4
Upper Upnor ME2 24 D4
Upper Victoria DD7 83 G4
Upper Vobster BA3 20 A7
Upper Wardington OX17 31 F4
Upper Waterhay SN6 20 D2
Upper Weald MK19 32 B5
Upper Weedon NN7 31 H3
Upper Welson HR3 28 B3
Upper Weston BA1 20 A5
Upper Whiston S60 51 G4
Upper Wick WR2 29 H3
Upper Wield SO24 11 H1
Upper Winchendon (Over Winchendon) HP18 31 J7
Upper Witton B23 40 C6
Upper Woodford SP4 10 C1
Upper Woolhampton RG7 21 J5
Upper Wootton RG26 21 J6
Upper Wraxall SN14 20 B4
Upper Wyche WR13 29 G4
Upperby CA2 60 F1
Uppermill OL3 49 J2
Upperthong HD9 50 D2
Upperton GU28 12 C4
Uppertown Derbys. S45 51 F6
Uppertown Ork. KW1 105 J1
Uppingham LE15 42 B5
Uppington TF6 38 E5
Upsall YO7 57 K1
Upsettlington TD15 77 G6
Upshire EN9 23 H1
Upstreet CT3 25 J5
Upthorpe IP31 34 D1
Upton Bucks. HP17 31 J7
Upton Cambs. PE28 32 E1
Upton Ches.W. & C. CH2 48 D6
Upton Cornw. PL14 4 C3
Upton Cornw. EX23 6 A5
Upton Devon EX14 7 J5
Upton Devon TQ7 5 H6
Upton Dorset BH16 9 J5
Upton Dorset DT2 9 G6
Upton E.Riding YO25 59 H4
Upton Hants. SP11 21 G6
Upton Hants. SO16 10 E3
Upton Leics. CV13 41 F6
Upton Lincs. DN21 52 B4
Upton Mersey. CH49 48 B4
Upton Norf. NR13 45 H4
Upton Northants. NN5 31 J2
Upton Notts. DN22 51 K5
Upton Notts. NG23 51 K7
Upton Oxon. OX11 21 J3
Upton Oxon. OX18 30 D7
Upton Pembs. SA72 16 D5
Upton Peter. PE5 42 E5
Upton Slo. SL1 22 C4
Upton Som. TA4 7 H3
Upton Som. TA10 8 D2
Upton W.Yorks. WF9 51 G1
Upton Wilts. SP3 9 H1
Upton Bishop HR9 29 F6
Upton Cheyney BS30 19 K5
Upton Cressett WV16 39 F6
Upton Crews HR9 29 F6
Upton Cross PL14 4 C3
Upton End SG5 32 E5
Upton Grey RG25 21 K7
Upton Hellions EX17 7 G5
Upton Lovell BA12 20 C7
Upton Magna SY4 38 E4
Upton Noble BA4 9 G1
Upton Park E13 23 H3
Upton Pyne EX5 7 H6
Upton St. Leonards GL4 29 H7
Upton Scudamore BA12 20 B7
Upton Snodsbury WR7 29 J3
Upton upon Severn WR8 29 H4
Upton Warren B61 29 J2
Upwaltham GU28 12 C5
Upware CB7 33 J1
Upwell PE14 43 J5
Upwey DT3 9 F6
Upwick Green SG11 33 H6
Upwood PE26 43 F7
Uradale ZE1 107 N9
Urafirth ZE2 107 M5
Urchany IV12 97 F7
Urchfont SN10 20 D6
Urdimarsh HR1 28 E4
Ure ZE2 107 L5
Urgha HS3 93 G2
Urlay Nook TS16 63 F5
Urmston M41 49 G3
Urpeth DH2 62 D1
Urquhart High. IV7 96 C6
Urquhart Moray IV30 97 K5
Urra TS9 63 G6
Urray IV6 96 C6
Ushaw Moor DH7 62 D2
Usk (Brynbuga) NP15 19 G1
Usselby LN8 52 D3
Usworth NE37 62 E1
Utley BD20 57 F5
Uton EX17 7 G6
Utterby LN11 53 G3
Uttoxeter ST14 40 C2
Uwchmynydd LL53 36 A3
Uxbridge UB8 22 D3
Uyeasound ZE2 107 P2
Uzmaston SA62 16 C4

V
Valley (Y Fali) LL65 46 A5
Valley Truckle PL32 4 B2
Valleyfield D. & G. DG6 65 G5
Valleyfield Fife KY12 75 J2
Valsgarth ZE2 107 Q1
Vange SS16 24 D3
Vardre SA6 17 K5
Varteg NP4 19 F1
Vatersay (Bhatarsaigh) HS9 84 B5
Vatsetter ZE2 107 P4
Vatten IV55 93 H7
Vaul PA77 78 B3
Vaynor CF48 27 K7
Vaynor Park SY21 38 A5
Veaullt HR5 28 A3
Veensgarth ZE2 107 N8
Velindre Pembs. SA41 16 D2
Velindre Powys LD3 28 A5
Vellow TA4 7 J2
Veness KW17 106 E5
Venn TQ7 5 H6
Venn Ottery EX11 7 J6
Venngreen EX22 6 B4
Vennington SY5 38 C5
Venny Tedburn EX17 7 G6
Venterdon PL17 4 D3
Ventnor PO38 11 G7
Venton PL7 5 F5
Vernham Dean SP11 21 G6
Vernham Street SP11 21 G6
Vernolds Common SY7 38 D7
Verwood BH31 10 B4
Veryan TR2 3 G5
Veryan Green TR2 3 G4
Vickerstown LA14 54 E3
Victoria PL26 3 G2
Vidlin ZE2 107 N6
Viewfield KW14 105 F2
Viewpark G71 75 F4
Vigo WS9 40 C5
Vigo Village DA13 24 C5
Villavin EX19 6 D4
Vinehall Street TN32 14 C5
Vine's Cross TN21 13 J5
Viney Hill GL15 19 K1
Virginia Water GU25 22 C5
Virginstow EX21 6 B6
Virley CM9 34 D7
Vobster BA3 20 A7
Voe Shet. ZE2 107 N6
Voe Shet. ZE2 107 M4
Vowchurch HR2 28 C5
Voy KW16 106 B6
Vron Gate SY5 38 C5

W
Waberthwaite CA18 60 C7
Wackerfield DL2 62 C4
Wacton NR15 45 F6
Wadbister ZE2 107 N8
Wadborough WR8 29 J4
Waddesdon HP18 31 J7
Waddeton TQ5 5 J5
Waddicar L31 48 C3
Waddingham DN21 52 C3
Waddington Lancs. BB7 56 C5
Waddington Lincs. LN5 52 C6
Waddingworth LN10 52 E5
Waddon Devon TQ13 5 J3
Waddon Gt.Lon. CR0 23 G5
Wadebridge PL27 3 G1
Wadeford TA20 8 C3
Wadenhoe PE8 42 D7
Wadesmill SG12 33 G7
Wadhurst TN5 13 K3
Wadshelf S42 51 F5
Wadworth DN11 51 H3
Wadworth Hill HU12 59 J7
Waen Denb. LL16 47 K6
Waen Denb. LL16 47 H6
Waen Aberwheeler LL16 47 J6
Waen-fâch SY22 38 B4
Waen-wen LL57 46 D6
Wag KW7 105 F6
Wainfleet All Saints PE24 53 H7
Wainfleet Bank PE24 53 H7
Wainfleet St. Mary PE24 53 H7
Wainford NR35 45 H6
Waingroves DE5 41 G1
Wainhouse Corner EX23 4 B1
Wainscott ME2 24 D4
Wainstalls HX2 57 F7
Waitby CA17 61 J6
WAKEFIELD WF 57 J7
Wakerley LE15 42 C6
Wakes Colne CO6 34 C6
Walberswick IP18 35 J1
Walberton BN18 12 C6
Walbottle NE15 71 G7
Walcot Lincs. NG34 42 D2
Walcot Lincs. LN4 52 E7
Walcot N.Lincs. DN15 58 E7
Walcot Shrop. SY7 38 C7
Walcot Tel. & W. TF6 38 E4
Walcot Green IP22 45 F7
Walcote Leics. LE17 41 H7
Walcote Warks. B49 30 C3
Walcott NR12 45 H2
Walcott Dales LN4 52 E7
Walden DL8 57 F1
Walden Head DL8 56 E1
Walden Stubbs DN6 51 H1
Walderslade ME5 24 D5
Walderton PO18 11 J3
Walditch DT6 8 D5
Waldley DE6 40 D2
Waldridge DH2 62 D2
Waldringfield IP12 35 G4
Waldron TN21 13 J5
Wales S26 51 G4
Walesby Lincs. LN8 52 E3
Walesby Notts. NG22 51 J5
Waleswood S26 51 G4
Walford Here. SY7 28 C1
Walford Here. HR9 28 E6
Walford Shrop. SY4 38 D3
Walford Staffs. ST21 40 A2
Walford Heath SY4 38 D4
Walgherton CW5 39 F1
Walgrave NN6 32 B1
Walhampton SO41 10 E5
Walk Mill BB10 56 D6
Walkden M28 49 G2
Walker NE6 71 H7
Walker Fold BB7 56 B5
Walkerburn EH43 76 B7
Walkeringham DN10 51 K3
Walkerith DN21 51 K3
Walkern SG2 33 F6
Walker's Green HR1 28 E4
Walkford BH23 10 D5
Walkhampton PL20 5 F4
Walkingham Hill HG3 57 J3
Walkington HU17 59 F6
Walkwood B97 30 B2
Wall Cornw. TR27 2 D5
Wall Northumb. NE46 70 E7
Wall Staffs. WS14 40 D5
Wall End LA17 55 F1
Wall Heath DY6 40 A7
Wall Houses NE45 71 F7
Wall under Heywood SY6 38 E6
Wallacehall DG11 69 H6
Wallacetown KA19 67 G3
Wallasey CH45 48 B3
Wallaston Green SA71 16 C5
Wallend ME3 24 E4
Waller's Green HR8 29 F5
Wallingford OX10 21 K3
Wallington Gt.Lon. SM6 23 F5
Wallington Hants. PO16 11 G4
Wallington Herts. SG7 33 F5
Wallington Wrex. LL13 38 D1
Wallingwells S81 51 H4
Wallis SA62 16 D3
Wallisdown BH12 10 B5
Walliswood RH5 12 E3
Walls ZE2 107 L8
Wallsend NE28 71 J7
Wallyford EH21 76 B3
Walmer CT14 15 J2
Walmer Bridge PR4 55 H7
Walmersley BL9 49 H1
Walmley B76 40 D6
Walmsgate LN11 53 G5
Walpole IP19 35 H1
Walpole Cross Keys PE34 43 J4
Walpole Highway PE14 43 J4
Walpole Marsh PE14 43 H4
Walpole St. Andrew PE14 43 J4
Walpole St. Peter PE14 43 J4
Walrond's Park TA3 8 C2
Walrow TA9 19 G7
WALSALL WS 40 C6
Walsall Wood WS9 40 C5
Walsden OL14 56 E7
Walsgrave on Sowe CV2 41 F7
Walsham le Willows IP31 34 E1
Walshford LS22 57 K4
Walsoken PE13 43 H4
Walston ML11 75 J6
Walsworth SG4 32 E5
Walter's Ash HP14 22 B2
Walterston CF62 18 D4
Walterstone HR2 28 C6
Waltham Kent CT4 15 G3
Waltham N.E.Lincs. DN37 53 F2
Waltham Abbey EN9 23 G1
Waltham Chase SO32 11 G3
Waltham Cross EN8 23 G1
Waltham on the Wolds LE14 42 A3
Waltham St. Lawrence RG10 22 B4
Walthamstow E17 23 G3
Walton Bucks. HP21 32 B7
Walton Cumb. CA8 70 A7
Walton Derbys. S42 51 F6
Walton Leics. LE17 41 H7
Walton M.K. MK7 32 B5
Walton Mersey. L9 48 C3
Walton Peter. PE4 42 E5
Walton Powys LD8 28 B3
Walton Shrop. SY7 28 D1
Walton Som. BA16 8 D1
Walton Staffs. ST15 40 A2
Walton Suff. IP11 35 H5
Walton Tel. & W. TF6 38 E4
Walton W.Yorks. WF2 51 F1
Walton W.Yorks. LS23 57 K5
Walton Warks. CV35 30 D3
Walton Cardiff GL20 29 J5
Walton East SA63 16 D3
Walton Elm DT10 9 G3
Walton Highway PE14 43 H4
Walton Lower Street IP11 35 G5
Walton on the Hill KT20 23 F6
Walton on the Naze CO14 35 G6
Walton on the Wolds LE12 41 H4
Walton Park D. & G. DG7 65 H3
Walton Park N.Som. BS21 19 H4
Walton West SA62 16 B4
Walton-in-Gordano BS21 19 H4
Walton-le-Dale PR5 55 J7
Walton-on-Thames KT12 22 E5
Walton-on-the-Hill ST17 40 B3
Walton-on-Trent DE12 40 E4
Walwen Flints. CH8 47 K5
Walwen Flints. CH6 48 B5
Walwick NE46 70 E6
Walworth DL2 62 D5
Walworth Gate DL2 62 D4
Walwyn's Castle SA62 16 B4
Wambrook TA20 8 B4
Wanborough Surr. GU3 22 C7
Wanborough Swin. SN4 21 F3
Wandel ML12 68 E1
Wandon NE71 71 F1
Wandon End LU2 32 E6
Wandsworth SW15 23 F4
Wandylaw NE67 71 G1
Wangford Suff. NR34 35 J1
Wangford Suff. IP27 44 B7
Wanlip LE7 41 J4
Wanlockhead ML12 68 D2
Wannock BN26 13 J6
Wansford E.Riding YO25 59 G4
Wansford Peter. PE8 42 D6
Wanshurst Green TN12 14 C3
Wanstrow BA4 20 A7
Wanswell GL13 19 K1
Wantage OX12 21 G3
Wapley BS37 20 A4
Wappenbury CV33 30 E2
Wappenham NN12 31 H4
Warblebank CA7 60 D2
Warbleton TN21 13 K5
Warblington PO9 11 J4
Warborough OX10 21 J2
Warboys PE28 43 G7
Warbreck FY2 55 G6
Warbstow PL15 4 C1
Warburton WA13 49 F4
Warcop CA16 61 J5
Ward End B8 40 D7
Ward Green IP14 34 E2
Warden Kent ME12 25 G4
Warden Northumb. NE46 70 E7
Warden Hill GL51 29 J6
Warden Street SG18 32 E4
Wardhouse AB52 90 D1
Wardington OX17 31 F4
Wardle Ches.E. CW5 49 F7
Wardle Gt.Man. OL12 49 J1
Wardley Gt.Man. M27 49 G2
Wardley Rut. LE15 42 B5
Wardley T. & W. NE10 71 J7
Wardlow SK17 50 D5
Wardsend SK10 49 J4
Wardy Hill CB6 43 H7
Ware Herts. SG12 33 G7
Ware Kent CT3 25 J5
Wareham BH20 9 J6
Warehorne TN26 14 E4
Waren Mill NE70 77 K7
Warenford NE70 71 G1
Warenton NE70 77 K7
Wareside SG12 33 G7
Waresley Cambs. SG19 33 F3
Waresley Worcs. DY11 29 H1
Warfield RG42 22 B4
Wargrave Mersey. WA12 48 E3
Wargrave W'ham RG10 22 A4
Warham Here. HR4 28 D5
Warham Norf. NR23 44 D1
Wark Northumb. NE48 70 D6
Wark Northumb. TD12 77 G7
Warkleigh EX37 6 E3
Warkton NN16 32 B1
Warkworth Northants. OX17 31 F4
Warkworth Northumb. NE65 71 H3
Warland OL14 56 E7
Warleggan PL30 4 B4
Warley Essex CM14 23 J2
Warley W.Mid. B68 40 C7
Warley Town HX2 57 F7
Warlingham CR6 23 G6
Warmfield WF1 57 J7
Warmingham CW11 49 G6
Warminghurst RH20 12 E5
Warmington Northants. PE8 42 D6
Warmington Warks. OX17 31 F4
Warminster BA12 20 B7
Warmlake ME17 14 D3
Warmley BS30 19 K4
Warmley Hill BS15 19 K4
Warmsworth DN4 51 H2
Warmwell DT2 9 G6
Warndon WR4 29 H3
Warners End HP1 22 D1
Warnford SO32 11 H2
Warnham RH12 12 E3
Warningcamp BN18 12 D6
Warninglid RH17 13 F4
Warren Ches.E. SK11 49 H5
Warren Pembs. SA71 16 C6
Warren House PL20 6 E7
Warren Row RG10 22 B3
Warren Street ME17 14 E2
Warrenby TS10 63 G4
Warren's Green SG4 33 F6
Warrington M.K. MK46 32 B3
WARRINGTON Warr. WA 49 F4
Warroch KY13 82 B7
Warsash SO31 11 F4
Warslow SK17 50 C7
Warsop Vale NG20 51 H6
Warter YO42 58 E4
Warthill YO19 58 C4
Wartle AB31 90 D4
Wartling BN27 13 K6
Wartnaby LE14 42 A3
Warton Lancs. LA5 55 J2
Warton Lancs. PR4 55 H7
Warton Northumb. NE65 71 F3
Warton Warks. B79 40 E5
Warton Bank PR4 55 H7
Warwick CV34 30 D2
Warwick Bridge CA4 61 F1
Warwick Wold RH1 23 G6
Warwick-on-Eden CA4 61 F1
Wasbister KW17 106 C4
Wasdale Head CA20 60 C6
Wash SK23 50 C4
Wash Common RG14 21 H5
Washall Green SG9 33 H5
Washaway PL30 4 A4
Washbourne TQ9 5 H5
Washbrook BS28 19 H7
Washfield EX16 7 H4
Washfold DL11 62 B6
Washford Som. TA23 7 J1
Washford Warks. B98 30 B2
Washford Pyne EX17 7 G4
Washingborough LN4 52 D5
Washington T. & W. NE38 62 E1
Washington W.Suss. RH20 12 E5
Washmere Green CO10 34 D4
Wasing RG7 21 J5
Waskerley DH8 62 B2
Wasperton CV35 30 D3
Wasps Nest LN4 52 D6

Was - Wes


Wass YO61 58 B2
Watchet TA23 7 J1
Watchfield Oxon. SN6 21 F2
Watchfield Som. TA9 19 G7
Watchgate LA8 61 G7
Watcombe TQ1 5 K4
Watendlath CA12 60 D5
Water BB4 56 D7
Water Eaton M.K. MK2 32 B5
Water Eaton Oxon. OX2 31 G7
Water End Bed. MK44 32 E4
Water End Cen.Beds. MK45 32 D5
Water End E.Riding YO43 58 D6
Water End Essex CB10 33 J4
Water End Herts. AL9 23 F1
Water End Herts. HP1 32 D7
Water Newton PE8 42 E6
Water Orton B46 40 D6
Water Stratford MK18 31 H5
Water Yeat LA12 55 F1
Waterbeach CB25 33 H2
Waterbeck DG11 69 H6
Watercombe DT2 9 G6
Waterend HP14 22 A2
Waterfall ST10 50 C7
Waterfoot E.Renf. G76 74 D5
Waterfoot Lancs. BB4 56 D7
Waterford SG14 33 G7
Watergate PL32 4 B2
Waterhead Cumb. LA22 60 E6
Waterhead D. & G. DG7 68 C5
Waterheath NR34 45 J6
Waterhill of Bruxie AB42 99 H6
Waterhouses Dur. DH7 62 C2
Waterhouses Staffs. ST10 50 C7
Wateringbury ME18 23 K6
Waterlane GL6 20 C1
Waterloo Aber. AB42 91 J1
Waterloo Derbys. S45 51 G6
Waterloo Gt.Man. OL7 49 J2
Waterloo High. IV42 86 C2
Waterloo Mersey. L22 48 C3
Waterloo N.Lan. ML2 75 G5
Waterloo Norf. NR10 45 G4
Waterloo P. & K. PH1 82 B4
Waterloo Pembs. SA72 16 C5
Waterloo Poole BH17 10 B5
Waterloo Cross EX15 7 J4
Waterloo Port LL55 46 C6
Waterlooville PO7 11 H3
Watermeetings ML12 68 E2
Watermillock CA11 60 F4
Waterperry OX33 21 K1
Waterrow TA4 7 J3
Waters Upton TF6 39 F4
Watersfield RH20 12 D5
Watersheddings OL4 49 J2
Waterside Aber. AB36 90 B3
Waterside Aber. AB41 91 J2
Waterside B'burn. BB3 56 C7
Waterside Bucks. HP5 22 C1
Waterside E.Ayr. KA6 67 J3
Waterside E.Ayr. KA3 74 C6
Waterside E.Dun. G66 74 E3
Waterstock OX33 21 K1
Waterston SA73 16 C5
Waterthorpe S20 51 G4
WATFORD Herts. WD 22 E2
Watford Northants. NN6 31 H2
Watford Park CF83 18 E3
Wath N.Yorks. HG4 57 J2
Wath N.Yorks. HG3 57 G3
Wath Brow CA25 60 B5
Wath upon Dearne S63 51 G2
Watley's End BS36 19 K3
Watlington Norf. PE33 44 A4
Watlington Oxon. OX49 21 K2
Watnall NG16 41 H1
Watten KW1 105 H3
Wattisfield IP22 34 E1
Wattisham IP7 34 E3
Watton Dorset DT6 8 D5
Watton E.Riding YO25 59 G5
Watton Norf. IP25 44 D5
Watton at Stone SG14 33 G7
Watton Green IP25 44 D5
Watton's Green CM14 23 J2
Wattston ML6 75 F4
Wattstown CF39 18 D2
Wattsville NP11 19 F2
Waughtonhill AB43 99 H5
Waun Fawr SY23 37 F7
Waun y Clyn SA17 17 H5
Waunarlwydd SA5 17 K6
Waunclunda SA19 17 K2
Waunfawr LL55 46 D7
Waun-Lwyd NP23 18 E1
Wavendon MK17 32 C5
Waverbridge CA7 60 D2
Waverton Ches.W. & C. CH3 48 D6
Waverton Cumb. CA7 60 D2
Wavertree L15 48 C4
Wawne HU7 59 G6
Waxham NR12 45 J3
Waxholme HU19 59 K7
Way Gill BD23 56 E3
Way Village EX16 7 G4
Way Wick BS24 19 G5
Wayford TA18 8 D4
Waytown DT6 8 D5
Wdig (Goodwick) SA64 16 C2
Weachyburn AB45 98 E5
Weacombe TA4 7 K1
Weald OX18 21 G1
Wealdstone HA3 22 E2
Weardley LS17 57 H5
Weare BS26 19 H6
Weare Giffard EX39 6 C3
Wearhead DL13 61 K3
Wearne TA10 8 D2
Weasenham All Saints PE32 44 C3
Weasenham St. Peter PE32 44 C3
Weathercote LA6 56 C2
Weatheroak Hill B48 30 B1
Weaverham CW8 49 F5
Weaverthorpe YO17 59 F2
Webheath B97 30 B2
Webton HR2 28 D5
Wedderlairs AB41 91 G1
Weddington CV10 41 F6
Wedhampton SN10 20 D6
Wedmore BS28 19 H7
Wednesbury WS10 40 B6
Wednesfield WV11 40 B6
Weedon HP22 32 B7
Weedon Bec NN7 31 H3
Weedon Lois NN12 31 H4
Weeford WS14 40 D5
Week Devon EX18 7 F4
Week Devon TQ9 5 H4
Week Som. TA22 7 H2
Week Orchard EX23 6 A5
Week St. Mary EX22 4 C1
Weeke SO22 11 F1
Weekley NN16 42 B7
Weel HU17 59 G6
Weeley CO16 35 F6
Weeley Heath CO16 35 F6
Weem PH15 81 K2
Weeping Cross ST17 40 B3
Weethley B49 30 B3
Weeting IP27 44 B7
Weeton E.Riding HU12 59 K7
Weeton Lancs. PR4 55 G6
Weeton N.Yorks. LS17 57 H5
Weetwood LS16 57 H6
Weir Essex SS6 24 E3
Weir Lancs. OL13 56 D7
Weir Quay PL20 4 E4
Weirbrook SY11 38 C3
Weisdale ZE2 107 M7
Welbeck Abbey S80 51 H5
Welborne NR20 44 E5
Welbourn LN5 52 C7
Welburn N.Yorks. YO60 58 D3
Welburn N.Yorks. YO62 58 C1
Welbury DL6 62 E6
Welby NG32 42 C2
Welches Dam PE16 43 H7
Welcombe EX39 6 A4
Weldon NN17 42 C7
Welford Northants. NN6 41 J7
Welford W.Berks. RG20 21 H4
Welford-on-Avon CV37 30 C3
Welham Leics. LE16 42 A6
Welham Notts. DN22 51 K4
Welham Green AL9 23 F1
Well Hants. RG29 22 A7
Well Lincs. LN13 53 H5
Well N.Yorks. DL8 57 H1
Well End Bucks. SL8 22 B3
Well End Herts. WD6 23 F2
Well Hill BR6 23 H5
Well Street ME19 23 K6
Well Town EX16 7 H5
Welland WR13 29 G4
Wellbank DD5 83 F4
Wellesbourne CV35 30 D3
Wellhill IV36 97 G5
Wellhouse W.Berks. RG18 21 J4
Wellhouse W.Yorks. HD7 50 C1
Welling DA16 23 H4
Wellingborough NN8 32 B2
Wellingham PE32 44 C3
Wellingore LN5 52 C7
Wellington Cumb. CA20 60 B6
Wellington Here. HR4 28 D4
Wellington Som. TA21 7 K3
Wellington Tel. & W. TF1 39 F4
Wellington Heath HR8 29 G4
Wellington Marsh HR4 28 D4
Wellow B. & N.E.Som. BA2 20 A6
Wellow I.o.W. PO41 10 E6
Wellow Notts. NG22 51 J6
Wells BA5 19 J7
Wells Green B92 40 D7
Wellsborough CV13 41 F5
Wells-next-the-Sea NR23 44 D1
Wellstyle Green CM6 33 K7
Wellwood KY12 75 J2
Welney PE14 43 J6
Welsh Bicknor HR9 28 E7
Welsh End SY13 38 E2
Welsh Frankton SY11 38 C2
Welsh Hook SA62 16 C3
Welsh Newton NP25 28 D7
Welsh St. Donats CF71 18 D4
Welshampton SY12 38 D2
Welshpool (Y Trallwng) SY21 38 B5
Welton B. & N.E.Som. BA3 19 K6
Welton Cumb. CA5 60 E2
Welton E.Riding HU15 59 F7
Welton Lincs. LN2 52 D4
Welton Northants. NN11 31 G2
Welton le Marsh PE23 53 H6
Welton le Wold LN11 53 F4
Welwick HU12 59 K7
Welwyn AL6 33 F7
Welwyn Garden City AL8 33 F7
Wem SY4 38 E3
Wembdon TA6 8 B1
Wembley HA0 22 E3
Wembley Park HA9 22 E3
Wembury PL9 5 F6
Wembworthy EX18 6 E4
Wemyss Bay PA18 73 K4
Wenallt Cere. SY23 27 F1
Wenallt Gwyn. LL21 37 J1
Wendens Ambo CB11 33 J5
Wendlebury OX25 31 G7
Wendling NR19 44 D4
Wendover HP22 22 B1
Wendover Dean HP22 22 B1
Wendron TR13 2 D5
Wendy SG8 33 G4
Wenfordbridge PL30 4 A3
Wenhaston IP19 35 J1
Wenlli LL22 47 G6
Wennington Cambs. PE28 33 F1
Wennington Gt.Lon. RM13 23 J3
Wennington Lancs. LA2 56 B2
Wensley Derbys. DE4 50 E6
Wensley N.Yorks. DL8 57 F1
Wentbridge WF8 51 G1
Wentnor SY9 38 C6
Wentworth Cambs. CB6 33 H1
Wentworth S.Yorks. S62 51 F3
Wenvoe CF5 18 E4
Weobley HR4 28 C3
Weobley Marsh HR4 28 D3
Weoley Castle B29 40 C7
Wepham BN18 12 D6
Wepre CH5 48 B6
Wereham PE33 44 A5
Wergs WV6 40 A5
Wern Gwyn. LL49 36 E2
Wern Powys SY21 38 B4
Wern Powys NP8 28 A7
Wern Shrop. SY10 38 B2
Wernffrwd SA4 17 J6
Wern-olau SA4 17 J6
Wernrheolydd NP15 28 C7
Wern-y-cwrt NP15 19 G1
Werrington Cornw. PL15 6 B7
Werrington Peter. PE4 42 E5
Werrington Staffs. ST9 40 B1
Wervil Grange SA44 26 C3
Wervin CH2 48 D5
Wesham PR4 55 H6
Wessington DE55 51 F7
West Aberthaw CF62 18 D5
West Acre PE32 44 B4
West Acton W3 22 E3
West Allerdean TD15 77 H6
West Alvington TQ7 5 H6
West Amesbury SP4 20 E7
West Anstey EX36 7 G3
West Ashby LN9 53 F5
West Ashford EX31 6 D2
West Ashling PO18 12 B6
West Ashton BA14 20 B6
West Auckland DL14 62 C4
West Ayton YO13 59 F1
West Bagborough TA4 7 K2
West Barkwith LN8 52 E4
West Barnby YO21 63 K5
West Barns EH42 76 E3
West Barsham NR21 44 D2
West Bay DT6 8 D5
West Beckham NR25 45 F2
West Benhar ML7 75 G4
West Bergholt CO6 34 D6
West Bexington DT2 8 E6
West Bilney PE32 44 B4
West Blatchington BN3 13 F6
West Boldon NE36 71 J7
West Bourton SP8 9 G2
West Bowling BD5 57 G6
West Brabourne TN25 15 F3
West Bradford BB7 56 C5
West Bradley BA6 8 E1
West Bretton WF4 50 E1
West Bridgford NG2 41 H2
West Bromwich B70 40 C6
West Buckland Devon EX32 6 E2
West Buckland Som. TA21 7 K3
West Burrafirth ZE2 107 L7
West Burton N.Yorks. DL8 57 F1
West Burton W.Suss. RH20 12 C5
West Butsfield DL13 62 B2
West Butterwick DN17 52 B2
West Byfleet KT14 22 D5
West Cairncake AB53 99 G6
West Caister NR30 45 K4
West Calder EH55 75 J4
West Camel BA22 8 E2
West Carbeth G63 74 D3
West Carr Houses DN9 51 K2
West Cauldcoats ML10 74 E6
West Chaldon DT2 9 G6
West Challow OX12 21 G3
West Charleton TQ7 5 H6
West Chevington NE61 71 H4
West Chiltington RH20 12 D5
West Chiltington Common RH20 12 D5
West Chinnock TA18 8 D3
West Chisenbury SN9 20 E6
West Clandon GU4 22 D6
West Cliffe CT15 15 J3
West Clyne KW9 97 F1
West Coker BA22 8 E3
West Compton Dorset DT2 8 E5
West Compton Som. BA4 19 J7
West Cowick DN14 58 C7
West Cross SA3 17 K7
West Crudwell SN16 20 C2
West Curry PL15 4 C1
West Curthwaite CA7 60 E2
West Dean W.Suss. PO18 12 B5
West Dean Wilts. SP5 10 D2
West Deeping PE6 42 E5
West Derby L12 48 C3
West Dereham PE33 44 A5
West Ditchburn NE66 71 G1
West Down EX34 6 D1
West Drayton Gt.Lon. UB7 22 D4
West Drayton Notts. DN22 51 K5
West Dullater FK17 81 G7
West Dunnet KW14 105 H1
West Edington NE61 71 G5
West Ella HU10 59 G7
West End Bed. MK43 32 C3
West End Brack.F. RG42 22 B4
West End Caerp. NP11 19 F2
West End Cambs. PE15 43 H6
West End E.Riding YO25 59 G3
West End Hants. SO30 11 F3
West End Herts. AL9 23 F1
West End Kent CT6 25 H5
West End Lancs. LA4 55 H3
West End Lincs. DN36 53 G3
West End N.Som. BS48 19 H5
West End N.Yorks. HG3 57 G4
West End Norf. NR30 45 J4
West End Norf. IP25 44 D5
West End Oxon. OX29 21 H1
West End Oxon. OX10 21 J3
West End S.Lan. ML11 75 H6
West End Suff. NR34 45 J7
West End Surr. KT10 22 E5
West End Surr. GU24 22 C5
West End Wilts. SN15 20 C4
West End Wilts. SP7 9 J2
West End Wilts. SP5 9 J2
West End Green RG7 21 K5
West Farleigh ME15 14 C2
West Farndon NN11 31 G3
West Felton SY11 38 C3
West Firle BN8 13 H6
West Fleetham NE67 71 G1
West Flotmanby YO14 59 G2
West Garforth LS25 57 J6
West Ginge OX12 21 H3
West Glen PA21 73 H3
West Grafton SN8 21 F5
West Green Gt.Lon. N15 23 G3
West Green Hants. RG27 22 A6
West Grimstead SP5 10 D2
West Grinstead RH13 12 E4
West Haddlesey YO8 58 B7
West Haddon NN6 31 H1
West Hagbourne OX11 21 J3
West Hagley DY9 40 B7
West Hall CA8 70 A7
West Hallam DE7 41 G1
West Halton DN15 59 F7
West Ham E15 23 G3
West Handley S21 51 F5
West Hanney OX12 21 H2
West Hanningfield CM2 24 D2
West Hardwick WF4 51 G1
West Harnham SP2 10 C2
West Harptree BS40 19 J6
West Harrow HA1 22 E3
West Harting GU31 11 J2
West Hatch Som. TA3 8 B2
West Hatch Wilts. SP3 9 J2
West Head PE34 43 J5
West Heath Ches.E. CW12 49 H6
West Heath Gt.Lon. SE2 23 H4
West Heath Hants. GU14 22 B6
West Heath Hants. RG26 21 J6
West Heath W.Mid. B31 30 B1
West Helmsdale KW8 105 F7
West Hendon NW9 23 F3
West Hendred OX12 21 H3
West Heslerton YO17 59 F2
West Hewish BS24 19 G5
West Hill Devon EX11 7 J6
West Hill E.Riding YO16 59 H3
West Hill N.Som. BS20 19 H4
West Hoathly RH19 13 G3
West Holme BH20 9 H6
West Horndon CM13 24 C3
West Horrington BA5 19 J7
West Horsley KT24 22 D6
West Horton NE71 77 J7
West Hougham CT15 15 H4
West Howe BH11 10 B5
West Howetown TA24 7 H2
West Huntspill TA9 19 G7
West Hyde WD3 22 D2
West Hythe CT21 15 G4
West Ilsley RG20 21 H3
West Itchenor PO20 11 J4
West Keal PE23 53 G6
West Kennett SN8 20 E5
West Kilbride KA23 74 A6
West Kingsdown TN15 23 J5
West Kington SN14 20 B4
West Kington Wick SN14 20 B4
West Kirby CH48 48 B4
West Knapton YO17 58 E2
West Knighton DT2 9 G6
West Knoyle BA12 9 H1
West Kyloe TD15 77 J6
West Lambrook TA13 8 D3
West Langdon CT15 15 J3
West Langwell IV28 96 D1
West Lavington W.Suss. GU29 12 B4
West Lavington Wilts. SN10 20 D6
West Layton DL11 62 C6
West Leake LE12 41 H3
West Learmouth TD12 77 G7
West Lees DL6 63 F6
West Leigh Devon EX17 6 E5
West Leigh Devon TQ9 5 H5
West Leigh Som. TA4 7 K2
West Leith HP23 32 C7
West Lexham PE32 44 C4
West Lilling YO60 58 C3
West Lingo KY9 83 F7
West Linton EH46 75 K5
West Liss GU33 11 J2
West Littleton SN14 20 A4
West Lockinge OX12 21 H3
West Looe PL13 4 C5
West Lulworth BH20 9 H6
West Lutton YO17 59 F3
West Lydford TA11 8 E1
West Lyn EX35 7 F1
West Lyng TA3 8 C2
West Lynn PE34 44 A4
West Mains TD15 77 J6
West Malling ME19 23 K6
West Malvern WR14 29 G4
West Marden PO18 11 J3
West Markham NG22 51 K5
West Marsh DN31 53 F2
West Marton BD23 56 D4
West Melbury SP7 9 H2
West Melton S63 51 G2
West Meon GU32 11 H2
West Meon Hut GU32 11 H2
West Mersea CO5 34 E7
West Milton DT6 8 D5
West Minster ME12 25 F4
West Molesey KT8 22 E5
West Monkton TA2 8 B2
West Moors BH22 10 B4
West Morden BH20 9 J5
West Morriston TD4 76 E6
West Morton BD20 57 F5
West Mostard LA10 61 J7
West Mudford BA21 8 E2
West Muir DD9 83 G1
West Ness YO62 58 C2
West Newbiggin DL2 62 E5
West Newton E.Riding HU11 59 H6
West Newton Norf. PE31 44 A3
West Norwood SE27 23 G4
West Ogwell TQ12 5 J4
West Orchard SP7 9 H3
West Overton SN8 20 E5
West Panson PL15 6 B6
West Park Aber. AB31 91 F5
West Park Mersey. WA10 48 E3
West Parley BH22 10 B5
West Peckham ME18 23 K6
West Pelton DH9 62 D1
West Pennard BA6 8 E1
West Pentire TR8 2 E2
West Perry PE28 32 E2
West Porlock TA24 7 G1
West Prawle TQ8 5 H7
West Preston BN16 12 D6
West Pulham DT2 9 G4
West Putford EX22 6 B4
West Quantoxhead TA4 7 K1
West Raddon EX17 7 G5
West Rainton DH4 62 E2
West Rasen LN8 52 D4
West Raynham NR21 44 C3
West Retford DN22 51 J4
West Rounton DL6 63 F6
West Row IP28 33 K1
West Rudham PE31 44 C3
West Runton NR27 45 F1
West Saltoun EH34 76 C4
West Sandford EX17 7 G5
West Sandwick ZE2 107 N4
West Scrafton DL8 57 F1
West Shepton BA4 19 K7
West Shinness Lodge IV27 103 H7
West Somerton NR29 45 J4
West Stafford DT2 9 G6
West Stockwith DN10 51 K3
West Stoke PO18 12 B6
West Stonesdale DL11 61 K6
West Stoughton BS28 19 H7
West Stour SP8 9 G2
West Stourmouth CT3 25 J5
West Stow IP28 34 C1
West Stowell SN8 20 E5
West Stratton SO21 21 J7
West Street Kent ME17 14 E2
West Street Med. ME3 24 D4
West Street Suff. IP31 34 D1
West Tanfield HG4 57 H2
West Taphouse PL22 4 B4
West Tarbert PA29 73 G4
West Tarring BN13 12 E6
West Thirston NE65 71 G3
West Thorney PO10 11 J4
West Thurrock RM20 23 J4
West Tilbury RM18 24 C4
West Tisted SO24 11 H2
West Tofts Norf. IP26 44 C6
West Tofts P. & K. PH1 82 C4
West Torrington LN8 52 E4
West Town B. & N.E.Som. BS40 19 J5
West Town Hants. PO11 11 J5
West Town N.Som. BS48 19 H5
West Town Som. BA6 8 E1
West Tytherley SP5 10 D2
West Walton PE14 43 H4
West Wellow SO51 10 D3
West Wembury PL9 5 F6
West Wemyss KY1 76 B1
West Wick BS24 19 G5
West Wickham Cambs. CB21 33 K4
West Wickham Gt.Lon. BR4 23 G5
West Williamston SA68 16 D5
West Winch PE33 44 A4
West Winterslow SP5 10 D1
West Wittering PO20 11 J5

Wes - Wic


West Witton DL8 57 F1
West Woodburn NE48 70 D5
West Woodhay RG20 21 G5
West Woodlands BA11 20 A7
West Worldham GU34 11 J1
West Worlington EX17 7 F4
West Worthing BN11 12 E6
West Wratting CB21 33 K3
West Wycombe HP14 22 B2
West Yatton SN14 20 B4
West Yell ZE2 107 N4
West Youlstone EX23 6 A4
Westbere CT2 25 H5
Westborough NG23 42 B1
Westbourne *Bourne.* BH4 10 B5
Westbourne *W.Suss.* PO10 11 J4
Westbourne Green W2 23 F3
Westbrook *Kent* CT9 25 K4
Westbrook *W.Berks.* RG20 21 H4
Westbrook *Wilts.* SN15 20 C5
Westbury *Bucks.* NN13 31 H5
Westbury *Shrop.* SY5 38 C5
**Westbury *Wilts.* BA13 20 B6**
Westbury Leigh BA13 20 B6
Westbury on Trym BS9 19 J4
**Westbury-on-Severn GL14 29 G7**
Westbury-sub-Mendip BA5 19 J7
Westby *Lancs.* PR4 55 G6
Westby *Lincs.* NG33 42 C3
**Westcliff-on-Sea SS0 24 E3**
Westcombe BA4 9 F1
Westcot OX12 21 G3
Westcott *Bucks.* HP18 31 J7
Westcott *Devon* EX15 7 J5
Westcott *Surr.* RH4 22 E7
Westcott Barton OX7 31 F6
Westcourt SN8 21 F5
Westcroft MK4 32 B5
Westdean BN25 13 J7
Westdowns PL33 4 A2
Westend Town SN14 20 A4
Wester Aberchalder IV2 88 C2
Wester Badentyre AB53 99 F5
Wester Balgedie KY13 82 C7
Wester Culbeuchly AB45 98 E4
Wester Dechmont EH52 75 J3
Wester Fintray AB51 91 G3
Wester Foffarty DD8 83 F3
Wester Greenskares AB45 99 F4
Wester Gruinards IV24 96 C2
Wester Hailes EH14 76 A4
Wester Lealty IV17 96 D4
Wester Lonvine IV18 96 E4
Wester Newburn KY8 83 F7
Wester Ord AB32 91 G4
Wester Quarff ZE2 107 N9
Wester Skeld ZE2 107 L8
Westerdale *High.* KW12 105 G3
Westerdale *N.Yorks.* YO21 63 H6
Westerfield *Shet.* ZE2 107 M7
Westerfield *Suff.* IP6 35 F4
Westergate PO20 12 C6
**Westerham TN16 23 H6**
Westerhope NE5 71 G7
Westerleigh BS37 19 K4
Westerloch KW1 105 J3
Westerton *Aber.* AB31 91 F5
Westerton *Angus* DD10 83 H2
Westerton *Dur.* DL14 62 D3
Westerton *P. & K.* PH5 81 K6
Westerwick ZE2 107 L8
Westfield *Cumb.* CA14 60 A4
Westfield *E.Suss.* TN35 14 D6
Westfield *High.* KW14 105 F2
Westfield *N.Lan.* G68 75 F3
Westfield *Norf.* NR19 44 D5
Westfield *W.Loth.* EH48 75 H3
Westfield *W.Yorks.* WF16 57 H7
Westfield Sole ME14 24 D5
Westgate *Dur.* DL13 62 A3
Westgate *N.Lincs.* DN9 51 K2
Westgate *Norf.* NR21 44 D1
Westgate *Northumb.* NE20 71 G6
Westgate Hill BD4 57 H7
**Westgate on Sea CT8 25 K4**
Westhall *Aber.* AB52 90 E2
Westhall *Suff.* IP19 45 J7
Westham *Dorset* DT4 9 F7
Westham *E.Suss.* BN24 13 K6
Westham *Som.* TA7 19 H7
Westhampnett PO18 12 B6
Westhay *Devon* EX13 8 C4
Westhay *Som.* BA6 19 H7
Westhead L40 48 D2
Westhide HR1 28 E4
**Westhill *Aber.* AB32 91 G4**
Westhill *High.* IV2 96 E7
Westhope *Here.* HR4 28 D3
Westhope *Shrop.* SY7 38 D7
Westhorp NN11 31 G3
Westhorpe *Lincs.* PE11 43 F2
Westhorpe *Notts.* NG25 51 J7
Westhorpe *Suff.* IP14 34 E2
Westhoughton BL5 49 F2
Westhouse LA6 56 B2
Westhouses DE55 51 G7
Westhumble RH5 22 E6
Westing ZE2 107 P2
Westlake PL21 5 G5
Westlands ST5 40 A1
Westlea SN5 20 E3
Westleigh *Devon* EX39 6 C3
Westleigh *Devon* EX16 7 J4
Westleigh *Gt.Man.* WN7 49 F2
Westleton IP17 35 J2
Westley *Shrop.* SY5 38 C5
Westley *Suff.* IP33 34 C2
Westley Heights SS16 24 C3
Westley Waterless CB8 33 K3
Westlington HP17 31 J7
Westlinton CA6 69 J7
Westloch EH45 76 A5
Westmancote GL20 29 J5
Westmarsh CT3 25 J5
Westmeston BN6 13 G5
Westmill SG9 33 G6
Westminster SW1H 23 F4
Westmuir DD8 82 E2
Westness KW17 106 C5
Westnewton *Cumb.* CA7 60 C2
Westnewton *Northumb.* NE71 77 H7
Westoe NE33 71 J7
Weston *B. & N.E.Som.* BA1 20 A5
Weston *Ches.E.* CW2 49 G7
Weston *Devon* EX12 7 K7
Weston *Devon* EX14 7 K5
Weston *Dorset* DT5 9 F7
Weston *Halton* WA7 48 E4
Weston *Hants.* GU32 11 J2
Weston *Here.* HR6 28 C3
Weston *Herts.* SG4 33 F5
Weston *Lincs.* PE12 43 F3
Weston *Moray* AB56 98 C4
Weston *N.Yorks.* LS21 57 G5
Weston *Northants.* NN12 31 G4
Weston *Notts.* NG23 51 K6
Weston *S'ham.* SO19 11 F3
Weston *Shrop.* SY4 38 E3
Weston *Shrop.* TF13 38 E6
Weston *Shrop.* SY7 28 C1
Weston *Staffs.* ST18 40 B3
Weston *W.Berks.* RG20 21 H4
Weston Bampfylde BA22 9 F2
Weston Beggard HR1 28 E4
Weston by Welland LE16 42 A6
Weston Colville CB21 33 K3
Weston Corbett RG25 21 K7
Weston Coyney ST3 40 B1
Weston Favell NN3 31 J2
Weston Green *Cambs.* CB21 33 K3
Weston Green *Norf.* NR9 45 F4
Weston Heath TF11 39 G4
Weston Hills PE12 43 F3
Weston in Arden CV12 41 F7
Weston Jones TF10 39 G3
Weston Longville NR9 45 F4
Weston Lullingfields SY4 38 D3
Weston Patrick RG25 21 K7
Weston Point WA7 48 D4
Weston Rhyn SY10 38 B2
Weston Subedge GL55 30 C4
Weston Town BA4 20 A7
Weston Turville HP22 32 B7
Weston under Penyard HR9 29 F6
Weston under Wetherley CV33 30 E2
Weston Underwood *Derbys.* DE6 40 E1
Weston Underwood *M.K.* MK46 32 B3
Westonbirt GL8 20 B3
Westoning MK45 32 D5
Weston-in-Gordano BS20 19 H4
Weston-on-Avon CV37 30 C3
Weston-on-the-Green OX25 31 G7
Weston-on-Trent DE72 41 G3
**Weston-super-Mare BS23 19 G5**
Weston-under-Lizard TF11 40 A4
Westonzoyland TA7 8 C1
Westow YO60 58 D3
Westport *Arg. & B.* PA28 66 A1
Westport *Som.* TA10 8 C2
Westra CF64 18 E4
Westray KW17 106 D3
Westray Airfield KW17 106 D2
Westridge Green RG8 21 J4
Westrigg EH48 75 H4
Westruther TD3 76 E6
Westry PE15 43 G6
Westside AB12 91 G5
Westvale L32 48 D3
Westville NG15 41 H1
Westward CA7 60 D2
Westward Ho! EX39 6 C3
Westwell *Kent* TN25 14 E3
Westwell *Oxon.* OX18 21 F1
Westwell Leacon TN27 14 E3
Westwick *Cambs.* CB24 33 H2
Westwick *Dur.* DL12 62 B5
Westwick *N.Yorks.* YO51 57 J3
Westwick *Norf.* NR10 45 G3
Westwood *Devon* EX5 7 J6
Westwood *Peter.* PE3 42 E6
Westwood *S.Lan.* G75 74 E5
Westwood *Wilts.* BA15 20 B6
Westwood Heath CV4 30 D1
Westwoodside DN9 51 K3
Wetham Green ME9 24 E5
Wetheral CA4 61 F1
**Wetherby LS22 57 K5**
Wetherden IP14 34 E2
Wetherden Upper Town IP14 34 E2
Wetheringsett IP14 35 F2
Wethersfield CM7 34 B5
Wethersta ZE2 107 M6
Wetherup Street IP14 35 F2
Wetley Abbey ST9 40 B1
Wetley Rocks ST9 40 B1
Wettenhall CW7 49 F6
Wettenhall Green CW7 49 F6
Wetton DE6 50 D7
Wetwang YO25 59 F4
Wetwood ST21 39 G2
Wexcombe SN8 21 F6
Wexham Street SL3 22 C3
Weybourne *Norf.* NR25 45 F1
Weybourne *Surr.* GU9 22 B7
Weybread IP21 45 G7
Weybread Street IP21 35 G1
**Weybridge KT13 22 D5**
Weycroft EX13 8 C4
Weydale KW14 105 G2
Weyhill SP11 21 G7
**Weymouth DT4 9 F7**
Whaddon *Bucks.* MK17 32 B5
Whaddon *Cambs.* SG8 33 G4
Whaddon *Glos.* GL4 29 H7
Whaddon *Glos.* GL52 29 J6
Whaddon *Wilts.* SP5 10 C2
Whaddon *Wilts.* BA14 20 B5
Whaddon Gap SG8 33 G4
Whale CA10 61 G4
Whaley NG20 51 H5
Whaley Bridge SK23 50 C4
Whaley Thorns NG20 51 H5
Whaligoe KW2 105 J4
Whalley BB7 56 C6
Whalsay ZE2 107 P6
Whalsay Airport ZE2 107 P6
Whalton NE61 71 G5
Wham BD24 56 C3
Whaplode PE12 43 G3
Whaplode Drove PE12 43 G4
Whaplode St. Catherine PE12 43 G4
Wharfe LA2 56 C3
Wharles PR4 55 H6
Wharley End MK43 32 C4
Wharncliffe Side S35 50 E3
Wharram le Street YO17 58 E3
Wharram Percy YO17 58 E3
Wharton *Ches.W. & C.* CW7 49 F6
Wharton *Here.* HR6 28 E3
Whashton DL11 62 C6
Whatcote CV36 30 E4
Whateley B78 40 E6
Whatfield IP7 34 E4
Whatley BA11 20 A7
Whatlington TN33 14 C6
Whatsole Street TN25 15 G3
Whatstandwell DE4 51 F7
Whatton NG13 42 A2
Whauphill DG8 64 E6
Whaw DL11 62 A6
Wheatacre NR34 45 J6
Wheatcroft DE4 51 F7
Wheatenhurst GL2 20 A1
Wheatfield OX9 21 K2
Wheathampstead AL4 32 E7
Wheathill *Shrop.* WV16 39 F7
Wheathill *Som.* TA11 8 E1
Wheatley *Hants.* GU34 11 J1
Wheatley *Oxon.* OX33 21 K1
Wheatley *W.Yorks.* HX3 57 F7
Wheatley Hill DH6 62 E3
Wheatley Lane BB12 56 D6
Wheatley Park DN2 51 H2
Wheaton Aston ST19 40 A4
Wheddon Cross TA24 7 H2
Wheedlemont AB54 90 C2
Wheelerstreet GU8 22 C7
Wheelock CW11 49 G7
Wheelock Heath CW11 49 G7
Wheelton PR6 56 B7
Wheen DD8 90 B7
Wheldale WF10 57 K7
Wheldrake YO19 58 C5
Whelford GL7 20 E2
Whelley WN1 48 E2
Whelpley Hill HP5 22 C1
Whelpo CA7 60 E3
Whelston CH6 48 B5
Whenby YO61 58 C3
Whepstead IP29 34 C3
Wherstead IP9 35 F4
Wherwell SP11 21 G7
Wheston SK17 50 D5
Whetley Cross DT8 8 D4
Whetsted TN12 23 K7
Whetstone *Gt.Lon.* N20 23 F2
Whetstone *Leics.* LE8 41 H6
Whicham LA18 54 E1
Whichford CV36 30 E5
Whickham NE16 71 H7
Whiddon EX21 6 C5
Whiddon Down EX6 6 E6
Whifflet ML5 75 F4
Whigstreet DD8 83 F3
Whilton NN11 31 H2
Whim EH46 76 A5
Whimble EX22 6 B5
Whimple EX5 7 J6
Whimpwell Green NR12 45 H3
Whin Lane End PR3 55 G5
Whinburgh NR19 44 E5
Whinny Hill TS21 62 E5
Whinnyfold AB42 91 J1
Whippingham PO32 11 G5
Whipsnade LU6 32 D7
Whipton EX1 7 H6
Whirlow S11 51 F4
Whisby LN6 52 C6
Whissendine LE15 42 B4
Whissonsett NR20 44 D3
Whisterfield SK11 49 H5
Whistley Green RG10 22 A4
Whiston *Mersey.* L35 48 D3
Whiston *Northants.* NN7 32 B2
Whiston *S.Yorks.* S60 51 G3
Whiston *Staffs.* ST10 40 C1
Whiston *Staffs.* ST19 40 A4
Whiston Cross WV7 39 G5
Whiston Eaves ST10 40 C1
Whitacre Fields B46 40 E6
Whitacre Heath B46 40 E6
Whitbeck LA19 54 E1
Whitbourne WR6 29 G3
Whitburn *T. & W.* SR6 71 K7
Whitburn *W.Loth.* EH47 75 H4
Whitby *Ches.W. & C.* CH65 48 C5
**Whitby *N.Yorks.* YO21 63 K5**
Whitbyheath CH65 48 C5
Whitchurch *B. & N.E.Som.* BS14 19 K5
Whitchurch *Bucks.* HP22 32 B6
Whitchurch *Cardiff* CF14 18 E3
Whitchurch *Devon* PL19 4 E3
**Whitchurch *Hants.* RG28 21 H7**
Whitchurch *Here.* HR9 28 E7
Whitchurch *Pembs.* SA62 16 A3
**Whitchurch *Shrop.* SY13 38 E1**
Whitchurch *Warks.* CV37 30 D4
Whitchurch Canonicorum DT6 8 C5
Whitchurch Hill RG8 21 K4
Whitchurch-on-Thames RG8 21 K4
Whitcombe DT2 9 G6
Whitcott Keysett SY7 38 B7
White Ball TA21 7 J4
White Colne CO6 34 C6
White Coppice PR6 49 F1
White Cross *Cornw.* TR8 3 F3
White Cross *Devon* EX5 7 J6
White Cross *Here.* HR4 28 D4
White Cross *Wilts.* BA12 9 G1
White End GL19 29 H6
White Hill BA12 9 H1
White Houses DN22 51 K5
White Kirkley DL13 62 B3
White Lackington DT2 9 G5
White Ladies Aston WR7 29 J3
White Lund LA3 55 H3
White Mill SA32 17 H3
White Moor DE56 41 F1
White Notley CM8 34 B7
White Ox Mead BA2 20 A6
White Pit LN13 53 G5
White Rocks HR2 28 D6
White Roding CM6 33 J7
White Waltham SL6 22 B4
Whiteacen AB38 97 K7
Whiteash Green CO9 34 B5
Whitebirk BB1 56 C7
Whitebog AB43 99 H5
Whitebridge *High.* KW14 105 H1
Whitebridge *High.* IV2 88 B3
Whitebrook NP25 19 J1
Whiteburn TD2 76 D6
Whitecairn DG8 64 C5
Whitecairns AB23 91 H3
Whitecastle ML12 75 J6
Whitechapel PR3 55 J5
Whitechurch SA41 16 E2
Whitecote LS13 57 H6
Whitecraig EH21 76 B3
Whitecroft GL15 19 K1
Whitecrook DG9 64 B5
Whitecross *Cornw.* TR20 2 C5
Whitecross *Cornw.* PL27 3 G1
Whitecross *Dorset* DT6 8 D5
Whitecross *Falk.* EH49 75 H3
Whiteface IV25 96 E3
Whitefield *Aber.* AB51 91 F2
Whitefield *Devon* EX32 7 F2
Whitefield *Dorset* BH20 9 J5
Whitefield *Gt.Man.* M45 49 H2
Whitefield *High.* IV2 88 C2
Whitefield *High.* KW1 105 H3
Whitefield *P. & K.* PH13 82 C4
Whiteford AB51 91 F2
Whitegate CW8 49 F6
Whitehall *Devon* EX15 7 K4
Whitehall *Hants.* RG29 22 A6
Whitehall *Ork.* KW17 106 F5
Whitehall *W.Suss.* RH13 12 E4
**Whitehaven CA28 60 A5**
Whitehill *Aber.* AB42 99 H5
Whitehill *Hants.* GU35 11 J1
Whitehill *Kent* ME13 14 E2
Whitehill *Midloth.* EH22 76 B4
Whitehill *N.Ayr.* KA24 74 A5
Whitehills AB45 98 E4
Whitehouse *Aber.* AB33 90 E3
Whitehouse *Arg. & B.* PA29 73 G4
Whitehouse Common B75 40 D6
Whitekirk EH42 76 D2
Whitelackington TA19 8 C3
Whitelaw TD11 77 G5
Whiteleen KW2 105 J4
Whitelees KA1 74 B7
Whiteley PO15 11 G4
Whiteley Bank PO38 11 G6
Whiteley Green SK10 49 J5
Whiteley Village KT12 22 D5
Whiteleys DG9 64 A5
Whitemans Green RH17 13 G4
Whitemire IV36 97 G6
Whitemoor PL26 3 G3
Whiteness ZE2 107 M8
Whiteoak Green OX29 30 E7
Whiteparish SP5 10 D2
Whiterashes AB21 91 G2
Whiterow KW1 105 J4
Whiteshill GL6 20 B1
Whiteside *Northumb.* NE49 70 C7
Whiteside *W.Loth.* EH48 75 H4
Whitesmith BN8 13 J5
Whitestaunton TA20 8 B3
Whitestone *Aber.* AB31 90 E5
Whitestone *Arg. & B.* PA28 73 F7
Whitestone *Devon* EX4 7 G6
Whitestreet Green CO10 34 D5
Whitestripe AB43 99 H5
Whiteway GL6 29 J7
Whitewell *Aber.* AB43 99 H4
Whitewell *Lancs.* BB7 56 B5
Whitewell *Wrex.* SY13 38 D1
Whiteworks PL20 5 G3
Whitewreath IV30 97 K6
Whitfield *Here.* HR2 28 D5
Whitfield *Kent* CT16 15 J3
Whitfield *Northants.* NN13 31 H5
Whitfield *Northumb.* NE47 61 J1
Whitfield *S.Glos.* GL12 19 K2
Whitford *Devon* EX13 8 B5
Whitford (Chwitffordd) *Flints.* CH8 47 K5
Whitgift DN14 58 E7
Whitgreave ST18 40 A3
Whithorn DG8 64 E6
Whiting Bay KA27 66 E1
Whitkirk LS15 57 J6
Whitlam AB21 91 G2
**Whitland (Hendy-Gwyn) SA34 17 F4**
Whitland Abbey SA34 17 F4
Whitleigh PL5 4 E4
Whitletts KA8 67 H1
Whitley *N.Yorks.* DN14 58 B7
Whitley *Read.* RG2 22 A5
Whitley *W.Mid.* CV3 30 E1
Whitley *Wilts.* SN12 20 B5
**Whitley Bay NE26 71 J6**
Whitley Chapel NE47 62 A1
Whitley Heath ST21 40 A3
Whitley Lower WF12 50 E1
Whitley Row TN14 23 H6
Whitlock's End B90 30 C1
Whitminster GL2 20 A1
Whitmore *Dorset* BH21 10 B4
Whitmore *Staffs.* ST5 40 A1
Whitnage EX16 7 J4
Whitnash CV31 30 E2
Whitnell TA5 19 F7
Whitney-on-Wye HR3 28 B4
Whitrigg *Cumb.* CA7 60 D1
Whitrigg *Cumb.* CA7 60 D3
Whitsbury SP6 10 C3
Whitsome TD11 77 G5
Whitson NP18 19 G3
**Whitstable CT5 25 H5**
Whitstone EX22 4 C1
Whittingham NE66 71 F2
Whittingslow SY6 38 D7
Whittington *Derbys.* S41 51 F5
Whittington *Glos.* GL54 30 B6
Whittington *Lancs.* LA6 56 B2
Whittington *Norf.* PE33 44 B6
Whittington *Shrop.* SY11 38 C2
Whittington *Staffs.* DY7 40 A7
Whittington *Staffs.* WS14 40 D5
Whittington *Worcs.* WR5 29 H3
Whittlebury NN12 31 H4
Whittle-le-Woods PR6 55 J7
Whittlesey PE7 43 F6
Whittlesford CB22 33 H4
Whittlestone Head BL7 49 G1
Whitton *Gt.Lon.* TW2 22 E4
Whitton *N.Lincs.* DN15 59 F7
Whitton *Northumb.* NE65 71 F3
Whitton *Powys* LD7 28 B2
Whitton *Shrop.* SY8 28 E1
Whitton *Stock.* TS21 62 E4
Whitton *Suff.* IP1 35 F4
Whittonditch SN8 21 F4
Whittonstall DH8 62 B1
Whitway RG20 21 H6
Whitwell *Derbys.* S80 51 H5
Whitwell *Herts.* SG4 32 E6
Whitwell *I.o.W.* PO38 11 G7
Whitwell *N.Yorks.* DL10 62 D7
Whitwell *Rut.* LE15 42 C5
Whitwell Street NR10 45 F3
Whitwell-on-the-Hill YO60 58 D3
Whitwick LE67 41 G4
Whitwood WF10 57 K7
Whitworth OL12 49 H1
Whixall SY13 38 E2
Whixley YO26 57 K4
Whorlton *Dur.* DL12 62 C5
Whorlton *N.Yorks.* DL6 63 F6
Whygate NE48 70 C6
Whyle HR6 28 E2
**Whyteleafe CR3 23 G6**
Wibdon NP16 19 J2
Wibsey BD6 57 G6
Wibtoft LE17 41 G7
Wichenford WR6 29 G2
Wichling ME9 14 E2
Wick *Bourne.* BH6 10 C5
Wick *Devon* EX14 7 K5
**Wick *High.* KW1 105 J3**
Wick *S.Glos.* BS30 20 A4
Wick *Som.* TA5 19 F7
Wick *Som.* BA6 8 E1
Wick *V. of Glam.* CF71 18 C4
Wick *W.Suss.* BN17 12 D6
Wick *Wilts.* SP5 10 C2
Wick *Worcs.* WR10 29 J4
Wick Airport KW1 105 J3
Wick Hill *Kent* TN27 14 D3
Wick Hill *W'ham* RG40 22 A5
Wick St. Lawrence BS22 19 G5
Wicken *Cambs.* CB7 33 J1
Wicken *Northants.* MK19 31 J5

## Wic - Woo

Wicken Bonhunt CB11 33 H5
Wickenby LN3 52 D4
Wicker Street Green CO10 34 D4
Wickerslack CA10 61 H5
Wickersley S66 51 G3
Wicketwood Hill NG4 41 J1
Wickford SS12 24 D2
Wickham Hants. PO17 11 G3
Wickham W.Berks. RG20 21 G4
Wickham Bishops CM8 34 C7
Wickham Heath RG20 21 H5
Wickham Market IP13 35 H3
Wickham St. Paul CO9 34 C5
Wickham Skeith IP23 34 E2
Wickham Street Suff. CB8 34 B3
Wickham Street Suff. IP23 34 E2
Wickhambreaux CT3 15 H2
Wickhambrook CB8 34 B3
Wickhamford WR11 30 B4
Wickhampton NR13 45 J5
Wicklewood NR18 44 E5
Wickmere NR11 45 F2
Wickstreet BN26 13 J6
Wickwar GL12 20 A3
Widcombe BA2 20 A5
Widdington CB11 33 J5
Widdop HX7 56 E6
Widdrington NE61 71 H4
Widdrington Station NE61 71 H4
Wide Open NE13 71 H6
Widecombe in the Moor TQ13 5 H3
Widegates PL13 4 C5
Widemouth Bay EX23 6 A5
Widewall KW17 106 D8
Widford Essex CM2 24 C1
Widford Herts. SG12 33 H7
Widford Oxon. OX18 30 D7
Widgham Green CB8 33 K3
Widmer End HP15 22 B2
Widmerpool NG12 41 J3
Widnes WA8 48 E4
Widworthy EX14 8 B5
WIGAN WN 48 E2
Wiganthorpe YO60 58 C2
Wigborough TA13 8 D3
Wiggaton EX11 7 K6
Wiggenhall St. Germans PE34 43 J4
Wiggenhall St. Mary Magdalen PE34 43 J4
Wiggenhall St. Mary the Virgin PE34 43 J4
Wiggenhall St. Peter PE34 44 A4
Wiggens Green CB9 33 K4
Wigginton Herts. HP23 32 C7
Wigginton Oxon. OX15 30 E5
Wigginton Shrop. SY11 38 C2
Wigginton Staffs. B79 40 E5
Wigginton York YO32 58 C4
Wigglesworth BD23 56 D4
Wiggonby CA7 60 E1
Wiggonholt RH20 12 D5
Wighill LS24 57 K5
Wighton NR23 44 D2
Wightwizzle S36 50 E3
Wigley SO51 10 E3
Wigmore Here. HR6 28 D2
Wigmore Med. ME8 24 E5
Wigsley NG23 52 B5
Wigsthorpe NN14 42 D7
Wigston LE18 41 J6
Wigston Parva LE10 41 G7
Wigthorpe S81 51 H4
Wigtoft PE20 43 F2
Wigton CA7 60 D2
Wigtown DG8 64 E5
Wike LS17 57 J5
Wilbarston LE16 42 B7
Wilberfoss YO41 58 D4
Wilburton CB6 33 H1
Wilby Norf. NR16 44 E6
Wilby Northants. NN8 32 B2
Wilby Suff. IP21 35 G1
Wilcot SN9 20 E5
Wilcott SY4 38 C4
Wilcrick NP26 19 H3
Wilday Green S18 51 F5
Wildboarclough SK11 49 J6
Wilde Street IP28 34 B1
Wilden Bed. MK44 32 D3
Wilden Worcs. DY13 29 H1
Wildhern SP11 21 G6
Wildhill AL9 23 F1
Wildmoor B61 29 J1
Wildsworth DN21 52 B3
Wilford NG11 41 H2
Wilkesley SY13 39 F1
Wilkhaven IV20 97 G3
Wilkieston EH27 75 K4
Wilksby PE22 53 F6
Willand Devon EX15 7 J4
Willand Som. TA3 7 K4
Willaston Ches.E. CW5 49 F7
Willaston Ches.W. & C. CH64 48 C5
Willaston Shrop. SY13 38 E2
Willen MK15 32 B4
Willenhall W.Mid. WV13 40 B6
Willenhall W.Mid. CV3 30 E1
Willerby E.Riding HU10 59 G6
Willerby N.Yorks. YO12 59 G2
Willersey WR12 30 C5
Willersley HR3 28 C4
Willesborough TN24 15 F3
Willesborough Lees TN24 15 F3
Willesden NW10 23 F3
Willesleigh EX32 6 D2
Willesley GL8 20 B3
Willett TA4 7 K2
Willey Shrop. TF12 39 F6
Willey Warks. CV23 41 G7
Willey Green GU3 22 C6
William's Green IP7 34 D4
Williamscot OX17 31 F4
Williamthorpe S42 51 G6
Willian SG6 33 F5
Willimontswick NE47 70 C7
Willingale CM5 23 J1
Willingdon BN20 13 J6
Willingham CB24 33 H1
Willingham by Stow DN21 52 B4
Willingham Green CB8 33 K3
Willington Bed. MK44 32 E3
Willington Derbys. DE65 40 E3
Willington Dur. DL15 62 C3
Willington Kent ME15 14 C2
Willington T. & W. NE28 71 J7
Willington Warks. CV36 30 D5
Willington Corner CW6 48 E6
Willisham IP8 34 E3
Willitoft YO8 58 D6
Williton TA4 7 J1
Willoughbridge TF9 39 G1
Willoughby Lincs. LN13 53 H5
Willoughby Warks. CV23 31 G2
Willoughby Waterleys LE8 41 H6
Willoughby-on-the-Wolds LE12 41 J3
Willoughton DN21 52 C3
Willow Green CW8 49 F5
Willows Green CM3 34 B7
Willsbridge BS30 19 K4
Willslock ST14 40 C2
Willsworthy PL19 6 D7
Willtown TA10 8 C2
Wilmcote CV37 30 C3
Wilmington B. & N.E.Som. BA2 19 K5
Wilmington Devon EX14 8 B4
Wilmington E.Suss. BN26 13 J6
Wilmington Kent DA2 23 J4
Wilmslow SK9 49 H4
Wilnecote B77 40 E5
Wilney Green IP22 44 E7
Wilpshire BB1 56 B6
Wilsden BD15 57 F6
Wilsford Lincs. NG32 42 D1
Wilsford Wilts. SP4 10 C1
Wilsford Wilts. SN9 20 E6
Wilsham EX35 7 F1
Wilshaw HD9 50 D2
Wilsill HG3 57 G3
Wilsley Green TN17 14 C4
Wilsley Pound TN17 14 C4
Wilson DE73 41 G3
Wilstead MK45 32 D4
Wilsthorpe E.Riding YO15 59 H3
Wilsthorpe Lincs. PE9 42 D4
Wilstone HP23 32 C7
Wilton Cumb. CA22 60 B5
Wilton Here. HR9 28 E6
Wilton N.Yorks. YO18 58 E1
Wilton R. & C. TS10 63 G5
Wilton Sc.Bord. TD9 69 K2
Wilton Wilts. SN8 21 F5
Wilton Wilts. SP2 10 B1
Wiltown EX15 7 K4
Wimbish CB10 33 J5
Wimbish Green CB10 33 K5
Wimblebury WS12 40 C4
Wimbledon SW19 23 F4
Wimblington PE15 43 H6
Wimborne Minster BH21 10 B4
Wimborne St. Giles BH21 10 B3
Wimbotsham PE34 44 A5
Wimpole SG8 33 G3
Wimpole Lodge SG8 33 G4
Wimpstone CV37 30 D4
Wincanton BA9 9 G2
Winceby LN9 53 G6
Wincham CW9 49 F5
Winchburgh EH52 75 J3
Winchcombe GL54 30 B6
Winchelsea TN36 14 E6
Winchelsea Beach TN36 14 E6
Winchester SO23 11 F2
Winchet Hill TN17 14 C3
Winchfield RG27 22 A6
Winchmore Hill Bucks. HP7 22 C2
Winchmore Hill Gt.Lon. N21 23 G2
Wincle SK11 49 J6
Wincobank S9 51 F3
Windermere LA23 60 F7
Winderton OX15 30 E4
Windhill IV4 96 C7
Windle Hill CH64 48 C5
Windlehurst SK6 49 J4
Windlesham GU20 22 C5
Windley DE56 41 F1
Windmill SK17 50 D5
Windmill Hill E.Suss. BN27 13 K5
Windmill Hill Som. TA19 8 C3
Windmill Hill Worcs. WR7 29 J4
Windrush OX18 30 C7
Windsor SL4 22 C4
Windsor Green IP30 34 C3
Windy Nook NE10 71 H7
Windygates KY8 82 E7
Windy-Yett KA3 74 C5
Wineham BN5 13 F4
Winestead HU12 59 J7
Winewall BB8 56 E6
Winfarthing IP22 45 F7
Winford I.o.W. PO36 11 G6
Winford N.Som. BS40 19 J5
Winforton HR3 28 B4
Winfrith Newburgh DT2 9 H6
Wing Bucks. LU7 32 B6
Wing Rut. LE15 42 B5
Wingate TS28 62 E3
Wingates Gt.Man. BL5 49 F2
Wingates Northumb. NE65 71 F4
Wingerworth S42 51 F6
Wingfield Cen.Beds. LU7 32 D6
Wingfield Suff. IP21 35 G1
Wingfield Wilts. BA14 20 B6
Wingfield Green IP21 35 G1
Wingham CT3 15 H2
Wingham Well CT3 15 H2
Wingmore CT4 15 G3
Wingrave HP22 32 B7
Winkburn NG22 51 K7
Winkfield SL4 22 C4
Winkfield Row RG42 22 B4
Winkhill ST13 50 C7
Winkleigh EX19 6 E5
Winksley HG4 57 H2
Winkton BH23 10 C5
Winlaton NE21 71 G7
Winlaton Mill NE21 71 G7
Winless KW1 105 J3
Winmarleigh PR3 55 H5
Winnard's Perch TR9 3 G2
Winnersh RG41 22 A4
Winnington CW8 49 F5
Winscombe BS25 19 H6
Winsford Ches.W. & C. CW7 49 F6
Winsford Som. TA24 7 H2
Winsham Devon EX33 6 C2
Winsham Som. TA20 8 C4
Winshill DE15 40 E3
Winsh-wen SA7 17 K6
Winskill CA10 61 G3
Winslade RG25 21 K7
Winsley BA15 20 B5
Winslow MK18 31 J6
Winson GL7 20 D1
Winsor SO40 10 E3
Winster Cumb. LA23 60 F7
Winster Derbys. DE4 50 E6
Winston Dur. DL2 62 C5
Winston Suff. IP14 35 F2
Winston Green IP14 35 F2
Winstone GL7 20 C1
Winswell EX38 6 C4
Winterborne Came DT2 9 G6
Winterborne Clenston DT11 9 H4
Winterborne Herringston DT2 9 F6
Winterborne Houghton DT11 9 H4
Winterborne Kingston DT11 9 H5
Winterborne Monkton DT2 9 F6
Winterborne Stickland DT11 9 H4
Winterborne Whitechurch DT11 9 H4
Winterborne Zelston DT11 9 H5
Winterbourne S.Glos. BS36 19 K3
Winterbourne W.Berks. RG20 21 H4
Winterbourne Abbas DT2 9 F5
Winterbourne Bassett SN4 20 E4
Winterbourne Dauntsey SP4 10 C1
Winterbourne Earls SP4 10 C1
Winterbourne Gunner SP4 10 C1
Winterbourne Monkton SN4 20 E4
Winterbourne Steepleton DT2 9 F6
Winterbourne Stoke SP3 20 D7
Winterbrook OX10 21 K3
Winterburn BD23 56 E4
Wintercleugh ML12 68 E2
Winteringham DN15 59 F7
Winterley CW11 49 G7
Wintersett WF4 51 F1
Wintershill SO32 11 G3
Winterslow SP5 10 D1
Winterton DN15 52 C1
Winterton-on-Sea NR29 45 J4
Winthorpe Lincs. PE25 53 J6
Winthorpe Notts. NG24 52 B7
Winton Bourne. BH9 10 B5
Winton Cumb. CA17 61 J5
Wintringham YO17 58 E2
Winwick Cambs. PE28 42 E7
Winwick Northants. NN6 31 H1
Winwick Warr. WA2 49 F3
Wirksworth DE4 50 E7
Wirksworth Moor DE4 51 F7
Wirswall SY13 38 E1
Wisbech PE13 43 H5
Wisbech St. Mary PE13 43 H5
Wisborough Green RH14 12 D4
Wiseton DN10 51 K4
Wishaw N.Lan. ML2 75 F5
Wishaw Warks. B76 40 D6
Wisley GU23 22 D6
Wispington LN9 53 F5
Wissett IP19 35 H1
Wissington CO6 34 D5
Wistanstow SY7 38 D7
Wistanswick TF9 39 F3
Wistaston CW2 49 F7
Wiston Pembs. SA62 16 D4
Wiston S.Lan. ML12 75 H7
Wistow Cambs. PE28 43 F7
Wistow N.Yorks. YO8 58 B6
Wiswell BB7 56 C6
Witcham CB6 33 H1
Witchampton BH21 9 J4
Witchburn PA28 66 B1
Witchford CB6 33 J1
Witcombe TA12 8 D2
Witham CM8 34 C7
Witham Friary BA11 20 A7
Witham on the Hill PE10 42 D4
Withcall LN11 53 F4
Withcote LE15 42 A5
Withdean BN1 13 G6
Witherenden Hill TN19 13 K4
Witherhurst TN19 13 K4
Witheridge EX16 7 G4
Witherley CV9 41 F6
Withern LN13 53 H4
Withernsea HU19 59 K7
Withernwick HU11 59 H5
Withersdale Street IP20 45 G7
Withersfield CB9 33 K4
Witherslack LA11 55 H1
Witherslack Hall LA11 55 H1
Withiel PL30 3 G2
Withiel Florey TA24 7 H2
Withielgoose PL30 4 A4
Withington Glos. GL54 30 B7
Withington Gt.Man. M20 49 H3
Withington Here. HR1 28 E4
Withington Shrop. SY4 38 E4
Withington Staffs. ST10 40 C2
Withington Green SK11 49 H5
Withington Marsh HR1 28 E4
Withleigh EX16 7 H4
Withnell PR6 56 B7
Withnell Fold PR6 56 B7
Withybrook Som. BA3 19 K7
Withybrook Warks. CV7 41 G7
Withycombe TA24 7 J1
Withycombe Raleigh EX8 7 J7
Withyham TN7 13 H3
Withypool TA24 7 G2
Witley GU8 12 C3
Witnesham IP6 35 F3
Witney OX28 21 G1
Wittering PE8 42 D5
Wittersham TN30 14 D5
Witton Angus DD9 90 D7
Witton Norf. NR13 45 H5
Witton Worcs. WR9 29 H2
Witton Bridge NR28 45 H2
Witton Gilbert DH7 62 D2
Witton Park DL14 62 C3
Witton-le-Wear DL14 62 C3
Wiveliscombe TA4 7 J3
Wivelsfield RH17 13 G4
Wivelsfield Green RH17 13 G5
Wivenhoe CO7 34 E6
Wiveton NR25 44 E1
Wix CO11 35 F6
Wixford B49 30 B3
Wixhill SY4 38 E3
Wixoe CO10 34 B4
Woburn MK17 32 C5
Woburn Sands MK17 32 C5
Wokefield Park RG7 21 K5
Woking GU22 22 D6
Wokingham RG40 22 B5
Wolborough TQ12 5 J3
Wold Newton E.Riding YO25 59 G2
Wold Newton N.E.Lincs. LN8 53 F3
Woldingham CR3 23 G6
Wolfelee TD9 70 A3
Wolferlow HR7 29 F2
Wolferton PE31 44 A3
Wolfhampcote CV23 31 G2
Wolfhill PH2 82 C4
Wolfpits LD8 28 B3
Wolf's Castle SA62 16 C3
Wolfsdale SA62 16 C3
Woll TD7 69 K1
Wollaston Northants. NN29 32 C2
Wollaston Shrop. SY5 38 C4
Wollaston W.Mid. DY8 40 A7
Wollaton NG8 41 H2
Wollerton TF9 39 F3
Wollescote DY9 40 B7
Wolsingham DL13 62 B3
Wolston CV8 31 F1
Wolsty CA7 60 C1
Wolvercote OX2 21 J1
WOLVERHAMPTON WV 40 B6
Wolverley Shrop. SY4 38 D2
Wolverley Worcs. DY11 29 H1
Wolvers Hill BS29 19 G5
Wolverton Hants. RG26 21 J6
Wolverton M.K. MK12 32 B4
Wolverton Warks. CV35 30 D2
Wolverton Wilts. BA12 9 G1
Wolverton Common RG26 21 J6
Wolvesnewton NP16 19 H2
Wolvey LE10 41 G7
Wolvey Heath LE10 41 G7
Wolviston TS22 63 F4
Womaston LD8 28 B2
Wombleton YO62 58 C1
Wombourne WV5 40 A6
Wombwell S73 51 F2
Womenswold CT4 15 H2
Womersley DN6 51 H1
Wonastow NP25 28 D7
Wonersh GU5 22 D7
Wonford EX2 7 H6
Wonson EX20 6 E7
Wonston SO21 11 F1
Wooburn HP10 22 C3
Wooburn Green HP10 22 C3
Wood Bevington B49 30 B3
Wood Burcote NN12 31 H4
Wood Dalling NR11 44 E3
Wood Eaton ST20 40 A4
Wood End Bed. MK43 32 D4
Wood End Bed. MK44 32 D2
Wood End Bucks. MK17 31 J5
Wood End Herts. SG2 33 G6
Wood End W.Mid. WV11 40 B5
Wood End Warks. CV9 40 E6
Wood End Warks. B94 30 C1
Wood End Warks. CV7 40 E7
Wood Enderby PE22 53 F6
Wood Green Essex EN9 23 H1
Wood Green Gt.Lon. N22 23 G2
Wood Green Norf. NR15 45 G6
Wood Lane SY12 38 D2
Wood Norton NR20 44 E3
Wood Seats S35 51 F3
Wood Stanway GL54 30 B5
Wood Street NR29 45 H3
Wood Street Village GU3 22 C6
Woodacott EX22 6 B5
Woodale DL8 57 F2
Woodall S26 51 G4
Woodbastwick NR13 45 H4
Woodbeck DN22 51 K5
Woodborough Notts. NG14 41 J1
Woodborough Wilts. SN9 20 E6
Woodbridge Devon EX24 7 K6
Woodbridge Dorset DT10 9 G3
Woodbridge Suff. IP12 35 G4
Woodbury Devon EX5 7 J7
Woodbury Som. BA5 19 J7
Woodbury Salterton EX5 7 J7
Woodchester GL5 20 B1
Woodchurch Kent TN26 14 E4
Woodchurch Mersey. CH49 48 B4
Woodcombe TA24 7 H1
Woodcote Oxon. RG8 21 K3
Woodcote Tel. & W. TF10 39 G4
Woodcote Green B61 29 J1
Woodcott RG28 21 H6
Woodcroft NP16 19 J2
Woodcutts SP5 9 J3
Woodditton CB8 33 K3
Woodeaton OX3 31 G7
Woodend Aber. AB51 90 E3
Woodend Cumb. CA18 60 C7
Woodend High. IV13 88 E2
Woodend High. PH36 79 J1
Woodend Northants. NN12 31 H4
Woodend P. & K. PH15 81 J3
Woodend W.Suss. PO18 12 B6
Woodend Green CM22 33 J6
Woodfalls SP5 10 C2
Woodfield Oxon. OX26 31 G6
Woodfield S.Ayr. KA8 67 H1
Woodfoot CA10 61 H5
Woodford Cornw. EX23 6 A4
Woodford Devon TQ9 5 H5
Woodford Glos. GL13 19 K2
Woodford Gt.Lon. IG8 23 H2
Woodford Gt.Man. SK7 49 H4
Woodford Northants. NN14 32 C1
Woodford Som. TA4 7 J2
Woodford Bridge IG8 23 H2
Woodford Green IG8 23 H2
Woodford Halse NN11 31 G3
Woodgate Devon EX15 7 K4
Woodgate Norf. NR20 44 E4
Woodgate W.Mid. B32 40 B7
Woodgate W.Suss. PO20 12 C6
Woodgate Worcs. B60 29 J2
Woodgreen SP6 10 C3
Woodhall Inclyde PA14 74 B3
Woodhall N.Yorks. DL8 62 A7
Woodhall Hills LS28 57 G6
Woodhall Spa LN10 52 E6
Woodham Bucks. HP18 31 H7
Woodham Dur. DL17 62 D4
Woodham Surr. KT15 22 D5
Woodham Ferrers CM3 24 D2
Woodham Mortimer CM9 24 E1
Woodham Walter CM9 24 E1
Woodhaven DD6 83 F5
Woodhead Aber. AB53 91 F1
Woodhead Staffs. ST10 40 C1
Woodhey CH42 48 C4
Woodhey Green CW5 48 E7
Woodhill Shrop. WV16 39 G7
Woodhill Som. TA3 8 C2
Woodhorn NE63 71 H5
Woodhouse Cumb. LA7 55 J1
Woodhouse Leics. LE12 41 H4
Woodhouse S.Yorks. S13 51 G4
Woodhouse W.Yorks. LS2 57 H6
Woodhouse W.Yorks. WF6 57 J7
Woodhouse W.Yorks. HD6 57 G7
Woodhouse Down BS32 19 K3
Woodhouse Eaves LE12 41 H4
Woodhouse Green SK11 49 J6
Woodhouses Gt.Man. M35 49 H2
Woodhouses Staffs. DE13 40 D4
Woodhouses Staffs. WS7 40 C5
Woodhuish TQ6 5 K5
Woodhurst PE28 33 G1
Woodingdean BN2 13 G6
Woodington SO51 10 E2
Woodland Devon TQ13 5 H4
Woodland Dur. DL13 62 B4
Woodland Kent CT18 15 G3
Woodland Head EX17 7 F6
Woodlands Dorset BH21 10 B4
Woodlands Hants. SO40 10 E3
Woodlands N.Yorks. HG2 57 J4
Woodlands Shrop. WV16 39 G7
Woodlands Som. TA5 7 K1
Woodlands Park SL6 22 B4
Woodlands St. Mary RG17 21 G4

Woo - Zou

Woodlane DE13 40 D3
Woodleigh TQ7 5 H6
Woodlesford LS26 57 J7
Woodley Gt.Man. SK6 49 J3
Woodley W'ham RG5 22 A4
Woodmancote Glos. GL7 20 D1
Woodmancote Glos. GL52 29 J6
Woodmancote Glos. GL11 20 A2
Woodmancote W.Suss. BN5 13 F5
Woodmancote W.Suss. PO10 11 J4
Woodmancott SO21 21 J7
Woodmansey HU17 59 G6
Woodmansterne SM7 23 F6
Woodmanton EX5 7 J7
Woodmill DE13 40 D3
Woodminton SP5 10 B2
Woodmoor SY15 38 B5
Woodnesborough CT13 15 J2
Woodnewton PE8 42 D6
Woodperry OX33 31 G7
Woodplumpton PR4 55 J6
Woodrising NR9 44 D5
Woodrow DT10 9 G3
Wood's Corner TN21 13 K5
Woods Eaves HR3 28 B4
Wood's Green TN5 13 K3
Woodseaves Shrop. TF9 39 F2
Woodseaves Staffs. ST20 39 G3
Woodsend SN8 21 F4
Woodsetts S81 51 H4
Woodsford DT2 9 G5
Woodside Aberdeen AB24 91 H4
Woodside Brack.F. SL4 22 C4
Woodside Cen.Beds. LU1 32 D7
Woodside Cumb. CA15 60 B3
Woodside D. & G. DG1 69 F6
Woodside Fife KY8 83 F7
Woodside Fife KY7 82 D7
Woodside Gt.Lon. SE25 23 G5
Woodside Hants. SO41 10 E5
Woodside Herts. AL9 23 F1
Woodside N.Ayr. KA15 74 B5
Woodside P. & K. PH13 82 C4
Woodside Shrop. SY7 38 C7
Woodside W.Mid. DY5 40 B7
Woodside Green ME17 14 E2
Woodstock Oxon. OX20 31 F7
Woodstock Pembs. SA63 16 D3
Woodthorpe Derbys. S43 51 G5
Woodthorpe Leics. LE12 41 H4
Woodthorpe Lincs. LN13 53 H4
Woodthorpe S.Yorks. S2 51 F4
Woodton NR35 45 G6
Woodtown EX39 6 C3
Woodvale PR8 48 C1
Woodville DE11 41 F4
Woodwall Green ST21 39 G2
Woodwalton PE28 43 F7
Woodwick KW17 106 C5
Woodworth Green CW6 48 E7
Woodyates SP5 10 B3
Woofferton SY8 28 E2
Wookey BA5 19 J7
Wookey Hole BA5 19 J7
Wool BH20 9 H6
Woolacombe EX34 6 C1
Woolage Green CT4 15 H3
Woolage Village CT4 15 H2
Woolaston GL15 19 J1
Woolaston Slade GL15 19 J1
Woolavington TA7 19 G7
Woolbeding GU29 12 B4
Woolcotts TA22 7 H2
Wooldale HD9 50 D2
Wooler NE71 70 E1
Woolfardisworthy Devon EX17 7 G5
Woolfardisworthy Devon EX39 6 B3
Woolfold BL8 49 G1
Woolfords Cottages EH55 75 J5
Woolgarston BH20 9 J6
Woolgreaves WF2 51 F1
Woolhampton RG7 21 J5
Woolhope HR1 29 F5
Woolland DT11 9 G4
Woollard BS39 19 K5
Woollaton EX38 6 C4
Woollensbrook EN11 23 G1
Woolley B. & N.E.Som. BA1 20 A5
Woolley Cambs. PE28 32 E1
Woolley Cornw. EX23 6 A4
Woolley Derbys. DE55 51 F6
Woolley W.Yorks. WF4 51 F1
Woolley Green W. & M. SL6 22 B4
Woolley Green Wilts. BA15 20 B5
Woolmer Green SG3 33 F7
Woolmere Green B60 29 J2
Woolmersdon TA5 8 B1
Woolpit IP30 34 D2
Woolpit Green IP30 34 D2
Woolscott CV23 31 F2
Woolsgrove EX17 7 F5
Woolstaston SY6 38 D6
Woolsthorpe NG32 42 B2
Woolsthorpe by Colsterworth NG33 42 C3
Woolston Devon TQ7 5 H6
Woolston S'ham. SO19 11 F3
Woolston Shrop. SY10 38 C3
Woolston Shrop. SY6 38 D7
Woolston Warr. WA1 49 F4
Woolston Green TQ13 5 H4
Woolstone Glos. GL52 29 J5
Woolstone M.K. MK15 32 B5
Woolstone Oxon. SN7 21 F3
Woolton L25 48 D4
Woolton Hill RG20 21 H5
Woolverstone IP9 35 F5
Woolverton BA2 20 A6
Woolwich SE18 23 H4
Woonton HR3 28 C3
Wooperton NE66 71 F2
Woore CW3 39 G1
Wootten Green IP21 35 G1
Wootton Bed. MK43 32 D4
Wootton Hants. BH25 10 D5
Wootton I.o.W. PO33 11 G5
Wootton Kent CT4 15 H3
Wootton N.Lincs. DN39 52 D1
Wootton Northants. NN4 31 J3
Wootton Oxon. OX20 31 F7
Wootton Oxon. OX1 21 H1
Wootton Shrop. SY7 28 D1
Wootton Shrop. SY11 38 C3
Wootton Staffs. ST21 40 A3
Wootton Staffs. DE6 40 D1
Wootton Bassett SN4 20 D3
Wootton Bridge PO33 11 G5
Wootton Common PO33 11 G5
Wootton Courtenay TA24 7 H1
Wootton Fitzpaine DT6 8 C5
Wootton Green MK43 32 D4
Wootton Rivers SN8 20 E5
Wootton St. Lawrence RG23 21 J6
Wootton Wawen B95 30 C2
WORCESTER WR 29 H3
Worcester Park KT4 23 F5
Wordsley DY8 40 A7
Wordwell IP28 34 C1
Worfield WV15 39 G6
Worgret BH20 9 J6
Work KW15 106 D6
Workhouse End MK41 32 E3
Workington CA14 60 B4
Worksop S80 51 H5
Worlaby Lincs. LN11 53 G5
Worlaby N.Lincs. DN20 52 D1
World's End Bucks. HP22 22 B1
Worlds End Hants. PO7 11 H3
World's End W.Berks. RG20 21 H4
Worlds End W.Mid. B91 40 D7
Worle BS22 19 G5
Worleston CW5 49 F7
Worlingham NR34 45 J7
Worlington IP28 33 K1
Worlingworth IP13 35 G2
Wormald Green HG3 57 J3
Wormbridge HR2 28 D5
Wormegay PE33 44 A4
Wormelow Tump HR2 28 D5
Wormhill SK17 50 D5
Wormiehills DD11 83 H4
Wormingford CO6 34 D5
Worminghall HP18 21 K1
Wormington WR12 30 B5
Worminster BA4 19 J7
Wormiston KY10 83 H7
Wormit DD6 82 E5
Wormleighton CV47 31 F3
Wormley Herts. EN10 23 G1
Wormley Surr. GU8 12 C3
Wormley West End EN10 23 G1
Wormshill ME9 14 D2
Wormsley HR4 28 D4
Worplesdon GU3 22 C6
Worrall S35 51 F3
Worsbrough S70 51 F2
Worsley M28 49 G2
Worstead NR28 45 H3
Worsted Lodge CB21 33 J3
Worsthorne BB10 56 D6
Worston BB7 56 C5
Worswell PL8 5 F6
Worth Kent CT14 15 J2
Worth W.Suss. RH10 13 F3
Worth Matravers BH19 9 J7
Wortham IP22 34 E1
Worthen SY5 38 C5
Worthenbury LL13 38 D1
Worthing Norf. NR20 44 D4
Worthing W.Suss. BN11 12 E6
Worthington LE65 41 G3
Worting RG23 21 K6
Wortley Glos. GL12 20 A2
Wortley S.Yorks. S35 51 F3
Wortley W.Yorks. LS12 57 H6
Worton N.Yorks. DL8 56 E1
Worton Wilts. SN10 20 C6
Wortwell IP20 45 G7
Wothersome LS23 57 K5
Wotherton SY15 38 B5
Wotter PL7 5 F4
Wotton RH5 22 E7
Wotton Underwood HP18 31 H7
Wotton-under-Edge GL12 20 A2
Woughton on the Green MK6 32 B5
Wouldham ME1 24 D5
Wrabness CO11 35 F5
Wrae AB53 99 F5
Wrafton EX33 6 C2
Wragby LN8 52 E5
Wragholme LN11 53 G3
Wramplingham NR18 45 F5
Wrangaton PL21 5 G5
Wrangham AB52 90 E1
Wrangle PE22 53 H7
Wrangle Lowgate PE22 53 H7
Wrangway TA21 7 K4
Wrantage TA3 8 C2
Wrawby DN20 52 D2
Wraxall N.Som. BS48 19 H4
Wraxall Som. BA4 9 F1
Wray LA2 56 B3
Wray Castle LA22 60 E6
Wrays RH6 23 F7
Wraysbury TW19 22 D4
Wrayton LA6 56 B2
Wrea Green PR4 55 G6
Wreay Cumb. CA11 60 F4
Wreay Cumb. CA4 60 F2
Wrecclesham GU10 22 B7
Wrecsam (Wrexham) LL13 38 C1
Wrekenton NE9 62 D1
Wrelton YO18 58 D1
Wrenbury CW5 38 E1
Wrench Green YO13 59 F1
Wreningham NR16 45 F6
Wrentham NR34 45 J7
Wrenthorpe WF2 57 J7
Wrentnall SY5 38 D5
Wressle E.Riding YO8 58 D6
Wressle N.Lincs. DN20 52 C2
Wrestlingworth SG19 33 F4
Wretham IP24 44 D6
Wretton PE33 44 A5
Wrexham (Wrecsam) LL13 38 C1
Wrexham Industrial Estate LL13 38 C1
Wribbenhall DY12 29 G1
Wrightington Bar WN6 48 E1
Wrightpark FK8 74 E1
Wright's Green CM22 33 J7
Wrinehill CW3 39 G1
Wrington BS40 19 H5
Writhlington BA3 19 K6
Writtle CM1 24 C1
Wrockwardine TF6 39 F4
Wroot DN9 51 K2
Wrose BD18 57 G6
Wrotham TN15 23 K6
Wrotham Heath TN15 23 K6
Wrotham Hill Park TN15 24 C5
Wrottesley WV8 40 A5
Wroughton SN4 20 E3
Wroxall I.o.W. PO38 11 G7
Wroxall Warks. CV35 30 D1
Wroxeter SY5 38 E5
Wroxham NR12 45 H4
Wroxton OX15 31 F4
Wstrws SA44 17 G1
Wyaston DE6 40 D1
Wyberton PE21 43 G1
Wyboston MK44 32 E3
Wybunbury CW5 39 F1
Wych Cross RH18 13 H3
Wychbold WR9 29 J2
Wychnor DE13 40 D4
Wychnor Bridges DE13 40 D4
Wyck GU34 11 J1
Wyck Rissington GL54 30 C6
Wycliffe DL12 62 C5
Wycoller BB8 56 E6
Wycomb LE14 42 A3
Wycombe Marsh HP11 22 B2
Wyddial SG9 33 G5
Wye TN25 15 F3
Wyesham NP25 28 E7
Wyfordby LE14 42 A4
Wyke Devon EX17 7 G6
Wyke Dorset SP8 9 G2
Wyke Shrop. TF13 39 F5
Wyke Surr. GU3 22 C6
Wyke W.Yorks. BD12 57 G7
Wyke Champflower BA10 9 F1
Wyke Regis DT4 9 F7
Wykeham N.Yorks. YO13 59 F1
Wykeham N.Yorks. YO17 58 E2
Wyken Shrop. WV15 39 G6
Wyken W.Mid. CV2 41 F7
Wykey SY4 38 C3
Wylam NE41 71 G7
Wylde Green B72 40 D6
Wyllie NP12 18 E2
Wylye BA12 10 B1
Wymering PO6 11 H4
Wymeswold LE12 41 J3
Wymington NN10 32 C2
Wymondham Leics. LE14 42 B4
Wymondham Norf. NR18 45 F5
Wyndham CF32 18 C2
Wynford Eagle DT2 8 E5
Wynnstay Park LL14 38 C1
Wynyard TS22 63 F4
Wyre Piddle WR10 29 J4
Wyresdale Tower LA2 56 B4
Wysall NG12 41 J3
Wyson SY8 28 E2
Wythall B47 30 B1
Wytham OX2 21 H1
Wythburn CA12 60 E5
Wythenshawe M22 49 H4
Wyton Cambs. PE28 33 F1
Wyton E.Riding HU11 59 H6
Wyverstone IP14 34 E2
Wyverstone Street IP14 34 E2
Wyville NG32 42 B3
Wyvis Lodge IV16 96 B4

## Y

Y Bala (Bala) LL23 37 J2
Y Bryn LL23 37 H3
Y Drenewydd (Newtown) SY16 38 A6
Y Fali (Valley) LL65 46 A5
Y Fan SY18 37 J7
Y Felin Newydd (New Mills) SY16 37 K5
Y Felinheli LL56 46 D6
Y Fenni (Abergavenny) NP7 28 B7
Y Fflint (Flint) CH6 48 B5
Y Ffôr LL53 36 C2
Y Fron (Upper Llandwrog) LL54 46 D7
Y Gelli Gandryll (Hay-on-Wye) HR3 28 B4
Y Trallwng (Welshpool) SY21 38 B5
Y Tymbl (Tumble) SA14 17 J4
Y Waun (Chirk) LL14 38 B2
Yaddlethorpe DN17 52 B2
Yafford PO30 11 F6
Yafforth DL7 62 E7
Yalberton TQ4 5 J5
Yalding ME18 23 K7
Yanley BS41 19 J5
Yanwath CA10 61 G4
Yanworth GL54 30 B7
Yapham YO42 58 D4
Yapton BN18 12 C6
Yarburgh LN11 53 G3
Yarcombe EX14 8 B4
Yardley B25 40 D7
Yardley Gobion NN12 31 J4
Yardley Hastings NN7 32 B3
Yardro LD8 28 B3
Yarford TA2 8 B2
Yarkhill HR1 29 F4
Yarlet ST18 40 B3
Yarley BA5 19 J7
Yarlington BA9 9 F2
Yarm TS15 63 F5
Yarmouth PO41 10 E6
Yarnacott EX32 6 E2
Yarnbrook BA14 20 B6
Yarnfield ST15 40 A2
Yarnscombe EX31 6 D3
Yarnton OX5 31 F7
Yarpole HR6 28 D2
Yarrow Sc.Bord. TD7 69 J1
Yarrow Som. TA9 19 G7
Yarrow Feus TD7 69 J1
Yarrowford TD7 69 K1
Yarsop HR4 28 D4
Yarwell PE8 42 D6
Yate BS37 20 A3
Yatehouse Green CW10 49 G6
Yateley GU46 22 B5
Yatesbury SN11 20 D4
Yattendon RG18 21 J4
Yatton Here. HR6 28 D2
Yatton N.Som. BS49 19 H5
Yatton Keynell SN14 20 B4
Yaverland PO36 11 H6
Yawl DT7 8 C5
Yaxham NR19 44 E4
Yaxley Cambs. PE7 42 E6
Yaxley Suff. IP23 35 F1
Yazor HR4 28 D4
Yeabridge TA13 8 D3
Yeading UB4 22 E3
Yeadon LS19 57 H5
Yealand Conyers LA5 55 J2
Yealand Redmayne LA5 55 J2
Yealand Storrs LA5 55 J2
Yealmbridge PL8 5 F5
Yealmpton PL8 5 F5
Yearby TS11 63 H4
Yearsley YO61 58 B2
Yeaton SY4 38 D4
Yeaveley DE6 40 D1
Yeavering NE71 77 H7
Yedingham YO17 58 E2
Yelford OX29 21 G1
Yell ZE2 107 N4
Yelland Devon EX31 6 C2
Yelland Devon EX20 6 D6
Yelling PE19 33 F2
Yelvertoft NN6 31 G1
Yelverton Devon PL20 5 F4
Yelverton Norf. NR14 45 G5
Yenston BA8 9 G2
Yeo Mill EX36 7 G3
Yeo Vale EX39 6 C3
Yeoford EX17 7 F6
Yeolmbridge PL15 6 B7
Yeomadon EX22 6 B5
Yeovil BA20 8 E3
Yeovil Marsh BA21 8 E3
Yeovilton BA22 8 E2
Yerbeston SA68 16 D5
Yesnaby KW16 106 B6
Yetholm Mains TD5 70 D1
Yetlington NE66 71 F2
Yetminster DT9 8 E3
Yettington EX9 7 J7
Yetts o'Muckhart FK14 82 B7
Yew Green CV35 30 D2
Yielden MK44 32 D2
Yieldshields ML8 75 G5
Ynys LL47 36 E2
Ynys Enlli (Bardsey Island) LL53 36 A3
Ynys Môn (Anglesey) LL 46 B4
Ynys Tachwedd SY24 37 F6
Ynysboeth CF45 18 D2
Ynysddu NP11 18 E2
Ynyshir CF39 18 D2
Ynyslas SY24 37 F6
Ynysmaerdy CF72 18 D3
Ynysmeudwy SA8 18 A1
Ynystawe SA6 17 K5
Ynyswen CF42 18 C2
Ynysybwl CF37 18 D2
Yockenthwaite BD23 56 E2
Yockleton SY5 38 C4
Yokefleet DN14 58 E7
Yoker G14 74 D4
Yonder Bognie AB54 98 E6
YORK YO 58 C4
Yorkletts CT5 25 G5
Yorkley GL15 19 K1
Yorton SY4 38 E3
Yorton Heath SY4 38 E3
Youldon EX22 6 B5
Youldonmoor Cross EX22 6 B5
Youlgreave DE45 50 E6
Youlthorpe YO41 58 D4
Youlton YO61 57 K3
Young's End CM3 34 B7
Yoxall DE13 40 D4
Yoxford IP17 35 H2
Yr Wyddgrug (Mold) CH7 48 B6
Ysbyty Cynfyn SY23 27 G1
Ysbyty Ifan LL24 37 H1
Ysbyty Ystwyth SY25 27 G1
Ysceifiog CH8 47 K5
Ysgubor-y-coed SY20 37 F6
Ystalyfera SA9 18 A1
Ystrad CF41 18 C2
Ystrad Aeron SA48 26 E3
Ystrad Meurig SY25 27 G2
Ystrad Mynach CF82 18 E2
Ystradfellte CF44 27 J7
Ystradffin SA20 27 G4
Ystradgynlais SA9 27 G7
Ystradowen Carmar. SA9 27 G7
Ystradowen V. of Glam. CF71 18 D4
Ystumtuen SY23 27 G1
Ythanwells AB54 90 E1
Ythsie AB41 91 G1

## Z

Zeal Monachorum EX17 7 F5
Zeals BA12 9 G1
Zelah TR4 3 F3
Zennor TR26 2 B5
Zouch LE12 41 H3

# INDEX TO NORTHERN IRELAND

**Administrative area abbreviations**

| | | | | | | | |
|---|---|---|---|---|---|---|---|
| *B'mena.* | Ballymena | *Cooks.* | Cookstown | *Dungan.* | Dungannon | *Maghera.* | Magherafelt |
| *Banbr.* | Banbridge | *Craig.* | Craigavon | *Ferm.* | Fermanagh | *New. & M.* | Newry & Mourne |
| | | | | | | *Newtown.* | Newtownabbey |
| | | | | | | *Strab.* | Strabane |

## A

| | | |
|---|---|---|
| Acton BT35 | 109 | G6 |
| Aghadowey BT51 | 109 | F2 |
| Aghagallon BT67 | 109 | G5 |
| Aghalee BT67 | 109 | G5 |
| Aghanloo BT49 | 108 | E2 |
| Ahoghill BT42 | 109 | G3 |
| Aldergrove BT29 | 109 | G5 |
| Annaclone BT32 | 109 | G6 |
| Annahilt BT26 | 109 | H6 |
| Annalong BT34 | 109 | H8 |
| Annsborough BT31 | 109 | H7 |
| **Antrim** BT41 | 109 | G4 |
| Ardboe BT80 | 109 | F5 |
| Ardglass BT30 | 109 | J7 |
| Ardmillan BT23 | 109 | J5 |
| Ardstraw BT78 | 108 | C4 |
| **Armagh** BT60 | 109 | F6 |
| Armoy BT53 | 109 | G2 |
| Arney BT92 | 108 | C7 |
| Articlave BT51 | 108 | E2 |
| Artigarvan BT82 | 108 | C3 |
| Attical BT34 | 109 | H8 |
| Aughamullan BT71 | 109 | F5 |
| **Augher** BT77 | 108 | D6 |
| **Aughnacloy** BT69 | 108 | E6 |

## B

| | | |
|---|---|---|
| Ballinamallard BT94 | 108 | C6 |
| Ballintoy BT54 | 109 | G1 |
| Ballybogy BT53 | 109 | F2 |
| Ballycarry BT38 | 109 | J4 |
| Ballycassidy BT94 | 108 | C6 |
| **Ballycastle** BT54 | 109 | G1 |
| **Ballyclare** BT39 | 109 | H4 |
| Ballyeaston BT39 | 109 | H4 |
| Ballygalley BT40 | 109 | H3 |
| Ballygawley BT70 | 108 | E6 |
| Ballygowan BT23 | 109 | J5 |
| Ballyhalbert BT22 | 109 | K5 |
| Ballyhoe Bridge BT53 | 109 | G2 |
| Ballyholme BT20 | 109 | J4 |
| Ballyhornan BT30 | 109 | J7 |
| Ballykeel BT25 | 109 | H6 |
| Ballykelly BT49 | 108 | E2 |
| Ballykinler BT30 | 109 | J7 |
| Ballyleny BT61 | 109 | F6 |
| Ballyloughbeg BT57 | 109 | F2 |
| Ballymackilroy BT70 | 108 | E6 |
| Ballymagorry BT82 | 108 | C3 |
| Ballymartin BT34 | 109 | H8 |
| **Ballymena** BT43 | 109 | G3 |
| **Ballymoney** BT53 | 109 | F2 |
| Ballynahatty BT78 | 108 | D5 |
| **Ballynahinch** BT24 | 109 | H6 |
| Ballynakilly BT71 | 109 | F5 |
| Ballynamallaght BT82 | 108 | D4 |
| Ballyneaner BT82 | 108 | D3 |
| Ballynoe BT30 | 109 | J7 |
| Ballynure BT39 | 109 | H4 |
| Ballyrobert BT39 | 109 | H4 |
| Ballyronan BT45 | 109 | F4 |
| Ballyroney BT32 | 109 | H7 |
| Ballystrudder BT40 | 109 | J4 |
| Ballyvoy BT54 | 109 | G1 |
| Ballywalter BT22 | 109 | K5 |
| Ballyward BT31 | 109 | H7 |
| Balnamore BT53 | 109 | F2 |
| **Banbridge** BT32 | 109 | G6 |
| **Bangor** BT20 | 109 | J4 |
| Bannfoot BT66 | 109 | F5 |
| Belcoo BT93 | 108 | B7 |
| **BELFAST** BT | | |
| Belfast City Airport BT3 | 109 | H5 |
| Belfast International Airport BT29 | 109 | G4 |
| Bellaghy BT45 | 109 | F4 |
| Bellanaleck BT92 | 108 | C7 |
| Belleek *Ferm.* BT93 | 108 | A6 |
| Belleek *New. & M.* BT35 | 109 | J4 |
| Belmont BT38 | 109 | J4 |
| Benburb BT71 | 109 | F6 |
| Bendooragh BT53 | 109 | F2 |
| Beragh BT79 | 108 | D5 |
| Bessbrook BT35 | 109 | G7 |
| Blackwatertown BT71 | 109 | F6 |
| Blaney BT93 | 108 | B6 |
| Bleary BT63 | 109 | G6 |
| Boho BT74 | 108 | B6 |
| Bolea BT49 | 108 | E2 |
| Bovedy BT51 | 109 | F3 |
| Boviel BT47 | 108 | E3 |
| Bready BT82 | 108 | C3 |
| Brookeborough BT94 | 108 | C6 |
| Broughshane BT42 | 109 | G3 |
| Bryansford BT33 | 109 | H7 |
| Burnside BT39 | 109 | H4 |
| Burren BT34 | 109 | G7 |
| **Bushmills** BT57 | 109 | F1 |
| Butterlope BT79 | 108 | D4 |

## C

| | | |
|---|---|---|
| Caddy BT41 | 109 | G4 |
| **Caledon** BT68 | 108 | E6 |
| Camlough BT35 | 109 | G7 |
| Cappagh BT70 | 108 | E5 |
| Cargan BT43 | 109 | G3 |
| Carland BT71 | 108 | E5 |
| Carncastle BT40 | 109 | H3 |
| Carnduff BT54 | 109 | G1 |
| Carnlough BT44 | 109 | H3 |

| | | |
|---|---|---|
| Carnteel BT69 | 108 | E6 |
| **Carrickfergus** BT38 | 109 | J4 |
| Carrickmore BT79 | 108 | E5 |
| Carryduff BT8 | 109 | H5 |
| Castlecaulfield BT70 | 108 | E5 |
| Castledawson BT45 | 109 | F4 |
| **Castlederg** BT81 | 108 | C4 |
| Castlereagh BT6 | 109 | H5 |
| Castlerock BT51 | 108 | E2 |
| Castleroe BT51 | 109 | F2 |
| **Castlewellan** BT31 | 109 | H7 |
| Chapeltown BT41 | 109 | G4 |
| Charlemont BT71 | 109 | F6 |
| Church Ballee BT30 | 109 | J6 |
| Church Hill BT93 | 108 | B6 |
| Churchtown BT30 | 109 | J6 |
| City of Derry Airport BT47 | 108 | D2 |
| Clabby BT75 | 108 | D6 |
| Clady *Maghera.* BT44 | 109 | F3 |
| Clady *Strab.* BT82 | 108 | C4 |
| Clady Milltown BT60 | 109 | F7 |
| Clanabogan BT78 | 108 | D5 |
| Clare BT62 | 109 | G6 |
| Claudy BT47 | 108 | D3 |
| Clogh BT44 | 109 | G3 |
| Cloghcor BT82 | 108 | C3 |
| **Clogher** BT76 | 108 | D6 |
| Cloghy BT22 | 109 | K6 |
| Clonelly BT93 | 108 | B5 |
| Clonoe BT71 | 109 | F5 |
| Clough BT30 | 109 | J6 |
| Cloughmills BT44 | 109 | G3 |
| Cloughreagh BT35 | 109 | G7 |
| Cloyfin BT52 | 109 | F2 |
| Coagh BT80 | 109 | F5 |
| Coalisland BT71 | 109 | F5 |
| **Coleraine** BT52 | 109 | F2 |
| Comber BT23 | 109 | J5 |
| Conlig BT23 | 109 | J5 |
| **Cookstown** BT80 | 109 | F5 |
| Cooneen BT75 | 108 | D6 |
| Corkey BT44 | 109 | G2 |
| Cox's Hill BT62 | 109 | F6 |
| Craig BT47 | 108 | D4 |
| Craigantlet BT23 | 109 | J5 |
| Craigavole BT51 | 109 | F3 |
| **Craigavon** BT65 | 109 | G6 |
| Craigdarragh BT47 | 108 | D3 |
| Craigs BT42 | 109 | G3 |
| Cranagh BT79 | 108 | D4 |
| Creagh BT94 | 108 | C7 |
| Creggan *New. & M.* BT35 | 109 | F8 |
| Creggan *Omagh* BT79 | 108 | E5 |
| Crilly BT69 | 108 | E6 |
| Cromkill BT42 | 109 | G4 |
| Crossgar BT30 | 109 | J6 |
| Crossmaglen BT35 | 109 | F8 |
| **Crumlin** BT29 | 109 | G5 |
| Culcavy BT26 | 109 | H5 |
| Culkey BT92 | 108 | C6 |
| Cullaville BT35 | 109 | F8 |
| Cullybackey BT42 | 109 | G3 |
| Cullyhanna BT35 | 109 | F7 |
| Culmore BT48 | 108 | D2 |
| Culnady BT46 | 109 | F3 |
| Curragh BT23 | 109 | J6 |
| Curran BT45 | 109 | F4 |
| Cushendall BT44 | 109 | H2 |
| Cushendun BT44 | 109 | H2 |

## D

| | | |
|---|---|---|
| Damhead BT52 | 109 | F2 |
| Darkley BT60 | 109 | F7 |
| Darragh Cross BT30 | 109 | J6 |
| Derry (Londonderry) BT48 | 108 | D3 |
| Derrychrin BT80 | 109 | F5 |
| Derrygonnelly BT93 | 108 | B6 |
| Derrylin BT92 | 108 | C7 |
| Derrymacash BT66 | 109 | G5 |
| Derrytrasna BT66 | 109 | F5 |
| Dervock BT53 | 109 | F2 |
| Desertmartin BT45 | 109 | F4 |
| Doagh BT39 | 109 | H4 |
| Dollingstown BT66 | 109 | G6 |
| Donagh BT92 | 108 | C7 |
| **Donaghadee** BT21 | 109 | J5 |
| Donaghcloney BT66 | 109 | G6 |
| Donaghmore BT70 | 108 | E5 |
| Donemana BT82 | 108 | D3 |
| Downhill BT51 | 108 | E2 |
| **Downpatrick** BT30 | 109 | J6 |
| Draperstown BT45 | 108 | E4 |
| Dromara BT25 | 109 | H6 |
| **Dromore** *Banbr.* BT25 | 109 | H6 |
| Dromore *Omagh* BT78 | 108 | C5 |
| Drumahoe BT47 | 108 | D3 |
| Drumaness BT24 | 109 | H6 |
| Drumaroad BT31 | 109 | H6 |
| Drumbo BT27 | 109 | H5 |
| Drumcard BT92 | 108 | B7 |
| Drumduff BT78 | 108 | C5 |
| Drumlegagh BT78 | 108 | C4 |
| Drummacrabranagher BT92 | 108 | C7 |
| Drumnakilly BT79 | 108 | D5 |
| Drumquin BT78 | 108 | C5 |
| Drumsurn BT49 | 108 | E3 |
| Dunaghy BT53 | 109 | F2 |
| Dundonald BT16 | 109 | J5 |
| Dundrod BT29 | 109 | H5 |
| Dundrum BT33 | 109 | J7 |
| **Dungannon** BT70 | 108 | E5 |
| Dungiven BT47 | 108 | E3 |

| | | |
|---|---|---|
| Dunloy BT44 | 109 | G3 |
| Dunmurry BT17 | 109 | H5 |
| Dunnamore BT80 | 108 | E4 |
| Dyan BT68 | 108 | E6 |

## E

| | | |
|---|---|---|
| Eden BT38 | 109 | J4 |
| Ederny BT93 | 108 | C5 |
| Eglinton BT47 | 108 | D2 |
| Eglish BT70 | 108 | E6 |
| **Enniskillen** BT74 | 108 | C6 |
| Ervey Cross Roads BT47 | 108 | D3 |
| Eshnadarragh BT92 | 108 | D7 |
| Eskragh BT78 | 108 | D6 |

## F

| | | |
|---|---|---|
| Feeny BT47 | 108 | E3 |
| Fintona BT78 | 108 | D5 |
| Finvoy BT53 | 109 | F3 |
| **Fivemiletown** BT75 | 108 | D6 |
| Foreglen BT47 | 108 | E3 |
| Forkhill BT35 | 109 | G8 |

## G

| | | |
|---|---|---|
| Gamblestown BT66 | 109 | G6 |
| Garrison BT93 | 108 | A6 |
| Garvagh BT51 | 109 | F3 |
| Garvaghy BT70 | 108 | D5 |
| Garvary BT74 | 108 | C6 |
| Gilford BT63 | 109 | G6 |
| Glarryford BT44 | 109 | G3 |
| Glebe BT82 | 108 | C4 |
| Glenanne BT60 | 109 | F7 |
| Glenariff BT44 | 109 | H2 |
| Glenarm BT44 | 109 | H3 |
| Glenavy BT29 | 109 | G5 |
| Glengormley BT36 | 109 | H4 |
| Glenhead BT49 | 108 | E3 |
| Glenhull BT79 | 108 | E4 |
| Glenoe BT40 | 109 | H4 |
| Glynn BT40 | 109 | J4 |
| Gortaclare BT79 | 108 | D5 |
| Gortin BT79 | 108 | D4 |
| Gortnahey BT47 | 108 | E3 |
| Gracehill BT42 | 109 | G3 |
| Grange Corner BT41 | 109 | G4 |
| Granville BT70 | 108 | E5 |
| Greencastle BT79 | 108 | D4 |
| Greenisland BT38 | 109 | H4 |
| Greyabbey BT22 | 109 | J5 |
| Greysteel BT47 | 108 | D2 |
| Groomsport BT19 | 109 | J4 |
| Gulladuff BT45 | 109 | F4 |

## H

| | | |
|---|---|---|
| Hamilton's Bawn BT60 | 109 | F6 |
| Hannahstown BT17 | 109 | H5 |
| Helen's Bay BT19 | 109 | J4 |
| Hillhall BT27 | 109 | H5 |
| **Hillsborough** BT26 | 109 | H6 |
| Hilltown BT34 | 109 | H7 |
| Holywell BT93 | 108 | B7 |
| **Holywood** BT18 | 109 | J5 |

## I

| | | |
|---|---|---|
| Inishrush BT44 | 109 | F3 |
| Irvinestown BT94 | 108 | C6 |

## J

| | | |
|---|---|---|
| Jonesborough BT35 | 109 | G8 |

## K

| | | |
|---|---|---|
| Katesbridge BT32 | 109 | H6 |
| Keady BT60 | 109 | F7 |
| Kearney BT22 | 109 | K6 |
| Keeran BT93 | 108 | C5 |
| Kells BT42 | 109 | G4 |
| Kesh BT93 | 108 | B5 |
| Kilcoo BT34 | 109 | H7 |
| Kilkeel BT34 | 109 | H8 |
| Killadeas BT94 | 108 | C6 |
| Killagan Bridge BT44 | 109 | G2 |
| Killen BT81 | 108 | C4 |
| Killeter BT81 | 108 | C4 |
| Killinchy BT23 | 109 | J5 |
| Killough BT30 | 109 | J7 |
| Killowen BT34 | 109 | G8 |
| Killyclogher BT79 | 108 | D5 |
| Killylea BT60 | 109 | F6 |
| Killyleagh BT30 | 109 | J6 |
| Kilmood BT23 | 109 | J5 |
| Kilmore BT30 | 109 | J6 |
| Kilraghts BT53 | 109 | G2 |
| Kilroa BT71 | 109 | F3 |
| Kilskeery BT78 | 108 | C6 |
| Kilwaughter BT40 | 109 | H3 |
| Kinallen BT25 | 109 | H6 |
| Kircubbin BT22 | 109 | J5 |
| Kirkistown BT22 | 109 | K6 |
| Knockcloghrim BT45 | 109 | F4 |
| Knocknacarry BT44 | 109 | H2 |

## L

| | | |
|---|---|---|
| Lack BT93 | 108 | C5 |
| Lackagh BT49 | 108 | E3 |
| Lagavara BT54 | 109 | G1 |

| | | |
|---|---|---|
| Laghy Corner BT71 | 109 | F5 |
| **Larne** BT40 | 109 | H3 |
| Laurelvale BT62 | 109 | G6 |
| Lawrencetown BT63 | 109 | G6 |
| Leggs BT93 | 108 | B5 |
| Leitrim BT31 | 109 | H7 |
| Letter BT93 | 108 | B5 |
| Letterbreen BT74 | 108 | B6 |
| Lettershendony BT47 | 108 | D3 |
| Ligoniel BT14 | 109 | H5 |
| **Limavady** BT49 | 108 | E2 |
| Lisbane BT23 | 109 | J5 |
| Lisbellaw BT94 | 108 | C6 |
| **Lisburn** BT28 | 109 | H5 |
| Liscloon BT82 | 108 | D3 |
| Liscolman BT53 | 109 | F2 |
| Lislea BT44 | 109 | F3 |
| Lisnarrick BT94 | 108 | B6 |
| Lisnaskea BT92 | 108 | C7 |
| Lissan BT80 | 108 | E4 |
| Listooder BT30 | 109 | J6 |
| Loanends BT29 | 109 | H4 |
| **Londonderry (Derry)** BT48 | 108 | D3 |
| Loughbrickland BT32 | 109 | G6 |
| Loughgall BT61 | 109 | F6 |
| Loughguile BT44 | 109 | G2 |
| Loughinisland BT30 | 109 | J6 |
| Loughmacrory BT79 | 108 | D5 |
| Lower Ballinderry BT28 | 109 | G5 |
| **Lurgan** BT66 | 109 | G6 |
| Lurganare BT34 | 109 | G7 |

## M

| | | |
|---|---|---|
| McGregor's Corner BT43 | 109 | G3 |
| Mackan BT92 | 108 | C7 |
| Macosquin BT51 | 109 | F2 |
| Maghaberry BT67 | 109 | G5 |
| Maghera *Down* BT31 | 109 | H7 |
| **Maghera** *Maghera.* BT46 | 109 | F3 |
| **Magherafelt** BT45 | 109 | F4 |
| Magheralin BT67 | 109 | G6 |
| Magheramason BT47 | 108 | C3 |
| Magheraveely BT92 | 108 | D7 |
| Maghery BT71 | 109 | F5 |
| Magilligan BT49 | 108 | E2 |
| Maguiresbridge BT94 | 108 | C7 |
| Mallusk BT36 | 109 | H4 |
| Markethill BT60 | 109 | F7 |
| Martinstown BT43 | 109 | G3 |
| Mayobridge BT34 | 109 | G7 |
| May's Corner BT32 | 109 | G7 |
| Mazetown BT28 | 109 | H5 |
| Meigh BT35 | 109 | G7 |
| Middletown BT60 | 108 | E7 |
| Mill Town BT41 | 109 | G4 |
| Millbay BT40 | 109 | J4 |
| Millbrook BT40 | 109 | H3 |
| Millford BT60 | 109 | F6 |
| Millisle BT22 | 109 | J5 |
| Milltown *Banbr.* BT32 | 109 | G7 |
| Milltown *Craig.* BT62 | 109 | F5 |
| Minerstown BT30 | 109 | J7 |
| Moira BT67 | 109 | G5 |
| Monea BT74 | 108 | B6 |
| Moneydig BT51 | 109 | F3 |
| Moneyglass BT41 | 109 | G4 |
| Moneymore BT45 | 109 | F4 |
| Moneyneany BT45 | 109 | F4 |
| Moneyreagh BT23 | 109 | J5 |
| Moneyslane BT31 | 109 | H7 |
| Monteith BT32 | 109 | G6 |
| Moorfields BT42 | 109 | G4 |
| Moortown BT80 | 109 | F5 |
| Mossley BT36 | 109 | H4 |
| Moss-side BT53 | 109 | G2 |
| Mount Hamilton BT79 | 108 | E4 |
| Mount Norris BT60 | 109 | F7 |
| Mountfield BT79 | 108 | D5 |
| Mountjoy *Dungan.* BT71 | 109 | F5 |
| Mountjoy *Omagh* BT78 | 108 | D5 |
| Moy BT71 | 109 | F6 |
| Moyarget BT54 | 109 | G2 |
| Moygashel BT71 | 109 | F5 |
| Mullaghbane BT35 | 109 | F8 |
| Mullaghmassa BT79 | 108 | D5 |
| Mullan BT92 | 108 | B7 |
| Murley BT75 | 108 | D6 |

## N

| | | |
|---|---|---|
| New Buildings BT47 | 108 | D3 |
| New Ferry BT45 | 109 | F4 |
| **Newcastle** BT33 | 109 | H7 |
| Newmill BT39 | 109 | H4 |
| Newmills BT71 | 109 | F5 |
| **Newry** BT34 | 109 | G7 |
| Newtown Crommelin BT43 | 109 | G3 |
| **Newtownabbey** BT36 | 109 | H4 |
| **Newtownards** BT23 | 109 | J5 |
| Newtownbutler BT92 | 108 | D7 |
| Newtownhamilton BT35 | 109 | F7 |
| Newtownstewart BT78 | 108 | D4 |
| Nutt's Corner BT29 | 109 | H5 |

## O

| | | |
|---|---|---|
| **Omagh** BT79 | 108 | D5 |
| Oritor BT80 | 108 | E5 |

## P

| | | |
|---|---|---|
| Park BT47 | 108 | D3 |
| Parkgate BT39 | 109 | H4 |

| | | |
|---|---|---|
| Pettigo BT93 | 108 | B5 |
| Plumbridge BT79 | 108 | D4 |
| Pomeroy BT70 | 108 | E5 |
| Portadown BT62 | 109 | G6 |
| Portaferry BT22 | 109 | J6 |
| Portavogie BT22 | 109 | K6 |
| Portballintrae BT57 | 109 | F1 |
| Portglenone BT44 | 109 | F3 |
| **Portrush** BT56 | 109 | F1 |
| **Portstewart** BT55 | 109 | F2 |
| Poyntz Pass BT35 | 109 | F7 |
| Prehen BT47 | 108 | D3 |

## R

| | | |
|---|---|---|
| Raffrey BT30 | 109 | J6 |
| Raholp BT30 | 109 | J6 |
| Randalstown BT41 | 109 | G4 |
| Rathfriland BT34 | 109 | G7 |
| Ravernet BT27 | 109 | H5 |
| Richhill BT61 | 109 | F6 |
| Ringboy BT22 | 109 | K6 |
| Ringsend BT51 | 109 | F2 |
| Riverside BT34 | 109 | H8 |
| Rosscor BT93 | 108 | A6 |
| Rosslea BT92 | 108 | D7 |
| Rostrevor BT34 | 109 | G8 |
| Rousky BT79 | 108 | D4 |
| Roxhill BT41 | 109 | G4 |
| Rubane BT22 | 109 | K5 |

## S

| | | |
|---|---|---|
| Saintfield BT24 | 109 | J6 |
| Sandholes BT80 | 108 | E5 |
| Saul BT30 | 109 | J6 |
| Scarva BT63 | 109 | G6 |
| Scollogstown BT30 | 109 | J7 |
| Scotch Street BT62 | 109 | F6 |
| Scribbagh BT93 | 108 | A6 |
| Seaforde BT30 | 109 | J6 |
| Seapatrick BT32 | 109 | G6 |
| Seskinore BT78 | 108 | D5 |
| Shoptown BT42 | 109 | H4 |
| Shrigley BT30 | 109 | J6 |
| Sion Mills BT82 | 108 | C4 |
| Sixmilecross BT79 | 108 | D5 |
| Soldierstown BT67 | 109 | G5 |
| Spamount BT81 | 108 | C4 |
| Springfield BT74 | 108 | B6 |
| Staffordstown BT41 | 109 | G4 |
| Stewartstown BT71 | 109 | F5 |
| Stonyford BT28 | 109 | H5 |
| **Strabane** BT82 | 108 | C4 |
| Straid *B'mena* BT42 | 109 | G4 |
| Straid *Newtown.* BT39 | 109 | H4 |
| Strangford BT30 | 109 | J6 |
| Stranocum BT53 | 109 | G2 |
| Swatragh BT46 | 109 | F3 |

## T

| | | |
|---|---|---|
| Tamlaght BT74 | 108 | C6 |
| Tamlaght O'Crilly BT46 | 109 | F3 |
| Tamnamore BT71 | 109 | F5 |
| Tandragee BT62 | 109 | G6 |
| Tassagh BT60 | 109 | F7 |
| Teemore BT92 | 108 | C7 |
| Templepatrick BT39 | 109 | H4 |
| Tempo BT94 | 108 | C6 |
| The Bush BT71 | 109 | F5 |
| The Diamond *Cooks.* BT71 | 109 | F5 |
| The Diamond *Omagh* BT78 | 108 | D5 |
| The Drones BT53 | 109 | G2 |
| The Loup BT45 | 109 | F4 |
| The Rock BT70 | 108 | E5 |
| The Sheddings BT42 | 109 | H3 |
| The Six Towns BT45 | 108 | E4 |
| The Spa BT24 | 109 | H6 |
| The Temple BT27 | 109 | H5 |
| Tobermore BT45 | 109 | F4 |
| Toome BT41 | 109 | F4 |
| Trillick BT78 | 108 | C6 |
| Trory BT94 | 108 | C6 |
| Tully BT92 | 108 | C7 |
| Tullyhogue BT80 | 109 | F5 |
| Tynan BT60 | 108 | E6 |

## U

| | | |
|---|---|---|
| Upper Ballinderry BT28 | 109 | G5 |
| Upperlands BT46 | 109 | F3 |

## V

| | | |
|---|---|---|
| Victoria Bridge BT82 | 108 | C4 |
| Vow BT53 | 109 | F3 |

## W

| | | |
|---|---|---|
| Waringsford BT25 | 109 | H6 |
| Waringstown BT66 | 109 | G6 |
| Warrenpoint BT34 | 109 | G8 |
| Whitecross BT60 | 109 | F7 |
| Whitehead BT38 | 109 | J4 |